"The 2000 presidential election wa[s] a close call—how does that happen? I wonder if it has happened before."

"How am I going to be sure I know all this material for the test? I feel confident now, but..."

"I understand that the bill of rights is important, but how is it used in real life?"

mypoliscilab™

Where participation leads to action!

with LongmanParticipate.com 3.0 insid[e]

This TIMELINE ACTIVITY examines other close-call elections in our history.

PRE-TESTS, POST-TESTS, CHAPTER EXAMS and **STUDY GUIDES** for each chapter of your book help students prepare for exams.

This SIMULATION ACTIVITY helps students judge whether a police officer who is breaking and entering is violating civil rights.

Available in CourseCompass™, WebCT, & Blackboard

mypoliscilab™
Where participation leads to action!

with LongmanParticipate.com 3.0 inside!

From **simulations** that place students in the role of campaign manager to **timeline activities**, from **pre- and post-chapter tests** to a fully integrated **Ebook**, MyPoliSciLab brings together an amazing collection of resources for both students and instructors. See a demo now at **www.mypoliscilab.com**!

Here's what's in MyPoliSciLab—

 PRE-TEST   POST TEST   EXAM

Pre-Test, Post Test, and Chapter Exam.
For each chapter of the text, students will navigate through a pre-test, post-test, and a full chapter exam—all fully integrated with the online Ebook so students can assess, review, and improve their understanding of the material in each chapter.

Ebook.
Matching the exact layout of the printed textbook, the Ebook contains multimedia icons in the margins that launch a wealth of exciting resources.

 REVIEW

Chapter Review.
For each chapter, students will find additional resources, such as a complete study guide, learning objectives, a summary, and Web explorations.

Research Navigator™.
This database provides thousands of articles from popular periodicals like *Newsweek* and *USA Today* that give students and professors access to topical content from a variety of sources.

New York Times Online Feed & The New York Times Search by Subject™ Archive.
Both provide free access to the full text of *The New York Times* and articles from the world's leading journalists of the *Times*. The online feed provides students with updated headlines and political news on an hourly basis.

LongmanParticipate.com 3.0
Our well-known and highly respected online tool is now fully updated. Students will find over 100 simulations, interactive timelines, comparative exercises and more—all integrated with the online ebook. Available inside MyPoliSciLab or as a website alone.

LongmanParticipate.com 3.0
Inside! →

Go to mypoliscilab.com for a free demo.

The New American Democracy

FOURTH EDITION

Morris P. Fiorina
Stanford University

Paul E. Peterson
Harvard University

Bertram Johnson
Middlebury College

D. Stephen Voss
University of Kentucky

PEARSON

Longman

New York • Boston • San Francisco
London • Toronto • Sydney • Tokyo • Singapore • Madrid
Mexico City • Munich • Paris • Cape Town • Hong Kong • Montreal

Dedication

To George Cole, John Kessel, Wayne Merrick, and other members
of the Allegheny College Political Science Department, circa 1966

To Harding C. Noblitt, Concordia College

To Richard Keiser and Steven Schier, Carleton College

And to Paul Paskoff, Jay Perkins, and Wayne Parent, Louisiana State University

In appreciation for their teaching excellence

Executive Editor: Eric Stano
Acquisitions Editor: Edward Costello
Development Editor: Barbara A. Conover
Senior Marketing Manager: Elizabeth Fogarty
Media and Supplements Editor: Kristi Olson
Senior Media Editor: Patrick McCarthy
Production Manager: Joseph Vella
Project Coordination, Text Design, and Electronic Page Makeup: Thompson Steele, Inc.
Cover Design Manager: Wendy A. Fredericks
Cover Designer: Kay Petronio
Cover Photos: *Capitol Building:* Doug Armand/Stone/Getty Images, Inc. *Crowd:* Dia Max/Taxi/
   Getty Images, Inc.
Manufacturing Manager: Mary Fischer
Senior Manufacturing Buyer: Alfred C. Dorsey
Printer and Binder: Courier Corp.—Westford
Cover Printer: Coral Graphics Services

For permission to use copyrighted material, grateful acknowledgment is made to the copyright holders on p. 680, which are hereby made part of this copyright page.

Library of Congress Cataloging-in-Publication Data
The new American democracy / Morris P. Fiorina ... [et al.].-- 4th ed.
     p. cm.
   Rev. ed. of: The new American democracy / Morris P. Fiorina, Paul E. Peterson with Bertram
Johnson. 3rd ed. c2003.
    Includes bibliographical references and index.
    ISBN 0-321-21000-X (main ed. ch1-20 : alk. paper)
   1. Democracy--United States--Textbooks. 2. United States--Politics and government--Textbooks. I.
Fiorina, Morris P. II. Fiorina, Morris P. New American democracy.
JK1726.N45 2005
320.473--dc22
                                        2004022541

Please visit our Website at http://www.ablongman.com

ISBN 0-321-21000-X (The New American Democracy, Fourth Edition)
ISBN 0-321-21001-8 (The New American Democracy, Alternate Fourth Edition)

1 2 3 4 5 6 7 8 9 10—CRW—07 06 05 04

Brief Contents

PART 1
The Foundations of a New American Democracy

PART 2
The Ingredients of the New American Democracy

PART 3
Campaigns and Elections

Detailed Contents

PART 1

THE FOUNDATIONS OF A NEW AMERICAN DEMOCRACY

Chapter 4   American Political Culture   85

PART 2

THE INGREDIENTS OF THE NEW AMERICAN DEMOCRACY

Chapter 7 — Interest-Group Participation in American Democracy   171

PART 3

CAMPAIGNS AND ELECTIONS

Chapter 10   Electing the President   253

PART 4
THE GOVERNMENT

PART 6
PUBLIC POLICY

Appendices

To the Students

This text grew out of a decade of teaching the introductory course together. As we listened to each other's lectures each year we noticed that our course was evolving into one whose underlying theme was both more specific than, and different from, the themes that could be found in other American government textbooks. Specifically, elections and their repercussions gradually became the primary connecting thread that tied together our lectures and discussions. In part, this emphasis reflected our own backgrounds and interests. Morris Fiorina has devoted his professional career to the study of elections—both narrowly, in the sense of why people vote the way they do, and more broadly, in the sense of how elections affect politicians, political institutions, and the policies they produce. Paul Peterson began his career with a focus on citizen participation in the War on Poverty and later studied the way the federal system limited what local officials could do. In recent years, he has examined the ways elections shape government response to budget deficits, welfare needs, race relations, educational issues, and the changing foreign policy environment.

It was not just our own research interests, however, that brought election issues to the fore. Both of us attempt to keep our lectures connected to present-day government and politics, and as a reflection of a changing reality, we found our lectures increasingly infused with the connections between elections and the work of government. From experience we know that students are keenly aware of the way elections affect the strategies of politicians and the decisions of policy-makers, as well as a great many other things that happen in government. As a result, we have written a different kind of American government textbook, one that gives a central place to elections and their consequences.

Level and Tone of This Textbook

Some educators think that today's students are less proficient in certain skills and less motivated than were students of a generation ago. Our view is that you may be different from those earlier students, but that does not mean that you are any less capable. In fact, you also have skills that were nonexistent years ago. (We bet that on average you are better at surfing the Internet than your professors!) As for motivation, that is something not purely your responsibility. It is our job as teachers to make the material as stimulating to you and as relevant to your lives as possible. Our premise is that undergraduate students are fully capable of understanding information and analyses that are clearly expressed. For this reason, this book emphasizes meaning and significance. It contains considerable interpretation in addition to the essential facts.

We do not shy away from controversy. Some individuals in American higher education would protect students from intellectual discomfort. The consequences of such beliefs include well-intentioned efforts to place some subjects and arguments outside the boundaries of classroom discussion. We do not agree with this approach. Our view is that politics is fundamentally about conflict. People have conflicting interests and, even more seriously, conflicting values. Politics is the nonviolent resolution of such conflicts. People can settle their disagreements and rise above their dislikes through political deliberation, or they can choose weapons, as so many have over the course of human history.

We believe that you need to learn to engage in such political deliberation. Within the bounds of civil discourse, you should be challenged, even at times provoked. Education proceeds by defending one's viewpoints and by learning to understand those of others. Thus, in the chapters that follow, we consider arguments that some of you may find uncomfortable. In the realm of education, a better, clearer understanding supersedes all other values.

Although the study of American politics is far more than the study of current events, a book that emphasizes the importance of elections can make its points come to life by placing them in the context of contemporary politics. This fourth edition is a careful revision of the third edition, updated to include information about important recent events such as the war against terrorism, the arrival of a new era in international politics, the latest Supreme Court decisions, and the 2004 campaign and elections. Of course, these stories—like politics generally—continue to evolve, and we hope this text provides you with the information you need to understand future developments.

Specific Features

This book has a number of specific features, many related to our elections theme. We call your attention to the following:

- Each chapter introduces you to the subject matter with an **opening vignette** on a high-interest issue or incident. Some vignettes are classics from American history, while others are based on current events. Examples include a discussion of the 2004 presidential election (Chapter 1—Democracy in the United States); a discussion of national reaction to "suspect" minorities in the wake of wars (Chapter 4—American Political Culture); the Supreme Court's "unsought responsibility" in the 2000 election (Chapter 9—The Courts); and the redefinition of George W. Bush's presidency in the wake of terrorism (Chapter 13—The Presidency: Powers and Practice). Following each vignette is a list of the questions and topics that the chapter covers.
- To illustrate the book's focus on electoral forces, some chapters include a box entitled **Election Connection,** describing the relationship between elections and institutions or policies. For instance, Chapter 4's box describes Republican efforts to court Hispanic voters; Chapter 6's discusses the controversy over nonvoters in 2000 who actually turned out; and Chapter 19's reports on the electoral calculations behind Bush administration trade policies.

- Many chapters contain an **International Comparison** box that compares a feature of American government with a similar feature in other countries. These boxes will give you a better understanding of the strengths and limitations of American democracy by letting you think about real alternatives, not just unattainable ideals. Chapter 2's feature box looks at the making of a constitution in Iraq; and Chapter 4's compares citizenship requirements in Europe to those in the United States. Chapter 10's explains why campaign financing isn't such a big issue in other countries and Chapter 18's illustrates the differences in student learning and expenditures between the United States and several European countries and Japan.

- You are given an opportunity to exercise your own critical thinking by considering a **Democratic Dilemma** in some chapters. Are there instances in which democratic values are in conflict? Will policy changes or institutional reforms actually achieve the goals their proponents claim? This box presents arguments pro and con, poses questions, and invites students to grapple with them. Examples include Chapter 3's comparison between categorical and block grants, Chapter 6's reflection on whether voters can speak for those who abstain; Chapter 8's discussion of gridlock and the impact of divided government; and Chapter 16's query as to whether campus speech codes unduly restrict free speech.

- **Critical thinking questions** accompany figures, photographs, and boxes to provoke discussion and thought about the issues at hand.

- Each chapter includes full **marginal definitions** for key terms that are boldfaced in the text and included in the end-of-book Glossary.

- At the end of each chapter we include an **On the Web** feature to direct readers to Web sites where they can find more information on the topics discussed.

- Also included at the end of each chapter are a **Chapter Summary, Key Terms** (alphabetized at the end of the chapter, with page references), and annotated **Suggested Readings.**

- Throughout the text, icons appearing in the margins refer readers to websites available with this text, MyPoliSciLab and LongmanParticipate.com 3.0. Each icon appears next to a particular topic and indicates that a simulation, visual literacy exercise, interactive timeline, participation activity, or comparative government exercise related to that topic exists on the sites. Each activity provides feedback, helps the reader better understand the concepts presented in the text, and makes learning fun. See the front of this text for more information on these exciting, interactive, and valuable resource.

In addition, the fourth edition feature, **Voices of the Permanent Campaign**, further emphasizes the election theme and concludes each major part of the text.

- Based on important current events, each Voices presents a thought-provoking issue and then illustrates how that issue plays out in the permanent campaign. Every Voices includes a brief review of the issue at hand, consideration of opposing viewpoints, references to pertinent Web sites, and critical thinking questions. For example, the Voices that concludes Part 3 (Campaigns and Elections) describes the complex politics of campaign finance. The Voices that concludes Part 6 (Public Policy) considers the U.S. politics of the Arab-Israeli conflict. We are confident that each Voices will stimulate students' intellect, drive home the relevance of the text's material, and help foster lively, thoughtful debates.

New to This Edition

The text has been carefully revised since its third edition. This fourth edition includes substantive rewrites, extensively revised features, and the inclusion of the latest information and examples on key topics. For example:

- The 2004 campaigns and elections
- The concern about terrorism and the treatment of immigrants
- Recent developments in the area of campaign finance including 527 committees
- Recent developments in state and local politics, including growing financial crises
- The latest Supreme Court decisions concerning federalism, civil liberties, and other issues, including discussion of the *Lawrence v. Texas* decisions.
- The politics of gun control
- The civil rights of Latinos, Asian Americans, and gays and lesbians
- The War Powers Resolution Act after 9/11

Supplements for Students of Qualified College Adopters

- **NEW! MyPoliSciLab for American Government with Longman Participate.com updated 3.0 version inside!** MyPoliSciLab is a state-of-the-art, interactive online solution for your course. Available in CourseCompass, Blackboard, and WebCT, MyPoliSciLab offers students a wealth of simulations, interactive exercises, and assessment tools—all integrated with an online e-book version of this text. For each chapter of the text, students will navigate through a pre-test, post-test, chapter review, and a full chapter exam, so they can assess, review, and improve their understanding of the concepts within the chapters. In addition to the online chapter content and assessment, students will have access to **Longman Participate.com 3.0,** Longman's best-selling interactive online tool providing over 100 interactive exercises for students. **LongmanParticipate.com 3.0** is also available as a website alone, independent of a course management system. To find out more, go to **MyPoliSciLab** at **www.mypoliscilab.com**. To find out more about **LongmanParticipate.com 3.0**, go to **longmanparticipate.com**.
- **Companion Website (www.ablongman.com/fiorina).** This text-specific, online study guide includes: Practice tests with feedback (multiple-choice, true/false, and fill-in-the-blank); Web Destinations; Chapter Summaries; Chatroom; Simulations; and Flash Cards.
- **Study Guide.** Written by Dennis Plane of Juniata College. The printed study guide features chapter outlines, key terms, practice tests, and critical thinking questions.
- **Research Navigator and Research Navigator Guide.** Research Navigator is a comprehensive Web site comprising three exclusive databases of credible and reliable source material for research and for student assignments: EBSCO's ContentSelect Academic Journal Database, the *New York Times* Search-by-Subject Archive, and "Best of the Web" Link Library. The site also includes an extensive help section. The Research Navigator Guide provides your students with access to the Research Navigator Web site and includes reference material and hints about conducting online research. **Free to qualified college adopters.**

- *New York Times* **Discount Subscription.** A 10-week subscription for only $20! Contact your local Allyn & Bacon/Longman representative for more information.
- *Culture War? The Myth of a Polarized America* **by Morris P. Fiorina, Stanford University, with Samuel J. Abrams, Harvard University, and Jeremy C. Pope, Stanford University.** The first book in the "Great Questions in Politics" series, *Culture War? The Myth of a Polarized America* combines polling data with a compelling narrative to debunk commonly-believed and currently prevalent myths about American politics—particularly the claim that Americans are deeply divided in their fundamental political views.
- *You Decide! Current Debates in American Politics,* **2005 Edition.** Edited by John T. Rourke, University of Connecticut, this exciting new debate-style reader examines provocative issues in American politics today. The topics have been selected for their currency, importance, and student interest, and the pieces that argue various sides of a given issue come from recent journals, congressional hearings, think tanks, and periodicals.
- *Voices of Dissent: Critical Readings in American Politics,* **Fifth Edition.** Edited by William F. Grover, St. Michael's College, and Joseph G. Peschek, Hamline University, this collection of critical essays goes beyond the debate between mainstream liberalism and conservatism to fundamentally challenge the status quo. Available at a discount when ordered packaged with this text.
- *American Government: Readings and Cases,* **Sixteenth Edition.** Edited by Peter Woll, Brandeis University, this best-selling reader provides a strong, balanced blend of classic readings and cases that illustrate and amplify important concepts in American government, alongside extremely current selections drawn from today's issues and literature. Available at a discount when ordered packaged with this text.
- *Ten Things That Every American Government Student Should Read.* Edited by Karen O'Connor, American University. We asked American government instructors across the country to vote for ten things beyond the text that they believe every student should read and put them in this brief and useful reader. Free when ordered packaged with the text.
- *Choices: An American Government Database Reader.* This customizable reader allows instructors to choose from a database of over 300 readings to create a reader that exactly matches their course needs. Go to **www.pearsoncustom.com/ database/choices.html** for more information.
- **Discount Subscription to** *Newsweek* **Magazine.** Students receive 12 issues of Newsweek at more than 80% off the regular price. An excellent way for students to keep up with current events.
- **Penguin–Longman Value Bundles.** Longman offers 25 Penguin Putnam titles at more than a 60% discount when packaged with any Longman text. A totally unique offer and a wonderful way to enhance students' understanding of concepts in American Government. Please go to **www.ablongman.com/penguin** for more information.
- *Writing in Political Science,* **Third Edition, by Diane Schmidt.** Take students step-by-step through all aspects of writing in political science. Available at a discount when ordered packaged with any Longman textbook.
- *Getting Involved: A Guide to Student Citizenship* **by Mark Kann, Todd Belt, Gabriela Cowperthwaite, and Steven Horn.** A unique and practical handbook

that guides students through political participation with concrete advice and extensive sample material—letters, telephone scripts, student interviews, and real-life anecdotes—for getting involved and making a difference in their lives and communities.

- *Texas Politics Supplement,* **Third Edition, by Debra St. John.** A 90-page primer on state and local government and issues in Texas. Free when shrink-wrapped with text.
- *California Politics Supplement,* **Third Edition, by Barbara Stone.** A 70-page primer on state and local government and issues in California. Free when shrink-wrapped with text.
- *Florida Politics Supplement,* **by John Bertalan.** A 50-page primer on state and local government and issues in Florida. Free when shrink-wrapped with text.

To Our Colleagues

The chapters that follow speak directly to students in down-to-earth language. In this preface we address their teachers, our colleagues, in more professional terms, about the reasons we decided to write this text.

More than a generation ago, one of the leading political scientists of the century, Robert Dahl, published a textbook entitled *Pluralist Democracy in the United States*.[1] Dahl was the acknowledged leader of the pluralist school of American political science, which viewed American politics as a collection of arenas in which leaders of organized interest groups bargained over the substance of public policies, with public officials involved both as brokers and as representatives of broader societal interests. Political institutions, in turn, were viewed as regularized bargaining arenas in which leaders were constrained by formal rules. *Groups, bargaining, leaders,* and *representation* were the operative terms for understanding American politics.

American politics has changed a good deal since Dahl wrote. Indeed, Dahl himself notes a number of these changes:

> Without intending to do so, over the past thirty years or so Americans have created a new political order. Although it retains a seamless continuity with the order it has displaced, in its present form it constitutes something so new that journalists, commentators, scholars, and ordinary citizens are still struggling to understand it.[2]

Dahl argues that this new political order is more fragmented and more plebiscitary than the old one. The proliferation of interest groups combined with the deterioration of traditional party organizations has strengthened divisive forces and weakened unifying ones. Such political developments, along with social and technological changes, have exposed public officials to popular pressures more than in the past. As a consequence, Dahl contends, representation and deliberation have suffered. He worries that these changes might create "a pseudo-democratic facade on a process manipulated by political leaders to achieve their own agendas."[3]

Another leading political scientist of Dahl's generation, Gabriel Almond, weighs in with similar sentiments:

> Television and radio have largely preempted the print media and the primary opinion leaders. . . . Domestic and international events are brought into the living room with powerful visual and emotional impact—a telepopulism that constrains and distorts public policy. The deliberative processes of politics are diluted and heated by this populism, and by "instant" public opinion polls based on telephone samples.[4]

Although we do not agree with every particular of these indictments, they serve to emphasize that something has happened to American government since the days when an earlier generation of scholars characterized it as a pluralist democracy. For better or for worse, it has become something closer to a popular democracy. In the pages that follow we describe the forces that have brought about these changes as well as their impact on contemporary politics, institutions, and policies. But, we are getting ahead of ourselves here.

Each year as we considered the range of texts available for the introductory American government course, we decided that available books, however worthy, did not match our views. In the first place, many gave less emphasis than we would like to topics that are essential parts of contemporary American politics—elections, most obviously, but also closely related topics such as public opinion, political participation, and the media. Second, in many texts the role of prime mover implicitly is assigned to the courts, whereas we see electoral context as an important influence on judicial activity and judicial outcomes. Third, contemporary textbooks typically separate the study of elections from other major headings: constitutional fundamentals, bureaucratic politics, the courts, and the formation of public policies. As James Stimson comments:

> In our texts public opinion is a chapter or two. The various branches of government are usually a chapter each. And the connection between what the public wants and what the government does is on the page fold between them. Public opinion is conceptualized as a set of measures and processes that do not speak to government. Governing institutions are studied in a manner which doesn't deny public opinion influence, but doesn't permit its active study. When citizens of Washington, DC, could not vote the analogy was complete; all opinion was outside the beltway, all government was inside.[5]

This book breaks down the artificial and unfortunate separation identified by Stimson. Rather than discuss public opinion in one self-contained chapter, political participation in a second, and elections in a third, then move on to a series of institutional and policy chapters, we give public opinion and electioneering their due in individual chapters devoted to those topics, but we continue to trace their effects on other political and institutional processes, culminating in discussions of why American public policies have the shape they do. Thus, the chapters of this text bear the familiar titles, but they are linked by an extended discussion of the pervasiveness of electoral influences in the new American democracy.

When we began writing the first edition of this book almost 15 years ago, we knew that our argument for the contemporary dominance of electoral forces would meet with some resistance. Most of the developments we described were fairly recent and we understood that some colleagues might not see as sharp a break with the pre-1960s era as we did. But the passing of the years has lessened the novelty of our argument. Under the "horse race" presidencies of Bill Clinton and George W. Bush, the line between electioneering and governing all but disappeared, as the techniques of the campaign moved to the very pinnacle of government.[6] Under George W. Bush, political adviser Karl Rove became a symbol of the permanent campaign, dividing his time between offering advice to the president and such tasks as selecting Republican precinct coordinators for the 2004 race.[7] Our view that contemporary American politics is a "permanent campaign" is now common. In fact, the Pew Charitable Trusts recently organized a consortium of public-policy think tanks to study the permanent campaign—how it has affected the range of American institutions and the policy process, with what consequences, and whether a line between electioneering and governing might once again be drawn.[8] This fourth edition now lies squarely in the mainstream of thinking about American politics.

We emphasize that to say that public opinion, political campaigns, and elections are of great import is to offer neither a celebrationist nor a cynical interpretation of

American politics. On the one hand, the shift to a more popular democracy is associated with a greater role for previously disadvantaged voices in the population. As the scramble to register new voters in 2004 illustrates, those who had been left out in the past can now exercise electoral power. On the other hand, the shift to a more popular democracy grants greater access to special interests and limits opportunities for reflective consideration of the long-range consequences of policy choices. But there is no reason to rush to a critical judgment. Future generations of scholars can judge whether the new order does more or less to advance the welfare of the American people than the old one.

Nor should our emphasis on elections suggest a focus on anything so narrow as what happens on election day or in the campaigns that precede it. When we say that elections play a dominant role, we are thinking not only of their direct effects but also of the indirect ways in which they affect the thinking of interest groups, parties, and public officials, both elected and appointed. It is not so much elections themselves as their anticipation that provides so much of the motive power in contemporary political life in the United States.

Finally, we understand that our colleagues will be understandably skeptical of any attempt to squeeze the study of American government into any single thematic frame—even one defined as broadly as our understanding and interpretation of electoral influence. The subject matter of American government is voluminous, and an introductory course must touch on its many aspects. We do not believe that elections explain all that needs to be known about all aspects of American government and politics. Our general approach is to consider the incentives at work in any situation. If electoral incentives are often a major force, they certainly are not the only one. Some leaders risk their reputations with the public for the good of the country. Some act out of ideological commitments, regardless of their electoral consequences. Some realize that foreign policies must take into account the interests of nations throughout the world. Where these and other nonelectoral factors are important, we recognize that fact and proceed accordingly. The result is a book that is more focused than most American government texts, but not one that forces the whole subject into a single theme.

In sum, we do not believe this book could or should have been written even as recently as a generation ago. For although elections have always been central to American politics, we believe, with Dahl, that American politics became significantly more plebiscitary in the late twentieth century. The contributing factors are widely recognized. Transformations in the process of nominating and electing candidates produced an individualistic politics in which each candidate forms his or her own organization rather than relying on a common party organization. Transformations in communications technology—survey research, phone, fax, and the Internet—made it possible for politicians to learn the political impacts of their decisions almost instantaneously. Transformations in the media generated a seemingly insatiable demand for news material—a demand often satisfied by stories about political conflict. In this context, interest groups mushroomed, polls and primaries proliferated, and the permanent campaign arrived on the scene. Older concepts used to characterize pluralist politics—groups, bargaining, leaders, and representation—are still important, but a full and accurate account of American politics today must also include careful consideration of the roles played by the media, polls, and campaigns and elections.

Approach and Organization

This book cuts across the old categories that characterize existing American government texts: historical development, political "inputs," institutions, and policy "outputs." Although we discuss all these aspects of American politics, we approach them in a more integrated manner. Following are a few illustrations of our approach:

- Contemporary practices are compared and contrasted with those existing in earlier periods, making the historical material more relevant to today's readers.
- Chapters on so-called political inputs focus on the choices of individuals, groups, parties, and the media as a response to the incentives they face.
- Analyses of Congress, the presidency, the bureaucracy, and the judiciary do not just describe the main institutions of government; they also show how elections shape the behavior of officeholders within these institutions.
- Civil liberties and civil rights are treated not simply as the result of judicial decisions, but also as the product of electoral forces. These chapters are placed in the policy section of the book, instead of at the beginning as part of the historical foundations of American government, in order to highlight the extent to which basic constitutional rights are themselves shaped by public opinion and electoral outcomes.
- Discussions of public policies do not just list policy problems or classify types of policies, but show how elections in particular and politics in general shape the way policies are addressed and adopted.

Finally, the book offers a critical but fair picture of American government and politics. Any objective observer must recognize that American government and politics have numerous shortcomings. We point out many of them and explain why they exist. But throughout the text we show that, judged against realistic standards, American politics and government are not nearly as blameworthy as the evening news and tabloid shows often suggest.

Instructor Supplements for Qualified College Adopters

- **Companion Website** (www.ablongman.com/fiorina). This Companion Website provides a wealth of resources for students and instructors using *The New American Democracy,* Fourth Edition. Students will find the site serving as a useful, online study guide with chapter summaries, practice tests, Web links, simulations, a guide to researching online, and a variety of other learning tools. Instructors will have access to the Instructor's Manual, PowerPoint® slides, and teaching links via a link to the Supplements Central Web site.
- *Digital Media Archive for American Government,* **First Edition.** This cross-platform CD-ROM for instructors contains hundreds of images, maps, audio and video clips ready for classroom presentation or downloading into PowerPoint or any other presentation software (ISBN: 0-321-27068-1).
- **Instructor's Manual.** Prepared by Tom Caiazzo of Collin County Community College, each chapter of this resource manual contains a Chapter Overview, Key Concepts and Objectives, Chapter Outline, Terms for Review, and Teaching Suggestions.

- **Test Bank with Practice Tests.** This test bank, prepared by Cecilia Manrique of University of Wisconsin-La Crosse, contains hundreds of multiple-choice, true/false, short answer, and essay questions, all accompanied by an answer key.

- **TestGen-EQ Computerized Testing System.** This flexible, easy-to-use computer test bank includes all the test items in the printed test bank. The software allows you to edit existing questions and add your own items. Tests can be printed in several formats and can include figures such as graphs and tables.

- **Text-specific Transparency Acetates.** Full-color transparencies drawn from *The New American Democracy* are available.

- **Interactive AmericanGovernment Video.** Contains 27 video segments on topics ranging from the term-limit debate, to Internet porn, to women in the Citadel. Critical thinking questions accompany each clip, encouraging students to "interact" with the videos.

- *Politics in Action* **Video.** Eleven "lecture launchers," covering broad subjects such as social movements, conducting a campaign, and the passage of a bill, are examined through narrated videos, interviews, edited documentaries, original footage, and political ads. *Politics in Action* is accompanied by an extensive user's manual, which provides background on the segments, links topics to textbooks, and discussion questions.

- **Longman American Government Video Archive.** These videos from a broad range of sources include famous debates, speeches, political commercials, and congressional hearings. The archive also includes series such as "Eyes on the Prize" and "The Power Game." Ask your Longman sales representative for more information.

- *MyPoliSciLab and LongmanParticipate.com 3.0 Faculty Teaching Guide,* **First Edition.** Contains chapter-by-chapter detailed summaries for each of the site's interactive activities, as well as a list of concepts covered, recommendations about how to integrate the site into coursework, and discussion questions and paper topics for every exercise. Instructors may use the table of contents in the front of the guide to locate information on a given activity icon that appears in the margin of their adopted textbook. This guide also provides faculty with detailed instructions and screen shots showing how to use MyPoliSciLab, how to register on the site, and how to set up and use the administrative features. The introductory chapter describes the numerous additional resources included on the Website. Written by Scott Furlong of University of Wisconsin (ISBN: 0-321-31689-4).

Acknowledgments

We want to thank the many people who helped us with the preparation of this book. Our deepest gratitude goes to the many undergraduate students whose questions forced us to refine our thinking about American government over the past ten years. We also thank numerous cohorts of teaching fellows for their perceptive comments, questions, and criticisms. We are also especially grateful to Bruce Nichols, who first argued with us the need for a new-century approach to the introductory text on American government. The Center for Advanced Study in the Behavioral and Social Sciences provided generous support for Paul E. Peterson's work on the first edition of the text during his academic year there.

Harding Noblitt of Concordia College read the entire first edition manuscript in search of errors of fact and interpretation, saving the authors much embarrassment. In addition, portions were read by Danny Adkison, Sue Davis, Richard Fenno, Gary Jacobson, Barry Rabe, and Chris Stamm, whose comments helped with fact checking. We especially appreciate John Ferejohn and the undergraduate students at Stanford University who took his course and tested an early draft of the entire manuscript, and Jay Greene and his students at the University of Texas at Austin who used subsequent page proofs. Larry Carlton supplied important factual material. Research assistance was provided by Ted Brader, Jay Girotto, Donald Lee, Jerome Maddox, Kenneth Scheve, Sean Theriault, and Robert Van Houweling—as well as William Howell who, in addition to making many other contributions, helped write the regulatory policy section in Chapter 18. Rebecca Contreras, Alison Kommer, Shelley Weiner, and Sarah Peterson provided staff assistance. Bert Johnson wishes to thank several classes of American Politics students at Carleton College, as well as professors Sharon Navarro, Kanishkan Sathasivam, Steven Schier, and Kim Smith for their helpful suggestions. Steve Voss thanks the Pool Night regulars, who sustained him through the dark hours, and Kathleen Elliott, who sustained the family.

We would like to extend our special thanks to Martin West of Harvard University and Jeremy Pope and Sam Abrams at Stanford University for the multitude of tasks they undertook to see this fourth edition into publication, and improved upon the third.

In the course of writing this book, we benefited from the advice of many instructors across the country. We deeply thank all the following, but we are especially grateful for the expert advice of Stephen Ansolabehere, Richard Fenno, John Ferejohn, Bonnie Honig, William Mayer, and Diana Owen.

The following are reviewers who assisted in the preparation of the second and third editions of the text: Danny M. Adkison, Oklahoma State University; Donald P. Aiesi, Furman University; Michael Bailey, Georgetown University; Gordon Bennett, University of Texas; Mark Berger, State University of New York at Stony Brook; William Bianco, Penn State University; Nancy Bond, Ranger College; Michael

Caldwell, University of Illinois, Urbana–Champaign; Thomas A. Chambers, Golden West College; Mark A. Cichock, University of Texas at Arlington; Louis DeSipio, University of Illinois, Urbana–Champaign; Richard E. Dunn, College of Charleston; Christine Fastnow, University of Michigan; Jon Hurwitz, University of Pittsburgh; Robert Jacobs, Central Washington University; Carlos Juarez, Hawaii Pacific University; David Leal, State University of New York at Buffalo; Brad Lockerbie, University of Georgia; William Lyons, University of Tennessee; Cecilia Manrique, University of Wisconsin, La Crosse; William P. McLauchlan, Purdue University; Michael E. Meagher, University of Missouri, Rolla; Charles Menifield, Murray State University; David S. Meyer, City College of New York; Timothy Nokken, University of Houston; John H. Parham, Minnesota State University; Curt Reithel, University of Wisconsin, La Crosse; Mankato; James A. Rhodes, Luther College; Todd M. Schaefer, Central Washington University; Theodore M. Vestal, Oklahoma State University; Shirley Anne Warshaw, Gettysburg College; Linda Faye Williams, University of Maryland; Jeremy Zilber, College of William and Mary.

The following are reviewers who assisted in the preparation of this fourth edition: Chris W. Bonneau, University of Pittsburgh; Audrey Haynes, University of Georgia; Eric Herzik, University of Nevada; Madhavi McCall, San Diego State University; Sarah Miller, Lourdes University; Beth Rosenson, University of Florida.

M. P. F.
P. E. P
B. J.
D. S. V.

About the Authors

Morris P. Fiorina

Morris P. Fiorina is Wendt Professor of Political Science and Senior Fellow of the Hoover Institution at Stanford University. He received a B.A. from Allegheny College in Meadville, Pennsylvania, and a Ph.D. from the University of Rochester. Before moving to Stanford, he taught at the California Institute of Technology and Harvard University.

Fiorina has written widely on American government and politics, with special emphasis on representation and elections. He has published numerous articles, and five books: *Representatives, Roll Calls, and Constituencies; Congress—Keystone of the Washington Establishment; Retrospective Voting in American National Elections; The Personal Vote: Constituency Service and Electoral Independence* (coauthored with Bruce Cain and John Ferejohn); and *Divided Government*. He has served on the editorial boards of a dozen journals in the fields of political science, economics, law, and public policy, and from 1986 to 1990 he served as chairman of the Board of Overseers of the American National Election Studies. He is a member of the National Academy of Sciences and is a Wendt *Family* Professor of Political Science.

In his leisure time, Fiorina favors physical activities, including hiking, fishing, and sports. Although his own athletic career never amounted to much, he was a successful youth baseball coach for 15 years. Among his most cherished honors is a plaque given by happy parents on the occasion of an undefeated Babe Ruth season.

Paul E. Peterson

Paul E. Peterson is the Henry Lee Shattuck Professor of Government and Director of the Center for American Political Studies at Harvard University. He received his B.A. from Concordia College in Moorhead, Minnesota, and his Ph.D. from the University of Chicago.

Peterson is an author or editor of twenty books and numerous articles on federalism, urban politics, race relations, and public policy, including studies of education, welfare, and fiscal and foreign policy. He received the Gladys Kammerer Award from the American Political Science Association for his book, *School Politics, Chicago Style* (1976) and the Woodrow Wilson Award for his book *City Limits* (Chicago, 1981). In 1996 his book *The Price of Federalism* (Brookings, 1995) was given the Aaron Wildavsky Award for the best book on public policy. He is a member of the American Academy of Arts and Sciences.

It is not only when writing a textbook that Peterson makes every effort to be as accurate as possible. On the tennis courts, he always makes correct line calls and has seldom been heard to hit a wrong note when tickling the ivories.

Bertram Johnson

Bert Johnson teaches political science at Middlebury College in Middlebury, Vermont. He received his B.A. from Carleton College and his Ph.D. from Harvard University.

Johnson has written on federalism, intergovernmental relations, and campaign finance. When not investigating new ideas about American politics, he can be found exploring prime rock climbing spots throughout the United States.

D. Stephen Voss

D. Stephen Voss is Associate Professor of Political Science at the University of Kentucky. He received his Ph.D. from Harvard University, and specializes in voting and elections with a particular focus on racial politics in the U.S. South. A New Orleans native, Voss also has two bachelor's degrees from Louisiana State University—one in history and one in print journalism.

Voss spends his dwindling leisure time shooting pool, listening to loud music, and playing Grand Theft Auto with his kids.

CHAPTER 1

* * * * * * * * * * * * * * * * *

Democracy in the United States

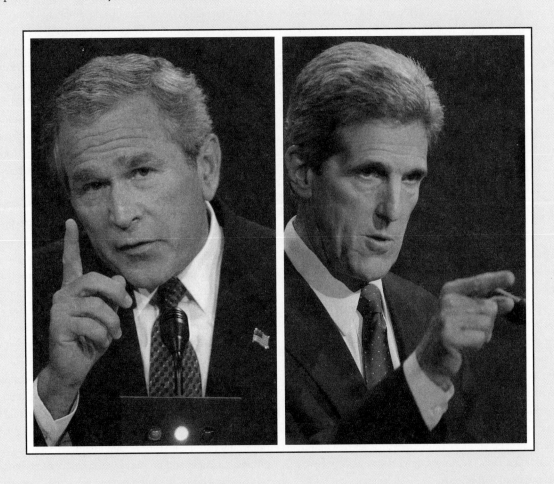

The Permanent Campaign Goes into Overtime

George W. Bush became president of the United States in one of the most closely contested elections in American history—and also one of the most controversial. Unlike any other president in the 20th century, Bush received several hundred thousand fewer votes than the man he defeated. He squeaked out a victory only because of the Electoral College, a 200-year-old method of selecting the chief executive (see Chapter 10). Bush picked up 271 out of 538 electoral votes.

Nor was Bush's victory simply a matter of old-fashioned rules giving him a bit of luck. The vote margin in Florida was so razor-thin that state law required a recount.

Whoever won Florida was going to win the presidency, and it quickly became clear that Florida's electoral procedures were not precise enough to resolve such a close contest in a manner satisfactory to everyone. Bush came out on top weeks after the election, when a favorable Supreme Court ruling ended the vote counting (see Chapter 15). Bush's ascension to the presidency therefore was not widely accepted as legitimate.

Voters were polarized over the Bush presidency, with roughly half disapproving of the new chief executive. Bush could not take the American public for granted if he wanted to be a viable president. Despite promises that he would make "decisions based upon principle, not based upon polls or focus groups," Bush had to stay in campaign mode and constantly weigh policy choices for their likely political consequences. The White House reportedly polled voters twice a month.[1]

Bush brought to the Oval Office a clever political operative named Karl Rove. Rove became Bush's domestic adviser but his true role, observers concluded, was to serve as chief political strategist. Rove reportedly played a significant role in public policies. For example, many observers attributed Bush's decision to halt Navy bombing on the Puerto Rican island of Viecques and his proposal to grant amnesty to as many as 3 million illegal Mexican immigrants to Rove's ambition to attract more of the Hispanic vote.[2]

Bush received a huge burst in popularity after the 9/11 terrorist attacks. Indeed, his job approval ratings reached unprecedented levels. But Bush's father had attained similarly impressive ratings during the Gulf War without being able to win reelection. The younger Bush knew that his newfound popularity would fade. He moved quickly against two nations thought to harbor terrorists—Afghanistan and Iraq—and his administration sent upbeat images and messages back to the American people (see Chapter 5). Bush also worked quickly to set up a new Homeland Security apparatus, a dramatic change in the federal bureaucracy (see pp. 427–432).

Numerous other White House policy decisions seemed to reflect political calculations. Bush agreed to raise barriers against foreign steel, contrary to Republican free-trade principles, in apparent recognition that the party needed votes in steel-producing states (see Chapter 19). Bush reluctantly caved in to farm-state demands for large agricultural subsidies, shoring up the rural vote (see Chapter 12). Bush and his congressional allies never stopped campaigning for reelection.

Nor were the Democrats sleeping during this time. Many liberals expected that anger about the nature of Bush's victory would mobilize Democrats four years later and sweep Bush out of office after only one term.

Commentators began speculating on likely Democratic candidates before Bush entered the Oval Office. Nine Democratic candidates had entered the presidential race by early 2003, only halfway into Bush's term. U.S. Sen. John Kerry of Massachusetts, the eventual nominee, was already dropping by key nomination states.

After Kerry won the nomination, his former rivals began working for his victory. New campaign-finance reforms had weakened the ability of the national parties to fund hard-hitting campaign ads on behalf of their candidates. Into this void appeared new organizations—called "527 Committees"—that would collect political donations and independently run ads to influence the election (see pp. 306–310). Anti-Bush 527 committees attracted the most money.

Senator Kerry, meanwhile, strove to connect with campaign audiences. He smiled a lot, took vacations that showed off his athleticism, and named a youthful running mate. He sharpened his political positions, which had evolved from the intricacies of congressional politics, so that they would be easier to communicate. When Kerry's spunky wife seemed too outspoken, their large brood of well-mannered children spread around the country to campaign.[3]

Overall, it was a presidential campaign of great energy, some positive, some negative. The American voter could hardly feel neglected. Two well-funded and capable presidential candidates had spent years wooing them, offering plans and proposals, passion and promises (see Chapter 6). Americans turned out to vote at a rate not seen since the crisis year of 1968. It was the new American democracy at work.

MAKING THE CONNECTION

The 2004 election illustrates important features of contemporary American democracy and how it differs from democratic practice elsewhere. The campaign was long and drawn out. Huge sums of money were spent. The mass media were deeply involved in the process. Some of the candidates' policy positions reflected their personal commitments and party principles, while others played to public opinion as revealed through the polls.

Elections underlie many of the most important developments in American government at the beginning of the twenty-first century. Indeed, the central theme of this book is that elections are the key to understanding contemporary American democracy. Not only are elections more important in the United States than in other democracies, but they are more important today than they were in most earlier periods of our history. In this chapter we address the following questions:

- Why are elections more important in the United States than in other democracies?

- Does it matter that American governments are freely elected rather than chosen in some other way?

- Why has American politics become a "permanent campaign" in recent decades?

- How can minorities exert influence in a system based on majority rule?

- How do elections produce a reasonably good government?

* * * * * * * * * * * * * * *

Elections in America

More than in any other democracy, politics in the United States is driven by electoral influences. To avoid any misunderstanding, we emphasize three points at the outset. First, our notion of electoral influence is very broad. We refer not just to what happens on election day or even just to what goes on during the formal campaigns. Rather, when we write about the importance of elections, we include the anticipation of and the preparation for future elections—what we call the permanent campaign. (You can learn more about the permanent campaign on pages 11-16.) Looking ahead to the next election affects what presidents propose, what they sign, and what they veto; what Congress passes and what it kills; whom groups support and whom they oppose; whom and what the media cover and whom and what they ignore. Just as the winner of an Olympic event may have been determined on the training fields years earlier, so the outcomes of elections may be determined far in advance of the actual campaigns by the anticipatory actions of candidates, groups, contributors, the media, and other political actors.

Second, when we emphasize the importance of elections, we are not making a naïve claim that "the people" rule. On the contrary, elections are not always accurate expressions of popular preferences. Elections give more power to some groups than to others. Sometimes elections allow special interests to block actions desired by the majority. And even if every election reflected the preferences of a majority, leaders elected by different majorities at different times might deadlock. Elections can be tremendously important without necessarily giving the public what it wants. Whether elections are truly representative and whether they generally work to produce good government are questions that spark debate and disagreement.

Finally, to say that elections are a key ingredient in American democracy—even the key ingredient—is not to deny that other elements are important as well. Elections are part of a very complicated political system. They are closely bound up with the historical evolution of American government, the political behavior of Americans, the workings of the country's basic institutions, and the policies that the governmental process generates. All of these topics receive thorough treatment in the chapters that follow.

Because Americans take elections so much for granted, we begin by calling attention to the sheer amount of electioneering that occurs in the United States.

Half-a-Million Elected Officials

The United States has more elections that choose more officials for public offices than any other country on Earth. Unbelievable as it may seem, more than half-a-million people in the United States are elected officials, about 1 for every 500 Americans. If all these elected officials lived in one place, the population would exceed that of Cleveland.[4]

National elections, in which voters choose the officials of the federal government, are held every two years. These important elections determine the president, the vice president, 100 senators, and 435 members of the House of Representatives. Although national elections get most of the media's attention, hundreds of thousands of elections occur at other levels of government.

In *state elections* the citizens of the 50 states choose their state public officials. Voters elect the governor and the state legislature in every state, and in nearly all states they elect a handful of other statewide offices such as the lieutenant governor, the treasurer, the state's attorney general and the auditor. Finally, voters in some states elect state railroad and public utility commissioners.

The number of elections explodes when we move to *local elections,* in which officials for all governments below the state level are chosen. Voters in cities elect mayors and city councils. Voters in the more than 3000 counties elect sheriffs, county treasurers, and county boards, among other officials. Voters select the membership of 90 percent of the nation's 16,000 school boards, as well as numerous officials responsible for the governance of towns, villages, and special districts.

Even the judicial system, which is often viewed as insulated from political pressure, is permeated by elections. In 37 states, voters elect at least some judges.[5] Altogether, Americans elect more than 1000 state judges and about 15,000 county, municipal, and other local judges and officers of the court.[6] Moreover, in recent years judges have been increasingly subject to **recall elections,** in which dissatisfied citizens try to remove incumbents from office during their terms.

recall election
Attempt to remove an official from office before completion of the term.

Nominating Candidates and Deciding Issues

Although half-a-million elected officials sounds like a lot, there are far more elections than there are elected officials. First, many officials must win two elections before they can take office. In the **primary election,** each party chooses a nominee who then squares off against the other parties' nominees in the **general election.** In *nonpartisan elections,* where candidates do not run with party labels, primaries are sometimes used to narrow the field of candidates. A place on the primary ballot is open to anyone who

primary election
Preliminary election that narrows the number of candidates by determining who will be the nominees in the general election.

general election
Final election that selects the office holder.

has the supporters to gather the required number of signatures and the money to pay the filing fees.

Second, to the extensive list of elections that choose office holders, we must add those elections in which the people directly decide public issues. In 27 states and the District of Columbia, citizens express themselves by voting on initiatives, referenda, or both. An **initiative** is a proposed law or amendment to a state constitution placed on the ballot in response to a citizen petition. A **referendum** is a law or state constitutional amendment that is proposed by a legislature or other elected body but goes into effect only if approved by a specified majority of voters. Often lumped together as **propositions,** initiatives and referenda enable citizens to bypass or overrule elected officials and decide budgets, taxes, laws, and amendments to state constitutions directly.[7] Some states, such as California, frequently have more propositions on the ballot than elected offices to be filled.

Americans have become accustomed to the frequency and variety of elections, but observers from other countries are struck by Americans' repeated trips to the polling places. (See International Comparison, page 6.) Noted British analyst Anthony King argues that "American exceptionalism"—the distinctive shape of American democracy when seen from an international perspective—arises not from our culture or from our institutions, as many have argued, but rather from the multitude and frequency of our elections. King observes that

> Americans take the existence of their elections industry for granted. Some like it; some dislike it; most are simply bored by it. But they are all conscious of it, in the same way that they are conscious of Mobil, McDonald's, *Larry King Live,* Oprah Winfrey, the Dallas Cowboys, the Ford Motor Company, and all the other symbols and institutions that go to make up the rich tapestry of American life. In a meaningful sense, America is about the holding of elections.[8]

The Initiative and the Referendum

initiative
Proposed laws or state constitutional amendments placed on the ballot via citizen petition.

referendum
A law or state constitutional amendment that is proposed by a legislature or city council but does not go into effect unless the required majority of voters approve it.

proposition
A shorthand reference to an initiative or a referendum.

INTERNATIONAL COMPARISON

Elections in Other Democracies

In contrast to Americans, many of whom can vote more than a dozen times for scores of candidates and issues in any given four-year period, citizens of other democracies vote for fewer offices and vote less frequently. Consider Great Britain, which elected Tony Blair Prime Minister in 1997 and re-elected him in 2001. In each of these elections, Britons voted for only one person—a candidate for parliament. Between these two elections, Britons voted on only two other occasions, for only two offices—their local councilor and their representative to the European Community. Most of the other European democracies vote more often than Britain does but far less often than does the United States.

The United States even looks peculiar when compared to our North American neighbors. In Mexico a presidential election is held every six years. Congressional elections are held every three years. Some Mexican states hold state and municipal elections at the same time as congressional elections, and others hold them at a different time. But at most a Mexican citizen votes four times in a four-year period: in presidential, congressional, state, and municipal elections.

In Canada, too, provincial and municipal elections may or may not be coordinated with national elections. If the elections are not so coordinated, a Canadian votes at most three times (national, provincial, and municipal) in a four-year period, except for an occasional referendum, such as Québec's vote on secession in 1995. Canadian officials are well aware of the contrast between the two systems. Former Prime Minister Jean Chrétien ruffled some American feathers when he commented that "In your system, you guys campaign for 24 hours [a day] every [day for] two years. You know, politics is one thing, but we have to run a government."[a]

[a]David Shribman, "In Canada, the Lean Season," *Boston Globe,* May 23, 1997: p. A3.

Government and Politics

Ironically, although Americans choose hundreds of thousands of their public officials in elections, and although they use initiatives and referenda to make specific policy decisions, many Americans are frustrated by government. As illustrated in Figure 1.1, despite an increase in confidence in recent years, Americans do not trust government as much as they did in the early 1960s. Citizens believe that government costs too much, delivers too little, and wastes their tax dollars. They think politics is needlessly contentious and often corrupt. Many are unenthusiastic about major-party presidential candidates like George Bush and John Kerry and yearn for new leaders like former POW John McCain or actor Arnold Schwarzenegger. Many are suspicious about the established TV networks and major newspapers and turn to alternative information providers such as talk show hosts and cable television comics. Many are frustrated with existing political processes and support radical reforms such as constitutional amendments to limit the number of terms elected officials may serve.[9]

To some extent, suspicion of government is healthy. By their very nature, governments threaten human liberty. The great German sociologist Max Weber defined **government** as the institution in society holding a "monopoly of the legitimate use of physical force."[10] Government is the only institution that *legally* can appropriate people's property (by taxing them and by invoking eminent domain), restrict their movements (by imprisoning them), and even take their lives (by executing them). As George Washington put it a century before Weber, "Government is not reason, it is not eloquence—it is force."[11]

Because government has the power to coerce, people have good reasons to distrust and fear it. Those who participate in politics generally do so because they want to see

government
The institution in society that has a "monopoly of the legitimate use of physical force."

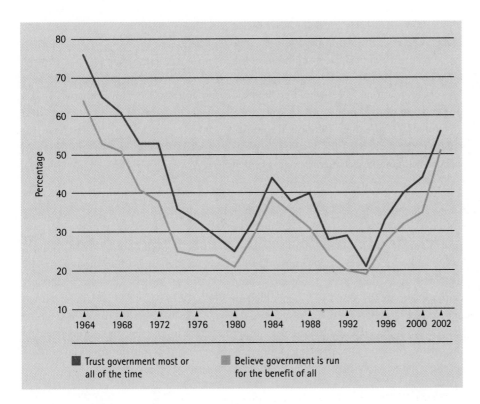

FIGURE 1.1

Americans Are More Skeptical of the National Government than in the early 1960s

Note: Data on the 1986 responses to the second question do not exist.

SOURCE: The American National Election Studies, University of Michigan.

the powers of government used for some particular purpose. At times the purposes are noble, as when Abraham Lincoln drafted soldiers to fight to save the Union. At times the purposes are less honorable, as when Richard Nixon tried to use the Internal Revenue Service to punish his political critics. Most of the time, the purposes are mixed. John Kerry offers a good example. No one would deny that he entered politics partly to satisfy his personal ambitions, which had been on display since high school.[12] But only his most bitter enemies would deny that he also hoped his leadership could improve the nation.

Because governmental power is fearsome and the motives of those who use it are mixed, citizens understandably do not trust it. Why, then, do we have governments at all? Do we really need them? When campaigning for president, Jimmy Carter professed that "All I want is . . . to have a nation with a government that is as good and honest and decent and competent and compassionate and as filled with love as are the American people."[13] These are admirable sentiments, but with all due respect to the former president, government is necessary precisely because such qualities are often missing from human behavior. As another former president, James Madison, put it earlier, "If men were angels, no government would be necessary."[14]

Governments are designed less for the times when people agree—when they are decent and compassionate and filled with love—than for the times when they disagree. No matter who you are, what you believe, what you want, or how you behave, it is an unfortunate fact of life that some of your fellow citizens dislike you for exactly that reason. People can settle their disagreements and rise above enmity through peaceful

One Man's Good Government
When campaigning for president, Jimmy Carter said, "All I want is . . . to have a nation with a government that is as good . . . as are the American people."
• *How good would such a government be?*

political means, or they can kill each other, as Americans did in the Civil War and as so many peoples of the world have done before and since.

The great political theorist Thomas Hobbes made the most basic case for government and politics. A world without government, he said, would be nothing less than "a war of all against all." Life would be "nasty, brutish and short."[15] Government is not a perfect solution to human conflicts, so citizens *should* be suspicious of its powers. But government is the best solution for human conflicts that human beings have yet contrived, and civilized life is unimaginable without it. Of course, that still leaves an important question: What *kind* of government?

Types of Government

British author Samuel Johnson once commented that "I would not give half a guinea to live under one form of government rather than another. It is of no moment to the happiness of an individual."[16] Johnson's comment is silly—at best. Lives can be terribly damaged or greatly improved, depending on the type of government under which people live. Twenty-three centuries ago, Aristotle classified governments into three general types: government by one person, government by the few, and government by the many. Although others have proposed more complex classifications, Aristotle's simple scheme remains a useful place to begin our study of government.

Government by One Person

Historically, pharaohs, emperors, kings, tsars, and other monarchs ruled by hereditary right or religious appointment (although, like modern dictators, they usually needed the support of an army or police force as well). The quality of government by a single ruler depends on who is in charge. The ruler can put the welfare of the people first, last, or anywhere in between. But placing the coercive power of government in the hands of one person requires unlimited trust in that person, and no one is so deserving. As another political theorist, Lord Acton, observed, "power tends to corrupt and absolute power corrupts absolutely." In the twentieth century alone, millions of people died at the hands of rulers who gained near-absolute power—tyrants such as Germany's Hitler, the Soviet Union's Stalin, China's Mao, and Cambodia's Pol Pot.

Government by the Few

aristocracy
Government by a few leaders made eligible by birthright.

oligarchy
Government by a few who gain office by means of wealth, military power, or membership in a single political party.

Government by the few is called **aristocracy** if leaders are chosen by birth or **oligarchy** if leaders are chosen on the basis of wealth, military power, or membership in a political party. Aristocracies ruled many countries in the past, but in the modern world birthright no longer seems an acceptable justification for ruling over others. Oligarchies still exist, however. The most important one governs China, where a small group of Communist party leaders has remained in power since 1946. Oligarchies have some advantages over dictatorships; to a limited extent, members of the oligarchy can check and balance each other. But here, too, power tends to corrupt, as the few take advantage of their position to acquire wealth at the expense of the rest of society.

Government by the Many

Government in which all citizens share power is called **democracy.** The word derives from the Greek word *demos,* which means "people." In its purest form, **direct democracy,** all citizens participate directly in making government decisions. In Aristotle's time, direct democracy was practical because citizenship was limited to free adult men with property, who in many Greek cities numbered no more than a few thousand. Direct democracy still exists in a few small New England towns where community decisions are made at town meetings in which all residents can participate.

Direct democracy is not practical in large countries such as the United States. Even with such modern communications as cable television, fax, e-mail, and the Internet, every citizen cannot participate in every governmental decision. People would have to spend their entire lives attending meetings, deliberating, and voting in order to decide all the questions that come up.

Because direct democracy is impractical in the modern world, government by the many generally takes the form of **representative democracy,** an *indirect* form of democracy in which citizens choose *representatives* who decide what government does. Free elections are the key feature of representative democracy, as its opponents well understand. Soviet dictator Joseph Stalin once commented, "The disadvantage of free elections is that you can never be sure who is going to win them."[17]

Although they generally agree on the importance of free elections, political theorists disagree about many other aspects of representative democracy.[18] As shown in Table 1.1, most of the arguments can be summarized by distinguishing between two general types or models of representative democracy, the popular model and the responsible model.

In the popular model of democracy, citizens take an active role in government. Popular democracy strives to be as open and responsive as representative democracy can be. Elections express the *popular will,* thus providing elected officials with *mandates*—instructions from the voters to adopt specific policies. In order for elections to work this way, citizens must be well informed about public issues, and they must engage in **prospective voting.** That is, they must look to the future while voting, taking into account each candidate's campaign promises. Each election becomes an occasion to decide the direction of public policies.

Those who favor the popular model say that democracy is more than a mechanical process for producing outcomes; it is also an educational forum in which individuals become better citizens by participating in democratic deliberation. Through participation, the public can reach consensus and make better decisions. Thus, popular democracy is expected to produce both better citizens and better policies. The process of participation transforms "private into public," "conflict into cooperation."[19]

Critics say that popular democracies are inefficient and can even be dangerous if uninformed citizens vote for poor public policies. These critics favor instead the responsible model of democracy, in which citizens play a more passive role. Citizens choose public officials but do not tell them what to do. Elected officials have the responsibility to govern and must answer to the people for the decisions they make. In this model, elections are occasions on which citizens grant or deny *popular consent* rather than grant or deny popular mandates. According to the responsible model, citizens need

Government by One Person
Pol Pot murdered millions of his fellow Cambodians—all in the name of progress.

democracy
System in which governmental power is widely shared among the citizens, usually through free and open elections.

direct democracy
Type of democracy in which ordinary people are the government, making all the laws themselves.

representative democracy
An indirect form of democracy in which the people choose representatives who determine what government does.

prospective voting
Voting on the basis of a candidate's policy promises for the future.

TABLE 1.1

TWO MODELS OF DEMOCRACY

The Popular Model	The Responsible Model
Elections determine policies.	Elections determine leaders.
Citizens vote prospectively.	Citizens vote retrospectively.
Direct democracy is preferred.	Representative democracy is preferred.
Popular participation is necessary for effective democracy.	Clear accountability of leaders is necessary for effective democracy.
Democratic politics should advance the civic education of citizens.	Democratic politics should produce effective governance.

retrospective voting
Voting on the basis of the past performance of the incumbent politician.

not be particularly well informed because they engage in **retrospective voting,** looking more to the past than to the future. In other words, they decide whether incumbents have done a good or a bad job. If the voters approve, they reelect incumbents; if the voters disapprove, they vote in a new group of leaders.

Critics of the responsible model say that it is hardly democracy at all.[20] In fact, critics sometimes refer to the responsible model as "elitist democracy" because elites—those who hold office, manage the parties, and lead the interest groups—dominate the political process. Those who favor the responsible model concede that it gives ordinary citizens a modest role—but they claim that direct popular participation in government is unnecessary, or even harmful, because people often are poorly informed.

Popular and Responsible Democracy in the United States

In the real world, of course, pure types do not exist; every real-world democracy has both popular and responsible features. Yet democracies differ in the degree to which they tend toward one or the other model. Britain, for example, more closely resembles the responsible model. British voters elect members of Parliament, but in the normal five-year period between elections, the governing party has great freedom to undertake independent action—including fairly radical action such as nationalizing or denationalizing entire industries, or going to war.

The United States has always been a more popular democracy than its European counterparts. When the French scholar Alexis de Tocqueville visited the United States during the 1830s, he was astounded by the extent of popular participation. "It must be seen to be believed," he exclaimed to his fellow French citizens. "No sooner do you set foot on American ground than you are stunned by a kind of tumult. . . . Almost the only pleasure an American knows is to take part in the government and discuss its measures."[21]

From the earliest days of the republic, the principles of popular democracy were an important part of American politics. "Where annual elections end, there slavery begins," said the second president, John Adams, arguing that citizens must have frequent opportunities to instruct and judge their representatives.[22] The third president, Thomas Jefferson, wanted to "divide the country into wards," so that "free men could control their own political destinies."[23]

The framers believed that rules written down on paper, which they called parchment barriers, were no guarantee of good government. Words alone would not prevent elected officials from abusing power, especially if unscrupulous officeholders were backed by a majority of voters. The framers thought that tyranny could best be prevented by "buttressing" constitutional rules with something firmer: a system of checks and balances that divided power among different representatives chosen in different elections.[24] Each national office was assigned a separate **constituency**—a set of people entitled to vote for the holder of that office—and office holders were to be chosen by these different constituencies at different times. In this way, the framers constructed a responsible democracy, even while including many popular features. Leaders have the interest and capacity to resist both popular passions and attempts by would-be tyrants to seize power.

constituency
Those legally entitled to vote for a public official.

The New American Democracy

When the Constitution was adopted, a small proportion of Americans had the right to participate in politics, but American politics has evolved in the direction of greater popular participation. Over the course of two centuries, more and more of the population have gained full rights of citizenship, the connection between representatives and the public has become increasingly direct, national institutions have become more open to popular influence, and the number and frequency of elections (coupled with the more extensive campaigning that accompanies them) have increased. These trends have accelerated dramatically in recent decades—to the extent that it is no exaggeration to title this book *The New American Democracy*.

The Permanent Campaign

The new American democracy is marked by a **permanent campaign.**[25] On the surface, this term means that campaigning literally never ends: The next election campaign begins as soon as the last one has finished, if not before. The dust from the 2002 elections had barely settled before discussion turned to which party would win control of the Senate in 2004. And even before the 2004 presidential campaign had run its course, pundits were speculating about who would run for president in 2008.

permanent campaign
Condition that prevails when the next election campaign begins as soon as the last has ended and the line between electioneering and governing has disappeared.

The deeper meaning of the term *permanent campaign* is that the line between campaigning and governing has disappeared. To some extent governing becomes a part of the campaign; in effect, it is a campaign strategy. Every action undertaken—or not undertaken—by the 108th Congress (2003–2004) was viewed as a potential issue in the upcoming presidential campaign. At its worst, the permanent campaign can be harmful. According to Professor Hugh Heclo, campaign values corrupt the governmental process: Public officials sacrifice the long-term good for short-term electoral advantage, they adopt adversarial rather than collaborative mindsets, and they abandon deliberation and education in favor of persuasion and selling.[26] Nevertheless, officials who are constantly concerned with pleasing voters are relatively likely to be responsive ones.

At least seven developments have contributed to the permanent campaign: the separation of election days, the decay of party organizations, the spread of primary elections, advances in mass communications, the explosion of interest groups, the proliferation of polling, and the increasing need for money (see Table 1.2). Together these factors have moved American democracy in a significantly more popular direction.

TABLE 1.2

SEVEN KEY DEVELOPMENTS HAVE CONTRIBUTED TO THE PERMANENT CAMPAIGN

Development	Effect
Separate election days for federal, state, and local elections	Increased number of elections, shortened time between elections
Spread of primary elections	Increased number of elections, shortened time between elections
Decay of traditional party organizations	Candidates must build individualized, personal campaign organizations almost from scratch
Rise of mass communication	Candidates may communicate directly with voters, but their mistakes are easily publicized
Profusion of interest groups	Elected officials constantly being watched and mistakes quickly publicized
Proliferation of polls	Provide constant feedback about potential election outcomes
Role of campaign money	Elected officials must spend more time fundraising

Separation of Elections   Imagine that all public officials were elected on the same day and served the same four-year term of office. There would be a long span of time between electoral contests during which no one had to think much about campaigning. Most other democracies are closer to this hypothetical scenario than to the electoral chaos that exists in the United States.

A century ago, American officials usually *were* elected on the same day. A graduate student named Woodrow Wilson wrote in 1885 that "This is preeminently a country of frequent elections, and few states care to increase the frequency by separating elections of state from elections of national functionaries."[27] In Wilson's time, citizens of most states cast votes simultaneously for president, senator, representative, governor, mayor, state representative and state senator, city council, and so forth. In a few states today, voters still fill most offices on the same day, but the trend in the past half century has been to separate election days.[28] Most Americans now turn out to vote for president at one general election, for governor at another, and for mayor at another still. Primary elections, as well as those for local offices, are held earlier in the election year. Initiatives and referenda may be scheduled on yet other occasions.

Thus, Americans today are called to the polls repeatedly. Rather than our imaginary election day held every four years, a conscientious citizen in California, for example, generally has to go to the polls on 16 separate occasions in each four-year presidential election cycle. As election dates have proliferated, electioneering has become a pervasive feature of American politics. There is some campaign going on somewhere, nearly all the time. There is very little "quiet time" during which there are no campaigns.

Decay of Party Organizations   Many political scientists think political parties are essential to the workings of representative democracy. Although we cannot always detect clear differences between Republicans and Democrats, the two parties give voters a choice by offering different political philosophies. The Republican Party leans in

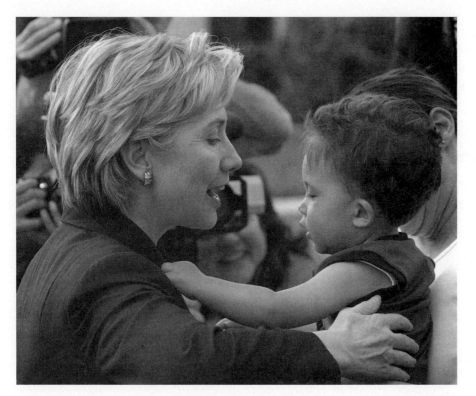

a conservative direction, generally favoring smaller government, lower taxes, less regulation of business activity, and greater support for traditional family values. The Democratic Party leans in a liberal direction, usually favoring a strong federal government, more extensive social programs, more regulation, and legal accommodation for alternative lifestyles. Because party positions on issues shift only gradually, parties give continuity and familiarity to political life, making it easier for voters to make choices.

A century ago, many state and local party organizations were powerful, disciplined structures that could mobilize large numbers of voters on election day. Public officials relied on the parties to conduct their campaigns when election time rolled around. But governmental reforms and various social changes killed off these types of organizations (see Chapter 8). As a consequence, today's parties do not deliver the vote for all the candidates running under their label. Instead, elected officials must build individual organizations and develop *personal* constituencies to achieve election and reelection.[29] Such personalized support is less reliable than the partisan support shared by numerous candidates in earlier eras.[30] Thus, incumbents today must constantly campaign to maintain their base of electoral support.

Spread of Primaries   In most countries, small groups of party leaders select candidates for office. A century ago this was the standard procedure in the United States as well. Candidates were picked in "smoke-filled rooms" by party "bosses." To eliminate the corruption that often accompanied such deal making, reformers passed laws giving voters the right to select party nominees in primary elections.

Although they came into being about a century ago, primaries did not become a significant part of the presidential nominating process until after World War II. The first presidential candidate who owed his nomination in any significant degree to winning primaries was Dwight D. Eisenhower, elected in 1952. As late as 1968, the Democratic nominee, Hubert Humphrey, did not enter a single primary.

Primaries contribute substantially to today's permanent campaign. While in 1968, fewer than 20 states held presidential primaries, now the number is over 40. Primaries shorten the time between one election and the next. Behind-the-scenes planning for the presidential election of 2004 began in 2001, and the campaign was well under way by mid-2003, more than six months before the primaries began and only two and a half years into George W. Bush's term. Nor is the permanent campaign limited to the campaign for the White House. Some members of the House of Representatives face primaries more than six months before their two-year terms end. On April 9, 1996, for example, a Texas Republican was defeated in a primary, scarcely 15 months after he had taken the oath of office.

Major Technological Innovations that Have Changed the Political Environment

Rise of Mass Communications   Technological progress also has helped to make campaigns continuous. Today's candidates constantly work to get their names in the papers and their faces on television. Moreover, cheap phone rates, fax, and e-mail give more opportunities for citizens and politicians to talk to each other. Dozens of cable television channels enable candidates to communicate with small, specialized audiences. C-SPAN provides continuous coverage of congressional debates, giving people outside Washington a chance to observe public officials directly. Radio talk shows have increased in popularity. Candidate and interest-group Web sites have proliferated. Conversation on the Internet, although often conspiratorial and inaccurate, is perhaps the fastest-growing mode of political communication.

The effects of technological change have been intensified by changes in the culture of the mass media. The demand for content has been greatly increased by 24-hour news services. Any move a politician makes might end up on television, and virtually every move a prominent politician makes is now evaluated for its political motivations and its electoral implications. Partly as a consequence of the media's insatiable appetite for news, the distinction between public and private life has eroded. The financial and medical histories of elected officials are treated as public knowledge, and reporters ask candidates almost any question imaginable, no matter how tasteless or unrelated to politics and government. Democratic presidential candidate John Kerry's Vietnam War service came under particularly close scrutiny during the 2004 election, even though he was a decorated war hero. As one communications professor put it, "We like to know the character of a candidate."[31]

Profusion of Interest Groups   The personal organizations that today's candidates construct to support them through the permanent campaign are based in large part on the numerous interest groups that have formed during the past generation. Many of the newer groups are spin-offs of the social movements of the 1960s (the antiwar, civil rights, women's, and environmental movements) which cut across and compete with traditional economic interests. Computer technology has played a role in the formation of other kinds of groups. In the snail-mail era, it was far more difficult for small

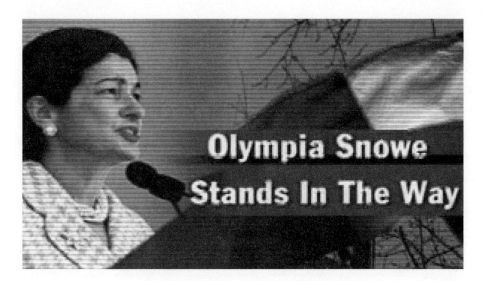

economic interests even to locate each other, let alone to organize. Today, interest groups can monitor the actions of elected officials electronically and then post information on their Web sites or send blanket e-mails to their members.

The most recent development is for interest groups to run critical ads well before a campaign ever begins. For example, a group calling itself the Club For Growth ran a series of advertisements criticizing four moderate Republican senators who seemed poised to vote against president Bush's tax cut proposals in 2003.[32] Two of these senators would not have to face voters formally for another three years, but for them the campaign was already under way.

Proliferation of Polls   Polling contributes to the permanent campaign. When an issue or problem arises, politicians no longer wonder about the state of public opinion—the newspapers and TV channels report it within days or sometimes hours. Even if elected officials wanted to make decisions without thinking about their political implications, it would be difficult to do so: They are bombarded with information about political implications at every turn. As Figure 1.2 shows, the media have made public opinion a much more important part of their coverage both by sponsoring polls and by incessant reporting of polling results.

Leaders always have been concerned about public opinion, of course. In the closing days of the Constitutional Convention in 1787, George Washington proposed a major change in the representational scheme for the House of Representatives so that the new Constitution would stand a better chance of being ratified by the elected state conventions. Abraham Lincoln waited for a military victory before he issued the Emancipation Proclamation abolishing slavery in the Confederate states, so that a happy northern public would be more inclined to support it. Politicians traditionally are portrayed as having their "ear to the ground" and their "finger to the wind." Until the introduction of modern polling in the 1930s, however, beliefs about the state of public opinion were only guesses.

FIGURE 1.2

Today's Media Conduct Their Own Polls

Bars represent the number of questions, mentioning one or both of the major-party presidential candidates, that selected media-sponsored polls asked.

SOURCE: Compiled by authors from Lexis-Nexis database.

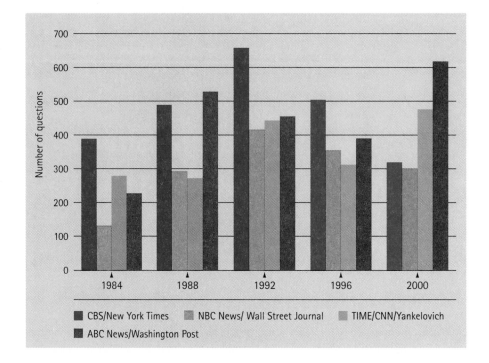

Rising Campaign Costs   Campaigning today is expensive. Polls, political consultants, and TV ads cost a great deal of money. As Figure 1.3 shows, the total costs of election campaigns have increased dramatically in the past three decades. Campaigns for the House of Representatives, for example, were more than three times more expensive in 2002 than in 1976, even after adjusting for inflation.[33]

Although elections may occur only every two, four, or six years, the quest for money is continuous. Nearly all governors serve four-year terms, but current estimates are that incumbents in large states must raise an average of $50,000 *every week of their terms* to fund their campaign for reelection.[34] U.S. senators serve six-year terms, but most contemporary observers believe that the Senate today is just as electorally sensitive as the House.[35] One reason is that Senate races are expensive; on average, senators must raise over $15,000 every week of their six-year terms to run for reelection. Thus, the effect of the six-year term has been partially offset by the constant quest for money.

Minorities and Elections

American democracy may have moved in a popular direction, but majorities do not get their way consistently. Elections by themselves do not guarantee that all citizens exert equal influence on the government. On the contrary, it is easy to show how special-interest groups and other numerical minorities influence elections, and to cite examples of how elected officials sometimes act contrary to popular wishes. The factors that give such minorities an advantage include unequal participation, the nominating process, unequal campaign resources, and misinformed citizens.

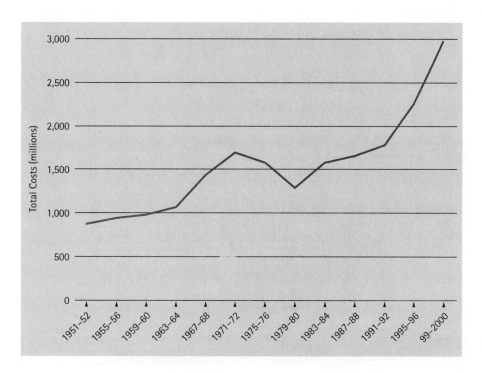

FIGURE 1.3

The Total Costs of American Elections Have Increased Dramatically in the Last Five Decades

Note: All figures have been adjusted for inflation in terms of 2001 CPI constant dollars.

SOURCES: Common Cause, the Center for Responsive Politics; and respective volumes of Herbert E. Alexander, *Financing the 1951–1952* [and 1955–2000 vols.] *Election* (Washington, DC: CQ Press.)

Voter Participation   In nearly all elections, most people do *not* vote (see Chapter 6). Even in the 2004 presidential election, only 59 percent of the adult population voted. Only 36 percent voted in the 2002 congressional elections. Turnout rates in other elections are much lower—even under 10 percent in some local elections!

One vote does not count for much, but collectively the vote is an important political resource. The simple fact is that groups of people who vote at higher rates have more influence. For example, older people vote more frequently than the young or the poor.[36] Not surprisingly, programs for the elderly are much better funded than programs that serve the young and the needy. Turnout is not the only explanation, of course, but elected officials naturally tend to pay greater heed to the demands of frequent voters than to those of people who do not bother to vote.

How to Satisfy Aunt Martha

Nominating Candidates   Although primary elections were intended to enhance popular control, only party members can vote in these elections in many states, and the turnout for primaries everywhere is much lower than for general elections. Those who vote in primaries are usually more involved and more committed than citizens who do not vote. Republican primary voters tend to be more conservative than the typical American, and Democratic primary voters tend to be more liberal. To win primary elections, candidates are therefore tempted to appeal to the more extreme elements of their parties. As a result, elections may give middle-of-the-road Americans a choice between two unappealing candidates.

Campaign Resources   As we have noted, modern campaigns increasingly rely on expensive hired help: consultants, pollsters, and other campaign professionals.

Playing Hooky

In 2004, despite massive get-out–the-vote efforts and higher turnout than usual, people ages 18–29 barely increased their voting rates outside of the swing states.

• *Why don't young people vote?*

single-issue voter
Voter who cares so deeply about some particular issue that a candidate's position on this one issue determines his or her vote.

Higher-level campaigns that rely on TV advertising are especially expensive. Consequently, the first job nearly every candidate faces is raising money.

Only about a quarter of the adult population has ever given to a campaign, and a much smaller percentage regularly gives substantial amounts.[37] Most fund-raising is done by groups who have special political interests they wish to promote. Liberal and conservative groups, economic and environmental groups, women's groups, minority groups, or whatever—all have a perfectly legitimate right to participate in politics. But all have a point of view, usually one that is narrower than the point of view of the typical nonmember.

Moreover, even in today's technologically advanced world, campaigns require workers as well as money. This is particularly true of lower-level campaigns. Volunteers circulate petitions, stuff envelopes, knock on doors, make phone calls, stage rallies and other photo ops, and drive voters to the polls. To attract volunteers, candidates may appeal to **single-issue voters,** people who care so deeply about some particular issue that the candidates' positions on this one issue determines their vote. For example, many members of the National Rifle Association (NRA) are prepared to work against any candidate who supports gun control. Pro-life and pro-choice activists are other familiar examples of single-issue voters. Candidates naturally give greater weight to the intense views of single-issue voters, who make up a large proportion of the activists from whom they recruit campaign workers.

Uninformed or Misinformed Citizens   Most Americans are not highly attentive to politics (see Chapter 5). Politics often seems remote from people's everyday interests

Local Politics
Candidates for local office can rarely afford expensive television advertising. Here, the father of a candidate volunteers his time.

• *Does a lack of media attention (and money to buy attention) mean that such races are unimportant?*

and concerns, and political controversies often are complicated and confusing. Moreover, nearly all of the players in politics present information and arguments that are biased; they are like opposing lawyers trying to win a lawsuit. Even the media exhibit well-known biases, as we discuss in Chapter 9. Thus, there are frequent opportunities to manipulate public opinion and elections.

Majorities and Elections

Although single-issue voters and other kinds of special interests at times wield disproportionate influence, such groups lose much of their clout when a clear majority of the voters take a strong interest in a highly visible subject. For example, Americans hold moderate views on the abortion issue (see Chapter 5). Thus, the Democratic Congresses of 1990–1994 did not pass the "Freedom of Choice Act," strongly supported by pro-choice forces, nor did more recent Republican Congresses adopt a constitutional amendment to outlaw abortion, as pro-life forces urgently sought.

Moreover, majorities have the potential to be powerful even when the public is uninformed about or unaware of an issue. Elected officials realize that the media spotlight might suddenly shine into what seemed to be a dark corner. Additionally, challengers pore over the incumbent's record, searching for unpopular votes cast, positions taken, or statements made. If found, such matters become campaign issues. Most of the time, incumbents think twice before taking actions in back rooms if those actions cannot be defended once the doors are opened.[38]

Thus, elected officials cannot routinely take positions contrary to those of their constituents and expect to escape the wrath of the electorate indefinitely. Because leaders are never sure which issues will become central to election campaigns, they tend to be cautious in handling all of them. Hence, the power of minorities is limited by the potential threat that the majority will become aroused. Ordinarily, majorities rule not so much because they actively articulate their views as they do because public officials anticipate majority opinion long before it asserts itself.

Reform?

The United States pays a price for the pervasiveness of its elections. Continuous electioneering creates a governmental system that is unattractive in many respects. Scandals—real and trumped up—are common; inefficiency and stalemate are widespread; important problems are ignored; and effective actions are delayed or compromised into ineffectiveness.[39]

Even though many citizens understandably are frustrated by American government, we should view proposals for radical reform cautiously. In particular, reforms often call for further movement toward popular democracy—more opportunities for constituencies to influence government, such as more elections (primaries, initiatives and referenda, recalls), more opportunities to exert popular pressure (open public meetings, electronic town halls), or more power for elected officials (oversight of independent boards and commissions). Americans apparently believe, with John Dewey, that "The cure for the ailments of democracy is more democracy."[40]

Such reforms overlook the tremendous popular pressure that political leaders are already under. Indeed, some scholars argue that popular influence on government may be part of the problem, not the solution.[41] Each public official answers to a somewhat different constituency. If all constituencies were similar, representatives would find it easier to reach agreement. But America is a diverse country, and the constituencies of elected officials reflect that diversity. People have conflicting interests and (even more important) conflicting values. Even if hundreds of officials were personally in agreement, which is unlikely, their views of governmental programs and policies often would conflict because they have an **electoral incentive**—the desire to be elected and reelected—that compels them to represent the views of their different constituencies. It is impossible to reach decisions without resolving differences generated by these constituencies. Political leaders must either persuade their opponents or bargain for their support.

Reforms that shift American politics in a still more popular direction may make problems worse rather than solving them. Louder demands from an increasingly diverse public will only make problem solving more elusive. If reformers are to be effective, they must take into account the electoral incentives that public officials face, and either identify reforms that permit negotiation, bargaining, and compromise or actually change the political system so that agreement is easier to reach. All too often, reformers forget that fact and substitute good intentions and rosy scenarios for realistic analysis.

electoral incentive
Desire to obtain or retain elected office.

Benefits of an Electoral Democracy:
A Pretty Good Government

As mentioned earlier, an irony of the new American democracy is that although citizens have more opportunities than ever before to influence their government, they have been growing increasingly unhappy with it. In our view, a significant part of the sour national mood is difficult to justify on the basis of objective conditions. Serious problems and unresolved conflicts obviously exist, but there is more that is right with the United States than political commentators may suggest. Too often, critics apply unrealistic standards of evaluation.

An old maxim states that "the best is the enemy of the good." Any policy or institution falls short when judged against some abstract standard of perfection. Perfection does not exist in the real world, but the wish for perfection in politics makes people unhappy with their government and their leaders. The search for perfection causes harm when people abandon the "pretty good" for something worse. As the great American judge Learned Hand once commented, "even though counting heads is not an ideal way to govern, it is at least better than breaking them."[42]

If American politics and government are so blameworthy, why are the governments of so many new democracies adopting institutions similar to those found in the United States? And why, throughout history and continuing today, have so many people left family and country behind to start over in the United States? Historically, most countries have posted border guards to keep people in; the United States has them to keep people out!

Across the entire sweep of human history, most governments have been controlled by one or a few. Many were tyrannical: A government that did not murder and rob its subjects was about as good a government as people could hope for. Nor are tyrannical governments just a matter of ancient history. Only a bare majority of the world's population today lives under governments that can reasonably be considered democratic, and in the twentieth century, governments caused the deaths of 170 million people, *not including wars*.[43] In recent years Americans have watched in horror as civil war or genocide has erupted in Iraq, Afghanistan, Sudan, Northern Ireland, Cambodia, Azerbaijan, Bosnia, Rwanda, Burundi, Chechnya, Albania, Zaire, Kosovo, East Timor, and Sierra Leone. Official tyranny—and worse—remains a contemporary reality.

To be sure, Americans should not set too low a standard for their political life. No one would seriously argue that Americans should be satisfied just because their country has not dissolved into warring factions. But Americans should have realistic standards for evaluating their political system. Critics selectively cite statistics showing that the United States is worse than Germany in one respect, worse than Japan in another respect, worse than Sweden in some other respect, and so on. But can one conclude with confidence that any other government of a large country works better? Probably not. This judgment should not discourage us from continuing to strive for a better government, but it should remind us that we are striving for levels of achievement never yet attained by real governments responsible for large populations. Only when comparing the United States with other countries do we see that American democracy, for all its faults, has extraordinary strengths as well.

Comparative

Comparing Political
Landscapes

Defenders of democracy often cite Winston Churchill's remark that "democracy is the worst form of government except all those other forms that have been tried."[44] Churchill's observation applies with special force to the new American democracy, which carries this form of government toward its popular extreme. Citizens in the United States enjoy rights and privileges that citizens in other lands only dream of. Not only can American citizens vote more often, but Americans also can speak their minds more freely, find out more easily what their government is doing, and deal with a government less likely to discriminate against them on the basis of race, religion, gender, social status, sexual preference, or anything else.

Citizens of the United States have enjoyed a government that has a better record than most at protecting them against foreign aggression while usually avoiding unwise involvement in foreign conflicts. On average, citizens of the United States are wealthier than citizens of any other comparably large country. They are better housed, better fed, and better clothed. Compared with residents of most other countries, they enjoy better communications, a superior national transportation system, better medical services, and safer working conditions. Their physical environment is more protected against degradation. Even the large fiscal deficits that have caused political controversies since the 1980s compare favorably to the deficits of most other industrial countries. The United States, for all its problems, has as good a government as exists anywhere, and a better one than most.

Of course, the United States is not the best at everything. Economic inequality and poverty rates are higher in the United States than in countries with comparable living standards. More homeless people are visible on our city streets than in other industrialized countries—a sign that the safety net has gaping holes (although it may also be a sign that poor people in the United States move about more freely than the poor of other nations).[45] More people lack access to adequate medical care than in other developed democracies. More people are murdered and more are imprisoned in the United States than in almost any other industrialized country. Just why the United States does poorly at some things and well at others will be considered in the pages that follow.

In coming chapters, we trace the effects of the permanent campaign through the institutions and processes that make up American government, finishing with the policies that government produces. The remainder of Part 1 discusses the Constitution, the federal system, and the underlying cultural predispositions that provide the foundations for the country's political life. Part 2 examines the people, groups, parties, and news media that constitute the elements of electoral politics. Part 3 looks closely at contemporary campaigns and elections. Part 4 turns to the central political institutions: Congress, the presidency, the bureaucracy, and the courts. Part 5 discusses civil liberties and civil rights—not in the standard way, as the foundations of democratic politics, but as rights and privileges that democratic politics regularly changes. Finally, Part 6 treats a broad range of important public policies, domestic and foreign.

Chapter Summary

Elections are a more prominent part of democracy in America than in other countries because there are so many elective offices in the United States, because terms of office generally are shorter, and because Americans select candidates in primaries and vote directly on propositions as well. If free elections are the essence of democracy—of government by the people—as democratic theorists believe, then politics in the United States is indisputably democratic.

American democracy is more open to popular influence today than ever before. It is characterized by a permanent campaign. Changing technologies helped bring this situation about, especially developments in mass communications and public-opinion polling. Institutional changes also contributed, especially the weakening of political parties, the proliferation of primary elections, and the separation of election days. Social changes, such as the explosion of organized interests, also played a role. And the increased need for money has contributed to the permanent campaign. Electoral considerations are never far from the minds of elected officials.

When weighing the costs and benefits of this movement toward a more popular democracy, it is not easy to decide which way the balance tips. Pervasive elections and electioneering change the way the government does business: It is more difficult to plan for the long run, and it seems harder to find acceptable compromises. Yet the advantages of more widespread participation are clear as well. The needs of once-excluded groups now are given at least some consideration. Citizens' concerns quickly become public issues. Imperfect as they are, American political institutions are still the envy of much of the world.

Key Terms

aristocracy, p. 8
constituency, p. 11
democracy, p. 9
direct democracy, p. 9
electoral incentive, p. 20
general election, p. 4

government, p. 6
initiative, p. 5
oligarchy, p. 8
permanent campaign, p. 11
primary election, p. 4
proposition, p. 5

prospective voting, p. 9
recall election, p. 4
referendum, p. 5
representative democracy, p. 9
retrospective voting, p. 10
single-issue voter, p. 18

Suggested Readings

Of General Interest

Blumenthal, Sidney. *The Permanent Campaign.* New York: Simon & Schuster, 1982. Describes the electioneering side of the new American democracy.

Bok, Derek. *The Trouble With Government.* Cambridge, MA: Harvard University Press, 2001. Comprehensive analysis of the pros and cons of modern government in the U.S.

Downs, Anthony. *An Economic Theory of Democracy.* New York: Harper, 1957. Seminal theoretical discussion of how elections shape the activities of voters, candidates, parties, and interest groups.

King, Anthony. *Running Scared: Why Politicians Spend More Time Campaigning Than Governing.* New York: Free Press, 1996. Provocative study by a British political scientist who shows how elections shape contemporary American politics.

Morone, James A. *The Democratic Wish.* New York: Basic Books, 1990. Brilliant historical analysis that shows how Americans have long tried to cure the ills of democracy by extending citizen participation.

Stanley, Harold, and Richard Niemi. *Vital Statistics on American Politics,* 9th ed. Washington, DC: CQ Press, 2003. Indispensable source of facts and figures about American government and politics.

Focused Studies

Chubb, John, and Paul Peterson, eds. *Can the Government Govern?* Washington, DC: The Brookings Institution, 1989. Collection of essays on problems of governing a democracy that is moving in the popular direction.

Cronin, Thomas. *Direct Democracy: The Politics of Initiative, Referendum, and Recall.* Cambridge, MA: Harvard University Press, 1989. Takes a generally positive view of direct democracy in the United States.

Dahl, Robert. *Who Governs?* New Haven, CT: Yale University Press, 1961. Although it is a study of politics in New Haven, Connecticut, the book shows more generally how elections shape power and influence.

Lowi, Theodore. *The End of Liberalism.* New York: Norton, 1969. Classic study of the way in which special interests have gained power over government.

Schier, Steven E. *By Invitation Only: The Rise of Exclusive Politics in the United States.* Pittsburgh: University of Pittsburgh Press, 2000. Argues that parties, interest groups, and candidates have switched in recent years from broad-based mobilization of voters to targeted "activation" of select portions of the public.

On the Web

The Internet allows citizen activists, interest groups, and government agencies to disseminate more and more political information. Given that elections are the main focus of this textbook, here are four sites that can help citizens make sense of the vast amount of information in elections.

www.dnet.org

www.vote-smart.org

The Democracy Network and Project Votesmart are excellent, nonpartisan resources for learning about federal candidates' positions and records of public service. The Votesmart surveys of candidate positions (NPAT) are particularly helpful for determining where your representatives stand on the issues.

www.fec.gov

The Federal Election Commission is responsible for monitoring federal elections. Its site links to candidate and interest-group financial filings, analysis of recent spending and fund-raising in elections, and descriptions of current campaign-finance law.

www.tray.com

Political Moneyline is a private watchdog organization that links to much the same information as the FEC, though in a somewhat more user-friendly—and opinionated—fashion. It is particularly useful for finding donors to campaigns and how much they donated.

CHAPTER 2

★ ★ ★ ★ ★ ★ ★ ★ ★ ★ ★ ★ ★ ★ ★ ★ ★

Establishing a Constitutional Democracy

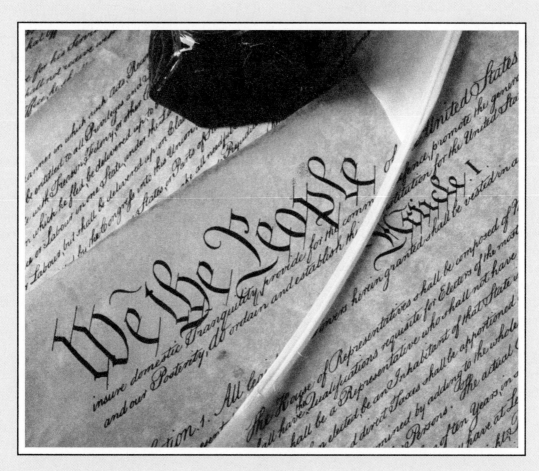

The First National Election

Though the United States Constitution is revered today, many Americans were skeptical of the document when it emerged from the secretive Constitutional Convention in September 1787. Those who supported the new plan were by no means assured of success, and victory was achieved only because they provided strong leadership, mobilized voters, sidestepped obstacles, and crafted powerful arguments in favor of ratifying (approving) the document.

In 1787 and 1788, in what might be called the first U.S. national election, voters chose delegates to ratification conventions in each of the 13 states. If 9 of the 13 states approved the document, its supporters asserted, it would become the law of the land. In newspaper editorials, debates, and public rallies, the **Federalists** (page 27), those who wrote and campaigned for ratification of the Constitution, clashed with opponents, who called themselves **Anti-Federalists** (page 27). Each side argued that its position was in the best interests of the voters.

Anti-Federalists appealed to voters' suspicions about the new system. They claimed that a strong national government would lead to suppression of the rights of states and of individual citizens. In Virginia the eminent American patriot Patrick Henry sounded the alarm. "I conceive the republic to be in extreme danger," he warned. "Here is a revolution as radical as that which separated us from Great Britain . . . [O]ur rights and privileges are endangered, and the sovereignty of the States [shall] be relinquished . . . The rights of conscience, trial by jury, liberty of the press, all pretensions to human rights and privileges, are rendered insecure, if not lost . . . "[1]

Like Henry, many opponents of ratification claimed to represent the interests of average people. Some wrote anonymous pamphlets and editorials under humble pseudonyms such as "A Federal Farmer," "A Son of Liberty," "A Citizen," and "A Countryman."[2] Federalists, while never conceding that the plan was bad for common farmers, appealed to different concerns of the voters, stressing that the new system would resolve costly economic conflicts among states and would enable the United States to negotiate more effectively with foreign countries.

Without a strong union, Alexander Hamilton of New York argued, even as minor an issue as payment of the nation's Revolutionary War debt could lead to disaster. "The citizens of the States interested would clamour, foreign powers would urge for the satisfaction of their just demands; and the peace of the States would be hazarded to the double contingency of external invasion and internal contention."[3]

With energy and organization on their side, the Federalists easily won the first rounds in the ratification struggle. Conventions in four of the smaller states (Delaware, New Jersey, Georgia, and Connecticut) ratified the document by an overwhelming vote within four months of its signing in September 1787.[4] Influenced by elder statesman Ben Franklin's prestige and some strong-arm tactics, Pennsylvania also quickly approved. Massachusetts signed on as well, after Federalists promised to add a Bill of Rights. By the end of 1788, Federalists had persuaded 11 of the 13 states to ratify the Constitution, and Revolutionary War hero George Washington was elected president in February 1789. North Carolina ratified later that year. Rhode Island, which had refused even to send delegates to the Constitutional Convention, finally gave its grudging approval on May 29, 1790 (see Table 2.1).

At the time the Constitution was adopted, the United States was not a modern democracy. For example, only male property owners ("freeholders") could vote in the election of delegates to most ratifying conventions. Yet the provisions in the Constitution had to win the approval of a wide variety of these voters. Those who wrote the Constitution had to be sensitive to regional differences, immediate governmental needs, and inherited political traditions. In this sense, the Constitution was not the product of a secretive meeting of men in Philadelphia but was, rather, the work of all those who voted in the first national election. As James Madison, a key participant in the Constitutional Convention, said years later, "Whatever veneration might be entertained for the body of men who formed our Constitution, . . . it was nothing more than the draft of a plan, nothing but a dead letter, until life and validity were breathed into it by the voice of the people, speaking through the several State Conventions."[5]

MAKING THE CONNECTION

The Constitutional Convention delegates designed the **Constitution,** the basic governing document of the United States, to appeal to the particular voters asked to select representatives who ratified it. Given this focus, the document had to be based on well-known political theories, on the colonial experience, and on the specific interests of those eligible to vote. In this chapter, we review the circumstances that led to the Constitution's writing and ratification, and answer the following questions:

- What experiences did colonists have with democracy prior to independence?

- What kinds of democratic ideals were spread during the Revolution?

- Why were the Articles of Confederation unsatisfactory as a system of government?

- How did the Constitutional Convention come about, what were the major points of contention there, and what compromises did delegates make?

- What kind of government did the Constitution create, and how well has it withstood the test of time?

- How can the Constitution be changed?

★ ★ ★ ★ ★ ★ ★ ★ ★ ★ ★ ★ ★ ★

The Colonial and Revolutionary Era

When delegates to the state conventions debated the Constitution in 1787, they drew lessons from nearly two centuries of colonial history. Beginning in the 1600s, European settlers had brought with them political theories and methods of governance that later colonists adapted and extended on the basis of their own needs and experiences. In this section, we review the nature of early colonial political systems, discuss how democratic ideals spread before and during the Revolution, and describe the state of political thought at the dawn of U.S. independence.

The Colonial Experience with Democracy

Although the United States would become the world's first large, stable democracy of the modern era, no sign of democracy is to be found in the first British plans for government in America. At the time when Queen Elizabeth encouraged Sir Walter Raleigh to explore America in 1584, British rulers claimed to govern by **divine right,** a doctrine stating that God selects the sovereign for the people. Queen Elizabeth delegated her authority over the Colony of Virginia to Raleigh. But just a few years after the first permanent settlement in Jamestown, Virginia, the colonists forced the formation of a representative assembly. Relations between the settlers and the company that owned Raleigh's charter grew so strained that King James, who had succeeded Elizabeth in 1603, withdrew the charter. Virginia became a **royal colony,** one governed by the king's representative with the assembly's advice.

A small group of religious dissenters, now remembered as the Pilgrims, intended to sail to Virginia in 1620. After their ship, the *Mayflower,* was blown off course and arrived in what today is Provincetown, Massachusetts, the Pilgrims found that they lacked a clear governmental framework. Rejecting the divine right of kings, they

Constitution
Basic governing document of the United States.

Federalists
Those who wrote and campaigned on behalf of ratification of the Constitution.

Anti-Federalists
Those who opposed ratification of the Constitution.

divine right
Doctrine that says God selects the sovereign for the people.

royal colony
Colony governed by the king's representative with the advice of an elected assembly. See *proprietary colony.*

TABLE 2.1

VOTING OF DELEGATES AT CONSTITUTIONAL RATIFYING CONVENTIONS

Article VII of the Constitution provided that "The Ratifications of the Conventions of nine States, shall be sufficient for the Establishment of this Constitution."

• *Why do you think the founders settled on 9 states instead of all 13? Or just 7?*

State	Date	"Yes" Votes/"No" Votes
Delaware	Dec. 7, 1787	30/0
Pennsylvania	Dec. 11, 1787	46-23
New Jersey	Dec. 18, 1787	38-0
Georgia	Jan. 2, 1788	26-0
Connecticut	Jan. 9, 1788	128-40
Massachusetts	Feb. 6, 1788	187-168
Maryland	Apr. 26, 1788	63-11
South Carolina	May 23, 1788	149-73
New Hampshire	June 21, 1788	57-47
Virginia	June 25, 1788	89-79
New York	July 26, 1788	30-27
North Carolina	Nov. 21, 1789	194-77
Rhode Island	May 29, 1790	34-32

SOURCE: Lauren Bahr and Bernard Johnson, eds., *Collier's Encyclopedia,* Vol. 7 (New York: P. F. Collier, 1992), p. 239.

believed that individuals should decide both religious and political matters for themselves. Their first political decision is still revered as the very beginning of the democratic experiment in America. Before leaving the ship, the Pilgrims signed the **Mayflower Compact,** the first document in colonial America in which the people gave their expressed consent to be governed. The Pilgrims promised to "covenant and combine ourselves together into a civil Body Politick, for our better Ordering and Preservation." The principle that government resulted from the people's consent was thus established from the very beginning of colonial settlement.[6]

Governance of the Colonies   As European settlement spread across the eastern shores of the North American continent, so did issues of politics and governance. Many colonies were initially organized as **proprietary colonies,** governed either by a prominent English noble or by a company. Settlements organized by companies, such as the Jamestown colony, were founded almost exclusively for economic gain, including the search for gold. But several of the most successful colonies, like the Pilgrims' settlement in Massachusetts and the Maryland colony established for Catholics by Lord Baltimore, were founded as havens for the practice of particular religious beliefs. The more economically motivated of the proprietary colonies often ran into political difficulties and were eventually reorganized as royal colonies. On the eve of the Revolution, 9 of the 13 had become royal colonies.

In both proprietary and royal colonies, power was divided between the governor and a two-chamber legislature. The **colonial assembly** was the lower legislative chamber elected by male property owners in the colony. The **colonial council** was the

Mayflower Compact
First document in colonial America in which the people gave their expressed consent to be governed.

proprietary colony
Colony governed either by a prominent English noble or by a company. See *royal colony.*

colonial assembly
Lower legislative chamber elected by male property owners in a colony.

colonial council
Upper legislative chamber whose members were appointed by British officials on the recommendation of the governor.

upper legislative chamber appointed by British officials, upon the recommendation of the governor. Governors were appointed by either the proprietor or the king.

Governors could veto any legislation passed by the legislature, but usually, instead of vetoing legislation, they maintained support in the assembly by means of their **patronage** power—the power to hand out jobs and benefits. Governors appointed their political supporters as sheriffs, judges, justices of the peace, militia officers, magistrates, and clerks. In Massachusetts, for example, 71 percent of the members of the 1763 assembly were simultaneously justices of the peace, giving "the Governors vast Influence."[7]

Although the governors' patronage influenced colonial assemblies, the assemblies held the power to levy taxes. They used this key authority to achieve broader influence, often obtaining financial control of the salaries of the governor and his appointed officials.[8] In most cases, the members elected to assemblies were esteemed members of the community. For example, Thomas Jefferson won both public respect and election to the Virginia assembly after persuading his fellow farmers to work together and clear the Rivanna River, making it navigable for their common benefit.[9] As the power of the elected colonial assemblies grew, the colonial councils appointed by the governors lost position and prestige, gradually becoming little more than advisory bodies.

Voting Qualifications   Although the assemblies were gaining control over colonial affairs, they were not democratic in the modern sense of the word. From the very beginning, women, slaves, and indentured servants were excluded from the voting rolls. Even male white voters usually had to meet certain property qualifications: In Virginia they had to own 25 acres and a house. In Maryland and Pennsylvania, voters needed to be worth 50 acres or 40 pounds. And in Connecticut prospective voters not only had to own property, but also had to demonstrate that they were "civil in conversation."[10] By 1750 these and other restrictions denied the vote to as much as one-quarter to one-half of the male population.[11]

Spread of Democratic Ideals During the Revolutionary War

The democratic practices that evolved during the colonial period were reinforced by the struggle for independence.[12] Liberties that the colonists had taken for granted now had to be defended against the fearsome power of the British king. The revolutionary struggle was set in motion with opposition to a tax, swelled into a question of rights and representation, and finally led to a Declaration of Independence cast in language that would shape American politics for centuries to come.

Taxation Without Representation   The revolutionary movement would eventually become a struggle for citizen rights and liberties, but it began as a tax revolt. Because military expenses were rising, the British government decided to ask the colonists to pay the cost of keeping troops in the colonies—troops that were needed to defend against potential attacks by both Indian tribes and French and Spanish soldiers. In 1765 the British government announced its intention to impose a **stamp tax,** which required that people purchase a small stamp to be affixed to pamphlets, playing cards, dice, newspapers, marriage licenses, and other legal documents. To the British, the stamp tax seemed reasonable—after all, colonial taxes were lower than those the British

patronage
Appointment of individuals to public office in exchange for their political support. Widely practiced in the eighteenth and nineteenth centuries and continues to present day.

stamp tax
Passed by Parliament in 1765, it required people in the colonies to purchase a small stamp to be affixed to legal and other documents.

themselves paid. But to the colonists, who had never before paid a direct tax, it was an outrageous imposition by King George III on a free people.

Colonial leaders opposed what they called **taxation without representation,** the levying of taxes by a government in which the people are not represented by their own elected officials. To organize their protest, nine colonies sent delegates to a **Stamp Act Congress** in New York, which became the first political organization that brought together leaders from throughout the colonies.

The Stamp Act Congress gave clear expression to the American demand for representative government. One of its resolutions boldly proclaimed "that the only Representatives of the People of these Colonies are Persons chosen therein by themselves, and that no Taxes . . . can be Constitutionally imposed on them, but by their respective Legislature."[13] In Boston, a group of citizens calling themselves the Sons of Liberty decided to enforce the resolutions of the Stamp Act Congress. They hung in effigy the city's proposed tax collector and then looted his home—and that of the lieutenant governor for good measure. As violence spread throughout the colonies, some tax collectors resigned their positions, others refused to take their places, and colonial assemblies banned the importation of English goods, making homespun clothes fashionable. Patrick Henry, who was one of the more outspoken members of the Virginia assembly, shouted, "Caesar had his Brutus; Charles the First his Cromwell; and George the Third [here the speaker of the assembly cried "Treason!"] may profit by their example. If this be treason, make the most of it." In the face of a tax revolt inspired by rhetoric that compared King George with rulers who were overthrown and killed, the Stamp Act became unenforceable, and within a year Parliament repealed the legislation.[14]

The British ignored the American demands for representation. They also unwisely replaced the stamp tax with a tax on tea, arousing passions even further. Colonists were urged on by such leaders as John Hancock and Samuel Adams, who began calling themselves **Patriots,** a political group defending American liberties against British infringements. In 1773 many Patriots organized the Boston Tea Party, a nighttime foray in which protesters disguised as American Indians dumped chests of tea into the city's harbor. Outraged at such lawlessness, Parliament punished the Bostonians by shutting down democratic institutions in the Massachusetts colony. It withdrew the colony's charter, closed its colonial assembly, banned town meetings, blockaded Boston's harbor, and strengthened the armed garrison stationed in the city.

The Continental Congresses   The Patriots responded by calling, in 1774, the **First Continental Congress,** the first quasi-governmental institution that spoke for nearly all the colonies. Attended by delegates from 12 of the colonies, the Continental Congress issued a statement of rights and called for a boycott of British goods, a measure the Patriots hoped would hurt the British economy. In Massachusetts, Patriots assembled guns and trained volunteers in military exercises.

To put down the rising insurrection, British soldiers marched from Boston harbor on April 19, 1775, in search of weapons hidden in the nearby countryside. Warned by Boston silversmith Paul Revere that British redcoats were approaching, 600 Patriots at Concord fired shots that poet Ralph Waldo Emerson would later write were "heard round the world." Certainly, word of the shots spread rapidly throughout the colonies, even to the Virginia assembly, where Patrick Henry cried, "Give me liberty, or give me

taxation without representation
Levying of taxes by a government in which the people are not represented by their own elected officials.

Stamp Act Congress
A meeting in 1765 of delegates from nine colonies to oppose the Stamp Act; the first political organization that brought leaders from several colonies together for a common purpose.

Patriots
Political group defending colonial American liberties against British infringements.

First Continental Congress
The first quasi-governmental institution that spoke for nearly all the colonies (1774).

death." Delegates from all 13 colonies soon journeyed to Philadelphia to participate in the **Second Continental Congress,** the political authority that, beginning in 1775, directed the struggle for independence. On July 4, 1776, the Continental Congress issued a **Declaration of Independence,** the document asserting the political independence of the United States of America from Great Britain. For seven long years the Patriots valiantly fought the British soldiers. Many **Tories,** colonists who opposed independence, lost their property and were imprisoned or chased from the colonies; some 80,000 fled to London, Nova Scotia, or the West Indies. In 1783 the British recognized American independence in the Treaty of Paris.

Second Continental Congress
Political authority that directed the struggle for independence beginning in 1775.

Declaration of Independence
Document signed in 1776 declaring the United States to be a country independent of Great Britain.

Tories
Those colonists who opposed independence from Great Britain.

Theory of Rights and Representation

The democratic experiment had officially begun, the new nation having committed itself to government by the people. Americans transformed colonial practice into a political doctrine stating that if governments are to be legitimate, they must be headed by leaders who have been chosen in elections.

No single document better expresses the democratic spirit that animates American politics than the Declaration of Independence. Written mainly by Thomas Jefferson, the document both denounced King George III and expressed the country's commitment to certain democratic principles. The Declaration asserts that God gave people the rights to "life, liberty, and the pursuit of happiness." To preserve those rights, the people form a government. But the people's consent is given on the condition that the ruler must safeguard these inalienable rights. If a ruler violates these rights, the people may and should form a new government. (See Appendix 1 for the full text of the Declaration of Independence.)

The Declaration of Independence "epitomizes and summarizes" a train of political thought that originated in England.[15] By the time of the Revolution, political thinkers who influenced the Patriots had long discarded the notion that kings had a God-given right to rule. In place of divine right stood three principles:

1. Government arises from the consent of the governed.
2. Power should be divided among separate institutions.
3. Citizen rights must be protected.

Each of these principles would shape the writing of the Constitution.

Consent of the Governed   As early as 1651, Thomas Hobbes, England's greatest political theorist, said that kings governed not by divine right but by the consent of the governed. People form a government because without a government, they live in a chaotic state of nature in which there is a "war of all against all." Without a government, everyone must resort to violence simply to avoid being a victim. Life becomes "solitary, poor, nasty, brutish and short." Hobbes argued that only a sovereign king with absolute power can prevent the war of all against all. If power is divided among more than one person, conflict among them becomes inevitable.[16] As a result, people consent to be governed by one all-powerful ruler.

Separation of Powers   Hobbes was ruthlessly logical. Accept his premise that individuals are selfish and shortsighted, and his conclusion that the people readily consent

Leviathan
Thomas Hobbes (1588–1679) thought that humans are by nature warlike and selfish. His treatise *Leviathan* held that the only way to maintain human society was for individuals to consent to rule by a single, all-powerful leader or government.
• *Do you think that people are basically selfish? If so, does democracy function in spite of, or because of, this basic selfishness? How did Locke modify Hobbes's theory?*

separation of powers
A system of government in which different institutions exercise different components of governmental power.

Whigs
Political opposition in eighteenth-century England that developed a theory of rights and representation.

to be ruled by an absolute sovereign seems almost inevitable. But the English, more pragmatic than consistent, shunned Hobbes's uncompromising defense of absolute kingly power. Instead, John Locke's ideas became popular. Writing in 1690, Locke agreed with Hobbes that government arises from the consent of the people, but Locke did not think it was necessary for this power to be concentrated in the hands of one absolute and all-powerful ruler.[17] Instead, Locke argued that governmental power took several different forms, each requiring a different institution. A country's founders should create a **separation of powers,** a system of government in which different institutions exercise the various components of governmental power. Locke thought each institution should be constituted as follows:

1. *Legislative power,* the making of law, to be exercised by an assembly with two chambers, the upper chamber consisting of the aristocracy and the lower chamber chosen by the people.
2. *Executive power,* the enforcement of law, to be exercised by a single person, often a king.

Nearly 60 years after Locke's writings, the French philosopher Charles de Secondat, Baron de Montesquieu, added a third institution:

1. *Judicial power,* the application of law to particular situations, exercised by independent judges.

Great political theorists often come to conclusions that differ very little from existing governmental practice. So it was with Locke, who set forth a theory that closely resembled English government. England had a legislature or parliament consisting of two chambers: the House of Lords (representing the aristocracy) and the House of Commons (representing the people). Executive power was exercised by the king. The House of Lords appointed the judges.

Cynics have said that the English discovered Locke's wisdom before he set it down on paper. More accurately, Locke's genius consisted of making theoretical sense of English practice, giving the English an enlightening way of thinking about a government that had evolved haphazardly over many centuries.

Citizen Rights and Representation   Not long after Locke wrote, British practice changed. Power, instead of being separated among the three branches, was concentrated in a small group of ministers drawn from Parliament but appointed by the king. These ministers, who owed their livelihoods to the monarch, were reluctant to be critical of the king's wishes.[18]

This system provoked intense opposition from a group known as **Whigs,** who attacked it as hopelessly corrupt and developed a counter-theory of citizen rights and representation. To the Whigs, a formal division of powers was not enough to ensure the security of the people. After all, in Great Britain, powers were divided in principle, but concentrated in practice. Instead, Whigs argued, citizens themselves should be given increased power over the government. The most important political thinker among the Whigs was James Harrington. In place of parliamentary control over a large nation, Harrington favored small self-governing republics (small cities governed by virtuous citizen leaders), each of which would protect the freedoms of its own citizens. In place of officeholders beholden to the king, he called for the election of virtuous citizens for short periods of time. In place of an aristocracy of birth, he said ordinary citizens should choose leaders from the most noble among them.[19]

Whig criticism of the British government made sense to many American colonists. The rough equality of colonial America stood in sharp contrast to the court intrigues in London. Colonial leaders thought of themselves as a natural aristocracy distinct from the inherited nobility in Britain. The more Parliament imposed taxes and interfered in colonial affairs, the more apparent became English corruption. The more the English government insisted on the ultimate sovereignty of the king, the more obvious it became to Americans that taxation without representation was illegitimate.

The Whig theory of rights and representation was explained forcefully in *Common Sense,* written by Thomas Paine, a native Englishman who had immigrated to the colonies.[20] The book, which was widely read by colonial Americans in the months before the Declaration of Independence, declared kingship to be "the most bare-faced falsity ever imposed on mankind." Instead of contributing to peace, as Hobbes had claimed, a hereditary monarchy "makes against it." Peaceful government is better achieved by representatives "who . . . have the same concerns at stake" as the people. If elections were frequent, representatives would establish a "common interest with every part of the community."

Still, the Whigs and their American followers were not modern-day democrats. Although they advanced a more participatory doctrine of rights and representation than previous theorists, they were of the opinion that only male property owners had the necessary virtues to be good citizens. Few philosophers took the time to explain why women could not also serve as good citizens. Not everyone was as frank as the philosopher and poet Alexander Pope, who blithely observed that "Most women have no characters at all." But such views were so widespread that English author Mary Wollstonecraft, writing in 1787, the year the Constitution was drafted, was moved to lament, "It would be an endless task to trace the variety of meannesses, cares, and sorrows into which women are plunged by the prevailing opinion that they were created rather to feel than reason."[21]

Only many years later would the theory of rights and representation come to include women, the propertyless, former slaves, and other previously excluded groups.

Government After Independence

Independence had been won, but the hard work of governance lay ahead. The Revolution had united the colonies in one cause, but it remained to be seen whether there was cause enough to keep them united in the absence of the British threat. The new states were slow to reorganize their own governments during the war years, and the loose confederation plan that the Second Continental Congress had assembled remained in place after the Treaty of Paris ended the conflict. But changes were afoot in two arenas. First, participation in government began to broaden. And second, the **Articles of Confederation,** the first basic governing document of the United States and forerunner of the Constitution, proved increasingly unsatisfactory as a governing system for the new nation.

Articles of Confederation
The first (1781–1789) basic governing document of the United States and forerunner to the Constitution.

Broadening Participation

The Patriots in America gave voice to sweeping participatory ideals during the seven years they fought for independence from England. During the war the colonies, now calling themselves "states," constructed governments of their own. For the most part, the 13 new states kept their colonial institutions much as they were, except "with Parliament and the King left out."[22] But the pace of democratization began to accelerate. Eight of the 13 states eased the property qualifications for voters, and 5 lowered them for candidates for the lower house of the state legislature.[23] The percentage of state legislators who had great wealth declined, giving new political opportunities to those from more modest backgrounds. Ten states required that governors be elected annually, and 6 limited the number of terms they could serve.[24]

Some believed that the Whig theory of the rights of man should apply to women. In a letter to her Patriot husband, Abigail Adams proposed giving women their rights and liberties as well: "In the new code of laws . . . I desire you would remember the ladies, and be more generous and favorable to them than your ancestors. . . . If . . . attention is not paid to the ladies we are determined to foment a rebellion, and will not hold ourselves bound by any laws in which we have no voice, or representation." But many of those who espoused Whig theory were unwilling to come to terms with all of its implications. Even Abigail Adams's husband, John, who later became the nation's second president, argued against making any changes in voting qualifications. If changes are made, "there will be no end of it," he said. "Women will demand a vote; lads from twelve to twenty-one will think their rights not enough attended to; and every man, who has not a farthing, will demand an equal voice."[25]

The Articles of Confederation (1781–1789)

The new country needed, above all, a sense of national unity. In one of its more inspired decisions, the Second Continental Congress helped bring the nation together by appointing George Washington, a Virginia plantation owner, as commander of a continental army—even though most soldiers initially came from northern colonies.

Although the Continental Congress was quick to take the needed military steps, reaching constitutional decisions took much longer. The idea of creating a national government was so foreign to the colonial experience that it took the Continental Congress nearly five years after declaring independence to write and win ratification for the country's first constitution, the Articles of Confederation. In the meantime, the Continental Congress did its best to govern by means of its own cumbersome procedures.

Provisions of the Articles Ratified in 1781, the Articles of Confederation amounted, in its own words, to little more than a "firm league of friendship" in which "each state retains its sovereignty, freedom and independence." The Articles granted the Continental Congress only limited powers. Although it could declare war, it could raise an army only by requesting states to muster their forces. Congress could not tax citizens directly; instead, it had to rely on voluntary contributions from the states. The Continental Congress could coin money, but it could not prevent states from also doing so. As a result, the country was flooded with many different currencies. Congress could negotiate tariffs with other countries, but so could each state. Most significant, Congress could not prevent states from interfering with interstate commerce. In fact, states

A League of Friendship
The Articles of Confederation, proposed in 1775, were finally ratified in 1781—eight years before the Constitution. Those eight years were marked by government instability.

• *How does the Constitution differ from the Articles of Confederation?*

imposed trade barriers on one another. New York, for example, taxed New Jersey cabbage and Connecticut firewood.[26]

Members of the Continental Congress were elected annually by state legislatures. Each state, no matter how large or small, was equally represented. On all important issues, a supermajority of 9 states (out of 13) had to agree before action could be taken. Even if this supermajority could agree on a policy, individual states frequently ignored Congress's wishes. This prompted a frustrated Alexander Hamilton to point out that national laws were "in practice . . . mere recommendations which the States observe or disregard at their option."[27]

The Articles of Confederation did not create a system of divided powers along the lines Locke had envisioned. Instead, the Continental Congress wielded all national powers, such as they were. There was no independent executive. A congressional Committee of the States could make decisions between meetings of the Continental Congress, but this was an unwieldy body because each state had representation. Again, 9 of the 13 delegates had to agree before the committee could take action. Judicial functions were left to the states, except that disputes between states were settled by ad hoc panels of judges selected by Congress. The Articles could be amended by Congress only with the approval of all the state legislatures.

Government Under the Articles   The unsatisfactory quality of the Articles became evident almost immediately. Virginia delegate James Madison recognized the need for a new constitution when he found it impossible, as a member of the Continental Congress, to keep states from issuing their own money. Trade among the states was impeded by constant quarrels over the relative worth of the coins of New York, Pennsylvania, and Virginia.

In addition to these trade difficulties, events were making it clear that the Articles had difficulty even keeping the peace. **Shays's Rebellion,** an armed uprising in western Massachusetts in 1786 led by Revolutionary War captain Daniel Shays, was especially disruptive. A group of impoverished, back-country farmers, unable to pay their taxes or mortgages, tried to intimidate the courts into forgiving their debts. Because it took months to suppress the rebellion, many prominent leaders felt that this episode proved that state governments were too weak. Even more embarrassing was an incident in which a group of ex-soldiers from the continental army descended on Congress in 1783, demanding their rightful back pay. Members of the Congress appealed to the State of Pennsylvania for help, but when none was forthcoming, they fled to Princeton College in New Jersey.

Domestic unrest raised serious questions about political stability, but threats from foreign countries were especially disturbing. The British disputed the boundary between its Canadian colonies and the United States. Also, the British navy routinely intercepted American ships and dragooned U.S. sailors into service, claiming that anyone who spoke English must be British unless he could prove otherwise. Spain, in possession of Florida and the lands west of the Mississippi river, claimed large segments of what are today the states of Mississippi and Alabama (see Figure 2.1). Even France, a Revolutionary War ally, blocked U.S. trade with its islands in the West Indies and demanded repayment of money advanced during the Revolution. The Continental Congress found it difficult to resolve these disputes, because it could not prevent individual states from undermining the Congress by engaging in independent negotiations with foreign countries.

Debtors Revolt
Scuffles broke out in western Massachusetts during Shays's Rebellion, when poor farmers and Revolutionary War veterans joined in an uprising.
• *How did this rebellion influence the writing of the Constitution?*

Shays's Rebellion
Uprising in western Massachusetts in 1786 led by Revolutionary War captain Daniel Shays.

FIGURE 2.1

Map of Competing Claims

This map shows only some of the competing claims being made in North America in 1787. Because the British had a superior navy, the United States was, in a sense, surrounded by foreign powers.

• *How did this threat influence the debates over the Constitution?*

SOURCE: Edgar B. Wesley, *Our United States: Its History in Maps* (Chicago: Denoyer-Geppert Co., 1965), p. 37.

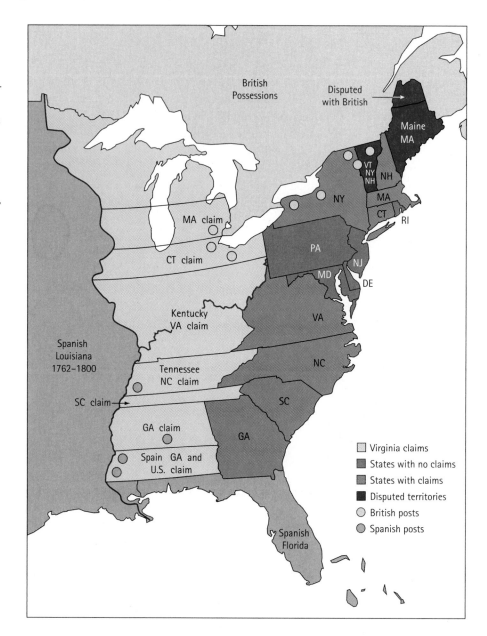

Drafting and Adopting a New Constitution

In light of the fragility of the American government in the 1780s, it is remarkable that the end of that decade produced a document that has, for the most part, remained intact for over 200 years. No less a figure than James Madison pronounced it "a miracle" that agreement on a new constitution was reached at all.[28] In this section we review the key events that led to this agreement and discuss the major components of the Constitution itself. We then turn to the important debates between Federalists and Anti-Federalists that set the stage for ratification.

The Constitutional Convention

None felt the deficiencies in the Articles more keenly than George Washington and James Madison. An avid speculator in land west of the Appalachian Mountains, Washington was frustrated by the inability of the states to work together to build canals and roads that would help develop the country's interior. Madison despaired at Congress's inability to raise money.

Alexander Hamilton, Madison, and other reformers met to discuss needed constitutional reforms in 1786 at what became known as the **Annapolis Convention,** but inasmuch as they represented only five states, they were unable to propose major constitutional changes. Later that year, however, in the aftermath of Shays's Rebellion, Madison persuaded Congress to ask each state legislature to elect delegates to a convention in Philadelphia for the "sole and express purpose of revising the Articles of Confederation."[29] Every state legislature but Rhode Island's agreed to do so. Rhode Islanders were fearful that any revisions in the Articles would reduce the powers of their small state.

For the most part, states sent political leaders who favored major constitutional change; most of those opposed to changing the Articles stayed away. Patrick Henry, when asked to be a delegate, refused, saying he "smelt a rat." True, ten delegates abandoned the convention before the Constitution was completed, and another three refused to sign the document, but the great majority of those in Philadelphia agreed that the national government needed to be strengthened.

The delegates to the Constitutional Convention did not constitute a cross section of the population. The people who met in Philadelphia were bankers, merchants, plantation owners, and speculators in land west of the Appalachians.[30] Yet the delegates had not gone to Philadelphia just to protect the interests of their social class. They believed the country as a whole needed a stronger government that could provide political stability, effectively mediate conflicts among the states, and defend the nation from foreign threats.[31]

Nor were the delegates in agreement on all issues. Chosen by their own state legislature, each had strong political bonds at home, which inevitably led to conflicts among the delegates. Two divisions were paramount. Delegates from big states often found themselves disagreeing with delegates from small states. And delegates from southern slave states opposed those from northern states, whose economies did not depend on slavery.

These differences were less apparent during the opening weeks of the convention, when a spirit of unity and reform filled the Philadelphia hall. But as the four-month convention progressed, differences among the delegates caused the convention to pull back from some of the more far-reaching proposals for reform in favor of compromises that would produce a document that could be ratified.[32]

The Virginia Plan   Three general decisions were made at the very beginning of the convention:

- Hold discussions behind closed doors. If debates were held in public, disagreements could be exploited by Anti-Federalists.
- Write an entirely new constitution instead of simply following Congress's instruction to suggest amendments to the Articles of Confederation.
- Use the **Virginia Plan** as the basis for initial discussions.

Annapolis Convention
1786 meeting to discuss constitutional reform.

Virginia Plan
Constitutional proposal supported by convention delegates from large states.

The Virginia Plan, which would win the support of most delegates from the larger states, had been prepared by Madison (with Washington's active involvement) prior to the gathering in Philadelphia. It proposed massive changes in the design and powers of the national government, creating a separation of powers along the lines that Locke had recommended. To win popular support for the new constitution, the Virginia Plan called for ratification by state convention delegates "expressly chosen by the people."[33]

Instead of a single Congress like that of the Articles, Madison proposed two chambers. The lower chamber—the future House of Representatives—would be elected by the voters. The upper chamber—the future Senate—would be nominated by state legislatures and elected by the lower house.

The Virginia Plan changed representation in Congress dramatically from the pattern that prevailed under the Articles of Confederation. Instead of each state's having one vote, the number of both representatives and senators would depend on a state's population. In short, Virginia, Pennsylvania, and other more populous states would have much more power under this plan than under the Articles.

The Virginia Plan also gave the national government vast powers far beyond those enjoyed by the old Congress. The new Congress could legislate on all matters that affected "the harmony of the United States" and could negate "all laws passed by the several states."[34] It could also use force to ensure that states fulfilled their duties.

According to the Virginia Plan, the weak executive power under the Articles was to be replaced by a president chosen by Congress. A Supreme Court would have the authority to resolve disputes among individuals from different states, something that could not be done under the Articles of Confederation. The Virginia Plan received strong support from two of the most populous states—Virginia and Pennsylvania—as well as from states that expected to grow rapidly in population in the next few years—North Carolina, South Carolina, and Georgia.

The New Jersey Plan   Delegates from smaller states, especially New Jersey and Delaware, were uneasy about the Virginia Plan. About two weeks into the convention, these states offered an alternative design prepared by New Jersey's William Paterson that became known as the **New Jersey Plan,** the small-state proposal for constitutional reform (see Table 2.2).

New Jersey Plan
Small-state proposal for constitutional reform.

The New Jersey Plan also separated powers into three branches, but instead of creating a House and Senate, it kept a one-chamber Congress in which each state had

TABLE 2.2

THE VIRGINIA AND NEW JERSEY PLANS

The differences between the Virginia Plan and the New Jersey Plan illustrate the disagreements between large and small states at the time of the convention.

• *Why were both large and small states willing to accept the Connecticut Compromise?*

Virginia Plan (favored by larger states)	New Jersey Plan (favored by smaller states)
Key Difference	
Each state is represented in proportion to its population.	Every state has the same number of representatives in Congress.
Other Differences	
Congress has general power.	Congress has only limited, defined powers.
Supreme Court settles disputes among individuals.	Judiciary settles only certain disputes (for example, those involving foreigners).

a single vote. It also envisioned a more limited national government. Unlike the Virginia Plan, it did not grant Congress general legislative power. Instead it gave Congress specific powers, including the power to levy taxes on imported goods, the power to compel states to pay their share of taxes, and the power to regulate "trade & commerce with foreign nations" and among the states. The judicial branch could hear only specific types of cases, such as those involving treaties or foreigners.[35]

Despite these limitations, the New Jersey Plan still granted the national government power far in excess of what existed under the Articles. The supporters of the New Jersey Plan were not so much opposed to a stronger government as afraid that the big states would control such a government. As one delegate observed at the time, "Give New Jersey an equal vote, and she will dismiss her scruples, and concur in a National system."[36]

The Connecticut Compromise   The convention nearly collapsed when a majority of the delegates rejected the New Jersey Plan. Representatives from the small states considered walking out of the convention, which would have killed all hope of successful ratification. The large states flirted with the idea of forming their own union and then using economic pressure to force the small states to join. To calm these unsettled waters, Benjamin Franklin proposed beginning each session with prayer, although the idea was rejected on the grounds that no money was available to pay a chaplain.

To temper the debate, the most divisive issues were turned over to a committee controlled by moderates. The committee came back with a split-the-difference compromise offered by delegates from the medium-sized state of Connecticut. Proposing a Congress along the lines we know today, the **Connecticut Compromise** called for a House proportionate to population and a Senate in which all states were represented equally (see Figure 2.2). Small states were placated by their strong representation in the Senate; large states were placated by the requirement that representation in the House of Representatives be proportionate to a state's population.

Connecticut Compromise
Constitutional Convention proposal that created a House proportionate to population and a Senate in which all states were represented equally.

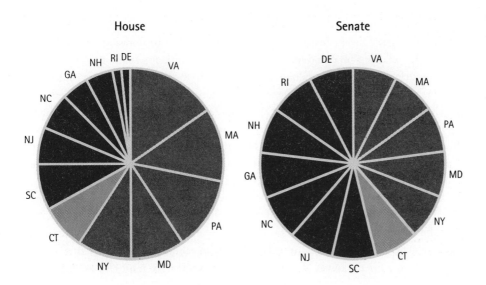

House   Senate

FIGURE 2.2
The Connecticut Compromise
• *On the basis of the pie graphs shown here, why do you think Connecticut was the state that proposed the compromise?*

TABLE 2.3

THE CONSTITUTION AND THE ARTICLES OF CONFEDERATION COMPARED

Many provisions of the Constitution directly address the failures of the Articles of Confederation.
• *Are there problems with the previous system that were not addressed by the Constitution? Why do you think these problems were not addressed?*

Weaknesses of the Articles of Confederation	How They Are Addressed in Constitution
Congress could not levy taxes.	Congress has power to levy taxes (Article I, Section 8).
States could restrict commerce among states.	States cannot regulate commerce without the consent of Congress (Article I, Section 10).
States could issue their own currency.	States are prohibited from coining money (Article I, Section 10).
Executive was not independent of Congress.	An independently elected president holds the executive power (Article II).
There was no national judicial system.	The Supreme Court was created, and Congress was granted the power to establish lower federal courts. (Article III, Section 1).
Amendments to Articles had to have unanimous approval of states.	Large majorities are necessary to amend the Constitution, but there are several different ways to do so (Article V).

A Government of Separated Powers

Once the delegates accepted the Connecticut Compromise, they found it relatively easy to broker other differences between the Virginia and New Jersey Plans. Following the Virginia Plan, they created a government with three branches, legislative, executive, and judicial, dividing powers among them. But in a step consistent with the New Jersey Plan, they limited the powers of all three branches.

Congress   As was called for in the New Jersey Plan, the convention delegates gave Congress a number of specific powers, including the powers to tax, coin money, regulate commerce, declare war, and maintain an army (see Table 2.3). But to address the concerns of the proponents of the Virginia Plan, they included the **necessary and proper clause,** which says that Congress has the power to "make all laws which shall be necessary and proper for carrying into Execution" its other powers. What is the definition of *necessary and proper?* Some delegates thought it meant only what was absolutely essential. Others s thought it meant anything convenient and useful. The phrasing was ambiguous enough that all delegates could interpret the language to their own liking.

The delegates were also influenced by the Whig theory on rights and representation that had proved so powerful during the Revolutionary War. Following Whig theory, the Constitution said that members of the House of Representatives were to be chosen by the voters and were to be subject to reelection every two years. Still, the democracy that was created was more of a responsible than a popular type (see Chapter 1). It departed from the Whig theory by not establishing a limit on the number of terms that a member could serve. The delegates modified Whig theory even further in regard to the Senate. Senators were to be elected not by voters but by state legislatures, and they would serve six-year terms of office.

The delegates settled on a delicate political solution to the question of voter qualifications. They said states could establish their own requirements, except that anyone eligible to vote for the lower chamber of the state legislature must also be allowed to

necessary and proper clause
Says Congress has the power to "make all laws which shall be necessary and proper for carrying into Execution" its other powers.

vote in elections for the House of Representatives. By wording the Constitution in this way, the delegates avoided changing state voting requirements but still guaranteed the vote to everyone already eligible. This open-ended language also permitted the gradual, state-by-state extension of the right to vote to many who were excluded from the electorate in 1787.

The Executive   Some analysts have claimed that many convention delegates secretly harbored a desire to create an executive who had powers comparable to those of a British king.[37] The delegates, however, were too practical to treat such an idea seriously—except for Alexander Hamilton, who actually made a proposal along these lines. They knew that voters would reject out of hand a Constitution that threatened the return of anyone comparable to King George.

Instead, the Constitution keeps presidential power under tight congressional control. The president is made commander in chief of the armed forces, but only Congress can declare war. Presidents can call Congress into session and speak to Congress, but they cannot dismiss Congress or prevent it from meeting. Presidents are given the power to veto legislation, but Congress can override a presidential veto with a two-thirds vote. (See Chapter 13 for a full discussion of how the constitutional system shapes the relationship between Congress and the president.)

Other presidential powers can be exercised only with senatorial **advice and consent**—support for a presidential action by a designated number of senators. For example, the president can sign treaties with foreign countries, but treaties can take effect only if two-thirds of the Senate approves. Also, the president can appoint both judges and executive branch officers, but appointees must be confirmed by a **majority** (50 percent plus one) of the Senate.

The impeachment clause makes clear the president's ultimate dependence on political support from Congress. The House of Representatives can impeach the president for "Treason, Bribery, or other high Crimes and Misdemeanors." If impeached, the president is tried in the Senate. If convicted by a two-thirds vote, the president is removed from office. Although no president has ever been removed in this way, in 1999 Bill Clinton was tried but not convicted, in 1974 Richard Nixon chose to resign in the face of almost certain impeachment and conviction, and in 1868 Andrew Johnson avoided conviction by only one vote.

The Electoral College   Although the Constitution sharply checked presidential power, delegates to the Constitutional Convention still expected the president to be a powerful political figure. As a consequence, they debated at great length on the method of presidential selection. Once again, the dispute divided the big states from the small ones. If the president were chosen by popular vote, big states would prevail because most people lived in big states. If the choice were made by the House of Representatives, big states would once again dominate. If the choice resided in the Senate, the small states would have extra clout.

The delegates finally agreed on a compromise that created the **electoral college**—those electors chosen to cast a direct vote for president by a process determined by each state. The electoral college is part of a complicated two-stage procedure that remains in effect today. The first stage involves selection of the electoral college and gives an advantage to larger states. Each state chooses the same number of electors as it has senators and representatives in Congress. For example, Texas now has 34 electoral

advice and consent
Support for a presidential action by a designated number of senators.

majority
Fifty percent plus one.

electoral college
Those chosen to cast a direct vote for president by a process determined by each state.

votes, because it elects 2 senators and 32 representatives. (In addition, as a result of the passage of the Twenty-Third Amendment, the District of Columbia casts three electoral votes.) If a candidate receives a majority of the electoral votes, that person is elected president.

If no candidate receives a majority in the electoral college, the action moves to the House of Representatives. In this stage, smaller states have an advantage, because each state delegation has a single vote.

The Constitution does not require that the members of the electoral college be chosen by the voters. Instead, the manner of selecting electors was left up to the states. Constitutional silence on this key matter was not an accident. Some delegates thought the president should be elected by the people; others felt this could lead to mob rule. The Constitutional Convention compromised on the question, as it did on so many, by leaving the issue up to the states. Not until 1864 did the last state, South Carolina, give voters the power to vote directly for its electors (though by the 1820s, electors were chosen by the voters in the great majority of states).[38]

Some think the electoral college compromise has proved to be less of a success than the Connecticut Compromise. For example, in four elections (1824, 1876, 1888, and 2000), the candidate who won the most popular votes was not selected president. Some scholars favor eliminating the electoral college altogether, on the theory that the candidate receiving the most popular votes should win the election. Others think that the electoral college, for all its faults, helps to maintain the two-party system and provides representation for both the states and the people.

The Judicial Compromise   Most convention delegates thought the country needed a Supreme Court to adjudicate conflicts between the states. They also found it fairly easy to agree that justices should be nominated for lifetime positions by the president and confirmed by a majority of the Senate.

The delegates differed over whether the Supreme Court needed lower federal courts to assist it. Advocates of the Virginia Plan thought lower federal courts were needed because state courts "cannot be trusted with the administration of the National Laws."[39] Advocates of the New Jersey Plan said the state courts were sufficient and protested that "the people will not bear such innovations" as a national court system.[40] The delegates compromised on the issue by leaving it to Congress to decide whether lower federal courts were needed. The first Congress created a system of lower federal courts, whose essentials remain intact today. The court system is described in Chapter 15.

The delegates also seem to have disagreed on whether the Supreme Court should be given the power of **judicial review,** court authority to declare laws null and void on the grounds that they violate the Constitution. Although Madison's account of the debate over judicial review is sketchy, many delegates, it seems, favored judicial review as a check on the power of state legislatures. Yet there is no record of anyone having risen to its defense when two delegates opposed judicial review. Although scholars have puzzled over the relative silence at the convention about an issue that would loom large in later years, this lack of debate is probably best explained by political expediency. Judicial review had provoked controversy in North Carolina and Rhode Island, and convention delegates avoided the issue because taking a clear position might have jeopardized ratification.

judicial review
Court authority to declare laws null and void on the grounds that they violate the Constitution.

Instead of calling for judicial review, convention delegates inserted into the Constitution an ambiguous phrase that has become known as the **supremacy clause,** which says the Constitution is the "supreme Law of the Land," to which all judges are bound. To some, this phrase simply told state judges to be mindful of the Constitution when interpreting state laws. To others, it gave the Supreme Court the power to declare both state and federal laws unconstitutional. The issue was not settled until 20 years later, when, as we shall see in Chapter 15, the Supreme Court interpreted the supremacy clause as giving the Court the power of judicial review over both federal and state laws.

supremacy clause
Part of the Constitution that says the Constitution is the "supreme Law of the Land," to which all judges are bound.

Compromising on the Issue of Slavery   The delegates never seriously contemplated eliminating slavery under the Constitution, although one delegate contended that it was their moral duty to do so. Many delegates were slave owners themselves, and the convention participants knew that southern states would not ratify the Constitution if it abolished slavery. The debate over the question of slavery took other forms instead. Northerners wanted to end the international slave trade. Most southerners argued that the slave trade, however despicable, was necessary to fuel economic growth in unsettled parts of the South. The two sides compromised by agreeing not to abolish the slave trade for 20 years. Abiding by this provision, Congress waited until 1808 before taking that step.

Northern delegates did not want to count slaves when figuring state representation in the House of Representatives. Southerners thought they should be counted. The two sides came up with the expedient, if disreputable, **three-fifths compromise,** which counted each slave, for purposes of representation, as "three-fifths" of a person. The three-fifths clause identified slaves not as such but as "other persons." Failing to talk about slavery in explicit terms was yet another way of reaching compromise. Not until after the Civil War did the Fourteenth Amendment repeal the three-fifths clause.

three-fifths compromise
Constitutional provision that counted each slave as three-fifths of a person when calculating representation in the House of Representatives; repealed by the Fourteenth Amendment.

North and South also split over tariffs. Northerners wanted to give Congress the right to impose tariffs on imports; southerners were afraid this provision would be used to protect northern manufacturing at southern expense. In exchange for the three-fifths compromise, southerners agreed to let Congress impose tariffs on foreign goods.

The Bill of Rights

The delegates to the Constitutional Convention made one mistake so serious that it nearly ruined their chances of securing ratification: They failed to include within the Constitution clauses that clearly protected the liberties of the people. It is surprising that the delegates to the Philadelphia Convention, who in other respects showed excellent political judgment, made such a serious political miscalculation. Ever since the Revolutionary War, the Whig concept of rights and representation had been part and parcel of American constitutional thinking. Quite apart from the Declaration of Independence, with its ringing endorsement of the "right to life, liberty, and the pursuit of happiness," the Virginia assembly—also in 1776—had passed a Bill of Rights protecting free speech, the right of the propertied to vote, the right to a trial by jury, the right not to be compelled to testify against oneself, and other civil liberties.[41] Similar provisions were approved by statute or were incorporated into the first constitutions adopted by most of the other states. Yet at the Constitutional Convention, when South

Each State a Pillar
At the time of this cartoon's publication, only 11 states had ratified the Constitution. The cartoonist eagerly awaited North Carolina ("Rise it will") and Rhode Island ("The foundation good—it may yet be saved") joining the new Union.

• *Why was Rhode Island the last state to ratify the Constitution?*

Carolina's Charles Pinckney offered a motion to guarantee freedom of the press, a majority voted the proposal down—on the grounds that regulation of speech and press was a state responsibility.[42]

The convention majority may have been technically correct, but they failed to appreciate how powerfully the demand for the protection of civil liberties would resonate with the voters. To win popular acceptance, the Constitution needed to contain an explicit expression of the Whig theory of rights and representation that the country had taken to heart during the Revolutionary War. When it failed to do so, Thomas Jefferson, author of the Declaration of Independence, wrote to Madison from his diplomatic post in Paris, saying that he thought a Bill of Rights needed to be added.

Bill of Rights
The first ten amendments to the Constitution, which protect individual and state rights.

Eventually, the Federalists recognized their mistake. To win ratification in Massachusetts, Virginia, and New York, they promised to enact, as a series of amendments to the Constitution, a **Bill of Rights** that would guarantee civil liberties. Two states, North Carolina and Rhode Island, wanted to make sure the Federalists made good on their promise. Although they probably would have ratified the Constitution at some point simply to avoid becoming isolated, they withheld their approval until after the first Congress fulfilled the Federalist promise to add a Bill of Rights (see Table 2.4). The Bill of Rights, which comprises the first ten amendments to the Constitution, has played such a central role in the country's constitutional development that all of Chapter 16, on civil liberties, is devoted to it.

The Anti-Federalist–Federalist Debate

Although the absence of a Bill of Rights gave Anti-Federalists powerful ammunition for their assault on the Constitution during the ratification campaign, their critique of the document was more broadly based. Drawing on the Whig theory of rights and

TABLE 2.4

KEY CIVIL LIBERTIES PROTECTED BY THE BILL OF RIGHTS

Responding to criticism by Anti-Federalists, proponents of the Constitution agreed to add a Bill of Rights soon after ratification.

• *Why is a Bill of Rights important in a democracy?*

• *What rights can you think of that are not in the Bill of Rights but should be?*

Freedom of speech, press, and assembly (Amendment I)

Free exercise of religion (Amendment I)

Right to bear arms (Amendment II)

Protection against soldiers being quartered in private homes (Amendment III)

Home security against unreasonable searches and seizures (Amendment IV)

Cannot be deprived of life, liberty, or property without due process of law (Amendment V)

Cannot be forced to testify against oneself (Amendment V)

Trial by jury (Amendments VI and VII)

No cruel or unusual punishment (Amendment VIII)

Assurance that people retain other rights not explicitly stated (Amendment IX)

Powers not delegated to national government are retained by states or people (Amendment X)

representation, which valued decentralized, popular government, they attacked the Constitution for laying the groundwork for a national tyranny. They said the shift in power from the states to the national government took power from the people. The number of representatives in Congress was too small to include a wide variety of citizens from all parts of the United States. In essence, presidents could become kings, because they could be reelected again and again for the rest of their lives. The reelection of senators and representatives would create a political aristocracy.[43]

Three Federalists—Alexander Hamilton, James Madison, and John Jay—wrote a series of newspaper columns to answer these Anti-Federalist arguments. Now known as the ***Federalist Papers,*** these essays are generally regarded as the finest essays on American political theory ever written.[44] The authors argued that tyranny could come from either outside or inside the country. The external danger came from European countries, which were eager to divide the new nation so that each section could be controlled. The Constitution would help prevent such divisions by creating a stronger national government that could defend the country.

Threats to liberty could also come from factions inside the country seeking to impose their will on others. The greatest threat to liberty came from a majority faction, because it could so easily impose its will on minorities. There were several ways of preventing majority factions from arising, or, if they did arise, of preventing them from tyrannizing over the rights of others. The authors of the *Federalist Papers* said that the large size of the new nation would help to prevent majority factions from arising because of the "greater variety of parties and interests" that a bigger nation would necessarily include.[45] The Constitution would prevent majority tyranny by creating a system of **checks and balances,** a division of governmental power among separate institutions, giving each institution the power to block the actions of the others. In the

You Are James Madison

Federalist Papers
Essays that were written in support of the Constitution's ratification and have become a classic argument for the American constitutional system.

The American System of Checks and Balances

checks and balances
Constitutional division of power into separate institutions, giving each institution the power to block the actions of the others.

James Madison (1751–1836), left, and Alexander Hamilton (1755–1804), right, the authors of the *Federalist Papers*
• *How did the Federalists respond to the Anti-Federalist claim that the new constitution would produce tyranny?*

first place, power was split between the states and a national government. Then, at the national level, power was divided among three branches: legislative, executive, and judicial. Finally, the legislative branch was divided into two chambers, a Senate and a House of Representatives. Each was elected in a different way, which would make it more difficult for any momentary majority to seize total power.

In retrospect, the Federalists seem to have had the better argument. The Federalists had a plan for the future; the Anti-Federalists had little to offer but the unsatisfactory status quo. When the Anti-Federalists claimed that the Constitution stripped the people of their rights and liberties, they relied on the not very convincing argument that the government of any large nation was likely to trample the liberties of the people. The writers of the *Federalist Papers* analyzed the situation more accurately; by creating a system of checks and balances that divided power into different branches and different levels, and by grounding each level in separate elections, they hoped to ensure that the ambitions of one group of politicians would restrain those of other groups. (See Appendix III and IV for two *Federalist Papers* that explain this argument in more detail: Federalist 10 and Federalist 51.)

Amendments to the Constitution

The delegates to the Constitutional Convention, realizing that the document they were writing was not perfect and that unforeseen circumstances could arise, considered ways in which the Constitution might be amended. Small states wanted to require unanimous consent of state legislatures. Big states felt that a unanimity rule would lead to stagnation and protracted conflict. Southern states were afraid that slavery would be endangered if amendments could be made easily.

To obtain agreement, Convention delegates designed a complicated formula that allowed amendment by any one of four different procedures, as shown in Figure 2.3. The simplest and most frequently used way to amend the Constitution requires a two-thirds vote in both Houses of Congress and then ratification by three-quarters of the

The History of Constitutional Amendments

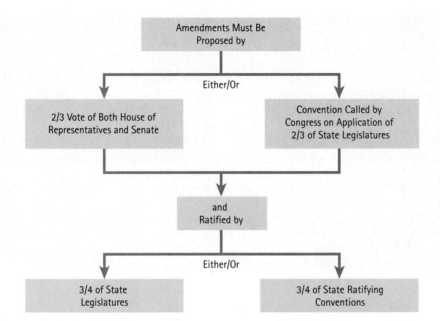

FIGURE 2.3

Amending the Constitution: A Two-Stage Process

• *Why did the founders make the amendment process so complicated?*

state legislatures. Of the 27 amendments to the Constitution, 26 have been enacted by this procedure. On one occasion, the amendment that repealed prohibition, the state legislatures were bypassed in favor of state ratifying conventions attended by delegates chosen by the voters (the same procedure used to ratify the Constitution itself).

Amending the Constitution requires such overwhelming majorities that only 17 amendments have been enacted since ratification of the Bill of Rights—less than one amendment every 12 years. Thousands of amendments have been proposed over the decades, but nearly all have failed to win approval. The hurdles a proposed amendment must jump are so high that even popular amendments that have the endorsement of both political parties are not necessarily approved. For example, many people thought that the Equal Rights Amendment, which said that men and women had "equality of rights under the law," would win approval in the 1970s. The amendment received overwhelming support in both houses of Congress and was quickly ratified by 34 states. But when the proposed amendment became intertwined with abortion and other disputed issues, it failed to win ratification by the final three state legislatures necessary to provide the required three-quarters approval.[46]

The single kind of amendment that seems capable of jumping the several high hurdles needed to achieve adoption is one that extends democratic electoral practices. Despite the complicated procedures that are in place, many amendments since the Bill of Rights have tightened the electoral connection well beyond what was originally envisioned by the Constitution—by broadening the electorate, by extending civil liberties, or by making more direct the connections between leaders and voters. Five amendments specifically extended the suffrage to citizens previously excluded from voting: African Americans, women, young people (ages 18–21), residents of the District of Columbia, and those unwilling or unable to pay a poll tax. Other amendments have

You Are Proposing a Constitutional Amendment

ELECTION CONNECTION

Amendments to the Constitution Have Extended Liberties and Tightened the Election Connection

Amendment	Year Ratified	Provision
XIII	1865	Abolishes slavery.
XIV	1868	Defines "citizens" to include African Americans. Guarantees citizens the right of due process and equal protection before state law. Removes the three-fifths compromise from the Constitution.
XV	1870	Extends suffrage to African Americans.
XVII	1913	Institutes direct election of senators. Up to this point, senators had been selected by state legislatures.
XIX	1920	Extends suffrage to women.
XXII	1951	Imposes two-term limit on presidents, an idea discussed but not implemented by the founders.
XXIII	1961	Extends presidential suffrage to residents of the District of Columbia; grants the District three electoral votes in presidential elections.
XXIV	1964	Abolishes taxes on voting, which had barred many African Americans from the polls.
XXVI	1971	Extends suffrage to 18-year-olds.

corrected procedural deficiencies thought to be inconsistent with democratic practice. (See the accompanying Election Connection.)

The Constitution: An Assessment

The debate over the Constitution did not end with its ratification in 1788. The influential historian Charles Beard wrote in 1913 that the Constitution represented a victory for the propertied classes against the masses of the people.[47] Beard pointed out that wealthy people wrote the document and that only people with property were allowed to vote in the ratification campaign. But modern-day historians Bernard Bailyn and Gordon Wood see it as moving the country toward the ideals of citizen rights and representation that motivated the revolutionary patriots.[48] In their view, the Whig ideals that spurred the war of independence were given practical expression in the Constitution.

A Step Backward?

Both sides of this debate probably overstate their case. The adoption of the Constitution consolidated changes in citizen participation and representation that had already taken place in many states. The adoption of the Constitution did not extend the right to vote, but neither did it further restrict it. The Constitution divided powers that had been lodged in a single representative body under the Articles of Confederation, but each of the new entities—House, Senate, Congress, and the courts—was ultimately grounded in the people. Senators were elected by the legislatures of each state, but the members of each state legislature were chosen in popular elections. Presidents were chosen by electors, but the electors were chosen according to state rules, which since the 1830s have generally called for direct elections by the voters. Judges were appointed for life, but they were selected by the president and confirmed by the Senate. If the U.S. government under the Constitution was a limited, responsible democracy in 1789, a more popular democracy evolved within the framework the Constitution set forth, though it took a Civil War to incorporate all races into the democratic process.

There remains much in the Constitution to criticize. The powers of the Supreme Court are poorly defined. The electoral college, though praised by some for representing both states and people, is thought by others to be a haphazard contraption that has more than once failed to work well. Many important issues are papered over with vague, ambiguous wording.

Certain clauses in the Constitution are especially disturbing to the modern eye. Written by 55 prosperous gentlemen, the document falls far short of expressing contemporary democratic ideals. The Constitution explicitly permitted the slave trade to continue until 1808, even though many delegates thought it an evil practice. Nothing was done to extend voting rights to women, indentured servants, slaves, youths, or those without property. Until the Bill of Rights was added, nothing was said about basic freedoms of speech, religion, and assembly, which are now taken for granted.

But we cannot judge eighteenth-century decisions by twenty-first-century principles. Most of what we see as flaws were written into the Constitution not to frustrate voters but to achieve ratification. Delegates compromised on the issue of slavery because that was the only way to get the support of voters in both northern and southern states. Even when slavery made its way into the Constitution, references to the practice were so vague and oblique that reasonable people could disagree on the Constitution's aim. Famed abolitionist and escaped slave Frederick Douglass even argued that "If that Constitution had dropped down to us from the blue overhanging sky, and we had read its contents, there [is] not a man who could reasonably suppose it was intended to sanction and support the slave system, but on the contrary . . . everything in it was intended to support justice and equality between man and man."[49]

The Constitution says nothing about the right to vote, because every state had its own voting rules. Had the Constitution proposed changing them, the states would have seen such provisions as violations of their sovereignty. The procedures for electing the president were designed to reduce conflicts between large and small states. The one big mistake the convention could most certainly have avoided—neglecting to include a Bill of Rights—was corrected by the first Congress.

If we want to censure the Constitution for its undemocratic features, we must first criticize the limits on suffrage imposed by state voting laws inherited from the colonial period. Historians estimate that only 20 percent of the electorate and 5 percent of the adult population voted.[50] The country was no longer ruled by King George III, but it was hardly a full-fledged democracy. The Constitution was written to win the support of the white, male, property-owning population. That it could do so—and still leave open the possibility for greater democratization in the centuries to come—is to the honor, not the discredit, of those who met in Philadelphia.

Achievements

Although it is easy to disparage the Constitutional Convention for what it failed to achieve, the delegates wrote a document that contributed to the solution of two of the most immediate and pressing problems facing the United States under the problematic Articles of Confederation. First, it created a unified nation capable of defending American sovereignty from foreign threats. True, the United States would fight an unsuccessful war against Britain in 1812. But the Constitution kept the country from disintegrating at a time when Britain, France, and Spain were all looking for a piece of the action in the New World. Instead of falling prey to European ambitions, the United States profited from European divisions by seizing, in 1803, the opportunity to make the Louisiana Purchase, which doubled the size of the country. This land was eventually incorporated into the Union as new member states.

Second, the new Constitution facilitated the country's economic development by outlawing the separate state currencies and state tariffs that had proliferated under the Articles. As a result, trade among states flourished, and the United States grew into an economic powerhouse more rapidly than any had expected.

The Constitution also created a presidency that was first filled by George Washington, the country's most beloved political leader. His great prestige gave the national government the additional strength it needed to overcome the many difficulties the new nation encountered.

The Constitution Today

In addition to solving immediate problems, the Constitution created a framework that facilitated an ever more popular democratic experiment. The document's durable but peaceful division of power, in which one branch can check another, would have surprised Thomas Hobbes, who said that a country could avoid chaos only by vesting power in a sovereign king. If a constitution separates powers into many parts and each part represents a different set of interests, then liberty can be preserved by giving minorities the opportunity to protect themselves from tyrannical majorities. The many compromises at the Constitutional Convention produced this kind of separation of powers that set competing interests against one another. The interests of big states, small states, northerners, southerners, commercial entrepreneurs, farmers, property owners, and debtors were all woven into the constitutional fabric.

In the two centuries that followed, the main lines of conflict have changed. People no longer worry much about divisions between big and small states or differences between commerce and agriculture. The country today has quite different ethnic, gender, cultural, income, and generational issues to resolve. But the Constitution still gives the many different groups and interests clear opportunities to voice their concerns.

Constitutional Ambiguity: A Virtue   The very ambiguities embedded in the Constitution have also been a plus. Written as compromises among conflicting interests, such vague phrases as "necessary and proper" and "supreme Law of the Land" have had the elasticity necessary to accommodate powerful social and political forces that the founders could not have anticipated. Over the centuries, the Supreme Court has interpreted ambiguous constitutional phrases in ways that have allowed the Constitution to

INTERNATIONAL COMPARISON

Constitution Making in Iraq

After the U.S.-led overthrow of Saddam Hussein's government in 2003, Iraqis were faced with the daunting task of setting up a democratic system of government. After a brief period of rule by a U.S. administrator and an appointed 'governing council,' Iraqis set to work in spring 2004 to create a lasting constitution. They came up with a system that was similar in many respects to that of the United States. It included protections of fundamental rights, as well as a federal system of government, for example. Despite superficial similarities between the United States and Iraqi constitutions, however, the situation in Iraq is very different from that which faced the U.S. in its early days. Each of these differences may affect whether the constitution ultimately succeeds or fails.

1. The U.S. Constitution was written by revolutionary leaders who had won the country's independence. In Iraq, a dictatorship was overthrown by an outside power. Some Iraqis also questioned whether exiles who had not been in the country for years should be included in the process of rebuilding the nation.
2. George Washington was revered as a military hero. There is no such consensus choice for a leader in Iraq.
3. In the United States, brief uprisings such as Shays's Rebellion, while alarming, were quickly quelled. In Iraq, an ongoing anti-U.S. insurgency has sought to disrupt the reconstruction efforts.
4. While there were religious and cultural differences in the early United States, the authors of the constitution were willing to compromise on them. In Iraq, religious differences between Sunni and Shiite Muslims, as well as cultural differences between Kurds and other Iraqis, were so intense as to threaten final agreement.
5. In the early United States, women were excluded from politics. In Iraq, women sought guaranteed representation in a new legislature.

• *In light of the experience in Iraq, do you believe that the success of the United States constitution was mostly due to careful planning or mostly due to favorable circumstances?*

SOURCE: Annia Ciezadlo, "Iraqi Women Raise Voices – For Quotas," *Christian Science Monitor*, December 17, 2003, p. 1.

remain relevant to the issues of the day. In subsequent chapters we shall discuss ways in which the compromises of 1787 have been redefined and given new meaning in response to changing political circumstances.

The Constitution's extraordinary adaptability over a prolonged period of time testifies to the framers' stunning accomplishment. Although the United States is often thought of as a relatively new country, its governing arrangements have remained intact for much longer than those in most other countries. Of all the great industrial democracies, only the British system comes close to enjoying basic governing arrangements that date back as far as those of the United States. And even the democratic features of British government are newer than those of the United States. Not until 1867 did most British men get the right to vote.

Most other countries have much newer constitutions. Iraq struggled with drafting a new constitution in 2004 (see the accompanying International Comparison). The latest Russian constitution was adopted in 1993. The current Spanish constitution was approved in 1978, the French constitution dates back only to 1958, the Danish to 1953, and the German, Italian, and Japanese constitutions to the late 1940s.

Comparing Constitutions

The Stain of Slavery Despite everything positive that can be said for the Constitution, the stain of slavery remains indelible. The Constitution validated the slave trade and stated that each slave could be counted as three-fifths of a person. The Constitution also explicitly required free states to return escaped slaves to the place from which they had fled.

Dividing and checking concentrations of power prevented the tyranny of the majority. But it also prevented a majority from undoing the tyranny of slavery. By denying the national government the capacity to bring slavery peacefully to an end, separation of powers helped perpetuate the slave system at a time when the practice was disappearing throughout the rest of the world. Perhaps it is too much to ask of any constitution that it provide the tools for resolving what had become an intractable problem. Perhaps it was, as Abraham Lincoln once said, only providential that "every drop of blood drawn with the lash shall be paid by another drawn with the sword."[51] It is not easy to imagine how the delegates to the Constitutional Convention could have designed a constitution that would have both freed slaves and won ratification by the voters of 1788.

Chapter Summary

The colonists who settled the eastern coast of North America established incomplete but meaningful rules of democracy through such institutions as the Mayflower Compact and elected colonial assemblies. These democratic institutions were reinforced by the spread of philosophical ideals during the Revolutionary War. Of critical importance was the concept that legitimate governments get their power from the consent of the governed. This principle formed the basis for the U.S. Constitution.

The Constitution was written to rectify difficulties the country experienced under the Articles of Confederation. The national government could not raise its own army, levy its own taxes, or regulate commerce among the states. Many leaders believed the country was too weak to fend off potential threats from Britain, Spain, and France.

When drafting a new Constitution designed to address needs unmet by the Articles of Confederation, the delegates to the Constitutional Convention designed a new basic law acceptable to the voters who were asked to ratify it. As a result, they prepared a document built both on their own colonial experience and on political theories popular at the time. They also incorporated many of the ideals expressed during the revolutionary struggle against King George III.

The Constitution curbed the powers of state governments, gave Congress additional authority, created a presidency of limited powers, and established a Supreme Court as the head of the judicial system. By dividing power between the states and the national government and by further dividing the power of the national government among the legislative, executive, and judicial branches, the Constitution provided an enduring system of limited government well designed to protect the liberties of the citizens.

To win ratification of the Constitution by voters in all parts of the country, the delegates to the Constitutional Convention had to reach many compromises. Congress was given not general power but a set of specific powers, along with the capacity to do anything "necessary and proper" to carry out these specific powers. Differences of opinion between delegates from big and small states were resolved by creating a Senate that gave equal representation to all states and a House of Representatives wherein states were represented in proportion to their population. Presidents were selected via a complicated two-stage system, which included a cumbersome electoral college arrangement. The Supreme Court was neither given nor denied the power of judicial review. Differences between the North and South were settled via a compromise: preserving the slave trade for 20 years and counting each slave as three-fifths of a person for purposes of representation.

The convention delegates erred in not including a Bill of Rights in the Constitution. But during the ratification campaign, Anti-Federalists insisted on, and the Federalists finally agreed to, ten amendments to the Constitution that became known as the Bill of Rights. Although the procedures for amending the Constitution are complicated, 17 additional amendments have been approved since the Bill of Rights was drafted, and 13 of these have shifted American democracy in a popular direction.

Key Terms

advice and consent, p. 41

Annapolis Convention, p. 37

Anti-Federalists, p. 27

Articles of Confederation, p. 33

Bill of Rights, p. 44

checks and balances, p. 45

colonial assembly, p. 28

colonial council, p. 28

Connecticut Compromise, p. 39

Constitution, p. 27

Declaration of Independence, p. 31

divine right, p. 27

electoral college, p. 41

Federalist Papers, p. 45

Federalists, p. 27

First Continental Congress, p. 30

judicial review, p. 42

majority, p. 41

Mayflower Compact, p. 28

necessary and proper clause, p. 40

New Jersey Plan, p. 38

Patriots, p. 30

patronage, p. 29

proprietary colony, p. 28

royal colony, p. 27

Second Continental Congress, p. 31

separation of powers, p. 32

Shays's Rebellion, p. 35

Stamp Act Congress, p. 30

stamp tax, p. 29

supremacy clause, p. 43

taxation without representation, p. 30

three-fifths compromise, p. 43

Tories, p. 31

Virginia Plan, p. 37

Whigs, p. 32

Suggested Readings

Of General Interest

Commager, Henry Steele, ed. *Documents of American History.* 6th ed. New York: Appleton-Century-Crofts, 1958. Collection of key primary documents in American history.

The Federalist Papers. New York: New American Library, 1961. Powerful defense of the proposed constitution by Alexander Hamilton, James Madison, and John Jay under the pseudonym Publius.

Morgan, Edmund S., and Helen M. Morgan. *The Stamp Act Crisis: Prologue to Revolution.* Chapel Hill: University of North Carolina Press, 1953. Readable account of key events leading to the revolution.

Rakove, Jack. *Original Meanings: Politics and Ideas in the Making of the Constitution.* New York: Random House, 1996. Pulitzer Prize-winning examination of the ideologies and political factors behind the drafting of the Constitution.

Storing, Herbert J., ed. *The Anti-Federalist.* Chicago: University of Chicago Press, 1986. Selection of Anti-Federalist writings.

Tuchman, Barbara W. *The First Salute: A View of the American Revolution.* New York: Ballantine, 1988. Shows how the struggle for power among European countries affected the outcome of the Revolutionary War.

Focused Studies

Adams, Willi Paul. *The First American Constitutions: Republican Ideology and the Making of the State Constitutions in the Revolutionary Era.* Chapel

Hill: University of North Carolina Press, 1980. Reveals that much of what seems original in the Constitution was already in place in many states.

Bailyn, Bernard. *The Origins of American Politics.* New York: Knopf, 1968. Identifies the sources of the American Revolution in colonial thought and practice.

Beard, Charles A. *An Economic Interpretation of the Constitution of the United States.* New York: Free Press, 1913. Interprets the writing of the Constitution as an effort by the wealthy to protect their property rights.

Elkins, Stanley, and Eric McKitrick. *The Age of Federalism.* New York: Oxford University Press, 1993. Authoritative account of political life during the first decade after the adoption of the Constitution.

Hartz, Louis. *The Liberal Tradition in America.* New York: Harcourt, 1955. A difficult but rewarding book that describes the distinctive quality of the American political tradition.

Roche, John P. "The Founding Fathers: A Reform Caucus in Action." *American Political Science Review* 55 (December 1961): 799–816. Identifies the election connection at the Constitutional Convention.

Wood, Gordon S. *The Radicalism of the American Revolution.* New York: Knopf, 1992. Portrays the unleashing of a democratic ideology during the struggle for independence.

On the Web

In this chapter, we examined the events that led to the drafting of the U.S. Constitution and the political struggles surrounding its ratification.

http://www.archives.gov/national_archives_experience/constitution.html
The text of the Constitution appears in the Appendix, and a high-resolution digital picture of the document itself is available at the National Archives and Records Administration Web site.

www.earlyamerica.com
The early American colonists brought with them traditional European ideas and forms of government. They also developed new ways of thinking by adapting these concepts to their own new world experiences. To learn more about the colonists, visit the Web site.

www.utm.edu/research/iep/l/locke.htm
www.utm.edu/research/iep/h/hobbes.htm
To learn more about one of the major political theories that influenced colonial thought, see the Internet Encyclopedia of Philosophy entries on John Locke and Thomas Hobbes.

www.pbs.org/ktca/liberty/
For a comprehensive account of the Revolutionary War, including time-lines, accounts of battles, and biographies of key figures, see the companion Web site to the PBS "Liberty!" series on the American Revolution.

www.yale.edu/lawweb/avalon/avalon.htm
The Avalon Project at Yale Law School is an excellent resource for major documents in law, history, and diplomacy. For the project home-page, see the Web site.

www.yale.edu/lawweb/avalon/federal/fed.htm
For Avalon's transcription of all 85 *Federalist Papers,* which can be searched by keyword, see the Web site.

http://www.usconstitution.net/constam.html
http://www.usconstitution.net/constamfail.html
As this chapter shows, the Constitution has been repeatedly amended, but this is a difficult and time-consuming process. To view a list of proposed amendments to the Constitution, go to the Web site. You can also go to see a list of amendments that did not make it through the approval process.

CHAPTER 3

* * * * * * * * * * * * * * *

Federalism: Division of Power Among National, State, and Local Governments

School Gun Violence:
A National or a State Problem?

In December 2001, Massachusetts police arrested five high school students on charges that they had conspired to massacre their classmates and teachers at New Bedford High School. According to authorities, the students planned to kill as many as they could and then climb to the school roof to "smoke pot and swill booze," before finally committing suicide.[1] Such a plot, which would have been unheard of only a few years before, seemed all too familiar to Americans. The late 1990s and the early years of the new century saw a series of violent incidents involving children and guns, of which the 1999 shooting spree at Columbine High School in Littleton, Colorado, was only the most deadly. Experts confirmed that multiple shootings at schools were more common than ever and were continuing to increase.[2]

Naturally, many activists turned to Congress for action on the issue of school gun violence, but what many failed to recall was that the national government had already acted: In 1990, Congress passed, and President George H. W. Bush signed, the Gun Free School Zones Act. Enacted in response to public concerns about high crime rates, this law made it a federal crime to carry unauthorized weapons near a public school, but it was declared unconstitutional by the Supreme Court in 1995.

In *U.S. v. Lopez,* a case involving a young man with no criminal record who foolishly brought a .38 caliber handgun to school, the Court said that regardless of the national government's clear intention to do what voters wanted, Congress did not have the power to enact this law. State governments, said the Court, had the authority to regulate this type of activity. "We do not doubt," wrote Chief Justice Rehnquist, "that Congress has authority . . . to regulate numerous commercial activities that . . . affect the educational process. That authority, though broad, does not include the authority to regulate each and every aspect of local schools."[3]

Because of the Court's ruling in this case, the Columbine killers and other perpetrators of school violence committed no *federal* crime when they carried guns onto school grounds. Was Congress wrong to pass such a law? Or did the Supreme Court make a mistake?

Answers to these questions go to the heart of the current debate over the proper division of powers between national and state governments in the U.S. federal system. On one side, supporters of the gun-free school law said Congress had clear authority to prohibit dangerous weapons on school grounds. On the other side, defenders of the powers and rights of the states emphasized that gun toting in school was already against state law; by passing a law on a subject that was a state responsibility, Congress was intruding where it did . . . sure to "do something" to stop school violence.

MAKING THE CONNECTION

The Lopez decision raises many questions. What does the Court mean when it says that some policy areas are beyond the reach of the national government? How is power divided among the national, state, and local governments? What does this division of power—called federalism—mean in practice? In this chapter we consider what federalism means and how its meaning has changed over the course of American history. In doing so, we answer the following questions:

- How is the contemporary debate over federalism related to debates on the topic at the time the Constitution was ratified?

- What did federalism mean prior to the Civil War?

- How did Supreme Court interpretations of federalism change following the Civil War?

- How has Congress influenced the nature of federalism through its power to spend money?

- What roles do state and local governments play in the United States?
- How have electoral forces and political conflicts shaped American federalism?

* * * * * * * * * * * * * * * *

The Federalism Debate: It's New But It's Old

Federalism is defined in terms of **sovereignty**—that is, fundamental governmental authority. **Federalism** divides sovereignty between at least two different levels. In the United States, the fundamental units are the *national government* and the *state governments,* and each has the power to act independently of the other. For a democratic government to be called a federal system, each fundamental level of government must have:

1. Its own set of elected officials;
2. Its own capacity to raise revenues by means of taxation;
3. Independent authority to pass laws regulating the lives of its citizens.

Local governments, such as cities, counties, towns, and school districts, are also important institutions of government in the United States, but *they are not fundamental units in the U.S. federal system* in the same way that the national and state governments are. According to a long-standing legal doctrine known as **Dillon's rule** (after the 19th century Iowa judge John Dillon), local governments are, in legal terms, mere "creatures of the state." A state legislature can, at any time, alter the boundaries of any local government, expand or narrow its power, or abolish it altogether. As a result, local governments are not considered fundamental components of the federal system, as defined by the Constitution. However, they play a major role in the day-to-day practice of federalism.

Federalism in Context

As a principle of government, federalism has had a dubious history. Simón Bolívar, the great fighter for Venezuelan independence, once observed, "Among the popular and representative systems of government, I do not approve of the federal system: It is too perfect; and it requires virtues and political talents much superior to our own."[4] Even today, the vast majority of countries in the world have **unitary governments,** in which all authority is held by a single, national government. In unitary arrangements, local governments are simply administrative outposts of the national government. In Britain, for example, Parliament has the power to abolish all local governments, a power it has often used to redesign the country's municipal and county governments. Even though Britain has granted some powers to local Scottish and Northern Irish parliaments, it could abolish or override these parliaments at any time. (See the accompanying International Comparison.)

Although most countries have unitary forms of government, federalism has long been thought to be ideally suited to U.S. conditions. Federalism was an essential part of the Constitution because the document could not have been ratified had the identity of the existing states not been retained. Federalism also facilitated the admission of new territory to the union, helped government adapt to ethnic and cultural diversity, and helped promote the nation's extraordinary economic development. As early as the

sovereignty
Fundamental governmental authority.

federalism
Division of sovereignty between at least two different levels of government.

Dillon's rule
Legal doctrine that local governments are mere creatures of the state.

unitary government
System under which all authority is held by a single, national government.

INTERNATIONAL COMPARISON

Great Britain and the United States: Unitary and Federal Governments

In Great Britain, which has a unitary government, the national government (Parliament) can reorganize regional and local governments whenever it wishes. In 1998, to put into effect a peace agreement reached between warring factions within the Catholic and Protestant communities in Northern Ireland, the British Parliament reorganized the government of Northern Ireland, granting it an autonomous assembly. Parliament has also created assemblies for Scotland and Wales. But Parliament, if it so desires, can at any time eliminate the regional governments of Wales, Scotland, and Northern Ireland, and it can pass legislation to override their policies. As it is, the new assemblies have power only over such "secondary" policy areas as health, agriculture, education, local government, and economic development. The leader of the Welsh government even joked that policy discussions in the local assembly are seldom more consequential than the debate over the "Sheep and Goats Identification Order of 2001."

In the United States, which has a federal system of government, Congress cannot change the constitutional powers of states, reorganize state government, or change state boundaries without the state's consent.

• *In your view, what are the advantages and disadvantages of a federal system with regard to (1) political accountability, (2) efficient administration, and (3) cultural identity?*

Britain: A Unitary Government
Regional and local boundaries can be changed by the British national government at any time.

SOURCE: Frank Millar, "Broadening Vision of New Wales," *The Irish Times*, May 24, 2001: 16.

Comparing Federal and Unitary Systems

1830s, the keen French observer of American politics Alexis de Tocqueville noted, "One can hardly imagine how much [the] division of sovereignty contributes to the well-being of each of the states that compose the Union. In these small communities . . . all public authority [is] turned toward internal improvements."[5]

Long before federalism had gained international respectability, Americans had reached almost universal agreement on its worth. But the exact distribution of powers between the national and state governments has been a subject of great conflict over the course of the nation's history. Individual protagonists in this debate have often made forceful arguments based on fundamental principles of governance. But the larger political divisions over these issues have reflected the practical consequences of the distribution of power for policy and for elections. Political parties have gradually shifted their positions over time as their bases of electoral strength and their policy concerns have shifted from national to local and back again.

Federalism and the Ratification of the Constitution

THE CONSTITUTION, TENTH AMENDMENT: *"The powers not delegated to the United States by the Constitution, nor prohibited by it to the States, are reserved to the States respectively, or to the people."*

The earliest debate over federalism divided the Federalists and the Anti-Federalists at the time the Constitution was being ratified. The Federalists (some say they should have been called Nationalists) were especially concerned with the military strength and economic vitality of the United States as a whole.[6] They took a position in favor of a strong national government, arguing that centralized power was needed to overcome the rivalries among the states and to defend the nation against foreign powers. The Anti-Federalists included many who were suspicious of the potential threat of national power to the independence of states and localities.[7] They wanted to keep the central government as limited as possible, fearing that a powerful national government would trample the liberties of the people.

The Constitution itself represents a compromise between these competing groups. To appease those who wanted a weak national government, the Constitution denied Congress a general legislative power, instead giving it only specific, delegated powers, such as the powers to levy taxes and regulate interstate commerce. It also gave states independent authority, such as the responsibility for appointing officers in the militia (today known as the National Guard). In addition, it guaranteed existing state boundaries, saying that no state can be stripped of its territory or divided into parts without its consent. The Anti-Federalists also won (as part of the Bill of Rights) the Tenth Amendment, which reserved to the states and to the people all powers not delegated to the federal government.

To satisfy the Federalists, the Constitution gave Congress, in addition to its delegated powers, the authority to undertake all activities "necessary and proper" to carry out its enumerated powers. It also enacted a **supremacy clause** stating that national laws "shall be the supreme Law of the Land . . . any Thing in the . . . Laws of any State to the Contrary notwithstanding," a statement that comes close to saying (yet does not quite say) that only the national government is truly sovereign. Table 3.1 summarizes the allocation of powers between the national and state governments.

The debate over federalism continues today, and the two major political parties hold very different views about how power ought to be distributed. Each political party tends to have a distinctive conception of the best way to organize American government. Although differences between the parties are not always sharp and clear, Republicans tend to think that as many government responsibilities as feasible should be left in the hands of state and local governments. They believe that much that is now paid for by the national government should be delegated to states and localities. These Republicans reason that state and local governments are closer to the people, more in touch with their needs, and less likely to waste taxpayer dollars. Conversely, many Democrats think that such policy areas as pollution control, ensuring educational opportunity, and providing care for the sick and the poor are too big and affect the population too broadly to be settled at state and local levels. They think the national government must also play a role. However, some Democrats favor selective delegation of some federal programs to state and local governments.

supremacy clause
Constitutional provision that says the laws of the national government "shall be the supreme Law of the Land."

Is Federalism Dead and Should It Be?

TABLE 3.1

CONSTITUTIONAL DIVISION OF POWER BETWEEN NATIONAL AND STATE GOVERNMENTS

• Why are both the national government and the state governments given vague grants of power (in the necessary and proper clause) and why are states given the right to exercise powers not granted to the national government?

Powers Granted to the National Government	Powers Granted to the State Governments
Conduct foreign affairs	
Raise armies and declare war	Maintain state militias (the National Guard)
Regulate imports and exports	
Regulate interstate commerce	Regulate commerce within the state
Regulate immigration and naturalization	
Establish and operate federal court system	Establish and operate state court systems
Levy taxes	Levy taxes
Borrow money	Borrow money
Coin money	
Provide for the general welfare	
Make laws "necessary and proper" to accomplish the above tasks	Exercise powers not granted to the national government

The Evolution of the Federalism Debate

Because the authors of the Constitution compromised on many of the differences between Federalists and Anti-Federalists, the issues raised at the time of the ratification campaign have never disappeared from American politics. Instead, the shape of American federalism has fluctuated over the course of American history, as the events in Figure 3.1 illustrate and the following discussion amplifies.

The driving force behind this fluctuation in the meaning of federalism has been political conflict between those who would benefit most from centralized power and those who would benefit most from local control. As the issues of the day changed, the coalitions favoring national power and local power shifted along with them. Changes in control of Congress and the presidency often had direct and immediate effects on the federal system.

Political conflict over the meaning of federalism has also often found its way to the Supreme Court, as the federal government, states, and individuals have engaged in legal battles, hoping that the courts will validate friendly interpretations of the Constitution. Supreme Court decisions have had a fundamental impact because the Supreme Court has the power of **judicial review,** the authority to declare laws null and void on the grounds that they violate the Constitution (see Chapter 15). When the Supreme Court declares a law of Congress unconstitutional, as it did in the Lopez case with which we began this chapter, it not only limits congressional power but also often expands the arena in which states are considered sovereign. The Supreme Court may also declare state laws unconstitutional, a power necessary for preserving national unity. In the pages that follow, we shall see how political conflict, elections, and the Supreme Court have often altered the shape of federalism.

judicial review
Court authority to declare laws null and void on the grounds that they violate the Constitution.

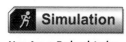

You Are a Federal Judge

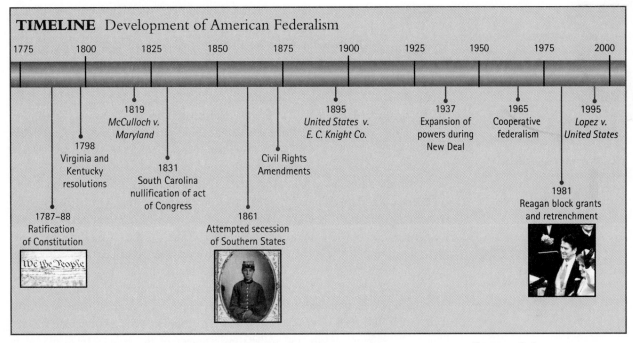

TIMELINE Development of American Federalism

FIGURE 3.1

Development of American Federalism

Nationally elected leaders, state legislators, and courts have all shaped the evolution of American federalism.

Dual Sovereignty and Nullification

Much of the legal debate over federalism, both historical and contemporary, concerns the doctrine of **dual sovereignty,** which says that both the national and state governments have final authority over their own policy domains. As a legal and political doctrine, dual sovereignty is an American invention that challenges Thomas Hobbes's powerful argument stating there could be only one sovereign (see Chapter 2). If governmental power is divided, Hobbes said, the competing sovereigns will inevitably come into conflict with one another, driving the country into a state of civil war.

The authors of the *Federalist Papers* defended dual sovereignty by turning Hobbes's argument on its head. Whereas Hobbes said that divided sovereignty would lead to war, they argued that ensuring the division of power was the *best* way of preserving liberty. If power is concentrated in any one place, it can be used to crush individual liberty. Even in a democracy a **tyranny of the majority** (a suppression of rights by those voted into power by the majority) may arise—and that is the worst kind of tyranny because it is stifling, complete, and seemingly legitimate. Dividing power between the national and state governments reduces the possibility that any single majority will be able to control all centers of governmental power.

Dual-sovereignty theory was an entrenched part of constitutional understanding during the first decades after the adoption of the Constitution. Some supporters of states' rights thought state sovereignty so complete that they propounded the doctrine of **nullification,** which says that state legislatures can invalidate acts of Congress that threaten state or individual liberties. States first used this doctrine in 1798 in response to the passage of the Alien and Sedition Acts, national laws that outlawed criticism of government officials. A Federalist-controlled Congress enacted the legislation to suppress the growing power of the Democratic–Republican party, led by Thomas Jefferson.

dual sovereignty
A theory of federalism saying that both the national and state governments have final authority over their own policy domains.

tyranny of the majority
Suppression of rights imposed by those voted into power by a majority.

nullification
A doctrine that says that states have the authority to declare acts of Congress unconstitutional.

Opposition newspaper editors were imprisoned, and even a Congressman was arrested and prosecuted under these laws. Invoking the doctrine of nullification, outraged Jeffersonian legislators in Virginia and Kentucky passed resolutions voiding the law within their states. Their defense of the right of free speech was praiseworthy, yet by using the theory of nullification to defend free speech, Jefferson and his allies proposed a legal doctrine that would eventually help tear the country apart.

At first, the doctrine of nullification had no serious consequences for national unity. On the contrary, the idea that states could undermine or overrule national policy was firmly rejected in **McCulloch v. Maryland,** a sweeping Supreme Court decision handed down in 1819 that is among the most important the Court has ever made.[8] The issue involved a dispute over the Bank of the United States, an institution that national commercial interests thought was vital to economic prosperity but that many local farmers, small businesses, and debtors blamed for causing a recent financial crisis. Responding to popular opinion, the State of Maryland levied a tax on the bank. James McCulloch, an officer of the bank's Maryland branch, refused to pay this tax.

A unanimous Court found in favor of McCulloch. In his opinion, Chief Justice John Marshall dismissed Maryland's argument that the national government possessed only those powers delegated to it by the sovereign states. Individual citizens, not the states, were the source of national power, he wrote. "The government of the Union . . . is, emphatically and truly, a government of the people. In form and in substance, it emanates from them." Because the people were the source of the central government's authority, a state could not override a national law. Although Marshall admitted that Maryland's tax was not a direct attempt to negate a law, as the Virginia and Kentucky resolutions had been, he said it was still unconstitutional because the "power to tax involves the power to destroy."[9] If a state government could tax a federal agency, then states could undermine the sovereignty of the federal government, just as if they had asserted that a national law was null and void. In declaring this state law unconstitutional, Marshall cast profound doubt on the power of the states to nullify acts of Congress.

Despite the *McCulloch* decision, the doctrine of nullification was not dead. The issue next arose shortly after the tumultuous 1828 election of Andrew Jackson as president. His vice-president, John Calhoun, formerly a senator from South Carolina, claimed that states had the power to nullify federal laws. A controversy developed over a tariff (a tax on imports) that was favored by northern manufacturers as a way of protecting the region's industries from foreign competition. Southerners opposed the tariff, because they wanted to sell their cotton to Europe and buy cheap manufactured products in return.

Calhoun's supporters in South Carolina called a special state convention, which declared the tariff null and void in the state. The state even threatened to secede from the union if the federal government tried to collect the tariff by force. President Jackson prepared to use armed force to crush the dissidents, but cooler heads prevailed. Congress passed a lower tariff less objectionable to southern interests, and South Carolina agreed to pay it.

Although the overt issue was tariffs, the underlying, long-term question involved African Americans. Afraid that northerners would abolish slavery, southern leaders continued to espouse the doctrine of nullification as well as the right to secede peacefully from the Union. The issue came to a head with the election of Abraham Lincoln

McCulloch v. Maryland
Decision of 1819 in which the Supreme Court declared unconstitutional the state's power to tax a federal government entity.

 Visual Literacy

Federalism and Regulations

in 1860. Lincoln was the candidate of the new Republican party, which opposed the extension of slavery into the western territories and favored its eventual abolition. Seeing the Republicans as a direct challenge to slavery, white southerners invoked what they saw as their right of secession, and the United States experienced what Hobbes had most feared: a war between competing sovereigns. Only after half a million soldiers had died and the southern countryside had been laid waste was the doctrine of nullification finally repudiated. After the Civil War, it was clear that whatever dual sovereignty meant, it did *not* mean that state legislatures could declare null and void the decisions of the federal government.

The Supreme Court and the Meaning of Dual Sovereignty

Once the doctrine of nullification had been laid to rest, it was up to the federal courts, not state legislatures, to decide the constitutional meaning of dual sovereignty. For over sixty years following the Civil War, the Supreme Court generally defended the sovereignty of the states against national power. While the war had settled the issue of whether states could secede, the Court preserved state autonomy in such areas as economic regulation and, distressingly, racial segregation (see Chapter 17). In the 1930s, after a political battle that could have reshaped the Supreme Court, the Court began to side most often with those who argued for broader national authority. The Court soon interpreted the Constitution's commerce clause and necessary and proper clause, which define the boundaries of national power, as allowing much more federal intervention into areas that were previously the domains of the states. Since the mid-1990's, however, a more conservative Court has used a series of key cases to reassert states' rights under these clauses. The Court has also invoked the doctrine of state sovereign immunity, found in the Eleventh Amendment, to expand state authority in the federal system.

Timeline

Federalism and the Supreme Court

The Commerce Clause and the Court-Packing Episode

CONSTITUTION, ARTICLE I: *"Congress shall have power . . . to regulate commerce . . . among the several states."*

In 1932, Democrat Franklin D. Roosevelt defeated Republican incumbent Herbert Hoover in a bitter presidential election that foreshadowed a period of expansion of federal power. Campaigning in the midst of the Great Depression, Roosevelt promised to use the power of the federal government to make the country prosperous again. He and his Democratic party allies in Congress enacted a series of governmental policies known as the **New Deal,** a wide array of programs that expanded the power of the federal government for the purposes of stimulating economic recovery and creating a national safety net for those in need. Many Republicans opposed these New Deal policies, arguing that they violated long-standing principles of federalism.

A majority of the Supreme Court, appointed by previous presidents, felt that the Court was duty-bound to reject much of Roosevelt's New Deal. In several key cases, the Court struck down New Deal legislation because, in the Court's view, it exceeded the power of the national government under the Constitution's **commerce clause,** which gives Congress the power to regulate commerce among the states.

New Deal
Programs created by the Franklin Roosevelt administration that expanded the power of the federal government for the purpose of stimulating economic recovery and establishing a national safety net.

commerce clause
Constitutional provision that gives Congress power to regulate commerce "among the states."

The courts have generally distinguished *interstate* (between-state) commerce, which Congress may regulate, from *intrastate* (within-state) commerce, which can be regulated only by the states. In the nineteenth century, intrastate commerce was defined as including all commerce that did not overtly cross state lines. Thus, for example, the Supreme Court in 1895 said, in *United States v. E. C. Knight Co.,* that Congress could not break up a monopoly that had a nationwide impact on the price of sugar, because the company that enjoyed the monopoly refined its sugar solely within the state of Pennsylvania.[10] The fact that the sugar was to be sold nationwide was said to be only "incidental" to its production.

The Supreme Court used this distinction to invalidate several key components of the New Deal. In the critical case of *Schechter Poultry Corp. v. U.S.,* for example, the Court declared unconstitutional the National Recovery Administration's regulation of economic activity inside individual states (see page 404 in Chapter 15). In trying to regulate the manner in which animals were slaughtered and sold within states, said the Court, Congress had gone beyond its authority to regulate interstate commerce.[11]

Democrats were furious at this and other decisions that restricted their ability to enact programs that they saw as necessary to combat the Depression. Roosevelt mocked the Court for using an outdated "horse-and-buggy definition of interstate commerce."[12] Never before had federalism placed the Supreme Court in such direct conflict with the president and Congress.

After his landslide reelection victory in 1936, Roosevelt believed he had the public mandate he needed to move against the Court. Early the following year, he surprised Congress with a proposal to add up to six new justices, one for each sitting justice over the age of 70. The resulting larger Court would be more efficient and more effective, argued the president. And—of course—it would be dominated by Roosevelt appointees. "The people are with me," FDR confidently told visitors to the White House.[13]

Many politicians and members of the public were uneasy with the president's proposal. They worried that the sudden increase in the size of the Court would upset the separation of powers between the branches of government. Roosevelt's court-packing scheme met stern opposition in Congress and was killed in the Senate Judiciary Committee.

While Roosevelt lost the battle, he won the war. Less than two months after he announced his court-packing plan, Chief Justice Charles Evans Hughes and Justice Owen Roberts, who had previously voted to restrict federal power, changed their views. This time the issue involved the recently passed Wagner Act, a New Deal law that protected union organizers. Despite the fact that the new law regulated activities within a state, a Court majority, in a 5 to 4 vote, declared it constitutional. Chief Justice Hughes declared: "When industries organize themselves on a national scale, . . . how can it be maintained that their industrial labor relations constitute a forbidden field into which Congress may not enter?"[14] Relations between employers and their workers, once said to be local, were now found to be part of interstate commerce.

The change of heart by Hughes and Roberts has been called "the switch in time that saved nine." In fact, the court-packing episode both illustrates the Court's susceptibility to political pressure and represents a critical shift in the dominant conception of federalism. With new appointments to the Court by President Roosevelt, the definition of interstate commerce continued to expand. In 1942 a farmer violated crop quotas imposed under New Deal legislation by sowing 23 acres of wheat. The Court ruled the quota law a constitutional regulation of interstate commerce, even though the farmer was feeding all the wheat to his own livestock. The Court reasoned that the farmer, by not buying wheat and instead producing his own, was depressing the worldwide price of grain.[15] With such an expansive definition of interstate commerce, hardly anything could be characterized as simply local or beyond the scope of Congress to regulate.

This broad interpretation of the commerce clause remained unquestioned until the 1995 case *U.S. v. Lopez,* discussed at the beginning of this chapter. The Lopez decision opened up an opportunity for a more conservative Supreme Court to place new limits on Congress's ability to intervene in state and local affairs. In 2000 the Court expanded the sweep of the Lopez decision by invalidating a federal law that gave battered spouses and rape victims the power to sue their attackers. This 1994 law, the Violence Against Women Act, could not stand, said the Court, because the law could not be said to regulate interstate commerce. "The Constitution requires a distinction between what is truly national and truly local," argued Chief Justice Rehnquist in his majority opinion.[16]

Necessary and Proper Clause

CONSTITUTION, ARTICLE I: *"Congress shall have power . . . to make all laws which shall be necessary and proper for carrying into Execution the . . . Powers vested by this Constitution in the government of the United States."*

The delegated powers of Congress include those items specifically mentioned in the Constitution, such as the power to tax, borrow money, and establish a currency. The **necessary and proper clause** gives Congress the authority to "make all laws which shall be necessary and proper for carrying to execution" its delegated powers. Justice John Marshall first analyzed the words *necessary and proper* in the same decision that challenged the doctrine of nullification, *McCulloch v. Maryland.* Maryland argued that Congress had no authority to establish a national bank, because a bank was not *necessary* for Congress to carry out its delegated power to coin money; it was only a *convenient* way of doing so. But Justice Marshall rejected such an interpretation as annihilating Congress's ability to select an appropriate means to carry out a task.

"Let the end be legitimate," Marshall said. "Let it be within the scope of the Constitution, and all means which are appropriate, which are plainly adapted to that end, which are not prohibited, but consistent with the letter and spirit of the Constitution, are constitutional."[17] Since this decision, the courts have generally found that almost any means selected by Congress are "necessary and proper." As a result, the necessary and proper clause has come to be known as the *elastic clause:* Over the centuries it has been stretched to fit almost any circumstance.

Even though an elastic interpretation of the necessary and proper clause has given Congress broad powers, the Supreme Court said in 1992 that these powers are not without limit. Adding its voice to the rising political concern in Congress over increasing federal power, the Supreme Court, in *New York v. U.S.,* declared that Congress cannot give direct orders to states. Though discussed in the arcane language of dual sovereignty, this case involved one of the most modern of political issues: the disposal of radioactive waste.

Disposal of radioactive waste—even so-called "low-level" waste from medical research, radiation detection equipment, and cleaning materials in power plants—has

necessary and proper clause
Constitutional clause that gives Congress the power to take all actions that are "necessary and proper" to the carrying out of its delegated powers. Also known as the *elastic clause.*

Congress Dumps a Problem on the States, But the Supreme Court Says No

Citizens organized protests and demonstrations whenever a town was named as a potential site for a waste dump.

• *Why did the Supreme Court reject Congress's response to this "Not in My Back Yard" (NIMBY) problem?*

NIMBY problem
Everyone wants the problem solved, but "Not In My Back Yard."

state sovereign immunity
Legal doctrine, based on the Eleventh Amendment, that says states cannot be sued under federal law by private parties.

become a particularly annoying political problem. Millions of cubic feet of such waste needs to be buried someplace where it cannot be disturbed for thousands of years.[18] The problem has become an elected official's nightmare: Something needs to be done, and there is no way of doing it without making some people extremely angry. Easily alarmed at the very word *radioactive,* citizens organize protests and demonstrations whenever a near-by area is mentioned as a potential radioactive dump. Everyone knows the stuff has to go somewhere, but everyone also says, "Not In My Back Yard." This is generally known as the **NIMBY problem.**

After stewing fitfully over the NIMBY problem for several years, Congress discovered a politically painless solution: It required each state either to find an adequate burial site for its waste or to become legally responsible for any damages the waste might cause. Rather than making tough decisions themselves, Congress decided to place an unfunded mandate on governors and state legislatures.

As a result, the debate over domestic radioactive waste shifted to the states. In no state was the issue more hotly debated than in New York. Often, when state officials identified a potential dump,[19] angry voters ran them off the site and burned them in effigy.[19] Under the pressure of the federal law, New York state officials decided to ignore the opposition and dump the waste in Cortland and Allegany counties. But the elected boards for the two counties, to keep faith with county voters, filed a suit claiming that the federal law was unconstitutional. Justice Sandra Day O'Connor, writing for the majority of the Supreme Court, said Congress could not force states or local governments to bury their nuclear waste; such direct orders to a state violated its sovereignty.[20]

With the radioactive waste case, the old doctrine of dual sovereignty was clearly revived. All doubts seemed to vanish in 1997 when the Supreme Court invalidated a portion of a national gun control law that required local police to check the backgrounds of gun buyers. If such a law were allowed to stand, said the Court, it would "compromise the structural framework of dual sovereignty."[21] Even though the Court has marked out a new direction for American federalism, many observers now believe further movement in this direction will be slowed by the terrorist attacks of September 11, 2001, which underlined the need for a strong national government.

State Sovereign Immunity

CONSTITUTION, ELEVENTH AMENDMENT: *"The Judicial power of the United States shall not be construed to extend to any suit in law or equity, commenced or prosecuted against one of the United States . . ."*

The necessary and proper clause and the commerce clause give power to the national government, but the Eleventh Amendment, ratified in 1795, explicitly restricts it. Since the mid-1990s, the Supreme Court has used the Eleventh Amendment to reinforce, and in some cases expand, the concept of **state sovereign immunity,** a doctrine that says that states cannot be sued under federal law by private parties.

Whereas cases involving state sovereign immunity may seem arcane and technical, they can have wide-reaching implications because private lawsuits are sometimes the main means by which certain laws are enforced. For example, the Indian Gaming Regulatory Act of 1988 established rules for states to negotiate gambling regulations with local Native American tribes. If states negotiated in "bad faith," the act gave Indians the right to sue. But the Supreme Court said in 1996 that this portion of the act was unconstitutional.[22]

Similarly, the Americans With Disabilities Act of 1990 allowed disabled employees to sue their employers if they were mistreated because of their disabilities. But when breast cancer sufferer Patricia Garrett sued her employer—the state of Alabama—charging discrimination, the Supreme Court ruled that her lawsuit, too, was invalid. Because of their immunity, "[s]tates are not required . . . to make special accommodations for the disabled," wrote Chief Justice Rehnquist in his 2001 opinion.[23]

In 2002, the Court ruled that a cruise line could not seek relief from the Federal Maritime Commission on a complaint that one of its ships was denied a berth by the state-owned port of Charleston, South Carolina. In his majority opinion, Justice Thomas argued that South Carolina had a right to conduct its business free of federal interference, saying that "Dual sovereignty is a defining feature of our constitutional blueprint."[24]

The doctrine of state sovereign immunity has the potential to create a broad range of independent power for states, but the Court is far from unanimous on its usefulness. Each major case on the issue since 1996 has divided the justices on a vote of 5 to 4, and some have written angry dissents. In 2003, the Court found that the Eleventh Amendment did not exempt states from being sued under the Family and Medical Leave Act, a law that requires employers to grant up to 12 weeks of unpaid leave to employees caring for a new child or seriously ill relative. Because the law was designed to ensure the civil rights of women (see Chapter 16), the Court found that Congress was within its constitutional authority to enact the law. The fate of the doctrine of state sovereign immunity may hinge on future presidential appointments to the Supreme Court.

Cooperative Federalism

The commerce clause, the necessary and proper clause, and the doctrine of state sovereign immunity work to define the boundaries between the domains of the states and of the federal government. These provisions therefore establish a constitutional basis for dual sovereignty. The congressional power to tax and spend, on the other hand, provides the constitutional basis for what has become known as the theory of **cooperative federalism,** or **marble-cake federalism.** According to this theory, first propounded by political scientist Morton Grodzins, all levels of government should—and in fact do—perform all governmental functions together. Because the Supreme Court has established a broad interpretation of Congress's spending power, the most serious political conflicts over national powers to tax and spend have occurred not in courtrooms, but in Congress and the state legislatures. These battles have often revolved around the nature of federal grants to state and local governments.

marble-cake federalism
The theory that all levels of government can work together to solve common problems. Also known as *cooperative federalism.*

Spending Clause

CONSTITUTION, ARTICLE I: *"Congress shall have power . . . to lay and collect taxes, duties, imposts and excises, to pay the debts and provide for the . . . general welfare of the United States."*

The **spending clause** grants Congress the power to collect taxes to provide for the general welfare. The New Deal Supreme Court considered the meaning of this clause when it ruled on the constitutionality of the social security program for senior citizens that was enacted in 1935. A taxpayer challenged the program on the grounds that tax

spending clause
Constitutional provision that gives Congress the power to collect taxes to provide for the general welfare.

dollars were being spent for the specific welfare of the elderly, not for the general welfare. But the Supreme Court, now in tune with Roosevelt's enlarged conception of federal power, said it was up to Congress, not the Court, to decide whether any particular program was for the general welfare. "[T]he discretion belongs to Congress," said the Court, "unless the choice is clearly wrong."[25] So far, the Court has never found Congress "clearly wrong."

Not only did the Supreme Court refuse to restrict the purposes for which Congress could tax and spend money, but it also conceded to Congress the right to attach any reasonable regulation to the money it spends. In 1984 Congress provided a grant to state governments for highway maintenance but withheld some of the funding unless states raised the drinking age from eighteen to twenty-one. South Dakota challenged the constitutionality of this mandate on the grounds that teenage drunkenness had only a remote connection to road repair. The Supreme Court rejected this argument.[26] State sovereignty was not violated, the Court concluded, because any state could choose not to accept the money. The regulation proved effective, inasmuch as every state has now accepted its full share of federal dollars and has raised its drinking age to twenty-one.

The congressional power to tax and spend has remained one of the broadest federal powers, because it allows Congress to attach whatever regulations it deems appropriate to the money it gives to states. Nevertheless, it is not beyond the realm of possibility that the Supreme Court could restrict this authority in its future decisions. In the South Dakota case, Chief Justice Rehnquist pointed out that "the spending power is of course not unlimited," and several judges have argued that the Court should begin to narrow its interpretation of the spending clause to safeguard some "sovereign rights" of the states.[27]

A Government of Shared Functions

You Are a Restaurant Owner

Political scientist Morton Grodzins criticized proponents of dual sovereignty for viewing government as a layer cake, each level independent of and separate from the others.[28] He pointed out that Congress has established many programs in which the agencies established to operate them must work together with other levels of government, combining and intertwining their functions to such an extent that the intergovernmental system resembles a marble cake.

In all policy realms, Grodzins said, one finds many levels of government working together on similar tasks. For example, law enforcement requires cooperation among the Federal Bureau of Investigation, state highway traffic control, the county sheriff's office, and local police departments. According to Grodzins, all levels of government should work together for three reasons:

1. Cooperative federalism is democratic. The involvement of all levels of government ensures that many different interests in society are represented.
2. Compromises are reached among officials elected by different constituencies. Federal officials listen to state and local officials, because the latter have influence with members of Congress. Similarly, state officials listen to community leaders, because to stay in office state legislators must pay attention to local needs.
3. Professional administrators usually share many values, no matter what level of government they work for. Law enforcement officials have numerous things in common, whether they work for the FBI or the local police. Most educational administrators, whether federal, state, or local, were once schoolteachers.

The 1964 election of Lyndon Johnson, together with an overwhelming Democratic majority in Congress, provided an opportunity to test more fully Grodzins's theory of cooperative federalism. Over the next few years, Congress passed a broad range of legislation that greatly enlarged the number, size, and complexity of **intergovernmental grants,** programs funded in part by the federal government but administered by state and local governments. State and local governments are often required to provide matching funds for a program in order to receive the grant. The typical "match" is 50 percent of total costs, but it can be as much as 90 percent or as little as 10 percent. Intergovernmental grants have become a key feature of the federal system. In 1930 only $97.1 million was spent on intergovernmental grants to local governments.[29] As Figure 3.2 on page 73 indicates, grants to state and local governments had grown to $49.1 billion by 1962, and by 1982 they had more than tripled to $166 billion. (Unless otherwise indicated, all amounts in this chapter are in 2003 dollars.)

Growth in the number and size of intergovernmental grants was facilitated by their popularity with most members of Congress. Many found they could profit handsomely from new projects begun in their home districts. As Senator Barry Goldwater said, "I don't care what the piece of equipment is—or how bad it is—if it's done in his state, the senator has to stand up and scream for it."[30] Such grants are often criticized as mere **pork barrel projects**—special legislative benefits targeted toward the constituents of particular members of Congress that have little or no general value. In 2003, Senator John McCain attacked his colleagues for continuing to "spend money like drunken sailors" for grants such as one designed to help the state of Hawaii contain its population of brown tree snakes.[31]

Most grants are, of course, well received by the city or town lucky enough to get the money, and this goodwill can improve the chances of reelection for the members of Congress responsible for the grants. "I make no excuses for the fact that, representing the district that I do, I can get dollars for specific programs," said Representative Jose Serrano, Democrat of New York City.[32] Former Speaker of the House Thomas Foley once pointed out that "One person's pork barrel project is another person's wise investment in the local infrastructure."[33] For example, an embankment protecting West Fargo from floods, constructed at the behest of a North Dakota senator, was originally condemned as sheer pork. But in the great 1997 flood of the Red River, the embankment saved the town from disaster.

Categorical Grants

In the 1960s and 1970s, the theory of cooperative federalism was particularly well suited to the Democratic Party. It fit well with the Democrats' philosophy, and was not difficult to pursue as a policy, since Democrats usually controlled Congress. Many Democrats saw federal grants as vehicles that could help the country address needs that state and local governments had long ignored. To ensure that grants were properly used, Democrats generally favored **categorical grants**—grants that include regulations that specify how the money is to be spent. Although some of these categorical grants fund basic government services, such as the construction of transportation and sanitation systems, most have had social welfare purposes. Categorical grants provide compensatory education for those coming from disadvantaged backgrounds, fund special educational programs for the disabled, and train the unemployed. They have also been used

intergovernmental grant
Grant from the national government to a state or local government.

pork barrel projects
Special legislative benefits targeted toward the constituents of particular members of Congress.

categorical grants
Federal grants to a state and/or local government that impose programmatic restrictions on the use of funds.

Head Start
Three decades after the
War on Poverty launched a variety of such initiatives, Head Start
remains one of the most visible
and successful early-intervention
programs for disadvantaged
preschoolers.

War on Poverty
One of the most controversial of the
Great Society programs, designed to
enhance the economic opportunity
of low-income citizens.

Great Society
Series of programs enacted under
President Lyndon Johnson, designed
to address social ills in the nation's
poor, elderly, and minority
communities.

implementation
The way in which grant programs
are administered at the local level.

to construct housing for low- and moderate-income groups and to provide food stamps for the poor. Rapid-transit operations are subsidized to help reduce commuting costs.

The **War on Poverty,** a wide-ranging set of programs designed to enhance the economic opportunity of low-income citizens, became the most famous and controversial of all categorical grant programs. It was one of a series of initiatives by President Lyndon Johnson, dubbed the **Great Society,** that aimed to address social ills among the nation's poor, elderly, and minority communities. Enacted in 1964 at the height of the civil rights movement, the War on Poverty required involvement of the poor in program design and implementation to the greatest extent feasible.

Several accomplishments of the War on Poverty remain evident four decades later. The popular Head Start program for preschoolers anticipated and paved the way for a nationwide system of child care and nursery school programs. Job Corps, a residential education and training program, paid off in better wages and employment prospects. Most notably, these antipoverty programs incorporated many minority leaders into the political process. From the ranks of the warriors on poverty emerged many minority mayors, state legislators, and members of Congress elected in the 1980s and 1990s.

Despite these achievements, the War on Poverty is better remembered for the warring factions that it generated than for its substantive results. An annual budget of just $23 billion was simply not capable of financing a "war" against poverty. In addition, efforts to coordinate local social services suffered from repeated dismal failures. Finally, most of the job search, worker readiness, summer job, and other short-term training programs had only limited long-term benefits.

The main political objection to the War on Poverty, however, was its emphasis on community mobilization. In many cities, poverty warriors antagonized local agencies and elected officials by encouraging protests, demonstrations, legal action, and minority electoral involvement. Local officials questioned why federal monies should be used to fund political opposition. Some blamed the program for the wave of civil violence that swept through American cities in the two years following its adoption. In 1974, Republican President Richard Nixon, who had campaigned against the War on Poverty, persuaded Congress to transfer its most popular components to other agencies and to shut down the remainder.

Problems of Implementation

The War on Poverty was only one of many categorical grant programs associated with the Great Society that came under tough scrutiny from those who studied their **implementation**—the way in which grant programs are actually administered at the local level. Aaron Wildavsky, Martha Derthick, and other implementation scholars gave three reasons for doubting that many intergovernmental grants were as effective as Grodzins had said:[34]

1. National and local officials, serving different constituencies, often block and check one another, making it impossible to get much done. For example, when President Johnson tried to build "new towns" for the poor on vacant federal land, he encountered the opposition of local officials who objected to the program's adverse effects on local property values.[35] Virtually no new towns were built.

2. When many participants are involved, delays and confusion are almost inevitable. It took over four years to get a job-creation program in Oakland, California, under

Unnecessary Complexity?

Some think that the intergovern-mental grant system is as convo-luted as the pencil sharpener shown here.

• *Does it have to be this compli-cated?*

Pencil Sharpener

Professor Butts gets his think-tank working and evolves the simplified pencil sharpener.

Open window (**A**) and fly kite (**B**). String (**C**) lifts small door (**D**), allowing moths (**E**) to escape and eat red flannel shirt (**F**). As weight of shirt be-comes less, shoe (**G**) steps on switch (**H**) which heats electric iron (**I**) and burns hole in pants (**J**).

Smoke (**K**) enters hole in tree (**L**), smoking out opossum (**M**) which jumps into basket (**N**), pulling rope (**O**) and lifting cage (**P**), allowing wood-pecker (**Q**) to chew wood from pencil (**R**), expos-ing lead. Emergency knife (**S**) is always handy in case opossum or the woodpecker gets sick and can't work.

way. Jeffrey Pressman and Wildavsky pointed out that the long delay was caused, at least in part, by the sheer number of agencies involved in the decision. The program required 70 separate clearances. Even if each took an average of only 3 weeks (not an unreasonable length of time), the total delay would be 210 weeks—or over 4 years.[36]

3. Federal policy makers often raise unrealistic expectations by using exaggerated rhetoric, thereby guaranteeing disappointment. It was a mistake to equate the poverty programs with a "war" when only limited resources were available.

The difficulty of achieving intergovernmental cooperation may have been exag-gerated by these implementation theorists. Most implementation studies focused on problems that federal grant programs had experienced during their first two or three years. More recent work has shown that many administrative problems were reduced with the passage of time. For example, the federal compensatory education program initially stigmatized disadvantaged students by separating them from their classmates in order to make sure that federal funds were concentrated on the most needy. But once this requirement was found to be counterproductive to education, federal administra-tors eliminated it.[37]

Block Grants

Despite these more positive findings from recent research, the criticism of categorical grants by implementation theorists proved quite influential. To simplify federal policy,

TABLE 3.2

CATEGORICAL GRANTS AND BLOCK GRANTS: SOME EXAMPLES

Type of Grant	Restrictions on Use of Funds?	Examples
Categorical grant	Significant	Food stamps (created 1971): Provides funds to states and localities to supply food to eligible low-income residents.
		Medicaid (created 1965): Provides health insurance to low-income and disadvantaged citizens.
Block grant	Minimal	Housing and Community Development Block Grant (created 1974): Provides funds to states and localities for general development purposes.
		Temporary Assistance to Needy Families (created 1996): Provides funds to states to design and implement their own welfare programs.

block grants
Federal grants to a state and/or local government that impose minimal restrictions on the use of funds.

general revenue sharing
The most comprehensive of block grants, which gives money to state and local governments to be used for any purpose whatsoever.

Congress replaced many categorical grants with **block grants,** intergovernmental grants with a broad set of objectives, a minimum of federal restrictions, and maximum discretion for local officials. Table 3.2 illustrates the difference between categorical and block grants and gives some examples of each.

The surge toward block grants has had three distinct waves, each prompted by Republican victories in national elections. Republicans were naturally hostile to categorical grants because many of these grants funded programs that Republicans had opposed in the first place, and believed were unnecessary or counter-productive in practice. The first wave of block grants began after President Nixon won election to the White House in 1968. The most comprehensive, **general revenue sharing,** gave state and local governments a share of federal tax revenues to be used for any purpose whatsoever. During this first wave, block grants did not replace categorical grants so much as supplement them. To win support for general revenue sharing and other block grants, Nixon was forced to agree to continue many of the categorical programs that Democrats in Congress favored. As a consequence, the total size of the intergovernmental grant program continued to grow throughout the administrations of Nixon and Gerald Ford. By the late 1970s, as the top line in Figure 3.2 shows, they cost more than $176 billion.

The second wave of block grants came after Ronald Reagan's 1980 defeat of Democrat Jimmy Carter. President Reagan's administration, unlike the Nixon administration, enjoyed a Republican majority in the Senate. Reagan succeeded in converting a broad range of categorical grants in education, social services, and community development to block grants and public health programs. During this second wave, the new block grants not only had fewer restrictions than the older categoricals,[38] but their funding levels were also reduced to comply with the administration's overall policy of "shrinking government." The amount spent on block grants fell from about $106 billion in 1977 to only $72.6 billion in 1998, and most of this reduction occurred in the early 1980s. General revenue sharing was eliminated in 1985, and the community development block grant, a major grant program for cities across the country, was cut from $8.7 billion in 1980 to $6.7 billion in 2003.[39]

The third wave of block grants took place after the congressional election of 1994, when Republicans captured control of Congress. Earlier block grant initiatives had not touched large social programs, such as Medicaid and Aid to Families with Dependent

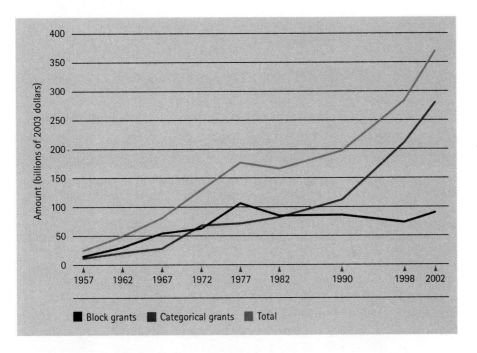

FIGURE 3.2

Growth and Change in Federal Grants to States and Localities

Expenditures for categorical grants continue to rise, whereas expenditures for block grants have remained stable in recent years.

• *Why do you think expenditures for block grants have not increased?*

Note: Totals exclude defense expenditures. Deriving precise estimates of block and categorical grants is difficult. Here we have employed grants used mainly for developmental purposes as a proxy for block grants, and grants used mainly for redistributive purposes as a proxy for categorical grants.

SOURCES: Paul E. Peterson, *The Price of Federalism* (Washington, DC: The Brookings Institution, 1995), chap. 5; and U.S. Bureau of the Census, *Federal Aid to the States for Fiscal Year 1998,* U.S. Bureau of the Census, *Federal Aid to the States for Fiscal Year 2002.*

Children (AFDC). But in 1996 Congress transformed the AFDC program, commonly called "welfare," into a block grant that gave states broad discretion over the way monies could be used (see Chapter 18). Congress also tried to transform the Medicaid low-income health insurance program into a block grant, but this was forestalled by President Clinton's veto. As a result, expenditures on categorical grants have continued to rise (see Figure 3.2).

Since the 1994 election, the debate over categorical and block grants has become a matter of intense political conflict. Each side can make a compelling case for its point of view. (See Democratic Dilemma, page 75.) Perhaps the best argument against both categorical and block grants is that even though they are often defended as a way of equalizing resources across the country,[40] federal grants in fact do not have this effect. Instead, wealthier states often receive more federal dollars than poorer states. Figure 3.3 shows that on average, the ten richest states in the country get much more money from block grants, per resident, than other states.

Perhaps the best argument in favor of federal grants is that they are necessary to maintain properly funded social programs. Federal categorical grants, such as Medicaid, food stamps, and other social welfare programs are especially important, because states, when not subject to federal regulation, try to shift to other states the burden of serving the needy, the sick, and the poor. In Minnesota, a state with generous programs for the poor, the proportion of new welfare recipients coming from out of state increased from 19 to 28 percent between 1994 and 1995, a time when other states were placing limits on welfare benefits. "We're really concerned," a county official said.[41] Fearful of migration from other places, many states feel pressured to offer fewer benefits than their sister states, creating a vicious cycle of cuts that President Clinton called a "race to the bottom." Between 1970 and 1993, welfare benefits in the average state fell by 42 percent.[42] From 1997 to 2000, in the wake of the reform of welfare that allowed states more flexibility, overall spending dropped further, and the number of people receiving welfare

FIGURE 3.3

Richer States Get More Per Capita Aid

Richer states get as much or more grant money than poorer states from the federal government, controlling for population.

• *Is this unfair, or do rich states deserve more because they pay more to the federal government in taxes?*

Note: State "wealth" defined as Gross State Product per capita.

SOURCES: Calculated by authors from U.S. Bureau of the Census, *Federal Aid to the States for Fiscal Year 2000,* April 2001, Table 1; and Statistical Abstract of the United States, 2001, Tables 18 and 644.

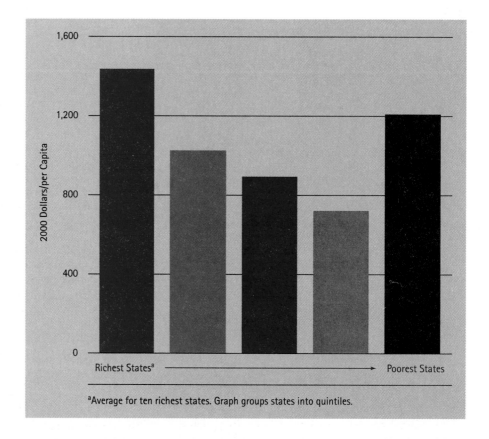

[a]Average for ten richest states. Graph groups states into quintiles.

shrank by 45 percent.[43] It is not yet clear, however, whether this decline is due to a race to the bottom or to the economic prosperity of the late 1990s that created job opportunities for the previously unemployed.

Although the debate over grants has polarized between those in favor of a wide variety of intergovernmental grants and those opposed to all of them, the most sensible solutions may lie somewhere in the middle. In areas where state and local governments have traditionally concentrated their efforts, including transportation, sanitation, and education, it may be appropriate to keep the federal role to a minimum, because states and localities can be expected to provide these services whether they receive federal aid or not. But in other areas, such as Medicaid and food stamps, it may be important to establish federal standards so that states do not "race to the bottom." In 1996 Congress and the president in fact found it possible to reach compromises at this middle position. They made the biggest cuts in traditional programs. They also changed the AFDC program into a block grant welfare program. But the largest social programs, Medicaid and food stamps, remained federally funded categorical programs.[44]

The Contemporary Debate

With the election of George W. Bush and a Republican consolidation of control in the House of Representatives, Republicans have modified their long-standing opposition to increased federal regulation of intergovernmental grants. Although in the past Republicans had opposed categorical grant programs, they now favored such grants when they required states and cities to spend money in ways that Republicans

DEMOCRATIC DILEMMA

Categorical or Block Grant: Which Is Better?

The intense debate over categorical and block grants strikes at the heart of how broad we understand federalism to be. Because of the restrictions Congress places on their use, categorical grants reserve more power for the national government. Block grants, on the other hand, relinquish more responsibility to the states.

A supporter of block grants might make the following arguments against categorical grants:

1. Categoricals are *inefficient.* Federal regulations tie the hands of state and local governments, who have a better understanding of local conditions. Categorical grants for public housing—designed with urban areas in mind—may be tied to inflexible regulations that are impractical for rural states, such as Montana and Idaho.

2. Categoricals create *powerful interest groups.* Categorical grants typically contain restrictions that focus services on specific groups. These groups support powerful lobbies that perpetuate unnecessary policies.

3. Categoricals impose *unfunded mandates.* Federal funds do not cover the full cost of the rules that accompany them. In effect, this forces states to raise the extra money through taxes. By forcing states to raise and spend this money, categorical grants sap their independence.

A supporter of categorical grants might make the following arguments:

1. Categoricals are *necessary to achieve national purposes.* For example, many environmental problems are national in scope. If a state does not clean up its radioactive waste or allows its factories to spew smoke into the air, the resulting pollution can spread far beyond its own boundaries. The federal government needs to attach regulations to its grants to ensure that all states comply with the effort to achieve national policy goals.

2. If grants are not categoricals that include regulations, states will *"race to the bottom."* Federal supervision of Medicaid, food stamps, and other welfare programs is especially important, because states, when not subject to federal regulation, often try to lower the benefits they make available, hoping that the needy and sick will move to other states.

3. Block grants are *wasteful.* If the federal government provides the money, it has every right and responsibility to make sure the funds are used for federal purposes. Block grants are a dream for local politicians—"free" money to be spent however they want without being held accountable to local taxpayers. When money is "free," it is likely to be wasted.

4. Block grants are simply the first step toward *eliminating needed federal programs.* After a program has been converted from a categorical to a block grant, its constituency is less well defined and it becomes harder to sustain the program's political base of support. Once the states are in charge of making policy decisions, it is easier for the federal government to abandon responsibility for the program altogether.

- *Which of these points makes the most sense to you? Why? Which position do you find more persuasive?*

---

preferred. In 2001 President Bush enthusiastically signed into law a new education reform that required all states, in exchange for federal dollars, to test students annually so that their educational progress could be monitored. Certain penalties are scheduled for those schools that fail to keep up.

The parties also appear to have modified their positions on **unfunded mandates,** the imposition of federal regulations on state and local governments without the appropriation of enough money to cover their cost. By 1993, mostly Democratic congresses had enacted countless mandates.[45] For example, state and local governments had to ensure equal access to public facilities by disabled persons but were given little money to cover the new construction costs. Clean-air legislation asked state and local governments to reduce air pollution but skimped on the funding necessary to do the job.[46] Medicaid required expanded services for low-income recipients, but for many states the law funded only half the cost of the program.[47]

Critics of unfunded mandates had high hopes that after the 1994 elections, mandates would be a thing of the past. That year, Republican candidates campaigned in

unfunded mandates
Federal regulations that impose burdens on state and local governments without appropriating enough money to cover costs.

devolution
Return of governmental responsibilities to state and local governments.

favor of governmental **devolution,** the return of governmental responsibilities to state and local governments. But Republican lawmakers soon proved that they were not immune to the practice. The Bush education bill required states and school districts to set standards, but critics said it provided little money to help them do so. After 2001 new antiterrorism rules also placed severe strain on state and local governments, as law enforcement officials were required to step up their monitoring of potential terrorist targets around the country. With the shoe on the other foot, Democrats began complaining about unfunded mandates. "I find it ironic [that] . . . the party that talks about being opposed to unfunded mandates is giving us a very significant unfunded mandate," said West Virginia Governor Robert Wise, a Democrat, about the education program.[48] Calling for a "new era of responsibility to our public schools," Democratic presidential candidate John Kerry called for increased education funding to eliminate unfunded mandates.[49]

Whether they are Democrats or Republicans, members of Congress have strong incentives to impose mandates on state and local governments, and to leave them unfunded. When a mandate is imposed, members of Congress get the credit for helping constituents. When it is left unfunded, Congress, safe at a distance, evades the taxpayers' wrath.

Local Government

State and local governments now play a more prominent role in the federal system than they have for several decades. Even before the most recent devolution, a large proportion of all domestic government expenditure was paid for by taxes raised by state and local governments. This pattern, shown in Figure 3.4, is in keeping with long-standing

FIGURE 3.4

Domestic Expenditure of Governments

State and local governments spend almost as much as the national government does.

• *Why did national government spending increase relative to state and local spending in the 1970s?*

Note: Figures on national government spending do not include defense expenditures.

SOURCES: Statistical Abstract of the United States, 1999, Tables 1434 and 1443; Office of Management and Budget, United States Budget for Fiscal Year 2004, Historical Tables, Table 3.1; United States Department of Commerce, Bureau of Economic Analysis, www.bea.doc.gov (GDP Figures).

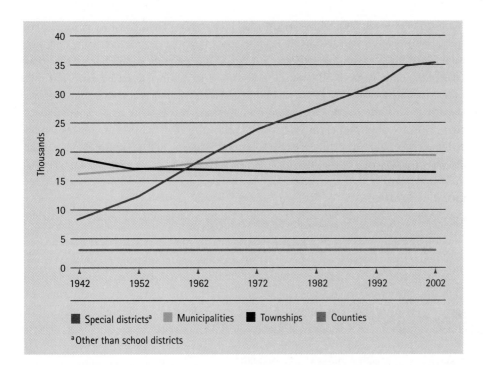

FIGURE 3.5

Number of Local Governments, 1942–2002

• *Why do you think the number of special districts has increased so much over the last 50 years?*

SOURCE: U.S. Bureau of the Census, *Statistical Abstract of the United States, 202,* Table 405.

American traditions. Nearly a century ago, the British scholar James Bryce identified the key role played by local governments in the American federal system:

> It is the business of a local authority to mend the roads, to clean out the village well or to provide a new pump, to see that there is a place where straying beasts may be kept till the owner reclaims them, to fix the number of cattle each villager may turn out on the common pasture, [and] to give each his share of timber cut in the common woodland.[50]

The nature of the work has been modernized since Bryce observed it, but the basic functions remain much the same. Local governments maintain roads; take care of parks; provide police, fire, and sanitation services; run the schools; and perform many other functions that affect the everyday lives of citizens.

The Number and Types of Local Governments

In sheer numbers, local governments constitute an overwhelming and growing presence; there were over 74,000 in 2002, up from about 46,000 in 1942 (see Figure 3.5).[51] There are several different major types of local governments, each of which has responsibilities that vary from state to state. Though the basic unit in most states is the county, not all counties are alike. In some states they manage school systems, welfare programs, local roads, sanitation systems, a sheriff's office, and an array of other governmental activities. In other states they have hardly any duties. Many counties are divided into townships—there are 16,500 of them nationwide—whose duties generally include local road maintenance and other small-scale activities.

As the population has become concentrated in urban areas, the total number of municipalities—cities, suburbs, and towns—has increased to nearly 20,000. In most states, these municipal governments have assumed many of the responsibilities once performed by counties.

Comparing State and Local Government

States, counties, and municipalities have also created an extraordinary array of special districts—over 35,000 in all. Each special district has responsibility for only one or a few specific governmental functions. Such governments are unique in that they overlap the boundaries of other local governments, sometimes spanning many different municipal jurisdictions. As Figure 3.5 shows, special districts account for most of the increase in the number of local governments over the last 50 years. Some special districts run schools, others manage parks, and still others administer transportation systems or garbage collection.[52] Even as humble a task as mosquito abatement can be the responsibility of a special district.

Local Elections

Most local governments are run by elected officials, although special district heads are sometimes appointed by other local governments. In the United States as a whole, the total number of elected local officials approaches half-a-million people. But despite the large number of local elections, actual rates of citizen participation in them are surprisingly low. When a particularly colorful candidate runs for mayor, or when ethnic or racial issues are raised, large numbers of voters can show up at the polls, but much of the time the local electorate is no more than half the size of the presidential electorate.[53]

The near invisibility of local elections helps to reduce local participation rates.[54] The sheer number of elected officeholders often makes local government elections confusing to many voters. Newspaper coverage is haphazard. Local governments often hold their elections at times that coincide with neither state nor national elections, which further reduces turnout rates.[55] When asked about the hotly contested 2001 Los Angeles mayoral race, one potential voter gave a typical response: "I don't really care too much. All I know is that there is a lot of bashing going on. One guy was like the D.A. or something like that and the other guy worked for him . . . I don't know."[56]

Surprisingly, local governments also oversee the administration of national elections. This local responsibility became a key issue in the close 2000 presidential election, when some voters in Palm Beach County, Florida, claimed that the county's confusing ballot design had led them to vote for the wrong candidate. The following summer, a nationwide commission of state and local election officials asked the federal government to provide procedural guidelines and standards—but not mandates—to prevent such confusion from occurring again.[57]

You Are the Director of Economic Development for the City of Baltimore, Maryland

Popularity of Local Government

One might think that this diverse, complicated, only half-democratic, and seemingly irrational system could not possibly succeed. Yet local government remains very popular. According to one survey, 37 percent of the population trust their local government more than other levels of government, compared to the only 19 percent who trust the federal government the most. Only 8 percent feel their local government is most wasteful of their tax dollars, as compared to 66 percent who feel this way about the federal government.

One explanation for the apparent popularity of local government, despite the low profile of its elections, is the ability of people to "vote with their feet"—that is, to move from one community to another—if they are unhappy with their local government. Americans are a mobile people: Over 15 percent move each year.[58] Every local government has to remember that if it is inefficient or unresponsive, its city or town will suffer a decline in population and property values. As a result, most local governments have good reason to be mindful of their constituents' needs, despite low voting rates.

The wide variety of local governments also gives people a choice. Some people favor sex education programs and condom distribution in school; others do not. Some people think refuse collection should be publicly provided; others prefer to recycle their own garbage. Some people think police protection should be intensive; others think an intrusive police presence violates the civil liberties of citizens. By giving people a choice, the diversity of local governments reduces conflict and enhances citizen satisfaction.

Limits on Local Government

For all the strengths of local governments, they often do not have the resources to meet the needs of the poor, the sick, and the disabled. If a local government tries to provide substantial services to the needy, it runs the risk of attracting more poor people and driving away those who are better off. For example, in the early 1990s, Framingham, Massachusetts, provided a broad range of social services to disadvantaged residents, including group homes for recovering drug and alcohol abusers, halfway houses for juvenile offenders, counseling centers, and other programs for the poor. Although the programs were well administered, the growing number of clients provoked complaints from town leaders that the community was becoming "a magnet for everyone else's problems." Complaining that taxpayers were being asked to foot the bill for the education, security, and fire protection of low-income nontaxpayers, one candidate appealed effectively to local voters by insisting, "We can't afford this anymore."[59] Most other cities agree; local governments nationwide spend only about 12 percent of their budgets on social programs, compared to around 29 percent for the state governments and about 59 percent for the federal government.[60] (But such is the variety of local governments that one can find exceptions to this as to any other rule. San Francisco and New York City, for example, provide a broad range of social services for needy groups.)

Local governments also compete with one another to attract businesses. Although such competition usually has positive benefits in that it keeps local governments sensitive to the community's economic needs, sometimes the competition can get out of hand. With state help, one county in Kentucky outbid its neighbors for a Canadian steel mill employing 400 people. It ended up costing the state $350,000 for every job created. Such bidding wars have spread across the country. As one Michigan official put it, "Right now, all we are doing is eating each other's lunch. At some stage we have to start thinking about dinner."[61]

In other cases, cities compete to secure or retain professional sports teams. In 1995 Cleveland Browns owner Art Modell abruptly decided to move the football team to Baltimore, which had promised him a new stadium, permanent seat licenses, and other financial incentives. Baltimore's mayor and Maryland's governor participated in the negotiations for the team and helped announce the move. Meanwhile, Cleveland officials were incensed. Mayor Michael White likened the move to "a kick in the teeth."[62] Undaunted, the city of Cleveland worked with major financial backers to bring professional football back to the city, this time as an expansion team. In 1999 the expansion Cleveland Browns played their first season in a brand new $283 million stadium.

A Local Election Campaign
• *Why do Americans vote at lower rates in local elections?*

Explore Your State Constitution

governor
State chief executive whose responsibilities roughly parallel those of the president.

laboratories of democracy
Doctrine that state and local governments contribute to democracy by providing places where experiments are tried and new theories tested.

State Government

When the Constitution was written, the design of the federal government was adapted from that which existed in many states. Thus, it is not surprising that the basic organization of most state governments bears a strong resemblance to that of the national government. Just as Congress has the Senate and the House of Representatives, the legislatures in all states except Nebraska have an upper and a lower chamber (Nebraska has only one). All states have multitiered court systems roughly comparable to that of the federal system. And every state has an independently elected **governor,** the state chief executive whose responsibilities roughly parallel those of the president.

State governments vary in many important ways, however. State legislatures vary greatly in size. Most lower houses have around 100 representatives, but in Alaska, Delaware, and Nevada they have as few as 40 members each, whereas in New Hampshire, with a similarly small population, the lower house includes 400 legislators. Some state governments hold their elections in even-numbered years, in conjunction with federal races; others do not. In some states, state administrative officers from the secretary of state to the attorney general are elected, whereas in other states, the governor appoints these officials.

State policies vary as well. State governments may serve as **laboratories of democracy**—places where experiments are tried and new theories about government are tested. If successful, an experiment may be copied by other states or by the national government. If it fails, the experiment is soon abandoned. For example, scholars have shown that states are more likely to establish state lotteries if their neighbors have their own lottery programs.[63] There is also significant state-by-state variation in the legality of assisted suicide, the rules governing a woman's access to an abortion, and social welfare policies. In South Dakota most consumer fireworks are permitted, but in Georgia even sparklers are against the law. In Nevada gambling is legal, but in Idaho it is a misdemeanor.

Some scholars believe the reason for many of these differences lies in variations in state political cultures. Citizens from different backgrounds and historical traditions form governments and elect officials that reflect these traditions. Minnesota and Massachusetts voters, for example, hold more positive views toward active government than voters in Texas or Florida.[64] It is no surprise, then, that Minnesota and Massachusetts have larger governments with more responsibilities than other states.[65]

State Elections

Despite policy differences among states, state elections bear a strong resemblance to national elections. The same two political parties—Republican and Democratic—are the dominant competitors in nearly all state elections. For many decades following the Civil War, the party of Lincoln, the Republicans, dominated the North, whereas the South was solidly Democratic. These regional patterns of party dominance have broken down in recent years as a result of the civil rights movement and population shifts. Republicans now often win as many southern elections as Democrats do. A new trend toward competitive politics and divided government has developed in most states. Democrats have had the advantage in state legislative races; Republicans have more often elected governors. The voters may like it this way: Each party can act as a check on the other, and government does not drift to either political extreme.[66]

Variation in State Government Responsibilities

The size and range of state responsibilities have grown dramatically in recent decades. As a percentage of GNP, state expenditures increased by over 60 percent between 1960 and 2003. States bear heavy responsibilities for financing elementary and secondary education, as well as for funding state colleges and universities. They maintain state parks, highway systems, and prisons. They manage welfare and Medicaid programs that serve low-income populations. They give grants to local governments to help pay for police, fire, and other basic governmental services.

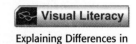

Visual Literacy

Explaining Differences in State Laws

The amount spent on government services varies from state to state. For one thing, wealthier states spend much more on public services. In 2000 the state and local governments in the ten richest states spent an average of $5524 per person on public services, whereas in the ten poorest states they spent, on average, less than $4080.[67] Many liberals say these differences in spending for education, health, and other public services are inequitable and should be rectified by federal grants. Many conservatives say that it is only to be expected that wealthier people will spend more on public services, just as they spend more for clothes, houses, and cars. In any case, federal grants have done very little, if anything, to reduce interstate fiscal inequalities.

Expenditures are also affected by elections. Each party has its favorite type of public service. The more often Democrats are elected to the legislature, the higher the expenditure for social services. The more Republicans who win, the higher the expenditure for traditional government services.[68]

Recent Developments at the State Level

In recent years, state governments have evolved in several important ways. State political institutions have become more modern, the role of governors has grown, and states have begun to develop their own economic policies.

State Financial Crisis   After a decade of rising budgets and a booming economy, state and local governments suffered greatly from a serious financial crisis prompted by the recession of 2001. As most states drafted their 2002 and 2003 budgets, they faced significant shortfalls due to declining tax revenues and increasing governmental responsibilities. In June 2003, the executive director of the National Governor's Association declared that the budget crisis was the worst for the states since the War of 1812.[69] Local governments suffered too, as states reduced aid to their cities to help fill the budget gaps. Many voters blamed politicians for these budget woes, just as in national elections economic problems often harm the president's reelection chances. Most memorably, Democratic Governor Gray Davis of California, whose state faced a $38 billion budget shortfall in 2003, lost a special recall election to actor-turned-politician Arnold Schwarzenegger.

The degree to which governors manage to cope with the economic crisis successfully may have broad repercussions for national politics. Being governor of a medium-sized or large state has historically been one of the best ways to position oneself for national office. Four of the last five U.S. presidents have been governors, and former governors have been major candidates in every presidential election campaign since 1976. George W. Bush's popularity as governor of Texas, coupled with the advantages of a well-known family name, quickly catapulted him into the presidential limelight. In 2004 Democratic presidential candidate and former Vermont governor Howard Dean reminded voters that his state was one of the few that did not face a budget shortfall during the crisis.[70]

Reapportionment and Professionalization   When the state constitutions were written, many of them included provisions freezing the boundaries of their legislative districts. In many other states, legislatures did not bother to change district boundaries to reflect shifts in population. Because the country became more urbanized in the first half of the twentieth century, by the early 1960s these rigid district boundaries meant that rural areas were grossly over-represented in state legislatures. Soon legal challenges brought these issues before the Supreme Court. In 1962 and 1964, the Court ruled that states must regularly redraw their districts so that all districts have similar numbers of residents,[71] a process known as **reapportionment.**   In the wake of these decisions, turnover in state legislatures rose significantly as they became more representative. In the longer term, the reapportionment requirements have sparked regular partisan battles in many states, as Democrats and Republicans compete to draw district boundaries in the way most favorable to their party.[72]

reapportionment
Redrawing of electoral district lines to reflect population changes.

After the 2000 census, reapportionment battles began again in earnest. A Colorado state representative complained that his state's reapportionment process had been "submerged in a morass of partisan haranguing."[73] A local official in Louisiana protested that his constituents were "being shifted around like the red-headed stepchild."[74] In the most extreme case, 51 Democratic legislators in the state of Texas fled the state in 2003 in an effort to prevent Republicans from passing a redistricting plan that would deliver more U.S. House seats to the GOP. Without the 51 legislators present, the House did not have enough members to conduct business legally. As the Democrats huddled at the Holiday Inn in Ardmore, Oklahoma, just beyond the reach of Texas state troopers, the standoff drew national attention. A network news correspondent described the situation as "like an old Western: a band of outlaws headed for Oklahoma with the Texas Rangers hot in pursuit."[75] After a second walkout and three special sessions of the legislature, Texas lawmakers finally passed the Republican plan. In 2004, several lawsuits challenging the plan were pending.[76]

Not all politicians were unhappy with their state's reapportionment process, however. "I believe [the new apportionment plan] gives us control for the next 10 years," said Pennsylvania's state House Republican Leader John Perzel. "I'm very very happy. I'm ecstatic."[77]

As state government has become more complicated, state legislatures have also become more professional. Scholars associate higher legislative "professionalization" with lower turnover rates, higher salaries, more staff, and longer sessions. In 2000 California's legislature was among the most modern. Its members remained in session throughout the year, receiving $99,000 in salary, retirement benefits, and handsome per diem expense pay, as well as the services of a full-time staff. By contrast, Wyoming paid its legislators only $125 dollars a day and limited its legislative sessions to a maximum of 40 working days in odd-numbered years and 20 days in even-numbered years.[78]

During the 1990s, voters reacted against the professionalization of state government, as many states limited the terms of legislators, cut their staffs, and reduced their salaries and benefits. In California, a 1990 term limit referendum caused legislative turnover to jump significantly, although its effects on other aspects of professionalization are unclear.[79] Term limit laws are now on the books in 19 states, but the trend to limit legislative terms appears to have slowed.[80]

State Economic Action   In the nineteenth century, state governments played an active role in their states' economies, granting charters to private corporations and investing their resources to assist in the development of key industries. After the New Deal, the federal government became predominant, and states relaxed their economic roles. Then, toward the end of the twentieth century, many states again became more active players in their economic development. States especially hard-hit by a decline in manufacturing jobs and by the economic recession of the early 1980s sought to reinvigorate their business climate through tax incentives and active recruitment of firms from out of state.

States with large economies and significant international exports, such as California and Texas, arranged trade missions to countries such as Mexico, Japan, and Canada. Some of these missions met with greater success than most observers thought possible. In 1987 California's governor George Deukmejian traveled to Japan to promote the sale of California rice. Most experts scoffed at his efforts, arguing that native Japanese rice was central to the country's national pride, culture, and self-sufficiency. "Negotiating for rice is like negotiating for Mt. Fuji," said one trade consultant. Nevertheless, the governor's efforts did not go unrewarded: By the late 1990s, Japan imported $100 million worth of rice from California, accounting for 20 percent of the state's rice crop.[81] More recently, California's attention has turned to its new top trading partner, Mexico. When Arnold Schwarzenegger won election as governor in 2003, one of his first meetings was with Mexico's secretary of foreign affairs.[82]

Chapter Summary

Federalism divides sovereignty between the states and the national government. Its existence in the United States is the result of a compromise between Constitutional Convention delegates who believed that a strong national government was necessary to preserve stability, and those who feared that centralized power would lead to tyranny.

Because the federal structure was a compromise, the Constitution does not clearly define the powers of the federal and state governments. As a result, the nature of American federalism has changed in response to electoral forces and Supreme Court decisions. Much of the debate over federalism has revolved around the meaning of dual sovereignty. The most extreme interpretation of dual sovereignty, the doctrine of nullification, was rejected with the end of the Civil War.

The power of the states was further eroded with the election of Franklin Roosevelt and the enactment of New Deal legislation that greatly enhanced the power of the federal government. Three provisions in the Constitution facilitated the expansion of federal power: the necessary and proper clause, the commerce clause, and the spending clause. The state sovereignty amendment has recently been used to restrict its expansion.

With the election of strong Democratic majorities in the 1960s, there emerged a new theory of federalism known as cooperative or marble-cake federalism, which holds that all levels of government can and should work together. In accordance with this theory, many new federal grants were given to state and local governments. The majority of these grants were categorical in nature; they contained restrictions that specified how the money should be spent. In response to criticism of the implementation of categorical grants, Republican leaders called for their replacement with block grants that have few federal mandates or restrictions. The two parties remain divided over the merits of categorical and block grants, although disagreements over these topics have shifted as Republicans gained the upper hand in Congress and the presidency.

Despite the expansion of federal power, state and local governments remain vital components of the federal system. Nearly half the domestic expenditures of the government are paid for with state and local tax dollars. Even though few citizens participate in local elections, local governments are the most popular of all governmental levels, in part because people can "vote with their feet"— that is, they can choose to live in the local community they like best.

State governments can play key roles in economic development, and governors are often well positioned to seek the presidency. Despite legal and structural variation, partisan battles on the state level can resemble those on the national level, as legislatures become more professional and voters increasingly choose "divided government" wherein neither party dominates all policy making.

Key Terms

block grants, p. 72
categorical grants, p. 69
commerce clause, p. 63
cooperative federalism, p. 67
devolution, p. 76
Dillon's rule, p. 57
dual sovereignty, p. 61
federalism, p. 57
general revenue sharing, p. 72
governor, p. 80
Great Society, p. 70

implementation, p. 70
intergovernmental grant, p. 69
judicial review, p. 60
laboratories of democracy, p. 80
marble-cake federalism, p. 67
McCulloch v. Maryland, p. 62
necessary and proper clause, p. 65
New Deal, p. 63
NIMBY problem, p. 66
nullification, p. 61
pork barrel projects, p. 69

reapportionment, p. 82
sovereignty, p. 57
spending clause, p. 67
state sovereign immunity, p. 66
supremacy clause, p. 59
tyranny of the majority, p. 61
unfunded mandates, p. 75
unitary government, p. 57
War on Poverty, p. 70

Suggested Readings

Of General Interest

Conlan, Timothy. *From New Federalism to Devolution: Twenty-Five Years of Intergovernmental Reform.* Washington, DC: The Brookings Institution, 1998. Excellent analysis of changing federal policy.

Dahl, Robert. *Who Governs?* New Haven, CT: Yale University Press, 1961. Classic study of local politics in New Haven.

Dye, Thomas R. *American Federalism: Competition Among Governments.* Lexington, MA: D.C. Heath, 1990. Comprehensive account of the way state and local governments work.

Peterson, Paul E. *The Price of Federalism.* Washington, DC: The Brookings Institution, 1995. Contrasts the responsibilities of national, state, and local governments.

Riker, William H. *Federalism: Origin, Operation, Significance.* Boston: Little, Brown, 1964. Theoretical treatise on federalism.

Focused Studies

Elazar, Daniel. *American Federalism: A View from the States.* New York: Harper & Row, 1984. Discussion of various regional political cultures in the United States.

Elkins, Stanley, and Eric McKitrick. *The Age of Federalism.* New York: Oxford University Press, 1993. Account of the first decades of the federal system under the Constitution.

Fiorina, Morris, *Divided Government.* New York: Macmillan, 1992. Explains why control of many state governments is divided between the Democratic and Republican parties.

Grodzins, Morton. *The American System: A New View of Government in the United States.* Chicago: Rand McNally, 1966. Classic study of cooperative federalism.

Pressman, Jeffrey L., and Aaron Wildavsky. *Implementation.* 3rd ed. Berkeley: University of California Press, 1973. Readable, fascinating account of the implementation of a federal program in Oakland, California.

Rivlin, Alice. *Reviving the American Dream.* Washington, DC: The Brookings Institution, 1992. Calls for reorganization of the American federal system.

Smith, Jean E. *John Marshall: Definer of a Nation.* New York: Henry Holt, 1996. Excellent biography of the chief justice who helped define American federalism.

On the Web

State and local governments have formed a variety of organizations to make their voices heard on the federal level.

www.nlc.org
www.ncsl.org
www.nga.org
The National League of Cities, the National Conference of State Legislatures, and the National Governor's Association provide information and policy priorities for state and local governments.

newfederalism.urban.org/
The Urban Institute's "Assessing the New Federalism" project provides a variety of studies on the impact of recent devolutionary programs.

www.federalismproject.org
The American Enterprise Institute's Federalism Project advocates devolution of more rights and responsibilities to the states.

CHAPTER 4

* * * * * * * * * * * * * * * *

American Political Culture

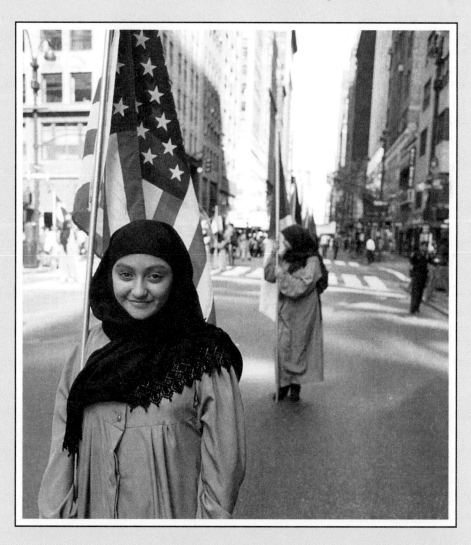

A Hard Test for American Diversity

The United States experienced the most serious act of terrorism in its history on September 11, 2001. Followers of Muslim extremist Osama bin Laden hijacked four jetliners, crashing two into New York City's World Trade Center, another into the Pentagon, and a fourth into the Pennsylvania countryside. Almost 3000 people died in this horrible tragedy.

All 19 of the terrorists came from Arab countries. None of them was American. Yet Arab Americans began to suffer widespread persecution in the wake of the attacks. Some incidents were as minor as school children fighting at recess. Others were dangerous, even deadly. One attacker shot a sleeping Yemeni American in the back 12 times, shouting his desire for revenge. A Yemeni shopkeeper, father of eight, was gunned down within sight of the American flag hanging in his store window. In all, Arab Americans faced an estimated 270 violent assaults within a month of 9/11. Five resulted in deaths.[1] California alone generated 73 official hate crimes against people perceived to be Arabs in 2001 (compared to three the year before). More than half of these were violent.[2]

All these sad tales of misdirected hostility resulted from the actions of individual Americans. However, many Americans began to call for the institution of anti-Arab discrimination on a wider scale. Survey respondents overwhelmingly endorsed subjecting those of Arab descent to special security checks at airports. A majority favored requiring Arabs to carry special identification cards, and more than a third supported placing them under "special surveillance."[3] As often is the case in the New American Democracy, officials partially responded to the public's demands. They cracked down on foreign visitors and on potential immigrants, both legal and illegal—especially Muslims and those from Arab nations.

Security in airports became more intrusive and, according to critics, more discriminatory. Many Arab Americans claimed to have been escorted off planes simply because of their ethnicity.[4] New helicopters and lights appeared along the border with Mexico. States beefed up their scrutiny of applicants for driver's licenses and other government documents.[5] Federal officials slowed the rate at which foreigners received permission to visit the United States and made the process more intrusive, such as taking fingerprints from applicants. They also reversed years of neglect by aggressively tracking down those who had overstayed their visas. They asked colleges to ensure that international students had their paperwork in order (one reason enrollment from abroad stagnated for two years running). Federal officials instituted a policy requiring more than 80,000 males from 25 mostly Middle Eastern countries to register at U.S. immigration offices. Law-enforcement officers seized hundreds of foreigners, from U.S. Army privates to pizza delivery boys, for minor legal violations that they once ignored. In some cases, officials detained people for months, obstructing their access to lawyers and even abusing them.[6]

This government crackdown on Arabs may sound excessive, but it pales in comparison to the treatment of perceived outsiders after previous national tragedies. Two generations ago, when the Japanese attacked Pearl Harbor, the government rounded up 120,000 Americans of Japanese ancestry and held them for up to three years in concentration camps. Detainees often lost their property and their jobs. Citizenship offered them no protection.[7] A generation earlier, after the United States entered World War I, German Americans suffered considerable abuse.[8] Social pressures became so great that immigrants abandoned their family names to downplay their ethnic origin. German-American children intentionally pricked their fingers "to let the German blood out."[9] In short, compared to the nation's historical experience, recent hate crimes have been relatively isolated and discrimination has been relatively mild.

Perhaps even more unusual, though, is the amount of energy that powerful Americans have devoted to suppressing anti-Arab sentiment. For every legislator who worried about Arabs running "all the convenience stores across the country," dozens increased their outreach to Arab-American constituents who felt vulnerable as a result of the backlash. One member of Congress dismissed Middle Easterners as "diaper heads," but using the slur brought him ridicule. President Bush, by contrast, received extensive praise for demanding unity and instructing citizens: "Islam is peace." The American media also showed little inclination to stir up ethnic hatreds, as they had during previous crises. Instead, journalists carefully documented the many injustices caused by new government policies. They also ran repeated stories conveying a simple message: that the country's immigrant communities were filled with loyal Americans, just as horrified by the terrorist attacks as anyone else.

These efforts did not go to waste. Anti-Islamic hate crimes dropped in 2002 to less than a third their previous rate. Policies that singled out people by religion or ethnicity lost

Border Protections Increased After 9/11

public support. The newly formed Department of Homeland Security stopped requiring special registration for Middle Easterners. Officials promised that, in the future, they would target individuals rather than "broad categories." [10] In other words, the message that Arabs could be loyal Americans seemed to find a receptive audience.

It is easy to take this insight for granted. "Of course Arabs can be good Americans," you might be thinking. "What does citizenship have to do with race or religion?" This reaction makes perfect sense in the United States, but it would be far from obvious in most countries. Carl Friedrich, a professor who immigrated to the United States from Germany, once wrote that "To be an American is an ideal, while to be a Frenchman is a fact." [11] Friedrich was pointing out that, in most of the world, **citizenship** is indeed defined by race or ethnicity. Nationality is a question of fact. Either you are German or you are not (see International Comparison, page 88.).

Instinctively, we recognize that the word *American* differs from labels applied to other nationalities—and we use it differently. It is not surprising to encounter a Muslim of Palestinian descent who claims to be a loyal American. But do you think you could move to Finland and ever credibly tell people you were Finnish? Can you imagine a Roman Catholic seriously claiming to be a loyal Iranian, in a country where the government operates under Islamic law? Probably not. If we rule out race or religion, though, what does it mean to be an American? Friedrich provides a clue. He calls it "an ideal." America's national identity is not an ethnic heritage, but a set of fundamental values and beliefs that anyone can adopt. Americanism is a matter of choice.

MAKING THE CONNECTION

The values held by a nation's people shape their political system. These core beliefs are more fundamental than the opinions citizens might hold about particular issues or public officials (see Chapter 5). Rather, they represent a broad orientation toward how government should and should not operate, a set of expectations about how it should treat them and how it should treat others. These assumptions define what leaders consider possible and what they rule out as unacceptable. Because such broad expectations are rather durable—a long-lasting tradition not unlike cultural preferences for certain foods or certain clothing—scholars often refer to them as the nation's **political culture.**

As this chapter will show, America's political culture stands out for the extent to which it defines the nation. It is exceptionally uniform, given the large land mass it unites and the varied population it integrates, and it distinguishes the United States from other advanced democracies. When you finish reading the chapter, therefore, you should understand why other U.S. citizens would accept that Arab-American Muslims could belong to the same nation as they do. More generally, you should be able to formulate an answer to the following questions:

- What core beliefs set Americans apart from citizens elsewhere?

- What influences caused these values to develop and spread?

- How have they stayed strong after more than 200 years?

- Do immigrants threaten America's political culture?

★ ★ ★ ★ ★ ★ ★ ★ ★ ★ ★ ★ ★ ★ ★ ★

INTERNATIONAL COMPARISON

Citizenship in Europe and the United States

Any child born in the United States is a U.S. citizen. A child born outside the United States is a U.S. citizen if either parent is a U.S. citizen and that parent has lived in the United States for 10 years—including two years after the age of 14. Legal immigrants can become "naturalized" citizens after 5 years of residence: They must learn English, demonstrate knowledge of American history and government, renounce their previous citizenship, and swear allegiance to the Constitution and laws of the United States. Naturalized citizens may not serve as U.S. president, because of a constitutional prohibition, but otherwise they possess almost every right and privilege possessed by native citizens.

Practices in other countries differ considerably. In Germany, for example, citizenship historically has been based on ethnicity. The constitution of the new German republic created after World War II carried over a 1913 law defining a German as "a refugee or expellee of German stock or as the spouse or descendant of such a person." As a consequence, Eastern European and Russian residents whose ancestors left Germany centuries ago can migrate to Germany today and quickly assume the rights and privileges of citizenship (as can Americans of German descent if they can make a case for hardship). But the children of Turkish "guest workers," born in Germany and speaking German as their first language, typically face enormous bureaucratic obstacles to becoming citizens because they are not Germans by blood.

Political cultures that emphasize ethnicity often produce conflict when the interests of different groups collide. In Germany, the new government of Social Democrat Gerhard Schroder attempted to liberalize immigration laws in 1999, but the proposals met strong resistance. A compromise reduced the residency requirement before an immigrant was eligible for citizenship from 15 years to 8 years and granted citizenship to any child born in Germany whose parents had resided there for 8 years or longer. France, meanwhile, contains the largest Muslim population of any European country. Ethnic tensions in 2004 led to a widely popular government crackdown on religious head coverings that obviously targeted the Islamic *hajib* or head scarf—a sort of religion-based regulation similar to one that the U.S. Supreme Court declared unconstitutional in a 1993 case called *Hialeah v. Lukumi Babalu.*

- *Why has the United States historically determined citizenship by beliefs rather than by ethnicity or nationality?*

- *Could countries like Germany or France define citizenship more as we do in the United States? Or is there something about other countries that naturally leads them to define citizenship in terms of ethnicity or nationality?*

- *More generally, some people argue that citizenship is an outmoded concept in today's globally integrated world where many people live for significant periods in other countries. Do you agree?*

- *Should citizens have any more privileges than people who are legal residents? Should legal noncitizens subject to taxes and other national obligations be permitted to vote?*

SOURCE: *The Economist,* April 5, 1997: 45–46; January 9, 1999: 17.

Americans: A Contradictory People?

citizenship
Status held by someone entitled to all the rights and privledges of a full-fledged member of a political community.

political culture
Collection of beliefs and values about the justification and operation of a country's government.

Americans are more ethnically and religiously diverse than the citizens of other democracies. Most long-lasting multicultural countries have featured authoritarian governments that could suppress cultural divisions, as in the Austro-Hungarian and Soviet empires. By contrast, most of the world's multicultural democracies have been short-lived—Yugoslavia being one recent, especially tragic, example. The United States is the exception, an unusual example of diverse people coexisting peacefully under a long-lasting democratic government. [12]

At the same time, many foreign observers have noticed an odd consistency in political beliefs across the United States, a uniformity that seems to contradict the cultural diversity. More frequently than in other democracies, Americans agree on fundamentals and share basic assumptions about the nature of a good society; they tend to value liberty, individual responsibility, equality, and religious faith. On first hearing, this claim strikes many Americans as exaggerated, if not wrong. The United States certainly knows its share of political conflict. Republicans clash angrily with Democrats in the halls of government. Liberals argue angrily with conservatives in the media. But the range of disagreement is much narrower than that found in other advanced democracies, which may contain political parties hoping to restore a royal family, to establish an official church, or to lead a workers' rebellion. Beliefs considered valid in other cultures operate outside the mainstream of debate in the United States.

How might such a contradiction arise? How does an ethnically and religiously heterogeneous society develop a political culture more homogeneous than most? To answer this question, we must know more about both the makeup of the American population and the core beliefs that Americans share. The next section therefore considers the diversity produced by new immigrants continuously entering the United States. The one that follows it then discusses the philosophy that unifies American beliefs and values.

Social Diversity

In "Federalist 2," John Jay described Americans as a "united people" who were "descended from the same ancestors, speaking the same language, professing the same religion, attached to the same principles of government, very similar in their manners and customs." Jay was exaggerating American unity, downplaying divisions that threatened ratification of the U.S. Constitution. In fact, no "united people" colonized the so-called New World.

The Dutch settled New York, and Swedes settled along the Delaware River. The French were present on the northern and western borders, and a small Spanish population lived in the south. The British were most numerous, of course, but they were not all of a kind. Religious dissenters called Puritans settled in New England, but Virginia's colonists remained loyal to the Church of England. Maryland was a grant to Lord Baltimore, who welcomed his fellow Catholics, whereas Pennsylvania accepted Quakers, who were unwelcome almost everywhere else. Moreover, after 1700, British immigration came increasingly from Scotland, Wales, and Ireland.

Indentured servants—who made up half the population of Pennsylvania, New York, and New Jersey—included thousands of Germans, Scandinavians, Belgians, French, and Swiss. And these were only the voluntary immigrants; the involuntary immigrants—slaves—were from Africa. (Native Americans, whose numbers had been decimated by wars and disease, were viewed as separate nations altogether.) All in all, historians estimate that on the eve of the American Revolution, only 50 percent of the population of the colonies was English and that nearly 20 percent was African American.[13]

You may react skeptically to this description of colonial diversity: a bunch of European Christians and their slaves. In the contemporary United States, debates over **multiculturalism** do not revolve around whether Catholics and Calvinists should get along, or whether the British should tolerate the Dutch. Instead, we debate whether people with nontraditional lifestyles should enjoy the same rights and privileges as those who are more traditionally oriented, or we struggle to identify policies that will allow people of color to live in peace among a white majority. But notions of diversity are relative to time and place. A few centuries ago, Protestants and Catholics looked upon each other with no more understanding (and possibly with less) than that with which a Christian looks upon a Muslim today—and the cultural distance between them often turned just as deadly.

multiculturalism
The idea that ethnic and cultural groups should maintain their identity within the larger society and respect one another's differences.

During the Thirty Years War (1618–1648), European Christians raped, tortured, and murdered each other on a monumental scale over religious differences. One-third of the population of what is now Germany died. Near the end of that period, Puritan dissenters from the Church of England fought against Royalist defenders of church and crown in the English Civil War (1642–1653). Ultimately, the king and the archbishop both lost their heads. For perhaps the most appalling contradiction of the notion that northern European Christians were all alike, consider the St. Bartholomew's Day Massacre that began on August 24, 1572. French Catholics moved methodologically from door to door and farm to farm, killing 30,000 French Calvinists with swords, axes, and crude firearms. The diversity of the past was quite capable of straining a government to the breaking point.

Relative to other countries, and to the times, America has always been diverse. The national motto imprinted on the United States Seal and on several coins, *E Pluribus Unum* ("out of many, one"), explicitly recognizes our diversity. It is a key ingredient of the nation's historical experience. In fact, the existence of distinct ethnic and religious groups and their desire to preserve some part of their distinctiveness underlie much of the history of political conflict in America. For this reason, the nation's continued success at absorbing waves of immigrants represents one of its proudest accomplishments, despite the controversies that have almost always sprung up after the arrival of new peoples.

A Nation of Immigrants Then

After the successful campaign for ratification of the Constitution, the new federal government maintained the states' policies of unrestricted immigration, although not everyone was happy about it. One of the most cosmopolitan Americans of the time, Benjamin Franklin, expressed his resentment of Germans in various letters:

> Why should *Pennsylvania,* founded by the *English,* become a colony of Aliens, who will shortly be so numerous as to Germanize us instead of our Anglifying them, and will never adopt our Language or Customs any more than they can acquire our Complexion? [emphasis in original].[14]

Despite such misgivings, land was plentiful and labor scarce. The quicker the territory could be populated, the quicker economic development would follow. Immigration gradually increased, until by mid-century immigrants from England, Ireland, and Germany were arriving in numbers as high as 400,000 per year. Irish immigration became a major political issue. Many Protestants feared that Irish Catholics would put their allegiance to the Pope above their loyalty to the United States and that they might even plot to overthrow the government. Cartoonists of the period depicted the Irish as dark, hairy, ape-like people. In the 1854 elections, the anti-Catholic "Know-Nothing" party won 43 seats in the House of Representatives, or almost a fifth of the chamber at the time. (The party's name came from its secret password, "I know nothing about it.")

Immigration increased considerably in the 1860s and continued at a high rate until World War I. In the 1860s and 1870s, the first of an eventual half-million French Canadians crossed the northeastern border of the United States, and several million Scandinavians joined a continuing stream of English, Irish, and Germans (see Figure 4.1). Political conflict in the late nineteenth century increasingly became "ethnocultural." [15] In the Midwest and much of the East, the Republican base lay in native Protestant communities, whereas the Democrats sank roots in the immigrant Catholic

ST. PATRICKS DAY 1867.

RUM. BRUTAL ATTACK ON THE POLICE. "THE DAY WE CELEBRATE." IRISH RIOT. Th. Nast BLOOD.

Bigotry on St. Patrick's Day c.1867

Thomas Nast portrays the Irish (celebrating a national holiday) as violent, ape-like brutes that riot and attack the police.

• *Would you be likely to see such a cartoon today? How would racism be expressed today?*

communities. Politics revolved around such issues as the prohibition or regulation of alcohol, public funding of parochial schools, bilingual schools (mostly German, but French in New England), and Sunday "blue laws"—laws that restricted commercial and recreational activities on Sundays. German Lutherans were an important "swing" group in some midwestern states; they generally voted Republican but cultural conflict sometimes swung them to the Democratic side. In Wisconsin, for example, the Republicans lost only two statewide elections between 1858 and 1890. One came after the party raised liquor license fees, the second after it passed a measure requiring English language instruction in the schools.[16]

The Chinese were the first Asians to immigrate on a significant scale. More than 20,000 Chinese participated in the California Gold Rush, which began in 1849. (Only two-thirds of the "forty-niners" were Americans, and only two-thirds of those Americans were white; large numbers of Cherokee Indians and African Americans panned for gold.[17]) More than 100,000 Chinese laborers helped build the western links of the transcontinental railroads. At first these newcomers were viewed positively as peaceful, hard-working (and cheap) labor. Soon, however, a virulent backlash set in. During the congressional debate on the Chinese Exclusion Act of 1882, California Senator John Miller characterized the Chinese as

> machine-like . . . of obtuse nerve, but little affected by heat or cold, wiry, sinewy, with muscles of iron; . . . automatic engines of flesh and blood; . . . patient, stolid, unemotional, and persistent, with such a marvelous frame and digestive apparatus that they can dispense with the comforts of shelter and . . . grow fat on less than half the food necessary to sustain life in the Anglo Saxon.

How could white Californians (even in the nineteenth century!) compete with such immigrants? In the eyes of Senator Miller, they couldn't:

> The experiment now being tried in California is to subject American free labor to competition with Chinese servile labor, and so far as it has gone, it has put in progress the displacement of American laborers, and the substitution of Chinese for

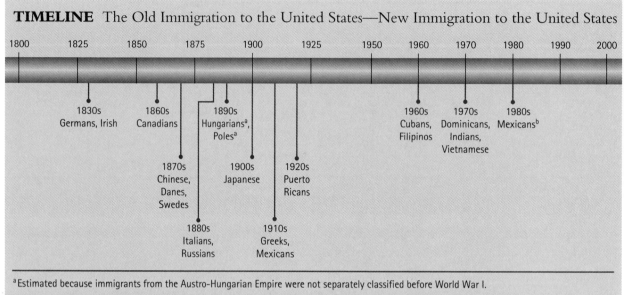

FIGURE 4.1

Immigration to the United States

The quantity and origin of immigration to the United States has changed sharply over time.

• *Why might interest in emigrating to the United States rise and fall?*

SOURCE: Stephanie Bernado, *The Ethnic Almanac* (Garden City, NY: Doubleday, 1981): 22–140;
The U.S. Immigration and Naturalization Service (http://www.ins.gov).

white men. The process will continue if permitted until the white laborer is driven out into other fields, or until those who remain in the contest come down to the Chinese level.[18]

Such charges were as common then as now: Cheap foreign labor will undercut the standard of living of "real" Americans—a charge that has repeatedly been leveled at immigrants through the decades.

Beginning in the 1880s the character of immigration changed, as millions of people from southern and eastern Europe followed their northern and western European predecessors. Again, these new immigrants were threatening to many "real" Americans, who by now believed that pre-1880 immigrants "were drawn from the superior stocks of northern and western Europe, while those who came later were drawn from the inferior breeds of southern and eastern Europe."[19] A best-selling book by Madison Grant of the American Museum of Natural History, published in 1916, reflects the sentiments of the time. Grant charged that European governments were unloading on the United States "the sweepings of their jails and asylums." He described new immigrants as "the weak, the broken, and the mentally crippled of all races drawn from the lowest stratum of the Mediterranean basin and the Balkans, together with hordes of the wretched, submerged populations of the Polish ghettoes." [20]

Reflecting widespread popular concern, a government commission was established in 1907 to study the immigration situation. Three years later, the U.S. Immigration Commission issued an immense report. The following observations, lifted from that report, illustrate how Americans of the time period viewed outsiders, and also how quick they were to prejudge entire immigrant groups:

> [Greeks]: *"There is no doubt of their nimble intelligence. They compete with the Hebrew race as the best traders of the Orient."*
>
> [Southern Italian]: *"excitable, impulsive, highly imaginative, impracticable . . . an individualist having little adaptability to high organized society."*
>
> [Persian]: *"is rather brilliant and poetical than solid in temperament. Like the Hindu he is more eager to secure the semblance than the substance of modern civilization."*
>
> [Poles]: *"are more high strung than are the most of their neighbors. In this respect they resemble the Hungarians farther south."*
>
> [Romanians]: *"more emotional than the Slav, less stolid and heavy than the Bulgarian."*
>
> [White Russians]: *"are said by travelers to be a distinctly weaker stock than the Great Russians and less prepossessing in appearance."*
>
> [Serbo-Croatians]: *19th century "savage manners" persist, "illiteracy is prevalent and civilization at a low stage. . . ."* [21]

Such ethnic stereotyping displays official insensitivity on a scale undreamed of today. No one should ever think that the American "melting pot" in any way resembled a community of harmony and love.

Not all opposition to immigration reflected ethnic or religious bigotry. Some opposed further immigration for economic or political reasons. Although immigrants joined the industrial unions, union leaders believed that continued immigration undercut the bargaining power of workers. And indeed, American business did encourage immigration as a source of cheap labor. The Progressives, a reformist political movement, opposed further immigration because immigrants were viewed as the foundation of corrupt urban political machines (see Chapter 8). The Progressives believed that shutting off immigration would shut off the supply of uninformed, ignorant voters whom the machines could manipulate.

For many reasons, then, anti-immigration sentiment grew. After two decades of advocacy, a national literacy test was adopted in 1917 (as we shall see in Chapter 17, such a device had earlier been used to disfranchise African Americans and poor whites in the South). Supporters of the test did not disguise their motives. The noted Massachusetts senator Henry Cabot Lodge observed that the test "will bear most heavily on the Italians, Russians, Poles, Hungarians, Greeks, and Asiatics, and very lightly, or not at all upon English-speaking emigrants or Germans, Scandinavians, and French."[22]

Contrary to what Senator Lodge believed, many would-be immigrants knew how to read or quickly learned, so stronger legislation was needed to close the door. A series of laws passed in the 1920s restricted immigration both quantitatively (the total was limited) and qualitatively (quotas gave northern and western Europeans preference over people from other areas).[23] The Japanese and other Asians were added to the Chinese as groups that were excluded altogether. By 1930 the era of the open door had ended, although Mexicans continued to enter the southwestern states to work in American agriculture (joining those who had been incorporated when the United States seized the territory from Mexico), and after World War II Puerto Ricans in significant numbers emigrated to New York City. But before the United States closed its doors to immigrants, more than 35 million people had left hearth and home to come to America. These immigrants and their children were a large component of the growth

**Chinatown Across
Half a Century**

Immigration helped create overwhelmingly Asian neighborhoods
in some American cities, as illustrated by these street scenes from
Manhattan. Although often
called "Chinatown" because of
attempts by immigrants to
preserve the tastes, sights, and
sounds of their past, these urban
neighborhoods actually created a
unique melange of the Asian and
the American.

Visual Literacy

Understanding Who
We Are

of the United States from a country of about 10 million inhabitants in 1820 to one of
more than 100 million in 1920.

Restrictions on immigration were part of a general reactionary movement that
broke out after World War I. In the "Red Scare," immigrants were persecuted as carriers
of Bolshevik, anarchist, and other subversive foreign ideologies. Anti-Catholic and Anti-
Jewish sentiments energized the Ku Klux Klan in the 1920s; it counted 25–30 percent
of the adult male Protestant population in its membership. [24] Not surprisingly, the 1928
Democratic presidential nomination of Catholic Al Smith caused a virulent reaction.[25]

Several bigoted radio demagogues were popular in the 1930s, and discrimination
against Catholics and Jews was still widespread. Indeed, not until 1950 did Ivy League
universities eliminate informal quotas on admissions of Jewish students. Gradually,
however, ethnocultural tensions died down. The cumulative effects of economic depression, World War II, revulsion at the Holocaust, and the Cold War led to a general reduction in ethnic and racial tensions that lasted approximately a generation. However, this
short period from the early 1930s to the mid-1960s, during which ethnic and religious
issues were relatively dormant, was the exception, not the norm. From the founding to
the 1930s, the kinds of issues now discussed under the heading of multiculturalism were
an important part of American politics.

A Nation of Immigrants Now

The Immigration Act of 1965 opened the door to the largest surge of immigration
since the 1890s. Congress abandoned the national-quotas system favoring northern
Europeans, with the result that immigration from Latin America and the West Indies
increased rapidly. In addition, hundreds of thousands of new immigrants from Vietnam,
Korea, Cambodia, India, Iran, the Philippines, and other countries became the first
numerically significant Asian groups to arrive since the Japanese in the early years of
the twentieth century (review Figure 4.1).

In the 1980s the absolute number of immigrants—about 9 million—was higher
than in any previous decade, although it was lower as a proportion of the population
than it had been at the turn of the century. Three million came from Mexico, Central
America, and the Caribbean, and nearly as many from Asia. Nearly half a million came
from South America and almost 200,000 from Africa. These figures include only legal
immigrants; an estimated 7 million people now live in the United States illegally. [26]

As a result of this newest wave of immigration, non-Hispanic whites dropped to
less than 70 percent of the population by the 2000 census. Soon afterward, Hispanics
surpassed African Americans as the nation's largest minority group. The population of
European origin is projected to fall to less than two-thirds in the next two decades (see
Figure 4.2). In many large cities, whites of European origin are already a minority. This
dramatic social change gave rise to the contemporary debates over issues such as bilingual education and the provision of social services to immigrants.

Immigration as a Contemporary Issue

Today, immigration once again is a political issue. In 1994, California voters overwhelmingly passed Proposition 187, an initiative that denied state services to illegal
immigrants and their children. The question of eligibility for governmental services has
remained a matter of intense controversy at the national level ever since. Welfare

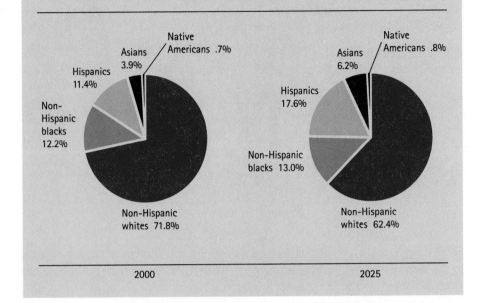

The two fastest-growing population groups are Asians and Hispanics. The Census Bureau projects that this will result in a significant shift in the composition of the American population over the next two decades.

2000

Native Americans .7%
Asians 3.9%
Hispanics 11.4%
Non-Hispanic blacks 12.2%
Non-Hispanic whites 71.8%

2025

Native Americans .8%
Asians 6.2%
Hispanics 17.6%
Non-Hispanic blacks 13.0%
Non-Hispanic whites 62.4%

FIGURE 4.2
U.S. Population by Race and Ethnicity, 1995 and 2025
The population of the United States is growing more Hispanic and more Asian, but less European.

SOURCE: U.S. Census Bureau, *Resident Population of the United States: Middle Series Projects, 1996–2050,* www.census.gov.

reforms enacted in 1996 denied legal immigrants access to food stamps, a measure that remained in effect until President Bush reversed it in his 2003 budget. Bush's 2004 proposal to grant amnesty to undocumented Mexicans working in the United States was less popular; it faced harsh criticism from Democrats with labor union ties as well as Republicans who considered the proposal a reward for lawbreakers.

Much of the contemporary debate over immigration would sound very familiar to Americans of earlier eras. Does providing services to immigrants impose a burden on native citizens? Do immigrants take jobs from native workers? Do hard-working immigrant entrepreneurs drive "native" shopkeepers out of business? As we have seen, such fears are not new, but that does not mean they are totally groundless. There are four tangible reasons why immigration today differs from that encountered in the past.

First, in contrast to earlier periods in American history, immigrants are not entering an economy hungry for unskilled labor. There is no exploding railroad industry to absorb today's immigrants as it absorbed the Irish and the Chinese. No expanding steel industry sends representatives to southern and eastern Europe to recruit laborers. The American economy is moving away from manufacturing to a globally integrated service and information economy. Many Americans, especially those who lack technical skills, face severe difficulties in the transition. Research indicates that competition from immigrants undercuts the wages of low-skilled Americans who already are struggling to make ends meet.[27]

Second, there are mismatches between the costs and benefits of immigration. In recent decades, more than 75 percent of new immigrants went to six states: California, New York, Texas, Florida, New Jersey, and Illinois. Studies show that immigrants strengthen the national economy and pay nearly as much in taxes as they consume in government services. But most of the taxes paid by immigrants are federal income and

Participation

The Debate over Immigration

Ambivalent As Always

Since the nation's founding, Americans have had a love/hate relationship with immigration. Newcomers have been feared for the cultural, economic, and political changes that they might bring. At the same time, the nation has always relied on the energy and ambition of new arrivals to drive economic development—for example, by providing goods and services cheaply. Once groups assimilate into American society, they are celebrated as part of the nation's proud immigrant heritage.

www.cartoonistgroup.com

social security taxes, revenue that goes to the national government rather than directly to the states where immigrants concentrate. Moreover, within states, it is the localities that are responsible for providing educational and social services to new immigrants, although they do not directly receive the taxes immigrants pay. [28] Disparities like these focus the costs of immigration much more narrowly than the benefits. Heavy immigration forces local and state governments to cut services, raise taxes, and beg for money from higher levels of government, options that elected officials naturally view as unpleasant.

Third, both the United States and the world face environmental problems tied to an expanding population. The fertilizers and pesticides popular for commercial farming eventually contaminate water used for drinking or for recreation. Chemicals needed to produce consumer goods, and fuels used to transport people and products, all cause health problems. Trees are cut down and unpopulated areas devastated to make room for housing developments and roads. Isolated locales once treasured for vacations, for outdoor sports, or just for their natural beauty may not be so isolated any more. Providing energy and water sometimes strains communities, as does disposing of garbage and other wastes. All of these concerns worsen as the population increases, and immigrants account for half of the country's current population growth. Obviously, many sorts of policies can address the declining quality of life associated with overcrowding, and shifts in population from one country to another may not worsen global problems. But concern with the environment does lead some Americans to question the wisdom of admitting even more people.[29]

Finally, whereas late-nineteenth-century law barred persons "likely to become a public charge," the immigration law adopted in 1965 gives preference to those with relatives already in the country: Two-thirds of all immigrants today are relatives of those already here. In consequence, a higher proportion of dependent persons—especially older people—have been admitted in recent years than in previous eras. [30] Thus, current U.S. immigration policy admits fewer taxpayers and more people in need of services than did earlier laws that gave first preference to productive workers. Even if immigrants as a group pay as much in taxes as they consume in services, many American taxpayers ask why they should admit *anyone* likely to be dependent on government programs.

Appropriate changes in public policy might be able to address these concrete reasons why some Americans oppose immigration. However, some Americans would still oppose immigration because they regard it as a different sort of risk, not an economic risk but one that threatens the American political culture. They believe that immigrants who speak different languages, believe in different religions, and practice different customs threaten American unity. They urge the United States to close the door before too much *pluribus* destroys the *unum*.[31] To evaluate such a claim, we need to understand the source of American unity. That is the subject of the next section.

Philosophical Unity

From the French visitor Alexis de Tocqueville in the 1830s to the Swede Gunnar Myrdal in the 1940s, foreign observers have claimed that Americans agree on a common core of values. These fundamental beliefs usually are described as *liberal*—but the term means something different when applied to political philosophy than it does when applied to current events.[32] Classical **liberalism** is a philosophy that emerged in Europe as medieval thought disintegrated in the religious wars of the seventeenth century. It sought to liberate individuals from a society structured by heredity and religious privilege, and to empower them at the expense of the nobility and the clergy. Roughly speaking, liberal thinkers wanted people to make political and religious choices for themselves. Modern-day American conservatives, who champion keeping government out of economic decisions, and modern-day American liberals, who champion keeping government out of moral decisions, are both outgrowths of a "liberal" political culture.

Focusing on individuals rather than groups gave liberal thinkers a unique perspective on society and government. They did not view people as a product of their society, a view that goes back to the Greeks. Rather, they considered society a creation of the individuals who made it up. Perhaps the best example of this perspective would be the "social contract" theorists, such as Thomas Hobbes, John Locke, and Jean-Jacques Rousseau. These philosophers tried to imagine what human life would be like in a natural state, without society or government, so that they could deduce why people would have created social and political institutions in the first place. That is, their whole approach started from an assumption that people can exist as isolated beings. They imagined government as nothing more than a creation of the individuals who chose to develop and perpetuate it, an agreement much like a contract in which both rulers and ruled accept certain rights, duties, and obligations.

Locke developed a string of specific political principles out of this line of reasoning. First, individuals have basic rights—life, liberty, and property—that precede the existence of government and that government therefore may not violate. Second, individuals are equal under the law; there are no distinctions based on heredity or religion. Third, to safeguard rights, government must be limited. Fourth, governments are instrumental, nothing more than tools people use to ensure their own safety—so a state succeeds only when it serves the citizenry. It is not an end or value in itself. Fifth, and

liberalism
A philosophy that elevates and empowers the individual as opposed to religious, hereditary, governmental, or other forms of authority.

finally, when a government threatens rights or fails to protect citizens, they may replace it with another.

The preceding paragraph should have a familiar ring. American colonists read social-contract theorists such as Locke in the years before rebelling against England. Liberalism provided the philosophical foundation for their democratic experiment. Thomas Jefferson encapsulated the spirit of classical liberalism in the *Declaration of Independence:*

> We hold these truths to be self-evident: That all men are created equal, that they are endowed by their Creator with certain inalienable Rights, that among these are Life, Liberty, and the Pursuit of Happiness.
>
> That to secure these rights Governments are instituted among Men, deriving their just powers from the consent of the governed;
>
> That whenever any Form of Government becomes destructive of these ends, it is the Right of the People to alter or to abolish it, and to institute new Government, laying its foundation on such principles and organizing its powers in such form, as to them shall seem most likely to effect their Safety and Happiness. .

These eloquent sentences capture the five tenets of liberal philosophy: political equality, rights, instrumental government, limited government, and the right to rebel. The Constitution and its Bill of Rights followed on this liberal tradition by laying out in detail the rights of citizens, the limits on government, and rules for changing leaders that would make future rebellion unnecessary.

To some degree, philosophers and historians have exaggerated the extent to which all Americans ascribe to a coherent political philosophy. Many writers refer to the American "creed" and the American "ethos." Terms like these suggest a more unified and well-defined set of beliefs than actually exists. In fact, at the time of the American Revolution, liberalism coexisted with a rival, civic republican tradition.[33] According to Gordon Wood, **civic republicanism** placed more emphasis on the welfare of the community relative to the rights of the individual.[34] Called "communitarian" today, this tradition faded over time but certainly has not disappeared—as illustrated by President John F. Kennedy's famous exhortation: "Ask not what your country can do for you; ask what you can do for your country!"

Critics also point out that the rights and privileges exalted in the liberal tradition extended only so far. In particular, they did not extend to the Native American tribes that were destroyed by the American settlers, and they did not extend fully to African Americans until a century after the Civil War. Full rights and privileges did not extend to women until even later.[35] And the rights of other minority groups such as homosexuals remain matters of political disagreement today. But even if the "liberal tradition" has been less than all-encompassing, there is plenty of evidence that Americans agree on certain basic "liberal" principles and that Americans differ in systematic ways from the citizens of other democracies.

American Individualism

Perhaps the most striking way in which Americans differ from people elsewhere lies in the balance they prefer between individual responsibility on the one hand, and collective—especially governmental—responsibility on the other. Figure 4.3 compares the responses of citizens of 13 democracies to a question about the responsibility of the

civic republicanism
A political philosophy that emphasizes the obligation of citizens to act virtuously in pursuit of the common good.

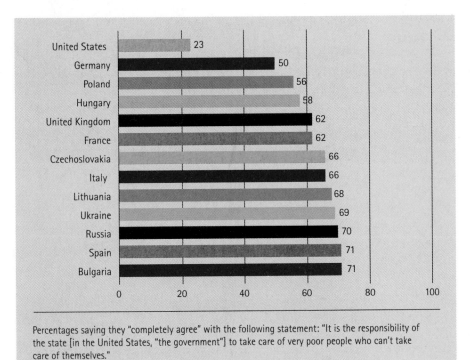

FIGURE 4.3
Americans Emphasize Individual Responsibility Much More Than People Elsewhere

SOURCE: Everett Carll Ladd, *The American Ideology* (Storrs, CT: The Roper Center, 1994), p. 79.

Percentages saying they "completely agree" with the following statement: "It is the responsibility of the state [in the United States, "the government"] to take care of very poor people who can't take care of themselves."

state. Note that less than a quarter of the American respondents completely agreed, "It is the responsibility of the government to take care of very poor people who can't take care of themselves." The proportion of Americans opting for governmental responsibility is only half as large as that in the next closest country (Germany) and barely a third as large as the average of the other 12 democracies.

Another survey of six long-established Western democracies found Americans to be similarly one-sided in their belief that individuals are responsible for their own welfare. As shown in Figure 4.4, just over a quarter of Americans supported a government-guaranteed income, whereas majorities of Germans, British, Italians, and Dutch supported it. Little more than one-fifth of Americans felt that the government should provide a decent standard of living for the unemployed, compared to an average of two-thirds in the four European democracies. A majority of Americans even rejected the mildly egalitarian notion that the government should reduce income inequality. Australia seems to occupy a middle position between the individual responsibility favored by Americans and the governmental responsibility favored by Europeans. Australia, too, is a society of immigrants, and its citizens seem to share some of the beliefs and values of Americans.

Americans are suspicious of governmental power and skeptical about governmental competence, attitudes that reinforce their emphasis on individual responsibility. In Samuel Huntington's view, "the distinctive aspect of the American creed is its anti-government character. Opposition to power and suspicion of government as the most dangerous embodiment of power are the central themes of American political thought."[36] If people doubt the motives and abilities of government, they can hardly be expected to grant it expansive powers and responsibilities. Americans also believe that

FIGURE 4.4

Americans Are Far Less
Supportive Than People
Elsewhere of Government
Actions to Reduce Economic
Inequality

SOURCE: Ladd, *The American
Ideology* (1994), p. 75.

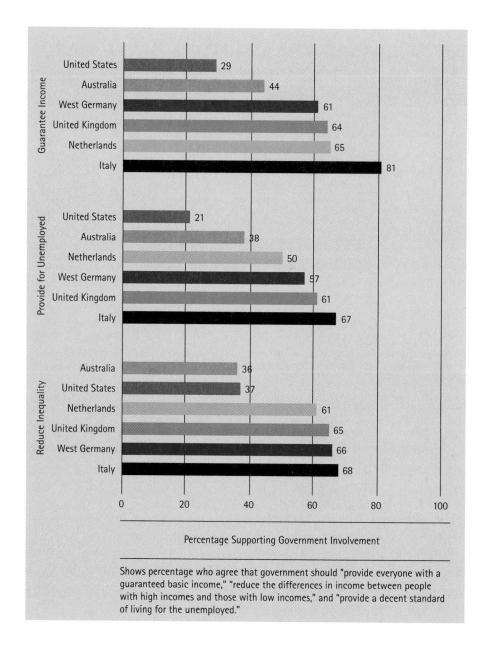

Percentage Supporting Government Involvement

Shows percentage who agree that government should "provide everyone with a
guaranteed basic income," "reduce the differences in income between people
with high incomes and those with low incomes," and "provide a decent standard
of living for the unemployed."

individual responsibility works, that hard work and perseverance pay off. People elsewhere are less likely to see personal effort as a sure means to better one's life, and therefore less likely to be optimistic about getting ahead (see Figure 4.5). Once again,
Australians are more similar to Americans than are Europeans.

One of the most striking features of the American belief in individual achievement
and responsibility is that it is not closely tied to the actual social and economic circumstances in which Americans find themselves. We might think that those at the bottom
of the economic ladder would be far less individualistic and optimistic than those at the
top, but that expectation has been contradicted repeatedly. Even the very poorest
Americans reject a government-guaranteed income, and only the very poorest feel that
the government should reduce income differences. There is little or no relationship

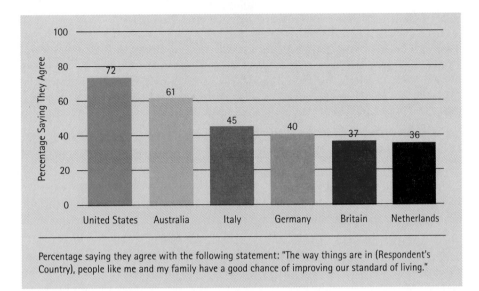

FIGURE 4.5
Americans Are Much More Optimistic About Their Chances of Getting Ahead Than People Elsewhere

SOURCE: Ladd, *The American Ideology* (1994), p. 76.

Percentage saying they agree with the following statement: "The way things are in (Respondent's Country), people like me and my family have a good chance of improving our standard of living."

between income and belief in the benefits of hard work: Two-thirds of the poorest Americans subscribe to this belief, just as do two-thirds of the most affluent.[37]

Other studies reveal that poor Americans are as likely as others to embrace the "work ethic" and equally likely to take personal responsibility for their condition.[38] The poor dislike the progressive income tax almost as much as the rich (see Chapter 19).[39] Perhaps the most powerful illustration of American individualism lies in the attitudes of minorities. African Americans and Latinos clearly share less in the American dream than do whites. On average, they earn less, work in less prestigious occupations, and suffer discrimination in many forms. It comes as no surprise, then, that they are a bit less likely than whites to embrace the individualist ethic, but it does come as a surprise that they embrace as much of it as they do. In terms of their belief in hard work and individual responsibility, black and Latino Americans are more like white Americans than like Europeans (see Figure 4.6). In sum, even those Americans who are faring poorly in an individualist social order still support its basic premises.[40]

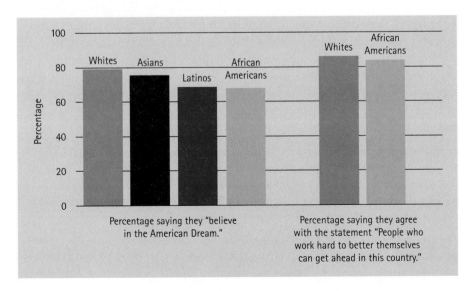

FIGURE 4.6
Even Racial and Ethnic Minorities Share the Individualist Values of the Larger Society

SOURCE: Adapted from data reported in "People, Opinions and Polls: An American Dilemma (Part II)," *The Public Perspective* (February/March 1996): 19–35.

The Tension Between Individualism and Equality

The findings on American individualism raise an important question: What about equality? Liberal philosophy attaches great importance to equality, and writers in the liberal tradition typically mention it just after liberty. Yet great inequalities exist in the United States. For example, not only has the income distribution changed little during the past six decades, it has actually become less egalitarian since the early 1970s.[41] Nevertheless, Americans do not demand that such inequalities be eliminated or even lessened. Most Americans do not regard economic and social inequality as justification for government action.

At one time there was no great incompatibility between liberty and equality. Indeed, Tocqueville and other early nineteenth-century visitors were struck by the extent of social and economic equality in the United States. Liberty and equality were thought to be complementary in the sense that free people would use their liberty to achieve economic success, and an economically secure middle class would use its resources to promote liberty. Economic development weakened the association between liberty and equality after the Civil War. The Industrial Revolution produced great concentrations of private wealth on the one hand and masses of low-wage workers on the other. Under such conditions, liberty and equality became detached.

Some Americans grew disillusioned with a political system that could tolerate such massive social and economic inequalities. Nevertheless, American reform movements typically focus on curbing the worst abuses of corporate power; they do not attack the foundations of the economic system generating such great inequality. Their limited demand for change might suggest that Americans actually do not value equality very much. The explanation for this apparent inconsistency, though, is that America's political culture requires only a limited kind of equality. Liberalism emphasized equality before the law, regardless of heredity or religious faith or personal connections; it did not demand economic equality. It guaranteed freedom to pursue happiness; it did not promise that everyone would achieve happiness. Americans regard economic inequality as not only inevitable but also fair—those who produce more for society deserve to receive more, even if they get rich. Americans therefore reject aggressive government action to erase such inequalities.

Today, it is customary to talk about this distinction in terms of the difference between **equality of opportunity** and **equality of condition.** Americans strongly support equality of opportunity: Everyone should have a fair chance. After the competition starts, though, may the best person win! Americans just as strongly reject attempts to bring about equality of condition, because that may involve rewarding people who are undeserving at the expense of those who work harder. Survey data probing attitudes about affirmative action reflect this distinction. Americans favor affirmative action for women and minorities when the survey questions are clear that equal opportunity is the goal:

> Ninety-four percent agree that "Our society should do what is necessary to make sure that everyone has an equal opportunity to succeed."
>
> Seventy-nine percent agree that "After years of discrimination, it is only fair to set up special programs to make sure that women and minorities are given every chance to have equal opportunities in employment and education."

But Americans just as strongly oppose affirmative action when the survey questions indicate that equality of outcome is the goal:

equality of opportunity
The notion that individuals should have an equal chance to advance economically through individual talent and hard work.

equality of condition
The notion that all individuals have a right to a more or less equal part of the material goods that society produces.

Eighty-six percent don't think "blacks and other minorities should receive preference in college admissions to make up for past inequalities."

Eighty percent don't think "blacks and other minorities should receive preference in hiring to make up for past inequalities."[42]

Simulation

What Are American Civic Values?

As far as most Americans are concerned, equality of opportunity should be sufficient. The rest is up to the individual. This belief also shows up in government policy. As social critics have pointed out, the United States spends a smaller proportion of its national income on social welfare than most other democracies—and spends especially little on the young (see Chapter 18). But the United States historically has spent a larger proportion of its national income on education than other democracies. Education is not "welfare." It is a means for creating equal opportunity, a way for individuals to improve their skills and become better economic competitors. That idea resonates with Americans.[43]

One Nation, Under God?

The American political culture stands out in one other notable way, which is the widespread importance of religion and religiosity. Americans are more likely to believe in God, to attend religious services, and to report that religion plays an important role in their lives. In short, as Figure 4.7 shows, American citizens are more involved with religion than citizens in other democracies.

To a certain extent, the visibility of religious faith traces back to the nation's founding. The original settlement of the United States was carried out in part by people seeking the freedom to practice their religion. These deeply, even radically, spiritual people sought to escape oppression and persecution by the established churches of Europe.

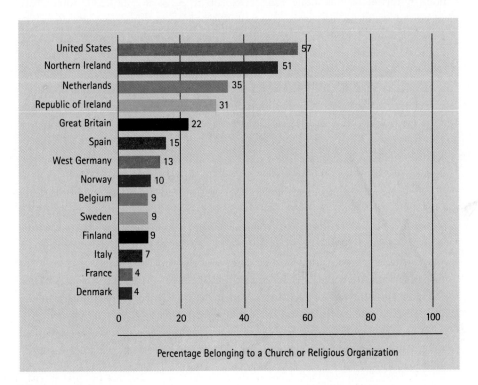

Percentage Belonging to a Church or Religious Organization

FIGURE 4.7

Americans Are Far More Involved with Religion Than People Elsewhere

SOURCE: Ladd, *The American Ideology*, p. 71.

Furthermore, the nation periodically has replenished its store of religious energy through great spiritual "awakenings" that wash over the country: the first in the 1730s and 1740s, the second around 1800 and into Jackson's presidency (1828–1836), the third starting in the 1890s and lasting about two decades.

Religion has always colored the political life of the United States. Political and religious institutions usually remain separate, with a "wall between church and state" (although there have been exceptions, such as the Congregational Church, which was the established church of Connecticut until 1818 and of Massachusetts until 1833). Rather, religion and morality usually operate in politics through the actions of individual voters and leaders. For example, aside from archaic provisions in a few state constitutions, no law requires political leaders to believe in a deity.[44] Such a provision is unnecessary, however, because a majority of Americans report that they will not vote for an otherwise qualified candidate who happens to be an atheist.[45] More generally, Americans tend to evaluate their politicians in more moralistic terms than do the citizens of other countries—although voters occasionally tolerate moral lapses, as they did with Bill Clinton.[46]

Church leaders cannot impose laws on American citizens and punish them for immoral behavior, as they can in some countries. Nevertheless, most outside observers agree that American politics is highly moralistic. (Critics may use the word *puritanical* instead, but they are using the term inappropriately.) Throughout history, religiously motivated Americans have attempted to use government to improve the character of their fellow citizens—that is, "to legislate morality"—more so than people in other democracies. At various times and places, laws have restricted recreational activities on Sundays, prohibited people from drinking, and censored what people can read or watch.

The continual rebirth of religion in the United States puzzles many observers. The nation's historical origins alone cannot explain it. After all, numerous forces have changed American society since the founding: westward expansion, the Industrial Revolution, immigration, and great wars, to name a few. Other democracies have an "established" church, an official religion that is often supported by the state. The Anglican Church is the established church in Great Britain, the Catholic Church in Italy, the Lutheran Church in Norway, and the Eastern Orthodox Church in Greece. In the United States, no religious institution receives direct government support. Instead, the nation contains a diverse assortment of religions, denominations, branches, and sects.

Furthermore, religiosity does not seem to fit well with American values. Christian faith, for example, may impose various burdens on members, such as an obligation to their fellow human beings or a duty to help create heaven on earth. That is, it calls on individuals to believe that they are part of something bigger than themselves. This orientation does not seem terribly compatible with a political culture that exalts the individual, that encourages personal autonomy. By calling Americans to reflect on spiritual matters, religion also seems to clash with the American reputation for practicality. Americans stereotypically focus on problem solving, on material success. They are supposed to show a distinctive trust in logic, in science, in technology, in the evidence before their eyes (a way of thinking that philosophers call "positivism"). How can we explain the robustness of religious faith in a country with no established church, with a reputation for individualism, and with a people known for their hard-headed pragmatism?

One explanation points to the diversity of religion. In April 2000, 1600 groups were listed on "house church" Web sites.[47] This wide range of options may make it easier to find a comfortable match with some religion in America than in other countries, where citizens typically have a much smaller range of choices. If a person doesn't like one religion, there are numerous others from which to choose, and exceptionally hard-to-please worshippers can always start their own churches. Similarly, church leaders know that they do not have a captive audience. They compete to retain the loyalty of members. Clergy adapt their "product" to the changing interests and values of their members. They provide services and auxiliary activities (youth clubs, sports clubs, and even singles clubs) that members value. Just as the free market in economics encourages economic enterprise, a free market in religion may encourage religious enterprise: The clergy act as entrepreneurs and actively "sell" their respective religions. Thus, Americans may be more involved with religion than people in other countries because, stimulated by competition, American religion offers them more reasons to be.

Perhaps the most intriguing explanation for the persistence of religiosity in the United States has been proposed by Robert Booth Fowler, who argues that the liberal tradition and religiosity do not conflict at all. He maintains, in fact, that just the opposite is true—that the liberal tradition creates a deep need for religion. People steeped in the liberal tradition jealously guard their rights and hold themselves personally responsible for their successes and failures. They create a society characterized by social and geographic mobility and by rapid social and economic change.

Fowler suggests that many people find life in such a society precarious, or at least somewhat lonely. He sees religion as filling a gap in American lives. Whereas citizens in communal cultures already feel part of something bigger than themselves, individualism leaves Americans with a greater need for a religious dimension in their lives:

> Religion has aided liberalism by being a *refuge* from liberalism. . . . [I]t provides an escape from liberal culture, a place of comfort where individualism, competition,

this-worldly pragmatism, and relentless rationalism do not hold sway. In a liberal country with liberal citizens, religion is a place where one can come home . . . and *then* emerge refreshed for the battles of life in the liberal world.[48]

If true, this argument would explain the periodic occurrence of religious awakenings. They should result whenever the prosperity created by individualism draws Americans too far from the spiritual ideals that they hold dear.[49] People eventually begin to wonder whether there is something more to life than money and success. Others are appalled by the self-serving behavior of their fellow individualists. Thus people turn to religion as an alternate avenue to personal satisfaction and as a means of correcting the destructive behavior of others.

Some observers believe that the United States is in the middle of its fourth religious awakening, for reasons similar to those implied by Fowler's theory. Evangelical Protestantism surged in the 1980s, they suggest, as a reaction to the excesses of the 1960s, a period of great economic growth during which the baby boomers—the individualistic "me generation"—came of age. Such sweeping historical claims are difficult to prove. Nevertheless, the last several decades only reinforce an indisputable fact about the American political culture: Along with individualism and belief in equality of opportunity, religiosity is a long-standing trait of the American public.

Why a Liberal Political Culture?

The time has now come to answer the question posed at the start of this chapter: How can we explain the apparent contradiction between a population that is strikingly heterogeneous in its ethnic, racial, and religious makeup but surprisingly homogeneous in the beliefs and values which constitute its political culture? Historically, opponents of immigration have feared that influxes of new, diverse peoples would alter or destroy the American political culture. Why have the opponents of multiculturalism been wrong in the past? Only if we can answer that question will it be possible to determine whether the new immigration threatens America's political culture today.

Traditional Explanations of American Liberalism

Early American colonists tended to come from what, looking back, we might call the European "middle class." They usually were not impoverished peasants, but they also were not powerful nobles. In short, they were the very merchants, professionals, and artisans among whom liberal ideas tended to flourish. They carried their political philosophy with them to North America, where they found little to resist it. According to scholar Louis Hartz, the American colonies lacked a feudal tradition to parallel the established social structure of Europe. There was no hereditary aristocracy or established church to defend or to resist, nor was there an oppressed peasant class that might rise up.[50] Dissenters aside, the United States formed among a white population for whom classical liberalism could be taken as "self evident." (Extending liberal ideals across racial lines took much longer.)

Perhaps as important as what the United States lacked, however, is what it had. In particular, it had a great deal of land. North America was a sparsely populated continent over which the United States steadily expanded.[51] Some historians suggest that the frontier operated like a social safety valve: Rather than revolt against intolerable conditions, the only option in the settled countries of Europe, struggling Americans found it easier to pack up their belongings, move west, grab some land (perhaps from Mexico or an indigenous tribe), and start again.

A plentiful supply of land and a scarcity of labor meant that ambitious individuals could and did succeed. Conditions in the new country therefore reinforced the individualistic values that early settlers brought with them. And with little competition from alternate value systems, a liberal political order and a market economy thrived. Generations of radical critics of American society have plaintively asked, "Why no socialism in America?"[52] Many complex philosophical and historical answers have been offered, but the simplest answer is that Americans never saw much need for socialism. Under the conditions that prevailed, individual effort usually was enough to provide an acceptable life for most people; they did not require governmental solutions (let alone revolutionary ones).

Still, questions remain. The frontier was officially closed more than a century ago, and labor shortages have not been of much concern for more than half a century. So even if social conditions in the nineteenth century reinforced the beliefs and values of the early settlers, how relevant is that today? Slaves freed after the Civil War certainly had little experience with liberty or equality. Moreover, the millions of immigrants who arrived after the Civil War were not from liberal societies. Most of them came from authoritarian states with established churches and had lived their lives in communal peasant societies that *did* have feudal traditions. What is the basis for *their* adherence to the individualist values of the liberal tradition?

Perhaps the answer lies in a process of **political socialization** that continues to instill liberal values long after the objective support for those values—social equality, an unsettled land, a frontier—has eroded. Certainly, material conditions are not the only factor that determines how people think and view the world; different cultures socialize their children in different ways of thinking and different ways of viewing the world, even under similar material circumstances. Beginning in the family and continuing in schools, churches, and other organizations, societies instill certain values and patterns of thinking in their members. Thus, the explanation for the persistence of the liberal tradition may be a simple one: Socialization perpetuates a consensus established in the eighteenth century, a consensus so dominant that it was able to integrate the children of slaves as well as tens of millions of immigrants.

Many scholars find such an explanation insufficient. For one thing, one of the principal means by which immigrants were integrated into American society was through the efforts of political parties, particularly the urban machines discussed in Chapter 8. The machines were interested in controlling government; to do that they had to win elections, and immigrant votes counted just as much as those of the native-born. Thus the machines organized each arriving group: In some eastern cities the Democrats gained an edge by organizing the Irish, so the Republicans countered by organizing the Italians, and so on. But the urban machines were not the embodiment of liberal, individualist values. On the contrary, the machines were something of an anomaly in the larger American political culture; they were collectivist and clannish—with an emphasis on obedience and loyalty, not independence. Because machine politics and immigration are closely associated in American history, we might expect political socialization to have pushed immigrants in a direction different from the liberal tradition.

political socialization
The set of psychological and sociological processes by which families, schools, religious organizations, communities, and other societal units inculcate beliefs and values in their members.

Renewing the Tradition

Immigration is a difficult process that tends to attract people with a greater sense of individualism and independence than found among those who stay in their home countries.

Newer Explanations

Recent research suggests other explanations for why classical liberalism survived over a long period, despite the influx of millions of diverse people from contrary traditions. Sven Steinmo argues that scholars have misunderstood the liberal tradition. Rather than maintaining that liberal ideas shape American government and politics, Steinmo argues the opposite—that the government and politics of the United States create and recreate the ideas.[53] Specifically, he argues that American government is so fragmented and decentralized that it can rarely act in a positive way to improve society. Often it is "gridlocked" or unable to act, and when it does act, it often does so via the exchange of political favors among special interests. In consequence, successive generations of Americans learn the same basic lesson: Rely on yourself because you cannot rely on government, and best keep government limited because it will usually act in support of special interests. Given their institutions, Americans would have learned this lesson whether they were originally liberal individualists or not. Steinmo's key insight is that, once established, institutions that originally *reflected* particular values may come to *generate* those values.

Even more important for understanding the impact of immigration, though, is the possibility that social diversity and the liberal tradition never contradicted each other in the first place. Rather than posing a threat to American traditions, in fact, the flow of diverse peoples to America may have reinforced and strengthened American traditions. How could that be the case? The answer lies in what statistical analysts refer to as *self-selection*. With the notable exception of African Americans, immigrants came to the United States voluntarily. True, many came when crops failed, when they could not find work, or when they faced political persecution at home. Emigration under such circumstances might not seem to have occurred by choice, *but not everyone chose to emigrate.* Only a small fraction of the potential immigrants—less than 1 percent—actually left their own countries. Furthermore, not all of them chose to stay in the United States; perhaps a third of immigrants eventually return to their home countries.

What kind of person would have been most likely to adopt a new nation, leaving family, friends, and village behind? Remember that immigration through most of history was not a matter of taking a train to Dublin, Frankfurt, or Rome and catching a flight to New York or Chicago. Before the Civil War, the journey usually took months, as immigrants walked to a port and then suffered through a long, miserable journey below deck on a sailing ship. Even after the Civil War, when the steamship shortened the ocean voyage and the railroad shortened the journey overland, it still took weeks. Many (if not most) of the people who booked passage knew that they would never see their relatives or their homes again.[54] What kind of people made such a decision?

In all probability the people who immigrated already were—relative to their own societies—unusually individualistic. They were more motivated to break free from the traditions of their communities. They were more ambitious, more willing to run risks in the hope of bettering themselves—in Hartz's words, more likely to possess "the spirit which repudiated peasantry and tenantry."[55] Prejudiced as it was, even the Immigration Commission in 1911 recognized that "emigrating to a strange and distant country, although less of an undertaking than formerly, is still a serious and relatively difficult matter, requiring a degree of courage and resourcefulness not possessed by weaklings of any class."[56] In short, even if they had never heard of the liberal tradition, immigrants already embodied much of its spirit.

Given this inherent independent spirit, immigration and the resulting diversity never were a threat to American values. On the contrary, successive waves of immigrants rejuvenated those values. People who were willing to endure hardships, eager to work hard, and convinced that they could have a better life were more than compatible with the American way of life. We have no reason to believe that today's immigrants are any different. They too have left homes and families. They have endured hardships to come to a new land with a different culture and language. In some extreme cases, they have risked life and limb to emigrate, as did the "boat people" of southeast Asia—who braved pirates, sharks, and storms—and the Cubans who swam from rafts to the Florida coast. Such people display a kind of individual initiative that can fairly be considered "American," regardless of their nationality.

By reputation, Republicans are supposed to be unsympathetic to the poor and disadvantaged. Furthermore, partisan interests would seem to encourage them to oppose immigration, because minority-group members typically vote for Democrats. Yet Republican leaders sometimes champion immigrants. During the 1994 battle over California's Prop. 187, which denied government services to illegal immigrants and their children, prominent Republicans William Bennett and Jack Kemp raised eyebrows by publicly opposing the initiative.[57] Similarly, in 1996 Rudolph Giuliani, the Republican mayor of New York, made news by denouncing congressional attempts to limit immigrant eligibility for welfare and other governmental services.[58] In the 2000 presidential campaign, George W. Bush appealed directly for support in immigrant communities, and as president he has continued to do so. (See Election Connection, page 110.)

Why would Republican leaders resist both their party's image and its short-term interests? They appeared to be betting that the earlier pattern of American history will continue in the future. They are gambling on an assumption that Mexican laborers, Korean grocers, and Middle Eastern service-station operators are today's successors to the Irish laborers, Italian grocers, and Jewish shopkeepers of generations past. They are betting that although ethnic activists often are allied with the Democratic Party, most members of those ethnic groups are focused more on economics than on politics. Over time, such people will become middle-class Americans concerned about their tax rates, their schools, and their property values—and willing to consider Republican appeals.

Regardless of their motivations, these leaders are acting in a fashion consistent with the research evidence. There are indications that, in the long term, today's immigrants will only reinforce the distinctly "American" political culture. For example, on the basis of extensive surveys, de la Garza reports that the children of Puerto Rican immigrants hold values almost indistinguishable from those native English speakers in similar socioeconomic conditions.[59] De la Garza's studies of Mexican immigrants reach very similar conclusions.[60] A 1995 Gallup survey found that immigrants, even those who have been in the country ten years or less, are virtually indistinguishable from native-born Americans—both in their beliefs about economic opportunity and in their general attitudes toward assimilation.[61]

ELECTION CONNECTION

Bush Courts the Latino Vote

Immigrants to America historically have met with prejudice and hostility—and often official discrimination at the hands of government as well. But in virtually all cases, discrimination eventually fades and immigrants join the mainstream of American society. Usually this assimilation occurs when politicians begin to see the immigrants in a different light: as potential voters.

The party machines of the late nineteenth century played an important role in the incorporation of the millions of new immigrants of that era. Although there are few machines around these days, public officials continue to seek support among communities of new immigrants, promising favorable policies in return. President George W. Bush provides the latest example.

In the 1990s the positions of Republicans in states like California gave the national party an anti-immigrant image, an image that Bush has worked hard to erase. The president speaks Spanish tolerably well, his brother Jeb is married to a Mexican American, and in the president's Texas gubernatorial campaigns he received significant support from voters of Mexican extraction. Building on this record, Bush appealed for Latino support during the 2000 presidential campaign—but more important, he has continued to do so as president.

On the symbolic front, President Bush invited President Vicente Fox of Mexico to be the guest at his first state dinner. The two presidents held a series of well-publicized discussions, but the president went well beyond symbolism. Bush provoked considerable controversy within his own party when he expressed support for an amnesty for undocumented workers who had entered the country from Mexico. He antagonized some conservatives by declining to have the Justice Department join in an appeal that might have brought an end to affirmative action. He disappointed the Navy by ordering a halt to the unpopular use of Vieques, a Puerto Rican island, for bombing practice. And Bush nominated Miguel Estrada to a powerful federal appeals court (although Estrada withdrew his candidacy after Democrats filibustered to block Senate confirmation of the appointment).

The president believes that Republicans should court Latino support. Latinos are culturally conservative on many issues, unlike the Democratic party. They have no history binding them to the Democrats, as African Americans do. And most Latinos work in the private sector, including many small businesspeople, so they seem a promising constituency. In the years to come, it will be interesting to watch Republicans court the Latino vote and Democrats attempt to fend them off. Republicans have already begun airing a Spanish-language TV news magazine—*Abriendo Caminos* (Opening Pathways)—and explicitly urging officials to learn Spanish. The outcome could determine control of Congress and of the presidency for decades to come.

This is just the latest example of a continuing struggle for votes that characterizes American politics.

• *Which do you think will prove more important in the parties' contest for Latino votes—the Latino community's identity as a disadvantaged minority (a traditionally Democratic appeal) or their economic interests as ambitious, individualistic workers (a traditionally Republican appeal)?*

• *What other groups are—or could be—courted on the basis of a cultural appeal?*

SOURCE: Greg Gireaux, "Pursuing the Political Prize of America's Hispanic Vote," *CQ Weekly*, June 24, 2002: 1711.

Demographic data suggest similar conclusions. One widely noted study reports that on the basis of standard measures of assimilation (citizenship, home ownership, English acquisition, and intermarriage), today's immigrants "overwhelmingly do what immigrants have always done: slowly, often painfully, but quite assuredly, embrace the language, cultural norms and loyalties of America."[62] Other studies suggest that the use of English as a principal language is occurring *more* rapidly among the children of today's immigrants than in the past.[63] And educational and economic progress among Latinos is occurring faster than among earlier European immigrants.[64]

In sum, the evidence is mounting that American society is evolving along a path that does not support the fears of the opponents of diversity. Ethnic, racial, and religious diversity can coexist with agreement on basic values. Although the process is not easy, Americans seem to be working their way through today's conflicts just as they worked through them in the past. On balance, today's diversity is more likely to reinforce than to undermine the American political culture.

Chapter Summary

For more than two centuries, the United States has been a study in contrasts. On the one hand, this country always has been socially diverse, containing a wider array of ethnic and religious groups than most other lands. On the other hand, the diverse citizenry of the United States has long shown a higher level of agreement on fundamental political principles than is found in other democracies. The fundamental political principles that are so widespread in the United States grew out of a classical liberal political philosophy that stresses the rights and liberties of individuals.

Native-born citizens have always feared that immigration was a threat to the distinctly American political culture. Much of today's multiculturalism debate is thus reminiscent of debates that have taken place throughout American history. Recent immigrants want to maintain some part of their cultural distinctiveness; so did previous waves of immigrants. "Native citizens" worry that the new immigrants are too different to fit easily into American society; so did native-born Americans a century ago. Such fears have proved unfounded in the past, and they probably will prove unfounded in the future. Immigrants usually reinforce rather than weaken the spirit of individualism in the United States. The very fact of their immigrating suggests that they possess the ambitious, individualistic outlook that is such a prominent part of the American political culture.

Key Terms

citizenship, p. 88
civic republicanism, p. 98
equality of condition, p. 102

equality of opportunity, p. 102
liberalism, p. 97
multiculturalism, p. 89

political culture, p. 88
political socialization, p. 107

Suggested Readings

Of General Interest

Fuchs, Lawrence. *The American Kaleidoscope: Race, Ethnicity, and the Civic Culture.* Hanover, NH: University Press of New England, 1990. Dispassionate discussion of the problems and prospects of contemporary immigrants and African Americans. Prefers "kaleidoscope" to "melting pot" as a metaphor for the history of ethnicity in America.

Lipset, Seymour Martin. *American Exceptionalism.* New York: Norton, 1996. A recent work on the American political culture by an eminent senior scholar who has spent much of his career studying it.

Mills, Nicolaus, ed. *Arguing Immigration: Are New Immigrants a Wealth of Diversity . . . Or a Crushing Burden?* New York: Simon & Schuster, 1994. This collection of essays provides a good overview of the contemporary immigration debate.

Portes, Alejandro, and Ruben G. Rumbaut. *Immigrant America: A Portrait.* Berkeley, CA: University of California Press, 1997. A sympathetic account of the post-1965 wave of immigration. Like much contemporary writing, it exaggerates the differences between immigration today and that of a century ago.

Focused Studies

Borjas, George. *Heaven's Door: Immigration Policy and the American Economy.* Princeton, NJ: Princeton University Press, 1999. Argues that immigration has hurt the poorest native-born workers, especially African Americans. Calls for restricting immigration and limiting it to better-educated and more highly skilled people.

Hartz, Louis. *The Liberal Tradition in America.* New York: Harcourt, 1955. A classic, if impenetrable, discussion of the liberal tradition. Argues that the absence of feudalism allowed liberal ideas to spread without resistance in the United States.

Kleppner, Paul. *The Cross of Culture.* New York: Free Press, 1970. This example of the "ethnocultural" school of political history provides a detailed account of political conflict in the Midwest from the rise of the Republican party to the end of the nineteenth century.

Lee, Kenneth K. *Huddled Masses, Muddled Laws: Why Contemporary Immigration Policy Fails to Reflect Public Opinion.* Westport, CT: Westview Press, 1998. Institutional analysis that questions why immigration policy remains liberal despite growing sentiment to restrict migration into the United States.

Menendez, Albert. *Religion at the Polls.* Philadelphia: Westminster Press, 1977. Survey of the association between religion and voting since the founding of the country.

Simon, Julian. *The Economic Consequences of Immigration.* 2nd ed., Ann Arbor, MI: University of Michigan Press, 1999. Argues that the U.S. economy would benefit from an increase in legal immigration.

On the Web

Anyone with an interest in diversity can find it on the Internet.

http://uscis.gov
The Department of Homeland Security's Web site on immigration and naturalization explains the naturalization process for aspiring citizens and provides statistical reports on the history of immigration to the United States.

www.cic.gc.ca
www.immi.gov.au
www.germany-info.org
Information on the immigration laws of some other countries (Canada, Australia, and Germany, respectively) can be found at these Web sites.

www.diversityinc.com
DiversityInc.com tries to take advantage of American diversity. Sponsored by several major corporations and public interest organiza-tions, the site provides original content on many subgroups of the American population, with a particular focus on the advantages of diversity in the workplace.

www.academicinfo.net
Academia has responded to the call for more diversity by promoting new areas of study, including women's studies, African-American studies, and gay and lesbian studies. The Academic Information Gateway contains bibliographies and guides for these subjects. Of course, these specific subpopulations—and any others you can think of—are repre-sented by many interest groups or clubs, most of them with Web sites. A good search engine can find hundreds of pages, illustrating the diversity of the Internet.

VOICES

OF THE PERMANENT CAMPAIGN

The Racial Politics of Affirmative Action

"Give every citizen the full equality which God enjoins and the law requires, whatever his belief, or race, or the color of his skin."

—President Johnson, May 22, 1964

THE ISSUE

Is affirmative action a justifiable policy for erasing unfair differences among racial groups? Or do affirmative action policies threaten the American belief in equal opportunity by legalizing racial and ethnic favoritism?

Background

African Americans entered the twentieth century lacking almost all of the rights enjoyed by other citizens, including basic equality before the law. Public policy was riddled with racially discriminatory practices, shutting African Americans out of the electoral process, out of employment opportunities, and out of real-estate markets. They could not serve on juries in many courtrooms and faced unequal standards when accused of crimes or when trying to enforce their property rights through lawsuits. Often they were neglected by government programs or services that assisted other citizens. Not surprisingly, then, the United States suffered from chronic and widespread racial inequalities for most of the century—in income, wealth, education, housing, health care, life expectancy, infant mortality, unemployment, occupational prestige, and numerous other quality-of-life indicators.

Over the course of the twentieth century, attitudes about race evolved. American elites came to view racial inequality as embarrassing, unproductive, maybe even immoral—and laws eventually changed to reflect the evolving attitudes. The electoral system increasingly allowed, and sometimes even encouraged, widespread participation by African Americans. Government agencies stopped promoting racial discrimination and moved toward eradicating it. The federal government aggressively worked to end racial segregation (see Chapter 17).

Policy is easier to change than society is, however. Antidiscrimination laws could attack open forms of unfairness, but they could not stop the perpetuation of racial stereo-types—which remained to influence the socially important decisions that both public officials and private individuals made every day. Banning discrimination therefore drove it underground and almost certainly reduced its severity, but lingering prejudices still slowed the pace of progress.

Nor was it realistic to expect that racial group differences would suddenly disappear when elected officials stopped reinforcing them. Rising up from poverty is seldom easy and rarely swift. It can take generations as families move up the occupational ladder, collect educational resources and financial assets, and learn how to exploit new opportunities that have opened up. For African Americans, this process may be especially frustrating if it takes place in a context filled with echoes of the nation's discriminatory past—such as unconscious slights or even intentional insults from white employers and coworkers. In such a demoralizing environment, the path to prosperity can seem obscured, if not impassable.

The Policy Solution

Many civil rights activists in the 1960s despaired at the sluggish rate of racial change. Simply removing barriers to the advancement of individual African Americans no longer seemed sufficient to erase economic imbalances. Activists argued that black-white differences might never disappear unless they were attacked directly and aggressively. They called for active policies that would take affirmative steps to promote minority advancement. One Urban League official, testifying before a congressional committee, worded the perception in this way: "Being color-blind for an official of government is no longer a virtue. What we need is to be positively color conscious and go to work on this job of color."[1]

Racial differences were not the only ones that troubled activists. Racial barriers were uniquely strong after a long history of slavery, Civil War, and segregation—but discrimination has never been exclusive to the African-American experience. At one time or another, with more or less severity, American society has discriminated among people according to their gender, sexuality, language, religion, family organization, national origin, complexion, health, wealth, age, weight, perceived physical attractiveness, and a host of other identifiable traits. Because some of this discriminatory legacy lingers in the form of measurable group differences in life outcomes, a policy to erase inequalities might embrace other

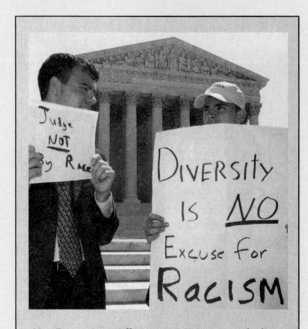

Hot-Button Issue Affirmative action is a severely divisive issue. Opposition to the policy has been especially strong in states with a lot of ethnic diversity—including Asians (who are especially harmed by the policy) and Hispanics (who may gain from the policy even if their families immigrated fairly recently.

disadvantaged groups as well—such as Hispanics, Native Americans, and women.

President Lyndon B. Johnson gave the effort important support in 1965, when he issued Executive Order 11246 requiring federal contractors to take "affirmative action to ensure that applicants are employed . . . without regard to their race, color, religion, sex, or national origin." At first, minorities received preferential treatment quietly, but in the 1970s the Nixon administration made the government's antidiscrimination policies more explicit, by endorsing "goals and timetables" for establishing minority integration into government agencies and minority representation among government contractors.[2] The effort spread to state and local governments during those years as well.

Today, affirmative action constitutes a wide-ranging set of policies carried out by numerous government agencies (as well as initiatives conducted by private organizations), all intended to equalize people by race, ethnicity, or gender. Institutions of higher education provide a useful illustration. Public universities actively recruit minority faculty and administrators, such as by setting aside funds to supplement minority salaries. Administrative units may have to fill out extra paperwork when hiring someone if the chosen candidate is not a minority. Universities also actively recruit minority students, sending representatives to predominantly black high schools or building minority cultural centers on campus. Many establish programs focused on African-American, Latino, Native American, Gay and Lesbian, and/or Women's studies, partly with the hope that such programs will help increase student diversity. They may take minority status into account when evaluating student applications—for example, by viewing potential students more favorably if they come from a disadvantaged group. Finally, they may provide special scholarships and other financial inducements to attract qualified minority students.

Political Dilemmas

Affirmative action poses a severe challenge to American individualism, a core component of the nation's political culture (see Chapter 4). On the one hand, lingering group differences in wealth, income, education, and occupational prestige violate the belief that people should rise or fall based on their individual traits rather than according to the involuntary categories into which they are born. American values provide no justification why the average black child, for example, should enter life with fewer opportunities than the average white child. From this perspective, government must honor the nation's individualistic heritage by compensating for widespread but hidden forms of discrimination. The faster it erodes the advantages that some Americans seem to enjoy over others, the faster the country reaches true equality of opportunity. Affirmative action therefore seems fundamentally consistent with American ideals.

On the other hand, affirmative action seeks to erase social differences by treating people unequally. If a woman can achieve employment with a record that would be insufficient for a male applicant, or if wealthy black students from good high schools can get into university programs with test scores that would be insufficient for impoverished white students from weak high schools, then government is not evaluating the applicants as individuals. It is treating citizens as though they are defined by their involuntary group memberships. From this perspective, affirmative action turns minorities into a privileged class that receives better treatment from government institutions than others do. Furthermore, racial equality is a societal goal, but society as a whole does not appear to pay the costs. Instead, group preferences seem to place the tangible burden on select individuals: those who barely miss out on a good job, a valuable contract, or acceptance to a prestigious school. Affirmative action therefore appears to violate American ideals.

The ambiguous position of affirmative action within the nation's political culture allows well-meaning Americans to take either side in debates over its fairness or constitutionality and to feel that justice is on their side. Conversely, angry conflict over affirmative action frequently springs up because it is so easy for people to believe that their opponents are betraying American values—either by ignoring persistent and offensive racial inequalities, or by implementing policies of "reverse discrimination" against nonminorities.

The uncertainty about who should receive affirmative action places supporters of the policy in a particularly difficult position. Allowing preferential treatment for a wide range of social groups means that more voters have a personal incentive to support it. Hispanics, for example, represent a growing portion of the U.S. population; they surpassed African Americans numerically around 2001. They form a potent voting bloc in southwestern states as well as in many large cities. Women, meanwhile, are not even a "minority" in numerical terms; they outnumber men. When affirmative action includes these politically powerful groups, group members have a self-interested reason to back it. The political coalition broadens.

Inclusive affirmative action policies bring political costs, however. At least three distinct arguments have been offered for giving African Americans preferential treatment. One is that American society must redress the historical mistreatment that African Americans have faced. Black citizens lack opportunities today because of past discrimination, whereas other American citizens have profited from the sins of their fathers and mothers, so it is fair to implement a policy that repairs the lingering damage. Another justification is that society still discriminates by skin color, even though the methods are more subtle than in the past. Without a policy to compensate for this hidden unfairness and level the playing field, black citizens will be less likely to receive the rewards earned by their abilities and effort. The third justification is that American institutions benefit from diversity. For example, schools might do a better job preparing students for life in a multicultural nation if they enroll a racially varied student body.

These arguments do not necessarily apply with equal strength to other minority groups. Consider the first, historical argument. Many Hispanics are recent immigrants whose ancestors did not face discrimination in the United States, let alone segregation or slavery. High rates of intermarriage across ethnic groups also make it much harder to generalize about the conditions that a Hispanic citizen's ancestors likely faced. Women, meanwhile, necessarily have male ancestors. Many are (or have been) married to men, perhaps even incredibly wealthy men. Giving either group preferential treatment therefore risks diluting the morally powerful historical claims that African Americans can offer, and may increase opposition by making affirmative action more widespread. The other arguments for affirmative action also may lose some of their persuasiveness when applied to other minority groups.

What the Public Believes

Reflecting the ambiguous nature of affirmative action policies and their uncomfortable fit within the nation's cultural and legal traditions, the American public is highly conflicted about giving minorities preferential treatment. Americans committed to individualism and individual achievement are especially likely to oppose racial preferences, but opposition is widely distributed across people with different ideologies and different party affiliations.[3]

PRO

Civil Rights.org: A pro-affirmative action Web site that offers a great deal of information on specific programs and recent issues.

www.civilrights.org

American Association for Affirmative Action: Founded in 1974, this association of professionals who manage affirmative action programs runs conferences on affirmative action and dispenses information about programs and opportunities across the country.

www.affirmativeaction.org

NOW: The National Organization for Women promotes affirmative action for all disadvantaged groups but pays special attention to programs for women.

www.now.org

CON

American Civil Rights Institute: An antipreferences organization founded by Ward Connerly to support Proposition 209 in California. The institute continues to oppose racial and gender preferences in several states.

www.acri.org

Center for Individual Rights: A nonprofit public interest law firm that argues many cases in an effort to end preferences in hiring and admissions.

http://www.cir-usa.org

A prominent libertarian public interest law firm, the Institute for Justice, opposes affirmative action as a violation of individual rights.

www.ij.org

Public opinion about affirmative action generally depends on how policies are described in surveys (see Figure 1). The public is most hostile to "quotas"—that is, the reservation of specific jobs, positions, or money for minorities only. Americans prefer a more-flexible system. A 2001 opinion poll found that about 7 out of 10 Americans oppose "preferences." Yet 7 out of 10 Americans support giving minorities "assistance" when they seek jobs or college admission. Overwhelming numbers endorse affirmation action when it is limited to intangible encouragement, such as making a special effort to advertise opportunities or to assure that qualified minorities are considered for those opportunities.[4]

The underlying motives for opposing affirmative action are unclear. Heavily publicized research by political scientist Martin Gilens argues that the whites who oppose welfare are significantly more likely to hold negative racial stereotypes than are welfare supporters. In particular, one powerful predictor of a white person's stand is whether he or she believes that blacks are "lazy."[5] Such studies encourage some scholars to argue that racism fuels the backlash against racially tinged policies such as affirmative action.

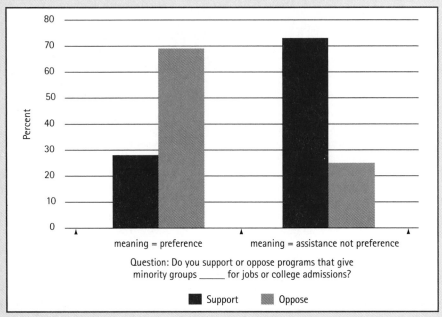

FIGURE 1

Public Support for Affirmative Action Depends on the Meaning of Affirmative Action
Note: Margin of error 2.5%
SOURCE: *ABC News/Washington Post poll released January 17, 2001.*

Other evidence challenges this assumption, however. For one thing, minorities feel conflicted about affirmative action in much the same way as the white majority, even though they may stand to benefit financially from the policies. According to a recent *Washington Post* survey, only 12 percent of blacks (and similarly low numbers of Hispanics and Asians) believed that race should be a factor in admissions or hiring decisions, although they overwhelmingly thought institutions should make an extra effort to find "qualified" applicants from among minority populations.[6]

An older survey, one focused specifically on racial policies, also undermines any broad-brush conclusion that opposition to affirmative action stems from racial hostilities (see Table 1). Some respondents to the 1995 Kaiser Race Poll were asked whether they wanted Congress to limit affirmative action, but also were allowed to clarify who they thought benefited from the policy.[7] Whites who knew that affirmative action helped African Americans were no more likely to want it cut than those who were unaware of this fact. It made much more of a difference whether Hispanics benefited, a group that respondents considered less likely to be held back by discrimination than blacks are. If whites did not believe that the policy helped Hispanics, only 58 percent wanted Congress to limit it, compared to 70 percent of those who believed that the policy applied to Hispanics. Affirmative action therefore may have lost political support because it was extended to groups with less-persuasive claims of deservedness—which would explain why

the most aggressive attempts to limit affirmative action have appeared in states with large Hispanic populations such as California and Texas.

The Kaiser poll also asked questions that tapped into each of the justifications for affirmative action: historical discrimination, current discrimination, and diversity (see Table 1). White respondents did not seem sympathetic with arguments on behalf of diversity: almost 9 out of 10 thought merit should be more important. Affirmative action is on stronger ground when defended in terms of overcoming either past discrimination or present racism, justifications that policy makers have deemphasized recently. More than a third of whites consider racism a major social problem, and they are significantly more likely than other whites to endorse affirmative action. Similarly, more than a third of whites believe the United States has an obligation to make up for past discrimination, an orientation that leads them to be sympathetic with racial preferences.

How the Courts Have Ruled

The U.S. Constitution's Fourteenth Amendment guarantees citizens "equal protection" of the law, so the permissibility of minority preferences is at root a question for the courts. However, judges and legal scholars disagree sharply about the constitutionality of affirmative action when it is used to compensate for societal discrimination (rather than as a remedy

TABLE 1

PUBLIC OPINION AND ARGUMENTS FOR AFFIRMATIVE ACTION

White survey respondents overwhelmingly reject diversity as a defense for racial and ethnic preferences.
Justifications based on current racism or past discrimination seem more persuasive.

Statement Wording	Number of Whites Asked	Percentage Agreeing	Percentage of Those Agreeing Who Want Congress to Limit Affirmative Action
PRESENT DISCRIMINATION Racism is not "a big problem" in "our society today."	670	62%	72.8%
PAST DISCRIMINATION Whites "have not benefitted" from discrimination and "have no responsibility to make up for these wrongs."	194	66%	73.4%
DIVERSITY "Hiring, promotion, and college admissions should be based strictly on merit and qualifications other than race and ethnicity."	664	87%	73.1%

SOURCE: Authors' analysis from 1995 Washington Post/Kaiser Family Foundation/Harvard University Race Poll.

for discrimination conducted by the institution itself). No Supreme Court majority has ever been able to deliver a clear statement on how minority preferences fit into the nation's constitutional law.

For many decades, the landmark Supreme Court opinion on the matter stemmed from a case brought by Alan Bakke, a white applicant to the UC–Davis medical school. He was denied admission in 1978 even though several minority applicants with lower grades and test scores had been accepted, and so sued the university for using an affirmative action policy based on quotas. The eventual ruling sided with Bakke but did little to establish a clear judicial standard. Four justices endorsed affirmative action, four others opposed it, and Justice Lewis Powell sat in the middle. The court opinion, which in effect spoke only for Powell, declared racial quotas unconstitutional but allowed race as one of a multitude of factors to be used in admissions or hiring decisions.

The *Bakke* case remained the authoritative statement for decades, despite its limited usefulness. The Supreme Court periodically revisited affirmative action during those years, sometimes accepting programs and sometimes rejecting them, but the opinions did little more than add details to the vague case law. Both sides of the affirmative action debate therefore watched tensely as two more cases made their way to the high court in 2003. The respondent in each lawsuit was Lee Bollinger, who had served as president of the University of Michigan as well as dean of its law school. One suit had been filed by Jennifer Gratz, denied admission as an undergraduate under a 150-point scoring system that automatically gave

members of "underrepresented" minority groups 20 points. The other came from Barbara Grutter, rejected under a law school admissions process that gave "substantial weight" to diversity considerations.

Once again, the Supreme Court included two stark groupings: justices consistently supportive of racial and ethnic preferences (Stevens, Ginsburg, and Souter) and those consistently offended by them (Rehnquist, Scalia, Thomas, Kennedy). However, the two swing justices (O'Connor and Breyer) saw a substantial difference in how the two policies treated individual applicants. The hazy law school policy passed constitutional muster because it was "flexible enough to ensure that each applicant is evaluated as an individual and not in a way that makes an applicant's race or ethnicity the defining feature of his or her application." The rigid undergraduate point system, in contrast, was unconstitutional because it "ensures that the diversity contributions of applicants cannot be individually assessed."[8] Michigan therefore won the *Grutter* case but lost the *Gratz* case.

The 2003 University of Michigan cases may not have moved the law far from where Justice Powell left it in 1978. Nonetheless, in both cases the swing justices articulated the same principle: Diversifying the student body in a university program is a compelling governmental interest that permits treating applicants differently depending in part, but only in part, on racial characteristics. The Supreme Court in 2003 therefore managed to find a middle ground not unlike the one favored by contemporary public opinion—it allowed race to influence, but not dominate, government decisions. An important unanswered question is whether shifting the defense for affirmative action from discrimination to diversity, as the Michigan cases did, will hurt public support for racial preferences in the long run.

What Do You Think?

1. Are affirmative action policies necessary to realize the American belief in individualism? Do they violate that belief?

2. Which justification for affirmative action is most persuasive when applied to blacks? To Hispanics? To women?

3. Would political support for affirmative action increase or decrease if it only applied to African Americans?

4. Is there an important distinction between "quotas" and more-flexible racial preferences? Should the courts place so much emphasis on how rigid policies are?

5. Is there some sort of middle ground on this issue that would satisfy both supporters and opponents of affirmative action?

[1] Quoted in Herman Belz, *Equality Transformed: A Quarter-Century of Affirmative Action,* New Brunswick, NJ: Transaction Publishers (1991), p. 20.

[2] Belz, *Equality Transformed,* p. 34.

[3] Martin Gilens, Paul M. Sniderman, and James H. Kuklinski, "Affirmative Action and the Politics of Realignment," *British Journal of Political Science* 28:1 (January): 159–183.

[4] Paul Sniderman and Edward G. Carmines, *Reaching Beyond Race,* Cambridge, MA: Harvard University Press (1997), pp. 23–27.

[5] Martin Gilens, "Racial Attitudes and Opposition to Welfare," *Journal of Politics* 57 (November, 1995): 994–1014.

[6] *Washington Post*/Kaiser Family Foundation/Harvard University, "Race and Ethnicity in 2001," Menlo Park, CA: Henry J. Kaiser Family Foundation, August 2001.

[7] Analysis comes from authors. For details on the poll, see Mollyann Brodie, *The Four Americas: Government and Social Policy Through the Eyes of America's Multi-racial and Multi-ethnic Society,* The *Washington Post*/Kaiser Family Foundation/Harvard University Survey Project (1995), or Richard Morin, "A Distorted Image of Minorities," *Washington Post* (October 8, 1995), p. 1.

[8] *Grutter v. Bollinger* (2003), 123 S. Ct. 2342; *Gratz v. Bollinger* (2003), 123 S. Ct. 2432.

CHAPTER 5

* * * * * * * * * * * * * * * *

Public Opinion

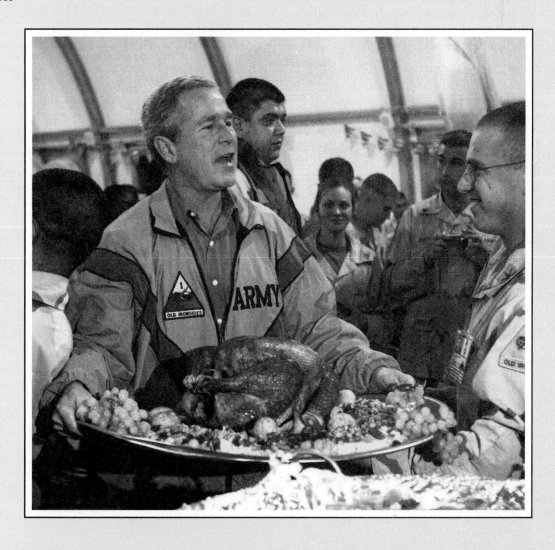

Public Opinion and War

Americans initially were divided over George W. Bush's presidency, with little more than half approving of his performance. Television comics regularly ridiculed the nation's leader, implying that he lacked intelligence. Other critics were less humorous. They dismissed Bush as an illegitimate leader—one who rose to wealth using family connections and shady stock manipulations, who rose to political prominence based on his father's name, and who rose to the land's highest office in a coup staged by Republican justices on the Supreme Court. The prospects of a popular Bush Administration seemed rather dim.

President Bush's public standing changed rapidly, however, in the wake of 2001's terrorist attacks against the nation. All of a sudden, citizens rallied behind their chief executive. Almost 9 out of 10 Americans reported to pollsters that they were satisfied with the job he was doing, the largest popularity increase ever recorded for a U.S. president. Judging from the polls, President Bush had become trusted, admired, even loved.

A presidential administration with limited political experience might have sat back and soaked up the admiration. Bush and his advisers knew better, though, because the President's father had been in much the same position just a decade before. After the Gulf War of 1991, President George H. W. Bush's popularity ratings reached levels very similar to those of his son—but American voters abandoned him over the next year as they became concerned with the nations' economic performance (see Figure 5.1). The elder Bush entered the 1992 election year as one of the least popular presidents in the last 50 years and lost his reelection effort to Bill Clinton, a previously obscure Arkansas governor.

Ten years later, his son and his son's advisers were painfully aware that they could not rely on public opinion to remain behind their administration. Their position was especially delicate because the administration's surge in popularity came at a serious cost. President George W. Bush faced overwhelming expectations after the 9/11 tragedy, including consoling the bereaved, increasing protections at home, exacting revenge abroad, shoring up the economy, and building international coalitions. Americans expected quick performance.

Wearing Down the Public

The Bush administration initially enjoyed strong public support for its handling of the war on terrorism, but upbeat presidential photo opportunities had to compete with more somber images returning from the front—such as this simple but haunting memorial to 15 American soldiers killed when their helicopter went down in November 2003 in Iraq. By the start of the 2004 presidential election season, public opinion of Bush's performance was mixed at best.

Bush's decision to initiate wars against Afghanistan and Iraq, two nations that harbored terrorists, carried perhaps the most-serious political risks. In the short term, of course, successful military action could sustain Bush's high popularity levels. But wars cost money, which would limit the president's flexibility in both domestic and economic policy. Furthermore, wars that go sour can help undermine a presidency, as the Korean War did to President Truman's and the Vietnam War did to President Lyndon Johnson's.

The Bush administration therefore worked aggressively from the start to maintain voter interest in and support for the president's foreign policy. In particular, they continually fed the media upbeat stories to compensate for the usual journalistic tendency to seek out bad news (see Chapter 9). Bush's advisers made frequent appearances on TV news shows to explain the administration's actions. Bush himself visited American forces in ways almost guaranteed to generate hopeful images—donning a flight suit and landing on an aircraft carrier in one instance, attending a secret Thanksgiving dinner with troops on another.

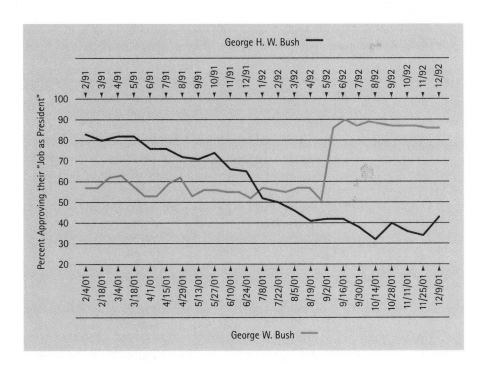

FIGURE 5.1

Wartime Presidents, Father and Son

George H. W. Bush's extraordinarily high approval rating declined steadily after the media shifted its focus to the economy (rather than Desert Storm). His son, George W. Bush, saw an enormous jump in approval rating after September 11, 2001. It subsequently eroded, but not before the 2002 elections, when the Republicans gained in both the House and the Senate.

SOURCE: Gallup Organization

War, Peace, and Public Opinion

Journalists were allowed unprecedented access to the troops in the field—they could bring their audiences along and make them feel part of the military effort. Iraq's organized armies were defeated with few American casualties. A spin campaign turned one captured American soldier, Jessica Lynch, into a national hero. Journalists also received extensive detail about the capture of Iraqi leader Saddam Hussein and the slaying of his two sons.

Nevertheless, the wars dragged on. Soldiers began to face deadly attacks from terrorists and guerrillas within the countries they had conquered. Tragic reports filtered home almost daily: young soldiers killed by enemy actions, American civilians held captive or killed horribly, brutal treatment of detained Iraqis in military-operated prisons, the liberated populations of Afghanistan and Iraq growing to resent American troops, and Europeans refusing to cooperate with efforts to rebuild the captured nations. Despite all of its public-relations efforts, therefore, the Bush administration could not sustain overwhelmingly positive public opinion for very long. By early 2004, a mere 49% of poll respondents approved of his job performance—with the result that Bush won reelection with only 51% of the popular vote.

MAKING THE CONNECTION

In the era of the permanent campaign, public opinion probably is more important than it has ever been.[1] Certainly, modern politicians have more information about it than ever before—but the role that public opinion plays in determining what government does continues to be complicated and unpredictable.

The failure of both George H. W. Bush and George W. Bush to maintain their popularity after an international crisis illustrates how hard it is for even the most visible politicians to cultivate public support. Opinions may be rooted in stable, underlying values—but they respond to social change, political debate, and the way journalists portray social problems. In this chapter we investigate public opinion by focusing on these questions:

- What is public opinion and how is it formed?
- How do we measure—and mismeasure—public opinion?
- What are some important characteristics of public opinion?
- Does public opinion determine public policy?

* * * * * * * * * * * * * * * * *

What Is Public Opinion?

public opinion
The aggregation of people's views about issues, situations, and public figures.

Public opinion is the aggregation of people's views about issues, situations, and public figures. Although conceptions of democracy differ (see Chapter 1), public opinion is an essential element of all of them—either determining policy outcomes directly or setting the bounds within which elected officials must operate when they choose public policies.

Political scientist V. O. Key, Jr. captures the importance of public opinion when he defines it as "those opinions held by private persons which governments find it prudent to heed."[2] Democratic governments find it "prudent" to heed the opinions of private persons, of course, because of elections. Note that, in Key's conception, public opinion need not be actively expressed. Even if public opinion is silent, or "latent," public officials may act or fail to act because they fear arousing it. This is the so-called law of anticipated reactions, whereby public opinion influences government even though it does so indirectly and passively.[3] When we say, "Public opinion wouldn't stand for that," we are referring to this latent, constraining function of public opinion.

Sources of Public Opinion

If public opinion is nothing more than the aggregated opinions of individual people, the first step in understanding public opinion is to figure out where individuals get their political ideas. Most of the sources of political attitudes fall into several broad categories. These categories are not mutually exclusive; often they overlap.

Socialization

socialization
The end result of all the processes by which social groups give individuals their beliefs and values.

People learn political beliefs and values in their families, schools, communities, religious institutions, and workplaces—a process called **socialization.** Sometimes socialization occurs directly and explicitly, as when schools teach citizenship and patriotism. Catholic doctrine condemns abortion, and church-going Catholics are indeed less accepting of abortion than are mainline Protestants and Jews.[4] Most fundamentalist Protestant churches officially condemn homosexuality, and rank-and-file members are indeed less tolerant of homosexuality than are mainline Protestants.[5] Labor unions typically endorse Democratic candidates, and union members are indeed more Democratic in their voting than other blue-collar workers.[6]

Sometimes socialization occurs indirectly, when someone observes or imitates others—a form of socialization that is no less powerful for being unplanned. Children begin to form political attitudes at an early age. Research carried out in the 1950s and 1960s usually concluded that the single most important socializing agent was the family (although a few scholars argued that schools carried more weight).[7] Within the family, studies generally found that the mother was most important; she spent more time with the children. Not surprisingly, then, studies have found that many children will identify themselves as Democrats or Republicans well before they have any idea what the parties stand for.[8] Older children are especially likely to share the party affiliation of their parents.[9] Different socializing agents may be dominant today, however, because of changes in American family life. Increases in single parenthood and in the divorce rate have left many children in one-parent families. Moreover, the proportion of mothers who work outside the home has doubled since the 1960s; even children in two-parent families spend more time with service providers and less time with the members of their household.

Participation

Are You a Liberal or a Conservative?

Personal Experiences

Although people form many of their attitudes in childhood, political views continue to develop over the course of a lifetime. Childhood socialization can be modified or even reversed by adult experiences. The horrors of the Great Depression focused many Americans on the importance of economic issues and, after the depression lifted, cemented their loyalty to the Democratic Party. On the other hand, the stagflation of the 1970s left a younger generation of Americans disenchanted with the Democrats and later encouraged their identification with the Republican party of Ronald Reagan. The ill-fated war in Vietnam made many people skeptical about getting U.S. troops involved in foreign wars.

Not all experiences are historical ones that change entire generations. Some life experiences differ from person to person within a single generation, perhaps because of the place in which one lives or the groups one chooses to join. Life experiences may differ because of how a community treats different sorts of people: men vs. women, youths vs. the elderly, people of different races, the poor, the handicapped, fat people or thin people, tall people or short people. These varying life experiences can profoundly influence not only how someone thinks about specific parties or policy proposals, but also how they feel about fundamental concepts such as fairness, authority, freedom, or justice.

Self-Interest

Public policies seldom affect everyone equally. Usually some people will benefit from a policy proposal and others will suffer. Some people profit from a political party's initiatives; others do not. Ordinary citizens show a rather impressive ability to determine where their bread is buttered, as the old saying puts it, when they approach public affairs.[10]

Voters do not always behave in a fashion that directly benefits them. People rarely abandon their party loyalties, for example, simply because one candidate or one policy position contradicts their personal tastes. Nevertheless, people's interests often determine where they stand in a political debate.[11] For example, blue-collar workers are more sensitive to a rise in unemployment that throws them out of work, and

FIGURE 5.2

Higher Education Is Associated with Greater Tolerance of Diversity

Individuals with a college education are less likely to express negative feelings toward Hispanics, blacks, and gays.

SOURCE: American National Election Study, 2000.

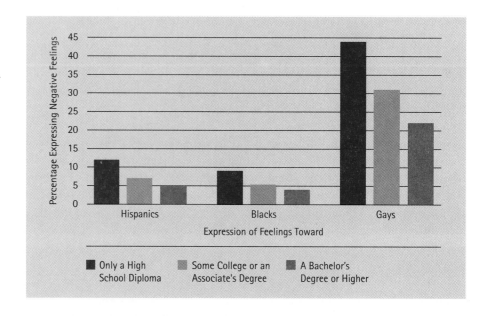

professionals and managers are more sensitive to a rise in inflation that drives up interest rates and depresses the overall business climate. Women working outside the home, who must balance the conflicting demands of home and workplace, are more supportive of gender equality than are stay-at-home mothers.[12]

Education

Although schools are socializing agents and one's training certainly affects self-interest, education belongs in something of a separate category—especially higher education. In general, education is associated with a somewhat more tolerant outlook. Highly educated people are especially tolerant of minority groups and practices.[13] Apparently, values emphasized in higher education predispose college graduates to think about political issues differently; they are more likely to accept people different from them and practices different from theirs (see Figure 5.2). They are also more likely to view political involvement as a duty to carry out rather than as a chore to be avoided. And higher education is associated with a greater sense of **political efficacy** (the belief that the citizen can make a difference by acting politically).

political efficacy
The belief that one can make a difference in politics by expressing an opinion or acting politically.

Reference Groups

Members of various social groups often differ significantly in the opinions they hold, as indicated by Figure 5.3. Weekly churchgoers show more hostility to homosexuality than those with less religious involvement. African Americans endorse government involvement in health care at a higher level than whites customarily do. Women support banning pornography at much higher rates than men do.

To a certain extent, group differences likely result from the same sources of public opinion that we've already discussed: different interests, life experiences, forms of socialization, and levels of schooling. Churches may socialize members to believe that homosexuality is wrong, for example. African Americans may be more likely to need improved health care, or they may be more likely to witness cases in which someone

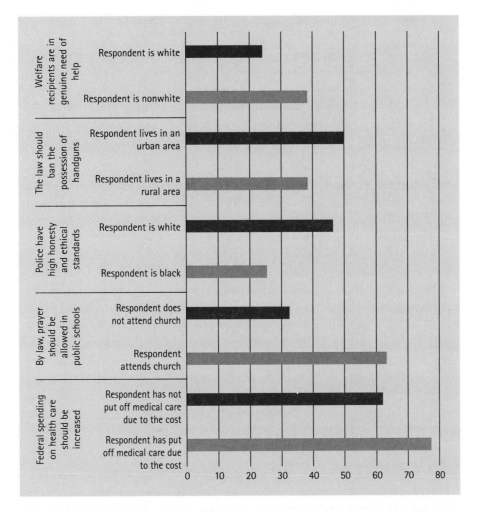

FIGURE 5.3

Examples of Group Differences in Public Opinion

People with different life experiences hold different views about politics.

SOURCE: Calculated from the National Election Studies and the Gallup Poll Cumulative Index.

lacks adequate care. Women may be socialized against consuming pornography, leaving them little reason to support keeping it legal.

On the other hand, individuals may look to the groups of which they are a part to determine where they ought to stand in a political debate. Even if their experiences or their interests push them to oppose a proposed law, they may become friendlier toward it if they notice that folks like them tend to number heavily among the supporters. Individuals are especially likely to stick with their reference group when they identify closely with its fate, or if they tend to hear about public affairs through word of mouth, from the perspective of other group members. Some groups even attempt to enforce solidarity, as when union members disparage the "scabs" who cross their picket lines or African Americans dismiss those who break ranks as "Uncle Toms." In short, the pushes and pulls of group identity can shape people's political attitudes beyond what one might expect given the other influences on their thinking.

The Media

In recent years, many people have expressed a fear that public opinion is increasingly shaped by the mass media. This substantial issue is steeped in controversy (see Chapter 9). Suffice it to say that under some circumstances the media can sway public opinion, while under other circumstances the media are surprisingly ineffectual. Overall, little evidence supports the worst fears of the media's critics. For example, an extensive study of opinion change during a presidential campaign found that, in the aggregate, TV and newspaper exposure had only marginal effects on preexisting views.[14] And more generally, despite the overwhelmingly negative coverage that President Clinton received during the Monica Lewinsky scandal, his job performance ratings scarcely budged. At best, the media represent only one influence on public opinion out of many.

Measuring Public Opinion

You Are a Polling Consultant

For most of the nation's history, figuring out what voters wanted was more art than science. Politicians attended public gatherings, scanned influential newspapers, or consulted with powerful local officials to gauge the popular mood. Often they made mistakes and paid the price on election day.

Estimating public attitudes requires much less guesswork in modern times. A whole industry has sprung up dedicated to contacting individuals, asking them questions, and collecting the responses. Firms range from specialized campaign-consulting operations to highly reputable research and marketing companies (such as Gallup, Roper, and Chilton). These companies sometimes divulge their poll results to the media. So do the various academic institutions and nonprofit foundations that conduct intensive surveys on particular public-affairs issues. Journalistic organizations, meanwhile, have formed alliances to survey public opinion for their own news coverage (examples include CBS News/*New York Times* and ABC News/*Washington Post*).[15] Both politicians and voters therefore have much more information about public opinion than in the past.

Sampling Error

sampling error
The error that arises in public opinion surveys as a result of relying on a representative, but small, sample of the larger population.

Americans sometimes express doubt about the reliability of all these opinion polls. They recognize that surveys rarely report the exact truth. Part of the problem with opinion polls is that even properly administered surveys contain **sampling error**—chance variation that results from using a small sample to estimate the characteristics of a larger population. People may not think about the problem in such technical terms, but they understand the idea intuitively. If you flip a coin, you expect that the chance of having it come up heads is the same as the chance of having it come up tails—which is why it is a fair method for deciding who gets to go first in a game or who gets the last piece of pie. If you flip a coin ten times, though, you would not be shocked by a result other than five heads and five tails. Coin tosses will vary by chance alone. Polling results also contain such sampling error. A survey of randomly selected people can tip this way or that through the luck of the draw.

The variability that results from sampling error makes people suspicious about polls. "I refuse to believe," they sometimes protest, "that the opinions of 1500 people can speak for a nation of 210 million adults." This skepticism is misplaced, however. Sampling error is not the reason that public opinion polls often are unreliable or even contradictory. A properly administered survey of national opinion should not require more than 1500 people (nor would increasing the number of participants do anything to redeem an *improperly* administered survey). A small sample of people can mirror a much larger population reasonably well.

THE WIZARD OF ID   parker and hart

Polling Wizardry

Surveys often provide inaccurate results because of errors in measurement, such as when the options available to respondents do a poor job of capturing the actual range of opinions. Pollsters who wish to avoid biased research must shape the wording of their questions carefully.

Furthermore, statistical theory provides a means to determine how reliable a given survey should be, at least as regards sampling error. If every reader of this book flipped a penny 1500 times, 95 percent of you would fall somewhere between 705 and 795 heads—that is, between 47 and 53 percent, within 3 points of the average. Bigger deviations are possible but they will occur rarely, one time out of 20. Similarly, the answers provided by a random sample of 1500 Americans on any political question would fall within 3 percentage points of national opinion 95 percent of the time. That is a statistical fact. It is what pollsters mean when they report that their survey has a "margin of error" of 3 percent. The natural variation caused by taking a random sample therefore does not explain most instances of misleading survey results. Two other sources of inaccuracy—selection bias and measurement error—usually account for misleading survey results.

Selection Bias

Survey researchers use a bewildering variety of techniques to ensure that their samples will mirror the larger population. However, the trait that unites most sampling methods is that they are devised to avoid **selection bias**—distortion caused when a method systematically includes or excludes people with certain types of attitudes. Surveys that fail to guard against selection bias usually offer nothing of value; results they report will not be *representative* of the larger population. For example, if we were to poll attendees at a hockey game, a heavy-metal concert, or even a political-science lecture, the results would say very little about public opinion because these events attract audiences that differ from other Americans in politically relevant ways.

Perhaps it seems obvious that the political attitudes held by heavy-metal fans would reveal little about national opinion. Yet real-life organizations regularly conduct polls just as likely to induce selection bias. Interest groups and magazines conduct mail surveys. Their samples are not representative, because their members and readers differ from the population at large. Moreover, those who bother to fill out and return the questionnaires are a biased sample of those who receive the survey—they are people who care more than others about the subject of the poll. The same is true for call-in surveys conducted by radio and TV stations. These may be good ways of generating audience interest, but they have little or no scientific value.

selection bias
The error that occurs when a sample systematically includes or excludes people with certain attitudes.

The latest craze is online surveys, but few such polls take adequate care to ensure a proper sample. Most tap only the opinions of people with existing World Wide Web connections who happen to find their way to the poll site and who have their own motivations for taking part in the exercise—hardly a representative group. The problem with Internet polls was highlighted by a mildly embarrassing experience suffered by the Democratic National Committee (DNC) in January 2000. At that time, the DNC Web site offered a weekly opinion feature. One question noted that the United States anticipated a large budget surplus and asked people to vote for one of two ways to use the surplus:

> "saving Social Security, strengthening Medicare, and paying down the debt," or
> "implementing George W. Bush's $1.7 trillion risky tax scheme that overwhelmingly benefits the wealthy."

Surprisingly, when the results were tabulated, 72 percent of the respondents favored "risky" tax cuts for "the wealthy"—mischievous Republicans monitoring the opposition had swamped the Democrats' poll![16] This amusing episode graphically illustrates the problem with allowing a sample to determine itself.

In a scientific poll, the investigator must control who is included in the sample and who is not. Pollsters typically select sampling methods that somehow choose participants *randomly,* with minimal differences from person to person in the chance of being picked. For example, telephone polls customarily rely on "random-digit dialing," in which a computer randomly selects some portion of the number being called. People with unlisted telephone numbers may be surprised and irritated when they answer their phone and hear a pollster, but no one has given out their personal information—the computer has found them by chance.

Not all selection bias results from flaws in the sampling method. Even if pollsters devise an approach that avoids favoring some sorts of people over other sorts, potential respondents still control whether to participate in the research. In a typical telephone poll, more than half the original sample either never answers the phone or refuses to be interviewed.[17] Research shows that, as a result, survey samples tend to contain too few men, whites, young adults, and wealthy people.[18] Although pollsters try to adjust their numbers to compensate for unequal rates of participation, they may not succeed at eliminating the bias. In 1996, pre-election polls overestimated Bill Clinton's margin over Robert Dole. Some conservative commentators claimed that the error occurred because pro-Democratic groups were more likely than pro-Republican groups to respond to the polls.[19]

Some tools for exploring public opinion do not seek to eliminate selection bias. Researchers using these tools care less about getting a representative sample than they do about reaching a complex and detailed understanding of certain kinds of people. For example, political consultants increasingly rely on **focus groups,** small groups of people brought together to talk about issues or candidates at length and in depth. These groups are too small to provide good estimates of public opinion, but they are useful for testing the appeal of ads, campaign slogans, symbols, and so forth. President Clinton's 1996 campaign slogan, "a bridge to the twenty-first century"—which later influenced the architectural design of his presidential library—was selected after it tested well in focus groups.

focus groups
Small groups used to explore how ordinary people think about issues and how they react to the language of political appeals.

Measurement Error

Media accounts of poll results routinely report sampling error. They also often describe the method for gathering the sample, and may even report the rate of participation among the people interviewers contacted. If sampling error and selection bias were the only two sources of inaccuracy in opinion polls, an attentive reader could judge their reliability fairly well. Unfortunately, sampling is a relatively unimportant source of error in most professional surveys. Various kinds of **measurement error** are much more troublesome.

An individual's opinion is not an objective fact like the length of a box. Ask ten people to measure a box and, if a ruler is handy, they will all do it about the same way. Unless they are careless, all ten will report approximately the same length. Opinions do not have such obvious physical properties; they are intangible. No obvious tool, such as a ruler, exists to measure them (although pollsters do sometimes settle on particular questions that they like to ask repeatedly). Opinions are hard to quantify.

Answers can vary dramatically depending on how a question is asked. For example, poll responses vary according to the choices provided.[20] People tend to give more consistent answers to questions that allow graduated responses (agree strongly, agree somewhat, neither agree nor disagree, disagree somewhat, disagree strongly) than to either/or questions (agree/disagree). More people will choose a "don't know" or "not sure" answer when it is explicitly offered to them. Survey responses also depend on the larger context. People respond differently if earlier questions in a survey prompt them to think along certain lines, or if the interviewer lists arguments on each side of an issue before asking about it. People also respond differently when surveyed after significant social, economic, or political developments than when surveyed beforehand.[21]

Opinions are particularly hard to pin down when citizens are unfamiliar with an issue. Just to take one example: A flurry of public opinion polls taken in the summer of 2001 probed whether citizens supported federal funding of embryonic stem cell research. Most Americans had not given much thought to this technical question, nor did pollsters have an established way to ask about it. Not surprisingly, polls reported anywhere from 24 percent to 70 percent in favor of the funding.[22] Sampling error certainly did not produce this much variability.

The wording of survey questions may be the most important source of measurement error. Even if people have fairly fixed opinions, the answers they provide pollsters will depend on exactly what they think a question is asking. Question wording may (1) confuse respondents, (2) prompt respondents to think about an issue in a certain way, or (3) oversimplify complex social issues. Let's consider examples of each problem.

Confusing Questions: The Holocaust Poll Fiasco   Germany's Nazi leaders executed millions of innocent civilians during World War II. Although they targeted gypsies, homosexuals, and Poles—among others—Nazi officials put most of their genocidal efforts into exterminating European Jews. They relocated Jewish men, women, and children to concentration camps within Nazi-controlled territory, where victims either were worked to death or were executed outright. Careful research indicates that at least 5 million Jews died as a result of the Holocaust, including almost the entire Jewish populations of Czechoslovakia, Poland, and the Baltic states. Aside from a fringe group of conspiracy theorists, who deny that such large-scale genocide really took place, scholars uniformly count the Holocaust as one of the worst horrors in a global war filled with terrible tragedy.

Just before the opening of the Holocaust Memorial Museum in Washington, DC, a respected commercial polling organization called Roper Starch Worldwide tried to determine whether Holocaust deniers were making headway among the American public. Roper's survey, commissioned by the American Jewish Committee, produced

measurement error
The error that arises from attempting to measure something as subjective as opinion.

Embarrassed by a Poll

The opening of the Holocaust Memorial Museum was accompanied by a polling embarrassment that underscored the necessity of keeping public-opinion-poll questions clear and simple.

• *Why might a person have answered yes to the following: "Does it seem possible, or does it seem impossible to you that the Nazi extermination of the Jews never happened?"*

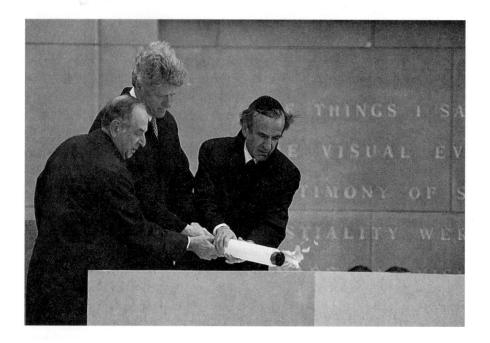

some distressing results. It indicated that 22 percent of the American public believed it "possible the Nazi extermination of the Jews never happened" and that another 12 percent were unsure.

The news media jumped on the story. Editorialists in particular pondered what might be wrong with the American public, that they would give such shocking survey responses. Had anti-Jewish prejudice grown so strong that a third of Americans embraced the views of the lunatic fringe? Was the educational system failing so miserably that, just 50 years after World War II, the American public could have forgotten one of the best-documented tragedies of that global crisis? What did the Holocaust poll say about the American people?

Very little, it turned out. Social scientists knowledgeable about prejudice and public opinion were immediately suspicious of the poll findings, which contradicted other research on American attitudes. The Gallup organization—a Roper business competitor—soon demonstrated that the Roper poll was seriously in error because it had asked a confusing question. The exact wording of Roper's question was:

> Does it seem possible, or does it seem impossible to you that the Nazi extermination
> of the Jews never happened?

One of the first rules of survey research is to keep questions clear and simple. The Roper question fails that test because it contains a double negative (*impossible . . . never happened*)—a grammatical construction long known to confuse people.

Gallup conducted a new poll in which half of the sample was asked the Roper question with the double negative and the other half an alternative question:

> Does it seem possible to you that the Nazi extermination of the Jews never
> happened, or do you feel certain that it happened?

This change in the question's wording may seem minor, but it made a great deal of difference. In the half of the sample that was asked the Roper question, one-third of the respondents again replied that it was possible the Holocaust never happened or that they were unsure, but in the half that were asked Gallup's alternative question, less than 10 percent of the sample were Holocaust doubters. The whole episode had been the product of a simple verbal mistake.[23] Roper asked a poorly constructed question, but its survey provided an accurate estimate of how Americans would react to the question, as verified by the Gallup poll.

Leading Questions: The Welfare Policy Mystery   What looks like minor variation in question wording can elicit significantly different answers. These are especially likely to occur when questions use emotionally or politically "loaded" terms. A classic example comes from the policy area of government spending on the poor. Consider the following survey question:

> We are faced with many problems in this country, none of which can be solved
> easily or inexpensively. I'm going to name some of these problems and for each one
> I'd like you to tell me whether you think we're spending too much money, too little
> money, or about the right amount.[24]

When the public was asked about "welfare," the responses showed that a large majority of Americans believed that too much was being spent:

Too little: 13%
About right: 25%
Too much: 62%

Conservatives might interpret such a poll to mean that Americans want to slash aid to the poor. But when the *same people* in the *same poll* were asked about "assistance to the poor," a similarly large majority responded that too little was being spent:

Too little: 59%
About right: 25%
Too much: 16%

Liberals could use the poll to argue that welfare spending should rise.

Although *welfare* and *assistance to the poor* may appear to mean the same thing—welfare is the policy used to provide assistance to poor families—the terms evidently tap into different attitudes. *Welfare* carries negative connotations; it seems to prompt people to think of lazy and undeserving recipients—the stereotypical welfare cheats. But *assistance to the poor* does not evoke these negative stereotypes. Careless (or clever) question wording can produce contradictory findings on a major public issue. Reputable survey organizations work constantly to identify and eliminate loaded questions.

Oversimplified Questions: Public Opinion on Abortion   In 1973, the Supreme Court handed down its *Roe v. Wade* decision, striking down any restrictions on a woman's right to terminate a pregnancy in the first trimester and limiting restrictions on that right in the second trimester. The issue has never left the national agenda since then, and there is reason to believe that most Americans long ago decided where they stood on the issue. Indeed, when the *same* survey question is repeated over time, public opinion is strikingly constant. Yet support for abortion rights varies widely from one poll question to another—prompting both pro-choice and pro-life spokespersons to claim that a majority of Americans support their position. Unless the laws of arithmetic fail to hold in the case of this issue, one side or both must be wrong, but neither side makes up its figures. How can this be?

As with welfare policy, part of the inconsistency comes from the use of leading questions.[25] One *Los Angeles Times* poll in the late 1980s asked,

> Do you think a pregnant woman should or should not be able to get a legal abortion, no matter what the reason?

By a heavy margin (57 percent to 34 percent), Americans said no. As pro-life spokespersons claimed, Americans were pro-life. Should Democratic campaign consultants have advised their clients to flip-flop to the pro-life side? Well, probably not. A few months later, a CBS News/*New York Times* survey asked,

> If a woman wants to have an abortion, and her doctor agrees to it, should she be allowed to have an abortion or not?

By more than a 2:1 margin (58 percent to 26 percent), Americans said yes. As the pro-choice spokespersons claimed, America had a pro-choice majority. Should Republican campaign consultants have advised their clients to flip-flop to the pro-choice side?

Which poll was right? Probably neither. Upon close examination, both survey questions are suspect. Each contains words and phrases that predispose people to answer in one direction. The first question uses the phrase "no matter what the reason." If forced to choose yes or no unconditionally, some generally pro-choice people will say no, believing that some circumstances are just not sufficiently serious to justify abortion. The CBS/*NYT* question leans in the opposite direction. A doctor's approval suggests a considered decision based on medically justifiable grounds. Some generally pro-life people might agree to abortion in such a case.

In addition, Americans distinguish between the morality of behavior and the legality of behavior. A CBS News/*New York Times* poll asked people whether they agreed or disagreed with the stark claim that "abortion is the same thing as murdering a child." Americans were deeply split (46 percent agreed, 41 percent disagreed). Similarly, a plurality or majority of Americans regularly agrees that "abortion is morally wrong" (51 percent agreed, 34 percent disagreed in the aforementioned CBS News/*New York Times* poll).[26] On the other hand, a CBS/*NYT* poll asked the following question:

> Even in cases where I might think abortion is the wrong thing to do, I don't think the government has any business preventing a woman from having an abortion.[27]

By close to a 3:1 margin (69 percent to 24 percent), Americans agreed with that sentiment. Individualistic Americans favor freedom of choice, especially when it involves preventing government interference. Many Americans who are troubled by abortion nonetheless will not support making it illegal.

Opinions on abortion are especially likely to change depending on the way pollsters ask about the issue, suggesting that the use of leading questions may be insufficient to explain the volatility. More likely, opinions on abortion are too complex for pollsters to capture in a single, simple question. Evidence that pollsters often oversimplify the abortion issue appears in surveys taken by the National Opinion Research Center, which use a more complex question. The NORC question reads as follows:

> Please tell me whether or not you think it should be possible for a pregnant woman to obtain a legal abortion if
>
> 1. the woman's health is seriously endangered?
> 2. she became pregnant as a result of rape?
> 3. there is a strong chance of serious defect in the baby?

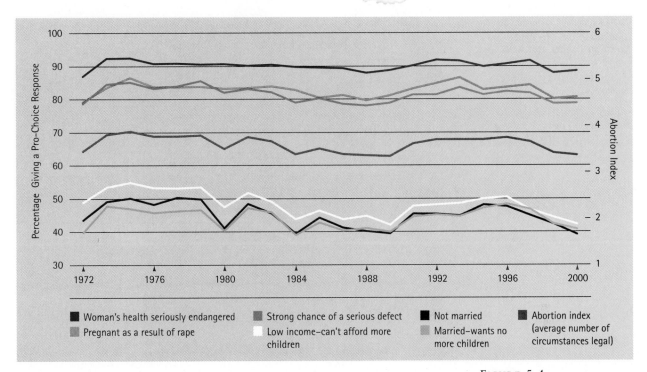

Woman's health seriously endangered   **Strong chance of a serious defect**   **Not married**   **Abortion index (average number of circumstances legal)**

Pregnant as a result of rape   **Low income–can't afford more children**   **Married–wants no more children**

FIGURE 5.4

Popular Attitudes Toward Abortion Have Been Remarkably Stable Since *Roe v. Wade* (1973)

Note: Respondents who answered "don't know" are included in the calculation.

SOURCE: Calculated by Sam Abrams from the General Social Survey 1972–2000 Cumulative Data File.

4. the family has low income and cannot afford any more children?
5. she is not married and does not want to marry the man?
6. she is married and does not want any more children?

As Figure 5.4 shows, after moving in a liberal direction in the late 1960s, opinion stabilized at the time of the 1973 *Roe v. Wade* decision, stayed remarkably constant for two decades, and then moved a bit in a conservative direction in the late 1990s. These trends across time vary much less than responses do across circumstances.[28] Americans are pragmatic, not ideological, when it comes to abortion. They favor the right to choose, but not an unconditional right to choose in every possible circumstance.

In the late 1990s, some pro-life groups began to focus media attention on a procedure called "partial-birth abortion," in which the fetus is destroyed after it has been partially delivered. Pictures and verbal descriptions of this process, disseminated by pro-life groups, are quite gruesome. The publicity surrounding this particularly distressing form of abortion probably explains why support for pro-choice positions declined during the period (review Figure 5.4). Majorities of Americans have consistently registered opposition to the procedure. The debate over partial-birth abortion reminded Americans of the conditions under which they opposed abortion rights, underscoring the fact that most Americans hold complicated opinions about when abortion should and should not be legal.

Figure 5.5 shows this complexity in a different way. It indicates that very few Americans hold absolute positions on abortion; only a fifth want abortion "always illegal" and only a quarter wish to keep it "always legal." The majority of Americans hold a more complicated set of preferences that would make abortion legal in some circumstances and illegal in others. Thus, although opinion on abortion has been stable over

FIGURE 5.5

Americans Tend to Favor Abortion Rights, But with Restrictions

Note: N = 1,001 adults nation-wide. Margin of error +/- 63.

SOURCE: CNN/USA Today/Gallup Poll

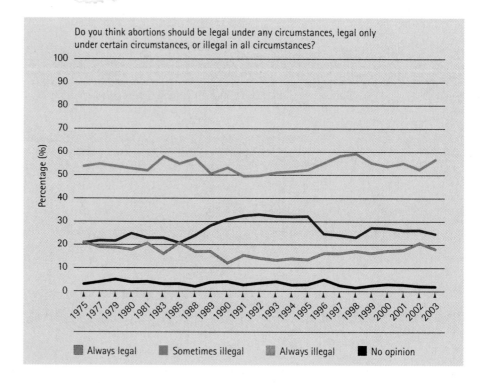

Do you think abortions should be legal under any circumstances, legal only under certain circumstances, or illegal in all circumstances?

■ Always legal   ■ Sometimes illegal   ■ Always illegal   ■ No opinion

time—suggesting that it is not the result of haphazard poll responses—it does not accommodate the oversimplified questions that pollsters customarily ask about it.

Characteristics of Public Opinion

Why should the results of measuring public opinion be so sensitive to *how* it is measured? The characteristics of public opinion often make it very hard to obtain reliable measurements.

Public Opinion Is Uninformed

On many issues, people have little or no information. The extent of popular ignorance is most obvious when surveys pose "factual" questions. As shown in Figure 5.6, only a third of adults over age 36 could identify the political party controlling their state legislatures in 2003. Less than a quarter could identify the Speaker of the U.S. House of Representatives; more than a third could not even identify the political party in charge. Young adults exhibited even less political knowledge.

Elections are not SAT tests, of course; it is not necessary to know the answers to all sorts of factual questions in order to vote intelligently. But widespread ignorance extends beyond such factual questions to important matters of government and public policy. During the 1995 federal government shutdown, 40 percent of Americans were unaware that the Republicans controlled both houses of Congress (and 10 percent did not know that the president was a Democrat). By more than a 2:1 margin, Americans believed—absolutely wrongly—that the federal government spent more on foreign aid

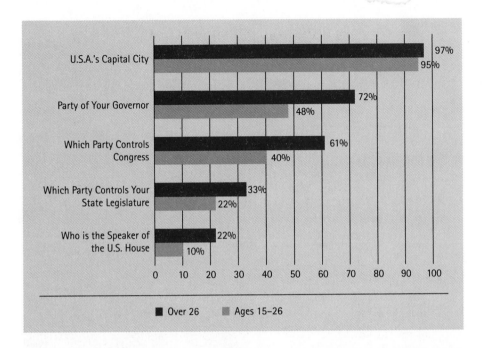

FIGURE 5.6
**Americans Are Not Very
Knowledgeable About the
Specifics of American
Government**
Young people know even less
about government than relatively
ill-informed older Americans.

SOURCE: Representative
Democracy in America Project,
2003.

than on Medicare. In fact, the United States was spending four times as much on Medicare as on foreign aid.[29] Most people pay little attention to politics.

Upon learning the full extent of popular ignorance, some politically involved students react critically, jumping to the conclusion that ordinary Americans are irresponsible people who fall far short of the democratic ideal. Such reactions are understandable, but unjustified. The simple fact is that most people have little time for politics. They work hard to take care of life's necessities, such as paying bills, caring for families, and nurturing personal relationships—leaving little time or energy to work through the *New York Times.* Nor do Americans stand out for their inattentiveness to public affairs. Citizens in other countries usually lack political and historical knowledge as well. A British Gallup poll, for example, found that only 40 percent of Britons know that the United States once was part of their empire![30]

Those who criticize ordinary citizens for their lack of attention to public affairs often have jobs that enable them to stay informed with little effort. For example, political conversation is a common diversion on university campuses. In such a context, professors and students find it easy to stay informed. Likewise, the jobs of many journalists involve following politics: If they are not informed, they are not doing their job. If everyone worked in a university or for the news media, no doubt we would all be much better informed. But most people do not—a fact that social critics tend to forget.

The general point is that gathering, digesting, and storing information is neither effortless nor free; it is costly. For most Americans, bearing such **information costs** brings them few immediate benefits.[31] Citizens doubt that they can make much difference when earthquakes strike Iran or riots erupt in Venezuela. When faced with a costly activity that has no obvious benefit, many of them quite rationally decide to minimize their costs. Thus, from a logical standpoint, the puzzle is not why so many Americans are ill informed; the puzzle is why so many are as well informed as they are.[32]

Comparing Public
Opinion

information cost
The time and mental effort required
to absorb and store information,
whether from conversations, personal
experiences, or the media.

Spending Time With Friends
Many Americans have little time or energy to devote to staying informed after a busy day working and tending to their families and personal relationships. They prefer to spend their remaining time on leisure and light entertainment.

Information costs do not fall equally on all people. Education makes it easier to absorb and organize information; thus it comes as no surprise that more-educated Americans are better informed than less-educated ones (see Figure 5.7). In addition, the benefits of information are not the same for all people on all issues. Most people will be better informed on issues that directly affect their lives or livelihoods. Parents and teachers are especially knowledgeable about school operations and budgets. Steelworkers have strong views on foreign imports. Farmers keep track of cotton and wheat subsidies. Such **issue publics** are different from the large mass of citizens in that they find relevant information particularly valuable and can gather it more cheaply.[33]

issue public
Group of people particularly affected by, or concerned with, a specific issue.

Of course, some people will bear information costs even when they get little direct benefit from doing so. They may consider it their duty as citizens to be informed, so they stay attuned to public affairs simply because they believe it is the "right thing" to do. Other people follow public affairs because they find it intrinsically interesting in the same way that some follow sports or the arts. For such people, following public affairs is a recreational activity, a luxury. Probably most citizens know as much as they do because they enjoy staying informed, not because they derive any tangible benefit from doing so.[34]

Why does American ignorance hinder attempts to measure public opinion? Americans are an accommodating people. If a pollster asks us a question, many of us will cooperate by giving an answer, even if we have not thought about the question or have no basis on which to arrive at an answer. An extreme example occurred in a survey asking people to rate 58 ethnic groups. Although one nationality included in the list ("Wisnians") was fictitious, 29 percent of the sample ranked them anyway.[35] Surveys that collect meaningless answers will obscure public opinion rather than clarify it.

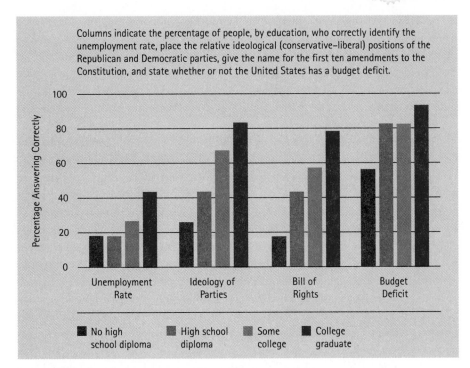

Columns indicate the percentage of people, by education, who correctly identify the unemployment rate, place the relative ideological (conservative–liberal) positions of the Republican and Democratic parties, give the name for the first ten amendments to the Constitution, and state whether or not the United States has a budget deficit.

Legend:
- No high school diploma
- High school diploma
- Some college
- College graduate

FIGURE 5.7

Higher Education Is Strongly Associated with Greater Knowledge of Politics and Government

SOURCE: Data are taken from Michael Delli Carpini and Scott Keeter, *What Americans Know About Politics and Why It Matters* (New Haven: Yale University Press, 1997: 189).

Public Opinion Is Not Ideological

Another characteristic of public opinion that makes it easy to misinterpret is that even when people have reasonably firm views on issues, those views usually are not connected to each other. In other words, few Americans are ideological.

An **ideology** is a system of principles and beliefs that ties together a person's views on a wide range of particular issues. For example, if you are told that Representative Smith is a "liberal" Democrat, it is a safe bet that Smith is pro-choice on abortion, favors gun control, and supports a strong government role in health care. Conversely, if you are told that Representative Jones is a "conservative" Republican, you might guess that she is pro-life, opposes gun control, and thinks that health care should be left to the private sector as much as possible. Such assumptions will seldom be wrong. The reason is that **political elites**—people who are deeply involved in politics, whether as activists or as office holders—tend to have well-structured ideologies that bind together their positions on different policy issues.

Ordinary citizens are another matter. People with little direct involvement in politics—a group traditionally called the **mass public**—usually are not ideological.[36] Their views on specific issues do not cluster together like those of elites, nor do their evaluations of party leaders or of political groups.[37] Rather than believe consistently in either activist or minimal government, citizens favor federal spending in some areas but oppose it in others. They like some Democratic politicians but dislike others. They favor toleration for some groups in some situations, but not for other groups in other situations.

Even when the standards for ideological thinking are rather low, the evidence indicates that few people follow conventional political ideologies. For example, *when given*

ideology
System of beliefs in which one or more organizing principles connect the individual's views on a wide range of issues.

political elite
Activists and office holders who are deeply interested in, and knowledgeable about, politics.

mass public
Ordinary people for whom politics is a peripheral concern.

the option, one-quarter to one-third of the population will not classify themselves on a liberal–conservative scale, and another one-quarter put themselves exactly in the middle: "moderate, middle of the road."[38] Furthermore, Americans seem unaware of the ideologies that structure the decisions made by their leaders. During the 2000 campaign, for example, only 59 percent of Americans considered the Republicans the more conservative of the two parties, while 9 percent thought the Democrats were, and 32 percent didn't know.[39]

Here again, there is a tendency to disparage regular citizens. Critics assume that ordinary Americans form their political attitudes haphazardly or thoughtlessly simply because their preferences do not follow conventional patterns. Here again, we disagree with such judgments. In our view, ideologies are *social* constructions. Personal views aside, can anyone explain why a person who prefers lower taxes and a strong military necessarily should oppose abortion but not the death penalty and should support strip-club regulations but not gun control? Such issue positions may go together when people polarize across an ideological divide—that is, when they view the political world as a struggle between liberals and conservatives and adopt the many traits that characterize their side—but no comprehensive political philosophy ties all these issue positions together. Indeed, ideologies change over time.[40] Maybe it is political elites who should be viewed critically for conforming to a laundry list of policy preferences that have no logical connection to each other.

Whether you regard ideological thinking as good or bad, however, you should bear one point in mind. Because they presume that ideological thinking is the norm, party and issue activists, media commentators, and many public officials will conclude too much on the basis of opinion polls and voting returns. Support for one variety of government action may indicate nothing about support for another, seemingly similar government action. Support for a candidate's position on one issue may suggest little or nothing about that candidate's "mandate" to act on seemingly related issues. The nonideological nature of public opinion means that elites often hear more than the voters are saying.

Visual Literacy

Who Are Liberals and Conservatives? What's the Difference?

Public Opinion Is Inconsistent

Given that people often have not thought about issues, and given that most of them do not think ideologically, perhaps it is inevitable that public opinion will send contradictory messages. For example, in 1980, when Ronald Reagan defeated Jimmy Carter and the Republicans made striking gains in Congress, many observers interpreted the election results as a "resurgence of conservatism" or a "turn to the right" in American politics. In fact, the data were confusing.[41]

Polls reported that large majorities of the citizenry felt that the federal government was spending too much money and doing too much regulating. Popular sentiments like these seemed to explain Reagan's victory. But the same polls asked the *same people* which domestic programs they favored cutting and which areas of business activity they favored deregulating. Surprisingly, pluralities—and often majorities—felt that most domestic activities deserved *higher* funding or warranted *more* regulation. Their sentiments about particular spending reductions and regulatory changes did not match the principles they claimed to endorse. Americans were inconsistent.

Just What Is Permitted?
Americans are supportive of free speech in general, but many are willing to restrict hate groups.

• *If rights are considered as part of a trade-off, rather than as inalienable rights, what will the consequences be for the substance of those rights? What sorts of limits on extreme groups are permissible? For instance, is it fair to allow the individuals shown here to march, but not in a town filled with Holocaust survivors?*

Findings like these are not unusual. In recent decades, the American people have never delivered a clear mandate either for the Republicans to cut and retrench or for the Democrats to tax and expand.[42] After the Republicans took control of Congress in 1994, for example, most Americans wanted to balance the budget but opposed cutting expensive entitlement programs that accounted for much of the government's deficits. President George W. Bush pushed a tax-cut plan early in his administration that a plurality of voters supported in early polls at the same time they endorsed increasing spending on social security and education.[43] Such contradictory views may be amusing—they recall the old maxim that "everybody wants to go to heaven but nobody wants to die"—but they confuse political debate. One consequence was the gridlock and deficits of the 1980s and 1990s. Both parties could refuse to compromise or to adapt their platforms, firm in the belief that public opinion supported much of what they stood for.

Why is public opinion so inconsistent? Ignorance explains some of the contradictions. People think that the federal budget lavishes money on unpopular programs such as "welfare" and foreign aid, even though such policies account for relatively little federal spending. They also believe that government agencies waste so much money that elected leaders could slice funding without harming essential services. Citizens therefore unrealistically expect painless budget cuts.

Not all examples of inconsistency reflect insufficient and inaccurate information, however. People oppose amending the Constitution but they endorse numerous amendment proposals. They support various fundamental rights, but not for groups they oppose.[44] As Figure 5.8 shows, most citizens favor free speech "for all"—but half would prevent a member of their most disliked group from giving a speech. They favor freedom of the press and freedom of assembly—with "reasonable" exceptions. And they believe in the separation of church and state—but favor prayer in schools. In short, citizens are so consistently inconsistent when applying general principles to specific cases that explanations other than ignorance must be at work.

FIGURE 5.8

Americans Tend to Endorse General Principles but Make Numerous Exceptions to Them

SOURCE: Data are taken from John Sullivan, James Piereson, and George Marcus, *Political Tolerance and American Democracy* (Chicago: University of Chicago Press, 1982).

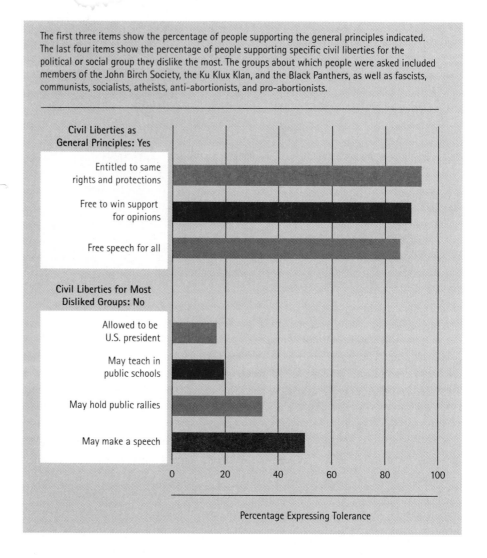

The first three items show the percentage of people supporting the general principles indicated. The last four items show the percentage of people supporting specific civil liberties for the political or social group they dislike the most. The groups about which people were asked included members of the John Birch Society, the Ku Klux Klan, and the Black Panthers, as well as fascists, communists, socialists, atheists, anti-abortionists, and pro-abortionists.

Civil Liberties as General Principles: Yes
- Entitled to same rights and protections
- Free to win support for opinions
- Free speech for all

Civil Liberties for Most Disliked Groups: No
- Allowed to be U.S. president
- May teach in public schools
- May hold public rallies
- May make a speech

Percentage Expressing Tolerance

Some social critics contend that Americans are hypocrites. Americans pay lip service to fine-sounding principles, but they do not really believe in these values. They abandon them whenever it is convenient to do so. A more positive interpretation is possible, however. Law professors, newspaper editors, and political activists tend to view rights inflexibly—as rules that government officials must respect at all times. Once leaders start making exceptions, they can water down rights until they provide no protection whatsoever. Few Americans accept such an absolutist perspective, though. They tend to be more practical, to be pragmatists. Rights are good things, but at times they conflict with other values.[45]

Most citizens are prepared to make trade-offs on a case-by-case basis,[46] relaxing rights when they threaten to produce "unreasonable" outcomes that violate "common sense." Yes, free speech is a good thing—but perhaps not enough to justify allowing Nazi rallies in a neighborhood where Holocaust survivors live. Yes, people should be treated equally—but perhaps it does little harm to favor historically disadvantaged groups when they apply for college as a way to erase social differences. Yes, police

The Irrational Public?

The inconsistencies in public opinion may suggest that voters are buffoons who think that government can provide anything they want. However, what seems like inconsistency may grow from the public's desire to avoid extremes and seek a practical balance between competing principles.

should not search someone's home without a good reason—but that does not necessarily mean murderers should go free just because police failed to obtain a search warrant before collecting evidence. To adults familiar with life's complexities, the realm of real-world politics has to be flexible. They may feel no contradiction in treating rights as guidelines rather than as ironclad rules.[47]

Governing by Public Opinion?

Never before have American politicians had so much data about public opinion. Indeed, critics regularly complain that politics and government today are "poll-driven." As we have seen, however, given the characteristics of public opinion, trying to measure and interpret it is far from an exact science. At times it is more like reading tea leaves! Furthermore, even when public opinion is fairly clear, there is no guarantee that policy makers will follow it. Political scientists have tried to determine if public opinion influences policy, and if so, when it does or does not do so.

The Power of Public Opinion

Public opinion may be uninformed, nonideological, and inconsistent—but that does not mean elected officials can ignore it. The public as a whole generally possesses enough information about the political system to understand the choices voters need to make. For example, the public at large understands that the Democrats are to the left of the Republicans on most issues.[48] Moreover, even within the same party, the public knew that Ronald Reagan was farther to the right than Richard Nixon and that George McGovern was farther to the left than Jimmy Carter. Political scientist James Stimson has shown that, when numerous survey questions are analyzed together, researchers can find distinct shifts in the general direction of "mood" of the public. For example, after analyzing hundreds of questions, he found that the electorate in fact did shift to the right in the years leading up to Ronald Reagan's election.[49]

In the same vein, noted political scientists Benjamin Page and Robert Shapiro have argued that, viewed *collectively*, the public is reasonably "rational." Analysis of thousands of poll questions asked repeatedly over more than a 40-year period shows that in the aggregate, public opinion is far more stable than the opinions of individual members of the public. When it does shift, public opinion generally reacts to new events and conditions in natural ways. For example, when federal spending goes up, public preferences for continued increases go down, an effect that indicates some broad public recognition of the direction in which government policy has moved.[50]

Given the stability and sensibility of overall public opinion, elected officials usually feel compelled to give voters what they want. Page and Shapiro have used their long-term survey research to confirm that American policies follow public opinion. When trends in opinion are clearly moving in one direction, public policy generally follows. The more pronounced the trend in opinion, the more likely policy is to follow it.[51] Such findings illustrate the problem with assuming that an uninformed, nonideological, and inconsistent public will be unable to exercise their rights in a democracy.

Why can a limited public nonetheless guide the behavior of their government? The answer lies in the distinction between individuals and aggregates. Even if particular voters have little grasp of public affairs, as a group they may be much more capable—with the process of aggregation canceling out individual error and enabling overall public preferences to emerge. Think of a grade school orchestra. Individually, the young musicians are so unsteady that it is difficult to identify the tune each is playing, but put them all together and the audience can make out "Twinkle, Twinkle Little Star." So it is with public opinion. On some issues and at some times, public opinion and public policy may not be closely aligned, but looking at the general direction of public policy over the long run reveals that it tends to follow public opinion.

The Limits of Public Opinion: Gun Control

Gun Rights and Gun Control

Policy makers may consider voter preferences when they shape policy, but the public does not always get what it wants. Even if individual politicians are highly responsive to public opinion, the system as a whole need not be. The Columbine shootings provide a stark illustration. On April 20, 1999, two deranged students at Columbine High School in Colorado killed a teacher and 12 of their schoolmates. They wounded more than 20 others. The killers used two shotguns, a semi-automatic pistol, and a semi-automatic rifle in their murderous spree. This was the fourth high-profile school shooting in the United States in little more than a year. Whether because of the cumulative impact or the sheer scale of the rampage, the Columbine tragedy energized elected officials.

In the Senate, a juvenile-crime bill had been going nowhere fast. Anti-gun legislators decided to use this bill as a vehicle for passing new gun control measures, sensing that the Columbine shootings might allow them to get a bill through the law-making process. They proposed an amendment to the bill that tightened restrictions on sales at gun shows. In a highly publicized climax to the renewed debate, the Senate adopted the amendment only after Vice-President Al Gore cast a tie-breaking vote (under the Constitution, the vice-president votes when the Senate is tied). By much wider

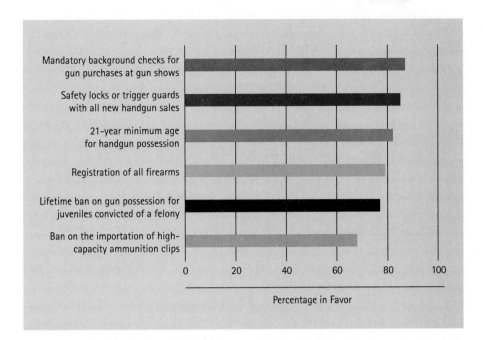

FIGURE 5.9
**Most Americans Support Gun
Control Proposals**

SOURCE: "Bear Arms—But
More Regulation," *Public
Perspective,* June/July 1999: 34.

margins, the Senate adopted other provisions mandating trigger locks or lock boxes with every handgun sale, outlawing imports of high-capacity ammunition clips, and raising the age at which juveniles could buy handguns and assault weapons. The amended bill easily passed the Senate.

In the House, Republican leaders agreed that the aroused state of public opinion required some response. Speaker Denny Hastert (R-IL) commented, "This is one of those rare times when the national consensus demands that we act." He promised that the House would pass a gun control measure.[52] But the issue was now thoroughly entangled in partisan politics. Vice-President Gore obviously believed that his highly visible gun control stance would aid his 2000 presidential bid, and congressional Democrats hoped to use the issue to take over Congress. The key target group was suburban voters—especially women, whom polls showed to be more in favor of gun control than were men.[53] To appeal to them, Democrats framed the issue as one of protecting children by restricting access to guns.

The Democrats were not united, however. A senior Democrat, John Dingell of Michigan, was an avid hunter and a former National Rifle Association board member. Dingell worked with Republican leaders to develop an amendment that would soften the Senate's gun-show restrictions. Forty-five Democrats followed Dingell, helping pass the alternative provision. Then, angry liberals who believed the weakened legislation did not go far enough joined angry conservatives who felt it still went too far. Together, they defeated the bill. Gun control was dead!

At first glance, this story seems to be one of irresponsible or even corrupt behavior by the Congress. The story line offered by the media was simple: Public opinion counted less than the campaign contributions and arm twisting of the NRA. Certainly the media interpretation was correct in one respect: The U.S. public favors limits on guns. As Figure 5.9 indicates, large majorities favor the specific provisions—background checks, trigger locks, restrictions on magazine size—that were part of the rejected bill.

FIGURE 5.10

Rural Members Are Far More Opposed to Gun Control Than Urban Members

SOURCE: Don Carney, "Beyond Guns and Violence: A Battle of House Control," *CQ Weekly,* June 19, 1999; and *Roll Call Votes,* pp. 1496–1497.

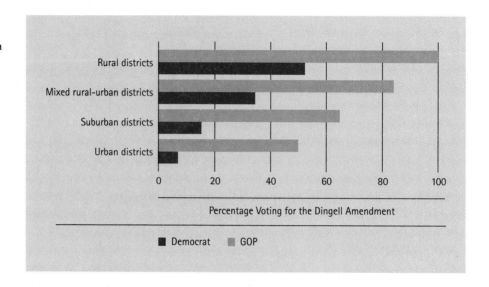

Different polls showed a high degree of agreement on these questions. How, then, could representatives of the people fail to pass gun control? The answer has two parts, one institutional, the other behavioral.

Institutionally, members of Congress represent congressional districts of approximately 630,000 people. The national distribution of opinion is of little importance to members of Congress. What counts is the distribution of opinion in their home districts, especially among the voters who elected them. Many of these district electorates differ significantly from the country as a whole. Opinion on gun control varies according to whether someone lives in an urban or rural environment, for example, with rural residents far more supportive of gun rights. Not surprisingly, therefore, 81 percent of the representatives from rural districts voted for Dingell's amendment, including a majority of Democrats (see Figure 5.10).[54] Although no detailed study is available, we think it likely that most representatives who voted against gun control voted in accordance with the sentiments of voting majorities *in their districts.*

Still, given the extremely high level of support for the gun-control provisions, it is likely that some representatives did vote against district preferences. Was this the NRA at work? To some extent, perhaps. But remember that interest-group endorsements and campaign contributions don't vote. There have to be voters in the district who will act on the group's support. That is the second part of the explanation for the failure of gun control. Behaviorally, supporters of gun control feel less strongly about it than do opponents. As Democratic Minority Leader Richard Gephardt (D-MO) conceded, "The 80 percent that are for gun safety just aren't for it very much. They're not intense."[55]

Indeed, although most polls registered a high level of support for gun control after Columbine, the same polls indicated that the public did not regard it as one of the more important issues facing the country. Gun control ranked relatively low compared to issues such as social security, health care, Medicare, and education. One national poll had gun control 12th in importance as a voting issue in the next election.[56] Not many supporters of gun control are intense, single-issue voters (if they vote at all), but opponents of gun control are classic single-issue voters. Indeed, Representative Dingell pointed out that popular support for gun control was at least as high earlier in the decade as it was after Columbine. Despite that fact, Democrats lost their congressional majority in 1994 in part because of the party's support for the ban on assault weapons.

Why are gun-control supporters less intense about the issue than its opponents are? Part of the explanation seems to be cultural. Guns are essential to rural culture, especially in the South and West.[57] For many rural voters, guns are a part of everyday life; they are not alien and frightening mechanical devices as they may seem to suburban voters. As former Senator Alan Simpson of Wyoming once commented, "Where I come from, people think gun control means how steady can you hold your rifle."[58] Such voters view gun control laws as government interference with their way of life, an attack on their values.

By contrast, gun-control supporters see restricting guns as little more than one method to reduce violence. They have relatively low expectations for gun control, believing that dangerous criminals will find ways to get around restrictive laws.[59] It is hard to feel passionate about laws that would have such a minor impact. Gun-control supporters are so doubtful about the effectiveness of restrictions that they seldom retaliate against elected officials who stand on the other side. They lack intensity. This example therefore illustrates the imperfect connection between aggregate public opinion and national public policy.

Chapter Summary

Public opinion is a basic element of democratic politics. For the people to "rule," their opinions must translate into public laws and policies. However, measuring public opinion is an inexact science at best. Sample design and question wording make interpreting opinion polls very tricky. And on many issues—among them abortion—the public truly does not have an answer that is easily quantified.

Even when public opinion seems relatively clear, governing by opinion poll may not be a good idea. Citizens tend to be uninformed, so polling data may not represent firmly held opinions. Preferences can change with little notice, and the public may not connect two issues that elected officials consider clearly related. Thus, leaders often misinterpret poll results. Politicians cannot stick too closely to short-term fluctuations in the polls if they wish to remain in office.

Rather, public opinion exerts its influence largely through the calculations of officials who try to anticipate what they must do to win reelection. Clearly, elected officials will hesitate to defy the will of an aroused public—but they pay more attention to the wishes of their own voters than they do to the wishes of the American public as a whole.

Key Terms

focus groups, p. 128
ideology, p. 137
information cost, p. 135
issue public, p. 136

mass public, p. 137
measurement error, p. 129
political efficacy, p. 124
political elite, p. 137

public opinion, p. 122
sampling error, p. 126
selection bias, p. 127
socialization, p. 122

Suggested Readings

Of General Interest

Herbst, Susan. *Numbered Voices: How Opinion Polling Has Shaped American Politics.* Chicago: University of Chicago Press, 1993. An informative survey of the growth of opinion polling, with a critical examination of its impact on contemporary politics.

Mayer, William. *The Changing American Mind: How and Why American Public Opinion Changed Between 1960 and 1988.* Ann Arbor: University of Michigan Press, 1992. Masterful survey of the changing contours of public opinion over the past generation, with careful dissection of the sources of opinion change.

Page, Benjamin, and Robert Shapiro. *The Rational Public.* Chicago: University of Chicago Press, 1992. Prize-winning study of public opinion from the 1930s to the 1990s. The authors argue that, viewed as a collectivity, the public is rational, however imperfect the individual opinions that members of the public hold.

Schuman, Howard, and Stanley Presser. *Questions and Answers in Attitude Surveys.* New York: Sage Publications, 1996. A comprehensive study of the effects of question wording, form, and context on survey results.

Focused Studies

Cook, Elizabeth, Ted Jelen, and Clyde Wilcox. *Between Two Absolutes: Public Opinion and the Politics of Abortion.* Boulder, CO: Westview, 1992. Although more than a decade old, this careful, disinterested description and explanation of American attitudes toward abortion is still accurate today.

Geer, John. *From Tea Leaves to Opinion Polls.* New York: Columbia University Press, 1996. Thoughtful consideration of a democratic dilemma: Do politicians lead public opinion or follow it? Concludes that rational leaders always follow on salient issues but often lead on less salient ones.

Jacobs, Lawrence and Robert Shapiro. *Politicians Don't Pander: Political Manipulation and the Loss of Democratic Responsiveness.* Chicago: University of Chicago Press: 2000. Provocative argument that today's politicians follow their own strongly held preferences and that polls are only a tool used to determine how best to frame the positions that the politicians personally favor.

Schuman, Howard, Charlotte Steeh, and Lawrence Bobo. *Racial Attitudes in America: Trends and Interpretations.* Cambridge, MA: Harvard University Press, 1985. Thoughtful examination of racial attitudes. The authors find that Americans have come to accept principles of equal treatment but remain quite divided on government policies designed to bring about racial equality.

Stimson, James. *Public Opinion in America: Moods, Cycles, and Swings.* Boulder, CO: Westview Press, 1991. Statistically sophisticated examination of American public opinion from the 1960s to the 1990s. The author finds that public opinion was moving in a conservative direction in the 1970s, but reversed direction around the time of Reagan's election.

Zaller, John. *The Nature and Origins of Mass Opinion.* New York: Cambridge University Press, 1992. An influential reinterpretation of public opinion findings that argues that people do not have fixed opinions on many subjects. Rather, their responses reflect variable considerations stimulated by the question and the context.

On the Web

Academic organizations archive a great deal of public opinion data on political and social topics.

www.aapor.org

www.ropercenter.uconn.edu

www.norc.uchicago.edu

Some of the best sites are the American Association for Public Opinion Research, the Roper Center, and the National Opinion Research Center. The AAPOR site links to the best scholarly journal of public opinion, *Public Opinion Quarterly.* The world's largest collection of public opinion data can be found at the Roper Center for Public Opinion Research. This collection includes a huge amount of commercial and academic poll data. The Roper Center's service—iPoll—requires subscription, but your university may be able to help you gain access. The National Opinion Research Center site contains the 23 General Social Surveys (GSS) carried out since 1972.

www.pollingreport.com

The Polling Report summarizes recent media polls from major media outlets such as CNN/Gallup and the *New York Times,* among others. This site will have more current information than the academic sites, but because news organizations polling about trendy issues sometimes use inconsistent or inadequately tested question wordings, the findings are more subject to question and interpretation.

CHAPTER 6

∗ ∗ ∗ ∗ ∗ ∗ ∗ ∗ ∗ ∗ ∗ ∗ ∗ ∗ ∗ ∗ ∗

Individual Participation

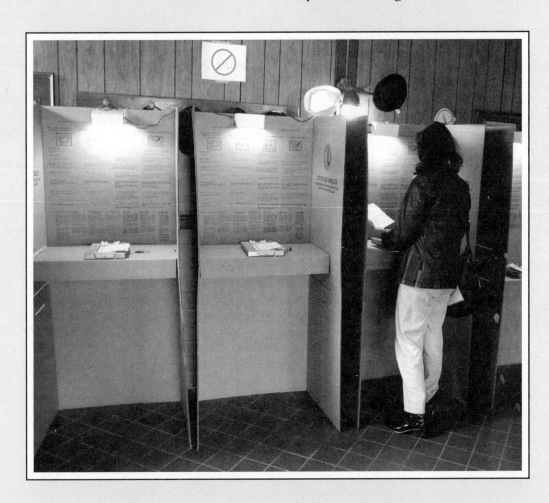

Nonvoting in 2000

The 2000 presidential election was one of the most competitive contests in American history. It featured Al Gore, the incumbent vice president serving as standard bearer for the popular but scandal-tainted Clinton administration, squaring off against George W. Bush, a rising star in the Republican party and son of the president Clinton had sent packing just eight years earlier. The two candidates seesawed back and forth in the polls for months as they fought a grudge match in which neither one could keep an advantage for long—leaving the race wide open as Americans went to the polls on Election Day.

The 2000 election crackled with political excitement for other reasons as well. Gore's running mate, Senator Joe Lieberman of Connecticut, advertised his Jewish faith in interviews and on the stump—energizing not only voters who shared his beliefs, but also those of other faiths grateful to see a candidate unapologetic about his religious convictions. The presidential field also included third-party candidates who could appeal to voters unhappy with politics as usual. The most important of these was Green Party nominee Ralph Nader, a long-time activist who mobilized the nation's disaffected liberal voters (including many college students). In addition, partisan control of Congress hung in the balance, as Democrats fought to regain control of the Senate and Republicans fought to protect their narrow majority in the House of Representatives.

The eventual election outcomes underscored that the 2000 elections were as competitive as they get. After the results were in, the two major parties each held fifty seats in the U.S. Senate, so leadership of the chamber depended on whether the vice president would use his tie-breaking vote to place Democrats or Republicans in charge. In the presidential election, meanwhile, the party with the most votes failed to win a clear-cut victory in the Electoral College—for the first time since 1888. Gore attracted more votes, in part thanks to energetic mobilization campaigns in urban areas, but too much of his electoral support was concentrated in a few big states like California and New York. Bush's voters appeared in a wider variety of locales, giving him critically close victories in important swing states.

The closest call of the presidential campaign came in the state of Florida, where Bush and Gore received almost the same number of votes. The initial tally gave Florida's electoral votes (and therefore the White House) to Bush, but the margin of victory was so small that state law required a recount. Legal teams for each side clashed repeatedly, in both state and federal courts, to influence the rules of the recount. The controversy took weeks to resolve. George W. Bush won out only after the U.S. Supreme Court intervened with a 5-4 ruling that terminated the vote counting. The new chief executive's official margin of victory in Florida amounted to a mere 537 votes.

Despite so much political drama, despite close contests that a few hundred voters could tip one way or the other, despite a series of hard-fought battles that would determine control of the nation's political institutions for years, the federal elections of 2000 failed to attract much more than half of the adult population. Approximately 100 million eligible Americans did not vote—and in Florida, where the vote margin was less than 1000 using almost any recount method, nearly 6 million eligibles stayed away from the polls. Nonvoters were 400 times more numerous than Gore's margin in the country as a whole, and in every state nonvoters exceeded the difference between the Bush and Gore tallies—typically many times over.

The 2004 elections attracted much higher levels of participation than four years earlier. Nationally, turnout increased to 59%, a rate of participation unmatched since 1968. Some states saw large increases in the rate of voting—including swing states like Florida, Nevada, New Hampshire, Ohio, Pennsylvania, and Wisconsin. But the numbers still fell far short of turnout rates in most other democracies.

MAKING THE CONNECTION

Many Americans are concerned about turnout levels in the United States, because voting is widely regarded as the fundamental form of democratic participation. Indeed, in modern democracies, voting is the *only* form of participation for the bulk of the population. About one-third of Americans report having signed a petition, and a similar number claim to have contacted a government official at one time or another, but substantially fewer make financial contributions to a party or candidate, attend a political meeting or rally, or work in a campaign. Two-thirds of Americans do nothing beyond voting.[1]

For most people, then, failure to vote means failure to participate at all. And if a bare majority—or even fewer people—vote, how representative are the public officials they elect, and how legitimate are the actions these officials take? Not very, in the view of some. Benjamin Barber charges that "In a country where voting is the primary expression of citizenship, the refusal to vote signals the bankruptcy of democracy."[2]

Should Americans worry about the dismal rate of voter participation in their country's elections? Answering that question requires a close look at the historical, personal, and institutional reasons why Americans fail to turn out. It also compels us to evaluate other forms of participation besides voting, to see if Americans have evolved alternate ways of communicating with their government. This chapter therefore provides the background necessary to analyze political participation, offering answers to the following questions about the New American Democracy:

- How did the **franchise**—or right to vote—spread in the United States, and did that historical process contribute to when and how people exercise their voting rights today?

- Why is turnout lower in the United States than in other democracies?

- Why has turnout declined in the United States over time?

- Have Americans developed alternate forms of participation that compensate for their failure to turn out on Election Day?

With that background, we can reach a clearer understanding of whether low participation levels threaten the legitimacy of American government.

★ ★ ★ ★ ★ ★ ★ ★ ★ ★ ★ ★ ★ ★ ★

A Brief History of the Franchise in the United States

By 1824, the political system in America's young republic had stagnated. Economic depression, cultural instability, and popular discontent all shook American society, but only one viable party remained to address social problems: the Democratic-Republicans. Their congressional caucus routinely nominated presidential and vice-presidential candidates, who were elected as a matter of course by those with voting rights. National politics therefore was in the hands of a congressional elite elected by a minority of white male property owners.

The caucus could not unite behind a single candidate for president in 1824, though. Four influential men vied for the office, including House Speaker Henry Clay of Kentucky and Secretary of State John Quincy Adams, son of the second president. But the candidate to beat was General Andrew Jackson, hero of the Battle of New Orleans and champion of the common man. Jackson attracted far more support than his rivals did—indeed, his closest competitor received only two-thirds as many votes— but his support was not sufficient to deliver a majority in the Electoral College. As specified by the Constitution (see Chapter 10), the election then went to the House of Representatives, where Clay delivered the victory to Adams. The new president later appointed Clay secretary of state, a position once considered a stepping-stone to the

franchise
The right to vote.

Demonstrating for Women's Suffrage

The suffragists put considerable pressure on President Woodrow Wilson to support the Nineteenth Amendment, even though women initially received the franchise in only a few western states.

• *How did that increase the pressure on politicians to support an amendment to the Constitution?*

presidency—leading General Jackson's supporters to suspect a "corrupt bargain" between the two politicians.

Outraged, Jackson's followers redoubled their efforts to break the long-term grip of the Democratic–Republican elite. For example, they pushed for favorable changes in the nation's electoral laws. In 1824, 6 of the 24 states did not allow voters to pick their presidential electors; the state legislatures selected them. That number fell to 2 states by 1828. Jackson's supporters also extended their campaign outward to the newly settled West and downward to the grass roots of the country. As a result, turnout exploded between the two elections. More than three times as many men voted in 1828 as had voted four years earlier, and Jackson easily defeated Adams the second time around.[3]

Despite the tripling of voter turnout, only about 56 percent of the adult male population voted in 1828— in part because of property qualifications that excluded the poor. Although restrictions varied from state to state and were unevenly enforced, they continued to exclude citizens from voting into the 1830s. Most states also limited the franchise to taxpayers until the 1850s.[4] Moreover, not all voter qualifications were economic. Until the 1830s, a few states limited voting to those who professed belief in a Christian god. Not until the eve of the Civil War could it be said that the United States had universal white male **suffrage** (another term for the right to vote).

suffrage
Another term for the right to vote.

Voting Rights in the Amendment Process

By 1860, even white aliens sometimes were permitted to vote, whereas free black citizens usually were not.[5] White men eventually lost their monopoly over voting rights, however. A series of constitutional amendments gradually expanded electoral access until, by the 1960s, most Americans of voting age held the legal right to participate in federal elections.

The Fifteenth Amendment to the Constitution, adopted in 1870, extended the franchise to black males. Within a few decades, though, violence, intimidation, and other discriminatory procedures disenfranchised African Americans in many states (see

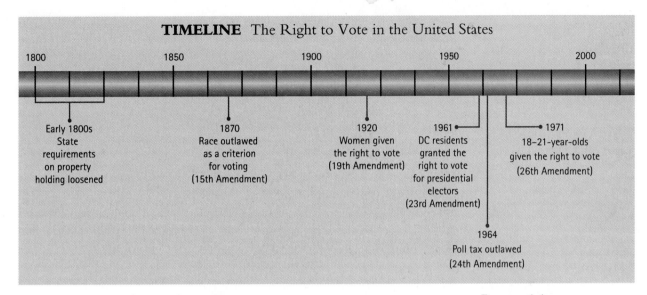

TIMELINE The Right to Vote in the United States

1800 — 1850 — 1900 — 1950 — 2000

Early 1800s
State requirements on property holding loosened

1870
Race outlawed as a criterion for voting
(15th Amendment)

1920
Women given the right to vote
(19th Amendment)

1961
DC residents granted the right to vote for presidential electors
(23rd Amendment)

1971
18–21-year-olds given the right to vote
(26th Amendment)

1964
Poll tax outlawed
(24th Amendment)

FIGURE 6.1

The Right to Vote in the United States Has Been Steadily Expanded

The right to vote in the United States has been a story of continual, if uneven, expansion.

• *Can still more groups be enfranchised? Which ones?*

Chapter 17). Black men could not exercise their voting rights in many parts of the South until the 1960s, when the Voting Rights Act reestablished federal oversight of southern elections. The result has been a steady increase in voting among African Americans.

Women's suffrage also progressed slowly.[6] Many Americans thought women did not require a voice in the political arena because they could depend on their more worldly husbands to speak on their behalf. The first state that explicitly allowed women to vote in national elections, Wyoming, did not do so until 1890. Eleven other states had expanded the franchise to women by 1916. Most were western states, where frontier conditions often required women to be more independent than those living nearer to the eastern seaboard. The Suffrage Movement won its crowning victory in 1920 when the Nineteenth Amendment granted women voting rights in every state.[7]

A small extension of the franchise occurred in 1961 when the Twenty-third Amendment to the Constitution was ratified. This amendment granted residents of the District of Columbia the right to vote for presidential electors. By law (if not in practice), all mentally competent, law-abiding Americans of voting age had gained the right to vote for president. The District of Columbia still lacks representation in the U.S. Senate, however, and its delegate to the House of Representatives may not vote on legislation.

The next and, to date, the last extension of the franchise came in 1971 with the adoption of the Twenty-sixth Amendment to the Constitution, which lowered the official voting age to 18.[8] Prior to the amendment, the federal Constitution did not guarantee voting rights to those under 21 (although individual states could use a lower limit). During the Vietnam War, however, Americans began to question why people old enough to die on a foreign battlefield were not old enough to vote.[9] Support for lowering the voting age grew until Republican President Richard Nixon announced his backing for a constitutional amendment, even though many Republicans feared it would help the Democrats.

In sum, the trend over the course of American history has been steady expansion of the franchise (see Figure 6.1). Today most adult U.S. citizens may vote if they wish.

Convicted felons are not eligible in many states, but some critics argue that even this restriction ought to be abolished because it falls especially heavily on African Americans. About one-eighth of black males are ineligible to vote, and this proportion rises to one-third in states such as Alabama and Florida.[10] Others have argued, presumably tongue-in-cheek, that voting rights should be expanded to include children, perhaps by giving extra weight to the choices of their parents.[11]

How Voting Rights Spread

The uneven expansion of the franchise reflects a compromise adopted by the Constitutional Convention: Voting rights were left up to the separate states, which extended the suffrage in different ways at different times. During times of war, for example, a disenfranchised group usually could expect to receive the suffrage in at least some states as a reward for their service—a process that opened the door for immigrants, for those who did not own property or pay taxes, and for young adults who were considered "old enough to fight, old enough to vote."[12] Once a group gained voting rights in one state, however, national candidates and political parties seeking their support had an incentive to go on record as supporting similar expansions in other states. Electoral pressures, therefore, often caused voting rights to spread quickly, a dynamic that was most apparent in the case of women's suffrage.

Woodrow Wilson won the 1912 presidential election after a three-way race in which he received only 42 percent of the popular vote. At that time, he had avoided taking a clear position on women's suffrage because many of his fellow Democrats opposed it. They believed that women would vote against labor unions, against liquor interests, and against machine politicians—all key Democratic constituencies. Southern Democrats worried, moreover, that granting voting rights to women would raise the aspirations of African Americans for similar rights. Nevertheless, by the time Wilson had to run for reelection women had gained the right to vote in 12 states, including California (1910) and Illinois (1913). The president, therefore, signaled his moderate support for women's suffrage by promising to vote for a related referendum in New Jersey, his home state.

Wilson's change of heart reflected the fact that his Republican opponent in 1916, Charles Evans Hughes, supported a constitutional amendment to let women vote. Had Hughes won the electors for every state with women's suffrage, their support would have moved him a third of the way to an Electoral College majority. Wilson's political position was precarious and he could not afford to surrender the West to Hughes, so he adopted a moderate stance on women's suffrage. Wilson carried 10 of the 12 states where women could vote and narrowly won reelection.

World War I stalled the suffrage movement, but only temporarily. As victory approached, suffragists pressed hard for congressional passage of the proposed constitutional amendment. The National American Women's Rights Association encouraged women to write letters, make campaign contributions, and use other conventional political strategies, while more militant suffragists engaged in confrontational tactics such as protests and demonstrations.

Women's suffrage soon looked inevitable, so politicians fearful of being left behind jumped on the bandwagon. Congress approved the suffrage amendment and sent it to the states, which ratified the provision within three years—in time for women in all 48 states to vote in the 1920 presidential election. Interestingly, the United States was far ahead of most of the world in granting full rights of citizenship to women. France did not allow women to vote until 1945, and the last Swiss canton did not enfranchise women until 1990![13]

Why People Participate: Costs and Benefits

Voting rights have steadily expanded in the United States, but extending the franchise need not lead to increased voter participation. Even in presidential elections, as much as half the potential electorate stays home. After the election, some editorialists criticize the nonvoters for being lazy while others criticize the candidates for being uninspiring— but the question of why eligible voters abstain is more complicated than newspaper editorials usually imply.[14]

Voting is costly. If you are paid by the hour and you take time off in order to vote, you lose a portion of your wages. Even if you are a professional who can leave work early or arrive late, you may do less work on election day if you take the time to vote. Moreover, not all costs are tangible. You may have to wait in long lines to be able to vote before or after work. In 2004, people at some polling places were still waiting in line to vote hours after the polls were supposed to have closed. The time you spend at the voting precinct is time that you may not spend on other activities, some of which may seem more fulfilling. For some people with little information about politics, the entire voting situation can be uncomfortable; staying home enables them to avoid the discomfort. If you are surprised that such seemingly small considerations could lower turnout, consider that turnout generally falls when the weather is rainy or very hot.[15]

There also are benefits to voting, of course. The most obvious is likely the least important: the possibility that your vote might swing an election. Your vote affects an electoral outcome only if it creates or breaks a tie.[16] Otherwise, you could stay home and the election would come out the same way. The chance that a single voter will swing a state or national election is very low indeed, even when turnout falls to its lowest ebb. In the 1996 presidential election, which attracted the lowest turnout rate of any presidential election in the twentieth century, almost 100 million Americans voted. In the 1998 elections for the U.S. House of Representatives, which featured the lowest midterm election turnout in half a century, an average of 141,000 citizens voted in each congressional race. Given numbers like these, a desire to determine who wins the election cannot be a very powerful individual motivation for turning out. From a purely practical standpoint, the puzzle is not that turnout is so low in the United States but, rather, that turnout is as high as it is.

Late in the nineteenth century, when turnout levels were especially high (usually over 75 percent outside the South), some voters had a compelling reason to show up at the polls: They were paid to do so. Historians estimate that the going price of a vote in New York City elections could soar as high as $25 in particularly competitive circumstances (as expressed in 1990s dollars).[17] Material rewards are a much rarer benefit of voting today, but direct payments for voting (sometimes called "walking-around money") still exist here and there, mainly in the poorer areas of eastern cities. Citizens also may feel compelled to vote in elections because the outcome can directly affect their material interests. For example, government employees vote at higher rates than people employed in the private sector, other things being equal—especially in low-turnout local elections.[18]

Today, however, most of the individual motivations for voting are not material but psychological. For example, some people feel a civic duty to vote. They avoid guilt by showing up at the polls. Americans are highly individualistic, though, so they are not especially prone to place much emphasis on civic duty (see Chapter 4). Perhaps the most compelling benefit of voting is the pleasure it can bring. Some Americans take satisfaction in expressing their preference for a candidate or an issue position, much as they might enjoy cheering for an athletic team.[19] Psychological benefits are an important incentive for voting. Whereas your vote makes no difference unless it affects the outcome, you receive the psychological benefits regardless of the closeness of an election. Indeed, voters may take even more satisfaction when they can be part of a political team that wins big, much as sports teams gain in popularity when they enjoy a particularly good season.

Another reason people vote goes beyond simple individual motivations. Sometimes people participate in elections because they have been encouraged to vote by others who have personal incentives to increase turnout. **Voter mobilization** consists of the efforts of parties, groups, and activists to turn out their potential supporters. Campaign workers provide baby sitters and rides to the polls, thus reducing the individual costs of voting. They apply social pressure by contacting citizens who haven't voted and reminding them to do so. Various groups and social networks to which individuals belong also exert social pressures, encouraging the feeling that one has a responsibility to vote. Although pressures and benefits like these may seem small, remember that the costs of voting are relatively small as well.

Armed with some understanding of the general reasons why people vote or fail to vote, we can now address an important question raised in the introduction to this chapter: Why do Americans vote at lower levels than citizens in other countries?

voter mobilization
The efforts of parties, groups, and activists to encourage their supporters to turn out for elections.

International Comparisons of Voter Turnout

Americans vote at much lower levels than people in most other countries, even countries such as Italy whose citizens are exceedingly cynical about politics (see Table 6.1). That being said, procedures for calculating turnout differ from country to country. These differences systematically lower American turnout figures relative to those in other democracies.

Turnout would seem to be simple enough to measure. The U.S. Census Bureau calculates official turnout in presidential elections as:

 Comparative

Comparing Voting and Elections

Number of people voting for president /

Number of people in the voting-age population

TABLE 6.1

AMERICANS ARE LESS LIKELY TO VOTE THAN THE CITIZENS OF OTHER DEMOCRACIES

The following figures represent the average turnout (in percentages) in elections to the lower house of the legislature or parliament in 37 countries, 1960–1995.

Australia (14)[a]	95	Greece (10)	86	France (9)	76
Malta (6)	94	Lithuania (1)	86	United Kingdom (9)	75
Austria (9)	92	Latvia (1)	85	Ireland (11)	74
Belgium (12)	91	Czech Republic (2)	85	Spain (6)	73
Italy (9)	90	Brazil (3)	83	Japan (12)	71
Luxembourg (7)	90	Netherlands (7)	83	Estonia (2)	69
Iceland (10)	89	Costa Rica (8)	81	Hungary (2)	66
New Zealand (12)	88	Norway (9)	81	Russia (2)	61
Denmark (14)	87	Israel (9)	80	India (6)	58
Venezuela (7)	85	Portugal (9)	79	United States (9)	54
Bulgaria (2)	80	Finland (10)	78	Switzerland (8)	54
Germany (9)	86	Canada (11)	76	Poland (2)	51
Sweden (14)	86				

[a] Number of elections.

SOURCE: Adapted from Mark Franklin, "Electoral Participation," in *Comparing Democracies,* ed. Lawrence Le Duc, Richard Niemi, and Pippa Norris (Thousand Oaks, CA: Sage, 1996), p. 218.

Rock the Vote
Efforts to mobilize young voters have increased. In 2004 they had some success in swing states, although nationwide the impact on turnout reportedly was modest.

This definition seems straightforward, but it lowers American turnout as much as 5 percent relative to other countries.

Why? Consider the numerator of the ratio. If you believe that all the candidates are bums and do not vote for president, you are not counted as having voted, an **undervote.** Election officials in many jurisdictions also ignore frivolous write-in votes (actual examples from U.S. elections: Rambo, ZZ Top, Batman), registering them as undervotes. In France, for example, there is a long tradition wherein disaffected voters scribble an offensive suggestion across their ballots (the English translation has initials "F. Y."). French election officials count such ballots, whereas most American officials would not.[20] Vote-counting machines, meanwhile, occasionally fail to register a person's vote, especially in counties using paper ballots—yet another source of undervotes (see the accompanying Election Connection). If you spoil your ballot by voting for more than one candidate, an **overvote,** you also do not appear when officials compute the turnout rate. Procedures differ in other countries. Such decisions lower U.S. turnout figures by 1 to 2 percent per election.[21]

Factors that affect the denominator of the ratio are even more significant. The **voting-age population** refers to the number of people over the age of 18, a number that includes some groups legally ineligible to vote: felons, people confined to mental or correctional institutions, and (most important) noncitizens. Counting the entire voting-age population rather than only the eligible voting-age population lowers U.S. turnout figures by another 3 percent.[22] And this underestimate appears to be growing because ineligible adults such as felons and immigrants make up an increasing proportion of the voting-age population.[23]

Personal Costs and Benefits: Registration

Far more important than the inclusion of ineligible felons and noncitizens in the U.S. voting-age population, however, is that other countries use an entirely different denominator in their turnout calculations. Their denominator is the registered population.

undervotes
Ballots that indicate no choice for an office (e.g., for president in 2000), whether because the voter abstained or because the voter's intention could not be determined.

overvotes
Ballots that have more than one choice for an office (e.g., for president in 2000), whether because the voter voted for more than one candidate or wrote in a name as well as making a mark.

voting-age population
All people in the United States over the age of 18, including those who may not be legally eligible to vote.

ELECTION CONNECTION

Nonvoters Who Actually Turned Out

The need to recompute Florida's 2000 presidential election returns focused media attention on the large number of attempted votes that never appear in an official tally. As the Bush and Gore camps jockeyed to influence the recount, their legal battle mostly revolved around which unrecorded votes should be counted the second time around.

Floridians who turned out on Election Day 2000 were counted as nonvoters for a variety of reasons. Some failed to communicate a preference, either because their ballot confused them or because they neglected to indicate a choice clearly on the ballot. Others communicated a preference but the voting machines failed to register it. These were the undervotes. Some accidentally voted more than once, either selecting more than one presidential candidate or recording both a regular vote and a write-in vote. These were the overvotes. The whole situation was especially confusing because Florida counties used a variety of voting technologies, from paper ballots to sophisticated machines, with widely differing rates of undervotes and overvotes.

The Supreme Court ended the official counting, but media organizations funded subsequent recounts to determine what really happened in Florida. They used various rules for counting undervotes and overvotes. The process took months and, when it was done, the results only partly clarified the election returns. Media organizations concluded that President Bush won the presidential election under most methods of counting, but some approaches would have given the election to his rival. The outcome fell somewhere between a margin of 1665 votes for Bush and 3 votes for Gore.[a]

The state's voting procedures may have been imperfect, but in an ironic way their haphazard nature actually made them difficult to manipulate. Neither Bush's legal team nor Gore's legal team managed to demand self-serving rules. Bush's margin would have been larger if the limited recount with liberal standards advocated by the Gore campaign had been adopted, and Gore would have won by 3 votes if the statewide recount with strict standards advocated by the Bush campaign was adopted! A later, even more extensive recount concluded that Gore might have won narrowly if overvotes had been counted. His campaign never asked that overvotes be counted, perhaps because they are routinely discarded by election authorities across the nation.[b]

• *Whose responsibility is it to make sure that a vote is recorded properly? Is that the voter's problem, or do election officials have a special obligation to correct for voter mistakes that lead to overvotes and undervotes?*

• *Reformers often demand uniform elections technologies because they fear that some voters will suffer if resources vary. But do the virtues of uniformity outweigh the costs of developing a system that might be easier to manipulate wholesale?*

[a] Tom Fiedler, "Introduction: The Encore of *Key Largo*," in *Overtime*, ed. Larry Sabato (New York: Longman, 2002), pp. 12–13.
[b] Dan Keating and Dan Balz, "Florida Recounts Would Have Favored Bush," *Washington Post*, November 12, 2001, p. A1.

---

registered voters
Those legally eligible to vote who have registered in accordance with the requirements prevailing in their state and locality.

The Prepared Voter Kit

More than 30 percent of the American voting-age population has not registered. When turnout is measured as the number voting among **registered voters,** U.S. figures jump to the middle of the range of turnout in industrial democracies.

Registration is automatic in most of the world. It is a function performed by the central government, like maintaining social security records in the United States. Virtually everyone eligible is registered, so turnout rates are essentially the same whether they are measured as a percentage of the voting-age population or as a percentage of those registered. American practice differs in making registration entirely the responsibility of the individual (although the difficulty of registering varies from state to state). Statistical simulations suggest that liberalizing state voting laws could boost national turnout about 9 percent higher than it is at present.[24]

Dropping individual registration requirements would not erase the participation gap between the United States and other industrialized democracies, though. A few states have no registration or allow registration at the polling stations on election day. In these states turnout is higher than the national norm, but it still falls well below the levels in many European countries.[25] Similarly, the national government enacted a proposal to ease registration requirements in 1993. Customarily called the "motor

Compulsory Voting
Many countries force citizens to vote by imposing fines or other penalties on those who abstain. Voting is compulsory in the Philippines, for example—the setting of this photograph.

voter" law, it required states to allow people to register to vote when they renewed driver's licenses and car registrations, among other things. Research suggests that such reforms had little impact, though.[26]

In sum, requiring voter registration does raise the individual costs of participating for Americans, but it is not the only reason for lower U.S. turnout levels.

Personal Costs and Benefits: Compulsion

The personal registration system makes voting relatively costly in the United States. By contrast, some countries attach costs to *nonvoting*. Would you believe that voting is compulsory in many countries? In Australia and Belgium, for example, nonvoters are subject to fines. Greek electoral law provides for imprisonment of nonvoters for up to 12 months, although that penalty is never applied. Other democracies do penalize nonvoters, at least sometimes. Australian law allows for fines of up to $50 for not voting (without a valid excuse), and estimates are that 4 percent of nonvoters pay fines. In Italy, nonvoters are not fined, but "Did Not Vote" is stamped on their identification papers, threatening nonvoters with the prospect of unsympathetic treatment at the hands of public officials should they get into trouble or need help with a problem. Italian nonvoters also have their names posted on community bulletin boards. Turnout in democracies with compulsory voting is almost 15 percent higher than in democracies without it.[27] American turnout figures would undoubtedly increase greatly if people were compelled to vote, although such a policy shift might not solve the fundamental problem posed by low electoral interest (see the accompanying Democratic Dilemma).

Other Personal Costs and Benefits

Several additional institutional variations raise the costs of voting for Americans. Elections in America traditionally are held on Tuesdays, an ordinary workday. In most of the rest of the world, either elections are held on Sundays or election days are proclaimed official holidays. Italian workers receive free train fare back to their place of registration, which is usually their hometown. In effect, the government subsidizes family reunions.

Some observers argue that U.S. turnout is low because Americans are called on to vote so often (see Chapter 1).[28] In most European countries, citizens vote only two or three times in a four-year period: once for a member of Parliament, once for a representative to the European Union, and perhaps once for a small number of local officials. In contrast, Americans vote for numerous national, state, and local officials—usually twice, once in a primary or caucus, and once in a general election. They also may vote for numerous ballot propositions or in a recall election. These elections can occur at different times. Some have suggested, not completely tongue-in-cheek, that turnout in the United States should be calculated as the percentage who vote at least once during a four-year period. In fact, the only European country where voters are called upon to vote frequently, Switzerland, has a turnout rate comparable to that in the United States.

Finally, some states use voter registration lists to select people for jury duty. The fear of losing a day's work, or more if a trial is extended, probably is sufficient to motivate some citizens to forfeit their right to vote. One study concluded that, in such jurisdictions, turnout could be as much as 5 to 10 percent lower than it otherwise would be.[29] Voters in other jurisdictions also sometimes avoid registering because they believe, wrongly, that they might end up with jury duty as a result.

All in all, both intentionally and incidentally, American practices raise the costs of voting relative to those in other countries. When some citizens understandably react to those costs by failing to vote, editorialists criticize them for their lack of public spirit.

Mobilization and Turnout

Not only do Americans face higher costs of voting and lower costs of nonvoting, but they also have less help compensating for these discouraging incentives. The chief mobilizing agent in modern democracies is the political party. Parties have incentives to mobilize their supporters; indeed, they have often undertaken that task with excessive enthusiasm, as when urban machines cast fraudulent votes on behalf of the dead or reported more votes for their candidates than there were residents in their cities. Political scientists Steven Rosenstone and Mark Hansen observe that

> party mobilization underwrites the costs of political participation. Party workers inform people about upcoming elections, tell them where and when they can register and vote, supply them with applications for absentee ballots, show them the locations of campaign headquarters, and remind them of imminent rallies and meetings. Campaigns drop by to pick up donations, telephone reminders on the day of the election, and drive the lazy, the harried, the immobile, and the infirm to the polls.[30]

It certainly is no accident that American turnout levels peaked in the late nineteenth century, when the efficiency of American parties was at a maximum and their ethics at a minimum. During this period the patronage system was strong. With hundreds of thousands of government jobs at stake in elections, the parties had little trouble motivating workers, not to mention their relatives and friends. And, unconstrained by conflict-of-interest or sunshine (open-government) laws, the parties were quite willing to do whatever it took to gain or keep control of government.

American parties have declined since the nineteenth century, at least as mobilizing agents (see Chapter 8). Voters are not as attached to them as in the past, and the parties have less in the way of inducements to turn out the dwindling numbers of faithful.[31] Progressive reforms instituted around a century ago undercut the mobilizing resources once enjoyed by political parties. The personal registration system discouraged voter fraud. Primary elections weakened the parties' control of nominations for office. Civil-service reforms took away much of the patronage that parties once used to buy loyalty. A significant part of the reason why turnout is lower in the United States than in other democracies is that parties are (on average) stronger and more active elsewhere than they are here.

Political parties are not the only mobilizing agent in democracies. Interest groups and associations also bring supporters to the polls (see Chapter 7). However, these organizations are not so deeply rooted in American politics as their counterparts elsewhere. Unions and churches form the very foundations of some political parties in Europe, but the same is not true in the United States. Thus, here too, Americans receive less support from collective political actors than do citizens in other democracies.

Several analysts have dissected statistically the difference in turnout levels between the United States and other countries.[32] All other things being equal, American turnout should actually be somewhat higher than in Europe because of higher educational levels and American civic attitudes that encourage popular participation. But other things are far from equal. Bingham Powell, for example, estimates that differences in electoral institutions (especially registration systems) depress American turnout between 10 and 15 percent relative to Europe. Weaker mobilization efforts depress turnout by about 10 percent. In sum, it costs Americans more to vote, and they receive less support for voting than do citizens in most other countries.

FIGURE 6.2

Turnout in the United States Seldom Reaches 1960s Levels

• *What are the causes of declining turnout? Why the difference between presidential and off-year elections?*

SOURCE: The Committee for the Study of the American Electorate and the Census Bureau.

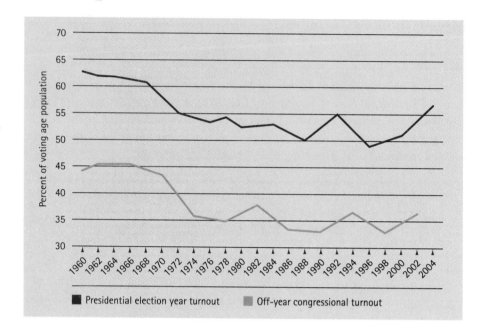

Why Has American Turnout Declined?

For many people the turnout problem is not only that levels in the United States are lower than in other advanced democracies but also that turnout has tended to be low during the past generation. Figure 6.2 shows that in presidential elections, turnout for presidential elections fell steadily between 1960 and 1988, before hitting a half-century low in 1996. In off-year elections, turnout declined more erratically, but it is significantly lower now than a generation ago.[33]

The decline in turnout is especially puzzling because developments late in the twentieth century led to an expectation of *rising* turnout. First, court decisions, federal legislation such as the Voting Rights Act, and the Twenty-fourth Amendment to the Constitution have removed numerous institutional and procedural impediments to voting and thus reduced the personal costs. Legal changes abolished poll taxes and literacy tests, shortened state and local residency requirements, simplified registration, permitted bilingual ballots, and eased the procedures for absentee voting. Such reforms were especially effective in the South, where they helped to overcome the terrible legacy of racial discrimination. Figure 6.3 shows how turnout among African Americans in the South increased sharply between 1960 and 1968.

Second, socioeconomic change should have raised turnout in the post-1964 period. That the potential electorate was getting younger as the baby boom generation came of age should have lowered turnout, because young people traditionally vote at lower levels than older people. But that effect should have been more than offset by rising educational levels. Education is the single strongest predictor of turnout. Higher educational levels produce a keener sense of civic duty and help people deal with the complexities of registering and voting. Ruy Teixeira estimates that, other things being equal, the net effect of socioeconomic changes should have been to raise national turnout by about 4 percent.[34]

What, then, explains the decline in turnout? There is not so much agreement on why voting has declined over time as there is on the explanation of turnout differences

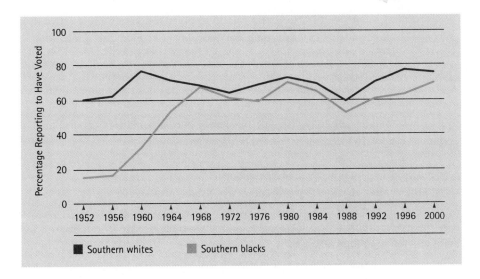

FIGURE 6.3

The Civil Rights Revolution Opened Southern Politics to African Americans

The turnout gap between African American and white voters narrowed as a result of the civil rights movement of the 1950s and 1960s.

• *Given that politicians respond to voters, how did this narrowed gap matter for public policy changes?*

SOURCE: American National Election Studies.

between the United States and other democracies (where, as we have seen, registration and political parties dominate the answer). Several factors clearly have contributed to the decline in American turnout, but their precise importance is a matter of debate.

Declining Personal Benefits

One reason why the decline in voting costs did not increase voting is that the benefits of voting may have declined at an even faster rate. Studies show that Americans today are not so interested in politics, don't care so much about who wins elections, and don't believe that government is as responsive as in times past.[35] Thus they do not see as much riding on their decisions as in years past, and they probably get less intrinsic satisfaction from supporting an admired candidate or party. One must be extremely careful in interpreting such findings, however. Lack of interest in elections and government could be another symptom of the problem, rather than the actual cause of nonvoting.

Another political factor that has lowered the benefits of voting is that elections have become less competitive. As we discuss in Chapter 11, the advantage of incumbency in congressional elections increased greatly after the mid-1960s. A similar process occurred more slowly in state legislative elections. Many presidential elections in the 1970s and 1980s were landslides, and gubernatorial elections had become less competitive as well. When candidates win by large margins, the notion that one's vote actually makes a difference must seem more outlandish than ever. Nor do blowout elections provide much incentive for campaign organizations to get out the vote. Rosenstone and Hansen find that in states with competitive gubernatorial campaigns, turnout is 5 percent higher, other things being equal.[36] Notably, turnout increased dramatically in 2004, when both the presidential election and a handful of Senate elections were especially close.

Declining Mobilization

Statistical studies reveal that personal costs and benefits account for less than half of the decline in turnout. The larger part of the decline reflects the decreased mobilization efforts of parties, campaigns, and social movements since the turbulent 1960s.

Parties still are active, of course, and candidate organizations are more active than ever. But polling and media advertising are probably not good substitutes for the pound-the-pavement, doorbell-ringing workers who used to dominate campaigns. Voters may be motivated by the coaxing of a campaign worker standing at the front door or telephoning late in the afternoon of election day, but those same voters may not be motivated by an impersonal TV spot urging them to vote.[37] Thus, a change in style from labor-intensive to high-tech campaigning may have indirectly contributed to declining turnout. In fact, political parties trying to attract additional votes recently have started returning to the old methods of voter mobilization, such as phone calls and personal visits from politically active neighbors.[38]

The fact that elections have become less competitive would further lower the motivation of campaigns to engage in difficult, time-consuming activity. When the result of an election is a foregone conclusion, the winning side grows complacent, and the losing side sees little reason to make a serious effort.

Declining Social Connectedness

You might interpret a turnout line trending downward to mean that any given citizen is less likely to vote today than a generation ago. Political scientist Warren Miller has shown that such a view is incorrect.[39] The decline in voter turnout is what social scientists call a **compositional effect**—an aggregate shift that results from a change in group composition rather than a change in the behavior of individuals already in the group. Older Americans learned to vote at high rates when they were young and they continue to do so. The turnout rates of middle-aged Americans (the baby boomers), by contrast, were low when they entered the electorate and remain low. Turnout is declining because of the simple fact that those accustomed to voting at high rates are dying and being replaced by habitual nonvoters. Robert Putnam argues that the younger generation is less likely to participate in other ways as well.[40]

Why are younger adults cut off from the political world? Stephen Knack suggests that common thinking about voting is misconceived.[41] Rather than voting being the fundamental political act, voting may be a form of social behavior. People will vote when they are integrated into their communities through connections such as extended families, neighborhoods, churches, and other social units. These forms of **social connectedness** are common among older Americans, who grew up in a simpler time when Americans were less mobile, more religious, and more trusting of their fellow citizens. Younger Americans have grown up in a highly mobile, worldly society where cynicism about their fellow citizens is widespread. They may not feel the social connections that prompt individuals to participate in political life.

This argument can be taken too far. Arguments based on social connectedness veer perilously close to sounding like nostalgia for the "good old days," which often were not so good when experienced first hand. After all, many social ties are built on exclusion, on a sense of being right while outsiders are wrong. Young people may stay out of politics because they have less desire to impose their will on others. As *Newsweek* columnist Fareed Zakaria writes, "Today's young . . . are less sure that they have the grand solutions for society's problems."[42] Younger adults also often experience their own forms of connectivity, such as through Internet news groups or chat rooms. These "electronic communities" may not be as satisfying emotionally as real-life ties, but there

compositional effect
A shift in the behavior of a group that arises from a change in the group's composition, not from a change in the behavior of individuals in the group.

social connectedness
The degree to which individuals are integrated into society—families, churches, neighborhoods, groups, and so forth.

is no reason they must be apolitical—especially because many of them link people with fairly similar personal interests, perhaps more similar than the interests of family or church members.

Nevertheless, a body of research does support looking to social explanations for the generational gap in voter participation. Voting is related to social involvement such as giving blood, donating to charities, and doing volunteer work.[43] Similarly, turnout is not related to trust in *government,* but it is significantly related to trust in *people.*[44]

Investigators have explored the relationship between turnout and measures of social connectedness. Even relying on such crude indicators as marriage rates, home ownership, church attendance, and length of residence in a community, recent studies find that decreased social connectedness accounts for as much as one-quarter of the decline in presidential turnout.[45] (One interesting tidbit from this body of research: Although being married is associated with higher turnout, being *newly* married lowers the odds of voting; apparently, getting to the polls is not high on the priority list of the newly married.[46])

Who Votes and Who Doesn't?

Low voting rates probably would not stimulate as much discussion as they do if all social and economic groups in America exhibited the same voting rates. But people differ in their ability to bear the costs of voting, in the strength of their feeling that voting is a duty, and in how often they are the targets of mobilization. Consequently, as Figure 6.4 indicates, turnout rates differ considerably across social and economic groups.[47]

Highly educated people are far more likely to vote than people with little formal education. Education instills a stronger sense of duty and gives people the knowledge,

Voter Turnout: Who Votes? Do Americans Vote as Much as Other Citizens?

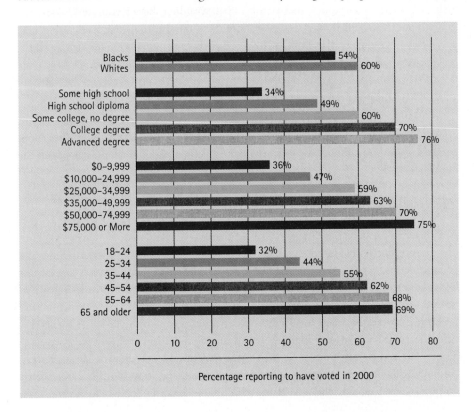

Percentage reporting to have voted in 2000

FIGURE 6.4

Do these differences influence public policy?

• *What appears to be the strongest predictor that someone will vote? Do these differences make a difference for public policy?*

SOURCE: Current Population Survey.

analytic skills, and self-confidence to meet the costs of registering and voting. Over and above education, income also has a significant effect. The wealthy are far more likely to vote than the poor. Affluence, too, reflects a set of skills and personal characteristics that help people overcome barriers to voting.

Studies of turnout in the 1970s concluded that, once disadvantages in education and income were factored out and their younger age in the population was considered, blacks were at least as likely to vote as whites.[48] But more recent research finds that blacks are somewhat less likely to vote than whites, even taking into account differences in income and educational levels.[49] One suggestion is that African Americans were disillusioned by the failure of the Jesse Jackson campaigns in 1984 and 1988.[50] Other minorities, such as Latinos and Asians, still face language barriers, although the situation is gradually improving.[51]

Turnout increases with age, until very old age when the trend reverses. People presumably gain experience as they age—experience that makes it easier for them to overcome any barriers to voting. They also become more socially connected, as well as more settled down in a life situation that clarifies their political preferences.

Notably, the relationships between socioeconomic characteristics and turnout are consistently stronger in the United States than in other democracies. Indeed, in some countries there is almost no relationship between education and income on the one hand and voting on the other.[52] Parties elsewhere are much more effective at mobilizing their supporters. In particular, European Social Democratic parties do a far better job of getting their less advantaged potential voters to the polls than does the Democratic party in the United States.

In sum, there is no question that the low turnout rates that exist in the United States result in an electorate that is somewhat wealthier, better educated, older, and whiter than the population at large. What are the implications of that fact?

Is Low Turnout a Problem?

Given who votes and why, should the relatively low turnout rate in the United States be a cause for concern? Quite a few answers have been offered on both sides of this question. To a considerable degree, these differing views hinge on different beliefs about people's motives for voting. We will briefly sketch three arguments on each side of the debate.

Three Arguments Why Low Turnout Is Not a Problem

A Conservative (with a Small "C") Argument   Many people concerned about low turnout implicitly assume that high turnout indicates enthusiasm about politics and commitment to making the political order work. Maybe not. Some skeptics suggest that high turnout may indicate tension or conflict, coupled with a belief that losing would be unacceptable. They cite the experience of Austria and Germany as their democratic governments crumbled and the Fascist parties took power in the 1930s.[53] Turnout in those elections reached very high levels, but this mobilization probably reflected disillusionment and desperation more than commitment and enthusiasm. More recently, Anthony King observes that the highest British turnouts occur in Northern Ireland, the home of centuries-old religious strife.[54] The 2004 U.S. presidential election is a less extreme case in point. Turnout rose, but did this increase indicate a healthier political system? On the contrary, by many indications people were frustrated and upset with their government, either its war on terrorism or its neglect of "moral values." Similarly, "angry white males" reportedly drove up turnout in 1994. Generalizing from examples like these, some argue that low turnout indicates contentment, not alienation—a sign of political stability.

An Elitist Argument   On average, nonvoters are less educated than voters. Studies also show them to be less informed, less interested in politics, and less concerned about it. Given these facts, some writers argue that the quality of electoral decisions is higher if no special effort is made to increase turnout. For example, David Reisman once remarked, "Bringing sleepwalkers to the polls simply to increase turnout is no service to democracy."[55] Columnist George Will provides a more succinct example of this elitist point of view: "Smaller is smarter."[56] Of course, this argument assumes that nonvoters would remain ignorant and unconcerned even after they decided to vote. If, instead, the process of encouraging people to vote also informed them and raised their interest in politics, their preferences might well change.

A Cynical or Radical Argument   Some radicals contend that it is not the nonvoters but the voters who are a cause for concern. According to this viewpoint, elections don't matter—they are charades. Real decisions are made by power elites far from the popular arena. If so, voting is merely a symbolic act. It makes the masses feel they have a say in how they are governed. Turnout doesn't matter because elections don't matter.

This is the one argument about the implications of low turnout that the evidence cannot support. Elections matter a great deal—in some cases, too much. They have enormous impact on public policies that directly affect the quality of American life.

Three Arguments Why Low Turnout Is a Problem

The Voters Are Unrepresentative   The most obvious concern arising from low turnout is that it produces an unrepresentative electorate. The active electorate is wealthier, whiter, older, and better educated than the potential electorate. People naturally assume that such an electorate is more Republican and more conservative than the voting-age population at large. Consequently, elections are biased, and public policies adopted by the winners are correspondingly biased. Plausible as the argument seems, though, research suggests that it is overstated. Numerous studies have compared the policy views and the candidate preferences of voters and nonvoters. Typically, they differ little. Some studies have even found that at times, contrary to the usual expectation, the conservative candidate was more popular among nonvoters (Ronald Reagan in 1984, for example).[57]

Given differences in voting rates across various social groups, why do the preferences of nonvoters and voters differ so little? Minorities and the poor vote less often than whites and the affluent, but the difference is only a matter of degree. Yes, blacks are less likely to vote than whites, but only about one-eighth of all the nonvoters are black. Similarly, the more highly educated are more likely to vote, but 25 percent of nonvoters have some college education. Nonvoters are not all poor, uneducated members of minority groups. Plenty of nonvoters are affluent, well educated, and white—especially those who do not vote because they've recently moved residences

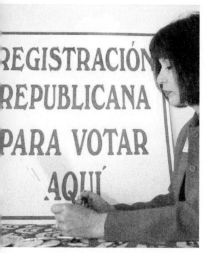

Minority Voting
Potential voters who do not speak English as their primary language turn out at particularly low rates. Both parties have worked hard to mobilize these nonvoters.

social issues
Issues (such as abortion, obscenity, gay rights, capital punishment, gun control, and prayer in schools) that reflect personal values more than economic interests.

(according to the U.S. Census Bureau, nearly one in five Americans moves during the two-year interval between national elections).

In the second place, few groups are as one-sided in their political inclinations as African Americans, who vote more than 8:1 Democratic. If turnout among most other groups were to increase, the Democrats would get somewhat more than half the additional votes, but the Republicans would get a fair proportion as well.

Teixeira provides a striking illustration of these points. According to his calculations, if all the Hispanics and African Americans in the country had voted in 1988 at levels 10 percent higher than whites, and all the white poor had voted at levels 10 percent higher than the white rich, the Democratic candidate, Michael Dukakis, would still have lost by two and a half million votes.[58] It is doubtful that plausible increases in turnout would produce a sea change in American politics—unless joining the political system produced a sharp change in the political outlook of former nonvoters.

Low Turnout Reflects a "Phony" Politics   This argument emphasizes the character of political issues in present-day America. Social critics assert that low turnout among working-class Americans results because the party system fails to address "real" issues of concern to such people. What are real issues? Basically, they are economic issues: jobs, health care, housing, income distribution, and education. What the United States has is two middle-class parties obsessed with "phony" issues: flag burning, gun control, feminism, school prayer, capital punishment, gay rights. (Political scientists refer to such issues as **social issues** to distinguish them from pocketbook worries and other practical personal concerns.)

Basic public opinion data seem to reinforce this criticism. A Gallup Organization poll from April 2004 asked respondents what they considered the most important problem faced by the United States. Economic issues topped the list; 43 percent of respondents mentioned unemployment, the economy's overall performance, or some other economic worry. Another 39 percent selected the war in Iraq or terrorism as the nation's most important problem. Very few people listed the hot-button issues that often dominate partisan debate, such as guns or racism (targeted by liberal politicians) or gay marriage, abortion and other morality issues (targeted by conservative politicians).[59] Voters concerned with "moral issues" therefore turned out in large numbers, but those with economic concerns were more thinly represented. Nor is concern with economics and foreign affairs unique to recent times. Since Gallup began asking the question in 1935, one of those two issue areas has almost always ranked at the top—foreign affairs during wartime, economic issues in times of peace.[60] In short, typical Americans usually worry about more practical concerns than the symbolic battles that make up the lifeblood of electoral competition. They perceive politics as a luxury interest irrelevant to their daily lives.

Low Turnout Discourages Individual Development   The final claim is in some respects a counterargument to the elitist argument that low turnout is not a problem. Classical political theorists from Aristotle to John Stuart Mill emphasized that democracy has an important educational component. Participation in democratic politics stimulates individual development. Because participants become better citizens and better human beings, they take politics to a higher level. Low turnout therefore signifies a lost opportunity to improve both the nonparticipants and politics itself.

Some are skeptical that political participation is such an ennobling experience. Attending an intensive face-to-face political event like a school board or city council meeting might improve a citizen. Pulling a few levers in a voting booth is unlikely to do so.[61] But the argument makes a valid point: Voting may affect not only who wins and what they do but also the voters themselves—what manner of people they are and what they want.

Evaluating the Arguments

There is considerable disagreement about whether low turnout in the United States is a problem and, if so, how serious a problem it is. Well-intentioned and well-informed people disagree and offer persuasive arguments in support of their positions. Our view is that nonvoters and voters have diverse motives. Some nonvoters are content whereas others are alienated, and the same goes for voters. High turnout can indicate either high approval of the political order or serious dissatisfaction with it. Nonvoters don't have much political information, but neither do many voters—so raising turnout will not "dilute" the electorate very much. Low turnout does make the actual electorate some-what less representative than the potential electorate, but not so much as critics often assume. Some potential voters undoubtedly are discouraged by a politics that discusses social issues of little relevance for them, but other citizens turn out to vote precisely because of their concern with such issues. And, although participation fosters citizen-ship, we are doubtful that the impersonal act of casting a vote will foster it very much. In short, we find some validity in each of the arguments presented above. We reject in its entirety only the argument that elections don't matter. Low turnout is a cause for concern, yes; a cause for despair, no.

Beyond the Voting Booth

One reason that low voter turnout should not cause Americans to despair for their nation's future is that citizens often participate actively outside of the voting booth. As Figure 6.5 shows, Americans vote much less often than citizens in Austria, Germany, the United Kingdom, and the Netherlands. However, they are significantly more likely to work in campaigns, contact public officials, or volunteer for work in their communi-ties. They also attend political meetings at a fairly high rate.

Americans participate actively in other ways as well, some that require a great commitment to candidates or causes, and others that take citizens outside the bounds of conventional politics. For example, an estimated one-quarter of Americans contribute money to political campaigns, judging from a survey analysis conducted by Sidney Verba and his associates. Around 14 percent attend local board meetings. Six percent of their survey respondents even admitted engaging in some form of political protest.[62] All of these sorts of activities require much greater sacrifice from participants than the simple act of voting, yet Americans apparently accept such sacrifices at relatively high rates.

Why would alternate forms of participation be so popular? Ironically, for many of the same reasons that voter turnout is so low.

- The frequency of elections in the United States opens up many opportunities for campaign involvement. Americans also have an easier time contacting public offi-cials and attending government board meetings, because they have so many elected officials and so many boards and commissions. Even if Americans are less likely to take advantage of any particular participatory opportunity, the sheer number of openings would give them a higher level of political participation than in other

FIGURE 6.5
**Americans Participate in Ways
More Demanding Than Voting**
• *Why might Americans not vote
at rates as high as citizens of other
democracies and yet participate at
higher rates than others in rela-
tively more demanding ways?*
SOURCE: Adapted from Sidney
Verba, Kay Lehman Schlozman,
and Henry Brady, *Voice and
Equality* (Cambridge, MA:
Harvard University Press, 1995),
p. 70.

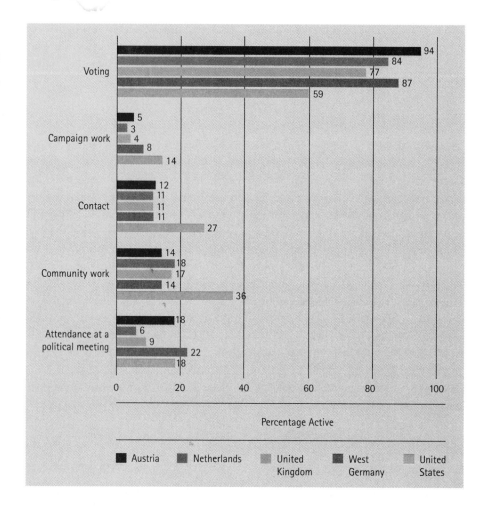

countries where opportunities are more limited. Indeed, as American elections have increased in frequency and as governmental bodies have increased in number, some studies have found increases in some kinds of campaign participation.[63]

• Our individualistic political culture may suppress the sense of civic duty that promotes voter turnout. The political culture's emphasis on rights and liberties, however, encourages Americans to contact their public officials and to protest government actions. In contrast, the political cultures of most other democracies are more deferential to authority and discourage ordinary citizens from taking as active a role in politics as in the United States. Citizens elsewhere are less likely to protest government decisions—and when they do, their governments are more likely to ignore them.

• Because American political parties are weaker today than in earlier eras, candidates construct numerous personal organizations, many of whose members are temporary. In other countries a small cadre of committed party workers shoulders most of the burden of campaigning year in and year out, but in the United States campaigns are fought by much larger groups of "occasional activists." These are enthusiastic amateurs who drift in and out of political campaigns, depending on whether particular candidates or issues arouse their enthusiasm.[64] As a result, overall involvement in campaign activity brings in a wider variety of individuals.

- The United States gained independence through revolution, and protests have remained a regular feature of American politics ever since. In the 1850s militant abolitionists fought slavery so aggressively that their actions resembled what we today call terrorism, as when John Brown and his abolitionist supporters seized a federal arsenal. Similarly, Carrie Nation brought her battle against Demon Liquor in the 1900s straight into the taverns carrying an axe, which she used to bust open casks of beer and whiskey. In the 1960s the civil rights movement fought for racial equality using marches, sit-ins, and boycotts. Direct action may not always be healthy for democracy. When a political movement resorts to taunting police and throwing rocks, one columnist suggests, "it is trying to achieve, through intimidation and scare tactics, what it has not been able to get through legislation."[65] Nevertheless, protests are as American as apple pie.

Political Protest
The war on terrorism, and especially the war in Iraq, resulted in increasing levels of unconventional political participation.

Protests aside, American participation outside the voting booth suggests a much healthier political system than the turnout rates alone might have implied. Americans would not donate their money, their time, and their energy to a political system that only grappled with "phony" politics or that failed to nurture citizens into full community members. Of course, those who engage in alternate forms of participation may be just as unrepresentative as voters are. Indeed, they likely are more so. But most of the legal barriers to voting—such as registration laws, election scheduling, fear of jury duty, and disenfranchisement caused by a felony conviction—would not apply to these alternatives. The availability of a wide variety of options for participation, each with its own costs and benefits, provides some reassurance that citizens who entirely abstain from political life do so because they prefer not to get involved.

Often Americans do not speak to their elected officials directly. Rather, they join organizations that can communicate with government on their behalf. These interest groups often mobilize Americans to participate: soliciting their signatures for petitions, their contributions for fundraising drives, their attendance at group meetings, and so forth. Organized groups also can be an encouragement for unconventional (or contentious) forms of participation: protests, demonstrations, and civil disobedience. There are far more groups and associations active in American politics than are found in other countries. They provide extensive opportunities for participation. Because group participation differs significantly from individual participation, we treat interest groups at length in the next chapter.

Chapter Summary

Popular participation in democratic elections is the essence of democracy. But in most elections, a majority of the American electorate stays away from the polls. Only in presidential elections does a majority usually turn out—and usually a bare majority at that. When it comes to participation in more demanding ways, far fewer people get involved.

American turnout levels are significantly lower than in other modern democracies, and they are lower than they were at the start of the century. The international difference is not hard to explain. In many ways the United States makes voting more costly than it is in other countries: Registration is left to the individual, voting is less convenient, and citizens are called on to vote much more often. In addition, mobilizing agents such as parties and unions are weaker in the United States than in other modern democracies, so Americans get less encouragement to vote from larger organizations.

The 2004 elections saw a dramatic increase in voter turnout, to levels not seen since the late 1960s. Nonetheless, the recent experience in America has been low levels of participation, despite reforms that have lowered the costs of voting and educational levels that have gone up. Americans seem less interested in politics and less inclined to think that voting makes a difference. The explanations for such disenchantment are a matter of much debate. Nevertheless, nonvoters differ from each other more, and from voters less, than is usually presumed.

Key Terms

compositional effect, p. 162
franchise, p. 149
overvote, p. 155
registered voters, p. 156

social connectedness, p. 162
social issues, p. 166
suffrage, p. 150

undervote, p. 155
voter mobilization, p. 154
voting-age population, p. 155

Suggested Readings

Of General Interest

Keyssar, Alexander. *The Right to Vote.* New York: Basic Books, 2000. A comprehensive history of the evolution of the suffrage in America.

Putnam, Robert. *Bowling Alone.* New York: Simon & Schuster, 2000. Monumental study of the decline of participation in social and political life. Argues that American life is less healthy because of the decline in civic engagement.

Verba, Sidney, Kay Schlozman, and Henry Brady. *Voice and Equality: Civic Volunteerism in American Politics.* Cambridge, MA: Harvard University Press, 1995. Fascinating discussion of the development of political skills in nonpolitical contexts such as churches. Strong on attention to differences involving race, ethnicity, and gender.

Focused Studies

Ansolabehere, Steven, and Shanto Iyengar. *Going Negative.* New York: Free Press, 1995. Based mostly on experiments, this important study finds that negative ads discourage moderates from voting.

Piven, Francis, and Richard Cloward. *Why Americans Don't Vote.* New York: Pantheon, 1988. This critical commentary on nonvoting in the United States contends that "have-nots" are systematically discouraged from voting.

Rosenstone, Steven, and John Mark Hansen. *Mobilization, Participation, and Democracy in America.* New York: Macmillan, 1993. Statistical study of electoral and governmental participation from the 1950s to the 1980s, with particular emphasis on the decline in turnout.

Wolfinger, Raymond, and Steven Rosenstone. *Who Votes?* New Haven, CT: Yale University Press, 1980. A statistical study that relies on huge Census Bureau samples, thus providing the best estimates of the relationships between demographic characteristics and voting, though in a limited number of elections (1972 and 1974).

On the Web

There are lots temporary organizations designed to increase voter turnout (usually for a specific candidate). These are usually closely tied to or run by a specific campaign. Organizations committed to a broader vision of democracy are not nearly so common.

www.lwv.org
Perhaps the oldest and most respected is the League of Women Voters, born out of the suffrage movement around the turn of the century. This nonpartisan group works to encourage informed and active participation.

www.rochester.edu/SBA
A useful summary of the suffrage movement, including its history and important documents, can be found via the University of Rochester.

www.vote-smart.org
One of the most useful sites for citizens interested in how to participate, and in information on candidates, is Project Vote Smart. It is also a nonpartisan site with a wealth of information on candidate backgrounds, positions, and records.

CHAPTER 7

✦ ✦ ✦ ✦ ✦ ✦ ✦ ✦ ✦ ✦ ✦ ✦ ✦ ✦ ✦ ✦ ✦

Interest-Group Participation in American Democracy

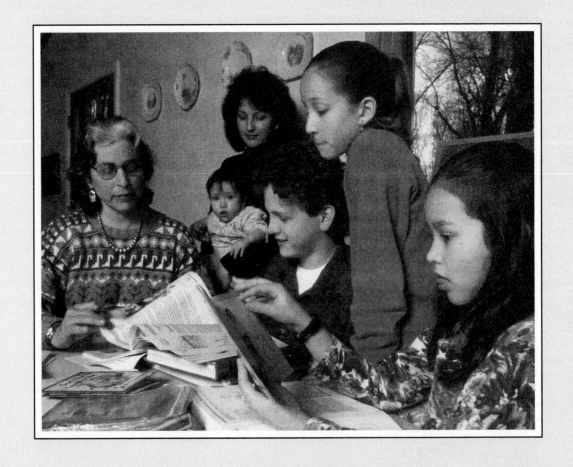

How One Group Challenged Congress

Members of the House Education Committee were hard at work on a major bill in February 1994, when California Democrat George Miller offered what appeared to be an acceptable amendment.[1] Miller's proposal would have withheld federal grant money from school districts that employed teachers who were not officially certified in their subjects. Approving the amendment must have been an easy decision. Committee members could claim that they had taken affirmative steps to improve teacher qualifications, without spending any additional money.

Miller's amendment promised other political advantages to the Democrats who controlled the committee. The mandate was sure to please two groups whose members frequently support their party: unions and universities. Teachers' unions favor certification requirements because they reduce competition from skilled, but uncertified, teachers. Education schools favor certification requirements because professionals, no matter how skilled, would have to go through one of their programs before being allowed to teach. But these eyes were not the only ones watching.

Unbeknownst to many people, including most members of Congress at the time, between 500,000 and 1 million American children are educated at home—many by conservative Christian parents opposed to the secular values of the educational profession. A homeschool advocate who had been following these obscure committee proceedings contacted U.S. Representative Richard Armey (R-TX) to inquire whether the amendment would affect parents who teach their own children. Uncertain about the impact of the proposal, Armey sought the advice of the Home School Legal Defense Association. The association's lawyers suggested that, given the tendency of the courts to interpret legislative mandates broadly, the proposal did threaten parents educating their children at home.

The reaction was fierce and immediate. In a letter to Congress that illustrates the fevered pitch of political rhetoric today, the Home School Legal Defense Association charged that the House proposal was "the equivalent of a nuclear attack upon the homeschooling community." Employing modern communications technologies, the interest group set out to mobilize the potential constituency of homeschoolers and their sympathizers.

Electronic communications carried the warning to every corner of the United States, and in a matter of days the echoes came back loud and clear. The homeschool constituency generated more than half-a-million communications, tying up Capitol Hill switchboards and overwhelming fax machines. A few days later, a second wave of electronic thunder rolled across Capitol Hill after the homeschool coalition convinced groups representing private schools that they, too, were endangered by the proposed mandate.

Many members of Congress—blithely unaware of what was going on in one of 275 committees and subcommittees—went home for the President's Day recess and were caught in the blast of a constituency explosion. Some of them were verbally ambushed at town meetings by constituents incensed that Congress might be planning to destroy homeschools. And when members tried to reach their offices to figure out what was going on, they found the lines jammed. Armey could not get through from Texas, and other members had to call staff at their homes to learn the nature of the problem.

In the face of such an outcry, the House sounded a full retreat. Before galleries packed with homeschool advocates, the committee offered a floor amendment to kill the Miller provision and add statutory language specifically exempting homeschools from the legislation's scope. It passed 424 to 1; Representative Miller stood alone. Not completely satisfied, Armey introduced a further amendment declaring that the legislation did not "permit, allow, encourage or authorize any federal control over any aspect of any private, religious or homeschool." To be on the safe side, the House passed this amendment too, 374 to 53.

MAKING THE CONNECTION

This episode graphically illustrates all the perceived ills of interest-group democracy. It shows large organizations trying to use federal power to reduce competition and steer people into paying for training they may not need. It shows a small, but intense, minority able to send the nation's entire legislative branch scrambling for cover. It shows the extent to which public policies emerge from fear and political calculation rather than from careful deliberation. On the other hand, it also shows how interest groups can enhance democracy. Most citizens do not participate actively in politics as individuals, but many are associated with groups that are active. By mobilizing citizens who ordinarily are uninvolved, these interest groups can be an effective way for the public to express its will—especially now that they have adopted state-of-the-art communications technologies that keep the public informed and amplify voter concerns in Washington, D.C.

In this chapter we examine interest groups and how they influence government. Specifically, we consider these questions:

- How do interest groups organize to communicate their views?

- What problems do interest groups face in mobilizing their members and how do they overcome these obstacles?

- How do interest groups influence government and how successful are they?

- Do interest groups contribute to or detract from democratic government?

★ ★ ★ ★ ★ ★ ★ ★ ★ ★ ★ ★ ★ ★ ★ ★ ★

Interest Groups in the United States

Americans are joiners, more so than the citizens of most other democracies (see Table 7.1). More than three-quarters of Americans belong to at least one group; on average they belong to two and they make financial contributions to four.[2] Many of these associations allow citizens to participate indirectly in politics because they are **interest groups**—organizations or associations of people with common interests that participate in politics on behalf of their members.

Of course, not all the groups with which people are associated are political groups—many are social clubs, charities, service organizations, church groups, and so forth—but literally thousands of groups do engage in politics. Even seemingly nonpolitical groups often engage in political activity. For example, parent-teacher organizations often are active in school politics. Neighborhood associations lobby about traffic, crime, and zoning policies. Hobby or recreation groups mobilize when they perceive threats to their favored activities—witness the National Rifle Association!

> **interest group**
> Organization or association of people with common interests that engages in politics on behalf of its members.

Growth and Development of Groups

Americans have a long-standing reputation for forming groups. In his classic book *Democracy in America,* Alexis de Tocqueville, a nineteenth-century French visitor to the United States, noted that Americans

> . . . are forever forming associations. . . . [A]t the head of any new undertaking, where in France you would find the government or in England some territorial magnate, in the United States you are sure to find an association.[3]

This tendency to form groups has never faded. In fact, there are more organized groups in the United States today than ever before. One study found that 40 percent of the associations with Washington offices were formed after 1960.

Group formation in the United States has not been a steady process, however. It has occurred in waves.[4] Before the Civil War, there were few national organizations in

TABLE 7.1
AMERICANS TEND TO BE JOINERS

Of nine democracies surveyed to assess their level of group membership, only the Netherlands rivaled the United States as a nation of joiners. The Dutch, like the Americans, are particularly likely to participate in religious groups.

	Percent Belonging to No Groups	Percent Belonging to Four or More Groups
Netherlands	15	31
United States	18	19
Germany	33	8
Canada	35	16
Britain	46	9
Italy	59	4
France	61	4
Mexico	64	4
Spain	70	2

SOURCE: Figures drawn from the World Values Surveys, 1990–1993, reported in *The Public Perspective,* April/May, 1995: 21.

single-issue group
An interest group narrowly focused to influence policy on a single issue.

America. Life in general was local. The social organization of the United States was one of "island communities" with few social and economic links among them.[5] As the railroads connected the country after the Civil War, however, a national economy developed—and national associations were not far behind. The first two decades after the war saw the birth of national agricultural associations like the Grange and of trade unions like the Knights of Labor and the American Federation of Labor.

Another major wave of group organization occurred during the Progressive era, roughly 1890 to 1917. Many of today's most broad-based economic associations date from that era: the Chamber of Commerce, the National Association of Manufacturers, and the American Farm Bureau Federation, for example. Other sorts of associations sprang up as well. For example, the National Association for the Advancement of Colored People (NAACP) formed as part of a strategy to promote equality for black Americans, and the National Audubon Society was established to promote conservation.

The 1960–1980 wave of group formation was by far the largest and the most diverse. Thousands of additional economic groups formed, but these tended to be more narrowly based than earlier ones. The American Soybean Association, the National Corn Growers Association, the Rocky Mountain Llama and Alpaca Association, and numerous other specialized organizations joined the more general agricultural associations. Similarly, in the commercial and manufacturing sectors, numerous specialized groups joined the older, more broad-based groups.

What are sometimes called "government interest groups" proliferated as older national associations of mayors, governors, teachers, and social workers were joined by newer, more specialized associations such as the National Association of State and Provincial Lotteries, the Association of State Drinking Water Administrators, and the U.S. Police Canine Association. Similarly, nonprofit groups now include all kinds of specialized occupational associations. Examples of particular relevance to likely readers of this book include the National Association of Student Financial Aid Administrators and the National Association of Graduate Admissions Professionals.

Innumerable shared-interest groups have formed in recent decades, some so narrowly focused that they are called **single-issue groups.** These groups may openly embrace a particular political ideology. Liberal groups such as the National Organization for Women (NOW, a feminist group) and People for the American Way (a civil-liberties group) are deeply involved in politics, as are such conservative groups as the Christian Coalition (a group promoting traditional morality) and Operation Rescue (an anti-abortion group). "Citizens" groups, on the other hand, purport to promote the interests of everyone by seeking the public good—even though their policy goals often are just as controversial as those of the ideological groups. Examples include Common Cause (a political reform group), Greenpeace (an environmental

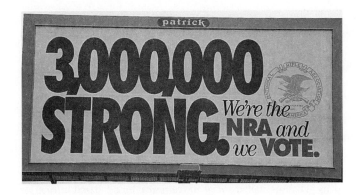

A Recreational Group Turns Political

The NRA was founded shortly after the Civil War to promote marksmanship among hunters, target shooters, and gun collectors. By the mid-twentieth century, the NRA operated safety programs and trained law enforcement officers. It is now known, however, as the chief opponent of gun-control legislation. Its PAC is usually one of the top ten contributors to congressional elections, and it employs some 80 lobbyists.

• *Why would a recreational group like the NRA become so intensely involved in political activities?*

group), the National Taxpayers' Union (an antitax and antispending group), and numerous other "watchdog" organizations, most less than a generation old.

Nearly every significant interest or activity in American society has groups that represent it—and under the right circumstances almost any group may become involved in politics. Associations representing sport fishers monitor regulations affecting natural resources, especially those pertaining to waterways. Associations representing snowmobilers and mountain bikers mobilize when government threatens to restrict their use of public lands. The American Association of Retired Persons (AARP), established in 1958, has become the largest voluntary association ever. It boasts upwards of 33 million members—and is still growing! AARP is a major player whenever social security or Medicare is on the political agenda, as it was in 2003.

Interest groups exploded during the past generation because of changes in both politics and technology. Increased government activity has given people more reasons to form groups. Businesses, for instance, organized to protect themselves from new taxes and regulations or to seek new government grants and contracts. Advances in communications technology, meanwhile, made groups easier to form. Computer databases permit the generation of all kinds of specialized mailing lists—and once they have located each other, people with common interests can communicate easily and cheaply via the Internet. Furthermore, once new groups organize, they may stimulate the formation of other groups opposed to them. The pro-life movement formed at least in part because of the activities of the pro-choice movement.[6] Similarly, ranching, mining, lumber, and sporting interests launched a "Sagebrush rebellion" in reaction to the successes of the environmental movement.

The Nature and Variety of "Interest Groups"

Robert Salisbury has called attention to the variety of groups, associations, and organizations included under the term *interest groups*.[7] Some have elaborate formal organizations with membership dues, journals, meetings, conventions, and so forth; the American Medical Association is a well-known example. Others are little more than an address where sympathizers send contributions. One study found that of 83 public interest groups examined, 30 had no membership.[8]

Some associations, like Common Cause, are "membership groups" composed of numerous private individuals who make voluntary contributions. Others are associations consisting of corporate or institutional representatives who pay regular dues; trade groups provide one example. Some large corporations maintain their own Washington offices for political reasons, as do hundreds of state, city, and county governments and even universities.

One researcher has estimated that almost 80 percent of the interest groups in existence in the 1980s represented professional or occupational constituencies.[9] For such groups, economic matters are of crucial concern—but these groups are about equally divided between those representing profit-seeking constituencies and those representing public and non-profit constituencies, so they do not exert a uniform influence on government taxing and spending policies. The other 20 percent of American interest groups reflect the activities of citizens with shared political goals, including those spawned by what are called social movements: broad-based reform or protest movements that bring new issues to the agenda. The civil rights movement, the environmental movement, the women's movement, and the religious right are important contemporary examples. We shall have more to say about these later in the chapter.

Forming and Maintaining Interest Groups

That so many people belong to so many groups and associations often leads people to overlook the difficulties many groups face.[10] But consider these facts:

There are about 107 million women over the age of 18 in the United States. Polls indicate that more than half have feminist sympathies. But the largest feminist group, NOW, has fewer than 300,000 members.

There are approximately 36 million African Americans in the United States, but the NAACP has only about 500,000 members—including whites.

About 40 million American households have at least one gun, but membership in the NRA is only 2.8 million.

Majorities of Americans consistently support spending more on the environment, but the combined membership of the seven large environmental groups is only about 6.5 million (even after counting multiple times those who belong to more than one organization).[11]

As these examples suggest, millions of people do *not* join or support associations whose interests they share. In many cases, groups and associations include 1 percent or less of their potential membership. Thus, common interest may be a necessary condition for joining a group, but it is far from a sufficient one.

Why, then, do people join or decline to join groups? The question is important, because the answer bears on how well or how poorly interest groups represent the American citizenry. If some kinds of interests are not fairly represented, politics may be biased, despite the existence of thousands of groups with millions of members.

Like voting, joining or supporting a group requires some investment of *resources*. It is a costly activity. Contributing money or paying dues is the most obvious example, but the time required for group activities also can be a significant cost. People who have more resources will find participation easier. Thus it is no surprise that the affluent contribute more than the poor and that two-worker families with small children participate less than people with more free time.[12] Regardless of the personal resources available, however, an individual will surrender them only if the *incentive* to do so—the expected benefit—justifies the investment.

Incentives take many forms and different groups rely on different incentives. James Q. Wilson divides incentives into three categories.[13] The first he calls *solidary*. Some people join a group for social reasons: They simply wish to associate with particular kinds of people. Religious groups and campus Greek organizations are examples. Where solidary incentives are dominant, membership in the group is an end in itself. Most such groups are nonpolitical, however—people who wish to socialize with each other usually do not need politics as an excuse. Conversely, it is unlikely that people join the National Taxpayers' Union to enjoy the company of other taxpayers, and people certainly do not send checks to such associations for social purposes!

A second category of incentives is *material*. Such incentives are economic rather than social: Some people join a group because membership confers tangible benefits. This is obviously the dominant incentive in economic groups and associations. Microsoft does not belong to various trade associations because its executives like to socialize with other computer executives—they have plenty of other opportunities to do that. Microsoft belongs because the trade associations are seen as a way of protecting and advancing corporate interests. Material incentives also play a role in some political groups. Those who join taxpayers' associations hope to reduce their taxes. Those who join groups that support government subsidies or services for people like themselves (realtors, the handicapped, the old, farmers) similarly hope to gain material benefits.

Finally, some people join groups for *purposive* reasons: People are committed to and wish to advance the group's social and political goals. They want to save the whales, to end abortion or to preserve freedom of choice, to bring about a liberal or conservative Congress. Given that politically active groups usually publicize their purposive goals, such incentives would appear to be the dominant factor underlying the formation and persistence of most of the groups that are active in politics. Things are not so simple as they appear, however.

The Free-Rider Problem

Groups that rely on purposive incentives face what is known as the **free-rider problem:** People can enjoy the benefits of group activity without bearing any of the costs. Thus, they have an incentive to "free-ride" on the efforts of others.[14] This problem arises when individuals perceive that attainment of the group goal has little relationship to their personal contribution. If you donate $20 to Greenpeace, does your contribution guarantee the survival of some identifiable baby seal? If you donate several hours of your time to march for the end of hunger, does your contribution measurably reduce the amount of malnutrition in the world? Although most well-meaning people are reluctant to admit it, in each case the truthful answer is no.

free-rider problem
Problem that arises when people can enjoy the benefits of group activity without bearing any of the costs.

These examples have two common elements. First, on reflection, people realize that their personal impact is so small as to be unnoticeable. If you don't contribute, just as many baby seals will live or die, just as many children will starve. So if your contribution makes no difference, why contribute? The second element makes matters worse: Individuals receive the benefit whether they contribute or not. If other people manage to save some seals or reduce world hunger, you enjoy those outcomes even if you did nothing to help out. So if you get the same benefit regardless of your actions, why contribute? These two conditions are major obstacles to group formation and survival. They encourage individuals to free-ride on the contributions of others, a dynamic that prevents some interests from organizing and hinders the efforts of groups that do form.

Two considerations affect the severity of the free-rider problem. First, other things being equal, the larger the group, the greater the problem. A few neighbors can pool their efforts to clean up a vacant lot that borders their properties. It is easy to identify those who don't show up and subject them to social pressure. It would be unthinkable, however, for a large city to rely on volunteer effort to maintain city parks. Social pressure is less effective where people do not know each other. Thus, cities pay city employees or private contractors to maintain their parks.

Second, other things being equal, the free-rider problem is more serious the greater the distance and abstractness of the benefit the group seeks to achieve. It is much easier to see one's personal impact on cleaning up a vacant lot than on cleaning up the atmosphere. It is much easier to see one's personal impact on feeding the poor in a specific locale than on reducing world hunger.

At issue here are what economists call **public goods,** as distinct from private goods. A tomato is a private good. If you consume it, others cannot. Clean air is a public good. If the air is clean everyone benefits from breathing it. Economists believe that because free riders can enjoy or consume public goods even if they make no contribution to their provision, such goods typically are provided at lower than optimal levels.[15]

public goods
Goods enjoyed simultaneously by a group, as opposed to a private good that must be divided up to be shared.

Economic goods can be public goods, too, so interest groups with an economic orientation also face free-rider problems. If General Motors lobbies successfully for a tariff or quota on Korean cars, Ford will enjoy the benefits (lower competition, higher prices) even if Ford did not aid GM in the lobbying effort. If members of the Corn Growers Association pool their efforts to get a higher corn subsidy, even growers who are not members of the association reap the benefit of the higher subsidy. The free-rider problem is widespread.

The most important implication of the free-rider problem for democratic politics lies in the kinds of groups best able to overcome it. Our discussion suggests that—again, other things being equal—small groups organized for narrow purposes have an organizational advantage over large groups organized for broad purposes. For example, a small number of corporations will find it relatively easy to organize an association to lobby for regulations that raise prices; the millions of consumers who buy the products the corporations sell will find it much more difficult to organize an association to lobby against such anticompetitive regulations. The free-rider problem implies that democratic politics will favor narrow "special" interests at the expense of the broader "public" interest.

Overcoming the Free-Rider Problem

On first learning about the free-rider problem, some idealists protest, "What if everyone felt that way?" Well, a great many people do; that is why so many groups mobilize such a small proportion of their potential constituencies. Still, there are groups that represent broad purposive interests. How do these groups manage to overcome the free-rider problem? History reveals a number of useful strategies.

Coercion If members of a labor union strike for higher wages, how can they prevent nonunion workers from enjoying the results? Historically, the answer has been coercion. Social pressure and even violence have been used to compel reluctant workers to join unions or prevent them from crossing union picket lines. Because violence is costly to inflict and often brings violence in return, unions preferred to rely on a

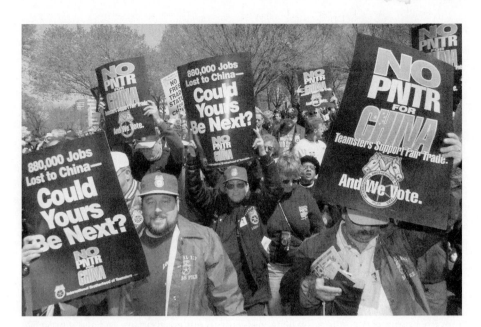

Teamsters Protest
Unions once relied heavily on violence to maintain collective action among workers. A turn to more peaceful tactics may help explain declining union membership.

strategy of negotiating "closed shops" with management. Such agreements permit only union members to work, and they require workers to join the union as a condition of employment.

Milder forms of coercion are still widespread, although they are often unrecognized. For example, professional and occupational associations may lobby governmental jurisdictions to hire, approve, or certify only their members, thus making membership a condition of working or practicing in that jurisdiction. Alternately, they may coerce members indirectly through their influence over professional or occupational qualifications. Practicing law usually requires membership in the state bar. Engaging in specialized trades such as plumbing, or professions such as teaching, may require a state license or official certification. Such requirements deny group benefits to potential free riders and reward those connected to professional and occupational networks.

Although it has been very effective historically, coercion appears to be a declining means of overcoming the free-rider problem. Society no longer tolerates the informal violence associated with strikes, and state governments no longer regulate many of the occupations and professions they once did. As a result, occupational interest groups have lost members and influence. The union movement in particular has fallen on hard times, its membership declining from more than one-third of the workforce to less than one-sixth.[16]

Social Movements   At times people do not think individualistically, as they do when they free-ride. In these instances, large numbers of people get swept up in a social cause. Such **social movements**—broad-based demands for government action on a problem or issue—have a long history in American politics. The abolitionist movement is one of the best known. Dedicated to ending slavery, the abolitionists forced the issue onto the national agenda. Their activism played a role in the political upheaval of the 1850s and, ultimately, in the outbreak of the Civil War. Other nineteenth-century social

social movement
Broad-based demand for government action on some problem or issue, such as civil rights for blacks and women or environmental protection.

movements included the Populist and labor movements in the 1880s and 1890s and the women's suffrage movement, which culminated in passage of the Nineteenth Amendment in 1920.

The civil rights movement is probably the best-known example of a social movement in modern times. As discussed in Chapter 17, the massive demonstrations of the 1960s evolved from a few sit-ins and boycotts in the 1950s. The movement culminated with the adoption of landmark federal legislation: the Civil Rights Act of 1964 and the Voting Rights Act of 1965.

Other movements soon followed. On April 22, 1970, Earth Day marked the sudden eruption of an environmental movement. Within the year, the United States had an Environmental Protection Agency and a Clean Air Act. The women's movement took off at about the same time, flexing its muscle in the 1972–1982 campaign for ratification of the Equal Rights Amendment (ERA), which succeeded in 35 states, 3 short of the three-fourths majority needed to adopt a constitutional amendment (see Chapter 17).[17] On the other side of the political spectrum, the ranks of the religious right swelled in the late 1970s and contributed to Ronald Reagan's presidential victories in the 1980s and to the Republican congressional resurgence of the last decade.[18] The movement supports constitutional amendments to outlaw abortion and allow prayer in schools, but, like the feminists, the religious right has been unable as yet to achieve constitutional change.

Social movements build on emotional or moral fervor. Many of those active within such movements dedicate themselves to what they see as a higher cause. When individuals think more collectively than individually, they may ignore the considerations that normally would lead them to free-ride. Still, social movements typically mobilize only small proportions of the population. Some people can be induced to think in moral or collective terms, but not many. Moreover, most people cannot sustain political passions for long, especially once demands for reform get bogged down in the tedious details of legislation and bureaucratic regulations. Thus, a social movement has a tendency to "run down" as its emotional basis subsides. For a social movement to exert long-term influence, it must find a way to "institutionalize" itself—to spin off organized groups and formal associations that will continue to work for its political goals. At that point, it faces the same free-rider problem as any other organized interest.

Selective Benefits   Many groups that work to achieve collective goods also provide their members with valuable private goods. Professional associations publish journals that contain occupationally useful information but restrict subscriptions to members. Trade associations inform their members—and only their members—about important technological advances. Agricultural associations provide their members—and only their members—with the latest information about new varieties of crops and new growing methods. In short, people, corporations, and institutions may join associations less to support the collective goods that the association supports than for the specific private goods that the association provides—selectively—to members: its **selective benefits.**

The American Association of Retired Persons (AARP) offers the most notable example of this strategy for overcoming the free-rider problem. For a mere $12.50 per year, members gain access to the world's largest mail-order pharmacy (where volume

You Are an Environmental Activist

selective benefits
Side benefits of belonging to an organization that are limited to contributing members of the organization.

buying keeps prices low); low-cost auto, health, and life insurance; discounts on hotels, airfares, and car rentals; and numerous other benefits. Even a senior citizen who disagrees with the political positions of AARP finds it hard to forgo membership!

Selective benefits are not limited to direct economic ones or to information that indirectly produces economic benefits. Anything that people like and that can be selectively provided may be a selective benefit. Some environmental groups produce magazines full of beautiful pictures, organize outings and activities, rate outdoor clothing and equipment, and so forth. These and other benefits of membership often are sufficient to induce people to pay the modest amounts that membership requires. In short, what seems to be the principal reason for a group's existence may not be the principal reason why many people belong.

Patrons and Political Entrepreneurs   Discussions of the free-rider problem typically reflect a bottom-up notion of how groups form. The implicit assumption is that individual people, corporations, or institutions band together and form associations. Recent research, however, indicates that the process of group formation often is more top-down than bottom-up. Many groups owe their existence to a **political entrepreneur,** an individual or a small number of individuals who take the lead in setting up and operating the group.[19]

In the first place, some individuals, institutions, or corporations are so influential that they do not face the free-rider problem. Their contributions to a group effort are not futile; they make a measurable difference. Large corporations also can have a large stake in the health of their industries. Their share of any group benefit is so great that they are not likely to consider political gains to be a public good. Microsoft, for example, has its own Washington office staffed by paid employees. When the interests of software manufacturers are at risk, Microsoft may be willing to mobilize its team of lobbyists to protect the industry even if smaller firms free-ride. Sometimes a large firm will bear most of the costs to support an industry association, which gives the appearance of a broad base of support. Ralston-Purina in the feed industry is an example.

Similarly, a rich individual with a deep commitment to the group goal may be able to make a difference. Your $20 contribution to Greenpeace may have no measurable impact, but if you are in a position to give a million dollars, you can probably save some seals. Foundations also support interest groups with grants and contracts. The W. Alton Jones Foundation and the Ford Foundation give millions of dollars a year to environmental groups.[20] Similarly, conservative foundations help to fund the Wise Use Movement which opposes traditional environmental groups.

In the second place, political entrepreneurs often set up and maintain a group for their own reasons. Their motives are varied. Some feel so strongly about a goal that they are willing to let others free-ride on them. We call such people either fanatical or dedicated, depending on whether we sympathize with their goals. An ascetic lawyer, Ralph Nader, did more than anyone else to organize the consumer movement and has devoted his life to it. Candy Lightner formed Mothers Against Drunk Driving after a man on bail from his third drunken-driving charge killed her daughter. Ross Perot founded and subsidized his own political party. Many (though not all) such individuals have passed up opportunities to parlay their visibility into riches or political office, and this restraint suggests that their commitment to broader goals is genuine.

political entrepreneurs
People willing to assume the costs of forming and maintaining an organization even when others may free-ride on them.

Of course, some political entrepreneurs do have ulterior motives. They may be aspiring politicians who see an opportunity to use new groups as the basis of future constituencies. Candidates for city and state offices often emerge from neighborhood associations and local protest groups. They may enjoy the celebrity or power that comes from leadership positions. They may be able to convert their fame into board appointments, consulting contracts, or book royalties. In short, self-seeking political entrepreneurs may invest their resources in interest-group organization the same way that profit-seeking business entrepreneurs invest their resources founding companies—taking on greater personal risk than others in the hope of reaping disproportionate personal gains if they succeed.

The government itself did much to organize the new groups of the 1960s and 1970s. As the role of government expanded, federal bureaucracies needed new ways to implement programs through a decentralized federal system. One strategy was to stimulate and subsidize organizations for that could be used to help develop standards and regulations, and to publicize them and carry them out. These groups were politically useful as well because they often promoted funding government programs generously. Not surprisingly, groups and associations that receive federal funds are more than twice as likely to support expanded government activity—and, by implication, the elected officials who expand it—as groups that do not.[21]

The available evidence suggests that the top-down activities of patrons and political entrepreneurs are a more important means of overcoming the free-rider problem than the provision of selective benefits, AARP notwithstanding.[22] Wealthy individuals, government agencies, corporations, and private foundations have been important sources of support for nonprofit-sector groups, especially citizens groups. About 90 percent of the latter have received such subsidies.

How Interest Groups Influence Government

The variety of groups, associations, and institutions that make up the interest-group universe engage in a wide array of political activities. We first discuss these political activities, which include government lobbying, grassroots lobbying, electioneering and political action committees, persuading the public, direct action, and litigation. We then focus on why groups choose particular tactics over others.

Lobbying

lobbying
Interest-group activities intended to influence directly the decisions that public officials make.

Many interest groups attempt to influence government the old-fashioned way: by lobbying public officials. **Lobbying** consists of interest-group activities intended to influence directly the decisions that public officials make. Groups and associations draft bills for friendly legislators to introduce, testify before congressional committees and in agency proceedings, meet with elected officials and present their cases (sometimes at posh resorts where the official is the guest), and provide public officials with information. In these and other ways, group representatives try to influence those who make governmental decisions.

lobbyist
One who engages in lobbying.

People who engage in lobbying are called **lobbyists,** although the term is usually reserved for those who do it as their primary job. Some lobbyists are so-called hired guns, people who will use their contacts and expertise in the service of just about anyone willing to pay their price, but some of the best known are closely associated with one party or the other. Many large groups and associations have their own staff lobbyists. Others hire lobbyists on a part-time basis or share a lobbyist with other groups. Some groups simply have their own leaders engage in lobbying, although these individuals typically are not called lobbyists.

Lobbying to ensure favorable national policies and prevent unfavorable ones has become a massive American industry. Spending on lobbying activities has spiraled upward; it reached $154 million per month by the end of 2002. Corporations account for the lion's share of traditional lobbying. Health-care industries alone spent $264 million in 2002. Lobbying operations vary widely in scope. The U.S. Chamber of Commerce and its Institute for Legal Reform together spent almost $29 million in the last half of 2002. The largest lobbying firm, Cassidy and Associates, reported spending $14 million. Miller Brewing Company, in contrast, spent less than $2 million during the 2002–2003 fiscal year, even though it spent more than any other beer company. Other lobbyists and lobbying groups spend almost nothing at all.[23]

You Are a Lobbyist

There are federal and state laws that require lobbyists to register, but because of disagreement about what lobbying is and who is a lobbyist, as well as lack of enforcement, those who register are only a fraction of those engaged in lobbying.[24] For example, the Center for Responsive Politics counted approximately 20,000 registered lobbyists in Washington, but reports that the true numbers are many times higher than that.[25]

The term *lobbyist* has negative connotations; few parents dream that their child will grow up to be one. Movies, novels, and even the newspapers often portray lobbyists as unsavory characters who operate on the borders of what is ethical or legal—and often step across them. Research suggests that this view is an exaggeration. Although there are examples of shady or corrupt behavior by lobbyists, such transgressions are less widespread today than in previous eras of American history. Numerous conflict-of-interest laws and regulations, along with an investigative media ever on the lookout for a hint of scandal, make outright corruption in today's politics relatively rare.

For the most part, lobbyists provide public officials with information and supporting arguments. They tend to deal with officials already sympathetic to their position and to support those officials' activities. Lobbyists have little incentive to distort information or lie; to do so would destroy their credibility and undermine their future effectiveness. Of course, they emphasize arguments and information favorable to their viewpoint, but they do not want to hurt their political allies by lying, concealing information, or otherwise exposing them to an embarrassing counterattack. Many political scientists think that lobbyists serve a useful purpose, injecting valuable information into the legislative process. As former Senator and President John Kennedy observed,

> Competent lobbyists can present the most persuasive arguments in support of their positions. Indeed, there is no more effective manner of learning all important arguments and facts on a controversial issue than to have the opposing lobbyists present their case.[26]

With the explosive growth of interest groups during the past generation, there is undoubtedly more old-fashioned lobbying than ever before. The number of corporate and trade-association offices in Washington doubled between 1970 and 1980. Membership in the District of Columbia Bar Association more than tripled between

1973 and 1983. Registered lobbyists increased sixfold between 1960 and 1980.[27] The democratization of Congress and the expansion of government helped stimulate such developments. In 1950 a group might have to lobby only one powerful committee chair or a key staffer, but by 1980 it had to lobby numerous subcommittee chairs as well as the rank and file and many of their staff (see Chapter 12).

Grassroots Lobbying

grassroots lobbying
Efforts by groups and associations to influence elected officials indirectly, by arousing their constituents.

Whereas lobbying consists of attempts to influence government officials *directly,* **grassroots lobbying** consists of attempts to influence officials *indirectly* through their constituents. The homeschooling example that opened this chapter illustrates the process. A Washington association communicates with its grassroots supporters, who in turn put pressure on their elected representatives.

Some scholars believe that grassroots lobbying has grown in importance and the effectiveness of traditional lobbying has faded. As one health care lobbyist put it,

> One of the perceptions about lobbying is that you go out drinking, and the guy's your buddy so he does you favors. . . . Those days are long gone. That sort of thing may work on tiny things like a technical amendment to a bill, but on big, important issues personal friendships don't mean a thing.[28]

One reason that friendships may not sway policy is that Congress is more decentralized than it once was. When only a few leaders need to be persuaded, a personal approach may suffice. When dozens need to be persuaded, reaching out and touching their constituents through grassroots lobbying may be more effective—especially given the advent of modern communications technology. Also, government in general is more open than in the past. It is not so easy for Washington insiders to make private deals. It is more important than ever to show that there is popular support for a group's position. Grassroots mobilization can create an image of popularity.

One of the newest innovations in grassroots lobbying is "grass-tops" lobbying.[29] In this variation, an interest group makes an ad featuring a prominent local personality—especially one who is an important supporter of a member of Congress—and then plays the ad in the member's district. Such ads signal members in no uncertain terms that powerful people back home stand behind the group's goals.

By no means should anyone think that grassroots lobbying is a new tactic, however; it has been around for a long time. In a classic study of the Anti-Saloon League (a prohibition group), Peter Odegard noted that this group had more than 500,000 names on its mailing list nearly a century ago—long before dependable long-distance telephone service, let alone computers, the fax, and e-mail![30] Influencing government officials' views by reaching out to their constituents is nothing new, but decentralized political institutions and rapid advances in communications technology have made such a strategy more attractive than ever.

Electioneering and PACs

Personal and grassroots lobbying influence the views of public officials on specific matters. One way to affect the views of public officials more generally is by influencing who gets elected in the first place. Groups have always been involved in the electoral process, supporting some candidates and opposing others—but as the role of party organizations in campaigns and elections has eroded, and as campaigns have become

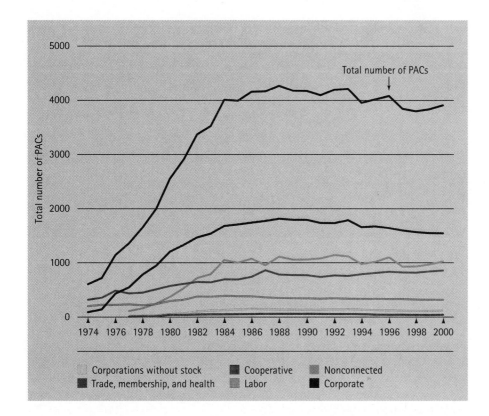

FIGURE 7.1

PACs Formed Rapidly After the 1974 Federal Election Campaign Act (FECA) Reforms

SOURCE: Paul Herrnson, *Congressional Elections,* 2nd ed. (Washington, DC: CQ Press, 1998), p. 106.

more expensive, groups have become more active than ever before. Electioneering is probably the fastest-growing group tactic, and a principal vehicle of this tactic is the political action committee.

Political action committees (PACs) are specialized organizations for raising and spending campaign funds. Many are associated with an interest group or association. They come in as many varieties as the interests they represent.[31] Some, such as the realtors' RPAC and the doctors' AMPAC, represent big economic interests. Others represent thousands of smaller interests—the beer wholesalers, for example, have SixPAC. Not all PACs represent economic interests. Supporters of Israel donate to AIPAC and NATPAC. Supporters of abortion rights send money to NARAL-PAC, while their pro-life adversaries send money to National Right to Life PAC. (Pro-choice Republicans uncomfortable with the liberal positions of NARAL can give money to WISH LIST.) Scores of individual politicians have established personal PACs.[32]

Like interest groups in general, PACs have enjoyed explosive growth in the past few decades. From a mere handful in 1970, they proliferated rapidly in the 1980s, as Figure 7.1 shows. Reflecting the overall contours of the interest-group system, far more PACs represent business and commercial interests than represent labor or citizen interests.

As their numbers have proliferated, PACs have played an increasingly prominent role in congressional campaign finance. Most PACs tend to give *instrumentally,* which means donating to the members of key committees regardless of party. When the Democrats were in the majority in Congress, some of their members became highly dependent on business contributions, and critics charged that this dependence affected their legislative judgment.[33] When Democrats became a minority after the 1994

political action committee (PAC)
Specialized organization for raising and contributing campaign funds.

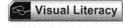

PACs and the Money Trail

TABLE 7.2

BUSINESS PAC CONTRIBUTIONS TEND TO FOLLOW POLITICAL POWER—WHEN CONTROL OF CONGRESS CHANGED, SO DID THE PATTERN OF BUSINESS CONTRIBUTIONS

	Percentage of Contributions to Republicans Jan.–Feb. 1993 (Democratic majority)	Percentage of Contributions to Republicans Jan.–Feb. 1995 (Republican majority)
American Dental Association	27	90
American Bankers Association	52	87
American Hospital Association	53	81
Ameritech	35	79
AT&T	36	79
American Institute of CPAs	45	87
Home Builders	45	71
Realtors	75	91
RJRNabisco	69	81
United Parcel Service	55	78

SOURCE: Jonathan Salant and David Cloud, "To the 1994 Election Victors Go the Fundraising Spoils," *Congressional Quarterly Weekly Report,* April 15, 1995: 1057.

Interest Groups and Campaign Finance

elections, they became much more favorably disposed toward campaign-finance regulation that restricted PACs (see Table 7.2).

There is widespread public dissatisfaction with the role of PACs in campaign finance. The popular perception of campaign contributions is that they buy elections or buy support from elected officials. The PAC problem is somewhat exaggerated by the popular media, however. Most research has failed to establish a significant relationship between contributions and legislative votes.[34] PAC contributions tend to be small and are intended as a way of gaining access to public officials. Moreover, there is evidence that politicians extort PACs, pressuring them to buy tickets to fund-raisers and otherwise to make contributions as a condition of continued access. For example, a former congressional staffer told one of us the following story:

> In our office we loved the FEC [Federal Election Commission] reports. We'd comb through them and list all the business groups who had contributed to our opponent. Then we'd call them up and say, "Hey, we noticed that you contributed to our opponent's campaign. The Congressman just wants you to know that there are no hard feelings. In fact, we're holding a fund-raiser in a few weeks; we hope you'll attend and tell us your concerns."

Thus, influence runs in both directions; elected officials are not just pawns to be moved around by interest groups. Furthermore, at the risk of sounding too complacent, we suggest that reformers have not identified a clear means to keep money out of politics. In fact, the proliferation of PACs is partly an unintended consequence of a previous attempt to reform campaign finance![35]

Persuading the Public

issue advocacy
Advertising campaigns that attempt to influence public opinion on an issue.

In recent years, what has come to be called **issue advocacy** has grown in prominence: Groups conduct advertising campaigns designed to move public opinion in regard to

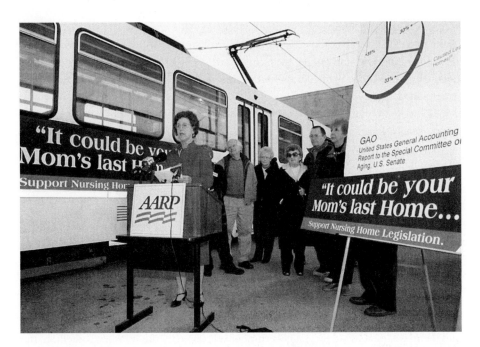

some policy proposal. This interest-group strategy overlaps somewhat with grassroots lobbying; the homeschool story was an example of interest groups persuading ordinary Americans that congressional actions directly threatened their interests. Estimates are that about $150 million was spent on issue advocacy in the 1996 presidential campaign and $260 million during the 1998 congressional campaigns. These amounts were greatly exceeded during the 2000 campaigns.[36]

Many groups communicate with citizens even when no specific legislation or regulation is at issue. Their goal is to build general support for the group and its interests so that it will be more successful in the long run. Thus, in the 1970s, the Mobil Oil Corporation began paying to have columns printed on the Op-Ed page of the *New York Times*. Sometimes these were "advocacy ads" directed specifically at a government activity or proposed law, but more often they were what are now called "infomercials"—attempts to convey information and arguments favorable to business in general and to the oil industry in particular.

Interest-group advocacy has become increasingly aggressive. Elected officials today rarely have the luxury of "down time" between campaigns. They never know when a group might launch an issue-advocacy campaign against them even if an election is far away. For example, during the California energy crisis in the spring of 2001, a group representing energy companies and Republicans ran attack ads against Governor Gray Davis, even though Davis was barely halfway through his term. They were attempting to "soften him up" long in advance of the Republicans' even choosing a candidate to oppose him. Davis won his reelection bid, but the critical ads may have contributed to his low popularity—which eventually resulted in a recall election that booted Davis from office.

One communications technique that is a product of modern electronic communications is **direct mail**.[37] Groups compile computerized mailing lists of people who might be favorably disposed toward their leader or cause and then send out printed material soliciting financial contributions. Often, in an attempt to scare or provoke the

direct mail
Computer-generated letters, faxes, and other communications to people who might be sympathetic to an appeal for money or support.

recipient into contributing, the mailing exaggerates the threat the group faces. Some groups depend almost completely on direct-mail fund raising for their budgets. The citizens group Common Cause, for example, prides itself on its dependence on small contributions.[38] Once again, the rise of the Internet makes the direct-mail strategy both easier and cheaper. Tabulating who visits various Web sites makes it possible to compile e-mail lists and contact prospective supporters for a much lower cost than that of traditional "snail mail" campaigns.[39]

Finally, any group likes to have favorable media coverage for its activities and points of view. Thus, groups are always on the lookout for opportunities to get such coverage—to plant stories, to associate themselves with popular issues and candidates, and to position themselves as opponents of unpopular issues and candidates. In sum, whether we call it public relations or education, communication with a wider audience is a significant concern for many interest groups.

Direct Action

direct action
Everything from peaceful sit-ins and demonstrations to riots and even rebellion.

As noted in Chapter 2, the original 13 colonies cast off British authority in a violent revolution, the Constitutional Convention was in part stimulated by Shays's Rebellion, and the newly established federal government was tested by the Whiskey Rebellion. But these early conflicts were by no means the end of **direct action** by citizens opposed to government policies. Urban workers rioted against the Civil War draft in 1863. In the 1880s and 1890s, state or federal troops battled strikers from West Virginia to Idaho and from Michigan to Texas. In 1932, more than 20,000 veterans marched on Washington and were dispersed by federal troops.[40]

Usually, tactics such as boycotts, sit-ins, marches, and demonstrations appeal to the members of social movements. They may be too disorganized to use established means of influencing government, or they may lack access to the resources needed to exploit other political strategies. Occasionally, however, organized interest groups do take advantage of the drama of direct action. Usually they do so in combination with attempts to persuade larger constituencies. The media—TV in particular—find direct action newsworthy. (See the accompanying Democratic Dilemma.)

Litigation

As we shall see in detail in Chapter 17, the modern civil rights movement followed a careful legal strategy, selecting cases to litigate that eventually led to the landmark 1954 ruling *Brown v. Board of Education of Topeka, Kansas*. Drawing lessons from the success of the civil rights movement, environmentalists, feminists, advocates for the handicapped, poor people, and other groups followed suit.[41]

Litigation strategies are by no means limited to groups ordinarily thought of as liberal. In the 1970s the Pacific Legal Foundation was set up to oppose environmental protection groups. The U.S. Chamber of Commerce established a National Chamber Litigation Center to support business interests in the courts. And the religious right founded the Christian Legal Society, which focuses on issues of church and state.[42] Liberal groups continue to be more active in the courts, perhaps because they tend to find a friendlier audience among the members of the legal profession, but conservatives sometimes win important courtroom victories.

DEMOCRATIC DILEMMA

Strange Bedfellows: The Battle for Seattle, 1999

Politics sometimes makes for strange bedfellows. One dramatic example came in the "Battle for Seattle" in December of 1999. The World Trade Organization (WTO), an organization dedicated to removing barriers to free trade, scheduled its "millennium round" of talks in Seattle. The meetings were expected to produce further trade agreements that would be a public-relations boon to the Clinton administration, which lobbied behind the scenes to have the talks called "the Clinton round." By the time the meetings adjourned in a shambles, however, they had become a public-relations disaster. Some critics suggested that they should be remembered as the "Tear Gas Round."[a]

Ten thousand protesters disrupted the meetings, and a few ran wild in the streets of Seattle, smashing windows and looting stores. The protesters were mobilized by an extremely diverse set of groups. Labor unions claimed that trade agreements exported American jobs to low-wage countries where workers were exploited. Although often opposed to labor, some environmental groups now joined forces with unions, contending that free-trade agreements in practice operated to override domestic environmental protection laws. Both attacked the WTO as a secretive international organization that operated in the shadows and threatened American sovereignty. This sort of argument normally is made by groups on the right wing of American politics, who at various times have charged that the United Nations, the Brookings Institution, and the Trilateral Commission are fronts for international conspiracies aimed at subjugating the United States. The WTO meetings brought all these strange bedfellows together. One militia member commented on the strangeness:

> "I'll be honest—I don't really know many people like the ones here," said Butch Razey, commander of the Yakima County Militia, who attended the protest on orders from superiors in Montana. "We're willing to die for our Constitution, and the patriots are all coming out because they know this is the beginning of world government. But I'll be honest—this will be the first time I'll be holding hands with a bunch of tree-huggers."[b]

Globalization Protest Garb

Not since the 1960s have Americans seen such militant protestors, obviously dressed to sharpen their message about the WTO.

Wrote one observer,

> As militia members milled with black-clad anarchists and topless environmentalists . . . , it was clear that American protest had entered uncharted territory.[c]

Encouraged by their success in Seattle, leaders of environmental and labor groups have continued their collaboration against globalization and free trade.

- *Do diverse protest coalitions present any particular challenge to the major political parties?*

- *Could an anti-globalization constituency be organized into an effective third party?*

- *Does this kind of protest represent democracy working or democracy breaking down?*

[a] Charles Pope, "Will Labor–Green Alliance Succeed in 2000?" *Congressional Quarterly Weekly Report,* December 11, 1999: 2959.
[b] Charles Duhigg, "Seattle Dispatch: Means of Dissent," *The New Republic,* December 20, 1999: 14.
[c] Ibid.

In addition to actually litigating cases, which is an expensive activity, interest groups engage in other activities intended to influence the course of litigation. Although it is improper to lobby judges directly, groups stage demonstrations in front of courthouses, generate letters and telegrams to judges, and file *amicus curiae* (a Latin term meaning "friend of the court") briefs in cases in which they are not otherwise directly involved.

Why Groups Use Particular Tactics

Different groups use different strategies or mixes of strategies. How they decide to allocate their resources depends both on their own characteristics and on the characteristics of the situation in which they are operating.

Group Characteristics   How a group decides to deploy its resources depends on what kind of group it is, what kind of resources it has, and how much it has in the way of resources. A trade association representing profitable corporations will have a Washington office with a full-time staff of experts. This gives such associations the wherewithal to maintain close personal contact with government decision makers. A mass-membership group may find grassroots lobbying a more effective use of its resources. A public-interest law firm with no citizen membership will naturally follow a litigation strategy; indeed, the group may have been formed by lawyers precisely because they wished to engage in such activities. A social movement representing a disadvantaged constituency such as the poor may find that direct action is the only means of calling attention to its cause. Wealthy groups of any size or type may find campaign contributions and media campaigns to be useful investments.

Some observers suggest that groups with a federal structure—local chapters under a national leadership—have a fund-raising advantage because contributions are solicited by people personally known to members rather than by an impersonal mailing. In addition, such groups have chapters in many communities and therefore are constituents of a large number of representatives, which may give them an advantage in grassroots lobbying. Interest groups representing realtors, doctors, and banks are good examples.

Situational Characteristics   One of the reasons why the civil rights movement adopted a litigation strategy was that more traditional strategies were unavailable. African Americans were disenfranchised in much of the South and were politically discriminated against elsewhere. In the Congresses of the 1940s and 1950s, the path of civil rights legislation was blocked by senior committee chairmen from the South. African Americans as a group were not wealthy, and they were a small minority of the population. By choosing to litigate, they made a virtue out of necessity. Then, as the movement gained support and won legal backing for its political activities, it was able to engage in direct action and later in electioneering to advance its goals further.

In contrast, an industry or corporation interested in the fine details of a bill or regulation may find it better to send an expert representative to discuss the matter with members of Congress and their staff or with regulators. Studies show that corporations spend much more on lobbying than they do on campaign contributions, probably reflecting their interest in legislative detail as opposed to their interest in the general ideological position of the legislator.[43]

Direct mail and other modern advertising and persuasion techniques were developed largely by conservative groups, probably because for 40 years Congress was controlled by Democrats who had little sympathy for their demands. Republicans have controlled the House since 1994, and the Senate for two years, so perhaps conservative groups will engage in more direct lobbying. Conversely, having lost some of their access to the congressional leadership, liberal groups may be forced to shift their resources to alternative methods of exerting influence.

In sum, various situational characteristics—party control of Congress and the presidency, the economic situation, the mood in the country, what the interest group seeks to achieve—interact with characteristics of interest groups to determine what mix of strategies is adopted.

How Influential Are Interest Groups?

The answer to this question is a matter of enormous disagreement. Some critics believe that interest groups dominate American politics. One charges that the United States suffers from "demosclerosis," a condition in which interest groups clog the veins and arteries of the body politic.[44] Another claims that Americans have the best Congress money can buy.[45] Certainly the number of groups, the volume of their activities, and their massive expenditure of resources amount to strong circumstantial evidence that groups and associations are very influential in politics.

On the other hand, academic research yields less clear conclusions. Indeed, some of the most expert students of interest-group politics contend that a great deal of what groups do is canceled out.[46] There are so many groups, and so many *opposed* groups, that the efforts of one association's high-priced lobbyist only offset the efforts of another's, one group's media campaign only counteracts the effects of another's, one group's direct-mail barrage only neutralizes the effects of another's, and so on.

Regardless, it seems fairly clear that, because changes in American politics have undermined the classic "subgovernments" that were dominated by particular interests, some "special interests" were more influential in the past than they are today.

Subgovernments

Observers of American politics in the 1940s and 1950s often concluded that "subgovernments" dominated important areas of public policy.[47] In the idealized **subgovernment** three collective actors worked hand in hand to determine policies:

- A *congressional committee* provided an executive agency with program authorization and budgetary support,
- The *executive agency* produced outcomes favored by an interest-group constituency, and
- The *interest groups* provided the members of the congressional committee with campaign contributions and votes.

Subgovernments allegedly dominated critical policy areas such as agriculture, public works, and business regulation. In the most extreme cases, subgovernments were called "iron triangles" (see Chapter 14) in recognition of the difficulty faced by outsiders who wished to break into the cozy relationship uniting legislative committees, executive agencies, and interest groups.

Interest groups played a central role in this story because they were the outside actors who worked with executive and legislative officials to achieve favorable policy. Whatever their importance in the past, however, subgovernments are less important today. First, as we shall see in Chapter 12, Congress has changed. The party caucuses and leadership are stronger and the committees weaker; particular committees no longer have strangleholds on their jurisdictions.

Comparative

Comparing Interest Groups

subgovernment
Alliance of a congressional committee, a bureaucratic agency, and a small number of allied interest groups that combine to dominate policy making in some specified policy area.

Second, there are many more groups now, including many who oppose other groups. In particular, citizens groups representing consumers, environmentalists, and taxpayers are much more active now than they were a half-century ago. They oppose the excesses of special-interest politics and publicize their opposition.

Third, as we discuss in Chapter 9, the focus of the media has changed with time. In particular, contemporary journalists are very much on the lookout for stories of special-interest profiteering at the expense of general interests. In the spring of 1996, for example, the media helped kill an attempt by the House Agriculture Committee to aid milk producers in raising prices by quietly including a helpful regulation in the agriculture bill then under consideration. Dan Rather discussed the "attempted rip-off of the consumer" on his evening news program, and in the wake of the publicity, the attempt collapsed.[48] Iron triangles thrived when they operated behind the scenes; they melt in the glare of publicity.

Issue Networks

issue network
A loose constellation of larger numbers of committees, agencies, interest groups and policy experts active in a particular policy area.

In the view of many scholars, subgovernments have been superseded by **issue networks**—bigger, broader, and much looser connections of interest groups, politicians, bureaucrats, and policy experts who have a particular interest in or responsibility for a policy area.[49] Given the enormous number and variety of interest groups today, the proliferation of legislative staff and other policy experts, and the interactions between policies in one area and those in another, issue networks are much more open than subgovernments and much less stable in their composition. Interests do not play such a central role in this new policy environment. They must compete with public officials and technical experts, as well as each other, in an effort to influence public policy.

The academic community today clearly leans toward thinking of policy environments as a network rather than as an iron triangle, but not everyone agrees with the conclusion, or with each other. On the one hand, some scholars suggest that even the term *network* may exaggerate the degree of organization that characterizes interest-group activity in Washington today.[50] On the other hand, some scholars emphasize that organized interests directly shape laws and regulations in new policy areas such as energy and social regulation.[51] In short, judgments about the general importance of interest groups remain as divided as ever.

Probably the safest conclusion about the power of interest groups is that influence is conditional: It ranges from weak to strong, depending on the conditions under which groups try to influence politics. Schlozman and Tierney conclude that groups are most influential when they act on low-profile issues, when they attempt to block action rather than originate it, when they are unopposed by other groups or politicians, and when they have plentiful resources.[52] Once again, the real world of American democracy is more complicated than many popular commentators suggest.

Interest Groups and Democratic Politics

Even the generic term *interest group* has a negative connotation, and terms like *pressure group, vested interest,* and *special interest* have pronounced negative connotations.[53] Why do contemporary Americans hold interest groups in such low regard? After all, the

Constitution protects the rights of citizens to work together to try to influence government. The First Amendment guarantees freedom of religion, speech, and the press, but it also prohibits any law abridging the "right of the people peaceably to assemble and to petition the government for a redress of grievances." Interest groups are the mechanism for exercising those rights.

Political scientists generally have not held interest groups in as low regard as ordinary citizens have. In fact, one mid-century school of thought, **pluralism,** celebrated the role of groups in American politics.[54] The pluralists believed that American politics should consist of an interplay of numerous interests. In this view, virtually everyone is represented in a dense network of groups, no single interest is dominant, and all are required to bargain and compromise. Moreover, groups exercise countervailing power; if one interest or set of interests becomes too powerful, others mobilize to counteract it. As a consequence, public policies tend to be moderate and to change incrementally. That is, the system tends to do a good job representing the broad range of interests in the country.

pluralism
A school of thought holding that politics is the clash of groups that represent all important interests in society and that check and balance each other.

Pluralism is out of fashion today. Critics cite several problems with the pluralist account. We have already discussed the first, the unrepresentativeness of the interest-group universe. As critic E. E. Schattschneider once observed, "The flaw in the pluralist heaven is that the heavenly chorus sings with a strong upper-class accent."[55] Because of the free-rider problem, small special interests have an advantage over large general interests. In particular, economic groups procure narrow economic benefits at the expense of the broader population of consumers and taxpayers. This is probably one reason why the term *interest group* has negative connotations in the popular mind; people see that most groups do not represent the general interests of Americans.

A second objection to the pluralist account would still apply even if interest groups were more representative: The interest of the whole nation is not equal to the sum of the interests of the parts. In our discussion of public opinion, we pointed out that majorities of Americans want to cut government spending and reduce government regulation, but majorities oppose specific cuts and reductions. Thus, if Congress heeds all the wishes of individual constituencies, it will displease the country as a whole by maintaining a bigger budget and more intrusive government than a majority desires.

Trade is another example. If the government erected a system of trade barriers to protect every American industry from foreign competition, the result would be retaliation against American exports, higher prices for consumers, and slower economic growth (if not worse). As Schattschneider long ago pointed out, a Congress operating according to pluralist principles enacted just such a trade policy in 1930—the Smoot-Hawley tariff, a policy that deepened and lengthened the Great Depression.[56] Simply adding up group interests is not enough. Ideally, politics harmonizes and synthesizes particular interests and incorporates them into the general interest of the nation.

A third criticism of pluralism is that a politics dominated by interest groups distorts political discussion and (ultimately) the political process. The reason is that groups reinforce extremism and undercut moderation. Ordinary citizens have multiple attachments and affiliations, which generally serve to moderate their outlooks. A retired couple, for example, might naturally favor higher social security and Medicare expenditures. But if they also are parents and grandparents, they might accept more modest benefits for themselves to avoid higher taxes on their children or lower government expenditures

TABLE 7.3

GROUP ACTIVISTS AND LEADERS
HOLD MORE EXTREME VIEWS

One study compared the views of 100 top leaders in environmental groups with the views of scientific experts—in this case, cancer researchers. Both sets of people were asked to rate various cancer risks on a scale of 1 to 10, with 10 being the highest. Relative to expert judgments, environmentalists systematically overstated the risks of cancer from environmental causes.

Carcinogen	Risk of Cancer	
	Environmentalists	Scientists
Dioxin	8.1	3.7
Asbestos	7.8	6.5
EDB	7.3	4.2
DDT	6.7	3.8
Pollution	6.6	4.7
Dietary fat	6.0	5.4
Food additives	5.3	3.2
Nuclear power	4.6	2.5
Saccharin	3.7	1.6

SOURCE: Stanley Rothman and S. Robert Lichter, "Environmental Cancer: A Political Disease," *Annals of the New York Academy of Sciences* 775 (1996): 234–235.

on their grandchildren's schools. Leaders of interest groups, by contrast, act in someone else's interest. Typically, they see their job as maximizing group benefits. Thus the leadership of a senior citizens group will be more supportive of higher benefits for the elderly than will many of its members. For example, AARP has been attacked as an organization composed of "tax-loving former teachers and government employees" who favor an "age-based welfare state."[57] This sharply worded attack was used by the National Taxpayers Union, an opposing interest group concerned with taxes.

This crowding out of moderate demands by more extreme ones is reinforced by the tendency of group activists and leaders to be more extreme in their views than are nonmembers or even rank-and-file members. Thus, they push their demands beyond the point where ordinary members and sympathizers would stop. Some activist supporters of the ERA suggested that it would send women into combat on the same basis as men: "[C]ombat duty, horrendous as it might seem to all of us, must be assigned to persons on a gender-neutral basis."[58] Most American women and men preferred something less than such full equality. Environmentalists exaggerate environmental threats (see Table 7.3) while their opponents discount real threats. The minorities on the extremes of the pro-choice and pro-life debate polarize the debate and drown out the three-quarters of the population who could satisfactorily compromise on it (see Chapter 5).

In the end, the general interests of a moderate population can get lost amid the bitter fighting of intense and extreme special interests. No one can deny that groups have a useful and legitimate role to play in articulating the interests of all components of American society, but many feel that groups somehow must be constrained. One of the first pluralists, James Madison, thought factions would be limited in an extended republic that covered a wide geographical area (as he explained in "Federalist 10" printed in Appendix III of this book). He did not foresee several modern developments.

First is the tremendous expansion of society that contributed to the explosion of groups. The range of interests active today probably would shock someone like Madison, who thought in terms of broad interests such as land, labor and commerce, or debtors and creditors. Second is the prevalence of logrolling. Rather than check and balance each other, interest groups often cooperate, forming coalitions to exploit the general interests of consumers and taxpayers by getting higher prices and tax breaks.[59] Logrolling among interests is facilitated by a third development, the rise of professional politicians who, in seeking reelection, broker the group deals in return for the electoral support that interest groups provide.

But what can be done? As the critics look over the experience of democratic governments, they see only one means of controlling group demands that is both democratic and effective. Ironically, it is an institution that George Washington warned the country about—political parties, the subject of the next chapter.

Chapter Summary

Only half the American citizenry votes in presidential elections, and only small minorities engage in other forms of political participation. But most Americans participate indirectly in politics by joining groups that attempt to influence government. In fact, Americans are more likely to participate indirectly through groups than are citizens of other democracies who vote at higher levels.

In the past generation, there has been a major increase in the number of interest groups. Successful groups have found ways to overcome the free-rider problem, the tendency of people to benefit from group activity without contributing to its costs. Some of the groups rely on selective benefits that are available only to group members, while others depend on the efforts of dedicated or wealthy members who will bear more than a proportionate share of the costs of group maintenance.

Group characteristics and their situations lead them to adopt a variety of political strategies. Grassroots lobbying involves attempts to influence elected officials indirectly by mobilizing constituents; traditional lobbying involves attempts to influence elected officials directly by speaking personally to them. Increasingly, groups engage in electioneering—contributing money to candidates and spending money independently to elect officials sympathetic to

their interests and views. Groups also attempt to persuade or educate the public, and some resort to direct action—demonstrations, protests, and the like—to call attention to their positions. Finally, some groups end-run the political process and attempt to influence government through the courts.

Despite extensive study of interest groups, there is wide disagreement about how influential they are. In general, popular commentators view them as more powerful than do academic researchers. There is no doubt that groups engage in an incredible amount of political activity and invest a great deal of money and other resources, but it is difficult to say how effective they are. For every issue that interest groups apparently dominate, skeptics can cite another issue on which interest groups seem to be ineffectual or to offset each other's efforts.

Many social critics worry about the overall effect of interest-group activity, though. First, special interests are better represented than general interests. Second, even if that were not so, the best interest of the nation as a whole is not merely the sum of the best interests of the particular parts. Third, interest groups support extreme positions in political debate and thus polarize political discussion, injecting excessive conflict into the political process.

Key Terms

direct action, p. 188
direct mail, p. 187
free-rider problem, p. 177
grassroots lobbying, p. 184
interest group, p. 173
issue advocacy, p. 186

issue network, p. 192
lobbying, p. 182
lobbyist, p. 182
pluralism, p. 193
political action committee (PAC), p. 185

political entrepreneurs, p. 181
public goods, p. 178
selective benefits, p. 180
single-issue group, p. 174
social movement, p. 179
subgovernment, p. 191

Suggested Readings

Of General Interest

Baumgartner, Frank, and Beth Leech. *Basic Interests.* Princeton, NJ: Princeton University Press, 1998. Comprehensive review, critique, and synthesis of the interest-group literature.

Heinz, John, Edward Laumann, Robert Nelson, and Robert Salisbury. *The Hollow Core: Private Interests in National Policy Making.*

Cambridge, MA: Harvard University Press, 1993. A major study of the Washington interest-group scene. Principal focus is on the characteristics and activities of group representatives and lobbyists.

Lowi, Theodore. *The End of Liberalism.* New York: Norton, 1969. Noted critique of "interest-group liberalism." Argues that a government of laws has been superseded by a process of bargaining between organized groups and public officials.

Schattschneider, E. E. *The SemiSovereign People.* New York: Holt, 1960. A delightful essay that remains timely. Argues that the pressure system of interest groups is biased and that the result is an artificially constricted range of political conflict in the United States.

Schlozman, Kay, and John Tierney. *Organized Interests and American Democracy.* New York: Harper & Row, 1981. Comprehensive study of the Washington interest-group universe circa 1980, as well as its expansion in the 1960s and 1970s.

Truman, David. *The Governmental Process.* New York: Knopf, 1951. Classic interpretation of American democracy as composed of the interplay of interest groups.

Walker, Jack. *Mobilizing Interest Groups in America.* Ann Arbor: University of Michigan Press, 1991. Explores the Washington interest-group universe. Noted for discussion of outside support for establishment of groups.

Hertzke, Allen. *Representing God in Washington.* Knoxville: University of Tennessee Press, 1988. Informative study of the lobbying activities of religious groups, including (but not limited to) members of the Christian right.

Mansbridge, Jane. *Why We Lost the ERA.* Chicago: University of Chicago Press, 1986. Thoughtful discussion of the narrow failure of the women's movement to win passage of the ERA. Argues that the movement overcame the free-rider problem by emphasizing the symbolism of the ERA, a strategy that precluded compromises.

Moe, Terry. *The Organization of Interests.* Chicago: University of Chicago Press, 1980. Analyzes the internal politics of groups and the strategies used by political entrepreneurs for organizing and maintaining groups.

Smith, Mark. *American Business and Political Power.* Chicago: University of Chicago Press, 2000. Argues that when business interests are united they are less influential, because the issues that unite business divide the political parties and arouse public opinion.

Focused Studies

Freeman, Jo, and Victoria Johnson. *Waves of Protest.* Lanham, MD: Rowman and Littlefield, 1999. Useful collection describing the social movements active since the 1960s.

On the Web

As we have noted, the Internet has been a valuable tool for interest groups. It has reduced organization and communication costs tremendously. It is no exaggeration to say that an interest group is probably not much of an interest group until it has its own Web page (The reverse is not true, however; it's so easy to have a Web page these days that merely possessing one does not qualify a group as an interest group). It would take too much space to list all of the interest groups with a presence on the Web.

www.aarp.org
www.aflcio.org
www.sierraclub.org
www.uschamber.org
www.now.org
www.cc.org

A sample of the most important interest groups with a presence on the Web are the American Association of Retired Persons, AFL-CIO, Sierra Club, U.S. Chamber of Commerce, National Organization for Women, and Christian Coalition of America.

www.vegan.org
www.deathwithdignity.org
www.anarchy.no
www.atheists.org

A few less prominent groups, the very existence of which testifies to the power of the Internet to reduce organizational costs, are Vegan Action (pro-vegetarian lifestyle), Death With Dignity National Center (pro-assisted suicide), Anarchy.org, and American Atheists.

CHAPTER 8

* * * * * * * * * * * * * * * *

Political Parties

A Tale of Two Conventions

The Democrats and the Republicans held spectacular national conventions in the summer of 2004 to pick their presidential nominees. Both parties spent millions of dollars to kick off the general election in style—filling their convention halls with red, white, and blue banners, with thousands of balloons, and with shouting delegates wearing colorful jackets and funny hats. A series of political celebrities marched to each convention podium and gave fiery speeches to stir up the party faithful and attract uncommitted voters. It was as close as political parties get to throwing the nation a real party.

Despite all the hoopla, few Americans watched the celebration. On average, the three major television networks gave the national conventions only three hours each over a four-day span. There is little reason to believe that this limited attention left hordes of Americans clamoring for more. Only 31 percent of respondents told pollsters with the Vanishing Voter Project that they intended to watch the upcoming conventions anyway.[1]

Voters cannot be blamed for skipping the national conventions. All the spectacle aside, the conventions offered minimal political drama. George Bush and John Kerry both had clinched their party's nominations five months earlier, after primary wins that gave each candidate a majority of his party's delegates. The vice-presidential candidates added little mystery; Kerry had named his running mate long before the convention and Bush was running with Vice President Dick Cheney again on the ticket. Nor did the events feature enough conflict to make up for the lack of surprise. Both campaigns kept a tight lid on dissident elements within the party. There were no floor fights over policy planks in the platform. No one contested the seating of any delegates. The conventions were basically long, expensive infomercials showcasing the party and its candidates.

Contrast these media events with the 1952 political conventions. That year, the three networks averaged 60 hours of convention coverage, essentially televising them from the opening gavel to the closing gavel (something only C-SPAN does now). There was no huge cable television industry in those days, so if families wanted to watch TV, they had only one feasible option: the nominating conventions. Why were earlier conventions deemed so newsworthy? Basically, they made more important decisions.

At the Democratic convention of 1952, four serious rivals vied for the nomination. Senator Estes Kefauver of Tennessee, who had achieved prominence investigating organized crime and who campaigned in a coonskin cap, led on the first two ballots, but he could not secure a victory. Some minor candidates then withdrew and delegates flowed to President's Truman's choice for the nomination, Governor Adlai Stevenson of Illinois. Stevenson, a northern liberal, won a narrow majority on the third ballot. Only afterward did Americans learn Stevenson's choice for the vice presidential nomination: Senator John Sparkman of Alabama, whose conservatism could balance the ticket.

The Republicans had a simpler choice. Senator Robert Taft of Ohio—known as "Mr. Republican" for his long service—faced a challenge from a man who had declared his GOP affiliation less than a year before: General Dwight Eisenhower, a popular World War II hero. Party insiders backed Taft, but the Republicans also wished to regain the White House after a 20-year absence. When Eisenhower's supporters challenged the seating of delegates from three pro-Taft states, they won the battle. Eisenhower still failed to attain a majority on the initial vote, but minor candidates threw him enough support that he won before a second official balloting became necessary. Eisenhower then named his running mate: a young anticommunist senator from California, Richard Nixon.

Why did no one know in advance who the nominees would be? In those days there was no permanent campaign. Few states held primaries and the existing primaries selected few convention delegates. The great majority of delegates were party officials, loyalists, contributors, and influential politicians appointed by state and local party leaders. They were free to wheel and deal at the conventions, exchanging their support for promises of future political payoffs. Thus, campaigns took shape more slowly. In contrast to today's candidates, who begin organizing in the early primary states 18 months before the election, Stevenson never entered a single primary. Eisenhower still served as Supreme Allied Commander of NATO six weeks before winning the nomination!

Today the labels are the same as they were in 1952: "Democrats" and "Republicans." In fact, they have not changed since the nineteenth century. But the Democratic and Republican parties of 1952 looked more like those of

1852 than they resemble the parties navigating today's permanent campaign. This chapter tells the story of how and why American parties changed so radically over such a short span of time.

MAKING THE CONNECTION

All modern democracies have parties. Traditionally defined as groups of like-minded people who band together in an attempt to win control of government, **political parties** serve as the primary connection between ordinary citizens and the public officials they elect. They nominate candidates for office. They mobilize voters. And after elections have determined the winners, parties coordinate the actions of elected officials in the government. In this chapter we address the following questions about political parties:

- Are parties essential to democratic politics?

- How have parties shaped the political history of the United States?

- Why does the United States have only two major parties?

- How do today's parties differ from those of earlier eras?

- How influential are parties today in American politics?

★ ★ ★ ★ ★ ★ ★ ★ ★ ★ ★ ★ ★ ★ ★

What Parties Do

To political commentators in most self-governed societies, democracy is unimaginable without parties. The European University Institute, a research arm of the European Community, published a four-volume study on political parties that called them "the central institutions of democratic governments," the "working mechanism" of liberal democracy.[2]

Many American professors hold similar views. Political scientist E. E. Schattschneider devoted much of his life to making the case for the vital role played by political parties. In introducing his classic work *Party Government,* he wrote, "This volume is devoted to the thesis that political parties created democracy and that modern democracy is unthinkable save in terms of the parties."[3]

For contemporary Americans, though, life without political parties is not so unthinkable. Americans rely on representative assemblies such as Congress to serve as the centerpiece of democratic government and are more likely to consider courts the heart of liberal democracy. They inhabit a political world populated by many institutions cut off from parties, such as direct ballot propositions, independent judges, and nonpartisan local elections. When asked directly about political parties, most Americans do not sing their praises. Indeed, surveys have shown that many Americans think government would be better without parties.[4] Could they be right, and the scholars and commentators wrong? To answer that question, this section describes both the positive and the negative functions performed by parties within the political system.

political parties
Groups of like-minded people who band together in an attempt to take control of government. Parties represent the primary connection between ordinary citizens and the public officials they elect.

How Parties Contribute to Democratic Politics

What do parties offer to make most Europeans and some Americans think they are essential for democratic government? The general answer is that, except at the local level, a democracy that relied on the activities of individuals and interest groups would be too disorganized to operate. Politicians create parties to *organize* political life, and parties do so by carrying on a series of activities.[5]

Organizing and Operating the Government   Parties coordinate the actions of hundreds, indeed thousands, of public officials. At each level of government, executives count on the support of their fellow partisans in the legislature, and legislators trust the information they get from their fellow partisans in the executive branch. Parties also coordinate activities across levels of government. In 1995, for example, Democratic governors convinced some Democratic members of Congress that they should support far-reaching welfare-reform proposals. Similarly, local officials appeal to their partisan allies in the state governments, and the latter appeal to their partisan allies in Congress. American government often appears disorderly, but many political scientists believe it would be absolutely chaotic without parties.

Focusing Responsibility for Governmental Action   Party labels operate much like brand names. Just as consumers might favor a reputable brand or avoid buying a brand that has sold poor merchandise in the past, voters judge Democrats and Republicans collectively.[6] The actions or performance of one leader influences the reputation of fellow party members seeking office. Parties therefore strive to fashion a record they can defend at the polls, which requires members to maintain a degree of unity. To paraphrase Ben Franklin, party members either hang together or they hang separately. President George W. Bush was able to rely on congressional support for his controversial tax-cut proposals in part because other Republicans recognized the need for his administration to create a record of accomplishment.

Developing Issues and Educating the Public   Parties engage in a continual battle for control of public offices, and they sharpen their issue positions as weapons in this struggle. They identify problems, publicize them, and advance possible solutions. Much of their motivation is adversarial, somewhat like a court proceeding in which the opposing lawyers present their cases, but the outcome of the competition can be beneficial. It generates information, educates the public, and shapes the policy agenda. Where parties are weak, as in the American South during the first half of the twentieth century, politics degenerates into a battle over private benefits rather than public issues.[7]

Political Parties: State Control and National Platforms

Synthesizing Interests   Good public policy must be more than the sum of various people's demands (see Chapter 7). Satisfying every specific interest can detract from the general interest. Also, some conflicting interests cannot be satisfied simultaneously; they require compromise. Translating societal demands into public policy therefore must go beyond simple addition to a more difficult and subtle kind of synthesizing or harmonizing. The major parties sometimes perform this critical role while trying to construct successful national coalitions. They develop platforms that offer a mix of benefits and burdens to all. When their platforms appear too focused on pleasing identifiable special interests, parties suffer electorally—as the Democrats did in 1984 and the Republicans did in 1996.

Recruiting and Developing Governmental Talent   There is an old adage in politics: "You can't beat somebody with nobody." Even if an elected official appears vulnerable, voters may continue to return that incumbent to office unless they are offered a plausible alternative—someone with the background and qualifications to hold the post.[8] Thus, parties are always on the lookout for promising candidates. They may make a special effort to recruit candidates who will improve the party's image, as the Republicans did in 2002 by trying to expand their pool of black candidates.[9] The parties keep track of the weak members in the opposition and bring along potential replacements from their own ranks. Like predators in the natural environment, parties help strengthen public service by weeding out the weak.

Simplifying the Electoral System   Imagine that there were no parties to winnow the field of candidates. Rather than choosing between two options for most offices, voters might be faced with a multitude of choices, each supported by a tiny slice of the electorate. Furthermore, the candidates would lack party labels, which otherwise help voters anticipate each candidate's beliefs. Neither major party is homogeneous, of course, but the labels *Democrat* and *Republican* do convey a good bit of information. Voters do not need to keep track of a candidate's various issue positions; they can concentrate on remembering the ones that differ from the party norm. In the absence of parties, therefore, Americans would have to work much harder before knowing how to vote.

How Parties Detract from Democratic Politics

Despite the valuable organizational functions that political parties can perform, Americans are traditionally suspicious of parties and, since the end of the nineteenth century, have held them in relatively low esteem. Part of this scorn results from the fact that parties do not always perform the valuable functions of which they are capable. After all, politicians do not organize parties because they want to simplify the electoral system, recruit talent, or synthesize interests. They give structure to political life only insofar as such activities help them gain power.[10]

Thomas Jefferson nurtured the Democratic-Republican party as a way to wrest power from the Federalists. Abraham Lincoln used the new Republican party to overthrow a Democratic majority. Theodore Roosevelt established the Bull Moose party because he could not win the GOP nomination. Once in office, public officials work to maintain their parties because parties help them govern. Andrew Jackson used the spoils of victory to consolidate his party's majority, as did the Republicans in the aftermath of the Civil War. Franklin Roosevelt used New Deal policies to strengthen the Democratic party in electorally critical locales.[11]

Although party leaders may view their partisan activities as furthering the public interest, their opponents seldom agree. But even voters on the winning side may be critical of parties, because party influence is a double-edged sword. Parties strong enough to perform beneficial functions are also strong enough to abuse their power. Each of the positive functions that parties can perform can be corrupted, and unfortunately, American history provides numerous such examples.

Presidential Primary Candidates

The 2004 Democratic presidential contenders offered party members a variety of ideologies and a variety of personal styles. Today's weak parties are not as capable of suppressing issues as the stronger parties of the nineteenth century were.

Capturing Governments and Dictating What They Do   At a certain point, co-ordination becomes control. A strong party that controls its members can force elected officials to stick with the desires of the leadership and ignore the wishes of voters back home (especially when candidates for the other party are equally unresponsive). At its extreme, party dominance becomes the equivalent of an elected dictatorship, a charge the Progressives leveled at the urban machines that ruled many American cities a century ago. The machines kept a stranglehold on elected offices, despite facing periodic elections, through the calculated distribution of jobs, contracts, and other patronage. When private payoffs failed, they often exploited illegal methods for maintaining power—such as vote fraud or police intimidation. They would even look the other way while their thugs beat up voters in strategically selected precincts.

Confusing Responsibility   Because credit for good times and blame for bad times are valuable political currencies, the parties attempt to "manufacture" responsibility. Opposition members may blame the incumbent administration for events over which it had no control. Incumbents, in turn, may take credit for positive outcomes not of their making. Worse, rather than helping to solve a public problem, opposition parties may concentrate on undercutting the governing party's proposed solutions. The Republicans used this tactic with President Clinton's health-care plan in 1994, and the Democrats used it with the Republican attempt to control entitlement spending in 1995. The temptation to torpedo the other party's initiatives is especially strong when **divided government** exists—when one party holds the presidency but does not control Congress—as was the case early in George W. Bush's presidency as well as for most of the 1990s. Under such conditions, voters are unsure how to assign responsibility for government inaction.[12]

divided government
Said to exist when a single party does not control the presidency and both houses of Congress.

Suppressing the Issues   For various reasons, parties may prevent the political system from addressing new issues. The leadership of both parties may fail to appreciate new developments in society because they have grown out of touch, or they may ignore issues that threaten the internal harmony of both parties. For example, the two major parties avoided the slavery issue during the first half of the nineteenth century, when they both contained members from the North as well as the South. Today, Democratic and Republican candidates almost uniformly resist reforming programs for the elderly, promising instead to "protect Social Security and expand Medicare," because neither party wishes to risk antagonizing senior citizens. Often it takes outsiders to force an issue onto the public agenda.[13]

Dividing Society   Rather than synthesize disparate interests into some larger whole, parties may do just the opposite. They may create or exacerbate social divisions as a means for gaining electoral advantage. President George Washington suggested as much

Celebrity Politician

Arnold Schwarzenegger has been famous for a long time. An immigrant from Austria, "Ahnold" went from body builder to movie star before becoming governor of California.

• *Although the California governor's office often furnishes presidential candidates, Schwarzenegger is constitutionally barred from the presidency because he is a naturalized citizen. Does that seem discriminatory, or is it a sensible precaution?*

two centuries ago. "The spirit of party," Washington warned during his farewell address, "agitates the community with ill-founded jealousies and false alarms, kindles the animosity of one part against another, [and] foments occasional riot and insurrection."[14] Since the 1980s, Democrats have charged that Republican campaigns subtly inflame racial resentments and homophobia. For their part, Republicans charge that Democrats divide the country by catering to disparate groups—African Americans, Hispanics, gays, feminists, labor—because they have no vision of a larger society.

Recruiting Candidates for the Wrong Reasons   Parties usually seek candidates who can win. In competitive environments, therefore, the desire for success may prompt parties to nominate seasoned leaders or to recruit accomplished political newcomers known for their intelligence, integrity, and good judgment. On the other hand, neither experience nor ability guarantees popularity—and sometimes potential candidates are popular for reasons that have nothing to do with their aptitude at governing. Celebrities, such as entertainers and former athletes, enjoy a distinct advantage in an electoral politics driven by media and money. California Governor Arnold Schwarzenegger may be the most obvious example, but Congress has seated movie actors (Sen. Fred Thompson), TV stars (Rep. Fred Grandy, Rep. Sonny Bono), and astronauts (Sen. John Glenn, Sen. Harrison Schmitt), as well as former stars of the NBA (Rep. Tom McMillan, Sen. Bill Bradley), the NFL (Rep. Jack Kemp), and major-league baseball (Sen. Jim Bunning). Well known? Yes. Qualified? Sometimes. In less competitive environments, meanwhile, parties may promote mediocre people characterized more by their unwavering partisanship than by their skills.

Oversimplifying the Electoral System   The voter who must choose between two candidates, one labeled Democrat and one labeled Republican, has a clearer and apparently easier choice than the voter who can choose among many candidates with no labels. But what if she doesn't like that clear but restricted choice? What if she is a pro-choice Republican or a pro-life Democrat? That's just tough. If there are only two major parties, she has only two serious alternatives. Her choice may be simple, but it also may be quite unsatisfactory.

The Balance Sheet

So who is correct—the scholars who champion political parties or the critics who think parties hinder democracy? Probably the safest answer is "both."

When evaluating party performance, scholars generally do not examine parties in the abstract. Rather, they usually use the standard "relative to having no parties." Functions performed by political parties are necessary for the successful operation of the political system, and scholars see no alternative institution prepared to take over those functions. They also are more likely to realize that parties inevitably act according to their political interests. They do not assume, naively, that a few legal changes suddenly will compel parties to promote the public good. Indeed, they recognize the danger of misconceived reforms, which may fail or even produce nasty unintended consequences.[15] Certainly scholars can risk becoming too complacent, confusing the way things are (which they may have devoted a lifetime to studying) with the way things ought to be. Nevertheless, they are right to value the important organizing role carried out by political parties.

Reformers focus on the failures of existing parties, the ways in which they detract from democratic government. Reformers run little risk of becoming complacent. Indeed, for many social critics, their fame and fortune depend on an ability to identify social problems. As part of this effort, reformers have publicized many real imperfections in how parties operate within the political system: abuses of power, gridlock that keeps problems unsolved, partisanship that makes political life unsavory, scandals and inefficiencies that alienate the public from their government. Certainly reformers can be too quick to demand radical change. They may not anticipate or care about the full consequences of the alterations they embrace. In particular, they do not bear the burden of identifying alternative institutions that could replace parties. Nevertheless, they are right to worry about the extent to which existing political parties undermine representation rather than promote it. As a result, the debate over party reform will continue.

Political Parties in American History

Contemporary Americans' comparative lack of enthusiasm for parties is somewhat ironic, given that the United States pioneered the mass parties that are an essential component of politics in modern Europe. Indeed, parties have organized American elections since the time of George Washington. At first the parties were composed of political notables who supported leaders like Jefferson and Hamilton. Such personal followings were the democratic counterparts of the "court" parties of monarchical governments—the groups of nobles who engaged in "palace intrigues" (and sometimes paid with their lives for their "treasonous" plotting).

American parties did not stay limited to national big shots for very long. During the administration of Andrew Jackson (1828–1836), the Democratic party spread outward from Washington and downward into the grassroots, a movement soon imitated by its adversaries, the Whigs. The kinds of mass parties that were contesting American elections by the 1840s and 1850s did not become common in Europe until half a century later. As late as 1889 Lord Bryce, the famous English political commentator, could observe that "In America the great moving forces are the parties. The government counts for less than in Europe, the parties count for more."[16] Today, of course, the first part of the statement remains true: The government counts for less than in Europe in the sense that the public sector in the United States is smaller. But the second part of Bryce's statement can be turned around: The parties also count for less than in Europe. American parties now are weaker than most of their European counterparts, and they are weaker than those of other economically developed democracies such as Japan and South Korea.

Still, above the local level, nearly all American public officials are elected as Democrats or Republicans (the Nebraska state legislature is formally nonpartisan). Unlike Europeans, Americans may not *believe* that parties are essential to democracy—but in practice parties seem to be as pervasive as in Europe. Indeed, political historians of the past generation have developed general accounts of American history organized around the concept of "party systems."[17] These accounts describe the important role the political parties, appreciated or not, have played in American history.

The Party-Systems Interpretation of American History

Political change usually occurs gradually. Individuals float in and out of the electorate, or from one party to another—actions that cause election results to vary—but the system as a whole remains fairly stable. The same people usually vote for the same parties each time. The same parties usually win in the same places. Occasionally, however, some sort of dramatic event can shock the political system, resulting in changes that are more sudden or more sweeping. Whole groups may enter or leave the electorate, or may swing their support from one party to another. Republican areas can become Democratic ones, and vice versa.

party alignment
The existence of social and economic groups that consistently support each party.

critical election
Election that marks the emergence of a new, lasting alignment of partisan support within the electorate.

realignment
Occurs when the pattern of group support for political parties shifts in a significant and lasting way.

"Realignment" scholars have tried to formalize the study of political change by breaking American political history into a series of distinct electoral eras, or "party systems."[18] Each era features stable **party alignments;** the social and economic groups that support each party remain consistent. The eras themselves are separated by one or more **critical elections,** or realigning elections, that alter the existing electoral alignment. Some scholars suggest that **realignments** naturally occur about once a generation, as society drifts away from the conditions that initially produced a party system. The realignment usually occurs in response to some crisis that may divide existing parties, increase voter turnout, or cause third parties to appear on the scene. Although defining "critical elections" or "electoral eras" is a tricky business, and some scholars doubt that it is possible to do so without oversimplifying political history too much,[19]

TABLE 8.1

THE PARTY-SYSTEMS INTERPRETATION OF AMERICAN ELECTORAL HISTORY

First (Jeffersonian) Party System: 1796–1824[a]
  7 Democratic-Republican presidential victories
  1 Federalist victory

Second (Jacksonian) Party System: 1828–1856
  6 Democratic victories
  2 Whig victories

Third (Civil War and Reconstruction) Party System: 1860–1892
  7 Republican victories
  2 Democratic victories

Fourth (National Republican) Party System: 1896–1928
  7 Republican victories
  2 Democratic victories

Fifth (New Deal) Party System: 1932–1964
  7 Democratic victories
  2 Republican victories

Sixth (Divided Government) Party System: 1968–???
  7 Republican victories
  3 Democratic victories

[a] Years are approximate.

the party-systems interpretation nevertheless provides a useful way to remember how party competition has changed over time (see Table 8.1).

The First Party System (Jeffersonian)   Some historians date the first party system from the early 1790s to about 1824. Commercial interests in the young republic, especially those located in New England, supported the Federalists. The party's leaders included Alexander Hamilton and John Adams. The agricultural interests, especially those located in the South and West, supported the Democratic-Republicans. Thomas Jefferson defined the party's public image, but James Madison also played a prominent role in its development.

The overriding issue during this period was the establishment of a national government and the delineation of its power. Jeffersonians wished to keep the national government small and, although Jefferson made an exception to allow the Louisiana Purchase, they generally interpreted the Constitution to limit federal power. Federalists preferred that government exert more authority. They supported higher taxes, government assistance for native industries, a centralized military, and ambitious public improvements such as roads and bridges. The two parties also divided over foreign policy. Federalists favored strong ties with the English, whereas Jeffersonians leaned toward the French.

In some ways, partisan competition has never been as bare-knuckled as it was early in this party system. The Federalists essentially tried to shut down Jefferson's 1800 presidential campaign by passing the Alien and Sedition Acts of 1798, which (among other things) allowed them to jail people who criticized incumbent Federalist leaders. Some prominent Federalist sympathizers even accused Jefferson of conspiring with Jesuit priests and hash-eating Arab assassins as part of a secret society called the Illuminati. The conspiracy's alleged purpose was "to root out and abolish Christianity, and overthrow all civil government."[20] These scurrilous efforts backfired. The Jeffersonians became the dominant political party, winning the presidency seven consecutive times from 1800 to

1824. The system splintered when Andrew Jackson won the popular vote *and* the electoral vote in 1824, but was denied the presidency in the House of Representatives (see Chapter 6).

Some historians object to characterizing the Democratic-Republican era as a party system. Party competition at this time did not involve many people. Property qualifications prevented a majority of white males from voting, and women and slaves could not vote. Political competition generally consisted of behind-the-scenes struggles among personal factions—especially once the Federalist Party withered after the War of 1812. In the view of these skeptical historians, no party system, strictly speaking, came into existence until the 1830s and the creation of parties with mass appeal.

The Second Party System (Jacksonian Democracy)   After his defeat in 1824, General Jackson and his allies laid the groundwork for another presidential campaign. In particular, they sought to mobilize more of their potential support. The strategy succeeded with a vengeance: Between 1824 and 1828, turnout in the presidential election tripled, sweeping Jackson into office. Jackson's victory over the congressional caucus was complete in 1832 when he had himself renominated by a **national convention** that also chose Martin Van Buren as the vice-presidential nominee. Ever since, party delegates have gathered in conventions to select presidential tickets and the platforms on which they run.

The Jacksonian Democrats often were called simply "the Democracy." This revitalized, greatly expanded successor to the Jeffersonian Democratic-Republicans was the world's first political party built on mass participation. Van Buren, one of its principal architects, is sometimes called the father of parties.[21] The Jacksonians believed in the adage "to the victors belong the spoils." They freely and openly passed out government jobs and contracts as a way to consolidate their hold on power. The Whigs, another mass party, formed to oppose "King Andrew" and his successors. They often used the same tactics as the Jacksonians. But the Democracy lost only two presidential elections to the Whigs, each time against a war hero (William Henry Harrison in 1840, Zachary Taylor in 1848). The Democracy also controlled Congress through much of this period.

During this second party system, the dominant issues were economic and territorial. The Democracy opposed tariffs and national banks, whereas they supported the territorial expansion of the Union. The Whigs generally thought otherwise; they wanted a national government that actively supported internal improvements. As the system matured, new issues arose and sectional differences over economics and slavery intensified. By the late 1840s, dissatisfied citizens were challenging the system under the banners of third parties. The "Free Soilers" opposed the expansion of slavery into the territories, and a few years later the "Know Nothings" opposed the immigration of Catholics.

Ultimately, in 1854–1856 a new party, the Republicans, displaced the Whigs as the second major party in the system. The Democracy, meanwhile, started to crumble. In 1860, it nominated both northern and southern candidates for president. Together with the Constitutional Union candidate, they received nearly 60 percent of the popular vote—but Abraham Lincoln led the race with nearly 40 percent, which was enough to give him an Electoral College majority.

The Third Party System (Civil War and Reconstruction)   The third party system was the most competitive electoral era in American history, a "period of no deci-

national convention
Quadrennial gathering of party officials and delegates who select presidential and vice-presidential nominees and adopt party platforms. Extension of the direct primary to the presidential level after 1968 has greatly reduced the importance of the conventions.

sion."[22] From 1876 to 1892, no presidential candidate received as much as 51 percent of the popular vote. In two elections (that of Rutherford Hayes in 1876 and that of Benjamin Harrison in 1888), the Electoral College even chose a president who had come in second in the popular vote. The Democrats maintained a base in the House of Representatives during the Civil War, and they took control of the House in 1874 following the South's readmission to the Union. Throughout the period, however, the Republicans controlled the Senate, partly through the strategy of admitting new western states to the Union. These states were very sparsely populated, but they dependably elected Republican senators.[23]

The dominant issue at the beginning of the period was Reconstruction in the South, but economic issues took center stage after 1876. The rise of large business organizations, industrialization and its associated dislocations, and a long agricultural depression generated the political issues of this party system. Party organizations reached their high point. Bitter memories of the Civil War left many people committed to the party of the Union (Republicans) or the party of the rebels (Democrats), and intense electoral competition encouraged these committed citizens to vote a straight party line. Indeed, independents often were viewed contemptuously as "traitors." With feelings so strong, the parties exerted tremendous effort in campaigns.[24] Parties reached such a high level of organization in many cities that they were referred to as **machines.**[25]

Once again, the party system was unable to contain or adapt to new pressures. Partisan divisions rooted in the Civil War seemed increasingly outmoded as the United States emerged as an industrialized nation. The excesses and corruption of the urban machines spawned reform movements aimed at destroying their influence. The Depression of the 1890s, during the administration of Democrat Grover Cleveland, plunged much of the country into misery. Agricultural protest, common throughout the period, gave rise to a Populist party that seriously challenged the major parties in the South and West and ultimately fused with the Democrats to nominate William Jennings Bryan for president in 1896.[26] But the 1896 election showed that the Populist vision of a worker-farmer alliance could not win the support of a national majority. Serious differences between Catholic workers and Protestant farmers, between the modernizing city and the traditional countryside, drove urban voters away from the Democrats. The period of no decision ended. Voters opted to try the Republican vision of a modern industrial state.

The Fourth Party System (Industrial Republican)   The critical election of 1896 inaugurated a period of Republican dominance.[27] The Democrats were reduced to their base in the old Confederacy, while the Republicans were in firm control in many areas of the North and West. No longer needing southern electoral votes for victory, the Republicans lost interest in their black supporters and allowed the South to erect a system of political disenfranchisement that persisted into the 1950s.[28] Voters tended to divide over religion and ethnicity, with Catholics and most immigrants preferring the Democrats and native Protestants siding with the Republicans—as demonstrated by the first-ever nomination of a Catholic major-party candidate, Democrat Al Smith, for the presidency in 1928.[29] The Democrats won the presidency only twice during the fourth party system: in 1912, when Woodrow Wilson emerged the victor in a three-way race with President William Howard Taft and ex-President Theodore Roosevelt, and

THE MILLENNIUM. THE TIGER AND THE LAMB LIE TOGETHER

The Tammany Tiger

Urban political machines often appeared to threaten the nation's democratic institutions. Here, a cartoonist portrays New York City's Tammany Hall machine as a tiger.

• *Political parties may be effective at organization, but at what point does the political system become too organized?*

machine
A highly organized party under the control of a boss, and based on patronage and control of government activities. Machines were common in many cities in the late nineteenth and early twentieth centuries.

again in 1916, when Wilson was narrowly reelected on a platform of keeping the United States out of World War I.

The fourth party system was a period of reform in American politics, during which wealthy and influential members of the Progressive movement tried to clean up both elections and government administration. Some commentators see a dark side to the reforms, though, because they often served to push ordinary citizens out of politics.[30] Turnout in elections plummeted, for example, after the **Progressives** instituted voter registration systems and the secret ballot.

The Progressives undermined two principal resources used by political parties to maintain power: control of public employment and control of nominations. Civil Service reforms begun at the national level with the Pendleton Civil Service Act of 1883 were extended wherever possible, diminishing the spoils the parties had available to distribute to their members. The **direct primary** system, which allowed voters instead of party leaders to choose nominees for office, weakened party control of nominations and hence the influence that parties could exercise over officeholders. The Progressives attacked the urban machines with demands for nonpartisan elections, and they provided tools of direct democracy such as the initiative, referendum, and recall as a way for voters to get around elected officials. The reforms targeted real corruption, but they also weakened the mobilizing agents that brought many low-income and low-status people into politics.

After World War I, the Progressives' influence declined. For a time the country appeared to have achieved a new, permanent state of prosperity. Then came the great stock market crash of 1929, followed by the Depression of the 1930s with unemployment levels over 20 percent. This terrible economic crisis almost immediately rearranged political loyalties. The Republicans lost the House of Representatives in the mid-term elections of 1930, and the critical elections of 1932 and 1936 established a new party system.

The Fifth Party System (New Deal)   The New Deal period instituted a class-based party system that resembled electoral alignments in modern European democracies. After Roosevelt's first term, the Democrats became the party of the "common" people (blue-collar workers, farmers, and minorities), while the Republicans became, more than ever, the party of business and the affluent. The former accounted for a lot more voters than the latter, leading to a period of Democratic dominance not seen since before the Civil War. Only Republican war hero Dwight Eisenhower was able to crack the Democratic monopoly, which he did in 1952 and 1956. Republicans controlled Congress for only one term, from 1952 to 1954.

During the New Deal party system, the United States fought to overcome the Great Depression, to defeat the Axis powers, and to lead democratic forces in the "Cold War" that followed. Foreign policy was formulated in a relatively nonpartisan fashion during this period, leaving politics to the domestic economic issues that favored Democrats. But racial divisions slowly eroded the Democratic Party's electoral coalition. In 1936 Roosevelt won repeal of the 104-year-old **two-thirds rule.** By requiring that the Democratic nominee receive a two-thirds majority of the delegates at the national convention, the rule had given the South a veto over racially liberal nominees. With its elimination, the South was increasingly unable to resist the growing national pressure for racial justice. Just as the inability to reconcile its northern and southern wings splintered the Jacksonian Democracy in the 1850s, the inability to reconcile its

Progressives
Middle-class reformers of the late nineteenth and early twentieth centuries who weakened the power of the machines and attempted to clean up elections and government.

direct primary
A method of choosing party candidates by popular vote of all self-identified party members. This method of nominating candidates is virtually unknown outside the United States.

two-thirds rule
Rule governing Democratic national conventions from 1832 to 1936. It required that the presidential and vice-presidential nominees receive at least two-thirds of the delegates' votes.

northern and southern wings splintered the New Deal Democrats a century later. By 1968 the Democratic party was at war with itself, and Republican Richard Nixon was elected president.

The Sixth Party System (Divided Government)   Most commentators believe that the New Deal party system is gone, but they are in less agreement about what sort of party system has replaced it—or even if one has. The electoral alignments that developed around Richard Nixon's presidency have puzzled scholars for much of the past generation because they do not resemble realignments of the past.

The end of the New Deal party system did not lead to dominance by either major party, as happened after voters rejected William Jennings Bryan in 1896 or abandoned the Republican Party during the Depression. Instead, Nixon's victory initiated decades of split election outcomes. For example, the Democrats lost five of the six presidential elections from 1968 to 1988, but they never lost control of the House between 1954 and 1994, and they lost the Senate only from 1980 to 1986. During earlier party systems, divided government control usually appeared during brief transitional periods between control by one major party and control by the other. Divided government after the fifth party system, however, resulted from a high rate of **ticket splitting**—that is, from voters supporting candidates of different parties in the same election. (See the accompanying Democratic Dilemma.) Three presidential elections in a row gave the White House to a candidate who lacked a majority of the popular vote: Clinton in 1992 and 1996, then Bush in 2000. Some scholars, such as Joel Silbey, interpret this evidence as an indication that American parties have grown too weak to structure a realignment and create a new party system.[31]

ticket splitting
Occurs when a voter does not vote a straight party ticket.

Nor can scholars identify a "critical election" of the sort that initiated previous realignments. The 1964 presidential election offers one possibility, because it marked the end of Democratic dominance in the South. Wedge issues such as race, religion, crime, and war led white southerners into the arms of Republican Senator Barry Goldwater. Yet the only effect of that election was to increase Democratic strength in Congress and return Lyndon Johnson to the White House—hardly a critical shift in the partisan control of American institutions. Outside the South, voting behavior did not realign dramatically until later.

The 1968 election, meanwhile, exhibits other features of a critical election. It occurred during a period of crisis, for example, following urban riots and protests against the Vietnam War—as well as the assassinations of civil rights protestor Martin Luther King, Jr., and presidential candidate Robert F. Kennedy. The election switched party control of the presidency, an important institutional shift. But Richard Nixon, the winning candidate, exploited the new wedge issues only indirectly and imperfectly. Instead, Alabama Governor George Wallace's third-party campaign thrived on racial and cultural resentments. Many blue-collar and urban whites joined southerners in abandoning Democratic presidential candidates and backing Wallace.

The inability to pin down a clear realignment has led many scholars to question the usefulness of a party-systems approach to political history. They cannot agree whether the current, sixth period of electoral history reflects a weak and confused realignment, or no durable set of alignments at all. Having such a closely divided electorate means that independents and swing voters enjoy an unprecedented amount of political influence, and that elections matter more than they have historically. Party control of the White House fluctuates more. As a result, even supporters of the party-

DEMOCRATIC DILEMMA

Is Gridlock Necessarily Bad?

Political scientists traditionally have viewed "party government" as superior to a more individualistic, candidate-centered politics. From this perspective, elections should consist of cohesive parties competing for control of public offices by offering distinct policy proposals. The electorate should compare the parties' platforms, choose the one that seems best suited for the time and conditions, and give it full control of our national elective institutions—both the presidency and Congress. Such unified control would enable parties to act vigorously and efficiently when they took office, and voters would know exactly whom to credit or blame for the actions of the government.

The American parties became increasingly cohesive and programmatic beginning in the late 1960s, but voters did not follow the professors' advice. Instead, as the major parties became more distinct and more cohesive, voters increasingly split their tickets. The country entered an era when, more often than not, control of national elected institutions was split between the two parties, with the Republicans generally winning the presidency and the Democrats the Congress.

Logic might suggest that divided governments should produce gridlock (because the institutions fight rather than cooperate) and irresponsibility (because the parties blame each other for inaction). Not every researcher agrees with this supposition. Yale University political scientist David Mayhew, for example, probed the legislative record and concluded that the national government was just as likely to pass major legislation under divided government as under unified government.[a] But the bulk of the evidence does seem to reinforce the traditional belief that divided authority hampers gover-

nance. For example, influential research by James Alt and Robert Lowry shows that divided state governments adjust their budgets more slowly and are less able to avoid deficits. They also appear to be less accountable for their economic policy failures.[b]

Why don't American voters take the professional advice available to them and regularly vote to install unified governments, as they did in 2002? Do they not realize that divided government might create gridlock? One possible explanation is that, unlike political writers inside and outside academia, the general public may not consider gridlock such a bad thing. Polls repeatedly report that majorities of Americans favor divided government. They view it as a way for one party to keep the other in check, preventing abuses of power, watching for scandalous or corrupt behavior, and vetoing the more extreme ideological indulgences of the opposition.

• *Do you think electoral politics should be guided by the clash of party ideologies and that candidates should take strong stands on the issues of the day?*

• *Do you think voters would support unified government more often if the parties nominated more middle-of-the-road candidates who offered moderate issue positions?*

• *Does divided government make it more difficult for voters to know whom to credit or blame?*

[a] David R. Mayhew, *Divided We Govern* (New Haven: Yale University Press, 1991).

[b] James E. Alt and Robert C. Lowry, "A Dynamic Model of State Budget Outcomes Under Divided Partisan Government," *Journal of Politics* 62:4 (November 2000): 1035–1069; Alt and Lowry, "Divided Government, Fiscal Institutions, and Budget Deficits," *American Political Science Review* 88:4 (December 1994): 811–828; Lowry, Alt, and Karen E. Ferree, "Fiscal Policy Outcomes and Electoral Accountability in American States," *American Political Science Review* 92:4 (December 1998): 759–774.

---

systems approach must concede that today's electoral patterns do not fit well into the framework that they have popularized (although they argue that the right issue or leader could realign voters in a way that resembles earlier party systems).[32]

Nevertheless, the United States entered a distinctly different electoral era after the 1960s, one unlike any that had preceded it. Like previous party systems, the era exhibits distinctive party alignments. Republicans tend to attract the support of small-town and rural voters. They thrive in the West and, increasingly, in the South. As U.S. Senator Zell Miller of Georgia described the situation, "Democratic leaders are as nervous as a long-tailed cat around a rocking chair when they travel south." Democrats dominate cities, university communities, and along the Atlantic and Pacific coasts. They receive solid support from racial and ethnic minorities. These patterns receive detailed attention in Chapter 10 but, for convenience, we can think of today's confusing and election-driven period as the sixth party system.

TABLE 8.2
THIRD PARTIES BY POPULAR SUPPORT

Year	Candidate	Party	Popular Vote %	Electoral Votes	Subsequent Events
1912	T. Roosevelt	Progressive	27.4	88	Supported GOP nominee in 1916.
1992	R. Perot	Independent	18.7	0	Created Reform Party, which faded.
1924	R. LaFollette	Progressive	16.6	13	Robert LaFollette died in 1925.
1968	G. Wallace	American Independent	13.5	46	Dropped from 1972 election after being maimed in assassination attempt.
1848	M. Van Buren	Free Soil	10.1	0	Supporters eventually merged with Republican Party.
1892	J.B. Weaver	Populist	8.5	22	Party supported Democratic ticket in 1896.
1996	R. Perot	Reform	8.5	0	Party collapsed in 2000 election.
1980	J. Anderson	National Unity	6.6	0	Candidate withdrew from politics.
2000	R. Nader	Green	3.0	0	Failed to qualify for 2004 federal funding.
1948	S. Thurmond	States' Rights	2.4	38	Democrats picked slate acceptable to South in 1952.
1948	H. A. Wallace	Progressive	2.4	0	Party disappeared.

NOTE: Candidates sorted by popular vote percentage.

Two-Party and Multi-Party Systems

Americans understandably regard a **two-party system** as a natural state of affairs. As the description of party systems showed, for the more than two centuries of the country's history, two major parties have dominated elections for national office, although third parties regularly arise (see Table 8.2). Several third parties, such as the Progressive party and the Green Party, have influenced the outcomes of some American elections, but nearly all third parties disappear.[33] Only once has a third party replaced a major party: The Republicans displaced the Whigs in the 1850s. Often third parties are a reaction to a particular problem, and they fade when the problem does. If the problem persists, the third party usually is absorbed or "co-opted" by a major party, as were the Populists in the 1890s, who joined with the Democrats.

Americans are in a minority as far as the rest of the world is concerned. Most democracies have multi-party systems. Canadians, for example, spread their votes across a number of significant alternatives—including conservative, liberal, and social democratic parties as well as a reform party and a strong regional party centered in the province of Québec. When the political system offers so many options, often no single party can win control of government; rather, two or more minority parties must ally together and form a coalition government based on their combined parliamentary

two-party system
System in which only two significant parties compete for office. Such systems are in the minority among world democracies.

 Timeline

Third Parties in American History

Not Enough Green

Ralph Nader's Green Party candidacy failed to attract enough votes in the 2000 presidential election to qualify for federal funding in 2004. Third parties are often hindered by their limited campaign resources.

majority. In the 2000 German Bund, for example, the Social Democrats and the Christian Democrats each held approximately 41 percent of the seats. Political control therefore depended on the disposition of the smaller parties, in particular the leftist Greens and the centrist Free Democratic Party.

Many scholars believe that the electoral system strongly affects how many parties a country can sustain. An **electoral system** is the way in which a country's constitution or laws translate popular votes into control of public offices.[34] The United States relies almost exclusively on the **single-member, simple plurality (SMSP) system.** Elections for office take place within geographic units (states, congressional districts, cities, and so on), and the candidate who wins the most votes wins the election. When only two candidates run, one candidate will win a majority; when more than two run, a simple plurality determines the winner. This electoral system is characteristic of the "Anglo-American democracies" (England and its former colonies). It is often called the "first past the post" system: Just as in a horse race, the winner is the one who crosses the finish line first, no matter how many others are in the race or how close the finish.

In most of the world's democracies, however, the electoral system is some version (there are many variations) of **proportional representation (PR).** In such systems, elections may (Germany) or may not (Israel) take place within smaller geographic units, but even if they do, each unit elects a number of officials, with each party winning seats in proportion to the vote it receives.

To illustrate the operation of these differing electoral systems, consider an example. Great Britain has a SMSP system, but for decades a small third party, currently called the Liberal Democrats, has survived. Suppose the vote were to be divided as follows within a parliamentary constituency:

Conservative: 40 %

Labour: 48 %

Liberal Democrat: 12 %

electoral system
A means of translating popular votes into control of public offices.

single-member, simple plurality (SMSP) system
Electoral system in which the country is divided into geographic districts, and the candidates who win the most votes within their districts are elected.

proportional representation (PR)
Electoral system in which parties receive a share of seats in parliament that is proportional to the popular vote they receive.

The Labour candidate, having won a plurality, would win the seat with a minority of the total vote. The Conservatives and the Liberal Democrats would have nothing to show for the 62 percent they won. This is not unusual: *SMSP electoral systems tend to manufacture majorities or at least to exaggerate their size.* In fact, the current Labour government, which holds 65 percent of the seats in Parliament, received only 41 percent of the nationwide vote in the 2001 elections.

When elections are conducted under PR arrangements, constituencies tend to be much larger and are assigned multiple representatives. For example, if the preceding distribution of the vote had occurred in a constituency assigned 10 members of Parliament, the Conservatives would have been given 4 seats, Labour 5, and the Liberal Democrats 1, an allocation of seats roughly proportional to the number of votes received. Under PR, seat majorities and vote majorities correspond very closely.

In the SMSP electoral system, winning is everything—finishing in any position but first achieves nothing. Thus, if small parties have more in common with each other than with the largest party, they have an incentive to join together in a single opposing party to challenge the plurality winner, because dividing the opposition among more than one candidate plays into the hands of the enemy. Citizens, in turn, realize that voting for a small party is tantamount to "wasting" their vote, because such a party has no chance of coming in first.[35] Thus they tend to support one of the two larger parties. These calculations by parties and voters work against third parties.

In PR systems, however, a party wins seats in proportion to its vote (as long as it finishes above some legally defined threshold). Because it is not necessary to finish first in order to win something, party leaders have more incentive to maintain their separate organizations. And, because only votes for tiny parties fail to count, voters are not motivated to abandon smaller parties. Thus a multi-party system persists.

As shown by the foregoing British example, the correlation between electoral system and number of parties around the world is not perfect, and third parties do survive in SMSP systems. The correlation is strong, however. One study found that the average number of parties in proportional representation systems was 3.7, while the average number in SMSP systems was 2.2.[36]

One factor that affects the survival of third parties in SMSP systems is whether their votes are geographically concentrated. If they receive, say, 20 percent of the nationwide vote but it is distributed evenly across the country, they win nothing. On the other hand, if their vote is regionally concentrated so that they are the first or second party in some constituencies, they may persist indefinitely. For example, modern Canadian elections have been dominated by two major parties, the Liberals and the Progressive Conservatives, which compete nationwide and ordinarily win most of the seats in Parliament. But in recent elections, two smaller parties have established regional footholds. In the French-speaking province of Québec, the Parti Québécois is the dominant party, and in some western provinces, Reform is the strongest party.

Comparing Political Parties

How Strong Are American Parties Today?

Given the dislike that many Americans express toward political parties, you may be surprised to learn that during the past three decades, observers have argued over whether the parties are declining or even dying.[37] Some of these writers have argued that genuine political parties are dead and the party system "decomposed."[38] Columnist David Broder titled his book on the subject *The Party's Over*.[39] Other writers responded with their own snappy titles. Two authors claimed that *The Party Goes On* and—not to be outdone—another writer boasted that *The Party's Just Begun.*[40] These observers differ sharply over whether the parties have really "declined" or just changed.[41] How can professional students of politics arrive at such widely differing viewpoints?

Part of the answer is that people have different conceptions of what a party is.[42] In most of the world, parties are well-defined organizations. People join them in the same way they join clubs in the United States: They pay dues, receive official membership cards, go to regularly scheduled meetings, and have a right to participate in various party-sponsored activities (such as nominating candidates). The term *party* also may refer to the public officials elected under the party's name. In most other countries party candidates run more centralized campaigns on behalf of their nominees than in the candidate-centered politics of the United States. They constitute "teams" that carry the names of the parties.

Historically, the United States did not have true national party organizations. Rather, what passed for national organizations were temporary alliances of state parties and local machines that joined together every four years to work for the election of a president. In the aftermath of the Progressive reforms, these state and local organizations themselves declined. Similarly, party members in government have generally not been terribly cohesive. Both parties (but especially the Democrats) have suffered from regional splits, and both parties have incorporated conflicting interests—agricultural versus commercial, moralistic versus worldly, and so forth (see Chapters 12 and 13).[43]

Neither party as a formal organization nor party as a unified team of elected officials fits the U.S. experience very well. As a result, modern American commentators have discussed *party* primarily in a third sense, as supporters in the electorate, the ordinary citizens who identify themselves as Democrats or Republicans.

For some decades it appeared that political parties in the United States were declining no matter how one defined them. State and local party organizations had withered by mid-century. Meanwhile, party cohesion and presidential support in Congress had declined.[44] The number of adherents to the two parties began dropping as well; in the mid-1960s the proportion of those calling themselves "independents" rose. To a certain extent, the parties have recovered. By the mid-1980s, party organizations were growing more active again, and party was becoming more important in government (the topic of the next section).[45] The trend to abandon parties has bottomed out as well, and many students of party affiliation note that even so-called independents usually vote consistently with one party or another (see Chapter 10).[46]

The Decline of Party Organizations

Party organizations were at their strongest at about the time the Progressive movement began. The decline of American party organizations was largely a consequence of deliberate public policies. As noted earlier, the two principal resources that party organizations depend on are control of patronage and control of nominations for office. The first was gradually eliminated by regular expansions of civil service protection and, after World War II, by unionization of the public sector, which gave government workers an additional layer of insulation from partisan politics. (Presently, the largest union in the AFL–CIO is the American Federation of State, County and Municipal Employees.) Today the president personally controls fewer than 4000 appointments.[47] At the height of the spoils system—and with a much smaller federal government—presidents controlled well over 100,000 appointments.[48] Similarly, governors and big-city mayors who once controlled tens of thousands of jobs now control only a few thousand.

Party control over nominations was greatly weakened by the spread of the direct primary, one of the most important Progressive reforms. As described in Chapter 10, the United States is the only world democracy that relies on open, popular elections to decide nominations. In all other democracies, much smaller groups of party activists and officials choose party nominees.

Deprived of their principal resources, modern American parties had few sticks and carrots to sway the behavior of members. Electoral defeat did not mean that tens of thousands of people would lose their jobs; hence they were less inclined to work for parties and support them through thick and thin. Similarly, outsiders could seek a party's nomination, and if they won, the party had no choice but to live with the fact. Controlling neither the livelihoods of ordinary voters nor the electoral fates of public officials, the party organizations atrophied.

However, deliberate political reforms do not entirely explain the weakening of American parties. Other factors also have contributed to their decline, independent developments that indirectly weakened the parties. For one thing, the communications revolution lessened the need for traditional parties. Candidates could raise funds through direct-mail appeals and then use these funds to reach voters directly by computer-generated mail and television. Elections have become less labor-intensive; they rely more on technology and money instead.[49] Technological developments have diminished the need for party workers and party support. Nor do the parties control their own TV networks, as the Christian Democrats, Social Democrats, and Communists all managed to do in Italy.

A second development that undercut U.S. parties was the increase in mobility—social, economic, and residential—that followed World War II. Better-educated voters had less need of parties to make sense of politics and guide their behavior. In a booming economy, voters had less need of parties to help them get jobs. And as the suburbs grew, the traditional, urban-based parties came to represent an ever-smaller proportion of the population, while the new, decentralized suburbs went largely unorganized.

The Revival of Party Organizations?

Through most of their 150-year history, the national committees were the weakest level of party organization. They became active only during presidential election years, when they organized the efforts of independent state and city organizations. Similarly, although powerful state organizations existed in some states, in many others the state organization was only a loose confederation of local organizations. That has changed greatly in the past quarter century. Creative politicians by the 1980s began to find new ways for party organizations to help them obtain and keep political power.

Most observers credit Republicans such as William Brock, chairman of the Republican National Committee (RNC) from 1976 to 1982, for leading the way to modern-day party politics. These Republican strategists raised large sums of money, passing them on to friendly candidates as well as local party organizations. It hired full-time political operatives and experts on polling, fund raising, campaigning, and the media. It retained lawyers versed in election law and specialists skilled in computers and other technologies. Such resources were made available at low cost to Republican campaigns nationwide. By the late 1980s, there were reports of Republican congressional campaign committees actively recruiting candidates for office, a level of national intervention that would have been unthinkable half a century ago. For their part, the Democrats eventually imitated the Republicans, especially starting with the Clinton campaign of 1992. Before the 2004 presidential election, the Democratic Party even planned to save their nominee from having to set up a campaign office in Washington, DC—they would provide a "nominee's room" with computers, phones, and staff space.[50]

State and local party organizations have become more active as well; indeed, there are data to suggest that the resurgence of local organizations began earlier, in the 1960s.[51] In contrast to a generation ago, most state parties have permanent headquarters, usually in the state capital, and they employ full-time directors and other staff. Many state organizations now conduct statewide polls. They, too, provide campaign aid and recruit candidates more actively than they did a few decades ago. A major study of party organization leaves no doubt that, in terms of personnel and activities, the state and local party organizations have a more tangible existence today than they did at mid-century.[52]

In sum, the national committees are active and well financed. They have been joined by senatorial and congressional campaign committees. Together these national committees have helped rejuvenate party organization at lower levels. Party increasingly matters for public officials. Republicans are increasingly conservative and Democrats increasing liberal, both in Congress and on the stump. Competition has become less civil, with both parties "increasingly waging the political equivalent of total war" through the use of devices such as recall elections, legislative redistricting, the blocking of judicial and bureaucratic nominees favored by the other party, even impeachment. The partisan ceasefire that followed terrorist attacks in 2001 lasted only 43 days.[53]

The debate, however, is far from over. Some knowledgeable observers remain skeptical of the party-resurgence thesis. John Coleman asks whether the parties are resurgent or "just busy."[54] Others grant that the parties are more active now than in earlier decades but argue that the newer activities do not make them stronger "parties" in any traditional sense. According to these critics, the party organizations essentially have become large campaign-consulting firms, taking advantage of economies of scale to provide electioneering services to their associates.

Today's parties still do not have the control over the candidates that they had in the United States a century ago or that they have in most other democracies today. They cannot deny candidates a nomination or demand their loyalty once they are elected. If a party-recruited candidate is defeated in a primary, the party normally supports the victor, and only rarely are "rebels" in office threatened with loss of party support. The reasons are obvious. Independence is highly valued in the United States. If a party tried to discipline a member, it would probably only ensure his or her reelection. Moreover, despite the impressive efforts of the newly constituted parties, they contribute only a fraction of the resources spent on electioneering. Candidates create personal organizations and raise their own war chests. Contributions by the parties to members of Congress, for example, make up under 10 percent of all congressional campaign expenditures, although the amount spent "independently" is growing.

Parties Versus Interest Groups

Some political theorists believe that the power of interest groups is negatively correlated with the power of parties—that when parties are strong, groups are weak, and vice versa.[55] The argument follows from two premises: first, that parties have incentives to synthesize narrow interests in order to make the broad appeals necessary to win elections; and second, that strong parties can provide electoral resources and deliver the vote, thus freeing their candidates from dependence on interest-group resources and insulating them from interest-group reprisals.

This argument implicitly assumes two-party politics rather than multi-party politics, because in the latter, parties often make very narrow appeals. Indeed, in multi-party systems, there may be little difference between parties and large interest groups such as labor unions. But within the two-party context, the argument has considerable plausibility. As we saw in Chapter 7, interest groups proliferated in the Progressive era, when the parties were systematically attacked by reformers, and again in the 1960s and 1970s, when American parties reached their nadir, before their recent recovery. Just as nature is said to abhor a physical vacuum, so it may be that political vacuums cannot persist. When parties do not fill them, groups or some other source of influence will.

If this argument is valid, then the real alternative to party domination of the electoral process is not popular influence but interest-group influence. Rather than reflecting the broad appeals of parties, elections will reflect the narrow views of special interests. Of course, interest groups are not the only competitors of parties in modern societies. As we will see in Chapter 9, another potential competitor is the media.

Chapter Summary

Although the Constitution makes no mention of them, political parties have been part of American politics since the colonial period. Indeed, American political history often is told in terms of "party systems," wherein each party has dependable support among particular social groups, so that elections tend to be similar within each system. At present, the United States has a party system that is less stable and more confusing than most of those systems that have preceded it.

The basic reason why parties have played such an important role in American history—as well as in the histories of all modern democracies—is that they perform coordinating functions that are essential in large-scale representative democracies. Parties coordinate the actions of numerous officeholders and focus responsibility for their actions. Parties develop issues, educate the public, and synthesize disparate interests. Parties recruit and develop governmental talent and simplify the choices of voters who would otherwise be overwhelmed by the task of choosing among numerous candidates for office.

Despite these important functions that parties perform, most Americans do not hold them in especially high regard. Parties constantly struggle for political supremacy. Thus, they act in accordance with partisan self-interest and historically have behaved dictatorially, corruptly, and divisively. The question reformers must face, however, is whether they can identify an alternative to party influence and activity.

The United States has the world's longest-lived two-party system. Parties in the United States are not so strong today as they were in earlier periods. Like other American institutions and processes, the parties have been democratized. Few "bosses" remain, party processes are open to all who register, and those elected under the party flag often go their own way when it suits them or their constituents. In short, political life is especially disorganized in modern America. Despite much discussion of party decline, though the Democratic and Republican parties continue to dominate American elections and structure governance. And, despite periodic third-party insurgencies, that dominance is likely to continue.

Key Terms

critical election, p. 206

direct primary, p. 210

divided government, p. 202

electoral system, p. 214

machine, p. 209

national convention, p. 208

party alignment, p. 206

political parties, p. 199

Progressives, p. 210

proportional representation (PR), p. 214

realignment, p. 206

single-member, simple plurality (SMSP) system, p. 214

ticket splitting, p. 211

two-party system, p. 213

two-thirds rule, p. 210

Suggested Readings

Of General Interest

Green, John C., and Paul Herrnson, eds., *Responsible Partisanship? The Evolution of American Political Parties Since 1950.* Lawrence, KS: University Press of Kansas, 2003. Comprehensive analysis of how well the political parties have served the American electorate, spread out over essays by some of the most influential researchers on the topic.

Jewell, Malcolm E., and Sarah M. Morehouse. *Political Parties and Elections in the American States.* 4th ed. Washington, DC: Congressional Quarterly, 2000. Textbook on parties and elections at the subnational level.

Key, V. O., Jr. *Politics, Parties and Pressure Groups.* 5th ed. New York: Crowell, 1964. A classic text. Although dated, it can still be read both for historical interest and for theoretical observations about party politics in a democracy.

Maisel, L. Sandy, ed. *Political Parties and Elections in the United States: An Encyclopedia.* New York: Garland, 1991. Useful reference that provides short discussions of specific topics in the history of party politics in America.

Focused Studies

Aldrich, John. *Why Parties?* Chicago: University of Chicago Press, 1995. Wide-ranging rational-choice account of how and why politicians form and transform political parties.

Layman, Geoffrey. *The Great Divide: Religious and Cultural Conflict in American Party Politics.* New York: Columbia University Press, 2001. Thorough look at the continuing importance of cultural differences in defining the major political parties.

Mayhew, David. R. *Placing Parties in American Politics.* Princeton, NJ: Princeton, 1986. Comprehensive study of state party organization in the twentieth century.

Sundquist, James. L. *Dynamics of the Party System.* Rev. ed. Washington, DC: The Brookings Institution, 1983. History of national politics since the 1840s told from a party-systems perspective.

On the Web

www.rnc.org

www.dnc.org

Both national party committees also employ Web sites that solicit contributions, attack their opponents, and generally advocate party-advocated policies.

www.greenparty.org

www.reformparty.org

www.natural-law.org

www.lp.org

Third-parties make tremendous use of the Web. The Green party USA, Reform party, Natural Law party, and Libertarian party have the most prominent minor-party sites.

CHAPTER 9

★ ★ ★ ★ ★ ★ ★ ★ ★ ★ ★ ★ ★ ★ ★ ★ ★

The Media

CHAPTER OUTLINE

The Media: 800-Pound Gorilla or 98-Pound Weakling?

More than three decades ago, hundreds of thousands of young Americans fought in the Vietnam War. More than 58,000 died, and ten times that number were wounded. Many Americans protested against the war, and especially against the military draft—the selection system that decided who would have to fight. Their protests sometimes won sympathy with journalists, but the public response to protesters was far more negative, a striking illustration of the way people resist media messages.

As the 1968 Democratic convention drew near, activists planned to gather in Chicago and protest the impending presidential nomination of the sitting vice president. Hubert Humphrey had not entered a single primary, but his influence within the Democratic party guaranteed that delegates would select him anyway. Most voters could not figure out exactly where Humphrey stood on the Vietnam conflict by 1968 (see Chapter 10), but his previous support for the administration still angered those committed to the antiwar movement.

The level of tension that existed at that time exceeds anything familiar to observers of contemporary politics. Mayor Richard Daley and the Chicago police force fully expected widespread violence on the streets. Rumors flew among the National Guard troops and law officers stationed outside that activists might lace the Convention water supply with hallucinogenic drugs or pose as cab drivers to kidnap Democratic officials.[1]

Daley refused to issue protest permits and warned that the city would deal harshly with those who spoiled the celebration. But some protest leaders were more than willing to provoke such reprisals.[2] A group calling themselves yippies even floated the rumor that they would fill a nearby lake with 10,000 nude bodies.[3] They never carried through on this threat, but they did help fill Chicago with roughly that number of demonstrators.

Many protestors flooded into Chicago's Grant and Lincoln parks, despite the lack of permits. They milled about on the grass, danced to provocative rock music, or chanted Buddhist mantras.[4] After some preliminary skirmishes, Daley's storm troopers finally decided to flush them out of the parks. They bathed the assemblies with tear gas, forcing many into the streets, where more tear gas and more police waited. The harshest confrontation occurred outside the Hilton Hotel, where the convention delegates stayed. As a mostly college-age crowd gasped and choked, armored troops formed into attack wedges and surged into the crowd, flailing about with stout clubs. Other officers hid their identities and attacked news reporters.[5] Ultimately, more than 500 victims needed medical attention. An investigative commission later described the explosion as a "police riot."

The attacks greatly disturbed many political elites. Inside and outside the convention, public figures used the harshest rhetoric. From the podium of the convention, Senator Abraham Ribicoff of Connecticut accused Mayor Daley of using Gestapo tactics to quash dissent—eliciting a string of obscenities from Mayor Daley that the microphones could not pick up. Hard-bitten British reporters who had covered the civil war in Northern Ireland wrote that the Chicago police had gone berserk.[6]

Media reporters clearly sympathized with the protesters. As Tom Wicker of the *New York Times* put it, "these were our children in the streets, and the Chicago police beat them up."[7] Over the course of the evening, the media lost all semblance of balance. Longtime NBC anchor Chet Huntley condemned the police. Walter Cronkite choked back tears.

It was exactly the sort of shocked reaction that many of the protest leaders had hoped to provoke when they exposed themselves to attack. They had uncovered the bankruptcy of "the establishment," which could combat disagreement only through brute force. As tear gas floated hazily before the cameras and sirens filled the background, the news footage carried a continuous taunt from the demonstrators: "The whole world is watching, the whole world is watching."

Indeed, much of the United States *was* watching. But what neither the protesters nor the journalists realized was that most in the audience were cheering on the storm troopers! Poll results that followed the Democratic National Convention stunned American elites: Popular majorities believed that the Chicago police had acted appropriately. In fact, many believed that the police should have used greater force.[8]

Protesters like those demonstrating in Chicago were familiar sights on college campuses, at public buildings such as draft offices, and in city streets. Many people had developed strong views about protesters. There was little opportunity for the media's interpretation of events in Chicago to alter such predispositions. The American people had tuned out the chatter, stared at their TVs, and rooted for the cops. So much for the awesome power of television.

MAKING THE CONNECTION

How powerful are the media, then? Are they an overwhelming force that even presidents must fear, or a lot of sound and fury that ordinary Americans ignore? The answer is that, depending on the circumstances, the media can be either of these, and everything in between. The media can have extremely powerful effects on public opinion, even to the extent of determining who wins elections and what governments do. But under other conditions, media effects are sharply limited. We begin our analysis of the role of the media by answering these questions:

- How did the media attain their present position as an important political actor?

- What kinds of media do Americans rely on for political information?

  Then we consider two important questions:

- In what ways do the media affect public opinion today?

- What types of bias characterize media reports?

  The relationship between the media and politics continually evolves. Politicians strive to use the media for their own ends, and the media cooperate or not, depending on the incentives they face. New developments in the political or technical realm can alter the equilibrium between these two important actors.

★ ★ ★ ★ ★ ★ ★ ★ ★ ★ ★ ★ ★ ★ ★ ★

Development of the Mass Media

The term **mass media** refers to affordable forms of communication capable of reaching an extensive audience. Such resources have existed for less than two centuries. Their development shaped American democracy because politicians engage in a never-ending struggle to control the information that reaches their constituents. Information is power, and politicians contend with media organizations for control of it. In this section we trace the development of the major forms of mass media used to spread political information: print (newspapers and magazines) and broadcast (radio and television). We also look at the emergence of such new media as cable TV and the Internet. In each case we focus on control of the message: Who is responsible for the information transmitted?

mass media
Means of communication that are technologically capable of reaching most people and economically affordable to most.

Newspapers and Magazines

At the time of the American Revolution, most of the colonies' newspapers were weeklies. These early papers were published by printers, like Benjamin Franklin, who also published books, almanacs, and official documents. They reprinted material from European newspapers and from each other, as well as offering letters and essays from their readers.[9]

As party politics developed, both fledgling parties realized the importance of having a means of communicating with their constituents. Hamilton and the Federalists established a "house" paper, the *Gazette of the United States,* and the Jeffersonians responded with the *National Gazette.* These newspapers were unabashedly one-sided. They printed the party line, viciously attacked the opposition, and depended for

Timeline

Three Centuries of
American Mass Media

economic survival on government printing contracts. So, although early presidents did not speak in their own voices, they have been "going public" to the extent that technology allowed since the beginning of the republic.[10]

Improvements in the manufacturing of paper and type and the invention of the steam-driven printing press made it cheaper and easier to publish newspapers. In 1833 the *New York Sun* began daily publication, selling for a mere penny. (Before that time the going price for a newspaper was an exorbitant six cents!) The rise of the penny press marks the birth of the mass media in the United States. Millions of ordinary people could purchase and read newspapers. Within two years the circulation of the *Sun* was third in the world, trailing only the two largest London newspapers.

As readership expanded, the newspapers began to acquire their modern characteristics. One is sensationalism. Then, as now, crime and sex sold newspapers. Politics and economics were left to the older weeklies. Still, the new penny papers were overwhelmingly partisan. According to the 1850 census, only 5 percent of the country's newspapers were neutral or independent.[11] Politicians worked hand in hand with the editors of friendly papers and withheld information from those allied with the opposition.

After the Civil War, an independent press began to develop. One-sided editorial positions remained common, but many publishers saw little point in alienating a large portion of their potential audience. Nor did political leaders need party organs any longer. This was the heyday of the political machine, when party bosses used their own networks of volunteers to communicate with constituents (see Chapter 8). Patronage jobs and government contracts cemented political alliances, not editorials.

The trend toward independence continued into the turn of the twentieth century, when many newspapers became large enterprises. Hearst, Scripps, and other companies bought up independent papers and consolidated them in great chains. Thus, the typical paper no longer was the voice of a lone editor. Journalists became more professional and even less partisan. Some newspapers were important participants in the Progressive movement, publishing "muckraking" exposés of shocking conditions in American industry and corruption in government. Magazines such as *The Nation* and *The Atlantic* that were aimed at the new, educated middle class also appeared.

You Are a News Editor

Today, newspapers and magazines continue to be an important part of the mass media: More than 10,000 newspapers and 12,000 periodicals are currently published. Large city papers like the *New York Times* and the *Los Angeles Times* have circulations of more than 1 million per day, and the *Wall Street Journal* reaches nearly 2 million. A relatively new entry, *USA Today,* has a circulation of about 1.5 million. *Time, Newsweek,* and *U.S. News and World Report* together sell about 10 million copies per week. These publications maintain their own Washington bureaus and send reporters all over the world. But even smaller city papers can get up-to-the-minute national and international news by subscribing to news services like the Associated Press (AP) and Reuters.

The most important development in the modern newspaper industry is the decline in diversity. Afternoon newspapers have all but disappeared. As a result of mergers, most cities are now being served by only one or two papers, down from several a half century ago, and chains such as Gannett and Knight-Ridder have continued to gobble up independent newspapers. Moreover, some media conglomerates own TV and radio stations, even networks, not just newspapers. Critics worry that the mass media are losing their value as they face increased pressure to generate corporate profits.

NAVAL OFFICERS THINK THE MAINE WAS DESTROYED BY A SPANISH MINE.

Hidden Mine or a Sunken Torpedo Believed to Have Been the Weapon Used Against the American Man-of-War---Officers and Men Tell Thrilling Stories of Being Blown Into the Air Amid a Mass of Shattered Steel and Exploding Shells---Survivors Brought to Key West Scout the Idea of Accident---Spanish Officials Protest Too Much---Our Cabinet Orders a Searching Inquiry---Journal Sends Divers to Havana to Report Upon the Condition of the Wreck. Was the Vessel Anchored Over a Mine?

Yellow Journalism

William Randolph Hearst's *New York Journal* went on the warpath after the explosion of the *Maine* in Cuba (ultimately leading to the Spanish-American War). Many people suspected that the Spanish were responsible, and Hearst's papers played on that fear.

• *Compare this newspaper's coverage to the coverage of the Gulf War. How is the coverage different? How is it similar?*

Radio

In the 1930s, the print monopoly of mass communications began to erode. The first radio stations appeared in the 1920s, the first radio news agencies in the 1930s. Politicians quickly made use of this exciting new technology. President Coolidge (1923–1928) was known as "Silent Cal," but to reach voters he took to the airwaves. Franklin Roosevelt helped calm a worried nation in the 1930s with his famous "fireside chats." Radio demagogues, such as the anti-Semitic Father Coughlin, exerted a less calming influence during the same period.

Radio spread rapidly throughout the country. Today there are approximately 16,000 radio stations that reach nearly 85 percent of the population at some time on an average day. Virtually every household has at least one radio; the average is more than five. And, of course, there are millions of cars on the road, nearly all of which contain radios. The growth in radios and radio stations has not produced a comparable growth in media voices, however. Media mergers have undercut diversity in radio programming just as they have eliminated variety in the print media. Less than a decade ago, the two largest radio chains owned 115 stations. By 2003 they owned 1400. Five owners reap more than half of all the revenues spent on local radio.[12]

Probably the most important political development in radio communications is the rapid increase in talk shows. The talk format is very popular, trailing only country-western and adult contemporary music programs in total listeners.[13] Sometimes local chat radio can wield dramatic political power. When Tennessee Governor Don Sundquist attempted to establish a state income tax in 2002, talk-show hosts helped generate massive protests against the proposal, a "tax war" they eventually won.[14] Satellite technology and low long-distance telephone rates have allowed national talk shows as well. Rush Limbaugh's radio show is perhaps the best-known example. This conservative commentator began broadcasting nationally in 1988 and by 2000, reached about 20 million listeners on more than 600 stations.[15]

Television and Presidential Campaigns

Television

To most people today, the term *mass media* means television. There are more than 1500 television stations in the United States, and 99 percent of all households have at least one TV set, the average being four. Like radio, TV is close to being a universal medium of communications.

The first TV station went on the air in 1939, but TV grew very slowly during World War II. Afterward it spread rapidly; by 1960, 90 percent of all households had TVs. Three large networks initially dominated the industry: ABC, CBS, and NBC. The networks pay local affiliates to carry programs the networks offer. The affiliates, in turn, make advertising time available for the networks to sell. Of course, the profit that networks make from their advertising sales depends critically on the popularity of their shows—which is why ratings are such an important consideration when it comes to programming decisions.

General Eisenhower's presidential campaign was the first to take advantage of TV, producing simple commercials that are amusing when viewed today. But John F. Kennedy was the first candidate to elevate TV above the print medium.[16] During his successful 1960 presidential bid, the Massachusetts Catholic used West Virginia's primary as his opportunity to convince Democratic leaders that he could attract Protestant votes. He ran a documentary film on TV emphasizing his past as a war hero and Pulitzer Prize winner, which helped produce a primary victory and eventually led to the party nomination. He then defeated his Republican opponent, Vice President Richard Nixon, after a televised debate in which the handsome young senator showed that he could hold his own against an experienced statesman. Later, during his short presidency, Kennedy regularly held televised press conferences that enabled him to communicate directly with voters. Kennedy once commented to a reporter, "When we don't have to go through you bastards we can really get our story to the American people."[17]

When network TV reached its height, about 85 percent of stations were affiliated with ABC, CBS, or NBC. But the network system began to fray after government deregulated the cable industry in the 1970s. The percentage of households with cable increased from 20 percent in 1980 to 67 percent in 2000, while prime-time network programming lost more than a quarter of its audience. Ratings for the big-three evening news telecasts fell 30 percent.[18]

Critics have complained that the networks responded to falling ratings by neglecting their news responsibilities. Nonetheless, the networks still seek ways to cut costs. For example, executives in charge of ABC and the Cable News Network (CNN) nego-

tiated in 2002 to merge their newsroom operations, which could have saved $100 mil-
lion but elicited widespread opposition.[19] Still, the networks continue to draw an audience of about 36 million people on an average weekday.[20] Network TV is still the
largest single source of information available to Americans.

New Media

Cable and Satellite TV are familiar examples of the **new media**.[21] Although CNN and
ESPN may seem no different from ABC and CBS to young Americans today, they are
relatively new, both having been established in 1979. MSNBC—a joint venture
between Microsoft and NBC—and Fox News were both established in the late 1990s,
adding to the choices available on cable and satellite networks. Despite their youth,
these new media outlets exhibit strong growth, eating into the audience for traditional
news coverage. In 2001 the Fox News audience grew by over 100 percent.[22]

During the 1992 campaign, Bill Clinton and Ross Perot irritated the establishment
media by appearing on popular television programs, including those on cable stations.
Clinton played his saxophone on the *Arsenio Hall Show,* for example, and Perot virtually announced his candidacy on *Larry King Live!* President George H. W. Bush even
appeared on *MTV* to compete with Clinton's growing popularity. By the 2004 presidential election, candidates regularly scheduled light-hearted TV appearances. Dr. Phil
analyzed the candidates and their wives, Bush went fishing on the Outdoor Life
Network and Kerry rode a Harley Davidson into Jay Leno's studio.[23] Younger viewers,
meanwhile, often receive their political news laced heavily with satire by entertainers
such as Jon Stewart on Comedy Central. Stewart's fake news program, *The Daily Show,*
not only featured interviews with 2004 presidential contenders but also was specifically
invited to cover the Democratic National Convention.[24]

new media
Cable and satellite TV, fax, e-mail,
and the Internet—the media that
have grown out of the technological
advances of the past few decades.

Web News

News agencies maintain Web pages that allow Americans to get world news immediately rather than waiting for the scheduled broadcast or for delivery of the daily paper.

• *How does this faster news cycle change the needs and expectations of consumers? As this outlet grows as a source, will it change what gets covered?*

Democracy and the Internet

The *Internet* is the newest example of the new media. Technically speaking, the Internet may not yet qualify as an example of mass media—especially as regards political news. During the 2000 election, for example, only about half the American population had access to the Internet.[25] One survey during the height of the 2000 primary season found that only 11 percent of Internet users had ever visited a candidate's Web site, a figure far lower than the number who had seen a candidate on network TV's evening news, or even on CNN.[26]

But the political importance of the Web has been growing. Neither presidential candidate had an official Web site in 1992 whereas, by 2000, Web sites were standard in campaigns as far down as the local level. Use of the Web for raising money has grown rapidly in recent campaigns as well. After McCain's upset victory in the New Hampshire primary, though, online contributions soared—in one month he raised $5.6 million, a quarter of his total fund raising.[27] Online contributions became even more important during the Democratic primary for 2004. Vermont Governor Howard Dean particularly excelled at on-line fundraising; in the third quarter of 2003 alone he had raised $74 million off of the Internet.[28]

The political significance of the new media is that they alter the nature of political appeals. Network TV has a large, relatively diverse audience. It encourages politicians to make general appeals. In contrast, the new media allow politicians to target specialized audiences with tailored appeals. Most Web surfers apparently stick to the sorts of sites that mirror their own political views. Of the 757,000 or so people who visited a presidential candidate's Web site during the 2000 general election, for example, only 60,000 visited both.[29]

TABLE 9.1

CITIZEN USAGE OF THE NEWS MEDIA, 1998

Percent of all Americans who regularly . . .

Read daily newspaper	68
Watch local evening news	64
Listen to radio news	52
Watch network news	38
Watch news magazines (such as *60 Minutes*)	37
Watch morning network news	23
Watch CNN	23
Go online to read news	20
Read news magazines (such as *Newsweek*)	15
Listen to NPR	15
Watch TV tabloids	14
Listen to talk radio	13
Watch CNBC	12
Watch MSNBC	8
Listen to Rush Limbaugh	5
Watch PBS *NewsHour* with Jim Lehrer	4
Watch C-SPAN	4

SOURCE: Adapted from Pippa Norris, *A Virtuous Circle* (Cambridge: Cambridge University Press, 2000), p. 268.

Once again, an innovation in the media realm is altering the existing equilibrium between politicians and the media, this time apparently in favor of politicians. The new media give them a greater capacity to communicate to voters without having their messages edited or interpreted by the traditional mass media. The struggle for control of information continues. Table 9.1 offers a snapshot summary of the wide variety of news sources now used by Americans.

Government Regulation of the Electronic Media

One of the reasons why newspapers spread so rapidly in the United States is that freedom of the press was closer to being an absolute doctrine here than in other countries. Press freedoms were not so expansive for radio and TV, however. After the invention of radio, it soon became apparent that if they were left to their own devices, stations would broadcast on the same frequencies and interfere with each other. To deal with this problem, Congress in 1927 created the Federal Radio Commission, followed by the Federal Communications Commission in 1934. These commissions were charged with regulating the industry. They issued licenses to operate and specified the conditions of operation. When television became commercially viable, Congress added regulation of television to the FCC's responsibilities.

Because the government was allocating a limited public resource, granting it to some and denying it to others, the courts upheld the right of government to regulate what was said over the airwaves in ways that never would have been allowed in the case of print.

equal-time rule
Promulgated by the FCC, it required any station selling time to a candidate to sell time to other candidates at comparable rates.

And politicians certainly had incentives to regulate: After all, to be denied access to radio (and later to TV) could severely handicap their electoral chances. And to restrict access to some points of view could keep those points of view from receiving a fair public hearing. Thus, the legislation creating the FCC established an **equal-time rule** specifying that if a station sells time to a legally qualified candidate, it must sell time to all such candidates. Later the rule was expanded, so that when the networks carry the president's State of the Union speech, for example, they must carry a reply from the opposition as well. From 1949 to 1987, the FCC also enforced a fairness doctrine that required stations to devote a reasonable amount of time to matters of public importance and to air contrasting viewpoints on those matters. Eventually the doctrine also required stations to give public figures who were criticized during programming an opportunity to reply.

In the 1970s technological advances undercut the rationale for government regulation. The courts broke up the Bell Telephone monopoly of telecommunications, and new technologies such as fiber optics and microwave transmission created a virtually unlimited number of radio and television channels, easing fears that a few large networks could deny a hearing to issues or candidates they opposed. In 1987 a deregulation-minded FCC staffed by appointees of President Reagan repealed the fairness doctrine. And more deregulation was to come.

By the mid-1990s technological developments had made the 1930s structure of communications regulation hopelessly obsolete. The Congress overwhelmingly approved a major telecommunications act in 1996 that sought to replace government regulation with competition. It created a giant national market for telecommunications services. The new legislation abolished the local phone monopolies, but allowed the local companies to compete in offering long distance. Cable rates were deregulated, but telephone companies were permitted to offer video services. As a result of the act's removal of long-standing barriers among sectors of the industry, far-reaching change in the telecommunications field is expected in the years ahead. Some of today's new media may become old media.

Despite this general trend toward deregulation, recent years have seen a rise in the number of proposals for regulation of the Internet. Some people would like to censor content, preventing both adults and children from reaching pornographic, hate-filled, violent, or otherwise objectionable Web sites, for example—although the First Amendment's free-speech guarantees often hinder their efforts. Various others would like to regulate e-commerce. For example, many state governors are unhappy that purchases made over the Internet are often not subject to state sales tax, which has the effect of denying their states revenue and giving online merchants a competitive advantage—but as of 2004, attempts to tax Internet purchases have stagnated in Congress.

What Information Sources Do Americans Rely On?

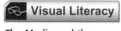

The Media and the American Public

Communication is a two-way street. No one can make people read newspapers, listen to radio, watch TV, or visit a home page.[30] Citizens are free to consume or ignore any message. These choices guide the information that becomes available, since media companies are profit-making enterprises. Their growth or decline should reflect the tastes of the popular audience.

Surveys show that TV supplanted newspapers as the public's principal source of information in the early 1960s. As shown in Figure 9.1, nearly 50 percent of Americans

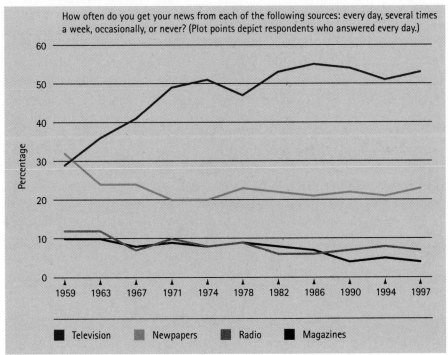

FIGURE 9.1

TV Is the Primary Source of News for Contemporary Americans

A majority of Americans watch TV news, and almost a majority rely exclusively on the television to learn about national politics.

SOURCE: Data are taken from the Roper Organization, *America's Watching: Public Attitudes Toward Television* (1997).

today rely *primarily* on television. A much smaller 20 percent rely primarily on news-papers, and the remaining 20 percent use both. A comparable percentage reports TV to be the most credible source of information.[31] In short, TV is America's dominant information provider.

Newspapers have slightly more influence over politics than over society as a whole.[32] In presidential campaigns, people rely more on TV than on newspapers by a margin of 3 to 1. But in statewide races for governor and senator, TV's edge is only 5 to 3. And in local election contests, newspapers have an edge over TV as the principal source of information. The national networks do not cover local races in small cities and towns, except under unusual circumstances. Whether newspapers can maintain their importance in this niche as local cable stations proliferate remains to be seen.

Individuals vary in their absorption of information.[33] Well-educated or older individuals are particularly likely to rely on newspapers, as are whites. Newspaper supporters argue that print is more informative than TV, but research fails to support that argument once the characteristics of the audience (such as education and race) are taken into account.[34] That is, people of comparable backgrounds tend to learn about the same amount, whether they rely on print or television.

Media Effects

People once feared the mass media as a great danger to democratic politics. The rapid spread of radio in the 1930s coincided with the rise of fascism in Europe. Some worried that this was more than coincidence. Before 1930, political leaders had communicated with constituencies indirectly, speaking and writing to lower-level leaders who in turn communicated with the grassroots. But demagogues like Hitler and Mussolini spoke directly to their audiences, sparking fears that radio created a "mass society" of lonely individuals susceptible to charismatic hate mongers.[35]

selective perception
Tendency to discount information that is inconsistent with one's prior predispositions in favor of information consistent with what one already believes.

Stimulated by such concerns, researchers conducted numerous studies of the media's ability to persuade. Contrary to expectations, research on the effects of mass communication turned up negative results. Americans, at least, were remarkably resistant to propaganda; media messages seldom altered the audience's views. Listeners apparently engaged in **selective perception,** absorbing information consistent with their predispositions and discounting the rest. Thus, exposure to communications tended to reinforce what people already believed.[36]

By 1960 many scholars accepted the idea that mass media had a minimal impact on American public opinion.[37] Younger generations of researchers took a new look at the subject, however, after the rapid spread of TV. This newer research—which took off in the 1980s and has continued to the present—identified important media effects, subtler than the kind of mass persuasion earlier studies had sought to document.

Agenda Setting

Public-opinion scholar Bernard Cohen argues that the media may not tell people *what* to think but do tell people what to think *about*.[38] The media can induce people to focus on an issue or problem by emphasizing it and whipping up concern. The media set the agenda, even if they do not determine how issues get resolved.

Catastrophes in Third World countries, for example, largely go unnoticed unless the media—particularly television—turn their attention to such events. Famine struck

Ethiopia in 1984, resulting in numerous front-page articles in powerful U.S. newspapers such as the *New York Times* and *Washington Post*. The Associated Press (AP) wire service carried 228 stories.[39] But it was not until television stations beamed heartrending footage into their living rooms that Americans became aware of the problem and supported governmental efforts to help.[40] Similar responses followed media coverage of tragedies in a series of countries around the world—including Somalia, Rwanda, and Kosovo. Media analysts have even given government responses like these a nickname, the **CNN effect,** after the tendency for a problem to be addressed once the Cable News Network covers it.

Agenda setting is well documented, although much of the evidence is not conclusive.[41] Say unemployment rises, the media focus heavily on unemployment, and people in growing numbers begin to think of unemployment as a major national problem. Is this agenda setting, or are the media and the people both responding to the same real conditions? Some careful studies conclude that the independent impact of the media has been exaggerated; astute government officials use the media to place problems on the national and international agendas.[42] A study of failed attempts to pass national health care plans concluded that "peaks in the volume and substantive focus of media reporting coincided with upsurges in discussions of real-world developments and fierce political debate over policy reforms."[43] Nevertheless, experimental studies that raise viewer concern about subjects *not* high on the national agenda have been able to provide some evidence of agenda setting.[44]

CNN effect
Purported ability of TV to raise a foreign tragedy to national prominence by broadcasting vivid pictures.

agenda setting
Occurs when the media affect the issues and problems people think about, even if the media do not determine what positions people adopt.

Priming and Framing

In the spring of 1991, following an impressive American victory in the Gulf War, President George H. W. Bush's approval ratings soared, reaching unprecedented levels. Journalists turned to other stories when the war ended, though. Gradually, Bush's ratings became dependent on the nation's economic performance, which voters judged negatively.[45] He lost the 1992 election to Bill Clinton. Similarly, Bush's son enjoyed soaring popularity ratings after 9/11 terrorist attacks. During the war in Iraq, though, media coverage dwelt on the administration's failings—including an inability to find "weapons of mass destruction" supposedly possessed by Iraq's government. Bush's ratings dropped steadily until the 2004 presidential campaign heated up, although he survived his reelection bid. These large shifts in public opinion are striking reflections of **priming**—altering in the standards that citizens use to evaluate their leaders.

priming
Occurs when the media affect the standards people use to evaluate political figures or the severity of a problem.

By what they choose to cover, the media can prime citizens to use some standards rather than others.[46] Obviously, the media do not have full control over which criteria Americans use to evaluate their presidents. War pushes everything else off the agenda of public opinion: All other concerns seem minor when husbands and wives and sons and daughters are in danger. Thus, both the media and the public react to the reality of war. Similarly, after war ends, both turn to other concerns.

Framing and priming are related notions.[47] In Chapter 5 we explained that Americans tend to shift their opinions on abortion depending on how pollsters frame the question. How issues are framed shapes more than just survey results, however; it also molds how the public thinks about issues more generally. For example, if crime is framed as a problem that presidents can and should do something about, it is more likely to have a political impact than if it is framed as an uncontrollable by-product of social breakdown. During the 2004 campaign, John Kerry attacked President Bush for allowing corporations to shift jobs overseas. He was attempting to frame the issue of global trade in a way that reflected negatively on the president. Inducing people to think along certain lines rather than others can affect their positions on issues and their evaluations of public officials.

framing
Occurs when the media induce people to think about an issue from one standpoint rather than from others.

Socialization

The *New Yorker* once published a famous cartoon in which a man sits up in bed and comments, with surprise, "I went to bed a Democrat, but woke up a Republican."[48] There is little evidence the media can cause such political conversions, at least not in large numbers. By setting the agenda, priming, and framing, media organizations influence people's views—but the effects usually are subtle.

For this reason, many critics worry less about media persuasion than about the role of media in socializing "impressionable youngsters." They anxiously document ways in which the mass media appear to distort reality—or at least to emphasize the seamy side of human nature—not only in news coverage but also in entertainment programs. The Henry J. Kaiser Family Foundation, for example, established a survey of sex on TV. Their 2003 results indicated that one in seven shows either depicted or strongly implied an act of sexual intercourse—and all but perhaps a third of shows aired between 7 AM and 11 PM contained some kind of sexual content.[49]

A variety of groups, both conservative and liberal, deride the omnipresence of violent behavior on television. A study by the Parents Television Council claimed that the six biggest broadcast networks aired 534 separate violent acts during their prime-time programming in early November 2002. Most of the networks had doubled the violence from four years earlier.[50] Documenting such developments in American entertainment, *Newsweek* proclaimed "The Death of Family TV" on a 2004 cover.

It is not clear how sex and violence influence American politics. They may help account for widespread concern with crime or for the increasing acceptance Americans show toward sexual practices once considered deviant. Such programming also may undermine the sense of "community" in modern life by encouraging more television watching,[51] since sex and violence seem to attract more viewers. The only obvious political impact of controversial programming is that it spurs groups who demand more broadcasting regulation. The FCC received more than 240,000 complains about radio and TV programs in 2003. Members of Congress angrily scheduled a hearing in 2004 after the Super Bowl halftime show let viewers glimpse singer Janet Jackson's exposed breast.[52]

Some media messages may have more direct political ramifications. Government agencies come across rather poorly in popular entertainment. The renegade hero may appear on the federal payroll—such as counterterrorist agent Jack Bauer on the TV series *24* or FBI agents Mulder and Scully on the syndicated *X-Files* program—but the leadership is usually corrupt and almost always stands in the way of justice. Generally speaking, media entertainment tends to mock or disparage authority figures, a portrayal that can influence political attitudes—including the level of trust in government.[53]

Scholars have long worried about the way in which mass media portray minorities, especially African Americans. One study that probed the network news found that journalists regularly talked to black sources about crime, sports, or entertainment—but almost never about elections, economics, or foreign affairs. A related analysis of the top movies of 1996 indicated that 9 out of 10 black female characters used vulgar language, compared to fewer than a fifth of the white women. More than half of the black women committed acts of physical violence; just over a tenth of the white females did. Such portrayals reinforce negative racial stereotypes.[54] Of course, programs regularly cast blacks in positive roles—as capable doctors, artists, attorneys, or criminal profilers. Movies such as *Bedazzled* and *Bruce Almighty* have even cast black actors as God. But these "all-knowing" characters may not encourage white viewers to identify with them. They're only "means to the white characters' salvation," one cultural scholar points out, "and not ends in themselves."[55]

How Strong Are Media Effects?

Effects like agenda setting, priming, and framing depend on both the characteristics of the audience and the nature of the information. People who are uninterested in and uninformed about politics are most susceptible to agenda setting. For example, political independents differ from partisans. Their concerns shift from one issue to another with the intensity of media coverage. Partisans, on the other hand, are inclined to think in terms of issues at the core of their party's concerns.[56]

The characteristics of the information being communicated are at least as important as the characteristics of the people receiving it. When the problem or event is far away—well beyond personal experience—the mass media provide the only information available. Their influence diminishes when information is closer to home and people have some personal basis for arriving at opinions.[57] The Vietnam War example introducing this chapter offers one illustration. The media eventually helped produce a backlash against President Lyndon Johnson for his administration's conduct of the war, about which journalists provided just about the only information available.[58] With the antiwar protests, though, TV was showing behavior about which most viewers held strong opinions. Thus the media *can* have a major impact on public opinion, but *whether* they do so depends on both whom they are reaching and what they are covering.

Media Biases

Are the Media Biased?

Modern journalists purport to be objective. They are supposed to report events and describe conflicts accurately so that voters can make informed judgments. If reporters and editors usually lived up to this ideal, then media effects would not be much cause for concern. But news organizations and other media corporations represent an important player in the political system, essentially an institution with its own interests, values, and operating procedures. Many observers believe that the media do skew the news. The most common charge is that the media show political bias, but academic critics believe that other sorts of bias may be even more serious.

Ideological Bias

Journalists clearly are more Democratic than the population at large. Majorities of journalists even supported George McGovern in 1972 and Walter Mondale in 1984, whose Republican opponents won by landslides. More recently, a survey of Washington bureau chiefs and congressional correspondents reported that in 1992, 89 percent voted for Clinton, compared to 43 percent of the electorate.[59] Journalists also hold views that are more liberal than those of other college-educated professionals, especially on issues such as abortion, drugs, crime, the death penalty, feminism, and gay rights.[60]

But how strongly do such beliefs affect the news? Conservatives often complain about the "liberal media." Even a respected nonpartisan election analyst, Charlie Cook, comments that "People who don't believe that there is a liberal or Democratic bias in the national media are kidding themselves."[61] Some studies do find evidence of partisan bias. For example, a team of researchers carefully watched tapes of the network evening news programs broadcast during the 1984 campaign. Their aim was to evaluate the **spin**—the positive or negative slant—that reporters and anchors put on their reports. They found that President Reagan got 10 seconds of bad spin for every second of good spin. In contrast, Democratic candidate Walter Mondale had a 3 to 2 ratio of good to bad spin.[62] On a less serious note, a study of the jokes told by late-night TV talk show hosts Johnny Carson and David Letterman during the 1988 campaign found that Republicans were skewered twice as often as Democrats.[63] As for the 2000 election, by mid-September George W. Bush had been the butt of 50 percent more late-night jokes than Al Gore.[64]

Although journalists do deviate from objectivity and Republicans suffer more than Democrats, lapses are not as common as critics imply. Newspaper readers do not perceive consistently liberal viewpoints.[65] More than three-fourths of the presidential election coverage on television in 1984 had no spin at all. More recently, a study of newspaper, television, and Web coverage of the 2000 campaign during October found that Al Gore received significantly more negative coverage than George W. Bush.[66] The media tend to be hard on incumbents, losers, and those caught up in scandals even when they are Democrats—as illustrated by the media-fueled scandals that plagued Bill Clinton from his initial presidential campaign until after he had left the White House. Similarly, late-night TV hosts focus on whoever offers the best material.

spin
The positive or negative slant that reporters or anchors put on their reports.

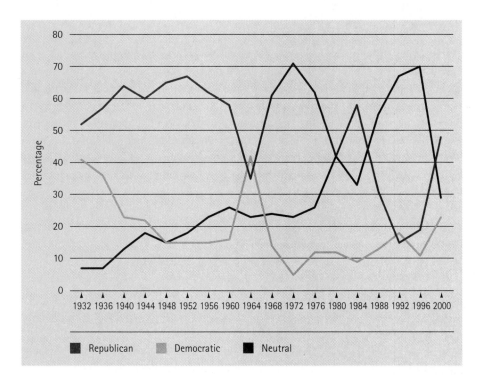

FIGURE 9.2

Newspapers Endorse Republican Presidential Candidates More Often than Democratic Candidates

SOURCE: Harold Stanley and Richard Niemi, *Vital Statistics of American Politics, 2001–2002* (Washington, DC: CQ Press, 2001), pp. 194–195.

They may be less vocal, but critics on the left of the political spectrum also charge that the media are ideologically biased—only they see a conservative slant. Whatever the personal views of rank-and-file journalists, their publishers tend to endorse Republicans, as shown in Figure 9.2.[67] Since 1930, only Lyndon Johnson and Bill Clinton have received more newspaper endorsements than their Republican opponents, although the larger urban newspapers are much more Democratic (counts for 2004 are not yet available). Journalists work for profit-making enterprises reliant on corporate advertising. They often collect impressive salaries and enjoy generous retirement benefits. Media celebrities also attract generous honoraria from corporate interests who invite them to give speeches, leading critics to call them "buckrakers" rather than muckrakers. All of these circumstances exert a conservative pull.[68]

Moreover, the weakening of the dominance of the big-three networks should reduce any existing liberal bias. In particular, media observers generally agree that the increasingly popular Fox News program leans to the right; some critics have attacked it as a propaganda outlet for Republicans.[69] Local news and public-affairs programs are more likely to reflect local sentiments, so they can be more conservative than network news operations headquartered in New York, Washington, and Los Angeles. Some cable channels feature programs produced by conservative and evangelical groups. Talk radio has a conservative slant. The Internet is open to all points of view, and libertarians are especially well represented there. Columnist John Leo even notes the rise of comedy that showcases "anti-liberal humor," including *Saturday Night Live* veteran Dennis Miller, Comedy Central's Colin Quinn, and the irreverent cable TV cartoon *South Park*.[70] In short, as communications outlets grow, mass media will be more open to alternative points of view than were the airwaves in the past. Other forms of bias may be more serious than the ideological kind.

Selection Bias

Periodically, frustrated citizens write to newspaper editors to complain that all their newspaper ever prints is bad news. Why not more good news? The answer is that to a considerable extent, the media *define* news as bad news.[71] A government program that works well is not news; one that is mismanaged or a failure *is* news. An elected official who is doing a good job is not newsworthy; one who is incompetent or corrupt is. People working hard and contributing to their communities is not news; one sociopath who runs amok is. Far more pervasive than ideological bias is a bias toward the negative in the media. An emphasis on the negative is a kind of **selection principle;** reporters and editors give a skewed perception of reality based on the way they make decisions.

Media critic Larry Sabato argues that the negative tone of the media has become much more prominent in recent decades. He contends that presidents from Franklin Roosevelt to John Kennedy enjoyed the support of a press with a "lapdog" mentality. Johnson and Nixon were subjected to far greater scrutiny by a press with a "watchdog" mentality. Succeeding presidents, he maintains, suffer mean treatment from a press with a "junkyard dog" mentality.[72] Some observers believe that the negative tone of press coverage has contributed to the increased cynicism of the American public about politics and government.[73] The claim is that politics today is no worse than in previous eras—perhaps it is better—but that media treatment makes things *seem* worse.

Another selection effect is that "news" must be new, must be exciting, and must be unusual. Gradual developments and persistent conditions do not lend themselves to the kind of hit-and-run coverage favored by the contemporary media. A crisis does. Senator Jay Rockefeller of West Virginia learned this point to his dismay in 1998 when he tried to hold a press conference on health-care reform and instead faced a deluge of questions about a Clinton administration sex scandal. Exasperated, he asked, "Is there anybody here that just, almost for the practice of it, has a question about the health care of children?"[74]

The media look for heroes and villains, not for abstract social developments. This bias is particularly characteristic of TV, which is even more fast paced than print. A frequently heard maxim to describe local TV news is "If it bleeds, it leads." TV needs dramatic events, colorful personalities, bitter conflicts, short and snappy comments (sound bites), and above all, compelling pictures. The result can be insufficient treatment of stories that do not fit the needs of the media and distorted treatment of stories to make them fit those needs.[75] For example, journalists lionized Private Jessica Lynch of West Virginia after she was injured, captured, and then rescued during the war in Iraq (to the point that critics charged reporters were helping the U.S. military fabricate "shamelessly trumped-up claims"). They paid far less attention to other members of the Army's 507th Maintenance Company, some of whom died, some of whom fought heroically, and some of whom (including another young woman, Shoshana Johnson) spent two weeks longer in captivity.

Numerous observers have pointed to such selection biases as a factor in the largest (in financial terms) policy debacle in American history—the Savings and Loan (S&L) disaster of the 1980s, with an estimated price tag of $200 billion.[76] Democrats and Republicans, Congress and the executive—all share the blame. As early as 1981, accountants, prominent economists, and a top government regulator began to issue

selection principle
Rule of thumb according to which stories with certain characteristics are chosen over stories without those characteristics.

Calvin and Hobbes

As the public gets more reports of scandal and problems, some worry that the electorate grows more cynical.

• *Does excessive coverage of scandal "packaged as a soap opera and horse race" lead the public to distrust government and politicians?*

warnings that the S&L industry was going bankrupt. The media provided only minimal coverage. Why? For one thing, the story was about financial policies that reporters found uninteresting. As one journalist commented, "It was a 'numbers' story, not a 'people' story."[77] Also, the issue was complex. Many reporters were ill-equipped to understand it, let alone to distill it into a short, simple story. The problem was particularly acute for TV, because initially the crisis offered few interesting pictures. Not until housing developments were being auctioned off for a song, S&L executives indicted, and members of Congress investigated did the media have the kind of story (and pictures) that it liked.

By the time the government started closing insolvent S&Ls, many had been operating recklessly for years, secure in the knowledge that their losses would be covered by taxpayers. Media neglect helped add to this cost. When journalists finally did pick up the story, they distorted it. They emphasized the rare cases of fraud and corruption, even though most of the problem came from the ordinary operation of the political process: generous campaign contributions, corporate lobbying, favorable legal changes, and regulators who did not watch the industry closely.[78] Thus, the media even missed the opportunity to articulate a useful lesson that might help avoid such a problem in the future.

Some critics charge that the media desire for heroism and action—along with their desire for popularity—especially distorts the coverage of war and foreign affairs. Such criticism is not new. As early as 1966, one detractor wrote:

> Our remaining correspondents fly from earthquake to famine, from insurrection to massacre. They land running, as we were all taught to do, and they provide surprisingly good coverage of whatever is immediately going on. . . . [But] we miss anticipation, thought, and meaning. Our global coverage has become a comic book: ZAP! POW! BANG-BANG.[79]

However, the recent war in Iraq has increased concerns about whether American journalists are "shirking their duty" to keep an eye on government and instead becoming boosters of military aggression. "Regardless of their own views on the war," according to Mark Weisbrot, co-director of the nonpartisan Center for Economic and Policy Research, "American journalists became the Bush administration's major means of promoting it." The director-general of the British Broadcasting Corporation, meanwhile, expressed his shock at "gung-ho" war coverage, charging that reporters had "wrapped themselves in the American flag and swapped impartiality for patriotism." Nonetheless, news coverage of the war on terrorism apparently improved public perceptions of the media.[80]

INTERNATIONAL COMPARISON

Al Jazeera—Questionable Sources?

As Americans tuned in during the fall of 2001 to follow the war on terrorism, they were introduced to the "The CNN of the Arab World": Al Jazeera.[a] In early 2001 Thomas Friedman of the *New York Times* had described Al Jazeera the "freest" cable network in the Arab world even though it received significant support from the government of Qatar. Aggressive marketing, lively debate and—according to Friedman—"uncensored" news stories attracted large blocs of viewers. Al Jazeera not only styled itself after Western news organizations, but actually was allied with CNN to provide content.[b]

After the terrorist attacks of September 2001, Al Jazeera began providing CNN with video footage of Al Qaeda training camps. The network's most controversial contribution, however, was a broadcast of Osama Bin Laden speaking in a very threatening manner toward the decadent West. Secretary of State Colin Powell denounced the Al-Jazeera's "vitriolic, irresponsible" statements. National Security Adviser Condoleezza Rice asked U.S. networks not to broadcast Bin Laden speeches.[c] Originally heralded for its unprecedented access to news sources unavailable to American media outlets, the station increasingly faced criticism because of the perception that it had become too closely tied to those same sources. Both Middle Eastern and Western governments criticized the media outlet as biased and potentially dangerous. The First Amendment means that little can be done about Al Jazeera—besides appealing to good taste—in the U.S. context. But Islamic culture, unencumbered by a tradition of protecting dissent, may be less kind to the organization.

Al Jazeera responded to this criticism by holding back video footage of Bin Laden. But its partner CNN obtained and broadcast the footage anyway (the two organizations have since severed their relationship).[d] Al Jazeera pushed the boundaries of acceptable news coverage in the Middle East, despite its reliance on government money, but continuing controversy over the station's editorial slant illustrates how news coverage depends in part on the information sources available to journalists.

[a]T. Straus, "The CNN of the Arab World," *Alternet*.org, October 26, 2001.
[b]T. Friedman, "The Fast Eat the Slow," *New York Times,* February 2, 2001.
[c]Straus, "The CNN of the Arab World."
[d]Associated Press, "Arab Network Cuts Ties with CNN," February 1, 2002.

Professional Bias

A third kind of media bias arises from the demands of the journalism profession today. A few journalists are experts who work specific "beats"—the business reporter, education reporter, health reporter, Supreme Court reporter, and so on. But most reporters and journalists are generalists who lack specific substantive expertise. They operate on tight deadlines and start from scratch on many stories. Thus, on subjects more complex than scandals and conflicts, they are dependent on experts and other outside sources for information and interpretation. Ironically, despite the familiar image of the investigative reporter, studies find that reporters uncover only a small fraction of the scandals they report—probably less than one-quarter.[81] Government agencies reveal the lion's share, and they generally do so officially, not through surreptitious "leaks." Reliance on government sources can make a big difference in news coverage and helps explain why U.S. news often differs sharply from the information available in other countries. (See the accompanying International Comparison.)

Moreover, as journalists themselves recognize, the news media have increased their emphasis on entertainment.[82] Especially in the case of TV, looks and personalities are more important today than a generation ago. With the growth of the new media, competitive pressures are greater than ever and have resulted in a race to the bottom, as network news becomes more like infotainment (a mixture of news and entertainment) and major newspapers become more like tabloids.

The lack of internal expertise and the competitive pressure for ratings and sales contribute to an unattractive feature of modern political coverage: "pack journalism," in which reporters unanimously decide something is the big story and attack it like

TABLE 9.2

EVALUATIONS OF THE MEDIA HAVE WORSENED

News Organizations Generall . . .

	1985 %	1999 %	2002 %
Are moral	54	40	39
Are immoral	13	38	36
Care about people they report on	35	21	30
Don't care	48	67	55
Are highly professional	72	52	49
Are not professional	11	32	31
Protect democracy★	54	45	60
Hurt democracy★	23	38	19
Care about how good a job they do★	79	69	78
Don't care★	11	22	14

★ Data are derived from 2001 survey data.
SOURCE: The Pew Research Center for the People and the Press.

wolves tearing apart wounded prey or sharks engaging in a feeding frenzy.[83] Comedian Jon Stewart prefers a different image: Small children playing soccer, all clumped together and thoughtlessly chasing a ball.[84] Normal people, observing such behavior, are puzzled by the media's pack behavior—but to journalists under great competitive pressure, there is safety in numbers. One can hardly be faulted for working on the same story as other prominent journalists. Far better to focus on what turns out to be an overblown, inconsequential story than to "run the risk of going down in history as 'the reporter who missed the next Watergate.'"[85] Indeed, there is every indication that the "pack" mentality extends to editorial offices, where each news show or newspaper fears missing the "next big thing."

Prospects for Change

However justified, criticisms of the media's coverage of politics and government miss an important point. The news media in the United States are not part of the public education system. Rather, most are private, profit-making enterprises. As one journalist commented, "What few people recognize is that the purpose of the media is not to educate, it is to impress—to make an impression. There isn't the time or space to educate."[86]

As to complaints that their coverage falls short of what many would like to see, defenders of the media generally respond that they try to provide the kind of coverage people want, to the point of using focus groups and other measures of reader interest to serve the audience better.[87] Nonetheless, Americans are not happy with media behavior today. As Table 9.2 shows, popular evaluations of the media have declined sharply since the mid-1980s. Growing percentages of people believe that the media are unprofessional, uncaring, immoral, and even harmful to democracy—although media evaluations have improved during the war on terrorism.

Furthermore, media representatives have always claimed that they are more than profit-making businesses. They claim to provide an essential public service. When they

Comparing News Media

publish sensitive or private information, they justify their behavior with more than a sprinkling of righteousness—using weighty terms such as "the public's right to know" or "the free flow of information in the marketplace of ideas." Such an exalted self-image may carry with it the responsibility to give the public what it needs as well as what it wants. Serving as guardians of the First Amendment may require more than 30-second sound bites.

Perhaps the main hope of critics is that media executives may underestimate the average American citizen. During the 1992 presidential campaign, people in the media were stunned by the ratings earned by Ross Perot's "infomercials"—as many as 10 million households tuned in.[88] TV producers defend sound-bite journalism with the observation that the average voter has a short attention span, but Perot treated voters as intelligent adults and held the interest of many for 30 minutes with lengthy expositions accompanied by charts and figures!

The Media and Electoral Politics

The mass media play an important role in democratic politics. Ideally, they transmit information about problems and issues, helping voters make intelligent choices among the candidates who compete for their votes. Many critics feel that the general biases discussed earlier cause media coverage of elections to fall far short of the ideal.

Campaign Coverage

Nowhere do critics of the mass media find more to criticize than in the coverage of political campaigns. Numerous studies report that the various media biases combine to produce campaign coverage that is characterized by sins of both omission and commission (see Chapter 10).

The media provide little coverage of policy issues: the nature of social and economic problems, the contrasts among the programs that candidates advocate, and so forth. Instead, critics charge, the media devote too much attention to "character" issues that have little to do with the ability of the candidates to govern. Thus, the press dwells on whether President Bush dodged military service as a young man or whether Senator Kerry earned his military commendations in Vietnam. Such matters have some relevance, to be sure, and may provide some indication of how a candidate would govern, but reporting on such matters should not crowd out more substantive election coverage.

Not only do the media concentrate on candidates' character at the expense of genuine policy and performance issues, but their interest primarily stems from a wish to handicap each race. Campaign coverage usually focuses on an election as though it were a horse race, reporting which candidate is leading, which candidate is dropping back, which one is coming up on the rail, what the latest polls say, who got what endorsement, and how a change in campaign personnel will affect public perceptions of the candidate. Even when the candidate announces a proposal or issue position, it is evaluated as a tactical move that can affect the candidate's standing in the larger horse race.

This tendency toward "horse-race coverage" has become much more pronounced over the past generation, as the attention devoted to substance has declined.[89] Increasingly, journalists interpret what candidates say rather than allowing candidates to speak for themselves. One study that compared network newscasts in 1968 with those in 1988 found that the average sound bite for presidential candidates who appeared on the news had fallen from 42 seconds to less than 10.[90] Although the media consciously tried to

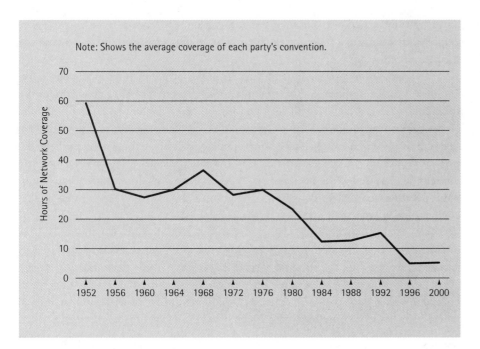

Note: Shows the average coverage of each party's convention.

FIGURE 9.3

The Networks Increasingly Ignore the National Political Conventions

SOURCE: Adapted by Sam Abrams from Harold W. Stanley and Richard G. Niemi, *Vital Statistics of American Politics 2001–2002,* 6th ed. (Washington, DC: CQ Press, 2001), p. 191.

make sound bites longer after 1988, the situation has improved little, and candidates still do not get enough time to explain their positions on complex issues. Modern candidates adapt to media needs and practices by simplifying their appeals accordingly.

Observers of contemporary political campaigns are not the only ones who are critical of media coverage. The candidates themselves are critical—so much so that they are finding ways to get around the contemporary media. As noted earlier, they have started appearing on popular television programs. They also make themselves available more frequently to state and local journalists. Reporters of national stature complain that the candidates are insulating themselves from the hard questioning of seasoned journalists, but the candidates seem to enjoy the opportunity to talk about issues rather than the trivia that often dominates national news coverage. The growth of alternative news sources also gives today's candidates the means to act on such sentiments.

The Conventions

Before presidential candidates were chosen in the primaries, national conventions were important political events. Party leaders came together, made deals, hammered out a platform, nominated candidates, and (if successful) left with a unified party prepared to battle the opposition. In recognition of the importance of the conventions, CBS and NBC provided gavel-to-gavel coverage from 1956 to 1976 and regularly assigned their top anchors and reporters to the events.

The process for nominating presidential candidates stabilized in 1972, removing the element of surprise from national party conventions (see Chapter 8). Since then, the conventions have not been nearly so important as in earlier eras, and media coverage has dropped accordingly (see Figure 9.3). As magazine writer Hendrik Hertzberg dryly put it, the "conventions are no longer troubled by the problem of being excessively interesting."[91] The parties now treat the conventions as huge infomercials in an attempt to take advantage of their diminishing time on the screen. Attractive speakers are slotted for prime time, and the entire convention schedule is arranged with the media in mind.

The parties showcase their candidates in hopes of producing a post-convention "bounce" upward in the polls. Recent conventions that produced large bounces for the candidates were the 2004 Republican convention (for President Bush) and the 2000 Democratic convention (for Vice President Gore).[92] Media coverage is a double-edged sword, however. If coverage emphasizes a divided party or unpopular elements of the party, it will cause the candidate to drop in the polls. The 1968 Chicago Democratic convention discussed at the beginning of this chapter is a classic example. Similarly, in 1992 Pat Buchanan gave an aggressive speech to the Republican convention that turned off many moderates.

The conventions probably will be even less important in the future. As one commentator observed after the 1996 events, "the more the party managers tried to package their message to please television, the less the major networks were interested."[93] In 1996 Ted Koppel and his *Nightline* team abandoned the Republican convention after two days, the networks cut coverage to about an hour a night, and ratings were off 25 percent from 1992. In 2000 MTV provided more convention coverage than the three major networks combined, and ABC pushed its coverage almost entirely to a program called *NBC News Now* available on its digital channels.[94] The networks appear to be abandoning convention coverage.

The Presidential Debates

One of the high points of modern presidential campaigns is the series of debates between the two—and sometimes three—major candidates. No other campaign events earn such high ratings. In fact, more people watch the debates than vote.

The first televised debates were held during the 1960 campaign between candidates Richard Nixon and John Kennedy. One of the surprising findings in studies of the debates was that people who listened to them on the radio evaluated Nixon's performance more favorably than people who watched them on TV, an indication that visual images could have impacts different from the words with which they were associated.[95] No debates were held in 1964, 1968, or 1972, but they have been held in every election since then. Although the format and arrangements usually are matters of considerable controversy, debates now appear to be an institutionalized part of presidential campaigns.

Studies show that performance in the debates can sway the undecided voter. For example, in 1984 President Reagan appeared tired and confused in his first debate with Walter Mondale. His unexpectedly poor performance raised the issue of his age (then 73) and resulted in a slight drop in the polls. Knowing how important the next encounter was, Reagan came in alert, prepared, and full of good humor. He dispelled the concerns raised in the first debate and gained 4 points in the polls.[96] As in campaign coverage generally, the first question the media raise about debates is "Who won?"

Most observers agreed that President Bush blew the first debate in 2004, turning what might have been an easy race into a neck-and-neck battle. Senator John Kerry failed to press his debating advantage in the two clashes that followed—Bush held his own in the town-hall format of the second debate and Kerry seemed too tired and ill-focused to sway voters in the final showdown.

Media Coverage of Government

Media coverage of government exhibits problems and biases analogous to those evident in media coverage of campaigns. From the standpoint of the mass media, much of the routine work of government is dull; hence the media focus on what they consider more exciting.

Emphasis on the President (and Other Personalities)

The president is a single individual with personality and character. Naturally, then, he (and, one day, she) will be inherently more interesting than a collectivity like Congress or an abstraction like the bureaucracy. The president receives the lion's share of the evening news coverage.[97] And not only does Congress play second fiddle in terms of media coverage, but coverage of the Congress has declined in recent decades.[98] The problem, of course, is that the president is only one part of the government, one with fairly limited powers (see Chapter 13). Thus, the media prime citizens to focus on the president to a degree that is out of proportion to his powers and responsibilities.

The exception to this generalization is one that proves the rule. For six months after the 1994 elections, the media virtually forgot about President Clinton as pack journalists turned their attention to House Speaker Newt Gingrich and the new Republican majority in Congress. For once, the media could represent Congress via a single personality. Now that the Republican leadership in Congress lacks a colorful personality like Gingrich, the media's former neglect of the institution has returned.

This focus of the media on personalities seems to be a universal tendency. It is similar to building military coverage around sympathetic war heroes or building sports coverage around professional superstars. An effective governmental team, like a winning sports team or a successful military unit, requires teamwork—but the media find individual heroics and failures to be more compelling stories. Unfortunately, in framing coverage in terms of individuals, the media probably discourage political entrepreneurs from building coalitions—and instead encourage them to promote themselves, to grandstand, to "hog the ball." Moreover, such media coverage primes citizens to think about government in terms of the heroic exploits and tragic failures of individuals rather than in terms of institutions and processes that are operating effectively or poorly.[99]

Emphasis on Conflict

Every time politicians make a controversial comment, they are assured of media coverage. Indeed, politicians who are more likely to make the kind of inflammatory remarks the media love, and to offer them up in convenient sound bites, can expect constant media attention.

In 1995, when President Clinton and Speaker Gingrich appeared on the same platform in New Hampshire and engaged in a mature discussion, citizens were receptive. Even the two rivals seemed to enjoy it. Journalists found it dull. How could they report an intelligent conversation? They would have been much more comfortable if the Speaker had leveled a serious charge or criticized the president personally in a 10-second sound bite.

Ironically, the journalistic preference for conflict can discourage politicians from doing anything really interesting. When reporters learn of an innovative proposal, the necessity to portray conflict leads them to search out the idea's likely enemies and

Rummey Under Fire
The media's taste for conflict means that congressional hearings get wide coverage. Here, Defense Secretary Donald Rumsfeld faces tough questions on military policies in Iraq.

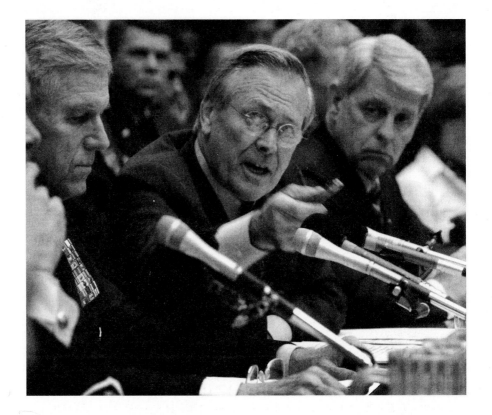

trumpet their hostile reaction. As a result, journalists "often lead the chorus of criticism of anyone who tries to upset the apple cart. In so doing, they implicitly side with the interest groups and old-line politicians whose prerogatives are being challenged." The clamor of opposition immediately threatens public perception of the proposal, but also threatens the person who floated it. The would-be reformer is likely to be portrayed "as naïve and politically unsophisticated" for taking the chance.[100]

Journalists especially like conflict when it revolves around some kind of scandal. The same study that found coverage of Congress to be declining also found that the focus of coverage had changed. Policy stories outnumbered scandal stories by 13 to 1 from 1972 to the mid-1980s, but since then the ratio has plunged to 3 to 1.[101] The Clinton administration faced repeated scandals, some sexual and some financial— culminating in incessant reports of Clinton's intimate relationship with a White House intern named Monica Lewinsky. George W. Bush, meanwhile, faced a number of controversies that approached scandal-like proportions, including charges that his administration falsely manufactured reasons for going to war in Iraq and that his polit- ical advisers leaked the name of a CIA operative because her husband had criticized the war effort.[102] News that military police had tortured detainees in Iraq's Abu Ghraib prison also tarnished the Bush administration's image. Given the media obsession with scandal and conflict, it is no wonder that politicians often try to tell journalists as little as possible. In 1998, White House spokesman Barry Toiv joked about this defense mechanism once when he was late for a news briefing: "It's not easy getting up here and saying nothing. It takes a lot of preparation."[103]

Emphasis on the Negative

Media on the lookout for conflicts, scandals, and mistakes naturally emphasize the negative. What government does well is less newsworthy than what government does badly. Quiet compromises that improve public policies are less newsworthy than noisy arguments that accomplish nothing. Thus, network coverage of Congress has gone from highly negative to almost completely negative. According to one count, 3 of every 4 evaluations of Congress were negative in 1972, and that ratio rose to 9 of 10 by 1992.[104] Has Congress become that much worse, or has the change been inside the media? As mentioned earlier, even entertainment shows now portray government officials more negatively than they did a generation ago.[105]

Exaggerated Concern with the Press

Because the press has become the principal link between citizens and their government, elected officials often lose sight of the people. Reflecting his concern about that link, President Franklin Delano Roosevelt established a press relations office in the White House, recognizing that an increasingly professional media required an equally professional political response—and every president has tried to manage the press since FDR. According to a former Clinton White House official,

> When I was there, absolutely nothing was more important than figuring out what the news was going to be. . . . There is no such thing as a substantive discussion that is not shaped or dominated by how it is going to play in the press. . . . When you put together a press that is only interested in "horse race" and "inside baseball" and a White House staff that is interested only in the press, you've got the worst of both worlds.[106]

Chapter Summary

The mass media are less than two centuries old. TV has superseded print as the most important form of mass communication—but recent technological developments have produced new media, such as cable TV and the Internet, that are weakening the traditional broadcast system. Nevertheless, the growing number of media options has not produced a comparable diversity in media voices. Mergers have consolidated mass communications into a smaller number of hands, including giant corporate conglomerates.

Although the mass media can have important effects on public opinion, such effects are not automatic. For example, where people have strong predispositions, the effects of the mass media are limited. Also, where people have alternative sources of information, such as their personal experience, media effects are limited.

Media effects on public opinion fall into several categories. Agenda setting occurs when media coverage affects what issues or problems people think about. Priming occurs when the media encourage people to evaluate political figures in terms of one set of considerations rather than another. Framing occurs when the media present problems or issues in such a way that people are stimulated to think about them in terms of one frame of reference rather than another. The media also may change attitudes more slowly through their role in political socialization.

Frequently, critics charge the media with one or another form of bias. Surveys show that reporters and editors are more liberal and more supportive of Democrats than the public at large, but research offers little reason to believe that political coverage has an overwhelming liberal bias. Moreover, other critics charge that professional considerations lead the media in a conservative direction on economic issues.

More important than ideological biases are biases that arise from the definition of what is news, and especially what is considered good TV news. The media reflect an emphasis on the negative and an emphasis on conflict. The media focus on dramatic incidents and colorful personalities rather than on more abstract forces and developments, even where the latter are far more important. The media oversimplify complex situations and reduce complicated arguments and positions to sound bites. Such media biases are understandable. Unlike the media in many other countries, the U.S. media are organized and operated from the private sector. The role of the mass media in serving the public interest exists in constant tension with their role as profit-making enterprises serving their stockholders.

Key Terms

agenda setting, p. 233
CNN effect, p. 233
equal-time rule, p. 230
framing, p. 234

mass media, p. 223
new media, p. 227
priming, p. 234

selection principle, p. 238
selective perception, p. 232
spin, p. 236

Suggested Readings

Of General Interest

Jamieson, Kathleen. *Packaging the Presidency.* New York: Oxford University Press, 1996. Critical survey of the evolution of presidential campaign advertising from the Eisenhower years to the present.

Neumann, W. Russell. *The Future of the Mass Audience.* Cambridge, England: Cambridge University Press, 1991. Thoughtful examination of the effects of technological change on mass communications. Concludes that new media will not fragment the audience as much as many think.

Norris, Pippa. *A Virtuous Circle.* Cambridge. Cambridge University Press. 2000. Hugely informative survey of politics and media in advanced industrial democracies. In general, Norris takes a more sanguine view of modern developments than many critics do.

Patterson, Thomas. *Out of Order.* New York: Vintage, 1994. A critical discussion of the way the print media define news when they cover presidential campaigns. Recommended by former President Clinton.

Sabato, Larry. *Feeding Frenzy.* Baltimore: Lanahan Publishers, 2000. Entertaining critique of the most extreme manifestations of "pack journalism."

Focused Studies

Iyengar, Shanto, and Donald Kinder. *News That Matters.* Chicago: University of Chicago Press, 1987. An exemplary experimental study that demonstrates the existence of agenda setting and priming.

Lavrakas, Paul, and Michael Traugott, eds. *Election Polls, the News Media, and Democracy.* New York: Seven Bridges Press, 2000. Comprehensive collection of essays on election polls. Suggests that the media make a significant contribution to American democracy through election polls, properly done.

West, Darrell. *Air Wars.* 2nd ed. Washington, DC: Congressional Quarterly, 1997. Readable study of the evolution and consequences of television advertising in campaigns since 1952.

On the Web

Virtually every news organization these days has a Web site.
abcnews.go.com/politics
www.cnn.com/allpolitics
www.nytimes.com/pages/politics
www.latimes.com/news/politics/
www.foxnews.com/politics/
www.washingtonpost.com
This list consists of some of the most prominent news organizations' politics Web sites. In addition to these news sites, commentary has become extremely important, particularly with respect to framing and priming issues. The editorial sections of these Web sites are also good sources for learning about elite debate and dialogue.

www.tnr.com
www.theweeklystandard.com
Magazines such as the left of center *New Republic* and the conservative *Weekly Standard* have become important outlets for policy ideas.

www.people-press.org
The Pew Research Center for the People and the Press conducts survey research on how the media conducts themselves. Its Web site is invaluable for understanding how the public reacts to the media.

VOICES

OF THE PERMANENT CAMPAIGN

Cultural Politics in America

"We have two massive colliding forces. One is rural, Christian, religiously conservative. [The other] is socially tolerant, pro-choice, secular, living in New England and the Pacific Coast."

—Republican pollster, Bill McInturff, The Economist, January 20, 2001

THE ISSUE

Many people in the media and contemporary politics believe that the United States is driven by cultural conflicts. In their view, politics today revolves around issues like abortion, gay rights, gun control, ethnic identity, morals, and religion—issues related to people's values rather than their material welfare. Others believe this picture is an exaggeration, if not an outright distortion.

Background

News coverage on election night 2000 and in the days that followed portrayed the electorate as deeply divided between the southern and midwestern heartland and the Northeast and West Coast. If the election had been held only in the dark gray states, shown in Figure 1 (p. 250), Al Gore would have won by more than 20 points, Democrats would have won the House by a large margin, and they would control the Senate by a three-fourths majority. Conversely, if the election had been held only in the light gray states, Bush would have won comfortably, and the Republicans would have controlled both the House and the Senate by large majorities. In 2004 the election returns were very similar, suggesting that the geographic division of states was more than the reflection of a particular presidential campaign.

As pollster Bill McInturff sees it, the divide between coastal states and heartland states is based on morals, rather than on such bread-and-butter issues as the economy. This view is consistent with those of politicians like Pat Buchanan and academics like James Davison Hunter, who argued in the 1990s that there is a "culture war" raging in the United States.[1] In an extensive follow-up report on the 2000 elections, *USA Today* visited two towns that it thought typified the cultural differ-

ences (Montclair, New Jersey and Franklin, Tennessee). The profiles of the two towns portray an America separated by both values and lifestyle.

Montclair, where Gore got three-quarters of the vote, is a bustling suburb. With jazz clubs, art museums, and coffee bars, it is "teeming with energy and interaction." According to the profile, the local interest groups and associations are prominently left of center: "Montclair has its own gun control, abortion rights and anti-war groups, its own chapters of Amnesty International and the NAACP." The Council for Secular Humanism recently opened up a "faith-free" Center for Inquiry in the small city of 39,000.

In contrast, Franklin, Tennessee, where Bush won by almost 30 points, has brick buildings on main street and "shops with such names as Pigg & Peach and Heart and Hands." A Confederate war memorial stands above the town square. The Christian-music industry is prominent, with gospel music associations looking for space in the town. Franklin's interest groups and associations are right-leaning: "It's home to the Middle Tennessee Home Education Association for home-schoolers and Christian World Broadcasting, which produces Christian programming in Russian and Chinese." The local colleges are mostly Christian.[2]

Cultural Issues and Electoral Politics

For the last several decades of the twentieth century, Republicans used cultural issues to pummel Democrats. As noted in Chapter 8, the disruptions of the 1960s gave Democrats an image of being out of step with "traditional" values—as being in favor of abortion rights, feminism, drug liberalization, gay rights, and as opposing any contact between church and state. Given that these were highly controversial positions within the larger society, Republicans adopted morally traditional positions and built a base in the mountain and southern states—the Republican "L" (see Chapter 10). The addition of only a few midwestern states to the "L" all but assures a Republican presidential candidate of victory. Bill Clinton cracked the Republican "L" in 1992 and 1996, in part by taking a page from the Republican playbook and adopting morally traditional positions, but Gore retreated from Clinton's centrism, a move that contributed to his defeat. Similarly, after the 2004 election Americans were subjected to a blizzard of commentary about how Democrats had lost the capacity to talk about values and connect with people of faith.

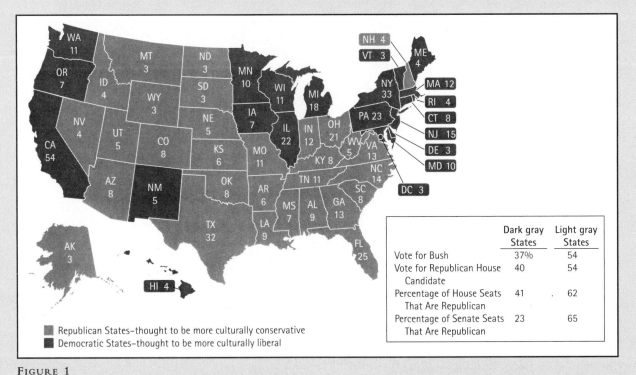

	Dark gray States	Light gray States
Vote for Bush	37%	54
Vote for Republican House Candidate	40	54
Percentage of House Seats That Are Republican	41	62
Percentage of Senate Seats That Are Republican	23	65

Republican States–thought to be more culturally conservative
Democratic States–thought to be more culturally liberal

FIGURE 1

The Cultural Divide

This map shows the breakdown between those states that voted Democratic (in dark gray)
and those that voted Republican (in light gray) in the 2004 elections.

• *What part did cultural issues play in the divide between dark gray and light gray states?*

Despite the importance of liberal constituencies to the party, Democratic candidates are aware of the electoral dangers posed by cultural issues in many areas of the country. At the 2001 Democratic Leadership Council meetings—held in the heartland state of Indiana—the moderates of the party vowed to push "values centrism." Senator Joe Liberman, a prominent member of the group (and an unsuccessful 2004 presidential candidate), said that the "challenge is to regain the public's confidence as a party that cares about and shares the mainstream values of the coutry."[3] When the 2004 outcome seemed to suggest that they had not met that challenge, disappointed Democrats wrung their hands over what they saw as a "God gap."

What Do Americans Believe?

Apparently, then, the United States consists of two groups at war culturally, a clash in which elections often serve as the arena of combat. But drawing this conclusion may not be warranted. Public opinion reveals few of the differences described in the media. At least at the mass level, the culture war appears to be greatly exaggerated. Remember that the vote is a blunt instrument. A voter cannot mark her ballot 55 percent for Kerry and 45 percent for Bush; she must mark it 100 percent for one of the candidates. Thus, *votes* are more divided than *voters*.

As shown in the top panel of Table 1, in 2000 36 percent of the citizens in the dark gray "coastal" states were Democrats, but the percentage of Democrats in the light gray "heartland" states was only 3 percent lower. Twenty-four percent of the people in the light gray states described themselves as conservatives, but the percentage of conservatives in the dark gray states was statistically indistinguishable—22 percent (Americans are ideological moderates, as discussed in Chapter 5).

What about cultural attitudes or values specifically? Can we find evidence of a culture war there? The middle panel in the table shows that on many such issues there was no difference. Similar numbers in both regions opposed immigration, favored protection of the environment even at the expense of jobs, favored school vouchers, favored English as the official language of the United States, and favored the death penalty. And citizens in the two regions did not differ in whether they believed that people should tolerate others' moral views—more than 60 percent in both regions advocated tolerance.

The lower panel in the table lists those issues where there were some differences between the two regions. People in the coastal states were more pro-choice and sympathetic with gay

TABLE 1

VOTER COMPARISONS BETWEEN COASTAL AND HEARTLAND STATES IN 2000

	"Coastal" States	"Heartland" States
Democrats[a]	36%	33%
Republicans	23	26
Self-Described Conservatives[b]	22	24
Self-Described Liberals	18	12
Questions with No Significant Differences		
Approve of Clinton's Job	71	64
Believe Immigration Should Be Decreased	44	47
Favor Protecting the Environment Over Protecting Jobs	41	42
Favor School Vouchers	56	57
Favor English as the Official Language	69	66
Favor the Death Penalty	73	75
Should Tolerate Others' Moral Views	64	62
Questions with Some Differences		
A Woman Should Always Be Able to Obtain an Abortion	50	36
For Gays Serving in the Military	58	46
Favor Gays Being Able to Adopt	51	40
Favor Eliminating Job Discrimination Against Gays	72	63
Favor Making It Harder to Obtain a Gun	64	55
Religion Is Important	70	82

SOURCE: 2000 American National Election Studies survey.

[a]Partisans counted if they were in the "strong" or "weak" categories. "Leaners" not collapsed.

[b]The ANES 2000 questionnaire did not ask the traditional liberal/conservative question. These data include only those who initially answered "liberal" or "conservative," not those who were later persuaded to "lean" toward a category.

rights. Religion was more important in the heartland states. But these differences should not be blown out of proportion—none of them reached 15 percent, and majorities in the two regions generally agreed. Although religion was less important in the coastal states, 70 percent of the respondents there still found it important. Over 60 percent of heartland respondents favored protecting gays from job discrimination. The heartland states are more sympathetic to the NRA than are the coastal ones, but a majority in each favored stricter gun control laws.

The notion that there is a "cultural chasm" or two massive colliding forces" was not supported by the evidence in 2000, and preliminary data indicate that the same was true in 2004.

Why the Emphasis on Differences?

At least three sets of actors have an interest in emphasizing differences among Americans rather than commonalities. One is the media. The media need good story lines and conflict is a good story line. Audiences cannot ignore culture wars raging in the schools and neighborhoods, dividing the United States into two hostile camps determined to undermine the core values cherished by their enemies. In contrast, "Americans mostly agree, prefer moderation" is not a headline that editors expect will sell newspapers.

Many interest groups that participate in electoral politics also perpetuate the notion of a culture war. Leaders of conser-

vative Christian groups allied with the Republican party genuinely believe they are fighting a dangerous enemy, as do leaders and activists in pro-choice and gay-rights groups allied with the Democratic party. They are small and unrepresentative minorities, but many interest-group members feel strongly about their issues and will make a lot of noise. By voting regularly, working to change the system, and contributing to candidates, such activists can dominate the nation's political discourse.

A third set of actors who have an interest in perpetuating the notion of a culture war are politicians themselves. Like the leaders of interest groups, some candidates and officeholders sincerely believe they are engaged in a war. Others see instrumental reasons to do so. Each party has a base, and members of the base may be particularly sensitive to cultural issues. Mobilizing one's base is an important component of a winning electoral strategy, so emphasizing cultural conflict may be an integral part of assembling a loyal electoral coalition. Scaring potential sympathizers is a good way to generate votes and donations. Some politicians and interest-group leaders defend their emphasis on cultural divisions. Interest-group leaders in particular sometimes claim that they are forcing the public to "address" their issues. They believe that the public is uninformed and unconcerned; it does not realize the significance of the issues at stake. Aggressive elections and campaigns shake people's complacency and force them to take a stand. Nonetheless, the effect of their efforts is to exaggerate conflict.

Web Sites on Cultural Issues

When it comes to social divisions in the United States, few states fall clearly on one side; most of them actually are "somewhere in between." Nonetheless, interest groups often stake out positions that allow them to be fit into the "culture war" metaphor. On the accompanying page are some Web sites of groups dedicated to social issues. Be sure to visit the Web sites of both culturally conservative and culturally liberal groups. What are some of the key differences between both groups?

Cultural Issues and the Courts

The courts have been deeply involved in the politics of cultural issues. For example, the controversy over abortion was greatly intensified by the Supreme Court's *Roe v. Wade* decision which made abortion a civil liberty for women. Similarly, the issue of gay marriage came to the forefront after a Massachusetts court decision in the spring of 2004. Court decisions on school prayer, gun control, flag burning, the death penalty, the Pledge of Allegiance, and other issues have also helped stoke the fires of cultural politics. If you are losing the battle in the electoral arena, seeking favorable court action is an especially attractive strategy. Critics argue, however, that the democratic process should be allowed to work out issues like these. Court involvement only antagonizes the losing side and makes political battles more intense.

What Do You Think?

1. Do the media seriously misrepresent the severity of cultural conflicts or the extent to which they divide Americans geographically? If so, why?

2. Why can the smallish differences between the two regions result in a big electoral difference?

3. Is it bad for the country to be divided? Is it damaging for the media to portray the country as divided when that is not actually the case?

4. Should the courts actively intervene in disputes over cultural issues, or should the courts take a hands-off approach?

5. What can a candidate or party do to bridge the differences in values across the nation?

CHAPTER 10

★ ★ ★ ★ ★ ★ ★ ★ ★ ★ ★ ★ ★ ★ ★ ★

Electing the President

CHAPTER OUTLINE

The Meaning of Elections

Tension ran high in the days before the 2004 presidential election. The contest between President Bush and Sen. John Kerry looked close, "too close to call" as the journalists like to say, leaving many Americans fearful of an election fiasco resembling the one that threatened the nation's political system in 2000. Wall Street's stock market was stagnant as investors fearful of a crisis held back their funds.[1]

Opinion polls in the months before the election only added to the confusion. They gave widely varying predictions, not only from one survey organization to another, but also across different polls conducted by the same people. Even the last-minute polls gave little guidance—some put Bush ahead and some put Kerry ahead, but in every case the predicted margin of victory was so tiny that the polls were, in the words of the *Washington Post,* "meaningless in attempting to predict the outcome."

Some sources confidently predicted a Kerry victory. Polls indicated that his performance in three presidential debates impressed voters, whereas Bush's conduct in the first debate strongly alienated viewers. "The effect of Kerry's debate sweep on the core undecided and persuadable voters has already been immense," concluded United Press International. Zogby International issued a bold prediction on election day, that the polling trends pointed to a Kerry victory with 311 electoral votes.

Other events also seemed to be going Kerry's way. For example, signs indicated—correctly, as it turned out—that voter turnout would surge. "A huge increase is likely to favor Kerry," the *Washington Post* surmised—wrongly, as it turned out. One polling firm saw the election tilting to Kerry because they expected minority turnout to jump, not realizing that Bush's support among minorities would jump too.

Polls conducted in key swing states indicated that, Bush would lose in the close races necessary to keep his job.

Meanwhile, the networks had spent $10 million to establish an "exit poll," in which voters at selected precincts would be asked their choices. Democrats, including younger voters, apparently cooperated at high rates. Preliminary figures thus promised Kerry victories in the key states of Florida and Ohio.

These numbers leaked onto the Internet, which caused investors to fear an election that would take weeks to resolve. The Dow Jones Industrial Average took a nosedive late in the afternoon, and British bookmakers reported a sudden surge in bets on Kerry. Journalists reported that President Bush had expressed a "rare sense of doubt," that he "appeared subdued." Bush's British ally, Prime Minister Tony Blair, reportedly said that he had "gone to bed thinking Mr. Kerry was the next president of the United States, only to wake up to learn otherwise."

Contrast all this flurry of activity with how political scientists approached the election.[2] Using statistical models refined over several presidential elections, scholars committed themselves to predictions long before most of the remarkable campaign events took place. Some of the most sophisticated attempts at forecasting the election came out in July and August, for example, around the time of the national party conventions and long before the first presidential debate.

Of the seven forecasts, only one described the election as too close too call. The other six predicted a Bush victory. In fact, one pair of scholars predicted in August that Bush would receive 51.7% of the major-party vote. He received 51.5%. Overall, the political scientists gave much clearer and much earlier predictions than all of the pundits, and they basically got it right.

MAKING THE CONNECTION

News coverage of presidential elections typically focuses on the short-term events of election campaigns: the strategies, the personalities, the mistakes. Someone who judged American elections simply on the discussion found in newspapers, in magazines, and on the airwaves would conclude that voters make snap decisions based on short-term (if not trivial) considerations. It is hard to reconcile this story of last-minute decision making with the ability of political scientists to forecast the presidential results accurately long in advance, before all of the fluctuations in the polls and before all the campaign events that supposedly drive the outcome. The purpose of this chapter is to offer an alternative view of what drives presidential elections, the one that scholars have constructed from studying elections scientifically. The chapter will begin with the nomination process:

- How are presidential candidates nominated in the United States?

- How did our unusual nominating process come to be?

- What are the pros and cons of the American nominating process?

It then turns to the general election:

- How does the Electoral College affect the nature of the campaign?

- How do Americans vote in presidential elections?

- Why is the importance of the media and the campaign often exaggerated?

- What issues and other factors have influenced the most recent presidential elections?

* * * * * * * * * * * * * * * *

Nominating a Presidential Candidate

In most democracies, nominees for chief executive are chosen by party activists—a small minority of dues-paying, card-carrying, meeting-attending members of the party. The United States is unusual for the lengthy public process used to determine presidential candidates, a process that one British correspondent calls "a bizarre ritual."[3] Every eligible voter can participate in a **caucus** (a meeting of candidate supporters) or **primary election** (a preliminary election) to choose the delegates who will select their party's presidential nominee. At the presidential level, nearly three-quarters of the states choose their delegates in primary elections, and the other quarter chooses them in caucuses. Because caucus states tend to be smaller, the lion's share of the delegates is chosen in primaries.

caucus
Meeting of candidate supporters who choose delegates to a state or national convention.

primary election
Preliminary election that narrows the number of candidates by determining who will be the nominees in the general election.

Caucuses

In caucus states, participants meet in each voter precinct to start the process of delegate selection. Generally they gather in public places such as town halls or public schools, but sometimes they hold meetings on private property such as in a restaurant. Voting in a precinct caucus is highly personal, as supporters of the various presidential candidates attempt to attract uncommitted voters to their side (see the accompanying Election Connection).

These precinct gatherings are only the beginning, however, because the process has a number of stages. For example, the Iowa caucuses early in the election year are the first major test for the candidates. But these caucuses only choose delegates to the county conventions that are held in March, which then choose delegates to the May congressional district conventions and the June state convention!

Democratic caucuses are constrained by national party rules that require proportional representation for the supporters of different candidates, as well as equal numbers of male and female delegates, where possible. Any registered Democrat is eligible to participate. Republican caucuses are less open. Some limit participation to party officials and workers. They are also freer to adopt their own rules; some use

ELECTION CONNECTION

A 2004 Caucus Experience

By Scott Peters, Assistant Professor,
University of Northern Iowa

Tonight I went to the local elementary school to attend my first Democratic precinct caucus. I arrived about 15 minutes before the 6:30 PM start time, and was confronted with a long line of people waiting to sign in. Much to my surprise, there was no ID check, even for people who were registering on-site.

We met in the school's cafeteria, and scattered among signs telling us to eat our vegetables were campaign signs from Dean, Edwards, and Kerry. I was surprised that I didn't see any Gephardt signs. I also didn't see very many stereotypically burly union guys, whom I could peg as traditional Gephardt supporters (although there were a few senior citizens present, a group that has provided Gephardt with staunch support in the past). Other than about a half-dozen teenagers attending with their parents, there were very few people there under 30, although I did see a few young hippies wearing Kucinich stickers. The rest of the people there were middle aged, and many of them were undecided, or at least claimed to be when asked.

We had 212 people in attendance. State party procedures demand that at 7 PM, the caucus split into preference groups—people literally walk to appointed spots in the room to demonstrate their support for a particular candidate. (It's a bit like a class splitting up to do group work, and it happens with about as much commotion, but considerably more pep.) I went to the Gephardt preference group. If influence were measured by median age, we would have been unstoppable. Unfortunately, what matters is numbers of people—if, after 30 minutes, a preference group fails to command at least 15% of the total number of attendees, it must disband and its members must migrate to another preference group. The magic number for our precinct was 32. After a few minutes, we had 17. The group leader started going around trying to appeal to other groups, but few of the rest of us made a similar effort. I stuck around to listen as representatives from other candidates came over to try to cherry-pick Gephardt's supporters.

The Kerry guy was very enthusiastic: "You know, Kerry's a friend of labor. He's got a 92% rating with AFL-CIO."

"Yeah, but he opposes the death penalty," said one 60-ish Gephardt supporter, consulting her cheat sheet with all the candidates' positions on key issues. "I don't want those criminals running around."

I eavesdropped on several conversations like this and was favorably impressed with people's knowledge of issues and desire to find a candidate they could support on issues. People were also very concerned with finding someone electable, someone who had a chance of beating Bush in November. Although along the way there was some harsh criticism of President Bush, for the most part the tone was serious but positive, and people really seemed to be having fun.

Occasionally a cheer would rise in one part of the room—it was a preference group welcoming new members who were abandoning their original choice once it became clear that it wasn't viable. First the Clark people broke up, most of them going to Kerry. Then, according to a deal the candidates had announced earlier in the day, most of the Kucinich supporters migrated over to Edwards. From what I could tell, the Edwards camp offered to give one of their county convention delegate positions to a Kucinich supporter if the group came over to Edwards. A few Kucinich people also went to Dean, which seemed to be the most natural second choice to a Kucinich supporter. Finally, the Gephardt supporters split pretty evenly between Kerry and Edwards.

When all was said and done, Edwards got 85 votes, and Kerry and Dean split the rest pretty evenly. The precinct's 13 delegates to the county convention were allotted accordingly: 5 to Edwards, and 4 each to Dean and Kerry. (The number of delegates per precinct depends, among other things, on levels of voter turnout in previous elections. One precinct near campus in which most of the residents are students, and therefore typically has very low voter turnout, was given only two delegates to the county convention despite the fact that over 200 people participated in the caucus.)

After that, the caucus broke up very quickly, a disappointment to me. One of the functions of the caucus is to propose platform planks, and I was really looking forward to observing the debate over them. But the chair of the caucus moved just to pass along all proposed planks to the county platform committee and let its members sort them out.

There was some other business the caucus had to take care of, mainly selecting various precinct officers. By my estimate, there were only about 40 people present during these discussions. The meeting ended at 8 PM, and when I got home I turned on the TV to watch the results.

variants of proportional representation and some continue to use winner-take-all voting procedures.[4]

Caucus turnout is extremely low, typically in single digits. About 6 percent of the state's voting-age population participated in the 2004 Iowa caucuses. This was not an unusually low figure. The 12 percent turnout in the 1988 Iowa caucuses, when both parties had competitive contests, is believed to be the highest caucus turnout ever recorded. Caucus participants of both parties are unrepresentative of the general population in terms of income and education, and ideologically they tend to be more extreme than their party's broader base of identifiers.

Primaries

Primaries take many forms across the states. In **closed primaries** only party members may vote—and only in the primary of the party in which they are registered. Independents cannot vote at all. Some of the most populous states, such as New York, Pennsylvania, and Florida, have closed primaries. In **semi-closed primaries** independents can vote in one of the party primaries. States with semi-closed primaries include Massachusetts, New Jersey, and Oregon. In **open primaries** any registered voter may vote in any party's primary. However, they must vote in the same party's primary for each contest on the ballot. California once allowed voters to switch from one party to another, office by office, but in 2000 the U.S. Supreme Court struck down this "blanket primary" as unconstitutional on the grounds that it violated the parties' rights of free association.

The type of primary that a state holds was significant in the 2000 primary season because of the candidacy of John McCain. McCain won in New Hampshire, a semi-closed-primary state, because he received heavy support among independents, who voted in the Republican primary. Then he gave George W. Bush a scare in South Carolina and won in Michigan—both open-primary states—where he received support among independents and even some Democrats. McCain's performance was notably weaker in states with closed primaries.

Evolution of the Nomination Process

Direct primaries are an American invention. Although they began as a progressive reform and swept across the states in the early twentieth century, primaries did not determine presidential nominations for another half-century.[5] Some states did hold presidential primaries, but they were treated as "beauty contests" in which potential nominees could demonstrate their popular appeal. Party leaders, not primaries, really controlled the process for selecting delegates to the nominating conventions.

The Republicans were the first major party to open up their delegate-selection process. Public participation weakened party leaders. In 1964 the candidate of the party establishment, New York Governor Nelson Rockefeller, lost to the insurgent candidate Senator Barry Goldwater of Arizona after Goldwater took the California primary.[6] The numerically dominant Democratic party did not change as quickly. As late as 1968, Vice President Hubert Humphrey won the Democratic nomination without entering a single primary.

Humphrey's nomination divided the Democratic party, however. Many Democratic activists had supported Eugene McCarthy or the late Robert F. Kennedy,

closed primaries
Primaries in which only party members can vote—and only in the party in which they are registered.

semi-closed primaries
Primaries in which independents can vote in one of the party primaries.

open primaries
Primaries in which any registered voter can vote in any party's primary.

Picking a Nominee

Rank-and-file members have direct influence on who receives their party's nomination. Caucuses are especially time consuming, however, and so are dominated by party activists. As a result, the system favors extreme candidates and candidates who conform more closely to the usual issue positions in their party.

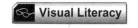 **Visual Literacy**

American Electoral Rules: How Do They Influence Campaigns?

both of whom opposed the war in Vietnam.[7] These candidates won most of the primaries that were held, driving President Lyndon Johnson from the race in the process, so their supporters—already stunned by Robert Kennedy's assassination—were outraged that the nomination went to Johnson's vice president.

The antiwar faction gained the upper hand in the party and adopted the current process.[8] Reforms instituted after the 1968 convention took power away from the party bosses, promoting the leftwing candidacy of Senator George McGovern in 1972 and allowing the rise of a previously unknown Georgia governor named Jimmy Carter in 1976. Carter probably was the first to recognize how the newly completed reform process had transformed presidential politics; in many ways his campaign became a model for those that followed.

The past two decades have seen much tinkering with the rules, but the broad outlines of the system have not changed. In 2000 about 80 percent of the Democratic delegates were chosen in primaries and caucuses, with the remaining slots reserved for elected officials and party leaders called *superdelegates*. Primaries and caucuses determined all of the Republican delegates. The general pattern today is that candidates build extensive organizations in the states where the first caucuses and primaries are held. The emphasis is on "retail politics," face-to-face contact with early voters, which resembles the dealings of neighborhood merchants with their customers. Candidates strive to exceed "expectations" and to build "momentum" so that they can raise money and thereby qualify for federal matching funds to continue their campaigns in later, more expensive contests.[9]

Financing Nomination Campaigns

The federal government provides public subsidies to candidates for the party nominations.[10] The money comes from the voluntary check-offs on Americans' income tax returns. The Federal Elections Commission (FEC) distributes the campaign subsidies as **matching funds.** Qualifying candidates have their fund raising matched, dollar for dollar, up to a prespecified maximum spending limit. To qualify, a candidate must raise at least $5000 in each of 20 states, in contributions no larger than $250, in the year in which he or she announces candidacy (or in the preceding year). Most serious candidates do not find it very difficult to raise $100,000 in this way. Even minor-party candidates have qualified, although they generally do not raise much money after they do.

    Staying eligible is harder than becoming eligible, however. To stay eligible, and to continue to receive matching funds throughout the primary season, candidates must comply with spending limits in each state, and they must be at least minimally successful during the voting. A candidate who fails to receive at least 10 percent of the vote in two consecutive primaries loses eligibility and can regain it only by getting 20 percent or more of the vote in a later primary. Thus, a struggling campaign may find itself deprived of funds just when it needs them most.

    Most candidates take matching funds, but there have been some notable recent exceptions. In 2000 the FEC spending limit for the nomination campaign was $40.5 million. George W. Bush had already raised $70 million before the primary season began, so he declined to accept matching funds and the associated restrictions. By the time he defeated John McCain and clinched the nomination, Bush had already spent $63 million, half again as much as he would have been permitted to spend had he accepted matching funds.[11] He opted out of the spending limits again in 2004, as did Vermont Governor Howard Dean and the eventual Democratic nominee, Senator John Kerry of Massachusetts.[12]

Strengths and Weaknesses of the Nomination Process

Despite its participatory nature, many observers criticize the presidential nomination process.[13] Their concerns fall into two broad categories, one procedural, the other political.

Procedural Concerns   As much as two years before the general election, candidates begin building their campaign organizations, first in the key primary states and then across the country. They start to raise money and to develop an initial strategy for capturing the nomination. A major goal at this stage is to scare off potential competitors—for example, by attracting high-profile endorsements or a formidable campaign war chest. Then, when the caucuses and primaries begin early in the election year, candidates try to secure enough early victories to sink their remaining competitors. They organize and campaign in one state, then pack up and move on to the next one.

    Critics complain that the campaign is too long and starts too early. Many voters simply do not pay attention to the campaigns until a month or two before the election. A poll taken over the Labor Day weekend in 2003, after Democratic presidential candidates had been campaigning 24/7 for months, reported that two-thirds of Democrats in the country could not name any of them.[14] Similarly, the town-hall debate between Bush and Kerry in 2004 drew an audience of less than 33 million homes, barely more than the typical audience for an episode of *CSI* or *CSI Miami*.[15] Candidates start sending messages to voters long before most voters are tuned in to receive them.

matching funds
Public moneys (from $3 check-offs on income tax returns) that the Federal Election Commission distributes to primary candidates according to a prespecified formula.

FIGURE 10.1

In 1996 and 2000 the Presidential Nominations Were Decided Earlier Than Ever

SOURCE: Data compiled by Sam Abrams through various news reports.

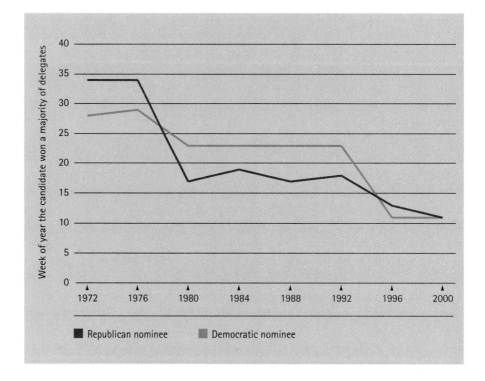

The perceived problem has worsened with time. The primaries have become increasingly "front-loaded" since 1996 (see Figure 10.1); many states have moved their primaries to earlier dates in the hope that the contests would take place while nominations still were up for grabs. Party leaders view front-loading favorably because the nomination contests are over more quickly and the winners have more time to unify their parties and plan for the fall election campaign.[16] Critics charge, however, that front-loading gives an advantage to well-known, establishment candidates who can raise large sums of money to pay for a national campaign.

By the time the process is over, the candidates may have been pounding on each other for months. Every personal flaw and any past mistakes have been exposed by the media and the attacks of campaign rivals. This scrutiny obviously provides attentive citizens with a great deal of information about their prospective leaders, although it also may account for the unhappiness voters express about the options available to them. Unfortunately, the lengthy scrutiny may deter good potential candidates who are unwilling to give up every shred of their personal privacy. Indeed, some have suggested—jokingly?—that anyone willing to expose every aspect of his or her life to media scrutiny is not the kind of person Americans should want to elect. As a result, some reformers have proposed compressing the nomination process into a few regional primaries or even into a single national primary held much closer to the general election.

Political Concerns   The reformers who instituted the modern nomination process claimed they were giving "power to the people"—the new process would empower ordinary citizens at the expense of the party "bosses." As we noted in the chapters on political parties and interest groups, however, taking power away from one group of elites seldom empowers unorganized citizens. Other elites are more often the beneficiaries. In the case of the nomination process, many commentators fear that taking power from party leaders and government officials may only have empowered two groups who are even more unrepresentative: political activists and the media.

Political activists gained influence from the changes in the nomination process. These are people who are more interested in and committed to political issues than are average citizens. As we have noted, caucus turnout is extremely low, and although turnout in primaries is higher, it is still much lower than turnout in general elections: In 2000, of the 18 states that voted while the nominations were still undecided, 12 set turnout records, but the average turnout was only 13.6 percent![17] Being more dedicated, activists naturally are more likely to vote in primaries than are ordinary citizens, so the current system gives their views more weight. Even more important, the activists work in campaigns and donate money to candidates, and they help mobilize other voters. None of this would be a cause for concern if the activists were like everyone else, but in some important respects the activists are different. Not only are their views more intense, but their views often are more extreme as well.

Because participation in primaries and (especially) caucuses is so low, small groups of dedicated activists can exert more influence in the nomination contests than they can in general elections, where turnout is much higher. Consequently, some analysts worry that the primary process confers an advantage to candidates who appeal to activists by taking positions far from the center of the political spectrum where the mass of Americans are located. Democratic candidates generally are more liberal, and Republican candidates generally more conservative, than the average voter. After they take office, candidates must choose between keeping the promises they made to party activists and adjusting their behavior to satisfy regular citizens.[18] Either way, someone is bound to face disappointment.

The preceding argument may be exaggerated. Primary electorates do not appear to be considerably different from other voters.[19] Even convention delegates, who do differ significantly from voters, apparently temper their views in the interests of winning.[20] Nonetheless, it seems likely that in the caucuses and in the fund-raising arena, unrepresentative activists exercise disproportionate influence.[21] The intense involvement of activists also apparently skews the political debate. Ordinary voters do not view as crucial the hot-button issues such as abortion and gun control that divide party activists. Yet these issues usually dominate nomination debates, at the expense of general and far-reaching issues such as education, taxes, and jobs.

The media are the second group that gained influence from the nomination process. Americans must look to television, radio, and newspaper reporters—as well as commentators and editors—to interpret confusing primary and caucus developments for them. Critics complain that the press focuses too much on the "horse race": who is ahead and by how far, who is coming up on the rail, and who is fading from contention. Professor Thomas Patterson has documented a striking shift in how the media "frame" campaigns. In the 1960s, before the primary era, media coverage was about evenly split between a policy orientation and a "game" orientation. In 1972, the first year of the new system, coverage shifted to the game frame by a proportion of 2 to 1. Since 1976, the game frame has had a 4 to 1 edge.[22] For the media, campaigns have become the political equivalent of "March Madness."

political activists
People who regularly participate in politics; they are more interested in and committed to particular issues and candidates than are ordinary citizens.

The media also tend to focus on scandals, gaffes, and campaign feuds. Critics charge that the media are more concerned with trivia and sleaze than with real questions of government policy. Of course, the media have a response to these criticisms of their behavior: Newspapers, news magazines, and television networks are profit-making enterprises that must compete for advertising dollars. They must print what sells, which is the horse race and the sleaze. What is the good of providing long, detailed policy coverage if the audience will just tune it all out?

Another criticism of the media is that they exaggerate the importance of many campaign events and developments. Iowa, the first caucus state, and New Hampshire, the first primary state, receive a disproportionate share of news coverage. Some critics ask whether two sparsely populated, rural states should play such an important role in determining whether candidacies are viable.[23] This particular criticism has become somewhat muted, though, given that both Iowa and New Hampshire ended up swing states in 2004.

Finally, some observers complain that the media no longer are mere reporters of the nomination process but have become important players in that process. In the 1960s, Patterson found that 20 percent or fewer of all campaign stories were "interpretive"; the rest were "descriptive." In 1972 the ratio shifted to 50:50, and in the 1988 and 1992 elections, the ratio shifted further to 80 percent interpretive and 20 percent descriptive.[24] Of course, all this extra interpretation also provides a useful service. The candidates and their managers usually work hard to shape public perceptions—for example, by pumping up their chances or by downplaying their failings. Interpretive reporting can counteract such self-interested "spin."

Whatever your view of the pros and cons of the American nomination process, it is now well established and is unlikely to change, except in marginal ways, in the foreseeable future. The system "works" in the sense that it determines a winner for each party, and it is democratic in the most basic sense: So far, the nominees have been the candidates who have won the most votes in their parties' primaries.

Who Nominates the Vice President?

Since 1968, one candidate in each party has won a majority of convention delegates by the end of the caucus and primary season. Consequently, the national conventions no longer are the important decision-making party meetings they were in earlier eras. Instead, they are media events (see Chapter 9). Party leaders today try to use the conventions to showcase their stars and to unify the party by compromising on the platform and giving the losers a chance to speak. Of course, realizing that the conventions have become relatively unimportant, the media increasingly ignore them.

Before the establishment of the contemporary nomination process, the conventions chose the vice presidential candidates as well as the presidential candidates. The choice usually was an effort to "balance" the ticket ideologically or geographically, and the convention often chose the runner-up for the presidential nomination—who, by definition, was supported by a significant fraction of the party. Today, the choice of vice presidential candidates is completely in the hands of the presidential nominees, although they still attempt to choose a nominee who will improve the ticket's chances.[25] The presidential nominees simply announce their choices, and the conventions accept them. Sometimes the presidential nominees keep the choice secret, hoping to inject some excitement into an otherwise dull convention, but in 2000 both Bush

A Ground-Breaking Choice
Vice Presidential nominee Joseph Lieberman was the first Jew to run on a major-party ticket.

and Gore made their choices before the convention. In 2004, President Bush asked Vice-President Dick Cheney to run again, while John Kerry announced his choice of Senator John Edwards of North Carolina before his party's convention as well.

The General Election for President

Labor Day traditionally marks the start of the fall campaign, although today's nominees do not take so much of a break after the summer conventions as they did in the past. From the start of the campaign until election day—the first Tuesday after the first Monday in November—the candidates maintain an exhausting pace, and the campaign dominates the news.[26]

Financing the General-Election Campaign

From the mid-1970s to the mid-1990s, presidential campaign funding was a very simple proposition. Under the terms of the 1974 Federal Elections Campaign Act (FECA), the general-election campaign is publicly funded. Unlike in the primaries, however, federal funds are not matching funds. Rather, the FEC gives major-party candidates a subsidy (Bush and Gore received approximately $67.5 million each in 2000), and in return the candidates agree not to raise and spend any more. Thus, from 1974 to 1992, most observers believed that the nominees of the major parties were adequately and equally funded.

In the 1990s, however, campaigns increasingly relied on soft money. Soft money is money contributed by interest groups, labor unions, and individual donors that is not subject to federal regulation. The reason why these contributions are not regulated is that the money is not given to the candidates, who are subject to FECA restrictions,

FIGURE 10.2

In the 1990s Reliance on Soft Money in Presidential Elections Increased Dramatically

Public funding declined in 2000 because Bush, Forbes, and the Republican party declined federal matching funds.

SOURCE: The Federal Election Commission. Note that the Federal Election Commission began requiring the parties to disclose their soft money in 1991. Figures for 1991 through 2000 are from the FEC. Figures for the 1984 and 1988 cycles are based on voluntary disclosures by the parties and on published estimates.

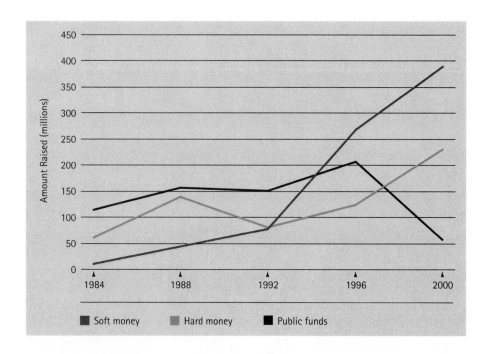

but to party committees with more flexibility in the contributions they may accept and how they may spend them. As Figure 10.2 demonstrates, soft-money contributions to the parties exploded in the 1990s, setting off one of the campaign financing controversies that periodically erupt in the United States (see the accompanying International Comparison). Congress passed campaign finance reform legislation in the spring of 2002 that banned soft-money contributions to the national parties, but state and local parties still may use such money. Furthermore, independent spending by party-aligned groups filled the void left by the soft money ban in 2004.

Spending in the General-Election Campaign

You Are a Presidential Campaign Consultant

Campaign consultants oversee the expenditure of the large sums of money raised by the campaigns—and they profit personally from such spending. These specialists in modern candidate-based campaigns have replaced the party leaders who supervised campaigns of earlier eras. Media consultants design the campaign ads or "spots," stage "media events" (appearances designed so that reporters get a story, not so candidates meet voters), and schedule the candidate's time so as to maximize coverage. Derided by critics as "handlers" and "hired guns," some campaign consultants have become celebrities in recent decades. Modern campaigns also retain pollsters capable of measuring surges and slumps in candidate support.

You Are a Media Consultant to a Political Candidate

The most important category of general-election spending is expenditures for "electronic media"—TV and radio advertising, with the lion's share going to television. Although campaign advertising is widely criticized, studies have consistently found that it is informative, in that those exposed to ads know more about the candidates and where they stand than those not exposed to ads.[27] Indeed, contrary to popular perceptions that everything is getting worse, research suggests that the issue content of ads actually has increased in recent years.[28]

INTERNATIONAL COMPARISON

Campaign Financing in Other Democracies

Campaign finance is rarely a major issue in democracies other than the United States. There are a number of reasons for this difference.

In the first place, much more money is spent in American elections—even relative to the size of the electorate—than in other countries. For example, nationwide, the total amount spent in the 2000 U.S. elections was about $3 billion. Only Japan comes close to spending as much (relative to the size of its electorate).

One reason American campaigns are so expensive is the candidate-centered electoral system. Each candidate constructs a personal organization that funds the campaign. In contrast to the United States (and Japan), most other democracies have party-centered elections. The national party and its leaders conduct a single campaign on behalf of all the party candidates. Rather than having hundreds of individual candidates running duplicate campaigns, the parties take advantage of what economists call economies of scale.

A second reason for the high cost of American campaigns is that they are increasingly fought over the airwaves, and TV time is expensive—as are the services of the consultants, ad people, and so forth.[a] In most other democracies, candidates still rely more on the campaign work of party members than on attempting to reach voters directly through broadcasting.

One reason why campaign finance is a lesser concern in other democracies is that spending is heavily regulated. In Britain individual candidates are not permitted to buy television or radio time! Even the parties cannot make media buys. They are limited to a small number of publicly financed addresses by national party leaders. In Germany the law requires TV networks to give the parties free airtime during campaigns, but it is illegal for candidates to buy any additional radio or TV ads.[b] If strict limits such as these were adopted in the United States, the courts would strike them down on First Amendment grounds.

Many other democracies provide at least some degree of public election financing.[c] For example, in Austria, Belgium, Denmark, Finland, Germany, Mexico, Sweden, and Turkey, the parties receive public subsidies in proportion to the number of votes they received in the last election or the number of seats they hold in parliament. In-kind subsidies, especially free media time, also are common. In the United States public financing has progressed only as far as presidential elections; attempts to extend it to Congress have failed.

In sum, candidate-centered media campaigns, the Constitution, and popular attitudes all interact to make campaign finance a more serious issue in the United States than elsewhere. Contrasts with other democracies raise a number of questions.

- *Should all legitimate candidates receive free TV time?*

- *Should all campaigns be publicly financed?*

- *Should the United States adopt a constitutional amendment that permits regulation of how much candidates can spend and what they can spend it on?*

[a] "Money and Politics," *The Economist,* February 8, 1997: 23.
[b] Charles Lane, "Kohl Train," *The New Republic,* February 14, 2000: 17.
[c] Richard Katz," Party Organizations and Finance," in *Comparing Democracies,* ed. Lawrence LeDuc, Richard Niemi, and Pippa Norris (Thousand Oaks, CA: Sage, 1996), pp. 129–132.

Another, less positive recent trend is in the tone of campaign advertising: It has grown increasingly negative.[29] Rather than make a positive case for themselves, candidates make a negative case against their opponents. However, not all negative ads are bad; pointing out the failures and flaws of an opponent is a perfectly legitimate part of the campaign.[30] But, too often, the campaign debate is filled with exaggerations, distortions, and, on occasion, outright lies.

Negative advertising seems to work, though, in the sense that people remember more of what they have seen from negative than from positive spots.[31] Candidates often succeed when they "go negative." What is good for individual candidates, of course, may have harmful consequences for the larger political process. Much of what people remember may be inaccurate, and attack ads might reduce turnout (especially among the independent, more moderate segment of the population). Candidates, then, are playing to the more committed and more extreme voters, making campaigns more polarized.[32]

Comparing Political Campaigns

The Electoral College

The Constitution stipulates that the president and vice president must be chosen by the Electoral College. Under this system, each state selects a number of electors equal to the sum of its House and Senate seats. (The District of Columbia gets three votes under the terms of the Twenty-Third Amendment for a total of 538 votes nationwide.) These electors then form the Electoral College and their **electoral vote** determines who will lead the country. Thus, the candidate who wins the most votes—the so-called **popular vote,** or the actual votes cast—does not necessarily become president. Rutherford Hayes in 1876, Benjamin Harrison in 1888, and George W. Bush in 2000 all became president despite coming in second during the popular vote. In 1960, the Democratic party won both the popular vote and the electoral vote, but the electors pledged to John F. Kennedy, Jr. actually received fewer popular votes than did electors committed to the loser, Richard Nixon.[33] If no one receives a majority of the electoral vote, then the election is decided by the House of Representatives, which is how John Quincy Adams defeated Andrew Jackson in 1824.

Because every state has two senators, whereas the number of House seats depends on the state's population, the Electoral College gives a theoretical advantage to small states. For example, with 2 senators but only 1 seat in the House, Wyoming has 3 electoral votes—approximately 1 per 165,000 residents. With 2 senators but 53 seats in the House, California has 55 electoral votes, approximately 1 per 617,000 residents. In the 2004 election, if a candidate had won a plurality in each of the 40 least populated states, which together included only 43 percent of the U.S. population, he would have won a majority of the Electoral College and become president.

Most observers agree, however, that in practice, the Electoral College has a bias in favor of large states that overwhelms the small-state bias just described. The reason is the traditional **winner-take-all voting** system. Under state laws, the candidate who wins the state receives *all* of the state's electoral votes (except in Maine and Nebraska, which give the winner of each congressional district one electoral vote and the statewide winner the two remaining votes). Thus, a candidate who carries a large state by a tiny margin receives a windfall of electoral votes, whereas those who win small states by a landslide get only a few. In 1996 Clinton won 49 percent of the popular vote but 70 percent of the electoral vote because of the winner-take-all system. And this is also the reason why, in a tight election like that of 2000, the popular-vote winner can lose in the Electoral College.

The confusion of 2000 has brought the Electoral College increased national attention, with reformers proposing its elimination. One reason for the increased scrutiny is that the distribution of voters across the country makes winning electoral votes somewhat more difficult for Democrats. More state electorates exhibit consistent loyalty to the Republican party. Between 1968 and 1988, 21 states with 191 electoral votes voted 6 consecutive times for the Republican candidate. Another 17 states with 176 electoral votes voted 5 times (with the single exception of 1976) for the Republicans. Only the District of Columbia, with 3 electoral votes, was as loyal to the Democrats. This base in the Electoral College—the Republican "L" depicted in Figure 10.3—led commentators in the 1980s to talk of a Republican "lock" on the presidency. Bill Clinton picked that lock twice in a row, breaking apart the Republican "L" in the process, but Bush's victories in both 2000 and 2004 built from solid support among the consistently Republican states.

electoral vote
Cast by electors, with each state receiving one vote for each of its members of the House of Representatives and one vote for each of its senators.

popular vote
The total vote cast across the nation for a candidate.

The Electoral College

winner-take-all voting
Any voting procedure in which the candidate with the most votes gets all of the seats or delegates at stake.

**And the Winner Is. . . .
Close Calls in
Presidential Elections**

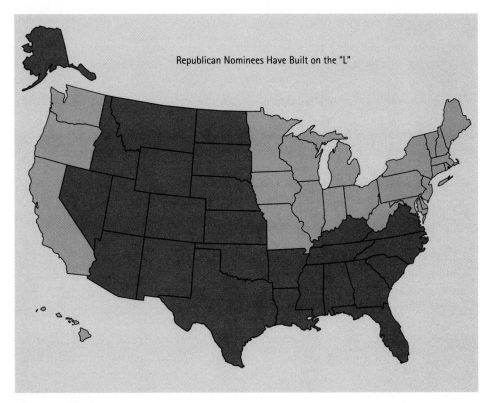

FIGURE 10.3

The Republican "L"

The base on which GOP majorities were built in presidential elections in the 1970s and the 1980s was a wide swath of states called "the Republican L." It takes in the Rocky Mountain region, the Plains states, and the entire South. With Alaska thrown in, these states have a total of 233 electoral votes (270 are needed to win). Bill Clinton cracked the "L," but only temporarily. President Bush won every one of the dark-gray states in 2004—as well as Iowa, Indiana, Missouri, Ohio, and West Virginia.

SOURCE: "Republican Nominees Have Built on the "L," *Congressional Quarterly Guide to the 1996 Republican National Convention,* August 3, 1996: 9.

Voting Behavior in Presidential Elections

In general, candidates concentrate on the states that are "up for grabs." They pay much less attention to states that they cannot win and those that they are almost guaranteed to win. Why do some states consistently support one party or the other for long periods of time? The reason is that there is considerable continuity in how citizens vote. This continuity, or "electoral inertia," not only explains why candidates know ahead of time how they will do in many states, it also explains why campaign organizations and the media enjoy limited impact on general election outcomes.

When Americans Decide

Many people decide how they will vote before the campaign begins. Typically, one-third to one-half of the electorate reports deciding how to vote *before the primaries.* This decision is easy enough for people who always vote the party line. It is also rather easy

TABLE 10.1

GROUPS DIFFER IN THEIR SUPPORT FOR THE PARTIES

Population Category	Percentage Voting Republican					
	Bush 2004	Bush 2000	Dole 1996	Bush 1992	Bush 1988	Reagan 1984
White	58	54	46	40	59	64
Hispanic	43	31	21	25	30	37
African American	11	8	12	10	12	9
Poor (<$15,000/year)	36	37	28	23	37	45
Affluent (>$50,000/year)	56	52	48	44	62	69
Union	40	37	30	25	42	46
White Protestant	67	63	52	47	66	72
Catholic	52	47	37	35	52	54
Jewish	25	19	16	11	35	31
Big-city resident (population>500,000)	39	26	25	28	37	n/a
Suburban resident	52	49	42	39	57	61
Rural resident	59	59	46	40	55	67
Lives in the East	43	39	34	35	50	53
Lives in the Midwest	51	49	41	37	52	58
Lives in the South	58	55	46	43	58	64
Lives in the West	49	46	40	34	52	61

SOURCE: Table accompanying Marjorie Connelly, "How Americans Voted: A Political Portrait," *New York Times* Week In Review, November 7, 2004.

for voters who know the identity of at least one of the nominees—usually an incumbent president who seeks reelection. Another portion of the electorate reports deciding how to vote between the start of the primaries and the end of the conventions. All told, from one-half to two-thirds of the electorate decides how to vote by the end of the conventions—before the fall campaign gets under way. The figure was 54 percent in 2000, when no incumbent ran, and 64 percent in 1996, when Clinton sought reelection.[34] Hence, a large fraction of the electorate (typically more than half) are not much affected by the campaign. They have already made up their minds!

How Americans Decide

Participation

Deciding on a Political Party

How can people make up their minds before policies and programs are debated in the fall campaign? The answer is simply that Americans decide how to vote not only on the basis of the short-term considerations that dominate campaign coverage (the candidates and the positions they advocate) but also on the basis of longer-term considerations that arise years before the campaign gets under way. The considerations that determine how Americans vote fall into four general categories: party loyalties, public policies, government performance, and the qualities of the candidates.

party identification
A person's subjective feeling of affiliation with a party.

Party Loyalties   About two-thirds of the American electorate view themselves as Democrats or Republicans, the remainder as independents. Political scientists call this allegiance to one party or the other **party identification,** or party ID for short.[35] Party ID is a long-term force that provides continuity from election to election. For example, the Civil War and Reconstruction created many "yellow dog" Democrats in the South—people who wouldn't vote for a Republican even if the Democratic nom-

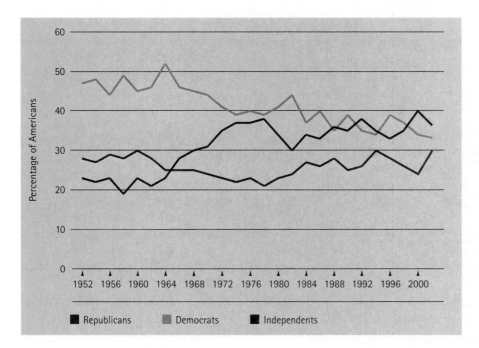

FIGURE 10.4
The Democratic Advantage in Party Identification Has Eroded

SOURCE: American National Election Studies.

inee were a yellow dog. Similarly, the Great Depression left many northerners intensely committed to the New Deal Democratic party of Franklin Roosevelt. Such deeply held allegiances underlie the "party systems" discussed in Chapter 8.

Party identification explains the well-known tendencies of various groups to support candidates of one party or the other. For example, Table 10.1 shows that African Americans and Jews are heavily Democratic in their voting. Union members, urban residents, and Catholics also have traditionally been Democratic groups, although the support of union members and Catholics has fluctuated in recent decades. On the other hand, the wealthy, rural residents, southerners, and Protestants—especially evangelicals—tend to vote Republican.

At one time, party ID was considered to be much like a religious affiliation. Not only was it resistant to change, but it was also learned early in childhood and had little policy or ideological content. Just as children learn to call themselves Catholics, Jews, or Muslims before they know the doctrines of their religion, so children learned to call themselves Democrats or Republicans before they knew what the party stood for. The traumatic events of the 1960s severely tested party loyalties, though, lessening the proportion of voters holding strong party identifications and increasing the number of independents. Thus, scholars generally recognize that party ID responds to political events and conditions, although slowly and gradually in most cases.[36]

As shown in Figure 10.4, between the 1936 and 1984 elections, more Americans consistently considered themselves Democrats than Republicans. Republican candidates such as Eisenhower and Nixon were able to win by capturing a majority of the independents and some Democrats. After Reagan's reelection in 1984, the gap between the parties began to close. Taking into account that Republicans are more likely to vote than Democrats, today's electorate contains about equal numbers of Democrats and Republicans. For the strongest partisans, the campaign is irrelevant—come hell or high water, they will vote their party ID.

Public Policies   For the most politically interested voters, policies and programs are the essence of politics. There are problems and conflicts in the United States and in the world. Problems cry out for solutions and conflicts for resolution. Elections decide these solutions and resolutions. For people with this view of politics, the campaign is a long-running debate—a chance to educate the electorate about alternative paths the country might choose and to persuade voters to follow one of them.

Surprisingly, research has found that although policy concerns are important, in most elections they are not the dominant influence on voting.[37] One reason is that public policy debates often are complex, and people have limited information. To cite one extreme example, President Clinton's 1993 health care proposal was 1342 printed pages long, and that was just one of the competing proposals! How could voters possibly be expected to have detailed views about such complex issues? Voters therefore seldom use elections as a means of giving public officials specific policy mandates. They select parties or party leaders, not policies.

Moreover, voters often are unsure where the candidates stand, because candidates equivocate and otherwise confuse voters about their positions. Research on the 1968 election, for example, found that views on U.S. policy in Vietnam (whether to escalate the war, maintain the status quo, or withdraw) were only minimally related to the presidential vote. How could that be true when intense disagreement about the war was tearing the country apart? The answer is that the positions of the candidates gave the voters no basis on which to choose. The Democratic nominee, Humphrey, supported the status quo, but he kept wavering. The Republican, Nixon, refused to reveal his position, saying that he had a "secret plan" to end the war. In the end, befuddled voters treated the two candidates as though they supported the same policy.[38] Again, voters uncertain about what candidates believe cannot use their vote to mandate specific policies.

There are some important exceptions to the finding that public policies are not the dominant factor in most elections. Social or cultural issues, for example, occasionally do play a significant role. Candidates announce that they favor prayer in schools or that they oppose allowing same-sex unions. Such issues are "easy" for voters to process because the policy proposals and the desired outcome are one and the same: Start praying in schools, ban gay marriages.[39] Such issues are different from policy issues such as health insurance or education, where a chain of actions is required to bring about a particular outcome.[40] Social issues are as much about values held by different groups in society as they are about specific public policies. Indeed, such values often are incorporated into the party identifications of citizens. They are part of the **party images,** the associations that voters make between the parties and particular issues.[41] Voters concerned with moral issues gave overwhelming support to Republicans in 2004, for example.

A second example of issues mattering is when voters are upset about a problem and eager for government to do *something* about it. Thus, candidates talk about "getting tough on crime," "cleaning up the welfare mess," and "getting guns out of the hands of children." These are important political issues, to be sure, but often they do not involve much in the way of specific policy proposals. Voters are merely asked to choose among different priorities or between general approaches such as "soft" and "tough." Moreover, such issues at least implicitly reflect voters' unhappiness with the government *performance* that has allowed such problems to fester.

party image
A set of widely held associations between a party and particular issues and values.

Watch What You Pray For

The party out of power usually profits from bad national news. Although the economy showed signs of weakness in 2004 and casualties in Iraq had mounted, voters were not particularly unhappy with government performance—which made the election an uphill battle for Democrats trying to regain power.

Government Performance Real elections are a mix of considerations, but a great deal of research confirms the influence of past government performance.[42] Performance voting demands less of voters than policy voting. To make judgments about performance, voters do not have to watch C-SPAN or read the *New York Times*. Voters can judge economic conditions from their own experiences and those of their friends and neighbors. They can judge other social conditions by observing daily life in their communities, schools, and workplaces.

Voting by looking backward at performance (often called **retrospective voting**) may outweigh voting by looking forward at policy promises (often called **prospective voting**). The 1984 campaign provided a classic illustration. Public opinion surveys showed that on many issues, voters were closer to the Democratic nominee, Walter Mondale, than to President Reagan. A majority believed that tax increases were inevitable (Mondale's position), expressed skepticism about "Star Wars" (the missile defense system dear to Reagan's heart), rejected Reagan's call for further increases in defense spending, and doubted Reagan's Central America policy.[43] Nevertheless, Reagan carried 49 states. Was this overwhelming support just an expression of his winning personality? Probably not. Analysis of the election returns showed that a majority of voters approved of Reagan's performance as president, regardless of many of the specific policies he followed.

Voters hardly can be blamed for adopting shortcuts like performance voting. The future is uncertain, the experts disagree, and time is limited, so how can one make an intelligent decision about complex policy alternatives? Moreover, candidates are not always clear about their intentions. At least good performance by government suggests competent leadership, so voters quite reasonably choose to stick with those in power when they are content.[44]

retrospective voting
Voting on the basis of the past performance of the incumbent administration.

prospective voting
Voting on the basis of the candidates' policy promises.

The important point to remember is that government performance is neither a long-term consideration nor a short one, but something in between. It refers to an assessment of leadership that reflects four years of activity, not something that suddenly arises when the campaign begins. Election-year campaign activity can attempt to put some "spin" on government performance, but it is difficult to make a bad economy or an unpopular war into a positive accomplishment for the incumbent administration, no matter how good the media experts and campaign consultants.

The Qualities of the Candidates   Not surprisingly, the individual candidates are the major source of change in how people vote from election to election.[45] Not since 1956, when Adlai Stevenson fought a rematch with Dwight Eisenhower, have Americans had the same choice of candidates in two presidential elections. In a country that exhorts voters to "support the person not the party," candidate quality is an extremely important influence on how people vote. Note, however, that *quality* is not the same thing as *personality*. Personality is overrated, especially by the losers. It is comforting for candidates or parties to blame failure on the foolishness of voters duped by an opponent's sparkling personality; they would rather not admit that voters rejected their beliefs or doubted their competence.

Even the importance of candidate quality can be exaggerated, though, because after an election there is a tendency to downgrade the loser's personal qualities and to upgrade the winner's. For example, after their defeat in 1996, many Republicans concluded that Robert Dole was a terrible candidate who had run an uninspired campaign. Although there is always some truth to such charges, his critics seemed to forget that Dole had been viewed much differently less than two years earlier. In the aftermath of the Republican takeover of Congress in 1994, Dole was viewed as the "grownup" in Washington, a mature, responsible, experienced public official who would fill the leadership vacuum, negotiate the necessary compromises, and keep the government functioning. Insider reports mentioned his quick wit and warm personality. Did Dole change in two years? No, he was the same Dole, but losing had hurt his political reputation even though he had taken on a popular incumbent with peace and prosperity behind him.

Al Gore provides a more recent example. After his defeat in a time of peace and prosperity, many Democrats preferred to attribute his loss to personality flaws rather than to his abandonment of the centrist stance that Bill Clinton had taken, or to a popular rejection of Bill Clinton's adulterous behavior, even though research showed those were the major reasons for Gore's loss.[46] Many in the party found it easier to blame their messenger than to admit that the electorate had rejected their message or the behavior of their most prominent officeholder.

There are some striking contrasts between what voters actually thought of the candidates in a given campaign and how popular history now views the candidates. The 1960 contest between John F. Kennedy and Richard Nixon is the most vivid example. Although historians have debunked much of the Kennedy mystique, you are probably familiar with the Kennedy legend—the charismatic leader of a new "Camelot." In fact, however, 1960 survey data show that Nixon was more favorably regarded as a candidate than Kennedy.[47] Kennedy owed his narrow victory primarily to the fact that he was a Democrat; at the time there were more Democrats than Republicans.[48] Did the data indicate that Nixon had a more attractive personality than Kennedy? No. Nixon was viewed as more experienced and better qualified for the job. But what lives on in political folklore about the candidates may bear little resemblance to the reality of citizens' opinions when they voted.

Ronald Reagan is a more recent example. When the former president died in the summer of 2004, commentators across the political spectrum praised his winning personality and admirable character, and hailed his accomplishments as president. Thousands of Americans stood in lines for hours to pass by his coffin, and the spectacle of the state funeral dominated the airwaves for days. Yet, before Reagan's election in 1980, voters evaluated Jimmy Carter's personal characteristics higher than Reagan's.[49] And average presidential approval ratings during his administration were not impressive—they were slightly below the average of the ten U.S. presidents between Truman and Clinton.[50] Memories of Reagan began to grow more positive after he left office, even before he became a victim of Alzheimer's disease. By the time he died, evaluations were considerably more positive than the views Americans had expressed at the time of his presidency. Thus, Ronald Reagan only became the beloved figure Americans remember after he had been elected and re-elected.

Finally, we should remember that what people think about the candidates is partly based on the other influences shaping their voting behavior. Most citizens with a strong Democratic party ID are going to like the Democratic candidate— any Democratic candidate. People with strong positions on certain policies probably are going to like any candidate who shares those policy commitments and to dislike any candidate who does not. People who think the president has performed very well probably are going to like him personally, although that affection is not guaranteed.

Public Display of Affection
Al Gore's aggressive kiss reportedly surprised wife Tipper at the 2000 Democratic National Convention. Whatever her reaction, "The Kiss" electrified some pundits, who credited it for Gore's bounce in the polls. But humorist Dave Barry thought Gore resembled an alien depositing an egg sac. Is it important to have an affectionate national leader, or is that relevant only to a personality contest?

Limited Media Influence on Presidential Elections

The media are less influential in the general-election campaign than in the primaries. The primaries, especially the early primaries, maximize the opportunity for media influence, but in the general election, media coverage runs up against voter predispositions. These consist of party identifications that many voters hold, and the impressions of government performance that voters have been forming for four (or even eight) years, not just the few months of the campaign.[51]

In the primaries, neither predisposition exists. Primary voters choose only among Democrats or only among Republicans, so party ID is not relevant. Nor is presidential performance of any use: Normally, all the candidates in the incumbent party's primaries defend the president's record, whereas all the candidates in the other party's primaries criticize that record. Consequently, citizens use other information to choose among the candidates, and the media in most cases provide it. The general election differs in that many voters have all the information they need: their own partisan identification, the candidate preferences of groups they like or dislike, and their impressions of government performance.

The importance of the campaign itself is similarly exaggerated. Contrary to what the media imply, many elections are practically "in the bag" before campaigning begins; conditions in the preceding four years and the government's response to them have determined the outcome. The 1972, 1984, and 1996 landslide reelections of incumbents are the clearest examples, but not the only ones. Political scientist James Campbell has calculated that between 1948 and 2000, the campaigns probably were decisive in 1948 and 1960, two exceedingly close elections. The campaigns may have been decisive in 1976, 1980, and 2000. In the other nine elections, the outcome was largely predetermined.[52]

Certainly campaigns do matter.[53] But campaigns are constrained by what goes on between elections. A card game provides a good analogy. Who wins a hand partly depends on the deal of the cards. No matter how skillfully you play, it may not be sufficient to overcome a bad draw. In politics, some cards are dealt years, even decades, before the election. The Democrats drew the Great Depression card in 1932 and played it successfully against Republicans until after World War II. The Republicans drew the "liberal special interest" card in the 1970s and were still playing it against Democrats in 2004. Other cards are drawn in the four years since the last election. Good economic conditions are aces dealt to the incumbent party; poor conditions are aces dealt to the opposition. The same is true for international embarrassments and costly wars.

The luck of the draw strongly affects the campaign. We praise and criticize campaigns, often forgetting that the candidates were limited in what they could do by social and economic realities. Did the fact that Michael Dukakis lost to Vice President Bush in 1988, whereas Clinton beat President Bush in 1992, indicate that Dukakis ran a poor campaign and Clinton a brilliant one? In retrospect, Dukakis surely could have done some things better, and Clinton had recruited some crack advisers.[54] But Clinton's brilliant campaign probably also reflects the fact that an economic recession made the Bush administration a much wider target in 1992 than the Reagan-Bush administration had been in 1988.

The importance of the campaign in presidential elections emerges in close contests. If, on the basis of party ID and presidential performance, the race is about even when the campaign begins, then the campaign will determine the outcome by winning over the marginal, or undecided, voters. Certainly with an election as close as the ones in 2000 and 2004, almost any success or any mistake or any candidate shortcoming could sway the results. Hundreds of choices "caused" the outcome. The tone of media coverage or the expertise of media advisers can win or lose the election. But the point to remember is that few elections begin as even contests. Rather, what elected officials have done between elections has largely determined the outcome.

The Contemporary Presidential Election Scene

The New Deal party system splintered in the 1960s. The racial and social turmoil created by the civil rights revolution and the war in Vietnam forced President Lyndon Johnson to withdraw from the race in 1968 and enabled Republican Richard Nixon to win two terms. It was the beginning of a Republican streak that saw them win five of the six presidential elections between 1968 and 1988. Not until the 1990s were the Democrats able to overcome the problems that first arose in the 1960s. We will survey these ups and downs in party fortunes in light of our discussion of American voting behavior in the previous section.

The 1970s and 1980s: Republican "Lock"

The so-called Republican lock on the presidency during the 1970s and 1980s reflected developments that gave Republicans a clear advantage on two of the four major factors that determine how Americans vote: performance and issues. This advantage forced

Democratic candidates to defend unpopular policies and eventually eroded the long-standing Democratic advantage in party ID. Although the Democrats enjoyed a brief recovery after the Watergate scandal, the extremely narrow margin of Jimmy Carter's victory suggested the severity of the Democrats' problems. The Carter administration only retained the White House for four years, after which Republicans won three consecutive elections: 1980, 1984, and 1988. During this period, Republican performance and policies beat the Democrats on each of the major fronts in contemporary politics: economic, foreign and defense, racial, and social.

For almost half a century, Americans viewed Democrats as the party of prosperity. But in the early 1970s, an inflationary era began that economists blamed on President Johnson's attempt to wage war in Vietnam while implementing major new domestic programs. The rising tide of inflation reached frightening levels (13 percent) under Democratic President Carter. As the party in power when economic conditions hit bottom, the Democrats took the blame.

Americans of the time also viewed Republicans as more capable in the international arena, a perception that the Vietnam War only reinforced. During the 1970s the United States faced a series of foreign challenges, and voters were not confident that the Democratic party could deal with them. The final humiliation came in 1979 when Iranian militants seized 90 hostages from the American embassy in Tehran and held them for more than a year. This hostage crisis destroyed any remaining hope for President Carter's reelection and reinforced the popular perception that the Democrats were unable to keep America strong internationally.

Racial politics also hurt the Democrats. The exact role that racial issues played is not clear. Some believe that white support of Republican candidates grew from lingering racism.[55] Others disagree, arguing many policies currently proposed to help minorities—such as affirmative action—are inconsistent with traditional American values.[56] Regardless, political attitudes are sharply polarized by race (see Figure 10.5). Democrats were caught in the middle of such disagreements between the white majority and the party's most loyal constituency.

Finally, social issues hurt the Democrats during this period. Starting in the 1960s, liberalism became associated in some voters' minds with controversial changes in American life—for example, sexual permissiveness, declining religious faith, family breakdown, and violent crime. A popular reaction arose in the late 1970s in the form of the "new right," a socially conservative movement connected to evangelical religious groups. These voters swelled the Republican ranks in many elections.

The 1990s: Democratic Resurgence

In 1992 Bill Clinton was elected with 43 percent of the vote in a three-way election. Even without Ross Perot in the contest, Clinton would have won.[57] How did the Democratic party revive? First, a recession rejuvenated the Democrats' image as the party of prosperity. The struggling economy was the foundation of Clinton's campaign. He promised to get the economy moving again, and he appealed to middle-class concerns with his support of universal health care. The end of the Cold War, meanwhile, meant that foreign threats did not distract voters from their preoccupation with the economy. With the collapse of the Soviet threat, national defense and foreign policy vanished from the list of voter concerns in 1992. Clinton also distanced himself from prominent black leaders, such as Jesse Jackson, and criticized the lyrics found in some

FIGURE 10.5

Blacks and Whites Differ Greatly in Their Views About Race Relations and Racial Policy

SOURCE: "An American Dilemma" (Part II), *The Public Perspective,* February/March 1996: 20, 23, 26.

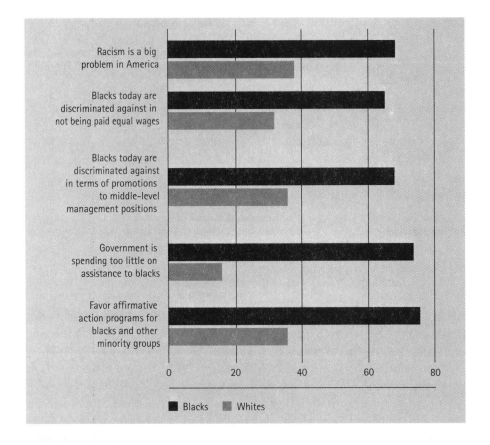

rap music. He prayed, talked about family values, promised "to end welfare as we know it," allowed capital punishment, and in other ways tried to dispel the cultural liberal image that had dogged the Democrats for a generation. Clinton was able to retain the presidency in 1996 even as his party suffered in the mid-decade congressional elections.

The economy grew steadily throughout Clinton's first term, and by the 1996 elections, most Americans were economically optimistic—indeed, as optimistic as they had been in 1984 when they overwhelmingly reelected Republican Ronald Reagan.[58] Incumbents who run during times of economic prosperity tend to be successful, and Clinton was no exception. Clinton also increased his support among moderates through a strategy of "triangulation"—positioning himself between liberal congressional Democrats and conservative Republicans.[59]

A growing gender gap also helped Clinton. Some polls reported that if only men had voted in 1996, Robert Dole would have won the election, the first time majorities of men and of women had voted for different candidates.

The gender gap is widely misunderstood. Many pundits understandably attributed the emergence of the gender gap to different male and female positions on "women's issues." On the contrary, men and women differ little in their views of abortion and issues related to equality of opportunity for women.[60] Rather, differences in voting appear to stem more from long-standing gender differences on issues of military force, the use of violence, and government activities in support of the disadvantaged (see

TABLE 10.2
WOMEN'S AND MEN'S ATTITUDES DIFFER

	Women	Men
Role of Government		
Consider self conservative	29%	43%
Government should provide fewer services	30	45
Poverty and homelessness are among the country's most important problems	63	44
Government should guarantee medical care for all	69	58
Favor affirmative action programs for blacks and other minority groups	53	41
Force/Violence		
American bombers should attack all military targets in Iraq, including those in heavily populated areas	37	61
Handguns should be illegal except for use by police and other authorized persons	48	28
Favor death penalty	76	82
Approve of caning the teenager in Singapore who committed acts of vandalism	39	61
Approve of the way the Justice Department took Elian Gonzalez from his Miami relatives	35	52

SOURCE: *The Public Perspective,* August/September 1996: 10–27; *The Public Perspective,* July/August 1994: 96. Gallup Tuesday Briefing, May 2, 2000.

Table 10.2).[61] There is considerable disagreement about why women and men differ on issues. Some argue that women's values are different from men's.[62] From an electoral standpoint, though, the origins of gender differences are less important than the fact that they exist.

Perhaps most important, the Republican Congress made a serious tactical error in shutting down the government in the winter of 1995–1996, when President Clinton would not accept their budget.[63] Polls indicated that voters sided with Clinton in the dispute, probably costing Dole any chance he had of winning the 1996 election. Clinton took the position that it was necessary to reelect him in order to check and balance the Republicans in Congress. Ironically, by the end of the campaign, the Republican party stopped seriously trying to defeat Clinton, instead running ads arguing that it was necessary to reelect congressional Republicans in order to check and balance the president![64]

The actions of the Republican Congress during 1995-1996 helped to widen the gender gap and reelect Bill Clinton. By adopting an approach to welfare that was viewed as punitive, by taking an aggressive stance on Medicaid and Medicare reform, and by proposing cutbacks in environmental and safety regulation—in these and similar ways, the Republicans drew attention to issues that divided men and women, naturally widening gender differences.[65] In addition, the close association between the Republican party and the religious right probably served to widen the gender gap. Because the religious right emphasizes family values, it sometimes alienates working women, as well as those who are unmarried or divorced. The gender gap is wider among single men and women than among married men and women—a marriage gap.[66]

George Bush Campaigning
Although the wealthy son of a former president, George W. Bush projects an earnestness and simplicity that helps regular voters identify with him—a crucial advantage under the permanent campaign.

The 2000 Election

Prophets of doom predicted that the U.S. economy would melt down when the calendar changed from 1999 to 2000. The economy did just fine, but no one anticipated that the polity might melt down later in the year. It took five weeks to determine that Republican George W. Bush had won the presidential election. President Bush headed the first unified Republican government since 1954 (although his party temporarily lost control of the Senate when James Jeffords of Vermont left the party in May 2001).

The 2000 election underscored the difference between primary and general-election campaigns. In the primaries, hot-button issues like abortion and gun control were prominent, but exit polls showed that such issues were of lesser importance in the general election. Gore had to back away from his primary position on guns because it was unpopular in many of the battleground states. Similarly, Bush downplayed his opposition to abortion. Instead, broad issues of concern to the great body of Americans—the economy, health care, and education—took center stage. The candidates talked long and in some detail about issues of concern to the American middle class: restructuring social security, reforming public schools, and what mix of taxing and spending they advocated.

To many political scientists the 2000 election was puzzling. Given the long-standing importance of government performance to voters, most political scientists expected Al Gore to win. During the Clinton administration the country enjoyed unprecedented prosperity and relative peace. As the election approached, President Clinton's approval ratings were exceptionally high by historical standards, consumers felt optimistic about the economy, and people thought that the country was on the right track. Supposedly, incumbent administrations do not lose during times of peace and prosperity. Why did Gore lose?

Detailed statistical analysis indicates that the vote for Gore was less closely tied to the administration's record than were the votes for incumbent-party candidates in the previous seven elections.[67] Some analysts argue that Gore did not receive credit because he ran the wrong campaign. Although the effects of campaigns often are exaggerated, in this case Gore's critics may be right. Gore did not emphasize the administration's record. As one critic sarcastically observed, Gore's theme was "You've never had it so good, and I'm mad as hell about it."[68] In trying to distance himself from a scandal-plagued president, Gore may have thrown away his trump card.

Gore also paid a penalty for being seen as farther from the average voter than Bush. Although polls showed that Gore was closer to people than Bush was on specific issues like education and social security, more people felt that Gore was too liberal than felt that Bush was too conservative.

Finally, there was the Clinton factor. Gore distanced himself from Clinton. Nonetheless, Clinton's personal ratings were much lower than his job ratings, and a majority of the country agreed that the country was on the wrong track morally, whatever the state of the economy. Statistical evidence indicates that Clinton's personal ratings helped drag Gore down. Independents and even Democrats who were dismayed by Clinton's personal behavior tended to favor Bush. Whether even more swing voters would have selected Bush had Gore tied himself more closely to Clinton is a question that statistics cannot answer.

The 2004 Showdown

Polls that showed a captivatingly close race in the final days of the 2004 campaign led many media commentators to speculate that the race would again be decided in the courts or in state-level recounts. Nevertheless, the result, while not an overwhelming victory for Bush, was at least a decisive one: for the first time since 1988, the winner of the presidency amassed a clear majority (51 percent) of the popular vote. Bush's victories in key states like Florida and Ohio, as well as Republican gains in Congress, frustrated Democrats who were convinced that economic stagnation and the Iraq war would swing undecided voters their way. In the days after the election, pundits made much of an apparent finding (based on exit polls) that significant numbers of voters based their decisions on "moral values." Some argued that Democratic candidate John Kerry ought to have placed greater emphasis on morality in his campaign speeches.

In reality, the 2004 election was not much different from past elections. Any "moral values" voters probably decided on a candidate long before election day. The economy, while not in great shape, was in better condition than it had been in past years when voters had thrown out incumbent presidents. The predictable criticisms of John Kerry's campaign fail to account for the fact that these and other critical factors were beyond the candidate's control.

Chapter Summary

The American nomination process is far more open than the nomination processes of other democracies. It gives rank-and-file voters more influence than in other countries where party leaders and elected officials dominate the process, and it gives "outsider" candidates a chance by enabling them to contest the early, smaller primaries and caucuses. The process begins long before the election itself and sometimes lasts months before a nominee is determined. It also heightens the influence of party issue activists and the media.

The presidential campaign is often misunderstood. It is not an independent force that determines election outcomes. Rather, the campaign itself is shaped by events and conditions in the years leading up to the election. Candidates perceived as running "good campaigns" are usually those who have good records that are easy to defend or those whose opponents have bad records that are hard to defend. Candidates who run "bad campaigns" are generally those who face uphill battles. The 2000 campaign of Al Gore, which did not try to capitalize on good government performance, may be an exception to these generalizations.

The reason why campaigns are limited in their impact is that most voters do not make up their minds on the basis of the campaign. Many of them decide well before the campaign ever begins. They do so on the basis of long-standing party identifications, evaluations of government performance, and the associations between the parties and particular values and positions. Only a minority decide how to vote late in the campaign and on the basis of the particular candidates and the particular things they say. In a case like the 2004 election, when neither campaign makes a serious blunder, party identification, government performance, and deeper issues will determine which candidate ends up on top.

Key Terms

caucus, p. 255
closed primaries, p. 257
electoral vote, p. 266
matching funds, p. 259
open primaries, p. 257

party identification, p. 268
party image, p. 270
political activists, p. 261
popular vote, p. 266
primary election, p. 255

prospective voting, p. 271
retrospective voting, p. 271
semi-closed primaries, p. 257
winner-take-all voting, p. 266

Suggested Readings

Of General Interest

Abramson, Paul, John Aldrich, and David Rohde. *Change and Continuity in the 2000 Elections.* Washington, DC: CQ Press, 2002. This quadrennial publication provides a comprehensive overview of voting behavior in national elections.

Mayer, William, ed. *The Making of the Presidential Candidates 2004.* Lanham, MD: Rowman & Littlefield 2004. An informative collection of essays covering all facets of the contemporary nominating process.

Pomper, Gerald, et al. *The Election of 2000.* Chatham, NJ: Chatham House, 1997. This quadrennial publication by a group of knowledgeable authors complements Abramson, Aldrich, and Rohde, offering less detail about voting behavior but a broader view of the campaigns and the activities of elites.

Focused Studies

Campbell, James. *The American Campaign.* College Station, TX: Texas A&M University Press, 2000. The most comprehensive scholarly study of presidential campaigns.

Carmines, Edward, and James Stimson. *Issue Evolution: Race and the Transformation of American Politics.* Princeton, NJ: Princeton University Press, 1989. An important argument about the importance of race for realigning American politics in the 1960s.

Holbrook, Thomas. *Do Campaigns Matter?* Thousand Oaks, CA: Sage, 1996. A scientifically rigorous study of the impact of presidential campaigns.

Miller, Arthur, and Bruce Gronbeck, eds. *Presidential Campaigns and American Self-Images.* Boulder, CO: Westview, 1994. This collection of essays presents a balanced and sophisticated view of campaigns.

On the Web

www.multied.com/elections/

A graphical history of presidential elections can be found through MultiEducator Incorporated.

www.archives.gov/federal_register/electoral_college/
The official National Archive Web site on the electoral college answers all basic questions about procedure, and it even includes an electoral college calculator.

www.umich.edu/~nes/
Perhaps the most comprehensive source of political science data is the National Election Study Archive at the University of Michigan. The site contains a wealth of data and also many charts and figures showing changes in American politics from election to election.

www.c-span.org

Some of the best Web sites for learning about a presidential campaign are the ones set up by the candidate themselves. Of course, the official 2004 campaign Web sites are mostly down now. But you can still see the major events of that election at C-SPAN's election archives.

www.netsol.com/cgi-bin/whois/whois

In fact, if you want to search the Web to see whether any domain names are still available, you can do so here. You may want to purchase one; perhaps you could sell it to a candidate.

CHAPTER 11

★ ★ ★ ★ ★ ★ ★ ★ ★ ★ ★ ★ ★ ★ ★ ★ ★

Choosing the Congress

How Not to Be Reelected to Congress

After digesting the results of the 1992 congressional elections, political pundits declared that 1992 was the "year of the woman." Four new female senators were elected, and the number of women representatives rose from 28 to 47. One of the newcomers to the House of Representatives was Democrat Marjorie Margolies-Mezvinsky, commonly known as MMM. She was the first Democrat in 76 years to be elected from an affluent suburban district near Philadelphia with a 2 to 1 Republican registration edge. A well-known local newscaster, MMM had jumped into the race when the Republican incumbent announced his retirement. She won the Democratic primary handily and squeaked by in the general election by less than 1 percent of the vote.

Normally, a member's first election is the hardest. Once in office, members launch themselves into the permanent campaign. They behave prudently, use the advantages of incumbency to expand their support among constituents, and avoid giving potential challengers a damaging issue to run on. By following these simple rules, incumbents win reelection with very high probability. MMM violated these rules, and the result was a rare incumbent defeat.

Eight months after her election, and sixteen months before the next one, the House of Representatives held the fate of the new Clinton presidency in its hands. The final version of the president's deficit reduction plan lay before the House. A sweeping package of spending cuts and tax increases, the plan would chart the course of governmental economic policy for the next five years. Earlier in the year, the House and Senate had passed the Clinton plan without a single Republican vote. Differences in the two chambers' versions of the legislation had been ironed out, and now final passage was at hand. Or was it?

Again, not a single one of the Republicans in Congress would support the plan: They considered the income tax increases unacceptable. Some Democrats also opposed the plan because it included small increases in gasoline taxes as well as other elements that they disliked. Democratic leaders worked frantically to muster a majority. Speaker Thomas Foley exhorted his troops, "Tonight is the time for courage. Tonight is the time to put away the old, easy ways. Tonight is the time for responsibility. Tonight is the night to vote."[1]

President Clinton himself worked the phones, calling undecided Democrats and telling them that he had to have their vote—his presidency was at stake. For Representative Margolies-Mezvinsky, the situation was a political nightmare. She already had voted against each of Clinton's three key economic proposals, including the deficit reduction package that was once again on the floor. On that earlier occasion she had announced, "I promised the voters of Montgomery County that I would not vote for an across-the-board tax increase—and tonight I kept that promise."[2] Since then she had reassured her constituents that she would continue to oppose the plan. Now she was under intense pressure from the president and Democratic leaders to reverse her stand. Which would prevail, party or constituency?

At the conclusion of electronic voting, the tally stood at 216 to 216. A majority of the full house (218 of 435) is required to pass the budget. Pat Williams, a Democrat from Montana, had agreed to support the president if necessary, so MMM's vote would decide the fate of the plan and, by implication, the fate of the Clinton presidency. Surrounded by supportive Democrats and "with the demeanor of someone being marched to her own hanging," she approached the well of the house to vote for the president's budget. Gleeful Republicans chanted "Goodbye, Marjorie!"[3] MMM may have saved the Clinton presidency, but the cost was her political life.

During the 1994 campaign the Democratic congressional leadership helped MMM raise more than $1.6 million in campaign funds, and President Clinton himself came to her district to support her reelection, but money and endorsements are not enough when a representative ignores the clear wishes of her constituency. The Republican she defeated in 1992 returned for a rematch in the next general election. He raised less than two-thirds as much money as MMM did, but she still lost with only 45 percent of the vote.

MAKING THE CONNECTION

Elections are never far from the minds of members of Congress. Members of the House of Representatives put their fates on the line every second November, but that two-year interval between elections is misleading. Many representatives face primaries in the spring of election years, so primary campaigns are under way a little more than a year after members have taken the oath of office. In response to such realities, representatives campaign for reelection more or less continuously. They are Exhibit A of the permanent campaign.

Surprisingly, the situation isn't much different for senators. Although senators are elected for six-year terms, a third of them are elected every two years, so at any given time one-third of the Senate is operating with the same short time horizon as members of the House. Moreover, Senate campaigns are so expensive that the average incumbent must raise an average of just over $15,000 every week for six years—a time-consuming, psychologically draining activity that keeps all of them aware of their need to maintain political support, even if their actual reelection campaign is years away.

The great majority of congressional incumbents win reelection, but as the unhappy experience of Representative Margolies-Mezvinsky illustrates, victory is never guaranteed. Even incumbent candidates who spend much more than their challengers can lose their seats after one politically damaging decision. That simple fact colors all aspects of congressional life.

This chapter focuses on the members of the United States Congress:

- How do they get elected and reelected?

- What is the advantage of incumbency?

- How do House and Senate elections differ?

- How have recent congressional elections changed?

- How representative is the body that congressional elections determine?

★ ★ ★ ★ ★ ★ ★ ★ ★ ★ ★ ★ ★ ★ ★

The Electoral Evolution of the Congress

The founders did not envision today's Congress. James Madison, for example, thought that frequent elections for the House of Representatives would cause the membership to consist of political amateurs closely tied to daily life in their districts. Madison wrote that the House should have "an immediate dependence on, and an intimate sympathy with, the people."[4] The founders also did not expect the Senate, with six-year terms, to be electorally sensitive—especially because the Constitution originally provided for senators to be chosen by state legislatures. According to Madison, the Senate would proceed "with more coolness, with more system, and with more wisdom, than the popular branch."[5] Not until adoption of the Seventeenth Amendment to the Constitution in 1913 did all senators face popular election.

In their broader operation, neither chamber developed exactly as the framers planned. At first, the House indeed was an amateur political body. Unstable in its membership and tumultuous in its operation, the House operated more or less according to plan. More than 40 percent of the members of the First Congress did not return

Young Representative Abraham Lincoln (Whig-IL) in 1846

for the Second. In fact, turnover levels often were as high as 50 percent until after the Civil War.[6] But contrary to Madison's argument, frequent elections were not the cause of high turnover. Until the late nineteenth century, many more representatives quit than were defeated. Job conditions were unattractive—especially after the national government moved to the uninhabited, swampy lands that became Washington, DC—and the national government was not particularly important in the early years of the republic.[7] Many members found that they had less comfort and less power living in Washington than they enjoyed in their home states.[8] Even those members willing to serve multiple terms sometimes were prevented from doing so by *rotation* practices, whereby a congressional district's political interests "took turns" holding the congressional seat. Abraham Lincoln, for example, was elected to the House in 1846 but stepped down after one term in accordance with local rotation agreements.[9] As a result of considerations like these, average service in the House of Representatives did not reach three years until after 1900.

Also contrary to Madison's expectations, the early Senate was far from being a stable body whose members served for long periods. In the first ten years of the republic, more than one-third of the senators failed to serve out their terms, and until 1820 more senators *resigned* during their term than were denied reelection by their state legislatures. Although they had the opportunity to stay longer than members of the House, many senators chose to pass it up for the same reasons that House members went home.[10]

professional legislature
Legislature whose members serve full-time and for long periods.

Today, things are much different. The Congress is the world's foremost example of what political scientists call a **professional legislature:** Its members are full-time legislators who stay for long periods, as shown in Figure 11.1. Relatively few members quit voluntarily, and many intend to remain in Congress indefinitely. In fact, many people in the United States think that the membership of Congress is *too* stable. They support institutional changes such as term limits in order to shake up what they see as an unresponsive institution.

Congressional unresponsiveness seems to clash with the overall claim of this book that American political institutions are electorally sensitive (if not hypersensitive). Given

FIGURE 11.1

Congress Became a Career in the Twentieth Century

SOURCES: Nelson W. Polsby, "The Institutionalization of the U.S. House of Representatives," *American Political Science Review*, March 1968: 146; and Norman J. Ornstein et al., eds., *Vital Statistics on Congress, 1995–1996* (Washington, DC: Congressional Quarterly, 1996), p. 60.

Fair Weather for Republicans
Population growth in the heavily Republican Sunbelt has outpaced that in the North, causing congressional districts to migrate southward. The Detroit area of Michigan, where this cartoon was first published, has been especially hard hit.

• *Do you think it is harder for a region to recover if it loses political power after the area has gone into decline?*

the electoral advantage that contemporary incumbents appear to enjoy, how is it possible to argue that Congress is an electorally sensitive institution? What critics of Congress overlook, however, is that contemporary incumbents fare so well precisely *because* they are so electorally aware; they anticipate threats to their reelection and act to avoid them. Before providing the evidence for this claim, though, the chapter must provide some background information on congressional elections.

Reapportionment and Redistricting

How are the constituencies that are represented in Congress determined? In the Senate, representation is simple and never changes. The Constitution gives every state two senators, regardless of population, and this provision can be amended only with the consent of every state (Article 5). Because smaller states will not give up their political advantage, the Senate's scheme of representation is essentially an amendment-proof feature of American democracy (see the Democratic Dilemma on page 286).

Representation is more complicated in the House. The Constitution requires that a census be held every decade. After the census, the 435 seats in the House of Representatives are apportioned among the states according to their populations—a process called **reapportionment.** In the past half-century, northeastern and midwestern states have lost more than 60 House seats to southern and southwestern states as population has shifted from the Frostbelt to the Sunbelt.[11] Given the different political leanings of these regions, the net effect has been to strengthen Republican representation in the House.

Currently, seven states have such small populations that they only receive one congressional seat, a minimum guaranteed by Article I. After the other states learn how many House seats they have received, they set to work **redistricting**—drawing the boundaries of the new districts. Congressional districts within individual states once

You Are Redrawing the Districts in Your State

reapportionment
The allocation of House seats to the states after each decennial census.

redistricting
Drawing new boundaries of congressional districts, usually after the decennial census.

varied widely in population, but now they must be of nearly equal population, the result of Supreme Court decisions beginning with *Wesberry v. Sanders* in 1964. Subsequent decisions have refined the standard to one of precise numerical equality (at least as indicated by census figures, which are only approximate, even on the day they are recorded). The principle has become "one person, one vote."

In most states the legislature drafts electoral maps, but in five states bipartisan commissions do the job, and in several others the lines are drawn by some combination of legislators and outside appointees. The redistricting process is often highly contentious, because political careers depend on which voters get placed in which districts. Charges of **gerrymandering**—drawing the lines for partisan or other political advantage—fly back and forth, and often the courts are drawn into the process.

gerrymandering
Drawing boundary lines of congressional districts in order to confer an advantage on some partisan or political interest.

The Congressional Nomination Process

The congressional nomination process is much simpler than the presidential one: A nominee for the House or Senate must win at most one primary election, not a sequence across many states. In a few states, party conventions can nominate candidates, but in most states the candidates are chosen in primaries. Some states hold their Senate and House primaries on the same day, and under the same rules, as their presidential primaries. Other states hold them at different times and/or under different rules.[12]

The dates of **filing deadlines** and primary elections also vary widely across states.[13] The filing deadline is the latest date on which a candidate who wishes to be on the ballot must file official documents and/or pay fees with state election officials. For the 2004 elections, California had the earliest filing deadline, December 5, 2003 (!), and Louisiana had the latest, August 6, 2004. The earliest primaries also took place in California on March 5, 2004, and the latest were in Hawaii on September 21, 2004. Thus, some candidates may know the identity of their opponent as much as six months earlier than others.

The hardest-fought primaries occur when there is an **open seat,** one without an incumbent running for reelection. If both parties have strength in the area, the primaries in both parties may be competitive. If only one party is strong, its primary will be hotly contested because the winner is likely to be the next member of Congress. When incumbents run, on the other hand, they seldom lose in the primary: Indeed, they seldom face tough races from other members of their party. This trend does not prove that primaries are unimportant. It may indicate instead that incumbents usually are pretty good about keeping members of their own party satisfied, thus discouraging a strong primary challenge.

Contemporary House Elections

Although journalists emphasize incumbency as the determining factor in House elections, party identification is more important. The Democrats maintained unbroken control of the House of Representatives between 1954 and 1994, even though all but three of their 1954 incumbents eventually departed.[14] In many House districts, it is almost inconceivable that the seat could change hands from one party to another; voters overwhelmingly prefer the incumbent party. Such districts are called **safe seats.**

Of course, the parties do not control campaigns as they did in earlier periods of American history, and voters are not so much influenced by party loyalties as in earlier times. Nevertheless, party organizations and party loyalties are still very important. One reason why party remains the most influential factor in House elections is that many voters know little, if anything, about the candidates. Only a third of the citizenry can recall the name of their representative, and even fewer can remember anything he or she has done for the district. Only 10 percent or so can remember how their representative voted on a particular bill. Challengers are even less well known. Having little information on which to base their vote, many people simply go by the brand name, voting for the candidate of the party with which they generally sympathize. In House elections, about three-fourths of all voters who identify with a party typically support the House candidate with the same affiliation.[15]

Although it is not the single most important factor in House elections, incumbency clearly is the second most important factor. Moreover, incumbency has grown in importance while party has declined. Statistical studies of House elections have revealed that, other things being equal, the electoral benefit of being an incumbent—that is, the **incumbency advantage**—has grown from about 2 percentage points before 1960 to as high as 12 in some recent elections.[16] The increase has not been smooth. Rather, as

filing deadline
The latest date on which a candidate for office may file official papers or pay required fees to state election officials.

open seat
A House or Senate race with no incumbent (because of death or retirement).

safe seat
A congressional district certain to vote for the candidate of one party.

You Are a Professional Campaign Manager

incumbency advantage
The electoral advantage a candidate enjoys by virtue of being an incumbent, over and above his or her other personal and political characteristics.

FIGURE 11.2

The Advantage of Incumbency Surged in the Mid-1960s and Peaked in the Mid-1980s

Note: The second election of each decade is not plotted because in those years decennial redistricting altered the districts of some incumbents, making incumbency advantage impossible to calculate.

SOURCE: Calculated by Sam Abrams, Stanford University, and Gary Jacobson, UC–San Diego, using the Gelman-King method.

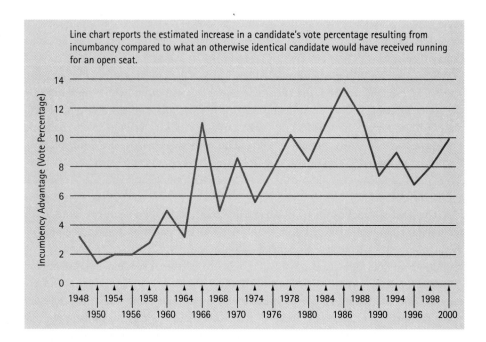

Line chart reports the estimated increase in a candidate's vote percentage resulting from incumbency compared to what an otherwise identical candidate would have received running for an open seat.

Visual Literacy

Why Is It So Hard to Defeat an Incumbent

shown in Figure 11.2, the incumbency advantage surged in the late 1960s, leveled off for a time, peaked in 1986, and then declined in the 1990s. At least five factors underlie this development: the weakening of parties, changes in the activities of representatives, the growth in resources available to incumbents, campaign funding disparities, and more responsive incumbents.

Party Decline

Although three-fourths of all party identifiers vote for the candidate of their party, that figure dropped somewhat in the 1960s and 1970s. Moreover, more voters had a party allegiance in the 1950s than do today. As party affiliations weakened, voters became more "available," more susceptible to other sorts of appeals.[17] Thus, the weakening of parties created an environment in which other factors, such as the incumbent's personal characteristics and activities, could exert a stronger influence on voter behavior.

Moreover, realizing that more voters were "up for grabs," incumbents adjusted their behavior accordingly. Their own partisan constituencies became less secure, but incumbents could use government programs to provide voters with additional, more personal reasons to support them. At the same time, voters who normally might have supported the other party had become receptive to a wider range of political appeals, so incumbents began to court them. In elections with an incumbent running, voters who identify with the opposition party defect to the incumbent almost half the time.[18]

Growth in Importance of "Representative" Behavior

You may think of members of Congress primarily as *lawmakers.* Indeed, making laws is the principal business of Congress and the major responsibility that the Constitution bestows on that body. But members of Congress do much more than write and vote on legislation. Most voters expect a wide range of activities from their representatives, so members of Congress must accommodate those demands.[19]

One activity that occupies a great deal of their time and effort is district service—making sure that their congressional districts get a fair share (or more) of federal programs, projects, and expenditures.[20] Some members of Congress are famous for their efforts to bring such economic benefits to their districts. Although critics of Congress often label such benefits "pork barrel spending," constituents generally approve when their representatives and senators "bring home the bacon"—and reward them at the ballot box for their successes.

Another activity to which modern representatives devote a great deal of attention is constituent assistance, usually called **casework.** Citizens, groups, and businesses frequently encounter difficulties in qualifying for government benefits or subsidies or in complying with federal regulations. When their problems are not solved through normal channels, they appeal to members of Congress for assistance. About one in six voters reports having contacted a representative for information or help with a problem. In overwhelming numbers, they report satisfactory resolution of their problems and, again, show their gratitude at the polls.[21]

District service and constituent assistance often are included together under the general term **constituency service.** They share an important characteristic that sheds some light on the advantage of incumbency, which is that they please voters back home regardless of party identification or ideology. Most voters express satisfaction with projects and grants funded by the federal government on their behalf. Similarly, Democratic incumbents willingly help Republican businesses deal with federal regulators, and Republican incumbents willingly help Democratic constituents qualify for federal benefits. These activities do not antagonize constituents, as is true when members of Congress take positions on controversial issues—so they carry significant electoral benefits but entail little if any electoral cost. It is hardly surprising that by a 5 to 1 margin in one survey, House administrative assistants ranked constituency service over their members' legislative records as the most important factor in maintaining their electoral base.[22]

Notably, both forms of constituency service have grown in scope. As the federal government expanded during the 1960s and 1970s, subsidizing and regulating more and more activity, the contacts of citizens, groups, and firms with the government multiplied. The opportunities for members of Congress to engage in constituency service increased correspondingly. Three times as many citizens in 1978 reported having contacted their representative for assistance as reported having done so in 1958.[23] Thus, at the same time that strength of party affiliation was declining, an expanding federal government was stimulating constituent demand for assistance that members of Congress were able and willing to provide. These activities enabled them to reinforce their own base and make inroads into that of the opposition, a tactic still used constantly today.

Expanding Member Resources

Some observers compare members of Congress to CEOs (chief executive officers) of small businesses.[24] Each member heads an office system—one in Washington and one or more in the district. The typical House member employs 18 personal staff assistants,

casework
Efforts of members of Congress to help individuals and groups when they have difficulties with federal agencies.

constituency service
The effort by members of Congress to secure federal funding for their districts and to help constituents when they have difficulties with federal agencies.

more than 40 percent of whom are assigned to district offices.[25] Senators have even bigger staffs, although office sizes depend on each state's population. These offices have many responsibilities, but no one doubts that much of their effort is directed toward the representative's reelection. Indeed, it has been said that Capitol Hill is the headquarters of 535 political machines.

Such was not always the case. In 1950 the average representative had three staff employees. And as late as 1960, nearly a third of the representatives lacked permanent district offices. The 1960s and 1970s were a period of great growth in congressional staff resources. Travel subsidies and other perks also expanded greatly.[26] In 1960 members were reimbursed for only three trips to their districts per year. By 1976 the number had increased to 26, and today there is no limit except the overall budget allocated to each member. Of course, before the jet plane, few members could go home every weekend, as they do today, and many went home only once or twice a session. Improvements in transportation made it possible for members of Congress to be "perpetual commuters," so Congress authorized the funds to support that change.[27]

Use of the **frank**—the free use of the U.S. mail for official business—has also grown. Although Congress has long subsidized communication with constituents, technological advances such as computerized mailing lists have allowed members to take greater advantage of the privilege in recent years. Congressional use of the frank increased much faster than the rate of population increase or the increase in incoming mail that required answering. Not surprisingly, congressional mailings to constituents are much higher in even-numbered (election) years than in odd-numbered years.

Representatives naturally take political advantage of new technologies as well. Today, nearly all members have homepages on the Web—a development led by younger members, Republicans, and members who represent highly educated constituents.[28] Although this technology has great potential for communicating information about legislation to constituents, thus far House offices appear to be using it mostly to advertise their members.[29]

Members of Congress are frequently criticized for providing themselves with these resources—often called perks, for "perquisites of office." But the increased resources enjoyed by incumbent representatives are related to the weakening of party and to the increase in constituency service. As traditional party organizations deteriorated, members voted themselves resources to substitute for the declining organizations. Similarly, as traditional partisan voting became unreliable, they voted themselves resources necessary to attract votes through constituency service. The resources controlled by incumbents are necessary for them to do their jobs well, of course, but these resources also help with self-promotion.[30]

Campaign Funds

Elections for Congress have become increasingly expensive: The average total spent by winning House candidates was almost $900,000 in 2002. The average victorious senatorial candidate spent almost $5 million.[31] Moreover, as Figure 11.3 shows, the gap between incumbents' spending and that of their challengers is wide and has grown wider since 1980. For many of today's reformers, the advantage of incumbency is simple and self-evident: money.

frank
Name given to representatives' and senators' free use of the U.S. mail for sending communications to constituents.

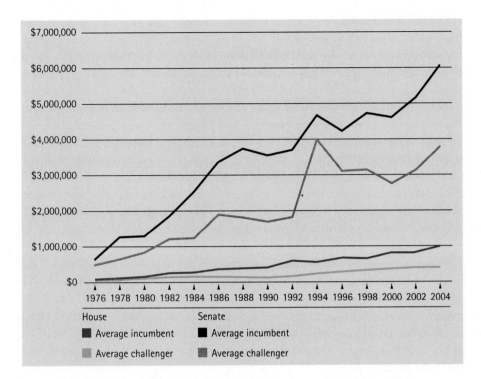

FIGURE 11.3
Congressional Campaign Funding

SOURCE: Norman J. Ornstein, Thomas E. Mann, and Michael J. Malbin, *Vital Statistics on Congress, 2001–2002* (Washington, DC: American Enterprise Institute, 2002), p. 81, 87 and the Federal Election Commission.

Money certainly affects candidate visibility, and congressional challengers are seriously underfunded. Nevertheless, research on the influence of money in congressional elections paints a surprisingly complicated picture. Although money contributes significantly to the electoral advantage that incumbents enjoy, its contribution probably is exaggerated.

First, researchers have found that campaign spending has what economists call *diminishing returns:* The more a candidate spends, the less impact an additional dollar of spending can have. In particular, for an incumbent who already has a vast budget for constituent outreach, an extra $100,000 has less impact than it would if it were spent by a challenger who lacked taxpayer-provided resources. Sophisticated advocates of campaign finance reform therefore oppose low limits on campaign spending. Such limits would hurt challengers, who have little name recognition, much more than incumbents, who already enjoy high visibility.[32]

Second, the surge in the incumbency advantage (the mid-1960s) did not occur at the same time as the explosion of spending in congressional campaigns. House elections in the late 1960s and early 1970s were not nearly so expensive as they are today. Indeed, heavy spending by an incumbent was regarded as a sign not of electoral strength but of weakness—a signal that an incumbent was in trouble.[33] That remains true today. For example, in 2002 the four losing incumbents on average spent more than $2 million, half a million more than their opponents and almost twice as much as spent by the average winner of an open seat.[34] Moreover, the growth of political action committees (or PACs) took place *after* the adoption of campaign finance reform laws in 1974, when incumbents had already developed a significant advantage.

An important effect of campaign spending today is one that is difficult to observe, let alone measure. Because it takes so much money for a challenger to mount a serious

The Debate Over
Campaign Finance
Reform

campaign, many potentially strong challengers never enter the race.[35] If the incumbent has a widely advertised million-dollar "war chest," the prospect of mounting a challenge is daunting and may scare potential opponents out of the arena.[36] This deterrent effect of campaign funds probably has been reinforced by the decline of local party organizations, too. In today's candidate-centered system, the individual candidate bears the risk of running and losing. A losing challenger may have taken time off from a lucrative job, run a campaign committee deeply into debt, and even tapped into personal savings to construct a campaign organization. Well-funded incumbents make this risk seem like a truly bad investment.

In recent years the topic of campaign finance reform has received enormous attention, and members of Congress have grappled with a wide variety of reform proposals. Citizens are disgusted with the present system of campaign finance and, as a result, are cynical about government in general and the Congress in particular. The problem is that the reforms likely to do the most good are the least likely to be adopted. Public financing of congressional elections, for example, would relieve candidates of the burden of fund raising, giving them time to spend on more productive activities. It also would insulate them from the influence of special interests. But setting subsidies high enough to make challengers credible—perhaps half a million dollars in House races, not counting primaries—would no doubt require expenditures too large for a cynical public to accept (even if incumbents were ever willing to give their opposition that much funding).[37]

All in all, the great advantage in campaign spending that incumbent representatives enjoy surely contributes to the extraordinary advantage of incumbency, but it is far from the only explanation. Even if spending disparities were wiped out overnight, incumbents would still do exceptionally well.

More Responsive Incumbents

Many critics of Congress believe that there is something wrong with high rates of reelection. This is true if members' electoral success reflects the operation of some illegitimate factor—selling out to PACs, for example. But, as we have noted, one reason for members' success is that they work very hard at helping their constituents and serving their districts. Another source of their success is that these legislators are extremely sensitive to the wishes of their constituents, perhaps even more so than members of Congress from earlier eras.

One reason for this sensitivity is that members of Congress today have more and better information than ever before. Not only do their offices have fax machines, e-mail, World Wide Web pages—technologies undreamt of a few decades ago—but the members also physically return to their districts 30 to 50 times a year. Only a generation ago, one often heard the derisive phrase "the Tuesday-to-Thursday Club" applied to a minority of East Coast members who lived close enough to Washington to go home to their districts on Friday and return to the capitol on Monday. Today, jet transportation enables most of the Congress to belong to the Tuesday-to-Thursday club. Important business is rarely scheduled for Mondays or Fridays, because so many members are traveling on those days. With members spending so much time in their districts, is it any surprise that they are highly attuned to the sentiments of constituents?

Moreover, members have access to survey research today. As recently as a generation ago, only a few well-funded interest groups ever conducted polls in congressional districts, and then usually only to gauge a candidate's chances. Today, with the growth of the survey research industry and the arrival of computer-assisted telephone interviewing, more members can afford to conduct surveys to learn the views of constituents. Today's members probably make fewer political mistakes than their predecessors did.

Contemporary members of Congress also may have greater incentive to act in accordance with the information they have. In the modern Congress, every vote is closely watched by interest groups who rate members. Moreover, years after a vote, opponents engaged in opposition research may bring it up in a campaign. In the House, more votes are public now than a generation ago. Until 1971, many votes were cast by standing, by voice (aye–nay), or by "tellers" (depositing colored cards in boxes)—procedures that hid the member's individual positions. But rules changes that year made it easy to demand a roll-call vote, and the number of roll calls in an average session more than doubled. A damaging roll-call vote need not be a highly visible one that saves a president, as in the Margolies-Mezvinsky case discussed in the chapter opener. Even an obscure vote may come back to haunt a member years later if the policy it supported proved a failure or had negative consequences.[38] More recorded votes mean more electoral danger.

A third reason why members may be more responsive today than in the past is that there are fewer constraints that might keep members from acting on the information and the incentives they have. Once again, party decline is an important factor here. Except under the most unusual situations, such as those that Representative Margolies-Mezvinsky encountered, members of Congress are not forced to cast votes that will damage them in their districts. When party and constituency collide, party leaders allow constituency to trump party—except under the direst circumstances.

You Are an Informed Voter

If members are forced to toe the party line, they are more likely to be defeated when constituents disagree with the party position. Today, members of Congress distance themselves from their party and president whenever they think the connection is politically dangerous.

Contemporary Senate Elections

The importance of incumbency in House elections contrasts with its importance in Senate elections. As Figure 11.4 shows, incumbent senators win more often than not, but they lose much more frequently than do representatives, and in a few elections (such as 1980) barely more than half survive. Despite their six-year terms, the average length of time a senator serves is the same as the average tenure of a representative: about 11 years.[39] Senate elections differ from House elections in party competition, in the information voters receive, in the quality of challengers, and in the ultimate ambitions of senators. Each of these differences makes the position of Senate incumbents less secure than that of House incumbents.

Party Competition

The two parties compete more evenly in Senate races than in House races.[40] Each senator has a state for a constituency; in general, states are more heterogeneous than the smaller congressional districts included in them. This difference is significant because social and economic diversity provides a basis for party competition.[41] For example, an urban, heavily minority House district will be dominated by the Democrats, and a rural, white district usually will be dominated by the Republicans. If a state includes both kinds of districts, however, each party has a natural base on which to compete for the Senate seats. Few states are reliably "safe" for either party, whereas a majority of the smaller, more homogeneous House districts are "safe" seats. Thus, part of the reason why senators lead less secure electoral lives than representatives is simply that they have larger, more diverse constituencies that are more difficult to please.

Uncontrolled Information

Senators receive far more media coverage than representatives. One study found that the average senator appeared on the network evening news 33 times over the course of a session, compared to 5 times for the average representative. Every senator had at least one appearance, whereas a quarter of the House got no coverage whatsoever.[42] Given the popular image of politicians as publicity seekers, greater media exposure might appear to benefit senators, but the source of the information is an important consideration. Nearly all the information that constituents receive about House incumbents comes *from* House incumbents—newsletters, press releases, and so forth.[43] Naturally, such information has an entirely positive slant: Representatives are not going to spread negative information about themselves! Senators also would like their constituents to receive nothing but positive information about them, but the media are not under Senate control. The media publicize controversial statements, personal embarrassments,

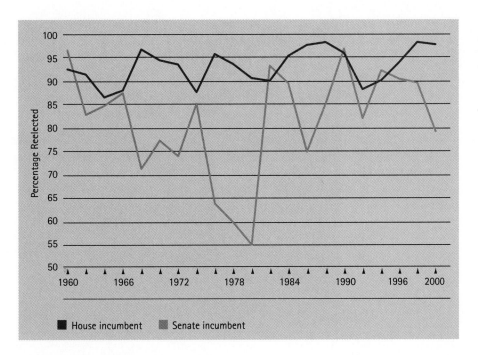

FIGURE 11.4
Representatives Get Reelected More Often Than Senators

SOURCE: Norman J. Ornstein, Thomas E. Mann, and Michael J. Malbin, *Vital Statistics on Congress, 2001–2002* (Washington, DC: American Enterprise Institute, 2002), pp. 69–70.

and fights with the president and other politicians. Such coverage inevitably puts the senator in a negative light in the eyes of at least some constituents.

Better Challengers

The office of senator enjoys a higher status than the office of representative. After all, the Senate is commonly referred to as the "upper" chamber, whereas the House is referred to as the "lower" chamber (reflecting sensitive House feelings, members of Congress refer to the "other" chamber). Naturally, high-quality challengers are more willing to risk a race for prestigious Senate seats than they are to seek House seats. Moreover, Senate seats are scarce. Every two years, all 435 House seats are available, compared to 33 or 34 Senate seats; a state with 20 House seats has 40 House elections in a four-year period, but only 2 Senate elections. Thus, far fewer credible challengers are needed to make Senate races competitive.

The combination of greater attractiveness and greater scarcity attracts Senate challengers with a serious chance of winning.[44] Senate challengers have more political experience, in terms of both campaigning and government service. They are better known and better liked than House challengers, and the funding gap between incumbents and challengers is smaller (review Figure 11.3). The combined effect of challengers who are more highly regarded and incumbents who are less highly regarded results in a limited incumbency advantage for those who sit in the Senate.

High Ambitions

Another reason why senators are associated with more controversial matters than representatives is that many of them have higher ambitions. Pundits have joked that every senator looks in the mirror and sees a president. The political system relies, of course,

Every senator sees a president
John Kerry of Massachusetts was one in a long line of senators who have tried unsuccessfully to move to the White House. The time spent pursuing their political ambitions is time that senators do not spend working for their constituents.

on ambitious office seekers putting themselves on the line.[45] But higher ambition has its risks. Senators cannot seek the presidential nomination solely on the basis of pork-barrel projects. Serving in a leadership position and jockeying for national power require senators to take positions on controversial issues, positions that are bound to offend some constituents. Moreover, involvement with broader national and international issues leaves senators vulnerable to the charge that they are neglecting their states. Senators have been defeated partly as a result of charges that they were "more interested in Africa than Iowa."[46] Notably, one Senate seat the Democrats lost in 2004 belonged to Tom Daschle of South Dakota, the party's minority leader in the chamber.

National Forces in Congressional Elections

Former Speaker of the House Thomas P. "Tip" O'Neill (D-MA) maintained that "all politics is local." In part, O'Neill's maxim reflected the parochial politics of Massachusetts, but it also reminds us that although members of Congress are national lawmakers, they are elected and reelected by people in thousands of localities, to whom they are ultimately responsible.

The tendency of representatives and senators to distance themselves from party and presidential positions that are unpopular in their districts makes modern congressional elections less subject to the kinds of *national forces* in politics and economics that would help or hurt a party's electoral chances across the board. Such forces were common in American history until the mid-twentieth century.[47] But in the late twentieth century, presidential **coattails**—the ability of presidents to carry their own party's candidates for Congress into office—declined in strength.[48] In recent decades more voters have split their tickets, voting for presidential and congressional candidates of different parties.[49] Moreover, as parties weakened and incumbency strengthened, fewer voters seemed to treat off-year elections as a means to express disappointment in the president they had

coattails
Positive electoral effect of a popular presidential candidate on congressional candidates of the party.

elected two years before. Until 1998, in every off-year election between the Civil War and 1994 except one (1934), the party of the president lost House seats—and usually Senate seats—but that cycle has broken down in the last few elections.

National Forces in the 1990s: A New Era?

Members of the House may appear to have insulated themselves from the kinds of national forces that in earlier times resulted in congressional turnover, but the 1994 elections serve as a prominent challenge to any such conclusion. In that election, Democrats suffered a 52-seat loss in the House, the largest since 1946. Coupled with an eight-seat loss in the Senate, the election results suggested that a strong national tide had swept aside the advantage of incumbency and destroyed the insulation of the Democratic Congress.

National forces clearly were more important in 1994 than in other recent elections. Nevertheless, the 1994 election did not vary from the norm of congressional insulation as much as pundits initially thought.[50] Even though incumbent losses in 1994 were severe and fell entirely on the Democratic side, 85 percent of the Democratic House incumbents who ran were reelected.

Some of the new Republicans announced that they intended to act as courageous lawmakers and not engage in mundane political activities like "bringing home the bacon." Representative Michael Flanagan (R–IL), who had upset a scandal-tainted incumbent, "practically bragged that he would bring home less federal largesse, saying, 'Pork has not served this district well.'"[51] A year later Representative Flanagan had changed his tune. His press release read, "These are good projects, not pork."[52] Flanagan's about-face did not save him in 1996—his district was too Democratic—but there is little doubt that the Republicans saved their majority in 1996 by time-honored practices such as constituency service.[53] Indeed, 91 Republican House candidates won districts carried by President Clinton in that year.

The 1998 elections also suggested that 1994 might have been exceptional. Both parties initially tried and failed to develop an issue that would capture the imagination of the electorate. Then, in late January, the Monica Lewinsky scandal erupted. Candidates and pundits everywhere began to reassess the situation. Republicans dreamed that popular revulsion toward the president would give them a landslide, and Democrats feared Republicans might be right. Many Democratic candidates distanced themselves from the president; some even canceled fund-raisers at which he was to appear.[54] But the president's approval ratings held. Congressional Republicans overplayed their hand, harping on Clinton's ethical lapses so much that they appeared too partisan for swing voters.[55] In a stunning surprise, Democrats actually gained five seats, the first time since 1934 that the president's party had gained in the mid-term election. Only one Democratic incumbent lost, as did four Republican incumbents, for an all-time record incumbent reelection rate of 98.5 percent. Not even a major presidential scandal disrupted congressional stability.

Congressional Elections in the 2000s: Neck and Neck

The Republicans retained their congressional majorities in the 2000 elections, but just barely. The Republican majority in the House was shaved to five seats and, for only the second time in American history, there was an exact tie in the Senate. Most observers felt that the elections had no national theme, and the parties selected candidates according to their chances of victory. For example, Democratic party committees backed some pro-life candidates, such as Robert Casey of Pennsylvania. Only eight House incumbents lost, out of 412 who had run. As usual, senators had a rougher time; five of 28 were defeated.

The next two congressional elections, like those in 1994, provided evidence that voters often approach congressional elections with national issues in mind. Republicans gained seats in both the House and the Senate in 2002, despite holding the White House—the second time voters flouted historical norms for midterm elections. It appears that Republican candidates got a boost from sharing a party affiliation with President Bush, who enjoyed unusually high approval ratings after the 9/11 terrorist attacks and who campaigned vigorously in the last weeks before the elections. Then, in 2004, President Bush's victory was accompanied by additional Republican gains in both chambers. In fact, Bush's chief political rival, Tom Daschle, lost his reelection bid after facing accusations that he had used his Senate leadership position to obstruct the President's efforts

Thus, since 1994 national forces seem to have more impact on congressional elections than they did in the 1970s and 1980s. Still, incumbents continue to do extremely well by conforming to the preferences of their own constituents. Congressional elections today exhibit both the strength of incumbency typical of the election in the 1970s and 1980s as well as the renewed importance of national forces that emerged in 1994.

Why Have National Forces Grown Stronger?

Although the changes represented by the 1994 elections may have been exaggerated, the evidence that has piled up since then confirms that congressional elections are more nationalized now than in Tip O'Neill's day when all politics was local. Two related developments contributed to this change. The first is more unified, and more distinct, political parties. The congressional parties are more unified today than they were a generation ago, and the differences between Republicans and Democrats are greater.[56] Thus, voters usually have a clear choice between two candidates who take distinct positions on national issues. Such clear differences are less likely to be overwhelmed by local factors or by the candidate's personal characteristics, which were more important in the preceding three decades.

The second reason lies in recent developments in campaign finance. In 2000 the parties raised nearly $500 million.[57] The parties spent much of this money on "issue advocacy," primarily TV commercials praising their own candidates or attacking the other party's candidates. Interest groups also engage in issue advocacy, often independent of the interests of the actual candidates running. In 1998, groups began running ads without the knowledge of (and sometimes in defiance of) the wishes of candidates. In a spring special election in California, for example, pro-life groups attacked the Democratic candidate even though the Republican candidate did not want to make abortion an issue in the race.[58] .

Although party issue advocacy in national elections has been severely curtailed by a campaign finance reform act passed in 2002, it is doubtful that issue advocacy by groups can be restricted much without violating rights to free expression. Numerous "527 committees" (named after the tax code that defines them) sprang up to fund independent campaign ads in the 2004 election. Most of these committees were clearly identified as either pro-Democratic or pro-Republican, although their temporary nature allowed them to fund nasty attack ads without undermining their party's reputation. The long-term implications of truly independent spending are significant. Candidates prefer to control the campaign agenda as much as possible. Both candidates may prefer that an issue not come up, either because the district is so split that neither candidate feels he or she can profit from the issue or, more innocently, because the issue is not important in their districts and needlessly muddies the political waters. Groups can force candidates—and voters—to address their issues.

Although many people are troubled by these developments, two things can be said in their favor. First, they help to redress the imbalance between incumbents and challengers. Parties and interest groups can inject large sums into campaigns where credible challengers are running, thus helping to offset the incumbency advantage. When Sen. Jim Bunning of Kentucky made a series of missteps in 2004, outside money helped a little-known state senator mount a credible campaign against the well-funded incumbent—although Bunning squeaked out a narrow victory. This may be one of the reasons why Congress was willing to ban soft money in 2002. Second, campaigns in which the parties and national interest groups actively participate will be more issue-oriented than those in which they are absent. Many people believe this is the way elections should be.

Do Congressional Elections Produce a Representative Body?

Members of Congress generally are qualified people. In contrast to times past, today's Congress contains few political "hacks"—people there only because of their connection to some political "boss." Of course, members today want to get reelected every bit as much as members did in the past, but current members are hard-working, well educated, bright, and personally interested in public policy. Moreover, despite media portrayals, today's members are less corrupt than ever before. Scandals are reported more commonly now than in the past, but these disclosures probably reflect changing perspectives in the media—the rise of the "junkyard dog" mentality—rather than increased corruption in the Congress.

Still, some people look at the membership of Congress and are troubled. They see a supposedly representative body that does not mirror the diversity of the United States. The Congress consists overwhelmingly of white male professionals. The 109th Congress elected in 2004 had only 65 women (14.9 percent of the House), 40 African American (9.2 percent) and 23 Hispanics (5.3 percent)—less than their proportions in the larger population. The numbers in the Senate, of course, are even lower: 14 women, 2 Hispanics, and one African American.[59] As shown in Figure 11.5, the numbers have been rising in recent decades, but the rate of increase, except for the 1992 surge, has been slow.

The subject of the gender, racial, and ethnic diversity of the Congress has been a matter of considerable controversy in recent years. The concept of representation means different things to different people. For some, personal characteristics such as the gender or race of a representative are unimportant: As long as he or she is responsive to the

FIGURE 11.5
Women and Minority
Members of Congress

SOURCE: Library of Congress—
Election Archive.

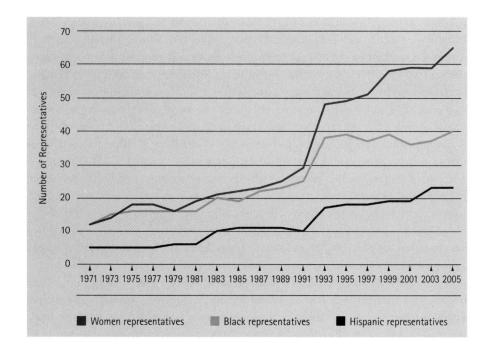

needs of constituents, they feel well represented.[60] Others disagree. They contend that
almost by definition, a male representative cannot be responsive to the needs and aspirations of women ("They just don't get it!") and that white representatives cannot truly
understand the needs and aspirations of African Americans. Those who hold such views
believe that Congress must be *descriptively* similar to the country in order to be a
successful representative body. Still others concede that white male representatives
might be able to represent women and minorities but believe nonetheless that women
and minority representatives have important symbolic value. A diverse presence in the
councils of government will enhance the legitimacy of government actions and provide
valuable role models for women and minorities in the population.[61]

    Those who believe in either the actual or the symbolic importance of diversifying
the Congress are not likely to see their frustration end soon. The Congress is not
like a business that hires employees or a university that admits students. Its members
are chosen by millions of citizens voting independently (and secretly) in hundreds of
elections. Voters can be urged to practice affirmative action, but such appeals are
unlikely to be very effective—partly because most serious congressional candidates
are white men, and partly because women and minorities who run face distinct
disadvantages.

Women

The United States ranks quite low among world democracies in the proportion of
women in the lower chamber of its national legislature. Indeed, politics is the most
prominent arena in which American women trail women in other countries. The
proportion of women elected to the House of Representatives is much lower than that
elected to the lower houses of most other countries. Of the advanced industrial democracies, the U.S. House contains a proportion of women comparable to that found in

Belgium, the United Kingdom, and Australia and significantly higher than the numbers in France and Japan. Otherwise, the United States trails.[62]

Undoubtedly there are many reasons for the differences. Gender prejudice does not seem to be among the major ones though. Societal prejudice against women serving in public office is low and has been diminishing.[63] On the other hand, a legacy of gender discrimination continues to operate. Winning a congressional seat is usually the result of a series of successful efforts, beginning with a local office or community organization and working up the political career ladder. Along the way, the member-to-be of Congress learns the art of politics, makes valuable political allies, becomes acquainted with those who bankroll campaigns, and generally acquires the experiences, characteristics, and resources that constitute the "qualifications" that someday will make her a "credible" challenger. Women have only recently gained admission to the networks that move politicians upward to higher office; men have had a long head start. As the pool of women in state legislatures and other lower offices grows, their representation in Congress should follow.

The electoral system found in the United States probably contributes to the slow rate of progress. The countries with the highest proportions of women tend to have some version or another of proportional representation (PR). In such systems, party leaders submit lists of candidates who will be elected in proportion to the party's vote. Judging by the results, these lists have significant numbers of highly ranked women. Women appear less successful where they have to contend with powerful men who live nearby for the same geographically defined seat.

Overall, the under-representation of women in Congress naturally will lessen as women's career patterns become more like those of men. Some feminists may reject this analysis, believing that women should strive to be elected as *women,* politicians with a "different voice," not because they have learned to play the electoral game in the same way men do. Because American women have a complex combination of identities, though, they are unlikely to vote as a bloc. The traditional pattern of political advancement is likely the best and fastest method available.

Minorities

The prospects for further increasing minority representation in Congress are less favorable than they are for women, especially the prospects for African Americans. The critical difference is that in ethnically diverse constituencies, **bloc voting**—in which groups vote as blocs—often occurs. When voting is racially polarized, for example, a black candidate is unlikely to win unless African Americans are a majority of the electorate. In the 103rd Congress, the first Congress after the 1990s redistricting, 32 of the 39 black members came from districts in which African Americans were in the majority, and in 5 of the remaining 7 districts, African Americans plus Latinos made up a majority. Similarly, 15 of the 17 Latino members of the 103rd Congress came from majority-Latino districts; none came from districts with a white majority. The 107th Congress was not much different from the 103rd: in the 107th, 30 of 36 African American members came from majority black districts, and all 17 Hispanic members came from majority Hispanic districts.

Given the historical tendency toward racially polarized voting, efforts to increase minority representation in Congress have been made largely through the redistricting process. The 1982 amendments to the Voting Rights Act and subsequent court decisions have required the creation of **majority-minority districts** wherever possi-

bloc voting
Voting in which nearly all members of an ethnic or racial group vote for the same candidate or party.

majority-minority district
District in which a minority group is the numerical majority.

Durable caucus

After the U.S. Supreme Court began targeting racial gerrymanders, critics warned that soon the Congressional Black Caucus would be able to meet in the back seat of a taxi cab. Their fears proved unfounded.

affirmative action redistricting
The process of drawing district lines to maximize the number of majority-minority districts.

ble. In such districts, a racial or ethnic minority constitutes a majority of the population so they are able to elect their representatives of choice. Given the lower turnout rates that prevail among minority groups, the rule of thumb often has been to create districts with at least a 65 percent minority population (a figure that political science research suggests is unnecessarily high).[64]

Efforts to create majority-minority districts—sometimes called **affirmative action redistricting**—have generated considerable controversy. Some of the districts that have been created have unusual shapes, uniting areas of different cities connected only by a highway. Such districts have provoked charges that they violate the constitutional guarantee that people will be treated equally regardless of race. In 1993 the Supreme Court ruled in *Shaw v. Reno* that majority-minority districting had limits: A district created on no basis other than to include a majority of minorities might raise constitutional questions. In later years the Court declared redistricting plans in Georgia, North Carolina, and Texas to be unconstitutional racial gerrymanders.

Even racial liberals are not all of the same mind on the issue of majority-minority districting. Those who support creating such districts value the increased representation of African American and Latino representatives. However, evidence strongly suggests that increasing descriptive representation for minorities simultaneously undercuts the electoral position of the Democratic party—the political party that minority voters tend to support—and therefore decreases the responsiveness of legislation to minority preferences. Research by political scientists David Lublin and D. Stephen Voss has traced this negative partisan impact at both the congressional and state legislative levels.[65] Recognizing the likely outcome, Republican leaders have tended to favor packing voters into majority-minority districts while Democratic leaders have tended to oppose it. During the 1990s redistricting, in particular, the Republican Justice Department aggressively pushed the creation of minority districts.

Whatever your view of such trade-offs, there is an upper limit on the number of majority-minority districts that can possibly be created: Racial minorities by definition consist of *minorities* of people, and electoral mapmakers cannot cross state boundaries to concentrate them. Indeed, given the recent court decisions, the United States may already be near that limit. If the maximum number of majority-minority districts that can be created is little more than the number that currently exist, then the upper limit for minority representatives will be correspondingly low unless minorities can break through and win in districts where they are not numerically dominant. Thus, many were encouraged when several black incumbents won in districts that had been redrawn so that they were no longer majority African American.[66]

Another potentially negative effect of affirmative action redistricting is less obvious: It may work to marginalize minority members of Congress, particularly black representatives. The homogeneity of African American views should not be overstated.[67] Nevertheless, blacks are overwhelmingly Democratic in their allegiance, more liberal in general, and far more supportive of federal social programs in particular.[68] Representatives of such a group are correspondingly liberal. Indeed, members of the Congressional Black Caucus (CBC) are among the most liberal members of Congress, as measured by numerous interest-group ratings. But liberal records compiled as U.S. representatives may prevent African Americans from being credible challengers in gubernatorial, senatorial, and ultimately presidential elections.[69] Extremely liberal candidates (as well as extremely conservative candidates) rarely win election in a diverse constituency, regardless of race.

In sum, the subject of minority representation in Congress is a difficult one, and existing court-imposed methods of encouraging more minority representation are controversial. Each person must decide whether the gains that accrue from ensuring some level of minority representation exceed the costs. Unfortunately, those costs are highly uncertain and, to a considerable extent, subjective. Thus, people of good faith may disagree.

Elections, Parties, and Group Representation

Some of the difficulty in increasing minority representation reflects the basic fact that the single-member, simple plurality (SMSP) electoral system is not designed to produce a descriptively representative legislative body. The SMSP system puts all minorities, racial and otherwise, at a disadvantage. If you receive fewer votes than the leading candidate—even if you get 49 percent of the vote—you win nothing. Republicans in Democratic districts and vice versa, liberals in conservative districts and vice versa, pro-lifers in pro-choice districts and vice versa—all are unrepresented when their side loses. In a sense, U.S. courts have been trying to coax a more proportional result, in terms of racial representation, from an electoral system not designed to be proportional. Not surprisingly, they have had only limited success. Recognizing these realities, some academic critics have raised questions about the electoral system itself.

It is conceivable that minorities (and women) would be better represented if the old-style party machines were still in existence. After all, the "balanced ticket" was a common strategy of the political party: To construct a coalition of diverse groups, the party recognized each group when they put together a slate of candidates.[70] Historians believe that because of racial prejudice, minorities generally did not fare so well as whites in the urban machines, which were based largely on white ethnic groups. But it is at least arguable that if every city in the United States still had a respectable machine, there would be more African Americans in government. Today, local party organization has weakened, and candidates fend for themselves. The demise of the machines and the rise of candidate-centered politics may be an additional disadvantage imposed on African Americans.

Chapter Summary

Members of the House of Representative are reelected at very high rates—more than 90 percent in all recent elections, including the Republican landslide of 1994. Upon close examination, this high level of incumbent success does not violate the founders' intention of an electorally sensitive House. On the contrary, because representatives are so electorally sensitive, they work very hard at serving their districts, try very hard to represent constituents' policy concerns, and in general attempt to eliminate any basis for a strong challenge against them. Contrary to the charges of many critics, electoral success does not lead members of the House to be lazy and unresponsive. Rather, members are reelected *because* they are so hard-working and responsive.

Senators, too, are hard-working and responsive (probably more responsive than the framers intended), although they do not enjoy the same electoral success as members of the House. On average, their constituencies—states—are more competitive than House districts; they face stronger challengers; and their ambitions and prominence make them the object of media coverage that they do not control and expose them to expectations and ambitions that carry risks as well as rewards.

For most of the past generation, the impact of national forces on congressional elections has been relatively low. Incumbents have managed to distance themselves from national leaders, de-emphasize potentially damaging issues, and emphasize their personal records. In recent elections, national forces have grown stronger, reflecting the greater distinctiveness of today's parties and the increased empha-

sis on national issues by parties and interest groups engaging in issue advocacy.

The single-member, simple-plurality electoral system provides strong incentives for representatives to be *responsive* to the wishes of majorities in their districts. But the system in no way ensures that the composition of Congress will be *descriptively representative* of the diversity of the country's population. On the contrary, if people vote as ethnic or racial blocs, the system will not elect a proportional number of ethnic and racial minorities. The courts have encouraged districting arrangements that would produce more proportional outcomes, but these efforts have met with limited success generally require the creation of majority-minority districts that are controversial and politically divisive. In the long run such procedures may work against minority representation by encouraging bloc voting and promoting the election of minority representatives who have limited experience or ability attracting white votes.

For women, the problems are different, and the most promising solution—though not one that many activists would like to hear—is time: As women increasingly win lower offices, the pool of qualified women candidates will inevitably expand. As the pool expands, the proportion of women candidates for Congress will increase. Otherwise, the solutions available to increase minority representation are not available for women: They are not segregated from men, so districts dominated by female voters are not feasible to draw, and women do not vote cohesively for female candidates.

Key Terms

affirmative action redistricting, p. 302

bloc voting, p. 301

casework, p. 289

coattails, p. 296

constituency service, p. 289

filing deadline, p. 287

frank, p. 290

gerrymandering, p. 286

incumbency advantage, p. 287

majority-minority districts, p. 301

open seat, p. 287

professional legislature, p. 284

reapportionment, p. 285

redistricting, p. 285

safe seat, p. 287

Suggested Readings

Of General Interest

Fenno, Richard. *Home Style.* Boston: Little, Brown, 1978. Classic study of how representatives interact with constituents, earning their trust.

Herrnson, Paul. *Congressional Elections.* 4th ed. Washington, DC: CQ Press, 2004. The most up-to-date study of congressional campaigns.

Jacobson, Gary. *The Politics of Congressional Elections.* 6th ed. New York: Longman, 2004. The definitive text on modern congressional elections.

Mayhew, David. *Congress—The Electoral Connection.* New Haven, CT: Yale University Press, 1974. Influential work which argues that much of congressional structure and behavior can be explained by the assumption that reelection is the most important goal of members.

Focused Studies

Brady, David. *Critical Elections and Congressional Policy Making.* Stanford, CA: Stanford University Press, 1988. Prize-winning account that ties together congressional elections, processes, and policy making.

Campbell, James. *The Presidential Pulse of Congressional Elections.* Lexington, KY: University of Kentucky Press, 1993. Detailed analysis of national forces operating in mid-term elections.

Cox, Gary and Jonathan Katz. *Elbridge Gerry's Salamander.* Cambridge, England: Cambridge University Press, 2002. Definitive Study of the "reapportionment revolution" of the 1960s.

Kahn, Kim, and Patrick Kenney. *The Spectacle of U.S. Senate Campaigns.* Princeton, NJ: Princeton University Press, 1999. Detailed study of how candidate strategies, media practices, and voter decisions interact in contemporary Senate campaigns.

The best place to learn about specific congressional races is either from the media (see Chapter 9) or from the candidates themselves.

On the Web

www.cookpolitical.com

One of the most famous handicappers of congressional races is Charlie Cook. To get all of his information, you have to subscribe, but a significant portion of his analysis is available free.

www.vis.org

If you are looking for more comprehensive discussion of election politics, Voter Information Services has a host of congressional report cards and records on voting.

www.lib.umich.edu/libhome/govdocs/psusp.html

The University of Michigan also has a site that includes links to historical and present-day resources about congressional elections about congressional elections.

VOICES

OF THE PERMANENT CAMPAIGN

The Funding of Election Campaigns

"As long as the wealthiest Americans and the richest organized interests can make six- and seven-figure donations to political parties and gain the special access to power that such generosity confers on the donor, most Americans will dismiss the most virtuous politician's claim of patriotism."

—John McCain, in the Senate,
March 19, 2001

THE ISSUE

Critics argue that money corrupts the electoral process. They advocate reforms that will limit the use of private campaign funds, such as by financing elections with public money or by tightening limits on the cash candidates can raise and spend. Others believe that such limitations violate free speech rights and argue that candidates should be able to raise and spend as much as they wish in order to publicize their campaigns.

Background

Americans have worried since the nation's founding that private money might corrupt their government. During the ratification battle over the U.S. Constitution, in fact, opponents argued that members of Congress would "associate with such company as will possess very little of the feelings of the middling class of people," becoming cozy allies of the rich and influential interests around them. To stay in office, one such writer explained, elected officials would use "their power to confer great favors" as a means to assemble a group of "numerous and powerful" friends.[1]

This anxiety with the corrupting power of money has never abated. During the late 1800s and into the next century, for example, social critics charged that the federal government had been bought out by "the trusts"—by which they meant deep-pocketed monopolies in industries such as banking, mining, railroads, and steel production. Newspapers of the time

"IF WILLIE IS A GOOD BOY, AND MINDS PAPA AND NURSIE, THEY WILL TRY TO LET HIM KEEP THE PRETTY HOUSE UNTIL HE IS EIGHT YEARS OLD."

Store-bought toy President
President William McKinley was sharply criticized for the support he received from industrial trusts, as organized by Republican businessman Mark Hanna.

lambasted the successful presidential campaigns of William McKinley, in particular, because they were guided by a wealthy businessman (Senator Mark Hanna of Ohio, who became chair of the Republican National Committee) and collected enough money to outspend McKinley's Democratic opponent 20 to 1.[2] President Dwight Eisenhower took office in 1952 promising to improve the nation's military preparedness, but by the time he stepped down eight years later he was warning Americans that a well-funded "military-industrial complex" had gained too much power.

Richard Nixon had perhaps the most notorious connections to big-money interests. During the 1952 election,

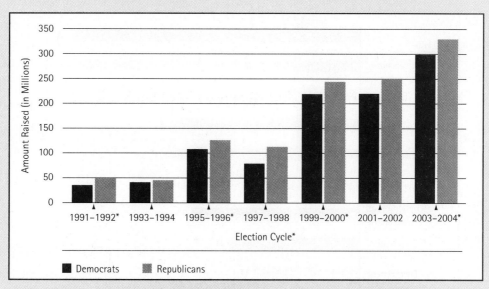

FIGURE 1

Soft Money Contributions to National Party Committees
NOTE: * indicates Presidential election year
SOURCE: Common Cause and the Center for Responsive Politics.

Eisenhower almost dropped Nixon as his vice-presidential nominee after a controversy erupted over $18,000 that Nixon had accepted from California business contributors for his political expenses. Nixon retained the nomination only after he went on television and explained that the fund was not secret, that he had not provided the donors with special favors, and that the only personal gift he had accepted was a cocker spaniel that his daughter had named Checkers. Directly addressing the public's fear of the corrupting influence of money in political campaigns, he assured listeners that "no contributor to this fund, no contributor to any of my campaign, has ever received any consideration that he would not have received as an ordinary constituent." Twenty years later, Nixon had become president and faced a similar set of charges. Critics in 1972 accused President Nixon of accepting more than a million dollars from wealthy contributors (a lot of money at the time), a charge that helped spur calls for reform.

The Shift to Soft Money

Reformers won an important legislative victory in 1974, after revelations of corruption fueled additional concern with campaign financing. The Federal Elections and Campaigns Act (FECA) limited contributions to candidates so that they could not exceed $1000, a regulation approved by the U.S. Supreme Court in the 1976 case *Buckley v. Valeo*. Despite this success, reformers watched in dismay as the campaign-finance system evolved new methods of funneling money into campaign coffers. FECA permitted the formation of political action committees, a method of bundling huge sums of cash

and passing them on to candidates—so PACs mushroomed in the 1980s.

Eventually, concern moved away from the direct contributions that individuals and interest groups made to candidates. Those contributions operated under FECA's limits and the limits grew increasingly restrictive as inflation eroded the value of $1000. Instead, the main irritant for those wishing to keep private money out of the electoral system is "soft money," a source of campaign financing distinct from the hard cash that donors contribute to a candidate's effort. Soft money goes to the political parties, who then use it for advertising campaigns and for get-out-the-vote efforts that indirectly benefit individual candidates.

These funds exploded in the late 1990s because they did not operate under FECA's contribution limits (see Figure 1). Often they were put to the same sorts of political uses that a candidate's own campaign managers would have chosen if the money had passed into their hands—such as distributing fliers promoting the quality of the party's nominee, buying television ads to criticize the other party's nominee, or organizing telephone banks to get party members to vote. The cash would flow into closely contested states and congressional districts during an election, saturating the media markets and the postal service with political advertising. Soft money certainly seemed to violate the spirit, if not the letter, of campaign-finance restrictions.

Finally, after the 1996 election cycle, many critics believed that the campaign-finance system was simply out of control. The news brought Americans images of Vice President Al Gore raising money at a Buddhist temple and reports of President Bill Clinton allowing donors to sleep in the White

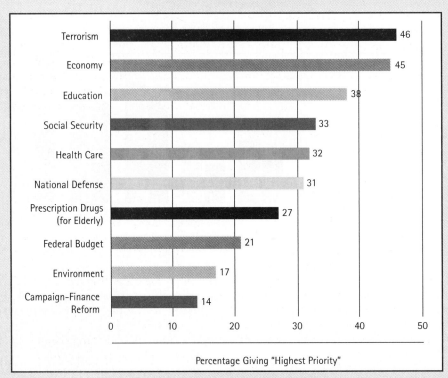

FIGURE 2
The Public Assigns Campaign-Finance Reform a Low Priority

House's prestigious Lincoln Bedroom. The Federal Election Commission eventually fined Democrats $719,000 as a result of fund-raising scandals from 1996, including steep fines for illegally accepting donations from Chinese nationals. The Republican party, meanwhile, was awash with big bucks, having raised more soft money than Democrats in every election cycle—an imbalance that lessened during the Clinton years but still led reformers to question the fairness of the electoral system.

The Policy Solution

The public takes a dim view of the political process—and a downright gloomy view of campaign fund-raising. Over 70 percent of Americans believe that politicians make public-policy decisions on the basis of their contributors' desires. The same poll found that 47 percent of the public thought Bush administration officials had done so (although, understandably, only 35 percent of Republicans felt this way).

These negative views might lead you to believe that the public has generated significant pressure to reform the campaign process. In fact, the public shows relatively little concern. Not even 15 percent want this issue to be given "highest priority" by lawmakers (see Figure 2). Issues such as terrorism, the economy, and education are perceived as need-

ing the most attention. But even less crucial issues, such as prescription drug benefits for the elderly, have outranked campaign finance in the list of voter priorities.

In fact, the impulse for change has been driven by a group of dedicated activists and politicians hoping to drum up public support. Senator John McCain of Arizona in particular has been able to energize the reformers. His 2000 campaign for the Republican presidential nomination publicized the effort to limit soft money, and corporate scandals that struck after the campaign (associated with company names such as Enron and Tyco) gave reformers the additional leverage they needed to get limits through Congress. In the spring of 2002 President George W. Bush quietly signed the Bipartisan Campaign Reform Act.

The BCRA, better known as the McCain-Feingold Act after its Senate sponsors, contains provisions that:

1. Ban soft-money contributions to national political parties.
2. Increase the limits on individual hard-money contributions.
3. Restrict the ability of corporations, labor unions, and non-profit organizations to run so-called "issue ads" close to an election.

Ironically, given that the main impulse for reform came from a sense that special interests dominate the political process, the most serious restrictions enacted by McCain-Feingold targeted political parties—the very institutions that historically have counterbalanced the power of interest groups (see Chapter 8). One unintended, but rather perverse, consequence of the reform therefore may be to strengthen exactly the sort of associations that spurred the public impulse for reform in the first place.

In particular, to fill the soft-money void left by the disempowerment of national parties, political activists quickly established a series of new nonprofit organizations—called Section 527 committees after the tax-code provision under which they were created—to bundle political contributions and use them for electioneering. Because many of the 527 groups are closely associated with particular politicians or particular political parties, critics of the McCain-Feingold bill have concluded that it only applied cosmetic changes to the electoral system rather than substantial reform. In the 2004 "election cycle," which ended before the year's national party conventions, the 527 committees spent almost $266 million. They tended to oppose President Bush. The best-funded committee, an anti-Bush group called the Joint Victory Campaign 2004 that was heavily patronized by film producer Stephen L. Bing, alone had its hands on more than $40 million. Sometimes contributors gave these groups huge sums. Twenty-nine people gave more than half-a-million dollars each to 527s. Almost $27 million entered the 527 networks from only two people: billionaires Peter Lewis, an insurance executive and owner of Progressive Corp., and George Soros, a financier.[3] Soft money quickly found new channels to flow into the electoral system.

Political Dilemmas

The battle over campaign-finance reform is not just about whether it works or how spending can be regulated successfully. Liberals, conservatives, and libertarians tend to disagree sharply over whether campaign financing ought to be regulated in the first place—with the liberals typically favoring far-reaching regulations, but the conservatives and libertarians opposing government control over campaigning. Both sides hold positions that are easily simplified to the point of appearing cartoonish, but the contradictory perspectives draw from core tenets of America's political culture and therefore have persuasive power when they are thoroughly understood. For this reason, the issue of campaign finance poses a serious legal and political dilemma.

From the liberal perspective, an electoral system ideally provides everyone with equal power. The nation's voting rights law guarantees "One Person-One Vote," but equality should be a central guiding principle for election policy in other ways as well. Private financing of election campaigns allows individuals with greater economic resources to use their wealth to spread political messages more widely than poorer people can. Campaign speech can never be "free speech" because advertisements are not cost free. Participation in the nation's political debate therefore is not equal. Furthermore, political parties

PRO

Many interest groups have taken strong stands on campaign-finance reform. Some interest groups are staunch supporters. Their only concern with legislation is usually that it does not go far enough.

> www.commoncause.org
> www.lwv.org
> www.publiccampaign.org
> www.citizens.org

CON

Opposition to campaign-finance regulation is concentrated among Republicans, but it is also opposed by some left-leaning libertarian groups, such as the ACLU, which worry about provisions that restrict the ability of outside groups to run "issue ads." Some of the strongest opposition comes from the congressional Republicans who are fighting the legislation in court.

> www.campaignfinancesite.org
> **Useful sources**
> Some Web sites provide useful background information on campaign finance issues.
> www.brokkings.org
> www.prospect.org

that articulate the interests of the rich will have an easier time financing campaigns than will political parties that speak to the needs of the poor, creating a bias in the party system—another source of inequality. Finally, because politicians rely on campaign funds to stay in office, they naturally reward generous donors with special attention, disproportionate access, and maybe even favorable laws. In political shorthand: Contributors are able to pay for an unjust influence over public policy. A fairer system therefore would cap campaign contributions low enough that most Americans would have the option of donating the maximum, or it would provide public financing according to how many voters supported a candidate or party.

Conservatives and libertarians disagree on many political issues, but when it comes to campaign finance they usually fall into the same camp. To each, election time is the most important part of the democratic process, the stage at which voters determine who will govern them. It is the central means through which citizens discuss the failings of their leaders and decide whether they would like to throw the rascals out. In particular, it is their opportunity to publicize actions by the nation's rulers that might threaten liberty. Allowing government to tamper with the free flow of campaign speech, by saying which sorts of messages are permitted and how individuals may work on behalf of their favored candidates, is therefore dangerous to the people's independence. The danger is particularly strong when we consider that the system's overall bias is (and the historical trend has been) toward growth of government power. The government can use tax laws and spending bills to cultivate groups that then advocate more government, a powerful message that taxpayers may wish to use their financial resources to counterbalance. And public financing of elections could worsen the problem, if it were implemented in such a way that citizens found their taxes being used by the federal government to subsidize candidates with whom they disagreed.

How the Courts Have Ruled

Although the debate over campaign-finance regulation can be conducted in terms of the nation's core principles, the legal debate is framed in terms of whether soft-money limits violated the constitutional guarantee to free speech. Led by U.S. Senator Mitch McConnell of Kentucky, opponents of McCain-Feingold charged that the law infringed on First Amendment rights. Regulating campaign communications, they argued, violates the Constitution's guarantee that citizens may express themselves freely—a guarantee that is supposed to be especially strong when it comes to political matters. Spending regulations prevent people from using their money to communicate with each other about politics, a choice that ought to be theirs to make.

The U.S. Supreme Court was able to rule on these claims in the 2003 decision *McConnell v. FEC.* Reflecting the public disgust with "big money" in campaign finance, the Supreme Court generally upheld the limits imposed by the McCain-Feingold Act. "The prevention of corruption or its appearance constitutes a sufficiently important interest to justify political contribution limits," Justice Stevens explained. "The idea that large contributions to a national party can corrupt or, at the very least, create the appearance of corruption of federal candidates and officeholders is neither novel nor implausible." In fact, Stevens argued, the close connection between candidates and the national parties "placed national parties in a position to sell access to federal officeholders in exchange for soft-money contributions that the party can then use for its own purposes."[4]

The issue is not settled, however. The Federal Election Commission must determine how to interpret McCain-Feingold's provisions, and so far the commissioners have not been inclined to exploit all the regulatory possibilities provided by the law's language. Reformers have charged the FEC with "gutting" McCain-Feingold by refusing to enforce the law properly. McCain himself has noted the limited effect of his reform and is gearing up for another attempt to crack down on campaign contributions. And the free-speech argument against limits on campaign messages has several supporters on the Supreme Court, justices who dissented in the *McConnell* case and eventually may attract enough allies to reverse the law. Justice Scalia, for example, disparaged the current campaign-finance law as one that "cuts to the heart of what the First Amendment is meant to protect: the right to criticize the government. For that is what the most offensive provisions of this legislation are all about." Concluded Scalia: "This is a sad day for the freedom of speech."

What Do You Think?

1. Should Congress try to limit soft-money expenditures by interest groups, as the McCain-Feingold law did for spending by the national parties?

2. Does the Constitution's free-speech guarantee allow Congress to limit whether and how people use their own money to communicate political messages?

3. Are there any options, other than campaign-finance regulations, that could limit the political influence of deep-pocketed campaign contributors?

4. In the long run, do you think soft-money limitations are most likely to hurt the Democrats or the Republicans?

[1] Brutus, "Essay XVI," in Herbert J. Storing (ed.), *The Anti-Federalists* (Chicago: University of Chicago Press, 1985), pp. 189–190.
[2] For this fact, and a general description of the election, see "Background Information on the 1900 Presidential Campaign" at http://www.graphicwitness.org/historic/opper.htm.
[3] Exact numbers from http://www.tray.com/fecinfo but see also Derek Wills, "The Money Pours In," distributed by the Center for Public integrity (April 20, 2004).
[4] McConnell v. FEC, 251 F. Supp. 2d 176.

CHAPTER 12

★ ★ ★ ★ ★ ★ ★ ★ ★ ★ ★ ★ ★ ★ ★ ★ ★

The Congress and Its Work

CHAPTER OUTLINE

Making Bad Policy Worse

Making public policy is a messy business. Side deals and legislative bargaining—often known by the colorful terms "logrolls" and "horse trades"—are critical to the process. Sometimes the backroom deals complement the policy-making process, helping to gather support for important public interest legislation. Occasionally, though, private interests gobble at the trough so greedily that they swallow the public good.

Such was the case with the farm bill passed by Congress and signed by President Bush in 2002, which commentators overwhelmingly criticized. The *New York Times* called the bill an "orgy of pandering to special interest groups." *USA Today* called it a "congressional atrocity." *The Economist*, a British news magazine, used the words *monstrous* and *lunacy* to describe the legislation.[1]

The problem did not start with this one bill. U.S. farm policy is an unmitigated disaster. Farmers have been subsidized and protected in various ways since the New Deal of the 1930s—when, in an effort to prop up prices, the national government began paying farmers to waste food at a time when city dwellers went hungry. They plowed fields under. They poured good milk into ditches and slaughtered pigs, leaving the meat to rot. Such policies were billed as "emergency measures," of course, but two generations later the entire industry remains addicted to unfair and wasteful handouts. Columnist Robert J. Samuelson calls it "the classic example of how unnecessary spending survives."[2]

Crop limits, price supports, guaranteed loans, and other agricultural subsidies hurt consumers twice: once through higher taxes, and once through higher prices on household staples such as bread and milk. Similarly, restrictions on importing agricultural goods keep food prices higher than they would otherwise be and provoke retaliation against American exports by potential trading partners.

Moreover, subsidies make a select group of farmers wealthy. No direct aid goes to the farmers responsible for producing meat, fruit, or vegetables. The money concentrates on special categories of farming, such as growing grains or producing dairy goods. A tenth of the nation's total farms receive more than two-thirds of the money. Because farm aid rewards the growing of specific crops in each region of the country, it distorts incentives, discouraging farmers from planting whatever is best for their lands or for the market. If you grow vegetables in California, the largest crop-producing state in the nation, you are out of luck. But California grows more rice than Japan. How can anyone profit from growing a swamp crop in desert conditions? Simple: California rice growers are among the 9 percent of the farmers in the state who receive cash subsidies. They also get huge amounts of subsidized water, another public policy scandal.

Of course, economic critiques of farm policy have stimulated efforts to reform the system. Most of these attempts have been unsuccessful. In 1996, for example, the Republican congressional majority teamed up with reform-minded Democrats to adopt a new farm policy, one that reduced federal payments and tried to equalize the distribution of benefits somewhat. Democratic President Bill Clinton quietly accepted the reforms. But they made little difference, because members of Congress quickly undermined them. In each of the next five years, Congress passed "emergency" appropriations bills, arguing that farmers had suffered a bad year. The assistance was a paltry $5.8 billion in 1998, but by 2000 it had ballooned to more than $30 billion.[3]

Five years after the reforms first passed, farm-state legislators initiated a move to revoke them altogether, to be replaced by a new ten-year, $190-billion commitment. President Bush initially balked, concerned with the rising governmental costs associated with a war on terrorism, but "it didn't take long before political calculation trumped the administration's alleged principles." The White House decided not to interfere with the "massive giveaways," allowing both the Republican House and the Democratic Senate to pass versions of the legislation enthusiastically.[4]

In the conference committee, where legislators from both chambers met to reconcile House and Senate versions of the bill, subsidy opponents initially tried to cap the benefit amounts available to individual farmers, but House conferees walked out of the negotiations in response.[5] California senators Barbara Boxer and Dianne Feinstein decided that the agricultural subsidies could not be stopped, so they hastened to secure larger payoffs for their state's rice farmers before the bill went to President Bush. Bush reluctantly signed the bill in May 2002.

How is this possible, you ask? How can agribusinesses use the force of government to take billions of dollars from American taxpayers, inflating their food prices and undercut-

Fields of green

Critics of the nation's agricultural policy liken generous farm subsidies to welfare for rural areas. However, the money is distributed according to politics, not according to need—some farmers growing some crops get nothing while others reap a bountiful harvest.

ting the economy? Well, for one thing, agricultural policy is not a sexy issue for most voters. Legislators are more likely to pander to special interests when voters are not paying attention. Also, the costs of farm subsidies are widely distributed; each person pays a few dollars here and a few dollars there, but no one loses enough to get worked up and start a crusade over it.

The farm population, on the other hand, pays close attention, because financial rewards are immense and benefits narrowly distributed. *Washington Post* reporter Dan Morgan provides one example: Westerfield Ranch, a farm three miles from President Bush's land in Crawford, Texas. That farm alone collected almost $1 million over five years, a third of all payments released to the Crawford area.[6] Beneficiaries of such a generous and focused program are going to feel intensely about it.

Humorist Dave Barry asks, "Wait a minute! Isn't this kind of like, I don't know . . . welfare?" But Barry ultimately decides the two policies are not quite the same. "Welfare is when the government gives money to people who produce nothing," he writes. "Whereas the farm-money recipients produce something that is critical to our nation: votes." The Farm Security Act of 2002 was merely one act in the drama called the permanent campaign. Neither political party can count on the votes from agricul-

tural areas, so legislators cannot afford to neglect their demands. Farm-state Democratic senators up for reelection in 2002 included nervous veterans like Max Baucus (Montana), Tom Harkin (Iowa), and Paul Wellstone (Minnesota), as well as vulnerable freshmen like Jean Carnahan (Missouri), Tim Johnson (South Dakota), and Max Cleland (Georgia). All enthusiastically supported the bill, as did House colleagues in a similar situation. It was a legal method of delivering "huge political bribes."[7]

Still, a majority of incumbents held safe seats in both chambers of Congress, and many members represent states or districts that receive almost no agricultural money at all. They did not need to endorse wasteful farm payments to save their own skins. What led Congress to pass the bill and President Bush to sign it was the struggle for control of Congress: Republicans controlled the House by only five seats, and Democrats controlled the Senate by a single vote. Neither party could afford to neglect rural districts if they wanted to remain on top. As one Bush aide commented after the president signed the bill, a veto would have been "political suicide in the November election."[8] Farm policy in 2002 not only affected farmers and their congressional representatives; it also affected the agendas of two major political parties.

MAKING THE CONNECTION

Farm policy illustrates how members of Congress shape their behavior to satisfy the voters back home. Although individual representatives and senators may care deeply about serving the nation, they can do nothing to address societal problems if they do not remain in office. The politics of lawmaking therefore always reflects electoral considerations, as members work not only to retain their own seats but also to capture and maintain majority status for their party. Even when they are focused on doing good, rather than on keeping power, members of Congress are likely to perceive political issues in terms of the needs of their own constituencies. They seek particular benefits to help the folks back home. The logrolling and deals that members of Congress demand before they will support policy changes can distort the purpose of legislation or make efforts to reform a public policy futile. This chapter examines the workings of our most powerful, most complicated, most democratic, most electorally sensitive, but least respected political institution. Specifically, we will consider:

- the party and committee organization that Congress has developed;

- the complex process of lawmaking;

- the ambivalent feelings that Americans have about Congress;

- attempts to reform Congress.

★ ★ ★ ★ ★ ★ ★ ★ ★ ★ ★ ★ ★ ★ ★ ★

**Farm Subsidies and
Democratic Policy**

Congress—The First Branch

Congress is called the first branch of government because the Constitution prescribes the powers and structure of Congress in Article I. Table 12.1 lists the powers that the Constitution gives to Congress. Historically, the most important have been the "power of the purse"—the power to tax and spend—and the "power of the sword"—the power to declare war. Additionally, through the "necessary and proper" clause, Congress has asserted broad powers over many different aspects of American life.

TABLE 12.1

THE PRINCIPAL POWERS OF CONGRESS

To levy taxes

To borrow money

To regulate commerce

To decide requirements for citizenship

To make monetary policy

To establish a postal system

To establish federal courts below the Supreme Court

To declare war

To raise an army and a navy

To call up the state militias

To make all laws that shall be necessary and proper for executing the other powers of Congress

SOURCE: U.S. Constitution, Article I.

Like many of the world's parliaments, Congress is **bicameral,** consisting of two chambers: an upper chamber called the Senate and a lower chamber called the House of Representatives. In other countries, the upper chamber of parliament typically has only ceremonial duties or, at most, powers that are much weaker than those of the lower chamber. The House and the Senate possess roughly equal powers, however, which can create a certain amount of interchamber rivalry. A Speaker of the House once called the Senate "a nice quiet place where good Representatives go when they die."[9] The Senate has a quick response to such jibes: In all of American history, only one senator (Henry Clay) has given up a Senate seat to run for the House, and that was in 1811.

The legislative branch includes tens of thousands of people in addition to the 535 members of the House and Senate. The members have personal staffs that total more than 7000 in the House and 4000 in the Senate, and each chamber hires thousands of staff members to support the committees. Many of these staffers are clerical workers; others are policy experts who play an important role in the shaping of legislation, especially long-time staff who speak for important members. Additional staff employees support the party leaders who coordinate the flow of bills through the legislative process. All in all, about 17,000 people are employed as congressional staff.

In addition to staff employed by members and committees, thousands of others work in various support agencies of Congress. The General Accounting Office (GAO), the watchdog agency of Congress that oversees the operation of the executive branch, employs more than 3000 people. A smaller number of people work for the Congressional Budget Office (CBO). This agency provides Congress with expert economic projections and budgetary information. In total, the legislative branch of government consists of many thousands of people. Table 12.2 provides a summary listing.

bicameral
Containing two chambers, as does a legislature such as the U.S. Congress.

TABLE 12.2

THE LEGISLATIVE BRANCH

Members of Congress are only a fraction of the legislative branch.

House	
Committee	1267
Personal staff	7216
Leadership staff	179
Officers of the House staff	974
Senate	
Committee staff	910
Personal staff	4272
Leadership staff	219
Officers of the Senate staff	990
Joint Committee Staffs	104
Support Agencies	
General Accounting Office	3275
Congressional Research Service	747
Congressional Budget Office	232
Miscellaneous	
Architect	2012
Capitol police	1251

SOURCE: Norman Ornstein, Thomas Mann, and Michael Malbin, *Vital Statistics on Congress, 1999–2000* (Washington, DC: Congressional Quarterly, 2000), pp. 129–130.

The Organization of Congress

The House and Senate are not undifferentiated collections of people who sit in their seats all day debating and voting as the urge strikes them. Like other large decision-making bodies, the two chambers have evolved an extensive division of labor—the committee system—as well as a means of organizing large numbers of people to make decisions—the party leadership structure. The Constitution says nothing about either the committee system or the party leadership structure; they developed to meet the needs of elected officials.[10] Both are more important in the House than in the Senate. The House is much larger, so it needs to be better organized. It operates in more of a follow-the-rules fashion than the Senate, which is small enough to operate by informal coordination and negotiation.[11]

The Congressional Parties

Although parties do not dominate Congress as much as they dominate the parliaments of other democracies, they are still the principal organizing force in Congress. (See the accompanying International Comparison.)

Speaker
The presiding officer of the House of Representatives; normally, the Speaker is the leader of the majority party.

The Power of the Speaker of the House

Speaker of the House   The Constitution stipulates that the House shall elect a **Speaker.** In practice, members consistently vote the party line in leadership elections, so the Speaker is always the leader of the majority party. Despite being a partisan leader, the Speaker ordinarily does not vote on legislation. Only in close contests involving matters vital to the party does the Speaker vote. In 1995, for example, even with the Republicans in control of the House for the first time in 40 years, Speaker Newt Gingrich participated in only 58 of 845 recorded votes.[12]

Until the late nineteenth century, the Speaker was the only formal party leader in the House. Indeed, from the end of Reconstruction to the turn of the century, the Speaker often rivaled the president as the most powerful public official in the United States. Powerful Speakers awarded the chairmanships of important committees to their close allies, made all committee assignments, and punished disloyal members by removing them from committees on which they had previously served.[13] Moreover, as the presiding officer of the House and chairman of the Rules Committee, which determines legislative procedure, the Speaker controlled the floor.

Joseph "Boss" Cannon was the last of the great Speakers. Pushing the envelope of all the powers he had inherited, Cannon dominated the House in the first decade of the twentieth century. But times were changing. The Republican party was split between regular and progressive wings, and maintaining party discipline led Cannon to an increasingly punitive use of his powers.[14] Dissident Republicans who chafed under the iron rule of the majority eventually joined with Democrats in a revolt that stripped the Speaker of his most important powers.[15] In 1910, the Speaker lost the power to make committee assignments and was removed from the Rules Committee.[16] Procedural reforms also guaranteed ordinary members some right to have their proposals considered. A year later, after the Democrats captured the House, they stripped the Speaker of the power to make committee assignments and vested that power in the House as a whole (practically speaking, in the majority party). The office of Speaker never regained the powers removed at this time. The era of the strong Speakers was over.

In the months immediately following the 1994 elections, which brought the Republican party to power in the House, Speaker Newt Gingrich moved boldly and

INTERNATIONAL COMPARISON

Congress in a Presidential System

Most world democracies are "parliamentary" in form. Voters rarely choose the chief executive under such a system. Instead, voters choose representatives to the national assembly, who in turn appoint ministers to execute law and policy for the nation's government. Having executives elected by the legislative branch might seem to give special influence to legislators, but in fact it makes them more dependent. They cannot afford to defect from the governing party coalition because doing so might undermine the leaders they have installed, handing political advantage to the opposition. Members of a parliament therefore usually do little more than rubber-stamp the executive's policy program. Indeed, in parliamentary systems, elected assemblies generally are not called legislatures, because they do little law making. They are called parliaments, because they do a lot of talking.

The United States is one of the exceptions, a democracy with a "presidential" form of government—a government in which the chief executive is elected directly by the people. Ironically, legislators can be more independent and therefore more influential in a presidential system. Their electoral fates are not tied as closely to the performance of the chief executive; unhappy voters can withdraw their support from a president without disrupting the membership of the legislative branch.

To highlight the legislative independence allowed by a presidential system of government, consider the case of the China Trade Bill passed by the U.S. House of Representatives in May of 2000. Although the China Trade Bill was strongly supported by President Clinton, a Democrat, the House's top-ranked Democratic leader opposed it. The number-two person, Democratic Whip David Bonior of Michigan, actually led the opposition. Few American commentators found this situation disturbing or even noteworthy.[a] Bonior's rust-belt district contained strong unions hostile to the legislation. The presidential system allowed Clinton and Bonior to go in opposite ways on an importance policy, each one following different electoral incentives.

Bonior's actions would have been unthinkable in a parliamentary system such as Britain's. Once the prime minister and cabinet decide on an important party policy, they expect virtually unanimous support from the rank and file in Parliament. High-ranking party members who opposed a key policy probably would be removed from their posts, assuming they did not resign voluntarily, and they might be threatened with other forms of political retribution.

One reason why the executive can impose such discipline is that, in most parliamentary systems, elections do not occur at fixed time intervals. Rather, new parliamentary elections often follow the legislative failure of a government's policy program, either because the opposition calls for a "vote of no confidence" or because the government itself chooses to dissolve Parliament and seek additional support from the nation's voters. Even if no new elections are called, the party's ministers may choose to step down if they cannot command sufficient legislative support. These various possibilities are all so dire to an executive's political allies that extreme party unity becomes the norm.

- *Do you think that members of Congress, rather than voters, should choose the president?*

- *Do you think that members of the party leadership in Congress should show greater loyalty to presidents from of their party?*

- *Do you think that the president should have the constitutional power to order new elections if Congress doesn't do what he or she wants?*

[a] "Key Democrat Ready to Oppose China Trade Bill," *San Francisco Chronicle*, April 18, 2000: p. A3.

---

decisively in a manner reminiscent of late-nineteenth-century Speakers. He elevated a few representatives to committee chairmanships even though other members had seniority over them. Some commentators explicitly likened Gingrich's behavior to that of Boss Cannon. But such comparisons ceased as the session wore on and the Speaker's ability to rule the House diminished.[17] When the Republicans unexpectedly lost seats in the 1998 elections, Gingrich took the fall; he resigned under pressure less than four years after some had proclaimed a "brave Newt world."

Party Leadership: House   Next in line to the Speaker, the House's presiding officer, comes the **majority leader.** Majority leaders are elected by the members of the majority party and lead them on the floor of the chamber. They are responsible for the day-to-day work necessary to build political coalitions and enact (or obstruct) laws:

majority leader
Title used for the Speaker's chief lieutenant in the House and for the most important officer in the Senate. Each is responsible for managing the floor of his or her chamber.

minority leader
Leader of the minority party who speaks for the party in dealing with the majority.

whips
Members of Congress who serve as informational channels between the leadership and the rank and file, conveying the leadership's views and intentions to the members and vice versa.

party caucus
All Democratic members of the House or Senate. Members in caucus elect the party leaders, ratify the choice of committee leaders, and debate party positions on issues.

party conference
What Republicans call their party caucus.

president pro tempore
President of the Senate, who presides in the absence of the vice president.

unanimous-consent agreement
Agreement that sets forth the terms and conditions according to which the Senate will consider a bill; these are individually negotiated by the leadership for each bill.

scheduling legislation; coordinating committee activity; and negotiating with the president, the Senate, and the minority. Unlike the Speaker, the majority leader votes on legislation. The minority counterpart of the majority leader is the **minority leader,** the floor leader of the minority party. Barbara Sinclair stresses that one important job of the leaders is to maintain "peace in the family." Different points of view flourish within parties, and it falls to the leadership to prevent minor spats and quarrels from developing into destructive feuds.[18]

The majority and minority leaders are assisted by **whips,** whose job is to link the leadership to the party's other representatives. The whip communicates leadership positions and strategies to the rank and file, counts votes, and reports rank-and-file opinions back to the leadership. The whip offices are rather large, with deputy, assistant, regional, and zone whips (upward of 25 in the Democratic party, about 20 in the Republican party). Their title conjures up an image of party leaders "whipping" their members into line (the title derives from "whippers-in" of the hounds in a fox hunt), but in practice the whips seldom use threats and coercion.

Many party members participate in the leadership via the whip organizations. Others participate via membership in party committees such as the Democratic Steering and Policy Committee, the Republican Policy Committee, and the Republican Steering Committee. These party committees provide a forum for discussing issues and developing a party program. Occasionally they endorse legislation. When the Democrats are in the majority, the Speaker chairs the Democratic Steering and Policy Committee and appoints many of its members. Thus, this committee serves as an important lever for influencing the behavior of members in their committees. In contrast, the Republicans elect a chair of their Policy Committee and also a chair of their Steering Committee, which makes committee assignments.

Finally, Democratic members belong to their **party caucus** and Republican members belong to their **party conference,** labels applied to meetings of the full party membership. These groups elect the party leadership and approve the slates of committees nominated by the Steering Committees. Sometimes they debate policies and attempt to develop party positions on policies. In Woodrow Wilson's time, they even adopted resolutions requiring party members to support particular policy proposals, a power that lies dormant today.

Party Leadership: Senate   Given that the Senate usually includes two members from each state—an even number—some tie-breaking mechanism is necessary. The Constitution obliges by giving vice presidents authority to preside over the Senate and to cast a tie-breaking vote *when necessary.* The Constitution also provides for a **president pro tempore,** who serves as Senate presiding officer in the vice president's absence (which is nearly all the time). This office is mainly honorific, without real power. Ordinarily it goes to the most senior member of the majority party. The Senate's majority and minority leaders are the true leadership of the chamber.

Although the Senate leadership also has a structure of whips and expert staff to assist them, Senate leaders are not as strong as those in the House. They spend much of their time negotiating compromises. Indeed, one of the main jobs of Senate leaders is to hammer out **unanimous-consent agreements** acceptable to all senators with any interest in a given proposal. These agreements specify the terms of debate—the amendments that will be in order, how long they will be debated, when votes will be taken, and so forth.[19] Such agreements are necessary because (unbelievable as it may sound) any Senator can delay consideration of a bill or resolution.

The Senate has a tradition of unlimited debate: the **filibuster.** According to present rules, a senator may speak indefinitely. The only way to silence a filibuster is for the Senate to adopt a **cloture** motion ending debate, which requires the support of 60 senators. The existence of the filibuster means that a simple majority of senators is not a winning coalition. A minority of 41 can prevent the Senate from acting on a measure. Unanimous-consent agreements represent one means of avoiding time-consuming filibusters; senators agree in advance to the terms under which they will consider legislation. These agreements require true unanimity, however, so a single senator may place a hold on debate or legislation by refusing to sign on. These practices allow minorities to obstruct legislation more easily in the Senate than in the House.

Ups and Downs of the Congressional Parties   It is difficult to measure the strength of congressional parties.[20] The power of congressional leadership has varied over time, though, and may be greater now than it was for half a century after the 1910 revolt against "Boss" Cannon.

One likely reason for the recent growth of party power is that congressional parties have become more homogeneous in their attitudes and policy preferences.[21] When parties are politically unified, leaders are likely to hold views consistent with those of the overall membership and members defer to their leaders. When the parties are more diverse, members are reluctant to give power to party leaders—who may act in ways objectionable, or even politically dangerous, to the rank and file.[22] As a result, institutional changes usually have followed changes in party unity (see Figure 12.1). The parties of the late nineteenth century represented distinct social groups, so Republican leaders in Congress were given immense power; but they lost influence when the party divided into progressive and regular wings. When Democrats swept into power during the Great Depression, they included both northern liberals and southern moderates, so leaders remained relatively weak.[23] The social revolutions of the 1960s, though, produced sharply divided parties that have grown increasingly unified and more ideologically extreme. Today's parties are exceptionally polarized. As a result, members of Congress have grown more willing to stick with strong leaders committed to the party's platform.[24]

Of course, just because a member of Congress usually agrees with the leadership does not mean that leaders will always do what the member wants. Being a leader often means making tough choices. Presumably some of those choices will be objectionable to portions of the party membership. Why would a member of Congress voluntarily pass decision-making authority over to leaders rather than retaining the right to "second guess" any decision?

Part of the answer is that an effective congressional party contributes to members' electoral prospects. Uninformed voters often choose among candidates on the basis of impersonal factors, including party images. Members of Congress wish to be part of an effective team, not part of a team that voters consider too divided to accomplish anything. As a result, they are willing to tolerate the limits imposed by their congressional leadership—indeed, to pass rules formalizing and strengthening such limits—because they cannot afford to undermine the party too often. The pressure for conformity can be especially strong when the president shares the member's party label.

Historic First
U.S. Rep. Nancy Pelosi became Minority Leader for the House Democrats in 2003, the first woman to lead a party caucus in Congress.

filibuster
Delaying tactic by which one or more senators refuse to allow a bill or resolution to be considered, either by speaking indefinitely or by offering dilatory motions and amendments.

cloture
Motion to end debate; requires 60 votes to pass.

FIGURE 12.1

The Congressional Parties Are More Unified Today Than a Generation Ago

The graph shows the percentage of all recorded votes on which a majority of voting Democrats opposed a majority of voting Republicans. Numbers for each year have been averaged over each Congress.

SOURCE: Norman Ornstein, Thomas Mann, and Michael Malbin, *Vital Statistics on Congress, 2001–2002* (Washington, DC: Congressional Quarterly, 2002), p.172.

A successful president can help members running for reelection. Conversely, as the Democrats found to their sorrow in 1994, an unsuccessful president can hurt the party, especially in mid-term elections. Members of the president's party thus have an incentive to work together to help him succeed.

Another source of party influence has grown in importance in recent years: The congressional parties are increasingly active in campaign funding. The House and Senate campaign committees are controlled by the leadership and most members of the leadership have established their own PACs.[25] Members who have received campaign contributions from party leaders naturally feel some obligation to support party leaders when they have enough political flexibility to do so.

Finally, members of Congress willingly accept some party discipline because they see it as necessary for attaining important policy goals. A representative might be able to dream up the perfect bill, one that would be immensely pleasing to voters back home, or perhaps one that would alter national policy until it was in perfect alignment with the member's preferences. But could the representative then turn that dream bill into law? Probably not. Sticking with the party's leaders increases the odds of real change. The representative may not like every detail of legislation that party leaders will negotiate, but they are likely to put together something better than current law—and, as powerful leaders, will actually have the ability to get it passed.

The Committee System

Members of Congress introduce thousands of bills and resolutions every year. Since 1980, for example, 6000 to 8000 bills have been introduced in each two-year session of the House of Representatives. Reviewing so many different pieces of legislation takes an immense amount of work. Rather than forcing everyone to master the details of so many bills, Congress has developed a screening process. Members of each congressional chamber are divided up into different committees specializing in particular policy areas. Each bill is referred to one or more committees, and the whole chamber usually only votes on legislation approved by the relevant committees. (In the House of Representatives, floor majorities can discharge a proposal from a recalcitrant committee via a discharge petition, but this process requires 218 signatures and is seldom used.) Of the thousands of bills introduced each year, only 10 to 15 percent eventually pass and most of the failed bills die at the committee stage.

Standing committees have fixed memberships and jurisdictions, and they persist from one Congress to another. The Appropriations, Commerce, and Foreign Relations Committees are examples. **Select committees,** by contrast, are temporary committees created to deal with specific issues. Both houses of Congress had standing committee systems in place by 1825.[26] The number of committees tends to expand until, at some point, the system is reorganized when majorities come to believe it has grown unwieldy and out of alignment with contemporary problems. The Legislative Reorganization Act of 1946 gave the committee system the shape it largely retains today, more than half a century later. In the 108th Congress (2003–2004), there were 19 standing committees in the House and 16 in the Senate (see Table 12.3). These "full" committees are subdivided into more than 150 subcommittees. There also are four "joint" committees, with membership from both houses, and a small number of select committees on special topics such as aging or national intelligence.

House Committees   House committees fall into three levels of importance. The top committees are Rules, Appropriations, Ways and Means, and Commerce. The Rules Committee is the right arm of the Speaker. It controls the flow of legislation to the floor and the conditions of debate. Appropriations and Ways and Means deal with spending and taxing, broad powers that enable them to affect nearly everything government does. Commerce has extensive jurisdiction over a wide variety of policy areas. A member who serves on one of these committees ordinarily is allowed no other assignment, except that he or she is eligible to serve on the Budget Committee. Committees at the second level of importance deal with nationally significant policy areas: agriculture, armed services, civil rights, and so forth. A member ordinarily serves on only one such major policy committee and on a third-level committee of lesser importance. These less important committees include "housekeeping" committees, such as Government Reform and Oversight, and committees with narrow policy jurisdictions, such as Veterans' Affairs. The Budget Committee has a special status. Members can serve for only four years in any ten-year period, and its membership is drawn from other committees and from the leadership.

Senate Committees   The Senate committee system is simpler than that of the House; it has just major and minor committees. Like their House equivalents, Appropriations and Finance are major committees, but the Senate Rules Committee is a minor committee with nothing like the power of its House counterpart (the Senate leadership itself discharges the tasks performed by the House Rules Committee). Budget is also a major committee, as is Foreign Relations, reflecting the constitutional responsibilities of the chamber in that area (advise and consent to treaties, confirm ambassadors).

standing committee
Committee with fixed membership and jurisdiction, continuing from Congress to Congress.

select committee
Temporary committee appointed to deal with a specific issue or problem.

TABLE 12.3

STANDING COMMITTEES OF THE 108TH CONGRESS

Committee	Size (party ratio)	Number of Subcommittees	Committee	Size (party ratio)	Number of Subcommittees
Senate			**House**		
Agriculture	21 (R11/D10)	4	Agriculture	51 (R27/D24)	5
Appropriations	29 (R15/D14)	13	Appropriations	65 (R36/D29)	13
Armed Services	25 (R13/D12)	6	Armed Services	61 (R33/D28)	6
Banking, Housing, and Urban Affairs	21 (R11/D10)	5	Budget	43 (R24/D19)	0
Budget	23 (R12/D11)	0	Education and Workforce	49 (R27/D22)	5
Commerce, Science, and Transportation	23 (R12/D11)	7	Energy and Commerce	57 (R31/D26)	6
Energy and Natural Resources	23 (R12/D11)	4	Financial Services	69 (R37/D32)	5
Environment and Public Works	16 (R10/D8/I1)	4	Government Reform	43 (R24/D19)	7
Finance	21 (R11/D9/I1)	5	House Administration	9 (R6/D3)	0
Foreign Relations	19 (R10/D9)	7	International Relations	49 (R26/D23)	6
Governmental Affairs	17 (R9/D8)	3	Judiciary	37 (R21/D16)	5
Health, Education, Labor, and Pensions	21 (R11/D9/I1)	4	Resources	52 (R28/D24)	5
Judiciary	19 (R10/D9)	6	Rules	13 (R9/D4)	2
Rules and Administration	19 (R10/D9)	0	Science	47 (R25/D22)	4
Small Business	19 (R10/D9)	0	Small Business	36 (R19/D17)	4
Veterans' Affairs	15 (R8/D6/I1)	0	Standards of Official Conduct	10 (R5/D5)	0
			Transportation	75 (R41/D34)	6
			Veterans' Affairs	31 (R17/D14)	3
			Ways and Means	41 (R24/D17)	6

SOURCE: Respective committee Web sites at the House homepage (www.house.gov) and the Senate homepage (www.senate.gov).

Committee power in the Senate is widely distributed: Chairs of major committees cannot chair any other committee or subcommittee, and chairs of minor committees can chair only one other panel. Each senator can serve on one minor and two major committees, and every senator gets to serve on one of the four major committees. On average, senators sit on more committees than do representatives—in part, a simple reflection of size difference: The Senate has nearly as many committees as the House with less than one-fourth as many members to staff them. But, in addition, senators represent entire states, which are typically more diverse than congressional districts; they cannot afford to limit their attention to one or two subjects, as many representatives can. Holding more committee assignments creates conflicting loyalties and makes it difficult for senators to specialize in a few subjects, as many House members do. As a result, senators' legislative lives are not so closely tied to a particular committee as are the lives of representatives.[27]

How Committees Are Formed   The committee system is formally under the control of the majority party in the chamber. Party committees nominate members for assignment and party caucuses approve those assignments. As a result, each committee has a ratio of majority to minority members at least as favorable to the majority as is the overall division of the chamber. The more important committees are stacked in favor of the majority. In the 108th Congress, for example, the Republicans had a 9 to 4 advantage over the Democrats on the House Rules Committee, a ratio far greater than their 229 to 205 edge in the chamber. In contrast, the party ratio on the less important Judiciary Committee was 21 to 16.

In practice, the committees exercise a considerable degree of independence. Part of the reason is the traditional use of **seniority** to choose committee chairs. Under seniority, the majority-party member with the longest continuous service on the committee chairs the committee. Often called a "norm" because the use of seniority is not an official rule yet is normally followed, seniority became the mode of selecting Senate committee chairs in the 1880s and House chairs after the 1910 revolt. The practice of seniority includes the right to continued reappointment to a committee. Thus, once a member is initially appointed to a committee, he or she automatically rises on its seniority ladder. Physically or mentally failing members sometimes are moved aside and, on occasion, the leadership or caucus rejects a nomination for chair, but the system gives committee chairs in particular, and committee members in general, a degree of independence or autonomy.

> **seniority**
> Practice by which the majority-party member with the longest continuous service on a committee becomes the chair.

The standard practice of seniority began to weaken in the 1970s when Democrats removed some senior chairs who were out of step with the caucus (including one who had addressed newly elected members as "boys and girls"). After the 1994 elections gave Republicans control of Congress for the first time in 40 years, Speaker Gingrich passed up the most senior committee member when he named the Republican chairs of Appropriations, Commerce, and Judiciary.[28] The Republican conference then adopted a three-term limit on committee chairs, which they enforced in 2000, indicating a major revision of the seniority system. Senate Republicans adopted an analogous rule in 1996. Whether either chamber will revert to the old system when the Democrats regain control remains to be seen.

Committee Reforms   In the 1950s, party influence in Congress had become so weak that many observers believed the chairs of the standing committees held the real power. A few of them behaved autocratically, creating and abolishing subcommittees and varying subcommittee jurisdictions, monopolizing subcommittee chairmanships, controlling committee staff and budgets, and even refusing to call meetings or to consider legislation they opposed. To make matters worse, because members from safe southern seats had built up considerable seniority, many of the chairs were more conservative than the younger, mostly northern Democrats who held more liberal views.[29]

Eventually, the rank and file membership, operating through party caucuses, curbed the power of the standing committee chairs and injected more democracy into the committee system. Much of this effort took place in the Democratic caucus.[30] In the early 1970s, a caucus resolution limited House committee chairs to holding one subcommittee chair. A "subcommittee bill of rights" guaranteed subcommittees their existence, jurisdictions, budgets, and staff. Moreover, power was distributed by allowing the Democratic members of a committee to choose among available subcommittee leadership positions in order of their seniority—subject to a vote of all committee

Democrats. The Senate had treated junior members somewhat better since the 1950s, but in recent decades it has moved in the same direction as the House, spreading power more evenly across the membership.

Many contemporary observers were unsure whether the preceding changes represented improvements. Did Congress simply decentralize power from approximately 40 standing committees to approximately 300 standing committees and subcommittees, many of them as small as eight or nine members? Had a period of "committee government" given way to a period of even more decentralized "subcommittee government"?[31] For more than a decade, political scientists debated the net impact of the reforms. Today the prevailing view is that the reforms adopted in the late 1970s to strengthen the party leadership offset the subcommittee reforms. The committee system appears to have been more subject to party influence in the last decade than it was a generation ago. An out-of-the-mainstream chair of an important committee would run a greater risk of being overthrown today than at any time since the revolt against Boss Cannon. Moreover, when the Republicans took control in 1995, their leadership acted to restrict the independence of subcommittees.

Purpose of Committees   Why does the standing committee system exist at all? Members of Congress are elected as equals. Why would a majority give to a minority exceptional influence in a policy area—the power to decide whether legislation should be considered, the power to shape the legislation if it is considered, and the power to review its implementation? Why not consider everything on the chamber floor (the so-called *Committee of the Whole*), where all members participate on an equal basis?

Members often use committee assignments to focus on district interests. For example, members from urban districts seek membership on committees that deal with banking, housing, or labor, whereas members from rural districts have little interest in such issues and opt instead for committees that deal with agriculture and natural resources. Members of these committees are in a position to bestow benefits on the voters back home. Studies have documented how districts and states whose members serve on particular committees receive a disproportionate share of the projects and grants that fall within the jurisdictions of those committees.[32] This distributive process is commonly called **logrolling,** because it implies that members defer to their colleagues on policies they care little about in exchange for particular influence on issues that deeply matter to them.[33] Such a system can result in spending bills larded with expensive projects. (See the accompanying Democratic Dilemma.)

An alternative interpretation is that committees primarily serve a knowledge function.[34] Members frequently are uncertain about the outcomes that policies will produce. Hence, they want some members to become experts in each subject area and share their knowledge with the broader membership. One way to encourage their hard work is to give committees disproportionate influence, subject to the condition that they do their job conscientiously and not abuse their power. Committee members can exploit their position to gain a bit extra for themselves, but only to the extent that they specialize and give the chamber useful, reliable information.

Still another theory holds that committees are the tools of the congressional parties.[35] Proponents of this partisan theory of committees argue that the party is so concerned with controlling public policy that it stacks committees with loyal members and shapes the jurisdictions of committees so that only reliable committees write and

logrolling
Colloquial term given to politicians' trading of favors, votes, or generalized support for each other's proposals.

DEMOCRATIC DILEMMA

Piles of Pork

Democratic Senator Robert C. Byrd of West Virginia chaired the Senate Appropriations Committee from 1989 until 1994, when the Democrats lost control of the Senate. He had vowed to steer $1 billion homeward after assuming the powerful chairmanship of the Appropriations Committee, and he needed only a little over two years to accomplish that goal. When Republicans took over the Congress in 1994, they vowed to slash pork barrel spending and by most accounts they did. But when difficult congressional races rolled around in 1998 and 2000, pork was back with a vengeance. Of course, "pork" is in the eye of the beholder. A program that seems pointless to an outsider may seem an essential investment of public money to recipients. Here are a few programs deemed worthy by members of the 107th Congress. You make the call.

Agriculture
$400,000 for manure-management research at the National Swine Research Center.

Commerce
$50,000 for a tattoo removal program in San Luis Obispo, California; $400,000 for exchange programs to build linkages between American and foreign musicians.

Interior
$2,500,000 for the Fort Benton visitor center in Lewiston, Montana; $650,000 for land acquisition for the Garnet Ghost Town, also in Montana.

Foreign Operations
$25,000,000 to the International Fund for Ireland (IFI). This U.S. contribution, intended to support the Anglo-Irish Accord, was to be spent on "those projects that hold the greatest potential for job creation and equal opportunity for the Irish people."

Labor and Education
$500,000 for exhibits on the Sullivan brothers at the Grout Museum in Waterloo, Iowa; $100,000 for Invent Iowa to encourage children to hold fairs displaying their inventions; and $61,000 for the State Historical Society to archive the history of Iowa workers.

Independent Agencies
$1,500,000 for the University of Missouri's Center for Gender Physiology in the area of gender-related issues in space flight crews.

• *Congress has the authority to tax and spend, a power it uses to engage in the sort of behavior illustrated here. Are there any checks on the abuse of that power? Can there be?*

• *Voters usually reward legislators for bringing home the bacon. What if the voters in a congressional district instead decided to elect a representative who would not fight to fund unnecessary programs? What could they reasonably expect to gain, such that it could compensate for all of the lost pork?*

SOURCES: "Byrd's Eye View," *Congressional Quarterly Weekly Report,* September 21, 1991: 2682; Daniel J. Parks, "Earmarks, Back with a Vengeance," *CQ Weekly Report,* December 1, 2001; Citizens Against Government Waste, *Pig Book* (Washington, DC: Citizens Against Government Waste, 2002).

revise important legislation. Proponents of partisan theory point out that the average ratio of majority to minority party members typically favors the majority party—sometimes by a lot.[36] And committee jurisdictions are influenced by party leaders. But there are many exceptions to these patterns. Sometimes committees behave in a bipartisan fashion, and the process of defining committee jurisdictions is extremely complicated, not clearly under the direct control of the leadership.[37]

Studies of committees are not conclusive about which of these three perspectives—distributive (or logrolling), informational, partisan—is the best explanation for the committee system. Committees likely promote all three of these purposes as members strive to balance their competing needs: to serve their local constituencies, to gain reliable information about public policy, and to accomplish partisan goals. It may also be that the type of committee matters a great deal. For instance, committees that hand out money for public projects or fund important programs seem to behave in distributive fashion. Other committees that deal with complex public policies such as environmental or telecommunications regulation may serve an informational function. Finally, some committees—such as the Rules Committee that controls the agenda and floor debate—seem dominated by the party leadership. The committee system probably reflects a mixture of the three theoretical purposes for committees, a mixture that varies over time and across committees.

Caucuses

caucus
A group within Congress, formed by members to pursue common interests.

In recent years voluntary groupings of members with common interests have become increasingly common, adding a third level of congressional organization. Called **caucuses,** but smaller than a party caucus, these groupings cross party, committee and even chamber lines. There were nearly 300 such groups in the 108th Congress, ranging from long-standing ones such as the Congressional Black Caucus and the Northeast-Midwest Congressional Coalition, to newer ones such as the Sportsmen's Caucus, the Wine Caucus, and the End-the-Death Tax Caucus.[38]

Caucuses are extremely varied in their concerns, their activities, and their effects. They can support the efforts of party or committee leaders but they also can pressure party or committee leaders on particular issues. Similarly, they can be a vehicle for cooperation across chambers, across parties, or across committees—or they can obstruct the proposals of chambers, parties, or committees because of some special interest they feel is being slighted or dealt with unfairly (such as wine or potatoes). Some caucuses are lavishly financed by outside interests while others subsist with modest contributions of office space, money, and staff from their members. The Sportsmen's Caucus, for example, had a 2003 budget of $860,000 provided by donations from the National Rifle Association and the sporting equipment industry.

There are few studies of caucuses and their activities as yet, but they appear to be increasingly important actors in the congressional process, another example of how congressional organization evolves to meet the needs of members in a changing political world.[39]

How a Bill Becomes a Law

You Are a Member of Congress

sponsor
Representative or senator who introduces a bill or resolution.

Congress makes the laws that govern the United States. In addition to the specific legislative powers set out in Article I, the "necessary and proper" clause authorizes Congress "to make all laws which shall be necessary and proper for carrying into execution the foregoing powers, and all other powers vested by this Constitution. . . ." How do the two parties in two chambers organized into over 200 committees and subcommittees get together and pass laws? Although no flowchart can possibly convey the complexity of getting a major bill through Congress, we will outline the process, describing the stages that important legislation goes through. Figure 12.2 lays out the process in idealized form, but any particular bill or resolution may have a different and even more complicated history as it loops over and over again through the various stages.

As a first step, a bill or resolution is introduced by a congressional **sponsor** and one or more co-sponsors. The House Speaker or Senate presiding officer, advised by the chamber's parliamentarian (an expert on rules and procedures), refers the proposal to an appropriate committee. In some cases, sponsors are not serious but are acting only to please some constituency or interest group. If they *are* serious, they may draft their bill

FIGURE 12.2
How a Bill Becomes a Law
Passing laws is a long and complicated process. Most bills fail to complete the journey.

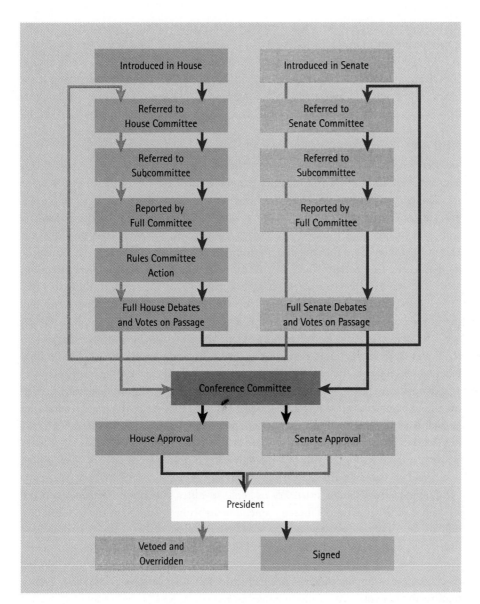

in such a way as to increase its chances of being referred to a friendly committee—often theirs. Sometimes the leadership decides on a **multiple referral,** sending the bill simultaneously to more than one committee or dividing it among several committees. Complex legislation and overlapping committee jurisdictions increase the likelihood of multiple referrals.

Once the bill goes to committee, the chair gives it to an appropriate subcommittee. Here the real work begins. If the subcommittee takes the bill seriously, the staff schedules hearings at which witnesses will speak in favor of the bill or in opposition to it. Witnesses can be other members of Congress, members of the executive branch, representatives of relevant interest groups, or ordinary citizens. Sometimes hearings are genuine attempts to gather information. More often, hearings are carefully

multiple referrals
Said to occur when party leaders give more than one committee responsibility for considering a bill.

choreographed: The subcommittee staff stacks the witness list in favor of the subcommittee chair's position.[40]

After hearings, the subcommittee begins **markup** of the bill—revising it, adding and deleting sections, and (assuming the bill enjoys majority support) preparing it for report to the full committee. The full committee may repeat the process, holding its own hearings and conducting its own markup, or it may largely accept the work of the subcommittee.[41] If a committee majority supports the bill after committee markup, the bill is nearly ready to be reported to the floor—but not quite.

Let's consider first what happens in the House. Bills that are not controversial, because they either are trivial or have extremely narrow impact, can be called up at specified times and passed unanimously with little debate. Somewhat more important bills are considered under a fast-track procedure called **suspension of the rules.** If a two-thirds majority of those voting agrees, the bill will be considered on the floor. Debate is limited to 40 minutes, no amendments are in order, and a two-thirds majority is required for passage. There is some risk in considering a bill under suspension: Even if a majority approves of it, the bill could fail to achieve two-thirds support. Indeed, a bill's opponents sometimes support the motion to suspend the rules precisely in order to raise the threshold for passage.

Legislation that is especially important, and therefore usually controversial, goes to the Rules Committee before going to the floor. The Rules Committee, too, may hold hearings, this time on the type of **rule** it should grant. In these hearings, only members of Congress may testify. The rule specifies the terms and conditions of debate, such as how long supporters and opponents will be allowed to speak. It may prohibit any amendments (a *closed rule*), allow any amendments (an *open rule*), or specify the amendments that are in order (a *restrictive rule*). In recent years, with the rise of stronger party leadership, three-quarters of all bills that have come from the Rules Committee have been granted restrictive rules.

Sometimes rules are unusual. For example, so-called *king of the mountain rules* allow a number of (frequently conflicting) amendments to be offered, but they specify that only the last amendment that receives a majority is adopted. Naturally, the committee orders the amendments so that the one it favors goes last. This kind of rule allows some members to play a little game with constituents. The members can vote for several conflicting amendments, thereby satisfying each of their supporters, all the while knowing that the last vote is the only one that matters.

If the Rules Committee recommends a rule, the floor then chooses to accept or reject it. In shaping the rule, the committee anticipates the limits of what the floor will accept. Thus, most rules receive approval—at which point the bill itself finally comes under consideration by the full chamber. The floor decides whether to adopt the "perfected" bill after any debate or amendment votes permitted by the rule.

The process in the Senate is a bit simpler to describe. For uncontroversial legislation, a motion to pass a bill by unanimous consent is sometimes all that is necessary. More important and controversial legislation requires the committee and party leaders to negotiate unanimous-consent agreements, which are complicated bargains analogous to the rules granted by the House Rules Committee. Assuming that such an agreement is successfully crafted and thereby avoids a filibuster, the bill eventually comes to a floor vote.

If a majority votes to adopt the bill, are we at the end of the process? Not at all. Before the bill can be sent for the president's signature, it must pass both chambers in

markup
Process in which a committee or subcommittee considers and revises a bill that has been introduced.

suspension of the rules
Fast-track procedure for considering bills and resolutions in the House; debate is limited to 40 minutes, no amendments are in order, and a two-thirds majority is required for passage.

rule
Specifies the terms and conditions under which a bill or resolution will be considered on the floor of the House—in particular, how long debate will last, how time will be allocated, and the number and type of amendments that will be in order.

identical form. A bill may have started in one chamber before going to the other, or it may have proceeded simultaneously through both. In either case, the House and Senate seldom pass exactly the same legislation. In fact, their versions may be in serious conflict. Unless one chamber is willing to defer to the other chamber, the two must iron out their differences. For major legislation, the usual method is that each chamber appoints representatives to a joint **conference committee** that can produce a compromise version.

In theory, each chamber's conferees are committed to the legislation approved by their colleagues, but in practice this allegiance is not likely. Conferences for some complex bills involve hundreds of members who support some parts of the bill, oppose other parts, and care little about still other parts. This complexity makes the situation ideal for bargaining. When a majority of each chamber's conferees agree to the final compromise, the bill is reported back to the parent chambers, where another floor vote in each chamber is required for passage.[42]

You may think that we have finally reached the end of the process. The bill will be sent to the president and, barring a presidential veto, will become law. Although it will formally become a law, there is no guarantee that the bill will have any effect. So far, we have been considering only the **authorization process.** All government action authorized by Congress—paying subsidies, issuing regulations, buying bombers, inspecting workplaces, whatever—also needs to have funds appropriated for it to be carried out.

The Constitution grants Congress the power of the purse and makes the House the lead actor: All tax bills must originate in the House, and by custom and tradition, all appropriations bills do, too. The **appropriations process** parallels the authorization process. Thirteen appropriations subcommittees in each chamber hold hearings and mark up the bill (the subcommittee chairs are commonly referred to as "the Cardinals of Capitol Hill").[43] The full committees may also do so, but they usually defer to their subcommittees. In the House, appropriations bills are privileged; they take precedence over other legislation, and a motion to take up an appropriations bill can be offered at any time. But in practice, appropriations bills, too, usually pass through the Rules Committee. Thus, appropriations subcommittees in both chambers must report spending bills, the rank and file in both chambers must pass them, and a conference committee must agree on every dollar before the government actually has any money to spend on the actions it has authorized.

Evaluating Congress

It is easy to get so wrapped up in the details of Congress and its operations that we lose sight of the reason for our interest in the institution. The reason, of course, is that Congress is the first branch, arguably the most powerful and most important of our three branches of government. It is the branch that bears primary responsibility for representing the needs and values of the American public and for developing legislation to improve its well-being. How well does Congress meet its responsibilities?

Criticisms of Congress

The most common criticism of the congressional process should be obvious: *It is lengthy and inefficient.* Legislation may take months or even years to wend its way through the process, and there is much duplication of effort—both within and between the

Star Power
Actress Julia Roberts testifies before the House Appropriations Committee, asking for more funding for the research of Rett Syndrome (a neurological disorder that mainly attacks women).

conference committee
Group of representatives from both the House and the Senate who iron out the differences between the two chambers' versions of a bill or resolution.

authorization process
Term applied to the entire process of providing statutory authority for a government program or activity.

appropriations process
Process of providing funding for governmental activities and programs that have been authorized.

Shoe on the Other Foot

Members of Congress usually view legislation in terms of the needs and interests of their own districts. They expect other districts to bear the brunt of any sacrifices.

chambers. Moreover, after all is said and done, Congress often produces a compromise that leaves no one satisfied. To those who want quick, decisive action, Congress-watching is enough to put their teeth on edge. And, of course, that is what the framers intended. They wanted to ensure that laws would pass only after they had been thoroughly considered and majorities were convinced that they were needed.

But that raises a second criticism: *The congressional process works to the advantage of policy minorities, especially those content with the status quo.* Proponents of legislation must build many winning coalitions—in subcommittee, in full committee, in appropriations committee, and on the floor, in both chambers, and perhaps in conference committee. Opponents have it much easier. A minority that controls only a single stage of the process may be able to block action. Of course, a determined majority cannot be stopped indefinitely, except by a Senate filibuster, but it can be held at bay for a long time or it can be forced to make undesirable compromises. Moreover, potential majorities sometimes decide not to act, calculating that the costs of overcoming all the obstacles are not worth the effort. Thus, the process hinders majorities who support change and helps minorities who are content to prevent change.

Two other criticisms focus on what Congress does when it acts, rather than on its failure to act. Given that members are trying to please constituencies, *they are constantly tempted to use their positions to extract constituency benefits,* even when important national legislation is at stake. President Jimmy Carter got so upset trying to deal with Congress on national energy policy that he wrote in his diary, "Congress is disgusting on this particular subject."[44] President Clinton's lobbying on behalf of the North American Free Trade Agreement (NAFTA) was likened to an "oriental bazaar," with members demanding special treatment for constituency interests or even trading their votes for concessions on unrelated issues. Many observers therefore charge that Congress defeats, distorts, and otherwise damages national interests in pursuit of its members' parochial interests. Such trading of favors may simply be the price of passing any general national legislation, however.[45]

Finally, the nature of the congressional process is such that *sometimes the very process of passing legislation ensures that it will not work.* This is especially true of proposals that, in order to correct a social problem, would need to concentrate resources on a small portion of the population. Representatives and senators are reluctant to pass up any opportunity to deliver local benefits, even if their district or state does not have the problem a program addresses or does not need federal money to address it. They therefore often pass bills that simply redistribute funds, and so are not targeted at the problem they originally were intended to correct. Consider, for example, the Economic

Development Administration, created in the 1960s to subsidize the construction of infrastructure such as roads, utilities, and industrial parks in depressed areas. By the time the program was killed by the Reagan administration, more than 80 percent of all the counties in the United States had been classified as "economically depressed" so that they would be eligible for the federal subsidies.[46] Everyone demanded a piece of the action.

Bashing the federal bureaucracy is a popular sport. Sometimes it is warranted— government programs may be poorly implemented or incompetently administered. But federal programs often fail because they were born to fail: Their enactment did not focus benefits where they would do the most good and did not concentrate resources sufficiently to have a major impact. Consequently, money is taken from some citizens and passed along to others but the nation has little to show for it. The failure does not result because government ignored the demands of voters. Quite the contrary: It results because members of Congress aggressively worked to promote the interests of their constituents.

Why Americans Like Their Members of Congress So Much More Than Congress Itself

More than people in other democracies, Americans are proud of their political institutions. They revere the Constitution, honor the law, and respect the presidency and the courts. But there is an exception to this generalization, and it is Congress. Congress is the butt of jokes. Congress has been defined as "a creature with 535 bellies, and no brain." Humorist Mark Twain once observed that "it could probably be shown with facts and figures that there is no distinctly native American criminal class except Congress."[47]

Disparaging quips like these reflect popular sentiments. As Figure 12.3 shows, Americans view their popularly elected representatives as having ethical standards well below those of most occupations. Congress as a whole also suffers from a particularly negative public image, even though it is the national government's most electorally sensitive institution.[48] Majorities of Americans doubt the competence and integrity of the legislative branch.[49]

Why, then, do members of Congress win reelection at a high rate (see Chapter 11)? Why do American voters not "throw the rascals out" and substitute better people? The answer is simple: Americans judge their own representatives by standards different from those by which they judge the collective Congress.[50] Voters like their own elected representatives. Citizens invariably rate their members of Congress far more favorably than they rate Congress as a whole, an observation that has become known as "Fenno's paradox" (after political scientist Richard Fenno, who popularized the observation).[51]

Polls show that Americans generally take a dim view of how well Congress solves national problems and meets national challenges. Congress, they believe, rarely meets its collective responsibilities. Citizens take an equally dim view of how they think Congress operates—sluggishly, conflictually, inefficiently, and sometimes corruptly. They therefore have little good to say about the institution or its membership. But citizens judge their own representatives and senators positively for doing the very things that make the collective Congress so ineffective. Members fight for what their constituents

Comparing Legislatures

A Congressional Debate
Disrespect for Congress is nothing new, as this 1798 print of the congressional floor shows.

FIGURE 12.3

The Public Rates the Honesty and Ethics of Members of Congress Lower Than Those of Other Occupations

SOURCE: The Gallup poll, November 13, 2000.

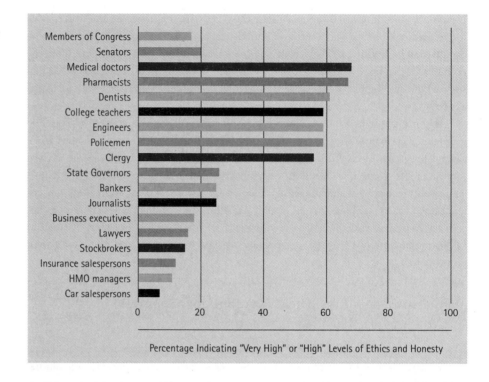

Percentage Indicating "Very High" or "High" Levels of Ethics and Honesty

want, even if it means blocking legislation, grabbing resources needed by others, or demanding unreasonable alterations in a government program.

Voters may resent such behavior when conducted on behalf of others, but they shower electoral rewards on the public officials who do it for them. That is, they would prefer other people's representatives to be **trustees**—legislators who use their own judgment to decide what is right—but demand that their own representatives serve as mere **delegates**—legislators who carry out the precise wishes of their constituents back home regardless of what they personally believe policy ought to be. However, because voters demand roughly the same sort of responsiveness everywhere, members of Congress typically work as delegates to the federal government charged with getting constituents the resources they want. An old saying states that "if you want to make an omelet, you've got to break some eggs." Voters want lots of omelets and reward legislators who deliver them to the table, then curse the kitchen for all the eggs it breaks in the process of feeding everyone.

Reforming Congress: Limit Their Terms?

In the early 1990s a reform movement swept over much of the United States. It proposed that public officials, especially legislators, be limited by law to some maximum number of terms (usually amounting to 6 to 12 years of service). By 1997, 21 states had limited the terms of their state legislators. Twenty-three states also tried to limit congressional service, but the Supreme Court held, in *U.S. v. Thornton* (1995), that such attempts were unconstitutional. Still, some candidates elected to Congress have pledged to support congressional term limits and congressional limits were the announced position of the Republican party for a time. The movement has waned somewhat, but its

trustee
Role a representative plays when acting in accordance with his or her own best judgment.

delegate
Role a representative plays when following the wishes of those who have elected him or her.

strength reflects popular frustration with American government in general and with legislative bodies in particular.

Whether Republican or Democratic, conservative or liberal, few political scientists favor term limits.[52] They generally believe that term limits would accomplish little and would probably do some harm. In their view, those who advocate term limits misunderstand what is wrong with Congress in particular and with legislatures in general. The argument for term limits assumes that incumbents are virtually unbeatable and that their electoral strength is illegitimate—a result of pandering to special interests. Reformers therefore select term limits as a means to turn incumbents out of office and increase legislative responsiveness to popular majorities. However, as this chapter has shown, incumbents work hard to please their constituents and usually succeed at doing so. They stay in office because they are responsive to the demands of their voters.

Reformers look to term limit as a means for replacing long-term governmental insiders with "citizen legislators" more familiar with the needs of regular Americans, representatives who could take a broad view of the public interest. Syndicated columnist George Will, for example, argues, "Term limits would increase the likelihood that people would come to Congress from established careers, with significant experience in the private sector."[53] But what sort of people can place their careers on hold for six to ten years while they serve in Congress? In all likelihood, Congress would still be populated with career politicians. Elected officials would circulate more rapidly among local, state, and federal offices, trading places as often as required. Would the responsiveness of such people to special interests—and local constituencies—be less than it is today? It might be even greater than now, because the professionals would be continually worried about their next positions.

Term limits would not be the end of the world—both advocates and opponents exaggerate the probable effects. But term limitation does not address the real problem with Congress. The real problem is that professional politicians chosen in single-member districts have compelling incentives to please the special interests within their districts and, as campaign funds become increasingly important, special interests outside their districts. They rarely need to consider the consequences of their activities for the larger, more general interests of the country.

Chapter Summary

The United States Congress is the world's most powerful legislature. It is also the most professionalized. Its members are full-time, career legislators. Congress has an extensive division of labor—the committee system—supported by a norm of party leadership focused on getting bills through the difficult lawmaking process. Nevertheless, citizens hold Congress in much lower esteem than they hold their individual representatives and senators, whom they reelect regularly.

This discrepancy arises because members of Congress depend for their election on specific constituencies. They act to satisfy those constituencies, even if doing so requires behavior that may not serve the larger interest of the nation. The result is that Congress is slow and inefficient, and what emerges from the complex legislative process may not be very effective. The structure of Congress is an uneasy compromise between what it takes to get the job done and what it takes to get reelected. Frustrated voters fail to see that members of Congress have powerful electoral incentives to behave as they do. The problem may not result from a lack of electoral responsiveness, but from an excess of it.

Key Terms

appropriations process, p. 329
authorization process, p. 329
bicameral, p. 315
caucus, p. 326
cloture, p. 319
conference committee, p. 329
delegate, p. 332
filibuster, p. 319
logrolling, p. 324

majority leader, p. 317
markup, p. 328
minority leader, p. 318
multiple referrals, p. 327
party caucus, p. 318
party conference, p. 318
president pro tempore, p. 318
rule, p 328
select committee, p. 321

seniority, p. 323
Speaker, p. 316
sponsor, p. 326
standing committee, p. 321
suspension of the rules, p. 328
trustee, p. 332
unanimous-consent agreement, p. 318
whips, p. 318

Suggested Readings

Of General Interest

Arnold, R. Douglas. *The Logic of Congressional Action*. New Haven, CT: Yale University Press, 1990. An excellent discussion of how the incentives that motivate members interact with the characteristics of public-policy problems to shape legislation.

Oleszek, Walter. *Congress and Its Members*. 9th ed. Washington, DC: CQ Press, 2003. A readable text that relates the electoral and institutional arenas.

Ornstein, Norman, Thomas Mann, and Michael Malbin. *Vital Statistics on Congress, 2001–2002*. Washington, DC: American Enterprise Institute, 2002. This biennial compilation of congressional statistics is to Congress-watchers what *The Bill James Baseball Sourcebook* is to baseball fans.

Smith, Steven, Jason Roberts, and Ryan Vander Wielen, *The American Congress*. 3rd ed., Online Version. http://congress.wustl.edu/ A comprehensive, up-to-date, and free (!) online textbook.

Focused Studies

Adler, E. Scott. *Why Congressional Reforms Fail*. Chicago: University of Chicago Press, 2002. Historical study which argues that member

desire for reelection consistently hampers efforts to reform the committee system.

Cox, Gary, and Mathew McCubbins. *Legislative Leviathan*. Berkeley: University of California Press, 1993. Challenges the perception that parties were unimportant during mid-century Congresses.

Hammond, Susan Webb. *Congressional Caucuses in National Policy Making*. Baltimore: Johns Hopkins Press, 2001. Discusses an increasingly important aspect of congressional organization that cuts across parties, committees, and chambers.

Oleszek, Walter. *Congressional Procedures and the Policy Process*. 6th ed. Washington, DC: CQ Press, 2003. An accessible treatment of the rules and procedures governing the congressional process.

Rohde, David. *Parties and Leaders in the Post-Reform House*. Chicago: University of Chicago Press, 1991. Important work that traces the strengthening of the congressional parties in recent decades.

Schickler, Eric. *Disjointed Pluralism*. Princeton, NJ: Princeton University Press, 2001. Focuses on the historical development of congressional rules and procedures.

On the Web

www.rollcall.com
Roll Call, the newspaper of Capitol Hill, is a definitive source of news on congressional affairs.

www.democrats.senate.gov
www.democrats.house.gov
www.gop.gov
These Web sites offer very current information on the partisan activities going on in Congress at any given time.

http://thomas.loc.gov
This Web site is the official source of information on Congress and has links to member offices, committee Web sites, historical documents, and

(most important) the congressional record and index. The information is not always easily organized, but it is comprehensive.

www.congress.org
This Web site by Capitol Advantage is an alternative, private source of congressional information. It chronicles the daily activities of Congress in committee and on the floor and makes it easy to contact the members who represent your state or district. You can even send a hand-delivered letter.

CHAPTER 13

* * * * * * * * * * * * * * * * *

The Presidency: Powers and Practice

CHAPTER OUTLINE ——————————————————————

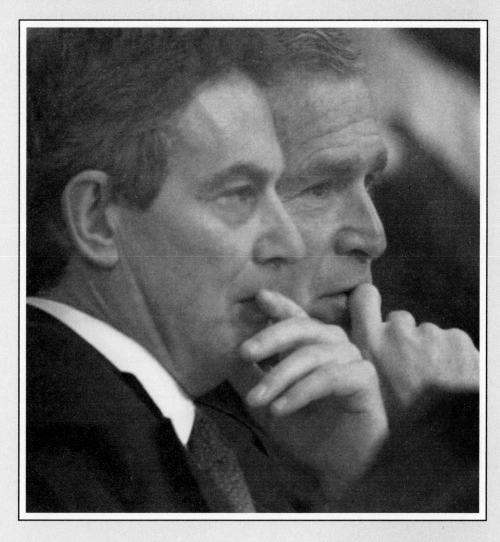

Terrorism Redefines the Bush Presidency

Unanticipated events can dramatically change presidential fortunes. Wars, depressions, disasters, and scandals can alter the way the public and those in politics look at a president—and even the way presidents look at themselves. Few episodes better illustrate the way in which traumatic moments shape a presidency than the terrorist attacks on the World Trade Center and the Pentagon.

George W. Bush had assumed the presidency in January 2001 with perhaps the slimmest electoral mandate in U.S. history. He had failed to carry the popular vote. His victory in the electoral college had hinged on fewer than 600 votes in Florida and was resolved only after a bitter court suit that had wound its way to the Supreme Court. Although a majority of Americans accepted the Supreme Court decision as final, many Democrats and African American voters did not. On inauguration day, one nationwide poll showed that only 19 percent of Democrats and 12 percent of African Americans viewed Bush's election as "legitimate." [1] His party controlled the House of Representatives by a small (nine-vote) margin, and the Senate was evenly divided, with Republican control dependent on the tie-breaking vote cast by Vice President Cheney. Even worse, Republicans lost control of the Senate just four months after Inauguration Day, as a moderate Republican, Vermont Senator James Jeffords, announced he was no longer a Republican and would henceforth vote with the Democrats. When Bush pushed through a tax cut with a narrow, mainly Republican majority, he seemed excessively partisan—even after making compromises to win the few Democratic votes he needed.

Most disconcerting, the president himself seemed to lack authority and a sense of direction. Controversial changes in environmental policy were proposed, then withdrawn. Attempts to adapt the military to meet new challenges were going nowhere. The American economy was drifting into recession.

The events of September 11, 2001 dramatically changed the picture. Soon after recovering from the immediate shock of the attack, the president acquired a force and conviction, a sense of purpose and mission that had previously not been evident in his public demeanor. He assembled a worldwide coalition against terrorism, launched a major attack on the al Qaeda terrorist network in Afghanistan, and mobilized domestic law-enforcement agencies in a massive effort to disrupt any terrorist cells that might still be operating within the United States. His popularity ratings shot upward from a bare majority of adults to over 90 percent. Even those most disturbed by the outcome of the election flocked to his support. The president scored major legislative victories on further tax cuts, education reform, Medicare, and homeland security. Bush had become truly a president of the nation as a whole, a symbol of the country's unity in the face of a foreign attack.

It would be an exaggeration to say that 9/11 silenced the president's critics. Bush's 2003 decision to wage a war against Iraqi dictator Saddam Hussein was controversial, and became a major issue in the 2004 election. Critics claimed that the administration's education reform was underfunded, and that the Medicare bill was unfair. But one thing was clear: As a result of the 9/11 tragedy, an elected official was transformed from a partisan politician into a respected national leader.

MAKING THE CONNECTION

Although President Bush faced a unique set of circumstances associated with the unprecedented 2000 election and the 9/11 attacks, his early frustrations and post-terrorism triumphs illustrate the pitfalls and promise of the modern presidency. Presidents may sometimes be seen as overly partisan, especially if they are elected in a close contest and if they face a Congress controlled, in part, by the opposite political party. At other times, they can be powerful symbols of national unity and resolve. This dual role is due both to the constituency pressures they face and to the nature of their powers. In this chapter, we consider the pressures on the office of the presidency and its strengths and weaknesses by focusing on the following questions:

- What are the president's constituencies, and how do they influence his actions?

- What constitutional powers do presidents exercise, and what are the limitations on these powers?

- What factors contribute to presidential success and failure in office?

* * * * * * * * * * * * * * * * *

Presidential Constituencies

Presidents often find it challenging to strike the right balance between their national constituencies, created by the general election, and their partisan constituencies, shaped by presidential primaries. Both national and partisan constituencies play a role in presidential decision making.

National Constituency

Presidents have one unique political asset: They fill a position elected by a national constituency. Only presidents can persuasively claim to speak for the country as a whole, and they can use this national constituency to powerful effect. In late 1995, after budget negotiations between the Democratic president and the Republican Congress deadlocked, much of the government was shut down for nearly a month. National parks were closed and government bills went unpaid. In the midst of the crisis, President Bill Clinton asked Congress to place the national interest above partisan objectives. Republican Speaker of the House Newt Gingrich replied by saying it was the president who should put the country's future ahead of his own. Each appealed to a national constituency, but the president, in part because he was the *president,* proved to be more persuasive. According to polls, most Americans sided with Clinton and blamed Congress for the deadlock. One Republican strategist acknowledged the president's advantages: "We've learned that it's nearly impossible to frame the national debate from the lower chamber of the legislative branch." [2]

In early 2003, President Bush proposed a "jobs and growth" plan that had as its centerpiece a cut on the taxes that investors paid on corporate dividends. "Lower taxes and greater investment will help the economy expand," reasoned Bush in his state of the union address.[3] Although Bush touted the plan as in the national interest, Democrats and liberal interest groups argued that it would be harmful to the economy and would increase the budget deficit. Democratic Senate leader Tom Daschle even pronounced the bill "dead on arrival" in that chamber.[4] Nevertheless, after a series of high-profile public appearances in states with wavering senators, Bush carried the day. Although smaller than what the president initially asked for, the $350 billion tax cut was still one of the largest in history. Once again, the president's ability to mobilize his national constituency gave him key advantages over his opponents in Congress.

Although the president's national constituency is a great political asset, it creates problems as well. Voters hold presidents responsible for many events and conditions over which they have little control. Presidents are expected to conduct foreign policy, manage the economy, administer a complex bureaucracy, promote desired legislation, respond to disasters, and address an endless variety of real and imagined social problems.[5]

Appealing to the Right
In the 2000 primary race, George W. Bush spoke at Bob Jones University, a conservative evangelical institution that at the time banned interracial dating.
• *Why do relatively small groups, such as strong conservatives or strong liberals, wield so much power in primary elections?*

commander in chief
The president in his constitutional role as head of the armed forces.

Presidents are sometimes given credit for prosperity and success, but they are more often blamed when things go bad. President George H. W. Bush, for example, enjoyed foreign policy triumphs equaled by only a few of his predecessors. Most notably, in his role as **commander in chief,** the constitutional head of the U.S. armed forces, he achieved a spectacular victory in the 1991 Persian Gulf War. Yet when the economy faltered, Bush was drummed from office.

Partisan Constituencies

In addition to a national constituency, presidents have a party constituency to which they must be responsive. They need to keep the support of those who work in and help finance their campaigns. If they do not satisfy their party constituency, they may encounter difficulties with the party faithful in presidential primaries.

A party constituency usually takes more extreme issue positions than does the national constituency. Presidents therefore have to find some way to balance the demands of their most ardent supporters with the more moderate concerns of the general-election voters who determine the outcome of national elections. At times, this balancing act proves unsuccessful. In the 2000 primaries, for example, George W. Bush stirred controversy when he appealed to his conservative base by speaking at Bob Jones University in South Carolina, an evangelical school that, at the time, banned interracial dating among its students.

Partisan Support in Congress

Even if presidents can balance their national and party constituencies, they usually cannot take action on their pledges without considering their level of support in Congress. On most issues, presidents gain more support from members of their own party than from the opposition (see Figure 13.1). As a consequence, when presidents

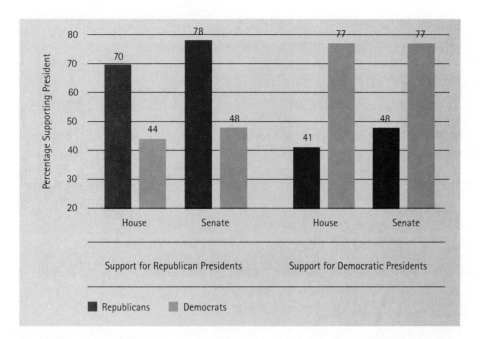

FIGURE 13.1

Partisan Support for the President in Congress

Each party in Congress supports its own president more often than a president of the opposing party.

• *What do you think happens when presidents face divided government?*

SOURCE: This figure is based on data for the period 1954–1998, taken from Norman Ornstein, Thomas E. Mann, and Michael Malbin, *Vital Statistics on Congress, 1999–2000* (Washington, DC: Congressional Quarterly, 2000).

have larger majorities in Congress, they are more likely to get their proposed legislation approved.[6]

The events surrounding the first Bush tax-cut bill provide a clear illustration of the importance to presidents of a party majority in Congress. When Bush entered office in 2001, the Senate had a bare majority of Republicans, whereas the GOP had a more comfortable—though still slim—margin in the House. Because of these differences in party margins, Bush's proposed tax cuts fared differently in the two chambers. In the House, the Republican majority not only gave the president most of the tax cuts he requested quickly, but added further tax breaks. In the Senate, Democrats and moderate Republicans combined to reduce the size of the cut by 25 percent.

Partisanship is not as pervasive in the United States as it is in many European countries. Still, political scientists have debated whether it is good or bad to have **divided government**—control of the presidency by one party and control of one or both houses of Congress by the other. (See the accompanying Democratic Dilemma.) In the 2002 election cycle, George W. Bush made a particularly aggressive effort to ensure unified Republican government and gain the support of his congressional partisans by becoming involved in fund raising and candidate selection for congressional races.[7] His success in securing a Republican Congress set the groundwork for 2003 Republican victories on taxes and Medicare reform.

divided government
The control of the presidency by one party and the control of one or both houses of Congress by the other.

Separate Institutions Sharing Power

In addition to frequent partisan divisions of government, presidents also face the fundamental divisions of power between the executive and legislative branches that are written into the Constitution. Presidents can seldom force members of Congress to support them; they usually have to coax, beg, plead, and compromise to gain the necessary votes. Even when the same party controls both the presidency and Congress, presidents do

DEMOCRATIC DILEMMA

Is Divided Government Good or Bad?

Scholars disagree on the issue of divided government. Some
see it as an unfortunate and harmful phenomenon, others as a
harmless or even beneficial result of popular elections.

James Sundquist argues that divided government often
prevents the government from taking necessary action
because it makes it harder for the president to enact his policy
agenda. "When the president sends a recommendation to the
opposition-controlled Congress," says Sundquist, "the legislators are virtually compelled to reject or profoundly alter it;
otherwise they are endorsing the president's leadership . . .
[and] strengthening him or his party for the next election."
Sundquist proposes a novel solution to this problem: four-year
House terms and eight-year Senate terms, with elections
coinciding with presidential elections. Sundquist claims that if
the president and Congress were elected at the same time,
divided government would be less likely.

Other scholars believe that the concern about divided
government is unwarranted and such radical solutions unnecessary. Morris Fiorina suggests that divided government may
be the result of conscious decisions by the voters to send
mixed signals. If this is so, "who are we to recommend that
they make a clear choice?" Perhaps voters believe that
Republicans are too extreme on some issues and Democrats
are too extreme on others. (For more on divided government,
see Chapter 8.)

Whom do you believe?

Unified Government?
President George W. Bush and Senate Majority Leader Bill
Frist

• *Do you think divided government produces harmful gridlock?
Or do you think it serves as a check against extreme action by
either party?*

• *Are good policies blocked?*

• *Are bad policies prevented?*

SOURCES: James L. Sundquist, *Constitutional Reform and Effective
Government* (Washington, DC: The Brookings Institution, 1986), pp.
75–76, 240; and Morris Fiorina, *Divided Government* (New York:
Macmillan, 1992), pp. 128–129.

not find it easy to get their proposals approved. For instance, Bill Clinton was unable
to persuade a Democratic Congress to enact his health care reform proposals.[8] Over 80
percent of the time, presidents either fail to secure passage of their major legislative
agendas or must make important compromises to win congressional approval.[9] As presidential scholar Charles Jones has observed, "Presidents don't pass laws; they work with,
alongside of, or against the House and Senate."[10]

When President Bush watched control of the Senate slip out of his party's hands
in 2001, he was not the first president to be frustrated by Congress. Theodore Roosevelt
sighed, "Oh, if I could only be president and Congress too for just ten minutes."[11]
Presidents find their position particularly exasperating because they feel they have a
duty to take decisive action. Facing a Republican Congress in 1995, President Clinton
angrily charged congressional leaders with trying "to destroy the ability of the federal
government to address the problems facing America—to move the country forward, to
move the country together."[12]

Those who wrote the Constitution ensured that presidents would govern only
with the help of Congress (see Table 2.3, p. 40). Most delegates to the Constitutional
Convention wanted to strengthen the executive branch beyond what was provided for

Tom Daschle, Senate Democratic Party Leader After 2002, Democrats grew frustrated with their minority party status.

• *In general, do you think divided government leads to inefficient gridlock, or is it a valuable check?*

by the Articles of Confederation. But the founders realized that voters would never ratify a constitution that created a strong executive who might become another King George. The result is a government of "separated institutions sharing powers."[13] We now turn to the many ways in which the Constitution has shaped presidential power and practice. (Our emphasis in this chapter will be on the president's powers with respect to domestic affairs.)

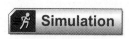

Presidential Leadership: Which Hat Do You Wear?

The Power to Inform and Persuade

> PRESIDENTIAL POWER: The President "shall from time to time give to the Congress Information of the State of the Union."

> CONGRESSIONAL CHECK: None

The Constitution requires presidents to give Congress information about the state of the Union. Presidents have interpreted this requirement as authority to persuade Congress and the public at large to support their policies. Modern presidents rely on hundreds of speeches each year to set forth their vision of the country's future, but the most prestigious and formalized address is the **State of the Union address,** which is given annually, usually in late January or early February. In this speech, the president usually outlines his legislative and foreign-policy priorities for the coming year.

State of the Union address Annual speech delivered by the president in fulfillment of the constitutional obligation of reporting to Congress on the state of the Union.

Early Use of Persuasion Power   The power to persuade is used much more publicly today than in times past, as Figure 13.2 illustrates. Early presidents seldom spoke in public, and when they did, their remarks were of a general nature. To fulfill their obligation to report on the state of the union, Thomas Jefferson and his nineteenth-century successors sent written messages to Congress. Early presidents found other ways of persuading Congress. Instead of using public rhetoric, Jefferson, a master politician,

FIGURE 13.2

Growth in Presidential Speech Making

• *Why have presidents made more public speeches in the last 50 years?*

SOURCES: Data on Washington through McKinley are taken from Jeffrey Tulis, *The Rhetorical Presidency* (Princeton, NJ: Princeton University Press, 1987), p. 64. For Theodore Roosevelt, see Robert V. Friedenberg, *Theodore Roosevelt and the Rhetoric of Militant Decency* (New York: Greenwood Press, 1990). For Taft, see *Presidential Addresses and State Papers of William Howard Taft,* Vol. 1, 1910 (New York: Doubleday). For Wilson, see Albert Shaw, ed. *Messages and Papers of Woodrow Wilson,* Vols. 1 and 2 (New York: Review of Reviews Corporation, 1924). For Coolidge, see Claude M. Feuss, *Calvin Coolidge: The Man from Vermont* (Hamden, CT: Archon Books, 1965). For Presidents Truman through Reagan, see Roderick Hart, *The Sound of Leadership* (Chicago: The University of Chicago Press, 1987). For Hoover, George H.W. Bush, Clinton, and George W. Bush, information is taken from *The Public Papers of the President,* various years, and the *Weekly Compilation of Presidential Documents.*

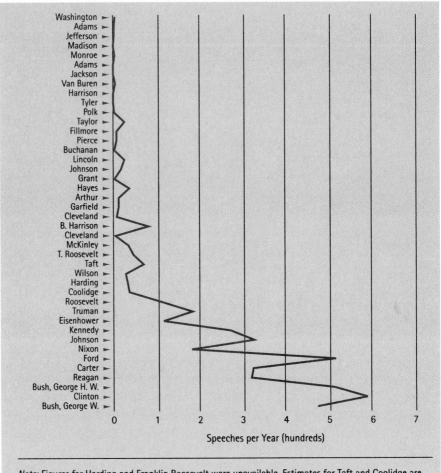

Speeches per Year (hundreds)

Note: Figures for Harding and Franklin Roosevelt were unavailable. Estimates for Taft and Coolidge are based on their first year in office only. Figures on George W. Bush are for 2001 only.

invited members of Congress to the Executive Mansion (later called the White House) for dinners at which he would persuade them to support his political agenda.[14] Not until Woodrow Wilson addressed a joint session of both houses of Congress in 1913 did it become a regular practice for presidents to report in person on the state of the union.[15]

In fact, the unwritten rule against presidential rhetoric was at one time so strong that it became a basis for presidential impeachment. President Andrew Johnson, who succeeded to the presidency upon the assassination of Abraham Lincoln, publicly criticized specific members of Congress. In the list of impeachment charges brought against Johnson, one seems particularly strange to modern Americans:

> That . . . Andrew Johnson, President of the United States, unmindful of the high duties of his office and the dignity and propriety thereof . . . did . . . deliver with a loud voice certain intemperate, inflammatory, and scandalous harangues, and did therein utter loud threats and bitter menaces . . . against Congress.

Today we would think that such a president, though perhaps not politically prudent, was merely exercising the right of free speech.[16]

Modern Persuasion Power   More than any other president, Theodore ("Teddy") Roosevelt changed the definition of what was permissible in presidential rhetoric. Roosevelt made frequent use of what he called the "**bully pulpit**" available to presidents. (*Bully* was nineteenth-century slang for "excellent.") Roosevelt suggested that, like a preacher, the president could use his position to move his "congregation"—the public—to action. He mobilized support through bold gestures, forceful speeches, presidential trips, and dramatic turns of phrase. As one historian has noted, "the number of laws [Roosevelt] inspired was certainly not in proportion to the amount of noise he emitted."[17] Yet Roosevelt's popular appeal was such that a cartoon depicting the president sparing the life of a bear cub while hunting resulted in the emergence of the term "Teddy Bear."

Presidents since Teddy Roosevelt have increasingly used the bully pulpit to persuade Congress and the public, as Figure 13.2 shows.[18] Franklin Delano Roosevelt's "fireside chats" over the radio enabled him to sidestep the print media, which he accused of being controlled by Republican publishers. John Kennedy had a compelling rhetorical style that both inspired and challenged his audience.[19]

President Reagan, the first president with experience as a professional actor, used television more effectively than any of his predecessors. He understood that there is but "a thin line between politics and theatricals."[20] As Reagan once said, "I've wondered how people in positions of this kind . . . manage without having had any acting experience."[21] Learning from Reagan's example, George W. Bush had his picture taken, on one occasion, while landing on an aircraft carrier off the coast of California, and, on another, carving a Thanksgiving turkey for U.S. troops in Iraq, shortly after arriving on a secret transatlantic flight. The Thanksgiving gesture proved especially popular, boosting the president's approval rating by five percentage points.

bully pulpit
The nature of presidential status as an ideal vehicle for persuading the public to support the president's policies.

A Popular President
Although President Theodore Roosevelt was an avid hunter, it was his decision to spare the life of a bear cub in 1902 that led to the emergence of the term "Teddy Bear."

• *How can symbolic actions like this one increase the power of the presidential "bully pulpit"?*

The Veto Power

> PRESIDENTIAL VETO POWER: Before any law "shall take effect," it must be "approved by" the president.

> CONGRESSIONAL CHECK: Unless "repassed by two-thirds of the Senate and House of Representatives."

veto power
Presidential rejection of congressional legislation. May be overridden by a two-thirds vote in each congressional chamber. Most state governors also have veto power over their legislatures.

override
Congressional passage of a bill by a two-thirds vote over the president's veto.

pocket veto
Presidential veto after congressional adjournment, executed merely by not signing a bill into law.

line item veto
Presidential authority to negate particular provisions of a law, granted by Congress in 1996 but struck down by the Supreme Court in 1998.

The president's **veto power** is more concrete than is the power to inform: It gives presidents the capacity to prevent bills passed by Congress from becoming law. Before the Civil War, presidents seldom used the veto. President Washington cast only two vetoes. The average number cast by presidents between Madison and Lincoln was only a little more than four. As Figure 13.3 shows, presidents from Franklin Roosevelt on have been much more willing to use the veto power.

This presidential power to say "No" can be checked. But Congress usually fails to muster the necessary two-thirds vote in each chamber to pass an **override,** which makes the bill a law despite the president's opposition. Since the Kennedy administration, Congress has overridden approximately only 1 out of every 10 vetoes.[22] Only 2 of President Clinton's 37 vetoes were overridden.[23]

Although the veto can seldom be used to initiate policy, it can be successfully employed as a weapon in negotiations with Congress. By 2004, George W. Bush had gone the longest without issuing a veto of any president since the early 1850s.[24] Still, he effectively used the threat of the veto in negotiations with Congress over such issues as homeland security legislation, reconstruction funds for Iraq, and telecommunications policy.[25]

If Congress enacts a law ten days before it adjourns, a president may exercise a **pocket veto** by simply not signing the bill into law. Congress has no opportunity to override a pocket veto. Because these vetoes could not be overridden, President Reagan made frequent use of them to convey the impression that he was a strong president. The pocket veto strategy works only at the very end of a congressional session, however; if Congress remains in session for more than ten days after passing a bill, the president must explicitly cast a veto to prevent the bill from becoming law. As the distinction between campaigning and governing has disappeared, Congress has remained in session virtually throughout the entire year, giving more recent presidents fewer opportunities to cast pocket vetoes.

Although Congress is sometimes able to override vetoes, it more often counters the president's veto power indirectly, by incorporating policies that presidents oppose into large bills that contain items presidents feel they must approve. When faced with such a package, the president finds it difficult to cast a veto. For example, Clinton reluctantly signed a bill requiring the discharge of HIV-positive soldiers from the armed services because the provision was incorporated into an important defense bill.

Because Congress can artfully package laws in this way, many people favor giving the president the **line item veto**—the authority to negate particular provisions of a law while letting the remainder stand. The presidential line item veto became a popular idea among congressional Republicans during the Reagan and first Bush administrations. In 1995, Congress passed legislation enacting a form of line item veto for the president, a measure that had President Clinton's wholehearted approval. But in 1998 the Supreme Court struck down the law. "If the Line Item Veto Act were valid," said Justice John Stevens, "it would authorize the president to create a different law, one

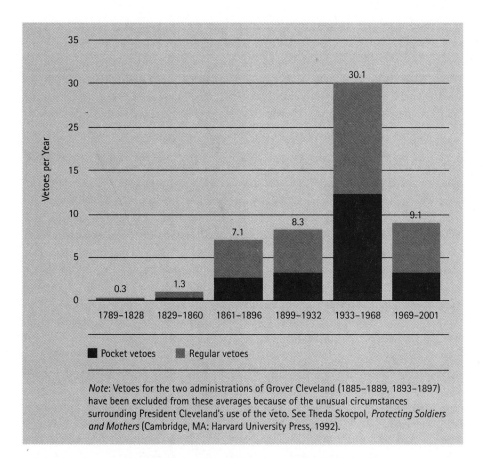

FIGURE 13.3

Trends in Presidential Use of the Veto Power

Currently presidents use the veto less than at mid-century, but more than in the 1800s.

• *Why did presidents become more assertive?*

SOURCES: Gary L. Galemore, "Presidential Vetoes, 1789–Present: A Summary Overview," Congressional Research Service Report for Congress, 98-148 GOV, November 4, 2000; and "Résumé of Congressional Activity: First Session of the One Hundred Seventh Congress," *Congressional Record Daily Digest,* January 29, 2002: D23.

Note: Vetoes for the two administrations of Grover Cleveland (1885–1889, 1893–1897) have been excluded from these averages because of the unusual circumstances surrounding President Cleveland's use of the veto. See Theda Skocpol, *Protecting Soldiers and Mothers* (Cambridge, MA: Harvard University Press, 1992).

whose text was not voted on by either house of Congress." This is contrary to the "procedures designed by the framers . . . of the Constitution."

The Appointment Power

> PRESIDENTIAL POWER: The president "shall appoint Ambassadors, other public Ministers and Consuls . . . and all other Officers of the United States."

> CONGRESSIONAL CHECK: Appointments are subject to the "Advice and Consent of the Senate," which is taken to mean that a majority must approve the nomination.

The appointment power enables presidents to appoint thousands of public officials to positions of high responsibility within their **administration,** which consists of those responsible for directing the executive branch of government.

The Cabinet   The president's **cabinet** consists of the key members of the administration. Most are heads of government departments and carry the title **secretary.** Originally, the president's cabinet had but four departments, and the secretaries met regularly with the president, giving him confidential political guidance on a broad range of policies. It was in cabinet meetings, for example, that Abraham Lincoln developed his strategy for fighting the Civil War.

administration
The president and his political appointees responsible for directing the executive branch of government.

cabinet
Top administration officials; mostly heads of departments in the executive branch.

secretary
Head of a department within the executive branch.

Over the years, government began to perform a much broader range of functions. As the number of departments grew from 4 to 14 (see Table 14.1, page 378), the cabinet lost its capacity to provide confidential advice to presidents. In President Nixon's words, "Cabinet government is a myth and won't work. . . . No [president] in his right mind submits anything to his cabinet."[26] Today the cabinet meets only occasionally, primarily for ceremonial purposes or to help the president make some kind of political statement.

The White House Staff   Many of the modern president's closest advisers are not cabinet secretaries but White House aides who deal in matters with utmost confidentiality. At one time the president's personal staff was small and informal. Abraham Lincoln had just two young assistants. Even President Franklin Roosevelt originally had only a handful of personal aides. To address organizational problems caused by the growing size of the federal government, Roosevelt in 1936 asked a committee of specialists in public administration headed by Louis Brownlow to study the issue. Saying "the President needs help," the Brownlow Committee recommended sweeping changes, including additional appointments to the president's personal staff. Brownlow said presidential staff members "should be possessed of high competence, great physical vigor, and a passion for anonymity." Although Congress rejected most of the other Brownlow recommendations, it agreed to enlarge the White House staff.[27]

Brownlow envisioned only a "small number of executive assistants," but the president's staff has steadily increased in size and complexity.[28] The number of aides has grown from 48 in 1944 to nearly 400 today.[29] Its organization is now complex enough to confuse even well-informed citizens. One basic distinction to remember is the difference between the **White House Office,** the main subject under discussion here, and the much larger **Executive Office of the President (EOP).** Although the names make it seem as though they are much the same thing, the White House Office is just one component of the EOP, which also includes other important coordinating bodies as well as operating agencies (see Table 13.1).

In Franklin Roosevelt's day, no single person headed the White House staff. Even as late as the Carter administration, White House aides worked together as "spokes in a wheel," each having direct access to the president. But today presidents usually place one person in charge.[30] This person, the **chief of staff,** meets with the president several times a day and communicates decisions to other staff, cabinet officers, and members of Congress.

The best chiefs are usually Washington insiders. Though little acclaimed, Ronald Reagan's 1987–1988 chief, Howard Baker, was one of the most powerful and effective. A former Senate majority leader and presidential aspirant, Baker helped boost Reagan's popularity, despite the fact that the aging president himself had lost much of his former vitality. When George W. Bush entered the White House, he appointed Andrew Card as his chief of staff. Card, who was deputy chief of staff and later Transportation Secretary under George H. W. Bush, had nearly two decades of experience in Washington politics.

Newcomers to Washington are usually less successful. Typically, they become lightning rods—people to be blamed when things go wrong. John Sununu, former governor of New Hampshire, was forced to leave the job of chief of staff when he was blamed for urging President George H.W. Bush to sign an unpopular tax increase.[31]

White House Office
Political appointees who work directly for the president, many of whom occupy offices in the White House.

Executive Office of the President (EOP)
Agency that houses both top coordinating offices and other operating agencies.

chief of staff
Head of White House staff. Has continuous, direct contact with the president.

TABLE 13.1
EXECUTIVE OFFICE OF THE PRESIDENT, BUDGET AND STAFF LEVELS

• *Why do you think the office of management and budget is the largest component of the EOP? (See Chapter 14.)*

	Budget (Millions)[a]	Staff[a]
Office of Management and Budget	$70.7	490
White House Office	54.6	369
Office of National Drug Control Policy	25.2	109
Office of Administration	46.9	182
Office of the U.S. Trade Representative	30.1	173
White House Residence/Operating Expenses	11.6	90
National Security Council	7.5	47
Office of Policy Development	4.1	31
Office of Science and Technology Policy	5.3	19
Council of Economic Advisers	4.2	30
Office of the Vice President	3.9	15
Council on Environmental Quality	2.9	22

[a]As of 2001.

SOURCE: Executive Office of the President, *Budget of the United States Government, Fiscal Year 2003,* Appendix.

Thomas McLarty from Arkansas resigned after the Clinton administration's poor beginning.[32]

Although Brownlow expected White House aides to have "no power to make decisions," modern presidents have regularly used their staffs to shape their public policy proposals.[33] Within the White House staff, more than anywhere else, presidents can count on the loyalty of those around them simply because, unlike the careers of department secretaries, those of staff members are closely intertwined with that of the president.

The White House staff is more potent than ever, in part because presidents have more need than ever for political help. Presidents today need pollsters who can keep them in touch with changes in public opinion.[34] They also need assistants who can help them communicate with the media, interest groups, and members of Congress. Once a major piece of legislation arrives for consideration on the chamber floor, White House aides are in regular contact with many legislators.[35] So intense is the work inside the White House that most staff jobs demand 7-day, 100-hour workweeks. As a result, many positions go to those young in years and spirit.

Quite apart from the president's genuine need for lots of political help, appointment to the White House staff is an excellent way to reward loyal campaign workers. After the presidency has been won, those who worked on the campaign often expect something in return. For example, when George W. Bush became president, he appointed his chief campaign strategist Karl Rove and his campaign spokeswoman Karen Hughes to key White House posts. The White House Office is also a convenient place for the president to put campaign workers, because the president has exclusive control over appointments to his personal staff. Not even the chief of staff must be confirmed by the Senate.

Scandals in the White House Office   The highly personal and partisan nature of the White House staff can be a weakness as well as a strength. A White House full of personal friends and fellow partisans has at times so shielded the president from external criticism that the chief executive has lost touch with political reality. And sometimes staff members have used the power of the presidential office for improper—even illegal—purposes, paving the way for scandals of presidential proportions.

Scandals are hardly new to American politics. When lawmakers discovered that Abraham Lincoln's wife and her assistants outspent housekeeping funds, the president successfully pleaded with Congress to appropriate more money secretly rather than carrying out an investigation.[36] But the intensity and significance of White House scandals have escalated in recent decades.[37] In addition to the Lewinsky scandal discussed later in this chapter, two major and many more minor scandals have captured the attention of the nation and carried the potential for presidential impeachment.

The most serious was the Watergate scandal during the Nixon administration. In 1972, at the instigation of members of the White House staff, five men broke into Democratic Party headquarters at the Watergate condominium complex in Washington, DC, apparently to obtain information on Democratic Party campaign strategies. Nixon's chief of staff, Bob Haldeman, knew that "hush money" was paid to keep the burglars from revealing White House involvement. When tapes of Nixon's own conversations indicated that the president himself had been involved in the "cover-up," the House initiated impeachment proceedings, and the president was forced to resign.

In the Iran–Contra scandal, staffers in the Reagan White House illegally sold arms to the Iranian government and gave the profits, also illegally, to a group of guerrillas known as Contras who were fighting to overthrow a left-wing government in Nicaragua. White House aides were prosecuted and some Democrats talked of impeachment, but no direct evidence implicating the president was found.

Certain factors make the White House staff particularly prone to scandal. News organizations and opposition leaders have a vested interest in uncovering a White House scandal. Any misdoing by the White House Office immediately embarrasses the president and could lead to presidential defeat, resignation, or impeachment. To guard against this propensity, George W. Bush surrounded himself with older and more experienced advisers than Clinton had relied on. The result was a more subdued, better-controlled White House staff. Said one former Clinton staffer, "If there's a mistake, staffers take the blame and insulate Bush from it. I'm not sure I could always say that about the Clinton White House."[38]

The Power to Recommend

PRESIDENTIAL POWER: The president may recommend to Congress for "their consideration such Measures as he shall judge necessary and expedient."

CONGRESSIONAL CHECK: Only Congress may enact measures into law.

The power to recommend gives the president the power of initiation—the power to set the political agenda.[39] Presidents can shut down old policy options, create new possibilities, and change the political dialogue. Bill Clinton placed major health care reform and welfare reform on the policy agenda; George W. Bush proposed tax cuts, education initiatives, and Medicare reform.

However, this power does not go unchecked. Congress can—and often does—ignore or greatly modify a presidential recommendation. Congress rejected Clinton's health care proposals and greatly modified his proposals on welfare reform. Nor is the power to initiate limited to the president. In 1994, congressional Republicans campaigned on a "Contract with America" that set the policy agenda for the next two years.

Early Use of the Power to Recommend   Presidential use of the power to recommend was exercised with great restraint in the decades preceding the Civil War.[40] Because the president was the symbol of the nation as a whole, and because the nation was divided into free and slave states, presidents dared not talk about slavery, the most important political question of the period. This principle of silence was extended to other issues as well; in general, presidents were expected to remain publicly mute on an issue once deliberations about it had begun on Capitol Hill.[41]

Modern Use of the Power to Recommend   Use of the presidential power to recommend expanded rapidly after the end of the Civil War. The country was growing swiftly, and many social and economic problems were becoming national in scope. The nation's strongest presidents have had their greatest impact not so much by making decisions as by opening up new possibilities. For example, Theodore Roosevelt made conservation a major public concern. Franklin Roosevelt called for a New Deal that would protect Americans from economic downturns and persuaded Congress to pass dozens of important bills within 100 days of his inauguration.

Timing Presidential Initiatives   Presidents make most new proposals at the very beginning of their first term. This is the time when presidential popularity is at a peak, and both Congress and the country are eager to hear what solutions the new president is bringing to the country's problems. As one of Lyndon Johnson's top aides noted, "You've got to give it all you can that first year. . . . You've got just one year when they treat you right. . . . You can't put anything through when half of the Congress is thinking about how to beat you."[42]

Because the beginning of a presidential term is so important, the **transition** period between the previous presidency and the new one is critical. The transition period consists of the approximately 75 days between election day and January 20, Inauguration Day. Incoming presidents do not yet have the burdens of office, but they have the time and resources to set the stage for a vigorous start. If the transition is well organized, this is the best of all times for building public support.

Despite the contested outcome of the 2000 election, George W. Bush enjoyed a surprisingly successful transition. Bush was able to nominate all of the members of his cabinet by Inauguration Day and won plaudits for appointing a diverse and well-qualified cabinet. However, the new president was not spared controversy. Former Missouri Senator John Ashcroft barely won Senate confirmation as Attorney General after many Democratic senators criticized his conservative record.[43]

The transition period is typically followed by the presidential **honeymoon**—the first several months of a presidency, when reporters are kinder than usual, Congress

transition
The period after a presidential candidate has won the November election, but before the candidate assumes office as president on January 20.

honeymoon
The first several months of a presidency, when reporters are more forgiving than usual, Congress more inclined to be cooperative, and the public receptive to new approaches.

Two Very Different Transitions

Presidents Bill Clinton and George W. Bush experienced very different transition and honey-moon periods. Clinton became bogged down with issues such as gays in the military (left), and Republicans lost control of the Senate less than four months after Bush took office. Bush had little time to prepare his administration because of the Florida election dispute.

• *What advice would you give a president who wanted to have a successful honeymoon period?*

Visual Literacy

Presidential Success in Polls and Congress

more inclined to be cooperative, and the public receptive to new approaches.[44] Franklin Roosevelt's successful first 100 days set the standard by which all presidential honey-moons have been judged.

Some analysts have wondered whether presidential honeymoons have gone the way of rotary-dial telephones and wooden tennis rackets. As public expectations have risen and presidents have become ever more exposed to media scrutiny, chief executives can no longer count on a period of goodwill before facing determined opposition.[45] Certainly, the example of Bill Clinton's honeymoon seems to support this point of view—it hardly lasted the time it took him to traverse the Inauguration Day parade route from the Capitol to the White House. "By Memorial Day," one scholar has noted, "Clinton gave an address at the Vietnam War memorial that was met by a highly vocal and hostile crowd."[46]

President George W. Bush had a very successful honeymoon period, however, especially considering the difficult circumstances under which he became president. He avoided controversies, passed a major tax cut, and used his subdued approach to governing to his advantage. "Bush's low-key style and staying out of the vortex on a lot of these swirling issues seems to work very effectively for him," admitted one Democratic consultant.[47] The contrast between Clinton's difficult honeymoon and Bush's relatively smooth one calls into question the argument that modern honeymoon periods are doomed to failure. Planning, unity of purpose, and learning from previous mistakes may increase the chances of presidential success. As one member of Congress said, "Bush's team is extremely competent, and the fact is that makes a difference."[48]

The President as Chief of State

PRESIDENTIAL POWER: The President "shall receive Ambassadors and other public Ministers . . . and shall Commission all the Officers of the United States."

CONGRESSIONAL CHECK: *None.*

In bestowing one of the very few unchecked powers granted to the president, this constitutional clause seems to say little more than that presidents may welcome visitors and administer oaths of office. Yet the words endow presidents with an invaluable political resource, the capacity to act with all the dignity countries accord their heads of state. In many countries, the political leader and the head of state are institutionally separated. (See the accompanying International Comparison.) In the United States, the president plays both roles.

According to Walter Bagehot, a nineteenth-century analyst of British politics, governments have both efficient and dignified aspects.[49] The **efficient aspect** of government involves the making of policy, administration of the laws, and the settling of political disputes. This is the nuts and bolts of day-to-day policy making, the kind of activity enjoyed by the Washington insider, often derisively called a "policy wonk." It is also hard work that frequently generates conflict. But government also has a **dignified aspect** that Bagehot thought equally important to its long-term effectiveness. Governments must express the unity of the people, their high moral purposes, their hopes for the future, and their capacity to defend themselves against foreign aggressors. Ceremonial occasions provide opportunities for expression of the dignified aspect of government that helps sustain public trust and loyalty.

Early American presidents were expected to play only a limited role in the efficient aspect of government so that they could enhance the dignity of the national government

Comparing Chief Executives

efficient aspect
According to Walter Bagehot, the aspect of government that involves making policy, administering the laws, and settling disputes.

dignified aspect
According to Walter Bagehot, the aspect of government, including royalty and ceremony, that generates citizen respect and loyalty.

An Informal President
President Jimmy Carter was uncomfortable with the formal trappings of the dignified aspect of the presidency, adopting a casual style even when meeting with chiefs of state. He donned his trademark sweater for negotiations with Egyptian President Anwar Sadat.

• *Does informality detract from the president's power?*

First Lady
Traditional title of the president's wife.

and serve as a unifying symbol for a far-flung country. By remaining aloof from day-to-day legislative politics, presidents tried to retain the respect and admiration of citizens throughout the nation. As presidents have become increasingly engaged in the efficient aspect of government, they have sometimes found it more difficult to maintain their dignity.

Presidents Richard Nixon and Ronald Reagan chose to accentuate the dignified aspect of the presidency, with markedly different results. Nixon enjoyed the pomp and circumstance of office, but as the Watergate scandal developed, many Americans began to feel that the president's vaguely royal pretensions were endangering democratic practices. Seven years after Nixon left office, Reagan worked assiduously to restore grandeur to the presidency. White House social events once again became formal affairs. The unveiling of a restored Statue of Liberty was carefully designed to celebrate the country's past and future. At the same time, Reagan withdrew from day-to-day legislative politics. By emphasizing the dignity of the office, Reagan acquired the title "the Teflon president," because bad news never seemed to stick to him.

Presidents Gerald Ford, Jimmy Carter, and Bill Clinton de-emphasized the splendor of the office. Ford adopted a folksy, informal manner that provided a noted contrast with his predecessor, Nixon. Carter wore a sweater, carried his own suitcases, and remained on a first-name basis with ordinary voters. At the same time, Carter became deeply involved in the efficient aspects of government, working late into the night on policy issues and foreign policy crises. Clinton likewise became known as a "policy wonk" who was engaged with specifics, sometimes at the expense of broader themes. After advisers warned him that this style left the public without a broad sense of what the president was fighting for, Clinton began to stress larger themes in his speeches.[50]

George W. Bush faced an agonizing conflict between the efficient and dignified aspects of the presidency on September 11, 2001. After the attacks on the World Trade Center and the Pentagon, security officials whisked Bush onto Air Force One from a Florida elementary school where he had been speaking, keeping his location secret for hours. Secret Service and military aides insisted that the president be kept safe to ensure a clear chain of command. But the nation clearly needed a dignified president to reassure the public and provide a sense of unified national response to the terrorism. Accordingly, Bush returned to the White House at 7 P.M. and delivered a televised address 90 minutes later. The symbolism of the White House address was as important as its substance. "It cannot look as if the president has been run off," said former White House official William Bennett, "or it will look like we can't defend our most important institutions."[51]

The First Lady   The historical role of the president's wife, traditionally called the **First Lady,** was to reinforce the dignified aspect of the presidency. In keeping with the traditional role women have played in American society, First Ladies typically hosted social events, visited the sick, promoted children's issues, and loyally stood by their husbands in times of trouble. Yet some were able to use this dignified role to make contributions that will long be remembered. Jacqueline Kennedy invigorated Washington art and culture, and restored the White House. Lady Bird Johnson committed herself to the beautification of Washington. Nancy Reagan's "Just Say No" educational program may have done more to reduce drug use than billions of dollars spent in antidrug enforcement efforts.[52]

Not all First Ladies have been content to confine themselves to the dignified aspect of the presidency, however. Eleanor Roosevelt promoted civil rights and other social causes supported only off-handedly by her husband.[53] But Hillary Rodham Clinton gave the role of the First Lady a dramatically new definition. At the beginning of President Clinton's first term, Hillary Clinton was appointed to lead the presidential health care task force.[54] Her policy involvement won the praise of some, but it took a toll on her popularity with the general public. To enhance her public image, she began de-emphasizing her policy responsibilities and enlarged her dignified role by concentrating on children's issues. In 2000, Hillary Clinton won election to the U.S. Senate, becoming the first First Lady to embark on her own political career.

When Laura Bush became First Lady in 2001, she restored to the role its traditional emphasis on reinforcing the dignified aspect of the presidency. In contrast to the overt involvement of Hillary Clinton in policy making, Laura Bush took no public stand on controversial issues. Instead, she emphasized her former career as a public school librarian by expressing support for teachers, and calling for the recruitment of additional teachers from those in business and the military who were seeking new careers.[55]

An Aide Informs Bush of the 9/11 Attacks
President Bush insisted on returning to the White House on September 11, 2001, to fulfill his role as national leader. But security officials worried about threats to the president's person and kept his location secret for much of the day.

• *In such a crisis, how should we weigh the president's safety against the need for visible national leadership?*

The Vice President   Traditionally, the vice president's impact on policy has been so limited that the dignity of the office suffered as well. The nation's first vice president, John Adams, wrote to his wife, "My country has in its wisdom contrived for me the most insignificant office that ever the invention of man contrived. . . . I can do neither good nor evil." Harry Truman, when vice president, allowed that the job was "about as useful as a cow's fifth teat."[56]

Jokes about the vice presidency have a basis in reality. The only formal responsibility of the office is to preside over the United States Senate and cast a vote in case of a tie. Otherwise, the vice president's duties and influence depend entirely on the will of the president. As Vice President Hubert Humphrey put it, "He who giveth can taketh away and often does."[57]

Presidents have traditionally been reluctant to delegate responsibility to vice presidents, because they constitute a potential political problem. Presidents cannot fire their vice presidents, as they can other aides. If a vice president decides to criticize the president or pursue an independent policy line, the president can do little about it. When Vice President Nelson Rockefeller pushed more liberal policies than those favored by Gerald Ford, he proved an embarrassment to the president and was not chosen to be Ford's running mate in 1976. Some analysts claim the Rockefeller controversy cost Ford his reelection.

The vice presidential selection process accentuates the potential for conflict, because vice presidents often come from a wing of the party different from that of the president.[58] An aide to John Kennedy admitted that Lyndon Johnson was picked for vice president because "he was the leader of that segment of the party where Kennedy had very little strength—the South."[59] In 2004, John Kerry of Massachusetts selected a southern senator, John Edwards of North Carolina as his running mate. Not only was Edwards from a different part of the country than Kerry, but, according to one observer, he had "the very attributes that some Democrats worry that Mr. Kerry lacks," such as an ability to personally connect with voters.[60] However, others wondered whether the right balance had been struck, because neither candidate had strong foreign policy experience and both came from the liberal side of the political spectrum.

Even if presidents have powerful incentives to limit the vice presidential role, one can no longer dismiss vice presidents as political lightweights. For one thing, no person is more likely to become president of the United States than the vice president, who can succeed to the office through death, via resignation, or by winning the next election. Twelve of the 43 presidents of the United States held the office of vice president, and no fewer than four of the last eight presidents were vice presidents.

Perhaps because of the greater awareness that the vice president may one day gain the highest office, the role of the vice president has steadily become more powerful. In 2001, no one questioned the influence of Vice President Richard Cheney. He had previously served as a leading conservative in the House of Representatives, as chief of staff under Gerald Ford, and as defense secretary for Bush's father. During Bush's presidential campaign, Cheney, age 59, had won the trust of the younger, less experienced candidate (age 54). After Cheney publicly foreswore any desire to run for president himself, Bush made the vice president his top adviser.

Inherent Executive Power

> PRESIDENTIAL INHERENT EXECUTIVE POWER: "The executive power shall be vested in a President."

inherent executive power
Presidential authority inherent in the executive branch of government, though not specifically mentioned in the Constitution.

Some scholars claim that this statement adds nothing to presidential power beyond the specific powers granted to the president. But many presidents have found in this clause the basis for a claim to additional rights and privileges. As we will see in Chapter 20, presidential claims to **inherent executive power** have been invoked most frequently in making foreign policy. But presidents have asserted inherent executive power on other occasions as well. Teddy Roosevelt placed 46 million acres of public land into the National Forest system just before signing a bill denying presidents the power to place any more land in the National Forest system.[61] After leaving office, Roosevelt admitted, "My belief was that it was not only the [president's] right but his duty to do anything that the needs of the Nation demanded unless such action was forbidden by the Constitution or by its laws."[62]

executive order
A presidential directive that has the force of law, though it is not enacted by Congress.

Executive Orders   One way in which presidents use their inherent executive powers is by issuing **executive orders**—directives that carry the weight of law even though they were not enacted by Congress. The Supreme Court ruled in 1936 that executive orders are constitutional, and since then they have increased in frequency and importance.[63] Executive orders were used by Harry Truman to desegregate the armed forces, by Lyndon Johnson to institute the first affirmative action program, by Ronald Reagan to forbid homosexuality in the military, and by George W. Bush to authorize military trials for suspected al Qaeda terrorists. Executive orders may not run counter to congressional legislation, and they may be overturned by Congress. When President Clinton proposed to issue an executive order reversing the ban on gays in the military, the threat of congressional action reversing such an order forced the president to reach an awkward "Don't ask, don't tell" compromise that distracted Clinton during his presidential honeymoon period. The use of executive orders among modern presidents has increased sharply, from about five major orders a year in the 1950s, to over a dozen in recent years.[64]

Timeline

With the Stroke of a Pen: The Executive Order

Executive Privilege   The most controversial invocation of inherent executive powers has been the doctrine of **executive privilege**—the right of the president to deny
Congress information it requests on the grounds that the activities of the executive
branch must be kept confidential. George Washington was the first to invoke executive
privilege when he refused to provide Congress information about an ill-fated military
expedition on the grounds that its "disclosure . . . would injure the public."[65] Ever since,
presidents have claimed authority to withhold from Congress information on executive
decision making. The Watergate scandal brought the question before the Supreme
Court, which sanctioned the doctrine of executive privilege, saying that private communication among aides to the president was "fundamental to the operation of government and inextricably rooted in the separation of powers under the Constitution." [66]

The Supreme Court went on to say that although Congress could not simply
demand access to any and all conversations taking place among the president's advisers,
executive privilege could not be invoked to cover up criminal conduct.
Communication that might be privileged under other circumstances loses that status
when wrongdoing occurs. Nor can it be left to the executive branch to decide whether
the communication is part of a cover-up. The disputed documents must be submitted
to a court for its examination behind closed doors. When the Supreme Court examined the Watergate documents, they found sufficient evidence of criminal conduct such
that President Nixon was forced to release the documents.

The Supreme Court's Watergate ruling did not halt presidents' invocation of inherent executive power, however. In 2002, Congress's General Accounting Office sued the
Bush administration in an effort to obtain records of White House energy-task-force
meetings. The task force, headed by Vice President Cheney, had been charged with
developing the administration's energy policy the previous year, and critics suggested
that failed energy company Enron had obtained undue access to the panel. The White
House fought the suit, arguing that "the GAO intends to intrude into the heart of executive deliberations . . . which the law protects to ensure the candor in executive deliberations necessary for effective government."[67] In 2004, the Supreme Court handed
Cheney a tentative victory in the case, delaying a final resolution until after the 2004
election.

The Power to Pardon   The constitution grants the president the "Power to Grant
Reprieves and Pardons for Offenses against the United States." The president may use
this power at his discretion, with the obvious exception of cases of impeachment.
Pardons have stirred major controversies throughout American history. During and after
the Civil War, Presidents Lincoln and Johnson pardoned many confederate soldiers, to
the consternation of radicals in Congress. President Ford pardoned former President
Nixon for any crimes committed in connection with the Watergate affair, and President
Carter granted a blanket amnesty to draft resisters after the Vietnam War.

More recently, President Clinton was accused of abusing his pardon power when
he pardoned an alleged tax evader whose ex-wife had donated hundreds of thousands
of dollars to the Democratic party and to Clinton's presidential library in Arkansas.

In light of the uproar surrounding this Clinton pardon, President George W. Bush
took special pains to avoid using the pardon for any purpose that might border on the
controversial. Bush pardoned a postal worker who had stolen $10.90 out of the mail in

executive privilege
The right of members of the
executive branch to have private
communications among themselves
that need not be shared with
Congress.

1971, a Jehovah's Witness who had refused to submit to the military draft in 1957, and a man who had altered the odometer of a motor vehicle.[68]

The Impeachment Power

> CONGRESSIONAL IMPEACHMENT POWER: Presidents may be impeached by a majority of the House of Representatives for "high crimes and misdemeanors." The president is removed from office if the Senate convicts by a two-thirds vote.

Nothing makes more clear the subordination of presidents to Congress than the fact that the House of Representatives can impeach and the Senate can convict and remove presidents from office. Though seldom used, the constitutional power of **impeachment** is no dead letter. Andrew Johnson was impeached in 1868, although the Senate, by one vote, failed to convict him.[69] Richard Nixon resigned in the face of almost certain impeachment in 1974. And President Clinton's affair with Monica Lewinsky, a White House intern, led to the first impeachment and trial of a president in over a century.

In 1994 a three-judge panel appointed Kenneth Starr as **independent counsel** with the authority to investigate charges related to the questionable Whitewater land deal in which Clinton had been involved while governor of Arkansas. Separately, an Arkansas public employee, Paula Jones, sued Clinton for sexual harassment. In 1998 the scandals merged. Starr concluded that Clinton had obstructed justice and committed perjury when, in the Jones case, he denied under oath having sexual relations with Lewinsky.

The president argued that his carefully worded denial did not constitute perjury, and the electorate seemed to take his side: Republicans lost ground in the 1998 congressional elections. But on December 19, 1998, the House voted (along mostly partisan lines) to impeach the president, making him only the second U.S. chief executive to be threatened with removal from office by Congress.

In early 1999 the Senate held its trial of the president, with Chief Justice William Rehnquist presiding. In considering their votes, most Senators believed that if they were to overturn a national election by removing Clinton from office, they needed a more serious cause. After all, polls showed that two-thirds of the public still thought the president should stay.[70] On February 12, the Senate voted for acquittal.

The Clinton scandals have altered the American presidency in important respects. First, presidents are now at risk of being sued by their political opponents. Addressing the Jones case, the Supreme Court ruled that presidents can be sued for alleged wrongful conduct that is not part of their presidential duties. In its opinion, the Supreme Court said that such lawsuits were unlikely to interfere with presidential responsibilities.

Second, it has become clear that the advice presidents receive from their government attorneys is not necessarily confidential. The president's attorney claimed the right to keep conversations about Lewinsky confidential. But the courts said that conversations between government attorneys and presidents were not protected unless they involved official duties. In the future, presidents can be expected to hire private legal advisers.

Finally, some scholars have argued that the partisan nature of Clinton's impeachment is a sign that the practice is more likely to be used in the future as a political weapon. Others disagree, however, noting that the circumstances of the scandal were unique. "If Watergate was a 'long national nightmare,'" suggests one presidential scholar, the Lewinsky scandal "seems more like a drug-induced hallucination."[71]

impeachment
Recommendation by a majority of the House of Representatives that a president, another official in the executive branch, or judge of the federal courts be removed from office; removal depends on a two-thirds vote of the Senate.

independent counsel
(Originally called **special prosecutor**) Legal officer appointed by a court to investigate allegations of criminal activity on the part of high-ranking members of the executive branch. Law expired in 1999.

In the last days of his presidency, Clinton admitted in a signed statement that he had given false information in the Lewinsky matter, apparently as part of an agreement that he would not be prosecuted after his departure from the presidency. Many presidential scholars have applauded the decisions not to prosecute either Presidents Nixon or President Clinton after they left office. To do otherwise might set precedents that in the long run could undermine the country's political stability.

Presidential Expectations and Presidential Performance

Presidents are expected to be strong, yet presidential powers are limited. As a result, presidents seldom satisfy the hopes and aspirations of the voting public. To sustain their reputation and effectiveness, presidents can sometimes act with Machiavellian cleverness. When Abraham Lincoln took office, seven Southern states had already seceded from the Union, and were threatening a Union outpost at South Carolina's Fort Sumter. Moving while Congress was out of session, Lincoln announced that he would order the U.S. Navy to send new supplies to the fort. After Confederates fired on Sumter as supply ships neared, Lincoln blamed the South for starting the war and received overwhelming support in the North. By forcing the South's hand, Lincoln created a situation that advantaged the Union cause.[72]

Presidents in the past were frequently able to cover ruthless actions with a cloak of dignity that the role of chief of state allowed them to wear. But as the life of the president becomes more open to the media, it gets harder to keep the cloak of dignity firmly in place. As Bill Clinton put it, "It is difficult for people to function in an environment in which they feel that their character, their values, and their motives are always suspect, and where the presumption here is against them."[73]

Presidential Reputations

To meet public expectations despite their limited power, presidents need to protect their professional reputation among members of Congress and other **beltway insiders,** the politically influential people who live inside the highway that surrounds Washington, DC.[74] Presidential reputations inside Washington are shaped by the quality of the people who serve the presidents and the frequency with which presidents win political contests. They also depend on the president's ability to let go of issues that cannot be won. As Lincoln put it, "When you have got an elephant by the hind legs and he is trying to run away, it is best to let him run." [75]

beltway insider
Person living in the Washington metropolitan area who is engaged in, or well informed about, national politics and government.

Presidential Popularity

In addition to guarding their professional reputation, presidents need to maintain their popularity with the general public. As Lincoln also shrewdly observed, "With public sentiment, nothing can fail; without it, nothing can succeed."[76] **Presidential popularity** is measured by asking the adult population how well they think the president is doing his job. Pollsters now ask the same question almost every week, so it provides a decent barometer of the public's current assessment of the president's performance.

All presidents experience fluctuations in their popularity over the course of their terms. But as a general rule, presidential popularity tends to decline over time as public

presidential popularity
Evaluation of president by voters, usually as measured by a survey question asking the adult population how well they think the president is doing the job.

expectations go unfulfilled.[77] A study of the first term of eight recent presidents indicates that apart from any specific economic or foreign policy events, their popularity fell by nearly 8 points in their first year in office and by 15 points by the middle of their third year. Their popularity recovered in their fourth year, when a presidential campaign was under way, probably because at that time, presidents make special efforts to communicate positive news about their administrations. Presidents regained popularity when reelected, but once again it trailed off.[78]

George W. Bush's approval ratings bucked the typical pattern, perhaps because of the unique circumstances of the 9-11 terrorist attacks and the Iraq War. They surged from about 52 percent to above 80 percent in the aftermath of the attacks and remained higher than average until early 2004, when negative news from Iraq prompted a decline.

Presidential popularity and professional reputation were at one time regarded as two quite separate phenomena. Unpopular presidents could still have the respect of beltway insiders if they husbanded their political resources carefully. But the distinction between popularity and reputation has become clouded.[79] Presidents are the focus of seemingly inexhaustible but utterly exhausting television, radio, and newspaper coverage. As soon as they have addressed one problem, they are urged to solve the next. As one commentator put it, "Getting the public's attention, particularly on a subject that the polls show is already gnawing at people, is no trick for a President. . . . The trick is holding that attention."[80]

The one kind of attention that presidents are likely to hold is the kind they don't want. When George H. W. Bush became nauseated at a state dinner in Tokyo, the embarrassing consequences were graphically reported in news headlines. President Clinton voiced exasperation over a "totally bogus story" that claimed he held up flights on a runway while getting a $200 haircut.[81] And George W. Bush endured criticism when his teenaged daughter Jenna was fined $500 for underage drinking.[82]

When these kinds of incidents cause a president's popularity to slip, weekly polling results transmit this information to beltway insiders. If the president's reputation is slipping in Washington, the news media just as quickly communicate insider opinions to the wider public. As a result, the president now has to work both the inside and the outside of the beltway at the same time.[83]

Great Presidents

Rate the Presidents

All presidents are challenged by problems and opponents both at home and abroad, and all find it difficult to preserve both professional reputation and public popularity throughout their terms. Yet some presidents are remembered as "great presidents," because they achieve many of the objectives they set for themselves; others are seemingly unable to tackle the problems they face. Why do some succeed and others fail?

In a study of presidential character, James Barber argued that certain personality traits make for successful presidents (see Table 13.2).[84] He said that effective presidents both like their job and readily adapt their policies to changing circumstances. He called these presidents "active-positives." For Barber, Franklin Roosevelt was the ideal active-positive president. He loved his job as president, and he brought great energy to it. He changed his mind frequently, but always with an eye to solving governmental problems. Clinton also seemed to have an active-positive approach to the job.

Barber argued that most other modern presidents lacked one or the other of these two character traits. President Eisenhower brought a positive attitude, but Barber

---

TABLE 13.2

PRESIDENTIAL CHARACTER

• *Does presidential effectiveness depend on presidential attitudes and energy?*

	PRESIDENT HAS **HIGH** ENERGY LEVEL.	PRESIDENT HAS **LOW** ENERGY LEVEL.
PRESIDENT ENJOYS THE JOB.	**Active-Positive** Examples Thomas Jefferson Franklin Roosevelt	**Passive-Positive** Examples James Madison Dwight Eisenhower
PRESIDENT IS DISCOURAGED BY THE JOB.	**Active-Negative** Examples John Adams Lyndon Johnson	**Passive-Negative** Examples George Washington Calvin Coolidge

---

SOURCE: Adapted from James Barber, *The Presidential Character: Predicting Performance in the White House,* 4th ed. (Englewood Cliffs, NJ: Prentice-Hall, 1992).

thought he was too passive. Instead of taking the initiative, he waited for others to propose solutions to problems. Barber claimed that both Lyndon Johnson and Richard Nixon brought an active-negative attitude to the job. Although both were energetic, neither could adapt to new circumstances. As a result, each pursued a policy position long after a more adaptive president would have changed course. Johnson led the country ever more deeply into the Vietnam War; Nixon tried to "cover up" Watergate misdeeds when he might have been better advised to let the problem come immediately to the surface.

Critics of Barber's schema say he placed too much emphasis on presidential activity.[85] Bill Clinton was an active policy wonk, but he was not always successful in achieving his goals. Eisenhower appeared to be passive, but presidential analyst Fred Greenstein shows that he governed with a "hidden hand."[86] Although Ike let others grab the headlines, he steered the ship from behind the scenes, staying out of controversy and preserving his popularity. Reagan was hardly an activist,[87] yet his use of the power of the dignified presidency, together with his focus on fundamental goals, made him a powerful political force.

Presidential success may depend less on personality than on the circumstances under which the newly elected come into office.[88] Presidential scholar Stephen Skowronek says that most are so hemmed in by the checks placed upon them that they simply cannot accomplish the job the public expects. As a result, presidents become "great" only when political circumstances allow them to repudiate the past and move in a sharply different direction. By rejecting the old way of doing things, they are able to discard political baggage that would limit presidential action.

A President's Resignation
The epitome of the active-negative president, grimly determined to do his duty until the end, Richard Nixon doggedly repeats his "V for victory" sign upon leaving office on August 9, 1974.

• *Were Nixon's difficulties due to his personality?*

Franklin Roosevelt is once again the archetypal effective president. Running for office in 1932 in the midst of the Great Depression, he declared, "these unhappy times call for . . . plans . . . that build from the bottom up and not from the top down, that put their faith once more in the forgotten man." After an election that realigned the American party system (see Chapter 8), Roosevelt pushed through a huge volume of important legislation in his first 100 days in office.

Roosevelt was not the first effective president who profited by breaking with the past (see Table 13.3). Thomas Jefferson discarded the program of John Adams and the Federalist Party. Republican Abraham Lincoln attacked slavery. Ronald Reagan halted the growth in government that had occurred under his predecessors, saying, "Government is not the solution to our problem. Government *is* the problem."[89] Whether a president is able to repudiate the past successfully is somewhat beyond the president's control, however. Congress and the public must also agree that a new direction is needed.

Skowronek's model is not perfect. Many people think Theodore Roosevelt was one of the country's most successful presidents, but he did not become president through a pivotal election or at a time of crisis. And some people think other presidents—Eisenhower (for managing the Cold War) and Johnson (for initiating the Great Society)—deserve inclusion at the top of the list of presidents. But Skowronek does show that presidents are often most effective when they exercise their power to initiate new approaches. It is often left to other, less effective presidents to try to follow this lead.

If Skowronek's theory is correct, the administration of George W. Bush faces significant obstacles to success. Bush was elected by a razor-thin margin to succeed a popular president from the opposing party. Moreover, many of Bush's most significant policy proposals, such as major tax cuts, are not new ideas, but are based on the agenda of a previous president: Ronald Reagan. Skowronek suggests that only one president has been successful under such circumstances: William McKinley. It is perhaps no surprise then, that Bush political adviser Karl Rove frequently cited McKinley as a role model for the Bush administration.[90]

TABLE 13.3

**DO FAILED POLICIES AND PRESIDENTS LEAD TO THE ELECTION
OF PRESIDENTS WHO SUCCEED BY REPUDIATING THE PAST?**

Year	Ineffective President	Leads to . . .	Very Successful President
1789	Articles of Confederation	→	George Washington
1800	John Adams	→	Thomas Jefferson
1828	John Q. Adams	→	Andrew Jackson
1860	James Buchanan	→	Abraham Lincoln
1932	Herbert Hoover	→	Franklin Roosevelt
1980	Jimmy Carter	→	Ronald Reagan

SOURCE: Based on Stephen Skowronek, *The Politics Presidents Make* (Cambridge, MA: Harvard University Press, 1993).

Chapter Summary

Presidents must meet the high expectations of their national and partisan constituencies, despite the fact that Congress checks many of their most important powers.

- Presidents can initiate legislation, but Congress often rejects or substantially modifies their proposals.
- Presidents can appoint executive and judicial officers, but the Senate must approve them.
- Presidents may invoke inherent executive power, including the right of executive privilege, but Congress can impeach them.
- Although the president can veto congressional bills, Congress may override the veto by a two-thirds vote.
- Presidential leadership depends most heavily on the power of the chief executive to initiate and persuade—capacities that derive as much from the dignity of the office as from any specific clauses in the Constitution.

To achieve their goals, presidents must preserve their professional reputation and their political popularity. Because their popularity tends to slip over time, it is at the beginning of their presidency—during the transition and honeymoon periods—that they have the most capacity to initiate change. Great presidents emerge not so much because they have the right personal qualities as because they come to office when the country thinks it is time for a change.

Key Terms

administration, p. 345

beltway insider, p. 357

bully pulpit, p. 343

cabinet, p. 345

chief of staff, p. 346

commander in chief, p. 338

dignified aspect, p. 351

divided government, p. 339

efficient aspect, p. 351

Executive Office of the President (EOP), p. 346

executive order, p. 354

executive privilege, p. 355

First Lady, p. 352

honeymoon, p. 349

impeachment, p. 356

independent counsel (originally called special prosecutor), p. 356

inherent executive power, p. 354

line item veto, p. 344

override, p. 344

pocket veto, p. 344

presidential popularity, p. 357

secretary, p. 345

State of the Union address, p. 341

transition, p. 349

veto power, p. 344

White House Office, p. 346

Suggested Readings

Of General Interest

Barber, James. *The Presidential Character: Predicting Performance in the White House.* 4th ed. Englewood Cliffs, NJ: Prentice-Hall, 1992. Argues that presidential character affects presidential success.

Jones, Charles. *The Presidency in a Separated System.* Washington, DC: The Brookings Institution, 1994. Examines the role of the president under divided government.

Kernell, Samuel. *Going Public: New Strategies of Presidential Leadership,* 3rd ed. Washington, DC: CQ Press, 1997. Describes the increasing tendency of presidents to use popular appeals to influence legislative processes.

Nelson, Michael, ed. *The Presidency and the Political System,* 7th ed. Washington, DC: CQ Press, 2002. Important contemporary essays on the presidency.

Neustadt, Richard E. *Presidential Power and the Modern Presidents.* New York: Free Press, 1990. Modern classic on the limits to presidential power.

Skowronek, Stephen. *The Politics Presidents Make: Leadership from John Adams to George Bush.* Cambridge, MA: Harvard University Press, 1993. Provocative analysis of the historical development of the presidency.

Focused Studies

Korn, Jessica. *The Power of Separation: American Constitutionalism and the Myth of the Legislative Veto.* Princeton, NJ: Princeton University Press, 1996. Identifies the many ways in which power is shared between Congress and the executive.

Mayer, Kenneth. *With the Stroke of a Pen: Executive Orders and Presidential Power.* Princeton, NJ: Princeton University Press, 2001. Study of how presidents use executive orders to make policy.

Moe, Terry. "The Politicized Presidency." In *The New Direction in American Politics,* ed. John Chubb and Paul E. Peterson Washington, DC: The Brookings Institution, 1985. Insightful essay on the evolution of the White House staff.

Rudalevige, Andrew. *Managing the President's Program: Presidential Leadership and Legislative Policy Formulation.* Princeton, NJ: Princeton University Press, 2002. Examines how presidents design policy initiatives.

Sundquist, James L. *The Decline and Resurgence of Congress.* Washington, DC: The Brookings Institution, 1981. Authoritative description of the growth in presidential powers and responsibilities, as well as congressional response to that trend.

Tulis, Jeffrey. *The Rhetorical Presidency.* Princeton, NJ: Princeton University Press, 1987. Contrasts modern presidential rhetoric with that of early presidents. Argues against a rhetorical presidency.

On the Web

www.whitehouse.gov
The official Web site of the White House offers current and historical information about U.S. presidents, as well as press releases and other policy statements.

www.thepresidency.org
Many political scientists study the factors that contribute to presidential success and failure. The Center for the Study of the Presidency publishes *Presidential Studies Quarterly* and showcases academic information and links.

www.archives.gov
Presidential libraries have been created for every president since Franklin Roosevelt. The National Archives and Records Administration (NARA) provides information about and links to these presidential libraries. NARA also provides a guide to presidential documents available online. These include executive orders, proclamations, speeches, and other materials.

www.vicepresidents.com
When Daniel Webster was offered the vice presidency, he famously demurred, saying "I do not propose to be buried until I am really dead." This Web site provides an online clearinghouse for information about this much-maligned post and its occupants.

CHAPTER 14

★ ★ ★ ★ ★ ★ ★ ★ ★ ★ ★ ★ ★ ★ ★ ★

The Bureaucracy

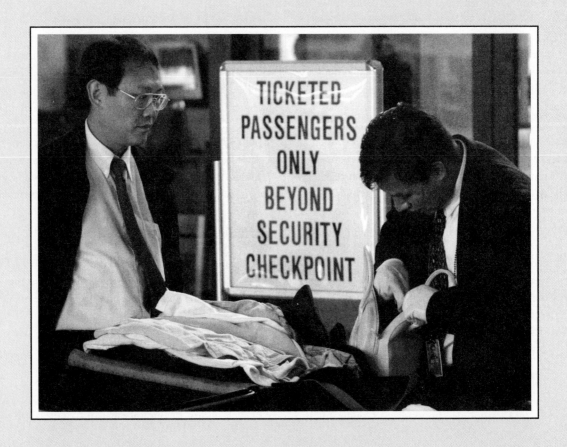

Organizing for Homeland Security

The unprecedented terrorist attacks of September 11, 2001, provoked feelings of shock, anger, and vulnerability that many Americans had never experienced before. But in the aftermath of the attacks, some channeled their reaction into a much more familiar argument: U.S. government agencies had failed to do their jobs well.

Even those loyal to these agencies agreed that they had botched the key task of protecting Americans from attacks from abroad. One former Federal Bureau of Investigation (FBI) official called the incident "the greatest counter-terrorism screw-up in U.S. history." The National Security Agency (NSA), the Central Intelligence Agency (CIA), and the FBI "are all tasked with getting this kind of information," he argued. "Billions and billions of dollars are spent on this. And if we can't get it, there's something very very wrong."[1]

Nine days after the attacks, George W. Bush moved to reform the way these agencies conducted the business of domestic security. In doing so, the president moved to implement the recommendations of a blue-ribbon commission that in February 2001 had called for greater coordination and planning among dozens of government organizations. The Bush plan was different from that of the commission in one respect, however: Whereas the panel had called for "a significant organizational redesign"—namely, a new cabinet-level agency charged with securing the U.S. from terrorism[2]—Bush was initially much more modest. He created a new White House Office of Homeland Security, headed by former Pennsylvania governor Tom Ridge.

Ridge, with his small staff of 100 operating from a corner of the executive mansion, was expected to coordinate the activities of agencies as diverse as the FBI in the Justice Department, the U.S. Customs Service in the Treasury Department, the Federal Aviation Administration (FAA) in the Transportation Department, and the Federal Emergency Management Agency (FEMA), an independent entity. Each of these agencies—and dozens of others that the Homeland Security office was supposed to keep track of—had separate budgets, separate directors, and separate organizational cultures. One national security expert likened Ridge's task to "getting a 40-mule team to be pulling in the right direction."[3] In his public appearances, Ridge admitted that the job was as difficult as "building the transcontinental railroad, fighting World War II, or putting a man on the moon"[4]

In the ensuing weeks, Ridge often appeared to be overshadowed by other administration officials. When authorities discovered that the deadly disease anthrax had been mailed to members of Congress and media outlets, Secretary of Health and Human Services Tommy Thompson took center stage. When a would-be terrorist was arrested after attempting to set off a bomb hidden in his shoes on a trans-Atlantic flight, FBI officials in Boston fielded media inquiries. And Transportation Secretary Norman Mineta was charged with ensuring that aviation screening met tough new federal standards. Ridge's most visible accomplishment was his invention of a color-coded national terrorism alert system. But even under this system it was the Attorney General—not Ridge—who would decide when to raise or lower the nation's state of alert.

After eight and one-half months of trying to manage the domestic security apparatus from the White House, and as members of Congress and the public expressed alarm at new revelations about pre-9/11 intelligence failures, the president admitted he needed to do more. In June 2002, Bush asked Congress to create a cabinet-level Department of Homeland Security that would have direct authority over nearly 170,000 government workers from eight departments. The Border Patrol, the Coast Guard, the Transportation Security Administration, and even the Secret Service moved to the new organization as part of the largest federal government shakeup in over 50 years (see Voices of the Permanent Campaign, p. 427). In a televised address to explain his reversal of course on this issue, Bush admitted that a more effective, unified structure was needed: "Right now, as many as a hundred different government agencies have some responsibilities for homeland security, and no one has final accountability."[5]

MAKING THE CONNECTION

Thomas Ridge was not the first presidential appointee to find it difficult to coordinate the departments and agencies of the federal government. Agency officials feel threatened by changes in their job descriptions, and Congress is also wary of such efforts. As one member of Congress observed, "We all know that the toughest things in Washington are the turf wars .... No [congressional] committee likes their authority cut back."[6]

The FBI, CIA, FAA, and FEMA are all part of the federal bureaucracy. **Bureaucracies** are hierarchical organizations of officials with responsibility for specific tasks. They are essential to government action but are often criticized as being inefficient or too large. In this chapter, we discuss how bureaucracies have developed and describe how they fit into modern American politics. In particular, we answer these questions:

- What role does the bureaucracy play in government, and what problems impede its performance?

- How has today's bureaucracy been shaped by the history of our nation, and what changes have been made to reform the bureaucracy?

- What influence do the president and Congress have on the bureaucracy?

- How is the bureaucracy organized, and how do elections affect its operation?

* * * * * * * * * * * * * * * * *

The Role of the Bureaucracy

Bureaucracies are essential to governmental action. Laws become effective only when a government agency enforces them. Without some kind of organization, agencies cannot build roads, operate schools, put out fires, fight wars, distribute social security checks, or do the thousands of other things Americans expect from their government.

As the range of governmental responsibilities has grown, the number of bureaucrats in the United States has also increased. The most growth has occurred at state and local levels, where the vast majority of civilian government workers are employed, including school teachers, police officers, and sanitation workers (see Figure 14.1). In addition, many private contractors perform tasks paid for by government agencies. Although the number of employees who work directly for the federal government is smaller, we shall focus most of our attention on federal bureaucracies, because their policies and regulations are far-reaching and their impact is felt throughout the country.

The **agency,** also known as the *office* or *bureau,* is the basic organizational unit of the federal government. It is the entity specifically assigned by Congress to carry out a task. There are hundreds of agencies within the federal government, but most are grouped under one of 14 **departments**—collections of federal agencies that report to a secretary who serves in the president's cabinet. Some 63 independent agencies are free-standing entities that report either to the president or to a supervisory board.[7] The Central Intelligence Agency and the Environmental Protection Agency are examples of independent agencies. Finally, there are 27 **government corporations**—independent organizations created by Congress to fulfill functions related to business.[8] Examples of government corporations include the Federal Deposit Insurance Corporation, which insures bank deposits, and the National Railroad Passenger Corporation, which runs Amtrak. Figure 14.2 illustrates how the federal bureaucracy is organized.

Bureaucracies can have great influence over policy because of their **administrative discretion,** the power to interpret their legislative mandates. Congress can enact general rules, but it cannot anticipate every circumstance, nor can it apply

bureaucracy
Hierarchical organization designed to perform a particular set of tasks.

agency
Basic organizational unit of federal government. Also known as *office* or *bureau.*

department
Organizational unit into which many agencies of the federal government are grouped.

government corporation
Independent organization created by Congress to fulfill functions related to business.

administrative discretion
Power to interpret a legislative mandate.

FIGURE 14.1

Government Employment, 1946–2001

The number of state and local employees has increased, but the number of federal employees has remained about the same.

• *Why do you think employment at the federal level has remained stable, despite budget increases and new government programs?*

Note: Federal government employment figures include civilians only. Military employment figures include only active-duty personnel.

SOURCES: U.S. Bureau of the Census, *Historical Statistics of the United States: Colonial Times to 1970* (Washington, DC: GPO, 1975), pp. 1100, 1141; *Statistical Abstract of the United States, 1999*, Tables 534 and 578; *Statistical Abstract of the United States, 2002*, Tables 446, 491; U.S. Office of Personnel Management, *Pay Structure of the Federal Civil Service, 2001*, Table 1; and U.S. Postal Service, *Annual Report of the Postmaster General, 2000*, p. 68.

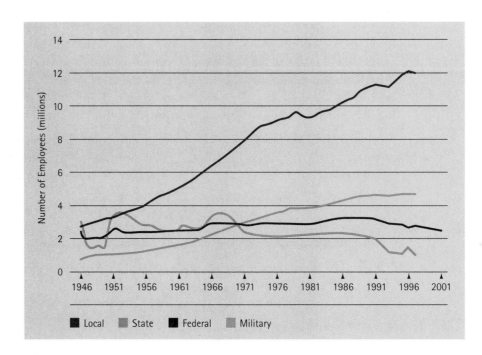

these rules to every individual case. Congress may decide to provide benefits to the disabled, but it is up to a bureaucrat (in this case, an official within the Social Security Administration) to decide whether a particular disability precludes employment.[9] Congress may decide to give loans to college students from families of moderate income, but it is up to a bureaucrat (in this case, an officer within the Department of Education) to determine what family resources count as income.

FIGURE 14.2

The Federal Bureaucracy Consists of Departments, Independent Agencies, and Government Corporations

SOURCES: *Statistical Abstract of the United States, 2000*, Table 537 (budget figures), Table 556 (employment figures); *United States Government Manual 2001–2002* (Washington, DC: GPO, 2001), structure of Department of Agriculture and FDIC; www.fdic.gov, accessed January 3, 2002 (budget data for FDIC); and www.ftc.gov, accessed June 26, 2002 (budget data for FTC).

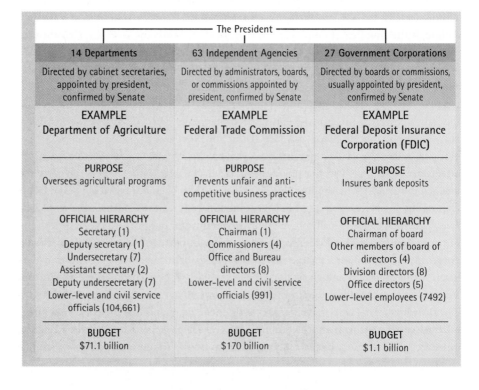

The Bureaucracy Problem

The ideal bureaucracy would be organized so that it could achieve its assigned task most efficiently. Selection of people hired to work in the bureaucracy would be based on their ability to do the job. Each would report to his or her superior via a clear chain of command, and ultimate authority would be exercised by the head of the bureau. Agency staff would supply each worker with the materials necessary to get the job done. The ideal is best exemplified by soldiers on parade, marching together in synchronized lockstep formation. When all works perfectly, bureaucracies exhibit unity, focus, and power.[10]

Although the ideal bureaucracy has tremendous potential, existing bureaucracies face competing demands that inhibit perfection by pulling bureaucrats in different directions at the same time. These competing demands lead to the difficulties that many critics recognize as characteristic of bureaucratic organizations. In many cases, bureaucracies must handle nearly impossible tasks. Meanwhile, their performance is difficult to measure, they have an awkward tendency to expand, they are slow to change, and they are often mired in red tape. Taken together, these factors create what is known as the bureaucracy problem.[11]

Impossibility of Tasks

Most governmental tasks are difficult to accomplish. If they were easy, someone other than the government would have undertaken the job! Not only can agency objectives be complicated, but goals themselves often remain vague and indefinite.[12] Schools are expected to teach students—but there is no end to what students might learn. Transportation agencies are expected to achieve smoothly flowing traffic—but to avoid all bottlenecks in most large cities, one would have to pave almost everything. The Environmental Protection Agency is charged with protecting the environment from pollutants—but nearly all human activity increases pollution in some way. Because their responsibilities are so complicated and the limits of their objectives are seldom well defined, bureaucracies are often blamed for problems even if they do the best possible job.

Difficulty Measuring Performance

It is often difficult to measure the performance of government bureaucracies.[13] If the streets and parks are strewn with garbage and litter, one is tempted to criticize the government. Yet city garbage collectors may be doing a good job but having trouble keeping up with the behavior of inconsiderate citizens. In 2003, many Californians criticized the U.S. Forest Service because its firefighters failed to stem the initial spread of the devastating Cedar Fire that destroyed over 2000 homes and caused 14 deaths. Forest Service officials argued that their response had been timely, however, and that they had done the best they could under the worst of possible circumstances.[14] Because it is hard to measure the performance of most government bureaucracies, it is difficult for supervisors, elected officials, and the public to tell whether work is being performed carefully and promptly. If officials are unsure how to gauge a bureaucracy's performance, they will have trouble trying to improve it. As a result, bureaucracies often have a reputation for inefficiency.

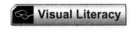

The Changing Face of
the Federal Bureaucracy

Expansionary Tendencies

Once they are created to address a problem, bureaucracies generally try to expand so they can address it better. Government agencies almost always feel they need more money, more personnel, and more time to perform their tasks effectively.[15] Bureaucrats experience policy problems up close, so they often sincerely believe that they need more resources to address these problems. But because they focus on specific issues, they can lose sight of the big picture. Congress cannot grant unlimited funds to every bureaucracy that wants them; trade-offs and choices have to be made.

There is nothing new about this debate between bureaucrats and Congress. "You may blame the War Department for a great many things," General Douglas MacArthur said back in 1935, "but you cannot blame us for not asking for money. That is one fault to which we plead not guilty."[16]

Slow to Change

Any large governmental organization has standard procedures through which it makes its decisions. And most standard procedures are essential if large numbers of people are to coordinate their work toward some common end. If procedures were not standardized, those working within the bureaucracy would be so confused that they would soon be unable to do anything.

Standard procedures nonetheless make bureaucracies sluggish and slow to adjust to new circumstances.[17] Schools still provide long summer holidays that were originally allowed so that children could help harvest crops on family farms. Despite massive increases in the use of energy in the United States, the Federal Energy Regulatory Commission has changed its approach to regulation of the electricity grid very little over the course of four decades.[18] After a catastrophic blackout in the northeastern part of the country in August 2003, former Energy Secretary Bill Richardson said, "We're a superpower with a third-world grid."[19] As one humorist observed, "Bureaucracy defends the status quo long past the time when the quo has lost its status."[20]

When events take unpredictable and catastrophic turns, existing guidelines can even lead to disaster. After New York's World Trade Center collapsed in 2001, killing hundreds of fire and emergency workers, some experts questioned standard procedures that called for fighting skyscraper fires from the inside. "We're going to rewrite the book as far as how we're going to handle incidents like that," said one firefighting authority.[21]

Red Tape

Everyone complains about governmental red tape, but as one analyst has observed, "One person's red tape may be another's treasured procedural safeguard."[22] People often complain, for example, that it takes forever to get a bridge repaired. But bridge repair can be politically complicated. The design of the replacement bridge must be acceptable to neighbors. If the bridge is regarded as an historical landmark—and a surprising number of bridges are so designated—the approval of an historical commission must be obtained. After the design is approved, the agency, when letting contracts, must advertise the job and allow time for the submission of bids. To avoid accusations of political favoritism, the choice of contractors must be made according to published criteria. And

Standard Operating Procedures
One of the drawbacks of standard procedures is that they may not work well in unprecedented circumstances, such as the 2001 terrorist attacks.
• *Will reorganization of the executive branch successfully adapt standard procedures to new terrorist threats?*

the repairs themselves must be subject to careful inspection to make sure the bridge does not collapse upon completion. Once again, a common bureaucratic problem is caused not by malice or ignorance but by important considerations of politics and safety.

At times, exceptions can be made. After the terrorist attacks of 2001, the Internal Revenue Service made a dramatic effort to speed up its approval of tax-exempt status for new disaster-relief charities. During this period, reviews of applications that normally would have taken 8 to 12 weeks were sometimes finished within 3 days.[23] Similarly, regulatory procedures were put to one side so that the Pentagon could be rebuilt as quickly as possible following the 9/11 tragedy. Progress was due not only to the more flexible regulatory climate but also to worker commitment. According to one reporter, "there's pride in the punishing schedule, and [in] the rapid progress."[24] But red tape was eliminated in these cases only because the public insisted that time was of the essence.

American Bureaucracies: Particularly Political

The bureaucracy problem exists in all countries, but American bureaucracies have special problems that are rooted in the country's unusual political history. As we discuss in this section, U.S. bureaucracies had a difficult beginning, were built with patronage, and were only slowly modernized by a "bottom-up" civil-service reform. Government workers today fall into two categories: career civil servants who are hired according to educational qualifications and who have job security, and political appointees at the highest level who can be dismissed at any time. Though the policy of reserving the top spots for political appointees makes the government more responsive to elections, it makes civil service jobs less attractive to bright young people.

Difficult Beginnings

Evolution of the Federal
Bureaucracy

American bureaucrats lack the noble heritage of their counterparts in Europe and Japan, where government departments evolved out of the household of the king, queen, or emperor. In the late 1600s, King Louis XIV constructed a great French administration within the Palace of Versailles. The extraordinarily efficient German administration, which became a model for the world, descended from the household of the King of Prussia. Japan's powerful bureaucracy owes its prestige to a time-honored relationship with the emperor. The lineage of federal bureaucrats in the United States is less distinguished. As one scholar has pointed out, "In England, France and Germany, . . . it is considered an honor simply to serve the state. . . . In the United States civil servants, instead of being regarded with honor, are often considered tax eaters, drones, grafters, and bureaucrats."[25]

The American Revolution was fought against King George's bureaucrats, who had been appointed to oversee the governments of the colonies. The resulting suspicion of appointed officials carried over to the time that the Constitution was written, when the framers could not even agree on a site for the people who were to run the new national government. Finally, as part of a compromise, they agreed to locate the District of Columbia, the new home of the federal government, on the Maryland–Virginia border near the small city of Georgetown.

Thomas Jefferson believed that the location would attract virtuous Virginians to federal jobs, leading to "a favourable bias in the Executive officers."[26] In fact, the land Congress had chosen was swampy and miserable. Visitors complained that it was thick with "contaminated vapour" and that its mud-spattered, ramshackle buildings gave it "the appearance of a considerable town, which had been destroyed by some unusual calamity."[27] If the government were to attract quality workers, its location would not be its main selling point.

Mountains of Patronage

patronage
Jobs, contracts, or favors given to
political friends and allies.

spoils system
A system of government
employment in which workers are
hired on the basis of party loyalty.

Not only did the disreputable living conditions in the District of Columbia diminish the prestige of the federal government, but bureaucrats were dealt a second blow after the election of 1828, when President Andrew Jackson handed out political **patronage**—government jobs, contracts, and other favors—to his supporters. Jackson reasoned that this practice made government more democratic, since it ensured that those who won elections were fully in control of the government. Furthermore, the quality of work would not suffer from political appointees, said Jackson, since "[t]he duties of all public officers are . . . so plain and simple that men of intelligence may readily qualify themselves for their performance."[28] The practice of hiring workers on the basis of party loyalty became known as the **spoils system** when New York Senator William Marcy attacked President Jackson for seeing "nothing wrong in the rule that to the victor belong the spoils."[29]

Politicians in both political parties quickly discovered that the spoils system suited their needs.[30] As barriers to participation fell in the mid-1800s, more and more Americans went to the polls to cast ballots (see Chapter 6). Because local, state, and national elections occurred frequently, mobilizing this growing electorate became a complicated and time-consuming task. Party politicians could use promises of government posts to enlist campaign workers to take on such thankless jobs as passing out pamphlets, organizing rallies, and transporting voters to the polls. The New York machine-politician George Washington Plunkitt explained the logic of patronage this way: "You can't keep an organization together without patronage. Men ain't in politics for nothin'. They want to get somethin' out of it."[31]

Patronage also made it easier for parties to raise large amounts of cash to fund their frequent election campaigns. Every Pennsylvania state employee during this period received the following letter from the Republican State Committee: "Two percent of your salary is—. Please remit promptly. At the close of the campaign we shall place a list of those who have not paid in the hands of the head of the department you are in."[32] These practices were not conducted in secret; politicians felt they were a natural and legitimate part of politics.

Plunkitt defended patronage, or graft, by making the fine distinction between its dishonest and honest varieties. Dishonest graft wasted the taxpayers' money or engaged in "blackmailin' gamblers, saloonkeepers, [and] disorderly people."[33] Honest graft simply paid a friend to build a bridge or roadway that needed to be constructed anyway. Or, as the patronage-prone Chicago Mayor Richard J. Daley once said when asked to explain why he had given the city's insurance business to one of his sons, "If a man can't put his arms around his sons, then what kind of a world are we living in? . . . I make no apologies to anyone. There are many men in this room whose fathers helped them, and they went on to become fine public officials."[34] Mayor Daley's sons did well for themselves. Richard M. Daley was elected to a fourth term as Chicago mayor in 1999, and William Daley served as Secretary of Commerce under President Clinton.

Advantages of the Spoils System

Looking back on American political history, many scholars have found much to praise in the old spoils system.[35] For one thing, it helped immigrants adjust to the realities of urban life in the United States. "I think there's got to be in every ward somebody that

FIGURE 14.3

Black Representation in State and Local Government Workforce Is Higher Than in Private Sector

• *Why are there different patterns of employment success for African-Americans and Hispanics?(See Figure 14.4.)*

Note: Government figures are from 1999; private-sector figures are from 2001.

SOURCE: *Statistical Abstract of the United States 2002,* Table 444 (government workers), Table 588 (private sector).

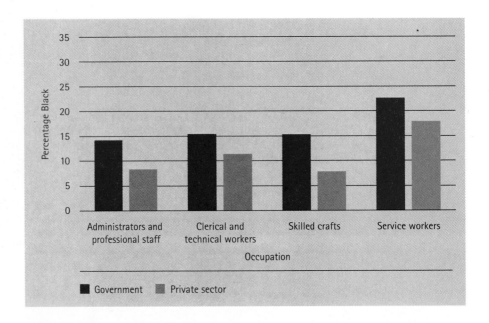

any bloke can come to—no matter what he's done—and get help," said one Boston politician. "Help, you understand; none of your law and your justice, but help."[36] Some of the help took the form of jobs in city government. Irish immigrants were particularly good at using politics as a way of getting ahead. In Chicago, the percentage of public-school principals of Irish background rose from 3 percent in the 1860s to 25 percent in 1914. In San Francisco, it climbed from 4 percent to 34 percent over a similar period.[37]

Contemporary affirmative-action programs have many of the same pluses and minuses as the old-fashioned spoils system. When African Americans became part of urban governing coalitions, they gained better access to government jobs by invoking the principle of affirmative action.[38] Nationwide, African Americans are more likely to get a job in government than in the private sector (see Figure 14.3), a sign that politics still seems to help some disadvantaged groups get a toehold on the ladder to success. However, government employment for Hispanics still lags behind their positions in the private sector (see Figure 14.4), probably because the percentage of Hispanics who vote and otherwise participate in politics remains comparatively low.

Disadvantages of the Spoils System

Even though the spoils system helped incorporate immigrants into American politics and society, it nonetheless contributed to the negative image of American bureaucracies. Education, training, and experience counted for little, and jobholders changed each time a new party came to power. As one Democratic leader joked after his party had been in power for years, a bureaucrat was "a Democrat who holds some office that a Republican wants."[39]

The many decades of patronage politics produced an anti-bureaucratic sentiment among members of the public that continues to the present day. Three-fourths of all Americans think "people in the government waste a lot of money we pay in taxes."[40]

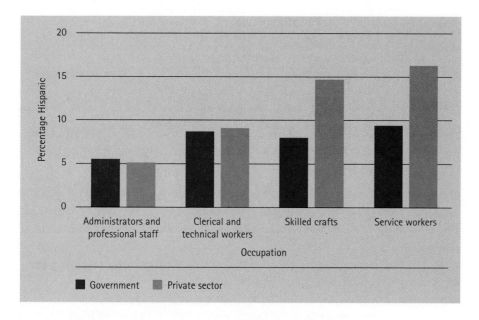

FIGURE 14.4

Hispanic Representation in State and Local Government Workforce Is Lower Than in Private Sector

Note: Government figures are from 1999; private-sector figures are from 2001.

SOURCE: *Statistical Abstract of the United States 2002,* Table 444 (government workers), Table 588 (private sector).

When Americans were asked how they would rate the credibility of federal government workers, only 20 percent found them credible. (Americans were otherwise quite lenient in their evaluations; even accountants scored above 50 percent!)[41]

Erosion of the Spoils System

The mountains of patronage created by the spoils system were gradually eroded by civil service reformers who, in the 1880s, were called **mugwumps.** A group of professors, journalists, clerics, and business leaders, mugwumps insisted that government officials should be chosen on the basis of merit, not for their political connections. Originally a sarcastic term of abuse, the name is a modification of a Native American word meaning "great man" or "chief." Mugwumps were also scorned for refusing to back either party. It was said that their "mugs" peered over one side of the fence while their "wumps" stuck out over the other. Mugwumps, in turn, accused politicians of appointing political hacks to crucial positions of public trust. One clergyman accused the mayor of Boston of appointing saloon keepers and bartenders to public office.

Even though the mountains of patronage did not erode easily, mugwumps won a succession of victories that gradually changed the system. Their first major breakthrough came in 1881 when President James Garfield was assassinated by a mentally disturbed man said to be a disappointed office seeker. Public scrutiny focused on the new president, Chester A. Arthur, who had once served as the New York customs collector and seemed the very personification of the spoils system. In 1883, as the demand for reform swept the country, Congress passed—and Arthur signed—the **Pendleton Act,** which created a Civil Service Commission to set up qualifications, examinations, and procedures for filling many government jobs.

Civil service reform occurred from the bottom up. In the first few years after the Pendleton Act, civil service requirements applied mainly to the lower-level, less skilled jobs performed by those who swept the floors and typed government forms. Gradually,

mugwumps
A group of civil-service reformers, organized in the 1880s, who maintained that government officials should be chosen on a merit basis.

Pendleton Act
Legislation passed in 1883 creating the Civil Service Commission.

civil service
A system in which government employees are chosen according to their educational qualifications, performance on examinations, and work experience.

higher-level positions were included in the civil service; such additions were especially plentiful when the party in power expected defeat in the next election. By making a job part of the civil service, soon-to-be-ousted presidents "blanketed in" their supporters, making it impossible for their successors to replace them with patronage workers from the other party. Civil service reform became nearly complete when, in 1939, Congress passed the **Hatch Act,** which barred federal employees from political campaigning and solicitation. The mountains of patronage were all but worn away.

Hatch Act
1939 law prohibiting federal employees from engaging in political campaigning and solicitation.

Political Appointees Today

In the arid expanses of Arizona and New Mexico stand mesas—often called islands in the desert—that tower over surrounding flatland. All that remain of ancient plateaus, long eroded by wind and water, mesas are ecologically distinct from the surrounding desert.

Just as one finds geological mesas in the deserts of the West, one can locate patronage mesas that have survived decades of civil-service reform. One of the most heavily populated patronage mesas is also the most prestigious, for it includes thousands of policy makers at the top levels of the federal government. It consists of most members of the White House staff, the heads of most departments and agencies, and the members of most government boards and commissions. Political appointees also predominate in the upper levels of individual agencies and departments, inhabiting offices that bear such titles as deputy secretary, undersecretary, deputy undersecretary, assistant secretary, deputy assistant secretary, and special assistant.

This high-level patronage mesa is becoming increasingly crowded. The estimated number of top-level agency appointees grew from less than 500 in 1960 to nearly 2500 in 1998.[42] Adding the White House staff, the total number of high-ranking patronage positions is estimated to be close to 3000.[43] No other industrialized democracy gives its leader as much patronage power. (See International Comparison, page 375.)

The president's ability to recruit political allies for the top echelon of government has both advantages and disadvantages. On the positive side, it allows newly elected presidents to enlist many new people with innovative ideas. For example, President Clinton drew on think-tank experts and leaders from interest groups to design his economic stimulus and health care reform proposals after taking office in 1993. The wholesale changeover in personnel also helps presidents introduce their political agendas with minimal resistance from an entrenched executive branch. President George W. Bush's tax-cut plan and education policies were developed without the aid or obstruction of leftover Clinton advisers. Indeed, it is the power of appointment that makes presidents the most dynamic element in the American political system.

Yet the prevalence of political appointees at the highest levels may result in administrators who have little knowledge of their own organizations. European and Japanese governments are marked by close, informal, long-time associations among leading administrators. In the United States, the average presidential appointee leaves office after only a little more than two years; almost a third leave in less than 18 months.[44] A member of Woodrow Wilson's cabinet once admitted that "the average head of a department is not highly competent and has not first-rate executive ability,"[45] a view echoed many years later by public-administration expert Leonard White, who observed, "The previous experience of federal Secretaries does not usually prepare them to exercise quick and effective leadership."[46]

INTERNATIONAL COMPARISON

Political Versus Professional Bureaucrats

Most high-level administrative positions in Europe and Japan are occupied by well-educated, highly experienced, professional civil servants who refrain from participating actively in politics. Most achieve their positions by studying in prestigious training programs. In France, for example, bureaucracies recruit new employees from the prestigious and highly selective Ecole Nationale D'Administration, which graduates only 150 students per year, and in Japan, about 80 percent of the nation's high-level bureaucrats attended Tokyo University. In these countries, high-level administrators have spent years—even decades—in dedicated government service.

In the United States, high government officials often get their jobs only after gaining prominence outside government in business, law, medicine, education, or a policy institute. Usually, they have worked in a presidential campaign, made financial contributions, or given other evidence of party loyalty. For example, President Clinton's secretaries of commerce were not long-time government experts on trade policy, but Ron Brown, Mickey Kantor, and William Daley, each of whom played key roles in the Clinton and Gore campaigns. Similarly, President George W. Bush, when selecting his secretary of energy, turned not to a long-time government servant who had worked on nuclear power or energy efficiency but to Spencer Abraham, a political supporter and former Michigan senator who had co-sponsored legislation to eliminate the department outright. Although some believed Abraham's management skills would be welcome at the Energy Department, others questioned his qualifications. "I don't see where he has much expertise in energy," said one activist. Another critic was more blunt: "The cabinet is a pension system for political allies."

More professionalized bureaucracies are not necessarily more popular with the general public. In 2002, for example, French Prime Minister Jean-Pierre Raffarin won popularity with proposals to streamline what he said was an inefficient and stagnant government workforce. But there is evidence that bureaucrats in other countries are less frustrated by political interference than are bureaucrats in the United States. According to one study, American civil servants have more negative views of political parties and are more likely to resent the interference of politicians than are Japanese civil servants.

This difference in attitude probably occurs because in the United States the bureaucracy must respond to both the president and Congress. In most other industrial democracies, the legislative branch has less direct influence over the bureaucracy. Where the bureaucracy has only one master, bureaucrats can be professionals instead of politicians.

- *Should the bureaucracy be reformed so that it has only one master?*

- *What would such reforms look like?*

- *What are the advantages and disadvantages of the tug of war between Congress and the president over the bureaucracy?*

SOURCES: "Toward the Multiversity," *The Economist,* July 11, 1987; Joel D. Aberbach, Ellis S. Krauss, Michio Muramatsu, and Bert A. Rockman, "Comparing Japanese and American Administrative Elites," *British Journal of Political Science,* 20:4 (October, 1990), pp. 461–488; Harry Eckstein, "The British Political System," in *Patterns of Government: The Major Political Systems of Europe,* ed. Samuel Beer and Adam Ulam (New York: Random House, 1962), pp.158–168; Hugh Heclo, *Modern Social Politics in Britain and Sweden: From Relief to Income Maintenance* (New Haven, CT: Yale University Press, 1974); Paul Pierson, *Dismantling the Welfare State* (New York: Cambridge University Press, 1994); and David Lazarus and John Wildermuth, "California Wants Abraham's Ear, But It's Unknown If He Can Ease Power Woes," *San Francisco Chronicle,* January 3, 2001: p.: A11; "Profligate France," *The Times* (London), October 9, 1992, p. 21.

The rapid turnover in high-level governmental personnel is so pervasive that it has been called a government of **in-and-outers**—people who come in, go out, and come back in again with each change in administration.[47] Because they cannot count on long-term employment with the government, most political appointees begin planning a way of making a satisfactory departure shortly after they arrive. For some people, this will mean returning to their old positions in the business, legal, or academic world. For others, it will be a matter of using connections inside the beltway to win new financial opportunities in the private or nonprofit sectors. When the new Bush administration came to Washington in 2001, a number of "outers" reentered government, including Vice President Dick Cheney, who had become CEO of an energy company after serving as secretary of defense in the first Bush administration, and Treasury Secretary Paul O'Neill, who had served in the Ford administration and later became head of a large aluminum firm. When O'Neill resigned as treasury secretary after two years of service, he took a job at an investment firm.

in-and-outers
Political appointees who come in, go out, and come back in again with each change in administration.

Comparing Bureaucracies

Who Wants to Be a
Bureaucrat?

These rapid changes in personnel create a government that lacks the continuity necessary for sustained policy focus. The newcomers bring energy and ideas, but by the time their ideas are turned into plans that can be brought to fruition, they themselves are gone, succeeded by another energetic group with an altogether different set of priorities. The newcomers also run the risk of trying to make too many changes at once. Clinton's inexperienced health-policy experts tried to introduce such massive changes that their efforts collapsed under the weight of their own ambitions.[48] Similarly, George W. Bush's inexperienced education advisers initially had difficulty designing an education policy that could withstand close scrutiny by experts in the field. New legislation was eventually passed, but the process was longer and more tortuous than originally anticipated.

With rapid change in personnel, governmental memory becomes as limited as that of an antiquated computer. One Japanese trade specialist who negotiated with the United States observed that the Japanese "look at politics in their historical perspective. . . . However, in the case of the U.S., almost all of their negotiators seem like they came in just yesterday."[49] At one point in 1994, the differing styles of top Japanese and U.S. bureaucrats created a relationship so abrasive that the two countries broke off trade negotiations on the eve of a summit meeting between their leaders.

Worst of all, the denial of most top-level positions to nonpolitical civil servants makes the civil service a less attractive career for intelligent, ambitious young people. In Japan, many of the top students graduating from the country's most prestigious law schools go directly into government service, and the most gifted reach the highest levels of government. But the peak of the U.S. government is not part of a large mountain that employees can gradually ascend over a lifetime career. Instead, the top-level mesa positions are ordinarily cut off from the surrounding civil-service desert, at elevations scaled only by a patronage-filled presidential helicopter.

If young people knew that years of work in the civil service could eventually be rewarded by promotion to high-level policy positions, many more might consider this an attractive career option. But the best advice that can be given to a young person who wants to achieve a high policy-making position in government is to do an internship with a member of Congress, build connections with a political party, achieve distinction outside the government, and wait for the right moment to make Washington a *temporary* home.

The President and the Bureaucracy

CONSTITUTION, ARTICLE II, SECTION 3: The President "shall take Care that the Laws be faithfully executed."

The Constitution charges the president with enforcement of the laws. Presidents fulfill this obligation by overseeing the federal bureaucracy, which is formally responsible to the chief executive. The president's cabinet is the most visible and long-standing connection between the president and the bureaucracy. However, the president also exercises power through appointments to independent agencies and through the powerful Office of Management and Budget.

Despite these means of control, even presidents can be frustrated by the bureaucracy problem. As an exasperated President Harry Truman once said, "I thought I was the president, but when it comes to these bureaucrats I can't do a d—ed thing."[50]

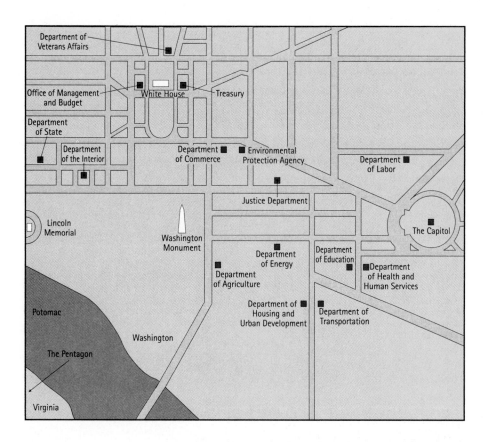

Where Are the Key Buildings in Washington?

The physical location of the headquarters of the inner cabinet suggests the comparatively close ties these departments have to the president. Treasury is located next door to the White House. The walks from State and Justice to the White House are also shorter than to Capitol Hill. Defense, almost a world unto itself, is headquartered in the Pentagon in nearby Virginia.

Many of the departments of the outer cabinet, such as Transportation, Education, Agriculture, Labor, and Housing and Urban Development are located at the foot of Capitol Hill. There they hunker, almost on bended knee, faceless and humorless, in the shadow of the magnificent Capitol building. The Office of Management and Budget (OMB), the nerve center of the executive branch, stands at the president's side, physically as well as metaphorically.

• *When purchasing a home, buyers are warned to think first about location. Why might this also be true in politics?*

The Cabinet

Most federal agencies are located in one of the major departments. The president appoints secretaries to head these departments. The secretaries, along with a few other top-ranking officials, form the president's cabinet (see Chapter 13). The four original departments are known as the **inner cabinet,** because their secretaries typically have ready access to the president.[51] Even the locations of their offices are close to the White House, as you can see from Figure 14.5. These departments are:

- *State,* responsible for foreign policy;
- *Defense,* originally called War, responsible for the military;
- *Treasury,* responsible for tax collections, payments, and debt service;
- *Justice,* headed by the attorney general, who is responsible for law enforcement.

A major function of the remaining departments of the cabinet, which are known as the **outer cabinet,** is to provide interest-group access to the executive branch of government.[52] The Interior Department's job was originally to regulate the use of federal land, particularly in the West. Today, it maintains close ties to ranchers, timber companies, mining interests, and others who depend on federal lands for their livelihood. The Agriculture Department serves farmers; the Commerce Department helps business and industry, especially firms with overseas contracts; Labor works closely with unions; Health and Human Services heeds the American Association for Retired Persons; and Education pays attention to teacher organizations (see Table 14.1).

inner cabinet
The four original departments (State, Defense, Treasury, and Justice) whose secretaries typically have the closest ties to the president.

outer cabinet
Newer departments that have fewer ties to the president and are more influenced by interest-group pressures.

TABLE 14.1
ESTABLISHMENT YEAR AND INTEREST-GROUP ALLIES OF EACH CABINET DEPARTMENT

• *Why have outer-cabinet departments formed alliances with outside groups?*

Department	Year	Interest-Group Allies
Inner Cabinet		
State	1789	
Treasury	1789	
Justice (attorney general)	1789	
Defense	1789 (as War)	
Outer Cabinet		
Interior	1849	Timber, miners, ranchers
Agriculture	1889	Farm bureau, other farm groups
Commerce	1913	U.S. Chamber of Commerce, other business groups
Labor	1913	Labor unions
Health and Human Services	1953	American Association of Retired Persons
Housing and Urban Development	1965	National League of Cities, Urban League
Transportation	1966	Auto manufacturers, truckers, airlines
Energy	1977	Gas, oil, nuclear power interests
Education	1979	Teachers' unions
Veterans Affairs	1987	American Legion, Veterans of Foreign Wars
Department of Homeland Security	2003	Airlines, state and local governments
Environmental Protection Agency	Not an official department	Sierra Club, other environmental groups

The connections between departments and interest groups can change overnight, however, if an event activates the public spotlight. Nowhere was this more evident than in the case of the corporate accounting scandals that arose in 2002. Companies such as energy conglomerate Enron and telecommunications giants Global Crossing and WorldCom had engaged in bookkeeping trickery to hide losses and inflate apparent earnings. The CEOs of these companies had traveled on Commerce Department-sponsored trade missions and enjoyed access to high-level policy makers. [53] When the scandals broke, however, Commerce Department officials distanced themselves from the now-bankrupt firms and took the lead in crafting President Bush's proposed corporate policy reforms. "Business leaders need to understand that they have responsibilities," said one Commerce official, "not just to shareholders, [but also] to creditors, to employees, to pensioners, and [to] government agencies."[54]

Presidents exercise their control over the cabinet departments primarily by appointing political allies to top positions. But once they become agency heads, allies often more closely identify with their turf than with the president's program. As FDR's top budget adviser put it, "Cabinet members are vice presidents in charge of spending, and as such they are the natural enemies of the President."[55] The bureaucracy problem, which tends to encourage sluggishness, red tape, and budgetary expansion, can be particularly frustrating for presidents, who are often interested in speed and efficiency.

Independent Regulatory Agencies

independent regulatory agencies
Agencies that have quasi-judicial responsibilities.

Not all agencies are members of cabinet departments. Some of the most important of these, the **independent regulatory agencies,** have quasi-judicial regulatory responsibilities, which are meant to be carried out in a manner free of presidential interference. These agencies are generally headed by a several-member board or commission appointed by the president and confirmed by the Senate. Independence from the pres-

TABLE 14.2

INDEPENDENT AGENCIES AND THEIR INTEREST-GROUP ALLIES

• *Do the alliances many agencies form with interest groups undermine their initial goals?*

Independent Agency	Board Size	Length of Term (years)	Interest-Group Allies
National Credit Union Administration	3	6	Credit unions
Federal Reserve Board	7	14	Banks
Consumer Product Safety Commission	5	5	Consumers Union
Equal Employment Opportunity Commission	5	5	Civil rights groups
Federal Deposit Insurance Corporation	5	3[a]	Banks
Federal Energy Regulatory Commission	4	4	Oil/gas interests
Federal Maritime Commission	5	5	Fisheries
Federal Trade Commission	5	7	Business groups
National Labor Relations Board	5	5	Unions
Securities and Exchange Commission	5	5	Wall Street
Tennessee Valley Authority	3	9	Regional farmers and utilities

[a] One member, the comptroller of the currency, serves a 5-year term.

ident, which is considered desirable to insulate such agencies from partisan politics, is achieved by giving board members appointments that last for several years (see Table 14.2). In a number of cases, presidents may not be able to appoint a majority of board members until well into their second term in office.

Most independent regulatory agencies were established by Congress in response to widespread public pressure to protect workers and consumers from negligent or abusive business practices. The Federal Trade Commission (FTC) was created in 1914 in response to the discovery of misbranding and adulteration in the meatpacking industry. The FTC was given the power to prevent price discrimination, unfair competition, false advertising, and other unfair business practices. Congress formed the Securities and Exchange Commission in 1934 to root out fraud, deception, and inside manipulation on Wall Street after the stock market crash of 1929 left many Americans suspicious of speculators and financiers.

When originally formed, most regulatory agencies aggressively pursued their reform mandates. But as the public's enthusiasm for reform fades, many agencies find their most interested constituents to be members of the very community they are expected to regulate. Thus the independent commissions, too, have tended to become connected to organized interest groups.[56] To protect against misleading business practices such as those undertaken by Enron, WorldCom, and Global Crossing, the Securities and Exchange Commission (SEC) has the responsibility for ensuring that publicly traded companies provide the stockholders with continually updated information about their true financial condition. Yet Enron was exempted from a key regulation in 1997 when its lobbyist, Joel Goldberg, a former high-level SEC staff member, convinced a current SEC official, Barry Barback (who previously had served under Goldberg), that an exemption from the usual rule was warranted. The close connection between SEC officials and those who lobby them, an all too common phenomenon, can have serious consequences for stockholders.[57]

Office of Management and Budget

Before 1921, every federal agency sent its own budget to Congress to be examined by an appropriations subcommittee. Without a single overseer to review all the requests at once, no one, not even the president, knew whether agency requests exceeded government revenues. When President Woodrow Wilson asked for a bureau to coordinate these requests, Congress at first refused to create one, saying such a bureau encroached on congressional authority. However, when federal deficits ballooned during World War I, Congress, under pressure to make government more efficient, relented and gave the president the needed help.

Originally known as the Bureau of the Budget, the agency is now called the **Office of Management and Budget (OMB),** a name that reflects its enlarged set of responsibilities. Although development of the president's budget is still its most important job, OMB also sets personnel policy and reviews every piece of proposed legislation that the executive branch submits to Congress to ensure that it is consistent with the president's agenda. Agency regulations, too, must now get OMB approval. Even preliminary drafts have to be reviewed by OMB before they are unveiled to the public. One bureau chief claimed that OMB has "more control over individual agencies than . . . [the departmental] secretary or any of his assistants [do]."[58]

OMB was once considered a professional group of technicians whose only goals concerned efficiency and frugality in budgeting. But OMB became more political during the 1980s and 1990s, when budgetary priorities starkly defined the differences between Democrats and Republicans.[59] Clinton's first OMB director, Leon Panetta, had been a Democratic member of Congress and later became the White House chief of staff, an admittedly political office. George W. Bush's first OMB Director, Mitchell Daniels, drew criticism for his advocacy of big tax cuts, and his second OMB director, Josh Bolton, helped negotiate congressional approval of a controversial $87 billion reconstruction aid package for Iraq.[60]

Although OMB has given presidents greater control over agencies, the latter can still make **end runs** around OMB by appealing to their allies on Capitol Hill. In 2001, for example, Democrats on congressional committees relied upon unapproved agency requests submitted to OMB to write legislation that increased funding to these agencies. The Coast Guard, the Customs Service, and the Department of Health and Human Services all stood to gain millions of dollars. Although Senate Republican leader Trent Lott denounced the proposal as a "political scheme," the legislation nearly won passage as part of a defense spending bill.[61]

To check OMB's growing power, Congress in 1974 created the **Congressional Budget Office (CBO),** an organization under the control of Congress that evaluates the president's budget as well as the budgetary implications of other legislation. CBO's sophisticated analyses of budget and economic trends have enhanced its influence in Washington to the point where it now stands as a strong rival to OMB. In the health care reform debate of 1994, for example, it proved to be a "critical player in the game" whose estimates of the costs of health care reform doomed both presidential and congressional proposals.[62] In 2003, CBO estimates of the cost of President Bush's Medicare reform legislation occasioned much debate in Congress over the affordability of the measure.[63]

Office of Management and Budget (OMB)
Agency responsible for coordinating the work of departments and agencies of the executive branch.

end run
Effort by agencies to avoid OMB controls by appealing to allies in Congress.

Congressional Budget Office (CBO)
Congressional agency that evaluates the president's budget as well as the budgetary implications of all other legislation.

Congress and the Bureaucracy

It is a truism that no one should have more than one "boss." When two or more people can tell someone what to do, signals get crossed, delays ensue, and accountability is undermined. Government bureaucrats in Japan and in most European countries generally abide by this rule. Members of the civil service report to the heads of their departments, who report to the head of the government. Members of parliament have little to say about administrative matters.

Officially, federal bureaucrats in the United States have only one boss—the president, who according to the Constitution is the head of the executive branch. But they also have many bosses in Congress. One House-subcommittee chair declared, quite frankly, "I've been running the Medicare system, or our committee has, for the past nine years. We're its board of directors."[64] With Congress divided into House and Senate, and with each chamber divided into many committees, bureaucrats often find themselves reporting to multiple committees, each of which considers itself a "board of directors." Further, the pressures on bureaucracies have intensified in an era of high exposure and perpetual campaigns. As Martha Derthick has observed, "[Although] the U.S. Constitution has not changed . . . the presidency ha[s] become much more vigilant and intrusive . . . [while] Congress has become more critical."[65]

Senate Confirmations

Congressional influence begins with the very selection of executive-department officers. The Senate's confirmation power has long given senators a voice in administrative matters, traditionally via the practice of **senatorial courtesy.** This custom consists of an informal rule that the Senate will not confirm nominees for positions within a state unless they have the approval of the senior senator of the state from the president's party. For example, there are 93 U.S. attorneys in the Department of Justice, appointed by the president to positions throughout the United States. A senator could block the approval of a U.S. attorney in his or her home state if for some reason the senator found the nominee unsatisfactory. Through the practice of senatorial courtesy, senators can protect their political bases by controlling patronage and shaping administrative practices within their states.

senatorial courtesy
An informal rule that the Senate will not confirm nominees within or from a state unless they have the approval of the senior senator of the state from the president's party.

In recent years, the mass media have linked senatorial confirmations and election strategies even more closely. In an age when strong visual images are needed for the television screen, confirmation processes make for good political theater. Nominees have private lives to be examined. They can be asked embarrassing questions during their confirmation hearings. Conflicts between nominees and senators can elevate a little-known senator to the national stage.

Because the confirmation process has greater potential to affect elections than ever before, senators want more than just the usual "courtesy" traditionally extended to senators from the nominee's home state. They now want to be assured that presidential nominees take acceptable policy positions, do not have private investments that conflict with their public duties, have not violated any laws, and have not acted contrary to conventional moral norms. In 2001, George W. Bush encountered difficulties when he submitted John Ashcroft's name for confirmation as attorney general. As a former Missouri senator, Ashcroft anticipated an easy confirmation process—mainly because

FIGURE 14.6

Average Time It Takes Presidential Appointees to Be Confirmed

• *Why has it taken longer in recent years for presidential appointees to be confirmed? What role might elections have played in this trend?*

SOURCES: Paul Light, *Thickening Government* (Washington, DC: Brookings, 1995), p. 68; and Brookings Institution Presidential Appointee Initiative Press Release, "Critical Posts in the Bush Administration Remain Vacant as Congressional Session Nears End," December 18, 2001.

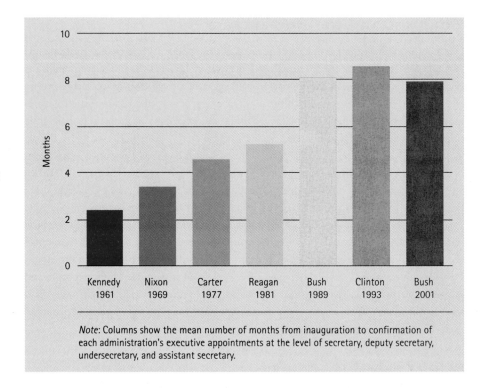

Note: Columns show the mean number of months from inauguration to confirmation of each administration's executive appointments at the level of secretary, deputy secretary, undersecretary, and assistant secretary.

senators seldom are critical of their colleagues, present or past. However, Ashcroft had a conservative record on abortion and civil rights issues, and as a senator, he had blocked Clinton's nomination of Ronnie White, an African American, to a judgeship. Although some Democrats alleged racial prejudice, Republican ranks held firm and Ashcroft was confirmed.

Senate rejections of presidential nominees are still the exception, not the rule. Yet because presidents know that nomination fights damage their standing with Congress and the public, the confirmation process has become more complicated and time-consuming. To decrease the likelihood that the Senate will reject a nominee, the prospective appointee must first survive ethics inquiries by the FBI, the IRS, the Office of Government Ethics (an independent agency), and the ethics official from the agency to which the nominee will be appointed.[66] The White House must then defend the nominee against exhaustive senatorial scrutiny. When John Kennedy was president, the average nominee was confirmed in less than two and a half months. The confirmation of George W. Bush's average nominee required nearly eight months (see Figure 14.6). Prolonging the confirmation process strengthens congressional control over administrative matters. As long as agency heads await confirmation, they hesitate before taking actions that might offend members of Congress. Bill Clinton was without half his administrative team throughout much of his first year as president, the very year in which he was expected to set the country on a new course.

recess appointment
An appointment made when the Senate is in recess.

Under Article II of the Constitution, presidents may make **recess appointments** without Senate confirmation "during the Recess of the Senate." Recess appointees may serve until the end of the next session of Congress, at which point they must resign if they have not been confirmed. Nothing in the Constitution precludes presidents from using the recess appointment repeatedly for the same person, even if that person is never confirmed. When Theodore Roosevelt could not secure confirmation of an African American as a customs collector in Charleston, South Carolina, the president reappointed him to the office during Senate recesses. Congress has since placed a check on the recess-appointment power by passing legislation prohibiting payment of salary to appointees who serve more than a year without Senate confirmation. As a result, presidents today seldom exercise this power over congressional objections.[67] One exception occurred in 2002, when President Bush used recess appointments to install Eugene Scalia (son of Supreme Court Justice Antonin Scalia) as Labor Department solicitor and Otto Reich as assistant secretary of state. The Bush administration believed the recess appointments were justified because the Democratic leadership had not yet allowed senators to vote either for or against the nominees on the Senate floor. Scalia, for example, had won approval from a majority of the Senate Judiciary Committee, and most observers thought he would have won confirmation, had a floor vote been taken.[68]

Agency Reorganization

Not only do presidents and Congress struggle over the appointment of agency officials, but Congress often opposes presidential proposals to reorganize executive agencies. Congress resists change because each agency reports to a specific congressional committee, and these committees are frequently protective of their power. They therefore typically resist governmental reorganization, no matter how duplicative or antiquated existing organizational structures might be.[69] For example, in the first Clinton administration, Vice President Gore proposed shifting the law-enforcement functions of the Drug Enforcement Administration (in the Department of Justice) and the Bureau of Alcohol, Tobacco and Firearms (in the Department of the Treasury) to the Federal Bureau of Investigation. Although the idea seemed logical in principle, because the agencies had similar functions, opposition from Congress and the agencies themselves killed the proposals.[70]

The Bush administration had to navigate similar opposition from some in Congress and executive agencies when it proposed the creation of a cabinet-level Department of Homeland Security. Members of the House Transportation and Infrastructure Committee, for example, argued that the Coast Guard should remain in the Department of Transportation, which the committee supervises. Members of the Senate Agriculture Committee objected to moving the Animal and Plant Health Inspection Service from the Agriculture Department to Homeland Security.[71]

The creation of a new department appeared so difficult that one expert likened the reorganization effort to a hypothetical attempt to merge the (baseball) Texas Rangers with the (hockey) New York Rangers.[72] (See Voices of the Permanent Campaign, p. 427.) Even after the Department of Homeland Security was created, many of the old divisions were still in place. Although the House chose to create a new Select Committee on Homeland Security to handle most issues concerning the new Department, the Senate divided oversight responsibilities among existing committees.

Legislative Detail

Congress also exercises its powers by writing detailed legislation outlining an agency's specific legal responsibilities. In European countries, most legislation is enacted in a form close to the draft prepared by the executive departments.[73] In Japan, 90 percent of all successful legislation is drafted by an executive agency.[74] In the United States, most legislation proposed by presidents is extensively revised by Congress, mainly by the committee with jurisdictional responsibility for the agency.[75] This route has been especially common in recent decades, when Congress and the presidency have more often been controlled by different parties. One study suggests that the average level of discretion that Congress grants the agencies fell by as much as 25 percent from the 1950s to the 1990s.[76]

Sometimes detailed but conflicting laws can have nonsensical results. For over a decade, critics have ridiculed laws that give the Agriculture Department the authority to regulate sausage pizzas but the Food and Drug Administration the authority to regulate cheese pizzas. The FDA operates under legislation authored by the House Commerce Committee and the Senate Human Resources Committee, whereas the Agriculture Department receives its mandates from the House and Senate Agriculture committees. Neither set of committees wishes to relax its control over its agency, so the peculiar division of responsibilities persists. The result, according to one report, "hinders the government's efforts to efficiently and effectively protect consumers from unsafe food."[77]

Even if the statute itself does not dwell on administrative issues, agency operations can be influenced by committee reports accompanying the legislation. These reports are considered by the courts to be evidence of congressional intent and have frequently been given the force of law. Even in the absence of court action, agencies pay attention to committee reports. In the words of one observer, "That language [in the reports] isn't legally binding, but the agencies understand very well what happens if they ignore it."[78]

The issue of legislative detail can be seen as a balancing act between administrative discretion, on the one hand, and congressional control, on the other. If the agency is mindful of congressional intent, Congress may allow it more freedom to act on its own. If an agency neglects a committee's wishes, Congress may enact legal restrictions or even use more forceful methods, such as its control over the agency's budget, to get its way.

Budgetary Control

Every year, each agency prepares a budget for the president to submit to Congress. Each agency must defend its budget before an appropriations subcommittee in both the House and the Senate, and those who offend committee members jeopardize their funding.

To ensure that agencies spend monies in ways consistent with congressional preferences, significant portions of many agency budgets are subject to an **earmark**—a very specific designation of the way money is to be spent, sometimes even specifying particular congressional districts. (See Election Connection, page 385.)

Earmarking seems to be on the increase. At one time, for example, Congress let the scientific-research community decide national research priorities, but between 1980 and 2001 the amount of research dollars earmarked for specific projects skyrocketed from $11 million to $1.7 billion,[79] often for pet projects at a representative's home university. In 2001, the House Transportation and Infrastructure Committee earmarked $423 million for specific highway projects in which members of Congress or their constituents were interested.[80]

The greatest "earmarker" of all time may be the former chair of the Senate Appropriations Committee, Robert Byrd, beloved by his constituents for earmarks requiring numerous agencies to locate their operations in his home state of West

You Are a Federal Administrator

earmark
A specific congressional designation of the way money is to be spent.

ELECTION CONNECTION

Congressional Legislation: A Matter of Detail

To help get reelected, members of Congress try to get what they want out of bureaucracies through the practice of earmarking—that is, designating specific ways in which money is to be spent. Here, in italics, is the specific language the Senate has substituted for the equally specific language of the House, which has been crossed out.

- *If you were an agency official, would you prefer more or less earmarking?*

- *Why do members of Congress care whether the money is spent for the Cumberland Gap tunnel or the Pittsburgh Busway?*

SOURCE: Department of Transportation Appropriations Act, Fiscal Year 1994, with the amendments of the Senate numbered H.R. 2750, 103rd Congress, 1st Session (GPO 1993), p. 40, as reprinted in Allen Schick, *The Federal Budget: Politics, Policy, Process* (Washington, DC: The Brookings Institution, 1995), p. 150.

```
9*   Additional Highway Projects
10   APPALACHIAN CORRIDOR IMPROVEMENT PROJECT
11   For 80 percent of the expenses necessary to continue
12   construction on (130) Kentucky Corridor B West Virginia
13   Corridor L of the Appalachian Development Highway Sys-
14   tem, as authorized by section 1069(y) of Public Law 192–
15   240, (131) $3,800,000 $62,200,000.
16   (132) CUMBERLAND GAP TUNNEL PROJECT
17   For 80 percent of the expenses necessary for the
18   Cumberland Gap Tunnel Project, as authorized by
19   1069(e) of Public Law 102-240, $10,000,000.
20   (133) Pittsburgh Busway
21   For 80 percent of the expenses necessary for the Pitts-
22   burgh Busway, as authorized by section 1069(e) of Public
23   Law 102-240, $28,000,000.
```
★ Numbers at left are line numbers in the actual congressional bill.

Virginia. For example, he once slipped into an emergency bill a provision that shifted the 2600-employee FBI fingerprinting center from downtown Washington to Clarksburg, West Virginia.[81] After the 9/11 attack in 2001, he tried to slip funding for an "aquaculture center"—that is, a swimming pool—into a homeland security bill, despite the apparent lack of relationship between swimming and security. When opposition developed, Byrd instead found room in the bill for $2 million to fund a virtual medical campus at West Virginia University, which, in the senator's words, "will link local doctors and emergency personnel . . . with specialists . . . in the event of a terrorist attack."[82]

Legislative Oversight

In addition to earmarking, committees hold hearings to ensure that agencies are not straying from their congressional mandates. The increase in such oversight hearings in recent decades has expanded committee control over administrative practice. The number of days each year that committees hold oversight hearings nearly quadrupled between the 1960s and the 1990s.[83] Although the number of oversight hearings fell in the late 1990s as a result of reforms instituted in 1995, they still far outnumber hearings called to consider specific legislation.[84]

At oversight hearings, members of the administration are often asked to testify about agency experiences and problems. Witnesses representing outside groups are given opportunities to praise or criticize the bureaucrats. Through the oversight process, committees obtain information that can be used to revise existing legislation or modify agency budgets, sometimes to the consternation of bureaucrats. Even when committees do not hold hearings, the threat of doing so is sometimes enough to cow agency officials into following congressional wishes.[85] According to one survey, nearly half of high-level agency officials complain of "a great deal" of congressional "micromanagement" of their jobs.[86]

Iron Triangles and Issue Networks

Congress has such power over bureaucracies that many agencies seek to build coalitions of allies among congressional committees and interest groups in order to survive. These connections have become so intimate that some political scientists have said that most federal government programs are run by **iron triangles**.[87] Interest groups form the base of the triangle, because they have the membership and money that can influence the outcome of congressional elections, and agencies listen to interest-group demands to obtain committee backing (see Figure 14.7a).

The relationship is said to be an *iron* triangle because the connections among the threesome remain a lot more stable than in the proverbial love triangle. In the case of the iron triangle, each of the three parties can deliver something the other needs. Compromises are readily arranged because interests are similar. Most oversight hearings are, in fact, three-way love fests. Interest-group representatives offer gracious testimony about agency work, and members of Congress chime in with words of endearment. When a congressional scholar asked congressional-committee staff whether they considered their committee to be agency advocates, nearly two-thirds said "yes." In response to this question, one staff person replied,

> I think any subcommittee . . . whatever its subject is, they're advocates. I mean the Aging Subcommittee is advocating for aging programs, the Arts for arts, you know, Education for education, Health for health. They wouldn't be doing their work if they weren't interested.

Added another,

> The trouble of it is we get in bed with agency people in some respects. We're hoping that they'll distribute good projects in our state, you know, and it's a kind of a working with them so that, you know, there'll be more, more and better of everything for everybody.[88]

These relationships often transcend partisan divisions. With the Republican takeover in 1995, the House leadership initially placed tight restrictions on committees in order to weaken the committee–agency relationship. Infuriated at the loss of committee power, Democrats on one committee complained that "the Republican leadership has decided that the considered judgment of expert committees no longer matters."[89] But within a year, the Republican leadership found it necessary to loosen its controls, and the natural tendency for committees to support "their" agencies reasserted

iron triangle
Close, stable connection among agencies, interest groups, and congressional committees.

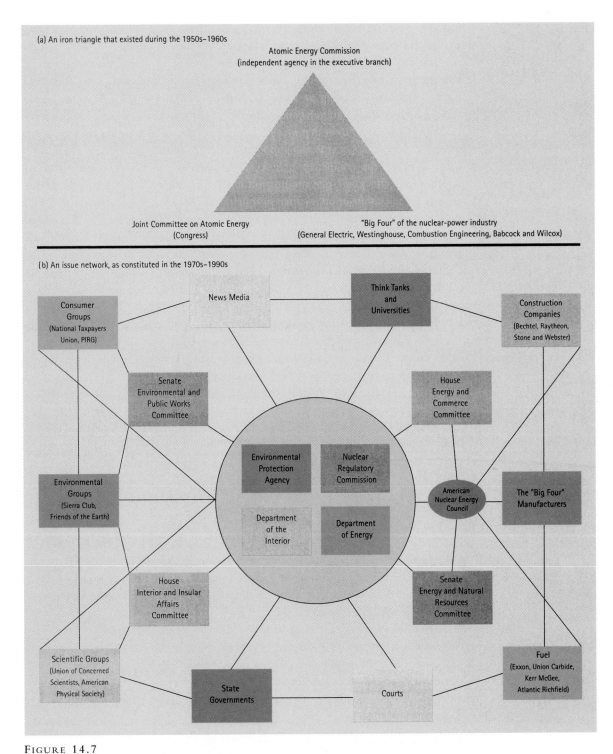

FIGURE 14.7
Change of Nuclear Energy Policy Arena from Iron Triangle to Issue Network
• *Why has the policy-making environment changed from a triangle to a web?*

SOURCES: Based on information in Seong-Ho Lim, "Changing Jurisdictional Boundaries in Congressional Oversight of Nuclear Energy Regulation: Impact of Public Salience," paper presented before the Annual Meeting of the American Political Science Association, 1992; and Frank R. Baumgartner and Bryan D. Jones," Agency Dynamics and Policy Subsystems," *Journal of Politics* 53 (November 1991): 1044–1074.

itself. For example, in 1995 House Republican leaders proposed elimination of all funding for the Public Broadcasting Corporation. "We were read our last rites," said the corporation's president. But after Republican members of the key congressional subcommittee were besieged by letters and faxes from constituents, who feared the demise of *Sesame Street* and *Mister Rogers' Neighborhood,* they voted to keep the agency alive, though at a reduced level of funding..[90]

Some iron triangles are no longer as rigid as they once were. As the number of interest groups and policy experts has expanded, congressional committees and government agencies have been bombarded with competing demands from multiple sides, which together form **issue networks** (see Figure 14.7b).[91] For example, nuclear energy policy was, at one time, of interest mainly to just four companies that built nuclear reactors and to the utility companies that used the electricity. After an accident at the Three Mile Island reactor in Pennsylvania, however, the subject attracted the attention of environmental, safety, and antinuclear groups, all of whom pressed for tighter regulation of nuclear reactors. With the interests of the groups divided, the media took greater notice of the issue, and conflict between congressional committees and the Department of Energy intensified.[92] By 2003, when Congress considered whether to subsidize nuclear power plants as a less-polluting alternative to oil, a wider variety of interest groups, companies, and even several U.S. states had become involved in the policy debate.[93] As this example illustrates, issue networks include more conflict, more players, and more publicity than iron triangles.

Many scholars argue that the concept of issue networks presents a more realistic picture of the way Washington works today than does the older concept of iron triangles. In past decades, the three points of the triangle provided a good image of the way many agencies, Congress, and interest groups did business, but increasingly, our current, more complicated politics looks less like a triangle and more like a web.

issue networks
Loose, competitive relationships among policy experts, interest groups, congressional committees, and government agencies.

Elections and the Bureaucracy

For more than a century, reformers have tried to separate politics from administration. Government should serve the people, they argue, not the special interests. Departments should make decisions according to laws and regulations, not in response to political pressure. Agencies should treat every applicant alike, not respond more favorably to those who contribute to political parties.

These reform principles are worthy of respect. When politics interferes, bureaucracies can be inefficient and ineffective. The customs service, its name once synonymous with political spoils, is still slow to report international economic transactions. The Department of Housing and Urban Development, always a political thicket, has at times so badly mismanaged its property that it has had to blow up buildings it constructed.[94]

Many of the more effective federal bureaucracies are less politically charged. The National Science Foundation, protected from political pressures by an independent board, is known for the integrity with which it allocates dollars among competing scientific projects. The Federal Bureau of Prisons does a better job than many state prisons of maintaining security without depriving prisoners of rights; it has succeeded in part because members of Congress, respectful of prison leadership, have left the agency alone.[95]

Even though agency autonomy has worked in some instances, electoral pressures have also played a positive role and in any case are an essential feature of modern bureaucracies.[96] Public pressure exerted through elections has affected the way bureaucracies keep secrets, enforce the law, manage their budgets, and make decisions. In the end, elections create pressures that force many agencies to balance competing interests by striking compromises.

Bureaucratic Secrecy

Bureaucracies like to protect their secrets. "Inside knowledge" is power. Secrecy can cover mistakes. In Europe, where administrators are less exposed to electoral pressure, they work hard to guard their private information. In Britain, it is a crime for civil servants to divulge official information, and political appointees swear themselves to secrecy upon taking office.

Electoral pressures have sharply curtailed the amount of secrecy in American government. In the view of one specialist, "secrecy has less legitimacy as a governmental practice in the United States than in any other advanced industrial society with the possible exception of Sweden," in large part because "Congress has done a great deal to open up the affairs of bureaucracy to greater outside scrutiny."[97] The **sunshine law,** passed in 1976, required that federal government meetings be held in public, unless military plans, trade secrets, or personnel questions are being discussed. Under the Freedom of Information Act of 1967, citizens have the right to inspect unprotected government documents. If the government believes the requested information needs to be kept secret, it must bear the burden of proof when arguing its case before a judge.

sunshine law
A 1976 law requiring that federal government meetings be held in public.

Even in the absence of new laws, the legislative and judicial branches can limit the degree to which executive agencies operate in secret. President Bush was furious when, in the aftermath of the terrorist attacks of 2001, members of Congress leaked classified information to the press.[98] And the president's executive order authorizing the trial of suspected terrorists by military tribunals was issued, in part, because of concern that secret intelligence information gathered by the FBI and CIA would be revealed during an ordinary trial. "We need to find some system of justice that allows us to punish guilty people without destroying our antiterrorism infrastructure around the world," said one law professor.[99]

Secrecy can sometimes be essential in pursuing national-security objectives. The Department of Homeland Security has often had to walk a delicate line between publicity, so as to keep the public adequately informed of threats, and secrecy, so as to more effectively detect or disrupt specific terrorist plotting. During the 2003 holiday season, Homeland Security Secretary Tom Ridge publicly announced a heightened terrorism alert status, advising travelers and law-enforcement officials to be on the lookout for suspicious behavior. Meanwhile, radiation experts from the Department of Energy were secretly placed on duty in five major cities across the United States, as a contingency in case a radioactive device was detonated.[100]

Despite the acknowledged benefits of some kinds of secrecy, many elected officials feel public pressure to force executive agencies to disclose as much information as possible. One survey found that, by a 3 to 1 margin, Americans believe that "too many" government documents are classified.[101] Voters seem to believe that, as one observer put it, "In order for people to direct their own government, they must have information about governance and be able to examine the performance of elected leaders and bureaucrats."[102]

Bureaucratic Coercion

Bureaucracies are often accused of using their coercive powers harshly and unfairly. Police officers stop young drivers for traffic violations that are often ignored when committed by older drivers. Bureaucratic zealots trap sales clerks into selling cigarettes to heavily bearded 17-year-olds. Disabled people are refused benefits because they do not fill out their applications correctly.

Although such abuses occur, they happen less frequently because agencies are held accountable to the electorate. In 1998, for example, Republican senators sensed popular discontent with the Internal Revenue Service (IRS), the government's tax collection agency. The agency's approval rating was an embarrassingly low 38 percent.[103] The Senate Finance Committee held a series of hearings that brought to light a litany of agency failings. The IRS had lost $150 billion in 1995 because of mistakes, unreported income, or improper deductions. Taxpayers were overbilled an average of $5 billion per year.[104] The technology the agency used was so outdated that IRS Commissioner Charles Rossotti himself admitted, "I have never seen a worse situation in a large organization."[105] And one rogue agent even tried to frame an ex-senator on money-laundering and bribery charges.[106] As a result of the hearings, Congress enacted a law restructuring the agency, making it harder for the IRS to accuse taxpayers of wrongdoing and bringing its tax collection systems up to date.[107] In the succeeding years, the IRS focused so much on customer service that some members of Congress ironically began to fear that the agency was not being tough enough in its enforcement actions.[108]

The example of the IRS illustrates a broader pattern in U.S. politics: if bureaucratic agencies make life difficult for the voting public, these agencies are more likely to be taken to task by elected officials.[109] Most agencies would prefer to avoid this painful scrutiny.

Agency Expansion

Agencies generally try to increase their budgets, but elections apply the brake to such tendencies, if only because politicians get blamed for raising taxes. "As a general rule," says analyst Martha Derthick, "Congress likes to keep bureaucracy lean and cheap."[110] The number of people working for the federal government, as a percentage of the workforce, has declined since the 1980s, in large part because elected officials are under public pressure to cut bureaucracy. The overall size of government grew during the Bush administration for the first time in years, as agencies added half-a-million new anti-terrorism jobs.[111] But President Bush also worked to shrink the bureaucracy by forcing some bureaucrats to compete with private companies for their jobs. This "competitive sourcing" initiative rankled some federal employees, who staged a protest outside the White House and called upon their allies in Congress to defend them.[112] "The long-term [government] employee is feeling devalued," said an anonymous U.S. Park Service worker.[113] In one survey, 59 percent of federal workers said their agencies only "sometimes" or "rarely" have "enough employees to do their jobs well."[114]

Administrator Caution

Federal agencies are sometimes accused of going beyond their legislative mandates. But most federal agencies are more likely to err on the side of caution. The worst thing any agency can do is make a major mistake that captures national attention. As one official explained, "The public servant soon learns that successes rarely rate a headline, but government blunders are front-page news. This recognition encourages the development of procedures designed less to achieve successes than to avoid blunders."[115]

In 1962 it was discovered, to widespread horror, that thalidomide, a sedative available in Europe, increased the probability that babies would be born with serious physical deformities. Congress immediately passed a law toughening the procedures the Food and Drug Administration (FDA) was to follow before approving prescription drugs for distribution.[116] Decades later, in keeping with this policy, the FDA refused to approve the sale of several experimental drugs to terminally ill people suffering from AIDS. Patients desperate to try anything that might help them did not share the FDA's concern for ascertaining proven effectiveness. When the FDA's refusal to allow experimentation became a public issue, the agency began to allow AIDS patients to try the untested drugs, once again responding to pressure from the voting public.

**You Are the President
of MEDICORP**

Compromised Capacity

Agency effectiveness is often undermined by the very terms of the legislation that created it. For legislation to pass Congress, a broad coalition of support is necessary. To build this support, proponents must strike deals with those who are at best lukewarm to the idea. Such compromise can cripple a program at birth.[117]

The politics of charter schools illustrates the restraint that compromises can place on organizational effectiveness. In the 1990s, school reform advocates began to establish charter schools—new schools free of most state regulations. Reformers expect charter schools to provide alternatives to, and competition for, traditional public schools. School boards and teacher organizations oppose the establishment of these schools, claiming they will attract students away from their local schools. Many state legislatures, under pressure from both sides, have compromised on the issue by passing legislation allowing charter schools but restricting their number, funding, and autonomy. It remains to be seen whether charter schools can prosper within the constraints imposed by these legislative compromises.[118]

Muddling Through

American bureaucracies do not perform as badly as most Americans think. One survey examines the actual experiences of clients encountering government bureaucracies and then compares their reactions to these experiences with the impressions that these same people have of government bureaucracies in general. The differences between actual experiences and general impressions are striking:

> Seventy-one percent of all the clients said that their [own] problems were taken
> care of, but only 30 percent think that government agencies [generally] do well at

taking care of problems. Eighty percent said that they were treated fairly, but only 42 percent think that government agencies treat most people fairly.

In other words, most Americans ... decide that their [good] experiences represent an exception to the rule. People who have had *bad* experiences, however, are likely ... to think that everyone else is getting unfair treatment too.[119]

The advent of the Internet has provided an opportunity for bureaucracies to communicate even more effectively with citizens. According to one study, over two thirds of visitors to government Web sites found them to be useful and easy to navigate.[120]

When all the pluses and minuses are added up, the average government bureaucracy probably deserves something like a B-minus grade. A few agencies, such as NASA during the race to the moon, merited an A-plus, although its reputation has since slipped. A few others, such as the customs service, don't deserve a passing grade. But the general tendency is toward a bland, risk-free mediocrity. Too much imagination generates too much controversy, which invites political retribution. One bureaucrat offered the following guidelines for his colleagues: "1) When in charge, ponder; 2) When in trouble, delegate; 3) When in doubt, mumble."[121] The best way to survive politically is to try to muddle through, making only gradual changes in policy and striving to satisfy everyone.[122]

The Forest Service, which is responsible for managing most of the millions of acres owned by the federal government, does a pretty good job of muddling through. Although its rangers are professionally trained, talented individuals, its political problems are vexing. Ranchers, miners, and timber companies want to exploit the land's natural resources. Others want to use the land for hiking, camping, and fishing. Environmentalists want to convert as much of the land as they can into wilderness areas for the benefit of future generations.

To balance these pressures, the Forest Service came up with the doctrine of multiple use. It proposed to manage the land in such a way that its multiple uses could be blended together and harmonized. Timber harvests should be accompanied by reforestation. Especially scenic areas should be preserved for recreational activities. Mining should be as inconspicuous as possible.

But the doctrine of multiple use did not so much resolve conflicts as institutionalize them. As a result, the Forest Service is under constant pressure. Ranching, timber, and mining interests have clout at the local level, where local political leaders make the potent claim that the local economy will suffer unless these interests are protected. Environmentalists, however, have the greatest influence on those chosen in elections affected by the national media, which dramatically depict the desecration of the American landscape.

Any attempt to balance these interests antagonizes one or more sides of the dispute. Only by muddling through can the Forest Service survive politically and manage the federal lands as well as it does.[123]

Chapter Summary

Government bureaucracies are essential, and bureaucratic problems are inevitable. But American bureaucracies have specific troubles that can be attributed to the electoral climate in which they have evolved. With the creation of the spoils system, bureaucrats were often regarded as slow, inefficient, corrupt political hacks. Gradually, civil-service reforms eliminated the worst of the abuses. But the reforms occurred in a bottom-up, not top-down fashion. The highest levels of government continue to be filled with political appointees—generally capable but not always experienced government administrators.

As chief executive, the president is nominally in charge of the bureaucracy, appointing key officials and exerting control through the Office of Management and Budget. But Congress also influences federal agencies via its confir-

mation of presidential nominees, detailed legislative enactments, the budget process, and legislative oversight. To survive, agencies build ties to key interest groups, who form the base of what are known as iron triangles. Today, some of these iron triangles are being transformed into more complex, unstable, and conflictual issue networks.

Elections influence agencies in diverse ways. On the one hand, they keep agencies from becoming too secretive and coercive. On the other hand, they can also make agencies too cautious or force them to operate under compromise-crafted laws that undermine their effectiveness. Most of the time, agencies respond to politics by muddling through, for which they deserve more credit than they usually get.

Key Terms

administrative discretion, p. 365
agency, p. 365
bureaucracy, p. 365
civil service, p. 373
Congressional Budget Office (CBO), p. 380
department, p. 365
earmark, p. 384
end run, p. 380

government corporation, p. 365
Hatch Act, p. 374
in-and-outers, p. 375
independent regulatory agencies, p. 378
inner cabinet, p. 377
iron triangle, p. 386
issue networks, p. 388
mugwumps, p. 373

Office of Management and Budget (OMB), p. 380
outer cabinet, p. 377
patronage, p. 370
Pendleton Act, p. 373
recess appointment, p. 382
senatorial courtesy, p. 381
spoils system, p. 370
sunshine law, p. 389

Suggested Readings

Of General Interest

Aberbach, Joel D., and Bert A. Rockman. *In the Web of Politics: Three Decades of the U.S. Federal Executive.* Washington, DC: The Brookings Institution, 2000. Traces controversies over the federal bureaucracy since the 1970s, including recent attempts to "reinvent" government.

Heclo, Hugh. "Issue Networks and the Executive Establishment." In *The New American Political System,* ed. Anthony King. Washington, DC: American Enterprise Institute, 1978. Describes the shift from iron triangles to issue networks.

Light, Paul. *Thickening Government: Federal Hierarchy and the Diffusion of Accountability.* Washington, DC: The Brookings Institution, 1995. Identifies and explains the growth in higher-level governmental positions.

Morone, James A. *The Democratic Wish: Popular Participation and the Limits of American Government.* New York: Basic Books, 1990. Account of the ways in which democratic movements have shaped the development of public administration in U.S. history.

Niskanan, William A. *Bureaucracy and Representative Government.* Chicago: Aldine-Atherton, 1971. Develops the argument that government bureaucracies seek to maximize their budgets.

Wilson, James Q. *Bureaucracy: What Government Agencies Do and Why They Do It.* New York: Basic Books, 1989. Comprehensive treatment of public bureaucracies.

Focused Studies

Chubb, John, and Terry Moe. Politics, Markets and America's Schools. Washington, DC: The Brookings Institution, 1990. Brilliant, controversial account of the way in which politics interferes with effective management of public schools.

DiIulio, John. *Governing Prisons: A Comparative Study of Correctional Management*. New York: Macmillan, 1990. Shows how politics affects the management of prisons.

Kaufman, Herbert. *The Forest Ranger*. Baltimore, MD: Johns Hopkins University Press, 1981. Classic study of a government agency.

Kettl, Donald F. *Reinventing Government: A Fifth-Year Report Card*. Washington, DC: The Brookings Institution, 1998. Evaluation of the Clinton–Gore "reinventing government" initiative.

Young, James. *The Washington Community 1800–1828*. New York: Harcourt, 1966. Engaging, insightful account of political and administrative life in Washington during the first decades of the nineteenth century.

On the Web

www.firstgov.gov

Most U.S. government agencies and departments have informative Web sites that can be reached through the federal government's central site, FirstGov.

www.whitehouse.gov/omb

The Office of Management and Budget, the president's main resource in controlling and organizing the federal bureaucracy, offers Web-accessible copies of budget documentation, testimony before Congress, and regulatory information.

www.opm.gov

The Office of Personnel Management calls itself "the federal government's human resources agency." It organizes the federal civil-service system, and its Web site provides information on federal pay scales, worker performance, and job opportunities.

www.gsa.gov

The General Services Administration sets acquisitions and management policies for much of the federal bureaucracy.

www.cbo.gov

The Congressional Budget Office, created in 1974 as Congress's counterpart to the Office of Management and Budget, produces reports on the economy, the budget, and the impact of current proposed legislation.

www.gao.gov

The General Accounting Office is the investigative arm of Congress and assists Congress in its oversight of the executive branch. It produces reports that evaluate the effectiveness of various federal agencies.

www.gpo.gov

The Government Printing Office provides the text of the Federal Register, where all new and proposed regulations are published.

CHAPTER 15

* * * * * * * * * * * * * * * *

The Courts

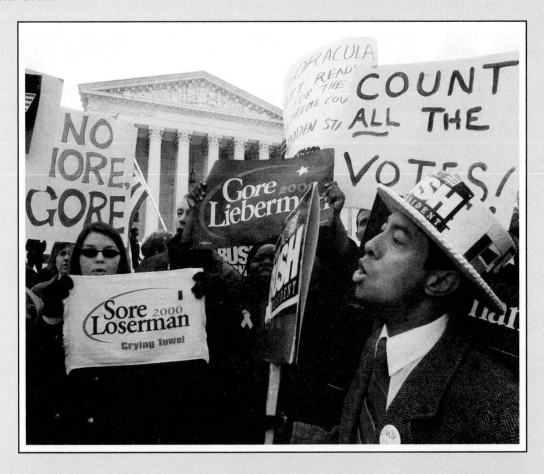

The Supreme Court's "Unsought Responsibility" in the 2000 Election

After dark on the evening of December 12, 2000, the entire nation waited in anxious anticipation for word from the Supreme Court. News agencies reported that lights still burned in the imposing granite building across from the U.S. Capitol, indicating that staffers had not yet gone home for the night. Then, with almost no fanfare, the Court's press office released the justices' **opinion,** the court's written justification of its decision, in the case of *Bush v. Gore*. As confused reporters stood outside the Court building, frantically paging through the opinion on live television, Gore staffers watching on the other side of town soon realized that the final hand had been dealt: They had lost the 2000 presidential election.

Over a month earlier, when voters had gone to the polls across the country, neither campaign could ever have anticipated that the election would be decided by the nation's highest court. But as the Bush and Gore campaigns began battling over Bush's tiny margin of victory in Florida, the case inexorably made its way there. After numerous challenges and counterchallenges to recounts by hand in various Florida counties, the Gore team finally, on December 8, secured an order from the State Supreme Court to allow recounts to proceed. Bush cried foul, saying the counting standard that the Florida court recommended was unconstitutionally vague. The Supreme Court granted Bush a stay of the count, pending a hearing, but in an unusual step four justices authored a stinging dissent to the stay. "To stop the counting of legal votes," they wrote, "the majority today departs from . . . rules . . . that have guided the Court throughout its history . . . Preventing the recount from being completed will inevitably cast a cloud on the legitimacy of the election."

On December 11, Bush and Gore attorneys made their case to the justices—Bush's team arguing that vague standards violated voters' rights to the equal protection of the laws,

Gore's team protesting that recounts were a state issue and should be left to Florida officials. The next day, a divided Court ruled in Bush's favor, noting the monumental and delicate nature of the case:

> None are more conscious of the vital limits on judicial authority than are the members of this Court, and none stand more in admiration of the Constitution's design to leave the selection of the President to the people, through their legislatures, and to the political sphere. When contending parties invoke the process of the courts, however, it becomes our unsought responsibility to resolve the federal and constitutional issues the judiciary has been forced to confront.[1]

The ruling provoked joy in some quarters, dismay in others. Critics charged that conservatives on the Court had departed from their legal principles to hand victory to their preferred candidate. The majority had "made it impossible for citizens of the United States to sustain any kind of faith in the rule of law as something larger than [the Court's] self-interested political preferences."[2] Others argued that the Supreme Court had taken a courageous step, bringing to an end what could have been a constitutional crisis. These observers said that the Court had done exactly what it was supposed to do: It had brought stability to American government. This view gained strength when later newspaper recounts revealed that the issue might never have been conclusively resolved. Such recounts indicated that Bush would still have won the election had the counting been conducted according to one standard, whereas Gore would have won if another procedure had been followed.

The fact that a presidential election had been decided by the nation's highest court prompted many to reexamine the Court's role in American politics. Did the Court "cast a cloud on the legitimacy of the election," or did it wisely exercise its "unsought responsibility"? More generally, what is the role of the courts in a nation run by elected officials?

MAKING THE CONNECTION

In recent years, the courts have been increasingly influenced by electoral considerations, even though the founders meant the courts to be more isolated than other political institutions from public pressures. This chapter describes the U.S. judicial system, which is headed by the Supreme Court and also includes other federal and state courts. In discussing the role the courts play in affecting public policy, we will answer the following questions:

- What is the role of state courts?

- What is the structure and what are the powers of the federal court system?

- How are people chosen to sit on the Supreme Court?

- How does the Supreme Court decide the outcome of specific cases?

- What are the checks on the power of the Supreme Court?

- How are the courts used to advance political agendas?

* * * * * * * * * * * * * * *

State Courts

The first American courts were state courts. Under the Articles of Confederation, there was no national judiciary, and virtually all disputes were handled by the various state legal systems. The Constitution created a national judicial branch, but most legal cases continued to be handled in the states, a practice that remains true today. The vast majority of judicial activity takes place within state trial courts under the control of state and local governments. In fact, 99 percent of all legal cases in the U.S. originate in these courts.[3]

Every state has its own judicial arrangements, but in most the basic structure has three tiers: trial courts, courts of appeals, and a court of last resort, usually called the state supreme court. Parties to a case may appeal from a trial court to a higher court if they believe the trial court has made an error in judgment. Decisions of state supreme courts may be appealed to the federal Supreme Court if the case involves a federal statute or the interpretation of the federal Constitution.

State Trial Courts: The Judicial Workhorses

As the name suggests, the main responsibility of the first tier of state courts is to hold trials. In all trials there are two sides: the **plaintiff,** the person bringing the suit, and the **defendant,** the person against whom the complaint is made.

Trials settle alleged violations of the civil and criminal codes. The **civil code** regulates the legal rights and obligations of citizens with regard to one another. Alleged violations of the civil code are stated by individuals, who ask the court to award damages and otherwise offer relief for injuries they claim to have suffered. For example, you can act as plaintiff and sue your landlord for not supplying heat to your apartment. You can ask for monetary damages and a guarantee that this will not happen in the future. People cannot be imprisoned for violating the civil code (although they *can* be imprisoned for noncompliance with a court order issued in conjunction with a civil suit).

Violations of the **criminal code** are offenses against society as a whole and are enforced by the government itself, acting as plaintiff and initiating charges against suspects. If convicted, the criminal owes a debt to society, not just to the injured party. The debt may be paid by fine, imprisonment, or (in the case of capital crimes) execution. Table 15.1 summarizes the differences between civil and criminal cases.

The same action can simultaneously be a violation of both the criminal and the civil code. After a jury found former football star O. J. Simpson not guilty of criminal

opinion
In legal parlance, a court's written explanation of its decision.

plaintiff
One who brings legal charges against another.

defendant
One accused of violating the civil or criminal code.

civil code
Laws regulating relations among individuals. Alleged violators are sued by presumed victims, who ask courts to award damages and otherwise offer relief.

criminal code
Laws regulating relations between individuals and society. Alleged violators are prosecuted by government.

TABLE 15.1

DIFFERENCES BETWEEN CIVIL AND CRIMINAL TRIALS

• *Why can a defendant be forced to testify in a civil case, but not in a criminal case?*

	Criminal Trial	Civil Trial
Plaintiff	The government	Private person or group
At issue	Duty of citizens to obey the law	Legal rights and obligations of citizens to one another
Type of wrongdoing	Transgression against society	Harm to private person or group
Remedy	Punishment (fine, imprisonment, etc.)	Compensation for damages
Standard of proof	Beyond a reasonable doubt	Preponderance of the evidence
Can defendant be forced to testify?	No	Yes

charges in conjunction with the murder of his ex-wife, Nicole Brown Simpson, her relatives filed civil charges, alleging that the family should be compensated for pain and suffering caused by her wrongful death. The plaintiffs were able to secure a guilty verdict in the civil suit and a monetary award, despite the finding of not guilty in the criminal prosecution, because in civil suits the accused can be forced to testify and the standards of proof are lower.

State courts are in a position to be significantly influenced by politics. In 37 of the 50 states, some judges are subject to election. In the remaining states, judges are appointed by the state legislature, the governor, or a governmental agency. Exactly which judges are elected varies from state to state. In New York, trial court judges are elected but appellate judges are appointed.[4] In Georgia it is the reverse. Studies show that, at least on a few issues, elected state judges are more likely to follow closely the opinions of their constituents.[5]

Although many state judges are subject to election, most judicial campaigns "are waged in obscurity, with the result that most voters are unfamiliar with the names, not to speak of the issues, involved in the campaign."[6] As a result, judicial elections have traditionally been dominated by organized groups and party politicians interested in controlling court patronage. Political scientist Milton Rakove described how the party-judicial connection worked in the 1960s:

> Without question the surest and safest road to a seat on the bench is through the party organization. Having a judge on the bench from [their] ward organizations gives the precinct captains access to the county judicial system which can be used on behalf of the ward's constituents. Many sitting judges continue to attend ward organization meetings and ward fund-raising affairs.[7]

Even today, Chicago observers bemoan "the political shenanigans that taint judicial elections and undermine public confidence in the justice system."[8] But parties seem to have a greater impact on court patronage than on judicial decisions; most studies find few differences between the decisions of Democratic and Republican state judges.[9]

Interest groups have also had a growing influence on judicial elections, especially as the cost of running campaigns for judgeships has increased. In 2000, for example, the thirteen candidates for five Alabama Supreme Court seats spent a combined total of over $13 million on the race.[10] Much of the money to fund judicial races is donated by single-issue groups that may have an interest in the way certain cases are decided. According to one observer, "The involvement of third parties has particularly intensified the battles over civil justice issues and the viciousness of judicial campaigns has clearly increased."[11]

Prosecuting State Cases

Upon receiving information from the police with respect to criminal wrongdoing, prosecutors in the office of the local **district attorney** determine whether the evidence warrants presentation before a grand jury for prosecution. In large cities the district attorney has enormous responsibilities. In Los Angeles, for example, the district attorney's office prosecutes 300,000 cases a year.

district attorney
Person responsible for prosecuting criminal cases.

Because they are responsible for the prosecution of all criminal cases, some of which have high visibility in local news media, many prosecutors earn recognition that wins them election or appointment to the judiciary. About 10 percent of all judges once worked in a district attorney's office.[12] Many local district attorneys are interested in moving to other elected offices as well.

In 2000 Paul Howard, a Georgia district attorney, was up for reelection. He pressed for the arrest and trial of Baltimore Ravens football star Ray Lewis for two murders outside a suburban Atlanta bar. But prosecutors could find no evidence linking Lewis to the crime, and Lewis's attorney criticized them for "indicting before investigating."[13] After prosecutors dropped the charges and released Lewis, some observers blamed the botched investigation on the district attorney's desire for notoriety. "Because Howard tried to ride to fame on the back of Ray Lewis," one critic wrote, "he has damaged—not enhanced—his chances for reelection."[14]

An Independent and Powerful Federal Judiciary

The case of the 2000 election described at the beginning of this chapter was a unique episode for the Supreme Court, but it illustrates two fundamental characteristics of the federal judiciary that the Constitution created in 1787. The Court was able to be decisive in this case because of the judiciary's independence from other political institutions, and because of its singular and long-established power to say what the Constitution means. The federal courts are independent from Congress and the presidency because of constitutional guarantees of life tenure and stable salaries. This independence does not set the courts apart from politics, however. On the contrary, the power to interpret the Constitution and laws passed by Congress has placed the judicial branch at the center of key political controversies throughout the country's history.

Tenure and Salary

> CONSTITUTION, ARTICLE III: "The Judges . . . shall hold their Offices during good behaviour and shall . . . receive for their Services a Compensation, which shall not be diminished during their Continuance in Office."

The original advocates of the Constitution believed the appointment of federal judges for life tenure (or "good behaviour") was essential to the system of separation of powers. As Alexander Hamilton expressed it, life tenure was an "excellent barrier to the encroachments and oppressions of the representative body."[15] The only way Congress may remove federal judges is through the impeachment process (see Chapter 13). Standards for impeachment are so high, however, that only thirteen federal judges have been impeached in U.S. history, and of these, only seven were removed from office.[16] The offenses in which these seven judges were found to have engaged included accepting bribes, committing perjury, and, in one case, applying for a job as a confederate judge during the Civil War.[17] If judges avoid such behavior, they are virtually assured their positions for as long as they wish to hold them.

The Constitution further protects judicial independence through its provision that fixes judicial salaries. Although Congress is permitted to increase the salaries of judges, it may not lower them for any judge, once that judge has taken office. Some legal scholars have argued that Congress has been less than diligent in raising judges' salaries to keep pace with inflation as well as with private sector salaries, and that the quality of the judiciary has suffered as a result. **Chief Justice** William Rehnquist, the head of the Supreme Court, has even gone so far as to argue that "Inadequate compensation seriously compromises the judicial independence fostered by life tenure."[18] Others point out, however, that, although pay is lower for judges than for many lawyers, the shorter work hours and job security are adequate to lure well-qualified people to the bench.[19]

chief justice
Head of the Supreme Court.

Judicial Review

CONSTITUTION, ARTICLE VI: "This Constitution, and the Laws of the United States which shall be made in Pursuance thereof . . . shall be the supreme Law of the Land."

The federal courts often find themselves at the center of major political controversies because their great political authority includes the power of **judicial review**—the power of the courts to declare null and void laws of Congress and of state legislatures that they find unconstitutional. This power can be exercised by any court, federal or state, but all lower-court decisions are subject to review by the Supreme Court, if it chooses to do so. The significance of the courts' power of judicial review can hardly be overestimated. Judicial review gives judges who are appointed for life the power to negate laws passed by the elected representatives of the people. As Senator George W. Norris complained, "The people can change Congress but only God can change the Supreme Court."[20]

judicial review
Power of the courts to declare null and void laws of Congress and of state legislatures that they find unconstitutional.

Although the Constitution affirms that it is the "supreme law of the land," it says nothing explicit about judicial review. The founders provided for a Supreme Court but offered few details about its powers (see Chapter 2, page 00). As political scientist Robert McCloskey once observed, "The United States began its history . . . with a Supreme Court whose birthright was most uncertain."[21]

Despite its uncertain status during the first years of the new republic, in 1803 the Supreme Court successfully asserted the power of judicial review for the first time in the most important of all its decisions, *Marbury v. Madison*. In this complex case, Supreme Court Chief Justice John Marshall used a dispute over patronage as an occasion to assert the Court's power to declare the acts of Congress null and void.

In 1801, before John Adams and the Federalists relinquished control of the White House and Congress to Thomas Jefferson's Democratic-Republicans, they appointed and confirmed 42 new justices of the peace for Washington, DC. The appointments had been so hastily arranged, however, that no one in the outgoing administration had time

Marbury v. Madison
Supreme Court decision (1803) in which the court first exercised the power of judicial review.

to deliver the official commissions to the appointees. Upon their arrival, Jefferson and his secretary of state, James Madison, declined to do so, making it impossible for the appointees to take office.

According to the Judiciary Act of 1789, the jilted appointees could request a court order to force the Jeffersonians to grant the appointments. Furthermore, said the act, the Supreme Court would have original jurisdiction in such cases—that is, it would be the first and only court to which such cases would be brought. On the basis of this law, one appointee, William Marbury, sued Madison for his job before the Supreme Court.

The case offered the Court no easy solution. The justices were sure that if they issued the order, the Jefferson administration would successfully ignore it, making the Court seem weak and ineffectual. On the other hand, if they declined to issue the order, they would appear to be caving in to pressure from the Jeffersonians.

Marshall solved this problem by asking an unexpected question: Was the Supreme Court the proper place to address Marbury's complaint? His stunning conclusion was that it was not—because the Constitution granted the Supreme Court original jurisdiction *only* in "all Cases affecting Ambassadors, other public Ministers and Consuls, and those in which a State shall be Party."[22] By giving the Court original jurisdiction in the case of the secretary of state (who did not qualify as a "public minister" in the accepted sense of the term), Section 13 of the Judiciary Act of 1789 had violated the Constitution and was therefore void.

Marshall's brilliant decision had transformed a situation that looked sure to sap the power of the federal courts into one that strengthened this power tremendously. By denying the Supreme Court's jurisdiction in the case, he invoked the power of judicial review for the first time. This authority has been acknowledged and accepted ever since.

In asserting the power of judicial review, Marshall's reasoning was simple and straightforward. Any new law overrides older laws on the same subject, except when the older law has been issued by a higher governmental entity. If a city passes a law declaring its speed limit to be 30 miles an hour, an older law that sets a speed limit of 40 miles an hour is automatically void, unless the old law was passed by a higher level of government, such as the state. Then the state law, even if it is from an earlier date, takes precedence. The highest law of the land, according to Marshall, is the Constitution. It was established by the people, and no entity subject to the Constitution—not even Congress itself—can enact legislation that contravenes the will of the people, as expressed in the Constitution.

Three Theories of Constitutional Interpretation

The reasoning is impeccable as long as one assumes that judges only examine a law of Congress, compare it to the Constitution, and determine whether the law runs counter to constitutional language. The simplest case, perhaps, would be a law that postponed a constitutionally mandated election day. But very few issues of constitutionality are that simple. To help decide which laws are unconstitutional, judges and legal scholars have developed three distinct theories of constitutional interpretation: original intent, living constitution, and plain meaning of the text. Each of these theories reflects a different conception of what the role of the courts ought to be in key political controversies.

The theory of **original intent** determines whether a law is constitutional by ascertaining the intentions of those who wrote the Constitution. To establish the intentions of the founders, judges examine such documents as the notes that James Madison

John Marshall
Appointed by John Adams to serve as chief justice (1801–1835), John Marshall was also a Revolutionary War soldier, a supporter of the Constitution at the Virginia ratifying convention, a Federalist member of Congress, and secretary of state.
• *Can you name another key court decision that Marshall wrote?*

original-intent theory
A theory of constitutional interpretation that determines the constitutionality of a law by ascertaining the intentions of those who wrote the Constitution.

wrote down at the Constitutional Convention, the *Federalist Papers,* and the speeches made during the ratifying campaign in 1787 and 1788. Among today's sitting Supreme Court justices, Justice Clarence Thomas relies most frequently on the theory of original intent. For example, he favors overturning the 1973 *Roe v. Wade* decision legalizing abortion because he finds nothing in the Constitution that gives women the right to choose an abortion. On the contrary, he says that at the time the Constitution was ratified, many states outlawed abortion, making it clear that the framers had no intention of denying the states this authority.

Those who favor original-intent theory tend to believe that the courts should play a very limited role in politics. As Justice Thomas puts it, "When struggling to find the right answer to a case, judges should adopt principles of interpretation and methods of analysis that reduce judicial discretion."[23] By refusing to go beyond what the founders had in mind, argues Thomas, original intent theory "places the authority for creating the legal rules in the hands of the people and their representatives, rather than in the hands of the judiciary."[24]

Critics of original-intent theory say that many issues upon which the courts must render decisions were never contemplated by those who wrote the Constitution. Additionally, constitutional language may be the result of compromises between those who held contradictory beliefs. And, even if the founders were united in their opinions, should the perspectives of 55 men gathered together in Philadelphia in the summer of 1787 constrain the actions of the U.S. government more than 200 years later?

living-constitution theory
A theory of constitutional interpretation that places the meaning of the Constitution in light of the total history of the United States.

Those who criticize original-intent theory offer instead a **living-constitution theory** of judicial review, which says that a law's constitutionality ought to be judged in light of the entire history of the United States as a nation. The determining factors should include not only the opinions expressed at the time the Constitution was written but also ideas and judgments shaped by American experience since then. In the words of Justice Oliver Wendell Holmes, Jr., constitutional questions must be "considered in the light of our whole experience and not merely in that of what was said a hundred years ago."[25]

Those who support living-constitution theory see a broader role for the courts to play in contemporary political controversies, especially when fundamental principles are at stake. "Our constitution," argued Justice William Brennan, "was not intended to preserve a preexisting society, but to make a new one, to put in place principles that the prior community had not sufficiently recognized."[26] Consequently, there may be public policy issues on which the other branches of government and the public feel one way, but on which justices are "bound, by a larger constitutional duty to the community . . . to point toward a different path."[27] For example, Brennan believed that the death penalty violates the Eighth Amendment's prohibition of "cruel and unusual punishment," despite evidence that the founders did not oppose capital punishment. (See Voices of the Permanent Campaign, p. 493.)

plain-meaning-of-the-text theory
A theory of constitutional interpretation that determines the constitutionality of a law in light of what the words of the Constitution obviously seem to say.

The living-constitution theory is practical and helps the Constitution adapt to modern circumstances; however, it may reduce constitutional interpretation to the judge's personal understanding of the meaning of American history. And because no two judges' interpretations of the country's history are likely to be the same, constitutional interpretation becomes highly subjective.

These difficulties have given rise to what has been called the **plain-meaning-of-the-text theory** of constitutional interpretation, which determines the constitutionality of a law in light of what the words of the Constitution obviously seem to say. Justice William Douglas pointed out that the First Amendment requires that "Congress shall make no law . . . abridging freedom of speech," adding, "The First Amendment is couched in absolute terms—freedom of speech shall not be abridged. . . . No leeway is granted."[28]

Plain meaning has several clear advantages. Like original intent theory, it suggests that the courts should be cautious in the scope of their decisions, and should not go beyond the printed word. But, unlike original-intent theory, it does not require extensive inquiry into debates undertaken in the distant past. The constitutional text itself is taken as a guide to action. Nor does this approach require that judges evaluate the meaning of the totality of the American experience.

But plain-meaning theory has its own limitations. The Constitution is a short document that left many issues undecided and used ambiguous language in order to win ratification. Words that appear plain do not always have a clear meaning. Even Justice Douglas agreed to some limitations on free speech—for example, he agreed that one private person cannot libel another with impunity (see Chapter 16).

Justice Sandra Day O'Connor relied on plain-meaning theory to overturn a federal law on the grounds that the federal government cannot order states to follow a regulatory program. She said no such power could be found in the Constitution, and the Tenth Amendment "made explicit" that all powers not delegated to Congress are reserved to the states. "Some truths," she wrote, "are so basic that, like the air around us, they are easily overlooked." But Justice John Stevens argued that O'Connor's interpretation of the law was far from a basic truth, pointing out that Congress, under the Articles of Confederation, had the authority to compel states to take certain actions. He said the Constitution was written to strengthen, not weaken, the powers of Congress. "The Tenth Amendment surely does not impose any limit on Congress' exercise of the powers delegated to it," he wrote.[29] If two noted jurists, O'Connor and Stevens, do not agree on the content of the Tenth Amendment, its meaning can hardly be plain and clear.

Judicial Review in Practice

The manner in which the courts interpret the Constitution can have serious consequences for the nation. In three celebrated instances, the Supreme Court created constitutional crises by declaring laws unconstitutional, thereby defying the declared will of Congress and the president.

The first case, *Dred Scott v. Sandford* (1857), declared unconstitutional the Missouri Compromise law passed in 1820.[30] The law drew a line coinciding with the Arkansas–Missouri border, north of which there could never be slavery (see Figure 15.1). Missouri, the exception, was allowed to legalize slavery. The Missouri Compromise had been so successful at preventing a breakup of the union that few even considered the possibility that the Supreme Court would dare call it unconstitutional. But instead of respecting Congress's capacity to find satisfactory compromises, the Supreme Court denied the power of Congress to prohibit slavery in the territories, claiming it was an unconstitutional restriction on property rights. Few, if any, court decisions have been more disastrous. The *Dred Scott* decision alarmed many northerners, who feared that slavery would, in practice, be extended throughout the Union.[31] And for southerners, the Court's arguments helped justify armed resistance.

Dred Scott

This painting depicts Dred Scott, a slave whose master had brought him outside slave-owning states. Scott sued for his freedom, arguing that when he set foot in a free state, he became free. In an infamous decision, the Supreme Court ruled that Scott had no right to sue and that Congress had no right to prohibit slavery in the territories.

• *How has the Dred Scott decision contributed to contemporary arguments against judicial review?*

FIGURE 15.1

The Missouri Compromise

The *Dred Scott* decision invalidated the Missouri Compromise, an 1820 agreement that averted a sectional crisis by fixing a line (pictured) south of which slavery would be permitted. Areas north of the line would be free.

• *Why was the Supreme Courts' invalidation of the compromise so destructive?*

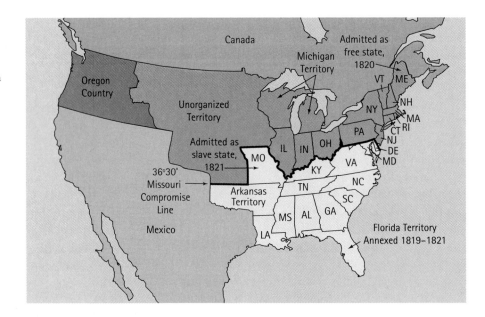

In the late nineteenth century, the Supreme Court once again unwisely used its power of judicial review to declare a law unconstitutional, this time to block legislation designed to curb the abuses of industrial capitalism. In *Lochner v. New York* (1905), the Court said the state of New York could not regulate the number of hours that bakers worked, because to do so deprived them of the "right" to work as long and as hard as they pleased. The New York legislature had passed the law at issue, limiting the work week to 60 hours to protect workers from unscrupulous employers. In his dissent from the Court's decision, Oliver Wendell Holmes insisted that the Constitution be interpreted as a living document:

> This case is decided upon an economic theory which a large part of the country does not entertain. A Constitution is not intended to embody a particular economic theory. It is made for people of fundamentally differing views.[32]

Holmes's dissent in *Lochner* eventually became the view of the Supreme Court. Today, it is accepted that government can regulate working conditions.

A third unfortunate use of the power of judicial review occurred after Franklin Delano Roosevelt became president in 1933. Coming to power in the midst of a depression, Roosevelt and his Democratic Party allies in Congress passed a host of new legislation, known as the New Deal, designed to stimulate economic recovery.

The Supreme Court, which included a majority of justices appointed by Republican presidents, declared many of the New Deal laws unconstitutional. In *Schechter Poultry Corp. v. United States* (1935), the Supreme Court found the National Industrial Recovery Act, which addressed labor and competition in the private sector, an unconstitutional intrusion on the power of the states to regulate commerce inside their own borders.[33] In what was known as the "sick chicken" case, the Court said the law regulated the sale of poultry *after* it arrived within the state of New York, not while the chicks were being transported across a state line. Because Congress could regulate only commerce between states, not commerce within a state, the Court declared the law unconstitutional (see Chapter 3, page 64). The decision placed the Supreme Court at odds with the president and Congress, creating a constitutional crisis that was not

INTERNATIONAL COMPARISON

Statutory Interpretation in the United States and Britain

When interpreting statutes, British judges have less leeway than American judges because they operate within a less fragmented governmental system. In Britain, the party of the prime minister exerts effective control over Parliament. Every piece of legislation passed by the party in power is carefully examined by specialists, who ensure that new legislation is internally coherent and consistent with existing laws. If a judge says government administrators have misinterpreted the law, the party in power can also, if it chooses, quickly pass new legislation. Political scientist Shep Melnick points out that as a result, "it is not surprising that British judges seldom question the interpretive authority of administrators."[a]

American judges work within a more decentralized governmental context. To get a majority when writing legislation, members of Congress are tempted to use ambiguous language that may include phrases that come close to contradicting one another. In Melnick's words, "The openness and messiness of the legislative process in the United States ensures that when judges scrutinize a statute and its history, they will seldom discover a single, coherent purpose or intent."[b] In the voting-rights legislation of 1982, for example, Congress forbade electoral arrangements that gave minorities "less opportunity than other members of the electorate to elect representatives of their choice" but, a few sentences later, said that nothing in the legislation required minorities to be elected "in numbers equal to their proportion in the population." The "less opportunity" forbidden in the first phrase seemed permitted by the second phrase which indicated that "equal numbers" need not be elected.[c]

When courts are asked to sort out the meaning of this kind of vague and potentially contradictory language, the office of the solicitor general may express the opinion of the presidential administration. But if the courts ignore the solicitor general, the administration must try to persuade Congress to enact a new law—a far more difficult task for American presidents than for British prime ministers. Knowing this, U.S. courts feel free to interpret laws in any way that is not plainly contrary to the intent of Congress. As Supreme Court Justice William Brennan once said, "the Court can virtually remake congressional enactments."[d]

- *The U.S. system is certainly more complex than the British one. Is it better?*

[a]R. Shep Melnick, *Between the Lines: Interpreting Welfare Rights* (Washington, DC: The Brookings Institution, 1994), p. 13 (ellipses deleted).

[b]Melnick, *Between the Lines,* p. 13.

[c]As quoted in Bernard Grofman, Lisa Handley, and Richard G. Niemi, *Minority Representation and the Quest for Voting Equality* (New York: Cambridge University Press, 1992), p. 39. (ellipses deleted).

[d]Melnick, *Between the Lines,* p. 13.

resolved until several justices switched their votes on such cases in the wake of Roosevelt's overwhelming reelection.

Cases such as *Dred Scott, Lochner,* and *Schechter Poultry* have led some legal theorists to argue that judicial review should be abandoned because it is anti-democratic. "If judicial review is a means to check encroachments," asks John Agresto, "what means exist to check the encroachments of the judiciary[?]"[34] But others see judicial review as a valuable protection against majority infringement on minority civil rights and civil liberties. Despite the controversy, judicial review has become a well-established practice in American government. It survives in part because it is seldom used to defy the strongly held views of the president and Congress. On only 151 occasions between 1803 and 2000 did the Supreme Court decide that a federal law was unconstitutional.[35] Most of these decisions affected old laws no longer supported either by a majority of Congress or by the president.

Political scientist Robert Dahl has gone so far as to claim that "The Supreme Court is inevitably a part of the dominant political leadership. The main task of the Court is to confer legitimacy on [the government's] fundamental policies."[36] Although some scholars think the Court is less sensitive to political pressure than Dahl claims, a recent study has identified changes in Supreme Court policy that parallel swings in public opinion. These policy shifts are not so pronounced as those in Congress, the study finds, but justices still seem to pay "attention to what the public wants."[37] The

A Federal District Court's Responsibility

In 2004, magazine publisher and television personality Martha Stewart appeared in federal district court to defend herself against allegations of insider stock trading.

• *How do federal district court responsibilities differ from those of a circuit court of appeals?*

Dred Scott and *Schechter Poultry* cases are the exception, not the rule. Bartender Mr. Dooley, the Irish cartoon figure, was not wide of the mark when he observed years ago that "th' supreme court follows th' illiction returns."

Statutory Interpretation

statutory interpretation
The judicial act of interpreting and applying ordinary laws, rather than the Constitution, to specific cases.

Judicial review is only the most sweeping and controversial of judicial powers. The courts also engage in **statutory interpretation,** the application of the laws of Congress and of the states to particular cases. American courts have great discretion in exercising this power, much more than their counterparts in Great Britain. (See the accompanying International Comparison.) For example, in 1973 Congress passed a vague and general law protecting endangered species. The Supreme Court gave this law teeth by saying that Congress intended to protect all species, the tiny snail darter as well as the eagle. In reaching this decision, Chief Justice Warren Burger wrote that "it may seem curious to some that the survival of a relatively small number of three-inch fish among all the countless millions of species extant would require the permanent halting of a virtually completed dam for which Congress has expended more than $100 million." But the law, Burger said, required "precisely that result."[38] Although dissenting Justice Powell thought it was "absurd" to assume Congress had any such intention, the Court majority argued that all it was doing in this instance was interpreting and applying an act of Congress.

The Federal Court System in Practice

CONSTITUTION, ARTICLE III, SECTION 1: "The judicial power . . . shall be vested in one supreme Court, and in such inferior Courts as the Congress may from time to time ordain and establish."

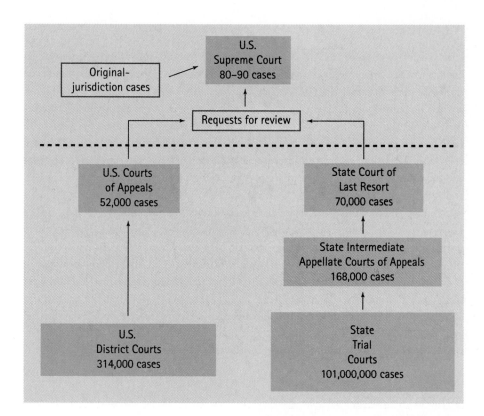

FIGURE 15.2
Federal and State
Court Systems
• *Why does the Supreme Court handle so few cases each year?*

Although the Supreme Court provides the linchpin for the nation's system of courts, resolving difficult questions of constitutional or statutory interpretation, most of the day-to-day work of the federal judicial branch is carried out at lower tiers. These lower courts are less visible institutions, but they are no less affected by political and electoral forces. In this section we describe the federal court system.

District Courts

The Constitution established a Supreme Court, leaving it to Congress to decide what lower federal courts were needed. The first Congress enacted the Judiciary Act of 1789, which, though it has been updated in many ways, still provides the basic framework for the modern federal court system.

Most federal cases are initially filed in one of the 94 **federal district courts,** the lowest tier of the federal court system. These courts are the trial courts of the federal system, and are similar to the trial courts that exist in each state. A variety of high-profile cases are heard in the district courts. In 2002, for example, a New York district court judge made headlines by ruling that the detaining of material witnesses to assist in grand jury investigations was unconstitutional. The ruling came after a college student, Osama Awadallah, had been detained for three months without being charged after the terror attacks of September 11, 2001.[39] In another highly publicized 2004 case, magazine publisher and television personality Martha Stewart was convicted in a federal district court for offenses connected to insider stock trading. As Figure 15.2 shows, the vast majority of federal legal proceedings begin and end in these district courts.

federal district courts
The lowest level of the federal court system and the courts in which most federal trials are held.

You Are a Young Lawyer

Appeals Courts

circuit court of appeals
Court to which decisions by federal district courts are appealed.

The federal district courts are organized into 13 circuits (including 11 numbered circuits, a DC circuit, and a federal circuit), each of which has a **circuit court of appeals,** the court to which all district court decisions may be appealed (see Figure 15.3). The name circuit, which means "a regularly traveled route around a given territory," recalls the early history of the courts, in which judges journeyed by stagecoach from district to district, listening to cases. Because of the deplorable state of roads in the early republic, riding the circuit could be a perilous duty. Judges complained of "heat and exposure to the sun, lack of drinking water in many areas, deep ruts, high water, and indifferent accommodations."[40]

plenary session
Activities of a court in which all judges participate.

Nearly all cases today are heard in the same building, usually by 3 of the 6 to 28 judges who serve on the court of appeals. The senior appeals-court judge assigns the 3 judges to each case. In most courts of appeals, they are chosen by lot. In exceptionally important cases, a **plenary session** may be held in which all of the appeals judges in the circuit participate. Courts of appeals confine their review to points of law under dispute; they ordinarily take as given the facts of the case, as stated in the trial record and decided by district judges. They do not accept new evidence or hear additional witnesses. Although decisions by the appeals court may be taken up by the Supreme Court, most appeals-court decisions are final.

Specialized Courts

Two trial courts have nationwide jurisdiction over specialized issues that do not fall within the purview of the district courts. The Court of International Trade handles cases concerning trade and customs. And the U.S. Court of Federal Claims hears suits concerning federal contracts, money damages against the United States, and other issues that involve the federal government. Cases originating in either of these courts may be appealed to the court of appeals for the federal circuit.

Selection of Federal Judges

senatorial courtesy
An informal rule that the Senate will not confirm nominees within or from a state unless they have the approval of the senior senator of that state from the president's party.

All federal judges hold lifetime positions after their nomination by the president and confirmation by the Senate. Because of long-standing agreements among senators, known as **senatorial courtesy,** any presidential nominee must be acceptable to the senior senator of the state involved who is of the same political party as the president. Political influences play a major role in the selection of federal judges. Most share the same partisan identification as the president who nominates them; 87 percent of Bill Clinton's nominees were Democrats, and 90 percent of George W. Bush's nominees have been Republicans.[41] Most judges would not acknowledge it publicly, but political loyalty is often the key to appointment. As one judge admitted,

> I worked hard for Franklin Roosevelt. . . . In 1939 I began running for the Senate, and the party convinced me it would be best if there wasn't a contest for the Democratic nomination. So I withdrew. . . . They gave this judgeship as sort of a consolation prize. . . .[42]

Although most lower-court nominees are confirmed, rejections do occur. Rejection is usually a result of some financial or personal problem uncovered during

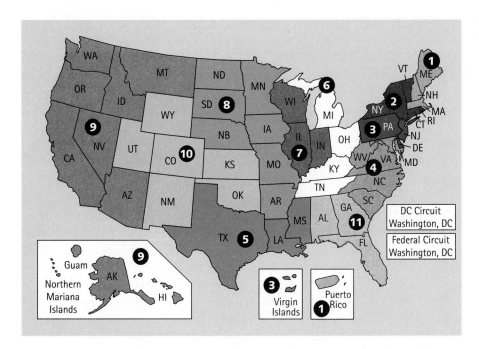

FIGURE 15.3

Courts of Appeals Circuit Boundaries

• *What is the role of the federal appeals court?*

SOURCE: Robert A. Carp and Ronald Stidham, *The Federal Courts,* 2nd ed. (Washington, DC: CQ Press, 1991), p. 18.

the confirmation process. Ideological and partisan considerations play a minor role. Conservative lawyer Robert Bork, for example, was easily confirmed as an appeals-court judge, even though he was later rejected as a nominee to the Supreme Court because of his right-wing views. But ideological battles over lower-court judges have become increasingly important. Clinton declined to nominate a liberal Washingtonian, Peter Edelman, as an appeals-court judge because Republicans in the Senate said they would block the appointment.

Short of rejection, opposition-party senators may exert their power by simply refusing to bring a nomination to a vote. In the late 1990s, President Clinton complained of congressional foot-dragging and Republicans criticized his judicial nominations as too liberal. This situation failed to improve after the election of George W. Bush: the now-Democratic Senate acted on only 43 percent of Bush's judicial nominees in 2001, delaying action on the rest.[43] Even after the Senate changed back to Republican hands, Miguel Estrada, Bush's choice for a seat on the U.S. Court of Appeals for the District of Columbia, withdrew his name from consideration in 2003 after a filibuster blocked a vote. Estrada was one of a handful of nominees that Democratic Senators argued were "extreme conservatives."[44]

One reason why parties are willing to do battle over nominations is that there are important ideological differences between potential judicial appointees. Overall, district judges' decisions reflect the political orientation of the president who nominated the particular judge—judges appointed by Democratic presidents are more likely than those appointed by Republican presidents to hand down liberal decisions.[45]

Deciding to Prosecute

Suspected violations of the federal criminal code are usually investigated by the Federal Bureau of Investigation, although other federal agencies, such as the Secret Service and the Bureau of Alcohol, Tobacco and Firearms, also exercise investigative powers. The

U.S. attorney
Person responsible for prosecuting violations of the federal criminal code.

evidence collected is given to prosecutors in the office of a **U.S. attorney,** who is responsible for prosecuting violations of the federal criminal code. Appointed by the president and confirmed by the Senate, the 93 U.S. attorneys act as the government's chief litigators. If persuaded that a prosecution is warranted, a U.S. attorney asks a grand jury consisting of 16 to 23 citizens to indict, or bring charges against, the suspect. Because accused people cannot defend themselves before a grand jury, the U.S. attorney's advice usually determines the outcome. As one wit observed, "Under the right prosecutor, a grand jury would indict a ham sandwich."[46] After the indictment, government prosecutors may find it more difficult to convince the trial jury to convict the defendant, however.

U.S. attorneys have a particularly high political profile. They usually share the president's party affiliation and, although they are expected to be incorruptible, they often are sensitive to the political needs of their superiors in Washington. Because routine law enforcement is left in the hands of state officials, U.S. attorneys concentrate on high-visibility, attention-grabbing crimes. If they are particularly successful, they may become candidates for higher office. For example, former New York Mayor Rudolph Giuliani achieved prominence as a federal attorney who successfully prosecuted Wall Street inside-trader Ivan Boesky and tax-evading hotel magnate Leona Helmsley, as well as several high-profile organized crime figures. Senator Ted Stevens of Alaska and Representatives Asa Hutchison of Arkansas and Howard Coble of North Carolina all began their careers as U.S. attorneys.

Relations Between State and Federal Courts

For the first few decades under the Constitution, the relationship between state and federal legal and judicial systems remained vague. Then, in an early key decision, *Martin v. Hunter's Lessee* (1816), the Supreme Court ruled that it had the power to review and, if necessary, to overturn the decisions of state courts. In that case, a Virginia court had argued that the decisions of state courts were final and could not be appealed to the national level. The Supreme Court disagreed, saying that "the importance, and even necessity of uniformity of decisions throughout the whole United States" made the Virginia court's argument untenable.[47] Three years later, in **McCulloch v. Maryland** (1819), the Supreme Court made it clear that the power of judicial review applied to state as well as federal laws (see Chapter 3, page 62). Maryland had imposed a tax on the congressionally chartered Bank of the United States. When a bank cashier, James McCulloch, refused to pay the tax, he was convicted of violating the law. But the Supreme Court overturned the conviction. Chief Justice Marshall argued that "the power to tax involves the power to destroy" and that no state had the power "to retard, impede, burden or in any manner control, the operations of the constitutional laws enacted by Congress."[48]

The Supreme Court's power to review state laws and the decisions of state courts is essential for maintaining basic uniformity in the laws of the United States. Over the decades, the Supreme Court has found over 1130 state statutes and state constitutional provisions contrary to the federal Constitution.[49] The judicial power to declare state laws unconstitutional is much less controversial than the power to declare laws of Congress unconstitutional. As Justice Holmes once said,

McCulloch v. Maryland
Decision (1819) in which the Supreme Court first declared a state law unconstitutional.

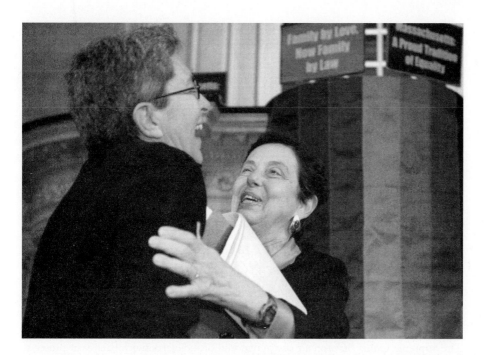

I do not think the United States would come to an end if we lost our power to declare an act of Congress void. I do think the Union would be imperilled if we could not make that declaration as to the laws of the several states. For one in my place sees how often a local policy prevails with those who are not trained to national views.[50]

Most cases are heard in state courts, but any case can be shifted to a federal court if it can be shown that a federal law or constitutional principle is involved. The federal courts have higher prestige than state courts; to become a federal judge is to hold a position of great honor. But as Justice Sandra Day O'Connor, a former state judge, acutely observed, "When the state court judge puts on his or her federal court robe, he or she does not become immediately better equipped intellectually to do the job."[51]

The same act can simultaneously be a violation of both state and federal laws. Although the Fifth Amendment to the Constitution forbids **double jeopardy**—one individual being tried twice for the same crime—something very close to double jeopardy can occur if a person is tried in both federal and state courts. In such cases, multiple trials are allowed if the same actions gave rise to distinct crimes. In 1897 the Supreme Court permitted dual prosecutions, saying that "an act denounced as a crime by both national and state sovereignties is an offense against the peace and dignity of both."[52]

double jeopardy
Placing someone on trial for the same crime twice.

Dual state and federal prosecutions remain unusual, however. Most of the time, federal and state officials reach an agreement allowing one or the other to take responsibility. Generally speaking, the federal government takes over the prosecution only when the case has national implications. For example, the 1995 bombing of a federal building in Oklahoma, in which 168 people lost their lives, constituted a violation of both state laws against murder and federal laws against conspiracy and manslaughter. Although state officials began the investigation, federal investigators quickly took charge and the accused, Timothy McVeigh and Terry Nichols, were convicted in a federal courtroom. Later, when Nichols failed to receive the federal death penalty for his role in the crime, state prosecutors brought state murder charges against him.

If the state prosecution fails to result in a conviction in a sensational case where a federal law has been broken, the federal U.S. attorney may also bring charges. In 1992 the state of California was unable to win a conviction in the trial of four police officers charged with beating African American motorist Rodney King, an event that had been videotaped. The failure to convict officers for what seemed to be a well-documented offense provoked three days of civil disorder in Los Angeles minority communities.

To help calm the city, the U.S. attorney decided to bring federal civil rights violation charges against the officers, despite the fact that the state had already tried them once for assault. After hearing all the evidence, the jury in the federal trial convicted two officers and acquitted the other two. The decision to hold a second trial was almost certainly affected by public and media pressure.

The Supreme Court

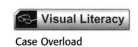

Case Overload

The Supreme Court sits atop a massive pyramid of judicial activity. Each year prosecutors and private citizens bring more than 27 million criminal trials and civil suits before the state and federal courts.[53] Yet in the 2003 term, the nation's high court heard only 87 cases.[54] In this section, we explain how the Court exerts its substantial influence through such a small number of cases and describe the practical process of how justices make decisions and write opinions. First, we discuss the process of Supreme Court appointments. Next, we consider two important rules of court procedure as well as the important players involved in the Court's activity. Finally, we consider the process of Supreme Court decision making itself.

The Politics of Supreme Court Appointments

> CONSTITUTION, ARTICLE II: "The President shall nominate . . . and by and with the Advice and Consent of the Senate, shall appoint . . . Judges of the Supreme Court."

The judicial system is supposed to be politically blind. Justice is expected to fall, like the rain, equally on rich and poor, Democrat and Republican, black, white, Latino, Asian, and Native American. Judges are appointed for life because they are expected to decide each case without any concern for the political consequences. Chief Justice Warren E. Burger went so far as to claim that "Judges . . . rule on the basis of law, not public opinion, and they should be totally indifferent to pressures of the times."[55]

Despite this ideal, however, the process by which justices are selected is a political one, and it has become more so in recent decades. Justices are nominated by the president, evaluated by the Senate Judiciary Committee, and confirmed by a vote of the full Senate. The Court's chief justice must also be nominated and confirmed in this manner, even if he or she is already a member of the Court. Because of this process, elected officials, as well as interest groups and the media, have a voice in choosing members of the Court. These players pay close attention to the electoral consequences of their actions, so elections inevitably affect nominations to the Court, and confirmation battles affect elections.

For at least the first half of the twentieth century, presidential nominations to the Supreme Court were confirmed by the Senate as a matter of course. Most nominees were approved quietly without even testifying before the Judiciary Committee. One of Harry Truman's nominees declined an explicit invitation to testify but was confirmed anyway.[56] Earl Warren, the Eisenhower appointee who would write the opinion in the landmark 1954 school desegregation decision, *Brown v. Board of Education* (see Chapter 17), was also confirmed without giving testimony.[57]

This long-time separation of Supreme Court nominations from political disputes owed a great deal to the efforts of William Howard Taft, the only person ever to serve both as president (1909–1913) and as chief justice of the Supreme Court (1921–1930). Before Taft, political factors openly affected confirmation decisions. In the nineteenth century, the Senate rejected a third of the presidents' nominees.[58] But Taft worked hard both as president and as chief justice to enhance the quality of nominees, minimize the significance of confirmation procedures, and elevate the prestige of the Court. He also made sure that the new Supreme Court building, eventually completed in 1935, was designed to resemble a Greek temple, so that Americans would respect their laws with the same reverence with which the ancient Greeks venerated their gods.

Taft was so successful that for nearly four decades, the Senate confirmed every nominee but one, most without significant dissent. But in recent years, the Senate has regained some of the power it had lost. Since 1955 every Supreme Court nominee has appeared before the judiciary committee, and since 1968 the Senate's propensity to reject presidential nominees has increased, as Table 15.2 indicates. One of the most celebrated cases involved Robert Bork, a Reagan nominee rejected by the Senate in 1987. A staunch conservative, Bork had produced a great many journal articles and

**You Are Appointing a
Supreme Court Justice**

TABLE 15.2

PRESIDENTIAL NOMINEES TO THE SUPREME COURT
NOT CONFIRMED BY THE SENATE, 1900–2002

• *Why have nominees faced more difficulties in the Senate in recent years?*

Nominee	Year	President	Main Reason for Rejection/Withdrawal
John Parker	1930	Hoover	Antilabor
Abraham Fortas (sitting justice nominated to be chief justice)	1968	Johnson	Too liberal; resigned from Court in 1969 over alleged financial abuses
Homer Thornberry	1968	Johnson	No vacancy when Fortas not confirmed for chief justice
Clement Haynesworth	1970	Nixon	Alleged financial abuses
G. Harrold Carswell	1970	Nixon	Racially conservative
Robert Bork	1987	Reagan	Controversial conservative record
Douglas Ginsburg	1987	Reagan	Smoked marijuana with students

borking
Politicizing the nomination process through an organized public campaign that portrays the nominee as a dangerous extremist.

speeches, which interest groups and Senate opponents used to attack him in a concerted national campaign.

Bork's rejection has, in fact, given American politics a new word, **borking,** which means politicizing the nomination process through an organized public campaign portraying the nominee as a dangerous extremist. Both Congress and the media now subject each nomination to scrutiny. (See the accompanying Election Connection.)

Not every Supreme Court nomination is subject to borking. If the same party controls both Congress and the presidency, borking becomes less likely. Thus, for example, Bill Clinton was able to appoint both Ruth Bader Ginsburg in 1993 and Stephen Breyer in 1994 without significant controversy. Even so, Clinton had to be careful to pick moderates rather than well-known liberals. Although Ginsburg was one of the first to develop a legal case against sex discrimination, as a lower-court judge she had taken moderate positions on other issues, making her acceptable to conservatives. Ginsburg was respectfully questioned by the Senate Judiciary Committee and confirmed by the overwhelming margin of 96 to 3.

Even if the Senate is controlled by the opposition, presidents may avoid borking by choosing a nominee whose views are unknown, a "stealth" strategy named after the bomber that cannot easily be detected by radar.[59] In 1990 President George H.W. Bush nominated stealth candidate David Souter, a New Hampshire state supreme court justice who had never written an opinion or treatise on any major constitutional question. Some legal scholars lamented such conflict avoidance, saying it made some brilliant intellects ineligible for consideration. But the bigger worry for presidents is that stealth candidates, however easy to appoint, can backfire upon taking office. Bush thought Souter would strengthen the conservative side of the Supreme Court, but the justice has proved to be one of the Court's most articulate liberals.

Although many critics think the increasing politicization of judicial appointments destroys "the public's belief in the fairness of those on the bench and . . . undermine[s] confidence in the Court,"[60] future trends seem clear. The United States is unlikely to go back to the older way of selecting Supreme Court justices. Modern technology and

ELECTION CONNECTION

The Thomas Nomination and the "Year of the Woman"

Thurgood Marshall, the Supreme Court's first black justice, once jested, "I have a lifetime appointment and I intend to serve it. I expect to die at 110, shot by a jealous husband." He nonetheless resigned in June 1991, reluctantly concluding that at age 83 he could no longer continue a civil rights struggle he had fought for decades. Asked by reporters why he was stepping down, an impatient Marshall declared, "I'm old! I'm getting old and coming apart."[a]

After days of public and media speculation about possible candidates, President George H.W. Bush nominated Clarence Thomas, an African American man who had brought a conservative definition of equal opportunity to his work as chair of the Equal Employment Opportunity Commission (EEOC). The Democrat-controlled Senate viewed the nominee with great suspicion, but at first it seemed that Thomas's political savvy would allow him to escape much criticism. He had not publicly expressed his views on controversial constitutional questions, thereby making it more difficult for his opponents to criticize his legal opinions.

But Thomas ended up being the center of a political uproar after all—as the result of testimony by a soft-spoken woman named Anita Hill. An attorney and former employee of Thomas's at the EEOC, Hill had left her job, she told a friend, because Thomas had sexually harassed her.

Judiciary Committee staffers approached Hill, who told them her story. Eventually, in hearings televised across the country, millions had an opportunity to hear Hill's account of the exact lewd and suggestive phrases she claimed to have heard from the mouth of a future justice of the Supreme Court. Thomas angrily denied all charges and called the Senate airing of the Hill allegations nothing less than a "high-tech lynching."[b]

For the fourteen Judiciary Committee senators forced to listen to the sensational testimony, it was a political nightmare. In some strange twist of politics, it was not just Thomas, but the Senate itself, that was on trial. When one senator explored Anita Hill's credibility through close cross-examination, women's groups attacked him for his aggressive style.

In the end, the Senate confirmed Thomas by a close vote. More Americans believed Thomas than Hill, and a clear majority continued to favor Thomas's confirmation.[c] The strong support Thomas received from African American voters was particularly significant.[d]

Although Thomas was confirmed, the process had a dramatic effect on the next election. The more women thought about the outcome, the more unhappy they became. The percentage of women who believed Thomas had harassed Hill increased from 27 to 51 percent over the course of the coming year.[e] The number of women elected to the House of Representatives increased by almost 70 percent in 1992, from 28 to 47, and four new women were elected to the Senate. In the presidential election, Bush's support among women was 5 percentage points less than his support among men, enough of a difference to cost Bush the election.[f] It was the costliest nomination to the Supreme Court a president had ever made.

- *Why did African Americans support Thomas, a conservative?*

- *Why do you think women's opinions about Thomas grew more negative over time?*

- *Why were members of the Senate caught by surprise by the intensity of feeling among women about the issue of sexual harassment?*

[a]Ruth Marcus, "Plain-Spoken Marshall Spars with Reporters," *Washington Post*, June 29, 1991, p. A1.
[b]Paul Simon, Advice and Consent (Washington, D.C.: National Press Books, 1992), chaps. 5–6.
[c]Ibid., p. 122.
[d]Ibid., p. 122.
[e]David Brock, *The Real Anita Hill: The Untold Story* (New York: Free Press, 1993), p. 66.
[f]Gerald Pomper, "The Presidential Election," in Gerald M. Pomper, et al., *The Election of 1992: Reports and Interpretations* (Chatham, NJ: Chatham House, 1993), p. 138.

the media ensure that presidents will choose justices with an eye to potential public controversies.

Stare Decisis

A small number of Supreme Court decisions can have a far-ranging impact because lower federal and state courts are expected to follow the principle of **stare decisis.** The phrase is Latin for "let the decision stand." This is to say that in deciding cases, judges should adhere to **precedents,** or prior decisions, as well as to the logic of

stare decisis
In court rulings, reliance on consistency with precedents. See also *precedent.*

precedent
Previous court decision or ruling applicable to a particular case.

their written opinions. Jonathan Swift used his biting satire to define *stare decisis* somewhat differently:

> Whatever has been done before may legally be done again; and therefore [judges] take special care to record all the decisions formerly made against common justice and the general reason of mankind. These, under the name of precedents, they produce as authorities, to justify the most iniquitous of opinions.[61]

Despite Swift's lampoon, *stare decisis* is a powerful judicial principle that can be ignored only at risk to the stability of the legal system. Only if court decisions are consistent with one another over time can a country live under a rule of law, where citizens know what it is that they are expected to obey. In the words of one judge, "We cannot meddle with a prior decision [unless it] strikes us as wrong with the force of a five-week-old unrefrigerated dead fish."[62]

When reaching a decision that seems contrary to a prior decision, courts try to find a **legal distinction** between the case at hand and earlier court decisions, usually by emphasizing that the facts of the current case differ. The process of drawing a legal distinction can sometimes become the refined art of perceiving a distinction when others can see no difference. As an attorney once bragged, "Law school taught me one thing: how to take two situations that are exactly the same and show how they are different."[63] If the legal distinctions drawn by a lower court seem unconvincing to the losing side, it may **appeal** the decision to the next-higher court. If the higher court thinks the lower court has strayed too far from legal precedents, it may decide on a **reversal,** or overturning, of the lower court's decision.

Certs

At one time the Supreme Court was required by law to review many appeals, but the workload became so excessive that in 1925 Congress gave the Court the power to refuse to review almost any case it did not want to consider. Today nearly all cases argued before the Court arrive upon the grant of what is known as a **cert** by court insiders. Cert is an abbreviation of the Latin phrase **writ of *certiorari,*** which means "to be informed of." When a cert is granted, it means the Court has agreed to consider the case.[64] The Court rejects most cert petitions because it is only practical to consider a fraction of the 8000 to 9000 cases appealed to it each year.[65] As one clerk for a Supreme Court justice put it, "You almost get to hate the guy who brings the cert petitions around. He is really a nice guy, but he gets abuse all the time."[66]

The number of certs granted by the Supreme Court has fallen markedly in recent years. In the 1970s the Supreme Court decided as many as 400 cases annually.[67] But as we have noted, only 87 cases were decided in the 2003 term. Certs are granted only for those cases that raise the most important legal or constitutional issues. As the old saying goes, the Supreme Court cares less about justice than about the law. In the words of one chief justice,

> The Supreme Court is not, and never has been, primarily concerned with the correction of errors in lower court decisions. . . . To remain effective the Supreme Court must continue to decide only those cases which present questions whose reso-

---

legal distinction
The legal difference between a case at hand and previous cases decided by the courts.

appeal
The procedure whereby the losing side asks a higher court to overturn a lower-court decision.

reversal
The overturning of a lower-court decision by an appeals court or the Supreme Court.

cert
See writ of *certiorari.*

writ of *certiorari* (cert)
A document issued by the Supreme Court indicating that the Court will review a decision made by a lower court.

lution will have immediate importance far beyond the particular facts and parties involved."[68]

To issue a cert requires the vote of four justices. The mere fact that an issue is controversial does not necessarily mean the Court will grant a cert. The justices may decide to let the issue percolate in the lower courts for a few years until the matter is ripe for decision.

The case for cert is strongest if two lower courts have reached opposite conclusions on cases in which the facts seem virtually identical. In such cases, the Supreme Court feels a responsibility to clarify the law so that its effect is uniform throughout the United States. In 1998, for example, the Wisconsin Supreme Court upheld a state law establishing a school voucher program in Milwaukee. Low-income families could receive state money and use it to attend a private school of their choice. Although many religious schools participated in the program, the Wisconsin court ruled that the law did not violate the constitutional clause prohibiting the establishment of religion (see Chapter 16). When a similar law was passed by the Ohio legislature for low-income families in Cleveland, a federal appeals court ruled that it unconstitutionally established religion. Because two lower courts had decided the same issue in contrary ways, the Supreme Court granted a cert and heard the Ohio case in early 2002. That summer, the Court finally decided the issue. In a landmark ruling, a slim majority found that vouchers did not violate the establishment clause because parents could decide whether the money went to religious institutions. Such a program of "true private choice," said Chief Justice Rehnquist, passed the constitutional test.[69]

The Role of the Chief Justice

The Supreme Court consists of eight **associate justices** and the chief justice, who heads the Court and is responsible for organizing its work. Although the chief justice has only one vote and many of the chief's tasks are of a ceremonial or housekeeping nature, certain responsibilities give the office added influence. For one thing, the chief justice, if voting with the majority, assigns the responsibility for writing the majority opinion. Because the Court's opinion is often as important as the actual decision, this assignment power can have far-reaching consequences; some cases are "destined for the history books, whereas others are, in [former Justice Lewis] Powell's term, 'dogs.'" Powell's biographer tells us that Warren Burger, not the most popular of chief justices, was suspected by his colleagues of voting with the majority, even when privately opposed, simply in order to exercise his assignment power.[70]

Some chief justices have used their position to facilitate compromise and achieve consensus. In the case of *Brown v. Board of Education of Topeka, Kansas* (1954), the landmark decision desegregating schools, Chief Justice Earl Warren was able to win the support of two judges who were initially inclined to dissent. To achieve the unanimity he thought crucial, Warren agreed to write a less-than-sweeping opinion. *Brown* banned segregation in schools but not in other public places, and it specified delay in the implementation of the ruling. Warren was willing to make these compromises because he thought that only a unanimous Court could order such a major social change—which at the time ran contrary to strongly held opinions of many southern whites.[71]

associate justice
One of the eight justices of the Supreme Court who are not the chief justice.

Timeline

The Chief Justice of the United States

Solicitor General Ted Olson
The solicitor general serves as the federal government's voice in many Supreme Court proceedings.
• *Why is the solicitor general known as the "tenth justice"?*

solicitor general
Government official responsible for presenting before the courts the position of the presidential administration.

law clerk
Young, influential aide to a Supreme Court justice.

You Are a Clerk to Supreme Court Justice Judith Ceray

The Role of the Solicitor General

A powerful figure who regularly appears before the Supreme Court is the **solicitor general,** the government official responsible for presenting before the Court the position of the presidential administration. Involvement of the solicitor general is a signal that the president and the attorney general have strong views on the subject, which enhances its visibility and political significance. Because the Court pays close attention to the position of the solicitor general, the person who holds this office is sometimes referred to as "the tenth justice." About 60 percent of the solicitor general's cert petitions are accepted by the Court.[72]

Solicitors general are employees of the Justice Department and as such report to the attorney general. However, they are always carefully selected by the president for their legal skills and are "in fact what the Attorney General is in name—the chief legal officer of the United States government as far as the courts are concerned."[73] The solicitor general presents the case for the government whenever it is party to a suit. In other important cases, the solicitor general may submit an *amicus curiae* brief—literally, a brief submitted by a "friend of the court." (*Amicus curiae* briefs can also be submitted by others who wish to inform the court of a legal issue presented by a particular case.) When the office of the solicitor general files an *amicus curiae* brief, it finds itself on the winning side approximately three-quarters of the time, a batting average envied by even the most successful private attorneys.[74] Several solicitors general, including William Howard Taft and Thurgood Marshall, have gone on to become Supreme Court justices themselves.[75]

The Role of Clerks

Much of the day-to-day work within the Supreme Court building is performed by **law clerks**—young, influential aides hired by each of the justices. Recently out of law school, most will have spent a year as a clerk with a lower court before being asked to help a Supreme Court justice. Each justice has between two and four law clerks.[76] Not only do clerks initially review certs, but they also draft many opinions. As a result, says one critic, "the standard opinion style has become that of the student-run [law] reviews: colorless, prolix, platitudinous, always error on the side of inclusion, full of lengthy citations and footnotes—and above all dull."[77] After one year of service to the Court at comparatively low salaries, law clerks move on to illustrious careers in the private sector, in legal academia, or perhaps on the bench. Three current justices (Rehnquist, Stevens, and Breyer) themselves once served as Supreme Court clerks.

Law clerks have become so important to the Court's routine that some observers claim that a junior Supreme Court of bright but unseasoned attorneys, unconfirmed by the Senate or anybody else, is the true "Supreme Court" of today. Others reply that well-trained graduates of the country's most prestigious law schools may be better judges than aging titans who refuse to leave office well beyond the age of normal retirement. The truth probably lies between these two extremes: The brilliance of the young clerks and the political and legal experience of the justices are probably better in combination than either would be without the other.[78] As Chief Justice Rehnquist has said of the clerk system, "The Justice may retain for himself control not merely of the outcome of the case, but the explanation for the outcome, and I do not believe this practice sacrifices either."[79]

Supreme Court Decision Making

Before reaching its decisions, the Supreme Court considers **briefs,** written legal arguments submitted by the opposing sides. (Unfortunately for judges, briefs are often anything but brief.) The justices then listen to oral arguments from attorneys on both sides in a plenary session—one attended by all justices—the chief justice presiding. During the half-hour allotted to each side to present its case, attorneys often find themselves interrupted by searching questions from the bench. Former law professor Antonin Scalia is especially well known for his willingness to turn the plenary session into a classroom seminar. Yet it is not always clear how closely the justices attend to the responses. As Chief Justice John Marshall said many years ago, "The acme of judicial distinction means the ability to look a lawyer straight in the eye for two hours and not hear a damned word he says."[80]

After hearing the oral argument, the justices usually reach a preliminary decision the same week in a private conference presided over by the chief justice. There are "three levels of elbow room about the conference table." The most ample is that for the chief justice and the senior associate justice, who sit at opposite ends. The next best is grabbed by the three most senior justices sitting on one side, leaving the four most junior crowded together across from them. No outsiders, not even a secretary, are permitted to attend. The only record consists of handwritten notes taken by individual justices.

From the outside, it may appear that the private conferences are opportunities for great minds to gather and discuss fundamental legal questions. But in most instances, the justices have already discussed the case with their law clerks and enter the conference room with their intentions fixed. The justices express their views and preliminary votes in order of seniority, beginning with the chief justice.[81] If the chief justice is in the minority, the writing of the opinion is assigned by the senior associate justice in the majority.[82]

The justice assigned the responsibility for preparing the court opinion circulates a draft version among the other eight. Revisions are then made in light of comments received from the other justices. On rare occasions, the justice writing the opinion has "lost a court"—that is, one or more justices who voted with the majority at the first conference have changed their minds. To keep a majority, the justice writing the opinion may produce a bland opinion that gives little guidance to lower-court justices. In the 1993 sexual harassment case *Harris v. Forklift Systems,* for example, the majority hardly created any precedent at all, saying only that courts should look at the "totality of the circumstances" in order to decide whether harassment in the workplace had occurred.[83]

Justices who vote against the majority may prepare a **dissenting opinion** that explains their disagreement. **Concurring opinions** may be written by those members of the majority who agree with the basic decision but disagree with some aspect of the reasoning included in the majority opinion or who wish to elaborate by raising further considerations. Two hundred years ago, when John Marshall was chief justice, the court

brief
Written arguments presented to a court by lawyers on behalf of clients.

dissenting opinion
Written opinion presenting the reasoning of judges who vote against the majority.

concurring opinion
A written opinion prepared by judges who vote with the majority but who wish either to disagree with or to elaborate on some aspect of the majority opinion.

The Justices of the Supreme Court
In this composite, the justices of the Supreme Court are pictured from left to right according to their judicial philosophies. On the left are John Paul Stevens, David Souter, Ruth Bader Ginsburg, and Stephen Breyer. In the middle are Sandra Day O'Connor and Anthony Kennedy. To the right are Chief Justice William H. Rehnquist, Antonin Scalia, and Clarence Thomas.

• *When the next justice is appointed, where do you think the new justice's picture will be positioned?*

was usually unanimous, and the chief justice wrote most opinions. Today, the Court is seldom unanimous in its judgments, and quite apart from the dissenting opinions, concurring opinions are filed often enough that it is sometimes difficult to ascertain exactly what the majority has decided. In the case of *Bush v. Gore,* the Court issued an unsigned "majority" opinion, a concurring opinion signed by three justices, and four separate dissenting opinions, each signed by a single justice. Many observers found both the concurring opinion and some of the dissenting opinions more persuasive than the unsigned majority opinion. Apparently it was difficult to write a cogent opinion when the time available was extremely limited, divisions within the Court were deep, and compromises had to be reached to obtain the signatures of a majority.

Although the proliferation of dissenting and concurring opinions has caused considerable confusion about overall Supreme Court rulings, these opinions themselves often have a clearer and more convincing style than majority opinions—in part because they are signed by only one or two justices, making compromise language unnecessary. In *Harris v. Forklift Systems,* the sexual harassment case mentioned above, Justice Ginsburg, although she agreed with the decision, wrote a crisp concurring opinion that proposed a simple, straightforward standard for ascertaining whether harassment had occurred: Harassment, she wrote, exists whenever discriminatory conduct makes it more difficult for a person to perform well at a job. Convincingly written concurring and dissenting opinions, such as Ginsburg's, sometimes become even more influential than majority opinions.

remand
To send a case to a lower court to determine the best way of implementing the higher court's decision.

Once the Court reaches a decision, it usually sends, or **remands,** the case to a lower court for implementation. Because the Supreme Court regards itself as responsible for establishing general principles and an overall framework, it seldom becomes involved in the detailed resolution of particular cases. This practice leaves a great deal of legal responsibility in the hands of lower courts.

Voting on the Supreme Court

Justices of the Court fall into quite predictable voting blocs. An exception to this pattern, Justice John Stevens, has "long been considered a maverick" who has often "confound[ed] the categorizers."[84] But the remainder of the judges currently serving on the Supreme Court can be divided into three fairly well-defined blocs.

The more liberal justices, consisting of Souter and the two Clinton appointees, Ruth Bader Ginsburg and Stephen Breyer, favor a certain amount of **judicial activism**—a doctrine that says that the principle of *stare decisis* should sometimes be sacrificed in order to adapt the Constitution to changing conditions. Ginsburg and Breyer contend that too rigid an application of the principle of *stare decisis* would place the country in a straitjacket and render it unable to adapt. Judicial activists also see the Court as a mechanism for preserving minority rights and fundamental freedoms that may be trampled upon by electoral majorities.

A second bloc of three conservative **restorationists,** including Thomas, Scalia, and Rehnquist, believe in overturning earlier liberal decisions. They think the only way the original meaning of the Constitution can be restored is by ignoring the doctrine of *stare decisis* until earlier liberal decisions have been reversed. For example, they favor reversing *Roe v. Wade,* the decision that declared laws forbidding abortion unconstitutional.

The moderates who hold crucial swing votes on the Court, Justices O'Connor and Kennedy, favor **judicial restraint,** a doctrine that says that courts should, if at all possible, avoid overturning prior court decisions. If the law is to be changed, it should be changed not by the courts but by the people's elected representatives. O'Connor and Kennedy are willing to uphold prior decisions even when they do not necessarily agree with them. Although they may not agree that *Roe v. Wade* was a correct decision, these justices have expressed a reluctance to reverse it.

Most of the time, justices vote along lines anticipated by those who nominated and confirmed them. Both statements made in testimony before Congress and other information available at the time the justice was confirmed generally provide a clear indication of the justice's future voting pattern. According to one study, information about the political views of Supreme Court justices at the time they were being confirmed by the Senate allows one to predict correctly the justices' decisions in civil liberties cases over 60 percent of the time.[85] That the future behavior of the typical justice is predictable may suggest that the justices do not decide each case on its facts and merits. But predictability does allow elected officials—both presidents and senators—to influence the future direction of the Supreme Court, thereby maintaining some degree of popular control of the courts.

Not every prediction of future behavior is correct, however. The justice who most surprised those who favored his selection was Harry Blackmun, thought to be a judicial conservative. Yet Blackmun wrote the famous opinion in *Roe v. Wade* declaring state laws forbidding abortion unconstitutional. Blackmun himself once said, "Having been appointed by a Republican president and being accused now of being a flaming liberal on the court, the Republicans think I'm a traitor, I guess, and the Democrats don't trust me. And so I twist in the wind . . . beholden to no one, and that's just exactly where I want to be."[86]

judicial activism
Doctrine that says the principle of *stare decisis* should sometimes be sacrificed in order to adapt the Constitution to changing conditions.

restorationist
Judge who thinks that the only way the original meaning of the Constitution can be restored is by ignoring the doctrine of *stare decisis* until liberal decisions have been reversed.

judicial restraint
Doctrine that says courts should, if at all possible, avoid overturning a prior court decision.

Checks on Court Power

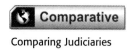

Comparing Judiciaries

Although the judicial system is more independent and powerful in the United States than in many countries, the consequences of court decisions can be limited by other political actors. As political scientist Jack Peltason has put it, "Judicial decision making is one stage, not the only nor necessarily the final one.[87] Alexander Hamilton, writing in the *Federalist Papers,* explained why this was to be expected under the Constitution:

> The judiciary will always be the least dangerous to the political rights of the Constitution. The executive not only dispenses honors but holds the sword of the community. The legislature not only commands the purse, but prescribes the rules. The judiciary, on the contrary, has no influence over either the sword or the purse. It may truly be said to have neither *force* nor *will,* but merely judgment.[88]

Other branches of government can alter or circumscribe court decisions in three important ways: by constitutional amendment, by statutory revision, and by nonimplementation.

Constitutional Amendment

The power to amend the Constitution is the formal constitutional check on the Supreme Court's power of judicial review. But this constitutional check has been used on only a few occasions. The Eleventh Amendment overturned an early Court decision that gave citizens of one state the ability to sue another state. The Sixteenth Amendment allowing an income tax was prompted by a Court decision that seemed to prohibit one. Many amendments under consideration by Congress today have been generated by court decisions, including proposed amendments to ban abortions, allow school prayer, and prohibit gay marriages. For amendments to pass, supporters must ordinarily win a two-thirds vote in Congress and the backing of three-quarters of the states. In practice, the complexities of the amendment process make it the weakest check on court power.

Statutory Revision

Congress can reverse court decisions without resorting to a constitutional amendment if the court decision involves only statutory interpretation. In such cases, Congress can simply pass a clarifying law that reverses a court interpretation of earlier legislation. In the case of *Wards Cove Packing Co. v. Atonio,* for example, the Supreme Court gave a narrow interpretation to a congressional law banning race and gender discrimination. The Court said that Congress intended that women and minorities bringing a discrimination complaint bear the burden of proof, a difficult assignment in these kinds of cases. Under pressure from women's groups and civil rights organizations, Congress responded in 1991 by passing a law that said the burden of proof had to be borne by the business, thereby reversing the Supreme Court decision.

Although passing new legislation is much easier than amending the Constitution, it may still be difficult and is ineffective if the Court decision involves constitutional interpretation.

Nonimplementation

Court decisions can also be checked simply by being ignored. When told of a Supreme Court decision he did not like, President Andrew Jackson reportedly replied, "Justice Marshall has made his decision, now let him enforce it."[89] Since Jackson's day, the prestige and authority of the Supreme Court has become deeply entrenched in American life. Outright refusal to obey a Supreme Court decision is now most unlikely. Even in the extraordinary *Bush v. Gore* controversy, the parties to the case readily obeyed the Court's decisions. When the Court ordered vote counters in Florida to stop counting ballots, it took less than an hour for ballot counting to come to a halt—despite the emotional intensity that had been aroused by the dispute. By contrast, earlier in the dispute, ballot counting in one Democratic-controlled county had continued for several hours after a deadline had been imposed by Florida's Republican secretary of state, even though her authority to set deadlines was written into state law.

Still, the power of courts to implement their decisions is not unlimited. State and local governments may mount strong resistance to lower-court decisions. After the Supreme Court declared Bible reading in public schools unconstitutional, the practice in most Tennessee school districts continued unchanged. As one school board attorney explained, "My personal conviction is that the Supreme Court decisions are correct, and I so told the Board and Superintendent, but I saw no reason to create controversy. If the Board had made public a decision abolishing devotional exercises, there would have been public outcry."[90]

To ensure implementation of judicial orders, courts sometimes appoint a **receiver,** an official who has the authority to see that judicial orders are carried out. For example, in 1996 a Massachusetts judge found the State Department of Mental Retardation guilty of willfully abusing its authority over a school that served severely disabled students. Because the state agency had a long history of misusing its authority over this school, the judge, to prevent future abuse, replaced state supervision of the school with that of a court-appointed receiver.

But even the monitoring power of the courts can be checked by elected officials. For two decades, the Correction Department of the city of New York had been overseen by a court monitor who enforced judicial orders ensuring respect for the civil rights of prisoners. Judge Harold Baer, Jr., reluctantly withdrew the monitor in 1995 after Congress and the president, concerned that the rights of the guilty were taking precedence over the rights of victims, enacted a law limiting court authority in such matters. "Although the court's [my] concerns with this new legislation are myriad," Judge Baer wrote, "I am constrained under the law to uphold it."[91]

receiver
Court official who has the authority to see that judicial orders are carried out.

Litigation as a Political Strategy

The courts have increasingly been used by interest groups to place issues on the political agenda, particularly when elected officials have not responded to group demands. This strategy was first used successfully by civil rights groups, a topic discussed in detail in Chapter 17. But the technique has since spread and become a common political phenomenon.[92] This development is fully consistent with Alexis de Tocqueville's observation over a century and a half ago that "there is hardly a political question in the United States which does not sooner or later turn into a judicial one."[93]

Disabled Americans owe many of their current legal rights in the United States to an extraordinarily successful use of litigation as a political strategy. As late as 1970, school officials told many parents of disabled children that their sons and daughters were not qualified to attend public school. Challenging such denial of equal educational opportunity, advocacy groups won, in 1972, two federal court rulings that gave the disabled a right to an "appropriate education." Anticipating further litigation, many school officials felt that a federal law might clarify the situation. In response, Congress within two years passed a law said to be the "most significant child welfare legislation" of the decade.[94]

class action suit
Suit brought on behalf of all individuals in a particular category, whether or not they are actually participating in the suit.

To advance an issue, advocacy groups often file a **class action suit** on behalf of all individuals in a particular category, whether or not they are actually participating in the suit. For example, in the late 1990s, groups of former smokers in several states filed class action suits against the major tobacco companies for lying to consumers about the harms caused by smoking. In the first such case to reach a verdict favorable to plaintiffs, a jury ordered the five major tobacco companies to pay millions of dollars in damages to up to 500,000 ill Florida smokers.[95] In 2002, investors and former employees sued the collapsed energy conglomerate Enron, claiming that the company had bilked them out of billions of dollars in stock and pensions.[96]

Attorneys have been accused of abusing their power to file class action suits by filing problematic claims and then reaching settlements that mainly benefit lawyers, not clients. A class action suit filed against the city of Chicago in 2001 on behalf of 5000 homeless people who claimed to have been harmed by the city's anti-begging law resulted in an average payment of less than $20 per plaintiff, and $375,000 for the lawyers.[97] But proponents justify class action suits on the grounds that often a legal issue affects many people in essentially the same way, and it would be costly and complicated for each member of the class to bring a separate individual suit in order to secure relief.

Chapter Summary

The courts are the branch of government most removed from political influences. Federal judges are appointed for life. They are expected only to apply the law, not to revise it. Constrained by the principle of *stare decisis,* they are expected to rely on legal precedents when reaching their decisions. They have been accused of sometimes using the power of judicial review to frustrate the popular will. In the famous *Dred Scott* and *Schechter Poultry* cases, the Supreme Court may well have done so.

Yet the courts are not immune to electoral pressures. Although many important political issues eventually reach the Supreme Court, the day-to-day work of the judiciary is carried out by state and lower federal court judges, who interpret the civil and criminal code. Many state judges and district attorneys are elected officials, and political factors also influence the operation of the lower courts in many other ways.

When justices are selected for the Supreme Court, their political and judicial philosophies are closely evaluated by both the president and Congress. Once appointed, most Supreme Court justices decide cases in ways that are consistent with views they were known to have at the time of their selection. Most of the time, court decisions are broadly responsive to contemporary political currents. If court decisions challenge deep-seated political views, they may be modified by new legislation, frustrated by nonimplementation, or even reversed by constitutional amendment.

The judicial system may not work perfectly, but it is probably better than most alternatives. If the law were more removed from politics, the law would control people instead of the reverse. But if federal judges did not have the distance from politics that lifetime appointment gives many of them, justice could be perverted to narrow, partisan ends.

Key Terms

appeal, p. 416

associate justice, p. 417

borking, p. 414

brief, p. 419

cert, p. 416

chief justice, p. 400

circuit court of appeals, p. 408

civil code, p. 397

class action suit, p. 424

concurring opinion, p. 419

criminal code, p. 397

defendant, p. 397

dissenting opinion, p. 419

district attorney, p. 399

double jeopardy, p. 411

federal district courts, p. 407

judicial activism, p. 421

judicial restraint, p. 421

judicial review, p. 400

law clerk, p. 418

legal distinction, p. 416

living-constitution theory, p. 402

Marbury v. Madison, p. 400

McCulloch v. Maryland, p. 410

opinion, p. 397

original-intent theory, p. 401

plain-meaning-of-the-text theory, p. 402

plaintiff, p. 397

plenary session, p. 408

precedent, p. 415

receiver, p. 423

remand, p. 420

restorationist, p. 421

reversal, p. 416

senatorial courtesy, p. 408

solicitor general, p. 418

stare decisis, p. 415

statutory interpretation, p. 406

U.S. attorney, p. 410

writ of *certiorari* (cert), p. 416

Suggested Readings

Of General Interest

Carp, Robert A., and Ronald Stidham, *The Federal Courts,* 4th ed. Washington, DC: CQ Press, 2001. Lucid description of the federal court system and its political context.

McCloskey, Robert G. *The American Supreme Court,* 3rd ed. Revised by Sanford Levison. Chicago: University of Chicago Press, 2000. Excellent analysis that shows the close connection between public opinion and court decisions.

Pritchett, C. Herman. *The American Constitution.* New York: McGraw-Hill, 1959. Dated, but still authoritative, account of constitutional issues.

Focused Studies

Agresto, John. *The Supreme Court and Constitutional Democracy.* Ithaca, NY: Cornell University Press, 1984. Makes a powerful case against judicial review.

Bork, Robert. *The Tempting of America.* New York: Free Press, 1990. Bork's defense of his legal position and his interpretation of the Senate confirmation process.

Bronner, Ethan. *Battle for Justice: How the Bork Nomination Shook America.* New York: Norton, 1989. Fascinating case study of the Senate refusal to confirm Robert Bork's nomination to the Supreme Court.

Jeffries, John C., Jr., *Justice Lewis F. Powell, Jr.: A Biography.* New York: Scribner, 1994. Superb biography by Powell's law clerk that provides inside information on the thinking that went into some of the most important Supreme Court decisions.

Melnick, R. Shep. *Between the Lines: Interpreting Welfare Rights.* Washington, DC: The Brookings Institution, 1994. Insightful analysis of the Court's role in the interpretation and elaboration of statutory law.

Murphy, Walter F. *Elements of Judicial Strategy.* Chicago: University of Chicago Press, 1964. A political analysis of the courts.

O'Brien, David M., Editor. *Judges on Judging: Views from the Bench,* 2nd Edition. Washington, DC: CQ Press, 2004. A fine selection of writings from Supreme Court justices and other judges.

Perry, H. W., Jr. *Deciding to Decide: Agenda Setting in the United States Supreme Court.* Cambridge, MA: Harvard University Press, 1991. Comprehensive explanation of the process by which the Supreme Court decides whether to review a case.

Simon, James F. *The Center Holds: The Power Struggle Inside the Rehnquist Court.* New York: Simon & Schuster, 1995. Describes the recent split between conservative and moderate justices.

On the Web

www.supremecourtus.gov

The official Web site of the U.S. Supreme Court contains information on the Court's docket, the text of recent opinions, the rules of the Court, and links to related Web sites. It also posts copies of Chief Justice Rehnquist's annual report on the federal judiciary.

www.usdoj.gov/osg/

Sometimes called "the tenth justice," the solicitor general participates in about two-thirds of Supreme Court cases. The Solicitor General's Office in the U.S. Department of Justice offers copies of briefs it has filed in federal court.

www.fjc.gov

In 1967 Congress created the Federal Judicial Center to produce research aimed at improving the administration of the judicial branch. Its reports, which are available online, cover general legal topics, such as antitrust law, as well as practical and institutional questions, such as media in the courtroom, caseloads, and the relationship between state and federal courts.

www.law.cornell.edu

The Legal Information Institute at Cornell Law School archives information on federal and state laws, and rules of civil and criminal procedure, and also provides a searchable database of Supreme Court decisions.

www.uscourts.gov

There is more to the federal court system than the Supreme Court. The Federal Judiciary homepage provides a concise guide to the federal court system, a regular newsletter, and annual reports on the state of the judiciary written by Chief Justice William Rehnquist.

http://www.ncsconline.org/

The National Center for State Courts showcases statistical information on the caseload of state court systems, as well as links to state-level legal associations.

VOICES

OF THE PERMANENT CAMPAIGN

The Politics of the New Department of Homeland Security

"This is going to be a tough battle, because we're going to be stepping on some people's toes. I understand that. You see, when you take power away from [people] in Washington, it tends to make them nervous."

—George W. Bush, remarks in Des Moines, Iowa, June 7, 2002

THE ISSUE

Is it impossible for government to reorganize itself or can public opinion push vested interests to one side?

Background

After the 9/11 tragedy, President George W. Bush appointed Tom Ridge as his White House homeland security adviser. But Ridge had difficulty building a coordinated system to combat potential terrorist attacks because he was only a member of the president's staff and did not run any department of the government.

After nine months of struggling to manage a coordinated homeland security effort from the White House, Bush and Ridge concluded that a new cabinet department had to be created (see the section "Organizing for Homeland Security" in Chapter 14). The administration realized that creating the department would be a challenge. The last time the United States had undergone a significant national security reorganization was in the late 1940s, after what President Truman called a "long hard battle" that lasted at least four years.[1]

Some present-day political scientists believe that in the United States, this kind of major governmental change is prohibitively difficult. Entrenched bureaucracies, allied with interest groups and key congressional committee members, have made it all but impossible to enact comprehensive changes.[2]

The battle over creating a new department of homeland security in 2002 provides proof that major change in the structure of government *can* occur, at least under certain circumstances.

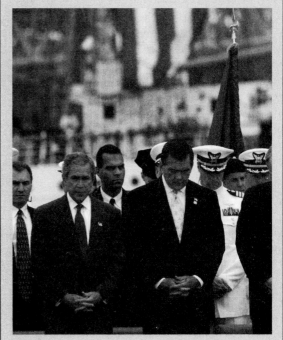

White House Homeland Security Adviser Tom Ridge with President Bush

• *Why did President Bush choose to exclude the cabinet from the process of drafting a plan for the new Homeland Security Department?*

The Administration's (Strategic) Advantages

The Plan for a New Department Was Drafted in Secret

Goal: Prevent interest groups and bureaucratic agencies from mustering opposition.

In late 2001 and again in April 2002, White House Homeland Security Adviser Tom Ridge circulated modest proposals for consolidating several executive-branch organizations responsible for homeland security. Agencies and interest

Organization of the Department of Homeland Security

FIGURE 1

Much Simpler, Right?

The picture on the right depicts the old organizational structure of agencies responsible for homeland defense. On the left is the Bush administration's original proposal for the structure of a new department.

• *Why isn't the FBI part of the new department?*

groups vigorously objected to these proposals in what the White House candidly called "obvious examples of bureaucratic inertia."[3]

Drawing a lesson from these aborted attempts at reform, in late April 2002 Bush directed four trusted aides to begin work on a proposal for a new department. "It's going to have to be something big or nothing at all," the president reportedly said.[4] Meeting secretly in an underground White House office, these four officials—Ridge, Chief of Staff Andrew Card, Office of Management and Budget Director Mitchell Daniels, and White House Counsel Alberto Gonzales—worked for six weeks to draft a plan. No one in Congress knew about the pending administration proposal and even Bush's cabinet was in the dark.[5]

As a result of this secrecy, instead of being nibbled to death by agency and interest-group complaints, Bush's proposal garnered immediate acclaim. Those in Congress who had been drafting less ambitious legislation to streamline homeland secu-

rity agencies swiftly embraced the Bush plan. "All of us agree the president's plan is better than what we have been working on," said one House member.[6]

The Plan for the New Department Incorporated Agencies That Were More Mobile and Left Others Alone

Goal: Avoid antagonizing the most powerful bureaucratic agencies.

The Bush plan called for the creation of a huge new agency, with 169,000 employees and a budget of $37.5 billion (see Figure 1). In terms of personnel, it would be the third largest department, after Defense and Veterans Affairs. But Bush's team selected the agencies to incorporate into the department very carefully. Those that were easier to shift became part of the final proposal; others were left alone.

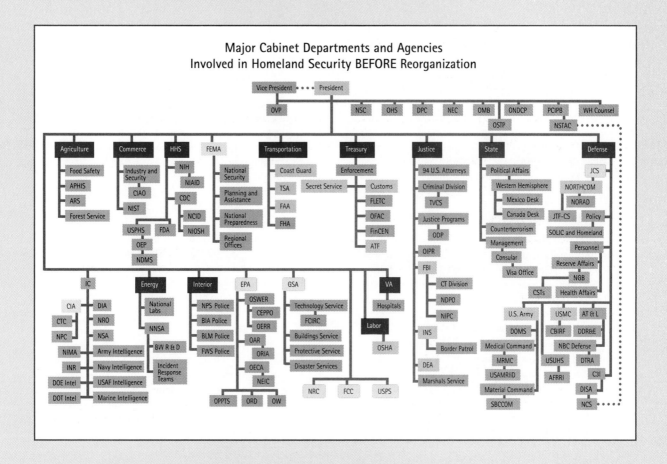

Major Cabinet Departments and Agencies Involved in Homeland Security BEFORE Reorganization

The administration chose to place in the new department the Federal Emergency Management Agency (FEMA), the Coast Guard, and the Transportation Security Administration—in part because these bureaucracies had less clout. FEMA, an independent entity, had only 2500 employees, many of whom were assigned to the agency's ten regional offices, far from Washington power centers. The Coast Guard was bigger, with 35,000 active duty personnel, but it had been moved among cabinet departments before. The Transportation Security Administration, although large, was brand new—it had been created in November 2001 to restructure airport security systems—so it had had little time to sink deep roots within the Department of Transportation.

Contrast these agencies with one other organization that many thought should have been included in the Bush proposal but was not: the Federal Bureau of Investigation (FBI). With a workforce of 27,000, a distinctive agency culture, and a history in the Justice Department that stretches back to 1908, the FBI would have been hard to change. According to one aide, if they were threatened Bureau officials would "throw a major fit and their friends in Congress would run us out of town for even proposing it."[7] Accordingly, despite its key role in investigating terrorists in the United States, the Bush team decided that "the organizational integrity of the FBI needs to be maintained."[8]

Obstacles to the Administration Plan

The Congressional Committee System

When Bush announced his plan, he pointed out that nearly 90 congressional committees and subcommittees had jurisdiction over some aspect of homeland security. The prospect of a brand new department raised the possibility that Congress would have to restructure its oversight committees—and the Bush administration urged legislators to do just that.[9] But existing committees resisted any organizational changes that would take power away from them (see the section "The Committee System" in Chapter 12). Congressman James Oberstar, top Democrat on the House Transportation and Infrastructure Committee, pointedly said, "Our committee is going to have to fight like hell to make sure that there's no Homeland Security Committee created."[10] Oberstar and committee chairman Don Young, a Republican, worried that the panel would lose its power to oversee the Coast Guard and the Transportation Security Administration. "Hell hath no fury like a committee chairman whose jurisdiction has been taken away," warned Republican Senator Robert Bennett.[11]

To avoid facing such fury, the new department's proponents postponed questions of committee jurisdiction until after Congress passed legislation creating the new department. The

Senate chose to debate the Bush proposal on the chamber floor rather than letting committees get their hooks into the plan, and House leaders created a temporary special committee, composed of House leaders, to consider the matter.

After the creation of the new department, the House gave jurisdiction over most homeland security matters to a select committee on homeland security, while the Senate chose to divide jurisdiction among existing committees. Still, in 2004 the report of the special commission appointed to investigate 9-11 called the congressional committee system "dysfunctional" and recommended major changes.[12]

The Public Employee Unions

The White House plan to create the Department of Homeland Security included a seemingly obscure provision that would allow the department to bypass ordinary civil service rules and use a merit-based management and promotion system. Homeland Security Adviser Tom Ridge argued that this policy was necessary to create a "motivated, high-performance, and accountable workforce."[13] But many of the 169,000 government workers who stood to be transferred into the new agency disagreed, and their allies in Congress protested. The job security of government workers was at stake (see the section "American Bureaucracies: Particularly Political" in Chapter 14). "We all want this process to succeed," said Democratic Representative Martin Frost of Texas, "But we should not begin the process by asking federal workers to be treated less well than they are now."[14]

The conflict over civil service rules turned out to be the most difficult and partisan controversy in the debate over a new department. Delays in the Democrat-controlled Senate over the issue prompted President Bush to assert that Senate Democrats were "not interested in the security of the American people."[15] In an emotional retort, Democratic Senator Tom Daschle denounced Bush's remarks as "outrageous."[16] Republicans won the day, and the final bill contained relaxed civil service provisions that largely mirrored those in the president's initial proposal. In the 2004 campaign, President Bush criticized his opponent, Senator John Kerry, for voting with his fellow Democrats on the matter.

The Department of Homeland Security and Elections

The plan for the new department received a critical boost from the high public regard for the proposal's sponsor. At the time, President Bush was enjoying a nearly unprecedented period of lofty approval ratings that outlasted the initial so-called "rally 'round the flag" boost after September 11. In addition, Bush had the advantage of being able to use his position as commander in chief to argue that his proposal was essential for public safety. As a result, according to one observer, "Bush is positioned to

For the official perspective on the new Homeland Security Department, see the following Web sites.

The Department of Homeland Security operates an official website with information about the department's current programs and activities, as well as Ready.gov, a practical web guide that informs citizens about how to prepare for possible terrorist attacks.

http://www.dhs.gov
www.ready.gov

Many thought that the FBI and CIA should have been placed in the new department, but the White House chose not to change their current status. To learn more about both of these organizations, visit their Web sites. Judging on the basis of what you have learned from material posted at these Web sites, do you think they should have been included within the new Department of Homeland Security?

www.fbi.gov
www.cia.gov

The House of Representatives created a Select Committee on Homeland Security to handle most homeland security matters, while the Senate divided oversight responsibilities among existing committees. For information on the committee system and links to committees, try the House and Senate Web sites.

www.house.gov/house/
www.senate.gov/

inflict grave political damage on a dilatory Congress that isn't doing what's necessary to make people safer."[17] Those who opposed the bill faced the prospect of having a popular president visit their districts and campaign against them.

Even though griping over congressional committee jurisdiction was significant, electoral considerations overcame this barrier as well. Members of Congress worried that if they held a new department hostage to concerns over turf, they would be punished by voters. As former senator Warren Rudman put it, "Are you going to tell 280 million American people, if something bad happens, that you voted against this reorganization because you wanted to be sure that you had your subcommittee on carrots and lettuce?"[18]

What Do Americans Believe?

As usual, elected officials were expert monitors of U.S. public opinion. As Figure 2 shows, the public overwhelmingly supported the Bush plan. More recent polls suggest that voters continue to support the new department and its mission, though with a few reservations.

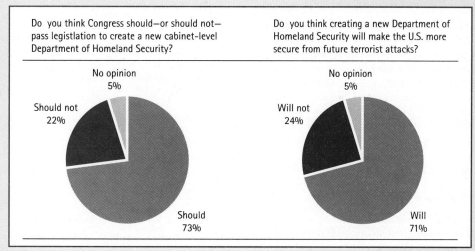

Do you think Congress should—or should not—pass legislation to create a new cabinet-level Department of Homeland Security?

No opinion 5%
Should not 22%
Should 73%

Do you think creating a new Department of Homeland Security will make the U.S. more secure from future terrorist attacks?

No opinion 5%
Will not 24%
Will 71%

FIGURE 2

Americans Supported the Bush Plan

Voters also believed the department would be a clear improvement over the present system.

• *Was Bush's popularity the decisive factor in winning congressional passage of the proposal?*

Opposing Viewpoints on the Department of Homeland Security

The Homeland Security bill passed Congress after the 2002 elections, and the new Department of Homeland Security (DHS) began operations shortly thereafter.

The Optimists

According to some, this case shows that, contrary to the views of pessimistic political scientists, the permanent campaign has not made governing impossible. From this perspective, the case of the Homeland Security Department shows that government can adapt to changing circumstances and, in so doing, act in the public interest:

> Many in Washington said it couldn't be done. But we had the will to unify. Separate bureaus that once seldom interacted now pool their strengths and pull their oars in the same direction....
>
> While we have been integrating, we have not stopped making America safer. Air security was improved from the curbside to the cockpit—with tens of thousands of highly trained screeners, hundreds of federal air marshals, random inspections of air cargo and secured cockpit doors. New layers of security were built around our ports and coastline—with Customs and Border Protection inspectors posted thousands of miles away at foreign ports, to safely screen and label U.S.-bound containers.

> "Smart border" agreements with Mexico and Canada were signed and new inspectors and new technology deployed to stop terrorists without slowing legitimate commerce and travel. A billion doses of antibiotics and vaccines were stockpiled and mobile "push-packs" deployed so our communities would never be left unprepared for a biological attack.

—Tom Ridge, Secretary of Homeland Security, "Remarks at the National Association of Counties Annual Legislative Conference," March 1, 2004
http://www.dhs.gov/dhspublic/display?content=3278

The Pessimists

Others argue that the new department represents more of the same: Bureaucratic squabbling limited the department's initial scope, the agency was slow to improve communications with state and local governments, and in May 2004, the Justice Department issued a new warning on potential terrorism, apparently without coordinating with DHS.[19]

> Far from being greater than the sum of its parts, DHS is a bureaucratic Frankenstein, with clumsily stitched-together limbs and an inadequate, misfiring brain. No one says merging 170,000 employees from 22 different agencies should have been easy. But, even allowing for inevitable transition problems,

DHS has been a disaster: underfunded, under-
manned, disorganized, and unforgivably slow-
moving. . . . DHS has failed to address some of our
most serious vulnerabilities, from centralizing intelligence to protecting critical infrastructure to
organizing against bioterror."

—Michael Crowley, "Playing Defense," *The New
Republic,* March 15, 2004, p. 17

What Do You Think?

1. Was the creation of the new Homeland Security
Department a substantive change or just a superficial one?

2. How was the Bush administration able to avoid major
obstacles to the restructuring?

3. Does this case study show that the politics of elections do not interfere with effective government? Or does it
illustrate the reverse?

[1] Harry Truman, *Memoirs,* Vol. 2: *Years of Trial and Hope* (Garden City,
NY: Doubleday, 1956), p. 51.
[2] See, for example, Theodore Lowi, *The End of Liberalism: Ideology,
Policy and the Crisis of Public Authority* (New York: Norton, 1969);
Mancur Olson, *The Rise and Decline of Nations: Economic Growth,
Stagflation, and Social Rigidities* (New Haven: Yale University Press,
1982); Jonathan Rauch, *Demosclerosis: The Silent Killer of American
Government* (New York: Times Books, 1994); and Haynes Johnson
and David Broder, *The System: The American Way of Politics at the
Breaking Point* (Boston: Little, Brown, 1996).
[3] David Von Drehle and Mike Allen, "Bush Plan's Underground
Architects; In Silence and Stealth, Group Drafted Huge Security
Overhaul," *Washington Post,* June 3, 2002: p. A1.
[4] Ibid.
[5] Ibid.
[6] William M. Thornberry (R-TX), quoted in Adriel Bettelheim and
Jim Barshay, "White House Proposal for Security Department Goes
Beyond Lawmakers' Request; Bush's Swift Sweeping Plan Is Battle
Order for Congress," *CQ Weekly,* June 8, 2002: 1498.
[7] Michael Kramer, "No Place Like Homeland for FBI, CIA," *New York
Daily News,* June 14, 2002: p. 26.
[8] Bill Miller and Mike Allen, "Homeland Security Dept. Could
Receive Raw FBI, CIA Data; Bush Still Opposes Merging FBI,"
Washington Post, June 19, 2002: p. A8.
[9] Bettelheim and Barshay.
[10] David Nather and Karen Foerstal, "Committee Chairmen Bristle at
Notion of Losing Some Jurisdiction; Proposal Presages Turf War," *CQ
Weekly,* June 8, 2002: 1505.
[11] Ibid.
[12] *Final Report of the National Commission on Terrorist Attacks Upon the
United States,* (New York: W. W. Norton, 204), p. 420.
[13] Nick Anderson and Richard Simon, "Democrats Attack Item in
Bush's Security Plan," *Los Angeles Times,* June 21, 2002: p. A26.
[14] David Firestone, "In Party-Line Vote, House Panel Approves
Security Department," *New York Times,* July 20, 2002: p. A8.
[15] "Daschle Says Bush Attack Politicizes Debate," *Seattle Post-Intelligencer,*
September 26, 2002: p. A1.
[16] Jim Vande Hei, "Daschle Angered by Bush Statement," *Washington
Post,* September 26, 2002: p. A1.
[17] Tod Lindberg, "The Homeland Security Two-fer; The Smart Politics
Behind Bush's New Cabinet Agency Proposal," *Weekly Standard,* June 24,
2002: p. 13.
[18] Adriel Bettelheim, "Lawmakers with a List of Concerns Are Sure to
Add Strings to Bush Proposal; Security Plan Gets Solid Backing But No
Rubber Stamp on Hill," *CQ Weekly,* June 15, 2002: 1577.
[19] Thomas Frank, "Terror Warnings not Coordinated," *Newsday,* May 28,
2004, p. A4.

CHAPTER 16

★ ★ ★ ★ ★ ★ ★ ★ ★ ★ ★ ★ ★ ★ ★ ★ ★

Civil Liberties

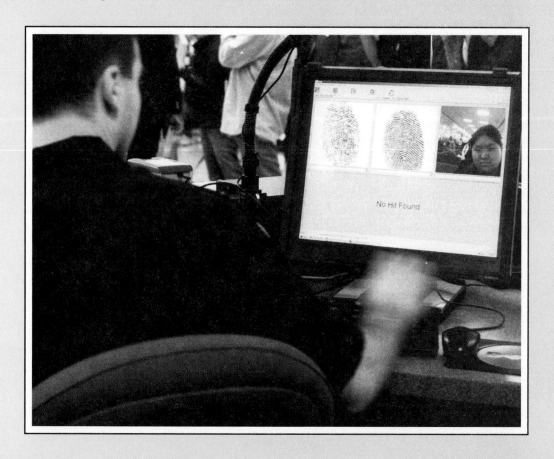

Terrorism, Privacy, and the Patriot Act

No law so divided politicians and the public in the years after the September 11 terrorist attacks as the USA Patriot Act. The name, an acronym for "Uniting and Strengthening America by Providing Appropriate Tools Required to Intercept and Obstruct Terrorism," seemed designed to reassure skeptics. But after receiving overwhelming initial support, the law became a target for those who argued that in moving to stamp out terrorism, Congress and the president had unduly restricted individual freedoms.

Members of Congress and administration officials, stunned that authorities had been unable to foresee or prevent the terrorist attacks on the World Trade Center and the Pentagon, clamored in the weeks after 9-11 to strengthen the power of law enforcement agencies to monitor and contain suspected terrorist activity. Polls showed that overwhelming majorities of voters favored giving new surveillance powers to government officials.[1] "Up to now there's really been no constituency to move with any of this," said Senator Dianne Feinstein (D-CA), who had pushed for broader antiterrorism laws in the past. "There was no critical mass to move a bill, and I don't think anybody believed the depth to which these terrorists would go."[2] A privacy advocate as a senator, Attorney General John Ashcroft now argued for broader law-enforcement powers.[3] "Each day that . . . passes is a day that terrorists have an advantage," Ashcroft warned.[4]

Congress overwhelmingly passed the Patriot Act in October 2001. The new law allowed law enforcement agencies to obtain a single search warrant to monitor all telephones or computers that might be used by a particular suspect. It permitted expanded CIA surveillance of terror suspects within the United States. And it allowed law enforcement to conduct so-called "sneak and peak" searches, in which the individuals whose property is searched do not have to be notified that the search has taken place. Other provisions in the law aimed to crack down on money laundering, counterfeiting, and credit-card fraud.

Soon afterward, internet privacy groups and civil libertarians began arguing that the law went too far. The American Civil Liberties Union (ACLU) claimed that it unduly discouraged free speech and association. "When average Americans hear about these new powers," said an ACLU spokesperson, "many realize that the Patriot Act is anything but patriotic."[5] The libertarian Cato Institute said that the act "abandons procedural norms and expands the power of the executive branch, which is already too powerful."[6] The liberal Center for Constitutional Rights charged that the government response to 9-11 represented a "deliberate, persistent, and unnecessary erosion of the basic rights that protect every citizen and non-citizen in the United States."[7]

Concern about the law was not limited to interest groups. Librarians across the country, upset with provisions in the Patriot Act that allowed federal law-enforcement organizations to secretly obtain the borrowing records of library users, resolved to keep fewer records on file.[8] Hundreds of cities and several states passed resolutions condemning the law, and some jurisdictions declared their unwillingness to cooperate with federal agents who tried to enforce it.

Still, many on both sides of the partisan aisle defended the act as a reasoned response to a serious threat. Criticism of the act is "ill informed and overblown", said Democratic Senator Joe Biden of Delaware.[9] As the 2005 date for reauthorization of the Patriot Act neared, the United States seemed poised for another debate about what steps the government should be allowed to take to ensure security from terrorist threats.

MAKING THE CONNECTION

For some, the antiterrorism legislation was an essential and appropriate response to a significant threat. To others, the new law represented an infringement of the rights of individuals driven by a desire to respond hastily to public demands. In this chapter we place such debates in a larger constitutional context by describing the evolution of civil liberties under the U.S. Constitution. The concept of **civil liberties,** the fundamental freedoms that together preserve the rights of a free people, is never mentioned in the Constitution, nor has it ever been explicitly defined by the Supreme Court. But specific rights that together make up the civil liberties of U.S. citizens are to be found in the Bill of Rights—the first ten amendments to the Constitution—and again in amendments added to the Constitution after the Civil War. These rights include the right to free speech, free association, and free exercise of religion.

Civil liberties should be distinguished from civil rights (considered in Chapter 17), which concern the rights of citizens to equal treatment under the law. This distinction may seem confusing, because at times both categories of protection may be referred to as "rights." But civil liberties are fundamental *freedoms* from government *interference,* whereas civil rights are fundamental *guarantees* of equal *treatment* by the government. In this chapter we focus on civil liberties and answer the following questions:

- How did civil liberties originate and evolve in the United States?

- What do the freedoms of speech, press, and assembly mean in practice?

- What are the two components of the Constitution's guarantee of freedom of religion, and how may they conflict with one another?

- What rights do accused criminals possess under the law?

- How do conflicting views of citizens' right to privacy shape modern court decisions and policy disputes?

* * * * * * * * * * * * * * * *

Origins of Civil Liberties in the United States

The evolution of civil liberties in the United States has been shaped by Supreme Court decisions. But as the controversy surrounding the Patriot Act reveals, these liberties have also been affected by political debates and election outcomes. Civil liberties have not been created simply by the actions of a small number of justices; rather, they reflect basic values shared by most citizens (see Chapter 4). In this section we discuss the constitutional beginnings of civil liberties and how Americans' understanding of these liberties has evolved since then.

civil liberties
Fundamental freedoms that together preserve the rights of a free people.

Balancing Liberty and Security in a Time of War

Origins of the Bill of Rights

The liberties of Americans were among the rallying cries of the American Revolution. Not only did the Declaration of Independence assert fundamental rights to "Life, Liberty and the pursuit of Happiness," but many states incorporated similar principles into their constitutions and statutes. For example, the Virginia Assembly passed a bill of rights a month before the proclamation of the Declaration of Independence. Among its provisions was the pronouncement that "freedom of the press" was "one of the great bulwarks of liberty."[10]

Despite their expressed commitment to basic freedoms, the colonial revolutionaries trampled on the liberties of the Tories, who opposed the revolution. They closed Tory newspapers, threatened well-known Tory editors, confiscated their property, and so intimidated the royalists that some 80,000 to 100,000 people fled to Canada, England, and the West Indies.[11] Even John Adams, a future president of the United States, vowed that "the [Tory] presses will produce no more seditious or traitorous speculations."[12]

Nor did those who drafted the Constitution include explicit protection for individual civil liberties. When Anti-Federalist Charles Pinckney offered a motion at the Constitutional Convention to guarantee freedom of the press, the Federalist majority voted the measure down—on the grounds that states should be responsible for regulating speech and the press.[13] Only when ratification of the Constitution seemed in danger did Federalists agree to add a bill of rights in the form of a series of amendments to the Constitution (see Chapter 2). The first Congress approved the ten amendments that make up the Bill of Rights in 1790 only at James Madison's insistence. Madison, then a member of the House of Representatives, felt significant pressure from his Virginia constituents to press for the amendments. Most others in Congress voted for the amendments, it seems, because they thought the provisions would have little practical effect.

Few Liberties Before the Civil War

The Bill of Rights initially applied only to the national government, not the states. The First Amendment, for example, focused solely on the national government, saying that "Congress shall make no law" abridging speech or religious practice. As a result, the Episcopal Church remained the official state church in Virginia, and the Puritanism remained the established religion in Massachusetts.

Other provisions in the Bill of Rights did not specifically mention either the national or the state governments, leaving open the possibility that they applied to both. For example, the Fifth Amendment said that "no person shall . . . be deprived of life, liberty, or property, without due process of law." But when the owner of Barron's Wharf complained that the City of Baltimore had deprived his company of property without "due process of law," the Supreme Court, in 1833, said the Fifth Amendment limited the powers of the federal government but not those of the states. The Bill of Rights, wrote Chief Justice John Marshall in *Barron v. Baltimore*, "contain[s] no expression indicating an intention to apply them to the state governments. This court cannot so apply them."[14]

It would have been difficult for Marshall to apply the Bill of Rights to the states prior to the Civil War, because doing so would have forced the country to confront the slavery issue head-on. Were slaves people who had liberties granted to them by the First Amendment, or were they property that belonged to their masters, according to the Fifth Amendment?

The main use of the Bill of Rights prior to the Civil War, ironically enough, was to justify continued enslavement. In the extraordinary *Dred Scott v. Sandford* decision, Chief Justice Roger Taney reached the conclusion that the Fifth Amendment precluded Congress from denying Dred Scott's master his right of property. As for Dred Scott, the slave, Taney ruled that he did not qualify as a "person" and therefore was entitled to no protections under the Fifth Amendment (see Chapter 15, p. 403).

Applying the Bill of Rights to State Governments

CONSTITUTION, FOURTEENTH AMENDMENT: "No State shall . . . deprive any person of life, liberty, or property, without due process of law."

The Civil War transformed the spirit, meaning, and application of the Bill of Rights. Once slavery had been abolished, the words in the first ten amendments could begin to be applied to all Americans. To give the Bill of Rights new meaning, the Constitution was altered by three **civil rights amendments,** the Thirteenth, Fourteenth, and Fifteenth Amendments, which abolished slavery, redefined civil rights and liberties, and guaranteed the right to vote to all adult male citizens, respectively.

Of all the provisions in the civil rights amendments, the one that has had the greatest significance for civil liberty is the **due process clause** of the Fourteenth Amendment, which says that a person cannot be deprived of life, liberty, or property without due process of law. As we have noted, the phrase already appeared in the Fifth Amendment, but the Fourteenth Amendment greatly expanded civil liberties by making one apparently minor change—saying that no *state* may "deprive any person of life, liberty, or property, without due process of law."

Despite the language in the Fourteenth Amendment applying the due process clause to the states, the Supreme Court did not immediately conclude that the states must abide by the entire Bill of Rights. The Fourteenth Amendment does not refer to the Bill of Rights, and the Court appeared to conclude that a sweeping decision applying the entire Bill of Rights to the states would create a "vast and perhaps unmanageable problem" of enforcement.[15] Instead, the Court has taken a gradual approach known as **selective incorporation,** a process by which it decides on a case-by-case basis whether a particular denial of a liberty listed in the Bill of Rights is also a violation of the due process clause of the Fourteenth Amendment.

Justice Benjamin Cardozo justified the Court's method of selective incorporation by arguing that there are some rights that are more important than others. Rights such as freedom of speech, for example, are so essential that "neither liberty nor justice would exist if they were sacrificed."[16] These rights may naturally fall under Fourteenth Amendment protection, while other less essential rights may not. Over the course of many decades, nearly all of the provisions in the Bill of Rights have been incorporated. But a few exceptions remain, such as the Second Amendment, which says that inasmuch as "a well-regulated militia" is necessary to "the security of a free state, the right of the people to keep and bear arms shall not be abridged." Although the National Rifle

civil rights amendments
The Thirteenth, Fourteenth, and Fifteenth Amendments, which abolished slavery, redefined civil rights and liberties, and guaranteed the right to vote to all adult male citizens.

due process clause
Found in the Fifth and Fourteenth Amendments to the Constitution; forbids deprivation of life, liberty, or property without due process of law.

selective incorporation
The case-by-case incorporation, by the courts, of the Bill of Rights into the due process clause of the Fourteenth Amendment.

Association (NRA) has argued that state laws banning or restricting the use of guns are contrary to the Constitution, the Supreme Court has maintained that this amendment guarantees only the state governments' right to have a militia.

Freedom of Speech, Assembly, and Press

CONSTITUTION, FIRST AMENDMENT: "Congress shall make no law . . . abridging the freedom of speech, or of the press; or the right of the people peaceably to assemble, . . . "

Of the liberties listed in the Bill of Rights, one trio is paramount: freedom of speech, press, and assembly. The three are closely intertwined. If free speech is to be effective, it must be communicated through a free press. Unless an audience can be assembled to listen, speakers might as well keep silent.

Even though the beginnings of these freedoms date back to the colonial period, the doctrine of free expression, as we know it today, is not so deeply entrenched in the American tradition as Fourth of July speakers often proclaim. Despite the First Amendment, people have been jailed for expressing controversial thoughts as long ago as 1798 and as recently as 1968. We spend the bulk of this section considering free speech, and then illustrate how the constitutional doctrines developed in free-speech cases have been applied to cases involving freedom of the press and free assembly. Finally, we point out key limitations of free expression in such areas as commercial speech, obscenity, and libel.

Free Speech and Majoritarian Democracy

Free speech is vital to the workings of free elections in a democratic society. In the absence of free speech, government officials could manipulate public opinion without fear of contradiction. Elections have little meaning when candidates cannot express their opinions without fear of punishment.

tyranny of the majority
Stifling of dissent by those voted into power by the majority.

Even so, elections are won by candidates backed by a majority of the voters, and majorities can at times be as tyrannical as single-minded despots. The greatest threat to the rights of the people, said James Madison, is the **tyranny of the majority**—the suppression of minority opinions by those voted into power by a majority.[17] The larger a majority gets, the more sure it is that its views are correct, and the more capable it is of punishing dissenters. As British historian Lord Acton said, "The one pervading evil of democracy is the tyranny of the majority, or rather of that party, not always the majority, that succeeds, by force or fraud, in carrying elections."[18]

Because of such fears about unscrupulous political coalitions, Madison believed that free speech should be placed outside the reach of even very powerful majorities. Accordingly, the Constitution's First Amendment specifically protects speech from regulation by Congress. Enshrining free-speech rights in the Constitution meant that majorities would have to tolerate dissent—at least until they could muster the strength to change the Bill of Rights.

The classic defense of free speech was provided by the English civil libertarian John Stuart Mill, who insisted that in the free exchange of ideas, truth would eventually triumph over error. This argument, said Mill, applied not just to politics but to many aspects of life. Galileo's declaration that the Earth was not at the center of the universe eventually became accepted as true, although informed opinion initially regarded his claims as preposterous. Modern events seem to bear out Mill's argument. Sixty years ago, geologists laughed at Alfred Wegener's suggestion that the world's continents gradually drifted over long distances. We now know that they do.

These examples illustrate the value of free speech in scientific debates, but must we tolerate even offensive and vicious error? It is not easy to accept the idea of people enjoying the freedom to spread doctrines of racial hatred. Are their beliefs not founded on false premises that could never be shown to be true? To such contentions, Mill replied that "he who knows only his own side of the case, knows little of that."[19] Mill argued further that error suppressed becomes more powerful by virtue of its suppression. Only if error is allowed to express itself can its proponents be denied the privilege of a false martyrdom.

From "Bad Tendency" to "Clear and Present Danger"

In colonial days, punishment for supposedly harmful speech was allowed under an English judicial standard known as the **bad tendency test,** a rule that held that expression could be punished if it could ultimately lead to illegal behavior. British courts developed the bad tendency standard to protect the monarchy from criticism, and also used it broadly to punish speech that was harmful to public morals and to the official church.[20] After the ratification of the Constitution, many Americans disagreed about whether the First Amendment simply restated the bad tendency test, or instead provided a much broader range of protection from government interference.

Unfortunately, an answer to this question would have to wait for many years. The courts did not enforce the Bill of Rights immediately, in part because until the ratification of the Fourteenth Amendment, it protected the right of free speech only against actions by Congress, not against those by state governments.

Even in more recent times, the Supreme Court has not been a leader in protecting those with unpopular opinions from the tyranny of the majority. Instead, the Supreme Court's view of what free speech entails has moved along at about the same speed as—or perhaps a little slower than—that of the rest of the country. In the words of one scholar, "the Court has seldom lagged far behind or forged far ahead of America."[21] Nonetheless, progress toward free speech in the United States can best be traced by noting the evolution in Court doctrine. The first major Supreme Court decision affecting freedom of speech arose out of the conscription of young men into the army during World War I. Wartime creates conditions that test the boundaries of civil liberties. As the country mobilizes to fight a common foe, elected officials are often under public pressure to identify pacifists or other dissenters as being in league with the enemy. As Alexis de Tocqueville wrote, "All those who seek to destroy the liberties of a democratic nation ought to know that war is the surest and shortest means to accomplish it."[22]

The occasion for the ruling was the conviction of Charles Schenck, a socialist who had mailed anti-conscription materials to draft-age men during the war. The jury decided that Schenck had violated the 1917 Espionage Act, which made it illegal to obstruct armed forces recruitment.

When asked to review Schenck's conviction, the Supreme Court, in *Schenck v. United States* (1919), enunciated the **clear and present danger doctrine**—the principle that people should have complete freedom of speech unless there is a "clear and present danger" that their language will provoke "evils that Congress has a right to

bad tendency test
Rule from English law saying that expression could be punished if it could ultimately lead to illegal behavior.

clear and present danger doctrine
The principle that people should have complete freedom of speech unless their language endangers the nation.

Civil Liberties and
National Security

prevent." The Supreme Court, which was no more sympathetic to socialists than Congress had been when it passed the Espionage Act, upheld Schenck's conviction. The Schenck case nevertheless marked the first time the Court moved to limit the regulation of speech by proposing a definite standard. Justice Oliver Wendell Holmes, author of the Court's opinion in the case, made the common-sense observation that no person has the right falsely to cry "Fire" in a crowded theater: Such a cry creates a clear and present danger to the public safety. In the same way, he argued, Congress could regulate speech only when there was a clear and present danger that the speech would provoke serious evils. His example seemed to capture succinctly the appropriate balance between the right of free speech and the need to maintain social order.

The meaning of clear and present danger, however, is open to different interpretations. A critical question is whether this standard simply restates the old bad tendency test (which allows limitations if speech *could* lead to illegal activities), or whether it instead defines a much narrower set of circumstances under which the government could legitimately limit speech (involving a determination about whether speech is *very likely* to lead to illegal activities). For example, many college campuses have sought to limit the use of so-called hate speech. (See the accompanying Democratic Dilemma.) Critics of such regulations might argue that in no sense does hate speech pose the kind of immediate peril that crying "Fire" in a crowded theater does. Others might reply that if racial and ethnic slurs came to be widely used, they would indeed constitute a clear and present danger to the safety of individuals, to the public order, and to the climate of intellectual growth; to keep that from happening, speech should be restricted before the danger becomes too present. Under this second interpretation, the clear and present danger standard seems to be equivalent to the bad tendency test.

Holmes himself took this second point of view in the *Schenck* case, appearing to argue that the clear and present danger test was the same as the bad tendency test. He said that Schenck's actions constituted a clear and present danger to the successful prosecution of the war because, if it achieved its ends, the mailing of anti-draft pamphlets to draft-age men could endanger the war effort.[23] Holmes ignored the fact that few prospective servicemen paid much attention to Schenck and his associates. In a very similar case, however, Holmes tried to separate his clear and present danger test from the bad tendency standard. In *Abrams v. United States* (1919), several activists were charged with violating the Espionage Act when they printed and distributed leaflets advocating socialism. Although the majority of the Court felt that the pamphlets had a tendency harmful enough for the government to jail the activists, Holmes dissented, arguing that the "publishing of a silly leaflet by an unknown man" posed no grave danger to the war effort.[24]

In numerous cases after *Abrams*, Holmes continued to argue for a clear and present danger test that allowed for fewer restrictions on speech than the bad tendency test did. Although the rest of the Court was at first reluctant to follow him, the doctrine became the foundation upon which a free-speech tradition was gradually built. During the 1930s, when the public was more tolerant of dissenting opinion, the Supreme Court, reflecting the changing political climate, explicitly defended the civil liberties of minorities. One case decided in 1931, *Stromberg v. California,* was particularly important, because for the first time it gave First Amendment protection to extremely unpopular opinions. Yetta Stromberg had encouraged children attending a camp operated by the Young Communist League to pledge allegiance to the flag of the Soviet Union, a viola-

DEMOCRATIC DILEMMA

Do Campus Speech Codes Unduly Restrict Free Speech?

College campuses are supposed to foster creativity and intellectual growth. But since the 1980s, a majority of the nation's colleges and universities have attempted to adopt speech codes that proscribe faculty members and students' uttering offensive words or promoting unacceptable ideas.

Some argue that such codes are essential for intellectual activity to thrive on campus. Racist or sexist language, say proponents of speech codes, only serves to stifle discussion and put many students on edge. Take, for example, the true story of a farm-science professor who used a *Playboy* centerfold to illustrate different cuts of meat. Is this a legitimate exercise of freedom of expression, or is it offensive and punishable behavior?

Or take another example provided by Sharon Gwyn of Stanford University, who speaks from personal experience:

When I was in sixth grade, my teacher gave us the word "slavery" in a spelling test. He recited a sentence to clarify its meaning: "Sharon is lucky she is not in slavery." As my stomach began to lurch, my hands held tighter to my pencil. . . . My teacher merely smiled; he never apologized.

. . . If I was hurt in a situation of that level, think of how the person who is the target of a racial epithet must feel.

Others maintain that offensive language and behavior, though sometimes painful, are part of intellectual growth. Says Jason Shepard, an openly gay student at the University of Wisconsin, "Racism, sexism, homophobia are all parts of our society, whether we like it or not. We can't erect a wall around our university and pretend those things don't exist." Philosophy professor Lester Hunt agrees:

Some people, like me, teach subjects that concern all the hot-button areas—race, gender, you name it—and what the [speech] code does is threaten you with punishment if you say the wrong thing. That makes it difficult or impossible to teach these subjects effectively.

- *Should colleges and universities restrict certain types of speech on campus?*

- *Which approach creates the best environment for learning?*

SOURCES: Gwyn's remarks are quoted from the *New York Times,* May 12, 1989: p. B12. Other material is from: Mitchell Zuckoff, "A New Word on Speech Codes; One School That Led Way Is Rethinking Its Rules," *Boston Globe,* October 21, 1998: p. A1; and Tom Mashberg, "Debates Rage on Campus Over Free-Speech Rules," *Boston Herald,* October 31, 1999: p. 1.

tion of California's "red-flag" law.[25] The Supreme Court overturned her conviction, saying that the California law limited "free political discussion." Because Stromberg did not constitute a clear and present danger, said the Court, her civil liberties should not be curtailed.

Fighting Words Doctrine

The toleration that emerged during the 1930s did not survive the onset of World War II. In 1940 Congress responded to public outrage against fascism by enacting the Smith Act, which forbade advocating the overthrow of the government by force. Even some university administrators prohibited demonstrations against the draft, arguing that such demonstrations would reflect poorly on their schools. Columbia University President Nicholas Butler justified the ban in these words: "Before academic freedom comes university freedom to pursue its high ideals, unembarrassed by conduct which tends to damage its reputation."[26]

Instead of acting as a bulwark against majority tyranny during World War II, the Supreme Court endorsed limitations on free speech. In the 1942 case of *Chaplinsky v. New Hampshire,* the court enunciated the **fighting words doctrine** that some words constitute violent acts and are therefore not protected under the First Amendment. Walter Chaplinsky, a member of the Jehovah's Witnesses religious group, had asked a policeman to guard him from a threatening crowd objecting to his pacifist address.

fighting words doctrine
The principle, endorsed by the Supreme Court in *Chaplinsky v. New Hampshire* (1942), that some words constitute violent acts and are therefore not protected under the First Amendment.

Senator Joseph McCarthy

Senator Joseph McCarthy, built a career in the 1950s on investigating alleged Communist sympathizers.

• *His methods outraged many, but should civil liberties be balanced against other important governmental interests, such as national security?*

balancing doctrine
The principle enunciated by the courts that freedom of speech must be balanced against other competing public interests at stake in particular circumstances.

When the policeman gave him no protection but instead cursed him and asked him to "come along," Chaplinsky called the policeman "a God damned racketeer" and "a damned Fascist." Enunciating the fighting words doctrine, the Supreme Court upheld Chaplinsky's conviction on the grounds that he had used threatening words that "are no essential part of any exposition of ideas" and that "by their very utterance inflict injury or intend to incite an immediate breach of the peace."[27] This new fighting words doctrine seriously qualified the Court's earlier inclination to protect most speech under the clear and present danger doctrine.

Balancing Doctrine

The end of World War II did not automatically restore civil liberties to dissident groups. Instead, those who were regarded as Communist sympathizers suffered harassment by government officials responding to public concern about the growing conflict between the United States and the Soviet Union. Republican Senator Joseph McCarthy of Wisconsin gained political popularity by accusing artists, teachers, and government officials of having ties to the Communist party. As part of the anti-Communist crusade, Congress voted to require that all employees of the federal government take an oath swearing loyalty to the United States. Students also had to take this oath when applying for student loans.

Once again, it was up to the courts to protect the free speech of minority dissidents. But, instead of taking special care to protect free speech, the Supreme Court enunciated the **balancing doctrine**—the principle that freedom of speech had to be balanced against other competing public interests at stake in particular circumstances. The Court developed this doctrine when considering a case in which 11 leaders of the Communist party had been convicted under the Smith Act for espousing the revolutionary overthrow of the government. In *Dennis v. United States* (1951), the Court said the convictions had been constitutional, arguing that the "balance . . . must be struck in favor" of the governmental interest in resisting subversion.[28] The balancing doctrine was used to reinterpret and place limits on the clear and present danger doctrine.

It was elected political leaders, not judges, who resisted the threat that McCarthyism posed to the country's civil liberties. A disgusted President Eisenhower refused to act on McCarthy's most outrageous accusations, and McCarthy's Senate colleagues finally inquired into the senator's methods of operation, later censuring him for his inappropriate conduct.

Fundamental Freedoms Doctrine

fundamental freedoms doctrine
Court doctrine stating that laws impinging on the freedoms that are fundamental to the preservation of democratic practice—the freedoms of speech, press, assembly, and religion—are to be scrutinized by the courts more closely than other legislation. These are also termed the *preferred freedoms.*

After an elected president and Congress had exposed and discredited McCarthy, public opinion became increasingly supportive of protecting the free-speech rights of all Americans, even radicals and Communists. While 70 percent of people surveyed in the 1950s said they would oppose allowing a Communist to speak in their community, this number fell to about 40 percent by 1975, and to 30 percent by the year 2000.[29] Reflecting these changes in public opinion, the Supreme Court gradually became committed to the **fundamental freedoms doctrine**—the principle that some constitutional provisions ought to be given special preference because they are basic to the functioning of a democratic society. The doctrine has its origins in a Supreme Court opinion written in 1938 by Justice Harlan Stone, who said that some freedoms, such as freedom of speech, have a "preferred position" in the Constitution; any law threatening these freedoms must be subject to strict scrutiny by the Supreme Court.[30]

Although no single court case specifically set forth the fundamental freedoms doctrine, it became the Supreme Court's governing principle during the 1960s in the midst of the Vietnam War. Under its guidance, the Court was more effective at defending dissenters against government repression than in any previous war. As one civil libertarian wrote in 1973, "The truly significant thing in recent years has not been the attempt of the current administration to suppress criticism, but rather the marked inability of the administration to do so effectively."[31] In virtually every case that came before it, the Court ruled against efforts to suppress free speech. For example, it overturned the expulsion from the University of Missouri of a student who had distributed a newspaper containing a picture of a policeman raping the Statue of Liberty. Said the Court, "The mere dissemination of ideas—no matter how offensive to good taste—on a state university campus may not be shut off" in the name of decency.[32]

The fundamental freedoms doctrine has now become firmly established. Nothing better illustrates the contemporary Supreme Court's strong commitment to this principle than its rulings with respect to flag burning.[33] During the 1984 Republican national convention in Dallas, Gregory Johnson was arrested for burning an American flag to protest the policies of the Reagan administration. Five years later, Johnson's case came before the Supreme Court. The Court, in *Texas v. Johnson* (1989), overturned his conviction, saying the principal purpose of free speech is to invite dispute and the mere burning of the flag was "expressive conduct" that did not breach the peace.[34]

Unlike earlier court decisions on the matter, the Supreme Court in the flag-burning case went well beyond popular opinion of the day. In a spirited dissent to the case, Chief Justice Rehnquist quoted Ralph Waldo Emerson and the national anthem, arguing that "For more than 200 years, the American flag has occupied a unique position as the symbol of our Nation, a uniqueness that justifies a governmental prohibition against flag burning."[35] President George H. W. Bush called for a constitutional amendment that would prohibit flag desecration, and over 70 percent of the public supported him. Almost immediately, Congress passed a law making it a federal offense to burn the flag. The very day the law was passed, activists set fire to flags in Seattle and Washington, DC, preparing the ground for another court decision. The next year the Supreme Court, in *United States v. Eichman* (1990), declared the new law unconstitutional.[36] Many thought it an indication that the commitment to free speech was now very broadly based when Antonin Scalia, one of the Court's most conservative justices, voted with the majority.

If anything, Supreme Court conservatives have become champions of free speech. In *R.A.V. v. City of St. Paul* (1990), Scalia wrote a majority opinion that gave protection to speech criticizing particular ethnic groups. The City of St. Paul had passed an ordinance forbidding the placement on public or private property of a symbol that "arouses anger, alarm or resentment in others on the basis of race, color, creed, religion or gender." When a group of teenagers was caught placing a "crudely made cross" made of "broken chair legs" inside the fence of the yard of a black neighbor and setting fire to it, the City of St. Paul charged them with violating the city ordinance. The Supreme Court unanimously ruled that the ordinance violated their right of free speech, saying that ordinary trespassing laws were adequate to deal with the alleged intrusion on a person's property.[37]

Gregory Johnson and the Flag
Gregory Johnson's conviction for torching the American flag in 1984 was overturned by the Supreme Court.

• *Is flag burning protected free expression, as the Court argued, or is the flag a unique national symbol that is worthy of special treatment?*

Freedom of the Press

Freedom of the press during the early colonial period was governed by the **prior restraint doctrine,** which said the government could not censor an article before it was published. However, the prior restraint doctrine did not prevent prosecution after the fact. Instead, the publisher could be convicted under the bad tendency test for bringing the government's "dignity into contempt," even if what he said were true. Thus in 1734, when John Peter Zenger published an accurate critique of an incompetent, unprincipled New York governor, the governor put Zenger in jail at excessive bail for ten months while he was awaiting trial. In one of the great early victories for freedom of the press, the jury found Zenger innocent after his attorney argued that the issue at stake was "the Liberty—both of exposing and opposing arbitrary Power . . . by speaking and writing Truth."[38]

Although the Zenger case was an important event in the history of press freedom, it was nearly two centuries later before the Supreme Court ruled that a publisher could not be punished for promoting a particular point of view. In 1931 the Supreme Court, in *Near v. Minnesota,* overruled a Minnesota law that prohibited newspapers from publishing "malicious, scandalous and defamatory" material. Even though a publication banned under the law had printed vicious anti-Semitic and racist harangues, the Court regarded the law as "the essence of censorship."[39]

In one of its most significant decisions, *New York Times v. United States* (1971), the Supreme Court rejected an attempt by the Nixon administration to prevent, on grounds of national security, the *New York Times* from publishing the "Pentagon Papers," a lengthy and detailed Defense Department document revealing many mistakes made by government officials in their conduct of the Vietnam War. Although the Court suggested that prior restraint might be permitted under particularly extreme circumstances if national security was endangered, it ruled in the newspaper's favor on the grounds that the "Pentagon Papers" did not, in fact, include highly sensitive material.

The Supreme Court has often treated freedom of the press as synonymous with freedom of speech. If speech is permitted in a certain case, a publication containing the same message is also permitted under the Constitution. On the one hand, newspapers, pamphlets, and the Internet enjoy the broadest First Amendment protections because they are, in theory, accessible to all. On the other, the Court has ruled that radio and television may be regulated by the government, since the airwaves are technically public property and comparatively few people have access to them (see Chapter 9). While prior restraint of radio and television programs is not permitted, the Federal Communications Commission may levy fines or refuse to renew a station's broadcast license if it fails to meet particular standards. After Janet Jackson bared a breast during the 2004 Superbowl halftime show, many in Congress and the general public called for increased penalties for broadcasters who aired offensive material.[40]

Freedom of Association

The freedom of association has long been considered to be inseparable from the freedoms of speech and of the press. Without the ability to assemble, the free exchange of ideas that John Stuart Mill advocated would be difficult if not impossible. Although the Court was willing to limit the activities of some fringe groups in the 1950s, as the *Dennis v. United States* case discussed above shows, the justices gradually broadened their interpretation of the rights of popular assembly in succeeding years. In the case of *NAACP v. Alabama* (1958), for example, the Court ruled that Alabama could not compel the National Association for the Advancement of Colored People to turn over its membership lists to the state. In this case, said Justice Harlan, a requirement of membership disclosure would be "as effective a restraint on freedom of association" as the direct governmental punishment in cases like *Near v. Minnesota*.[41]

Several recent rulings on freedom of association have been controversial because they concern the ability of private organizations to exclude particular members. In *Boy Scouts of America v. Dale* (2000), for example, the Court ruled that the Scouts could refuse to accept a prospective scoutmaster who was gay. Accepting gay scoutmasters, argued the Court, would infringe upon the Scouts' ability to convey their system of values to youth, one of the tenets of which is that "homosexual conduct is not morally straight."[42]

Limitations on Free Expression

Although free expression has now been firmly established as one of the country's fundamental freedoms, not all expression is free of government control. In particular, three types of speech are subject to regulation: commercial speech, obscenity, and libel.

Commercial speech—advertising or other speech made for business purposes—may be regulated. According to the Court, regulation of commercial speech is needed so that companies will not take advantage of consumers by providing false or misleading information. Also, commercial speech can be controlled to discourage the consumption of substances the government regards as harmful. For example, cigarette advertising on television and radio is forbidden, despite the complaints by tobacco companies that this prohibition interferes with their right to free speech.

Obscenity—publicly offensive language or portrayals with no redeeming social value—is not protected under the First Amendment. Whether explicit sexual material is obscene depends on whether it has some social or cultural purpose. The Court, in *Redrup v. New York* (1967), came close to saying that it would not uphold any obscenity conviction unless the obscenity involved a juvenile, was forced upon unwilling adults, or "pandered" to the most disgusting of prurient interests. But just a few years later, in *Miller v. California* (1973), a more conservative Court said that obscenity is a matter to be settled according to local community standards.[43] Overall, the Court seems to have said that local communities may ban hard-core pornography if they wish to do so. Less explicit sexual material may not be outlawed, particularly if presented within an artistic or literary context.

With the growth of the Internet, the distinction between national and local standards is rapidly disappearing, and sexually explicit material has become generally available. In 1996 Congress passed the Communications Decency Act, which prohibited posting or sending on the Internet obscene material that might be viewed by minors. The following year the Supreme Court struck down this law as unconstitutional, arguing that its restrictions were too broad.[44] But Congress responded by writing a narrower law targeting commercial pornographers. In 2002, a divided Court suggested that even this narrower statute might not meet constitutional standards, but it reserved final judgment until lower courts devoted more attention to the issue.[45]

Libel—a false statement defaming another—is not constitutionally protected if made by one private person about another. But what if press reports about public

commercial speech
Advertising or other speech made for business purposes; may be regulated.

obscenity
Publicly offensive language or portrayals with no redeeming social value.

 Visual Literacy

What Speech Is Protected by the Constitution?

libel
False statement defaming another.

figures are erroneous? Can a newspaper then be successfully sued? This issue was raised by a fund-raising advertisement placed in the *New York Times* on March 29, 1960, by a civil rights group. The advertisement reported on student demonstrations against segregation in Montgomery, Alabama. In addition to containing several relatively innocuous errors (student demonstrators sang the national anthem, not "My Country 'Tis of Thee," as claimed), the advertisement implied that the local police were part of a "wave of terror" directed at protesters. "When the entire student body protested to state authorities by refusing to reregister," read the advertisement, "their dining hall was padlocked in an attempt to starve them into submission."

Pointing out that the police had never padlocked the dining hall, the local official charged with supervising the police department, Montgomery County Commissioner J. L. Sullivan, sued for libel. An all-white Alabama jury found the *New York Times* and those who placed the ad guilty to the tune of half a million dollars per allegation.[46]

The Supreme Court's decision in this case reflected national public opinion, which at the time was supportive of the civil rights movement. In *New York Times v. Sullivan* (1964), the Court reversed the libel conviction, holding that untruthful statements made about public figures were not actionable for libel unless the errors were made knowingly or with reckless disregard for the truth. In the Court's view, the errors in the advertisement were reasonable mistakes.

Some critics wonder whether the *Sullivan* decision, by freeing the media from legal responsibility for "accidental" errors and falsehoods, granted them too much power. Certainly, the news media have adopted an aggressive, investigative style that at times has led them to make erroneous accusations. In 1992, ABC's *Primetime Live* had an employee with a hidden camera submit a fake résumé to get a job in the meat section of a grocery store that it accused of selling doctored and outdated fish. A federal jury found ABC liable for $5.5 million in damages due to fraud, but an appeals court threw out the award in late 1999, granting the grocery store only a symbolic $2 for trespassing and encouraging employee disloyalty.[47] Although these cases prompted some editorial writers to question journalistic ethics, legal efforts to restrain the media must still clear very high hurdles.

Freedom of Religion

CONSTITUTION, FIRST AMENDMENT: "Congress shall make no law respecting an establishment of religion, or prohibiting the free exercise thereof."

Freedom of religion is guaranteed by two clauses in the First Amendment. The **establishment of religion clause** denies the government the power to establish any single religious practice as superior. The **free exercise of religion clause** protects the right of individuals to practice their religion without government interference. When interpreting these clauses, the Supreme Court, as we shall see, has often been influenced by the political and electoral context in which its decisions have been made.

establishment of religion clause Denies the government the power to establish any single religious practice as superior.

free exercise of religion clause Protects the right of individuals to practice their religion without government interference.

Establishment of Religion Clause

The constitutional prohibition against government establishment of religion may seem stark, but one can point out many gray areas and seeming contradictions in the way it has been enforced. The motto "In God We Trust" appears on U.S. currency, yet courts have ruled against nativity scenes in village squares. Each session of Congress opens with a prayer, but public schools cannot begin their day in a similar fashion.

Religious issues often arise in conjunction with the provision of public education, in large part because many parents and policy makers think schools need to teach not only reading and arithmetic but morals and values as well. The issue is one of the oldest in American politics. Massachusetts passed the nation's first compulsory-schooling law in 1852, because many Protestants felt something had to be done about the waves of Catholic immigrants arriving in Boston from Ireland and Germany. Distressed by the changing composition of the city's population, the Boston School Committee urged,

> We must open the doors of our school houses and invite and compel them to come in. There is no other hope for them or for us. . . . In our schools they must receive moral and religious teaching, powerful enough if possible to keep them in the right path amid the moral darkness which is their daily and domestic walk.[48]

Catholic parents did not think they were allowing their sons and daughters to live in "moral darkness" and saw little reason why their children should acquire their moral and religious training in public schools run by Protestants, so they requested instead public monies to help fund Catholic schools. But Catholic demands for government financing only heightened Protestant fears of immigrants and "the power of the Catholic pope." The anti-Catholic forces were so strong that in 1875 they nearly succeeded in passing a constitutional amendment that explicitly forbade state aid to religious schools.[49]

Although the proposed amendment failed to pass, Supreme Court decisions interpreting the establishment of religion clause reflected the views of the Protestant majority, which opposed aid to religious schools. As a result, the Court has for the most part followed Thomas Jefferson's **separation of church and state doctrine,** which says that a wall should separate the government from religious activity. For example, in *Meek v. Pittenger* (1975), the Court struck down most forms of aid that Pennsylvania provided to religious schools as part of its federally funded compensatory education program.[50] The Court said public monies cannot be used for payment to religious-school teachers, for curricular materials, or for any other expense at such schools, except for textbooks and the cost of transporting students to school.

During the 1960s and 1970s, as the Court was reinforcing its commitment to broad interpretations of other parts of the Bill of Rights, the doctrine was applied quite rigorously to most forms of state-supported religious activity. School prayer, a sacred moment of silence, reading from the Bible as a sacred text, and the celebration of religious holidays in schools—all once widely practiced—were banned.[51] After evangelical religious groups protested these decisions in the 1980s and 1990s, however, a more conservative Supreme Court relaxed the ban on prayer in school somewhat, saying students may form Bible-reading or school prayer clubs as long as other clubs are allowed to use school property.[52]

Other recent decisions have also opened up windows in the wall of separation between church and state. In 2000 the Supreme Court ruled that states could provide private religious schools with computer equipment.[53] More important, in *Agostini v. Felton* (1997) the Supreme Court ruled that public school teachers can provide specialized remedial instruction in religious schools, so long as this instruction does not discriminate against students on the basis of religion, and any aid to religious

separation of church and state doctrine
The principle that a wall should separate the government from religious activity.

institutions occurs "only as a result of the genuinely independent and private choices of individuals."[54] By justifying its decision in terms of the "private choices of individuals," the Court showed a concern for the right to the free exercise of religion, the subject to which we now turn.

Free Exercise of Religion Clause

If the establishment of religion clause seems to bar state involvement in religion, the free exercise of religion clause seems to instruct states not to interfere with religious practices. Once again, this issue frequently arises in the context of education policy. The Supreme Court has often protected private religious schools from hostile action by state legislatures. For example, during the 1920s, anti-immigrant sentiments were so strong in Nebraska that the legislature tried to close private religious schools that provided instruction in foreign languages. In 1923 the Supreme Court ruled that the law violated the free exercise clause of the First Amendment, because it prevented parents from exercising "the right of the individual to . . . establish a home and bring up children [and] to worship God according to the dictates of his own conscience."[55] Extending this line of reasoning, the Court in *Wisconsin v. Yoder* (1972) disallowed the application of a compulsory public school attendance law to two Amish children, whose parents opposed their attendance on religious grounds.[56]

The guarantee of free exercise of religion has often forced the Court to draw fine distinctions about how the government can make its rules. In a 1993 case, the Court invalidated a Hialeah, Florida, city ordinance that banned animal sacrifices because it unduly infringed on the practices of the Santeria religion.[57] On the other hand, in *Oregon v. Smith* (1990) the Court ruled that members of a Native American church could be denied unemployment compensation under Oregon law after getting fired from their jobs as drug rehabilitation counselors because of their peyote use. Although the peyote was used as a sacrament, Justice Antonin Scalia wrote in his majority opinion that the state could enforce its ban on the drug in this case because the law was "not specifically directed at [Native American] religious practice."[58]

Establishment of Religion or Free Exercise?

The *Wisconsin v. Yoder* case involving the Amish children raises the issue of what the courts ought to do when the establishment clause and the free exercise clause come into conflict with one another. Some critics might argue that by allowing the Amish to be exempt from certain laws to ensure that they could exercise their religion freely, the Court was violating the establishment clause by giving the Amish preferential treatment. A similar quandary arises when one considers the case of overseas members of the armed services. Should the army hire chaplains to ensure soldiers' right of free religious exercise? Or does the army violate the establishment clause by employing religious leaders?[59]

The debate over school choice raises the question of whether the establishment clause is violated if families and students are given a choice of school, whether religious or secular. Many Republicans, including President George W. Bush, favor giving families vouchers that allow parents to choose among public schools and private schools, whether religious or secular. In their view, school vouchers do not violate the estab-lishment clause because it is the parent, not the government, that decides whether the child attends a religious school. But many Democrats say that the inclusion of private religious schools in any choice program is unconstitutional because the federal dollars flowing to religious schools could be used for any aspects of the school's program, even those aspects that are clearly religious in nature.

The issue was addressed by the Supreme Court in 2002 in *Zelman v. Simmon-Harris,* which found constitutional a small voucher program serving low-income families in Cleveland, despite the fact that most of the students using the program were attending religious schools. The Court reasoned that students had the option of either attending secular public schools or making use of the voucher opportunity.

Participation

The Courts and School Vouchers

Law, Order, and the Rights of Suspects

Elections also affect court interpretations of the procedural rights of the accused. These procedural rights are often thought to conflict with the need for government to main-tain social order. Many public officials believe procedural obstacles protecting the rights of suspects unduly handicap the efforts of the police to find and prosecute criminals. They seem to share the view of the ancient jurist who once said, "The judge is condemned when the criminal is absolved."[60] But others think that unless procedural safeguards are carefully observed, innocent people will be unjustly convicted. "I think it a less evil," said Justice Oliver Wendell Holmes, "that some criminals should escape than that the government should play an ignoble part."[61] In this section we first summa-rize the role that elections play in this debate and then review the rights of the accused, including the rights of suspects against unreasonable police intrusion, as well as their rights at and after criminal trials.

Participation

Privacy and Rights of the Accused

Election Politics and Criminal Justice

Politics affects criminal justice routines, because almost everyone worries about being a victim of a crime. According to the Federal Bureau of Investigation, 83 percent of all Americans will become crime victims at some point in their lifetimes.[62] Most of these crimes—thefts, burglaries, and robberies—take place at more or less the same rate in the United States as in other major industrial countries. But many people in the United States today are especially afraid of personal injury and violent death, and their fears are not unfounded. (See International Comparison, page 450.) After 2001, fears of further terrorist attacks on the United States were also widespread.

In response to public demands to solve these problems, politicians often feel they must "do something." As one senator remarked, "There is a mood here that if someone came to the floor and said we should barbwire the ankles of anyone who jaywalks, I suspect it would pass."[63]

The ways in which the police and the courts treat suspects were severely scruti-nized during the 1960s, when civil liberties and civil rights groups focused public atten-tion on the rights of the disadvantaged. Influenced by political currents at the time, the Supreme Court, under the leadership of Chief Justice Earl Warren, issued a series of decisions (discussed below) that interpreted the Bill of Rights as providing significant

INTERNATIONAL COMPARISON

United States Has Much Higher Murder, but Not Burglary, Rates Than Most Other Countries

Many Americans fear being the victim of a violent crime.

• *Why do you think the murder rate is so much higher in the United States than in other countries, while the rate of burglaries is about average?*

Note: Comparisons among nations should be interpreted with caution because of different definitions of crimes and methods of calculation.

SOURCES: Gordon Barclay and Cynthia Tavares, *International Comparisons of Criminal Justice Statistics, 2000,* (London: Research, Development, and Statistics Directorate, Home Office, July 12, 2002), Table 1.1, Table 2.

Comparing Civil Liberties

protections of the rights of the accused. Warren was a former governor of California who one of his colleagues described as holding "a simple belief in the things we now laugh at: motherhood, marriage, family, flag, and the like."[64] He also believed that the Court had a duty to actively adapt constitutional principles to modern circumstances, as the living constitution theory says (see Chapter 15). Warren guided the Court through what one historian calls one of the "great creative periods in American public law."[65]

As the rights of the accused were being extended by these Warren Court decisions, many law-enforcement officials claimed that the courts had forgotten about the rights of victims. An increasing number of voters agreed, favoring rigorous enforcement of

TABLE 16.1

KEY CHANGES IN THE RIGHTS OF THE ACCUSED

• *How did voter concerns affect court decisions on the rights of the accused from the 1960s to the 1980s?*

Constitutional Provision	Amendment	Extensions by Warren Court	Limitation by Post-Warren Court
Search and seizure	4	*Mapp v. Ohio*, 1961 Improperly collected evidence cannot be introduced in court.	*United States v. Leon* 1984. But such evidence can be used if officers collected it in "good faith" belief that search was legal.
No self-incrimination	5	*Miranda v. Arizona*, 1966 Officers must tell suspects their rights before questioning.	*Harris v. New York*, 1971 But if suspects testify, evidence obtained without their "rights" can be introduced. *Dickerson v. U.S.*, 2000 *Miranda* reaffirmed.
Impartial jury	6	*Sheppard v. Maxwell*, 1966 Establishes guidelines to protect jurors from biased news coverage.	*Nebraska Press Association v. Stuart*, 1976 But pretrial publicity does not necessarily preclude a fair trial.
Legal counsel	6	*Gideon v. Wainwright*, 1963 Poor defendants are guaranteed legal counsel.	No limitation
No double jeopardy	5	*Benton v. Maryland*, 1969 Applies to state as well as federal trials.	No limitation

laws and harsh punishments for criminals, including the death penalty. Court procedures soon became a campaign issue, and many who sought office called for tougher law enforcement. Richard Nixon's successful 1968 campaign was the first to become known as the "law and order" election. After that, the issue arose frequently in national and local campaigns.

After Warren's retirement in 1969, the Supreme Court, responding to changing political circumstances, began to temper its decisions on the rights of those accused of a crime. Yet, as we shall see in the remainder of this section, the post–Warren Court did not reverse but only qualified the major Warren Court decisions (see Table 16.1). Most debate over the rights of those suspected of criminal activity has focused on five constitutional provisions: (1) search and seizure, (2) immunity against self-incrimination, (3) impartial jury, (4) legal counsel, and (5) double jeopardy. These are the topics of the remainder of this section.

Visual Literacy

Race and the Death Penalty

Search and Seizure

> CONSTITUTION, FOURTH AMENDMENT: "The right of the people to be secure in their persons, houses, papers, and effects, against unreasonable searches and seizures, shall not be violated, and no Warrants shall issue, but upon probable cause."

Your house cannot be searched without your permission unless a search warrant, based on evidence that a crime has probably been committed, is properly issued by a court. Prior to the Warren Court era, police officers could conduct thorough searches of a suspect's property based only on arrest warrants. In 1969, however, the Court ruled, in

exclusionary rule
Legal standard that says that illegally obtained evidence cannot be admitted in court.

Mapp v. Ohio
Supreme Court decision saying that any evidence obtained without a proper search warrant may not be introduced in a trial.

You Are a Police Officer

Chimel v. California, that arrest warrants only allowed officers to search a suspect's person and his or her close proximity (to prevent the suspect from retrieving a weapon, for example).[66]

If law enforcement officers illegally search a suspect's belongings and discover incriminating evidence, a legal standard known as the **exclusionary rule** prohibits that evidence from being admitted in a court of law. First enunciated for federal trial proceedings in 1914, the exclusionary rule was firmly established as constitutional law and applied to the states in the case of ***Mapp v. Ohio*** (1961). In that case, Cleveland police officers had searched Dollree Mapp's property without a proper warrant and had arrested her for possession of "certain lewd and lascivious books, pictures, and photographs" that they found there.[67] Saying that "[t]here is no war between the Constitution and common sense," the Court ruled that Mapp could not be convicted on the basis of such illegally-obtained evidence.[68]

In the post-Warren Court years, there have been several significant conservative modifications of the principle enunciated in *Mapp.* In 1984 the Court heard a case in which a California police officer seized evidence based on a search warrant that was later discovered to be invalid. This evidence was admissible, said the Court majority, because the officer had acted in "good faith," believing the search was proper.[69] In 2000 a unanimous Court ruled that officers may sometimes stop and search people simply because they turn and run when they see police approaching. Running away, argued the Court, is cause for "reasonable suspicion," which can justify such a search. "Headlong flight—whenever it occurs—is the consummate act of evasion," Chief Justice William Rehnquist wrote in his opinion. "It is not necessarily indicative of wrongdoing, but it is certainly suggestive of such."[70]

Immunity Against Self-Incrimination

> CONSTITUTION, FIFTH AMENDMENT: "Nor shall [any person] be compelled in any criminal case to be a witness against himself."

Miranda v. Arizona
Supreme Court decision stating that accused persons must be told by police that they need not testify against themselves.

The Fifth Amendment protects individuals from torture and coerced confessions by saying that persons cannot be forced to testify against themselves. In ***Miranda v. Arizona*** (1966), the Warren Court gave teeth to this constitutional provision by requiring police officers to tell suspects, before questioning them, that they have the right to remain silent and that they may request the presence of an attorney. If suspects are not so "Mirandized," then any information obtained may not be presented in court. After Richard Nixon made the *Miranda* decision an issue in his 1968 presidential campaign, the Supreme Court softened the ruling when it decided, in *Harris v. New York* (1971), that information gathered in violation of the *Miranda* decision may be introduced in evidence if defendants testify in their own defense.

In 2000 the Supreme Court finally ruled on a 1968 law passed by Congress that some observers believed overturned the *Miranda* decision. In a 7 to 2 decision, the Court affirmed the *Miranda* ruling. Chief Justice Rehnquist, writing for the majority, pointed out that "*Miranda* has become embedded in routine police procedure to the point where the warnings have become part of our national culture." Reluctant to reverse earlier Supreme Court decisions and modern police practices, the majority chose judicial restraint in the case. Many commentators found it particularly interesting that Rehnquist, usually a judicial restorationist who had in the past specifically questioned the *Miranda* decision, joined the moderates on the Court in showing a reluctance to overturn prior decisions. In a heated dissent, Justice Antonin Scalia, who remained a judicial restorationist in this case as in others, objected that the *Miranda* requirements had no basis in the Constitution. He argued that according constitutional force to the original *Miranda* decision simply on the grounds that an earlier court had (in his view, wrongly) so decided would give the courts an "immense and frightening antidemocratic power." Priority was being given not to the Constitution but, instead, to a prior court decision.[71] (See the discussion of judicial restraint and restorationists in Chapter 15, p. 421.)

Ernesto Miranda

Ernesto Miranda, the namesake of the "Miranda rights" that are read to all suspects before questioning. The Supreme Court ruled that Miranda's confession was inadmissible in court because he had not been advised of his right not to answer questions.

• *Are Miranda rights now part of American culture?*

Impartial Jury

CONSTITUTION, SIXTH AMENDMENT: "The accused shall enjoy the right to a speedy and public trial, by an impartial jury."

The requirement that a jury be impartial is difficult to meet when a crime becomes newsworthy, because jurors may be biased by media accounts of the alleged crime both before and during the trial. The Warren Court considered these issues in *Sheppard v. Maxwell* (1966), a case that grew out of the trial of medical doctor Sam Sheppard, who was accused of murdering his wife. (The case became the basis for the television show and movie *The Fugitive*.) Sheppard complained about the excessive news coverage to which jurors were exposed, including the fact that the media were positioned in the courtroom in such a way that they could listen in on his conversations with his attorneys.[72] This complaint has been echoed in later years by such high-profile suspects as Oklahoma City bomber Timothy McVeigh and Washington, DC-area snipers John Muhammad and Lee Boyd Malvo. The Supreme Court overturned Sheppard's conviction and set forth the following guidelines in an effort to ensure impartial juries in the future:

1. Trials should be postponed until public attention has subsided.
2. Jurors should be questioned to screen out those with detailed knowledge or fixed opinions.
3. Judges should emphatically instruct jurors to consider only the evidence presented in the courtroom, not any evidence obtained from an external source.
4. A court may **sequester** jurors during a trial—that is, keep them away from all sources of information about the crime other than information presented in the courtroom.
5. Courts should consider changing the **trial venue**—the place where the trial is held—in order for the case to be heard by a jury less exposed to pre-trial publicity.[73]

sequester
To house jurors privately, away from any information other than that presented in the courtroom.

trial venue
Place where a trial is held.

Although these constitutional safeguards designed to prevent the jury from becoming biased have never been reversed, the post-Warren Court, in *Nebraska Press Association v. Stuart* (1976), handed down a decision reflecting the country's more conservative political mood. It said that "pre-trial publicity—even pervasive, adverse publicity—does not inevitably lead to an unfair trial."[74]

Legal Counsel

CONSTITUTION, SIXTH AMENDMENT: ". . . and to have Assistance of Counsel for his defense."

Gideon v. Wainwright
Supreme Court decision in 1963 giving indigent people accused of crimes the right to court-appointed counsel.

public defender
Attorney whose full-time responsibilities are to provide for the legal defense of indigent criminal suspects.

The Warren Supreme Court ruled in ***Gideon v. Wainwright*** (1963) that all citizens accused of serious crimes, even the indigent, are constitutionally entitled to legal representation. If the accused is too poor to hire an attorney, then the court must assign one.

As a result, most states have created the office of **public defender,** an attorney whose full-time responsibility is to provide for the legal defense of indigent criminal suspects. But this solution has had its problems. For one thing, the job of a public defender is thankless, pay is low, and defenders are forced to deal with "rotten case after rotten case."[75]

For another, public defender systems and standards vary widely from state to state and, in some cases, from county to county.[76] One felon, when asked by a judge whether he had had an attorney, replied, "No, I had a public defender."[77] Public prosecutors probably appreciate the work of the public defender more than anyone else. As fellow attorneys, they know that those working on the other side are just doing their job.

Double Jeopardy

CONSTITUTION, FIFTH AMENDMENT: "Nor shall any person be subject for the same offence to be twice put in jeopardy of life or limb."

double jeopardy
Fifth Amendment provision that prohibits prosecution for the same offense twice.

The Warren Court ruled in *Benton v. Maryland* (1969) that states cannot try a person twice for the same offense, thereby placing the defendant in **double jeopardy.** Despite this rule, the Supreme Court, in an old decision that has never been overturned, has said that a person can be tried in federal courts, even if acquitted in a state court. "An act denounced as a crime by both national and state sovereignties is an offense against the peace and dignity of both."[78] As noted in Chapter 15, the same conduct may constitute a violation of both state and federal criminal statutes, and both levels of government can prosecute without technically placing the defendant in double jeopardy.

Prosecution by both federal and state governments is most likely in high-visibility cases. For example, in 1992 when the state of California was unable to win a conviction in the trial of the four police officers charged with beating Rodney King, the officers were tried again under a federal law for violating King's civil rights.

Rights in Practice: Habeas Corpus

CONSTITUTION, ARTICLE ONE: "The privilege of the Writ of Habeas Corpus shall not be suspended, unless when in Cases of Rebellion or Invasion the public Safety may require it."

writ of habeas corpus
A judicial order that a prisoner be brought before a judge to determine the legality of his or her imprisonment.

If a prisoner believes his or her constitutional rights have been violated, he or she may file for a **writ of habeas corpus,** a judicial order that a prisoner be brought before a judge to determine the legality of his or her imprisonment. A prisoner may petition for such a hearing for a variety of reasons, usually having to do with violation of procedural rights, and may do so before trial, during a trial, or after conviction.

Legal scholars have called the writ of habeas corpus "the Great Writ" because it preserves the right of the accused to due process of law. Even after having been convicted of a crime and after having exhausted all normal appeals, a prisoner may still file for a writ of habeas corpus. Similarly, if a person is detained indefinitely without trial, he or she may file for a writ of habeas corpus, arguing that his or her right to a speedy trial has been violated.

After the 9/11 terrorist attacks, civil libertarians used writs of habeas corpus on a variety of occasions to challenge the Bush administration's detention of suspects. In 2004, in the most famous such case, the Supreme Court ruled that Yasser Hamdi, a United States citizen who had been imprisoned indefinitely as a so-called "enemy combatant," had the right to appear before a judge despite alleged ties to the Al Qaeda terrorist organization. In a similar case, the Court also said that non-citizens detained at the Guantanamo Bay naval base in Cuba must be granted an opportuinty to legally contest their detention.[79]

Rights in Practice: The Plea Bargain

If a case is newsworthy, constitutional procedures are generally observed: The public is looking on, and those participating in the trial must take political pressures into account. But the reality of justice in most criminal cases is very different. Hardly anyone accused of a crime is actually tried by a jury, and nearly all those convicted of a crime testify against themselves. The accused have their rights, to be sure, but very few of the accused actually choose to exercise them. Most of the time, it is to their advantage *not* to do so.[80]

Trial court judges depend on the willingness of prosecutors and defenders to settle cases before going to trial. The number of people accused of crimes is high, the list of cases on the court docket is seemingly endless, court personnel resources are limited, and court time is precious. To speed the criminal justice process, defenders and prosecutors are usually expected to try to arrange a **plea bargain**—an agreement between prosecution and defense that the accused will admit to having committed a crime, provided that other charges are dropped and a reduced sentence is recommended. The Supreme Court has approved of this transformation of the rights of the accused into bargaining chips that can be used "to cop a plea." In the words of Justice Burger, plea bargaining is "an essential component of the administration of justice. Properly administered, it is to be encouraged."[81]

plea bargain
Agreement between prosecution and defense that the accused will admit having committed a crime, provided that other charges are dropped and the recommended sentence is shortened.

Extensive use of the plea bargain has become an issue in electoral politics, and many candidates insist that those convicted should serve longer sentences. One popular proposal, enacted in a number of states, is known as "three strikes and you're out." After having been convicted of three felonies, a convict must receive life imprisonment, whether or not a plea bargain is struck. As a result of these tough new laws, incarceration rates are rising and prison costs are becoming one of the fastest-growing items in state budgets.

Whether a higher incarceration rate is the best way to reduce crime has become a subject of considerable debate. Even some judges now argue that the laws are too severe. In 2000 a Michigan judge rejected prosecutors' pleas to imprison, with adults, a boy who had killed at age 11. Handing down a seven-year sentence to be served in a juvenile facility, Judge Eugene Moore chastised the legislature for writing laws that were not "helping to prevent [crimes] and rehabilitate" criminals. The speaker of the Michigan House of Representatives told the judge, in effect, to mind his own business: "We don't need judges on a soapbox; we need judges who will uphold the law."[82]

The Right of Privacy

CONSTITUTION, NINTH AMENDMENT: "The enumeration in the Constitution, of certain rights, shall not be construed to deny or disparage others retained by the people."

right of privacy
Right to be free of government interference in those aspects of one's personal life that do not affect others.

The civil liberties discussed thus far are explicitly mentioned in the Bill of Rights. In addition, the Supreme Court has enunciated another liberty, the **right of privacy**— the right to be free of government interference in those aspects of one's personal life that do not affect others. Although the right of privacy is not explicitly mentioned in the Constitution, the Ninth Amendment says that some rights may be retained by the people even though they are not explicitly mentioned in the Constitution.

Some constitutional scholars believe that the judicial power to identify any right not explicitly mentioned in the Constitution should be exercised with great caution, because abuse of this power would give an unelected judiciary the authority to overrule the will of elected public officials. "Where constitutional materials do not clearly specify [a right]," judicial scholar Robert Bork has said, "the judge must stick close to the text and history, and their fair implications, and not construct any new rights."[83]

Nevertheless, in the 1960s and 1970s the Court went a long way toward recognizing a right to privacy. In this section we first consider the Court's rulings on this issue with regard to private sexual behavior and abortion. Finally, we consider the growing concerns about personal privacy in the information age.

Regulation of Sexual Behavior

The modern right to privacy owes its existence to the Supreme Court's ruling in *Griswold v. Connecticut* (1965).[84] Estelle Griswold, executive director of Planned Parenthood, was fined $100 for violating a Connecticut law prohibiting the use of any instrument for the purpose of contraception. Declaring the law unconstitutional, Justice William Douglas discerned "a right of privacy older than the Bill of Rights." "Would we allow the police to search the sacred precincts of marital bedrooms for telltale signs of the use of contraceptives?" asked Douglas. "The very idea is repulsive to the notions of privacy surrounding the marriage relationship." In a dissent, Justice Potter Stewart declared the Ninth Amendment "but a truism" that could hardly be used to "annul a law passed by the elected representatives of the people."[85]

Despite Stewart's objection, there is little doubt that a national majority agreed with the Supreme Court that a married couple should have the right to use contraceptives. But would the Supreme Court be equally protective of the right of privacy when the actions in question were not approved by a majority of the public? This question arose in 1986 in *Bowers v. Hardwick,* when the Court was asked to declare unconstitutional a Georgia law prohibiting sodomy under which two homosexuals had been convicted. Noting that laws against sodomy existed at the time the Constitution was written, the Court majority found no reason to think that its authors intended to exempt homosexual behavior from state regulation. In the 2003 case of *Lawrence v. Texas*, however, the Court revisited this issue and made an almost complete reversal. In a very unusual repudiation of a case so recently decided, Justice Kennedy wrote in the majority opinion that "*Bowers* was not correct when it was decided, and it is not correct today. It ought not to remain binding precedent."[86]

Although these rulings are clearly at odds with one another, they are consistent with one measure: public opinion. In 1986, when *Bowers* was decided, a majority of those surveyed believed that homosexual relations should be outlawed. But by 2001, polls found that Americans favored legalizing homosexual behavior by a margin of 54 to 42 percent. Similarly, 85 percent of people thought gays and lesbians should have equal rights in the workplace—a figure up over 25 percentage points from the early 1980s. In deciding the *Lawrence* case in favor of privacy rights, the Supreme Court once again has shifted with changing public sentiment.[87]

Abortion: Right to Life or Right to Choose?

Although the Court has left uncertain the range of sexual acts to which the right of privacy extends, it ruled, in *Roe v. Wade* (1973), that the right of privacy was broad enough to include at least a partial right of abortion. The case arose out of a request from Norma McCorvey, using the pseudonym Jane Roe. Roe, seeking to terminate a pregnancy, asked for a judgment declaring unconstitutional the Texas law prohibiting abortion. Writing for the Court majority, Justice Harry Blackmun said that the woman's right of privacy was so fundamental that it could be abridged only when the state interest in doing so was compelling. Dissenting justices objected to judicial interference with a state legislature's right to balance a woman's rights against the welfare of her unborn child.

Roe v. Wade launched two powerful political movements that have helped to shape American politics in the three decades since the Court's decision. The "right to life" crusade was organized by Catholic and other religious groups opposed to abortion on the grounds that inasmuch as human life begins at conception, abortion cannot be distinguished from infanticide.

These "right-to-life" supporters became actively engaged in state and national politics, lobbying legislatures to impose as many restraints on abortion as the courts would allow. Responding to "right-to-life groups," Congress in 1976 enacted legislation preventing coverage of abortion costs under government health insurance programs, such as Medicaid. In 1980 the Republican party promised to restore the "right to life," and in subsequent years, Republican presidents began appointing to the Supreme Court justices who were expected either to reverse *Roe v. Wade* or to limit its scope.

In response to these political pressures and to the change in its membership, the Supreme Court began to allow certain restrictions on abortion. The Court ruled in 1980 that the law Congress had enacted prohibiting the public funding of abortions was constitutional.[88] In 1989 it said that states could require a doctor to ascertain the viability of a fetus before permitting an abortion, if the woman was 20 or more weeks pregnant.[89]

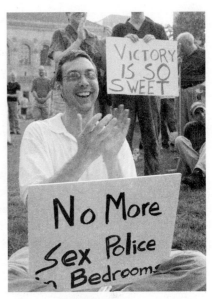

Celebrating a Landmark Ruling

Activists celebrate the Supreme Court's 2003 ruling in *Lawrence v. Texas,* which declared anti-sodomy laws unconstitutional.

• *Which provisions in the Constitution provide the basis for a right to privacy?*

Opposition to "right-to-life" groups was at first weak and uncertain, mainly because many of those who supported a woman's constitutional "right of choice" thought it had been permanently protected by the Supreme Court decision. But as the "right-to-life" movement gained momentum and it appeared more likely that *Roe v. Wade* would be overturned, the "right-to-choose" movement gained in strength and aggressiveness. Abortion-rights activists became an important force in Democratic Party politics.

Both sides of the controversy waited anxiously for the 1992 court decision in *Planned Parenthood v. Casey.*[90] The organization challenged a Pennsylvania law that placed a number of restrictions on the right to an abortion that went well beyond what seemed permissible under *Roe v. Wade.* The Court majority satisfied neither side entirely, finding a compromise that upheld some of the Pennsylvania restrictions on abortion but left intact the principle that states cannot simply outlaw all abortions.

The majority based its decision on nothing other than the principle of *stare decisis,* the rule stating that court decisions, once made, should be followed by subsequent judges if at all possible (see Chapter 15, page 415). To do otherwise, argued the Court, is to make a mockery of the law. In the words of Justice Sandra Day O'Connor, "Where . . . the Court decides a case in such a way as to resolve the sort of intensely divisive controversy reflected in *Roe* . . . the promise of constancy, once given, binds its maker for as long as . . . the understanding of the issue has not changed so fundamentally as to render the commitment obsolete."[91] In other words, the Court said it was not changing its mind.

In *Casey,* the Court majority once again adopted a position very close to that of the average American voter. It permitted restrictions (such as a requirement that teenagers obtain parental consent) endorsed by a majority of voters but rejected those most people think are not warranted (such as a requirement that a married woman obtain the consent of her husband). Even in matters as sensitive as the right of privacy, the Court seems to be influenced by majority opinion, as expressed in the outcome of recent elections.

Privacy in the Information Age

The Internet and related technologies have sparked an information revolution, but technology also reduces the privacy of individuals. A number of free or low-cost Web sites, for example, allow researchers to uncover all publicly available data about a person, from criminal records to property holdings to professional licensing information. Armed with such details, businesses can target consumers for nuisance appeals, or—much worse—unscrupulous outlaws can commit the growing crime of so-called "identity theft." Credit-card records and other financial data are protected by 1970s-era laws that allow customers to review their files and demand corrections, but some lawmakers and experts have called for strict new laws that would guarantee consumer privacy.

Private firms are, of course, not the only ones in the information business. Whereas some urge the government to protect personal privacy with new legislation, others fear that the government itself will be the biggest intruder into the private lives of average Americans. Passengers boarding planes at some airports now have their faces electronically scanned and checked against databases of known criminals.[92] The federal government and state agencies began work in 2002 to encode driver's licenses with data—such as fingerprints—that could create a de facto "national identity card" system.[93] And there are already over 2 million video cameras stationed in public places in the United States,

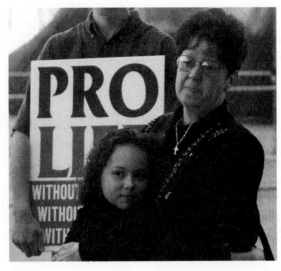

From Jane Roe to Pro-Life Activist

Norma McCorvey, who made history as litigant Jane Roe in the 1973 case that legalized abortion (left), later changed her views on the issue and became an anti-abortion activist (right).

• *Does the Supreme Court pay attention to activists and voters when considering cases on controversial issues such as abortion?*

from street corners to subway tunnels, which may soon be used to search for and apprehend dangerous suspects.[94]

Many supporters of these efforts argue that keeping track of outlaws in this way achieves the goal of protecting Americans from criminals and terrorists without compromising citizens' fundamental freedoms. As one expert put it, "We as a people are willing to trade a little less privacy for a little more security. . . . If using more intrusive technology is the only way to prevent horrible crimes, chances are that we'll decide to use the technology, then adjust our sense of what is private and what is not."[95] But critics fear that such technological innovations will lead to increased government suppression of dissent. One authority cautioned that "law enforcement has a history of snooping on 'enemies' that are a far cry from terrorists, such as Martin Luther King, Jr. and John Lennon."[96]

Because technology has advanced so quickly, the Supreme Court has not yet had time to establish a clear set of rules with which it will interpret the Constitution in cases involving information-age privacy. But unless the newfound concern with terrorism alters Supreme Court thinking, a 2001 ruling suggests that the Court remains concerned with protecting the privacy of individuals. In the case of *Kyllo v. United States,* the Court considered whether police departments could make use of thermal imaging equipment to examine a suspect's home without a search warrant. Officers suspected that the defendant, Danny Kyllo, was illegally growing marijuana in his home, and they used the thermal equipment to check for the hot halide lamps necessary to grow the plants indoors. Police argued that no violation of the Fourth Amendment's ban on "search and seizure" had occurred, because officers did not actually enter the suspect's home, but Kyllo argued that his home had for all practical purposes been unconstitutionally searched without a warrant. In a 5 to 4 opinion that surprised many observers, the Court sided with Kyllo. Justice Scalia, writing for the majority, argued that, although "It would be foolish to contend that the degree of privacy secured to citizens by the Fourth Amendment has been entirely unaffected by the advance of technology," nevertheless "we must take the long view, from the original meaning of the Fourth Amendment forward."[97]

Chapter Summary

The Bill of Rights remained pretty much a dead letter until the Civil War ended slavery. Only as key provisions of the Bill of Rights were gradually and selectively incorporated into the due process clause of the Fourteenth Amendment did they become effective components of the country's constitutional makeup.

Although the courts are expected to protect civil liberties against majority tyranny, most of the time the Supreme Court has followed, not led, public opinion. In 1919 the Supreme Court said speech could not be prohibited unless it created a clear and present danger to a peaceful society, but it initially applied the doctrine in a way consistent with the common law bad tendency test, convicting a socialist for his political speech. Although it protected minority dissent during the 1930s, it later elaborated the fighting words doctrine, which declared certain phrases to be the equivalent of violent acts. Not until McCarthyism had been rejected by elected officials did a Court majority say free speech was a fundamental freedom that required special protection.

Freedom of religion is protected by two separate clauses in the First Amendment. The establishment of religion clause prohibits the propagation of religious beliefs by public institutions and direct aid to churches, religious schools, and other religious institutions. The free exercise of religion clause prevents the government from interfering with the religious activities of citizens. At times the two clauses come into conflict, as the issue of school vouchers has shown

When balancing the rights of the accused against the need to maintain social order, Supreme Court decisions have fluctuated with changes in public opinion. During the 1960s the Warren Court expanded the rights of the accused by tightening the rules under which police and prosecutors could obtain evidence, question suspects, and hold trials. After "law and order" became a campaign issue, the Supreme Court modified, though it did not reverse, many of these decisions.

The Court has also discerned a right of privacy, despite the fact that no such right is mentioned explicitly in the Bill of Rights. This right of privacy is broad enough to include a woman's right to terminate a pregnancy as well as to cover private consensual sexual behavior. But it is not absolute. As interpreted by the Court, the right of privacy does not preclude regulation of abortions, especially among children and after the first trimester of pregnancy. The right of privacy discerned by the Court comes very close to the viewpoint held by most Americans. The country's definition of civil liberties seems to depend as much on the thinking of its citizens as on its judicial system.

Key Terms

balancing doctrine, p. 442
bad tendency test, p. 439
civil liberties, p. 435
civil rights amendments, p. 437
clear and present danger doctrine, p. 439
commercial speech, p. 445
double jeopardy, p. 454
due process clause, p. 437
establishment of religion clause, p. 446
exclusionary rule, p. 452

fighting words doctrine, p.441
free exercise of religion clause, p. 446
fundamental freedoms doctrine, p. 442
Gideon v. Wainwright, p. 454
libel, p. 445
Mapp v. Ohio, p. 452
Miranda v. Arizona, p. 452
obscenity, p. 445
plea bargain, p. 455

prior restraint doctrine, p. 444
public defender, p. 454
right of privacy, p. 456
selective incorporation, p. 437
separation of church and state doctrine, p. 447
sequester, p. 453
trial venue, p. 453
tyranny of the majority, p. 438
writ of habeas corpus, p. 454

Suggested Readings

Of General Interest

Abraham, Henry J. and Barbara A. Perry. *Freedom and the Court: Civil Rights and Liberties in the United States, 8th Edition.* Lawrence, KS: University Press of Kansas, 2003. Comprehensive discussion of the Constitution's protections of civil rights and civil liberties.

Casper, Jonathan D. *American Criminal Justice: The Defendant's Perspective.* Englewood Cliffs, NJ: Prentice-Hall, 1972. Discusses the day-to-day realities of the criminal justice system.

Friedman, Lawrence M. *Crime and Punishment in American History.* New York: Basic Books, 1993. Readable overview of the changing nature of the American system of criminal justice.

Goldstein, Robert. *Political Repression in Modern America: 1870 to the Present.* New York: Schenkman, 1978. Comprehensive account of violations of freedom of speech, press, and assembly in the United States.

Macedo, Stephen. *The New Right v. The Constitution.* Washington, DC: Cato Institute, 1987. Thoughtfully asserts the responsibility of the courts to protect all liberties, not just fundamental freedoms, from legislative intrusion.

Rehnquist, William H. *All the Laws but One: Civil Liberties in Wartime.* New York: Knopf, 1998. The chief justice of the Supreme Court considers instances in which civil liberties have been sacrificed for the sake of security, focusing on cases from the Civil War and World War II.

Focused Studies

Garrow, David J. *Liberty and Sexuality.* New York: Macmillan, 1994. Comprehensive account of the legal debate over abortion before and after Roe.

Goldstein, Robert. *Saving "Old Glory": The History of the Desecration Controversy.* Boulder, CO: Westview, 1995. Authoritative political and constitutional history of the flag-burning controversy.

Lessig, Lawrence. *The Future of Ideas: The Fate of the Commons in a Connected World.* New York: Random House, 2001. A law professor's view of the potential for, and dangers to, free expression on the Internet.

Lewis, Anthony. *Make No Law: The Sullivan Case and the First Amendment.* New York: Random House, 1992. Excellent, readable case study of the politics of the *Sullivan* decision and the evolution of the free-speech doctrine.

McIntyre, Lisa J. *The Public Defender: The Practice of Law in the Shadows of Repute.* Chicago: University of Chicago Press, 1987. Careful sociological study of this little-appreciated courtroom player.

Meiklejohn, Alexander. *Free Speech and Its Relation to Self-Government.* New York: Harper, 1948. Influential, early statement of the absolutist, fundamental freedoms position.

Skolnick, Jerome. *Justice Without Trial.* New York: Wiley, 1966. Classic study of the way in which police and courts resolve low-visibility criminal cases.

Wilson, James Q. *Thinking About Crime.* New York: Basic Books, 1975. Makes a persuasive, realistic, and conservative case for ways of controlling crime.

On the Web

www.aclu.org
The American Civil Liberties Union provides legal assistance to many who feel that their civil liberties have been violated. The sometimes-controversial organization has a detailed Web site outlining its agenda for promoting civil liberties, as well as describing the history and present status of civil-liberties law.

www.freedomforum.org
The First Amendment freedoms of speech and of religion may seem clear-cut, but some First Amendment issues remain controversial, as we have seen in this chapter. The Freedom Forum is a nonpartisan founda-tion that publicizes and analyzes current issues involving First Amendment freedoms.

http://religiousfreedom.lib.virginia.edu/
Thomas Jefferson, founder of the University of Virginia, argued for a "wall of separation" between government and religion. The University of Virginia's Religious Freedom Page carries on the Jeffersonian tradi-tion by providing analysis of many key Supreme Court decisions concerning religious freedom and by including links to other key religious freedom organizations.

www.naral.org

www.nrlc.org

Does a constitutional right of privacy protect a woman's right to have **an abortion?** The National Abortion and Reproductive Rights Action League (NARAL) says yes, whereas the National Right to Life Committee (NRLC) disagrees.

www.eff.org

www.cdt.org

As we have seen in this chapter, a growing area of controversy regarding civil liberties concerns issues of information technology and privacy on the Internet. The Electronic Frontier Foundation (EFF) and the Center for Democracy and Technology (CDT) follow issues and provide information about free speech and privacy in the information age.

CHAPTER 17

* * * * * * * * * * * * * * *

Civil Rights

CHAPTER OUTLINE ────────────────────────────

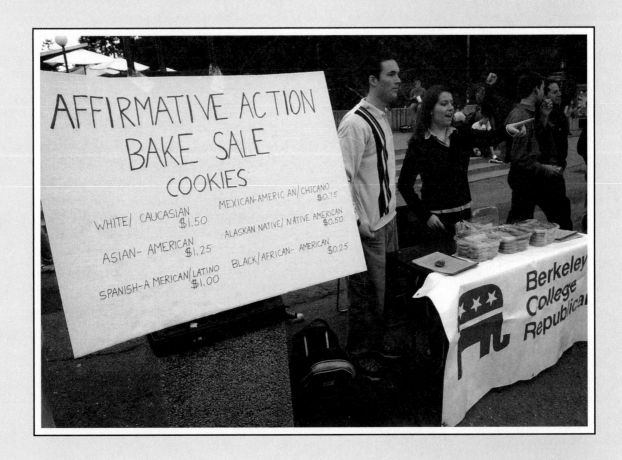

Affirmative Action in University Admissions

It was an unusual sight for a frigid, snowy day. In mid-February 2004, a small group of University of Colorado students made their way to the north side of campus, set up a table and several signs, and prepared to sell a variety of baked goods to passersby. The group drew a crowd—but not a crowd of customers. More than three dozen students, their mouths duct-taped shut in silent protest, held placards. Others argued with the pastry vendors in exchanges that grew heated at times. "I think it's disgusting," said one student leader, objecting to the event.[1] After several hours, someone grabbed a plate of baked goods without paying and passed it around. Someone else tore down a sign announcing the bake sale. "We're holding this sale to try to have an intelligent, academic dialogue, and you guys aren't willing to do that," complained one organizer.[2]

The controversial event was a so-called "Affirmative Action Bake Sale," organized by campus Republicans. Such bake sales had been held at other campuses, including the University of California-Berkeley and Texas A&M. The price of the cupcakes, donuts, and cookies that the students were selling depended upon the buyer's race. A cookie cost a white student $1, a Hispanic student, 50 cents, while an African American student would only have to pay a quarter.[3]

By varying prices in this way, the Republicans sought to dramatize their claim that the University of Colorado's policy of considering race as a factor in admissions decisions constituted unfair discrimination. "We're showing [that] the policy of the University of Colorado is racist," said one organizer.[4] Some of their classmates, however, felt the event was ill-conceived. "It is tasteless, what they are doing," said another student. "It seems they're not trying to prove a point as much as they are seeking to offend people."[5]

Americans as a whole seem just as divided as University of Colorado students over the policy of affirmative action, programs designed to enhance opportunities for race- or gender-based groups that have suffered discrimination in the past. A poll taken in March 2004, for example, found that the public was evenly split over the policy, with 41 percent in favor of it and 43 percent opposed. Even the Supreme Court crafted a delicate compromise over the issue in a key pair of cases in 2003, striking down a rigid system of allocating applicants "points" for being a member of a minority group, but allowing a more flexible consideration of race as one of a number of relevant factors. Uncertainty over the meaning of racial equality seems likely to persist in the United States for years to come.

MAKING THE CONNECTION

The debate over affirmative action in university admissions raises broader questions. What does it mean to say the Constitution is colorblind? When may people be legally classified by race, ethnicity, or gender? Do the courts define the issues, and then voters and elected officials follow? Or is it the other way around? In this chapter we shall discuss the struggle for civil rights for African Americans, other minority groups, women, and the disabled. In most cases we shall find that in characterizing the legal meaning of civil rights, the Supreme Court followed trends initiated by the public debates and coalition building that make up electoral politics. As Justice Ruth Bader Ginsburg once observed, "With prestige to persuade, but not physical power to enforce, and with a will for self-preservation, the Court generally follows, it does not lead, changes taking place elsewhere in society."[6] Nonetheless, the Court has played a major role by codifying civil rights policy into constitutional doctrine. We explore these issues by answering the following questions:

- How did African Americans begin their struggle for civil rights, and how did civil rights advocates persuade the Supreme Court to become involved?

- How has the Supreme Court's interpretation of the Fourteenth Amendment's equal protection clause shaped the development of civil rights?

- What steps have other groups, such as women and minorities other than African Americans, taken to ensure their civil rights, and how have the courts and elected officials responded?

* * * * * * * * * * * * * * * *

Origins of Civil Rights

CONSTITUTION, FOURTEENTH AMENDMENT: "No state shall . . . deny to any person within its jurisdiction the equal protection of the laws."

Although the terms *civil liberties* and *civil rights* are often used interchangeably, there is an important distinction between them. Civil liberties are the freedoms that together preserve the rights of a free people (see page 434). **Civil rights** embody the right to equal treatment under the law. In Chapter 16 we emphasized how important the due process clause of the Fourteenth Amendment has been to the protection of civil liberties in the United States. The civil rights of Americans are guarded by a no less important provision in the Fourteenth Amendment, the **equal protection clause,** which says that no state can deny any of its people equal protection under the law.

Although the equal protection clause has been a part of the Constitution since 1868, its legal and cultural meaning has changed over the years. These changes have most often been the result of one of two phenomena. First, minority groups with grievances have mobilized in electoral politics and other venues, such as protests or boycotts. By undertaking such activities, they unify their numbers so as to influence elections more effectively, and they win popular opinion to their side, broadening their impact on elected officials. "One of the difficult lessons we have learned," wrote Martin Luther King, Jr., "is that you cannot depend on American institutions to function without pressure. Any real change in the status quo depends on continued creative action to sharpen the conscience of the nation."[7]

Second, because minorities are seldom able to control the outcome of elections directly, and because at times in American history they have been prevented from freely exercising their right to vote, they have often pursued a legal strategy, bringing apparent violations of civil rights to the attention of the courts. But legal strategies do not always work. Judges, too, are concerned about preserving credibility with majorities. If judges defy public opinion regularly, they might undermine confidence in the courts. Also, if judges persist in deviating from the majority view, elected officials will eventually appoint judges willing to reverse direction. As a result, the Supreme Court has not provided steady leadership on civil rights questions. As one legal scholar has noted, "For every case destructive of racial segregation, other cases can be cited with greater force to support the view of judicial power as fundamentally unfriendly to civil rights, unnecessarily illiberal in its judgment, and oppressive in its results."[8]

Because most people have personal experience with the relationships among races, genders, and ethnic groups, differing interpretations of the meaning of the equal protection clause have generated intense political controversy.[9] In this section, we first describe actions taken in the years following the Civil War that affected the civil rights of African Americans, then review the Supreme Court's early rulings on these efforts,

civil rights
Specific rights that embody the general right to equal treatment under the law.

equal protection clause
Fourteenth Amendment clause specifying that no state can deny any of its people equal protection under the law.

and finally examine the changes in political power that led up to the Court's major rulings on civil rights in the mid-twentieth century.

Conflict Over Civil Rights After the Civil War

black codes
Restrictive laws that applied to newly freed slaves but not to whites.

At the end of the Civil War, some southern states passed **black codes,** restrictive laws that applied to newly freed slaves but not to whites. "Persons of color . . . must make annual written contracts for their labor," one of the codes read, adding that if blacks ran away from their employers, they had to forgo a year's wages.[10] Other black codes denied African Americans access to the courts or the right to hold property, except under special circumstances. Northern abolitionists, who thought the fight against slavery had been won, urged Congress to override these black codes. Congress responded by passing the Civil Rights Act of 1866, which gave citizens "of every race and color . . . the same right . . . to full and equal benefit of all laws." Almost the same words were incorporated into the equal protection clause of the Fourteenth Amendment, which won final ratification two years later.

Reconstruction
Period after the Civil War when southern states were subject to a federal military presence.

The federal government's civil rights stance was imposed on southern whites during **Reconstruction,** a period after the Civil War when southern states were subject to a federal military presence. During this period, blacks exercised their right to vote, while that right was denied to many whites who had served in the Confederate army. In addition, Congress established a Freedman's Bureau, which was designed to provide blacks with education, immediate food relief, and inexpensive land from former plantations.[11]

Many southern whites bitterly resented the federal Reconstruction policies, and some took violent action to resist them. The Ku Klux Klan, a fraternal organization founded in Tennessee, terrorized blacks and Republicans throughout the South from 1866 to the early 1870s. Hooded Klansmen burned black churches and schoolhouses, drove black elected officials from their homes, and lynched those who seemed to threaten white supremacy.[12] Whites became targets if they aided Republicans or blacks; blacks could fall under suspicion just by becoming educated. The Klan murdered one former slave in Georgia because "he can write and read and put it down himself."[13] In 1871 Congress passed the Force Act, which temporarily succeeded in disbanding the Klan, but similar organizations continued to terrorize African Americans for many years.

Reconstruction was motivated both by moral outrage at racial injustice and by northern postwar bitterness toward the Confederacy. But as the years passed, moral commitment evaporated and war memories faded. The programs of the Freedman's Bureau ultimately proved to be a disappointment to many blacks and abolitionists. Northerners were thrown on the defensive by charges of fraud, corruption, and mismanagement in the new southern state governments. Though not always justified, complaints were effectively leveled against both black elected officials and new arrivals from the North, who were derisively called carpetbaggers, after the luggage in which they kept their clothing.

The close election of 1876 brought Reconstruction to an end. Republican presidential candidate Rutherford B. Hayes claimed victory, but the outcome depended on allegedly fraudulent vote counts reported by several southern states. The compromise resolving the dispute gave each side what it most wanted. Republicans were given the presidency, but Democrats won removal of the federal army from the South and control of future southern elections.

With the end of Reconstruction, whites gradually restored many of the old racial patterns.[14] State legislatures enacted laws requiring voters to pass a literacy test, meet strict residency requirements, and pay a **poll tax,** a fee that allowed one to vote. Although the laws themselves avoided specific mention of African Americans, blacks were in fact the target. As the chair of the suffrage committee in Virginia bluntly admitted, "I expect the [literacy] examination with which the black men will be confronted to be inspired by the same spirit that inspires every man in this convention. I do not expect an impartial administration of this clause."[15] States also enacted what became known as a **grandfather clause,** a law that exempted men from voting restrictions if their fathers and grandfathers were eligible to vote before the Civil War. Of course, only whites benefited from this exemption.

The most successful restriction on the right to vote was the **white primary,** elections held by the Democratic party that excluded nonwhites from participation. Republicans were perceived by southerners as the hated instigators of Reconstruction, so Democrats won nearly all southern elections at that time. As a result, the winner of the white primary nearly always won the general election.[16] Because blacks were denied a meaningful vote, only 10 percent of adult African American males were registered to vote in most of the states of the old Confederacy in 1910.[17]

African Americans were also subject to **Jim Crow laws,** state laws that segregated the races from each other. (The name comes from a stereotypical, belittling characterization of African Americans in minstrel shows popular at the time.) Jim Crow laws required African Americans to attend segregated schools, sit in separate areas on public trains and buses, eat in separate restaurants, and use separate public facilities. The reason for these regulations was clear. As one (white-owned) New Orleans newspaper put it, "The quarter-century that has passed since the war has not diminished in the slightest degree the determination of the whites to prevent such dangerous doctrine as social equality, even in the mildest form."[18]

Early Court Interpretations of Civil Rights

With little public support for civil rights, the Supreme Court of the day took a very restrictive view of the Fourteenth Amendment's equal protection clause. Two Court decisions were of particular significance. In a decision that has been given the ironic title the *Civil Rights Cases* (1883), the Court declared the Civil Rights Act of 1875 unconstitutional.[19] This law, written just before Reconstruction came to an end, had abolished segregation in restaurants, train stations, and other public places. In declaring the law unconstitutional, the Supreme Court invoked the **state action doctrine**—the principle that only the actions of state and local governments, not those of private individuals, must conform to the equal protection clause. The Court said that Congress could prevent state and local governments from discriminating against blacks but that it had no constitutional authority to tell private individuals whom to serve in their restaurants, railroads, and hotels.[20]

A second major decision by the Supreme Court, ***Plessy v. Ferguson*** (1896), had even more sweeping consequences. It developed the **separate but equal doctrine,** the principle that laws mandating segregated facilities were constitutional as long as the

poll tax
Fee that one must pay in order to be allowed to vote.

grandfather clause
Racially restrictive provision of certain southern laws after Reconstruction, permitting a man to vote if his father or grandfather could have voted before the Civil War.

white primary
Primary elections, held by the Democratic party after Reconstruction, that excluded nonwhites from participation in many southern states.

Jim Crow laws
Laws, passed by southern states after Reconstruction, enforcing segregation.

state action doctrine
Rule stating that only the actions of state and local governments, not those of private individuals, must conform to the equal protection clause.

Plessy v. Ferguson
Court decision declaring separate but equal public facilities constitutional.

separate but equal doctrine
Rule stating that the equal protection clause was not violated by the fact of state mandated racial segregation alone, provided that the separated facilities were equal.

facilities were equivalent. Homer Plessy had challenged a Louisiana law that required "equal but separate accommodations" for white and black railroad passengers.[21] Plessy argued that his inability to use white facilities denied him equal protection before the law. But by a majority of 8 to 1, the Supreme Court said the Louisiana statute was constitutional, because the mere fact that the racial groups were being separated did not stamp African Americans with a "badge of inferiority." In a famous dissent, Justice Harlan protested that "Our Constitution is color-blind, and neither knows nor tolerates classes among citizens." Laws enforcing segregation, argued Harlan, violated this constitutional principle.[22]

Blacks Get Electoral Power

Because of the court decisions in the *Civil Rights Cases* and *Plessy v. Ferguson,* legally sanctioned segregation remained intact until well into the middle of the twentieth century. Black civil rights activists were by no means quiescent during this period. Between 1900 and 1910, for example, African Americans in over two dozen cities took part in organized boycotts of segregated streetcars.[23] But significant gains in dismantling the old system of segregation took place only after African Americans gained electoral clout by moving in large numbers from southern states, where they could not vote, to northern states, where they could. During World War I, industrial northern cities faced a labor shortage, and many African Americans gave up sharecropping in Mississippi and Alabama for factory work in the sweatshops of New York, Chicago, and Detroit. When World War II created another shortage of factory workers, blacks left southern farms for northern big-city tenements in even larger numbers.

Northerners were not much more tolerant of blacks than were southerners. Most northern blacks attended segregated schools, ate in segregated restaurants, and shopped in segregated stores. Housing was even more segregated than in the South. But at least African Americans in the North could vote.

Unlike those who governed the South, northern machine politicians who dominated big-city politics were not fussy about the color or religion of the voters they organized. The tough, shrewd, urban political organizer knew that black votes counted as much as the vote of any other resident of the city.[24] One Chicago newspaper assessed the situation in 1927: "Their solid vote is the Negroes' greatest weapon. They have a total vote in Chicago of about 40,000. This total vote is cast for the candidate who makes the best bargain with them."[25]

By the 1930s, African Americans used their votes to win a small place in the politics of a few big cities. African American politicians won election to city councils and became neighborhood leaders in party organizations, obtaining jobs and other benefits for their constituents.[26] By 1945, two African Americans, William Dawson of Chicago and Adam Clayton Powell of New York, held seats in the House of Representatives.[27] But the biggest political breakthrough for African Americans occurred in 1948, when many observers gave them credit for casting the decisive votes electing Harry Truman president. Recognizing the power of black voters in key states like Ohio, Illinois, and Michigan early in the campaign, Truman delivered the strongest civil rights message that any president had ever presented. He called for the abolition of poll taxes, more effective protection of voting rights, the creation of a Fair Employment Practices Commission with authority to stop racial discrimination, and an end to racial segregation within the armed forces. Some scholars have argued that the president's slim

Rosa Parks
• *Why did acts of civil disobedience prove so effective during the civil rights movement?*

margins of victory in several crucial states were due to his two-thirds support among African Americans.[28] This growing electoral clout, and the increasing rhetorical support President Truman gave to the cause of civil rights, lent added force to civil rights lawsuits that activists began to bring before the Supreme Court.

Awakening the Supreme Court to Civil Rights

The legal case against segregation was gradually developed by the **National Association for the Advancement of Colored People (NAACP),** a civil rights organization that relied heavily on a legal strategy to pursue its objectives. Formed in 1909, the NAACP bears a name that strikes readers today as odd but is rooted in the historical moment when it was established. After several failed attempts to persuade Congress to pass a law against lynching, the NAACP chose the courtroom strategy because its leaders concluded that the electoral strength of African Americans was too small to effect dramatic change.

But a legal strategy carried out without the support of black votes was not very effective. Despite the care with which cases were prepared by the NAACP's lead attorney, Thurgood Marshall (who later became the first black Supreme Court justice), the organization initially had but few successes in the courtroom. It could get neither the poll tax nor education requirements outlawed. For all of the legal efforts of the NAACP, only 12 percent of the southern black adult population was registered to vote in 1947.[29]

The NAACP's legal strategy gained strength as northern blacks became more politically potent. President Roosevelt took minor symbolic steps to court the black vote in the 1940 presidential race, and in 1941 the threat of a summer march on

National Association for the Advancement of Colored People (NAACP)
Civil rights organization, dating from 1909, that relied heavily on a legal strategy to pursue its objectives.

Washington by up to 100,000 African Americans drew a promise from the president to eliminate discriminatory employment practices in the defense industry.[30] Around this time, FDR appointed to the Supreme Court five justices who were known to be friendly to the NAACP's point of view.[31] Finally, this substantially new Court outlawed the white primary in the 1944 case *Smith v. Allwright,* saying that political parties were not private organizations but integral parts of a state electoral system.[32] After this decision, black voting in the South gradually began to increase.

In 1948, the very year blacks helped elect Harry Truman, the Court outlawed **restrictive housing covenants,** legal promises by those buying houses that they would not resell to an African American. Under the state action doctrine enunciated by the Court in the *Civil Rights Cases,* the contract seemed a private matter, not subject to constitutional scrutiny. But in its 1948 ruling in *Shelly v. Kramer,* the Court held that although the contracts themselves were indeed private, any state *enforcement* of such covenants was a public act that violated the equal protection clause.[33] By making this decision, the Court greatly narrowed the range of activities in which segregation could be legally practiced, laying the groundwork for a redefinition of the equal protection clause.

restrictive housing covenant
Legal promise by home buyers that they would not resell to an African American; enforcement declared unconstitutional by Supreme Court.

The Struggle for Equal Protection

Redefining the Equal Protection Clause

Although Harry Truman's election and the Court's decisions in *Smith v. Allwright* and *Shelly v. Kramer* offered some hope, the legal rights of African Americans in the United States had changed little from the 1890s to the 1940s. Most blacks lived in segregated neighborhoods, many could not vote, and violence and intimidation directed against blacks continued.

From the mid-1950s to the early 1970s, the status of African Americans changed dramatically, however, through both legal victories and popular mobilization. By no means were all problems solved in this period, but blacks made great advances in redefining and strengthening the constitutional guarantee of "equal protection of the laws." In this section, we review the history of the civil rights movement that began in the 1950s, consider the debate over affirmative action, and assess the current state of civil rights for African Americans.

Brown v. Board of Education of Topeka, Kansas

Civil rights groups tried hard to reverse the separate but equal doctrine set forth in *Plessy v. Ferguson,* but for decades the Supreme Court resisted. In one extraordinary case, the Court allowed a school district to operate with a white high school, but no black high school, saying that blacks would gain little from a decision to shut down the white school, and ignoring the possibility that blacks and whites might share the same facility.[34]

The NAACP seemed more successful in 1938 when it won a suit on behalf of a black law student denied access to Missouri's all-white law school.[35] Missouri had no black law school but offered to pay students' tuition to attend a law school in an adjacent state. When the Court ruled that this policy was unconstitutional, Missouri and other southern states responded by creating all-black law schools of inferior quality, leaving blacks worse off than they were before the decision.

After blacks demonstrated their electoral influence in 1948, the NAACP proved more effective in the courtroom, as the Supreme Court began to reconsider the separate but equal doctrine enunciated in *Plessy.* First, in 1950, the Court unanimously declared that requiring black law students to attend an all-black school was inherently unconstitutional because such a school could not be an effective "proving ground for legal learning and practice."[36] By focusing on law schools, the NAACP had shrewdly aimed at the weakest point in the separate but equal doctrine. Most Supreme Court justices were attorneys, and they knew from personal experience the importance of a law school's reputation for one's subsequent career.

Once the law-school decision provided an opening wedge, the NAACP attacked the separate but equal doctrine directly by encouraging Oliver Brown to file suit saying his daughter, Linda, was being denied equal protection by Topeka, Kansas, by being forced to attend an all-black school. The fact that the black schools in Topeka seemed to be just as good as the white schools was irrelevant, argued the NAACP. This suit led to the Supreme Court's ***Brown v. Board of Education of Topeka, Kansas*** decision in 1954 that finally declared racial segregation unconstitutional.[37]

Newly appointed Chief Justice Earl Warren, a former California governor, was keenly aware of the political significance of the Brown case, so he worked hard to convince the rest of the Court to issue a unanimous decision. At first it seemed that Warren would fail in this effort, because two members of the Court thought a decision to reverse *Plessy v. Ferguson* would violate the principle of *stare decisis,* a rule that says courts should adhere to the doctrines set forth in prior decisions (see Chapter 15, page 415). But Warren argued that the *Brown* decision could be distinguished from *Plessy* because the *Plessy* case had involved trains, not schools.

To distinguish segregation in school from segregation in transportation, Warren cited psychological studies provided by the NAACP to show that racial separation created a sense of inferiority among black children. One study showed, for example, that black children favored white dolls over black ones.[38] Focusing on the particularly harmful effects of segregation on children allowed Warren to limit his opinion to schools, thereby avoiding a direct repeal of *Plessy.* By so limiting the effect of the decision, Warren was able to obtain a unanimous vote from the justices, but in pursuing a legal doctrine Warren might have done better to have followed Harlan's dissent in *Plessy* that simply said, "the Constitution is color-blind." Since the *Brown* decision, many have argued that the constitutionality of racial segregation should depend not on its psychological effects, which may vary from person to person, but on whether racial criteria are valid grounds for classifying individuals.

Years later, the Supreme Court did provide this very rationale for its finding that segregation was unconstitutional. In 1973 it said that any legal distinction based on race or on membership in any other ethnic group that had been discriminated against in the past was a **suspect classification,** which required strict scrutiny by the courts to make sure that its use did not violate the Fourteenth Amendment's equal protection clause. This concept, which is now the standard tool with which the courts adjudicate civil rights cases, soon became crucial for ensuring that racial and ethnic minorities received equal protection before the law.[39]

In 1954, however, Chief Justice Warren realized he could not get a unanimous Court to back such a sweeping statement outlawing all forms of segregation, so, in *Brown,* he settled for less by focusing on segregation's psychological effects on young children. Also to preserve court unanimity, Warren postponed consideration of the exact way in which school boards were to rectify their segregated practices. The following

Brown v. Board of Education of Topeka, Kansas
1954 Supreme Court decision declaring racial segregation in schools unconstitutional.

suspect classification
Categorization of a particular group that will be closely scrutinized by the courts to see whether its use is unconstitutional.

year, the Court handed down a separate ruling on this enforcement issue, calling for school desegregation "with all deliberate speed," a phrase that appeared to have contradictory meanings. *Deliberate* implied a slow, methodical pace, whereas *speed* suggested a need for prompt compliance. Most southern school boards focused on deliberation, enacting as little desegregation as possible.

In spite of its defects, scholars believe *Brown* to be among the most important decisions the Supreme Court has ever made.[40] In this decision, the Supreme Court declared unconstitutional a system of racial segregation that from the earliest colonial settlements had organized social life in a large part of the United States. Within two years, the border states of Maryland, Kentucky, and Missouri, as well as Kansas and the District of Columbia, eliminated formal segregation in their schools.

Civil Rights After *Brown*

Brown also energized civil rights activists around the country. The impact on young people and church leaders was particularly noticeable. Immediately after the decision, three new civil rights organizations—the Congress of Racial Equality (CORE), the Student Nonviolent Coordinating Committee (SNCC), and the Southern Christian Leadership Conference (SCLC)—rose to prominence. Consisting mainly of college students and ministers, these groups held demonstrations, led boycotts, undertook voter registration drives, and appealed to the federal government for intervention into southern racial practices.[41]

One year after *Brown,* a more activist phase of the civil rights movement erupted. In December 1955, Rosa Parks of Montgomery, Alabama, engaged in an extraordinarily successful act of **civil disobedience**—a peaceful, well-publicized violation of a law designed to dramatize that law's injustice. Her arrest for refusing to vacate her seat in the white section of a segregated bus prompted a bus boycott led by a young Baptist minister, Martin Luther King, Jr., who had just earned his Ph.D. in theology. He was only 27 years old at the time, but he had the resourcefulness and rhetorical capacity to give the event national significance.[42] "If there is a victory [over segregation]," King wrote, "the victory will not be merely for the Negro citizens and a defeat of the white citizens, but it will be a victory for justice and a defeat of injustice. It will be a victory for goodness in its long struggle with the forces of evil."[43]

Using boycotts, protests, and acts of civil disobedience, the southern civil rights movement gained strength by winning sympathetic coverage in the northern press.[44] But activists met intense opposition from government officials at home. In March 1956, nearly every southern member of Congress signed the Southern Manifesto, committing themselves to resist the implementation of the *Brown* decision by "all lawful means."[45] Southern resistance to court-ordered integration was so consistent and complete that in the states of the old Confederacy, hardly any school desegregation actually occurred. When school began in the fall of 1964, ten years after the *Brown* decision, only 2.3 percent of black students in the states of the old Confederacy attended integrated schools.[46]

Yet the protests and demonstrations gradually had their effect. For one thing, southern African Americans were registering to vote. The percentage that were registered more than doubled from 12 percent in 1947 to 28 percent in 1960. At the same time, African Americans were becoming a more powerful political force in the large

civil disobedience
A peaceful, well-publicized violation of a law designed to dramatize that law's injustice.

Civil Rights Activist
• *Did these activists or the courts contribute more to the end of formal segregation?*

industrial states of the North. With civil rights demonstrators focusing national attention on racial issues, presidential candidates had to balance southern resistance against the need to get black votes in big northern states.

John Kennedy's victory over Richard Nixon in the breathtakingly close election of 1960 owed much to his success in attracting the black vote. When the 1960 campaign began, Kennedy realized that he needed to improve his civil rights credentials, especially because he had won the Democratic nomination by defeating two candidates with stronger civil rights records: Hubert Humphrey and Adlai Stevenson. To strengthen his support in the black community, Kennedy placed a well-publicized phone call to Coretta Scott King expressing sympathy for the plight of her husband, Martin Luther King, who had been jailed in Birmingham after participating in a student sit-in. That phone call took on great symbolic significance and helped generate support for Kennedy in the black community. Kennedy, who had begun the campaign with little support among African Americans,[47] captured enough black votes to win such crucial states as Ohio, Michigan, and Illinois.

Once in office, Kennedy introduced civil rights legislation that received vigorous support from civil rights demonstrators. In the largest of these demonstrations, over 200,000 black and white demonstrators marched on the Washington Mall in the summer of 1963, calling for congressional passage of the proposed legislation and other reforms. From the steps of the Lincoln Memorial, King delivered his powerful and moving "I Have a Dream" oration, in which he firmly connected the struggle for civil rights to mainstream American values. The dream of African Americans, he said, was "deeply rooted in the American dream that one day this nation will rise up and live out

I Have a Dream

Martin Luther King, Jr., delivers his "I Have a Dream" speech at the March on Washington in August 1963.

• *Why did the civil rights movement lose support just a few years later?*

the true meaning of its creed . . . that all men are created equal."[48] These appeals persuaded many ordinary voters. In the wake of the march, for the first time a plurality of Americans that were polled said they viewed civil rights as the country's most important problem.[49] Just a few months later, Kennedy's assassination generated an unprecedented outpouring of moral commitment to racial justice.

Elected political leaders responded quickly to this transformation in the public mood. The new president, Lyndon Johnson, though himself a southerner, called upon Congress to memorialize the dead president by enacting his civil rights legislation. After intense debate, majorities of both Republican and Democratic members of Congress voted in favor of the Civil Rights Act of 1964, the most sweeping civil rights legislation passed since Reconstruction. This act banned segregation in all places of public accommodation, prohibited federal money from being used to support segregated programs, and created the Equal Employment Opportunity Commission (EEOC) to guard against employment discrimination. The law brought about major changes in race relations throughout the South. Enticed by new federal funds facilitating desegregation, and intimidated by the new enforcement powers of federal officials, many southern schools desegregated. The percentage of black students in southern schools that included whites increased dramatically from 2.3 percent in 1964 to 91.3 percent in 1972.[50]

Buoyed by economic prosperity and his civil rights achievements, Lyndon Johnson won a sweeping election victory in the fall of 1964. Not one to rest on his accomplishments, Johnson soon engineered congressional passage of the Voting Rights Act of 1965, which guaranteed black voting rights by stationing federal examiners in south-

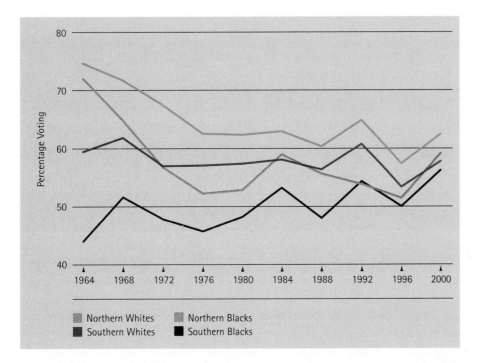

FIGURE 17.1

Changes in Black and White Participation in Presidential Elections, by Region

• *Why do you think blacks still vote at lower rates than whites? Why do southern and northern blacks now vote at similar rates?*

SOURCE: U.S. Bureau of the Census, *Current Population Survey Reports.* (*South* is defined as the states that formed the Confederacy.)

ern registration halls and polling places.[51] As a result, the percentage of voters among southern black adults jumped upward after 1964, as shown in Figure 17.1.[52] The number of elected officials of African American descent rose from less than 500 in 1965 to over 9000 in 2000.[53]

Decline in Strength of the Civil Rights Movement

Segregation and discrimination were not limited to the South. Most northern blacks lived in racially isolated neighborhoods, sent their children to predominantly black schools, and found it hard to get good jobs. Even as Congress was passing the Voting Rights Act of 1965, Martin Luther King shifted the focus of the civil rights movement by mounting a series of civil rights demonstrations in Chicago.[54] This decision changed the way the public viewed the civil rights movement. As school busing and job discrimination became a northern issue as well, support for civil rights protests among many northern whites dwindled.[55] At the same time, new black leaders, such as black nationalist Malcolm X, took a more militant position, affirming black culture, denying the value of integration, and suggesting that violent "self defense" might be needed. "If Negroes can get freedom nonviolently, good," said Malcolm X. "But that's a dream. Even King calls it a dream."[56]

Civil violence began to break out in black neighborhoods, beginning in Los Angeles in 1964 and spreading to other cities over the next three years. When King was assassinated by a white man in Memphis, Tennessee, in April 1968, violent racial disturbances broke out simultaneously in dozens of cities throughout the country.

After these events, the white majority began to view the problem of civil rights as less important. As long as civil rights issues were being addressed by nonviolent demonstrations in the South, African Americans appealed successfully to the moral instincts of northern whites. But once whites realized that the problem was national in scope, and that civil disobedience could turn violent, many had second thoughts. Opposition to busing, affirmative action, and other programs of racial integration split the biracial political coalition that had elected Harry Truman and John Kennedy.

Race issues then began to divide the two political parties further. When Senator Barry Goldwater voted against the Civil Rights Act of 1964, he was among a minority of Republicans to do so. But by 1968, Republicans were pursuing what was known as a "southern strategy," an appeal to those who thought the civil rights movement had gone too far. Meanwhile, blacks solidified their allegiance to the Democratic Party.[57] The percentage of delegates attending the Democratic convention who were black grew from 6.7 to 14.6 percent between 1968 and 1972.

Supreme Court No Longer Forges Ahead

de jure segregation
Racial segregation that is legally sanctioned.

de facto segregation
Segregation that occurs as the result of decisions by private individuals.

Encountering increasing popular resistance to further legislative initiatives, civil rights groups once again turned to the courts for assistance. But the courts, following the direction in which public opinion was moving, also adopted a more conservative attitude. For example, the Supreme Court drew a distinction between two types of segregation. ***De jure* segregation,** the legal separation of the races practiced in the South, was said by the Court to violate the equal protection clause of the Constitution. But segregation in the North was said to be ***de facto* segregation,** occurring as the result of private decisions made by individuals, such as their choice of residence.

In *Milliken v. Bradley* (1974), the Supreme Court considered the constitutionality of the most pervasive form of *de facto* segregation.[58] Bradley argued that the state of Michigan (under Governor William Milliken) tolerated racial segregation by allowing virtually all-white suburban school districts to surround the city of Detroit, whose schools were predominantly black. In rejecting Bradley's argument that the whole metropolitan area ought to be desegregated, the Court ruled that suburban school districts in the North had never practiced *de jure* racial segregation. The segregation that had occurred was *de facto*—simply the result of private decisions to live in Detroit or in its suburbs.

Writing for the majority, Warren Burger, who had replaced Earl Warren as chief justice, said that the lower courts, in siding with Bradley, were trying to produce "the racial balance which they perceived as desirable." But the Constitution only forbids segregation; it "does not require any particular racial balance." Dissenting from the decision, Justice Thurgood Marshall, the former NAACP attorney, responded, "Negro students will continue to perceive their schools as segregated educational facilities and this perception will only be increased when whites flee . . . to the suburbs to avoid integration." After the *Milliken* decision, little additional school desegregation took place in either the North or the South. In recent years, school segregation among African Americans and Latinos has actually increased, as Figure 17.2 illustrates.

Affirmative Action

Civil rights groups also called upon government agencies, universities, and businesses to rectify past discrimination by taking affirmative steps to provide increased educational and job opportunities for African Americans. In response to these demands, many

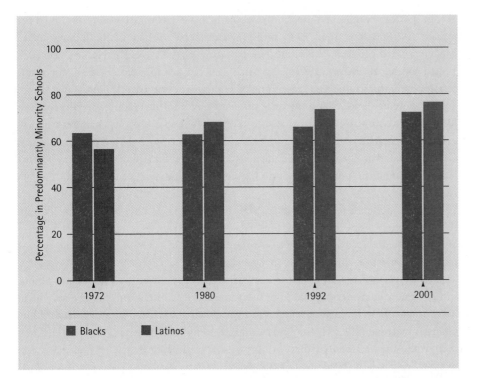

FIGURE 17.2

Percentage of African American and Latino Students in Segregated Schools, 1972–2001

• *In your opinion, why has segregation increased since the 1980s?*

SOURCE: Gary Orfield, *Schools More Separate: Consequences of a Decade of Resegregation,* (Cambridge, MA: The Civil Rights Project, Harvard University, July 2001), Table 9; Erika Frankenberg, Chungmei Lee, and Gary Orfield, *A Multiracial Society with Segregated Schools: Are We Losing the Dream?* (Cambridge, MA: The Civil Rights Project, Harvard University, January 2003) p. 33.

organizations have instituted policies of **affirmative action,** programs designed to enhance opportunities for race- or gender-based groups that have suffered discrimination in the past. In some cases, these programs may consist of nothing more than special advertising, recruitment, and counseling initiatives designed to help members of disadvantaged groups learn about available opportunities. In other cases, universities and employers may also take note of a person's membership in a disadvantaged group as one factor among many to be considered in admissions or hiring decisions. The strongest form of affirmative action involves setting aside a **quota,** or a specific number of positions, for members of disadvantaged groups.

The Supreme Court first considered the constitutionality of affirmative action programs in a 1978 case that involved Allen Bakke, a Norwegian American, who sued for admission to the medical school of the University of California at Davis.[59] Bakke argued that he had been denied admission because of the school's affirmative action policy, which set aside 16 spots in each entering class of 100 for minority applicants. In an unusually complex ruling, a divided Court found that strict quotas like Davis's were unconstitutional, but that affirmative action programs that used race as one among many factors were permissible. Justice Lewis Powell, the deciding vote in the case, argued that some kinds of affirmative action were justified if the goal was to create a diverse community that would benefit all.

During the 1990s, all forms of affirmative action came under increasing criticism. In 1995 the University of California's Board of Regents voted to end the use of race as a factor in its admissions policies, a decision that took on broader significance when the state later passed an initiative banning affirmative action. That same year, voters in Washington State passed a similar measure, and two years later, a federal court ordered Texas to eliminate race-based preferences from its state university admissions system.

affirmative action
Programs designed to enhance opportunities for groups that have suffered discrimination in the past.

quota
Specific number of positions set aside for a specific group; said by the Supreme Court to be unconstitutional.

Allen Bakke

Allen Bakke was admitted to medical school following the Supreme Court decision in his favor and is now a doctor.

• *Do you believe it is appropriate to consider race in university admissions?*

In 2003, the Supreme Court heard two affirmative action cases that prompted the justices to reexamine the *Bakke* decision. Both cases began at the University of Michigan. In the first, *Grutter v. Bollinger,* Barbara Grutter argued that she had been denied admission to the University of Michigan's law school because of an affirmative action system that considered race as one of a number of criteria in a process that placed great importance on creating a diverse student body.[60] In the second, *Gratz v. Bollinger,* Jennifer Gratz similarly argued that she had been refused a spot in Michigan's undergraduate program because of the school's affirmative action policy. Both Grutter and Gratz alleged that they had been denied equal protection under the law, and that Michigan's affirmative action programs should be struck down as a violation of the 14th Amendment.

The undergraduate admission system differed from the law school system, however. Law school admissions officers considered race as one "plus" factor in a "highly individualized, holistic review" of each candidate.[61] The undergraduate process operated under a "points" system, in which academic record, standardized test scores, high school quality, and other factors each garnered an applicant a set number of points. Prospective students needed 100 points or more to be admitted, and membership in an "underrepresented minority group" automatically secured an applicant 20 points.[62] The Court invalidated this points system because it was too blunt an instrument. Even though the Court admitted that diversity was a valid goal, the undergraduate system was not "narrowly tailored" to avoid undue discrimination.

The law school system, on the other hand, was acceptable, wrote Justice Sandra Day O'Connor for the majority in *Grutter.* O'Connor reaffirmed Powell's argument in *Bakke* that "diversity will, in fact, yield educational benefits," and argued further that affirmative action would help educational institutions train "a set of leaders with legitimacy in the eyes of the citizenry."[63]

In rejecting a rigid points system while allowing some forms of affirmative action, the Court again struck a compromise that placed it in the mainstream of public opinion. Perhaps recognizing this fact, George W. Bush, whose administration had urged the Court to ban all types of affirmative action, praised the Court "for recognizing the value of diversity on our nation's campuses." Still, Bush added, "I look forward to the day when America will truly be a color-blind society."[64]

Comparing Civil Rights

Elections, Courts, and Civil Rights: An Appraisal

Significant problems still beset African Americans in the United States as well as elsewhere. Chief among them is the persistence of poverty in the black community. Poverty rates among blacks remain about two and one half times those of whites.[65] Black unemployment is nearly double the national average.[66] And teen pregnancy and infant mortality rates are far higher among African Americans than among others.[67] Critics argue that although middle- and upper-class blacks have made progress, these successes have not translated into wide-reaching economic gains for all African Americans.[68]

But there is increasing reason for optimism about the status of African Americans in the United States. The victories of the civil rights movement have promoted advancement in almost every sector. The percentage of black men and women in professional and managerial positions increased markedly in the decades following the passage of the Civil Rights and Voting Rights Acts.[69] Blacks have also made political gains, winning an increasing number of mayoral elections, state legislative races, and seats in Congress, and they have made noticeable educational advances. The percentage of blacks between the ages of 18 and 24 who have dropped out of high school fell from over 27 percent in 1975 to less than 14 percent in 2001. And between 1977 and 1999 the math and science test scores of black high school seniors improved by 6 percent, while the scores of white students either remained unchanged or dropped over the same period.[70]

The economic expansion of the late 1990s also proved beneficial to blacks. Although the poverty rate among African Americans is still much higher than that of whites, it was 18 percent lower in 2002 than it was in 1995.[71] The unemployment rate among blacks fell even faster.[72]

Civil Rights of Other Minorities

Most of the civil rights issues and rulings discussed thus far apply as much to other racial and ethnic groups as they do to African Americans. The civil rights of other ethnic groups nonetheless assume distinctive legal and political significance under two circumstances: (1) when groups eligible for affirmative action need to be defined, and (2) when language or other group-specific issues arise.

The Supreme Court has never specifically delineated the groups in American society whose treatment over the course of U.S. history makes them eligible for affirmative action. Neither the 1964 nor the 1965 civil rights legislation identified any groups other than blacks as deserving affirmative action to redress historical grievances. But after the civil rights movement defined many issues in terms of equal protection under the Constitution, groups representing other ethnic minorities began to make similar civil rights claims, and Congress, through voting rights legislation, has given them recognition.

The pace of this process and the degree to which each group receives recognition in law have in large part depended on how effectively each group has been able to mobilize its members in elections. Latinos, Asian Americans, and gays and lesbians have recently begun to exert their influence on national electoral politics. But until very recently Native Americans remained a small, politically inactive voting bloc.

Latinos

Latinos are now the largest minority group in the United States. In 1980 they made up only 6.4 percent of the U.S. population, but by 2002 they had grown to 13.4 percent, surpassing the 13.3 percent that are African American.[73] In contrast to African Americans, who have been politically assertive for nearly 50 years, Latinos are only beginning to exercise their influence regularly in elections. There are several reasons for this difference. A sizable percentage of the Latino population lacks citizenship, and even among Latino citizens voting rates are much lower than among African Americans, partly because most Latinos have not experienced a prolonged—and unifying—civil rights struggle.[74] Many new Latino immigrants also may plan to return to their countries of origin and therefore care more about the politics of the home country than about politics in the United States.[75]

Building a broad-based political coalition is further complicated by the fact that Latinos come from many different countries and differ from one another in important

Courting the Latino Vote

George P. Bush, whose mother is of Mexican descent, campaigned for his uncle, George W. Bush, in the Latino community in 2004.

• *Why are parties paying closer attention to Latino voters?*

cultural and political respects. For example, Mexican Americans in California and Texas who are concerned about job discrimination and working conditions may have a hard time identifying with Cuban Americans in Florida who are primarily concerned with the restoration of democracy in their home country. Latino voters are also much less likely than African Americans to vote as a bloc. Whereas 83 percent of blacks consider themselves Democrats, only 57 percent of Latinos do.[76]

Like African Americans, Latinos have mobilized through both social protest and legal activism. In the late 1960s and early 1970s, Mexican Americans in the Southwest founded the Chicano Movement, which argued for cultural and social separatism from white America. But it was the United Farm Workers Union, under the leadership of César Chávez, that drew mainstream public attention to Latino concerns. In the late 1960s, Chávez organized a five-year national boycott of grapes to protest working conditions for migrant farm workers. The boycott, along with marches, strikes, and other nonviolent protest tactics, led to California legislation that guaranteed farm workers rights. In addition, Chávez's principled appeals drew respect from large numbers of Americans, just as the African American civil rights movement had. Reflecting on his uncle's legacy, Federico Chávez said, "He taught us to persevere in a nonviolent way so when you won, it would be a moral victory as well as an organizing victory. . . . In that way, I think, he was able to gain the support of the American people."[77]

In 1968, while Chávez was organizing California farm workers, Latinos in Texas founded the Mexican American Legal Defense and Education Fund (MALDEF), a legal advocacy organization that has focused on voting, education, and immigration issues (see Chapter 4 for discussion of immigration). In 1974, in response to MALDEF complaints, the Supreme Court interpreted the 1964 Civil Rights Act to mean that schools must provide special educational programs for those not proficient in the English language.[78] MALDEF and other groups also argued that Latinos and other language minorities were discriminated against because ballots and other voter registration materials were published only in English. Congress responded to these concerns in 1982 by requiring that ballots be printed in the language of any protected minority that constitutes more than 5 percent of a county's population, thereby extending protection not only to Latinos but also to Asian Americans and American Indians.[79]

Latinos have also begun to make their influence felt in elections—first in state and local politics, later in national campaigns—although their voter turnout remains low relative to other groups.[80] A key turning point came in 1994 when California voters passed Proposition 187, which would have denied state and local public services to illegal aliens. (See the Election Connection in Chapter 4.) Although courts blocked the measure before it could be implemented, the bitter campaign over its passage energized the California Latino community and caused many Latinos to support the Democratic Party, which had opposed the measure.[81]

Both national parties, anticipating that Latinos would make up nearly a tenth of the voting population in 2004, actively courted the Latino vote as the election approached.[82] George W. Bush stressed his support for some bilingual education programs and his opposition to English-only mandates. He also presided over aggressive efforts to appoint Latinos to many top government positions, including Mel Martinez as Secretary of Housing and Urban Development.[83] Finally, he suggested a limited amnesty for illegal immigrants with ties to those already in the United States, and he proposed a new guest-worker program for immigrants that would allow non-citizens to work legally in the United States for up to six years.[84]

Democratic presidential candidate John Kerry appealed to Latino voters as well, promising to allow undocumented immigrants to earn legal status if they had been in the United States for a long period of time, had been working, and could pass a background check.[85] Democrats saw Latino voters as crucial in key southwestern states, as well as Florida.[86]

Asian Americans

Like Latinos, Asian Americans have only recently begun to make their voices heard in national electoral politics. They constitute less than 4 percent of the population, and over 60 percent are foreign born.[87] Like Latinos, they represent many different nationalities and have differing—even conflicting—policy concerns. Asian Americans are also less likely to support affirmative action programs and more likely to vote Republican than other ethnic minorities.[88]

In 1996 activists in the Asian American community flexed their political muscle by mounting a coordinated national fund-raising and voter-registration drive.[89] That year, Gary Locke of Washington State was elected the first Asian American governor of a state other than Hawaii. But the Clinton campaign's fund-raising scandals, in which several Asians and Asian Americans were involved, caused many to worry about a backlash against the Asian American community. When, at the same time, a Chinese American scientist was jailed on thin evidence for alleged spying for the Chinese government, activists voiced public concern about stereotyping of Asian Americans and about a "chilling effect" on Asian American political participation.[90] Eventually, the government dropped all but one less serious charge against the scientist.

The major civil rights victory for Asian Americans in recent years has been the compensation paid to Japanese Americans for their internment in relocation camps during World War II. Responding to public concern that Japanese Americans on the West Coast might act as spies or saboteurs for Japan, President Franklin Roosevelt ordered 70,000 Japanese American citizens and another 40,000 resident Japanese to leave their homes and live in "relocation centers" for the duration of the war. Those who swore loyalty to the United States were released, but if they lived close to either coast, they were told they could not return home. Earl Warren, the California attorney general and later chief justice of the Supreme Court, gave a race-based rationale for these actions: "When we are dealing with the Caucasian race we have methods that will test the loyalty of them. . . . But when we deal with the Japanese . . . we cannot form any opinion that we believe to be sound."[91]

In *Korematsu v. United States* (1944), the Supreme Court went along with ferociously anti-Japanese public opinion and found the relocation centers constitutional. But in his dissent from the Court's decision, Justice Frank Murphy condemned the relocation as "one of the most sweeping and complete deprivations of constitutional rights in the history of this nation."[92] At the instigation of Japanese American activists organized as the National Coalition for Redress and Reparations, Congress agreed in 1988 to apologize for the incident and pay each internee (or the internee's heirs) $20,000.[93]

Because of the diversity of the Asian American community, a unified political agenda for the future has yet to take shape. Some Asian American activists and political organizations are concerned with issues such as immigrant rights and expanding the Supreme Court's definition of a suspect classification to include Asian language speakers.[94] However, other Asian Americans favor the elimination of quotas and affirmative action programs from which they are excluded.

**Civil Rights and
Gay Adoption**

Gays and Lesbians

Some of the most contentious political debates in the early twenty-first century surrounded the rights of gays and lesbians. It is no accident that at the same time, homosexuals were more engaged in electoral politics than ever before. Although the first local law protecting individuals against discrimination on the basis of sexual orientation was passed in 1973, and the first such state law in 1982, it has only been since the early 1990s that the gay and lesbian community has exerted significant influence in national elections.[95] In 1992, gay and lesbian donors gave an estimated $3.5 million to the Clinton campaign, persuading Clinton to promise, among other things, an end to the ban on gays in the military.[96] Congressional and media attention paid to gay and lesbian issues also rose around the same time, in part as a result of pressure from organized gay and lesbian interest groups.[97] Since the early 1990s the number of openly gay government officials has quadrupled, from 49 to over 200.[98]

In the last decade the American public grew to believe that gays deserve equal job opportunities, as Figure 17.3 shows. Laws barring employment discrimination on the basis of sexual orientation have been passed in fourteen states and have bipartisan support in Congress.[99] In 2000 Vermont became the first state legally to recognize same-sex civil unions. Three years later, the Massachusetts Supreme Judicial Court ruled

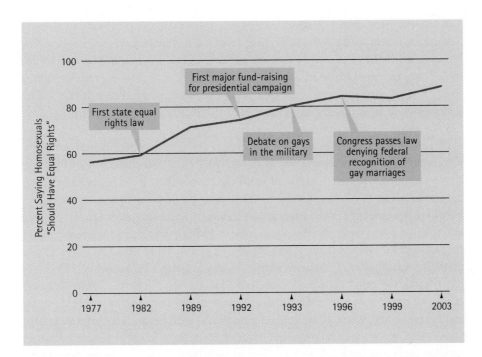

FIGURE 17.3

Public Opinion on Gay Rights Has Changed as Gay and Lesbian Political Activism Has Increased

• *Why do you think support for gay rights declined slightly in the late 1990s after rising steadily for so long?*

SOURCE: The Gallup Poll

that the state's constitution protected the right of gays to marry, and the first legal gay weddings began occurring there in May 2004. That same year, local officials in San Francisco, New Mexico, and upstate New York began marrying gay couples in the absence of a specific legal mandate to do so. San Francisco mayor Gavin Newsom said his decision to allow such marriages was risky, but justified: "Most politicians don't get away with doing the right thing at a time when society is not necessarily unanimously ready for that."[100]

Newsom is correct in his assessment that public opinion remains conservative on many issues regarding homosexuality. Large majorities disapprove of gay marriage and have serious reservations when asked whether gays should be allowed to serve as teachers or youth leaders.[101] Thirty-nine states have passed laws banning same-sex marriages.[102] Many in Massachusetts and around the country reacted negatively to that state's supreme court ruling, and the legislature swiftly moved to place a state constitutional amendment on the ballot that would restrict same-sex unions. President Bush voiced his support for an amendment to the U.S. Constitution defining marriage as heterosexual, while Democratic presidential candidate John Kerry voiced support for civil unions, but not for gay marriage.

Native Americans

The rights and liberties of descendants of indigenous tribes are not protected by the Bill of Rights, because at the time of the writing of the Constitution, these people were considered members of a foreign nation. As one authority on Indian rights has put it, "No constitutional protections exist for Indians in either a tribal or an individual sense."[103]

The relations between Native Americans and the government are instead governed by laws of Congress and by the many treaties that have been signed by the United States and American Indian tribes. Over the long course of American history, the United States government, under political pressure from those migrating westward, ignored or broke many of the treaties it made with indigenous tribes. Still, the Supreme Court today interprets some of these treaties as binding.[104] As a result, members of these tribes have certain rights and privileges not available to other groups. For example, Court interpretations of treaties have given tribes in the Pacific Northwest special rights to fish for salmon—rights that tribes view as vital in preserving their cultural and religious traditions. These exemptions can also be economically important for Native Americans, who suffer from the highest poverty rates of all U.S. racial and ethnic groups.[105]

Another economically significant tribal right recognized in recent years has been the authority to provide commercial gambling on tribal property. In several cases, tribes have used resources from these gambling operations to increase their political clout. For example, the Choctaw Native American tribe in Mississippi spends $3 million annually on Washington, DC, lobbyists. According to Choctaw Chief Philip Martin, "If you don't have some political influence in this country, you don't have anything."[106]

Most of the rights contained in the Bill of Rights have been applied to members of tribes through congressional legislation. To protect tribal religious freedom, Congress in 1978 passed the American Indian Religious Freedom Resolution. Tribal leaders have argued that the resolution gives them special access to traditional religious sites in national parks and other government-owned lands. But the federal courts have interpreted the resolution narrowly, saying it does not make indigenous Americans "supercitizens." Rather, it gives them religious freedoms comparable to those granted to other citizens.[107]

Women's Rights

Although gender is not mentioned in the equal protection clause of the Fourteenth Amendment, the meaning of the clause has been gradually redefined to refer to equal rights for women as well as for racial and ethnic groups. As one constitutional scholar has written, "It is in the very nature of ideas to grow in self-awareness, to work out all their implications over time. . . ."[108] Changes in the meaning of the equal protection clause were won as a result of a broad struggle for women's rights played out as much among the electorate as in the legal arena.

The first struggle for women's rights focused on the right to vote (see Chapter 6, page 150). Once the Nineteenth Amendment was passed in 1920, the women's movement became dormant for nearly 50 years, finally to be awakened in the late sixties by the civil rights movement.[109] Since then, women's groups have achieved four civil rights objectives: the right to equal treatment before the law, tough enforcement of this right, the right not to be sexually harassed in the workplace, and access to state-funded military academies. Achievement of these objectives required both electoral involvement and courtroom presentations.

The Right to Equality Before the Law

As unlikely as it may seem, it was a conservative southerner, Representative Howard Smith of Virginia, who proposed an amendment to Title VII of the Civil Rights Act of

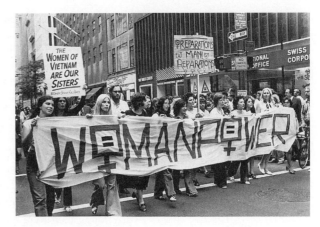

Women's Rights Across the Century
(left) Women's rights issues in the United States at first focused on women's right to vote.
(right) In August 1970, 50 years after women had won the franchise, 10,000 women's liberationists marched to a "Women's Strike for Equality" rally at New York City's Bryant Park.
• *Why did the women's rights movement begin in the 1970s, when women had voting rights as early as 1920?*

1964 that would prohibit discrimination on the basis of sex as well as race, religion, or national origin. Although the amendment passed overwhelmingly, the National Organization for Women (NOW) was formed because activist women became concerned that the gender provision in Title VII would not be enforced. To guarantee enforcement of women's civil rights, NOW, together with other women's organizations, backed the **Equal Rights Amendment,** a proposed amendment to the Constitution that banned gender discrimination. Proponents expected this amendment to give the courts the tools necessary to strike down gender inequities.

At first it seemed that women's groups would succeed in winning passage of this constitutional amendment. Responding to its female constituency, Congress passed the ERA by overwhelming majorities by the spring of 1972. Within a year a majority of states had voted to ratify it.[110] But at the very moment when the ERA was about to become a part of the U.S. Constitution, it encountered increasing resistance led by groups of conservative women who were concerned, among other things, that the amendment would require government funding of abortions and the application of the military draft to women.[111] With women divided, the amendment was ratified by 35 states but failed to win approval from the 3 additional legislatures necessary to achieve the three-fourths required to ratify a constitutional amendment.

As discouraging as the ERA defeat was for its supporters, in retrospect it seems that they won the war by losing the battle. Fifty years earlier, the women's movement had collapsed immediately following passage of the Nineteenth Amendment. This time, the women's movement continued to forge on, perhaps partly because the Equal Rights Amendment did not pass. In the 25 years after the ERA campaign began in earnest, women's place in politics changed more dramatically than in any previous quarter-century. More women were elected to public office in the 1990s than ever before.[112] In 2004 the House of Representatives included 62 women, the Senate had 14, and 2 of the 9 Supreme Court justices were female.

Equal Rights Amendment (ERA)
Proposed amendment to the Constitution that banned gender discrimination.

Initial Court Response to Women's Rights

The ERA also had an impact on Supreme Court decisions. Before the ERA campaign, the Court had done little for women's rights. As late as 1961, in an opinion ironically signed by the same chief justice who wrote the *Brown* decision, Earl Warren, the Court unanimously upheld a Florida law that made a clear gender distinction. It said that men were to be asked to serve on juries but that women were to serve on a jury only if they volunteered for duty.[113]

Court opinions changed after the House of Representatives voted overwhelmingly in favor of the ERA's passage. The Supreme Court, in *Craig v. Boren* (1976), declared unconstitutional an Oklahoma law that allowed women to drink at age 18 but denied that privilege to men until the age of 21. Oklahoma defended the law on the grounds that young men were more likely than young women to drive when drunk and were therefore more likely to have accidents. But the Supreme Court rejected this argument as irrelevant on the grounds that the law constituted "invidious gender-based discrimination" that constituted "a denial [to males] of equal protection of the laws in violation of the Fourteenth Amendment."[114] (Oklahoma subsequently made 21 the legal drinking age for both men and women.)

Although the Supreme Court said that gender discrimination violates the equal protection clause, it has never said that gender, like race, is a suspect classification that will be strictly scrutinized by the courts to see whether its use is constitutional. Instead, the Court has said only that it will rule against a law that includes gender distinctions unless those distinctions have "a substantial relationship to an important objective."[115]

National defense remains the most important arena in which classifications by gender remain intact. According to federal law, men must register for the draft but women need not, and men carry out combat assignments whereas women are not allowed to do so—although many "noncombat" positions now assigned to women may actually place women in danger of enemy fire. The Supreme Court ruled gender distinctions within the military constitutional in *Rostker v. Goldberg* (1981) on the grounds that on military matters, "Congress' constitutional power" is broad and "the lack of competence on the part of the courts is marked."[116] The ruling was consistent with the view of a majority of the voters, who favored certain restrictions on female participation in military combat.[117]

Discrimination in the Workplace

Employers sometimes argue that they have legitimate reasons for not hiring representative numbers of women and members of disadvantaged groups. Certain jobs might only be performed effectively by people of a particular gender. (The position of prison guard could be one example.) Qualified job applicants from disadvantaged groups may also be in short supply. In such cases of "business necessity," the Supreme Court has allowed employers to maintain unrepresentative workforces.[118] Furthermore, in *Ward's Cove Packing Co. v. Antonio* (1989), the Court also said that, under Title VII of the Civil Rights Act of 1964, workers who bring discrimination suits have a responsibility to prove that business necessity is not at issue in their cases.[119]

In a dissenting opinion, Justice Harry Blackmun denounced this interpretation of the Civil Rights Act as hostile to women and minorities. "One wonders," he said, "whether the majority [of the Court] still believes that . . . discrimination is a problem

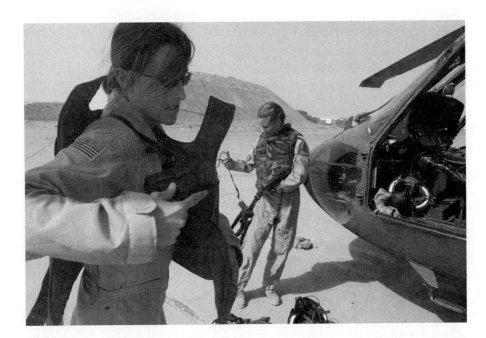

Women in the Military
Classifications by gender still exist in the military. Although women can serve as combat pilots, they may not serve in front line Army infantry units, for example.
• *Are these gender distinctions justified?*

in our society, or even remembers that it ever was."[120] Mindful of how important the burden of proof can be in discrimination cases, where evidence is sometimes sparse and inconclusive, women's groups and civil rights activists pressed Congress to take action. Congress did so in the Civil Rights Act of 1991, which was signed by President George H. W. Bush. This act reversed the *Ward's Cove* decision, placing the burden of proof on employers rather than on workers. In sum, it was elected officials, not the Court, who took the lead on this gender discrimination issue.

Sexual Harassment

The Supreme Court did not rule on the meaning of sexual harassment in the workplace until *Meritor Savings Bank v. Vinson,* a case decided in 1986.[121] In this case, Michelle Vinson said that she had been psychologically damaged as a result of sexually abusive language used in her presence. In deciding in Vinson's favor, Justice Rehnquist wrote a narrow opinion that strongly implied that sexual harassment would be considered illegal only if it caused psychological damage to the victim. In other words, the Court said sexual harassment had to be experienced as personally devastating before it constituted a violation of Title VII.

Sexual harassment became a major political issue in 1991, when Clarence Thomas was nominated to serve on the Supreme Court (see Chapter 15, page 415). The issue so energized the women's movement that 1992, the election year that followed, became known as the "year of the woman." NOW reported a dramatic jump in membership that year and presided over a 750,000-person march in Washington, DC.[122] The number of women elected to the House of Representatives increased by 19, and 4 more women were elected to the Senate. Responding to the change in the political atmosphere, the Supreme Court, in the unanimous 1993 decision *Harris v. Forklift Systems,* expanded its definition of sexual harassment.[123] Teresa Harris resigned her position at Forklift Systems Inc., a heavy equipment rental firm, because her employer called her "a dumb ass woman" and made other derogatory remarks. Lower courts denied her compensation, because no psychological damage could be shown. But Justice Sandra Day O'Connor wrote, in the majority opinion, that Title VII "comes into play before harassing conduct leads to a nervous breakdown." Once again, the Supreme Court moved forward in the wake of public pressure and political events.

Single-Sex Schools and Colleges

Single-sex schools have long been a significant part of American education. As late as the 1950s, well-known private colleges, such as Princeton and Yale, limited their admissions to men. Although these colleges now admit approximately equal numbers of men and women, single-sex education survives at some private women's colleges. These colleges assert that women learn more in an environment where many can assume leadership roles. Hillary Rodham Clinton, who graduated from Wellesley, a Massachusetts women's college, said it "was very, very important to me and I am so grateful that I had the chance to go to college at a place where women were valued and nurtured and encouraged."[124] Arguments have recently been made for all-male education as well. In 1989 the Dade County, Florida, school system established an all-male elementary school serving African American boys.[125] The school system claims that the school has succeeded in increasing student attendance and test scores, while reducing hostility among the students. In 2004, in response to such claims, the Bush administration drafted new regulations designed to make it easier to establish single-sex public schools.[126]

Although policy makers continue to debate the pros and cons of single-sex education, the Supreme Court in 1996 cast doubt on its constitutionality. In *United States v. Virginia,* the Court ruled that women must be admitted to Virginia Military Institute (VMI), even though the state had recently established a separate military education program for women.[127] The Court said the newly established military training program for women did not match the history, reputation, and quality of VMI. It remains unclear, however, whether the Court will extend its decision to private schools or to state programs beyond those that prepare young people for military careers.

The Future of Women's Rights

Despite many gains, the women's movement has not yet realized all of its civil rights agenda. Sexual harassment remains a burning issue within the military and in many business firms. Women still face difficulties breaking through what is known as the **glass ceiling**—the invisible barrier that has limited their opportunities for advancement to the highest ranks of politics, business, and the professions.[128] Few women are chosen as college presidents, as heads of major corporations, or as partners in major law firms. And no woman has yet been nominated for president by either major political party.

The changing American family has also left many women in difficult circumstances. The percentage of children raised in single-parent families headed by a woman has increased sharply in the past quarter-century, and these households are much more likely to be poor than households headed by males or couples. In 2002 the Bush administration announced plans to address this problem by promoting marriage through educational campaigns and counseling programs for poor women. But some women's advocates argued that federal money would be better spent on financial assistance. "To say that the path to economic stability for poor women is marriage is an outrage," argued

glass ceiling
The invisible barrier that has limited women's opportunities for advancement to the highest ranks of politics, business, and the professions.

NOW's president, Kim Gandy.[129] This and other debates suggest that women's issues are likely to remain an important feature in American politics in the twenty-first century.

Americans with Disabilities

According to the U.S. Census Bureau, disabled people constitute over 18 percent of the working-age population.[130] Ironically, they have one political advantage that both women and minorities lack: Every person runs the risk of someday becoming disabled. The rights of disabled people thus have broad appeal. Yet this advantage is offset by a number of factors that make coordinated political efforts more difficult: disabilities differ in kind and severity, the disabled are more scattered geographically and less visible than ethnic minorities, and the more severely mentally disabled neither vote nor engage directly in politics. The cost of helping people with disabilities is another drawback. It is estimated that the annual cost of disability payments and health care services for this group exceeds $300 billion.[131] Although many people are, in principle, sympathetic to the needs of the disabled, they do not necessarily like to pay the taxes needed to fund appropriate services.

You Are the Mayor

The needs of the disabled were first successfully cast in terms of civil rights not by an interest group but by one individual, Hugh Gallagher, a wheelchair-bound polio victim who in the mid-sixties served as a legislative aide to Alaska Senator E. L. Bartlett. Gallagher constantly faced great difficulty using public toilets and gaining access to such buildings as the Library of Congress. At his prodding, Congress in 1968—just four years after the 1964 Civil Rights Act—enacted a law requiring that all future public buildings constructed with federal monies provide access for the disabled. Similar language was subsequently inserted into transportation legislation in 1970.[132]

Once elected officials had responded to the demands of the disabled, the courts, too, became more sensitive. Previously, many developmentally disabled children were denied access to public education on the grounds that they were not mentally competent. But in the early seventies, federal courts required that states provide disabled children with equal educational opportunity.[133] These decisions generated a nationwide movement for disabled children, culminating in the passage in 1975 of the Education for All Handicapped Children Act. Reauthorized as the Individuals with Disabilities Education Act in 1990, this legislation guarantees children with special needs the right to an appropriate education.[134]

Encouraged by both judicial and legislative victories, disability rights groups became increasingly energetic and assertive. Legislative victories in education, transportation, and construction of public buildings finally culminated in the Americans with Disabilities Act of 1991, signed by President George H. W. Bush. This act made it illegal to deny employment to individuals on the grounds that they are disabled, unless the person's disability "pose[s] a direct threat to the health or safety of other individuals in the workplace."[135] In addition, workplaces and public accommodations must be adapted to the capacities of disabled persons, whenever feasible.

Because of these legislative changes, opportunities for the disabled have greatly increased. Twenty years ago, public toilets for the disabled hardly existed; sidewalks and staircases had no ramps; buses and trains were inaccessible to those in wheelchairs; colleges and universities were designed in ways that all but precluded attendance by the physically challenged; and developmentally disabled children were denied a public education. Unlike President Franklin Roosevelt, who 50 years ago felt it necessary to avoid being photographed in the wheelchair to which he was confined, Robert Dole referred constantly to his disabled arm during his 1996 campaign for the presidency. Meanwhile, Georgia voters elected wheelchair-bound, Vietnam veteran Max Cleland to the Senate, and President Clinton appointed David Tatel, who is blind, to a federal appeals court.

The courts themselves have shown considerable reluctance to interpret the rights of the disabled in sweeping terms. For example, in 2001 the Supreme Court ruled against an Alabama state employee who was punished for taking time off from her job to be treated for breast cancer. The employee, Patricia Garrett, argued that the Americans with Disabilities Act protected her from discrimination. But the Court said that state governments were not covered by the act because of their rights under federalism (see Chapter 3).[136] In 2002, a unanimous Court ruled that to qualify for protection under the ADA, a person must have a condition that impairs activities "central to daily life"—not just workplace activities.[137] In these and other cases, the disabled have found that legislators have been friendlier to their cause than judges.

Yet the disabled, too, have begun to encounter increasing political resistance. Educators complain that too many school dollars are set aside for special-education programs. Architectural changes in public buildings and adaptations in transportation are said to be far too expensive to justify the limited amount of usage they receive. One example of the controversy that accommodations for the disabled can stir occurred in 2001, when the Supreme Court ruled that disabled golfer Casey Martin should be allowed to use a golf cart in competition. Many golfers had argued that walking from hole to hole was fundamental to the game. "I don't think the Supreme Court is in a position to tell me what is or is not important to the game of golf," argued one golf pro who was upset with the decision. "They're not players."[138] It remains to be seen whether such complaints are a sign that the rights of the disabled are soon to be subjected to more limits or whether the extensions enacted in recent years will continue.

Chapter Summary

Civil rights groups have achieved many of their advances by persuading majority populations of the justice of their causes through participation in political demonstrations and electoral politics.[139] The 1954 *Brown* decision, to be sure, had an impact of its own, but even this decision came only after blacks had demonstrated political clout in the 1948 presidential election. Otherwise, the Supreme Court has usually followed the moods and trends of the rest of the country. When the country abandoned Reconstruction in the latter part of the nineteenth century, the Supreme Court, in the *Civil Rights Cases* and *Plessy v. Ferguson,* ruled against civil rights demands. When blacks moved north and thereby acquired the right to vote, the Supreme Court reversed these decisions and redefined the equal protection clause, banning discrimination against African Americans, Latinos, Asians, and members of other minority groups. Yet the most notable progress toward racial desegregation occurred as the result of legislation passed by bipartisan majorities in Congress in 1964 and 1965.

When civil rights groups called for metropolitan-wide desegregation and affirmative action programs in the North, many northern whites, no less than southern whites, felt threatened by racial change. Supreme Court decisions in the 1970s reflected this new mood. The Court said *de facto* segregation was not contrary to the Constitution, and the Court also forbade quotas as part of affirmative action programs.

Latinos, Asian Americans, gays and lesbians, and American Indians have achieved varying degrees of legal rights, and the differences have largely reflected their electoral clout. In general, these groups have only begun to exert their strength in national elections, although they were influential in some states and localities much earlier.

The modern women's rights movement grew out of the civil rights movement. Once women's groups became active, they achieved striking changes in legal doctrine, even though they did not succeed in securing passage of the ERA. The Supreme Court has outlawed most forms of

Former Senator Max Cleland Attends a Rally in Support of Democratic Presidential Candidate John Kerry

• *Are the rights of the disabled more effectively protected by the courts or by elected officials? Why?*

gender discrimination, but women are not allowed in combat positions within the military. The Court has declared gender discrimination and sexual harassment in the workplace contrary to the Civil Rights Act of 1964 and has ruled state-funded, single-sex military training unconstitutional.

The civil rights movement also helped focus attention on the rights of the disabled. Once again, the most important steps forward were taken not by the courts but by Congress, which acted in response to electoral-based political pressure.

Key Terms

affirmative action, p. 477

black codes, p. 466

Brown v. Board of Education of Topeka, Kansas, p. 471

civil disobedience, p. 472

civil rights, p. 465

de facto segregation, p. 476

de jure segregation, p. 476

equal protection clause, p. 465

Equal Rights Amendment (ERA), p. 485

glass ceiling, p. 488

grandfather clause, p. 467

Jim Crow laws, p. 467

National Association for the Advancement of Colored People (NAACP), p. 469

Plessy v. Ferguson, p. 467

poll tax, p. 467

quota, p. 477

Reconstruction, p. 466

restrictive housing covenant, p. 470

separate but equal doctrine, p. 467

state action doctrine, p. 467

suspect classification, p. 471

white primary, p. 467

Suggested Readings

Of General Interest

Browning, Rufus, Dale Rogers Marshall, and David H. Tabb. *Protest Is Not Enough: The Struggle of Blacks and Hispanics for Equality in Urban Politics.* Berkeley: University of California Press, 1984. Excellent analysis of the importance of electoral politics for black advances.

Lipsky, Michael. "Protest as a Political Resource." *American Political Science Review* LXII (December 1968): 1144–1158. Shows the limits of protest as a political bargaining tool.

Rosenberg, Gerald N. *The Hollow Hope: Can Courts Bring About Social Change?* Chicago: University of Chicago Press, 1991. Argues that courts are generally unable to act contrary to majority opinion.

Skocpol, Theda. *Protecting Soldiers and Mothers: The Political Origins of Social Policy in the United States.* Cambridge, MA: Harvard University Press, 1992. Analyzes the way women's groups have influenced U.S. social policy.

Focused Studies

Chang, Gordon H. *Asian Americans and Politics: Perspectives, Experiences, Prospects*. Stanford, CA: Stanford University Press, 2001. A series of articles detailing Asian Americans' engagement in U.S. politics.

Deloria, Vine, Jr., and David E. Wilkins. *Tribes, Treaties, and Constitutional Tribulations*. Austin: University of Texas Press, 1999. Discusses the constitutional status of the rights of indigenous peoples.

Garcia, F. Chris, ed. *Pursuing Power: Latinos and the Political System*. Notre Dame, Indiana: University of Notre Dame Press, 1997. A comprehensive series of essays concerning Latino politics.

Ginsburg, Ruth Bader. "Employment of the Constitution to Advance the Equal Status of Men and Women." In Shlomo Slonim, ed., *The Constitutional Bases of Political and Social Change in the United States*. New York: Praeger, 1990, pp. 186–196. Succinct overview of court interpretations of women's rights.

Higgenbotham, A. Leon, Jr. *Shades of Freedom: Racial Politics and Presumptions of the American Legal Process*. New York: Oxford University Press, 1996. A former jurist's sharp critique of the racial bias in American legal practice.

Hochschild, Jennifer L. *Facing Up to The American Dream: Race, Class and the Soul of the Nation*. Princeton, NJ: Princeton University Press, 1995. Discusses how whites and blacks think about one another and argues that racial divisions pose a threat to the American dream.

Katzman, Robert A. *Institutional Disability: The Saga of Transportation Policy for the Disabled*. Washington, DC: The Brookings Institution, 1986. Discusses the ways in which legislative and judicial policy making for the disabled have interacted.

Key, V. O., Jr. *Southern Politics*. New York: Random House, 1949. Classic study of the effects of racial conflict on southern politics.

Lublin, David. *The Paradox of Representation: Racial Gerrymandering and Minority Interests in Congress*. Princeton, NJ: Princeton University Press, 1997. Discusses dilemmas of affirmative action in redistricting.

Mansbridge, Jane J. *Why We Lost the ERA*. Chicago: University of Chicago Press, 1986. Insightful, readable case study.

Riggle, Ellen D. B. and Barry L. Tadlock, eds., *Gays and Lesbians in the Democratic Process: Public Policy, Public Opinion, and Political Representation*. New York: Columbia University Press: 1999. A series of sophisticated essays on gay and lesbian participation in politics.

Tate, Kathryn. *From Protest to Politics*. Cambridge, MA: Harvard University Press, 1993. Explains black political choices in the 1980s.

Wolbrecht, Christina. *The Politics of Women's Rights: Parties, Positions, and Change*. Princeton, NJ: Princeton University Press, 2000. Shows how divisions between Democrats and Republicans have been affected by debates over women's rights.

On the Web

www.usdoj.gov
In this chapter, we discussed several important pieces of civil rights legislation, such as the Voting Rights Act and the Americans with Disabilities Act. The U.S. Department of Justice's Civil Rights Division provides information on its enforcement of these and other civil rights laws.

www.usccr.gov
In 1957, one year after the Montgomery bus boycott, Congress created the U.S. Commission on Civil Rights. The commission remains active today, investigating complaints of discrimination in many sectors of American society.

www.stanford.edu/group/King/
Martin Luther King, Jr., effectively used nonviolent protest tactics to persuade the majority of Americans of the importance of civil rights. The Martin Luther King, Jr. Papers Project at Stanford University maintains a Web site with many of King's speeches and sermons, as well as several scholarly articles and book chapters.

www.naacp.org
The NAACP, the nation's oldest civil rights organization, successfully pursued the legal strategy that led to the *Brown v. Board of Education* decision.

www.now.org
Created to promote the Equal Rights Amendment, the National Organization for Women is the country's largest feminist organization, with over 500,000 members.

www.nclr.org
In the 2000 census, Latinos surpassed African Americans in population for the first time. This and other factors have convinced Democrats and Republicans that future victories may depend on the Latino vote. The National Council of La Raza monitors issues of concern to Hispanic Americans.

www.hrc.org
Gay and lesbian activists have achieved important goals, but public opinion on this group remains divided. Human Rights Campaign, a leading gay rights organization, monitors changes in public policy toward gays and lesbians at the local, state, and federal levels.

www.leap.org
Leadership Education for Asian Pacifics, Inc. (LEAP) houses the Asian Pacific American Public Policy Institute, which authors numerous reports on Asian Americans.

www.ncd.gov
The National Council on Disability is an independent federal agency that makes recommendations to the president and Congress regarding policy on Americans with disabilities. The agency's site provides links to other relevant federal agencies, press releases, and in-depth reports.

VOICES

OF THE PERMANENT CAMPAIGN

The Politics of the Death Penalty

Excessive bail shall not be required, nor excessive fines imposed, nor cruel and unusual punishments inflicted.
—*CONSTITUTION, Amendment VIII*

THE ISSUE

Is the death penalty a just and legitimate punishment for the most heinous of crimes? Or is it an unconstitutional and unworkable violation of the civil rights and liberties of Americans?

Background

In drafting his proposed bill of rights in 1789, James Madison relied in many respects on previous such declarations. In the case of what would become the Eighth Amendment, he lifted text almost verbatim from the English Bill of Rights of a century earlier, which said, "[E]xcessive bail ought not to be required, nor excessive fines imposed; nor cruel and unusual punishments inflicted." That pronouncement had been drafted in response to the reign of the widely hated King James II, whose enemies were sometimes "hanged, cut down before death, disemboweled, beheaded, and hacked to pieces."[1] For those who wonder what the founders meant by "cruel and unusual," this gruesome punishment would surely fit the bill.

But what about the modern death penalty? Although the number of people executed in the United States is lower now than it was in the 1930s, it has increased steadily since the 1970s, when several Supreme Court decisions made it clearer what kinds of capital-punishment statutes would survive legal scrutiny (see Figure 1). As of 2004, 38 states provide for a penalty of death for the most serious crimes, and criminals may be sentenced to death under federal law for crimes such as treason, grave drug offenses, terrorism, and, under extreme circumstances, murder.[2] In 2002, 71 convicted criminals were executed in the United States, and in 2003, 65 received the death penalty. Over 3700 prisoners sit on "death row," awaiting execution.[3]

Proponents of the death penalty argue that capital punishment is the best way to deter heinous crimes. As George W. Bush put it, "I support the death penalty because I believe, if

Timothy McVeigh

• *Does the example of Timothy McVeigh demonstrate that the death penalty is justified?*

administered swiftly and justly, capital punishment is a deterrent against future violence and will save other innocent lives."[4] Proponents also claim it offers closure to victims or their relatives. After serial killer Ted Bundy was executed in 1989, the father of one of his victims said "People said I even looked different. It took the black cloud out of my perspective."[5] Similarly, when Timothy McVeigh received his death sentence in 2001 for killing 168 people in the Oklahoma City bombing, few observers shed tears, and many victims expressed relief.

But many opponents argue that although it is perhaps not so abhorrent as the excesses of James II, the modern death penalty constitutes cruel and unusual punishment. One of the most eloquent critics of the death penalty, Supreme Court Justice William Brennan, argued that "the state, even as it punishes, must treat its citizens in a manner consistent with their intrinsic worth as human beings—a punishment must not be so severe as to be degrading to human dignity."[6]

In recent years, some anti-death-penalty groups have achieved success with a more practical approach, focusing on allegedly flawed state death penalty systems. In 2000, after a *Chicago Tribune* study convinced Governor George Ryan that the Illinois system was "fraught with error and [presented] innumerable opportunities for innocent people to be executed,"

FIGURE 1

Executions in the U.S. 1930–2003

• *Why do you think executions were more common in the 1930s than today?*

SOURCE: U.S. Department of Justice, Bureau of Justice Statistics, *Capital Punishment 2002* (December 2003).

Ryan—a death penalty supporter in principle—imposed a moratorium on executions in the state.[7] In 2002, Governor Parris Glendening did the same in Maryland. Concern centered on the possibility that the system did a poor job of protecting minorities and low-income defendants from undeserved execution. "The death penalty is typically about the poor, victims of child abuse, [and] people who had bad attorneys," said one expert. "If the only people on death row were the Bundys and McVeighs, the whole debate would be very, very different."[8]

The Death Penalty and Elections

Sensing that a majority of the public supports capital punishment, most politicians adopt that perspective as well. Both Bill Clinton and George W. Bush presided over controversial executions as governors of their respective states during their campaigns for president. In 1994, the last time Congress enacted changes to the federal death penalty law, about three-quarters of both the House and the Senate went on record in favor of it.[9] Despite a slight dampening of support in the late 1990s, large majorities of voters continue to be in favor of the death penalty for murder (see Figure 2).

In fact, the last time a presidential candidate expressed an anti-death-penalty view, in 1988, he became notoriously unpopular for it. Asked by CNN reporter Bernard Shaw during a televised debate whether he would favor capital punishment if his wife had been murdered, Democratic presidential hopeful Michael Dukakis offered an awkward and emotionless response, convincing many voters that he did not understand the suffering of crime victims.

Opposing Viewpoints on the Death Penalty

Against the Death Penalty

Opponents of capital punishment make two types of arguments. The first is that the death penalty in any form is fundamentally immoral:

> "We oppose capital punishment not just for what it does to those guilty of horrible crimes but for what it does to all of us as a society. Increasing reliance on the death penalty diminishes all of us and is a sign of growing disrespect for human life. We cannot overcome crime by simply executing criminals, nor can we restore the lives of the innocent by ending the lives of those convicted of their murders. The death penalty offers the tragic illusion that we can defend life by taking life."

> —United States Conference of Catholic Bishops," A Good Friday Appeal to End the Death Penalty," April 2, 1999

A second argument is that the death penalty, as applied, violates civil rights and liberties by being levied against certain groups—such as African Americans and the poor—more than others:

494

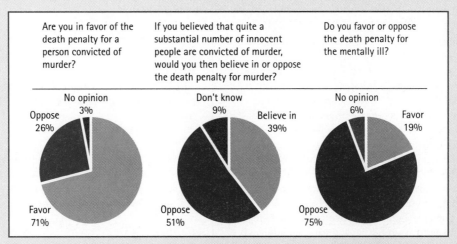

FIGURE 2

Most Americans Favor the Death Penalty, with Reservations

• *Should public opinion about the death penalty influence how the Supreme Court rules on the issue?*

SOURCES: Gallup Poll, May 2-4, 2004; Harris Poll, July December 10-16, 2003; and Gallup Poll, May 6-9, 2002.

"Minorities and the poor often cannot pay for adequate and competent [legal] representation. They cannot afford 'dream teams' who negotiate with prosecutors to eliminate the possibility of a death sentence before a trial begins. . . . Innocent people are often unable to adequately address their legal problems with definitive evidence of their innocence."

—Rep. Jesse L. Jackson Jr. (D-IL), *CQ Researcher,* November 16, 2001

For the Death Penalty

Death penalty critics do not have a monopoly on moral argument. Defenders of capital punishment appeal to justice as well:

"If a man steals your bicycle and society allows him to keep and ride around on that bicycle, most of us would find that profoundly unjust. Why, then, is it just to allow everyone who steals a life to keep his own? . . . [A]llowing all murderers to keep their lives diminishes the worth of human life. The way society communicates what it thinks about a crime is by the punishment it metes out."

—Dennis Prager, "Death Penalty Guards What Is Valued Most," *Milwaukee Journal–Sentinel,* June 9, 2001

They also argue that practical problems with state and federal systems are of minor significance and are being overcome:

"With the average time consumed by appeals between sentencing and execution now at about 10 years, and with the arrival of DNA testing in the 1990s, the likelihood of wrongful executions is less than ever. . . . Compelled to administer justice in an imperfect world, we should not allow a utopian yearning for perfect certainty to render us moral eunuchs."

—Eugene H. Methvin, "Death Penalty Is Fairer Than Ever," *Wall Street Journal,* May 10, 2000

What Do Americans Believe?

A majority of Americans appear to agree, more or less, with the voter who advised one pollster, "I'll tell you where I stand on the death penalty: right next to the switch!"[10] In 2004, 71 percent of Americans said that they favored the death penalty for those convicted of murder, and this number has remained high for many years.[11]

Nevertheless, when pollsters ask voters more complex questions, Americans' positions seem more conditional. Fully three-quarters of respondents oppose the death penalty for the mentally ill, and a majority also say they would oppose capital punishment if errors in the system led to the execution of innocents (see Figure 2). These qualifications explain how elected officials such as the governors of Illinois and Maryland may retain public support even as they enforce a halt in executions.

Is the Death Penalty Constitutional?

In 1972 the Supreme Court ruled in *Furman v. Georgia* that the death penalty, as it was then being applied in the states, violated the Constitution's guarantee against cruel and unusual punishment. The decision was confusing because each justice wrote a separate opinion, but the view of the majority seemed to be that existing death penalty laws were too likely to be unfairly applied across racial and income groups. Legislatures must "write penal laws that are evenhanded, nonselective, and nonarbitrary, and [must] require judges to see to it that general laws are not applied sparsely, selectively, and spottily to unpopular groups," wrote Justice William Douglas.[12]

States struggled for several years to rewrite their laws, and in the meantime they refrained from executing criminals, as Figure 1 illustrates. Then, in 1976, the Court ruled that a new Georgia law that included procedural safeguards against arbitrary executions did not violate the Constitution.[13] Since then, states have modeled their systems on this law, and the use of capital punishment has increased. Some states have gone even further—in Illinois, the legislature enacted a series of reforms in 2003 that was intended to make sure executions were only carried out when guilt was virtually certain.[14]

In 2002 the Supreme Court issued two important rulings on capital punishment that altered the way states administered the death penalty, but did not diverge from majority public opinion on the issue. First, it ruled that juries—not judges—must be responsible for deciding whether to apply the death penalty in any given case. Second, it declared that the execution of mentally retarded criminals constitutes cruel and unusual punishment. The Court explained that these rulings were necessary to safeguard the rights of individuals to a fair and unbiased sentencing process. In the case of the mentally ill, for example, "their impairments can jeopardize the reliability and fairness of capital proceedings."[15] As Figure 2 shows, the public agreed with the Court on this point.

What Do You Think?

1. Should the constitutional guarantee of no cruel and unusual punishment protect criminals from being executed, or does it apply only to sadistic violence such as that practiced by James II?

2. What standard should officials use to determine what constitutes cruel and unusual punishment?

3. Regardless of which position you take on the death penalty, which types of arguments are more convincing to you—moral arguments or practical arguments? Why?

The death penalty is a subject of heated national debate. For this reason, many interest groups have established significant Web sites. The Web sites listed below include information from both sides of the death penalty debate. To conscientiously investigate this controversial issue and the arguments involved, be sure to go to the Web sites of both those groups that are in favor of the death penalty and those groups that are opposed. In your opinion, which Web site(s) present the most convincing argument?

PRO

The Criminal Justice Legal Foundation is a pro-death-penalty organization that assists in a variety of legal cases.

http://www.cjlf.org/

Justice for All, a victims'-rights organization, maintains an extensive Web site containing pro-capital-punishment articles and links, as well as a database of the victims of death row inmates.

www.prodeathpenalty.com

CON

The American Civil Liberties Union condemns capital punishment as "barbaric" and argues that it disproportionately affects poor minority defendants.

www.aclu.org

The National Coalition to Abolish the Death Penalty provides reports, informational materials, and links to other organizations that share its views.

www.ncadp.org

The Death Penalty Information Center provides a variety of in-depth statistical information on the death penalty and its administration, arguing that there are serious practical difficulties with capital punishment.

www.deathpenaltyinfo.org

---

[1] Barry Latzer, *Death Penalty Cases: Leading U.S. Supreme Court cases on Capital Punishment* (Boston, MA: Butterworth-Heinemann, 1998), p. 2.

[2] For more details on the federal death penalty, see *The Federal Death Penalty: A Statistical Survey, 1988–2000* (Washington, DC: U.S. Department of Justice, September 12, 2000), available at http://www.usdoj.gov/dag/pubdoc/dpsurvey.html, accessed July 15, 2002.

[3] Amnesty International, "Facts and Figures About the Death Penalty," March 2002, available at http://www.amnestyusa.org/abolish/facts_fgures032002.pdf, accessed July 15, 2002.

[4] Quoted in John Aloysius Farrell, "Lethal Dilemma: Five of the Prisoners Scheduled for Execution in Texas Early Next Year Will Highlight Gov. George W. Bush's Death Penalty Role," *Boston Globe,* December 19, 1999: p. A1.

[5] Lois Romano, " 'It Took the Black Clout Out'; Families of Murder Victims Find Some Peace After Executions," *Washington Post,* August 8, 1996: p. A19.

[6] *Gregg v. Georgia,* 428 U.S. 153 (1976).

[7] "Illinois Governor Plans to Halt Death Penalty, a Report Says," *New York Times,* January 31, 2000: p. A14.

[8] Michael Radelet, quoted in Michael Kranish, "McVeigh Case Defies Views on Death in General, Support for Executions Down," *Boston Globe,* June 11, 2001: p. A1.

[9] U.S. Senate Roll Call Vote, 103rd Congress, 1st Session, Vote 379 on Levin Amendment to Violent Crime Control and Law Enforcement Act of 1993, www.senate.gov, accessed July 16, 2002; U.S. House of Representatives Roll Call Vote, 103rd Congress, 2nd Session, Vote 107 on Kopetski Amendment to Violent Crime Control and Law Enforcement Act, *Congressional Record,* April 14, 1994, p. H2330.

[10] Farrell.

[11] Gallup poll, June 2, 2004.

[12] *Furman v. Georgia,* 408 U.S. 238 (1972).

[13] *Gregg v. Georgia.*

[14] Monica Davey, "Illinois Governor in the Middle of New Death Penalty Debate," *New York Times,* March 15, 2004, p. A14.

[15] *Atkins v. Virginia,* No. 00-8452 (2002).

CHAPTER 18

* * * * * * * * * * * * * * * *

Domestic Policy

CHAPTER OUTLINE

Types of Public Policy
Stages of Policy Making

Social Policy
Social Insurance for Senior Citizens • Public
Assistance to Poor Families

Education Policy
Local Control • Development of Public Education
• Contemporary Issues in Education Policy •
Politics of Education

Regulation
The Rise of Federal Regulation • Justifications for
Regulation • Politics of Regulation • Deregulation

Medicare Reform and U.S. Domestic Policy

In January 2003, Congressional analysts and administration officials predicted that the government would spend significantly more money over the next year than it collected in taxes. Despite record-setting surpluses in 1999 and 2000, an economic downturn, terrorist attacks, and tax cuts had sent federal budget figures plunging back into the red. The Iraq War promised to deplete government resources even further. Meanwhile, the so-called "baby boom" generation, born from 1945 to the early 1960s, grew ever closer to retirement. When this large generation begins to leave the workforce and rely on social programs for the elderly sometime around 2010, policy experts warn of an unprecedented strain on the federal budget. "The collision course is pretty easy to see," said one economist.[1]

In the face of these budget pressures, it might have seemed that politicians in Washington would work to raise taxes or reduce spending on programs for the elderly in order to place the budget back on an even footing. In fact, the opposite occurred. In addition to enacting a significant tax cut in spring 2003, the president and nearly all of Congress supported increased spending on **Medicare,** the government health insurance program for Americans over the age of 65. In his January State of the Union Address, President George W. Bush promised to "commit an additional $400 billion over the next decade to reform and strengthen Medicare."[2]

Democrats opposed Bush only insofar as they preferred more generous new benefits, as well as limitations on the profits of drug companies. While Bush proposed to cover the cost of prescription drugs only for those Medicare recipients who chose to receive coverage through private insurance providers, Democrats pressed for drug coverage for all Medicare enrollees. Said Democratic Senate Leader Tom Daschle, "America's seniors should never be forced to choose between the doctor they trust and the prescriptions they need."[3]

By the end of the year, Republicans and some Democrats agreed on a compromise plan that would provide limited prescription drug coverage for all elderly Medicare recipients beginning in 2006. Supported by the American Association of Retired Persons (AARP), this bill was criticized as incomplete by Democratic leaders, but many others saw it as a major victory. As California Democratic Senator Dianne Feinstein put it, "I knew in my heart of hearts that the seniors in my great state are going to be better served by this bill than they are today."[4]

Meanwhile, the estimated cost of the plan swelled from $400 billion to more than $530 billion over ten years.[5] The federal budget deficit showed no signs of shrinking. "What's ever happened to my party's fiscal discipline?" complained Republican Senator John McCain.[6]

MAKING THE CONNECTION

Why did Congress rush to add benefits to Medicare even in the face of a growing budget shortfall? Are the needs of the elderly great enough to override concerns about fiscal discipline? Do older Americans have more urgent needs than other groups, such as low income families with children? Or are senior citizens and the middle class better organized and do they exercise more voting power?

To provide a way of thinking about these questions, this chapter examines the electoral and political forces that shape domestic policy. We discuss the various stages through which all domestic policies proceed and then consider three major types of domestic policy: social policy, education policy, and regulatory policy. For each, we examine the political factors that help shape policy outcomes. In doing this, we address the following questions:

- What is domestic policy and how is it made?

- What are the major social policies in the United States, how have they developed over time, and who are the major political actors in debates over these policies?

- How does politics shape education policy?

- What is regulatory policy and how is it formulated?

* * * * * * * * * * * * * * * *

Types of Public Policy

Public policy is a term applied to all government programs and regulations. Often policies are classified as foreign or domestic. Foreign policy involves relations with other nations (see Chapter 20). **Domestic policy** consists of all government programs and regulations that directly affect those living within a country. It includes everything from education and health care to transportation and garbage collection—hundreds of different kinds of governmental activity. However, the distinction between domestic and foreign policy is not always sharp and clear. Some domestic policies, such as immigration policy, affect relations with other countries. Some foreign policies, such as foreign trade regulations, have major domestic consequences. Of all the domestic policies, economic ones are among the most complex and important, and Chapter 19 is devoted to a discussion of economic policy. In this chapter we look at a variety of other domestic policies.

Stages of Policy Making

The making of policy is a complex, never-ending series of events. Most policies develop through a series of stages known as the policy-making round. To clarify what is often a very messy process, political scientists have divided the policy-making round into six stages; these are shown in Figure 18.1. At each stage, policy makers pay close attention to public opinion and try to estimate the consequences of their choices for the next election.

The first stage is **agenda setting,** making an issue visible enough that important political leaders take it seriously.[7] When elected officials think a problem is serious and

Medicare
Program that provides social security recipients a broad range of medical benefits.

domestic policy
Government programs and regulations that directly affect those living within a country.

agenda setting
Making an issue so visible that important political leaders take it seriously.

FIGURE 18.1
Policy-Making Stages
• *Can you match each stage with events in the development of welfare policy?*

policy deliberation
Debate and discussion by groups and political leaders over issues placed on the policy agenda.

policy enactment
Passage of a law by public officials.

policy implementation
Translation of legislation into a set of government programs or regulations.

policy output
Provision of services to citizens or regulation of their conduct.

policy outcome
Effect of policy outputs on individuals and businesses.

Temporary Assistance for Needy Families (TANF)
Welfare reform law passed by Congress in 1996.

Making a Difference: Welfare Reform

might even affect an election, the issue has reached the agenda stage. The second stage consists of **policy deliberation,** the debate and discussion over issues placed on the policy agenda.[8] At this stage, groups and policy experts try to convince leaders not only that their proposals are a good way to deal with the problem, but also that these proposals are popular with the electorate. Next comes **policy enactment,** the passage of a law by public officials. Enactment may involve passage by Congress, a state legislature, or a city council and signing into law by a president, governor, or mayor. Elected officials who vote for the law usually expect that its passage will enhance their popularity, although there have been a few celebrated instances in which political leaders have sacrificed their careers for what they see as the good of the country. The fourth stage is **policy implementation,** translation of the legislation into an actual set of government programs or regulations.[9] When fashioning the details, bureaucrats are expected to carry out the intentions of the legislative branch and not to stray too far from what is politically acceptable. At the fifth stage, government produces **policy outputs,** the provision of services to citizens or the regulation of their conduct. Beneficiaries usually think well of those who established the program; those who are hurt by the policy outputs probably feel otherwise. Finally, **policy outcomes** are the effects of policy outputs on individuals and businesses.[10] These outcomes often give rise to new issues, which are then placed on the policy agenda, completing the policy-making round.

The enactment of the 1996 welfare reform law, **Temporary Assistance for Needy Families (TANF),** illustrates the way politics affects the various stages of the policy round. The first stage, placing the issue on the policy agenda, occurred when Bill Clinton scored points in his 1992 campaign for president by promising to "end welfare as we know it." The second stage, policy deliberation, occurred when interest groups, policy experts, members of Congress, and the media debated many different ways of redesigning welfare policy. Throughout the debate, polls revealed that a majority of the public supported welfare reform, increasing the likelihood that something would be approved. The third stage, policy enactment, saw Congress shift responsibility for welfare policy from the federal to state governments. President Clinton signed the bill into law in part because voters supported the idea, even though he had expressed strong reservations about many of the bill's provisions. The fourth stage, policy implementation, began in early 1997 when many state governments started revising their welfare plans, often in response to electoral pressures at the state level. The fifth stage, policy outputs, took place when many families left or were removed from the welfare rolls.

After nearly ten years under the new law, analysts began to evaluate policy outcomes. Welfare rolls had declined dramatically; fewer than half as many people received assistance in 2004 as in 1994.[11] In fact, contrary to expectations, the number of Americans receiving benefits continued to decline even during the economic downturn of 2001 and the slow economy that followed.[12] Supporters of the reform argued that this proved the policy was a long-term success. But critics charged that this decline during economic hard times was a sign that welfare was not reaching those it was designed to help. "Falling caseloads amid rising poverty should be a cause for concern," argued one expert.[13] In 2004, Congress began debating an extension of the 1996 law, launching a new policy-making round.

The political forces that shape public policies differ from one policy to the next. In the remainder of this chapter we describe the political factors shaping three major types of public policy: social policy, education policy, and regulatory policy.

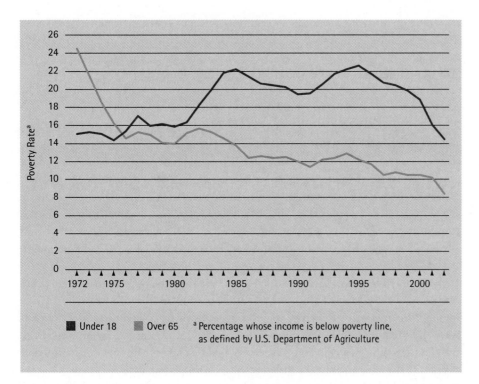

FIGURE 18.2
U.S. Poverty Rates for Senior
Citizens and Children,
1970–2002
• *Why are poverty rates higher for
children than for seniors?*
SOURCE: U.S. Census Bureau,
Historical Poverty Tables—People,
Table RDP-4: Poverty Status by
Age, Race and Hispanic Origin,
http://www.census.gov/hhes/
poverty/histpov/rdp04.html,
accessed March 30, 2004.

Social Policy

Social policy is a type of domestic policy that consists of programs designed to help those thought to be in need of government assistance. People may be regarded as needy because they are old, infirm, young, disabled, unemployed, poor, or some combination of these. One of the central issues in the making of social policy is finding an appropriate balance between government assistance to the elderly and to the young. As the chapter opening emphasizes, the elderly have done particularly well in securing government help.

One can observe the different effects of social policy on the young and the old by comparing some basic statistics concerning changes in the nation's poverty rate. As Figure 18.2 illustrates, poverty among senior citizens fell from 25 percent in 1970 to less than 9 percent in 2002, but child poverty did not decline over this same period of time. The poverty rate among families with children in the United States is twice as high as in most other advanced industrial societies;[14] the poverty rate among senior citizens is about the same in the United States as elsewhere.[15]

Poverty is not just a matter of money; it pervades many aspects of life. For example, the chances of being in good health are different for senior citizens and children. Of the seven countries with the largest economies, the United States has the highest infant mortality rate. But if one becomes a senior citizen, one has a better chance of living longer in the United States than in any of the other six countries. As one analyst put it, the United States is perhaps the "healthiest place to grow old but the riskiest [in which] to be born."[16]

social policy
Domestic policy programs designed to help those thought to be in need of government assistance.

Comparing Social
Welfare Policy

In the next two sections, we explain how this phenomenon came to be. First we describe the development of social programs for senior citizens and the powerful political support that sustains them. Then we describe the development of social programs for children and the more limited support that they enjoy.

Social Insurance for Senior Citizens

The improvement in the well-being of senior citizens today is due in large part to the country's social policy. As the population has aged, the government has expanded programs to meet the retirement income and medical needs of the elderly. The amount spent on social programs for senior citizens grew from around $9700 per senior citizen in 1971 to over $19,200 in 2000.[17] (Unless otherwise indicated, all dollar figures in this chapter are expressed in constant 2004 dollars so as to adjust for inflation.) In this section we describe the conditions that led to this dramatic increase in social insurance.

The Evolution of Social Policy

social insurance
Program that provides benefits in return for contributions made by workers.

social security
Social insurance program for senior citizens.

Origins and Development of Social Insurance Programs　Demands for aid to senior citizens escalated during the Great Depression of the 1930s, when poverty among the elderly was particularly acute. Approximately five million senior citizens rallied behind the proposals of Dr. Francis E. Townsend, a Californian who promised to end the depression by giving everyone over 60 years old the equivalent in today's dollars of $2700 a month, provided that they spent it immediately.[18] Always quick to recognize potential electoral threats, President Franklin Roosevelt checked Townsend's soaring popularity by appointing an advisory committee to recommend better ways of meeting the needs of the elderly. The committee recommended a program of **social insurance**, a program that provides benefits in return for contributions made by workers. In a response consistent with the committee's recommendations, in 1935 Congress enacted the landmark Social Security Act, which created a broad range of social programs, including a social insurance program for senior citizens generally known as **social security**.[19]

The social security program initially cost the government little. Most of those who first retired under the program received minimal benefits because they had paid into the program only for a limited number of their working years. Also, retirement costs were low because, in 1935, average life expectancy for those reaching the age of 65 was only an additional 12.6 years. In contrast, a worker retiring at 65 today is expected to live at least 17 more years.

Gradually, the program expanded. The number of people covered went up; so did the length of their retirement. Benefits increased in size and cost. Two major changes deserve particular attention. In 1965, the year after Democrats won an overwhelming election victory, Congress enacted Medicare, which provides social security recipients a broad range of medical benefits. In 1972, an election year, Congress gave senior citizens a large increase in their monthly social security check and linked, or indexed, this amount to the cost of living. If inflation goes up 10 percent, so does the paycheck.[20] Passed at a time when prices were rising, this new benefit soon became very popular.

The popularity of both social security and Medicare is due in part to the fact that they are based on the insurance principle—that is, the principle that people receive benefits in return for contributions they have made. In the case of social security, the insurance principle works in the following way: People become eligible for benefits by

Johnson Signs Medicare Bill
President Lyndon B. Johnson signs the Medicare bill in 1965 as Vice-President Hubert Humphrey and former President Truman look on.
• *Why did Congress and President Bush agree to expand Medicare benefits in 2003?*

paying a portion of their regular salary—a payroll tax—to social security during their working years. To get social security benefits, beneficiaries need only prove that they are over the age of 65. (This eligibility age will gradually increase to 67 for those born after 1959.) Because of the insurance principle, a retiree does not have to show a need. Upon reaching the age of 65, even billionaire Microsoft founder Bill Gates will be eligible to receive a social security check.

Although social security is called an insurance program, it differs from a true insurance program in one fundamental respect: It operates at a loss. In private insurance programs, most people pay more in initial payments and forgone interest than they receive in benefits; if this were not the case, the insurance company could not make a profit. From the beginning, however, social security has given most people more in benefits than they contributed in their social security tax. A couple who retired in 2000 can expect to receive about $290,000 in social security benefits over the remaining years of their lives, even though the worker in the family made tax contributions of only $148,300.[21]

How is this magic possible? How can benefits exceed contributions? Why have social security and Medicare not gone broke? Up until now, there have been three reasons:

1. Workers have grown in number, as women and "baby boomers" have entered the workforce and unemployment rates have fallen. Thus, more people are contributing to the social security program.
2. Workers today produce more and earn more than their predecessors did. As result, more money is available to distribute to retirees.
3. Workers today pay a higher percentage of their earnings in social security taxes than their predecessors did. Essentially, younger generations have been asked to pay more to cover the expenses of older ones. As economist Lester Thurow has pointed out, "the current generation of retirees . . . did not have to pay [much] into the system

FIGURE 18.3

Projected Cost of Social Insurance for Senior Citizens

• *Why will costs of programs for senior citizens rise rapidly in the coming years?*

Note: Figures after 2003 are estimates; projections are for an 'intermediate cost' scenario.

SOURCE: U.S. Department of Health and Human Services, Social Security Administration, "Status of the Social Security and Medicare Programs," A Summary of the 2004 Annual Reports, http://www.ssa.gov/OACT/TRSUM/trsummary.html, accessed May 25, 2004.

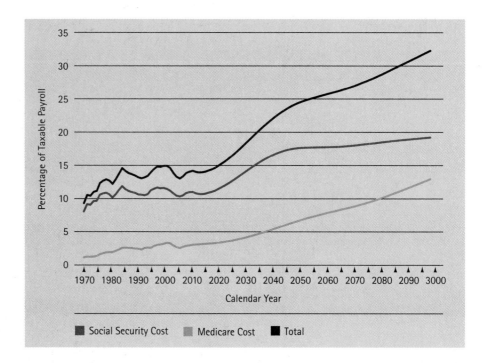

but gets benefits financed by those behind them."[22] The practice is not new. Jonathan Swift saw the same thing happening in England three centuries ago. "'Tis pleasant to observe," he said, "how free the present Age is in laying taxes on the next."[23]

Unfortunately, some of these circumstances may be changing:

1. Experts do not expect the number of workers to increase much in the next couple of decades. The massive baby boom generation will reach retirement age from 2010 to 2030. As they leave the workforce, the number of retirees will grow faster than the number of workers. As a result, the cost of retirement programs will increase, as Figure 18.3 shows.

2. Rates of growth in economic productivity may not always be as high as they were in the 1990s. In 2001, experts were reminded that a serious economic recession could quickly change the picture. Then workers in the future would not be producing enough to cover the higher cost of social security caused by the retirement of the baby boomers.

3. Workers may be less willing to pay higher taxes. It will be difficult to increase taxes to cover the retirement costs of the baby boomers.

For these reasons, a presidential panel declared in December 2001 that "the system is not sustainable as currently structured."[24] Politicians agreed on the problems with the program but disagreed over the varied proposals for reform. More than most other issues, changes in social security are politically excruciating to make, as we explain in the next section.

Politics of Social Insurance   Many subway systems use dangerous middle rails, or third rails, that provide the electricity that drives the trains. Social security and Medicare are said to be the "third rail" of American politics—"touch it and you die." Richard Morin put it another way: "The bottom line on the public's attitude is: Spend whatever is needed—particularly on me—just don't bill us for it."[25]

The Risks of Change to Social Security—Most public officials know they will be punished by the voters if they are perceived as threatening social security programs. Only once, in 1983, did Congress make significant cuts in social security benefits. A commission that included leaders from both political parties recommended cuts that would become effective, for the most part, only in the distant future.[26] Because the recommendations were bipartisan and because cuts were postponed into the next century, the reductions did not produce an electoral fallout. But almost without exception, political leaders since then have opposed cutting social security, even though it is the most costly single program in the entire federal budget. President George W. Bush advocated a partial privatization plan for social security, in which participants could direct that their contributions to the pension system be invested in the stock market. Although Bush stressed that this plan would not mean that the program would be cut, Democrats used the issue against his party in the 2002 elections, arguing that the proposal would endanger senior citizens' retirement funds.

Complexities of Medicare—The politics of Medicare are much the same, making it difficult to keep the cost of the program from growing rapidly. The cost of the program grew from little more than $34 billion in 1970 to over $300 billion by 2004.[27] Numerous factors contribute to the rapidly rising cost of Medicare. Although doctors and hospitals are often accused of profiteering, other factors play a more important role. The number of elderly is growing rapidly, increasing the demand for medical services. Doctors can use better technology to diagnose and treat more crippling injuries and life-threatening diseases. Finally, patients expect error-free medicine; when mistakes are made, lawsuits drive up doctors' insurance costs (and the fees doctors must charge to cover them).

In the late 1990s, Congress made efforts to control some of these costs. It placed limits on Medicare payments for doctor and hospital fees, moved to end the duplication of high-cost technologies, refused to pay for expensive, highly experimental treatments, and encouraged the formation of health maintenance organizations (HMOs), which have strong incentives to rein in costs. These actions only briefly slowed the rising cost of Medicare, however. In 1999 Medicare costs declined slightly from 1998 levels, but they increased by nearly 43 percent over the next five years—well above the rate of inflation.[28] At the same time, doctors complained that reductions in federal reimbursements squeezed them financially, and some refused to take on new Medicare patients. "My expenses go up and up and up every year," said one family doctor. "For the government to lower what it pays me when my expenses are rising—that doesn't make sense. It's an insult."[29]

Analysts expect Medicare costs to rise even faster when the baby boom generation retires and needs more medical services. Meanwhile, politicians have shied away from such cost-saving proposals as raising medical premiums and requiring patients to pay a larger share of the costs, and instead have moved in the opposite direction. As we discussed at the beginning of this chapter, new prescription drug benefits that President

Supporting Medicare
• *Why are there fewer public demonstrations in favor of programs for the poor?*

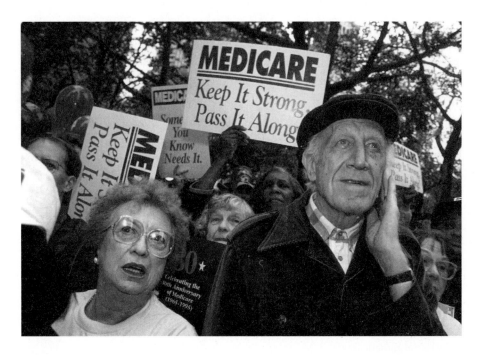

Bush and Congress enacted in 2003 will result in at least an additional $500 billion in Medicare expenses from 2005 to 2015.

The Influence of Senior Citizens—The electoral impact of the social security issue is likely to remain central to American politics. At a time when overall voter turnout has been declining, senior citizen turnout rates are high and have been climbing. Between 1972 and 2000, turnout among voters aged 18 to 24 dropped by 10 percent, while turnout among voters over 65 climbed by 4.1 percent.[30] Around 70 percent of voters over the age of 65 said they voted in the 2000 presidential election, but only 36 percent of those between the ages of 18 and 24 reported voting.[31]

Senior citizens are also much more likely than young people to back up their votes with other political actions, such as writing letters to elected officials and contributing money to political campaigns.[32] Over 35 million people have joined the American Association of Retired Persons (AARP), the largest interest group in the United States.[33]

AARP is a large and influential organization. Upon reaching the age of 50, any person can become a member of AARP for $12.50 per year. Members are eligible for a wide range of travel and other discounts worth much more than their annual dues. They also receive a magazine that keeps them up to date on policy proposals that might affect their social security and Medicare benefits. AARP employs more than 1800 people, works with over 160,000 volunteers, and has an annual budget that exceeds $620 million.[34]

Broad Support—AARP has the advantage of promoting a cause that few voters strongly oppose. In fact, young people are just about as likely to support benefits for senior citizens as those over the age of 65. When asked whether they would be willing to pay higher taxes to fund a prescription drug program for seniors, overwhelming majorities of both young and elderly voters say they would do so (see Figure 18.4).

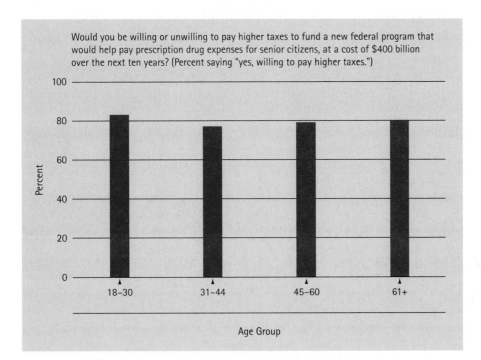

Would you be willing or unwilling to pay higher taxes to fund a new federal program that would help pay prescription drug expenses for senior citizens, at a cost of $400 billion over the next ten years? (Percent saying "yes, willing to pay higher taxes.")

FIGURE 18.4
Both Young and Old Support Senior Citizens' Programs
• *Why do the young support programs for the elderly even though they do not yet receive benefits from such programs?*
SOURCE: Washington Post/ABC News Poll, October 9-13, 2003.

There are three main reasons for the broad support that social security and Medicare enjoy. First, most people hope to benefit from these programs someday themselves. In addition, many have parents who currently receive these benefits, relieving their children of financial responsibility. Finally, most people think that because senior citizens contributed to social security, they now deserve the benefits they were promised, and few are aware that these benefits are usually in excess of the contributions.

Public Assistance to Poor Families

The interests of the elderly may be well protected by AARP and both political parties, but the same cannot be said for the interests of poor families with children. Programs designed for poor families are neither as lavish nor as user-friendly as those designed for the elderly. Neither political party is strongly committed to expanding them, and no association comparable to AARP defends the interests of poor families with children.

Origins and Development of Public Assistance Programs   **Public assistance** consists of programs that provide low-income households with limited income and access to essential goods and services. Together, the programs make up what is often known as the "safety net" that catches those who fall into financial difficulty. The sheer number of major public assistance programs actually exceeds the number of major programs for the elderly. Public assistance programs include Temporary Assistance for Needy Families, food stamps, the Earned Income Tax Credit, rent subsidies, and Medicaid.

Temporary Assistance for Needy Families (TANF)—As we noted earlier in this chapter, this program, enacted by Congress in 1996, gave the states the responsibility for designing income-maintenance programs for poor families. However, state programs are subject

public assistance
Programs that provide to low-income households a limited income and access to essential goods and services.

to certain limitations. For example, no family may receive more than two consecutive years of assistance, and no family may receive more than five years of assistance altogether.

TANF replaced the long-standing public assistance program known as Aid to Families with Dependent Children (AFDC), which was established in 1935 as part of the Social Security Act. AFDC was designed to serve widows, but as the number of unmarried women increased, the size of the program grew sharply and the social composition of beneficiaries changed markedly. Branded "the welfare program," AFDC was criticized by liberals and conservatives alike. Conservatives claimed that it discouraged recipients from working, an argument that became increasingly potent as the percentage of working women increased.[35] Liberals believed that the benefits were too low and that program eligibility and administrative restrictions were too harsh.[36] TANF has proved to be a more popular welfare program, because welfare rolls have fallen and poverty rates have not increased dramatically, as some critics predicted.

Food Stamps—This public assistance program provides recipients with coupons that can be used to purchase food. Enacted by Congress on an experimental basis in the early seventies, it has been gradually expanded, and today it is larger than TANF. Benefits depend on the recipient's income and household size, but the average is about $83 per person per month.[37] The **food stamps** program has been more popular than AFDC was, because most Americans believe everyone should be provided with enough food to avoid going hungry—especially when agricultural surpluses exist.

Earned Income Tax Credit (EITC)—This program uses the tax structure to benefit those who have little income. Initially proposed by Republicans in the early seventies as a way of simultaneously helping the poor and rewarding work, the **Earned Income Tax Credit** program was greatly expanded during the first year of the Clinton administration. An eligible person who fills out a tax return can receive an EITC reimbursement even if he or she has paid no taxes. In 2004, a family of four could receive a credit of as much as $4204 a year.[38]

Supplemental Security Income (SSI)—**Supplemental Security Income** provides disabled people of low income with income assistance. Created in 1972, SSI succeeds programs of aid to the blind and the deaf established by the Social Security Act of 1935. As of January 2003, the average monthly benefit for SSI's 6.4 million recipients was $381.[39]

Rent Subsidies—This policy provides low-income families with government vouchers to help pay their rent, provided that they select designated housing. The **rent subsidies** program was established in the early 1970s to replace public housing programs, which had been criticized for encouraging racial segregation and creating large concentrations of poverty.[40]

Medicaid—This program pays for medical services for the poor. A person becomes eligible only if he or she has no more than a minimal income and few assets other than a home. **Medicaid** was established in 1965, at the same time as Medicare, in response to Republican objections to Medicare on the grounds that it was designed to serve the middle class but not the poor. The cost of Medicaid benefits has risen rapidly—from around $13 billion in 1970 to $177 billion in 2004.[41]

---

food stamps
Public assistance program that provides recipients with stamps that can be used to purchase food.

Earned Income Tax Credit (EITC)
Provision that gives back tax payments to those who have little income.

Supplemental Security Income (SSI)
Program that provides disabled people of low income with income assistance.

rent subsidies
Help in paying rent for low-income families, provided that they select designated housing.

Medicaid
Program that provides medical care to those of low income.

Food Stamp Assistance
The food stamp program is more popular than AFDC was.
• *Why do you think it is the more popular program?*

Although Medicaid serves poor families regardless of age, over one-quarter of all Medicaid costs cover the medical expenditures of low-income senior citizens.[42] Thus, Medicaid is an important supplement to the better-known Medicare program discussed earlier.

Limitations on Public Assistance Programs   This list of public assistance programs that help poor families with children seems impressive, but actual expenditures are only one-tenth as much as what is spent on the elderly. Federal social programs for the elderly amounted to over $17,500 per capita in 2000, whereas public assistance programs for families with children amounted to little more than $1500 per capita (see Figure 18.5). In addition, programs for families with children are more restrictive than programs for senior citizens. Five factors make programs for families with children less user-friendly.[43]

Fewer Cash Benefits—In 2002 the elderly received about 64 percent of their benefits in cash,[44] whereas only 32 percent of the benefits received by poor families with children were cash benefits.[45] Because most people prefer cash income to benefits in the form of goods and services, senior citizens have the better arrangement. Cash income enables one to purchase what one wants and to purchase it when, where, and from whom one wishes.

Less Indexation—Nearly all benefits to the elderly, including social security and other retirement pensions, are indexed to changes in the cost of living. Although some programs for families with children are also indexed, the main welfare program, TANF

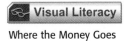

Where the Money Goes

FIGURE 18.5

Federal Entitlement Expenditures by Beneficiary Age Group, Per Capita, 1960–2000

• *Why is so much more spent on the elderly than on children?*

Note: Figures are in constant 2000 dollars.

SOURCE: Neil Howe and Richard Jackson, *2001 Chartbook: Entitlement and the Aging of America* (Alexandria, VA: National Taxpayers Union Foundation, 2001), Chart 2-3.

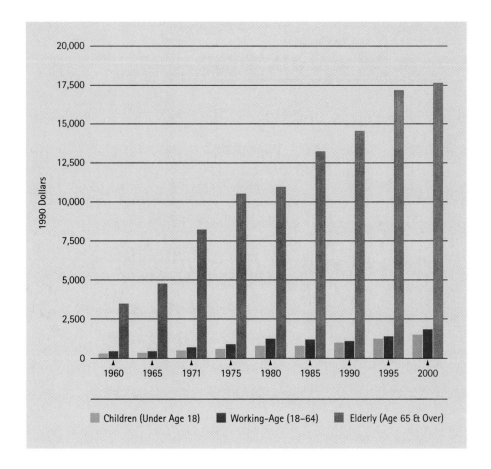

is not. Instead of keeping pace with increases in the cost of living, benefits under this program fell by 7 percent in real terms in the 5 years following the 1996 reform.[46]

Assistance, Not Insurance—Unlike social security, which distributes benefits automatically according to age and contributions made to an insurance fund, programs for families with children are paid out only after family income has been carefully scrutinized. To become eligible for benefits, a low-income family must demonstrate that it has virtually no other means of livelihood. To receive cash benefits, the potential recipient must document that the family does not own a home of any significant value, has virtually no savings, and has hardly any income. According to one survey, over 20 percent of charity food bank users hadn't even applied for food stamps because it was "too much hassle."[47]

State, Not National, Programs—Families with children receive benefits that vary from one state to another. Only EITC benefits are uniform throughout the country. For the other major programs—TANF, food stamps, SSI, housing assistance, and Medicaid—eligibility rules and benefit levels vary from state to state. In the case of TANF, the benefits can be over four times as much in one state as in another.[48]

Because public assistance programs are state-operated, families who have children and who move from one state to another must reconnect to public assistance programs.

As a result, poor families may not be able to respond quickly to job opportunities or changing family circumstances.[49]

These restrictions do not apply to senior citizens because social security is a national program. Senior citizens can move from New Jersey to Florida (or even overseas) without jeopardizing the amount or delivery of their social security check.

Benefits Cannot Supplement Income—The benefits that poor families with children receive are usually a substitute for other income; they do not supplement it. In many states, families are not eligible for income assistance if they have savings of more than $2000, a car worth more than $5000, or anything other than a very modest home (the exact value varies from state to state).[50] Under the old AFDC program, families lost a dollar in benefits for every dollar they earned. Under TANF, states have the flexibility to continue benefits for some working recipients,[51] but these benefits count toward a federal lifetime limit of five years of TANF participation.[52]

By comparison, senior citizen benefits supplement the recipient's own resources. Senior citizens may receive their Medicare and social security benefits even if they are working full-time, have savings, earn dividends and interest on their investments, and are homeowners. Before 2000, social security recipients between 65 and 69 years old lost $1 in benefits for every $3 they earned in wages above $17,000 per year. But Republicans and Democrats in Congress, eager to please elderly voters in an election year, repealed this "earnings penalty" unanimously.[53]

Politics of Public Assistance   Programs for poor families with children are poorly funded and restrictively designed because, unlike the elderly, children and the poor do not exercise direct political power. Instead, they are dependent on others who provide only limited help: policy analysts who offer competing explanations for the persistence of poverty, a weak network of interest groups that fight among themselves, a divided public, and opportunistic political parties.

Policy Debate—Before the government can design solutions, it has to decide what the problem is. But policy experts disagree about the causes of poverty among families with children. Three different theories have influenced the welfare debate.

Liberal theory argues that poverty rates among children have risen because the government has not maintained an adequate level of governmental assistance. Sociologist Theda Skocpol points out that lower poverty rates in European countries are due in part to government programs that aid low-income families.[54] She advocates the establishment of a similar family allowance program that would guarantee all families with children a basic stipend not unlike the social security checks that the elderly receive.

Conservative theory finds the explanation for rising poverty rates in what is identified as a "culture of poverty," in which young people are encouraged to place short-term pleasures ahead of long-term goals. Flashy clothes, adventure, crime, and sexual promiscuity are emphasized, to the detriment of the discipline, patience, and hard work necessary for long-term success. Policy analyst Charles Murray has argued that this culture of poverty has been strengthened and reinforced by welfare policies that reward sloth and irresponsibility. Because they can count on government aid, young people bear more children out of wedlock and think less about responsible parenting.[55]

Spokeswoman for Children
Marian Wright Edelman, founder of the Children's Defense Fund.
• *Why does Edelman have less clout in Washington than the head of AARP?*

Conservatives point out that between 1970 and 2002, the percentage of women with children who were living without a mate doubled—from 11 percent to 22 percent.[56] These female-headed families are particularly at risk of living in poverty. Many women find it difficult to both work and raise children. Mothers who do work find it hard to get full-time jobs at good wages. Nearly two-thirds of all children living in poverty are living in single-parent families headed by a woman.[57] Liberals respond by noting that poverty rates among families with children are much lower in other countries such as Great Britain, France, and Sweden, despite the fact that the frequency of out-of-wedlock births is often just as high or higher than that of the U.S.[58]

Offering a third explanation, sociologist William J. Wilson attributes a growing culture of poverty to *changes in the postindustrial economy.* Physically demanding blue-collar jobs, which can be performed by unskilled workers with minimal education, are declining in number. These jobs have been lost to technology or have moved overseas.[59] As a result, from 1975 to 2001, annual salaries for men without a high school degree plunged from 92 percent to 60 percent of the national average.[60] According to Wilson, when young men cannot find work, they refuse to take on the responsibilities of marriage and child rearing. Young women don't want to marry men with few prospects. Wilson believes his view was substantiated by trends that emerged in the late 1990s. As the economy grew, less-well-educated males found new job opportunities, marriage rates increased, and, at the same time, welfare rolls declined.

Group Organization—No group speaking on behalf of children has a mass membership of a size remotely comparable to that of AARP. Instead, many small, competing groups take stances as varied as the alternative explanations for rising poverty rates. The most significant pro-welfare group, the Children's Defense Fund, headed by Marion Wright Edelman, fought welfare reform to no avail. Although the group had a budget in 2004 of $13 million and a staff of 150, it lacks a large membership that can effectively lobby Congress.[61]

On the conservative side, Gary L. Bauer, a Republican candidate for president in 2000, built the Family Research Council into a 450,000-member organization committed to the protection of family values.[62] The group favored the welfare reform bill, a stance reflecting its conviction that welfare programs, by helping unwed mothers make ends meet, discourage family formation and allow fathers to neglect family responsibilities.

Other groups adopt positions on issues that affect children's welfare, but these groups typically have other objectives more central to their mission. For example, the Urban League has long emphasized the importance of youth programs, but its fundamental objective remains protection of the civil rights of African Americans. The AFL-CIO supports most legislation intended to promote child welfare, but its main concern is protection of the interests of labor. Although many women's groups care about children's issues, they tend to remain focused on issues of gender discrimination and sexual harassment. In short, the interest-group chorus on children's issues sings separate songs in different keys. They are unable to focus on a common cause in the way AARP does.

Public Opinion—The general public wavers between liberal and conservative beliefs about rising poverty rates. In 2001, when the country was entering a recession, the population was evenly divided on the question of whether poverty was due mainly to circumstances beyond a person's control or whether it was due mainly to a lack of effort. But in the mid-1990s, when the economy was booming, twice as many people thought poverty was due to a lack of effort than thought it was due to circumstances beyond a person's control.[63] This public uncertainty makes it difficult for policy makers to generate enthusiasm for public-assistance programs.

Political Parties—Because public opinion on welfare policy fluctuates, so do the positions of the political parties. Most of the time, the Democratic Party takes a more liberal position, the Republicans a more conservative one. Senator Hillary Clinton, for example, was once a member of the liberal Children's Defense Fund's board of directors. Gary Bauer of the Family Research Council is a former Reagan adviser and sought the Republican nomination for president in 2000.[64] Despite these underlying partisan differences, party leaders often search for the middle ground. As a result, their positions shift over time, and they do not always disagree.

When the country was building the Great Society in the 1960s and 1970s (see Chapter 3), Democrats took the lead, but Republicans were not far behind. Republican presidents signed into law several welfare programs for children. President Nixon proposed the food stamp and SSI programs. Republicans proposed, and President Ford signed, the law creating the Earned Income Tax Credit. Republicans in Congress initiated the Medicaid program.

As the public mood shifted in a conservative direction, the positions of both parties changed accordingly. In 1995 it was the Republicans who took the lead, proposing cuts in many of the programs they had once sponsored.[65] Although some Democrats opposed the cuts, a majority voted in favor of welfare reform, and President Clinton signed the bill into law. Today, both parties take credit for the passage of TANF.

Education Policy

Although social policy has long been one of the domestic policies of great interest to voters, education policy has recently become almost as significant in the public debate. Historically, Americans have supported a large, well-financed educational system. Equal opportunity meant equal access to good schools. But the commitment to public schools, though still strong, has been modified by increasing concern about the quality of education provided in traditional public schools. In this section we discuss the history of locally controlled public education in the United States, current policy on education, and the groups that shape this increasingly visible policy debate.

Local Control

Responsibility for education is divided among local school boards, state departments of education, and the federal Department of Education, but the bulk of control over education policy remains at the state and local level. Keeping control of public schools in the hands of local communities is an important issue for many parents and educators who do not want distant politicians making decisions about their children's lives. Former Secretary of Education Lamar Alexander provided a vehement expression of this point of view. Testifying before Congress, he accused those in favor of federal involvement of holding "the deeply erroneous belief that American parents, teachers, communities, and states are too stupid to raise their own children, run their own schools, and make their own decisions."[66]

Today, 93 percent of the cost of public education is paid for out of state and local budgets, each contributing approximately half the cost (although the exact percentage paid varies widely from one state to another). The 7 percent contribution by the federal government is spent mainly on programs enhancing equal opportunity, such as special education for the disabled and compensatory programs for disadvantaged children.[67] Core education programs are generally paid for with state and local dollars.

Development of Public Education

The public's commitment to its schools is deeply rooted. As early as 1785, Congress set aside the revenue from the sale of one-sixteenth of the land west of the Appalachian Mountains to help pay for "the maintenance of public schools."[68] Support for public schools intensified with the flood of immigrants that arrived in the nineteenth century. As immigrants gained the right to vote, they won access to public education. In Chicago and San Francisco, for example, children from immigrant backgrounds were no more likely to suffer from crowded classrooms than were children from native-born families. On the other hand, where racial minorities lacked adequate political representation, they were given second-class schools. Before gaining the right to vote, African Americans in the South and Chinese Americans in California were segregated into badly maintained, inferior schools.[69]

Despite the discriminatory treatment of racial minorities, public schools did much to build American democracy. The percentages of young people enrolled in American schools far surpassed those in European countries. Public schools helped foster a common language among people from disparate parts of the world. Open to most, if not all, citizens, they reinforced a distinctive American identity built around the concepts of liberty and equality. They also educated the workforce that operated the new machines that were to make the country the world's greatest industrial power.

Contemporary Issues in Education Policy

Despite the strength of the American educational tradition, Americans seem to be increasingly dissatisfied with traditional public schools. Within the United States itself, financial support for public elementary and secondary education (as a percentage of gross domestic product) has increased only slightly over the past 15 years.[70] And teacher salaries, relative to the average wage in the United States, have declined since 1970.[71]

Other nations, once far behind in school spending, have now nearly caught up. Governments in the United States spend 3.5 percent of the U.S. GDP on primary and secondary education. Although Japan and Germany still spend less than the United States, countries such as Canada, Sweden, and France spend more. (See International Comparison, page 515.)

American schools also seem to be doing an inferior job at converting dollars into schools that help students learn.[72] Students in American schools are learning less in reading, science, math, and geography than are students in most other industrial countries (see International Comparison). Not surprisingly, the public's assessment of the quality of its schools has slipped. The percentage of Americans who expressed "a good deal" or "quite a lot" of confidence in the public schools dropped from 58 percent in 1973 to 40 percent in 2003.[73]

INTERNATIONAL COMPARISON

Student Learning and School Expenditures

Student math scores are lower in the United States than in other industrial countries, yet Americans pay more for schools than many other countries.

• *Do you believe that test scores would improve if the United States spent more on education? Why or why not?*

SOURCE: U.S. Department of Education, National Center for Education Statistics, *Digest of Education Statistics, 2000,* March 2001 (NCES 2000-031), Table 396, p. 455; Table 412, p. 469.

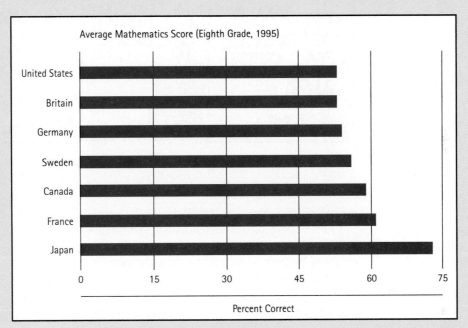

Average Mathematics Score (Eighth Grade, 1995)

Percent Correct

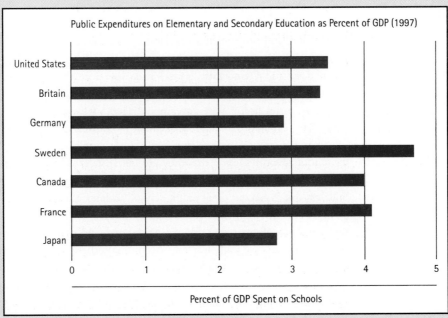

Public Expenditures on Elementary and Secondary Education as Percent of GDP (1997)

Percent of GDP Spent on Schools

Campaigning on Education
• *Can presidential decisions have a significant effect on school policies? Why or why not?*

You Are a State Legislator

As in other areas, different policy makers diagnose the problem differently and offer competing solutions. There are at least three major sets of proposals that seek to improve the system of education in the U.S.

First, some policy makers recommend redesigning the educational system so that students and parents have their choice of schools, just as senior citizens, under Medicare, have their choice of doctors and hospitals.[74] The government would give each family a voucher, which it could use to purchase education from any school the family preferred. Proponents say the resulting competition would prompt poorly performing schools to improve. Opponents argue that vouchers would increase disparities between schools, thereby broadening racial, religious, and ethnic divisions.[75]

In 2002 the Supreme Court opened the door to wider use of vouchers by ruling that a Cleveland program did not violate the constitutional separation of church and state (see Chapter 16). Controversy continues to surround vouchers, however, and some Republican and Democratic leaders have therefore turned to a proposal known as "charter schools" as an alternative. Charter schools are public schools in that they receive a charter from a state government agency. However, they are not subject to the same state regulations as traditional public schools, and only a few find their policies subject to negotiation with teachers' unions. Because of these minimal constraints, charter school advocates argue that they are better able to innovate and to adapt to each local community. In 2004 there were over 2600 charter schools operating in 37 states. Still, less that 2 percent of all public school students attend a charter school.[76]

A second set of policy makers suggests that the problem with public schools is that their educational goals are seldom well defined, and that they are often unable to tell whether students are really learning. Accordingly, these policy makers recommend a set of national standards, as well as a national curriculum.[77] Critics worry that rigid nationwide standards would rob states and school districts of flexibility and prevent adaptation to new conditions. In 2002 President George W. Bush signed the "No Child Left Behind Act," a new law that compromised on the issue. Under the new system, states must establish clear goals in math and reading, testing children in grades 3 through 8 to make sure that students meet these expectations. However, states may set their own standards and design their own tests and procedures for meeting them. At the same time, new federal funds assist students at poorly performing schools.

Critics of the bill argued that, while it was well intentioned, it was underfunded and thus did not give schools the resources necessary to improve themselves. Calling the act a "bait-and-switch," 2004 Democratic presidential candidate John Kerry proposed a national education trust fund that would "guarantee we fully fund our schools."[78]

This criticism of the No Child Left Behind Act leads to a third set of proposals for improving public education. Many liberals argue that schools could be more effective if they were given more resources. [79] These analysts point out that between 1985 and 2000, government spending on health care jumped over 40 percent—from 4.2 to nearly 6 percent of GDP.[80] But spending on elementary and secondary education inched up from only 3.2 percent to 3.5 percent of GDP over the same period.[81] In other words, government has committed itself to helping to pay more of the costs of medical care in order to extend the last years of life, while doing little more to enhance the capacities of those in the first years of life.

On the other hand, there are those who argue that money is neither the problem nor the solution. Replying to the critics of the No Child Left Behind Act, some scholars have pointed out that federal aid to schools increased by $300 per student between 2000 and 2004, while the cost of new testing that the bill required was only $20 per student.[82] These skeptics also cite studies showing that the amount that young people learn in school is seldom affected by the amount of money a school has.[83]

Politics of Education

In the past, public schools were, like baseball and apple pie, beyond partisan dispute. But in recent years, the two political parties have begun to disagree over a broad range of educational issues. Republicans have increasingly supported holding schools to high standards by testing students annually and giving parents greater choice through vouchers and charter schools, whereas Democrats have won strong support from the two largest teacher groups, the National Education Association and the American Federation of Teachers, by proposing higher levels of funding for traditional public schools.

Despite the partisan controversy, both parties remain strongly committed to public education. Both George W. Bush's No Child Left Behind Act and John Kerry's national trust fund proposal were directed primarily, if not exclusively, at the improvement of public schools. For all the current discontent, Americans still think schools are crucial for achieving the American dream. As long as the electorate feels this way, schools will continue to have bipartisan support.

Regulation

On December 23, 2003, as many American families headed home for the holiday season, the United States Department of Agriculture (USDA) announced that a case of bovine spongiform encephalopathy, otherwise known as "mad cow disease" had been discovered in one Washington State cow. The fatal disease, which rapidly destroys brain tissue, can spread from cattle to humans and is exceedingly difficult to eradicate from the environment.

This was the first case of the disorder in the United States, but it had not come without warning. Dr. Stanley Prusiner, a Nobel Prize-winning biologist who had studied the disorder, said he had recently warned Secretary of Agriculture Ann Veneman that her department's animal inspection procedures were too lax to determine even the extent of the problem.[84] In fact, many so-called "downer cows," animals that are too sick to walk, had been slaughtered and added to the country's meat supply.

The USDA acted swiftly to calm public fears and shore up the international market for American beef, banning the use of downer cows for food, stepping up inspections, and implementing several other safeguards. "The downer decision is a huge leap forward," said one consumer advocate "but it's really too bad USDA waited to take this step and others until after the first case was found. These are changes that many scientists and consumer advocates have been calling for for years."[85]

The case of mad cow disease raises questions about the government's regulatory policy making, an important and often overlooked component of domestic policy. Does the federal government have a responsibility to ensure public safety? What other kinds of activities should be regulated? How should this responsibility be exercised? In the remainder of this chapter, we discuss why and how the federal government regulates many aspects of our lives.

The Rise of Federal Regulation

regulation
Rules and standards that control economic, social, and political activities.

Government **regulation** consists of rules and standards that control economic, social, and political activities. Although Congress can itself pass regulations, usually it gives the responsibility to agencies within the executive branch, which issue rules within general congressional guidelines. Such rules affect the lives of average Americans at nearly every turn. For example, the Food and Drug Administration sets safety standards for medical devices, agricultural products, and nutrition; the Securities and Exchange Commission protects small investors by requiring companies to disclose standardized financial information; and the Consumer Products Safety Commission organizes the recall of products deemed to be hazardous.

Regulation dates back to feudal times. For example, businesses in sixteenth-century England "were required to set prices and render service in a socially responsible manner."[86] In the United States, the basis for federal regulation is found in the Constitution, which gives Congress the power "to regulate Commerce." Regulations under the authority of the commerce clause were originally applied to the railroad industry, with the passage of the Interstate Commerce Act of 1887. They have since been applied by Congress to regulate everything from civil rights to national insurance standards. Since the New Deal, the Supreme Court has generally found regulatory policies constitutional (see Chapter 3).[87]

Government regulations increased in number and significance at three distinct periods in the country's history: the progressive era, the New Deal era, and the 1960s and 1970s. Each period is marked by a strong political movement that identified major abuses in certain sectors of society, and each produced legislation that created a host of new government agencies with new regulatory powers.

During the progressive era of the 1890s and early 1900s, writers and journalists known as muckrakers exposed the worst abuses of industrialization. Initially, the spotlight was focused on the power of large corporations, such as Standard Oil Company, which exercised almost complete control over the oil industry. When the public demanded antitrust legislation, Congress enacted the Sherman Act (1890), which made it a crime to "restrain" or "monopolize" trade. This law still plays a major role in government–industry relations. Under this statute, for example, Microsoft, producer of computer operating systems and software, was found guilty of creating a monopoly and restraining trade. While the company was not required to break itself into pieces, as some had hoped, Microsoft did have to abide by an agreement with the Justice Department aimed at halting unfair business practices.[88]

The muckrakers also publicized other abuses, leading to the creation of additional regulatory agencies. For example, Upton Sinclair's best-selling novel *The Jungle* detailed horrible sanitation conditions in the meat-packing industry and resulted in the passage of the Meat Inspection Act of 1906.

The second regulatory wave occurred during the 1930s, when the government tried to prevent practices that were thought to have caused the Great Depression. The eight major regulatory agencies created at that time, including the Federal Deposit Insurance Corporation (FDIC), the Federal Communications Commission (FCC), and the Civil Aeronautics Board (predecessor to the modern Federal Aviation Administration), formed an important component of Franklin Roosevelt's New Deal.

A third wave of regulatory innovation took place in the 1960s and 1970s. During this period, the issues were consumer safety, occupational safety, and environmental protection. In 1965 Ralph Nader, an enterprising young lawyer, published a best-selling book, *Unsafe at Any Speed*, that revealed serious safety problems with a popular sports car, the Corvair. His efforts were so effective that General Motors halted production and new government regulations required manufacturers to install seat belts in all cars. Nader founded several consumer advocacy organizations, hiring young people who came to be known as "Nader's Raiders." In time, they found safety problems in many domains, including other consumer products, occupational environments, and industrial pollutants. In the ensuing years, Congress passed 61 significant pieces of new regulatory legislation and established or substantially enhanced the role of 9 regulatory agencies. Nader has remained politically active, running for president in 2000 and 2004.

The most important of the new agencies formed in this period was the **Environmental Protection Agency (EPA),** which has the main responsibility for issuing regulations designed to protect the environment from unwanted pollutants. Its controls on air and water pollution have done much to improve air and water quality throughout the United States. As one analyst has pointed out,

Environmental Protection Agency (EPA)
Agency responsible for issuing regulations designed to protect the environment from unwanted pollutants.

> Air pollution from lead, by far the worst atmospheric poison, declined 89 percent during the 1980s; pollution from carbon monoxide, also poisonous, went down 31 percent. In 1992, the number of Americans living in counties that failed some aspect of air-quality standards was only half [those] who lived in dirty air in 1982.[89]

Justifications for Regulation

As a result of these waves of regulatory expansion, the government now regulates many business and social activities. According to Murray Weidenbaum, a former chairman of the Council of Economic Advisers,

> No business, large or small, can operate without obeying a myriad of government rules and restrictions. Costs and profits can be affected as much by a directive written

by a government official as by a management decision in the front office or a customer's decision at the checkout counter.[90]

Why have the regulatory responsibilities of government expanded so dramatically during the past century? Scholars have identified three broad types of circumstances in which they find government regulation most easily justified: natural monopoly, externalities, and protection of the uninformed.

natural monopoly
A situation in which a public service is best provided by a single company.

Natural Monopoly   In a **natural monopoly** a public service is best provided by a single company. To make sure that the company does not take advantage of its monopoly power and charge consumers unnecessarily high prices, natural monopolies are usually subject to regulation. For example, regulations control the charges set by telephone companies that until recently have had exclusive rights in a particular region. Regulations also control the prices of gas, electricity, cable television, and other utilities that have exclusive rights in a particular state or locality. Otherwise, it is likely that these companies would charge excessively high rates.

externalities
Consequences affecting people who are not directly engaged in the activities that bring those consequences about.

Negative Externalities   An **externality** is any consequence of an activity that has an impact on those not responsible for the action. An externality may be positive or negative. If neighbors plant beautiful flowers in their front yard, then they provide those nearby with a positive externality. But if the same neighbors pile unsightly, reeking junk on their front lawn, then those nearby suffer a negative externality. Because neighbors—and corporations—may not care about the consequences of their actions for others, the government may regulate to prevent or adjust for externalities.

One of the best examples of an externality is air pollution. A company may try to keep its costs low by using cheap fuel, even though burning that fuel emits black soot into the air. The black soot does not seriously affect the company, although it both threatens the health of those living nearby and creates a nuisance for them. To prevent companies from imposing this externality on others by polluting their environments, the EPA has imposed numerous regulations on industry to control the emission of pollutants.

A recent controversy over government regulation of externalities took place over the use of U.S. national park land. Until 2000, over 180,000 snowmobile aficionados used the national parks each winter, sometimes racing through the woods at speeds in excess of 60 miles per hour. Environmentalists protested this use of public property, arguing that "the national parks should be places where the public can go to escape traffic. . . . And clearly these snow machines are loud, they're polluting, and they cause conflict with other visitors." In 2000 the National Park Service sided with the environmentalists, announcing a sweeping ban on snowmobile use in the national parks, with only minor exceptions. As in many other cases of regulation, those being regulated became very upset. Fumed one angry rider, "It's part of a planned campaign by this administration to limit access to public lands."[91] The Bush administration reversed most of these restrictive rules in 2001, but a federal judge blocked this move in 2003, denouncing it as "completely politically driven."[92] An exasperated pro-snowmobile spokesman admitted "We're totally confused."[93]

Protecting the Uninformed   Regulations are also used to protect those who cannot be expected to be well informed, most notably consumers. For example, many government rules forbid the marketing of unsafe products or the use of deceptive advertising and labeling.

Snowmobiling in Yellowstone
• *Do snowmobilers in U.S. national parks represent an externality-producing nuisance that must be regulated?*

The need for regulation is especially great in the case of medications. When citizens catch the flu, they cannot be expected to research the side effects of every cold medication on the market. Thus, government regulation is necessary to ensure that drugs sold over the counter meet specified safety standards.

Regulation of drugs began during the progressive era. In 1906 Congress created the Food and Drug Administration (FDA), granting it the power to regulate the production and labeling of goods sold in interstate commerce. The initial legislation gave the FDA only limited powers. To garner public support for stronger regulatory authority, in the 1920s the FDA established a museum known as the Chamber of Horrors that contained such atrocities as

> Samples seized from goods on public sale—samples of patent medicines to cure every known disease, with testimonials from their users, accompanied by copies of their death certificates; and samples of cosmetics—eye-lash beautifiers containing poisonous aniline dyes, hair removers containing thallium acetate, and hair tonics, freckle removers, ointments, and salves containing mercury or other dangerous ingredients—together with photographs of women who had been blinded, paralyzed, or permanently disfigured by their use.[94]

The museum effectively aroused public concern. The FDA now monitors the production of everything from drugs to cosmetics to therapeutic devices such as muscle developers and sun lamps.

Politics of Regulation

When and how regulations are imposed are political decisions. Regulations are thus shaped by election pressures on Congress, government agencies, and even the courts.

Congress   Members of Congress often create regulatory agencies in order to escape criticism when things go wrong. Laws frequently win passage in response to a well-publicized incident or disaster. After a series of accounting scandals at companies like Enron and WorldCom, for example, Congress passed the Corporate Accountability Act of 2002, which more strictly regulated corporations and corporate auditing firms. With each disaster or scandal, congressional representatives demonstrate their responsiveness to public concerns by passing another regulatory act. The end result is that regulations often duplicate and overlap one another.

Although regulation may help reassure the public after a crisis has occurred, it is inherently unpopular with at least some. Regulations require some people to follow restrictive procedures in order to avoid injuring others. For example, the regulations that prohibit snowmobiles in national parks may win the approval of environmentalists, but they almost certainly will alienate devotees of the sport. Because compelling people to do something is likely to make them upset or angry, members of Congress usually employ a strategy known as **blame avoidance,** a set of political techniques designed to disguise their actions and shift the blame to others. In the case of regulatory policy, Congress avoids blame by not directly imposing the regulations but handing that job off to a regulatory agency.

When creating a regulatory agency, Congress often defines its task in general terms. As one group of policy analysts has said about the EPA, its "discretion [is] truly enormous. It produce[s] hundreds of pages of regulations, embodying dozens of significant policy choices, all on the basis of the most elliptical statutory language and the sparsest of legislative records."[95] Congress justifies leaving the terms of reference vague on the grounds that the authors of the legislation cannot anticipate every circumstance requiring regulatory action. Legislators can correctly claim that only those who know the facts in detail can come up with the appropriate regulation. But Congress has also discovered that it can avoid "unpleasant truths" by keeping regulatory legislation broad and general.[96] Different members of Congress may then interpret the law in contrasting ways. Some may claim they have satisfied the concerns of environmentalists and consumers; others will insist they have not imposed undue burdens on business and industry.

In rare cases where the public has become upset at the vagueness of congressional legislation, Congress has taken further (though still less than specific) steps. One such measure is to set specific goals and then to include a **hammer**—a harsh penalty—to be imposed if these goals are not met somehow. For example, the Clean Air Act of 1990 says that if certain goals are not met in particular metropolitan areas by a specific deadline, then the "sale of all gasoline in the designated area must cease."[97] Such draconian penalties make Congress *appear* tough, but in fact they are typically so impractical that they would never be imposed, and the legislation still usually includes no guidelines regarding how the goals should be met.

Agency Discretion   Because of the very ambiguity of much congressional legislation, agencies often enjoy considerable freedom in deciding how to execute their mandates. When Congress charged the EPA with improving air quality in metropolitan areas, the agency had to decide the following kinds of questions: Should automobile manufacturers be required to build and sell some electric cars within ten years? Should every vehicle be checked at a state-run inspection station? Should inner-city highways be subject to a toll during rush hour? Should states be told they cannot build new roads? Although EPA officials have considered each of these difficult questions, nothing in the Clean Air Act of 1990 provides precise answers.

---

blame avoidance
Set of political techniques employed by political leaders to disguise their actions and shift blame to others.

hammer
Harsh penalty set by Congress to be imposed if a regulatory agency does not achieve a statutory objective.

The autonomy afforded to regulatory agencies is not limitless. There exists a **zone of acceptance**—a range within which Congress will accept whatever an agency decides is the correct interpretation of the statutes.[98] When an agency goes beyond this informal and ambiguous zone, political opposition arises and the agency backtracks. For example, all of the clean-air options mentioned here provoked controversy and, as a result, the EPA has been slow to implement them.

Courts   Although regulatory policies are enacted by Congress and executed by agencies, courts interpret the meaning of congressional statutes and decide whether their application in specific cases conforms to congressional intent. Courts exercise considerable discretion when performing this role, because they are often asked to interpret vague, and even contradictory, laws passed by Congress.

Court interpretations of the 1973 Endangered Species Act illustrate how federal judges influence public policy. The law protects any species on federal lands that is found by the U.S. Fish and Wildlife Service to be threatened with extinction. Such a species' natural habitat is to be safeguarded from human activity that threatens it, no matter what the economic consequences of such protection. In voting for this legislation, most members of Congress probably thought they were protecting large mammals and birds, such as wolves, whooping cranes, and eagles. And, indeed, the Endangered Species Act has been successful in protecting the American bald eagle. In 1963 there were only 417 nesting pairs; by 1999 the numbers had increased to 5800, and President Clinton announced that the animal would be removed from the endangered species list.[99] However, the Fish and Wildlife Service greatly expanded the scope of the legislation when it found nearly 1000 species to be in danger of extinction. And the federal courts have interpreted the law as applicable even to little-known species. Judges have halted the growth of suburbs in order to protect desert kangaroo rats; they have prevented the construction of a billion-dollar dam in order to save a tiny snail darter; and they have halted logging operations in order to safeguard the spotted owl.

Deregulation

Although regulation is an inevitable part of modern society, it can be carried to excess, and regulations intended to *protect* consumers may have the opposite effect. For example, regulating drugs may prevent some patients from getting the treatment they need. Furthermore, regulation is expensive. Salaries for bureaucrats, lawyers, and investigators generate an annual price tag that runs to billions of dollars. Regulatory policies may also limit the ability of businesses to compete effectively. The additional paperwork, inspections, procedures, and mandates imposed by regulatory agencies can spell the difference between a business that thrives and provides good jobs to Americans and one that cannot remain solvent and has to reduce its workforce.

To address these concerns, Congress has introduced in many areas policies of **deregulation,** the removal of government rules that once controlled an industry. It has systematically authorized the partial deregulation of the trucking, banking, and communications industries.[100] Banks may now provide customers with insurance and handle the purchase and sale of stocks. Regional telephone companies may now offer long-distance and cellular service.

Perhaps the most celebrated deregulation occurred within the airline industry. At one time, a government agency approved the airfare set for every route a plane flew.

zone of acceptance
Range within which Congress allows agencies to interpret and apply statutes.

deregulation
Removal of government rules that once controlled an industry.

Though it was originally enacted to prevent price gouging by airlines that had a monopoly in a particular city, many policy analysts claimed that the effect of the law was precisely the opposite of its intent: Regulators were letting airlines charge excessively high prices.

To address this and other problems, Congress enacted the Airline Deregulation Act of 1978. Most policy outcomes were favorable. Airline competition increased, companies became more efficient, service to remote areas increased, and air fares fell.[101] Although some worried about the effect on safety,[102] the number of deaths per passenger mile also declined. Yet many experts argue that some regulation must remain in place to ensure that airline companies, in their eagerness for profit, do not cut corners too closely.[103] Complete deregulation is unlikely, because the public will always expect government to act in the wake of disasters or to prevent costly externalities.

Chapter Summary

Domestic policy involves government spending on social policies, education, and other policies, as well as government regulation of these activities. The two political parties are divided on many domestic policies. Democrats typically want to spend more on social and education policy, and they usually favor more regulation. Republicans usually favor less spending and less regulation.

But beyond these partisan differences, there are also differences in the way these policies affect different interest groups and portions of the electorate. These cause the policy-making process to vary from one policy to another

and result in policy outcomes that at times seem self-contradictory. Social policies designed to aid the elderly are far more popular and more extensive than similar policies designed to aid poor children. The public wants national candidates to address education policy but does not want to relinquish local control over public schools. And Congress is quick to pass regulatory legislation in the wake of disasters, but otherwise tends to write vague legislation, leaving interpretation to the agencies and the courts. Only through a clear understanding of the policy process can one understand these complex, even contradictory outcomes.

Key Terms

agenda setting, p. 499
blame avoidance, p. 522
deregulation, p. 523
domestic policy, p. 499
Earned Income Tax Credit (EITC), p. 508
Environmental Protection Agency (EPA), p. 519
externalities, p. 520
food stamps, p. 508

hammer, p. 522
Medicaid, p 508.
Medicare, p. 499
natural monopoly, p. 520
policy deliberation, p. 500
policy enactment, p. 500
policy implementation, p. 500
policy outcome, p. 500
policy output, p. 500
public assistance, p. 507

regulation, p. 518
rent subsidies, p. 508
social insurance, p. 502
social policy, p. 501
social security, p. 502
Supplemental Security Income (SSI), p. 508
Temporary Assistance for Needy Families (TANF), p. 500
zone of acceptance, p. 523

Suggested Readings

Of General Interest

Kingdon, John. *Agendas, Alternatives and Public Policies.* Boston: Little, Brown, 1984. Discusses the policy-making process, paying special attention to how problems become issues on the political agenda.

Murray, Charles A. *Losing Ground: American Social Policy: 1950–1980.* New York: Basic Books, 1984. Makes the case that government welfare benefits help to create poverty. Suggests ending welfare.

Pierson, Paul. *Dismantling the Welfare State? Reagan, Thatcher and the Politics of Retrenchment.* New York: Cambridge University Press, 1994. Insightful analysis of political battles over cuts in welfare expenditure.

Skocpol, Theda. *Protecting Soldiers and Mothers: The Politics of Social Provision in the United States.* Cambridge, MA: Harvard University Press, 1993. Fascinating, comprehensive historical analysis of the evolution of the U.S. welfare state.

Focused Studies

Burtless, Gary, ed. *Does Money Matter? The Effect of School Resources on Student Achievement and Adult Success.* Washington, DC: The Brookings Institution, 1996. Excellent collection of essays that debate the current state of public education.

Derthick, Martha, and Paul Quirk. *The Politics of Deregulation.* Washington, DC: The Brookings Institution, 1985. Engaging accounts of the political circumstances that enable the federal government to eliminate existing regulations.

Howell, William, and Paul E. Peterson, with Patrick Wolf and David Campbell. *The Education Gap: Vouchers and Urban Public Schools.* Washington, DC: The Brookings Institution, 2002. Analysis of school choice initiatives by scholars sympathetic to vouchers.

Landy, Marc K., Marc J. Roberts, and Stephen R. Thomas. *The Environmental Protection Agency: Asking the Wrong Questions from Nixon to Clinton,* expanded edition. New York: Oxford University Press, 1994. Thorough, critical analysis of EPA policy making.

Weidenbaum, Murray L. *Business, Government and the Public.* Englewood Cliffs, NJ: Prentice-Hall, 1990. Examines when and how the government interferes with business affairs.

Whicker, Marcia. *Controversial Issues in Economic Regulatory Policy.* Newbury Park, CA: Sage Publications, 1993. Provides a comprehensive summary of the arguments for and against government regulation.

Wilson, James Q. *The Politics of Regulation.* New York: Basic Books, 1980. Comprehensive text on regulatory politics and policy.

Wilson, William J. *The Truly Disadvantaged: The Inner City, the Underclass, and Public Policy.* Chicago: University of Chicago Press, 1987. Argues that poverty has been caused by the internationalization of the economy and the disappearance of blue-collar jobs. Maintains that government should provide jobs.

On the Web

In this chapter, we discussed a variety of government programs and regulations. Many programs and regulatory agencies have Web sites that provide information to the public. They including the following:

www.medicare.gov
The official government information site for Medicare, the health insurance program for the elderly.

www.ssa.gov
The Social Security Administration (SSA), which administers the social insurance program that makes up a quarter of the federal budget.

www.acf.dhhs.gov
The Administration for Children and Families, which runs the federal side of the Temporary Assistance for Needy Families (TANF) program.

www.ed.gov
The U.S. Department of Education, which provides statistical information on the state of education in the United States and describes national education programs.

www.fda.gov
www.epa.gov
www.sec.gov
www.osha.gov
www.cpsc.gov
The Food and Drug Administration, the Environmental Protection Agency, the Securities and Exchange Commission, the Occupational Safety and Health Administration, and the Consumer Product Safety Commission, five major regulatory agencies.

In this chapter we also discussed a number of interest groups and organizations that affect the design and implementation of domestic policy in the United States. They include:

www.aarp.org

The American Association of Retired Persons (AARP), the large and influential lobby for senior citizens.

www.childrensdefense.org

The Children's Defense Fund, which works to provide "a voice for all the children of America who cannot vote, lobby or speak for themselves."

www.frc.org

The Family Research Council, a conservative foundation that "champions marriage and family."

www.educationnext.org

Education Next is a journal that discusses contemporary education policy issues.

www.aft.org

The American Federation of Teachers (AFT), one of the most powerful lobbying organizations on education issues.

www.publiccitizen.org

Ralph Nader's Public Citizen, which lobbies for consumer protection regulations.

www.regulation.org

The conservative Heritage Foundation's regulation project advocating deregulation.

CHAPTER 19

★ ★ ★ ★ ★ ★ ★ ★ ★ ★ ★ ★ ★ ★ ★

Economic Policy

CHAPTER OUTLINE

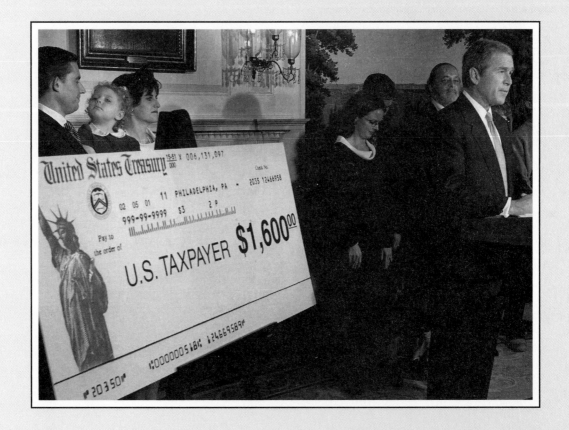

The Politics of the 2001 Tax Rebate

Bill Clinton left office after presiding over the longest economic expansion in American history. The **gross domestic product (GDP),** the official measure of the total value of economic activity in the United States, had grown by a yearly average of 5.8 percent during his tenure, more than double the average for the previous two decades.[1] Unemployment was the lowest it had been in thirty years,[2] and the value of stocks on Wall Street had tripled.[3] The scandal-ridden president's high approval ratings reflected the fact that the public gave him a great deal of credit for this prosperity, and Clinton made no effort to discourage this perspective. "I think all of us are very proud that we can leave that legacy to the incoming administration and to the children of this country," he said.[4]

No sooner had Bush taken office, however, than the economy began to sour. Technology stocks, already in trouble, drove stock markets relentlessly lower. Major employers from Amazon.com to Disney to DaimlerChrysler announced significant layoffs.[5] Growth in the GDP slowed to a crawl.

Bush aides worried that the president would be blamed for the shrinking economy—indeed, polls showed voters losing confidence in him on this issue.[6] Accordingly, Bush advisers threw their support behind a novel amendment to the tax cut bill that the Bush administration was shepherding through Congress: Taxpayers would get a one-time tax rebate of up to $600 to spend as they pleased. In theory, people would spend this unexpected cash on consumer goods, thus boosting the nation's flagging economy. Americans "need tax relief fast," Bush said. "In fact, they need it yesterday."[7] After the bill passed and rebate checks were mailed out, the White House anticipated immediate political gains. As one presidential aide put it, "People will open the mail and say, 'Holy cow, he really did do something!' "[8]

But if the political benefits of the plan were clear, its effect on the economy was widely debated.[9] Some experts said the tax cut gave the economy a boost just when it was needed, and indeed the economy began to recover shortly thereafter. The stock market revived, but gains in employment were slow to reappear, making the economy an important issue in the 2004 presidential election.

MAKING THE CONNECTION

Elected officials place great emphasis on formulating and implementing the policies that affect economic conditions. And elections are often decided on the basis of economic factors. But were the voters correct to base their assessments of Presidents Clinton and George W. Bush on the state of the economy? How much control do the president and Congress have over economic trends? What other governmental institutions besides the president are able to make economic policy and what powers do they have? To answer these and related questions, we consider the following specific topics:

- How does the state of the economy affect presidential elections?

- What kinds of policies does the government use to manage economic fluctuations?

- How have economic trends and government policies affected the budget and national policy debates?

- How does the U.S. tax system work?

- How does the relationship between the U.S. government and the economy compare to that in other nations?

* * * * * * * * * * * * * * *

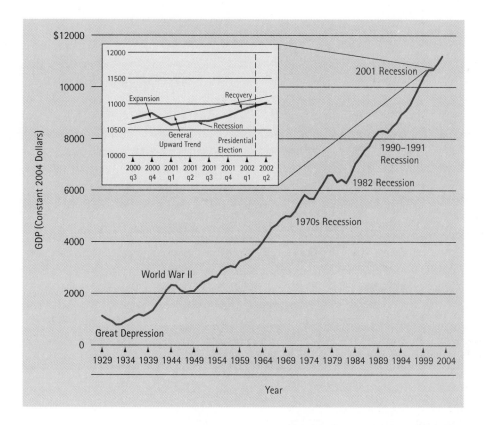

FIGURE 19.1

Long-Term Growth and the Business Cycle in the United States

Although the general economic trend may be upward over the long run, expansions and recessions that characterize the business cycle can—in the short term—harm both citizens and elected officials.

• *Can you name the president in office during each economic downturn labeled in the figure?*

SOURCES: *Statistical Abstract of the United States, 1999,* p. 881, Table 1434 and U.S. Department of Commerce, Bureau of Economic Analysis, "National Income and Product Accounts," http://www.bea.gov/bea/dn1.htm, accessed August 25, 2004

Economic Growth and the Business Cycle

Economies grow as the result of technological innovations, investments in physical capital (factories, agricultural production, communication systems, and so on), and investments in human capital (education, worker training, and the like). As a result of technological change and investments in physical and human capital, the U.S. economy has grown enormously, and many of those who have invested in American industry have reaped huge rewards. For example, if you had purchased $25 worth of stock in a cross section of American companies in the late 1920s, that stock would be worth about $1100 today.

In any given year, however, short-term fluctuations in the economy can adversely affect stock values. For example, that $25 investment would have lost over two-thirds of its value from 1929 to 1933, the early years of the Great Depression, and would not have regained its original value until the mid-1950s.

Few economic downturns are as severe as the Great Depression. But **recessions**— slowdowns in economic activity—occur relatively often, if unpredictably. Economists refer to these periodic episodes of economic slowdown, followed by recovery, renewed expansion, and rising prices, as the **business cycle.** Figure 19.1 provides an illustration of this phenomenon.

Governments try to set economic policies in such a way as to minimize the disruptions caused by the business cycle so that most people keep their jobs and prices remain stable. In other words, they try to avoid two major problems: inflation and unemployment.

gross domestic product (GDP)
The measure of the total value of economic activity in a nation in one year.

recession
A slowdown in economic activity, officially defined as a decline that persists for two quarters (six months).

business cycle
The alternation of periods of economic growth with periods of economic slowdown.

Herbert Hoover

Herbert Hoover, a Republican, was president when the United States plunged into the Great Depression.

• *How did this event affect Republican party fortunes? Why?*

inflation
A sustained rise in the price level such that people need more money to purchase the same amount of goods and services.

unemployment
The circumstance that exists when people who are willing to work at the prevailing wage cannot get jobs.

Inflation—a rise in the price level—makes consumers pay more money for an equal amount of goods and services. As a result, the general public becomes unhappy if inflation rates are high. **Unemployment**—which occurs when people willing to work at prevailing wages cannot find jobs—harms a smaller number of people but harms them in ways that are marked and visible. It also makes it difficult for many people who have jobs to change jobs or win wage increases.

Political leaders try to avoid both misfortunes, but they are not always successful. For a long time, the two conditions were thought to be closely related: Lower unemployment was assumed to mean higher inflation, and vice versa.[10] But economists no longer believe the relationship is so close. In fact, President Jimmy Carter had the misfortune to run for reelection at a time of "stagflation," when both inflation and unemployment were high. He suffered a humiliating defeat. For the next three elections, Republicans reminded the public of the economic chaos of the Carter years.

Economic Conditions and Political Fortunes

As Carter's experience shows, people tend to blame those in charge when times are hard. George W. Bush weathered criticism of his lax regulation of business in the wake of malfeasance at major corporations such as Enron, Global Crossing, and WorldCom. And during the 2004 campaign, Democratic presidential candidate John Kerry blamed Bush for disappointing employment figures, as well as for allowing corporations to "outsource" jobs to locations in other countries.

Bush and Carter have not been the only presidents to have lost popularity when the economy faltered. President George H. W. Bush also suffered from economic adversity in 1992. His popularity ratings fell 40 percentage points during a recession in

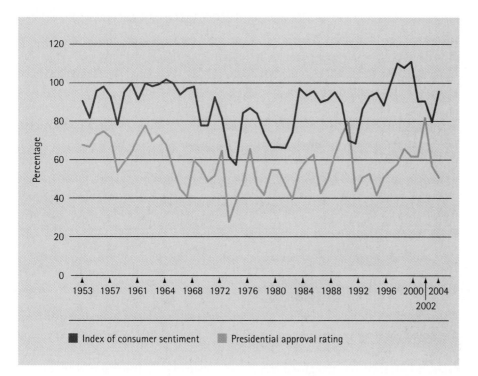

FIGURE 19.2

When Americans Feel Positively About the Economy, They Also Approve of the President

• *When does the economy not have a major impact on the public's view of the president?*

Note: The figure displays data for the first quarter of each year.

SOURCES: Index of Consumer Sentiment, Surveys of Consumers, University of Michigan; and Gallup polls, various years.

the second half of his administration—from 78 percent in July 1990, when the rate of unemployment first began to rise, to 38 percent two years later, when unemployment peaked. Presidents Eisenhower and Nixon suffered similar fates, losing significant public support when recessions hit. Some critics called Ronald Reagan the "Teflon president" because they believed that none of the usual political dirt and grease stuck to him; but even Ronald Reagan's popularity dropped precipitously during the 1981–1982 recession.[11]

Terrible economic times in American history are associated with massive election losses for the party of the president. The depression of the 1890s ushered in an era of Republican dominance, and the Great Depression of the 1930s did the same for the Democrats. Indeed, Republican President Herbert Hoover (1929–1933) became one of history's most unpopular presidents simply because he was in office when the Great Depression began. For decades afterward, Democrats ran against the party of Hoover, using the Depression issue to help them win the next five elections.

Prosperity, in contrast, strengthens a president's position in a bid for reelection, as Figure 19.2 illustrates. Riding booming economies, Lyndon Johnson trampled Barry Goldwater in 1964, Richard Nixon crushed George McGovern in 1972, Ronald Reagan trounced Walter Mondale in 1984, and Bill Clinton overwhelmed Bob Dole in 1996. Of course, a healthy economy does not guarantee presidential popularity. For example, prosperity did not keep Johnson's popularity from falling sharply in response to the rising casualty rate in Vietnam.[12] Nonetheless, presidents usually do better in elections when the economy is strong.

National economic conditions may influence congressional elections as well.[13] In 1930 Democrats captured control of Congress when voters blamed Republicans for the onset of the Great Depression. The Eisenhower recession of 1958 inflated the narrow

John Maynard Keynes
John Maynard Keynes, the economic theorist responsible for the school of macroeconomics that came to be called "Keynesianism."
• *Why is Keynesian thinking on fiscal policy less influential today?*

fiscal policy
The sum total of government taxing and spending decisions, which determines the level of the deficit or surplus.

deficit
The amount by which annual spending exceeds revenue.

surplus
The amount by which annual revenue exceeds spending.

budget
The government's annual plan for taxing and spending.

Keynesianism
Economic policy based on the belief that governments can control the economy by manipulating demand, running deficits to expand it, and surpluses to contract it.

Council of Economic Advisers (CEA)
Three economists who head up a professional staff that advises the president on economic policy.

Democratic majorities in the House and Senate. The huge Democratic majorities of 1974 were due both to the Watergate scandal and to an economic downturn.[14] When the economy dragged Carter under in 1980, the Republicans took control of the Senate and made large gains in the House. To be sure, economics is not the only force at work in congressional elections. The Democrats suffered serious congressional losses in 1966, even though the economy was fine. That election turned on Vietnam and racial tensions. Similarly, the Republicans captured control of both House and Senate in 1994, even though unemployment fell during Clinton's first two years.

But the economy is most critical for presidential elections, so it is the president who pays the closest attention to economic policy. Presidents may make narrow economic policies with an eye toward key groups of voters, as George W. Bush did with steel import policy in 2002. (See Election Connection, page 534.) Presidents may also try to shape overall economic conditions by using two major policy tools, fiscal policy and monetary policy. We discuss these policy tools in the next two sections.

Fiscal Policy

A government's **fiscal policy,** the sum total of government taxation and spending, determines whether government revenues exceed expenditures. When yearly spending exceeds tax receipts, the government runs a **deficit.** When the amount collected in taxes exceeds spending, the government enjoys a **surplus.** When the two are exactly the same, the budget is said to be balanced. The nation's fiscal policy is formulated in a **budget,** the government's annual plan for taxing and spending. The budget sets funding levels for all government programs. In 2004 the federal budget amounted to about $2.3 trillion, or about 21 percent of the nation's GDP.[15] Since the 1970s the president has proposed a budget to Congress each year, but Congress usually makes major changes to the president's plan before passing it. The largest portion of the federal budget—21 percent—goes to the social security program, as Figure 19.3 indicates. Medicare and Medicaid claim 19 percent, and national defense accounts for another 19 percent of the nation's spending. Interest paid on the sizable national debt consumes an additional 7 percent. Everything else the government spends money on—from highway funds and education programs to child nutrition, housing subsidies, and foreign aid—constitutes the remaining 34 percent of the budget.[16]

Use of the Budget Deficit

According to an influential English economist of the 1920s and 1930s, John Maynard Keynes, there is nothing sacred about a balanced government budget; on the contrary, he said, budget deficits can lift an economy out of a recession. If government spends money when no one else does, it can jump-start the economy, which then can begin to grow on its own. Following this line of reasoning, which came to be called **Keynesianism,** Franklin Roosevelt broke with the traditional belief in a balanced budget (a belief held by his predecessor Herbert Hoover) and ran large deficits during the 1930s in an attempt to get the country moving again.

After World War II, Keynesian thinking became widely accepted. In 1946 Congress established a **Council of Economic Advisers (CEA)** composed of three prominent economists who would advise the president about the state of the national and inter-

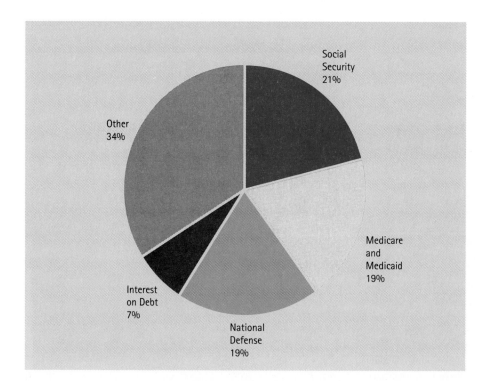

FIGURE 19.3
Major Components of the Federal Budget
• *Do these budget figures surprise you? Can you think of programs that deserve more spending? Less spending?*
SOURCE: Office of Management and Budget, *Budget of the United States Government, Fiscal 2005,* Table S-12, "Budget Summary by Category," p. 386.

national economy, present economic forecasts, and make recommendations about the budget. Because deficits were thought to create jobs, whereas surpluses held prices down, these expert economists tried to help presidents "fine-tune" the economy to ensure steady prosperity. On the recommendation of the CEA to stimulate a sluggish economy, John Kennedy urged Congress to pass a deficit-creating tax cut. Some credit the cut, passed in 1964, with stimulating the mid-1960s economic boom.[17] Conversely, to slow down the inflation rate, Lyndon Johnson followed CEA advice and persuaded Congress to pass a tax increase in 1968. Despite the tax, inflation continued. Some said that the cut failed to have the desired effect because the tax increase was not big enough.[18] Others said that the failure of the tax increase to stop inflation proved Keynes's theory wrong.

The CEA declined in importance in the 1980s and 1990s, as presidents relied more on White House staffers, treasury secretaries, and other political aides for advice on economic policy. Under George W. Bush, the CEA reclaimed some of the prestige and policy influence of years past, exerting influence over trade initiatives, tax policy, and even some aspects of homeland security.[19]

Decline of Fiscal Policy

Administrations today are much less likely to use fiscal policy as a tool for managing the economy than they were during the Kennedy-Johnson era. Several factors have contributed to the decline in the economic significance of fiscal policy. These factors include divided government, monetarism, budget deficits, and internationalization.

ELECTION CONNECTION

George W. Bush and United States Steel Policy

Republicans are supposed to be for free trade. At least, that has been the case since the mid-twentieth century, protectionists such as right-wing presidential candidate Pat Buchanan notwithstanding. According to most economists, free trade enables world markets to function with less distortion, leading to more robust and even economic growth for all.

Because most Republicans accept this argument, it surprised some observers when, in 2002, President George W. Bush approved a new system of tariffs on imported steel, affecting up to $8 billion of imports annually from around the world. Under the 3-year plan, steel entering the country could be taxed at a rate of up to 30 percent. Steel industry officials praised the new tariffs as necessary to enable U.S. manufacturers to compete with foreign producers, many of which had benefited from past subsidies from their own governments. But others scoffed at these justifications. According to one critic, the policy "is so wrong it makes other kinds of wealth-destroying [government] intervention feel inadequate."

Surprise at the Bush action was muted by a recognition of the electoral facts. The list of major steel-producing states reads like a list of the most hotly contested states in presidential elections: Pennsylvania, Ohio, Indiana, Maryland, West Virginia,

and Michigan. Three of these six states voted for Bush in 2000; three voted for Democrat Al Gore. Furthermore, in four of these states, the margin of victory was 6 percentage points or less. Bush and his advisers clearly recognized the potential benefits of paying attention to steel workers in these states. In one appearance at a steel plant in Pennsylvania, Bush assured an assembly of plant personnel that their product constituted "an important national security issue."

Bush lifted the steel tariffs in late 2003 after it appeared that they might prompt retaliation from other countries. While some Democrats argued that by doing so he "broke a promise" to steelworkers, his supporters argued that the tariffs, while brief, had given the troubled steel industry the "breathing space" it needed to get back on its feet.

• *Do electoral considerations lead to distorted economic policies, or are elected officials just doing a good job of representing their constituents?*

• *Do electoral considerations constitute a greater problem with economic policy than with other policy areas?*

• *Would the government's steel policy have differed if Al Gore had been elected in 2000?*

SOURCES: The "inadequate" quote, "George Bush, Protectionist," *The Economist,* March 9, 2002; Federal Election Commission 2000 election data; and the "national security issue" quote, "Romancing Big Steel," *The Economist,* February 16, 2002; "promise" and "breathing space," Edward Chen and Richard Simon, "Bush Rescinds Steel Tariffs, Says Aims Met," *Los Angeles Times,* December 5, 2003, p. A1.

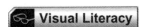

Visual Literacy

Evaluating Federal Spending and Economic Policy

Divided Government   Fiscal policy and divided government do not mix well together. An economic policy must be implemented quickly if it is to alleviate the economic conditions it is aimed at. But when government is divided between the two parties, it is difficult to enact fiscal policy quickly in response to changing economic conditions.

Fiscal policy is a product of the taxing and spending decisions recommended by presidents and passed by Congress. Even under the most favorable conditions, it takes considerable time for the two institutions to iron out their differences and adopt a budget. When George W. Bush proposed a tax cut in 2001, he justified the cut according to Keynesian principles, arguing that the cut was needed to stimulate a slowing economy. Responding to the president's urgent request, Congress moved quickly to pass a long-term tax cut and an immediate tax rebate for Americans. However, the bulk of the tax cuts took effect only several years later, too late to jump-start the faltering economy, and experts differed on whether 2001's one-time tax rebate provided much stimulus.

Similarly, in 2003, Bush pressed for the elimination of taxes on stock dividends, saying that "[l]ower taxes and greater investment will help this economy expand."[20] Although Congress enacted the bulk of his proposals, and the Bush administration claimed that his tax cuts had revived the economy, many economists remained skeptical of this claim.

Monetarism   The second factor that has reduced the significance of fiscal policy is the increased influence of **monetarism,** a school of economic thinking that says that the money supply, not the pattern of government taxing and spending, is the most important influence on the economy. Monetarists argue that the deficits that Keynesians favor in times of economic distress are paid for by borrowing money from investors. Thus, every dollar the government spends is one less dollar to be invested in other productive activities. Budget deficits do not add any extra stimulus—they just transfer available dollars from the private sector to the government. In the next section, we outline what steps monetarists favor in lieu of deficits.

Even Keynesians favor only temporary deficits; they do not believe that a government budget can be continuously in deficit. Over the long run, a nation's economy can grow only if people save money and invest it in productive enterprises. The problem is that when a government borrows money, it soaks up some of the country's savings, and with less savings-to-finance investment, economic growth slows. Thus, most economists today agree that persistent deficits result in lower long-term economic growth.

Growing Budget Deficits   Fiscal policy was also undermined by the large budget deficits of the 1980s and early 1990s. In the 1960s, when regulation of the economy by means of fiscal policy was a popular idea, the federal **debt**—the accumulation of annual deficits—was still declining from the peak to which it had climbed during World War II. Thus, modest adjustments in fiscal policy could be made from one year to the next without creating long-term problems. But in the 1970s, large defense expenditures, coupled with growing social welfare spending, regularly produced unbalanced budgets in which total expenditures exceeded tax revenues by significant amounts.

During the 1980s and most of the 1990s, the budget deficit gradually but inexorably became a major issue in American politics. In the 1980s, **supply-side economics,** implemented by the Reagan administration, further exacerbated the large deficits of the 1970s.[21] The central tenet of supply-side economics (called "Reaganomics" by its critics) held that lowering tax rates would stimulate so much additional productive economic activity that the government would raise more in revenues even if tax rates were lower. The theory proved incorrect. Large tax cuts enacted during the 1980s, coupled with increases in defense spending and continued high spending for social programs, led to sustained deficits unprecedented in American history (see Figure 19.4). Nevertheless, some experts argued that deficits were neither a substantive nor a political problem. "You just don't have people running through the streets to have the deficit cut," pointed out one Reagan administration official.[22]

But, by the 1990s, sustained voter concern about the deficit, coupled with the independent presidential candidacy of Ross Perot, provoked action on the issue. Perot made deficit reduction the centerpiece of his campaign for the presidency in 1992, and the 19 percent of the vote that he received convinced Bill Clinton that budgetary reform had popular backing. Still, elected officials struggled to find a way to satisfy public demands for a reduced deficit without angering voters by raising taxes or cutting spending. Stalemates between the president and Congress over how to balance the budget forced the federal government to shut down several times in the winter of 1995–1996.

In 1997 Clinton and a Republican Congress finally agreed on a balanced budget. But this achievement was due almost entirely to unexpected economic growth that by itself dramatically cut budget deficits. Suddenly it became easy to balance the budget while at the same time increasing social spending.

monetarism
An economic school of thought that rejects Keynesianism, arguing that the money supply is the most important influence on the economy.

debt
The accumulation of yearly deficits.

supply-side economics
Economic policy based on the belief that governments can keep the economy healthy by supplying the conditions (especially low taxes and minimal regulation) that encourage private economic activity.

 Timeline

Growth of the Budget and Federal Spending

FIGURE 19.4

The Federal Deficit or Surplus, 1950–2005

• *What accounts for the large deficits of the 1980s and the sudden surpluses of the late 1990s?*

Note: Figures for 2004–2005 are estimates.

SOURCE: Office of Management and Budget, *The Budget of Fiscal Year 2005, Historical Tables,* pp. 23-4, Table 1.2.

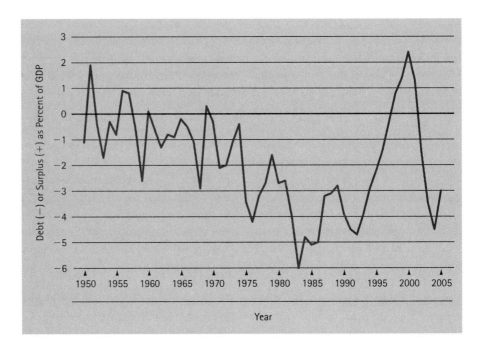

Predictably, when economic growth slowed, deficits moved back into the picture. Beginning in 2002, the federal government began running deficits again, and the budget shortfall in 2004 was expected to be over $500 billion.[23] The Bush tax cuts, as well as increased spending on the war in Iraq, homeland security, and Medicare, seemed likely to result in deficit spending for the foreseeable future. Although Americans no longer view the deficit as the most important problem facing the country, many policy analysts continue to view it as an important issue.[24] High deficits, coupled with public concern about their size, make it difficult for the president and Congress to consciously use deficit spending to affect the economy.

Internationalization   Fiscal policy has been further limited by the internationalization of the economy. Economic activity has become increasingly linked to overseas markets, so the reactions of economic actors to government policies are no longer limited to conditions in their own countries. If American investors think the government is spending too much, they can move billions of dollars to markets in Europe or Asia. Investors in other countries can do the same. Thus advances in communications have enabled investors in stocks and bonds to penalize governments for poor economic policies. If a government adopts taxation or spending policies that investors dislike, they can, for example, sell their bonds and their money to more accommodating countries, thus imposing economic costs on the government that adopts unfavorable policies. James Carville, President Clinton's 1992 campaign manager, made a humorous remark recognizing the power of investors in the stock and bond markets: "I used to think if there was reincarnation, I wanted to come back as the president or the Pope . . . but now I would like to come back as the bond market. You can intimidate everybody."[25]

These changes in the international economy gave rise to another school of economic thinking called "rational expectations." According to this theory, firms, investors, and other private economic actors rationally anticipate what government plans to do and then act in ways that offset what the government subsequently does.[26] For example, if the government plans to run a budget deficit in order to stimulate the economy, rational investors anticipate inflation and, to protect their investments, demand a higher interest rate on government bonds and other investments. But higher interest rates dampen economic growth, which offsets the intended stimulus effect of the budget deficit. In other words, government objectives are undermined by investors in the bond market.

Of course, people are not perfectly informed and even professional economic forecasters cannot predict economic developments very well, but rational-expectations arguments are sensible enough to raise doubts about the ability of government to manage the economy, especially when government plans become widely known during the lengthy public process of setting fiscal policy. By the beginning of the twenty-first century, governments appeared especially sluggish at a time when the communications revolution was making it possible for investors to react very quickly to changes in government policy.

Monetary Policy: The Federal Reserve System

Although fiscal policy was once a significant method of regulating the economy, today **monetary policy,** varying the supply of money to stabilize the business cycle, is the government's most important tool in this regard. When the supply of money is increased, it becomes cheaper for private citizens and investors to borrow and spend more of it (interest rates—the cost of borrowing money—go down). This increase in borrowing and spending in turn leads to economic growth and lower unemployment. If the supply of money increases too fast, however, inflation may result. Conversely, when the supply of money goes down, it becomes more costly to borrow and spend (interest rates go up). With less to spend and invest, the economy slows and inflationary pressures ease. If the economy contracts too rapidly, of course, unemployment may increase.

> **monetary policy**
> The actions taken by government to vary the supply of money in an effort to stabilize the business cycle.

Many believe that monetary policy is an effective tool for managing the economy because, unlike fiscal policy, it can be altered quickly in response to changing economic circumstances. This is due to the fact that decisions affecting the money supply are made not by Congress or even by the president, but by the **Federal Reserve System,** a government authority that manages U.S. monetary policy. Created in 1913, the Federal Reserve System (commonly known as the Fed) is headed by a board consisting of seven governors appointed by the president and confirmed by the Senate, each Fed governor holding office for 14 years. The Fed acts on the economy through the operations of its 12 regional banks, each of which oversees member banks in its part of the country. Figure 19.5 illustrates the structure of the Fed and its relationship to the federal government.

> **Federal Reserve System**
> The country's central bank, which executes monetary policy by manipulating the supply of funds that member banks can lend.

The most important decisions affecting the day-to-day workings of the economy are made by the Fed's Open Market Committee. This committee considers whether interest rates are too high or too low and what adjustments should be made. The committee consists of the 7 governors, all of whom vote, and the 12 regional bank presidents, only 5 of whom have a vote (the New York bank president always has a vote; the remaining 4 votes rotate among the other 11 banks). The Open Market Committee has three primary tools with which to affect the supply of money: it may buy and sell federal securities (treasury bills, notes, and bonds); it may change the interest rate it

FIGURE 19.5

The Structure of the Federal Reserve System

• *Do banks have too much say?*

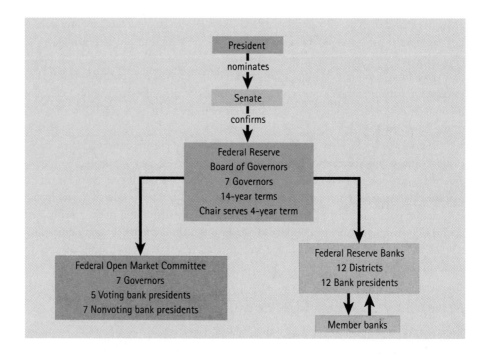

charges other banks; and it may change the percentage of deposits that banks are required to hold in reserve. In practice, the Fed usually makes policy through the first two methods.

Often the Fed is said to be the most powerful agency in the government after the Executive Office of the President. Its decisions affect interest rates, employment levels, and economic growth rates. The great American humorist Will Rogers once remarked that "two things can disrupt business in this country. One is a war and the other is a meeting of the Federal Reserve Board."[27] Surprisingly (given its importance), the Fed's activities are relatively unknown to many Americans.

The Fed Chair

If the Fed is the second most powerful agency in Washington, the chair of the Federal Reserve Board, currently Alan Greenspan, ranks among the most powerful persons in government. The chair's great power derives from close ties to the president, direct access to up-to-date economic information supplied by the Fed staff, and the power to approve the appointment of the 12 presidents of the Federal Reserve Banks (upon the recommendation of the member banks in each region). In addition, the chair inherits a job held in the past by powerful, prestigious people. Martin Eccles, head of the Fed during the 1930s, is acclaimed for taking actions to get the country out of the Great Depression, William McChesney Martin received credit for keeping the American economy on an even keel after World War II, and Paul Volcker is remembered for bringing the double-digit inflation of the late 1970s to an end.

Greenspan is adding to this tradition by becoming known as the person who managed the sustained economic growth of the 1990s. He also received plaudits for swiftly slashing interest rates less than a week after the September 11 terrorist attacks to shore up confidence in the financial system.

Alan Greenspan, Chairman of the Fed

• *Why is congressional influence over the Fed less than its influence over other agencies?*

Who Controls the Fed?

Surprisingly, in an elections-dominated political system, this key government agency is relatively insulated from electoral pressures. The Fed's power, independence, and objectivity are symbolized by its Washington home, a magnificent quasi-palace fronted by a remote—almost forbidding—facade and located two miles from Capitol Hill, adjacent to the National Academy of Sciences. Of course, the Fed is not immune to political pressure, but it is more insulated than most government agencies.

Congressional Influence   Like all other government agencies, the Fed was created and its powers defined by congressional statutes. Nominees to the Federal Reserve Board must be approved by the Senate, and the Fed must make quarterly reports to the banking committees of the House and Senate.

But despite these legal obligations to Congress, the Fed is remarkably free of congressional influence. For one thing, the Fed's budget is not congressionally determined. Instead, the Fed raises its own revenue by creating money (almost literally) and using this money to buy U.S. Treasury bonds, from which it earns interest. Creating money and buying Treasury bonds are a necessary part of the Fed's job—they are among the ways the Fed puts money into and takes money out of the economy. But Fed investments have a side benefit for the agency. Every year Fed investments earn billions of dollars (about $28 billion in 2001). Most of this money is turned over to the federal treasury, but the Fed keeps about a tenth for its own operations.[28] As a result, the Fed does not need to ask Congress for an appropriation the way most agencies do. The Fed owns squash courts in its building near the Washington Monument and bowling alleys on Wall Street, the most expensive real estate in the world—a reflection of the fact that it can almost literally manufacture its own money.

The Fed is also relatively free of congressionally determined salary schedules and personnel controls. Consequently, it is able to hire a better-trained, more professional, more prestigious staff than are other government agencies. In fact, the Fed is the one agency of the United States government that has a civil service that resembles the type found in Europe and Japan (see Chapter 14). Instead of political appointees who rotate in and out of office, the Fed staff consists of expert, career appointees.

In general, congressional influence on the Fed is exerted indirectly. Congress "jawbones" the Fed when it feels that monetary policy is not appropriate for prevailing conditions. Individual members make critical speeches and committees hold hearings at which the Fed chair is asked to testify. In these ways, some members make known their belief that monetary policy is too restrictive, and others announce their conviction that monetary policy is too loose. In these pronouncements there is an implied warning that if the Fed is not responsive, more serious attempts to influence it may be forthcoming. But members of Congress usually cannot agree on any specific course of action.

Although observers usually agree that Congress does not exert significant control over the Fed, there is less consensus on the influence of other groups and institutions. Three distinct interpretations of the source of influence over Fed operations have been offered: banker dominance, presidential control, and Fed independence.

Banker Dominance   The first interpretation, held by many liberal critics of the Fed, is that the banks control the Fed.[29] Just as interest groups underpin other iron triangles (see Chapter 14), so the banking industry, which has a huge stake in Fed decisions, forms the primary base of support for the Fed. Bankers influence the appointment of the Board of Governors, and they nominate the Federal Reserve Bank presidents, who cast five votes on the Open Market Committee.

As evidence of banker dominance, proponents point to the apparent policy bias of the Fed, which is generally viewed as being less concerned about reducing unemployment than about lowering inflation rates. To put it another way, the Fed seems to be more worried about avoiding rising prices than about staving off recessions. The Fed "can't stand prosperity." When jobs are plentiful and people are spending freely, the Fed typically responds by raising interest rates and slowing down the economy: "Just when the party gets going, the Fed takes away the beer."[30]

The Fed defends itself against such accusations of policy bias by saying that unless inflation is checked quickly, much stronger action will eventually have to be taken, creating more hardship in the long run. The Fed offers as evidence its policy in the late 1970s, when it mistakenly let inflation get out of control. Only after the deep and painful recession of 1981–1982 were inflation and interest rates brought down to acceptable levels.

Presidential Dominance   A second interpretation emphasizes not the bankers, but the president, as the main source of influence on the Fed. And indeed, most observers believe that the president, who appoints its members and chairs, has a great deal more influence than Congress.[31] But how much influence do presidents have, and to what ends do they use it?

Some political scientists suggest that presidents try to manipulate Fed policy for their own political purposes. These scholars note that the chair of the Federal Reserve Board, in order to win reappointment, must be sensitive to signals from the White House. Even more important, the Fed's very desire to appear nonpolitical creates a dependence on the president. If the president publicly criticizes the Fed, it becomes the subject matter of news commentaries and talk shows because the Fed's actions have become matters of partisan controversy. The best way for the Fed to appear independent is for its chair to listen carefully to suggestions coming from presidents and their advisers and to avoid acting in such a way as to provoke controversy.

There are two versions of the presidential-control interpretation—the partisan and the election-cycle interpretations.[32] The **partisan interpretation** distinguishes between the constituencies of Republican and Democratic presidents.[33] The Republican constituency includes more upper-income business and professional people, who traditionally are less worried about unemployment (which strikes them less frequently) than about inflation. The Democratic constituency includes more lower-income, blue-collar workers, who traditionally are more concerned about rising unemployment (which hits them hardest normally). Indeed, studies show that inflation rates tend to rise under Democratic presidents and fall under Republican presidents, and that stocks and bonds earn higher returns under Republican administrations.[34]

But there are reasons to doubt the more extreme version of the partisan interpretation. Most citizens, regardless of income, occupation, or partisan affiliation, dislike both rising unemployment and rising prices; they do not want to lose their jobs, but neither do they want to see the purchasing power of their wages eroded by inflation. Similarly, investors dislike inflation, but if growth slows and unemployment rises, their investments will earn lower returns. Thus, whatever their party, presidents are better off

partisan interpretation
The argument that Democratic administrations set economic policy to benefit lower-income, wage-earning groups and that Republican administrations set economic policy to benefit higher-income, business, and professional groups.

striking a balance between the two goals rather than focusing on either one and neglecting the other. Nevertheless, Democrats and Republicans strike different balances, reflecting their different constituencies. Republican administrations seem more willing to accept a little more unemployment in order to avoid inflation. Democrats strike the opposite balance. They appear more likely to accept somewhat higher inflation in order to avoid unemployment. To keep from provoking presidents, the Fed probably tends to slant its decisions in the direction of these well-known partisan preferences. But the effect is too small to call it presidential control.

The second version of the presidential dominance view, the **election-cycle interpretation,** says that presidents deliberately manipulate the economy to engineer their reelection. They tolerate slow growth, even a recession, early in their term of office so they can step on the gas and "rev up" the economic engine when the election payoff is greatest.

Richard Nixon's first term is a clear example of presidential manipulation. The Nixon administration pulled out all the stops and achieved a huge increase in household income during the election year 1972.[35] Nixon was reelected overwhelmingly.

If Nixon's first term fit the election-cycle interpretation, George H.W. Bush's single term directly contradicts it. The first president Bush also seems to have done things exactly backwards. In the beginning of his term the country enjoyed steady growth, but later the economy reversed, and Bush's fortunes shifted with it. Bush's timing could not have been worse. Bush's son, George W. Bush, appears to fall somewhere in between. The slowdown of 2001 occurred very early in the younger Bush's presidency, allowing plenty of time for recovery in advance of the 2004 elections. However, the effects of the economic slowdown were still evident in 2004, giving Bush's advisers cause to worry. According to one pollster, "The economy and jobs are the number one issue, in my polling and everyone else's polling that I have seen."[36]

Combining information for all years since World War II yields some evidence, but not a lot, that presidents manipulate the economy to their political advantage. In years when presidents themselves are running for reelection, growth rates are, on average, somewhat higher, but not a lot higher, than in other years.[37]

An Independent Fed   Fed supporters say the agency is independent of both politics and external pressure groups.[38] The independence of the Fed is guaranteed by the fact that board members are appointed for 14-year terms. They can be removed only through the impeachment process. Because board members serve such long terms, presidents may not be able to appoint a majority of the board until they themselves have been in office six years. And because the chair of the Fed serves a 4-year term, in the worst case a president may not be able to appoint a new chair until the fourth year of an administration.

There are other reasons for the Fed's independence. Business confidence in government economic policy is strengthened by the belief that Fed decisions are above politics. The board acts on the advice of a strong, independent staff. The chair is usually more knowledgeable about economic policy than any other presidential appointee. Monetary policy is too arcane to engage the general public; consequently, Fed-bashing is not a very effective campaign tactic.

Further, those who say the Fed is independent usually believe this is a good idea. They say that an independent Fed has improved the management of the economy. In

election-cycle interpretation
The argument that, whatever their party, presidents attempt to slow the economy early in their terms and then to expand it as their opportunity for reelection approaches.

particular, they emphasize that the country has had fewer and shorter recessions since the Fed was established than it had earlier in its history.

Perhaps it is impossible to conclude that anyone tightly controls the Fed. The Fed operates with a considerable amount of independence, mainly because it tries to achieve not only what presidents want but also what nearly everyone desires: steady, stable economic growth. Presidents need good economic news their first year, because that is when they are getting their political agenda off the ground. They need good economic news their second year to help the congressional candidates of their party. It is dangerous for a president to encourage a recession in the third year because it could spill over into the election campaign and, of course, no president wants a recession in the election year.

The Fed's emphasis on steady, moderate growth is pretty much what the president wants, so the president can usually leave the Fed alone. A case in point is the relationship President Clinton had with Fed chair Alan Greenspan. Ronald Reagan first appointed Greenspan as Fed chair, and Clinton sought to reassure financial markets in the election year of 1996 by renominating him.[39] Because both Greenspan and Clinton were interested in stable growth, each felt it was in his interest to leave the other alone. Perhaps the Fed is an example of the proposition that good public policy in a democracy is not necessarily produced by the most democratic processes.

The "T" Word: Taxes

Hardly anyone likes to pay taxes. As Figure 19.6 shows, most people think that their tax bill is too high. As a result, tax policy is a major topic of public concern, and various aspects of the American tax system are subject to heated debate.[40] In this section we discuss the three most important issues in this debate: the tax burden, the breadth of the tax base, and the progressivity of the tax structure.

The Tax Burden

tax burden
The total amount of tax that a household pays.

You Are Trying to Get a Tax Cut

In considering changes in tax policy, officials must take into account the **tax burden**— the total level at which Americans are taxed. Federal individual income tax receipts, as a percentage of the nation's GDP, rose by over 60 percent between 1950 and 1970.[41] Although they stabilized after 1970, the steep increase in the earlier period put the tax burden issue high on the country's political agenda. Some advocates of higher government spending argue that Americans have become selfish over the course of the past generation and are increasingly unwilling to tax themselves for good purposes. Others, writing in defense of taxpayers, point to the stagnation of personal incomes that began in the early 1970s. As long as standards of living were rising, people were willing to absorb higher taxes, but once living standards stagnated, frustrated citizens increasingly vented their unhappiness on the tax system. At any rate, many Americans came to feel that the tax burden was too high, and elected officials responded—from Reagan's tax cuts to President George H. W. Bush's 1988 campaign pledge of "no new taxes" to George W. Bush's two successful tax cut proposals.

The sizable budget surpluses that emerged in the late 1990s encouraged politicians to propose tax reductions. Almost immediately after taking office, George W. Bush guided the most extensive tax reduction in several decades through both houses of

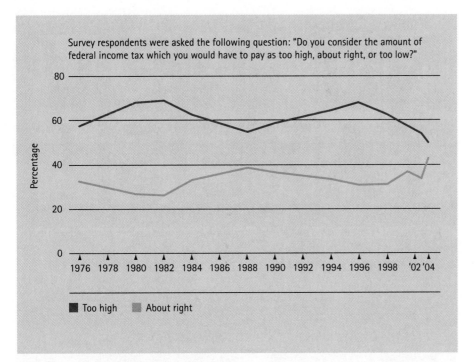

Survey respondents were asked the following question: "Do you consider the amount of federal income tax which you would have to pay as too high, about right, or too low?"

■ Too high   ▨ About right

FIGURE 19.6
Public Opinion About Taxes
• *Do you think taxes are too low or too high? Why?*
SOURCE: National Opinion Research Center, General Social Survey; 2003 and 2004 figures from identical question asked by Gallup, April 6–8, 2001, question ID USGALLUP.01APL06, R.21.

Congress. The bill, which included the one-time refund provision discussed at the beginning of the chapter, also cut tax rates gradually from 2002 to 2010, at an overall cost of nearly $1.4 trillion. Critics charged the president with "accounting gimmickry" and with allowing the cost of the tax cut to fall on future generations of Americans. "Our kids and grandkids are the real losers . . . ," said one member of Congress; "they will have to dig out of the hole that this tax bill causes."[42] But others saw the bill as a reasonable use of the budget surplus and as fulfilling Bush's promise to give the excess money "back to the people who earned it, the taxpayers."[43] Republicans praised Bush for making tax cuts central to his campaign and his presidency.

In 2003 Bush again proposed tax cuts, this time arguing for an elimination of the tax on stock dividends. The president claimed the measure would increase investment and would make the tax structure fairer, since taxing corporate profits as well as the dividends companies paid to shareholders constituted a type of "double taxation." Although the president did not get everything he wanted, Congress did pass a significant reduction in the dividend tax as part of a 10-year, $350 billion tax cut package.

In 2004 Democratic presidential candidate John Kerry responded to the Bush tax cuts by arguing that Bush had done too little to shift the tax burden off of average Americans. As part of what he called a focus on "middle class families who are working hard to cover the mortgage, pay the high cost of health care, child care and tuition, or just trying to get ahead," Kerry proposed new tax breaks for health care expenses and college tuition costs.[44]

The Tax Base

Even though the tax burden is the most frequently discussed tax-related topic, it is not necessarily the most important. At least as critical is the breadth of the **tax base:** the

tax base
Types of activities, types of property, or kinds of investments that are subject to taxation.

Protesting the Tax Burden

• *Why are antitax sentiments widespread in the United States, despite the fact that the country's taxes are lower than in many comparable nations?*

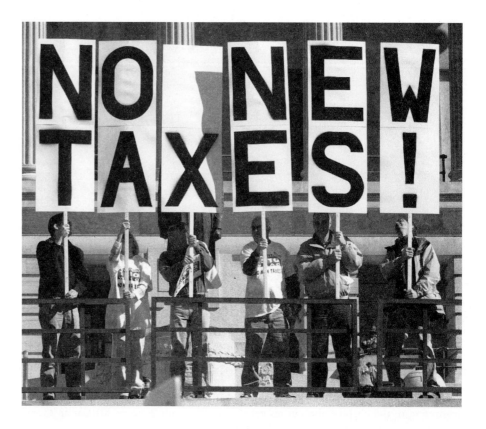

income, property, wealth, or economic activity that is taxed. Many economists argue that taxes are less intrusive if they are broad-based—that is, imposed on all economic activity at the same rate. Thus, the amount you pay in taxes should depend only on the amount you make, not on how you make it. Whether you make your money growing crops, making movies, writing wills, or running a charity should not matter. Nor should the amount you pay in taxes depend on whether you spend money on groceries, cars, beer, or medical insurance. If everything is taxed alike, then tax policy will not distort the economy. That is, it will not influence the choices people make.

Broad-based taxes are more easily recommended than enacted into law, however. Frequently, good reasons can be given for not taxing some particular activity, and there are numerous organized groups that offer good (and often not-so-good) reasons to persuade elected officials to give favorable treatment to the activities of their members. In response to these pressures, national and state legislators have enacted thousands of **tax preferences** that exempt particular types of economic activity from taxation. Critics say these tax preferences distort economic activity and cost the government billions of dollars in forgone revenues. Here are some major examples of tax preferences and the economic distortions that critics say they foster:

tax preferences
Special tax treatment received by certain activities, property, or investments.

- *Tax credits for college tuition* ($10 billion).[45] In 1997 Congress allowed a tax credit for college tuition, a tax break popular with college students. Critics say colleges, realizing that students have more tuition dollars, will simply boost tuition.
- *Deductions for mortgage interest on owner-occupied homes* ($63 billion). Developers and brokers claim that this tax preference encourages home ownership, which is said to be good for families and to boost community stability. Critics say the preference

primarily benefits higher-income people who can afford huge mortgages and subsidizes their over-investment in big houses and vacation homes.

- *Deductions for charitable contributions* ($34 billion). Defenders of this tax preference claim that it encourages public support for the arts, education, and the needy. But critics say many charities are actually businesses that provide services to those who "give" them money.

Tax preferences are the classic "slippery slope." Once government grants them to any group, it abandons the principle of neutral taxation and encourages other groups to lobby for their own preferences. Tax preferences distort the economy by encouraging people to make economic decisions on the basis of tax considerations. Moreover, granting preferences to some activities requires that taxes be higher on other activities that lack defenders strong enough to get their own tax break. Some economists argue that the only solution to this dilemma is somehow to restrict the government's ability to grant tax breaks to any activity or group.[46] Yet it is unlikely that all tax preferences will be eliminated. Some activities—home ownership, education, charities—are so popular that most people think they should get a tax break.

Not all special treatment is favorable. The government also sometimes imposes **sin taxes,** taxes intended to discourage unwanted behavior. The most prominent examples of sin taxes are the taxes on the consumption of cigarettes and alcohol. Critics of such measures argue that they fall primarily on the poorest segments of the population and fail to have a significant impact on the consumption of addictive products.

sin tax
A tax intended to discourage unwanted behavior.

Tax Progressivity

If some economists think the breadth of the tax base is the most important tax issue, others think tax progressivity is. Taxes are said to be **progressive taxes** if people with higher income pay a higher tax rate. The most important progressive tax is the federal income tax. In 2003, individual taxable incomes up to $7,000 were taxed at a 10 percent rate, while additional income between $7000 and $28,400 was taxed at a 15 percent rate. For example, if your annual income was $20,000, you paid 10 percent, or $700, in taxes on the first $7000, and then 15 percent, or $1950 on the remaining $13,000. Tax rates on additional income (called "marginal rates") increased up to a maximum rate of 35 percent for income over about $312,000.

progressive tax
A tax structured so that higher-income people pay a larger proportion of their income in taxes than do lower-income people.

Taxes that require low-income people to pay a higher rate are called **regressive taxes.** The payroll or social security tax is a regressive tax, because as of 2004 it was levied only on the first $87,900 that a person earns. Because all earnings in excess of that figure are exempt from the tax, higher-income people pay a smaller share of their income for social security than do lower-income people.

regressive tax
A tax structured so that higher-income people pay a smaller proportion of their income in taxes than do lower-income people.

For example, if you made $40,000 per year, you would pay 6.2 percent of your income, or $2480, in social security taxes. If you made $1 million, you would pay 6.2 percent in taxes on the first $87,900 you made, or $5449. In the second case, the amount paid is larger, but note that it makes up only half a percent of total income, whereas in the first case, 6.2 percent of total income goes for the tax.

There are numerous taxes levied in the United States. The federal personal income tax and some state personal income taxes are progressive. Social security and state sales taxes are regressive. Property taxes vary a great deal, but generally fall in between. When all taxes levied by federal, state, and local governments are taken into account, it is difficult to say whether the tax structure in the United States is progressive or not.[47]

Progressive taxes traditionally have been defended by liberals, who claim that progressive rates reduce income inequality in the society. Thus, Bill Clinton and the congressional Democrats pushed through an increase in the taxes paid by high-income taxpayers over united Republican opposition in 1993. Progressive taxes traditionally have been opposed by conservatives, who claim that progressive rates discourage investment and hard work by the most productive members of society. Thus, the Bush tax cut of 2001 made the tax system less progressive because the largest cuts in tax rates went to those with the highest incomes.

Tax Reform

Debates over tax reform traditionally focus on the breadth and progressivity of the tax system. In 1986 Congress passed a widely acclaimed reform that lowered individual income tax rates, raised corporate rates, and broadened the tax base by eliminating many tax preferences. The federal income tax burden for a typical family of four dropped from 10.5 to 8.9 percent of total income without reducing government revenue.[48]

flat tax
A tax that is neither progressive nor regressive; everyone pays at the same rate.

In recent years, many members of Congress have proposed even more sweeping tax reforms. The best known is the **flat tax,** a proposal that would eliminate progressive income tax rates and would tax all income groups above a certain minimum at the same rate.[49] Advocates argue that it is unfair to require some people to pay a higher percentage of their income in taxes than others. Supporters of a flat tax also defend it on the grounds of efficiency—the more progressive taxes are, the greater the incentive for the wealthy to hire accountants, lawyers, and lobbyists to help them avoid taxes. Indeed, the wealthy are not the only ones who pay: As of 2000, 54 percent of Americans used professional tax preparers,[50] and taxpayers spent over $150 billion a year on record keeping, filling out forms, complying with audits, and paying for accountants and lawyers.[51]

The debate over tax reform is likely to remain fractious and many-sided because people want to use the tax system to achieve different—often conflicting—goals. They want to raise revenue, to reduce income inequality, to discourage some kinds of behavior, and to give breaks so as to promote other kinds of activity, such as education and home ownership.

The U.S. Economy: An International Comparison

Comparing
Economic Policy

Even though we have focused on government and the economy, the truth is that the extent to which the economy can be controlled by government is limited—and has become much more so in recent years. When the Fed loosens or tightens the money supply, it is reacting to national and global economic forces that may overcome its best efforts. Indeed, all over the world, countries with very different political systems are struggling to meet economic challenges similar to those in the United States. Relative to other advanced democracies, the United States is dealing reasonably well with its economic challenges and difficulties. In this section we shall place U.S. taxes, national debt, and employment opportunities in comparative perspective.

Taxes

The tax burden in the United States compares very favorably with that in the world's other developed countries. As of 2002, the tax burden in the United States was among

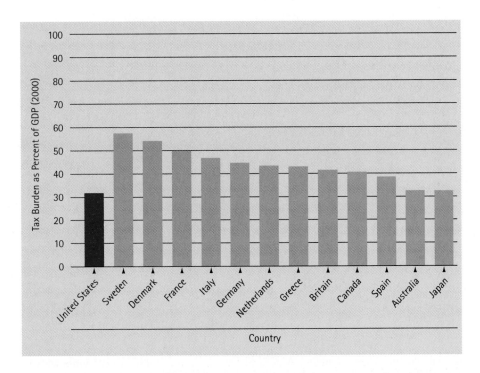

FIGURE 19.7

U.S. Tax Burden Is Less Than That in Many Other Democracies

• *Why are U.S. taxes lower than taxes in other countries?*

SOURCE: U.S. Bureau of the Census, *Statistical Abstract of the United States, 2001,* Table 1347.

the lowest of 13 major industrialized countries: about 32 percent of GDP. At the other extreme, the public sector in Sweden taxes away over 59 percent of the country's GDP. Taxes in Denmark, France, Belgium, Greece, and Italy all exceed 45 percent of GDP (see Figure 19.7).

To be sure, other countries provide more services in exchange for the money they extract in taxes. The most important example is health care; about half of it is paid for by the private sector in the United States, whereas it is almost entirely government-provided in other countries.

If their tax rates and the overall tax burden are the lowest in the developed world and are continuing to fall, why have Americans traditionally been so unhappy with taxes, and why did George W. Bush win so much praise for lowering taxes further in 2001?

We doubt that there is any single explanation for the American aversion to taxes. Part of the answer may lie in the nature of the American tax system. The United States relies more heavily than most other countries on income and payroll taxes to raise revenues; nearly two-thirds of total tax revenues come from such sources, a figure exceeded only by Switzerland and Belgium. Other countries rely more heavily on consumption taxes, such as a sales tax known as the value-added tax (VAT), which is hidden in the prices of goods and services. Thus, their voters may not realize the full tax cost of the services they receive, despite the fact that the VAT affects low-income families the most. Ironically, Sweden, Germany, and Italy—with their large welfare states—rely heavily on the VAT, a tax that American liberals view as regressive. Only Japan, with its minimal provision of social services, relies less on sales taxes than the United States.

U.S. historical experience is probably more important for explaining the views of Americans than the type of tax levied, however. In Chapter 4 we saw that, more than

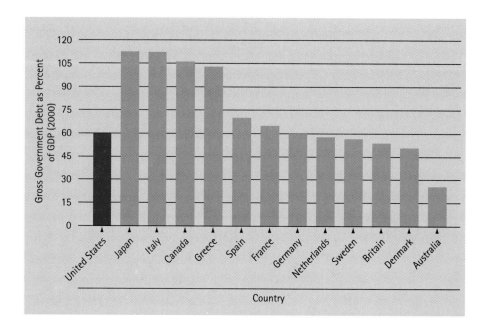

the citizens in other countries, Americans are economic individualists who wish to keep the role of government limited. They expect less from government, and they wish to keep more of their money for their own use.

National Debt

Seven and one-half trillion dollars, the size of the national debt in 2004, is an almost unimaginable number. But such numbers are meaningful only relative to baselines, and the natural baseline—the size of the American economy—was over $11 trillion. Relative to the size of the economy, the public debt in the United States is moderate. For example, as a proportion of GDP, France, Germany, and Canada all have larger national debts than the United States—and Japan and Italy have debts that are nearly twice as large (see Figure 19.8).

Certainly, this is not to say that historical and continuing concern about the debt was and is unwarranted. That so much debt has accumulated is worrisome, but the debt in other democracies has increased more rapidly than in the U.S. For example, between 1990 and 2000, the total U.S. debt declined as a percentage of GDP, while France's debt increased by nearly 65 percent.[52]

Employment Opportunities

The United States has done a better job than most countries of incorporating new workers into the economy. In late 2003, for example, the unemployment rate in western Europe was nearly 9 percent—significantly higher than the 5.9 percent rate in the United States, even as the U.S. continued to suffer from an economic slowdown.[53]

The situation in 2003 is the result of changes that date back to the 1980s. At that time, the workforce in the Western world expanded rapidly as the baby boom generation reached working age and as women moved into the workforce in greater numbers. The American economy absorbed these new workers far more successfully than did European economies, creating three times more new jobs per 1000 people than did France and West Germany. Moreover, European countries were able to keep their unemployment rates as low as they did only by introducing policies that would be unacceptable in the United States. For example, policies in Germany and Switzerland induced so-called guest workers to return to their countries of origin. The United States, in contrast, allowed immigration to increase during the 1980s. Some countries absorbed new workers by expanding their public sectors. Sweden, for example, dealt with the surge of women into the labor force by doubling public-sector employment.[54] In the United States, public-sector employment grew very slowly.

Some critics object that many of the jobs that have been created in the United States are low-skill, low-paying "McJobs," and that many good jobs have been exported abroad by U.S. companies, but the evidence suggests that such claims are at least somewhat exaggerated. According to several studies, much of the job growth in recent years has been in higher-paying occupations and industries—again, a performance far superior to Western European democracies.[55]

Compared to most other countries, the American economy is less restricted by government policies and regulations. This gives it a greater capacity to adapt to changing economic conditions. For example, changes in the world economy have had an adverse effect on workers in the manufacturing sector. In 1950 these industries accounted for 34 percent of U.S. jobs, and by 2000 this figure had shrunk to 15 percent. Amazingly, the United States produces no more steel today than it did in the early 1960s.[56]

But these adverse consequences have been offset by gains in the service, communications, and technology industries. In the late 1990s, the U.S. information technology sector grew at stunning rates, and officials estimated that by 2006, nearly half of the U.S. workforce would be employed by industries closely connected to the technology sector. The United States is better equipped than most of its European peers to handle this rapid transition to a high-technology economy. For example, the proportion of people with access to the Internet is about 50 percent higher in the United States than in the European Union.[57]

Inequality

The price of limited government seems to be greater social inequality. Compared to other advanced democracies, income inequality in the United States is higher (see Figure 19.9). Moreover, after declining between 1930 and 1970, inequality rose until, by the 1990s, it was higher than at any time since the 1930s. Some social critics see in such trends a "class war" of the rich against the poor,[58] but there seems to be no great popular demand for government to intervene directly to reverse the trend toward inequality. Candidates who advocate a greater role for government and a greater degree of income redistribution regularly run for office, but the American people have usually not elected them. Nor have they demanded such policies from their representatives in Congress and the state legislatures.

FIGURE 19.9

Income Inequality Greater in United States Than in Many Other Countries

• *Why is inequality greater in a wealthy country like the United States?*

Note: The bars represent the value of the Gini index for each country. A Gini index value of zero represents complete equality; a value of 100 represents complete inequality. Data were collected from 1991 to 1997.

SOURCE: *World Development Report 2000/2001* (Washington, DC: World Bank, 2000), Table 5, pp. 282–283.

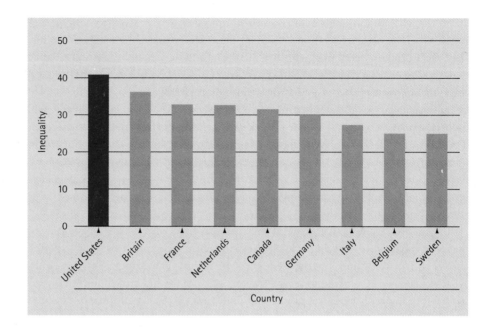

Chapter Summary

People care a lot about whether they can find a job and what they have to pay for the things they buy. When times are bad, the president takes the blame. When times are good, the president usually—but not always—gets the credit. Presidents' popular standing and their odds of reelection are significantly influenced by national economic conditions. To a somewhat lesser extent, this is also true of members of Congress and even of state-level elected officials.

Given these political facts of life, presidents give economic policy top priority. To achieve this objective, they grant the agency responsible for monetary policy, the Federal Reserve, a good deal of independence. Although they may try to shape policy on occasion, presidents generally realize that the Fed needs independence to do its job well. And when the Fed does a good job by keeping economic growth steady, the president usually gets the credit.

For half a century, presidents tried to use fiscal policy—the management of budget deficits and surpluses—to manage the economy. But the importance of fiscal policy for managing the economy has been reduced by a combination of factors, including divided government, declining faith in Keynesian theory, a rising public debt, and the globalization of economic activity.

Debates over tax reform typically involve discussion of the tax burden, whether tax preferences should be eliminated in order to broaden the tax base, and whether the progressivity of the tax system needs to be raised or lowered. Although the two parties fought for much of the 1980s and 1990s over whether to increase taxes to eliminate the deficit, in 2001 and 2003 President Bush pushed major tax cuts through Congress, arguing that the cuts would stimulate economic growth and propel the nation out of an economic slowdown.

The United States has a lower tax burden, a smaller national debt, and lower unemployment rates than many other countries. But Americans also seem more willing to tolerate economic inequality than people in other nations are.

Key Terms

Suggested Readings

Of General Interest

Krugman, Paul. *Peddling Prosperity.* New York: Norton, 1994. Written for the noneconomist, this critique of many of those who have influenced recent economic policy provides a comprehensible discussion of schools of economic thought and an overview of economic trends of the past several decades.

Weir, Margaret. *Politics and Jobs: The Boundaries of Employment Policies in the United States.* Princeton, NJ: Princeton University Press, 1992. Broad historical and political analysis of government efforts to guarantee full employment.

Woodward, Bob. *Maestro: Greenspan's Fed and the American Boom.* New York: Simon & Schuster, 2000. A diverting account of how Alan Greenspan managed monetary policy in the 1990s.

Yergin, Daniel, and Joseph Stanislaw. *The Commanding Heights: The Battle Between Government and the Marketplace That is Remaking the Modern World.* New York: Simon & Schuster, 1998. A Pulitzer Prize-winning writer and a business consultant examine the implications of globalization for the United States and other nations.

Stiglitz, Joseph. *The Roaring Nineties: A New History of the World's Most Prosperous Decade.* New York: W. W. Norton & Co., 2003. A Nobel Prize-winning economist critiques recent U.S. economic policy.

Focused Studies

Birnbaum, Jeffrey H., and Alan S. Murray. *Showdown at Gucci Gulch.* New York: Random House, 1987. Fast-paced case study of the passage of the 1986 tax reforms.

Hibbs, Douglas, A., Jr. *The American Political Economy.* Cambridge, MA: Harvard University Press, 1987. Provides detailed statistical evaluations of partisan and election-cycle interpretations of presidential management of the economy.

Kettl, Don. *Deficit Politics.* New York: Macmillan, 1992. Short, readable book on budget deficits.

Weaver, R. Kent. *Automatic Government: The Politics of Indexation.* Washington, DC: The Brookings Institution, 1988. Explains how government benefits came to be indexed.

On the Web

www.federalreserve.gov
Some claim that the Federal Reserve holds power second only to the president of the United States. The Federal Reserve System maintains an informative Web site, complete with publications, congressional testimony, and economic data.

www.commerce.gov
The Department of Commerce houses the Economics and Statistics Administration and the Bureau of Economic Analysis, which provide regular data and analysis on the U.S. economy.

www.nber.org
The National Bureau of Economic Research is considered the unofficial arbiter of many economic issues, such as when recessions begin and end. It publishes an excellent series of working papers by eminent economists.

www.publicdebt.treas.gov/
Debate over the budget deficit defined economic policy debates in the 1970s and 1980s and continues to affect discussions of new taxing and spending. The Bureau of the Public Debt, located in the Department of the Treasury, provides precise daily updates of how much the government owes. While there, you may peruse information on how to buy federal securities, thus helping to finance the national debt.

www.ctj.org
www.taxfoundation.org
The contentious debates over taxation in Washington have been enough to inspire a number of interest groups to people the barricades on both sides. Citizens for Tax Justice (CTJ) argues for progressive taxation, whereas the Tax Foundation promotes the idea of a flat tax.

CHAPTER 20

★ ★ ★ ★ ★ ★ ★ ★ ★ ★ ★ ★ ★ ★

Foreign and Defense Policy

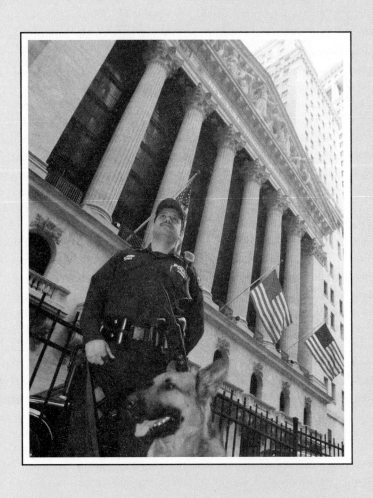

While America Slept

Democracies are not very good at solving problems until they turn into full-blown crises. While a college undergraduate, future President John F. Kennedy wrote a senior honors thesis titled "While England Slept." Later published as a book, the thesis described Britain's head-in-the-sand response to the threat Hitler posed. Today, students have the opportunity to write a similar senior honors thesis about the 1990s, this one titled "While America Slept."

It will require careful research to reveal the whole story, but some of the most telling points are already clear. In February 1993, more than eight years before September 11, 2001, terrorists bombed the World Trade Center, killing six people and wounding over a thousand, making it clear that this complex, including some of the world's tallest buildings, was seen by terrorist groups such as Osama bin Laden's al-Qaeda as the nerve center of the western economic order. Five years later, al-Qaeda bombs destroyed the U.S. embassies in Kenya and Tanzania. Even more worrisome, al-Qaeda wreaked serious havoc on a U.S. naval intelligence ship, the *U.S.S. Cole,* while it was docked in a Yemen seaport. That al-Qaeda could so closely approach a well-equipped vessel and wreak such devastating damage was a telling indication of the organization's growing strength and sophistication.

Any of these events could have spurred the president to mobilize political support for a sustained campaign against terrorism. But no effective response occurred. To be sure, in 1996, Congress passed and President Clinton signed into law counterterrorist legislation. And Clinton ordered one-time raids on Iraq, Sudan, and the bin Laden headquarters in Afghanistan. But President Clinton never visited the site of the first World Trade Center bombing, nor did the country's political leadership, in 1999, heed the warnings of the bipartisan Hart-Rudman Commission on National Security. In testimony before an investigating commission in 2004, current and former administration officials admitted that prior to 9/11, the George W. Bush administration felt no greater sense of urgency about the problem than Clinton had. As National Security Adviser Condoleezza Rice explained, "Historically, democratic societies have been slow to react to gathering threats, tending instead to wait to confront threats until they are too dangerous to ignore or until it is too late."[1]

We now know some of the steps that would have been taken in an energetic war on terrorism. The United States could have adopted tighter airline security practices. More effective controls over the manufacture and distribution of anthrax and other potential biological agents could have been put in place. Most important, the Federal Bureau of Investigation and other key agencies needed to be told that terrorist threats—not drug dealers—were to be given top priority. Even before 9/11, top-level intelligence officers were well aware of "the paucity of analytical [counterterrorist] resources in FBI field offices."[2] It was just this absence of sophistication at the field level that was evident when the FBI responded haphazardly to a call from instructors at the Pan Am Flight Academy in Eagan, Minnesota. The school reported suspicious behavior indicating that a student was a potential hijacker, but the FBI investigation was slipshod. After 9/11, the student, Zacarias Moussaoui, was indicted as one of the co-conspirators in the terrorist attacks. A congressional investigation and media reports revealed that this was only one of many intelligence lapses. Miscommunications between the FBI and the Central Intelligence Agency (CIA) caused officials to lose track of key terrorists in the months before the attacks. Perhaps most chilling, intelligence officers intercepted communications in early September indicating that 9/11 was "zero hour," but only translated them into English after the planes had hit their targets.

Although many have blamed the Clinton and Bush administrations for inaction, this conclusion is too simplistic. No other major political figures were pressing for action either. Robert Dole, the Republican candidate for president in 1996, introduced antiterrorist legislation in Congress, but his proposals were confined to modest changes in the criminal justice system.

In the early months of the Bush administration, Democrats criticized Bush's tax cuts, his withdrawal from a global-warming treaty, and his focus on a missile defense program, but rarely chastised him for lack of attention to terrorism. On September 10, 2001, Democratic Senator Joseph Biden accused Bush of neglecting the terror threat, but this point was buried in a larger critique of missile defense and administration policy on China, North Korea, and Russia, as well as a call for modernization of defense technology and higher military salaries.[3]

Two of the country's top intelligence officers, Joseph S. Nye, Jr., and James Woolsey, wrote an essay in 1995 lamenting the fact that "the very nature of U.S. society makes it difficult to prepare for this problem. We are unlikely to mount an adequate defense until we suffer an attack." The piece was published by the *Los Angeles Times,* but its authors were simply crying in the wilderness. The general attitude, Nye later reported, was simply "If it is so likely, why hasn't it happened?"[4]

MAKING THE CONNECTION

Democracies are slow to respond to problems until they become full-blown crises. Even presidents may not be able to mobilize public support for strong action until a foreign policy problem becomes urgent. Still, presidents play a preeminent role in the making of foreign policy, and they may be rewarded and punished accordingly by the voting public. In this chapter, we explore how America conducts foreign policy and examine the changing connections between foreign policy and electoral politics. In doing so, we answer the following questions:

- What characteristics of foreign policy enable presidents to exercise greater influence over it than over domestic policy?

- What constitutional responsibilities over foreign affairs are granted to the president and Congress?

- How do various agencies in the executive branch help design and coordinate foreign policy?

- How has the campaign against terrorism changed agency responsibilities?

- How has America's history shaped modern debates over the country's foreign policy goals?

- How has the campaign against terrorism changed this debate?

* * * * * * * * * * * * * * * *

Elections, Presidents, and Foreign Policy

Foreign policy is the conduct of relations among nation-states. The most important foreign policy issues involve war and peace. Of all foreign policy objectives, the most critical is to prevent the country from being attacked or invaded by a foreign power. But foreign policy also involves economic trade among nations, as well as such mundane matters as issuing passports to citizens who wish to travel abroad.

In a classic essay, political scientist Aaron Wildavksy developed the **two-presidency theory,** which explains why presidents exercise greater power over foreign affairs than over domestic policy.[5] On domestic matters, presidents are usually subject to pressure politics and congressional checks. On foreign policy questions, however, presidents have a degree of autonomy that enables them to manage the external relations of the country in relative freedom from short-term political pressures. In this section we describe four reasons why foreign policy differs from domestic policy: (1) the need for fast action, (2) the voters' focus on presidents, (3) the limited role of interest groups, and (4) the comparatively minor role of congress.

foreign policy
Conduct of relations among nation-states.

two-presidency theory
Theory that explains why presidents exercise greater power over foreign affairs than over domestic policy.

Patriotic Fervor

The Gulf War stirred a wave of patriotic fervor, boosting the first President Bush's approval ratings to the highest ever for a modern president.

• *Why did this support evaporate so rapidly that Bush lost the 1992 election?*

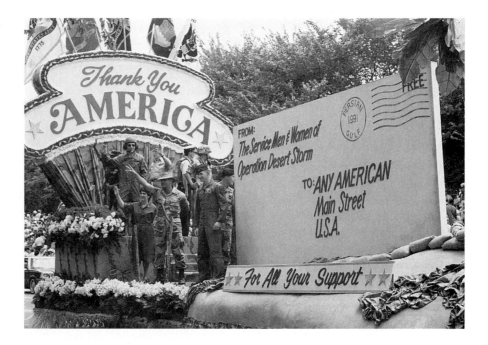

Need for Fast Action

On domestic issues, the president may negotiate with Congress over the course of several years, but foreign policy questions often require rapid, decisive action. As Alexander Hamilton observed, governments require a single executive leader in order to achieve "decision, activity, secrecy, and dispatch."[6] Or, in the words of nineteenth-century humorist Artemus Ward, "Thrice is he armed that has his quarrel just—And four times he who gets his fist in first."[7] Following this principle, President Bush sent marines to Haiti in 2004 to guard U.S. interests as the government of Haitian President Aristide crumbled. Secretary of State Colin Powell briefed Congress on the operation, but Bush did not seek lawmakers' approval for it.

Voters' Focus on Presidents

On key domestic issues, members of Congress know that voters hold them to account, but on foreign affairs, Wildavksy points out, voters "expect the president to act."[8] In the early days of a crisis, voters often ignore those who criticize presidential actions. After the 9/11 terrorist attacks, for example, President George W. Bush's popularity, which had been hovering around the 50 percent level, skyrocketed to above 90 percent.

"rally 'round the flag" effect
The tendency for the public to back presidents in moments of crisis.

The tendency among the public to back presidents in foreign crises, which is often called the **"rally 'round the flag" effect,** shows up in opinion polls in almost every instance in which the United States becomes involved in a foreign policy emergency.[9] Support for the president nearly always goes up in the first days of a conflict with another nation. Figure 20.1 shows the crises that presidents from Truman to Bush have faced and the changes in opinion polls that occurred after those crises broke. Between 1950 and 2004, public support for presidents increased by an average of 7 percentage points in the month after a foreign policy crisis occurred.

Although voters support presidents initially, they nonetheless demand quick results. When Iranian radicals took dozens of American embassy workers hostage in 1979,

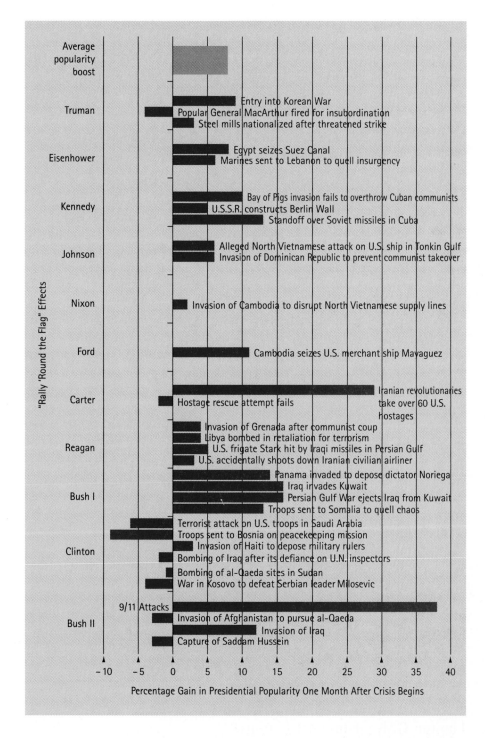

FIGURE 20.1

"Rally 'round the Flag" Effects

Presidents' gains in popularity average 7 percentage points in the months following a crisis.

• *Why do you think President Clinton did not experience as large a boost in public support after foreign policy crises as his predecessors?*

President Jimmy Carter's approval rating initially rose by nearly 20 points. But as the Tehran hostage crisis dragged on, Carter's support evaporated, and he was defeated in the 1980 election.

The public seems especially ready to hold presidents accountable when war breaks out and American casualties mount. The public supported U.S. entry into both the Korean War and the Vietnam War. But when the conflicts dragged on, both Harry

Truman, in the case of the Korean War, and Lyndon Johnson, in the case of Vietnam, lost so much public support that they announced they would not run for reelection. The opposition party won the next election in each instance.[10] Over two-thirds of the public approved of President George W. Bush's presidency during the initial phase of the 2003 Iraq War, but as casualties mounted and occupation forces failed to prevent repeated attacks by insurgents, the president's popularity suffered. By mid-2004, Democratic challenger John Kerry was using the Iraq issue to mobilize voters against Bush, a tactic that most political strategists would have seen as unthinkable only a year before.

Not only do voters demand quick results, but they also soon forget foreign policy victories. If the economy steadily improves, presidents receive credit for the progress year after year. But, unless a foreign policy accomplishment immediately precedes an election, there are few electoral dividends. Before too long, voters forget and turn to domestic concerns. For example, during the first three years of the George H. W. Bush presidency, the United States won both the Cold War and the Persian Gulf War. Yet one year later, the voters, deciding that domestic issues were more important, voted Bush out of office.

As media coverage has become more intense and technologically more sophisticated, pressure on presidents has increased. During the Iraq War, many journalists traveled into combat zones with troops, and news networks aired live video and audio feeds of battles taking place at remote desert outposts. Although in the early phases of the conflict the effect of this unprecedented access was to improve the president's stature by highlighting the armed forces' rapid progress, later events made journalistic scrutiny more problematic. When graphic photographs surfaced of prisoner abuse at Iraq's Abu Ghraib prison, President Bush was placed on the defensive, and repeatedly denied that he or other top administration officials had condoned the abuse. "We do not condone torture. I have never ordered torture. I will never order torture," the president said.[11]

As media pressures on presidents have increased, the political benefits of foreign policy action have become less predictable. President Clinton, for example, did not get the same "rally 'round the flag" boost enjoyed by his predecessors. During the major foreign policy crises of the Clinton administration, the president's popularity underwent a downward shift of an average of 3 points, rather than the average 8-point boost that previous presidents had enjoyed. President Bush received an overwhelming and sustained popularity boost after 9/11, but the capture of Saddam Hussein two years later generated only a minor surge in approval, lasting less than a month. Perhaps because of the uncertain nature of public support, presidents have sought to dampen high expectations in the foreign policy arena. In a spring 2004 speech, for example, President Bush predicted further violence in Iraq in the months to come, but urged Americans to place the events into a larger context of progress.[12]

Limited Role of Interest Groups

On domestic issues, many groups with large constituencies constantly mobilize voters and urge members of Congress to take action. But on foreign policy questions, "the interest group structure is weak, unstable, and thin."[13] The most important national membership organization influencing foreign affairs is the Council on Foreign

Relations, a prestigious group that includes former secretaries of state, former ambassadors, foreign policy experts, and prominent business leaders. But the organization influences government action by the quality of its advice, not by its ability to mobilize votes.

On some occasions, organized groups capable of mobilizing large numbers of voters play a role in foreign policy issues. For example, the hundreds of thousands of people living in Florida whose families fled Cuba in the 1950s when communist leader Fidel Castro came to power have persuaded the U.S. government not to recognize the legitimacy of the Castro regime, despite the fact that nearly every other country now does.

Participation

Economic Sanctions
and Cuba

Middle East policies are also shaped by group pressures. Former Secretary of State James Baker has observed that the conflict between Israel and the Palestinians is "a perpetual fixture of domestic politics" as a result of "the political power of the American Jewish community."[14] Because a strong domestic constituency is vitally interested, Congress regularly becomes actively engaged. The American Israel Public Affairs Committee (AIPAC) boasts on its Web site that *Fortune* magazine has ranked it the second most influential lobbying group in Washington, second only to the American Association of Retired Persons.[15] With strong support in Congress, Israel receives nearly 20 percent of all U.S. foreign aid (see Voices of the Permanent Campaign, p. 000). But although U.S. Middle East policies are, in the words of one former State Department official, influenced by "what we can get through [Capitol] Hill,"[16] they are also shaped by the country's interest in protecting access to oil reserves located in Arab countries. As a result, U.S. support for Israel seldom is as wholehearted as Jewish organizations would like, and relations between the United States and Israel are often uneasy.

The examples of Cuba and Israel are "exceptions that prove the rule," however. Most nationality groups are not large enough, or concentrated enough, or sufficiently attentive to events overseas to have influence over election outcomes and, thereby, a decisive effect on U.S. foreign policy.

Congressional Role

Although Congress plays a central role in the formation of domestic policy, when it comes to foreign affairs, members of Congress follow a "self-denying ordinance." They do not think it is their job to determine the nation's defense policies."[17] This was particularly true in the years immediately after World War II. During these years, Congress's prestige with respect to foreign policy was seriously damaged because it had left the country unprepared for the war. Just four months before the Japanese attacked Hawaii's Pearl Harbor, the incident that provoked U.S. involvement in the war, a bill requiring young men to register for service in the armed forces passed the House of Representatives by only a single vote. In the period after World War II, Congress, embarrassed by its earlier mistakes, let the president make most major foreign policy decisions.

Later, after the Vietnam War, Congress played a more assertive foreign policy role, and conflict between Congress and the president intensified.[18] But the victory in the Persian Gulf War in 1991 erased some of the bad memories from the Vietnam War and helped boost the prestige of the executive. For example, after 9/11 Congress for the most part allowed the Bush administration to develop antiterrorist policy on its own and approved military action in Afghanistan and Iraq.

Foreign Policy Responsibilities of the President and Congress

CONSTITUTION, ARTICLE I, SECTION 8: "The Congress shall have power to . . . declare war, . . . raise and support armies, . . . provide and maintain a navy, . . . [and] make rules for the government and regulation of the land and naval forces."

CONSTITUTION, ARTICLE II, SECTION 2: "The President shall be commander in chief of the army and navy."

CONSTITUTION, ARTICLE II, SECTION 1: "The executive power shall be vested in a President of the United States."

Although the president plays the dominant role in the making of foreign policy, the Constitution gives clear responsibilities to Congress as well. As a consequence, the constitutional debate over the power of Congress and of the presidency has continued from the early years of the republic down to the present day. In this section we review how the power to wage war has evolved through history, describe congressional attempts to limit presidential war powers, and consider the treaty-making power, which the Constitution divides between the president and the Senate.

War Power

From Stand-Alone to Superpower: The Evolution of Foreign Policy

The debate over which institution ought to control the nation's war power predates even the ratification of the Constitution. Writing in support of the new form of government, Alexander Hamilton argued that "Of all the concerns of government, the direction of war most peculiarly demands the exercise of power by a single hand."[19] Yet the Constitution gives Congress the authority to declare war and to raise and maintain the armed forces. The president's constitutional powers are less clearly defined; the Constitution says only that the president is commander in chief and exercises executive power. Chief Justice John Marshall interpreted these powers broadly: "The President is the sole organ of the nation in its external relations, and its sole representative with foreign nations."[20] But nineteenth-century Representative Thaddeus Stevens, a great defender of congressional prerogatives, proclaimed that "though the president is commander-in-chief, Congress is his commander, and God willing, he shall obey."[21] The issue has been debated ever since.

Prior to the Civil War, presidents seldom acted on their own on military matters. President James Madison refused to attack Great Britain in 1812 until Congress had declared war. And in 1846, President James K. Polk, although he provoked war by placing troops in disputed territory, did not actually order troops into battle against Mexico until Congress had declared war.

Faced with a national emergency, Abraham Lincoln was the first president to take action based on an expanded interpretation of the role of commander in chief. When the southern states seceded from the Union, Lincoln proclaimed a blockade of southern ports and enlisted 300,000 volunteers before Congress had a chance to convene. A few decades later, Theodore Roosevelt further broadened the role of commander in chief by exercising executive powers in a much less urgent situation. He sent naval ships to Japan even when Congress refused to appropriate enough money for the trip. He said that the president, in his role as commander in chief, would send the ships. Congress, if it wished, could appropriate enough funds to get them back. Congress did.

Following Lincoln and Roosevelt's lead, modern presidents have felt free to initiate military action even in the absence of congressional approval. Not since World War II has Congress officially declared war, and many presidential uses of force have never received nonbinding resolutions of support from Congress. President Truman fought the Korean War without any congressional declaration whatsoever. More recently, President Clinton ordered the bombing of Kosovo without securing congressional approval.

Two major Supreme Court decisions have set the boundaries within which presidents exercise their authority as commander in chief. In 1936 the Court was asked, in ***U.S. v. Curtiss-Wright,*** whether Congress could delegate to the president the power to determine whether arms could be sold to Bolivia and Paraguay, countries engaged in a border dispute. In his decision in favor of presidential power, Justice George Sutherland wrote that the authority of presidents on foreign affairs was greater than their discretion over domestic policy. Sutherland referred to "the very delicate, plenary and exclusive power of the president as the sole organ of the federal government in the field of international relations." He went on to say that the president had "a degree of discretion and freedom . . . which would not be admissible were domestic affairs alone involved."[22]

U.S. v. Curtiss-Wright
Supreme Court decision in which Congress is given the authority to delegate foreign policy responsibilities to the president.

Curtiss-Wright was qualified by the 1952 ***Youngstown Sheet and Tube Co. v. Sawyer*** case, in which the Supreme Court placed limits on the executive power of the president. At the height of the Korean War, trade unions in the steel industry announced that they would go on strike. Claiming that the steel industry was crucial for national defense, President Truman ordered the federal government to seize control of the steel mills and commanded union members to continue to work. In doing so, Truman ignored alternative procedures for handling labor disputes that had recently been enacted by Congress. When the steel companies challenged Truman's claim of executive power in this case, the Supreme Court ruled against the president, saying he should have instead observed the congressionally defined procedures. Justice Robert Jackson wrote that when a president "takes measures incompatible with the expressed or implied will of Congress, his power is at its lowest ebb."[23]

Youngstown Sheet and Tube Co. v. Sawyer
Case in which the Supreme Court placed limits on the executive power of the president.

When the *Curtiss-Wright* and *Youngstown* cases are considered together, the Court seems to have said that presidents have more constitutional discretion with respect to foreign than to domestic questions. However, presidents may not act contrary to the clearly expressed will of Congress.[24]

War Powers Resolution

The issue of executive authority arose again during the Vietnam War. Presidents Eisenhower and Kennedy had sent soldiers to Vietnam to serve as "advisers" to the South Vietnamese army, which was engaged in a war against communist guerrillas trained in North Vietnam. Neither Eisenhower nor Kennedy had received congressional authorization to send these advisers and, as the war intensified, U.S. military personnel became ever more directly involved. Then, in the summer of 1964, North Vietnamese torpedo boats apparently fired on several U.S. destroyers stationed in Tonkin Bay off the coast of Haiphong, Vietnam's second-largest city. President Lyndon Johnson denounced the action as an unlawful attack on U.S. ships that, he said, were sailing in international waters. He asked Congress for a resolution authorizing him to

Tonkin Gulf Resolution
Congressional resolution giving the
president the authority to send
troops to Vietnam.

War Powers Resolution
1973 congressional resolution
requiring the president to notify
Congress formally upon ordering
U.S. troops into military action.

respond with armed force. By a nearly unanimous vote, Congress passed the **Tonkin Gulf Resolution,** which gave the president the authority to "take all necessary measures" to repel any attacks and to "prevent further aggression."[25] The resolution became the legal basis for a war that would last for eight more years. Only much later was it revealed that Johnson had misled Congress by inaccurately claiming that the United States had not invaded North Vietnam's territorial waters.

The experience of a long and discouraging war in Vietnam prompted Congress to rethink its broad approval of the president's authority over military action. In 1970 it repealed the Tonkin Gulf Resolution. As a further precaution against presidential usurpation of congressional prerogatives, Congress in 1973 passed, over President Nixon's veto, the **War Powers Resolution,** which required that the president formally notify Congress any time he orders U.S. troops into military action. The resolution further specifies that troops must be withdrawn unless Congress approves the presidential decision within 60 days after notice of the military action has been received.

Before 9/11, only one president, George H. W. Bush, had asked for congressional authorization for military action. Bush asked—and received—authorization for using troops in the Persian Gulf War. However, President Reagan invaded Grenada, bombed Libya, and placed military troops in Lebanon without notifying Congress. President Clinton bombed Iraq, deployed troops in Bosnia, bombarded Serb positions in Kosovo, and struck at terrorist sites in Sudan and Afghanistan without notifying Congress as called for by the War Powers Resolution. On five separate occasions, individual members of Congress sued in federal courts, attempting to force the president to abide by that resolution. In each case, however, judges dismissed the suits.[26]

Some analysts believe that these failed legal efforts, coupled with presidential refusal to notify Congress of military engagements, have made the War Powers Resolution a dead letter without any legal significance. But other analysts have pointed out that Congress can, by majority vote, pass a resolution that takes formal notice of any military engagement. Once it has done so, the 60-day clock begins to tick, and after those 60 days, troops must be withdrawn. Although lawsuits have been filed by individual representatives, Congress as a whole has never been willing to challenge presidential refusal to observe the War Powers Resolution by passing this type of measure.

The War Powers Resolution, far from reigning in presidential power after 9/11, proved to be the vehicle by which President Bush mobilized congressional support on behalf of his policy. At the administration's request, Congress passed, with but one dissenting vote in the House of Representatives, a sweeping resolution that gave President Bush all the discretion he needed to carry out the war on terrorism. Congress authorized the president to "use all necessary and appropriate force against those nations, organizations, or persons he determines planned, authorized, committed, or aided the terrorist attacks that occurred on September 11, or harbored such organizations or persons, in order to prevent any future acts of international terrorism." Although the resolution limits the president to taking action against those involved in the 9/11 attacks, its definition of such individuals and entities is extraordinarily wide-ranging. The president alone is to determine who was involved, and action can be taken not only against those who committed the acts but also against those who planned or "aided" or "harbored" the terrorists. No limit is placed on the time period in which the president may act.[27]

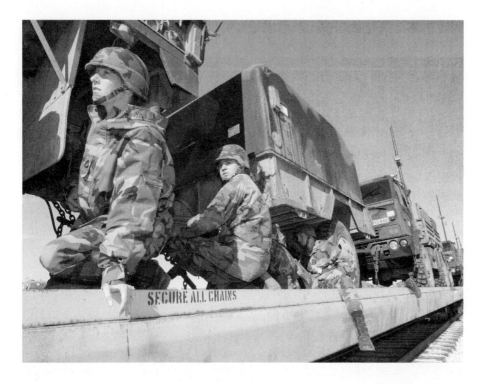

U.S. Troops in Iraq
A large majority of Congress voted for the resolution granting President Bush the authority to attack Iraq.
• *Why did President Bush seek Congressional approval of this military operation?*

A second resolution, authorizing the use of force to "defend the national security of the United States against the continuing threat posed by Iraq" passed Congress overwhelmingly in late 2002. The resolution gave President Bush crucial backing for the subsequent Iraq war, but also offered political cover for those members of Congress who were wary of military involvement: It required Bush to exhaust "diplomatic or other peaceful means" of resolving the conflict prior to resorting to force.[28] John Kerry, who voted for the resolution, argued during the 2004 campaign that Bush had conducted the war imprudently.

Treaty Power

> CONSTITUTION, ARTICLE II, SECTION 2: "[The President] shall have power, by and with the advice and consent of the Senate, to make Treaties, provided two-thirds of the Senators present concur."

The power of the president to negotiate **treaties**—official agreements with foreign countries that are ratified by the Senate—is the most circumscribed of all presidential powers. A treaty does not take effect until it wins approval by a two-thirds vote in the Senate. Because this super-majority can be difficult to achieve unless a treaty has overwhelming public support, presidents have often felt constrained by senatorial pressures when negotiating with foreign countries. Although the Senate has approved about 90 percent of the treaties that presidents have submitted to it from the 1780s to the present, this fact may simply indicate that presidents decline to negotiate or submit treaties that they feel have no chance of passage.[29]

No president was more frustrated than Woodrow Wilson by this constitutional check on presidential power. When negotiating the Versailles Treaty that ended World

treaties
Official agreements with foreign countries that are ratified by the Senate.

FIGURE 20.2

Growing Presidential Power: Executive Agreements Are Replacing Treaties

• *Why have presidents increasingly turned to executive agreements? Does this behavior deny the Senate its constitutional role in foreign policy?*

Note: Data for George W. Bush are for 2001–2002.

SOURCES: Gary King and Lynn Ragsdale, *The Elusive Executive: Discovering Patterns in the Presidency* (Washington, DC: CQ Press, 1988), pp. 131–140; Harold Stanley and Richard Niemi, *Vital Statistics on American Politics*, 2001–2002, (Washington, DC: CQ Press, 2001), p. 334; Data for George W. Bush calculated by authors from data on treaty actions available at Department of State, Office of the Legal Advisor, www.state.gov/s/1/, accessed August 26, 2004.

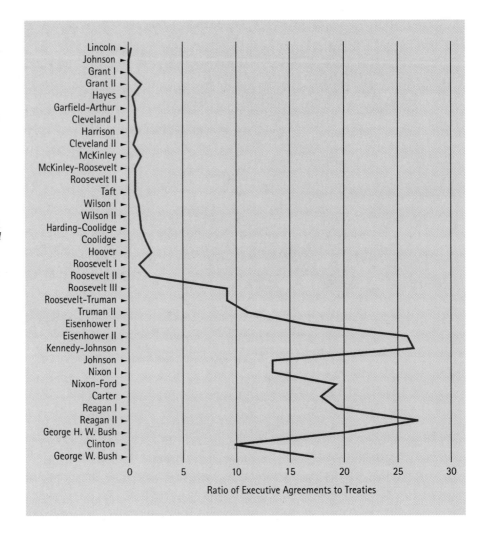

League of Nations
International organization created after World War I to settle international disputes; precursor of the United Nations.

War I, President Wilson pursued one objective above all others: the establishment of a **League of Nations,** an international organization created to settle international disputes, which became the precursor to the United Nations. Wilson felt that such an organization was essential if future world wars were to be avoided. The other nations at the Versailles conference and a considerable portion of the American public supported Wilson's ideas. But the Senate voted down the treaty, primarily because many members believed the League of Nations would undermine U.S. sovereignty.

Eighty years later, President Clinton faced similar difficulties with Congress. In October 1999 the Senate considered the Comprehensive Nuclear Test Ban Treaty, which was negotiated in 1996. The multinational agreement would have prohibited the testing of nuclear weapons and would have enacted more stringent monitoring systems to ensure compliance. Proponents of the treaty argued that it was essential to slowing the spread of nuclear weapons around the world. But critics, including many Senate Republicans, were skeptical of its effectiveness and worried that it would hamper the nation's ability to modernize its armed forces. After negotiations broke down between Republican leaders and the Clinton administration, the Senate voted against ratification, 51 to 48.

Because one-third-plus-one of the Senate can block passage of a treaty, presidents often negotiate **executive agreements,** legal contracts with foreign countries that require only a presidential signature. Nothing in the Constitution explicitly gives the president the power to make executive agreements, but the practice has long been established. The first executive agreement—limiting the size of the U.S. and Great Britain's naval forces on the Great Lakes—was signed by President James Monroe in 1817. In 1937 the Supreme Court affirmed the constitutionality of executive agreements.[30] Since that decision, presidents have increasingly relied on this method as a vehicle for negotiating with other nations. Most executive agreements either are extensions of treaties ratified by the Senate or involve routine presidential actions that have otherwise been authorized by Congress. But presidents sometimes use executive agreements to implement major foreign policy decisions. For example, President Clinton relied on an executive agreement to coax newly independent Ukraine into giving up its nuclear arsenal in exchange for economic aid.[31] In recent years about 20 executive agreements have been signed for every treaty submitted to the Senate for its approval (see Figure 20.2).

> **executive agreement**
> Agreement with foreign countries that requires only a presidential signature.

Foreign Policy Institutions: From Cold War to Homeland Defense

The critical institutions that are responsible for foreign policy today took shape in the early years of the **Cold War,** the 43-year conflict (1946–1989) between the United States and the Soviet Union. The modern Department of State, the Department of Defense, the Central Intelligence Agency, and the office of the National Security Adviser were all designed to meet the Cold War threat posed by the Soviet Union. The relationships of these organizations to one another and to the president are shown in Figure 20.3. In the wake of 9/11, policymakers reevaluated these institutions in light of the new threat posed from terrorist organizations, in some cases making significant changes. In this section we begin with a comparison of the Cold War world to the post-Cold War era, discuss the emergence of each of these institutions, and consider their revised role in responding to terrorist attacks.

> **Cold War**
> The 43-year period (1946–1989) during which the United States and the Soviet Union threatened one another with mutual destruction by nuclear warfare.

The Cold War and the Post-Cold War World

At the outset of the Cold War, U.S. officials recognized that it represented the greatest foreign policy challenge the country had yet faced. In the months following World War II, Germany was divided into eastern and western parts, and Korea was split into a North and South, one-half of each country under Western influence, the other within the communist domain. In short order, the Soviet Union consolidated its control over much of Eastern Europe, establishing communist governments in Poland, Hungary, Bulgaria, Romania, and Czechoslovakia. In 1961, pursuant to Soviet directives, East Germany constructed a huge concrete wall through the middle of Berlin, dramatically symbolizing the division of the world into communist and Western parts.

The Cold War began at a time when the prestige of the executive branch had been greatly enhanced by its successful prosecution of World War II. As a result, President Truman was able to mobilize bipartisan support for his foreign policy and recruit to key positions the most talented group of foreign policy advisers the country had ever assembled. These advisers saw the world as **bipolar,** divided between two major centers

> **bipolar**
> Cold War view of the world as divided into two centers of power, the United States and its allies, and the Soviet Union and its allies.

FIGURE 20.3

The Foreign Policy Institutions

• *Why does the Army Chief of Staff report both to the Joint Chiefs and to the Secretary of the Army?*

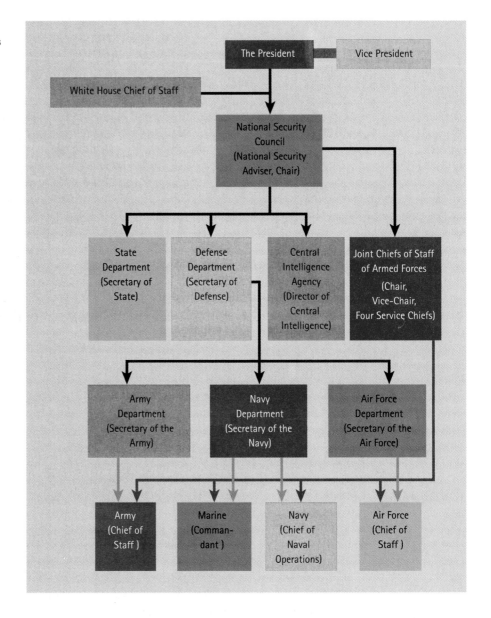

of power: the U.S. and its allies, and the Soviet Union and its allies. "The assault on free institutions is worldwide now," they wrote in a 1950 memo to the president, "and in the context of the present polarization of power a defeat of free institutions anywhere is a defeat everywhere."[32] Accordingly, they decided that the U.S. should use its military might to deter a direct attack from the Soviet Union, while at the same time countering aggression by the Soviets in other countries, when it occurred.[33] This overall strategy was called **containment,** a policy that attempted to stop the spread of communism in the expectation that this system of government would eventually collapse on its own. The policy, originally proposed by George Kennan, a brilliant State Department specialist, won bipartisan support.[34]

Although it took nearly 50 years, containment proved successful. Unrest began in the communist-dominated countries of Eastern Europe during the 1980s and spread to

containment

U.S. policy that attempted to stop the spread of communism in the expectation that this system of government would eventually collapse on its own.

The Berlin Wall
Built during the presidency of John F. Kennedy, the Berlin Wall (left) symbolized what British Prime Minister Winston Churchill called the Iron Curtain. The wall, and the curtain, crumbled in 1989 (right).

• *How has American foreign policymaking changed since the end of the Cold War?*

the Soviet Union by the end of the decade. When East Germany allowed demonstrators to tear down the Berlin Wall in 1989, the Cold War finally came to an end. Two years later, the Soviet Union officially dissolved itself.

At the end of the Cold War, some observers predicted an era of peace and security. But more astute experts cautioned that new and unpredictable conflicts might surface, leading to dangerous instability in key areas of the world. During the 1990s, presidents George H.W. Bush and Bill Clinton sought to lessen regional instability by intervening in important local conflicts. The first President Bush, for example, fought the 1991 Persian Gulf War in response to an Iraqi invasion of Kuwait, and sent troops to Somalia when it seemed that chaos in that country was creating a humanitarian and political crisis. For his part, Clinton led an international effort to defeat Serbian leader Slobodan Milosevic, who had engaged in years of destructive wars in the former Yugoslavia.

After 9/11, however, the George W. Bush administration reevaluated the nature of threats to the United States. Rather than the clear threat of a competing nation, as in the Cold War, or indirect political and economic threats resulting from regional instability, as in the 1990s, foreign policy-making officials now saw direct peril from secretive terrorist organizations that might not even be linked to specific countries. "Enemies in the past needed great armies and great industrial capabilities to endanger America," wrote the White House national security staff in 2002, "Now, shadowy networks of individuals can bring great chaos and suffering to our shores for less than it costs to purchase a single tank."[35]

You Are the President
John F. Kennedy

Leaders in both political parties agreed that the U.S. should dedicate itself to addressing this new environment. Because the major foreign policy-making institutions in the United States were developed to address the Cold War, however, the new threat required policy makers to critically examine the role that each of these institutions plays. Large organizations develop routines and standard operating procedures that are often difficult to alter, and are not always suited for unexpected circumstances, as we discuss in Chapter 14. On 9/11, for example, the pilot of a military jet that was ordered to Washington to defend U.S. airspace later told investigators, "I reverted to the Russian threat . . . I'm thinking cruise missile threat from the sea."[36] In the sections that follow, we examine each of the major U.S. foreign policy-making institutions, and discuss the challenges that each institution faces in the post-Cold War world.

State Department

It was during the Cold War that the modern professional State Department emerged out of the patronage-ridden entity that preceded it. However, the State Department itself—the agency responsible for conducting diplomatic relations—dates back to the administration of George Washington and his secretary of state, Thomas Jefferson.

secretary of state
Officially, the president's chief foreign policy adviser and head of the Department of State, the agency responsible for conducting diplomatic relations.

Ever since that time, the **secretary of state** has been the president's official foreign policy adviser. In most administrations, the secretary of state is also the nation's chief diplomat. For example, Colin Powell, the secretary of state during the George W. Bush administration, played a major role in mobilizing international support for the war against the Taliban and al-Qaeda in Afghanistan, as well as in arguing the case for an invasion of Iraq. The job of chief diplomat is extremely challenging. As former Secretary of State George Marshall once commented, "In diplomacy, you never can tell what a man is thinking. He smiles at you and kicks you in the stomach at the same time."[37] Or as one pundit put it, "Diplomacy is the art of saying 'nice doggie' until you can find a rock."[38]

ambassador
The head of a diplomatic delegation to a major foreign country.

embassy
The structure that houses ambassadors and their diplomatic aides in the capital cities of foreign countries.

Reporting to the secretary of state are **ambassadors,** who head the diplomatic delegations to major foreign countries. Ambassadors are responsible for the management of major U.S. **embassies** abroad, which house diplomatic delegations in the capital cities of foreign countries. Consulates are maintained in important cities that are not foreign capitals. If you wish to travel abroad, you must first obtain a passport from the State Department. If you encounter difficulty while traveling in a foreign country, your first phone call might well be made to the closest embassy or consulate.

Although embassies and consulates help American tourists and businesses, their most important political responsibility is to provide the State Department with detailed information on the government and politics, as well as the economic and social conditions, of the host country. The ambassador also conveys to the host country the views of the United States government, as instructed by the State Department. An ambassador must be able to listen to others carefully and communicate no more than what the president wants to convey. As the British diplomat Sir Henry Wotton put it, "an ambassador is an honest man sent to lie abroad" for his country.[39]

Before the Cold War, U.S. ambassadorial appointments were as important for rewarding those who helped presidents win election as for the diplomacy they carried out. The most prestigious ambassadorships were given to long-time political supporters who had raised large sums of money for the president's election. As one historian put

Colin Powell, Secretary of State under George W. Bush
• *How does a modern secretary of state use the resources of the State Department to influence U.S. foreign policy?*

it, "Most diplomats earned their appointments through party affiliation, personal wealth, or social position, seldom through training. Many lacked knowledge; some lacked dignity, although few were as tactless as John Randolph, who allegedly commented, when presented to the czar in 1830, 'Howaya Emperor? And how's the madam?' "[40] Even today, some ambassadorial positions remain frankly political. For example, President Bush, as of early 2002, had appointed 19 of his top fund-raisers as ambassadors, including those appointed to France, the Netherlands, New Zealand, Norway, Portugal, Spain, and Switzerland.[41]

But patronage today is more the exception than the rule. Those appointed to less prestigious diplomatic positions are nearly always trained career officers who are familiar with the language and customs of the host country.

Ever since the 1920s these officers have been organized into a **foreign service,** which consists of the diplomats who staff U.S. embassies and consulates. After World War II, the foreign service was strengthened as part of the effort to fight the Cold War. In particular, Dean Acheson, President Truman's secretary of state, did much to improve the professional caliber of the foreign service. A reporter at the time declared, "For the first time in the memory of living man, the American foreign office comes somewhere near being adequate to the needs of the country."[42]

foreign service
Diplomats who staff U.S. embassies and consulates.

Today, the State Department is responsible for holding together a worldwide coalition in the war against terrorism. Even the definition of terrorism poses diplomatic problems. Does the concept include any explicit attack on civilians and civilian property, regardless of circumstance? Or are there conditions under which civilians are appropriately treated as military targets? These questions pose problems for U.S. diplomats seeking to resolve the conflict between Israel and the Palestinians. In support of Israel, the United States has denounced as terrorism the attacks on civilians by Palestinian suicide bombers. But Arab leaders, in support of the Palestinians, contend that Israel illegally occupies Palestinian territory. They say the attacks against the occupying nation are simply military operations being carried out against an occupying power that has killed thousands of Palestinians. Inasmuch as the United States, while supporting Israel, still needs to maintain good relations with Arab governments in order to further its search for al-Qaeda terrorists, the State Department is constantly challenged to find new diplomatic ways to resolve these alternative definitions of terrorism.

Defense Department

Ever since the first decades of the country's independence, Americans have been concerned about the ill effects of a large military. The nation has sometimes looked to popular generals, such as George Washington, Andrew Jackson, Ulysses S. Grant, and Dwight Eisenhower, for political leadership. But generals must give up their military appointment when running for president. In general, Congress and the president have always made certain that the military was controlled by civilian appointees. As one analyst puts it, freedom "demands that people without guns be able to tell people with guns what to do."[43] The Cold War posed new challenges for this ideal of civilian control. To ensure the country's continued international leadership and to carry out the policy of containment, Congress provided for the largest military establishment in the nation's history. In an effort to better handle this large peacetime standing army, the military went through several major organizational changes.

Department of Defense
Cabinet department responsible for managing the U.S. armed forces.

secretary of defense
The president's chief civilian adviser on defense matters and overall head of the army, navy, and air force.

Joint Chiefs of Staff
The heads of all the military services, together with a chair and vice-chair nominated by the president and confirmed by the Senate.

Organization of the Defense Department   At the close of World War II, the army and navy were two separate departments, each with its own air force and each with its own seat in the president's cabinet. With the onset of the Cold War, to coordinate civilian control of the armed forces better, the 1947 National Security Act created a single **Department of Defense** that contained within it the Departments of the Army, Navy, and Air Force, each with its own civilian secretary appointed by the president. The secretaries for the army and the air force are responsible for their respective branches of the armed services. The secretary of the navy is responsible for both the naval forces and the marines. All three secretaries report to the **secretary of defense,** the president's chief civilian adviser on defense matters and the overall head of all three departments.

Subordinate to the civilian leadership of the secretary of defense and the other three appointed secretaries, military professionals direct the armed forces. At one time, each armed force had its own military leadership, and they acted more or less independently of each other. To achieve better coordination, Congress formally created the **Joint Chiefs of Staff** in 1947. The Joint Chiefs consist of the heads of all the military services—the army, navy, air force, and Marine Corps—together with a chair and vice-chair nominated by the president and confirmed by the Senate. Omar Bradley, the first chairman of the Joint Chiefs of Staff, suggested that the organization was essential if the country were to achieve a unified, effective military force: "Our military forces are one team—in the game to win regardless of who carries the ball. This is no time for 'fancy dans' who won't hit the line with all they have on every play unless they can call the signals." [44] (See the accompanying International Comparison.)

Rivalries among the armed services have been so intense that it took decades to achieve what Bradley promised in 1949, but eventually a unified command structure was created in each of the regions of the world. This unified structure proved extraordinarily effective during the 1991 Persian Gulf War when General Norman Schwarzkopf, an

International Comparison

United States Lucky in War

Isolationist sentiments have been fed by the country's wartime successes, which have fostered the belief that the United States is invincible. After the War of 1812 and until the Vietnam War, the United States had an impressive military record. The Mexican War, the Spanish–American War, and World Wars I and II all ended in overwhelming victories. Few, if any, other world powers have achieved such an unbroken string of successes. Japan and Germany can never forget their humiliating defeats in World War II. The French cannot forget the ease with which German troops captured Paris in both 1870 and 1940. The Russians cannot readily dislodge the memory of their defeat by Japan in 1905 or the collapse of their army in 1917. Only the British have nearly as enviable an historical record as the Americans, and even Britain suffered more than one defeat at the hands of the French.

Not only has the United States won its wars, but it has done so quickly. The Mexican War, though spread over three years, consisted of three short and decisive campaigns. The Spanish–American War was over in eight months. Even U.S. involvement in the two world wars was of relatively short duration. Within six months of the arrival of U.S. troops in Europe, an armistice brought World War I to an end. The

pattern was not altogether different in World War II. Little more than a year after U.S. troops landed in Normandy, Germany was defeated. Japan struggled for an additional two months until nuclear bombs dropped by the United States over Hiroshima and Nagasaki forced surrender. Before 9/11, American civilians rarely suffered significantly from foreign attack. Not since the British burning of Washington, DC, in 1814 has the mainland of the United States been invaded by foreign troops. Apart from the 9/11 attack and the bombing of Pearl Harbor, the United States has been free of aerial raids. During World War II, German tanks overran Europe and Russia, German airplanes bombed Britain, and U.S. airplanes all but destroyed German and Japanese cities. As the graph here shows, even U.S. troop casualties have been small.

• *What effect have the loss in Vietnam and the victory in the Persian Gulf had on U.S. foreign policy debates?*

SOURCES: R. Ernest Dupuy and Trevor N. Dupuy, *The Harper Encyclopedia of Military History: From 3500 B.C. to the Present* (New York: HarperCollins, 1993); Y. Takenob, *The Japan Year Book: 1919–1920* (Tokyo: Japan Year Book Office, 1921); B. R. Mitchell, *International Historical Statistics: Europe 1750–1988* (New York: Stockton Press, 1992); B. R. Mitchell, *International Historical Statistics of the Americas: 1750–1988* (New York: Stockton Press, 1993); B. R. Mitchell, *International Historical Statistics: Africa and Asia* (New York: New York University Press, 1982); and Raymond E. Zickel, ed., *Soviet Union: A Country Study* (Washington, DC: U.S. Government Printing Office, 1991).

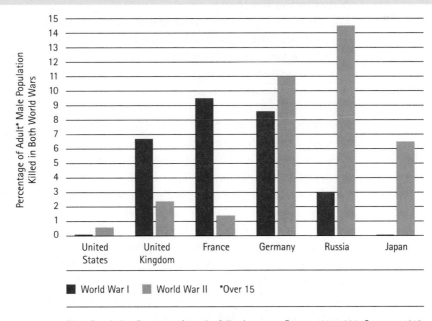

Note: Population figures are from the following years; France, 1911, 1936; Germany, 1910, 1939; United Kingdom (including Scotland), 1911, 1931; United States, 1910, 1940; Russia, 1930 (estimated), 1939; Japan, 1913, 1940.

army general, directly controlled not only the actions of the army but also those of the navy, air force, and marines, achieving one of the best-coordinated military attacks the United States has ever mounted.

Military Response to Terrorism   The military was given the central role in responding to the 9/11 terrorist attack in part because the Bush administration redefined U.S. counterterrorism policy in two important respects.[45] First, the president called upon government agencies to treat terrorist actions as acts of war that need to be anticipated and prevented, not criminal activities to be investigated and prosecuted. Second, the problem was defined not simply as consisting of private individuals or groups engaged in terrorist activities but, rather, as also including governments and states that allowed such activities within their borders. These governments and states had to be held accountable, just as much as the terrorists themselves.

The initial military response in Afghanistan was surprisingly effective—so effective that it surpassed the expectations of many commentators. The explanation for this fact illustrates some of the changes that have been underway in the armed forces since the end of the Cold War. While Cold War planners anticipated large-scale land attacks that placed a premium on heavy equipment and brute force, modern strategists are more likely to value lightweight, high-technology weapons. As a result, military campaigns can be executed with greater precision than ever before. In Iraq and Afghanistan, pilotless drones dropped bombs without risking the lives of American pilots. Heat sensors could detect movement within buildings and caves. Communication detection devices could pinpoint signs of enemy activity. Precision bombing reduced the amount of civilian damage. All in all, technology had advanced far beyond that employed at the height of the Vietnam War.

But technology is only part of the story. Just as important are the new governance structures that have been created within the U.S. armed forces. As in the case of the Persian Gulf War, one commander, General Tommy Franks, was assigned authority over all U.S. forces in Iraq and Afghanistan. Franks sought to reduce the use of large-scale attacks, and instead often favored elite specialized technical forces—Army Green Berets, Navy Seals, CIA operatives, the British Royal Marine Special Boat Service, and other highly trained personnel.

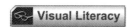

Evaluating
Defense Spending

But al-Qaeda terrorists remain scattered all over the globe, and a swift and successful war to depose dictator Saddam Hussein gave way to a costly occupation in Iraq, during which congressional critics complained that technology was no substitute for larger numbers of troops. To pursue the campaign against terrorism and the Iraq War, the Bush administration sought and received more Congressional funding for national defense. This reversed a decline in military spending that had been underway since the end of the Cold War. In the 1950s, during the height of the Cold War, the United States spent 10 percent of its total gross domestic product (GDP) on defense. Although the expenditure rate declined after the Vietnam War, it was still 6 percent as recently as the mid-1980s. But with the end of the Cold War, Congress began to cut the defense budget, responding to the decline in public concern about the communist threat. By 1999, as Figure 20.4 shows, defense expenditures had dropped to 3 percent of GDP—the lowest level since before World War II. The campaign against terrorism brought this downward trend to a halt.

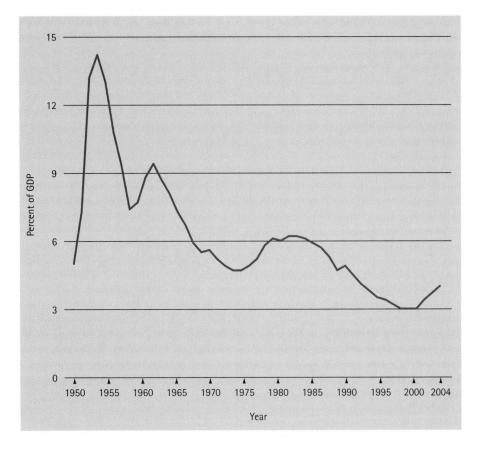

FIGURE 20.4
Defense Expenditures Have Declined as a Percentage of GDP, 1950–2004
• *What accounts for the increases in defense expenditures in the early 1950s, the late 1960s, and the mid-1980s?*

SOURCES: Office of Management and Budget, "Budget of the United States, Fiscal Year 2005," Historical Tables, Table 3.1, pp. 45–52.

Central Intelligence Agency

"I only regret that I have but one life to lose for my country," said the Revolutionary War hero Nathan Hale, after he had been caught spying and was about to be hanged by the British. A statue erected in Hale's memory stands at the entrance to the main offices of the **Central Intelligence Agency (CIA),** the agency primarily responsible for gathering and analyzing information about the political and military activities of other nations. The subject of many a spy novel, it is lovingly referred to as "the Company" or "the Pickle Factory" by members of the intelligence community.[46]

Central Intelligence Agency (CIA)
Agency primarily responsible for gathering and analyzing information about the political and military activities of other nations.

Formation of CIA   If spying is an ancient and honorable practice, its organization into an independent agency that reports directly to the president is of fairly recent vintage. The need for better-organized intelligence became clear during World War II, especially at Hawaii's Pearl Harbor on December 7, 1941, called a "day of infamy" by President Roosevelt. It was a day of particular disrepute for the intelligence community, inasmuch as naval officers at Pearl Harbor were completely unaware that Japan had both the capability and the intention of destroying half the U.S. naval force. (The chief naval official in Hawaii had an appointment with the Japanese envoy on that infamous day.)

The U.S. government made haphazard efforts to improve intelligence capabilities in the wake of the Pearl Harbor attack, but it was not until the Cold War began that Congress established a systematic, centralized system of intelligence gathering. The

National Security Act of 1947 created the CIA as a separate agency independent of both the Department of State and the Department of Defense. Although State and Defense (as well as other departments) continue to have their own sources of intelligence, the 1947 law made the CIA the main intelligence-collection agency. It also gave the CIA the authority to conduct secret operations abroad at the request of the president.

Covert Operations   It is the CIA's authority to conduct clandestine, or covert, operations that has been most controversial, because critics argue that only the armed forces ought to conduct secret military activities. The CIA's most notorious covert operation was the ill-fated attempt in 1961 to dislodge communist leader Fidel Castro from Cuba.[47] In an effort to overthrow Castro, the CIA helped Cuban exiles plan an invasion on the shores of Cuba's **Bay of Pigs** that was expected to foment a popular insurrection. President Kennedy approved the invasion attempt but decided against giving it naval or air support. The effort failed, leaving in doubt the CIA's ability to conduct large-scale military operations. Although the Bay of Pigs has been the CIA's most visible covert operation, the agency drew criticism for covert activities in Chile in the early 1970s, in Nicaragua and Afghanistan in the 1980s, and in other nations.

Bay of Pigs
Location of CIA-supported effort by Cuban exiles in 1961 to invade Cuba and overthrow Fidel Castro.

Response to Terrorism   To avoid such criticism, the CIA limited the scale of its covert operations, reducing the number of agents. In the period leading up to the 9/11 terrorist attack, it actually had "fewer Arabic-speaking case officers than in the cold war," making it difficult for the agency to interpret conversations that were intercepted. Agents who can penetrate terrorist groups have proved extremely difficult to recruit. Perhaps, as one former CIA official observed, it is not easy to find talented individuals willing to participate in "operations that include diarrhoea as a way of life."[48]

Just as important, the CIA in recent decades has not found it easy to work closely with the Federal Bureau of Investigation (FBI). Cooperation between the two agencies was curtailed because both had been criticized for illegal spying on U.S. citizens during the Vietnam War. As a result, intelligence operations within the United States were left solely to the FBI, which lacked information on the presence of foreign terrorists within the United States and could wiretap suspects only after obtaining a court order. Although these procedures helped safeguard the civil liberties of American citizens, they also contributed to a major intelligence failure. As one analyst pointed out, "At least 19 people worked for as long as five years, mostly in the United States, on a complex operation to crash multiple airliners into several targets. And America's $30-billion-a-year intelligence services hardly got a whiff of them."[49] In response to such failures, the special commission appointed to investigate the 9/11 attacks proposed creating a cabinet-level post to coordinate intelligence gathering among the CIA, the FBI, and a dozen other intelligence agencies. It remains to be seen how quickly the United States will build the intelligence capacity necessary to meet the new threat to U.S. security.

National Security Council

National Security Council (NSC)
White House agency responsible for coordinating U.S. foreign policy.

Because so many departments and agencies needed to work together to formulate U.S. Cold War policy, Congress created The **National Security Council (NSC)** in 1947. This organization, located inside the White House Executive Office of the President, is responsible for coordinating U.S. foreign policy. Meetings of the NSC are generally attended by the president, the vice president, the secretary of state, the secretary of

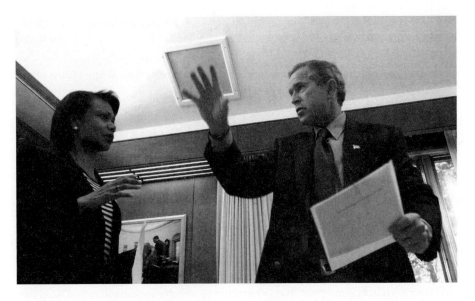

George W. Bush and National Security Adviser Condoleezza Rice
• *What role does the NSA play in foreign policy formulation?*

defense, the head of the Central Intelligence Agency, the chair of the military Joint Chiefs of Staff, the president's chief of staff, and such other individuals as the president designates.[50] The council is assisted by a staff located in the White House under the direction of the national security adviser (NSA). The NSA has often played simply a coordinating role by reconciling interagency disagreements or, if that proved impossible, reporting them to the president. Because it has no budget authority over other departments and agencies, its ability to control on-going policy operations is limited. But inasmuch as the NSA has more access to the president than any member of the foreign policy team, the adviser can wield great influence in crises. During the Nixon administration, National Security Adviser Henry Kissinger became the president's most influential aide, overshadowing the secretary of state. In the George W. Bush administration, NSA Condoleezza Rice has won the trust of the president and, as a result, has emerged as one of his most influential advisers.

The office of the NSA has not escaped controversy. The most notorious event in which it played a major part has become known as the **Iran-Contra affair,** an allegedly illegal diversion of funds from an Iranian arms sale to anticommunist rebels in Nicaragua known as the Contras. In this case, President Ronald Reagan's NSA office, which was officially responsible only for policy coordination, actually attempted to conduct a covert operation of the type ordinarily conducted by the CIA. In a clear violation of U.S. antiterrorist policy, National Security Adviser Robert McFarlane helped orchestrate a secret arms sale to Iran in an effort to secure the release of several American hostages in the Middle East. Profits from this sale were then diverted to the Contras, to whom Congress had cut off U.S. aid several years before.

In the Iran-Contra episode, the NSC staff appeared to have ignored both administration antiterrorist policy and clear congressional directives. Congress held hearings on the scandal, and an independent prosecutor conducted a thorough investigation, although the most significant convictions were overturned in courts of appeals. A specially appointed presidential commission recommended that, in the future, the office of the NSA limit itself to a coordinating role and not involve itself in covert operations. By following these guidelines, the NSA has since avoided political controversy.

Iran-Contra affair
An allegedly illegal diversion of funds, derived from the sale of arms to Iran, to a guerrilla group in Nicaragua during the Reagan administration.

You Are the President

The National Security Council initially served as an organizational model for the George W. Bush administration's homeland security efforts. Bush appointed Tom Ridge to serve as a "homeland security adviser" analogous to the NSA. Ridge was then expected to coordinate the activities of dozens of agencies from his White House office. As we discuss in Chapter 14, however, this proved to be an impossible task. President Bush finally proposed, and Congress created, the cabinet-level Department of Homeland Security to give Ridge the budgetary authority and political clout necessary to manage homeland defense (see Voices of the Permanent Campaign, p. 427).

Ideals, Interests, and the Worldwide Campaign Against Terror

The way in which the president and his advisers resolve foreign policy questions is shaped by a long-standing tension that exists between American philosophical ideals and the country's practical need to defend itself against foreign aggression. Alexander Hamilton, in the *Federalist Papers,* made the best case for placing the highest priority on the country's practical interests:"No Government [can] give us tranquility and happiness at home, which [does] not possess sufficient stability and strength to make us respectable abroad."[51] The idealist point of view was best expressed by Abraham Lincoln, who reminded his fellow citizens that one purpose of the American experiment was to spread liberty throughout the world. "The Declaration of Independence . . . [gave] liberty, not alone to the people of this country, but hope to the world for all future time."[52]

The tension between ideals and interests that has long been part of the American foreign policy tradition continues to shape policy debates today. On the one side, **idealists** say that U.S. foreign policy should be guided primarily by democratic principles—the spread of liberty, equality, human rights, and respect for international law throughout the world. On the other side, **realists** say that U.S. foreign policy best protects democracy when it guards its own economic and military strength.

One can find both idealists and realists in each political party and in all government agencies, and some people are idealistic on one issue yet realistic on another. In fact, many foreign policy makers use both idealist and realist arguments to make their points.

The events of 9/11 have changed the nature of the debate between idealists and realists in many ways, including their consideration of strategies for nation building, the role of international organizations, and the role of human rights in relations with Russia and China.

Strategies for Nation Building

Interventions designed to enhance democratic practices in other countries—actions known as **nation building**—have long been a point of contention between idealists and realists. According to realists, the United States should avoid getting involved in nation building unless U.S. interests are directly at stake. Realists opposed the first President Bush's decision to send troops into Somalia and Clinton's decision to send them to Bosnia and Kosovo. If the United States continues to involve itself in the internal political life of foreign countries, they argue, it will eventually find itself unprepared or unable to defend its true interests when they are threatened.

Nation building can at times be fraught with peril. For one thing, actions taken can have unanticipated consequences. Unjustified intervention in the internal affairs of

idealists
Those who say that U.S. foreign policy should be guided primarily by democratic principles—the spread of liberty, equality, human rights, and respect for international law throughout the world.

realists
Those who say that U.S. foreign policy best protects democracy when it safeguards its own economic and military strength.

nation building
Interventions designed to enhance democratic practices in another country.

other countries, moreover, runs contrary to international law, which regards each legitimate government as sovereign over its own citizens. Idealists nonetheless suggest that Americans should intervene to enhance democratic practices and safeguard human rights, especially if governments seek to deport or eliminate entire ethnic groups, a practice known as **ethnic cleansing.**

Differences between idealists and realists were evident after the collapse of Yugoslavia in Eastern Europe at the end of the Cold War. When the country split into pieces, armed struggle broke out among Bosnians, Serbs, and Croats. Idealists supported the Clinton administration's decision to send troops to separate the warring parties in Bosnia, and to conduct aerial bombing to end the Serbian invasion of Kosovo. By such actions, the United States tries to prevent violation of human rights by punishing governments that engaged in ethnic cleansing and by capturing war criminals and referring them to international tribunals.

When George W. Bush campaigned for president in 2000, he questioned the U.S. efforts to secure human rights and other efforts to enhance democratic practices in other countries. He doubted whether the United States should become engaged in the business of nation building. In the words of Condoleezza Rice, who was later appointed as Bush's national security adviser, "Carrying out civil administration policy functions is simply going to degrade the American capability to do the things America has to do. We don't need to have the 82nd Airborne escorting kids to kindergarten."[53]

But after the terrorist attack on 9/11, Bush administration policies changed sharply. If nation building had at one time seemed little other than dreamy-eyed idealism, it suddenly emerged as an important realist objective as well. Where foreign governments were weak and illegitimate, terrorists could roam unchecked. From Bush's perspective, the clearest examples of such weak governments were Afghanistan and Iraq. In Afghanistan, the al-Qaeda terrorist organization formed an alliance with the Taliban government and operated for years without hindrance. In Saddam Hussein's Iraq, the Bush administration argued, terrorists had also been granted safe haven and might have had access to dangerous weapons. The president stated the case for involvement in Iraq in both realist and idealist terms: "Our actions . . . are guided by a vision. We believe that freedom can advance and change lives in the greater Middle East, as it has advanced and changed lives in Asia, and Latin America, and Eastern Europe, and Africa. . . . And when that day comes, the bitterness and burning hatreds that feed terrorism will fade and die away. America and all the world will be safer when hope has returned to the Middle East."[54]

But Bush's critics, who had in many cases defended President Clinton's involvement in the former Yugoslavia, made the realist argument that the Iraq operation was contrary to our national interest. From this perspective, the war in Afghanistan was justifiable as retaliation for specific attacks on U.S. soil, but the war in Iraq was an unnecessary distraction. As former vice president Al Gore put it, "As the main body of our troops were deployed for the new invasion [in Iraq], those who had organized the attack against us escaped, and many are still at large."[55]

Role of International Organizations

At the end of World War II, the victorious nations agreed to establish the **United Nations,** an international organization whose purpose is to preserve world peace and foster economic and social development throughout the world. Although the United Nations has been more successful than its predecessor, the ill-starred League of Nations,

ethnic cleansing
Seeking to deport or eliminate entire ethnic groups from a country or region.

United Nations
Organization of all nation-states, whose purpose is to preserve world peace and foster economic and social development throughout the world.

idealists and realists within the United States often find themselves at odds concerning the usefulness of the United Nations and other international organizations as vehicles for the conduct of U.S. foreign policy.

Idealists recommend that the United States work through the United Nations and other international organizations to achieve closer international cooperation. Idealists argue not only that these goals place American foreign policy on a high ethical plane, but also that they are an important tool for promoting peace and stability. If countries work together in international organizations, they are less likely to engage in warfare.[56]

Realists are reluctant to give the United Nations or other international organizations responsibility for the conduct of U.S. policy. They insist that decisions to intervene in world affairs must be predicated not on some vague ideal but on a calculation of the extent to which the United States has a substantial and visible interest at stake.[57] These decisions must be made on a case-by-case basis by the United States alone. Realists point out, for example, that the United Nations has condemned Israel, a U.S. ally, for its treatment of Arab Palestinians. They also criticize U.N. officials for wasteful and inefficient administration of the organization.

Because of these administrative problems, Republican leaders in Congress opposed paying the dues that the United States annually owes to the United Nations. As a result, the United States was behind in its payments throughout the 1990s. But after improvements in U.N. administrative operations, the George W. Bush administration persuaded Republicans in Congress to pay the necessary dues. Bush also turned to the U.N. at key moments in the war against terrorism: the international body coordinated relief efforts in Afghanistan and helped set up an interim government in Iraq after the U.S. relinquished administrative control in July, 2004. But Bush conducted the war in Iraq without the U.N.'s approval, an action that drew criticism from Democrats.

Russia, China, and Human Rights

Comparing Foreign Policy

Idealists and realists also differ on what is the appropriate U.S. policy toward Russia and China, two of the world's leading countries. Because China crushed a democratic movement in Beijing's Tiananmen Square in 1989 and has jailed many dissidents and religious groups for their political and religious beliefs, idealists have argued that the United States should use economic and political means to force the Asian nation to alter its policies. Similarly, they argue that the United States must sanction Russia for its ongoing war in Chechnya, in which many civilians have been killed and allegations of atrocities are widespread. Realists recommend that the United States exercise caution before supplementing diplomatic efforts to promote human rights with economic or military pressure.

The campaign against terror has further altered U.S. policy toward the two countries. Some al-Qaeda members had fought against the Russians in Chechnya, and as a result, Russia firmly backed the U.S. attack on the al-Qaeda in Afghanistan. In return, the Bush administration has been reluctant to criticize strong actions taken by the Russian government in Chechnya. Similarly, China has seen the U.S. campaign against terrorism as an opportunity to conduct its own struggle against Muslim separatists in the western regions of the country. Realists say the antiterrorist campaign is more important than responding to specific violations of human rights by these countries. In the long run, they maintain, the idealistic goals of the United States can be better achieved by encouraging the spread of free markets and international trade, the subject to which we now turn.

The Politics of World Trade: New Alliances?

When the Cold War began, the Truman administration took the position that the growth of free markets would aid in the effort to contain communism. International banks were created to lend money to needy countries, United Nations organizations handled world health and refugee problems, and an international trade agreement reduced tariffs around the world. In late 1947, for example, 23 countries founded the General Agreement on Tariffs and Trade (GATT) in Geneva, Switzerland.

Believing that it might be difficult to persuade Congress to approve GATT, Truman signed on to the measure anyway, proclaiming that it was an executive agreement that did not need Senate approval. This action set the pattern for the conduct of trade policy ever since. The executive branch takes the lead in formulating trade policy, although Congress must approve the overall framework within which policies are determined.[58]

In recent years, trade policy has grown increasingly contentious, as labor and environmental groups have become concerned that firms in other countries need not follow the labor and environmental regulations to which U.S. firms are subject. First came the 1993 battle over the North American Free Trade Agreement (NAFTA), which eliminated trade barriers among the United States, Canada, and Mexico. Negotiated by President Bush and promoted by President Clinton, NAFTA won only a narrow majority in Congress after fierce lobbying by all sides.

More significant than the publicity surrounding NAFTA was the unusual profile of the coalitions on both sides of the debate. Although it was promoted by a Democratic president, only 40 percent of Democratic members of Congress supported the measure.[59] Opponents included not only some business interests but also labor unions, environmental groups, consumer groups, and isolationist politicians. They worried that trade agreements would cost jobs, harm the environment, and lead to the nullification of U.S. laws and standards. Proponents included business groups and those who favored greater ties with other nations.

The battle over NAFTA proved to be only the beginning of a very public debate over the status of world trade. In 1994, negotiators from 104 nations officially transformed GATT into the World Trade Organization (WTO), a trade body much more powerful than GATT, with enforcement and dispute resolution mechanisms. Opposition to the organization was significant and vocal and was led by the same groups that opposed NAFTA. Tens of thousands of protesters disrupted a meeting of WTO trade ministers in Seattle in 1999, blocking streets and preventing delegates from attending the meetings. World trade became the subject of public controversy as never before. As California State Senator Tom Hayden said, "the WTO, which was unknown in this country yesterday, is going to be a household word now. . . . This is a great turning point."[60]

In 2001 President Bush called for the expansion of NAFTA to include other Latin America countries, thereby greatly increasing its size and scope. He also asked for congressional backing for another round of world trade talks. But Congress has balked at these proposed relaxations of trade restrictions.

Election pressures limit congressional enthusiasm for increased free trade. Even the president is not free of them. In 2002 such pressures proved particularly significant for tariffs on steel. This industry has been subject to growing competition from steel companies in Japan, South Korea, and Europe. Because the U.S. steel industry is

Simulation

You Are the Leader of
Concerned Citizens for
Justice World

A Japanese Naval Vessel
The United States has worked with countries around the world to combat terrorism.

• *Are international coalitions more important or less important now than during the Cold War?*

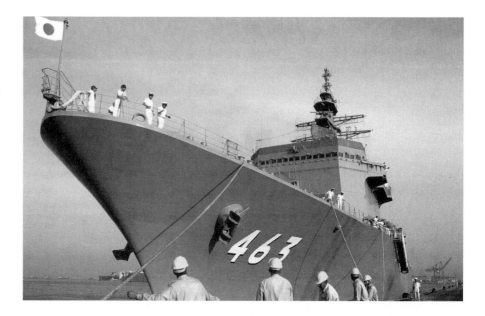

concentrated in Pennsylvania, Ohio, and Michigan, states that President Bush hoped to win in 2004, the president proved particularly sensitive to industry complaints of unfair competition by steel companies abroad. In response to these complaints, Bush briefly raised tariffs by as much as 30 percent on some steel products—a policy markedly at odds with his overall goal of increasing worldwide trade.

The pressures on members of Congress from these states are even greater. Many observers thought that unless the president raised steel tariffs, he would lose all hope of getting congressional support for NAFTA expansion and further world trade negotiations. Said one analyst, "This is the necessary step backward so the president can make two steps forward on what really matters."[61] However these issues are resolved, the Bush administration will need to balance its commitment to international free trade with strong political pressures from vulnerable domestic industries.

Chapter Summary

Electoral considerations help account for the fact that presidents dominate policy making on foreign policy questions more than on domestic ones. Voters expect presidents to take the lead. In the short run, they tend to support presidents in crises no matter what action is taken. Only later, if things do not turn out well, do voters penalize presidents for choosing the wrong policy.

Other factors reinforce the president's dominant role in foreign policy. Fast action is often needed; interest-group pressures are less intense than on domestic issues; the Supreme Court has interpreted the powers of the president broadly; and Congress tends to defer to the executive. In

the campaign against terrorism, Congress, acting under procedures set forth in the War Powers Resolution, authorized the president to take all military action necessary to find and punish those who aided or harbored the 9/11 terrorists, as well as to conduct action against Iraq as a last resort.

The three agencies that shape U.S. foreign policy, the Department of State, the Department of Defense, and the Central Intelligence Agency, together with the head of the Joint Chiefs of Staff, all sit on the National Security Council, which is managed by a national security adviser responsible to the president for overall coordination of foreign policy. These institutions took their modern shape during the early years of the Cold War, and are all seeking to adapt to the post-Cold War world of terrorist threats.

Both idealistic and realistic factors help shape American foreign policy. On the one hand, the United States feels responsible for promoting the democratic experiment abroad. On the other hand, the United States,

like any other country, has its own interests to protect. Idealist and realist considerations both play a role in current debates over international organizations, nation building, and the human rights records of Russia and China. But in the aftermath of 9/11, both realists and idealists believe it is important to help establish strong, legitimate governments throughout the world.

Key Terms

ambassador, p. 568

Bay of Pigs, p. 574

bipolar, p. 565

Central Intelligence Agency
(CIA), p. 573

Cold War, p. 565

containment, p. 566

Department of Defense, p. 570

embassy, p. 568

ethnic cleansing, p. 577

executive agreement, p. 565

foreign policy, p. 555

foreign service, p. 569

idealists, p. 576

Iran-Contra affair, p. 575

Joint Chiefs of Staff, p. 570

League of Nations, p. 564

nation building, p. 576

National Security Council
(NSC), p. 574

"rally 'round the flag" effect, p. 556

realists, p. 576

secretary of defense, p. 570

secretary of state, p. 568

Tonkin Gulf Resolution, p. 562

treaties, p. 563

two-presidency theory, p. 555

United Nations (U.N.), p. 577

U.S. v. Curtiss-Wright, p. 561

War Powers Resolution, p. 562

*Youngstown Sheet and Tube Co. v.
Sawyer,* p. 561

Suggested Readings

Of General Interest

Corwin, Edward S. *Total War and the Constitution.* New York: Knopf, 1947. Classic, if dated, discussion of constitutional arrangements as they affect foreign policy.

Daalder, Ivo and James Lindsay. *America Unbound: The Bush Revolution in Foreign Policy.* Washington, DC: Brookings Institution Press, 2003. Two foreign policy scholars argue that George W. Bush has made dramatic changes in U.S. foreign policy.

Peterson, Paul E., ed. *The President, the Congress, and the Making of Foreign Policy.* Norman, OK: Oklahoma University Press, 1994. Essays describing changes in presidential and congressional policy-making roles.

Pillar, Paul. *Terrorism and U.S. Foreign Policy.* Washington, D.C.: Brookings Institution Press, 2001. An assessment of U.S. policy by a former CIA official just prior to 9/11.

Wildavsky, Aaron. "The Two Presidencies." In Steven A. Shull, ed., *The Two Presidencies: A Quarter Century Assessment.* Chicago: Nelson-Hall, 1991, pp. 11–25. Explains how politics differs between foreign and domestic issues.

Focused Studies

Allison, Graham. *Essence of Decision.* Boston: Little, Brown, 1971. Fascinating account of the Cuban missile crisis, the closest the United States and the Soviet Union ever came to nuclear confrontation.

Anonymous. *Imperial Hubris: Why the West Is Losing the War on Terror.* Dulles, VA: Brassey's Inc., 2004. Informed, sometimes angry, account of U.S. policy on terrorism written by a top CIA analyst.

Huntington, Samuel. *The Clash of Civilizations.* New York: Simon & Schuster, 1996. Argues that future world conflicts will occur between clusters of nations that share a common cultural heritage.

Jeffreys-Johnes, Rhodri. *The CIA and American Democracy.* New Haven, CT: Yale University Press, 1989. A solid history of the CIA.

Johnson, Loch K. *America's Secret Power: The CIA in a Democratic Society.* New York: Oxford University Press, 1989. Informed critique of CIA power and tactics.

Leffler, Melvyn P. *A Preponderance of Power: National Security, the Truman Administration, and the Cold War.* Stanford, CA: Stanford University Press, 1992. Historical account of the establishment of U.S. Cold War strategy under Truman.

Silverstein, Gordon. *Imbalance of Powers: Constitutional Interpretation and the Making of American Foreign Policy.* New York: Oxford University Press, 1996. Argues that the president's constitutional authority over foreign policy has not been ceded to Congress.

Weissman, Stephen R. *A Culture of Deference: Congress's Failure of Leadership in Foreign Policy.* New York: Basic Books, 1995. Argues that Congress defers too much to presidential authority in foreign affairs.

On the Web

www.state.gov

www.defenselink.mil

The Department of State and the Department of Defense are the oldest and most important cabinet agencies with responsibility for conducting American foreign policy.

www.odci.gov (Central Intelligence Agency)

www.whitehouse.gov/nsc/

www.dtic.mil/jcs/

In this chapter we discussed the changes to the U.S. foreign policy-making agencies that occurred at the beginning of the Cold War. The Central Intelligence Agency, the National Security Council, and the Joint Chiefs of Staff all were created after World War II to conduct foreign affairs more effectively.

www.ustr.gov

The U.S. trade representative, located in the Executive Office of the President, is the U.S. government's chief trade negotiator.

www.un.org

www.wto.org

The United Nations and the World Trade Organization are two key international organizations that have at times weathered criticism from both realists and idealists in the United States.

www.cfr.org

www.aipac.org

www.canfnet.org

One of the reasons why the president has more authority over foreign affairs than over domestic affairs is the comparative lack of interest groups with a foreign policy focus. Nevertheless, there are at least several interest groups that pay close attention to foreign policy, including the Council on Foreign Relations (CFR), the American Israel Public Affairs Committee (AIPAC), and the Cuban American National Foundation (CANF).

www.senate.gov/~foreign/

Although Congress plays a smaller role in foreign affairs than in domestic politics, the U.S. Senate has the constitutional responsibility to approve or reject foreign treaties and confirm nominees for key posts. Such issues are handled by the Senate's Committee on Foreign Relations.

VOICES
OF THE PERMANENT CAMPAIGN
The U.S. Politics of the Arab–Israeli Conflict

"I have about come to the conclusion that the Palestine problem is insoluble, but I suppose we will have to keep working on it."

—President Harry S. Truman, letter to
Senator Elbert Thomas, November 9, 1947[1]

THE ISSUE

What should the United States do to end violence in the Middle East? Israel and Palestinian Arabs are unable to resolve their differences over their competing territorial claims. Should the U.S. back Israel, back the Palestinians, back neither, or impose a settlement?

Background

When Israel became a nation in 1948, the United States was the first country to recognize it. Arab states in the region, however, were upset by the creation of a Jewish nation on land that until the twentieth century had been occupied mainly by Arabs. As Jewish migration to the area increased during the 1930s, guerrilla skirmishes between Jews and Arabs intensified. In 1947 a United Nations partition proposal called for the creation of separate Jewish and Arab states. But when a provisional Israeli government declared itself to be a sovereign state, six Arab nations invaded Israel. Israel won that war, gained more territory than it lost, and then greatly expanded the territory under its control in successive wars with its Arab neighbors in 1956, 1968, and 1973. As a result, many Palestinians left Israel to live in refugee camps in neighboring countries.

Egypt and Jordan sought to make peace with Israel beginning in the late 1970s. But many Palestinian Arabs, especially those in refugee camps who longed to return to the land where they had once lived, resented their status and condemned the atrocities the Israelis were alleged to have committed. They especially resented the establishment of a large number of Jewish settlements within areas that had historically been settled by Arabs, but that Israeli armies occupied at the conclusion of the series of Arab-Israeli wars. Control of the ancient, religiously significant City of Jerusalem

was still another point of great controversy between the two sides, especially after Israel declared that Jerusalem, not Tel Aviv, was its capital. Many Palestinians engaged in strikes, civil disorder, and (in recent years) suicide bombings and other terrorist attacks to advance their cause. Meanwhile, Israel continued to occupy Palestinian regions captured in the wars, such as the West Bank and Gaza Strip areas (see Figure 1) and refused to allow millions of displaced Palestinians to return to their ancestral lands.

Despite the hostility between the two sides, at times peace seemed within reach. In 1993, then-prime minister Yitzhak Rabin signed a landmark U.S.-sponsored peace accord with Yasir Arafat, leader of the Palestinian Liberation Organization (PLO). This agreement paved the way for the West Bank and Gaza Strip to enjoy limited self-government under a so-called Palestinian Authority. But Rabin was assassinated by a Jewish extremist in 1995. Even more disconcerting, new Palestinian terrorists (said by the PLO to be operating illegally and beyond the control of the weak Palestinian Authority) stepped up their suicide bombings and other attacks. In 2002 the Israeli government, led by conservative Ariel Sharon, invaded the land under the control of the Palestinian Authority. Israeli tanks even surrounded Palestinian government offices, essentially holding captive Yasir Arafat, the head of the Authority. In 2004, Sharon's government moved to abandon Jewish settlements in the Gaza strip, but this plan came under attack from members of Sharon's own party, and seemed unlikely to resolve the overall conflict.

Options for U.S. policy included the following alternatives, each with its own drawbacks:

1. *Support Israel's crackdowns on Palestinians.* But would this position alienate Arab allies of the United States, such as Saudi Arabia, and complicate the war on terrorism?

2. *Support the rapid creation of a Palestinian state.* But would this position send the message that terrorist bombings are effective?

3. *Force the two parties to the bargaining table, taking a hands-on role in negotiations and in the implementation of whatever peace plan might result.* But would such an effort waste U.S. diplomatic energy, taking attention away from the nation's other international responsibilities? After all, President Clinton expended an extraordinary amount of energy on just such an effort, culminating in two weeks of intensive discussions at the Camp David presidential retreat in 2000, all to no avail.

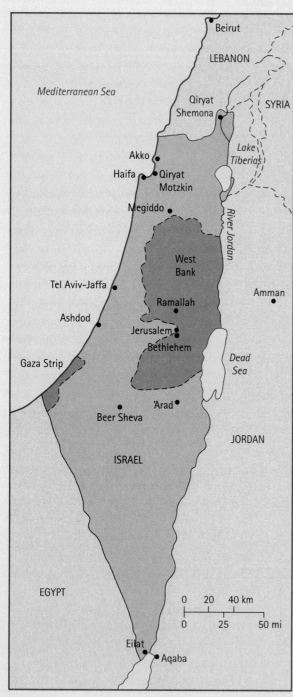

FIGURE 1

Israel

This map shows Israel, as well as the Palestinian regions of the West Bank and Gaza Strip.

• *Why is a permanent settlement so difficult to achieve?*

Elections and U.S. Policy Toward Israel

The United States has always been a key ally of Israel. In the aftermath of the Holocaust, Americans felt sympathy for the Zionists, advocates of a Jewish state in Palestine, many of whom had escaped from Europe and had endured great hardships under the Nazi regime. The case for a Jewish homeland, wrote one senator at the time, had been "written in blood and suffering."[2] During the Cold War, foreign policy experts saw Israel as strategically important because of its status as the only democracy in a region rich with oil. In the aftermath of the September 11 terrorist attacks, many in the United States felt renewed kinship with Israeli citizens, who had long lived their daily lives under the threat of terrorism.

Since 1976, Israel has been the number-one recipient of U.S. foreign aid (see Figure 2). American presidents have also often backed Israel in the United Nations, where it otherwise might have been outvoted by Arab states. During the 1991 Gulf War, when Saddam Hussein's Iraq launched Scud missiles at Israel, the U.S. government supplied state-of-the-art Patriot missiles to intercept the Scuds before they could hit their targets.

In recent decades, however, the U.S. alliance with Israel has become an uneasy one. Many critics in the United States and abroad have objected to the Israeli government's "aggressive behavior" in its responses to the suicide bombers. These responses have included such tactics as assassinating terrorist leaders, bulldozing the homes of terrorists' families, constructing a 450-mile "security fence" that would restrict travel between the West Bank and the rest of Israel, and engaging in retaliatory military incursions into Palestinian cities.[3] Nearly one thousand Israeli citizens were killed in the spate of conflict from 2000 to mid-2004, but three times as many Palestinians died during the same period.[4] Accordingly, the U.S. government has officially stated that, in George W. Bush's words, "A stable, peaceful [independent] Palestinian state is necessary to achieve the security that Israel longs for."[5]

Some in Congress criticized Bush for appearing indecisive on the issue of Israel—publicly scolding Sharon in early 2002 and then, only a few months later, appearing to back Sharon's aggressive policies and calling for the removal of Arafat as Palestinian leader. Whatever the merits of the issue, it can be perilous for U.S. elected officials to appear to be anti-Israel. Although Jewish Americans make up only 2 percent of the population,[6] several key interest groups are extremely well-organized advocates for Israel. In particular, the American Israel Public Affairs Committee (AIPAC) has over 65,000 members, meets with members of Congress over 2000 times a year, and is active on over 200 college campuses.[7] Participation in AIPAC surged after violence again erupted in Israel in 2000.[8] In addition to lobbying, political fund raising by pro-Jewish groups exceeds fund raising by pro-Arab groups by a factor of about 140 to 1.[9]

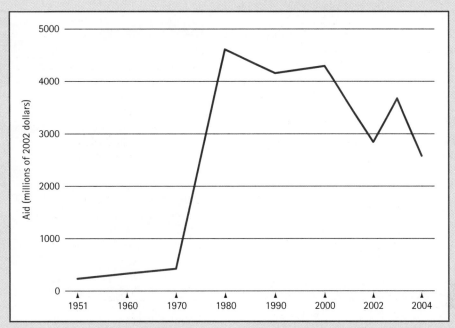

FIGURE 2

U.S. Aid to Israel, 1951–2004

Since 1976, Israel has been the recipient of more U.S. foreign aid than any other country.

• *Does this large amount of aid reflect the strategic interests of the United States or domestic political pressures?*

Note: 2003 and 2004 figures are estimates.

SOURCE: Clyde R. Mark, "Israel: U.S. Foreign Assistance" (Washington, DC: Congressional Research Service, October 3, 2003), Table 2, Table 3, p. 11.

Opposing Viewpoints on a Palestinian State

The West Bank and Gaza Strip, areas captured by Israel in its wars against its Arab neighbors, have disproportionately high Palestinian Arab populations and are collectively known as the "occupied territories."

For a Palestinian State

Advocates of a Palestinian state argue that the United States should act quickly to force Israel to accept a new nation of Palestine within these territories:

"There is, of course, only one solution to this appalling carnage, and that is to create a fully independent Palestinian state alongside Israel. Palestinians have suffered far too long from the most cruel and brutal occupation in recent history, and they will accept nothing less than freedom. . . . The solution is obvious and within reach, but given the ever-deteriorating cycle of violence in which the two parties are locked, a robust and courageous third party intervention is required. It is

up to the United States to play the role it has assigned itself, and which no other party could play, and act forcefully to bring the parties to the table without preconditions to negotiate a swift and complete end to the occupation."

—Ziad Asali, president, American–Arab Anti-Discrimination Committee, April 10, 1992 press release

Some who favor an independent Palestine also argue that to build a lasting solution, the United States should use its clout to help mend some of the destruction that the Middle East conflict has created:

"Provocation from the Israeli side will continue . . . until the U.S. moves to publicly challenge the [conservative] government's use of aggressive military force against the Palestinians. . . . To break this cycle of despair and violence that has gripped the Palestinians, the U.S., the European Union, and the Arab states should lead an international effort to help radically transform the West Bank and Gaza. . . . New roads and infrastructure, repaired buildings and restored services will create hope and invest people in the promise of peace."

—John Zogby, president, Arab American Institute, "The Steps We Must Now Take," May 20, 2002, www.aaiusa.org

Against a Palestinian State

Advocates of the Israeli position argue that PLO leader Arafat has either allowed terrorism to continue or even has encouraged it. Consequently, a Palestinian state would be a terrorist state if Arafat remained at the helm:

We are not opposed to a Palestinian state. We are opposed to a terror state. Certainly, U.S. goals in the region do not include the creation of a state that could be designated a 'state sponsor of terror.' Given Arafat's refusal to end incitement, apprehend terrorists or work to dismantle the terrorist infrastructure that has developed in his Palestinian Authority, a state under his leadership would be just that."

—Amy Friedkin, president, and Howard Kohr, executive director, AIPAC, June 13, 2002, www.aipac.org

"This rewarding of terrorism is not just a moral scandal. It is disastrous diplomacy. What does [an offer of a] provisional state say to the Palestinians? You can reject the state you were offered two years ago, start a war, murder daily, and then be re-offered a state—this time without even having to be asked to make peace.

For an American foreign policy whose major objective is stability and nonviolence (if for no other reason than to give us freedom of action elsewhere in the region to fight terrorism), one could not devise a worse policy. If two years of bloodletting gives the Palestinians an interim state . . . what possible disincentive do they have to continue the violence?"

—Charles Krauthammer, "Offering Statehood for Palestinians in the Absence of Peace is Utter Folly," *Pittsburgh Post–Gazette,* June 22, 2002: p. A10

What Do Americans Believe?

When asked whether they sympathize with Israelis or Palestinians, Americans have consistently expressed support for Israel over the years (see Figure 3). Nevertheless, they also feel that a Palestinian state is justified—especially if terrorist groups pledge to end the suicide bombings.[10]

Public sympathy for Israel, coupled with the active organization and fund-raising skills of pro-Israel organizations such as AIPAC, has successfully convinced many elected officials that

(a)

(b)

The Scene of a Palestinian Attack and of an Israeli Bombing

(A) Palestinian militant organizations make frequent use of terrorist bombings, as was the case in an August 2002 attack at Hebrew University that resulted in the deaths of seven people, including five Americans. (B) Critics accuse Israel of disregarding innocent lives in its retaliatory strikes, as in this July 2002 bombing that killed the leader of the military wing of the militant group Hamas—along with 14 civilians.

• *Would U.S. support for the Palestinian cause undermine or bolster the war on terrorism?*

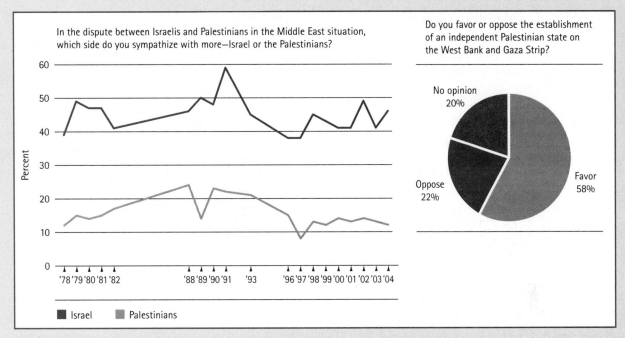

In the dispute between Israelis and Palestinians in the Middle East situation, which side do you sympathize with more—Israel or the Palestinians?

Do you favor or oppose the establishment of an independent Palestinian state on the West Bank and Gaza Strip?

No opinion 20%

Oppose 22%

Favor 58%

■ Israel   ■ Palestinians

FIGURE 3

Americans Express More Sympathy with Israel in the Arab–Israeli Conflict But Also Support Creation of a Palestinian State

• *Do you think Americans express support for Israel because of cultural affinities between the two countries, because Israel is a democracy, or for reasons of strategic national interest?*

SOURCES: Gallup, Harris, Pew Research Center polls, various years; and Gallup poll, May 30-June 1, 2003.

they oppose Israel at their peril. Members of Congress are reluctant to be seen as opposing the only democracy in the Middle East and, especially since 9/11, members who support the Palestinians risk appearing to be soft on terrorism. As a result, voices in support of the Palestinians are rare. As one Arab American expert lamented, "You see more criticism of Israel in Israeli newspapers than you do in Congress. I guess the newspaper editors aren't trying to get reelected."[11]

The following list of Web sites includes some that represent each side of this complex issue. To be better informed about this controversial issue and the arguments involved, be sure to go to the Web sites of both pro-Israel and pro-Palestinian groups. In your opinion, which Web sites(s) present the most convincing argument?

PRO-ISRAEL

The American Israel Public Affairs Committee (AIPAC) is the largest pro-Israel lobby in Washington, and conducts many outreach activities in the rest of the country as well. Browse its issue papers for a detailed defense of the Israeli perspective.

www.aipac.org

The American Jewish Committee publishes a variety of briefings and issue papers on the Arab–Israeli conflict and other issues.

www.ajc.org

The Israeli government, through its ministry of foreign affairs, sponsors an official website with the latest details on Israel's policies and actions in the conflict.

www.israel.org

PRO-PALESTINIAN

The Arab American Institute is a lobbying and outreach organization concerned with the Middle East conflict and with other issues of concern to Arab Americans.

www.aaiusa.org

The Palestine Solidarity Campaign is an activist organization dedicated to an independent Palestinian state.

www.palestinecampaign.org

The official Web site of the Palestinian Authority offers the Palestinian perspective on the conflict.

www.pna.gov.ps/

What Do You Think?

1. Should Americans become deeply involved in bringing the two parties to agreement, or would this waste energy that could be better expended elsewhere?

2. Should the fact that Israel is a democracy affect our foreign policy decisions related to the country? Why or why not?

3. Should elected officials pay much attention to public opinion on this issue, or are Americans' views on foreign policy too vague and ill-informed to be meaningful?

---

[1] Available at the Truman Presidential Museum and Library, Recognition of Israel Study Collection, www.trumanlibrary.org, accessed July 18, 2002.

[2] Letter from Senator Robert F. Wagner (D-NY) to President Harry S. Truman, June 20, 1946, Truman Presidential Museum and Library, Recognition of Israel Study Collection, www.trumanlibrary.org, accessed July 19, 2002.

[3] Laura King and Fayed abu Shammalah, "Israel Kills New Leader of Hamas," *Los Angeles Times,* April 18, 2004, p. A1; Patrick McMahon, "Terrorism Stirs Jews in USA to Activism," *USA Today,* June 25, 2002: p. 13A.

[4] "Conflict Statistics," Middle East Policy Council http://www.mepc.org/public_asp/resources/mrates.asp, accessed June 9, 2004.

[5] Robin Wright, "A Palestinian State Requires New Leadership, Bush Says," *Los Angeles Times,* June 25, 2002: p. A1.

[6] U. S. Bureau of the Census, *Statistical Abstract of the United States: 2001,* Table 66.

[7] American Israel Public Affairs Committee, www.aipac.org, accessed July 20, 2002.

[8] Patrick McMahon, "Terrorism Stirs Jews in USA to Activism," *USA Today,* June 25, 2002, p. 13A.

[9] David Lightman, "Arab Lobby Gains Clout; Fighting Image, History; Small Victories Add Up," *Hartford Courant,* May 26, 2002, p. A1.

[10] This is especially true if the establishment of such a state would lead to an end to terrorism. Fully 74 percent say "favor" when asked the question "Do you favor or oppose the establishment of an independent Palestinian state on the West Bank if the Palestinian government demonstrates that it can end the suicide bombings in Israel?" Gallup poll, June 21–23, 2002.

[11] Ibrahim Hooper, spokesman for the Council on American-Islamic Relations, quoted in Deirdre Shesgreen, "Gephardt Says Bush's Proposal for Palestinian State is 'Problematic,'" *St. Louis Post–Dispatch,* June 21, 2002: p. A7.

Appendix I

The Declaration of Independence

In Congress, July 4, 1776

The Unanimous Declaration of the Thirteen United States of America

WHEN IN THE COURSE of human events it becomes necessary for one people to dissolve the political bands which have connected them with another, and to assume, among the powers of the earth, the separate and equal station to which the Laws of Nature and of Nature's God entitle them, a decent respect to the opinions of mankind requires that they should declare the causes which impel them to the separation.

We hold these truths to be self-evident, that all men are created equal, that they are endowed by their Creator with certain unalienable Rights, that among these are Life, Liberty and the pursuit of Happiness. That to secure these rights, Governments are instituted among Men, deriving their just powers from the consent of the governed. That whenever any Form of Government becomes destructive of these ends, it is the Right of the People to alter or to abolish it, and to institute new Government, laying its foundation on such principles and organizing its powers in such form, as to them shall seem most likely to effect their Safety and Happiness. Prudence, indeed, will dictate that Governments long established should not be changed for light and transient causes; and accordingly all experience hath shewn that mankind are more disposed to suffer, while evils are sufferable, than to right themselves by abolishing the forms to which they are accustomed. But when a long train of abuses and usurpations, pursuing invariably the same Object evinces a design to reduce them under absolute Despotism, it is their right, it is their duty, to throw off such Government, and to provide new Guards for their future security.—Such has been the patient sufferance of these Colonies; and such is now the necessity which constrains them to alter their former Systems of Government. The history of the present King of Great Britain is a history of repeated injuries and usurpations, all having in direct object the establishment of an absolute Tyranny over these States. To prove this, let Facts be submitted to a candid world.

He has refused his Assent to Laws, the most wholesome and necessary for the public good.

He has forbidden his Governors to pass Laws of immediate and pressing importance, unless suspended in their operation till his Assent should be obtained; and when so suspended, he has utterly neglected to attend to them.

He has refused to pass other Laws for the accommodation of large districts of people, unless those people would relinquish the right of Representation in the Legislature, a right inestimable to them and formidable to tyrants only.

He has called together legislative bodies at places unusual, uncomfortable, and distant from the depository of their Public Records, for the sole purpose of fatiguing them into compliance with his measures.

He has dissolved Representative Houses repeatedly, for opposing with manly firmness his invasions on the rights of the people.

He has refused for a long time, after such dissolutions, to cause others to be elected; whereby the Legislative Powers, incapable of Annihilation, have returned to the People at large for their exercise, the State remaining in the mean time exposed to all the dangers of invasion from without, and convulsions within.

He has endeavored to prevent the population of these States; for that purpose obstructing the Laws of Naturalization of Foreigners; refusing to pass others to encourage their migration hither, and raising the conditions of new Appropriations of Lands.

He has obstructed the Administration of Justice, by refusing his Assent to Laws for establishing Judiciary powers.

He has made Judges dependent on his Will alone, for the tenure of their offices, and the amount and payment of their salaries.

He has erected a multitude of New Offices, and sent hither swarms of Officers to harass our people, and eat out their substance.

He has kept among us, in times of peace, Standing Armies without the Consent of our legislatures.

He has affected to render the Military independent of and superior to the Civil power.

He has combined with others to subject us to a jurisdiction foreign to our constitution, and unacknowledged by our laws, giving his Assent to their Acts of pretended Legislation:

For quartering large bodies of armed troops among us:

For protecting them, by a mock Trial, from punishment for any Murders which they should commit on the Inhabitants of these States:

For cutting off our Trade with all parts of the world:

For imposing Taxes on us without our Consent:

For depriving us in many cases, of the benefits of Trial by Jury:

For transporting us beyond Seas to be tried for pretended offences:

For abolishing the free System of English Laws in a neighboring Province, establishing therein an Arbitrary government, and enlarging its Boundaries so as to render it at once an example and fit instrument for introducing the same absolute rule into these Colonies:

For taking away our Charters, abolishing our most valuable Laws, and altering fundamentally the Forms of our Governments:

For suspending our own Legislatures, and declaring themselves invested with power to legislate for us in all cases whatsoever.

He has abdicated Government here, by declaring us out of his Protection and waging War against us.

He has plundered our seas, ravaged our Coasts, burnt our towns, and destroyed the lives of our people.

He is at this time transporting large Armies of foreign Mercenaries to compleat the works of death, desolation and tyranny, already begun with circumstances of Cruelty and perfidy scarcely paralleled in the most barbarous ages, and totally unworthy the Head of a civilized nation.

He has constrained our fellow Citizens taken Captive on the high Seas to bear Arms against their Country, to become the executioners of their friends and Brethren, or to fall themselves by their Hands.

He has excited domestic insurrections amongst us, and has endeavored to bring on the inhabitants of our frontiers, the merciless Indian Savages, whose known rule of warfare, is an undistinguished destruction of all ages, sexes and conditions.

In every stage of these Oppressions We have Petitioned for Redress in the most humble terms: Our repeated Petitions have been answered only by repeated injury: A Prince, whose character is thus marked by every act which may define a Tyrant, is unfit to be the ruler of a free people.

Nor have We been wanting in attention to our British brethren. We have warned them from time to time of attempts by their legislature to extend an unwarrantable jurisdiction over us. We have reminded them of the circumstances of our emigration and settlement here. We have appealed to their native justice and magnanimity; and we have conjured them by the ties of our common kindred to disavow these usurpations, which would inevitably interrupt our connections and correspondence. They too have been deaf to the voice of justice and consanguinity. We must, therefore, acquiesce in the necessity, which denounces our Separation, and hold them, as we hold the rest of mankind, Enemies in War, in Peace Friends.

We, therefore, the Representatives of the United States of America, in General Congress, Assembled, appealing to the Supreme Judge of the world for the rectitude of our intentions, do, in the Name, and by Authority of the good People of these Colonies, solemnly publish and declare, That these United Colonies are, and of Right ought to be Free and Independent States; that they are Absolved from all Allegiance to the British Crown, and that all political connection between them and the State of Great Britain, is and ought to be totally dissolved: and that as Free and Independent States, they have full power to levy War, conclude Peace, contract Alliances, establish Commerce, and to do all other Acts and Things which Independent States may of right do. And for the support of this Declaration, with a firm reliance on the protection of divine Providence, we mutually pledge to each other our Lives, our Fortunes and our sacred Honor.

JOHN HANCOCK

NEW HAMPSHIRE
Josiah Bartlett,
Wm. Whipple,
Matthew Thornton.

MASSACHUSETTS BAY
Saml. Adams,
John Adams,
Robt. Treat Paine,
Elbridge Gerry.

RHODE ISLAND
Step. Hopkins,
William Ellery.

CONNECTICUT
Roger Sherman,
Samuel Huntington,
Wm. Williams,
Oliver Wolcott.

NEW YORK
Wm. Floyd,
Phil. Livingston,
Frans. Lewis,
Lewis Morris

NEW JERSEY
Richd. Stockton,
In. Witherspoon,
Fras. Hopkinson,
John Hart,
Abra. Clark.

PENNSYLVANIA
Robt. Morris,
Benjamin Rush,
Benjamin Franklin,
John Morton,
Geo. Clymer,
Jas. Smith,
Geo. Taylor,
James Wilson,
Geo. Ross.

DELAWARE
Caesar Rodney,
Geo. Read,
Tho. M'kean.

MARYLAND
Samuel Chase,
Wm. Paca,

Thos. Stone,
Charles Caroll of Carollton.

VIRGINIA
George Wythe,
Richard Henry Lee,
Th. Jefferson,
Benjamin Harrison,
Thos. Nelson, jr.,
Francis Lightfoot Lee,
Carter Braxton.

NORTH CAROLINA
Wm. Hooper,
Joseph Hewes,
John Penn.

SOUTH CAROLINA
Edward Rutledge,
Thos. Heyward, Junr.,
Thomas Lynch, jnr.,
Arthur Middleton.

Appendix II

The Constitution of the United States of America

WE THE PEOPLE of the United States, in Order to form a more perfect Union, establish Justice, insure domestic Tranquility, provide for the common defence, promote the general Welfare, and secure the Blessings of Liberty to ourselves and our Posterity, do ordain and establish this Constitution for the United States of America.

ARTICLE I

SECTION 1. All legislative Powers herein granted shall be vested in a Congress of the United States, which shall consist of a Senate and House of Representatives.

SECTION 2. The House of Representatives shall be composed of Members chosen every second Year by the People of the several States, and the Electors in each State shall have the Qualifications requisite for Electors of the most numerous Branch of the State Legislature.

No person shall be a Representative who shall not have attained to the Age of twenty five Years, and been seven Years a Citizen of the United States, and who shall not, when elected, be an Inhabitant of that State in which he shall be chosen.

Representatives and direct Taxes shall be apportioned among the several States which may be included within this Union, according to their respective Numbers which shall be determined by adding to the whole Number of free Persons, including those bound to Service for a Term of Years, and excluding Indians not taxed, three fifths of all other Persons. The actual Enumeration shall be made within three Years after the first Meeting of the Congress of the United States, and within every subsequent Term ten Years, in such Manner as they shall by Law direct. The Number of Representatives shall not exceed one for every thirty Thousand, but each State shall have at Least one Representative; and until such enumeration shall be made, the State of New Hampshire shall be entitled to chuse three, Massachusetts eight, Rhode-Island and Providence Plantations one, Connecticut five, New-York six, New Jersey four, Pennsylvania eight, Delaware one, Maryland six, Virginia ten, North Carolina five, South Carolina five, and Georgia three.

When vacancies happen in the Representation from any State, the Executive Authority thereof shall issue Writs of Election to fill such Vacancies.

The House of Representatives shall chuse their speaker and other Officers; and shall have the sole Power of Impeachment.

SECTION 3. The Senate of the United States shall be composed of two Senators from each State chosen by the Legislature thereof, for six Years; and each Senator shall have one Vote.

Immediately after they shall be assembled in Consequence of the first Election, they shall be divided as equally as may be into three Classes. The Seats of the Senators of the first Class shall be vacated at the Expiration of the second year, of the second Class at the Expiration of the fourth Year, and of the third Class at the Expiration of the sixth Year, so that one third may be chosen every second Year and if Vacancies happen by Resignation, or otherwise, during the Recess of the Legislature of any State, the Executive thereof may make temporary Appointments until the next Meeting of the Legislature, which shall then fill such Vacancies.

No Person shall be a Senator who shall not have attained to the Age of thirty Years, and been nine Years a Citizen of the United States, and who shall not, when elected, be an Inhabitant of that State for which he shall be chosen.

The Vice President of the United States shall be President of the Senate, but shall have no Vote, unless they be equally divided.

The Senate shall chuse their other Officers, and also a President pro tempore, in the Absence of the Vice President, or when he shall exercise the Office of President of the United States.

The Senate shall have the sole Power to try all Impeachments. When sitting for that Purpose, they shall be on Oath or Affirmation. When the President of the United States is tried, the Chief Justice shall preside: And no Person shall be convicted without the Concurrence of two thirds of the Members present.

Judgment in Cases of Impeachment shall not extend further than to removal from Office, and disqualification to hold and enjoy any Office of honor, Trust or Profit under the United States; but the Party convicted shall nevertheless be liable and subject to Indictment, Trial, Judgment and Punishment, according to Law.

SECTION 4. The Times, Places and Manner of holding Elections for Senators and Representatives, shall be prescribed in each State by the Legislature thereof; but the Congress may at any time by law make or alter such Regulations, except as to the Places of chusing Senators.

The Congress shall assemble at least once in every Year, and such Meeting shall be on the first Monday in December, unless they shall by Law appoint a different Day.

SECTION 5. Each House shall be the Judge of the Elections, Returns and Qualifications of its own Members, and a Majority of each shall constitute a Quorum to do Business; but a smaller Number may adjourn from day to day, and may be authorized to compel the Attendance of absent Members, in such Manner, and under such Penalties as each House may provide.

Each House may determine the Rules of its Proceedings, punish its Members for disorderly Behaviour, and with the Concurrence of two thirds, expel a Member.

Each House shall keep a journal of its Proceedings, and from time to time publish the same, excepting such Parts as may in their judgment require Secrecy; and the Yeas and Nays of the Members of either House on any question shall, at the Desire of one fifth of those present, be entered on the Journal.

Neither House, during the Session of Congress, shall, without the Consent of the other, adjourn for more than three days, nor to any other Place than that in which the two Houses shall be sitting.

SECTION 6. The Senators and Representatives shall receive a Compensation for their Services, to be ascertained by Law, and paid out of the Treasury of the United States. They shall in all Cases, except Treason, Felony and Breach of the Peace, be privileged from Arrest during their Attendance at the Session of their respective Houses, and in going to and returning from the same; and for any Speech or Debate in either House, they shall not be questioned in any other Place.

No Senator or Representative shall, during the Time for which he was elected, be appointed to any civil Office under the Authority of the United States, which shall have been created, or the Emoluments whereof shall have been encreased during such time; and no Person holding any Office under the United States, shall be a Member of either House during his Continuance in Office.

SECTION 7. All Bills for raising Revenue shall originate in the House of Representatives; but the Senate may propose or concur with Amendments as on other Bills.

Every Bill which shall have passed the House of Representatives and the Senate, shall, before it become a Law, be presented to the President of the United States; If he approves he shall sign it, but if not he shall return it, with his Objections to that House in which it shall have originated, who shall enter the Objections at large on their journal, and proceed to reconsider it. If after such Reconsideration two thirds of that House shall agree to pass the Bill, it shall be sent, together with the Objections, to the other House, by which it shall likewise be reconsidered, and if approved by two thirds of that House, it shall become a Law. But in all such Cases the Votes of both Houses shall be determined by Yeas and Nays, and the Names of the Persons voting for and against the Bill shall be entered on the Journal of each House respectively. If any Bill shall not be returned by the President within ten Days (Sundays excepted) after it shall have been presented to him, the Same shall be a Law, in like Manner as if he had signed it, unless the Congress by their Adjournment prevent its Return, in which Case it shall not be a Law.

Every Order, Resolution, or Vote to which the Concurrence of the Senate and House of Representatives may be necessary (except on a question of Adjournment) shall be presented to the President of the United States; and before the Same shall take Effect, shall be approved by him, or being disapproved by him, shall be repassed by two thirds of the Senate and House of Representatives, according to the Rules and Limitations prescribed in the Case of a Bill.

SECTION 8. The Congress shall have Power To lay and collect Taxes, Duties, Imposts and Excises, to pay the Debts and provide for the common Defence and general Welfare of the United States; but all Duties, Imposts and Excises shall be uniform throughout the United States;

To borrow Money on the credit of the United States;

To regulate Commerce with foreign Nations, and among the several States, and with the Indian Tribes;

To establish a uniform Rule of Naturalization, and uniform Laws on the subject of Bankruptcies throughout the United States;

To coin Money, regulate the Value thereof, and of foreign Coin, and fix the Standard of Weights and Measures;

To provide for the Punishment of counterfeiting the Securities and current Coin of the United States;

To establish Post Offices and post Roads;

To promote the Progress of Science and useful Arts, by securing for limited Times to Authors and Inventors the exclusive Right to their respective Writings and Discoveries;

To constitute Tribunals inferior to the supreme Court;

To define and punish Piracies and Felonies committed on the high Seas, and Offences against the Law of Nations;

To declare War, grant Letters of Marque and Reprisal, and make Rules concerning Captures on Land and Water;

To raise and support Armies, but no Appropriation of Money to that Use shall be for a longer Term than two Years;

To provide and maintain a Navy;

To make Rules for the Government and Regulation of the land and naval Forces;

To provide for calling forth the Militia to execute the Laws of the Union, suppress Insurrections and repel Invasions;

To provide for organizing, arming, and disciplining, the Militia, and for governing such Part of them as may be employed in the Service of the United States, reserving to the States respectively, the Appointment of the Officers, and the Authority of training the Militia according to the discipline prescribed by Congress;

To exercise exclusive Legislation in all Cases whatsoever, over such District (not exceeding ten Miles square) as may, by Cession of particular States, and the Acceptance of Congress, become the Seat of the Government of the United States, and to exercise like Authority over all Places purchased by the Consent of the Legislature of the State in which the Same shall be for the Erection of Forts, Magazines, Arsenals, dock-Yards, and other needful Buildings;—And

To make all Laws which shall be necessary and proper for carrying into Execution the foregoing Powers, and all other Powers vested by this Constitution in the Government of the United States, or in any Department or Officer thereof.

SECTION 9. The Migration or Importation of such Persons as any of the States now existing shall think proper to admit, shall not be prohibited by the Congress prior to the Year one thousand eight hundred and eight, but a Tax or duty may be imposed on such Importation, not exceeding ten dollars for each Person.

The Privilege of the Writ of Habeas Corpus shall not be suspended, unless when in Cases of Rebellion or Invasion the public Safety may require it.

No Bill of Attainder or ex post facto Law shall be passed.

No Capitation, or other direct, Tax shall be laid, unless in Proportion to the Census or Enumeration herein before directed to be taken.

No Tax or Duty shall be laid on Articles exported from any State.

No Preference shall be given by any Regulation of Commerce or Revenue to the Ports of one State over those of another; nor shall Vessels bound to, or from, one State, be obliged to enter, clear, or pay Duties in another.

No Money shall be drawn from the Treasury, but in Consequence of Appropriations made by Law; and a regular Statement and Account of the Receipts and Expenditures of all public Money shall be published from time to time.

No Title of Nobility shall be granted by the United States: And no Person holding any Office of Profit or Trust under them, shall, without the Consent of the Congress, accept of any present, Emolument, Office, or Title, of any kind whatever, from any King, Prince, or foreign State.

SECTION 10. No state shall enter into any Treaty, Alliance, or Confederation; grant Letters of Marque and Reprisal; coin Money; emit Bills of Credit; make any Thing but gold and silver Coin a Tender in Payment of Debts; pass any Bill of Attainder, ex post facto Law, or Law impairing the Obligation of Contracts, or grant any Title of Nobility.

No State shall, without the Consent of the Congress, lay any Imposts or Duties on Imports or Exports, except what may be absolutely necessary for executing its inspection Laws: and the net Produce of all Duties and Imposts, laid by any State on Imports or Exports, shall be for the Use of the Treasury of the United States, and all such Laws shall be subject to the Revision and Controul of the Congress.

No State shall, without the Consent of Congress, lay any Duty of Tonnage, keep Troops, or Ships of War in time of Peace, enter into any Agreement or Compact with another State, or with a foreign Power, or engage in War, unless actually invaded, or in such imminent Danger as will not admit of delay.

ARTICLE II

SECTION 1. The executive Power shall be vested in a President of the United States of America. He shall hold his Office during the Term of four Years, and, together with the Vice President, chosen for the same Term, be elected as follows.

Each State shall appoint, in such Manner as the Legislature thereof may direct, a Number of Electors, equal to the whole Number of Senators and Representatives to which the State may be entitled in the Congress; but no Senator or Representative, or Person holding an Office of Trust of Profit under the United States, shall be appointed an Elector.

The Electors shall meet in their respective States, and vote by Ballot for two Persons, of whom one at least shall not be an Inhabitant of the same State with themselves. And they shall make a List of all the Persons voted for, and, of the Number of Votes for each; which List they shall sign and certify, and transmit sealed to the Seat of the Government of the United States, directed to the President of the Senate. The President of the Senate shall, in the Presence of the Senate and House of Representatives, open all the Certificates, and the Votes shall then be counted. The Person having the greatest Number of Votes shall be the President, if such Number be a Majority of the whole Number of Electors appointed; and if there be more than one who have such Majority, and have an equal Number of Votes, then the House of Representatives shall immediately chuse by Ballot one of them for President; and if no Person have a Majority, then from the five highest on the List the said House shall in like Manner chuse the President. But in chusing the President, the Votes shall be taken by States, the Representation from each State having one Vote; A quorum for this Purpose shall consist of a Member or Members from two thirds of the States, and a Majority of all the States shall be necessary to a Choice. In every Case, after the Choice of the President, the Person having the greatest Number of Votes of the Electors shall be the Vice President. But if there should remain two or more who have equal Votes, the Senate shall chuse from them by Ballot the Vice President.

The Congress may determine the Time of chusing the Electors, and the Day on which they shall give their Votes; which Day shall be the same throughout the United States.

No Person except a natural born Citizen, or a Citizen of the United States, at the time of the Adoption of this Constitution, shall be eligible to the Office of President; neither shall any Person be eligible to that Office who shall not have attained to the Age of thirty five Years, and been fourteen Years a Resident within the United States.

In Case of the Removal of the President from Office, or of his Death, Resignation, or Inability to discharge the Powers and Duties of the said Office, the Same shall devolve on the Vice President, and the Congress may by Law provide for the Case of Removal, Death, Resignation or Inability, both of the President and Vice President, declaring what Officer shall then act as President, and such Officer shall act accordingly, until the Disability be removed, or a President shall be elected.

The President shall, at stated Times, receive for his Services, a Compensation, which shall neither be encreased nor diminished during the Period for which he shall have been elected, and he shall not receive within that Period any other Emolument from the United States, or any of them.

Before he enter on the Execution of his Office, he shall take the following Oath or Affirmation—"I do solemnly swear (or affirm) that I will faithfully execute the Office of President of the United States, and will to the best of my Ability, preserve, protect and defend the Constitution of the United States."

SECTION 2. The President shall be Commander in Chief of the Army, and Navy of the United States, and of the Militia of the several States, when called into the actual Service of the United States; he may require the Opinion, in writing, of the principal Officer in each of the executive Departments, upon any Subject relating to the Duties of their respective Offices, and he shall have Power to grant Reprieves and Pardons for Offences against the United States, except in Cases of Impeachment.

He shall have Power, by and with the Advice and Consent of the Senate, to make Treaties, provided two thirds of the Senators present concur; and he shall nominate, and by and with the Advice and Consent of the Senate, shall appoint Ambassadors, other public Ministers and Consuls, Judges of the supreme Court, and all other Officers of the United States, whose Appointments are not herein otherwise provided for, and which shall be established by Law: but the Congress may by Law vest the Appointment of such inferior Officers, as they think proper, in the President alone, in the Courts of Law, or in the Heads of Departments.

The President shall have Power to fill up all Vacancies that may happen during the Recess of the Senate, by granting Commissions which shall expire at the end of their next Session.

SECTION 3. He shall from time to time give to the Congress Information of the State of the Union, and recommend to their Consideration such Measures as he shall judge necessary and expedient; he may, on extraordinary Occasions, convene both Houses, or either of them, and in Case of Disagreement between them, with Respect to the Time of Adjournment, he may adjourn them to such Time as he shall think proper; he shall receive Ambassadors and other public Ministers; he shall take Care that the Laws be faithfully executed, and shall Commission all the Officers of the United States.

SECTION 4. The President, Vice President and all civil Officers of the United States, shall be removed from Office on Impeachment for, and Conviction of, Treason, Bribery, or other high Crimes and Misdemeanors.

ARTICLE III

SECTION 1. The judicial Power of the United States, shall be vested in one supreme Court, and in such inferior Courts as the Congress may from time to time ordain and establish. The Judges, both of the supreme and inferior Courts, shall hold their Offices during good Behaviour, and shall, at stated Times, receive for their Services, a Compensation, which shall not be diminished during their Continuance in Office.

SECTION 2. The judicial Power shall extend to all Cases, in Law and Equity, arising under this Constitution, the Laws of the United States, and Treaties made, or which shall be made, under their Authority;—to all Cases affecting Ambassadors, other public Ministers and Consuls;—to all Cases of admiralty and maritime Jurisdiction;—to Controversies to which the United States shall be a Party;—to Controversies between two or more States;—between a State and Citizens of another State;—between Citizens of different States,—between Citizens of the same State claiming Lands under Grants of different States,—and between a State, or the Citizens thereof, and foreign States, Citizens of Subjects.

In all Cases affecting Ambassadors, other public Ministers and Consuls, and those in which a State shall be Party, the supreme Court shall have original Jurisdiction. In all the other Cases before mentioned, the supreme Court shall have appellate Jurisdiction, both as to Law and Fact, with such Exceptions, and under such Regulations as the Congress shall make.

The Trial of all Crimes, except in Cases of Impeachment, shall be by Jury; and such Trial shall be held in the State where the said Crimes shall have been committed; but when not committed within any State, the Trial shall be at such Place or Places as the Congress may by Law have directed.

SECTION 3. Treason against the United States, shall consist only in levying War against them, or in adhering to their Enemies, giving them Aid and Comfort. No Person shall be convicted of Treason unless on the Testimony of two Witnesses to the same overt Act, or on Confession in open Court.

The Congress shall have Power to declare the Punishment of Treason, but no Attainder of Treason shall work Corruption of Blood, or Forfeiture except during the Life of the Person attainted.

ARTICLE IV

SECTION 1. Full Faith and Credit shall be given in each State to the public Acts, Records, and judicial Proceedings of every other State. And the Congress may by general Laws prescribe the Manner in which such Acts, Records and Proceedings shall be proved, and the Effect thereof.

SECTION 2. The Citizens of each State shall be entitled to all Privileges and Immunities of Citizens in the several States.

A Person charged in any State with Treason, Felony, or other Crime, who shall flee from Justice, and be found in another State, shall on Demand of the executive Authority of the State from which he fled, be delivered up, to be removed to the State having Jurisdiction of the Crime.

No Person held to Service or Labour in one State under the Laws thereof, escaping into another, shall, in Consequence of any Law or Regulation therein, be discharged from such Service or Labour, but shall be delivered up on Claim of the Party to whom such Service or Labour may be due.

SECTION 3. New States may be admitted by the Congress into this Union; but no new State shall be formed or erected within the Jurisdiction of any other State; nor any State be formed by the Junction of two or more States, or Parts of States, without the Consent of the Legislatures of the States concerned as well as of the Congress.

The Congress shall have Power to dispose of and make all needful Rules and Regulations respecting the Territory or other Property belonging to the United States; and nothing in this Constitution shall be so construed as to Prejudice any Claims of the United States, or of any particular State.

SECTION 4. The United States shall guarantee to every State in this Union a Republican Form of Government, and shall protect each of them against Invasion, and on Application of the Legislature, or of the Executive (when the Legislature cannot be convened) against domestic Violence.

ARTICLE V

The Congress, whenever two thirds of both Houses shall deem it necessary, shall propose Amendments to this Constitution, or, on the Application of the Legislatures of two thirds of the several States, shall call a Convention for proposing Amendments, which, in either Case, shall be valid to all Intents and Purposes, as Part of this Constitution, when ratified by the Legislatures of three fourths of the several States, or by Conventions in three fourths thereof, as the one or the other Mode of Ratification may be proposed by the Congress; Provided that no Amendment which may be made prior to the Year One thousand eight hundred and eight shall in any Manner affect the first and fourth Clauses in the Ninth Section of the first Article; and that no State, without its Consent, shall be deprived of its equal Suffrage in the Senate.

ARTICLE VI

All Debts contracted and Engagements entered into, before the Adoption of this Constitution, shall be as valid against the United States under this Constitution, as under the Confederation.

This Constitution, and the laws of the United States which shall be made in Pursuance thereof; and all Treaties made, or which shall be made, under the Authority of the United States, shall be the supreme Law of the Land; and the Judges in every State shall be bound thereby, any Thing in the Constitution or Laws of any State to the Contrary notwithstanding.

The Senators and Representatives before mentioned, and the Members of the several State Legislatures, and all executive and judicial Officers, both of the United States and of the several States, shall be bound by Oath or Affirmation, to support this Constitution; but no religious Test shall ever be required as a Qualification to any Office or public Trust under the United States.

ARTICLE VII

The Ratification of the Conventions of nine States, shall be sufficient for the Establishment of this Constitution between the States so ratifying the Same.

Done in Convention by the Unanimous Consent of the States present the Seventeenth Day of September in the Year of our Lord one thousand seven hundred and Eighty seven and of the Independence of the United States of America the Twelfth. In witness whereof we have hereunto subscribed our Names,

Go. WASHINGTON
Presid't. and deputy from Virginia

Attest
WILLIAM JACKSON
Secretary

Articles in addition to, and amendment of the Constitution of the United States of America, proposed by Congress and ratified by the Legislatures of the several states, pursuant to the Fifth Article of the original Constitution.

(The first ten amendments were passed by Congress on September 25, 1789, and were ratified on December 15, 1791.)

AMENDMENT I

Congress shall make no law respecting an establishment of religion, or prohibiting the free exercise thereof; or abridging the freedom of speech, or of the press; or the right of the people peaceably to assemble, and to petition the Government for a redress of grievances.

AMENDMENT II

A well regulated Militia, being necessary to the security of a free State, the right of the people to keep and bear Arms, shall not be infringed.

AMENDMENT III

No Soldier shall, in time of peace be quartered in any house, without the consent of the Owner, nor in time of war, but in a manner to be prescribed by law.

AMENDMENT IV

The right of the people to be secure in their persons, houses, papers, and effects, against unreasonable searches and seizures, shall not be violated, and no warrants shall issue, but upon probable cause, supported by Oath or affirmation, and particularly describing the place to be searched, and the persons or things to be seized.

AMENDMENT V

No person shall be held to answer for a capital, or otherwise infamous crime, unless on a presentment or indictment of a Grand Jury, except in cases arising in the land or naval forces, or in the Militia, when in actual service in time of War or public danger; nor shall any person be subject for the same offence to be twice put in jeopardy of life or limb; nor shall be compelled in any criminal case to be a witness against himself, nor be deprived of life, liberty, or property, without due process of law; nor shall private property be taken for public use, without just compensation.

AMENDMENT VI

In all criminal prosecutions, the accused shall enjoy the right to a speedy and public trial, by an impartial jury of the State and district wherein the crime shall have been committed, which district shall have been previously ascertained by law, and to be informed of the nature and cause of the accusation; to be confronted with the witnesses against him; to have compulsory process for obtaining witnesses in his favor, and to have the assistance of counsel for his defence.

AMENDMENT VII

In Suits at common law, where the value in controversy shall exceed twenty dollars, the right of trial by jury shall be preserved, and no fact tried by a jury, shall be otherwise re-examined in any Court of the United States, than according to the rules of the common law.

AMENDMENT VIII

Excessive bail shall not be required, nor excessive fines imposed, nor cruel and unusual punishments inflicted.

AMENDMENT IX

The enumeration in the Constitution, of certain rights, shall not be construed to deny or disparage others retained by the people.

AMENDMENT X

The powers not delegated to the United States by the Constitution, nor prohibited by it to the States, are reserved to the States respectively, or to the people.

AMENDMENT XI
(Ratified on February 7, 1795)

The Judicial power of the United States shall not be construed to extend to any suit in law or equity, commenced or prosecuted against one of the United States by Citizens of another State, or by Citizens or Subjects of any Foreign State.

AMENDMENT XII
(Ratified on June 15, 1804)

The Electors shall meet in their respective states, and vote by ballot for President and Vice-President, one of whom, at least, shall not be an inhabitant of the same state with themselves; they shall name in their ballots the person voted for as President, and in distinct ballots the person voted for as Vice-President, and they shall make distinct lists of all persons voted for as President, and of all persons voted for as Vice-President, and of the number of votes for each, which lists they shall sign and certify, and transmit sealed to the seat of the government of the United States, directed to the President of the Senate;—The President of the Senate shall, in the presence of the Senate and House of Representatives, open all the certificates and the votes shall then be counted;—The person having the greatest number of votes for President, shall be the President, if such number be a majority of the whole number of Electors appointed; and if no person have such majority; then from the persons having the highest numbers not exceeding three on the list of those voted for as President, the House of Representatives shall choose immediately, by ballot, the President. But in choosing the President, the votes shall be taken by states, the representation from each state having one vote; a quorum for this purpose shall consist of a member or members from two-thirds of the states, and a majority of all the states shall be necessary to a choice. And if the House of Representatives shall not choose a President whenever the right of choice shall devolve upon them, before the fourth day of March next following, then the Vice-President shall act as President, as in the case of the death or other constitutional disability of the President.—The person having the greatest number of votes as Vice-President, shall be the Vice-President, if such number be a majority of the whole number of Electors appointed, and if no person have a majority, then from the two highest numbers on the list, the Senate shall choose the Vice-President; a quorum for the purpose shall consist of two-thirds of the whole number of Senators, and a majority of the whole number shall be necessary to a choice. But no person constitutionally ineligible to the office of President shall be eligible to that of Vice-President of the United States.

AMENDMENT XIII
(Ratified on December 6, 1865)

SECTION 1. Neither slavery nor involuntary servitude, except as a punishment for crime whereof the party shall have been duly convicted, shall exist within the United States, or any place subject to their jurisdiction.

SECTION 2. Congress shall have power to enforce this article by appropriate legislation.

AMENDMENT XIV
(Ratified on July 9, 1868)

SECTION 1. All persons born or naturalized in the United States, and subject to the jurisdiction thereof, are citizens of the United States and of the State wherein they reside. No State shall make or enforce any law which shall abridge the privileges or immunities of citizens of the United States; nor shall any State deprive any person of life, liberty, or property, without due process of law; nor deny to any person within its jurisdiction the equal protection of the laws.

SECTION 2. Representatives shall be apportioned among the several States according to their respective numbers, counting the whole number of persons in each State, excluding Indians not taxed. But when the right to vote at any election for the choice of electors for President and Vice President of the United States, Representatives in Congress, the Executive and Judicial officers of a State, or the members of the Legislature thereof, is denied to any of the male inhabitants of such State, being twenty-one years of age, and citizens of the United States, or in any way abridged, except for participation in rebellion, or other crime, the basis of representation therein shall be reduced in the proportion which the number of such male citizens shall bear to the whole number of male citizens twenty-one years of age in such State.

SECTION 3. No person shall be a Senator or Representative in Congress, or elector of President and Vice President, or hold any office, civil or military, under the United States, or under any State, who, having previously taken an oath, as a member of Congress, or as an officer of the United States, or as a member of any State legislature, or as an executive or judicial officer of any State, to support the Constitution of the United States, shall have engaged in insurrection or rebellion against the same, or given aid or comfort to the enemies thereof. But Congress may by a vote of two-thirds of each House, remove such disability.

SECTION 4. The validity of the public debt of the United States, authorized by law, including debts incurred for payment of pensions and bounties for services in suppressing insurrection or rebellion, shall not be questioned. But neither the United States nor any State shall assume or pay any debt or obligation incurred in aid of insurrection or rebellion against the United States, or any claim for the loss or emancipation of any slave, but all such debts, obligations and claims shall be held illegal and void.

SECTION 5. The Congress shall have power to enforce, by appropriate legislation, the provisions of this article.

AMENDMENT XV
(Ratified on February 3, 1870)

SECTION 1. The right of citizens of the United States to vote shall not be denied or abridged by the United States or by any State on account of race, color, or previous condition of servitude.

SECTION 2. The Congress shall have power to enforce this article by appropriate legislation.

AMENDMENT XVI
(Ratified on February 3, 1913)

The Congress shall have power to lay and collect taxes on incomes, from whatever source derived, without apportionment among the several States, and without regard to any census or enumeration.

AMENDMENT XVII
(Ratified on April 8, 1913)

The Senate of the United States shall be composed of two Senators from each State, elected by the people thereof, for six years; and each Senator shall have one vote. The electors in each

State shall have the qualifications requisite for electors of the most numerous branch of the State legislatures.

When vacancies happen in the representation of any State in the Senate, the executive authority of such State shall issue writs of election to fill such vacancies: Provided, That the legislature of any State may empower the executive thereof to make temporary appointments until the people fill the vacancies by election as the legislature may direct.

This amendment shall not be so construed as to affect the election or term of any Senator chosen before it becomes valid as part of the Constitution.

AMENDMENT XVIII
(Ratified on January 16, 1919)

SECTION 1. After one year from the ratification of this article the manufacture, sale, or transportation of intoxicating liquors within, the importation thereof into, or the exportation thereof from the United States and all territory subject to the jurisdiction thereof for beverage purposes is hereby prohibited.

SECTION 2. The Congress and the several States shall have concurrent power to enforce this article by appropriate legislation.

SECTION 3. This article shall be inoperative unless it shall have been ratified as an amendment to the Constitution by the legislatures of the several States, as provided in the Constitution, within seven years from the date of the submission hereof to the States by the Congress.

AMENDMENT XIX
(Ratified on August 18, 1920)

The right of citizens of the United States to vote shall not be denied or abridged by the United States or by any State on account of sex.

Congress shall have power to enforce this article by appropriate legislation.

AMENDMENT XX
(Ratified on February 6, 1933)

SECTION 1. The terms of the President and Vice President shall end at noon on the 20th day of January, and the terms of Senators and Representatives at noon on the 3d day of January, of the years in which such terms would have ended if this article had not been ratified; and the terms of their successors shall then begin.

SECTION 2. The Congress shall assemble at least once in every year, and such meeting shall begin at noon on the 3d day of January, unless they shall by law appoint a different day.

SECTION 3. If, at the time fixed for the beginning of the term of the President, the President elect shall have died, the Vice President elect shall become President. If a President shall not have been chosen before the time fixed for the beginning of his term, or if the President elect shall have failed to qualify, then the Vice President elect shall act as President until a President shall have qualified; and the Congress may by law provide for the case wherein neither a President elect nor a Vice President elect shall have qualified, declaring who shall then act as President, or the manner in which one who is to act shall be selected, and such person shall act accordingly until a President or Vice President shall have qualified.

SECTION 4. The Congress may by law provide for the case of the death of any of the persons from whom the House of Representatives may choose a President whenever the rights of choice shall have devolved upon them, and for the case of the death of any of the persons from whom the Senate may choose a Vice President whenever the right of choice shall have devolved upon them.

SECTION 5. Sections 1 and 2 shall take effect on the 15th day of October following the ratification of this article.

SECTION 6. This article shall be inoperative unless it shall have been ratified as an amendment to the Constitution by the legislatures of three-fourths of the several States within seven years from the date of its submission.

AMENDMENT XXI
(Ratified on December 5, 1933)

SECTION 1. The eighteenth article of amendment to the Constitution of the United States is hereby repealed.

SECTION 2. The transportation or importation into any State, Territory, or possession of the United States for delivery or use therein of intoxicating liquors, in violation of the laws thereof, is hereby prohibited.

SECTION 3. This article shall be inoperative unless it shall have been ratified as an amendment to the Constitution by conventions in the several States, as provided in the Constitution, within seven years from the date of the submission hereof to the States by the Congress.

AMENDMENT XXII
(Ratified on February 27, 1951)

No person shall be elected to the office of the President more than twice, and no person who has held the office of President, or acted as President, for more than two years of a term to which some other person was elected President shall be elected to the office of the President more than once. But this Article shall not apply to any person holding the office of President when this Article was proposed by the Congress, and shall not prevent any person who may be holding the office of President, or acting as President, during the term within which this Article becomes operative from holding the office of President or acting as President during the remainder of such term.

AMENDMENT XXIII
(Ratified on March 29, 1961)

SECTION 1. The District constituting the seat of Government of the United States shall appoint in such manner as the Congress may direct:

A number of electors of President and Vice President equal to the whole number of Senators and Representatives in Congress to which the District would be entitled if it were a State, but in no event more than the least populous State; they shall be in addition to those appointed by the States, but they shall be considered, for the purposes of the election of President and Vice President, to be electors appointed by a State; and they shall meet in the District and perform such duties as provided by the twelfth article of amendment.

SECTION 2. The Congress shall have power to enforce this article by appropriate legislation.

AMENDMENT XXIV
(Ratified on January 23, 1964)

SECTION 1. The right of citizens of the United States to vote in any primary or other election for President or Vice President, for electors for President or Vice President, or for Senator or

Representative in Congress, shall not be denied or abridged by the United States or any State by reason of failure to pay any poll tax or other tax.

SECTION 2. The Congress shall have power to enforce this article by appropriate legislation.

AMENDMENT XXV
(Ratified on February 10, 1967)

SECTION 1. In case of the removal of the President from office or of his death or resignation, the Vice President shall become President.

SECTION 2. Whenever there is a vacancy in the office of the Vice President, the President shall nominate a Vice President who shall take office upon confirmation by a majority vote of both Houses of Congress.

SECTION 3. Whenever the President transmits to the President pro tempore of the Senate and the Speaker of the House of Representatives his written declaration that he is unable to discharge the powers and duties of his office, and until he transmits to them a written declaration to the contrary, such powers and duties shall be discharged by the Vice President as Acting President.

SECTION 4. Whenever the Vice President and a majority of either the principal officers of the executive departments or of such other body as Congress may by law provide, transmit to the President pro tempore of the Senate and the Speaker of the House of Representatives their written declaration that the President is unable to discharge the powers and duties of his office, the Vice President shall immediately assume the powers and duties of the office as Acting President.

Thereafter, when the President transmits to the President pro tempore of the Senate and the Speaker of the House of Representatives his written declaration that no inability exists, he shall resume the powers and duties of his office unless the Vice President and a majority of either the principal officers of the executive department or of such other body as Congress may by law provide, transmit within four days to the President pro tempore of the Senate and the Speaker of the House of Representatives their written declaration that the President is unable to discharge the powers and duties of his office. Thereupon Congress shall decide the issue, assembling within forty-eight hours for that purpose if not in session. If the Congress, within twenty-one days after receipt of the latter written declaration, or, if Congress is not in session, within twenty-one days after Congress is required to assemble, determines by two-thirds vote of both Houses that the President is unable to discharge the powers and duties of his office, the Vice President shall continue to discharge the same as Acting President; otherwise, the President shall resume the powers and duties of his office.

AMENDMENT XXVI
(Ratified on July 1, 1971)

SECTION 1. The right of citizens of the United States, who are eighteen years of age or older, to vote shall not be denied or abridged by the United States or by any State on account of age.

SECTION 2. The Congress shall have power to enforce this article by appropriate legislation.

AMENDMENT XXVII
(Ratified on May 7, 1992)

No law varying the compensation for the services of Senators and Representatives shall take effect until an election of Representatives shall have intervened.

Appendix III

The Federalist No. 10

November 22, 1787
James Madison

TO THE PEOPLE OF THE STATE OF NEW YORK.

Among the numerous advantages promised by a well constructed Union, none deserves to be more accurately developed than its tendency to break and control the violence of faction. The friend of popular governments, never finds himself so much alarmed for their character and fate, as when he contemplates their propensity to this dangerous vice. He will not fail therefore to set a due value on any plan which, without violating the principles to which he is attached, provides a proper cure for it. The instability, injustice and confusion introduced into the public councils, have in truth been the mortal diseases under which popular governments have every where perished; as they continue to be the favorite and fruitful topics from which the adversaries to liberty derive their most specious declamations. The valuable improvements made by the American Constitutions on the popular models, both ancient and modern, cannot certainly be too much admired; but it would be an unwarrantable partiality, to contend that they have as effectually obviated the danger on this side as was wished and expected. Complaints are every where heard from our most considerate and virtuous citizens, equally the friends of public and private faith, and of public and personal liberty; that our governments are too unstable; that the public good is disregarded in the conflicts of rival parties; and that measures are too often decided, not according to the rules of justice, and the rights of the minor party; but by the superior force of an interested and over-bearing majority. However anxiously we may wish that these complaints had no foundation, the evidence of known facts will not permit us to deny that they are in some degree true. It will be found indeed, on a candid review of our situation, that some of the distresses under which we labor, have been erroneously charged on the operation of our governments; but it will be found, at the same time, that other causes will not alone account for many of our heaviest misfortunes; and particularly, for that prevailing and increasing distrust of public engagements, and alarm for private rights, which are echoed from one end of the continent to the other. These must be chiefly, if not wholly, effects of the unsteadiness and injustice, with which a factious spirit has tainted our public administrations.

By a faction I understand a number of citizens, whether amounting to a majority or minority of the whole, who are united and actuated by some common impulse of passion, or of interest, adverse to the rights of other citizens, or to the permanent and aggregate interests of the community.

There are two methods of curing the mischiefs of faction: the one, by removing its causes; the other, by controlling its effects.

There are again two methods of removing the causes of faction: the one by destroying the liberty which is essential to its existence; the other, by giving to every citizen the same opinions, the same passions, and the same interests.

It could never be more truly said than of the first remedy, that it is worse than the disease. Liberty is to faction, what air is to fire, an aliment without which it instantly expires. But it could not be a less folly to abolish liberty, which is essential to political life, because it nourishes faction, than it would be to wish the annihilation of air, which is essential to animal life, because it imparts to fire its destructive agency.

The second expedient is as impracticable, as the first would be unwise. As long as the reason of man continues fallible, and he is at liberty to exercise it, different opinions will be formed. As long as the connection subsists between his reason and his self-love, his opinions and his passions will have a reciprocal influence on each other; and the former will be objects to which the latter will attach themselves. The diversity in the faculties of men from which the rights of property originate, is not less an insuperable obstacle to a uniformity of interests. The protection of these faculties is the first object of Government. From the protection of different and unequal faculties of acquiring property, the possession of different degrees and kinds of property immediately results: and from the influence of these on the sentiments and views of the respective proprietors, ensues a division of the society into different interests and parties.

The latent causes of faction are thus sown in the nature of man; and we see them every where brought into different degrees of activity, according to the different circumstances of civil society. A zeal for different opinions concerning religion, concerning Government and many other points, as well of speculation as of practice; an attachment to different leaders ambitiously contending for pre-eminence and power; or to persons of other descriptions whose fortunes have been interesting to the human passions, have in turn divided mankind into parties, inflamed them with mutual animosity, and rendered them much more disposed to vex and oppress each other, than to cooperate for their common good. So strong is this propensity of mankind to fall into mutual animosities, that where no substantial occasion presents itself, the most frivolous and fanciful distinctions have been sufficient to kindle their unfriendly passions, and excite their most violent conflicts. But the most common and durable source of factions, has been the various and unequal distribution of property. Those who hold, and those who are without property, have ever formed distinct interests in society. Those who are creditors, and those who are debtors, fall under a like discrimination. A landed interest, a manufacturing interest, a mercantile interest, a monied interest, with many lesser interests, grow up of necessity in civilized nations, and divide them into different classes, actuated by different sentiments and views. The regulation of these various and interfering interests forms the principal task of modern Legislation, and involves the spirit of party and faction in the necessary and ordinary operations of Government.

No man is allowed to be a judge in his own cause; because his interest would certainly bias his judgment, and, not improbably, corrupt his integrity. With equal, nay with greater reason, a body of men, are unfit to be both judges and parties, at the same time; yet, what are many of the most important acts of legislation, but so many judicial determinations, not indeed concerning the rights of single persons, but concerning the rights of large bodies of citizens, and what are the different classes of legislators, but advocates and parties to the causes which they determine? Is a law proposed concerning private debts? It is a question to which the creditors are parties on one side, and the debtors on the other. Justice ought to hold the balance between them. Yet the parties are and must be themselves the judges; and the most numerous party, or, in other words, the most powerful faction must be expected to prevail. Shall domestic manufactures be encouraged, and in what degree, by restrictions on foreign manufactures? are questions which would be differently decided by the landed and the manufacturing classes; and probably by neither, with a sole regard to justice and the public good. The apportionment of taxes on the various descriptions of property, is an act which seems to require the most exact impartiality; yet, there is perhaps no legislative act in which greater opportunity and temptation are given to a predominant party, to trample on the rules of justice. Every shilling with which they over-burden the inferior number, is a shilling saved to their own pockets.

It is in vain to say, that enlightened statesmen will be able to adjust these clashing interests, and render them all subservient to the public good. Enlightened statesmen will not always be at the helm: Nor, in many cases, can such an adjustment be made at all, without taking into view indirect and remote considerations, which will rarely prevail over the immediate interest which one party may find in disregarding the rights of another, or the good of the whole.

The inference to which we are brought, is, that the causes of faction cannot be removed; and that relief is only to be sought in the means of controlling its effects.

If a faction consists of less than a majority, relief is supplied by the republican principle, which enables the majority to defeat its sinister views by regular vote: It may clog the administration, it may convulse the society; but it will be unable to execute and mask its violence under the forms of the Constitution. When a majority is included in a faction, the form of popular government on the other hand enables it to sacrifice to its ruling passion or interest, both the public good and the rights of other citizens. To secure the public good, and private rights, against the danger of such a faction, and at the same time to preserve the spirit and the form of popular government, is then the great object to which our enquiries are directed: Let me add that it is the great desideratum, by which alone this form of government can be rescued from the opprobrium under which it has so long labored, and be recommended to the esteem and adoption of mankind.

By what means is this object attainable? Evidently by one of two only. Either the existence of the same passion or interest in a majority at the same time, must be prevented; or the majority, having such co-existent passion or interest, must be rendered, by their number and local situation, unable to concert and carry into effect schemes of oppression. If the impulse and the opportunity be suffered to coincide, we well know that neither moral nor religious motives can be relied on as an adequate control. They are not found to be such on the injustice and violence of individuals, and lose their efficacy in proportion to the number combined together; that is, in proportion as their efficacy becomes needful.

From this view of the subject, it may be concluded, that a pure Democracy, by which I mean, a Society, consisting of a small number of citizens, who assemble and administer the Government in person, can admit of no cure for the mischiefs of faction. A common passion or interest will, in almost every case, be felt by a majority of the whole; a communication and concert results from the form of Government itself; and there is nothing to check the inducements to sacrifice the weaker party, or an obnoxious individual. Hence it is, that such Democracies have ever been spectacles of turbulence and contention; have ever been found incompatible with personal security, or the rights of property; and have in general been as short in their lives, as they have been violent in their deaths. Theoretic politicians, who have patronized this species of Government, have erroneously supposed, that by reducing mankind to a perfect equality in their political rights, they would, at the same time, be perfectly equalized and assimilated in their possessions, their opinions, and their passions.

A republic, by which I mean a government in which the scheme of representation takes place, opens a different prospect, and promises the cure for which we are seeking. Let us examine the points in which it varies from pure democracy, and we shall comprehend both the nature of the cure and the efficacy which it must derive from the union.

The two great points of difference, between a democracy and a republic, are, first, the delegation of the government, in the latter, to a small number of citizens, elected by the rest; secondly, the greater number of citizens, and greater sphere of country, over which the latter may be extended.

The effect of the first difference is, on the one hand, to refine and enlarge the public views, by passing them through the medium of a chosen body of citizens, whose wisdom may best discern the true interest of their country, and whose patriotism and love of justice, will be least likely to sacrifice it to temporary or partial considerations. Under such a regulation, it may well happen, that the public voice, pronounced by the representatives of the people, will be more consonant to the public good, than if pronounced by the people themselves, convened for the purpose. On the other hand the effect may be inverted. Men of factious tempers, of local prejudices, or of sinister designs, may by intrigue, by corruption, or by other means, first obtain the suffrages, and then betray the interest of the people. The question resulting is, whether small or extensive republics are most favorable to the election of proper guardians of the public weal, and it is clearly decided in favor of the latter by two obvious considerations.

In the first place, it is to be remarked that, however small the republic may be, the representatives must be raised to a certain number, in order to guard against the cabals of a few; and that however large it may be, they must be limited to a certain number, in order to guard against the confusion of a multitude. Hence, the number of representatives in the two cases not being in proportion to that of the constituents, and being proportionally greatest in the small republic, it follows, that if the proportion of fit characters be not less in the large than in the small republic, the former will present a greater option, and consequently a greater probability of a fit choice.

In the next place, as each Representative will be chosen by a greater number of citizens in the large than in the small Republic, it will be more difficult for unworthy candidates to practise with success the vicious arts, by which elections are too often carried; and the suffrages of the people being more free, will be more likely to center on men who possess the most attractive merit, and the most diffusive and established characters.

It must be confessed, that in this, as in most other cases, there is a mean, on both sides of which inconveniences will be found to lie. By enlarging too much the number of electors, you render the representatives too little acquainted with all their local circumstances and lesser interests; as by reducing it too much, you render him unduly attached to these, and too little fit to comprehend and pursue great and national objects. The Federal Constitution forms a happy combination in this respect; the great and aggregate interests being referred to the national, the local and particular, to the state legislatures.

The other point of difference is, the greater number of citizens and extent of territory which may be brought within the compass of Republican, than of Democratic Government; and it is this circumstance principally which renders factious combinations less to be dreaded in the former, than in the latter. The smaller the society, the fewer probably will be the distinct parties and interests composing it; the fewer the distinct parties and interests, the more frequently will a majority be found of the same party; and the smaller the number of individuals composing a majority, and the smaller the compass within which they are placed, the more easily will they concert and execute their plans of oppression. Extend the sphere, and you take in a greater variety of parties and interests; you make it less probable that a majority of the whole will have a common motive to invade the rights of other citizens; or if such a common motive exists, it will be more difficult for all who feel it to discover their own strength, and to act in unison with each other. Besides other impediments, it may be remarked, that where there is a consciousness of unjust or dishonorable purposes, communication is always checked by distrust, in proportion to the number whose concurrence is necessary.

Hence it clearly appears, that the same advantage, which a Republic has over a Democracy, in controlling the effects of faction, is enjoyed by a large over a small Republic—is enjoyed by the Union over the States composing it. Does this advantage consist in the substitution of Representatives, whose enlightened views and virtuous sentiments render them superior to local prejudices, and to schemes of injustice? It will not be denied, that the Representation of the Union will be most likely to possess these requisite endowments. Does it consist in the greater security afforded by a greater variety of parties, against the event of any one party being able to outnumber and oppress the rest? In an equal degree does the increased variety of parties, comprised within the Union, increase this security? Does it, in fine, consist in the greater obstacles opposed to the concert and accomplishment of the secret wishes of an unjust and interested majority? Here, again, the extent of the Union gives it the most palpable advantage.

The influence of factious leaders may kindle a flame within their particular States, but will be unable to spread a general conflagration through the other States: a religious sect, may degenerate into a political faction in a part of the Confederacy but the variety of sects dispersed over the entire face of it, must secure the national Councils against any danger from that source: a rage for paper money, for an abolition of debts, for an equal division of property, or for any other improper or wicked project, will be less apt to pervade the whole body of the Union, than a particular member of it; in the same proportion as such a malady is more likely to taint a particular county or district, than an entire State.

In the extent and proper structure of the Union, therefore, we behold a Republican remedy for the diseases most incident to Republican Government. And according to the degree of pleasure and pride, we feel in being Republicans, ought to be our zeal in cherishing the spirit, and supporting the character of Federalists.

Publius

Appendix IV

The Federalist No. 51

February 6, 1788
James Madison

TO THE PEOPLE OF THE STATE OF NEW YORK.

To what expedient then shall we finally resort for maintaining in practice the necessary partition of power among the several departments, as laid down in the constitution? The only answer that can be given is, that as all these exterior provisions are found to be inadequate, the defect must be supplied, by so contriving the interior structure of the government, as that its several constituent parts may, by their mutual relations, be the means of keeping each other in their proper places. Without presuming to undertake a full development of this important idea, I will hazard a few general observations, which may perhaps place it in a clearer light, and enable us to form a more correct judgment of the principles and structure of the government planned by the convention.

In order to lay a due foundation for that separate and distinct exercise of the different powers of government, which to a certain extent, is admitted on all hands to be essential to the preservation of liberty, it is evident that each department should have a will of its own; and consequently should be so constituted, that the members of each should have as little agency as possible in the appointment of the members of the others. Were this principle rigorously adhered to, it would require that all the appointments for the supreme executive, legislative, and judiciary magistracies, should be drawn from the same fountain of authority, the people, through channels, having no communication whatever with one another. Perhaps such a plan of constructing the several departments would be less difficult in practice than it may in contemplation appear. Some difficulties however, and some additional expense, would attend the execution of it. Some deviations therefore from the principle must be admitted. In the constitution of the judiciary department in particular, it might be inexpedient to insist rigorously on the principle; first, because peculiar qualifications being essential in the members, the primary consideration ought to be to select that mode of choice, which best secures these qualifications; secondly, because the permanent tenure by which the appointments are held in that department, must soon destroy all sense of dependence on the authority conferring them.

It is equally evident that the members of each department should be as little dependent as possible on those of the others, for the emoluments annexed to their offices. Were the executive magistrate, or the judges, not independent of the legislature in this particular, their independence in every other would be merely nominal.

But the great security against a gradual concentration of the several powers in the same department, consists in giving to those who administer each department, the necessary constitutional means, and personal motives, to resist encroachments of the others. The provision for defense must in this, as in all other cases, be made commensurate to the danger of attack. Ambition must be made to counteract ambition. The interest of the man must be connected with the constitutional right of the place. It may be a reflection on human nature, that such devices should be necessary to control the abuses of government. But what is government itself but the greatest of all reflections on human nature? If men were angels, no government would be necessary. If angels were to govern men, neither external nor internal controls on government would be necessary. In framing a government which is to be administered by men over men, the great difficulty lies in this: You must first enable the government to control the governed; and in the next place, oblige it to control itself. A dependence on the people is no doubt the primary control on the government; but experience has taught mankind the necessity of auxiliary precautions.

This policy of supplying by opposite and rival interests, the defect of better motives, might be traced through the whole system of human affairs, private as well as public. We see it particularly displayed in all the subordinate distributions of power; where the constant aim is to divide and arrange the several offices in such a manner as that each may be a check on the other; that the private interest of every individual, may be a sentinel over the public rights. These inventions of prudence cannot be less requisite in the distribution of the supreme powers of the state.

But it is not possible to give to each department an equal power of self defense. In republican government the legislative authority, necessarily, predominates. The remedy for this inconveniency is, to divide the legislature into different branches; and to render them by different modes of election, and different principles of action, as little connected with each other, as the nature of their common functions, and their common dependence on the society, will admit. It may even be necessary to guard against dangerous encroachments by still further precautions. As the weight of the legislative authority requires that it should be thus divided, the weakness of the executive may require, on the other hand, that it should be fortified. An absolute negative, on the legislature, appears at first view to be the natural defense with which the executive magistrate should be armed. But perhaps it would be neither altogether safe, nor alone sufficient. On ordinary occasions, it might not be exerted with the requisite firmness; and on extraordinary occasions, it might be perfidiously abused. May not this defect of an absolute negative be supplied, by some qualified connection between this weaker department, and the weaker branch of the stronger department, by which the latter may be led to support the constitutional rights of the former, without being too much detached from the rights of its own department?

If the principles on which these observations are founded be just, as I persuade myself they are, and they be applied as a criterion, to the several state constitutions, and to the federal constitution, it will be found, that if the latter does not perfectly correspond with them, the former are infinitely less able to bear such a test.

There are moreover two considerations particularly applicable to the federal system of America, which place that system in a very interesting point of view.

First. In a single republic, all the power surrendered by the people, is submitted to the administration of a single government; and usurpations are guarded against by a division of the government into distinct and separate departments. In the compound republic of America, the power surrendered by the people, is first divided between two distinct governments, and then the portion allotted to each, subdivided among distinct and separate departments. Hence a double security arises to the rights of the people. The different governments will control each other; at the same time that each will be controlled by itself.

Second. It is of great importance in a republic, not only to guard the society against the oppression of its rulers; but to guard one part of the society against the injustice of the other part. Different interests necessarily exist in different classes of citizens. If a majority be united by a common interest, the rights of the minority will be insecure. There are but two methods of providing against this evil: The one by creating a will in the community independent of the majority, that is, of the society itself, the other by comprehending in the society so many separate descriptions of citizens, as will render an unjust combination of a majority of the whole, very improbable, if not impracticable. The first method prevails in all governments possessing an hereditary or self appointed authority. This at best is but a precarious security; because a power independent of the society may as well espouse the unjust views of the major, as the rightful interests, of the minor party, and may possibly be turned against both parties. The second method will be exemplified in the federal republic of the United States. While all authority in it will be derived from and dependent on the society, the society itself will be broken into so many parts, interests and classes of citizens, that the rights of individuals or of the minority, will be in little danger from interested combinations of the majority. In a free government, the security for civil rights must be the same as for religious rights. It consists in the one case in the multiplicity of interests, and in the other, in the multiplicity of sects. The degree of security in both cases will depend on the number of interests and sects; and this may be presumed to depend on the extent of country and number of people comprehended under the same government. This view of the subject must particularly recommend a proper federal system to all the sincere and considerate friends of republican government: Since it shows that in exact proportion as the territory of the union may be formed into more circumscribed confederacies or states, oppressive combinations of a majority will be facilitated, the best security under the republican form, for the rights of every class of citizens, will be diminished; and consequently, the stability and independence of some member of the government, the only other security, must be proportionally increased. Justice is the end of government. It is the end of civil society. It ever has been, and ever will be pursued, until it be obtained, or until liberty be lost in the pursuit. In a society under the forms of which the stronger faction can readily unite and oppress the weaker, anarchy may as truly be said to reign, as in a state of nature where the weaker individual is not secured against the violence of the stronger: And as in the latter state even the stronger individuals are prompted by the uncertainty of their condition, to submit to a government which may protect the weak as well as themselves: So in the former state, will the more powerful factions or parties be gradually induced by a like motive, to wish for a government which will protect all parties, the weaker as well as the more powerful. It can be little doubted, that if the state of Rhode Island was separated from the confederacy, and left to itself, the insecurity of rights under the popular form of government within such narrow limits, would be displayed by such reiterated oppressions of factious majorities, that some power altogether independent of the people would soon be called for by the voice of the very factions whose misrule had proved the necessity of it. In the extended republic of the United States, and among the great variety of interests, parties and sects which it embraces, a coalition of a majority of the whole society could seldom take place on any other principles than those of justice and the general good; and there being thus less danger to a minor from the will of the major party, there must be less pretext also, to provide for the security of the former, by introducing into the government a will not dependent on the latter; or in other words, a will independent of the society itself. It is no less certain than it is important, notwithstanding the contrary opinions which have been entertained, that the larger the society, provided it lie within a practicable sphere, the more duly capable it will be of self government. And happily for the republican cause, the practicable sphere may be carried to a very great extent, by a judicious modification and mixture of the federal principle.

Publius

Appendix V

Presidents of the United States

President	Year	Party	Most Noteworthy Event
George Washington	1789–1797	Federalist	Establishment of Federal Judiciary
John Adams	1797–1801	Federalist	Alien-Sedition Acts
Thomas Jefferson	1801–1809	Dem.–Republican	First President to Defeat Incumbent/Louisiana Purchase
James Madison	1809–1817	Dem.–Republican	War of 1812
James Monroe	1817–1825	Dem.–Republican	Monroe Doctrine/ Missouri Compromise
John Quincy Adams	1825–1829	Dem.–Republican	Elected by "King Caucus"
Andrew Jackson	1829–1837	Democratic	Set up Spoils System
Martin Van Buren	1837–1841	Democratic	Competitive Parties Established
William H. Harrison	1841	Whig	Universal White Male Suffrage
John Tyler	1841–1845	Whig	Texas Annexed
James K. Polk	1845–1849	Democratic	Mexican-American War
Zachary Taylor	1849–1850	Whig	California Gold Rush
Millard Fillmore	1850–1853	Whig	Compromise of 1850
Franklin Pierce	1853–1857	Democratic	Republican Party Formed
James Buchanan	1857–1861	Democratic	Dred Scott Decision
Abraham Lincoln	1861–1865	Republican	Civil War
Andrew Johnson	1865–1869	Republican	First Impeachment of President
Ulysses S. Grant	1869–1877	Republican	Reconstruction of South
Rutherford B. Hayes	1877–1881	Republican	End of Reconstruction
James A. Garfield	1881	Republican	Assassinated by Job-seeker
Chester A. Arthur	1881–1885	Republican	Civil Service Reform
Grover Cleveland	1885–1889	Democratic	Casts 102 Vetoes in One Year
Benjamin Harrison	1889–1893	Republican	McKinley Law Raises Tarrifs
Grover Cleveland	1893–1897	Democratic	Depression/Pullman Strike
William McKinley	1897–1901	Republican	Spanish-American War
Theodore Roosevelt	1901–1909	Republican	Conservation/Panama Canal
William H. Taft	1909–1913	Republican	Judicial Reform
Woodrow Wilson	1913–1921	Democratic	Progressive Reforms/ World War I
Warren G. Harding	1921–1923	Republican	Return to Normalcy
Calvin Coolidge	1923–1929	Republican	Cuts Taxes/Promotes Business
Herbert C. Hoover	1929–1933	Republican	Great Depression
Franklin D. Roosevelt	1933–1945	Democratic	New Deal/ World War II
Harry S Truman	1945–1953	Democratic	Beginning of Cold War
Dwight D. Eisenhower	1953–1961	Republican	End of Korean War
John F. Kennedy	1961–1963	Democratic	Cuban Missile Crisis
Lyndon B. Johnson	1963–1969	Democratic	Great Society/Vietnam War
Richard M. Nixon	1969–1974	Republican	Watergate Scandal
Gerald R. Ford	1974–1977	Republican	War Powers Resolution
James Earl Carter	1977–1981	Democratic	Iranian Hostage Crisis
Ronald Reagan	1981–1989	Republican	Tax Cut/ Expenditure Cuts
George Bush	1989–1993	Republican	End of Cold War/Persian Gulf War
William J. Clinton	1993–2001	Democratic	Deficit Reduction
George W. Bush	2001–	Republican	U.S. Response to Terrorism

Refer to www.ablongman.com.fiorina

Glossary

administration   The president and his political appointees responsible for directing the executive branch of government.

administrative discretion   Power to interpret a legislative mandate.

advice and consent   Support for a presidential action by a designated number of senators.

affirmative action   Programs designed to enhance opportunities for groups that have suffered discrimination in the past.

affirmative action redistricting   The process of drawing district lines to maximize the number of majority-minority districts.

agency   Basic organizational unit of federal government. Also known as *office* or *bureau*.

agenda setting   Making an issue so visible that important political leaders take it seriously; occurs when the media affect the issues and problems people think about, even if the media do not determine what positions people adopt.

ambassador   The head of a diplomatic delegation to a major foreign country.

Annapolis Convention   1786 meeting to discuss constitutional reform.

Anti-Federalists   Those who opposed ratification of the Constitution.

appeal   The procedure whereby the losing side asks a higher court to overturn a lower-court decision.

appropriations process   Process of providing funding for governmental activities and programs that have been authorized.

aristocracy   Government by a few leaders made eligible by birthright.

Articles of Confederation   The first (1781–1789) basic governing document of the United States and forerunner to the Constitution.

associate justice   One of the eight justices of the Supreme Court who are not the chief justice.

authorization process   Term applied to the entire process of providing statutory authority for a government program or activity.

bipolar   Cold War view of the world as divided into two centers of power, the United States and its allies, and Soviet Union and its allies.

balancing doctrine   The principle enunciated by the courts that freedom of speech must be balanced against other competing public interests at stake in particular circumstances.

Bay of Pigs   Location of CIA-supported effort by Cuban exiles in 1961 to invade Cuba and overthrow Fidel Castro.

beltway insider   Person living in the Washington metropolitan area who is engaged in, or well informed about, national politics and government.

bicameral   Containing two chambers, as does a legislature such as the U.S. Congress.

bad tendency test   Rule from English law aying that expression could be punished it it could ultimately lead to illegal behavior.

Bill of Rights   The first ten amendments to the Constitution, which protect individual and state rights.

black codes   Restrictive laws that applied to newly freed slaves but not to whites.

blame avoidance   Set of political techniques employed by political leaders to disguise their actions and shift blame to others.

bloc voting   Voting in which nearly all members of one group (such as African Americans) vote for a candidate of their race, whereas nearly all members of another group (such as whites) vote against that candidate.

block grant   Federal grants to a state and/or local government that impose minimal restrictions on the use of funds.

borking   Politicizing the nomination process through an organized public campaign that portrays the nominee as a dangerous extremist.

brief   Written arguments presented to a court by lawyers on behalf of clients.

Brown v. Board of Education of Topeka, Kansas   1954 Supreme Court decision declaring racial segregation in schools unconstitutional.

budget   The government's annual plan for taxing and spending.

bully pulpit   The nature of presidential status as an ideal vehicle for persuading the public to support the president's policies.

bureaucracy   Hierarchical organization designed to perform a particular set of tasks.

business cycle   The alternation of periods of economic growth with periods of economic slowdown.

cabinet   Top administration officials; mostly heads of departments in the executive branch.

casework   Effort of members of Congress to help individuals and groups when they have difficulties with federal agencies.

categorical grant   Federal grants to a state and/or local government that impose programmatic restrictions on the use of funds.

caucus   Meeting of candidate supporters that chooses delegates to a state or national convention. All Democratic members of the House or Senate. Members in caucus elect the party leaders, ratify the choice of committee leaders, and debate party positions on issues.

Central Intelligence Agency (CIA)   Agency primarily responsible for gathering and analyzing information about the political and military activities of other nations.

cert   See *writ of certiorari*.

checks and balances   Constitutional division of power into separate institutions, giving each institution the power to block the actions of the others.

chief justice   Head of the Supreme Court.

chief of staff   Head of White House staff. Has continuous, direct contact with the president.

circuit court of appeals   Court to which decisions by federal district courts are appealed.

citizen duty   The belief that it is a citizen's duty to be informed and to participate in politics.

citizenship   Status held by someone entitled to all the rights and privileges of a full-fledged member of a political community.

civic republicanism   A political philosophy that emphasizes the obligation of citizens to act virtuously in pursuit of the common good.

civil code   Laws regulating relations among individuals. Alleged violators are sued by presumed victims, who ask courts to award damages and otherwise offer relief.

civil disobedience   A peaceful, well-publicized violation of a law designed to dramatize that law's injustice.

civil liberties   Fundamental freedoms that together preserve the rights of a free people.

civil rights   Specific rights that embody the general right to equal treatment under the law.

civil rights amendments   The Thirteenth, Fourteenth, and Fifteenth Amendments, which abolished slavery, redefined civil rights and liberties, and guaranteed the right to vote to all adult male citizens.

civil service   A system in which government employees are chosen according to their educational qualifications, performance on examinations, and work experience.

class action suit   Suit brought on behalf of all individuals in a particular category, whether or not they are actually participating in the suit.

clear and present danger doctrine   The principle that people should have complete freedom of speech unless their language endangers the nation.

closed primaries   Primaries in which only party members can vote—and only in the party in which they are registered.

cloture   Motion to end debate; requires 60 votes to pass.

CNN effect   Purported ability of TV to raise a distant foreign affairs situation to national prominence by broadcasting vivid pictures.

coalition government   Occurs when two or more minority parties must join together in order to elect a prime minister. Such governments are common in multi-party systems.

coattails   Positive electoral effect of a popular presidential candidate on congressional candidates of the party.

Cold War   The 43-year period (1946–1989) during which the United States and the Soviet Union threatened one another with mutual destruction by nuclear warfare.

colonial assembly   Lower legislative chamber elected by male property owners in a colony.

colonial council   Upper legislative chamber whose members were appointed by British officials on the recommendation of the governor.

commander in chief   The president in his constitutional role as head of the armed forces.

commerce clause   Constitutional provision that gives Congress power to regulate commerce "among the states."

commercial speech   Advertising or other speech made for business purposes; may be regulated.

communism   An extreme type of socialism based on the work of Karl Marx, who taught that history is a product of the struggle between those who exploit and those who are exploited.

compositional effect   A change in the behavior of a group that arises from a change in the group's composition, not from a change in the behavior of individuals in the group.

concurring opinion   A written opinion prepared by judges who vote with the majority but who wish either to disagree with or to elaborate on some aspect of the majority opinion.

conference committee   Group of representatives from both the House and the Senate who iron out the differences between the two chambers' versions of a bill or resolution.

Congressional Budget Office (CBO)   Congressional agency that evaluates the president's budget as well as the budgetary implications of all other legislation.

Connecticut Compromise   Constitutional Convention proposal that created a House proportionate to population and a Senate in which all states were represented equally.

constituency   Those legally entitled to vote for a public official.

constituency service   The totality of Congress members' district service and constituent assistance work.

Constitution   Basic governing document of the United States.

containment   U.S. policy that attempted to stop the spread of communism in the expectation that this system of government would eventually collapse on its own.

cooperative federalism   See *marble-cake federalism.*

corporatist   The official representation of important interest groups in government decision-making bodies.

Council of Economic Advisors (CEA)   Three economists who head up a professional staff that advises the president on economic policy.

criminal code   Laws regulating relations between individuals and society. Alleged violators are prosecuted by government.

critical election   Election that marks the emergence of a new, lasting alignment of partisan support within the electorate.

debt   The accumulation of yearly deficits.

Declaration of Independence   Document signed in 1776 declaring the United States to be a country independent of Great Britain.

de facto **segregation**   Segregation that occurs as the result of decisions by private individuals.

defendant   One accused of violating the civil or criminal code.

deficit   The amount by which annual spending exceeds revenue.

de jure **segregation**   Racial segregation that is legally sanctioned.

delegate   Role a representative plays when following the wishes of those who have elected him or her.

democracy   System in which governmental power is widely shared among the citizens, usually through free and open elections.

department Organizational unit into which many agencies of the federal government are grouped.

Department of Defense Cabinet department responsible for managing the U.S. armed forces.

deregulation Removal of government rules that once controlled an industry.

devolution Return of governmental responsibilities to state and local governments.

dignified aspect According to Walter Bagehot, the aspect of government, including royalty and ceremony, that generates citizen respect and loyalty.

Dillon's rule Legal doctrine that local governments are mere creatures of the state.

direct action Everything from peaceful sit-ins and demonstrations to riots and even rebellion.

direct democracy Type of democracy in which ordinary people are the government, making all the laws themselves.

direct mail Computer-generated letters, faxes, and other communications to people who might be sympathetic to an appeal for money or support.

direct primary A method of choosing party candidates by popular vote of all self-identified party members. This method of nominating candidates is virtually unknown outside the United States.

dissenting opinion Written opinion presenting the reasoning of judges who vote against the majority.

district attorney Person responsible for prosecuting criminal cases.

divided government Said to exist when a single party does not control the presidency and both houses of Congress.

divine right Doctrine that says God selects the sovereign for the people.

domestic policy Government programs and regulations that directly affect those living within a country.

double jeopardy Fifth Amendment provision that prohibits prosecution for the same offense twice.

dual sovereignty A theory of federalism saying that both the national and state governments have final authority over their own policy domains.

due process clause Found in the Fifth and Fourteenth Amendments to the Constitution; forbids deprivation of life, liberty, or property without due process of law.

earmark A specific congressional designation of the way money is to be spent.

Earned Income Tax Credit (EITC) Provision that gives back tax payments to those who have little income.

efficient aspect According to Walter Bagehot, the aspect of government that involves making policy, administering the laws, and settling disputes.

election-cycle interpretation The argument that, whatever their party, presidents attempt to slow the economy early in their terms and then to expand it as their opportunity for reelection approaches.

electoral college Those chosen to cast a direct vote for president by a process determined by each state.

electoral incentive Desire to obtain or retain elected office.

electoral system A means of translating popular votes into control of public offices.

electoral vote Cast by electors, with each state receiving one vote for each of its members of the House of Representatives and one vote for each of its senators.

embassy The structure that houses ambassadors and their diplomatic aides in the capital cities of foreign countries.

Environmental Protection Agency (EPA) Agency responsible for issuing regulations designed to protect the environment from unwanted pollutants.

equal protection clause Fourteenth Amendment clause specifying that no state can deny any of its people equal protection under the law.

Equal Rights Amendment (ERA) Proposed amendment to the Constitution that banned gender discrimination.

equality of opportunity The notion that individuals should have an equal chance to advance economically through individual talent and hard work.

equal–time rule Promulgated by the FCC, required any station selling time to a candidate to sell time to other candidates at comparable rates.

establishment of religion clause Denies the government the power to establish any single religious practice as superior.

ethnic cleansing Seeking to deport or eliminate entire ethnic groups within a country or region.

exclusionary rule Legal standard that says that illegally obtained evidence cannot be admitted in court.

executive agreement Agreement with foreign countries that requires only a presidential signature.

Executive Office of the President (EOP) Agency that houses both top coordinating offices and other operating agencies.

executive order A presidential directive that has the force of law, though it is not enacted by Congress.

executive privilege The right of members of the executive branch to have private communications among themselves that need not be shared with Congress.

externalities Consequences that affect people who are not directly engaged in the activities that bring those consequences about.

fascism Rule by a dictator supported by a strong party that permeates society; generally supports capital against labor and is associated with extreme nationalism.

federal district courts The lowest level of the federal court system and the courts in which most federal trials are held.

Federal Reserve System The country's central bank, which executes monetary policy by manipulating the supply of funds that lower banks can lend.

federalism Division of sovereignty between at least two different levels of government.

Federalist Papers Essays that were written in support of the Constitution's ratification and have become a classic argument for the American constitutional system.

Federalists Those who wrote and campaigned on behalf of ratification of the Constitution.

fiduciary Someone whose duty is to act in the best interest of someone else.

fighting words doctrine The principle, endorsed by the Supreme Court in *Chaplinsky v. New Hampshire* (1942), that some words constitute violent acts and are therefore not protected under the First Amendment.

filibuster Delaying tactic by which one or more senators refuse to allow a bill or resolution to be considered, either by speaking indefinitely or by offering dilatory motions and amendments.

filing deadline The latest date on which a candidate for office may file official papers or pay required fees to state election officials.

First Continental Congress The first quasi-governmental institution that spoke for nearly all the colonies (1774).

First Lady Traditional title of the president's wife.

fiscal policy The sum total of government taxing and spending decisions, which determines the level of the deficit or surplus.

flat tax A tax that is neither progressive nor regressive; everyone pays at the same rate.

focus groups Small groups used to explore how ordinary people think about issues and how they react to the language of political appeals.

food stamps Public assistance program that provides recipients with stamps that can be used to purchase food.

foreign policy Conduct of relations among nation–states.

foreign service Diplomats who staff U.S. embassies and consulates.

framing Stating an argument in such a way as to emphasize one set of considerations and deemphasize others.

franchise The right to vote.

frank Name given to representatives' and senators' free use of the U.S. mail for sending communications to constituents.

free exercise of religion clause Protects the right of individuals to practice their religion.

free-rider problem Problem that arises when people can enjoy the benefits of group activity without bearing any of the costs.

fundamental freedoms doctrine Court doctrine stating that laws impinging on the freedoms that are fundamental to the preservation of democratic practice—the freedoms of speech, press, assembly, and religion—are to be scrutinized by the courts more closely than other legislation. These are also termed the *preferred freedoms.*

general election Final election that selects the office holder.

general revenue sharing The most comprehensive of block grants, which gives money to state and local governments to be used for any purpose whatsoever.

gerrymandering Drawing boundary lines of congressional districts in order to confer an advantage on some partisan or political interest.

Gideon v. Wainwright Supreme Court decision in 1963 giving indigent people accused of crimes the right to court-appointed counsel.

glass ceiling The invisible barrier that has limited women's opportunities for advancement to the highest ranks of politics, business, and the professions.

government The institution in society that has a "monopoly of the legitimate use of physical force."

government corporation Independent organization created by Congress to fulfill functions related to business.

governor State chief executive whose responsibilities roughly parallel those of the president.

grandfather clause Racially restrictive provision of certain southern laws after Reconstruction, permitting a man to vote if his father or grandfather could have voted.

grassroots lobbying Efforts by groups and associations to influence elected officials indirectly, by arousing their constituents.

Great Society Series of programs enacted under President Lyndon Johnson, designed to address social ills in the nation's poor, elderly, and minority communities.

gross domestic product (GDP) The measure of the total value of economic activity in a nation in one year.

hammer Harsh penalty set by Congress to be imposed if a regulatory agency does not achieve a statutory objective.

Hatch Act 1939 law prohibiting federal employees from engaging in political campaigning and solicitation.

honeymoon Period early in a president's term when partisan conflict and media criticism are minimal.

idealists Those who say that U.S. foreign policy should be guided primarily by democratic principles—the spread of liberty, equality, human rights, and respect for international law throughout the world.

ideology System of beliefs in which one or more organizing principles connect the individual's views on a wide range of issues.

impeachment Recommendation by a majority of the House of Representatives that a president, other official in the executive branch, or judge of the federal courts be removed from office; removal depends on a two-thirds vote of the Senate.

implementation The way in which grant programs are administered at the local level.

incumbency advantage The electoral advantage a candidate enjoys by virtue of being an incumbent, over and above his or her other personal and political characteristics.

independent counsel (Originally called special prosecutor) Legal officer appointed by a court to investigate allegations of criminal activity on the part of high-ranking members of the executive branch. Law expired in 1999.

independent regulatory agencies Agencies that have quasi-judicial responsibilities.

individual motivations for voting The tangible and intangible benefits and costs of exercising one's right to vote.

inflation A sustained rise in the price level such that people need more money to purchase the same amount of goods and services.

information cost The time and mental effort required to absorb and store information, whether from conversations, personal experiences, or the media.

inherent executive power   Presidential authority inherent in the executive branch of government, though not specifically mentioned in the Constitution.

initiative   Proposed laws or state constitutional amendments placed on the ballot via citizen petition.

inner cabinet   The four original departments (State, Defense, Treasury, and Justice) whose secretaries typically have the closest ties to the president.

interest group   Organization or association of people with common interests that engages in politics on behalf of its members.

intergovernmental grant   Grant from the national government to a state or local government.

Iran–Contra affair   An allegedly illegal diversion of funds, derived from the sale of arms to Iran, to a guerrilla group in Nicaragua during the Reagan administration.

iron triangle   Close, stable connection among agencies, interest groups, and congressional committees.

issue advocacy   Advertising campaigns that attempt to influence public opinion on an issue.

issue network   Loose, competitive relationship among policy experts, interest groups, congressional committees, and government agencies.

issue public   Group of people particularly affected by or concerned with a specific issue.

Jim Crow laws   Laws passed by southern states after Reconstruction, enforcing segregation.

Joint Chiefs of Staff   The heads of all the military services, together with a chair and vice-chair nominated by the president and confirmed by the Senate.

judicial activism   Doctrine that says the principle of *stare decisis* should sometimes be sacrificed in order to adapt the Constitution to changing conditions.

judicial restraint   Doctrine that says courts should, if at all possible, avoid overturning a prior court decision.

judicial review   Power of the courts to declare null and void laws of Congress and of state legislatures they find unconstitutional.

Keynesianism   Economic policy based on the belief that governments can control the economy by manipulating demand, running deficits to expand it and surpluses to contract it.

laboratories of democracy   Doctrine that state and local governments contribute to democracy by providing places where experiments are tried and new theories tested.

law clerk   Young, influential aide to a Supreme Court justice.

League of Nations   International organization created after World War I to settle international disputes; precursor of the United Nations.

legal distinction   The legal difference between a case at hand and previous cases decided by the courts.

libel   False statement defaming another.

liberalism   A philosophy that elevates and empowers the individual as opposed to religious, hereditary, governmental, or other forms of authority.

line item veto   Presidential authority to negate particular provisions of a law, granted by Congress in 1996 but struck down by the Supreme Court in 1998; power (enjoyed by most governors) to reject specific components of legislation rather than rejecting entire bills.

living-constitution theory   A theory of constitutional interpretation that places the meaning of the Constitution in light of the total history of the United States.

lobbying   Interest-group activities intended to influence directly the decisions that public officials make.

lobbyist   One who engages in lobbying.

log-rolling   Colloquial term given to politicians' trading of favors, votes, or generalized support for each other's proposals.

machine   A highly organized party under the control of a boss, based on patronage and control of government activities. Machines were common in many cities in the late nineteenth and early twentieth centuries.

majority   50 percent plus one.

majority leader   Title used for the Speaker's chief lieutenant in the House and for the most important officer in the Senate. Each is responsible for managing the floor of his or her chamber.

majority-minority district   District in which a minority group is the numerical majority.

Mapp v. Ohio   Supreme Court decision saying that any evidence obtained without a proper search warrant may not be introduced in a trial.

marble-cake federalism   The theory that all levels of government can work together to solve common problems. Also known as *cooperative federalism*.

Marbury v. Madison   Supreme Court decision (1803) in which the court first exercised the power of judicial review.

markup   Process in which a committee or subcommittee considers and revises a bill that has been introduced.

mass media   Means of communication that are technologically capable of reaching most people and economically affordable to most.

mass public   Ordinary people for whom politics is a peripheral concern.

matching funds   Public moneys (from $3 check-offs on income tax returns) that the Federal Election Commission distributes to primary candidates according to a prespecified formula.

Mayflower Compact   First document in colonial America in which the people gave their expressed consent to be governed.

McCulloch v. Maryland   Decision of 1819 in which the Supreme Court declared unconstitutional the state's power to tax a federal government entity.

measurement error   The error that arises from attempting to measure something as subjective as opinion.

Medicaid   Program that provides medical care to those of low income.

Medicare   Program that provides social security recipients a broad range of medical benefits.

minimal-effects thesis Theory that the mass media have little or no effect on public opinion.

minority leader Leader of the minority party, who speaks for the party in dealing with the majority.

Miranda v. Arizona Supreme Court decision stating that accused persons must be told by police that they need not testify against themselves.

monetarism An economic school of thought that rejects Keynesianism, arguing that the money supply is the most important influence on the economy.

monetary policy The actions taken by government to vary the supply of money in an effort to stabilize the business cycle.

Monroe Doctrine Policy that declared the Western Hemisphere to be free of European colonial influence (1819).

mugwumps A group of civil service reformers organized in the 1880s who maintained that government officials should be chosen on a merit basis.

multiculturalism The idea that ethnic and cultural groups should maintain their identity within the larger society and respect one another's differences.

multi-party system System in which more than two parties compete for control of government. Most of the world's democracies are multi-party systems.

multiple referrals Said to occur when party leaders give more than one committee responsibility for considering a bill.

nation building Interventions designed to enhance democratic practices in another country.

National Association for the Advancement of Colored People (NAACP) Civil rights organization, dating from 1909, that relied heavily on a legal strategy to pursue its objectives.

national convention Quadrennial gathering of party officials and delegates who select presidential and vice-presidential nominees and adopt party platforms. Extension of the direct primary to the presidential level after 1968 has greatly reduced the importance of the conventions.

national forces Electoral effects felt across most states and congressional districts, most often generated by especially strong or weak presidential performance, party performance, or the state of the economy.

National Security Council (NSC) White House agency responsible for coordinating U.S. foreign policy.

natural monopoly A situation in which a public service is best provided by a single company.

necessary and proper clause Constitutional clause that gives Congress the power to take all actions that are "necessary and proper" to the carrying out of its delegated powers. Also known as the *elastic clause*.

New Deal Programs created by the Franklin Roosevelt administration that expanded the power of the federal government for the purpose of stimulating economic recovery and establishing a national safety net.

New Jersey Plan Small-state proposal for constitutional reform.

new media Cable and satellite TV, fax, e-mail, and the Internet—the media that have grown out of the technological advances of the past few decades.

NIMBY problem Everyone wants the problem solved, but "Not In My Back Yard."

nullification A doctrine that says that states have the authority to declare acts of Congress unconstitutional.

obscenity Publicly offensive language or portrayals with no redeeming social value.

Office of Management and Budget (OMB) Agency responsible for coordinating the work of departments and agencies of the executive branch.

oligarchy Government by a few who gain office by means of wealth, military power, or membership in a single political party.

open primaries Primaries in which any registered voter can vote in any party's primary.

open seat A House or Senate race with no incumbent (because of death or retirement).

opinion In legal parlance, a court's written explanation of its decision.

original-intent theory A theory of constitutional interpretation that determines the constitutionality of a law by ascertaining the intentions of those who wrote the Constitution.

outer cabinet Newer departments that have fewer ties to the president and are more influenced by interest-group pressures.

override Congressional passage of a bill by a two-thirds vote over the president's veto.

overvotes Ballots that have more than one choice for an office (e.g., for president in 2000), whether because the voter voted for more than one candidate or wrote in a name as well as making a mark.

partisan interpretation The argument that Democratic administrations set economic policy to benefit lower-income, wage-earning groups and that Republican administrations set economic policy to benefit higher-income, business, and professional groups.

party alignment The existence of social and economic groups that consistently support each party.

party caucus All Democratic members of the House or Senate. Members in caucus elect the party leaders, ratify the choice of committee leaders, and debate party positions on issues.

party conference What Republicans call their caucus.

party identification A person's subjective feeling of affiliation with a party.

party image A set of widely held associations between a party and particular issues and values.

Patriots Political group defending colonial American liberties against British infringements.

patronage Appointment of individuals to public office in exchange for their political support. Widely practiced in the eighteenth and nineteenth centuries and continues to present day.

Pendleton Act Legislation in 1883 creating the Civil Service Commission.

permanent campaign Condition that prevails when the next election campaign begins as soon as the last has ended and the line between electioneering and governing has disappeared.

plain meaning of the text theory A theory of constitutional interpretation that determines the constitutionality of a law in light of what the words of the Constitution obviously seem to say.

plaintiff One who brings legal charges against another.

plea bargain Agreement between prosecution and defense that the accused will admit having committed a crime, provided that other charges are dropped and the recommended sentence is shortened.

plenary session Activities of a court in which all judges participate.

Plessy v. Ferguson Court decision declaring separate but equal public facilities constitutional.

pluralism A school of thought holding that politics is the clash of groups that represent all important interests in society and that check and balance each other.

pocket veto Presidential veto after congressional adjournment, executed merely by not signing a bill into law.

policy deliberation Debate and discussion by groups and political leaders over issues placed on the policy agenda.

policy enactment Passage of a law by public officials.

policy implementation Translation of legislation into a set of government programs or regulations.

policy outcome Effect of policy outputs on individuals and businesses.

policy output Provision of services to citizens or regulation of their conduct.

political action committee (PAC) Specialized organization for raising and contributing campaign funds.

political activists People who voluntarily participate in politics; they are more interested in and committed to particular issues and candidates than are ordinary citizens.

political culture Collection of beliefs and values about the justification and operation of a country's government.

political efficacy The belief that one can make a difference in politics by expressing an opinion or acting politically.

political elite Activists and office holders who are deeply interested in and knowledgeable about politics.

political entrepreneurs People willing to assume the costs of forming and maintaining an organization even when others may free-ride on them.

political parties Groups of like-minded people who band together in an attempt to win control of government.

political socialization The set of psychological and sociological processes by which families, schools, religious organizations, communities, and other societal units inculcate beliefs and values in their members.

poll tax Fee that one must pay in order to be allowed to vote.

popular model of democracy Type of representative democracy in which ordinary people participate actively and closely constrain the actions of public officials.

popular vote The total vote cast for a candidate across the nation.

pork barrel projects Special legislative benefits targeted toward the constituents of particular members of Congress.

precedent Previous court decision or ruling applicable to a particular case.

president pro tempore President of the Senate, who presides in the absence of the vice-president.

presidential popularity Evaluation of president by voters, usually as measured by a survey question asking the adult population how well they think the president is doing the job.

primary election Preliminary election that narrows the number of candidates by determining who will be the nominees in the general election.

priming Occurs when the media affect the standards people use to evaluate political figures or the severity of a problem.

prior restraint doctrine Legal doctrine that gives individuals the right to publish without prior restraint—that is, without first submitting material to a government censor.

professional legislature Legislature whose members serve full-time and for long periods.

progressive tax A tax structured so that higher-income people pay a larger proportion of their income in taxes than do lower-income people.

Progressives Middle-class reformers of the late nineteenth and early twentieth centuries who weakened the power of the machines and attempted to clean up elections and government.

proportional representation (PR) Electoral system in which parties receive a share of seats in parliament that is proportional to the popular vote they receive.

proposition A shorthand reference to an initiative or a referendum.

proprietary colony Colony governed either by a prominent English noble or by a company. See *royal colony*.

prospective voting Voting on the basis of the candidates' policy promises.

public assistance Programs that provide to low-income households a limited income and access to essential goods and services.

public defender Attorney whose full-time responsibilities are to provide for the legal defense of indigent criminal suspects.

public goods Goods enjoyed simultaneously by a group, as opposed to a private good that must be divided up to be shared.

public opinion The aggregation of people's views about issues, situations, and public figures.

quota Specific number of positions set aside for a specific group; said by the Supreme Court to be unconstitutional.

"rally 'round the flag" effect   The tendency for the public to back presidents in moments of crisis.

realigning election   Another term for a critical election.

realignment   Occurs when the pattern of group support for political parties shifts in a significant and lasting way.

realists   Those who say that U.S. foreign policy best protects democracy when it safeguards its own economic and military strength.

reapportionment   Redrawing of electoral district lines to reflect population changes; the allocation of House seats to the states after each decennial census.

recall election   Attempt to remove an official from office before completion of the term.

receiver   Court official who has the authority to see that judicial orders are carried out.

recess appointment   An appointment made when the Senate is in recess.

recession   A slowdown in economic activity, officially defined as a decline that persists for two quarters (six months).

Reconstruction   Period after the Civil War when southern states were subject to a federal military presence.

redistricting   Drawing new boundaries of congressional districts, usually after the decennial census.

referendum   A law or state constitutional amendment that is proposed by a legislature or city council but does not go into effect unless the required majority of voters approve it.

registered voters   Those legally eligible to vote who have registered in accordance with the requirements prevailing in their state and locality.

regressive tax   A tax structured so that higher-income people pay a smaller proportion of their income in taxes than do lower-income people.

regulation   Rules and standards that control economic, social, and political activities.

remand   To send a case to a lower court to determine the best way of implementing the higher court's decision.

remedy   Court-ordered action designed to compensate plaintiffs for wrongs they have suffered.

rent subsidies   Help in paying rent for low-income families, provided that they select designated housing.

representative democracy   An indirect form of democracy in which the people choose representatives who determine what government does.

responsible model of democracy   Type of representative democracy in which public officials have considerable freedom of action but are held accountable by the people for the decisions they make.

restorationist   Judge who thinks that the only way the original meaning of the Constitution can be restored is by ignoring the doctrine of *stare decisis* until liberal decisions have been reversed.

restrictive housing covenant   Legal promise by home buyers that they would not resell to an African American; enforcement declared unconstitutional by Supreme Court.

retrospective voting   Voting on the basis of the past performance of the incumbent administration.

reversal   The overturning of a lower-court decision by an appeals court or the Supreme Court.

right of privacy   Right to keep free of government interference those aspects of one's personal life that do not affect others.

rotation   The practice whereby a member of Congress stepped down after a term or two so that someone else could have the office.

royal colony   Colony governed by the king's representative with the advice of an elected assembly. See *proprietary colony.*

rule   Specifies the terms and conditions under which a bill or resolution will be considered on the floor of the House—in particular, how long debate will last, how time will be allocated, and the number and type of amendments that will be in order.

safe seat   A congressional district certain to vote for the candidate of one party

sampling error   The error that arises in public opinion surveys as a result of relying on a representative but small sample of the larger population.

Second Continental Congress   Political authority that directed the struggle for independence beginning in 1775.

secretary   Head of a department within the executive branch.

secretary of defense   The president's chief civilian adviser on defense matters and overall head of the army, navy, and air force.

secretary of state   Officially, the president's chief foreign policy advisor and head of the Department of State, the agency responsible for conducting diplomatic relations.

select committee   Temporary committee appointed to deal with a specific issue or problem.

selection bias   The error that occurs when a sample systematically includes or excludes people with certain attitudes.

selection principle   Rule of thumb according to which stories with certain characteristics are chosen over stories without those characteristics.

selective benefits   Side benefits of belonging to an organization that are limited to contributing members of the organization.

selective incorporation   The case-by-case incorporation, by the courts, of the Bill of Rights into the due process clause of the Fourteenth Amendment.

selective perception   Tendency to discount information that is inconsistent with one's prior predispositions in favor of information consistent with what one already believes.

semi-closed primaries   Primaries in which independents can vote in one of the party primaries.

senatorial courtesy   An informal rule that the Senate will not confirm nominees within or from a state unless they have the approval of the senior senator of that state from the president's party.

seniority   Practice by which the majority party member with the longest continuous service on a committee becomes the chair.

separate but equal doctrine   Rule stating that the equal protection clause was not violated by the fact of racial segregation alone, provided that the separated facilities were equal.

separation of church and state doctrine   The principle that a wall should separate the government from religious activity.

separation of powers   A system of government in which different institutions exercise different components of governmental power.

sequester   To house jurors privately, away from any information other than that presented in the courtroom.

Shays's Rebellion   Uprising in western Massachusetts in 1786 led by Revolutionary War captain Daniel Shays.

sin tax   A tax intended to discourage unwanted behavior.

single-issue group   An interest group narrowly focused to influence policy on a single issue.

single-issue voter   Voter who cares so deeply about some particular issue that a candidate's position on this one issue determines his or her vote.

single-member, simple plurality (SMSP) system   Electoral system in which the country is divided into geographic districts, and the candidates who win the most votes within their districts are elected.

social connectedness   The degree to which individuals are integrated into society—families, churches, neighborhoods, groups, and so forth.

social insurance   Program that provides benefits in return for contributions made by workers.

social issues   Issues (such as abortion, obscenity, gay rights, capital punishment, gun control, and prayer in schools) that reflect personal values more than economic interests.

social movement   Broad-based demand for government action on some problem or issue, such as civil rights for blacks and women or environmental protection.

social policy   Domestic policy programs designed to help those thought to be in need of government assistance.

social security   Social insurance program for senior citizens.

socialism   A philosophy that supports government ownership and operation of the means of production, as well as government determination of the level of social and economic benefits that people receive.

socialization   The end result of all the processes by which individuals form their beliefs and values in their homes, schools, churches, communities, and workplaces.

solicitor general   Government official responsible for presenting before the courts the position of the presidential administration.

sovereignty   Fundamental governmental authority.

Speaker   The presiding officer of the House of Representatives; normally, the Speaker is the leader of the majority party.

spending clause   Constitutional provision that gives Congress the power to collect taxes to provide for the general welfare.

spin   The positive or negative slant that reporters or anchors put on their reports.

spoils system   A system of government employment in which workers are hired on the basis of party loyalty.

sponsor   Representative or senator who introduces a bill or resolution.

Stamp Act Congress   A meeting in 1765 of delegates from nine colonies to oppose the Stamp Act; the first political organization that brought leaders from several colonies together for a common purpose.

stamp tax   Passed by Parliament in 1765, it required people in the colonies to purchase a small stamp to be affixed to legal and other documents.

standing committee   Committee with fixed membership and jurisdiction, continuing from Congress to Congress.

stare decisis   In court rulings, reliance on consistency with precedents. See also *precedent*.

state action doctrine   Rule stating that only the actions of state and local governments, not those of private individuals, must conform to the equal protection clause.

State of the Union address   Annual speech delivered by the president in fulfillment of the constitutional obligation of reporting to Congress on the state of the Union.

state sovereign immunity   Legal doctrine, based on the Eleventh Amendment, that says states cannot be sued under federal law.

statutory interpretation   The judicial act of interpreting and applying the law to particular cases.

subgovernment   Alliance of a congressional committee, a bureaucratic agency, and a small number of allied interest groups that combine to dominate policy making in some specified policy area.

suffrage   Another term for the right to vote.

sunshine law   A 1976 law requiring that federal government meetings be held in public.

Supplemental Security Income (SSI)   Program that provides disabled people of low income with income assistance.

supply-side economics   Economic policy based on the belief that governments can keep the economy healthy by supplying the conditions (especially low taxes and minimal regulation) that encourage private economic activity.

supremacy clause   Constitutional provision that says the laws of the national government "shall be the supreme Law of the Land."

surplus   The amount by which annual revenue exceeds spending.

suspect classification   Categorization of a particular group that will be closely scrutinized by the courts to see whether its use is unconstitutional.

suspension of the rules   Fast-track procedure for considering bills and resolutions in the House; debate is limited to 40 minutes, no amendments are in order, and a two-thirds majority is required for passage.

tax base   Types of activities, types of property, or kinds of investments that are subject to taxation.

tax burden   The total amount of tax that a household pays.

tax preferences   Special tax treatment received by certain activities, property, or investments.

taxation without representation   Levying of taxes by a government in which the people are not represented by their own elected officials.

Temporary Assistance for Needy Families (TANF)   Welfare reform law passed by Congress in 1996.

three-fifths compromise   Constitutional provision that counted each slave as three-fifths of a person when calculating representation in the House of Representatives; repealed by the Fourteenth Amendment.

ticket splitting   Occurs when a voter does not vote a straight party ticket.

Tonkin Gulf Resolution   Congressional resolution giving the president the authority to send troops to Vietnam.

Tories   Those colonists who opposed independence from Great Britain.

transition   The period after a presidential candidate has won the November election but before the candidate assumes office as president on January 20.

treaties   Official agreements with foreign countries that are ratified by the Senate.

trial venue   Place where a trial is held.

trustee   Role a representative plays when acting in accordance with his or her own best judgment.

two-party system   System in which only two significant parties compete for office. Such systems are in the minority among world democracies.

two-presidency theory   Theory that explains why presidents exercise greater power over foreign affairs than over domestic policy.

two-thirds rule   Rule governing Democratic national conventions from 1832 to 1936. It required that the presidential and vice-presidential nominees receive at least two-thirds of the delegates' votes.

tyranny of the majority   Stifling of dissent by those voted into power by the majority.

unanimous-consent agreement   Agreement that sets forth the terms and conditions according to which the Senate will consider a bill; these are individually negotiated by the leadership for each bill.

undervotes   Ballots that indicate no choice for an office (e.g., for president in 2000), whether because the voter abstained or because the voter's intention could not be determined.

unemployment   The circumstance that exists when people who are willing to work at the prevailing wage cannot get jobs.

unfunded mandates   Federal regulations that impose burdens on state and local governments without appropriating enough money to cover costs.

unitary government   System under which all authority is held by a single, national government.

United Nations   Organization of all nation–states, whose purpose is to preserve world peace and foster economic and social development throughout the world.

U.S. attorney   Person responsible for prosecuting violations of the federal criminal code.

U.S. v. Curtiss-Wright   Supreme Court decision in which Congress is given the authority to delegate foreign policy responsibilities to the president.

veto power   Presidential rejection of congressional legislation. May be overridden by a two-thirds vote in each congressional chamber. Most state governors also have veto power over their legislatures.

Virginia Plan   Constitutional proposal supported by convention delegates from large states.

voter mobilization   The efforts of parties, groups, and activists to encourage their supporters to turn out for elections.

voting-age population   All people in the United States over the age of 18.

War on Poverty   One of the most controversial of the Great Society programs, designed to enhance the economic opportunity of low-income citizens.

War Powers Resolution   1973 congressional resolution requiring the president to notify Congress formally upon ordering U.S. troops into military action.

Whigs   Political opposition in eighteenth-century England that developed a theory of rights and representation.

whips   Members of Congress who serve as informational channels between the leadership and the rank and file, conveying the leadership's views and intentions to the members, and vice versa.

White House Office   Political appointees who work directly for the president, many of whom occupy offices in the White House.

white primary   Primary elections, held by the Democratic party after Reconstruction, that excluded nonwhites from participation in many southern states.

winner-take-all voting   Any voting procedure in which the side with the most votes gets all of the seats or delegates at stake.

writ of certiorari (cert)   A document issued by the Supreme Court indicating that the Court will review a decision made by a lower court.

writ of habeas corpus   A judicial order that a prisoner be brought before a judge to determine the legality of his or her imprisonment.

Youngstown Sheet and Tube Co. v. Sawyer   Case in which the Supreme Court placed limits on the executive power of the president.

zone of acceptance   Range within which Congress allows agencies to interpret and apply statutes.

Endnotes

PREFACE

1. *Pluralist Democracy in the United States: Conflict and Consent* (Chicago: Rand McNally, 1967).

2. Robert Dahl, *The New Political (Dis)Order* (Berkeley, CA: IGS Press, 1994): 1.

3. Ibid., 5.

4. "The Civic Culture: Prehistory, Retrospect, and Prospect," Center for the Study of Democracy Research Monograph No. 1, University of California, Irvine, 1996: 14.

5. James Stimson, "Opinion and Representation," *American Political Science Review* 89 (1995): 181.

6. James Barnes, "Clinton's Horse Race Presidency," *National Journal* (May 29, 1993): 1310.

7. Kenneth T. Walsh, "So, Why is This Man Laughing?" *U.S. News and World Report,* September 6, 204, p. 30.

8. The Transition to Governing Project, directed by Norman Ornstein and Thomas Mann.

CHAPTER 1

1. John F. Harris, "Campaign Promises Aside, It's Politics As Usual," *Washington Post Weekly Edition,* (July 2–8, 2001): 11.

2. On the importance of political consultant Karl Rove to George W. Bush's White House, see Dana Milbank, "The White House Lightning Rod: If Sparks are Flying, Karl Rove Is Probably at the Center," *Washington Post Weekly Edition* (July 23–29, 2001): 13–14; and Thomas B. Edsall, "Bush's Big Gamble: An Amnesty Proposal for Illegal Immigrants Angers GOP Conservatives," *Washington Post Weekly Edition* (July 23–29, 2001): 14.

3. Evelyn Nieves, "Heinz Kerry's Campaign Balancing Act," *Washington Post,* September 12, 2004: A1; *New York Times,* "Political Family Rules," August 1, 2004: Section 4, page 10.

4. "Half a Million Voters' Choices," *Governing,* April 1995: 15.

5. *The Book of the States, 2002* (Lexington, KY: Council of State Governments, 2002), pp. 209–211.

6. Herbert Jacob and Kenneth Vines, "Courts," in *Politics in the American States: A Comparative Analysis,* 4th ed., ed. Virginia Gray, Herbert Jacob, and Kenneth Vines (Boston: Little, Brown, 1983), p. 238.

7. Thomas Cronin, *Direct Democracy* (Cambridge, MA: Harvard University Press, 1989); and David Magleby, *Direct Legislation* (Baltimore, MD: Johns Hopkins University Press, 1984).

8. Anthony King, *Running Scared: Why America's Politicians Campaign Too Much and Govern Too Little* (New York: Free Press, 1996), pp. 2–3.

9. Joseph S. Nye, Jr., Philip D. Zelikow, and David C. King, eds., *Why People Don't Trust Government* (Cambridge, MA: Harvard University Press, 1997).

10. H. H. Gerth and C. W. Mills, trans., *From Max Weber* (New York: Oxford University Press, 1946), p. 78.

11. Chuck Henning, *The Wit and Wisdom of Politics: Expanded Edition* (Golden, CO: Fulcrum, 1992), p. 91.

12. Todd Purdom, "Prep School Peers Found Kerry Talented, Ambitious, and Apart," *New York Times,* May 16, 2004: p. A1.

13. Jimmy Carter, *A Government as Good as Its People* (New York: Simon & Schuster, 1977), p. 102.

14. "Federalist 51."

15. Hobbes, *Leviathan* (New York: Dutton, 1973), p. 65.

16. Henning, *Wit and Wisdom,* p. 89.

17. "How to Run a Referendum," *The Economist,* November 23, 1996: 66.

18. Good surveys of democratic theory include J. Roland Pennock, *Democratic Political Theory* (Princeton, NJ: Princeton University Press, 1979); and Giovanni Sartori, *The Theory of Democracy Revisited* (Chatham, NJ: Chatham House, 1987).

19. James Morone, *The Democratic Wish: Popular Participation and the Limits of American Government* (New York: Basic Books, 1990), p. 5. Morone is summarizing the claims of others; he himself is a critic of popular democracy.

20. Benjamin Barber, *Strong Democracy* (Berkeley, CA: University of California Press, 1984).

21. Alexis de Tocqueville, *Democracy in America,* 2nd ed., trans. Henry Reeve, 2 vols. (Cambridge, MA: Sever & Francis, 1863), I, pp. 318–319, as quoted in Morone, *The Democratic Wish,* p. 86.

22. John Adams, *The Political Writings of John Adams,* ed. George Peek, Jr. (New York: Macmillan, 1985), p. 89.

23. Morone, *The Democratic Wish,* pp. 5–6.

24. "Federalist 51."

25. Sidney Blumenthal, *The Permanent Campaign* (New York: Simon & Schuster, 1982).

26. Hugh Heclo, "The Permanent Campaign: A Conspectus," in *Campaigning to Govern or Governing to Campaign?* ed. Thomas Mann and Norman Ornstein (Washington, DC: The Brookings Institution, 2000).

27. Woodrow Wilson, *Congressional Government* (Cleveland, OH: Meridian Books, 1956), p. 39.

28. Richard Boyd, "Decline of U.S. Voter Turnout: Structural Explanations," *American Politics Quarterly* 9 (1981): 133–159.

29. Frank Sorauf, *Political Parties in the American System* (Boston: Little, Brown, 1964); and Martin Wattenberg, *The Decline of American Political Parties, 1952–1984* (Cambridge, MA: Harvard University Press, 1986).

30. Gary Jacobson finds that national swings in House elections are much more heterogeneous than at mid-century. See "The Marginals Never Vanished: Incumbency and Competition in Elections to the U.S. House of Representatives, 1952–1982," *American Journal of Political Science* 31 (1987): 126–141.

31. Susan Baer, "Candidates' Spouses Revisit Traditional Role," *Baltimore Sun,* January 23, 2004: p. 1A.

32. Carolyn Lochhead, "GOP Rebels Keep Bush's Tax Cut Bill on the Ropes," *San Francisco Chronicle,* May 14, 2003.

33. Joseph Cantor, *Congressional Campaign Spending, 1976–1996,* Congressional Research Service Report Number 97–793, (Washington, DC: Congressional Research Service, August 19, 1997), p. 2, Table 1; Center for Responsive Politics, www.crp.org, (accessed May 16, 2004).

34. John Broder, "Governors Join Ranks of Full-Time Campaign Money-Raisers," *New York Times,* December 5, 1999: p. 22.

35. John Alford and John Hibbing, "Electoral Convergence of the Two Houses of Congress," Paper presented at the Norman Thomas Conference on Senate Exceptionalism, Vanderbilt University, Nashville, TN, October 21–23, 1999.

36. Susan A. Macmanus, *Young v. Old: Generational Combat in the 21st Century* (Boulder, CO: Westview Press, 1996), chap. 2.

37. Sidney Verba, Kay Lehman Schlozman, and Henry Brady, *Voice and Equality* (Cambridge, MA: Harvard, 1995), pp. 50–54.

38. R. Douglas Arnold, *The Logic of Congressional Action* (New Haven, CT: Yale University Press, 1990).

39. Benjamin Ginsberg and Martin Shefter, *Politics by Other Means: The Declining Importance of Elections in America* (New York: Basic Books: 1990); and Terry Moe, "The Politics of Bureaucratic Structure," in *Can the Government Govern?* ed. John Chubb and Paul Peterson (Washington, DC: The Brookings Institution, 1989), pp. 267–329.

40. John Dewey, as quoted in Morone, *The Democratic Wish,* p. 322.

41. Morone, *The Democratic Wish.*

42. Henning, *Wit and Wisdom,* p. 94.

43. "A League of Evil," *The Economist,* September 11, 1999: 7.

44. Henning, *Wit and Wisdom,* p. 58.

45. Charles Masters, "Riviera Tramps Run Risk of 'Tourist Cleansing' Round-Ups," *Daily Telegraph,* July 27, 1996, International Section, p. 15.

CHAPTER 2

1. Herbert Storing, ed., *The Complete Anti-Federalist: Maryland and Virginia and the South,* vol. 5 (Chicago: University of Chicago Press, 1981), pp. 210, 212; selections from two speeches.

2. Herbert Storing, ed., with the assistance of Murray Dry, *The Complete Anti-Federalist* (Chicago: University of Chicago Press, 1981).

3. Alexander Hamilton, "Federalist 7," *The Federalist Papers* (New York: Bantam Books), p. 31.

4. Owen S. Ireland, *Religion, Ethnicity and Politics: Ratifying the Constitution in Pennsylvania* (University Park, PA: Pennsylvania State University Press, 1995).

5. Quoted in Jack Rakove, *Original Meanings: Politics and Ideas in the Making of the Constitution* (New York: Vintage, 1997), p. 17.

6. Thomas A. Bailey, *The American Pageant: A History of the Republic* (Boston: D.C. Heath, 1956).

7. Gordon S. Wood, *The Radicalism of the American Revolution* (New York: Knopf, 1992), p. 80.

8. Jack P. Greene, "The Role of the Lower Houses of Assembly in Eighteenth-Century Politics," in *The Reinterpretation of the American Revolution 1763–1789,* ed. Jack P. Greene, (New York: Harper & Row, 1968), pp. 86–109.

9. Merrill D. Peterson, *Thomas Jefferson and the New Nation* (New York: Oxford University Press, 1970), pp. 22–23.

10. Robert J. Dinkin, *Voting in Revolutionary America: A Study of Elections in the Original Thirteen States, 1776–1789* (Westport, CT: Greenwood Press, 1982) and Robert J. Dinkin, *Voting in Provincial America: A Study of Elections in the Thirteen Colonies, 1689–1776* (Westport, CT: Greenwood Press, 1977).

11. Wood, *Radicalism,* p. 55.

12. J. Franklin Jameson, *The American Revolution Considered as a Social Movement* (Princeton, NJ: Princeton University Press, 1926).

13. Edmund S. Morgan and Helen M. Morgan, *The Stamp Act Crisis: Prologue to Revolution* (Chapel Hill: University of North Carolina Press, 1953), p. 106.

14. Morgan and Morgan, *Stamp Act Crisis,* p. 106.

15. Bernard Bailyn, *The Origins of American Politics* (New York: Knopf, 1968), p. 12.

16. Thomas Hobbes, *Leviathan* (New York: Oxford University Press, 1996). Originally published in 1651.

17. John Locke, *Two Treatises on Civil Government* (London: Dent, 1924). Originally published in 1690.

18. J. H. Plumb, *The Origins of Political Stability* (Boston: Houghton Mifflin, 1967).

19. For a discussion of the influence of James Harrington on colonial thought, see Samuel H. Beer, *To Make a Nation: The Rediscovery of American Federalism* (Cambridge, MA: Harvard University Press, 1993).

20. Thomas Paine, *Common Sense* (New York: Penguin, 1986). Originally published in 1776.

21. John Bartlett, *Familiar Quotations,* 15th ed. (Boston: Little, Brown, 1980), pp. 334, 342, 414.

22. C. L. Becker, *Freedom and Responsibility in the American Way of Life* (New York: Knopf, 1945), p. 16, as quoted by Louis Hartz, *The Liberal Tradition in America* (New York: Harcourt, 1955), p. 61.

23. Robert J. Dinkin, *Voting in Revolutionary America: A Study of Elections in the Original Thirteen States,* 1776–1789 (Westport, CT: Greenwood Press, 1982); and Robert J. Dinkin, *Voting in Provincial America: A Study of Elections in the Thirteen Colonies, 1689–1776* (Westport, CT: Greenwood Press, 1977).

24. Willi Paul Adams, *The First American Constitutions: Republican Ideology and the Making of the State Constitutions in the Revolutionary Era* (Chapel Hill: University of North Carolina Press, 1980), pp. 245, 308-311.

25. Adams, *First American Constitution,* p. 207.

26. Bailey, *American Pageant,* p. 136.

27. Alexander Hamilton, James Madison, John Jay, *The Federalist Papers* (New York: Mentor Books, 1999 [1787]), p. 76 (Federalist 15).

28. James Madison, Letter to Thomas Jefferson, October 24, 1787, in James Madison, *Letters and Other Writings of James Madison* (Philadelphia: Lippincott, 1865).

29. "Report of Proceedings in Congress, February 21, 1787," The Avalon Project at Yale Law School, http://www.yale.edu/lawweb/avalon/const/const04.htm (accessed January 22, 2004).

30. Charles A. Beard, *An Economic Interpretation of the Constitution of the United States* (New York: Free Press, 1913).

31. Robert E. Brown, *Charles Beard and the Constitution* (Princeton, NJ: Princeton University Press, 1956); and Forrest McDonald, *We the People* (Chicago: University of Chicago Press, 1958).

32. John P. Roche, "The Founding Fathers: A Reform Caucus in Action," *American Political Science Review* 55 (December 1961): 799–816.

33. Winton U. Solberg, ed., *The Federal Convention and the Formation of the Union of the American States* (New York: Bobbs-Merrill, 1958), p. 78.

34. Solberg, *Federal Convention,* p. 78.

35. Solberg, *Federal Convention,* pp. 131–134.

36. Max Farrand, *The Framing of the Constitution of the United States* (New Haven: Yale University Press, 1913), p. 113.

37. Thornton Anderson, *Creating the Constitution: The Convention of 1787 and the First Congress* (University Park, PA: Pennsylvania State University Press, 1993).

38. Arthur M. Schlesinger, Jr., ed., *History of American Presidential Elections, 1789–1968,* vol.2 (New York: McGraw-Hill, 1971), p. 1244.

39. Anderson, *Creating the Constitution,* p. 148.

40. Anderson, *Creating the Constitution,* p. 148.

41. Henry Steele Commager, ed., *Documents of American History* (New York: Appleton-Century-Crofts, 1958), p. 104; and Willi Paul Adams, *The First American Constitutions: Republican Ideology and the Making of the State Constitutions in the Revolutionary Era* (Chapel Hill: University of North Carolina Press, 1980).

42. Arthur M. Schlesinger, *Prelude to Independence* (New York: Knopf, 1958), p. 299.

43. C.M. Kenyon, "Men of Little Faith: The Anti-Federalists on the Nature of Representative Government," in *The Reinterpretation of the American Revolution, 1763–1789,* ed. Jack P. Green (New York: Harper & Row, 1968), pp. 526–567; and Herbert J. Storing, ed., *The Anti-Federalist* (Chicago: University of Chicago Press, 1986).

44. John Jay, Alexander Hamilton, and James Madison, writing under the pseudonym Publius, *The Federalist Papers* (New York: New American Library, 1961).

45. James Madison, "Federalist 10," in John Jay, Alexander Hamilton, and James Madison, writing under the pseudonym Publius, *The Federalist Papers* (New York: New American Library, 1961).

46. Jane Mansbridge, *Why We Lost the ERA* (Chicago: University of Chicago Press, 1986).

47. Beard, *An Economic Interpretation of the Constitution of the United States.*

48. Bernard Bailyn, *The Ideological Origins of Revolution* (Cambridge, MA: Harvard University Press, 1967); and Gordon S. Wood, *The Creation of the American Republic, 1776–1787* (Chapel Hill: University of North Carolina Press, 1969).

49. Frederick Douglass, "Is the Plan of the American Union Under the Constitution Anti-Slavery or Not?" *The Frederick Douglass Papers,* ed. John W, Blassingame (New Haven: Yale University Press, 1979), vol. 3, p. 157.

50. Beard, *Economic Interpretation,* chap. 9.

51. Second Inaugural Address, 1865, as quoted in John Bartlett, *Familiar Quotations,* 16th ed. (Boston: Little, Brown, 1992), p. 450.

CHAPTER 3

1. Kevin Vaughan, "This Time Threats Brought Action," *Rocky Mountain News,* December 1, 2001: p. 1B.

2. Mark Anderson et al. "School Associated Violent Deaths in the United States, 1994–1999," *Journal of the American Medical Association* 286: 21 (December 5, 2001): 2695–2702.

3. *United States v. Lopez,* 514 U.S. 549 (1995).

4. John Bartlett, *Familiar Quotations: Revised and Enlarged,* 15th ed. (Boston: Little, Brown, 1980), p. 452.

5. Alexis de Tocqueville, *Democracy in America,* vol. I, ed. Philips Bradley (New York: Knopf, 1945), p. 169.

6. Gordon S. Wood, *The Creation of the American Republic, 1776–1787* (New York: Norton, 1972), pp. 483–499.

7. Wood, pp. 483–499.

8. Jean E. Smith, *John Marshall: Definer of a Nation* (New York: Henry Holt, 1996), pp. 440–446.

9. *McCulloch v. Maryland* (1819), 4 Wheaton 316, as reprinted in Henry Steele Commager, ed., *Documents of American History,* 6th ed. (New York: Appleton-Century-Crofts, 1949), p. 217.

10. *United States v. E. C. Knight Co.,* 156 U.S. 1 (1895).

11. *A. L. A. Schechter Poultry Corp. v. United States,* 295 U.S. 495 (1935).

12. James MacGregor Burns, *Roosevelt: The Lion and the Fox,* (New York: Harcourt Brace, 1956), p. 223.

13. Burns, p. 298.

14. *NLRB v. Jones & Laughlin Co.,* 301 U.S. 1 (1937).

15. *Wickard v. Filburn,* 317 U.S. 111 (1942).

16. *United States v. Morrison,* 99-5 (2000).

17. *McCulloch v. Maryland* (1819), as reprinted in Commager, p. 217.

18. Dan M. Berkovitz, "Waste Wars: Did Congress 'Nuke' State Sovereignty in the Low-Level Radioactive Waste Policy Amendments Act of 1985?" *Harvard Environmental Law Review* 11, (1987): 437–440.

19. *New York Times,* January 18, 1991.

20. *New York v. U.S.,* 488 U.S. 1041 (1992).

21. *Printz v. U.S.,* 521 U.S. 98 (1997).

22. *Seminole Tribe of Florida v. Florida et al.,* 517 U.S. 44 (1996).

23. *Board of Trustees of the University of Alabama v. Garrett,* 99-1240 (2001).

24. *Federal Maritime Commission v. South Carolina State Ports Authority,* 01-46 (2002).

25. *Helvering v. Davis,* 301 U.S. 548, 599 (1937).

26. *South Dakota v. Dole,* 483 U.S. 203 (1987).

27. Simon Lazarus, "The Federalist Society; Their Judicial Ideology Would Dismantle Accepted Social Policy," *Milwaukee Journal Sentinel,* July 1, 2001: 1J.

28. Morton Grodzins, *The American System: A New View of Government in the United States,* ed. Daniel J. Elazar (Chicago: Rand McNally, 1966).

29. Calculated from data in Ester Fuchs, *Mayors and Money* (Chicago: University of Chicago Press, 1992), p. 210.

30. Chuck Henning, comp., *The Wit and Wisdom of Politics: Expanded Edition.* (Golden, CO: Fulcrum, 1992), p. 208.

31. *Congressional Record,* July 16, 2003: p. S9476-7.

32. Carl Hulse, "Spending Bill Is Approved, With Its Storehouse of Pork," *New York Times,* February 14, 2003: p. A24.

33. Ibid.

34. Jeffrey L. Pressman and Aaron Wildavsky, *Implementation,* 3rd ed. (Berkeley: University of California Press, 1984); Martha Derthick, *New Towns in Town: Why a Federal Program Failed* (Washington, DC: Urban Institute, 1972); and Eugene Bardach, *The Implementation Game,* 4th ed. (Cambridge, MA: MIT Press, 1982).

35. Derthick, *New Towns in Town.*

36. Pressman and Wildavsky, *Implementation,* p. 118.

37. Paul E. Peterson, Barry Rabe, and Kenneth Wong, *When Federalism Works* (Washington, DC: The Brookings Institution, 1986).

38. Timothy Conlan, *New Federalism: Intergovernmental Reform from Nixon to Reagan* (Washington, DC: The Brookings Institution, 1988).

39. Executive Office of the President, Office of Management and Budget, *Budget for Fiscal Year 2004, Historical Tables,* Table 12.3.

40. David McKay, *Domestic Policy and Ideology: Presidents and the American State, 1964–1987* (New York: Cambridge University Press, 1989), chap. 4.

41. Lynda McDonnell, "Will Our State Be a Magnet for Poor from Across Nation?" *Pioneer Press,* December 31, 1995: pp. 1A, 10A.

42. Paul E. Peterson and Mark Rom, *Welfare Magnets: A New Case for a National Standard* (Washington, DC: The Brookings Institution, 1990).

43. Calculated from Table 2.3, *Temporary Assistance for Needy Families (TANF) Program: Third Annual Report to Congress,* (Washington, DC: U.S. Department of Health and Human Services), August 2000, p. 17. See also Judith Havemann, "Welfare Reform 'Surplus' is $4.7 Billion" *Washington Post,* September 8, 1998: p. A2.

44. Peterson, *The Price of Federalism.*

45. Timothy Conlan, "And the Beat Goes On: Intergovernmental Mandates and Preemption in an Era of Deregulation," *Publius* 21 (Summer 1991): 57.

46. On the costs of environmental mandates, see Richard C. Feiock, "Estimating

Political, Fiscal and Economic Impacts of State Mandates: A Pooled Time Series Analysis of Local Planning and Growth Policy in Florida." Paper prepared for the annual meeting of the American Political Science Association, 1994.

47. Colleen M. Grogan, "The Influence of Federal Mandates on State Policy Decision-Making." Paper prepared for the annual meeting of the American Political Science Association, 1994; Teresa Coughlin, Leighton Ku, and John Holahan, *Medicaid Since 1980* (Washington, DC: Urban Institute, 1994); and John Holahan et al., "Explaining the Recent Growth in Medicaid Spending," *Health Affairs* 12 (Fall 1993): 177–193.

48. Jim VandeHei, "Education Law May Hurt Bush; No Child Left Behind's Funding Problems Could Be '04 Liability," *Washington Post*, October 13, 2003: p. A01.

49. Patrick Healy, "Kerry Education Plan Would Add $20B In Federal Spending," *Boston Globe*, November 26, 2003: p. A4.

50. James Bryce, *Modern Democracies* (New York: Macmillan, 1921), vol. I, p. 132.

51. This figure excludes school districts. School districts have dramatically decreased in number, from over 108,000 in 1942 to about 14,000 today. This is, for the most part, the result of consolidation of rural school districts in the 1940s and 1950s. (See *Statistical Abstract of the United States, 2000,* Table 490.)

52. For more data on special districts, see *Finances of Special District Governments, 1997,* (Washington, DC: U.S. Census of Governments, 2000). For a study of how and why special districts form, see Nancy Burns, *The Formation of American Local Governments: Private Values in Public Institutions* (New York: Oxford University Press, 1994).

53. Robert R. Alford and Eugene C. Lee, "Voting Turnout in American Cities," *American Political Science Review* 62 (September 1968): 796–813; and Albert Karnig and B. Oliver Walter, "Decline in Municipal Voter Turnout: A Function of Changing Structure," *American Politics Quarterly,* 11: 4 (October, 1983): 491–505.

54. Village politics are well described in A. J. Vidich and J. Bensman, *Small Town in Mass Society* (New York: Harper & Row, 1972). For descriptions of courthouse gangs in the county politics of the South, see v. O. Key, *Southern Politics* (New York: Random House, 1949).

55. Paul E. Peterson, *City Limits* (Chicago: University of Chicago Press, 1981).

56. Soloman Moore, "A Heavy Turnout for Apathy," *Los Angeles Times,* May 25, 2001: p. 12.

57. Edward Walsh, "Report Urges Expanding Federal Role in Elections; Task Force Recommends Guidance, Not Mandates," *Washington Post,* August 10, 2001: p. A02.

58. *Statistical Abstract of the United States, 2000,* Table 28.

59. Greta Anand, "Circling of the Welcome Wagons: Selectman Candidates Rip Social Programs," *Boston Globe,* West Weekly Section, March 19, 1995: pp. 1, 8.

60. Calculated from *Statistical Abstract of the United States, 2000,* Tables 494, 513, 515, and 533. "Social programs" is defined for state and local governments as the U.S. census of government categories "public welfare" and "health and hospitals." For the federal government, "social programs" include Office of Management and Budget categories "health," "Medicare," "income security," "social security," and "veterans benefits and services."

61. "Money to Burn," *The Economist,* August 14, 1993: 23.

62. Steve Rushin, "The Heart of a City," *Sports Illustrated,* December 4, 1995.

63. Frances Stokes Berry and William D. Berry, "State Lottery Adoptions as Policy Innovations: An Event History Analysis," *American Political Science Review,* 84:2 (June, 1990): 395–415.

64. Daniel Elazar, *American Federalism: A View From the States* (New York: Harper & Row, 1984).

65. See, for example, John Kincaid, ed. *Political Culture, Public Policy, and the American States* (Philadelphia: Institute for the Study of Human Issues, 1982).

66. Morris Fiorina, *Divided Government* (New York: Macmillan, 1992).

67. Calculated from *Statistical Abstract of the United States, 2002,* Table18, 430, 635; and Department of Commerce, U.S. Bureau of the Census, State Government Finances, 2000, http://www.census.gov/govs/www/state01 .html (accessed January 24, 2004). Data are expressed in 2000 dollars and combine expenditures by state and local governments. Because the sharing of responsibilities by state and local governments varies widely from state to state, any interstate comparison that looks at state government expenditures alone can be quite misleading.

68. Peterson, *The Price of Federalism,* p. 105.

69. Jodi Wilgoren, "With Deadline Near, States Are in Budget Discord," *New York Times,* June 27, 2003: p. A14.

70. Jodi Wilgoren and David Rosenbaum, "Defying Labels Left or Right, Dean's '04 Run Is Making Gains," *New York Times,* July 30, 2003: p. A1.

71. *Baker v. Carr,* 369 U.S. 186 (1962); *Reynolds v. Sims,* 377 U.S. 533 (1964).

72. See Gordon E. Baker, *The Reapportionment Revolution* (New York: Random House, 1966); and Timothy G. O'Rourke, *The Impact of Reapportionment* (New Brunswick, NJ: Transaction Books, 1980).

73. John Sanko, "Boundary Map Favors Democrats," *Rocky Mountain News,* November 28, 2001: p. 23A.

74. Paul Bartels, "Plan to Redraw 11th District Opposed," *New Orleans Times-Picayune,* October 4, 2001: Metro 1.

75. Peggy Ficak, "Lights! Camera! Lawmakers!" *San Antonio Express News,* May 15, 2003: p. 9A.

76. Edward Walsh, "DeLay, Barton Subpoenaed in Texas Redistricting Case," *Washington Post,* November 22, 2003: p. A2.

77. John Bull, "Redistricting Critics Unappeased; Panel Finalizes Boundaries, But Court Challenge Likely," *Pittsburgh Post-Gazette,* November 20, 2001: p. B-1.

78. The Council of State Governments, *The Book of the States: 2000–2001 Edition* (Lexington, KY: Council of State Governments).

79. Patrick Basham, *Assessing the Term Limits Experiment: California and Beyond,* Cato Institute Policy Analysis No. 413, August 31, 2001, p. 8.

80. Alan Greenblatt, "Crash Course," *Governing,* November 2001: 54.

81. George Skelton, "Lessons from an Earlier Foreign Journey," *Los Angeles Times,* October 25, 1999.

82. Matea Gold, "Gov-Elect Rolls Up His Sleeves on Budget," *Los Angeles Times,* October 22, 2003: p. 1.

CHAPTER 4

1. Karen Breslau, "Hate Crime: He Wasn't Afraid," *Newsweek* (October 15, 2001): 8.

2. *Los Angeles Times,* "Rights and the New Reality" (September 21, 2002): part 2, p. 22.

3. Sam Howe Verhovek, "Americans Give in to Racial Profiling," *New York Times* (September 23, 2001): p. 1A; Sandra Tan, "Change of Heart," *The Buffalo News* (October 22, 2001): p. A1.

4. American Arab Anti-Discrimination Committee, press release, September 21, 2001.

5. Mary Jordan, "It's Harder to Cross the Mexican Border," *Washington Post Weekly Edition,* June 3-9, 2002: 17; Anne Hull, "A New Anxiety," *Washington Post Weekly Edition,* December 3-9. 200: 9.

6. Shannon McCaffrey, "Justice Report: Immigrants Held after 9/11 Abused," Knight Ridder News Service, June 3, 2003; *Lexington (KY) Herald-Leader,* "Fewer Foreign Students," November 3, 2003: p. A3; David J. Jefferson,

"Stopped at the Border," *Newsweek,* October 14, 2002: 59.

7. For background, go to http://www.oz.net/~cyu/internment/main.html.

8. Elizabeth Becker, "All White, All Christian, and Divided by Diversity," *New York Times,* June 10. 2001.

9. Recollection of Louise Bauer Ritschard, mother-in-law of Morris Fiorina.

10. Suzanne Gamboa, "Foreigners Won't Have to Register Any Longer," Associated Press, December 12, 2003; *Lexington* (KY) *Herald-Leader,* "Hate Crimes Decline," November 13, 2003: p. A3.

11. Carl J. Friedrich, *Problems of the American Public Service* (New York: McGraw-Hill, 1935), p. 12.

12. See Alvin Rabushka and Kenneth Shepsle, *Politics in Plural Societies* (Columbus, OH: Merrill, 1972).

13. John A. Garrity and Peter Gay, eds., *The Columbia History of the World* (New York: Harper & Row, 1972), p. 673.

14. Quoted in Marc Shell, "Babel in America; or, The Politics of Language Diversity in the United States," *Critical Inquiry* 20(1993): 109.

15. Richard McCormick, "Ethno-Cultural Interpretations of Nineteenth-Century American Voting Behavior," *Political Science Quarterly* 89 (1974): 351–377.

16. Richard Wayman, "Wisconsin Ethnic Groups and the Election of 1890," *Wisconsin Magazine of History* 51(1968): 273. More generally, see Paul Kleppner, *The Third Electoral System, 1853–1892: Parties, Voters, and Political Cultures* (Chapel Hill, NC: University of North Carolina Press, 1979).

17. On the multicultural character of California after it was annexed to the United States, see Ronald Takaki, *A Different Mirror* (Boston: Little, Brown, 1993), chap. 8.

18. John Miller, "Chinese Exclusion Act," *Congressional Record–Senate 1882,* 13, Pt. 2: 1484–1485.

19. This is Oscar Handlin's sardonic characterization. See his *Race and Nationality in American Life* (Boston: Little, Brown, 1957), p. 95.

20. Madison Grant, *The Passing of the Great Race* (New York: Scribner's, 1916), pp. 80–81.

21. *Abstracts of Reports of the Immigration Commission* (Washington, DC: U.S. Government Printing Office, vol. 1, 1911). The quoted passages can be found on pp. 244, 251, 259, 261, 265, and 229. The characterization of southern Italians is based on work by an Italian (presumably a northern Italian) sociologist, but the commission clearly agrees with the description.

22. Henry Cabot Lodge, "Immigration Restriction," *Congressional Record–Senate 1896,* 28, Pt. 3: 2817.

23. "Emergency" immigration restrictions passed in 1921 were fine-tuned and formalized in the National Origins Act of 1924 and the National Origins Quota Act of 1929.

24. Seymour Martin Lipset and Earl Raab, *The Politics of Unreason* (New York: Harper & Row, 1970), p. 111.

25. Alan Lichtman, *Prejudice and the Old Politics: The Presidential Election of 1928* (Chapel Hill, NC: University of North Carolina Press, 1979).

26. "Where illegal immigrants are," *USA Today*, January 8, 2004: p. 3A.

27. George Borhas, "The New Economics of Immigration," *Atlantic Monthly,* November 1996: 72–80.

28. National Research Council, *The New Americans: Economic, Demographic, and Fiscal Effects of Immigration* (Washington, DC: National Academy Press, 1977), chaps. 4–6.

29. Brad Knickerbocker, "Environment vs. Immigrants," *Christian Science Monitor,* April 27, 1998: p. 3; and William Branigin, "Sierra Club Votes for Neutrality on Immigration; Population Issue 'Intensely Debated,'" *Washington Post,* April 26, 1998: p. A16.

30. David Kennedy, "Can We Still Afford to Be a Nation of Immigrants?" *Atlantic Monthly,* November 1996: 67.

31. Arthur Schlesinger, Jr., *The Disuniting of America* (Knoxville, TN: Whittle, 1991).

32. Louis Hartz, *The Liberal Tradition in America* (New York: Harcourt, 1955).

33. Bernard Bailyn, *The Ideological Origins of the American Revolution* (Cambridge, MA: Harvard University Press, 1967).

34. Gordon Wood. *The Creation of the American Republic* (New York: Norton, 1972); and J. G. A. Pocock, *The Machiavellian Moment* (Princeton, NJ: Princeton University Press, 1975).

35. Rogers Smith, "Beyond Tocqueville, Myrdal and Hartz: The Multiple Traditions in America," *American Political Science Review* 87(1993): 549–566. These inconsistencies were not lost on earlier thinkers, to be sure. Recall Jefferson's pessimistic predictions in his *Notes on the State of Virginia 1781–1785*. Also see Alexis de Tocqueville, *Democracy in America,* ed. J. P. Mayer (New York: Harper, 1969), pp. 340–363.

36. Samuel Huntington, *American Politics: The Promise of Disharmony* (Cambridge, MA: Harvard University Press, 1981).

37. Everett Carll Ladd, *The American Ideology* (Storrs, CT: The Roper Center, 1994): 76.

38. I. A. Lewis and William Schneider, "Hard Times: The Public on Poverty," *Public Opinion,* June/July 1985: 2–8, 59–60.

39. "Income Tax Irritation." *Public Perspective* (July/August, 1990): 86.

40. Stanley Feldman, "Structure and Consistency in Public Opinion: The Role of Core Beliefs and Values," *American Journal of Political Science* 32 (1988): 416–440.

41. Paul Krugman, *Peddling Prosperity* (New York: Norton, 1994), chap. 5.

42. Ladd, *The American Ideology,* pp. 56–57.

43. Sidney Verba and Gary Orren, *Equality in America* (Cambridge, MA: Harvard University Press, 1985).

44. "In (Blank) We Trust," *The Economist,* October 12, 1996: 32.

45. Mariana Servin-Gonzalez and Oscar Torres-Reyna, "Trends: Religion and Politics," *Public Opinion Quarterly* 63 (1999): 613–614.

46. Seymour Martin Lipset, *American Exceptionalism* (New York: Norton, 1996).

47. Laurie Goodstein, "Search for the Right Church Ends at Home," *New York Times,* April 29, 2001: pp. 1, 16.

48. Robert Booth Fowler, *Religion and Politics in America* (Metuchen, NJ: American Theological Library Association, 1985), p. 27.

49. Huntington, *American Politics: The Promise of Disharmony.*

50. Louis Hartz, *The Liberal Tradition in America* (New York: Harcourt, Brace, and World, 1955).

51. Frederick Jackson Turner, *The Frontier in American History* (New York: Holt, 1920).

52. For a discussion, see Seymour Martin Lipset, "Why No Socialism in the United States?" in *Sources of Contemporary Radicalism,* ed. Seweryn Bialer and Sophia Sluzar (New York: Westview Press, 1977).

53. Sven Steinmo, "American Exceptionalism Reconsidered," in *The Dynamics of American Politics,* ed. Larry C. Dodd and Calvin Jillson (Boulder, CO: Westwood, 1994), pp. 106–131.

54. For a sympathetic description of the trials and ordeals of the immigrants, see Oscar Handlin, *The Uprooted,* 2nd ed. (Boston: Little, Brown, 1973).

55. Hartz, *The Liberal Tradition,* p. 18.

56. *Abstracts of Reports of the Immigration Commission,* p. 170.

57. William Bennett and Jack Kemp, "The Fortress Party?" *Wall Street Journal,* October 21, 1994: p. A14.

58. David Firestone, "Mayor Seeks Immigration Coalition," *New York Times,* October 11, 1996: p. B3.

59. "The Effects of Ethnicity on Political Culture," in *Classifying by Race,* ed. Paul Peterson (Princeton, NJ: Princeton University Press, 1995), pp. 351–352.

60. Rodolfo de la Garza, Angelo Falcon, and F. Chris Garcia, "Will the Real Americans Please Stand Up: Anglo and Mexican American Support of Core American Political Values," *American Journal of Political Science* 40 (1996): 335–351.

61. Lydia Saad, "Immigrants See United States as Land of Opportunity," *Gallup Poll Monthly,* July 1995: 19–33.

62. Gregory Rodriguez, quoted in Patrick McDonnell, "Immigrants Quickly Becoming Assimilated, Report Concludes," *San Francisco Chronicle,* July 7, 1999: p. A4.

63. Philip Martin and Elizabeth Midgley, *Immigration to the United States* (Washington, DC: Population Reference Bureau, June 1999), p. 37.

64. James Smith, "Assmilation Across the Latino Generations," *American Economic Review* 93(2003): 315–319.

CHAPTER 5

1. Paul Quirk and Joseph Hinchliffe, "The Rising Hegemony of Mass Opinion," *Journal of Policy History* 10 (1998): 19–50.

2. Valdimer Orando, *Public Opinion and American Democracy* (New York: Knopf, 1961).

3. Carl Friedrich, *Man and His Government* (New York: McGraw-Hill, 1963), pp. 199–215.

4. Elizabeth Cook, Ted Jelen, and Clyde Wilcox, *Between Two Absolutes: Public Opinion and the Politics of Abortion* (Boulder, CO: Westview Press, 1992).

5. David Leege, Kenneth Wald, and Lyman Kellstedt, "The Public Dimension of Private Devotionalism," in *Rediscovering the Religious Factor in American Politics,* ed. David Leege and Lyman Kellstedt (Armonk, NY: Sharpe, 1993), pp. 139–156; and Alan Hertzke and John Rausch, "The Religious Vote in American Politics: Value Conflict, Continuity, and Change," in *Broken Contract,* ed. Stephen Craig (Boulder, CO: Westview Press, 1996), p. 188.

6. Warren Miller and Santa Traugott, *American National Election Studies Data Sourcebook, 1952–1986* (Cambridge, MA: Harvard University Press, 1990), pp. 316, 332.

7. Robert Hess and Judith Horney, *The Development of Political Attitudes in Children* (Garden City, NY: Doubleday, 1967).

8. Fred Greenstein, *Children and Politics* (New Haven, CT: Yale University Press, 1969), chap. 4.

9. M. Kent Jennings and Richard G. Niemi, *Generations and Politics* (Princeton, NJ: Princeton University Press, 1981), p. 51.

10. Arthur Lupia, "Shortcuts versus Encyclopedias: Information and Voting Behavior in California Insurance Reform Elections," *American Political Science Review* 88 (1994): 63-76.

11. For a survey of positive and negative findings, see Jack Citrin and Donald Green, "The Self-Interest Motive in American Public Opinion," *Research in Micropolitics,* vol. 3 (Greenwich, CT: JAI Press, 1993), pp. 1–28.

12. David Sears and Leonie Huddy, "On the Origins of Political Disunity Among Women," in *Women, Politics, and Change,* ed. L. Tilly and P. Gurin (New York: Russell Sage, 1990), pp. 249–277.

13. Norman Nie, Jane Junn, and Kenneth Stehlik-Barry, *Education and Democratic Citizenship in America* (Chicago: University of Chicago Press, 1996).

14. Larry Bartels, "Messages Received: The Political Impact of Media Exposure," *American Political Science Review* 87 (1993): 267–285.

15. Details on how these polls are conducted appear in D. Stephen Voss, Andrew Gelman, and Gary King, "Preelection Survey Methodology: Details from Eight Polling Organizations, 1988 and 1992," *Public Opinion Quarterly* 59 (Spring): 98–132.

16. "Poll Leaves Democrats with Red Faces," Reuters, January 5, 2000.

17. Don Van Natta, Jr., "Polling's 'Dirty Little Secret': No Response," *New York Times,* November 21, 1999: sect. 4, pp. 1, 16.

18. John Brehm, *The Phantom Respondents* (Ann Arbor, MI: University of Michigan Press, 1993), chap. 2.

19. Everett Ladd, "The Pollsters' Waterloo," *Wall Street Journal,* November 19, 1996.

20. Jon Krosnick and Matthew Barent, "Comparisons of Party Identification and Policy Preferences: The Impact of Survey Question Format," *American Journal of Political Science* 37 (1993): 941–964.

21. On these topics, see Howard Schuman and Stanley Presser, *Questions and Answers in Attitude Surveys* (New York: Harcourt, Academic Press, 1981); and the essays in Thomas Mann and Gary Orren, eds., *Media Polls in American Politics* (Washington, DC: The Brookings Institution, 1992).

22. Adam Clymer, "The Unbearable Lightness of Public Opinion Polls," *New York Times,* July 22, 2001: p. 3.

23. For a full discussion, see David Moore and Frank Newport, "Misreading the Public: The Case of the Holocaust Poll," *Public*

Perspective, March/April 1994: 28–30; and Tom Smith, "Review: The Holocaust Denial Controversy," *Public Opinion Quarterly* 59 (1995): 269–295.

24. Tom Smith, "Public Support for Public Spending, 1973–1994," *The Public Perspective* 6 (April/May 1995): 2.

25. "Abortion: Overview of a Complex Opinion," *The Public Perspective,* November/December, 1989: 19, 20.

26. "Abortion," *The American Enterprise,* July/August 1995: 107.

27. Ibid., 20.

28. Cook, Jelen, and Wilcox, *Between Two Absolutes,* chap. 2.

29. For a comprehensive breakdown of federal spending, see "Where the Money Goes," *Congressional Quarterly,* December 11, 1993.

30. Anthony King, "Names and Places Lost in the Mists of Time," *Daily Telegraph,* August 26, 1997: 4.

31. Anthony Downs, *An Economic Theory of Democracy* (New York: Harper & Row, 1957), chaps. 11–13.

32. Morris P. Fiorina, "Information and Rationality in Elections," in *Information and Democratic Processes,* ed. John Ferejohn and James Kuklinski (Urbana: University of Illinois Press, 1990), pp. 329–342.

33. John Krosnick, "Government Policy and Citizen Passion: A Study of Issue Publics in Contemporary America," *Political Behavior* 12 (1990): 59–92; and Peter Natchez and Irvin Bupp, "Candidates, Issues, and Voters," *Public Policy* 1 (1968): 409–437.

34. Fiorina, "Information and Rationality in Elections."

35. Tamar Lewin, "Study Points to Increase in Tolerance of Ethnicity," *New York Times,* January 8, 1992: p. A12.

36. Philip Converse, "The Nature of Belief Systems in Mass Publics," in *Ideology and Discontent,* ed. David Apter (New York: Free Press, 1964), pp. 206–261.

37. M. Kent Jennings, "Ideological Thinking Among Mass Publics and Political Elites," *Public Opinion Quarterly* (1992): 419–441.

38. Miller and Traugott, *American National Election Studies Data Sourcebook,* p. 94.

39. *2000 American National Election Study,* as analyzed by the authors.

40. Vernon Van Dyke, *Ideology and Political Choice* (Chatham, NJ: Chatham House, 1995), chaps. 3–5.

41. James A. Davis, "Changeable Weather in a Cooling Climate Atop the Liberal Plateau," *Public Opinion Quarterly* 56 (1992): 261–306; and Morris P. Fiorina, "The Reagan Years: Turning to the Right or Groping

Toward the Middle?" in *The Resurgence of Conservatism in Anglo-American Democracies,* ed. Barry Cooper, Allan Kornberg, and William Mishler (Durham, NC: Duke University Press, 1988), pp. 430–459.

42. Morris P. Fiorina, *Divided Government,* 2nd ed. (Boston: Allyn & Bacon, 1995), pp. 173–177.

43. "Public Expects GOP Miracles," *Times-Mirror News Release,* December 8, 1994; CNN, "Gallup Poll: 50 Percent Americans Support, 33 Percent Oppose, Bush Tax Plan," February 27, 2001.

44. Samuel Stouffer, *Communism, Conformity, and Civil Liberties* (New York: Doubleday, 1955); and James Prothro and Charles Grigg, "Fundamental Principles of Democracy: Bases of Agreement and Disagreement," *Journal of Politics* 22 (1960): 176–194.

45. For evidence that people's opinions reflect a smaller number of "core beliefs" that may conflict with each other or situational characteristics, see Stanley Feldman, "Structure and Consistency in Public Opinion: The Role of Core Beliefs and Values," *American Journal of Public Opinion* 32 (1988): 416–440; and Stanley Feldman and John Zaller, "A Simple Theory of the Survey Response: Answering Questions Versus Revealing Preferences," *American Journal of Political Science* 36 (1992): 579–616.

46. R. Michael Alvarez and John Brehm, "American Ambivalence Toward Abortion Policy," *American Journal of Political Science* 39 (1995): 1055–1082.

47. On the effects of posing political conflicts as matters of conflicting rights, see Mary Anne Glendon, *Rights Talk: The Impoverishment of Political Discourse* (New York: Free Press, 1991).

48. "A Macro Theory of Information Flow," in *Information and Democratic Processes,* ed. John Ferejohn and James Kuklinski (Urbana: University of Illinois Press, 1990), pp. 345–368.

49. James Stimson, *Public Opinion in America: Moods, Cycles, and Swings* (Boulder, CO: Westview Press, 1991).

50. Christopher Wlezien, "The Public as Thermostat: Dynamics of Preferences for Spending," *American Journal of Political Science* 39 (1995): 981–1000.

51. Benjamin Page and Robert Shapiro, *The Rational Public* (Chicago: University of Chicago Press, 1992).

52. Dan Carney, "House GOP Embrace of Gun Curbs Not Yet Lock, Stock and Barrel," *CQ Weekly,* May 29, 1999: 1267.

53. Dan Carney, "Beyond Guns and Violence: A Battle for House Control," *CQ Weekly,* June 1999: 1426–1432.

54. Don Carney, "Beyond Guns and Violence: A Battle of House Control," *CQ Weekly,* June 19, 1999.

55. Kathy Keily, "After Failed Gun Legislation, Political Finger Pointing Begins," *USA Today,* June 21, 1999: p. 14A.

56. ABC News/*Washington Post* poll of August 30–September 2, 1999.

57. Francis X. Clines, "In a Bitter Cultural War, an Ardent Call to Arms," *New York Times,* June 17, 1999.

58. Personal communication.

59. "Increased Gun Control Not Necessarily a Cure-All," *Public Perspective,* June/July 1999: 35.

CHAPTER 6

1. Steven Rosenstone and John Mark Hansen, *Mobilization, Participation, and Democracy in America* (New York: Macmillan, 1993), p. 51.

2. Benjamin Barber, *Strong Democracy: Participatory Politics for a New Age* (Berkeley and Los Angeles: University of California Press, 1984), p. xiii.

3. John Aldrich, *Why Parties?* (Chicago: University of Chicago Press, 1995), pp. 106–107.

4. Chilton Williamson, *American Suffrage from Property to Democracy: 1760–1860* (Princeton, NJ: Princeton University Press, 1960); and Alexander Keyssar, *The Right to Vote* (New York: Basic Books, 2000), p. 29.

5. Ibid., p. 277.

6. Eleanor Flexner, *Century of Struggle,* rev. ed. (Cambridge, MA: Harvard University Press, 1975); and Anne Scott and Andrew Scott, *One Half the People* (Philadelphia: Lippincott, 1975).

7. For a history of the drive to enfranchise women, see Keyssar, *The Right to Vote,* chap. 6. On the strategies used by the suffrage movement, see Anna Harvey, "The Political Consequences of Suffrage Exclusion," *Social Science History* 20 (1996): 97–132.

8. "18-Year-Old Vote: Constitutional Amendment Cleared," *Congressional Quarterly Almanac* (Washington, DC: Congressional Quarterly, 1972), pp. 475–477.

9. Keyssar, *The Right to Vote,* pp. xxi, 14–15.

10. "Can the Black Vote Hold Up?" *The Economist,* April 3, 1999: 24.

11. Paul Peterson, "An Immodest Proposal," *Daedalus* 121 (1992): 151–174.

12. Keyssar, *The Right to Vote,* pp. xxi, 14–15.

13. For a comparative study of the American and Swiss suffrage movements, see Lee Ann Banaszak, *Why Movements Succeed or Fail* (Princeton, NJ: Princeton University Press, 1996).

14. Rosenstone and Hansen, *Mobilization, Participation, and Democracy,* chap. 2.

15. Jeffrey Jones, "Does Bringing Out the Candidate Bring Out the Votes?" *American Politics Quarterly* 26 (1998): 406.

16. John Ferejohn and Morris Fiorina, "The Paradox of Not Voting: A Decision Theoretic Analysis," *American Political Science Review* 68 (1974): 525–535.

17. John Milholland, "The Danger Point in American Politics," *North American Review* 164 (1897).

18. Raymond Wolfinger and Steven Rosenstone, *Who Votes?* (New Haven, CT: Yale University Press, 1980), p. 101.

19. A more sophisticated variant of this argument appears in Alexander A. Schuessler, *The Logic of Expressive Choice* (Princeton, NJ: Princeton University Press.

20. Howard Rosenthal and Subrata Sen, "Electoral Participation in the French Fifth Republic," *American Political Science Review* 67 (1973): 29–54.

21. Wolfinger and Rosenstone, *Who Votes?* p. 116.

22. Ruy Teixeira, *The Disappearing American Voter* (Washington, DC: The Brookings Institution, 1992), p. 10.

23. Michael McDonald and Samuel Popkin, "The Myth of the Vanishing Voter," *American Political Science Review* 95 (2001): 963–974.

24. Wolfinger and Rosenstone, *Who Votes?* p. 88.

25. Stephen Knack estimates that election-day registration boosts turnout by 3 to 6 percent on average. See his "Election Day Registration: The Second Wave," *American Politics Research* 29 (2001): 65–78.

26. Stephen Knack, "Drivers Wanted: Motor Voter and the Election of 1996," *PS: Political Science and Politics* 32 (1999): 237–243; and Michael Martinez and David Hill, "Did Motor Voter Work?" *American Politics Quarterly* 27 (1999): 296–315.

27. Mark Franklin, "Electoral Engineering and Cross-National Turnout Differences: What Role for Compulsory Voting? *British Journal of Political Science* 29 (1999): 205.

28. Richard Boyd, "Decline of U.S. Voter Turnout: Structural Explanations," *American Politics Quarterly* 9 (1981): 133–159.

29. Stephen Knack, "The Voter Participation Effects of Selecting Jurors from Registration Lists," Working Paper No. 91-10, University of Maryland, Department of Economics; and J. Eric Oliver and Raymond Wolfinger, "Jury Aversion and Voter

Registration." Paper presented at the 1997 Annual Meeting of the American Political Science Association, Washington, DC.

30. Rosenstone and Hansen, *Mobilization, Participation, and Democracy,* chap. 7, p. 175.

31. Martin Wattenberg, *The Decline of American Political Parties, 1952–1996* (Cambridge, MA: Harvard University Press, 1998). Interestingly, the percentage of voters who reported being contacted by a party rose from 1956 to 1982 but declined thereafter. Party efforts would appear to have met with very limited success, inasmuch as turnout was falling throughout the period. See Rosenstone and Hansen, *Mobilization, Participation, and Democracy,* p. 163.

32. G. Bingham Powell, "American Voter Turnout in Comparative Perspective," *American Political Science Review* 80 (1986): 17–43; and Robert Jackman, "Political Institutions and Voter Turnout in the Industrial Democracies," *American Political Science Review* 81 (1987): 405–423.

33. Rosenstone and Hansen, *Mobilization, Participation, and Democracy,* pp. 63–70. There is some conflict between their figures and those reported by Verba, Schlozman, and Brady in *Voice and Equality* (pp. 69–74). Part of the explanation may be that the survey items relied on by Rosenstone and Hansen generally have more specific referents (such as this year's elections), whereas the items relied on by Verba, Schlozman, and Brady ask more generally about activity in the last year or two years. Thus, the Verba, Schlozman, and Brady figures may reflect the increasing number of opportunities.

34. Teixeira, *The Disappearing American Voter,* p. 49.

35. Richard Brody, "The Puzzle of Political Participation in America," in *The New American Political System,* ed. Anthony King (Washington, DC: American Enterprise Institute, 1978), pp. 287–324; and Paul Abramson and John Aldrich, "The Decline of Electoral Participation in America," *American Political Science Review* 76 (1982): 502–521.

36. Rosenstone and Hansen, *Mobilization, Participation, and Democracy,* p. 183.

37. Marshall Ganz, "Motor Voter or Motivated Voter?" *The American Prospect,* September-October, 1996: 46–48; and Marshall Ganz, "Voters in the Crosshairs," *The American Prospect,* Winter 1994: 100–109.

38. David S. Broder, "Shoe-Leather Politicking," *Washington Post Weekly Edition,* June 25–July 1, 2001: 4.

39. Warren Miller, "The Puzzle Transformed: Explaining Declining Turnout," *Political Behavior* 14 (1992): 1–43.

40. Robert Putnam, "Tuning In, Tuning Out: The Strange Disappearance of Social

Capital in America," *PS: Political Science and Politics* 28 (1995): 664–683.

41. Stephen Knack, "Civic Norms, Social Sanctions, and Voter Turnout," *Rationality and Society* 4 (1992): 133–156.

42. Fareed Zakaria, "The Character of Our Campuses," *Newsweek,* May 28, 2001: 31.

43. Stephen Knack, "Civic Norms, Social Sanctions, and Voter Turnout," *Rationality and Society* 4 (1992): 133–156.

44. Eric Uslaner, "Faith, Hope, and Charity: Social Capital, Trust, and Collective Action" (College Park, MD: University of Maryland, unpublished manuscript).

45. Rosenstone and Hansen, *Mobilization, Participation, and Democracy,* chap. 7; and Teixeira, *The Disappearing American Voter,* chap. 2.

46. Laura Stoker and M. Kent Jennings, "Life-Cycle Transitions and Political Participation: The Case of Marriage," *American Political Science Review* 89 (1995): 421–433.

47. For detailed analyses of the relationship between demographic characteristics and voting, see Raymond Wolfinger and Steven Rosenstone, *Who Votes?* (New Haven, CT: Yale University Press, 1980), and Rosenstone and Hansen, *Mobilization, Participation, and Democracy,* chap. 5.

48. Verba and Nie, *Participation in America: Political Democracy and Social Equality* (New York: Harper & Row, 1972), pp. 170–171; and Wolfinger and Rosenstone, *Who Votes?* p. 90.

49. See, for example, Rosenstone and Hansen, *Mobilization, Participation, and Democracy in America,* chap. 5.

50. Katherine Tate, "Black Political Participation in the 1984 and 1988 Presidential Elections," *American Political Science Review* 85 (1991): 1159–1176.

51. On language and political participation, see Sidney Verba, Kay Schlozman, and Henry Brady, *Voice and Equality: Civic Volunteerism in American Politics* (Cambridge, MA: Harvard University Press, 1995).

52. Russell Dalton, *Citizen Politics in Western Democracies* (Chatham, NJ: Chatham House, 1988), pp. 51–52.

53. Herbert Tingsten, *Political Behavior: Studies in Election Statistics* (London: King & Son, 1937), pp. 225–226.

54. "Why Poor Turnout Points to a Healthy Democracy," *Gallup Poll Release,* May 23, 2001.

55. Quoted in Seymour Martin Lipset, *Political Man* (New York: Anchor, 1963), p. 228, note 90.

56. George Will, "In Defense of Nonvoting," in *The Morning After,* ed. George Will (New York: Free Press, 1986), p. 229.

57. Stephen Bennett and David Resnick, "The Implications of Nonvoting for

Democracy in the United States," *American Journal of Political Science* 34 (1990): 771–802.

58. Teixeira, *The Disappearing American Voter,* p. 92.

59. Joseph Carroll and Frank Newport, "A Quarter of Americans Say Iraq Nation's Most Important Problem; But Americans Still More Likely to Name Economic Issues as Top Problem Facing Country," Gallup Poll News Service, April 15, 2004.

60. Tom W. Smith, "America's Most Important Problem: A Trend Analysis, 1946–1976," *Public Opinion Quarterly* (1980): 164–180; and "America's Most Important Problems: Part I," *Public Opinion Quarterly* (1985): 264–274.

61. Political theorist Benjamin Barber refers to the former as an example of "strong democracy" and to the latter as an example of "thin democracy." See Barber, *Strong Democracy* (note 4).

62 Sidney Verba, Kay Schlozman, and Henry Brady, *Voice and Equality* (Cambridge, MA: Harvard University Press, 1995), p. 50.

63. Verba, Schlozman, and Brady, *Voice and Equality,* p. 72.

64. David Nexon, "Asymmetry in the Political System: Occasional Activists in the Democratic and Republican Parties, 1956–1964," *American Political Science Review* 65 (1971): 716–730; and Warren Miller and M. Kent Jennings, *Parties in Transition* (New York: Russell Sage, 1986), chap. 2.

65. Fareed Zakaria, "The New Face of the Left," *Newsweek,* April 30, 2001: 32.

CHAPTER 7

1. The following account is based on Phil Kunz, "Home Schooling Movement Gives House a Lesson," *Congressional Quarterly Weekly Report,* February 26, 1994: 479–480.

2. There is some controversy about how to measure group membership and consequently about the exact figures. For differing viewpoints, see Frank Baumgartner and Jack Walker, "Survey Research and Membership in Voluntary Associations," *American Journal of Political Science* 32 (1988): 908–928; Tom Smith, "Trends in Voluntary Group Membership: Comments on Baumgartner and Walker," *American Journal of Political Science* 34 (1990): 646–661; and Baumgartner and Walker, "Response to Smith's 'Trends in Voluntary Group Membership,'" *American Journal of Political Science* 34 (1990): 662–670.

3. Alexis de Tocqueville, *Democracy in America,* ed. J. P. Mayer (New York: HarperPerennial, 1969), p. 513.

4. Kay Schlozman and John Tierney, *Organized Interests and American Democracy* (New York: Harper & Row, 1981), p. 75.

5. Robert Wiebe, *The Search for Order, 1877–1920* (New York: Hill and Wang, 1967).

6. Kristen Luker, *Abortion and the Politics of Motherhood* (Berkeley: University of California Press, 1984), chaps. 5–6.

7. Robert H. Salsbury, "Interest Representation: The Dominance of Institutions," *American Political Science Review* 78 (1984): 64–76.

8. Jeffrey Berry, *Lobbying for the People* (Princeton, NJ: Princeton University Press, 1977).

9. Jack Walker, *Mobilizing Interest Groups in America* (Ann Arbor: University of Michigan Press, 1991), p. 10.

10. An excellent source of basic information about groups and associations in the United States is the *Encyclopedia of Associations,* ed. Carol Schwartz and Rebecca Turner (Detroit, MI: Gale Research, annual editions).

11. These figures represent the combined membership of the Sierra Club, Environmental Defense Fund, Friends of the Earth, the Audubon Society, the National Wildlife Federation, the Natural Resources Defense Council, and the Wilderness Society (Encyclopedia of Associations, 2000 edition).

12. Henry Brady, Sidney Verba, and Kay Schlozman, "Beyond SES: A Resource Model of Political Participation," *American Political Science Review* 89 (1995): 271–294.

13. James Q. Wilson, *Political Organizations* (New York: Basic Books, 1973), chap. 3.

14. Mancur Olson, *The Logic of Collective Action* (Cambridge, MA: Harvard University Press, 1965).

15. R. Cornes and T. Sandler, *The Theory of Externalities, Public Goods and Club Goods* (Cambridge, England: Cambridge University Press, 1986), chap. 6.

16. Documented in annual editions of U.S. Department of Labor, *Employment and Earnings* (Washington, DC: U.S. Government Printing Office, 1945–2001).

17. Jane Mansbridge, *Why We Lost the ERA* (Chicago: University of Chicago Press, 1986).

18. Kenneth Wald, *Religion and Politics in the United States,* 2nd ed. (Washington, DC: CQ Press, 1992), chap. 7.

19. The term is from Richard Wagner, "Pressure Groups and Political Entrepreneurs," *Papers in Nonmarket Decision Making* 1 (1966): 161–170. For extended discussions, see Norman Frolich, Joe Oppenheimer, and Oran Young, *Political Leadership and Collective Goods* (Princeton, NJ: Princeton University Press, 1971); and Terry Moe, *The Organization of Interests* (Chicago: University of Chicago Press, 1980), chaps. 3–4.

20. "As Green Turns to Brown," *The Economist,* March 5, 1994: 28.

21. Walker, *Mobilizing Interest Groups in America,* pp. 98–99.

22. Jack Walker, "The Origins and Maintenance of Interest Groups in America," *American Political Science Review* 77 (1983): 390–406.

23. PoliticalMoneyLine, "Health Care and Tort Reform Push Lobbying Expenditures over $154 Million a Month," www.political moneyline.com (2003); Frederick J. Frommer, "Miller Leads Beer Companies in Spending on Lobbying," Associated Press (October 5, 2003).

24. Carl Weiser, "Enforcement of Law Almost Non-existent," *USA Today,* November 16, 1999: p. 11A.

25. Center for Responsive Politics, various issues of *Influence, Inc.,* available at http://www.opensecrets.org.

26. Chuck Henning, *The Wit and Wisdom of Politics* (Golden, CO: Fulcrum Publishing, 1992), p. 137.

27. For figures see Mark Petracca, ed., *The Politics of Interests* (Boulder, CO: Westview Press, 1992), pp. 14–15; and Edward Laumann, John Heinz, Robert Nelson, and Robert Salisbury, "Washington Lawyers—and Others: The Structure of Washington Representation," *Stanford Law Review* 37 (1985): 465–502.

28. Lobbyist Michael Bromberg, quoted in Eleanor Clift and Tom Brazaitis, *War Without Bloodshed: The Art of Politics* (New York: Scribner, 1996), p. 100.

29. Jackie Koszczuk, "Hitting Them Where They Live," *Congressional Quarterly Weekly Report,* October 2, 1999: 2283–2286.

30. *Pressure Politics: The Story of the Anti-Saloon League* (New York: Columbia University Press, 1928), p. 76.

31. Frank Sorauf, *Inside Campaign Finance* (New Haven, CT: Yale University Press, 1992), chap. 4. A basic reference on PACs is *The PAC Directory* (Cambridge, MA: Ballinger, various editions).

32. Ross Baker, *The New Fat Cats: Members of Congress as Political Benefactors* (New York: Priority Press, 1989); and Eliza Carney, "PAC Men," *National Journal,* October 1, 1994: 2268–2273.

33. Thomas Ferguson and Joel Rogers, *Right Turn: The Decline of the Democrats and the Future of American Politics* (New York: Hill and Wang, 1986).

34. For a discussion, see Richard Hall and Frank Wayman, "Buying Time: Moneyed Interests and the Mobilization of Bias in Congressional Committees," *American Political Science Review* 84 (1990): 797–820.

35. See Edward Epstein, "Business and Labor Under the Federal Election Campaign Act of 1971," in *Parties, Interest Groups, and Campaign Finance Laws,* ed. Michael Malbin (Washington, DC: American Enterprise Institute, 1980), pp. 107–151.

36. Jim Drinkard, "Issue Ads Crowd Airwaves Before 2000 Election," *USA Today,* November 29, 1999: p. 11A.

37. R. Kenneth Godwin, *One Billion Dollars of Influence* (Chatham, NJ: Chatham House, 1988).

38. Andrew McFarland, *Common Cause: Lobbying for the People* (Chatham, NJ: Chatham House, 1984), pp. 74–81.

39. Ed Henry, "It's the '90s: Old Dogs, New Tricks," *Roll Call Monthly,* November 1997: 13.

40. For elaboration, see Hugh Graham and Ted Gurr, *The History of Violence in America* (New York: Bantam, 1969).

41. For an analysis of the expansion by the judiciary of federal programs for the handicapped and the poor, see R. Shep Melnick, *Between the Lines* (Washington, DC: The Brookings Institution, 1994).

42. Karen O'Connor and Bryan McFall, "Conservative Interest Group Litigation in the Reagan Era and Beyond," in *The Politics of Interests,* ed. Mark Petracca (Boulder, CO: Westview Press, 1992), pp. 263–281.

43. Jeffrey Milyo, David Primo, and Timothy Groseclose, "Corporate PAC Campaign Contributions in Perspective," *Business and Politics* 2(2000): 75–88.

44. Jonathan Rauch, *Demosclerosis* (New York: Random House, 1994).

45. Philip Stern, *The Best Congress Money Can Buy* (New York: Pantheon, 1988).

46. John Heinz, Edward Laumann, Robert Nelson, and Robert Salisbury, *Representing Interests: Structure and Uncertainty in National Policy Making* (in press).

47. J. Leiper Freeman, *The Political Process,* rev. ed. (New York: Random House, 1965); Grant McConnell, *Private Power and American Democracy* (New York: Knopf, 1966); and Theodore Lowi, *The End of Liberalism* (New York: Norton, 1969).

48. David Hosansky, "House and Senate Assemble Conflicting Farm Bills," *Congressional Quarterly Weekly Report,* February 3, 1996: 298.

49. Hugh Heclo, "Issue Networks and the Executive Establishment, in *The New American Political System,* ed. Anthony King (Washington, DC: The Brookings Institution, 1978), pp. 87–124.

50. Robert Salisbury, John Heinz, Robert Nelson, and Edward Laumann, "Triangles, Networks, and Hollow Cores: The Complex Geometry of Washington Interest Representation," in *The Politics of Interests,* ed. Mark Petracca (Boulder, CO: Westview Press, 1992), pp. 130–149.

51. John Chubb, *Interest Groups and the Bureaucracy* (Stanford, CA: Stanford University Press, 1983), pp. 249–265; and Richard Harris, "Politicized Management: The Changing Face of Business in American Politics," in *Remaking American Politics,* ed. Richard Harris and Sidney Milkiss (Boulder, CO: Westview Press, 1989), pp. 261–286.

52. Schlozman and Tierney, *Organized Interests and American Democracy,* pp. 314–317.

53. John Hibbing and Elizabeth Theiss-Morse, *Congress as Public Enemy* (New York: Cambridge University Press, 1995), pp. 63–65, 147.

54. Earl Latham, *The Group Basis of Politics* (New York: Cornell University Press, 1952); and David Truman, *The Governmental Process* (New York: Knopf, 1958).

55. E. E. Schattschneider, *The Semisovereign People* (New York: Holt, 1960), pp. 34–35.

56. *Politics, Pressures, and the Tariff* (New York: Prentice-Hall, 1935).

57. E. E. Schattschneider, "The Gerontocrats," *The Economist,* May 13, 1995: 32.

58. Mansbridge, *Why We Lost the ERA,* p. 73.

59. Peter Aranson and Peter Ordeshook, "A Prolegomenon to a Theory of the Failure of Representative Democracy," in *American Re-evolution,* ed. Aranson and Ordeshooks (Tucson: University of Arizona, 1977), pp. 23–46.

CHAPTER 8

1. Terence Smith, "Media Notebook on the Republican National Convention," PBS Online NewsHour, September 1, 2004; Shorenstein Center, "Election Interest Is Up Sharply But Convention Interest is Not," Cambridge, MA: John F. Kennedy School of Government.

2. The first phrase comes from Richard Katz, "Party Government: A Rationalistic Conception," in *Visions and Realities of Party Government,* ed. F. Castles and R. Wildenmann (Berlin: deGruyter, 1986), p. 31. The second comes from Geoffrey Smith, "The Futures of Party Government," p. 206 of the same volume.

3. *Party Government* (New York: Farrar and Rinehart, 1942), p. 1.

4. Martin Wattenberg, *The Decline of American Political Parties, 1952–1992* (Cambridge, MA: Harvard University Press, 1994).

5. John Aldrich, *Why Parties?* (Chicago: University of Chicago Press, 1995), chap. 2.

6. See, for example, James Campbell, *The Presidential Pulse of Congressional Elections* (Lexington: University Press of Kentucky, 1993).

7. V. O. Key, Jr., *Southern Politics* (New York: Knopf, 1949).

8. Richard Fenno, *Home Style* (Boston: Little, Brown, 1978), chap. 3.

9. Juliet Eilperin, "GOP, Trying to Expand, Aids Black Candidates," *Washington Post,* July 16, 2000: p. A6.

10. Anthony Downs, *An Economic Theory of Democracy* (New York: Harper & Row, 1957).

11. Gavin Wright, "The Political Economy of New Deal Spending: An Econometric Analysis," *Review of Economics and Statistics* 56 (1974): 30–38.

12. Morris Fiorina, *Divided Government,* 2nd ed. (Boston: Allyn & Bacon, 1996), pp. 107–110.

13. R. Michael Alvarez and Jonathan Nagler, "Economics, Issues, and the Perot Candidacy: Voter Choice in the 1992 Presidential Election," *American Journal of Political Science* 39 (1995): 714–744.

14. Discussed in James MacGregor Burns, *The Deadlock of Democracy* (Englewood Cliffs, NJ: Prentice-Hall, 1964), chap. 2.

15. Austin Ranney, *Curing the Mischiefs of Faction* (Berkeley: University of California Press, 1975); and Nelson Polsby, *Consequences of Party Reform* (New York: Oxford University Press, 1983).

16. James Bryce, *The American Commonwealth,* 4th ed. (London: Macmillan, 1910), vol. 2, p. 5.

17. See, for example, William Chambers and Walter Dean Burnham, eds., *The American Party Systems: Stages of Political Development* (New York: Oxford University Press, 1975).

18. The seminal contribution was V. O. Key, Jr., "A Theory of Critical Elections," *Journal of Politics* 17 (1955): 3–18. The most influential elaborations and extensions of the idea are Walter Dean Burnham, *Critical Elections and the Mainsprings of American Politics* (New York: Norton, 1970) and James Sundquist, *Dynamics of the Party System,* rev. ed. (Washington, DC: The Brookings Institution, 1983).

19. David R. Mayhew, *Electoral Realignments: A Critique of an American Genre* (New Haven, CT: Yale, 2002).

20. George Johnson, *Architects of Fear: Conspiracy Theories and Paranoia in American Politics* (Los Angeles: Tarcher/Houghton Mifflin, 1983), p. 59.

21. Robert Remini, *Martin Van Buren and the Making of the Democratic Party* (New York: Columbia, 1959); and Donald Cole, *Martin Van Buren and the American Political System* (Princeton, NJ: Princeton University Press, 1984).

22. For a recent history of the period, see Paul Kleppner, *The Third Electoral System, 1853–1892: Parties, Voters, and Political Cultures* (Chapel Hill: University of North Carolina Press, 1979).

23. Charles Stewart and Barry Weingast, "Stacking the Senate, Changing the Nation: Republican Rotten Boroughs, Statehood Politics, and American Political Development," *Studies in American Political Development* 6 (1992): 223–271.

24. Michael McGerr, *The Decline of Popular Politics* (New York: Oxford University Press, 1986).

25. Harold Gosnell provides a classic study of a machine. See his *Machine Politics: Chicago Model* (Chicago: University of Chicago Press, 1937). For a more recent study, see M. C. Brown and C. N. Halaby, "Machine Politics in America, 1870–1945," *Journal of Interdisciplinary History* 17 (1987): 587–612.

26. John D. Hicks, *The Populist Revolt* (Minneapolis: University of Minnesota Press, 1931).

27. E. E. Schattschneider, "United States: The Functional Approach to Party Government," in *Modern Political Parties,* ed. Sigmund Neumann (Chicago: University of Chicago Press, 1956), pp. 194–215.

28. Richard Vallely, "National Parties and Racial Disenfranchisement," in *Classifying by Race,* ed. Paul Peterson (Princeton, NJ: Princeton University Press, 1995), pp. 188–216.

29. Alan Lichtman, *Prejudice and the Old Politics* (Chapel Hill: University of North Carolina Press, 1979).

30. Richard Hofstadter, *The Age of Reform* (New York: Vintage, 1955); and Gabriel Kolko, *The Triumph of Conservatism* (New York: Free Press, 1963).

31. Joel Silbey, "Beyond Realignment and Realignment Theory," in *The End of Realignment?* ed. Byron Shafer (Madison: University of Wisconsin Press, 1991), pp. 3–23.

32. Walter Dean Burnham believes that a realignment did indeed occur in the early 1990s. See his "Realignment Lives: The 1994 Earthquake and Its Implications," in *The Clinton Presidency: First Appraisals,* ed. Colin Campbell and Bert Rockman (Chatham, NJ: Chatham House, 1996), pp. 363–395.

33. Steven Rosenstone, Roy Behr, and Edward Lazarus, *Third Parties in America*

(Princeton, NJ: Princeton University Press, 1981).

34. Maurice Duverger, *Political Parties: Their Organization and Activity in the Modern State* (New York: Wiley, 1963), book II, chap. 1.

35. Ibid. For elaboration, see Thomas Palfrey, "A Mathematical Proof of Duverger's Law," in *Models of Strategic Choice in Politics,* ed. Peter Ordeshook (Ann Arbor: University of Michigan Press, 1989), pp. 69–91.

36. Douglas Rae, *The Political Consequences of Electoral Laws,* rev. ed. (New Haven, CT: Yale University Press, 1971), p. 98. Compare Arend Lijphart, who argues that Rae's figures exaggerate the difference; see Lijphart, "The Political Consequences of Electoral Laws, 1945–1985," *American Political Science Review* 84 (1990): 481–496.

37. *Trans Action* 7 (1969): 12–22.

38. *Critical Elections,* chap. 5.

39. *The Party's Over: The Failure of American Politics* (New York: Harper & Row, 1971).

40. Xandra Kayden and Eddie Mahe, Jr., *The Party Goes On: The Persistence of the Two-Party System in the United States* (New York: Basic, 1985); and Larry Sabato, *The Party's Just Begun: Shaping Political Parties for America's Future* (Glenview, IL: Scott, Foresman, 1988).

41. Leon Epstein, *Political Parties in the American Mold* (Madison: University of Wisconsin Press, 1986); and Joseph Schlesinger, "The New American Party System," *American Political Science Review* 79 (1985): 1152–1169.

42. The following classification of parties as organizations, parties in the electorate, and parties in government is a standard one developed most fully in Frank Sorauf's text, *Party Politics in America* (Boston: Little, Brown, various editions).

43. Julius Turner, *Party and Constituency: Pressures on Congress* (Baltimore, MD: Johns Hopkins University Press, 1951).

44. *The Deadlock of Democracy.*

45. John C. Green and Paul S. Herrnson, eds., *Responsible Partisanship? The Evolution of American Political Parties Since 1950* (Lawrence, KS: University Press of Kansas, 2003).

46. Bruce E. Keith et al., *The Myth of the Independent Voter* (Berkeley, CA: University of California Press, 1992).

47. Writing in the 1970s, Hugh Heclo put the number at 3000. See his *A Government of Strangers* (Washington, DC: The Brookings Institution, 1977). By 1992 Thomas Weko put the number at about 3700. See *The Politicizing Presidency* (Lawrence: University of Kansas Press, 1995), p. 161.

48. Stephen Skowronek, *Building a New American State* (New York: Cambridge University Press, 1992), p. 69.

49. Stephen Frantzich, *Political Parties in the Technological Age* (New York: Longman, 1989).

50. *U.S. News & World Report,* "The Winner's Room," December 1, 2003: 8.

51. Cornelius Cotter, James Gibson, John Bibby, and Robert Huckshorn, *Party Organizations in American Politics* (New York: Praeger, 1984).

52. Ibid.

53. Dick Polman, "American Politics Circa 2003: Neither Kind nor Gentle," Knight-Ridder News Service, August 17, 2003; David S. Broder, "Fighting Over the Economy," *Washington Post Weekly Edition,* November 5–11, 2001: 4.

54. John Coleman, "Resurgent or Just Busy? Party Organizations in Contemporary America," in *The State of the Parties,* 2nd ed., ed. John Green and Daniel Shea (Lanham, MD: Rowman and Littlefield, 1996), pp. 312–326.

55. Robert Dahl, *Dilemmas of Pluralist Democracy* (New Haven, CT: Yale University Press, 1982).

CHAPTER 9

1. Allen J. Matusow, *The Unraveling of America* (New York: Harper and Row, 1984), p. 413; Jules Witcover, *The Year the Dream Died* (New York: Warner Books, 1997), p. 321; and Todd Gitlin, *The Sixties* (New York: Bantam, 1987), p. 322.

2. Ronald Radosh, *Divided They Fell* (New York: Free Press, 1996), p. 123; and Gitlin, *The Sixties,* p. 320.

3. Matusow, *Unraveling of America,* p. 413; and Gitlin, *The Sixties,* p. 322.

4. Radosh, *Divided They Fell,* pp. 124–128; and Matusow, *Unraveling of America,* pp. 418–419.

5. Witcover, *Year the Dream Died,* p. 327; and Matusow, *Unraveling of America,* p. 418.

6. On the British reporters, see Lewis Chester, Godfrey Hodgson, and Bruce Page, *An American Melodrama* (New York: Viking, 1969), p. 582. For an attempt to interpret Daley's verbal abuse of Ribicoff, see Gitlin, *The Sixties,* p. 334.

7. Chester, Hodgson, and Page, *American Melodrama,* p. 592.

8. John Robinson, "Public Reaction to Political Protest: Chicago 1968," *Public Opinion Quarterly* 34 (1970): 1–9.

9. Frank Luther Mott, *American Journalism* (New York: Macmillan, 1950).

10. Samuel Kernell, *Going Public: New Strategies of Presidential Leadership* (Washington, DC: CQ Press, 1986). Compare Mel Laracey, "The Presidential Newspaper: The Forgotten

Way of Going Public" (manuscript, Harvard University, 1993).

11. Mott, *American Journalism,* p. 216.

12. William Safire, "Media Mergers Limit Information Flow," New York Times News Service, January 22, 2003.

13. 1999 annual radio station survey by M Street Corporation of Nashville http://www.mstreet.net.

14. Tom Humphrey, "Talk Radio is Major Player in Tennessee Political Wars," *Knoxville* (TN) *News-Sentinel,* July 19, 2002.

15. Personal communication of Premier Radio, which manages and distributes the Limbaugh show, with research assistant Sam Abrams, March 28, 2000.

16. Theodore H. White, *The Making of the President, 1960* (New York: Signet, 1961), p. 128; Nelson Polsby and Aaron Wildavsky, *Presidential Elections* (New York: Scribner, 1964), pp. 119–121.

17. Mary Ann Watson, *The Expanding Vista: American Television in the Kennedy Years* (New York: Oxford University Press, 1990), p. 76.

18. Austin Ranney, "Broadcasting, Narrowcasting, and Politics," in *The New American Political System,* second version, ed. Anthony Kind (Washington, DC: AEI Press, 1990), pp. 175–201.

19. *Newsweek,* November 9, 2001, p. 23; Johnnie L. Roberts, "All the News That's Fit to Merge," *Newsweek,* October 7, 2002, p. 48.

20. Pew Research Center for the People and the Press (http://www.peoplepress.org/med98rpt.htm); Mediamark Research Inc., "Multimedia Audiences," 1999.

21. William Mayer, "The Rise of the New Media," *Public Opinion Quarterly* 58 (1994): 124–146.

22. *Atlanta Journal Constitution,* January 29, 2002.

23. Terence Smith, "Humanizing the Candidates," PBS Online NewsHour, October 7, 2004.

24. Marc Peyser, "Red, White, and Funny," *Newsweek,* January 5, 2004, pp. 71–77.

25. www.nua.ie/surveys/how_many_online/index.html.

26. Mark Gillespie, " 'Cyber-Politics' May be More Hype Than Reality . . . So Far," Gallup Poll Release, February 25, 2000.

27. Jim Puzzanghera, "Candidates Rake in Funds on Internet, *San Jose Mercury News,* January 5, 2000.

28. Bob Keefe, "Internet Levels Fundraising Field for Dean," GlobalSecurity.com, December 11, 2003.

29. *Newsweek,* "A Whole New Political Game," October 30, 2000, p. 90.

30. Markus Prior, "The Political Impact of Changes in the Media Environment," (Ph.D. dissertation, Stanford University, 2003).

31. Roper Organization, *America's Watching: Public Attitudes Toward Television* (1997).

32. William Mayer, "Trends in Media Usage," *Public Opinion Quarterly* 57 (1993): 597, 610.

33. For example, Doris Graber, *Mass Media and American Politics* (Washington, DC: CQ Press, 1993), chap. 7; and Pippa Norris, *A Virtuous Circle* (Cambridge: Cambridge University Press, 2000), p. 173.

34. Russell Neuman, Marion Just, and Ann Crigler, *Common Knowledge: News and the Construction of Political Meaning* (Chicago: University of Chicago Press, 1992); and Jeffrey Mondak, "Newspapers and Political Awareness," *American Journal of Political Science* 39 (1995): 513–527.

35. William Kornhauser, *The Politics of Mass Society* (New York: Free Press, 1959).

36. An example is the study of the 1940 presidential campaign reported in Paul Lazarsfeld, Bernard Berelson, and Hazel Gaudet, *The People's Choice* (New York: Columbia University Press, 1948).

37. Joseph Klapper, *The Effects of Mass Communication* (New York: Free Press, 1960).

38. Bernard Cohen, *The Press and Foreign Policy* (Princeton, NJ: Princeton University Press, 1963), p. 13.

39. Presentation by Steven Livingston at the John F. Kennedy School of Government, Harvard University, March 1996.

40. Robert Rotberg and Thomas Weiss, eds., *From Massacres to Genocide* (Washington, DC: The Brookings Institution, 1996).

41. M. McCombs and D. Shaw, "The Evolution of Agenda-Setting: Twenty-Five Years in the Marketplace of Ideas," *Journal of Communications* 43 (1993): 58–67.

42. Steven Livingston and Todd Eachus, "Humanitarian Crises and U.S. Foreign Policy: Somalia and the CNN Effect Reconsidered," *Political Communication* 12 (1995): 413–429.

43. Lawrence Jacobs and Robert Shapiro, *Politicians Don't Pander* (Chicago: University of Chicago Press, 2000).

44. Shanto Iyengar and Donald Kinder, *News That Matters: Television and American Opinion* (Chicago: University of Chicago Press, 1987).

45. Jon Krosnick and Laura Brannon, "The Impact of the Gulf War on the Ingredients of Presidential Evaluations," *American Political Science Review* 87 (1993): 963–975.

46. Marc Hetherington, "The Media's Role in Forming Voters' National Economic Evaluations in 1992," *American Journal of Political Science* 40 (1966): 372–395.

47. The most extensive study of framing is Shanto Iyengar's *Is Anyone Responsible?* (Chicago: University of Chicago Press, 1991).

48. *Public Opinion,* December/January 1985: 39.

49. Chicago Tribune, "TV Showing More Sex, More Safe-Sex Messages," published in the *Lexington* (KY) *Herald-Leader,* February 21, 2003, p. A17.

50. David Bauder, "Smash-Mouth Programming," Associated Press, December 10, 2003.

51. Robert D. Putnam, "Tuning In, Tuning Out: The Strange Disappearance of Social Capital in America," *PS: Political Science and Politics,* 27 (4): 664–683.

52. Marc Peyser, "Family TV Goes Down the Tube," *Newsweek,* February 23, 2004: pp. 52–54.

53. Allan McBride, "Television, Individualism, and Social Capital," *PS: Political Science and Politics,* September 1998: pp. 542–552.

54. Robert M. Entman and Andrew Rojecki, *The Black Image in the White Mind* (Chicago: University of Chicago Press, 2000).

55. Michael Eric Dyson, quoted in "Guess Who's Coming to the Rescue," *Newsweek,* November 13, 2000: p. 14.

56. Iyengar and Kinder, *News That Matters,* chaps. 6, 10.

57. Bernard Cohen, *The Press and Foreign Policy.* See also Lutz Erbring, Edie Goldenberg, and Arthur Miller, "Front-Page News and Real-World Clues: A New Look at Agenda-Setting by the Media," *American Journal of Political Science* 24 (1980): 16–49.

58. Don Oberdorfer, *Tet!* (New York: Doubleday, 1971); and Peter Braestrup, *Big Story,* Abridged Edition (New Haven, CT: Yale University Press, 1983).

59. S. Robert Lichter and Stanley Rothman, "Media and Business Elites," *Public Opinion:* October/November 1981: 43. Freedom Forum survey cited in Jill Zuckman, "Dole Says Media Overplay GOP View on Abortion," *Boston Globe,* June 25, 1996: p. 10.

60. William Schneider and I. A. Lewis, "Views on the News," *Public Opinion:* August/September 1985: 6–11; and "Ordinary Americans More Cynical Than Journalists: News Media Differs with Public and Leaders on Watchdog Issues" (Washington, DC: Times Mirror Center on People and the Press, May 22, 1995).

61. Charlie Cook, "It's More, Much More, Than Just a Kiss," *National Journal,* September 23, 2000: 2993.

62. Maura Clancy and Michael Robinson, "The Media in Campaign '84: General Election Coverage, Part I," *Public Opinion,* December/January 1985: 49–54, 59.

63. Daniel Amundson and S. Robert Lichter, "Heeeeeeree's Politics," *Public Opinion,* July/August 1988: 46.

64. Martha Moore, "Candidates Try to Reach Voters by Joking with Jay, Dueling with Dave," *USA Today* (March 1, 2000): p. 14A.

65. Schneider and Lewis note that in the *Los Angeles Times* study that they report on, "Views on the News," one-quarter of the readership thought their papers were conservative, one-quarter thought liberal, one-quarter thought moderate, and one-quarter didn't know.

66. Jeff Leeds, "More Negative Coverage for Gore Than Bush This Fall," *San Francisco Chronicle,* November 1, 2000: p. A2.

67. Harold Stanley and Richard Niemi, *Vital Statistics on American Politics,* 5th ed. (Washington, DC: CQ Press, 1995), p. 73.

68. Ben Bagdikian, *Double Vision* (Boston: Beacon Press, 1995), p. 48.

69. Harold Meyerson, "Misinformed? You May Be Getting Your News from Fox," *Washington Post,* printed in the *Lexington Herald-Leader,* October 17, 2003: p. A13.

70. John Leo, "A Surprising Jog to the Right," *U.S. News & World Report,* November 24, 2003: 64.

71. G. C. Stone and E. Grusin, "Network TV as Bad News Bearer," *Journalism Quarterly* 61 (1984): 517–523; R. H. Bohle, "Negativism as News Selection Predictor," *Journalism Quarterly* 63 (1986): 789–796; and D. E. Harrington, "Economic News on Television: The Determinants of Coverage," *Public Opinion Quarterly* 53 (1989): 17–40.

72. Larry Sabato, *Feeding Frenzy* (New York: Simon and Schuster, 1991).

73. Michael Robinson, "Public Affairs Television and the Growth of Political Malaise," *American Political Science Review* 70 (1976): 409–432. On TV making people more negative about human nature generally, see George Comstock, *The Evolution of American Television* (Newbury Park, CA: Sage, 1989), pp. 265–269.

74. *Newsweek,* September 28, 1998: 31.

75. A widely cited study of what constitutes news is provided by Herbert Gans, *Deciding What's News: A Case Study of CBS Evening News, NBC Nightly News, Newsweek and Time* (New York: Vintage, 1979).

76. The following account is based on Thomas Romer and Barry Weingast, "Political Foundations of the Thrift Debacle," in *Politics and Economics in the 1980s,* ed. Alberto Alesina and Geoffrey Carliner (Chicago: University of Chicago Press, 1981), pp. 175–214.

77. Ellen Hume, "Why the Press Blew the S & L Scandal," *New York Times,* May 24, 1990: p. A25.

78. Mark Rom, *Public Spirit in the Thrift Tragedy* (Pittsburgh: University of Pittsburgh Press, 1996).

79. Quoted in James Fallows, *Breaking the News* (New York: Pantheon, 1966), p. 137.

80. Mark Weisbrot, "Shirking Journalistic Duty," Knight Ridder/Tribune News Service, May 13, 2003; Greg Dyke, quoted in *Newsweek,* May 5, 2003, p. 25; and Howard Kurtz, "What's Blue and White and Red All Over?" *Washington Post Weekly Edition,* December 13–19, 2001: 34.

81. John David Rausch, Jr., "The Pathology of Politics: Government, Press, and Scandal," *Extensions: A Publication of the Carl Albert Congressional Research and Studies Center* (Norman, OK: Carl Albert Congressional Research and Studies Center, Fall 1990), pp. 11–12.

82. A Gallup survey of former Nieman Journalism Fellows found that more than three-quarters believe that traditional journalism is being replaced by tabloid journalism. See "The State of the Public Media Today" (Cambridge, MA: Nieman Foundation, April 1995).

83. Sabato, *Feeding Frenzy.*

84. Peyser, "Red, White, and Funny," p. 77.

85. Fallows, *Breaking the News,* p. 132.

86. John Kramer, vice president for communication, Institute of Justice, personal communication, September 9, 1999.

87. Alison Carper, "Paint-by-Numbers Journalism: How Reader Surveys and Focus Groups Subvert a Democratic Press" (Barone Center on the Press, Politics and Public Policy, Harvard University Kennedy School of Government, Discussion Paper D-19, April 1995).

88. Peter Canellos, "Perot Ad Announcement is Also-Ran Against Reruns," *Boston Globe,* September 13, 1996: p. A24.

89. Thomas Patterson, *Out of Order* (New York: Knopf, 1993), chap. 2.

90. Kiku Adatto, *Picture Perfect* (New York: Basic, 1993), chap. 25.

91. Quoted in Craig Lambert, "Hertzberg of the *New Yorker,*" *Harvard Magazine,* January–February 2003: 36.

92. Ibid.

93. Pippa Norris, "Editorial," *Press/Politics* 2 (1997): 1.

94. *Washington Post,* "Parties Take Their Conventions to the Web," July 14, 2000; Smith, "Media Notebook."

95. Elihu Katz and Jacob Feldman, "The Debates in the Light of Research: A Survey of Surveys," in *The Great Debates,* ed. Sidney Kraus (Bloomington: University of Indiana Press, 1962), pp. 173–223.

96. Thomas Holbrook, "Campaigns, National Conditions, and U.S. Presidential Elections," *American Journal of Political Science* 38 (1994): 973–998.

97. Michael Robinson and Margaret Sheehan, *Over the Wire and on TV* (New York: Russell Sage, 1983).

98. S. Robert Lichter and Daniel Amundson, "Less News Is Worse News: Television News Coverage of Congress, 1972–92," in *Congress, the Press, and the Public,* ed. Thomas Mann and Norman Ornstein (Washington, DC: American Enterprise Institute, 1994), pp. 131–140.

99. Iyengar, Shanto, *Is Anyone Responsible?* (Chicago: University of Chicago Press, 1991).

100. David Ignatius, "Did You Say Change?" *Washington Post Weekly Edition,* September 10–16, 2001: 27.

101. Lichter and Amundson, "Less News Is Worse News."

102. Kenneth T. Walsh, "A White House Whodunit," *U.S. News & World Report,* October 13, 2003: 18-20; Evan Thomas and Michael Isikoff, "Secrets and Leaks," *Newsweek,* October 13, 2003: 26–32.

103. *Newsweek,* August 17, 1998: 21.

104. Ibid.

105. S. Robert Lichter, Linda S. Lichter, and Daniel Amundson, "Government Goes Down the Tube, Images of Government in TV Entertainment, 1955–1998," *Press/Politics* 5 (2) (2000): 96–103.

106. Quoted in Fallows, *Breaking the News,* pp. 187–188.

CHAPTER 10

1. Information on polls and journalistic commentary comes from: Dan Balz and David S. Broder, "Election Day Dawns With Unpredictability," *Washington Post,* November 2, 2004: A1; Jim Rutenberg, "Report Says Problems Led to Skewed Survey Data," *New York Times,* November 5, 2004: 23; David Andreatta, "Swervy Surveys," *New York Post,* November 4, 2004: 9; Martin Sieff, "October Surprises Rock Bush," United Press International, October 14, 2004; Agence France Presse, "British Bookmakers Report Flurry of Bets on Kerry Victory," November 2, 2004; The Frontrunner, "Bush Maintains Small Edge in National Polls," October 29, 2004; The Frontrunner, "GOP Defectors May Give Kerry Victory in Iowa," November 1, 2004; William Raspberry, "'Unwanted, Unpolled' Voters Could Spur Kerry Victory," *Deseret Morning News,* November 1, 2004; Anatole Kaletsky, "Opinion Poll Tie Suggests Kerry Is On Course to Win," *The Times* (London), October 26, 2004: 50.

2. Information on political science predictions appears in the October 2004 issue of *PS: Political Science & Politics* as well as U.S. Newswire, "Political Scientists Forecast Bush Victory in 2004," October 15, 2004.

3. "Fresh Light on Primary Colors," *The Economist,* February 24, 1996: 23.

4. A good current description of the caucus system can be found in William Mayer, "Caucuses: How They Work, What Difference They Make," in *In Pursuit of the White House,* ed. William Mayer (Chatham, NJ: Chatham House, 1996).

5. On the history of the presidential primary, see James Davis, *Springboard to the White House* (New York: Crowell, 1967).

6. John Kessel, *The Goldwater Coalition* (Indianapolis: Bobbs-Merrill, 1968), chap. 3.

7. Nelson Polsby, *Consequences of Party Reform* (New York: Oxford University Press, 1983), chap. 1.

8. For a participant observer's account of the post-1968 reforms, see Austin Ranney, *Curing the Mischiefs of Faction* (Berkeley: University of California Press, 1975).

9. On primary dynamics, see John Aldrich, *Before the Convention* (Chicago: University of Chicago Press, 1980); and Larry Bartels, *Presidential Primaries and the Dynamics of Public Choice* (Princeton, NJ: Princeton University Press, 1988).

10. Stephen Wayne, *The Road to the White House, 1996* (New York: St. Martin's, 1997), chap. 2.

11. Jim Drinkard, "Let the Fundraising Begin—Again," *USA Today,* March 10, 2000: p. 14A; and Elizabeth Shogren, "Bush Cracks Records for Campaign Spending," *USA Today,* March 21, 2000: p. 13A.

12. Expenditures for 2004 documented at http://www.fec.gov/press/20031230 certification.html.

13. John Haskell, *Fundamentally Flawed* (Lanham, MD: Rowman and Littlefield, 1996).

14. "Many Voters Unable to Name Any Democratic Candidates, Poll Finds," Associated Press, August 31, 2003.

15. Nielsen Media Research, "Top 10 Primetime Broadcast TV programs," 10/25/04–10/31/04; Nielsen Media Research, "Presidential Debate—Day 2," October 11, 2004.

16. Larry Sabato, "Presidential Nominations: The Front-Loaded Frenzy of '96," in *Toward the Millennium: The Elections of 1996,* ed. Larry Sabato (Boston: Allyn & Bacon, 1997), pp. 37–91.

17. "A Good Fight Draws a Crowd," *New York Times,* March 12, 2000: section 4, p. 5.

18. On popular perceptions of Democratic and Republican presidential versus congressional candidates, see Robert Erikson, "Roll Calls, Reputations, and Representation in the U.S. Senate," *Legislative Studies Quarterly* 15 (1990): 630.

19. See John G. Geer, *Nominating Presidents* (New York: Greenwood Press, 1989), chap. 2; and Barbara Norander, "Nomination Choices: Caucus and Primary Outcomes, 1976–1988," *American Journal of Political Science* 37 (1993): 343–364.

20. James McCann, "Presidential Nomination Activists and Political Representation: A View from the Active Minority Studies," in *In Pursuit of the White House,* ed. William Mayer (Chatham, NJ: Chatham House, 1996), pp. 72–104.

21. On presidential fund raising, see Clifford Brown, Lynda Powell, and Clyde Wilcox, *Serious Money* (Cambridge, England: Cambridge University Press, 1995).

22. Thomas Patterson, *Out of Order* (New York: Vintage, 1994), p. 74.

23. "Once Again, 2 Small States Warp Political Process," *USA Today,* January 24, 2000: p. 18A.

24. Patterson, *Out of Order.*

25. Most research finds only small electoral impacts for the vice-presidential nominees. See Steven Rosenstone, *Forecasting Presidential Elections* (New Haven: Yale University Press, 1983), pp. 64–66 and 87–88.

26. During the last two months of the presidential campaigns of 1976–1988, about 40 percent of the lead stories on the CBS evening news were about the election, as were 20 percent of all the stories reported. See Stephen J. Rosenstone and John Mark Hansen, *Mobilization, Participation, and Democracy in America* (New York: Macmillan, 1993), p. 178, n. 26.

27. Thomas Patterson and Robert McClure, *The Unseeing Eye: The Myth of Television Power in National Elections* (New York: Putnam, 1976); and Stephen Ansolabehere and Shanto Iyengar, *Going Negative: How Attack Ads Shrink and Polarize the Electorate* (New York: Free Press, 1995).

28. Darrel West, *Air Wars: Television Advertising in Election Campaigns, 1952–1992* (Washington, DC: Congressional Quarterly, 1993).

29. Edwin Diamond and Stephen Bates, *The Spot,* 3rd ed. (Cambridge, MA: MIT Press, 1992).

30. William Mayer, "In Defense of Negative Campaigning," *Political Science Quarterly* 111 (1996): 437–455.

31. Craig Brians and Martin Wattenberg, "Campaign Issue Knowledge and Salience: Comparing Reception from TV Commercials, TV News, and Newspapers," *American Journal of Political Science* 40 (1996): 172–193.

32. Ibid. Not all scholars agree that negative ads are more effective than positive ones or that negative ads depress turnout. For a thorough airing of the issues, see the Forum in the December 1999 issue of the *American Political Science Review.*

33. Brian J. Gaines, "Popular Myths About Popular Vote-Electoral College Splits," *PS: Political Science and Politics* 34 (March, 2001): 71-75.

34. See the National Election Studies at www.umich.edu/~nes/.

35. Although the general notion of "partisanship" has been around for centuries, the social-psychological concept of party ID was advanced in the pioneering work of Angus Campbell, Philip Converse, Warren Miller, and Donald Stokes, *The American Voter* (New York: Wiley, 1960), chaps. 6–7.

36. Morris Fiorina, *Retrospective Voting in American National Elections* (New Haven, CT: Yale University Press, 1981); and Michael MacKuen, Robert Erikson, and James Stimson, "Macropartisanship," *American Political Science Review* 83 (1989): 1125–1142.

37. The classic demonstration appears in Chapter 8 of Campbell et al., *The American Voter,* although there is general agreement that the picture presented there is overstated. For balanced treatments of policy issues in recent campaigns, see the series of *Change and Continuity* volumes by Paul Abramson, John Aldrich, and David Rohde, published by CQ Press.

38. Benjamin Page and Richard Brody, "Policy Voting and the Electoral Process: The Vietnam War Issue," *American Political Science Review* 66 (1972): 979–995.

39. Edward Carmines and James Stimson, "The Two Faces of Issue Voting," *American Political Science Review* 74 (1980): 78–91.

40. Ibid. Also see R. Douglas Arnold, *The Logic of Congressional Action* (New Haven, CT: Yale University Press, 1990), chap. 2.

41. Richard Trilling, *Party Image and Electoral Behavior* (New York: Wiley, 1976).

42. Fiorina, *Retrospective Voting.*

43. Scott Teeter, "Public Opinion in 1984," and Gerald Pomper, "The Presidential Election," both in Gerald Pomper et al., *The Election of 1984* (Chatham, NJ: Chatham House, 1985).

44. Samuel Popkin, *The Reasoning Voter* (Chicago: University of Chicago Press, 1991), pp. 60–67.

45. Donald Stokes, "Some Dynamic Elements of Contests for the Presidency," *American Political Science Review* 60 (1966): 19–28.

46. Morris Fiorina, Samuel Abrams, and Jeremy Pope, "The 2000 US Presidential Election: Can Retrospective Voting Be Saved?" *British Journal of Political Science* 33 (2003): 163–187.

47. Stokes, "Some Dynamic Elements," p. 222.

48. Indeed, by some calculations, Kennedy ran worse than a "generic" Democrat for that time. See Angus Campbell, Philip Converse, Warren Miller, and Donald Stokes, "Stability and Change in 1960: A Reinstating Election," in *Elections and the Political Order* (New York: Wiley, 1966), pp. 78–95.

49. Fiorina, Abrams, and Pope, "The 2000 US Presidential Election," p. 180.

50. Frank Newport, Jeffrey Jones and Lydia Saad, "Ronald Reagan From the People's Perspective: A Gallup Poll Review," The Gallup Organization, June 15, 2004.

51. Thus, an important correlate of support for Bush in 1988 was what citizens thought of *Reagan's* performance as president. See Paul Abramson, John Aldrich, and David Rohde, *Change and Continuity in the 1988 Elections* (Washington, DC: CQ Press, 1990), chap. 7.

52. James Campbell, "When Have Presidential Campaigns Decided Election Outcomes?" *American Politics Research* 19 (2001): 437–460.

53. See Thomas Holbrook, *Do Campaigns Matter?* (Thousand Oaks, CA: Sage, 1996).

54. For a discussion, see Marjorie Hershey, "The Campaign and the Media," in Gerald Pomper et al., *The Election of 1988* (Chatham, NJ: Chatham House, 1989), chap. 3.

55. Donald Kinder and Lynn Sanders, *Divided by Color* (Chicago: University of Chicago Press, 1996).

56. Paul Sniderman and Thomas Piazza, *The Scar of Race* (Cambridge, MA: Harvard University Press, 1993).

57. Paul Abramson, John Aldrich, and David Rohde, *Change and Continuity in the 1992 Elections* (Washington, DC: Congressional Quarterly, 1994); and Herbert Weisberg and David Kimball, "Attitudinal Correlates of the 1992 Presidential Vote: Party Identification and Beyond," in *Democracy's Feast: Elections in America,* ed. Herbert Weisberg (Chatham, NJ: Chatham House, 1995), pp. 72–111.

58. Everett Ladd, "The Public's Views of National Performance," *The Public Perspective,* October/November 1996: 17–20.

59. Robert Merry, "A Rule for Presidents: Go Centrist or Perish," *Congressional Quarterly Weekly Report,* October 26, 1996: 3106.

60. Jane Mansbridge, "Myth and Reality: The ERA and the Gender Gap in the 1980

Election," *Public Opinion Quarterly,* 49 (1985): 164–178.

61. Emily Stoper, "The Gender Gap Concealed and Revealed," *Journal of Political Science* 17 (1989): 50–62; and Tom Smith, "The Polls: Gender and Attitudes Toward Violence," *Public Opinion Quarterly* 48 (1984): 384–396.

62. Rhodes Cook, "Race of Muted Differences Has the Nation Yawning," *Congressional Quarterly Weekly Report,* October 19, 1996: 2950.

63. Peter Canellos, "New TV Ad Mentions a GOP Unmentionable," *Boston Globe,* October 29, 1996: p. A23.

64. For discussions, see Pamela Conover, "Feminists and the Gender Gap," *Journal of Politics* 50 (1988): 985–1010; and Elizabeth Cook and Clyde Wilcox, "Feminism and the Gender Gap—A Second Look," *Journal of Politics* 53 (1991): 1111–1122.

65. "Where the Parties Are," *The Public Perspective,* March/April 1994: 78–79; and "Which Party Is Better on Which Issues?" *The Public Perspective,* June/July 1996: 65.

66. This was first noted by Herbert Weisberg, "The Demographics of a New Voting Gap: Marital Differences in American Voting Behavior," *Public Opinion Quarterly* 51 (1987): 335–343.

67. Morris Fiorina, Samuel Abrams, and Jeremy Pope, "The 2000 Elections: Can Retrospective Voting Be Saved? *British Journal of Political Science* 33 (2003).

68. Michael Kinsley, as quoted by Howard Kurtz, "The Premature Post-Mortems Are Starting," *Washington Post,* online extras, October 31, 2000.

CHAPTER 11

1. Quoted in George Hager and David Cloud, "Democrats Tie Their Fate to Clinton's Budget Bill," *Congressional Quarterly Weekly Report,* August 7, 1993: 2123.

2. Martha Angle, "Tallying Up the Thank-Yous," *Congressional Quarterly Weekly Report,* May 29, 1993: 1344.

3. Hager and Cloud, "Democrats Tie Their Fate to Clinton's Budget Bill," pp. 2125, 2127.

4. "Federalist 52," *The Federalist Papers,* ed. Clinton Rossiter (New York: Mentor, 1961), p. 327.

5. Max Farrand, ed., *The Records of the Federal Convention of 1787* (New Haven, CT: Yale University Press, 1966), vol. 1, p. 151.

6. Morris Fiorina, David Rohde, and Peter Wissel, "Historical Change in House Turnover," in *Congress in Change,* ed. Norman Ornstein (New York: Praeger, 1975), pp. 24–57; and Nelson Polsby, "The Institutionalization of the U.S. House of Representatives," *American Political Science Review* 62 (1968): 144–168.

7. James Young, *The Washington Community, 1800–1828* (New York: Harcourt, 1966) chap. 2.

8. The South was primarily agricultural and had fewer high-status career opportunities outside of politics. From the very beginning, southern members of Congress stayed longer than northerners. Fiorina, Rohde, and Wissel, *Historical Change in House Turnover,* pp. 34–38.

9. Robert Struble, Jr., "House Turnover and the Principle of Rotation," *Political Science Quarterly* 94 (1979–1980): 660.

10. Douglas Price, "The Congressional Career—Then and Now," in *Congressional Behavior,* ed. Nelson Polsby (New York: Random House, 1971), pp. 14–27.

11. Rhodes Cook, "The Rhodes Cook Letter," May 2001: 14.

12. A good overview of the variety of rules governing congressional primaries is contained in Kristin Kanthak and Rebecca Morton, "The Effects of Electoral Rules on Congressional Primaries," in *Nomination Politics and Congressional Representation,* ed. Peter Galdersis and Mike Lyons (Lanham, MD: Rowman and Littlefield, 2000).

13. "Congressional Primary Schedule," *Congressional Quarterly Weekly Report,* January 1, 2000: 16–17.

14. On the failure of incumbency to provide a complete explanation of Democratic dominance during this era, see Morris Fiorina, *Divided Government,* 2nd ed. (Boston: Allyn & Bacon, 1996), pp. 18–23.

15. Norman Ornstein, Thomas Mann, and Michael Malbin, *Vital Statistics on Congress, 1999–2000* (Washington, DC: American Enterprise Institute, 2000), pp. 70–71.

16. Robert Erikson, "Malapportionment, Gerrymandering and Party Fortunes in Congressional Elections," *American Political Science Review* 66 (1972): 1234–1245; and Gary King and Andrew Gelman, "Systemic Consequences of Incumbency Advantage in U.S. House Elections," *American Journal of Political Science* 35 (1991): 110–138.

17. John Ferejohn, "On the Decline of Competition in Congressional Elections," *American Science Review* 71 (1977): 172–174.

18. Gary Jacobson, *The Politics of Congressional Elections,* 4th ed. (New York: Longman, 1997).

19. Heinz Eulau, "Changing Views of Representation," in *The Politics of Representation,* ed. Heinz Eulau and John Wahlke (Beverly Hills, CA: Sage, 1978), pp. 31–53.

20. Morris Fiorina, *Congress—Keystone of the Washington Establishment,* 2nd ed. (New Haven, CT: Yale University Press, 1989).

21. Ibid., chap. 10. See also Bruce Cain, John Ferejohn, and Morris Fiorina, *The Personal Vote* (Cambridge, MA: Harvard University Press, 1987), chap. 2.

22. Richard H. Shapiro, *Frontline Management* (Washington, DC: Congressional Management Foundation, 1989), p. 94.

23. Morris Fiorina, "Congressmen and Their Constituents: 1958 and 1978," in *The United States Congress: Proceedings of the Thomas P. O'Neill, Jr. Symposium,* ed. Dennis Hale (Leominster, MA: Eusey Press, 1982), pp. 33–64.

24. Burdett Loomis, "The Congressional Office as a Small Business: New Members Set Up Shop," *Publius* 9 (1979): 35–55.

25. Ornstein, Mann, and Malbin, *Vital Statistics,* p. 133.

26. Glenn Parker, *Homeward Bound* (Pittsburgh, PA: University of Pittsburgh Press, 1986).

27. Juliet Eilperin, "The House Member as Perpetual Commuter," *Washington Post Weekly Edition* (September 10–16, 2001): 29.

28. E. Scott Adler, Chariti Gent, and Cary Overmeyer, "The Home Style Homepage: Legislator Use of the World Wide Web for Constituency Contact," *Legislative Studies Quarterly* 23 (1998): 585–595.

29. Diana Owen, Richard Davis, and Vincent James Strickler, "Congress and the Internet," *Press/Politics* 4 (1999): 10–29.

30. Peter J. Sepp, "Congressional Perks: How the Trappings of Office Trap Taxpayers," Policy Paper 131 (Alexandria, VA: National Taxpayers Union Foundation, 2000).

31. "The Price of Admission," from "The Big Picture" on www.opensecrets.org.

32. Gary Jacobson, "Practical Consequences of Campaign Finance Reform: An Incumbent Protection Act?" *Public Policy* 42 (1976): 1–32.

33. Gary Jacobson, *Money in Congressional Elections* (New Haven, CT: Yale University Press, 1980).

34. "Different Races, Different Costs," from "The Big Picture" on www.opensecrets.org.

35. Jacobson, *Politics of Congressional Elections,* p. 40.

36. Kenneth Bickers and Robert Stein, "The Electoral Dynamics of the Federal Pork Barrel," *American Journal of Political Science* 40 (1996): 1300–1326.

37. David Magleby and Kelly Patterson, "The Polls—Poll Trends: Congressional Reform," *Public Opinion Quarterly* 58 (1994): 420–421.

38. Douglas Arnold, *The Logic of Congressional Action* (New Haven, CT: Yale University Press, 1990), chap. 2.

39. Amihi Glazer and Bernard Grofman, "Two Plus Two Equals Six: Tenure in Office of Senators and Representatives, 1953–1983," *Legislative Studies Quarterly* 12 (1987): 555–564.

40. Alan Abramowitz and Jeffrey Segal, *Senate Elections* (Ann Arbor, MI: University of Michigan Press, 1992), pp. 34–35.

41. Morris Fiorina, *Representatives, Roll Calls, and Constituencies* (Lexington, MA: D.C. Heath, 1974), pp. 90–100.

42. Joe Foote and David Weber, "Network Evening News Visibility of Congressmen and Senators," paper presented to the Association for Education in Journalism and Mass Communication, August 1984.

43. Glenn Parker, "Interpreting Candidate Awareness in U.S. Congressional Elections," *Legislative Studies Quarterly* 6 (1981): 219–233.

44. Abramowitz and Segal, Senate Elections, pp. 228–231; and Jonathan Krasno, *Challengers, Competition, and Reelection: Comparing Senate and House Elections* (New Haven, CT: Yale University Press, 1995).

45. Joseph Schlesinger, *Ambition in Politics* (Chicago: Rand McNally, 1966).

46. This charge was leveled at Senator Dick Clark of Iowa in his losing 1978 race.

47. David Brady and Morris Fiorina, "Ruptured Legacy: Presidential Congressional Relations in Historical Perspective," in *Looking Back on the Reagan Presidency,* ed. Larry Berman (Baltimore, MD: Johns Hopkins University Press, 1989), pp. 268–287.

48. John Ferejohn and Randall Calvert, "Presidential Coattails in Historical Perspective," *American Journal of Political Science* 28 (1984), pp. 127–146.

49. Morris Fiorina, *Divided Government,* 2nd ed. (Boston: Allyn & Bacon, 1996), p. 14.

50. Ibid., pp. 135–139.

51. Janet Hook, "Freshmen in Congress Find Uses for Pork as They Seek Reelection, *Boston Globe,* July 2, 1996: p. 6.

52. Ibid.

53. Jon Healey, "Projects' Are His Project," Congressional Quarterly Weekly Report, September 21, 1996, 2672. Also see Jonathan Salant, "Some Republicans Turned Away from Leadership," *Congressional Quarterly Weekly Report,* December 7, 1996: 3352–3354; and Andrew Tayler, "GOP Pet Projects Give Boost to Shaky Incumbents," *Congressional Quarterly Weekly Report,* August 3, 1996: 2169–2173.

54. Karen Foerstel, "Slouching Toward Election Day, Democrats Are Anxious and Angry," *Congressional Quarterly Weekly Report,* September 12, 1998: 2383–2385.

55. Alan Abramowitz, "It's Monica, Stupid: The Impeachment Controversy and the 1998 Midterm Election," *Legislative Studies Quarterly* 26 (2001): 211–226.

56. David Rohde, *Parties and Leaders in the Postreform House* (Chicago: University of Chicago Press, 1991).

57. Karen Foerstel, "Campaign Finance Passage Ends a Political Odyssey," *CQ Weekly,* March 23, 2002: 800.

58. Donna Cassate, "'Independent Groups' Ads Increasingly Steer Campaigns," *Congressional Quarterly Weekly Report,* May 2, 1998: 1114.

59. *Associated Press,* "New Congress to Look More Like Real America," November 5, 2004.

60. Carol Swain, *Black Faces, Black Interests: The Representation of African Americans in Congress* (Cambridge, MA: Harvard University Press, 1993).

61. For a thoughtful treatment of these and related issues, see Jane Mansbridge, "In Defense of Descriptive Representation," working paper, Harvard University, 1997.

62. Pippa Norris, "Legislative Recruitment," in *Comparing Democracies,* ed. Lawrence LeDuc, Richard Niemi, and Pippa Norris (Thousand Oaks, CA: Sage, 1996): pp. 191–192.

63. "Americans Rate Their Society and Chart Its Values," *The Public Perspective,* February/March 1997: 25

64. See Charles Cameron, David Epstein, and Sharyn O'Halloran, "Do Majority-Minority Districts Maximize Substantive Black Representation in Congress?" *American Political Science Review* 90 (1996): 794–812.

65. David Lublin and D. Stephen Voss, "The Missing Middle," *Journal of Politics* 65 (February, 2003): 227–237; Lublin and Voss, "Racial Redistricting and Realignment in Southern State Legislatures," *American Journal of Political Science* 44 (October, 2000): 792–810; Lublin and Voss, "Boll-Weevil Blues," *American Review of Politics* 22 (Fall/Winter, 2000).

66. Juliana Gurenwald, "Incumbents Survive Redistricting," *Congressional Quarterly Weekly Report,* November 9, 1996: 3229; D. Stephen Voss and David Lublin, "Black Incumbents, White Districts: An Appraisal of the 1996 Congressional Elections," *American Politics Research* 29 (March, 2001): 141–182.

67. Lee Sigelman and Susan Welch, *Black Americans' Views of Racial Inequality* (Cambridge, England: Cambridge University Press, 1991).

68. Donald Kinder and Lynn Sanders, *Divided by Color* (Chicago: University of Chicago Press, 1996).

69. Former Representative Mike Espy (D-MS), who harbored gubernatorial or senatorial ambitions, openly espoused such beliefs.

More recently, the relatively moderate record of Representative Harold Ford (D-TN) has been explained by reference to his interest in being Tennessee's first black governor or senator. Nancy Zuckerbrod, "Tennessee Democrat Has His Sights Set High," *USA Today,* March 27, 2000: p. 29A.

70. Writing about politics in New Haven, then an old-style machine city, in the 1950s, Dahl observed that African Americans were much better represented in government jobs and political offices than in the private sector. See Robert Dahl, *Who Governs* (New Haven, CT: Yale University Press, 1961), p. 294.

CHAPTER 12

1. "Pushing the Limit," *New York Times,* May 19, 2002: p. 14; and "Bush the Anti-Globaliser," *The Economist,* May 11, 2002: 14.

2. Robert J. Samuelson, "A Sad Primer in Hypocrisy," *Newsweek,* February 11, 2002: 49.

3. Data found at www.cbo.gov.

4. Samuelson, "A Sad Primer"; and Paul Krugman, "Farm Bill Shows Rural States Can't Lay Claim to High Road," New York Times News Service, May 8, 2002.

5. Gebe Martinez, "Playing the Blame Game on Farm-Friendly Politics," *CQ Weekly,* April 20, 2002: 1008–1014.

6. Dan Morgan, "For Bush's Ranch Neighbors, Money Grows from Grain," *Washington Post Weekly Edition* (September 10–16, 2001): 12.

7. Dave Barry, "The Mohair of the Dog That Bites You," *Miami Herald,* June 23, 2002; and Samuelson, "A Sad Primer."

8. Quoted in David Sanger, "Bush OKs Farm Subsidies," *San Francisco Chronicle,* May 14, 2002.

9. Speaker Thomas Reed, as quoted in Neil McNeil, *Forge of Democracy* (New York: McKay, 1963).

10. David Mayhew, *Congress: The Electoral Connection* (New Haven, CT: Yale University Press, 1974), pp. 81–82; and John Aldrich, *Why Parties?* (Chicago: University of Chicago Press, 1995).

11. Richard Fenno, *The United States Senate: A Bicameral Perspective* (Washington, DC: American Enterprise Institute, 1982).

12. "Voting Participation: House," *Congressional Quarterly Weekly Report,* January 27, 1996: 256.

13. Nelson Polsby, Miriam Gallagher, and Barry Rundquist, "The Growth of the Seniority System in the U.S. House of

Representatives," *American Political Science Review* 63 (1969): 787–807. For a partial dissent, see Keith Krehbiel and Alan Wiseman, "Joseph Cannon: Majoritarian from Illinois," *Legislative Studies Quarterly* 26 (2001): 357–389.

14. Nelson Polsby, Miriam Gallagher, and Barry Rundquist, "The Growth of the Seniority System in the U.S. House of Representatives," *American Political Science Review* 63 (1969): 787–807.

15. Charles Jones, "Joseph G. Cannon and Howard W. Smith: An Essay on the Limits of Leadership in the House of Representatives," *Journal of Politics* 30 (1968): 617–646.

16. For a more extensive discussion, see Charles Jones, "Joseph G. Cannon and Howard W. Smith: An Essay on the Limits of Leadership in the House of Representatives," in *Congressional Behavior,* ed. Nelson Polsby (New York: Random House, 1971), pp. 203–224.

17. Jackie Koszczuk, "For Embattled GOP Leaders, Season of Discontent," *Congressional Quarterly Weekly Report,* July 20, 1996: 2019–2023; and Jackie Koszczuk, "Unpopular, Yet Still Powerful, Gingrich Faces a Critical Pass," *Congressional Quarterly Weekly Report,* September 14, 1996: 2573–2579.

18. Barbara Sinclair, *Majority Leadership in the U.S. House* (Baltimore, MD: Johns Hopkins University Press, 1983).

19. For a full discussion, see Steven S. Smith and Marcus Flathman, "Managing the Senate Floor: Complex Unanimous Consent Agreements Since the 1950s," *Legislative Studies Quarterly* 14 (1989): 349–374.

20. Keith Krehbiel, 1993. "Where's the Party?" *British Journal of Political Science* 23 (1993): 235–266.

21. David Rohde, *Parties and Leaders in the Postreform House* (Chicago: University of Chicago Press, 1991).

22. Barbara Sinclair, *Legislators, Leaders, and Lawmaking: The U.S. House of Representatives in the Postreform Era* (Baltimore, MD: Johns Hopkins University Press, 1995).

23. Gary Cox and Mathew McCubbins, *Legislative Leviathan* (Berkeley: University of California Press, 1993).

24. Gary Cox and Mathew McCubbins, *Setting the Agenda: Responsible Party Government in the U.S. House of Representatives* (in press).

25. Jim Drinkard, "Confident Candidates Share Campaign Wealth," *USA Today,* April 19, 2000: p. 10A.

26. Gerald Gamm and Kenneth Shepsle, "Emergence of Legislative Institutions: Standing Committees in the House and Senate, 1810–1825," *Legislative Studies Quarterly* 14 (1989): 39–66; and Joseph Cooper, *The Origins of the Standing Committees and the*

Development of the Modern House (Houston, TX: Rice University Studies, 1970).

27. Richard Fenno, *Congressmen in Committees* (Boston: Little, Brown, 1973), p. 172.

28. Karen Foerstel, "Gingrich Flexes His Power in Picking Panel Chiefs," *Congressional Quarterly Weekly Report,* November 19, 1994: 3326.

29. Mark Ferber, "The Formation of the Democratic Study Group," in *Congressional Behavior,* ed. Nelson Polsby (New York: Random House, 1971), pp. 249–267.

30. Norman Ornstein, "Causes and Consequences of Congressional Change: Subcommittee Reforms in the House of Representatives, 1970–1973," in *Congress in Change,* ed. Norman Orstein (New York: Praeger, 1975), pp. 88–114; and Roger Davidson and Walter Oleszek, *Congress Against Itself* (Bloomington: Indiana University Press, 1977).

31. Lawrence C. Dodd and Richard L. Schott, *Congress and the Administrative State,* (New York: John Wiley, 1979), p. 124; and Roger H. Davidson and Walter J. Oleszek, *Congress and Its Members,* 2nd ed. (Washington, DC: CQ Press, 1985), pp. 228–230.

32. John Ferejohn, *Pork Barrel Politics* (Stanford, CA: Stanford University Press, 1974); and R. Douglas Arnold, *Congress and the Bureaucracy* (New Haven, CT: Yale University Press, 1979).

33. Barry Weingast and William Marshall, "The Industrial Organization of Congress," *Journal of Political Economy* 91 (1988): 132–163.

34. Keith Krehbiel, *Information and Legislative Organization* (Ann Arbor: University of Michigan Press, 1991).

35. Cox and McCubbins, *Legislative Leviathan.*

36. Norman Ornstein, Thomas Mann, and Michael Malbin, *Vital Statistics on Congress: 1999–2000* (Washington, DC: American Enterprise Institution Press, 2001), see particularly chapter 4.

37. David King, *Turf Wars: How Congressional Committees Claim Jurisdiction* (Chicago: University of Chicago Press, 1997).

38. Alan Ota, "Caucuses Bring New Muscle to Legislative Battlefield," *CQ Weekly*, September 27, 2003: 2334–2341; and "Caucuses and Their Members Make Up a Large Contingent," *CQ Weekly,* September 27, 2003: 2379–2388.

39. The most comprehensive study to date is Susan Webb Hammond, *Congressional Caucuses in National Policy Making* (Baltimore, MD: Johns Hopkins University Press, 2001).

40. Jeffrey Talbert, Bryan Jones, and Frank Baumgartner, "Nonlegislative Hearings

and Policy Change in Congress," *American Journal of Political Science* 39 (1995): 391–392.

41. For a detailed study of how and why individual members participate at these various stages of the legislative process, see Richard Hall, *Participation in Congress* (New Haven, CT: Yale University Press, 1996).

42. On the conference committee in recent years, see Stephen Van Beek, *Post-Passage Politics: Bicameral Relations in Congress* (Pittsburgh: University of Pittsburgh Press, 1995).

43. Richard Munson, *The Cardinals of Capitol Hill* (New York: Grove Press, 1993).

44. Quoted in Stephen Skowronek, *The Politics Presidents Make* (Cambridge, MA: Harvard University Press, 1993), p. 389.

45. Diana Evans, "Policy and Pork: The Use of Pork Barrel Projects to Build Policy Coalitions in the House of Representatives," *American Journal of Political Science* 38 (1994): 894–917.

46. Harrison Donnelly, "Reagan Opposition Threatens EDA Development Program," *Congressional Quarterly Weekly Report* 40 (1982): 2295–2296.

47. Chuck Henning, *The Wit and Wisdom of Politics* (Golden, CO: Fulcrum, 1992), p. 39.

48. For institutional comparisons, see John Hibbing and Elizabeth Theiss-Morse, *Congress as Public Enemy* (New York: Cambridge University Press, 1995), chap. 2.

49. Kelly Patterson and David Magleby, "Trends: Public Support for Congress," *Public Opinion Quarterly* 56 (1992): 539–551.

50. Glenn Parker and Roger Davidson, "Why Do Americans Love Their Congressmen So Much More Than Their Congress?" *Legislative Studies Quarterly* 4 (1979): 52–61.

51. Richard Fenno, "If, As Ralph Nader Says, Congress is the 'Broken Branch,' How Come We Love Our Congressmen So Much?" in *Congress in Change,* ed. Norman Ornstein (New York: Praeger, 1975), pp. 277–287.

52. Mark Petracca, "Predisposed to Oppose: Political Scientists and Term Limitations," *Polity* 24 (1992): 657–672.

53. George F. Will, *Restoration: Congress, Term Limits, and the Recovery of Deliberative Democracy* (New York: Free Press, 1992).

CHAPTER 13

1. E. J. Dionne, Jr. "The Best of Bush . . . ," *Washington Post,* January 23, 2001: p. A17.

2. John F. Harris, "Both Sides Frustrated as Budget Wars End," *Washington Post,* November 15, 1999: p. A1.

3. George W. Bush, State of the Union Address, January 28, 2003, Washington, DC:

White House Office of the Press Secretary, http://www.whitehouse.gov/news/releases/2003/01/20030128-19.html (accessed January 8, 2004).

4. Jonathan Weisman, "Thomas Questions Dividend Tax Cuts," *Washington Post*, January 28, 2003: p. A4.

5. Terry Moe, "The Politicized Presidency," in *The New Direction in American Politics*, ed. John Chubb and Paul E. Peterson (Washington, DC: The Brookings Institution, 1985).

6. Mark Peterson, *Legislating Together: The White House and Capitol Hill from Eisenhower to Reagan* (Cambridge, MA: Harvard University Press, 1990), chap.6; and Jon R. Bond and Richard Fleisher, *The President in the Legislative Arena* (Chicago: University of Chicago Press, 1990), chap. 4.

7. Judy Keen, "Bush Isn't on the Ballot, But His Influence Is," *USA Today*, April 29, 2002: p. 7A.

8. Haynes Johnson and David Broder, *The System: The American Way of Politics at the Breaking Point* (Boston: Little, Brown, 1996).

9. Peterson, *Legislating Together*, p. 157.

10. Charles O. Jones, "Campaigning to Govern: The Clinton Style," in *The Clinton Presidency: First Appraisals*, ed. Colin Campbell and Bert A. Rockman (Chatham, NJ: Chatham House, 1996), p. 16. Also see Michael L. Mezey, *Congress, the President and Public Policy* (Boulder, CO: Westview, 1989).

11. As quoted in Chuck Henning, *The Wit and Wisdom of Politics: Expanded Edition* (Golden, CO: Fulcrum Publishing, 1992), p. 240.

12. Jack Nelson, "Angry Clinton Rebukes His Whitewater Critics," *Los Angeles Times*, December 21, 1995: p. A1.

13. Richard E. Neustadt, *Presidential Power and the Modern Presidents* (New York: Free Press, 1990), p. 29.

14. Benjamin Ginsberg and Martin Shefter, *Politics by Other Means: The Declining Importance of Elections in America* (New York: Basic Books, 1990).

15. Daniel Stid, *The Statesmanship of Woodrow Wilson: Responsible Government Under the Constitution* (Lawrence, KS: University Press of Kansas, 1998), chap. 6.

16. Jeffrey Tulis, *The Rhetorical Presidency* (Princeton, NJ: Princeton University Press, 1987), p. 91.

17. Thomas Bailey, *The American Pageant* (Boston: D.C. Heath, 1956), p. 669.

18. Samuel Kernell, *Going Public* (Washington, DC: CQ Press, 1986).

19. Inaugural Address, January 20, 1961, as quoted in *Bartlett's Familiar Quotations, Revised and Enlarged*, 15th ed. (Boston, MA: Little, Brown, 1980), p. 890.

20. Neustadt, *Presidential Power*, p. 274.

21. Henning, *Wit and Wisdom of Politics*, p. 240.

22. Norman C. Thomas, Joseph A. Pika, and Richard A. Watson, *The Politics of the Presidency*, 3rd ed. (Washington, DC: CQ Press, 1993), p. 204.

23. Office of the Clerk, U.S. House of Representatives, "Presidential Vetoes, 1789–2001," http://clerkweb.house.gov/histrecs/househis/lists/vetoes.htm, (accessed April 21, 2002).

24. Senate Library under the Direction of Walter J. Stewart, Secretary of the Senate, *Presidential Vetoes, 1789–1988*, S. Pub. 102-12, Washington, DC: U.S. Government Printing Office, 1992; Senate Library under the Direction of Jeri Thomson, Secretary of the Senate, *Presidential Vetoes, 1989–2000*, S. Pub. 107-10, Washington, DC: U.S. Government Printing Office, 2001.

25. Nick Anderson "Deal on Media Could Bring Passage of Spending Bill," *Los Angeles Times*, November 25, 2003: p. 23; Bill Miller, "Senators Take Up Homeland Security; Bush Strengthens Veto Threat," *Washington Post*, September 5, 2002: p. A29.

26. As quoted in James P. Pfiffner, *The Modern Presidency* (New York: St. Martin's, 1994), p. 114.

27. John Hart, *The Presidential Branch: From Washington to Clinton*, 2nd ed. (Chatham, NJ: Chatham House, 1995), pp. 26–30.

28. See Matthew Dickinson, *Bitter Harvest: FDR, Presidential Power, and the Growth of the Presidential Branch* (New York: Cambridge University Press, 1997).

29. Harold W. Stanley and Richard Niemi, *Vital Statistics on American Politics 1999–2000* (Washington, DC: CQ Press, 1999), pp. 250–251; and Office of Personnel Management, *Federal Civilian Workforce Statistics: Employment and Trends*.

30. Paul Quirk, "Presidential Competence," in *The Presidency and the Political System*, 4th ed., ed. Michael Nelson (Washington, DC: CQ Press, 1994), pp. 171–221; and John P. Burke, *The Institutional Presidency* (Baltimore, MD: Johns Hopkins University Press, 1992), pp. 40–42.

31. Colin Campbell, "Management in a Sandbox," in Colin Campbell and Bert A. Rockman, *The Clinton Presidency: First Appraisals* (Chatham, NJ: Chatham House, 1996), p. 60.

32. Charles O. Jones, "Campaigning to Govern: The Clinton Style," in Campbell and Rockman, *The Clinton Presidency*, p. 16.

33. Terry Moe, "The Politicized Presidency"; and Andrew Rudalevige, "The President's Program and the Politicized Presidency," paper presented at the Annual Meeting of the American Political Science Association, Atlanta, Georgia, September 2–5, 1999.

34. Bruce E. Altshuler, *LBJ and the Polls* (Gainesville: University of Florida Press, 1990); and Lawrence R. Jacobs, "The Recoil Effect: Public Opinion in the U.S. and Britain," *Comparative Politics* 24 (1992): 199–217.

35. *Wall Street Journal*, December 22, 1993: p. A4.

36. Jack Mitchell, *Executive Privilege: Two Centuries of White House Scandals* (New York: Hippocrene Books, 1992), pp. 89–90.

37. John Farrell, "Embattled Security Official Quits, Calls Getting FBI Files a 'Mistake,'" *Boston Globe*, June 27, 1996: p. 12.

38. Richard Berke, "Bush Is Providing Corporate Model for White House," *New York Times*, March 11, 2001: p. 1.

39. John W. Kingdon, *Agendas, Alternatives and Public Policies* (Boston: Little, Brown, 1981).

40. Tulis, *Rhetorical Presidency*, chap. 3.

41. Ibid.

42. Harry McPherson, *A Political Education* (Boston: Little, Brown, 1972), p. 268, as quoted in Paul C. Light, *The President's Agenda: Domestic Policy Choice from Kennedy to Reagan* (Baltimore, MD: Johns Hopkins University Press, 1991), p. 13.

43. Dana Milbank and Ellen Nakashima, "Bush Team Has 'Right' Credentials; Conservative Picks Seen Eclipsing Even Reagan's," *Washington Post*, March 25, 2001: p. A1.

44. Stephen Hess, *Organizing the Presidency* (Washington, DC: The Brookings Institution, 1988), pp. 11–18.

45. Richard Brody, *Assessing the President: The Media, Elite Opinion and Public Support* (Stanford, CA: Stanford University Press, 1991), p. 40.

46. Rockman, "Leadership Style and the Clinton Presidency," in Campbell and Rockman, *The Clinton Presidency*, p. 334.

47. Paul West, "Behind Bush's Low Key Style Is a Blueprint Drafted Well in Advance," *Baltimore Sun*, April 25, 2001: p. A8.

48. Rep. Robert Matsui (D-CA), quoted in David Westphal, "High Marks for a Solid Start," *Minneapolis Star Tribune*, April 29, 2001: p. 8A.

49. Walter Bagehot, *The English Constitution* (London: Fantana, 1993).

50. Gerald F. Seis, "Soul on High: Clinton Strikes Deeper Chords," *Wall Street Journal*, December 15, 1993.

51. Elisabeth Bumiller with David E. Sanger, "A Day of Terror: The President," *New York Times*, September 12, 2001: p. A1.

52. Lou Cannon, *President Reagan: The Role of a Lifetime* (New York: Simon & Schuster, 1991), p. 25.

53. Doris Kearns Goodwin, *No Ordinary Time: Franklin and Eleanor Roosevelt: The Home Front in World War II* (New York: Simon & Schuster, 1994).

54. Rockman, "Leadership Style and the Clinton Presidency," pp. 334–336.

55. Laurence McQuillan, "Laura Bush's Travel Agenda: Education First Lady Heads to California to Promote Teaching Careers," *USA Today,* March 22, 2001: p. 12A.

56. Henning, *Wit and Wisdom of Politics,* p. 261.

57. Paul C. Light, *Vice Presidential Power* (Baltimore, MD: Johns Hopkins University Press, 1984) p. 258.

58. Sidney Milkis, *The President and the Parties: The Transformation of the American Party System Since the New Deal* (New York: Oxford University Press, 1993), p. 81.

59. Theodore Sorensen, as quoted in M. Miller, *Lyndon: An Oral Biography* (New York: Putnam, 1980), p. 254.

60. Adam Nagourney, "A Partner with Contrasts That Complement," *New York Times,* July 7, 2004, p. A1.

61. Stephen Skowronek, *The Politics Presidents Make: Leadership from John Adams to George Bush* (Cambridge, MA: Harvard University Press, 1993), p. 250.

62. As quoted in James L. Sundquist, *The Decline and Resurgence of Congress* (Washington, DC: The Brookings Institution, 1981) p. 31.

63. *United States v. Belmont,* 301 U.S. 324 (1936); Harold Bruff and Peter Shane, *The Law of Presidential Powers: Cases and Materials* (Durham, NC: Carolina Academic Press, 1988), p. 88; and Joseph Paige, *The Law Nobody Knows: Enlargement of the Constitution—Treaties and Executive Orders* (New York: Vantage Press, 1977), p. 63.

64. William Howell, "The President's Powers of Unilateral Action: The Strategic Advantages of Acting Alone" (Ph.D. diss., Stanford University, 1999).

65. Louis Fisher, *Constitutional Conflicts Between Congress and the President,* 3rd ed., rev. (Lawrence: University of Kansas, 1991), p. 154.

66. *United States v. Nixon,* 418 U.S. 683, 709 (1974).

67. Michael Doyle, "U.S. Sues U.S. Over Cheney Files," *Chicago Sun-Times,* February 24, 2001: p. 21.

68. Mike Allen, "Bush Issues Pardons to Seven in First Exercise of Clemency Power," *Washington Post,* December 24, 2002: p. A2.

69. The man who cast the decisive vote provided subject matter for John F. Kennedy's *Profiles in Courage* (New York: Harper & Row, 1964).

70. *Washington Post/ABC* News Poll, January 28–30, 1999.

71. Robert J. Spitzer, "Clinton's Impeachment Will Have Few Consequences for the Presidency," *PS: Political Science and Politics* 32:3 (September 1999): 541–545

72. Harvey Mansfield, Jr., *Taming the Prince: The Ambivalence of Modern Executive Power* (New York: Free Press, 1989); and James McPherson, *The Battle Cry of Freedom: The Civil War Era* (New York: Oxford University Press, 1988), pp. 264–275, 505.

73. *Wall Street Journal,* December 22, 1993: p. A1.

74. Neustadt, *Presidential Power,* chap. 4.

75. Henning, *Wit and Wisdom of Politics,* p. 219.

76. As quoted in Henning, *Wit and Wisdom of Politics,* p. 222.

77. The effect of time on presidential support is stressed by Paul Brace and Barbara Hinckley, "The Structure of Presidential Approval: Constraints Within and Across Presidencies," *Journal of Politics* 53 (November 1991): 993–1017; and by John Mueller, "Presidential Popularity from Truman to Johnson," *American Political Science Review* (March 1970): 18–24. For contrasting views, which stress events rather than time, see Brody, *Assessing the President;* and Samuel Kernell, "Explaining Presidential Popularity," *American Political Science Review* (June 1978): 506–522. Also see Michael MacKuen, "Political Drama, Economic Conditions, and the Dynamic of Public Popularity," *American Journal of Political Science* (May 1983): 165–192; Charles Ostrom and Dennis Simon, "Promise and Performance: A Dynamic Model of Presidential Popularity," *American Political Science Review* (June 1985): 334–358; and James Stimson, "Public Support for American Presidents," *Public Opinion Quarterly* (1976): 401–421.

78. Paul Brace and Barbara Hinckley, *Follow the Leader: Opinion Polls and the Modern Presidents* (New York: Basic Books, 1992), p. 33, Figure 2.3.

79. Samuel Kernell, *Going Public,* 2nd ed. (Washington, DC: CQ Press, 1993), chap. 5.

80. Anthony Stephen King, *Running Scared: Why America's Politicians Campaign Too Much and Govern Too Little* (New York: Free Press, 1997).

81. "Los Angeles Times Interview: Clinton Sees 'A Lot of Insecurity in This Country,'" *Los Angeles Times,* December 5, 1993: p. A38.

82. "Bush Twin Gets Maximum Fine, License Penalty," *Houston Chronicle,* July 7, 2001: p. A29.

83. George C. Edwards III, *At the Margins: Presidential Leadership of Congress* (New Haven, CT: Yale University Press, 1989) pp. 120–124; Calvin Mouw and Michael MacKuen, "The Strategic Configuration, Political Influence, and Presidential Power in Congress" (paper prepared for the annual meeting of the Midwest Political Science Association, Chicago, 1989); and Terry Sullivan, "Headcounts, Expectations and Presidential Coalitions in Congress," *American Journal of Political Science* 32 (1988): 567–589.

84. James Barber, *The Presidential Character: Predicting Performance in the White House* (Englewood Cliffs, NJ: Prentice-Hall, 1972).

85. For criticism of Barber's analysis, see Michael Nelson, "The Psychological Presidency," in *The Presidency and the Political System,* 4th ed., ed. Michael Nelson (Washington, DC: CQ Press, 1994), pp. 198–224; Alexander George, "Assessing Presidential Character," *World Politics* 26 (January 1974): 234–282; Jeffrey Tulis, "On Presidential Character," in *The Presidency in the Constitutional Order,* ed. Jeffrey Tulis and Joseph M. Bessette (Baton Rouge: Louisiana State University Press, 1981); and Erwin C. Hargrove, "Presidential Personality and Leadership Style," in *Researching the Presidency: Vital Questions, New Approaches,* ed. George C. Edwards III, John H. Kessel, and Bert A. Rockman (Pittsburgh, PA: Pittsburgh University Press, 1993), pp. 93–98.

86. Fred Greenstein, *The Hidden-Hand Presidency: Eisenhower as Leader* (New York: Basic Books, 1982).

87. Charles O. Jones, "The Separated Presidency—Making It Work in Contemporary Politics," in *The New American Political System,* second version, ed. Anthony King (Washington, DC: American Enterprise Institute, 1990), p. 24.

88. Stephen Skowronek, *The Politics Presidents Make.*

89. Henning, *Wit and Wisdom of Politics,* p. 92.

90. Editorial, "George 'McKinley' Bush?" *Pittsburgh Post Gazette,* April 2, 2002: p. A-17.

CHAPTER 14

1. John Donnelly, "U.S. Security Aspects Familiar to Some," *Boston Globe,* September 12, 2001: p. A9.

2. *Road Map for National Security: Imperative for Change,* the Phase III report of the United States Commission on National Security for the 21st Century, February 15, 2001, p. 15.

3. Richard Simon and Charles Piller, "Security Chief Must Battle Bureaucracy," *Los Angeles Times,* October 8, 2001: p. A9.

4. Alison Mitchell, "Dispute Erupts on Ridge's Needs for His Job," *New York Times,* November 4, 2001: p. B7.

5. James Gerstenzong, "Response to Terror: Bush Proposes a Cabinet-Level Homeland Security Department," *Los Angeles Times,* June 7, 2002: p. 1.

6. *New York Times,* September 9, 1993: p. D20.

7. Committee on Government Reform and Oversight, U.S. House of Representatives, *U.S. Government Policy and Supporting Positions ("Plum Book")* (Washington, DC: U.S. Government Printing Office, 1996).

8. General Accounting Office, *Government Corporations: Profiles of Existing Government Corporations* (GAO/GGD-96-14) (Washington, DC: General Accounting Office, 1995).

9. Martha Derthick, *Agency Under Stress: The Social Security Administration in American Government* (Washington, DC: The Brookings Institution, 1990).

10. Max Weber, *Essays in Sociology* (New York: Oxford University Press, 1958); and Max Weber, *Economy and Society* (Berkeley: University of California Press, 1978).

11. James Q. Wilson, "The Bureaucracy Problem," *The Public Interest* (Winter 1967): 3–9.

12. Michael Lipsky, *Street-Level Bureaucracy: Dilemmas of the Individual in Public Services* (New York: Russell Sage, 1980).

13. Ibid.

14. Tony Perry, "Forest Service Official Defends Cedar Fire Response," *Los Angeles Times,* November 8, 2003: p. B14.

15. William A. Niskanen, *Bureaucracy and Representative Government* (Chicago: Aldine-Atherton, 1971), chaps. 2–4.

16. Aaron Wildavsky, *The New Politics of the Budgetary Process* (Boston: Little, Brown, 1988), pp. 84–85.

17. Graham Allison, *Essence of Decision: Explaining the Cuban Missile Crisis* (Boston: Little, Brown, 1971), chap. 3.

18. Tom McGinty and Dan Fagin, "One Tangled Web; Experts Agree: Nation's Electric System Aging, Byzantine," *Newsday,* November 17, 2003: p. A6.

19. Barton Gellman and Dana Millbank, "Blackout Causes Mass Disruption; Millions Struggle Without Power from N.Y. to Toronto to Detroit," *Washington Post,* August 15, 2003: p. A1.

20. Laurence J. Peter, as quoted in Chuck Henning, *The Wit and Wisdom of Politics: Expanded Edition* (Golden, CO: Fulcrum Publishing, 1992), p. 16.

21. Steve Berry, Mitchell Landsberg, and Doug Smith, "A New View of High-Rise Firefighting," *Los Angeles Times,* September 24, 2001: p. A1.

22. Kaufman, *Red Tape,* p. 434.

23. Jay Tokasz, "The I.R.S. Moves Rapidly to Process New Charities," *New York Times,* November 12, 2001: p. G12.

24. The Online News Hour: The Website of the News Hour with Jim Lehrer, http://www.pbs.org/newshour/, "Rebuilding the Pentagon," (accessed January 16, 2002).

25. Lucius Wilmerding as quoted in Herman Finer, "Better Government Personnel," *Political Science Quarterly* 50, 4 (1936): 577.

26. Stanley Elkins and Eric McKitrick, *The Age of Federalism* (New York: Oxford University Press, 1993), p. 170.

27. James Young, *The Washington Community 1800–1828* (New York: Harcourt, 1966), pp. 49, 23.

28. Robert v. Remini, *The Life of Andrew Jackson* (New York: Harper & Row, 1988), p. 185.

29. John Bartlett, *Familiar Quotations: Revised and Enlarged,* 15th ed. (Boston: Little, Brown, 1980), p. 455.

30. Seymour J. Mandelbaum, *Boss Tweed's New York* (New York: Wiley, 1965).

31. As quoted in Henning, *Wit and Wisdom of Politics,* p. 11.

32. A. James Reichley, *The Life of the Parties* (New York: Free Press, 1992), pp. 157–158.

33. William L. Riordon, *Plunkitt of Tammany Hall: A Series of Plain Talks on Very Practical Politics* (New York: E.P. Dutton, 1963), p. 3.

34. Eugene Kennedy, *Hurrah! The Life and Times of Mayor Richard J. Daley* (New York: Viking, 1978), pp. 255, 274.

35. Robert Dahl, *Who Governs?* (New Haven, CT: Yale University Press, 1961); Raymond E. Wolfinger, *The Politics of Progress* (Englewood Cliffs, NJ: Prentice-Hall, 1974), chap. 4; Edward Banfield and James Q. Wilson, *City Politics* (New York: Random House, 1963); and Robert K. Merton, *Social Theory and Social Structure* (Glencoe, IL: Free Press, 1957), pp. 71–81.

36. Quoted in Reichley, *Life of the Parties,* p. 212.

37. Paul E. Peterson, *The Politics of School Reform, 1870–1940* (Chicago: University of Chicago Press, 1985), pp. 86–87.

38. Rufus P. Browning, Dale Rogers Marshall, and David H. Tabb, *Protest Is Not Enough: The Struggle of Blacks and Hispanics for Equality in Urban Politics* (Berkeley: University of California Press, 1984), chap. 5.

39. Alben W. Barkley, vice president of the United States from 1949 to 1953, as quoted in Henning, *Wit and Wisdom of Politics,* p. 17.

40. National Election Study, 1948–2000 Cumulative Data File, conducted by the Center for Political Studies at the University of Michigan.

41. Gallup/Employee Benefit Research Institute Poll, April 1994 (USGALLUP .EBRI56).

42. Paul Light, *Thickening Government* (Washington, DC: The Brookings Institution, 1995), p. 9, Table 1-2; and Paul Light, "The Changing Shape of Government," Brookings Institution Policy Brief 45 (Washington, DC: The Brookings Institution, February 1999), p. 1.

43. Paul Light, *Thickening Government: Federal Hierarchy and the Diffusion of Accountability* (Washington, DC: The Brookings Institution, 1995), chap. 1.

44. G. Calvin MacKenzie, "The Presidential Appointment Process: Historical Development, Contemporary Operations, Current Issues" (background paper for the Twentieth Century Fund Panel on Presidential Appointments, March 1, 1994), p. 1.

45. David Houston, secretary of agriculture from 1913 to 1920 and secretary of the treasury from 1920 to 1921, as quoted in Richard F. Fenno Jr., *The President's Cabinet* (Cambridge, MA: Harvard University Press, 1959), p. 221.

46. Leonard White, *Introduction to the Study of Public Administration,* 4th ed. (New York: Macmillan, 1955), p. 80.

47. As quoted in G. Calvin MacKenzie, *The In-and-Outers: Presidential Appointees and Transient Government in Washington* (Baltimore, MD: Johns Hopkins University Press, 1987).

48. Haynes Johnson and David Broder, *The System: The American Way of Politics at the Breaking Point* (Boston: Little, Brown, 1996).

49. *Wall Street Journal,* February 9, 1994: p. 1.

50. Lyn Ragsdale, "Studying the Presidency: Why Presidents Need Political Scientists," in *The Presidency and the Political System,* 5th ed., ed. Michael Nelson (Washington, DC: CQ Press, 1998), p. 50.

51. Thomas E. Cronin, *The State of the Presidency,* 2nd ed. (Boston: Little, Brown, 1980).

52. Jefferson Cohen, *The Politics of the U.S. Cabinet* (Pittsburgh, PA: University of Pittsburgh Press, 1988).

53. Judy Keen, "Bush, Lay Kept Emotional Distance," *USA Today,* February 26, 2002: p. 6A; Joseph Kahn, "Contract Offers Look at How Global Played Influence Game," *New York Times,* February 28, 2002: p. C1.

54. Michael E. Kanell, "Business Scandals: Bush Official Seeks 'Severe' Action," *Atlanta Journal Constitution*, July 12, 2002: p. 5D.

55. Kermit Gordon, *Reflections on Spending* (Washington, DC: The Brookings Institution, 1967), p. 15.

56. Marver H. Bernstein, *Regulating Business by Independent Commission* (Princeton, NJ: Princeton University Press, 1955); Harold Seidman, *Politics, Position and Power: The Dynamics of Federal Organization,* 2nd ed. (New York: Oxford University Press, 1975); George J. Stigler, "The Theory of Economic Regulation," *Bell Journal of Economics and Management Science* 2 (Spring 1971): 3–21; Terry Moe, "Regulatory Performance and Presidential Administration," *American Journal of Political Science* 16 (May 1982): 197–224; B. R. Weingast and M. J. Moran, "Bureaucratic Discretion or Congressional Control? Regulatory Policymaking by the Federal Trade Commission," *Journal of Political Economy* 91, 5 (1983): 765–800; and B. R. Weingast, "The Congressional-Bureaucratic System: A Principal–Agent Perspective (with Application to the SEC)," *Public Choice* 44, 1 (1984): 147–191.

57. Stephen Labaton, "Exemption Won in '97 Set Stage for Enron Woes," *New York Times,* January 23, 2002: p. A1.

58. Herbert Kaufman, *The Administrative Behavior of Federal Bureau Chiefs,* p. 183, n. 8.

59. Hugh Heclo, "OMB and the Presidency—the Problem of 'Neutral Competence,'" *Public Interest* 38 (Winter 1975): 80–98; and Karen Hult, "Advising the President," in George C. Edwards, John H. Kessel, and Bert A. Rockman, *Researching the Presidency: Vital Questions, New Approaches* (Pittsburgh, PA: University of Pittsburgh Press, 1992), p. 126.

60. Richard W. Stevenson, "Bush's Budget Director Girds for a Tough Year," *New York Times,* December 31, 2001: p. A8; Esther Schrader and Janet Hook, "Bush's $87 Billion Request Detailed; Most of the Funding Sought by the White House Would Go to Iraq Military Operations," *Los Angeles Times,* September 18, 2003: p. A10.

61. Karen Masterson, "Defense Budget Flap Delays Funds for War," *Houston Chronicle,* November 24, 2001: p. A1; and Nick Anderson, "Senate OKs Defense Bill without NY, Domestic Security Extras," *Los Angeles Times,* December 8, 2001: p. A27.

62. Johnson and Broder, *The System,* p. 116.

63. David R. Francis, "Medicare Reform Carries Huge Fiscal Toll," *Christian Science Monitor,* October 17, 2003, p. 5.

64. Johnson and Broder, *The System,* p. 397.

65. Derthick, *Agency Under Stress,* p. 200.

66. *Staffing a New Presidential Administration: A Guide to Personnel Appointments in a Presidential Transition* (Washington, DC: The Presidential Appointee Initiative, a project of the Brookings Institution funded by the Pew Charitable Trusts), November 2000.

67. Frederic Ogg and P. Orman Ray, *Introduction to American Government,* 10th ed. (New York: Appleton-Century-Crofts, 1951), p. 405.

68. Paul Kane, "Senate Set for Recess Politics," *Roll Call* online edition, December 13, 2001, www.rollcall.com.

69. David King, "The Nature of Congressional Committee Jurisdictions," *American Political Science Review* 88 (March 1995): 48–62.

70. See *New York Times,* September 5, 1993: Sec. I, p. 39.

71. Paul Light, quoted in Janet Hook, "Turf Battles Could Snag Bush's Security Proposal," *New York Times,* June 15, 2002: p. A18.

72. Richard W. Stevenson, "Breaking Up Is Hard; Merging Is Harder," *New York Times,* June 23, 2002: Sec. 4, p. 3.

73. James Q. Wilson, *Bureaucracy: What Government Agencies Do and Why They Do It* (New York: Basic Books, 1989), pp. 295–314; and Ezra N. Suleiman, *Politics, Power and Bureaucracy in France: The Administrative Elite* (Princeton, NJ: Princeton University Press, 1974).

74. T. J. Pempel, "The Bureaucratization of Policymaking in Postwar Japan," *American Journal of Political Science* 18 (November 1974): 64. See also, Michio Muramatsu and Ellis S. Krauss, "Bureaucrats and Politicians in Policymaking: The Case of Japan," *American Political Science Review,* 78, 1 (March 1984): 126–146.

75. R. Shep Melnick, *Regulation and the Courts: The Case of the Clean Air Act* (Washington, DC: The Brookings Institution, 1983).

76. David Epstein and Sharyn O'Halloran, *Delegating Powers: A Transaction Cost Politics Approach to Policy Making under Separate Powers* (New York: Cambridge University Press, 1999), Figure 5.9, p. 116.

77. Dick Kirschten, "Slicing the Turf," *Government Executive,* April 1999.

78. Robert L. Park, director of the Washington office of the American Physical Society, as quoted in Graeme Browing, "Fiscal Fission," *National Journal,* June 8, 1996: 1259.

79. Graeme Browning, "Fiscal Fission," p. 1259; and Jeffrey Brainard and Ron Southwick, "A Record Year at the Federal Trough," *Chronicle of Higher Education,* August 10, 2001: 20. See also James D. Savage, *Funding Science in America: Congress, Universities and the Politics of the Academic Pork Barrel* (New York: Cambridge University Press, 1999).

80. "Young Blasts Funding Earmarks," *Engineering News-Record,* December 17, 2001: 9.

81. Bill McAllister, "Byrd's Big Prize: Bringing Home the FBI," *Washington Post,* March 13, 1991: p. A1.

82. Office of Senator Robert C. Byrd, News Release, "Byrd Funding for WVU Homeland Defense Effort Now Law," December 14, 2001.

83. Joel Aberbach, *Keeping a Watchful Eye* (Washington, DC: The Brookings Institution, 1990), p. 38; Policy Agendas Project, University of Washington, www.policyagendas.org, hearings data.

84. Policy Agendas Project.

85. Matthew McCubbins and Thomas Schwartz, "Congressional Oversight Overlooked: Police Patrols vs. Fire Alarms," *American Journal of Political Science,* 28, 1 (February 1984): 165–179.

86. Joel Aberbach and Bert Rockman, *In the Web of Politics: Three Decades of the U.S. Federal Executive* (Washington, DC: The Brookings Institution, 2000), p. 121.

87. Grant McConnell, *Private Power and American Democracy* (New York: Knopf, 1966); Theodore Lowi, *The End of Liberalism,* 2nd ed. (New York: Norton, 1979); and Mark P. Petracca, ed., *The Politics of Interests: Interest Groups Transformed* (Boulder, CO: Westview, 1992).

88. Joel Aberbach, *Keeping a Watchful Eye,* pp. 162–166.

89. Graeme Browning, "Fiscal Fission," p. 1260.

90. "Public Broadcasting Develops Dialogue with House GOP," *Congressional Quarterly Weekly Report,* March 23, 1996: 791.

91. Hugh Heclo, "Issue Networks and the Executive Establishment," in *The New American Political System,* ed. Anthony King (Washington, DC: American Enterprise Institute, 1978), pp. 87–124.

92. John E. Chubb, *Interest Groups and the Bureaucracy* (Stanford, CA: Stanford University Press, 1983); John Chubb "U.S. Energy Policy: A Problem of Delegation," in *Can the Government Govern?* ed. John Chubb and Paul E. Peterson (Washington, DC: The Brookings Institution, 1989); Seong-Ho Lim, "Changing Jurisdictional Boundaries in Congressional Oversight of Nuclear Energy Regulation:

Impact of Public Salience" (paper presented before the annual meeting of the American Political Science Association, 1992); and Frank R. Baumgartner and Bryan D. Jones, "Agenda Dynamics and Policy Subsystems," *Journal of Politics* 53 (November 1991): 1044–1074.

93. Bill Lambrecht, "Industries Have Pumped Millions Into Energy Bill," *St. Louis Post-Dispatch*, December 7, 2003: p. A1.

94. Paul E. Peterson, Barry G. Rabe, and Kenneth K. Wong, *When Federalism Works* (Washington, DC: The Brookings Institution, 1986), chap. 8; John J. Harrigan, *Political Change in the Metropolis,* 2nd ed. (Boston: Little, Brown, 1981), pp. 267–268, 350–351; and Rochelle L. Stanfield, "Communities Reborn," *National Journal,* June 22, 1966: 1371.

95. John Dilulio, *No Escape: The Future of American Corrections* (New York: Basic Books, 1991), pp. 19–26.

96. James A. Morone, *The Democratic Wish: Popular Participation and the Limits of American Government* (New York: Basic Books, 1990).

97. Francis Rourke, "Executive Secrecy: Change and Continuity," in Rourke, *Bureaucratic Power in National Policy Making,* pp. 536–537.

98. Todd Purdom and Alison Mitchell, "Bush, Angered by Leaks, Duels with Congress," *New York Times,* October 10, 2001: p. A1.

99. Robert Turner, quoted in Warren Richey, "Tribunals on Trial," *Christian Science Monitor,* December 14, 2001: 1.

100. John Mintz and Susan Schmidt, "'Dirty Bomb' Was Major New Year's Worry," *Washington Post,* January 7, 2004: p. A1.

101. Department of Defense Personnel Security Research Center poll, cited in *Secrecy & Government Bulletin,* 48, May 1995 (Washington, DC: Federation of American Scientists).

102. Martin Halstuk, "New Privacy Policy Hinders Public's Right to Know," *Los Angeles Times,* November 19, 2001: part 2, p. 11.

103. Jeffrey Birnbaum, Eileen Gunn, et al., "Unbelievable! The Mess at the IRS *Is* Worse Than You Think," *Fortune,* April 13, 1998.

104. Ibid.

105. Ibid.

106. Albert B. Crenshaw, "Witnesses Say IRS Agent Tried to Frame Ex-Senator," *Washington Post,* May 1, 1998: p. A1.

107. Albert B. Crenshaw, "IRS Overhaul Set for Passage; Measure Gives Taxpayers New Rights, Includes Capital Gains Break," *Washington Post,* June 25, 1998: p. A1.

108. Jonathan Weisman, "GAO Finds Increases in Tax Evasion; Report Says IRS Needs More Resources," *Washington Post,* December 19, 2003: p. E1.

109. Matthew McCubbins and Thomas Schwartz, "Congressional Oversight Overlooked: Police Patrols vs. Fire Alarms," *American Journal of Political Science,* 28, 1 (February 1984): 165–179.

110. Martha Derthick, *Agency Under Stress,* p. 87.

111. Christopher Lee, "Federal Workforce Is Largest Since 1990," *Washington Post,* September 5, 2003: p. A19.

112. Christopher Lee, "Federal Case; Government Workers Protest Outsourcing," *Washington Post,* May 21, 2003: p. A31; Christopher Lee, "Outsourcing Shield Weakened; Appeals Rights Stripped as Worker Raises Are Approved," *Washington Post,* November 26, 2003: p. A23.

113. Blaine Harden, "Cuts Sap Morale of Parks Employees; Many Fear Losing Jobs to Outsourcing," *Washington Post,* June 10, 2003: p. A19.

114. Paul Light, "To Restore and Renew: Now is the Time to Rebuild the Federal Public Service," *Government Executive,* November 2001: 32–47.

115. Former Bureau of the Budget director Kermit Gordon, as quoted in Kaufman, *Administrative Behavior,* p. 443.

116. Paul J. Quirk, "Food and Drug Administration," in James Q. Wilson, *The Politics of Regulation* (New York: Basic Books, 1980), p. 199.

117. Terry Moe, "The Politics of Bureaucratic Structure," in John E. Chubb and Paul E. Peterson, *Can the Government Govern?* (Washington, DC: The Brookings Institution, 1988).

118. Brian Hassel, "Charter Schools: Designed to Fail?" (Ph.D. dissertation, John F. Kennedy School of Government, Harvard University, 1997).

119. Robert L. Kahn, Barbara A. Gutek, Eugenia Barton, and Daniel Katz, "Americans Love Their Bureaucrats," *Psychology Today* (1975), as reprinted in Rourke, *Bureaucratic Power in National Policy Making,* p. 290.

120. John Clayton Thomas and Gloria Streib, "The New Face of Government: Citizen-Initiated Contacts in the Era of E-Government," *Journal of Public Administration Research and Theory,* 13:1 (January 2003): 92.

121. James H. Boren, quoted in Antony Jay, *The Oxford Dictionary of Political Quotations,* (New York: Oxford University Press, 2001), p. 48.

122. Charles Lindblom, "The Science of 'Muddling Through,'" *Public Administration Review* XIX (Spring 1959): 79–88.

123. Herbert Kaufman, *The Forest Ranger: A Study in Administrative Behavior* (Baltimore, MD: Johns Hopkins University Press, 1960). For recent confirmations of this analysis, see Warren Wolfe, "A Milestone for the BWCA: 25 Years of Nature and Fighting," *Minneapolis Star Tribune,* October 11, 2003: p. 1A; Charles Seabrook, "Forest Use Rules May Relax; Logging Expected to Increase," *Atlanta Journal-Constitution,* November 28, 2002: p. 3A; Glen Martin, "Cattlemen Prod Forest Service; Federal Land Use Policies to Come Under Review, Again," *San Francisco Chronicle,* July 5, 2002: p. A3; Jim Robbins, "Logging Plan for West's Burned Forests Incites a Debate," *New York Times,* July 22, 2001: p. 23; Douglas Jehl, "Forest Officials Address Unusual Uses of Land," *New York Times,* July 5, 2001: p. A12.

CHAPTER 15

1. *Bush v. Gore,* 531 U.S. 98 (2000).

2. Jeffrey Rosen, "The Supreme Court Commits Suicide," in *Bush v. Gore: The Court Cases and the Commentary,* ed. E. J. Dionne and William Kristol (Washington, D.C.: The Brookings Institution, 2001), p. 312.

3. Melinda Gann Hall, "State Judicial Politics: Rules, Structures, and the Political Game," in *American State and Local Politics: Directions for the 21st Century,* ed. Ronald Weber and Paul Brace (New York: Chatham House, 1999), p. 114.

4. Herbert Jacob and Kenneth Vines, "Courts," in *Politics in the American States: A Comparative Analysis,* 4th ed., ed. Virginia Gray, Herbert Jacob, and Kenneth Vines (Boston: Little, Brown, 1983), p. 238.

5. Melinda Gann Hall, "Justices as Representatives: Elections and Judicial Politics in the American States," *American Politics Quarterly* 23 (October 1995): 485–503.

6. Jacob and Vines, "Courts," p. 239.

7. Excerpted with ellipses deleted. Milton Rakove, *Don't Make No Waves; Don't Back No Losers* (Bloomington: Indiana University Press, 1975), pp. 223–225.

8. "Process Has No Merit," *Chicago Sun Times,* January 3, 2000: p. 21.

9. Jamie B. W. Stecher, "Democratic and Republican Justice: Judicial Decision Making in Five State Supreme Courts," *Columbia Journal of Law and Social Problems* 13 (1977): 137–181.

10. Mark Hansen, "A Run for the Bench," *ABA Journal,* October 1998: 68; Deborah Goldberg, Craig Holman, and Samantha Sanchez, *The New Politics of Judicial Elections* (New York: The Brennan Center for Justice and the National Institute on Money in State Politics), February 2002, p. 11.

11. Professor Anthony Champagne, quoted in Jerry Crimmins, "Experts: Negative

Ads Erode Confidence in Judges," *Chicago Daily Law Bulletin,* November 9, 2001: 1.

12. John Paul Ryan, Allen A. Ashman, Bruce D. Sales, and Sandra Shane-Dubow, *American Trial Judges* (New York: Free Press, 1980), p. 125.

13. "Investigate, Then Prosecute; Bungled Lewis Trial: Atlanta Prosecutors, Police Rushed to Indict Before They Had All the Evidence," *Baltimore Sun,* June 14, 2000: p. 22A.

14. Cynthia Tucker, "Murder Acquittals: Running for Glory, Fulton DA Fumbles," *Atlanta Constitution,* June 14, 2000: p. 14A.

15. Alexander Hamilton, James Madison, and John Jay, *The Federalist Papers* (New York: Bantam Books, 1982 [1787]), "Federalist 78," p. 393.

16. American Judicature Society, http://www.ajs.org/cji/cji_impeachment.asp (accessed February 7, 2004).

17. Ibid.

18. William Rehnquist, *2002 Year-End Report on the Federal Judiciary* (Washington, DC: U.S. Supreme Court, January 1, 2003), p. 2.

19. Richard A. Posner, *The Federal Courts: Challenge and Reform* (Cambridge, MA: Harvard University Press, 1996), Chapter 1, pp. 29–33.

20. Henning, *The Wit and Wisdom of Politics: Expanded Edition* (Golden, CO: Fulcrum Publishing, 1992), p. 250.

21. Robert G. McCloskey, *The American Supreme Court* (Chicago: University of Chicago Press, 1960), p. 14.

22. U.S. Constitution, Article 3, Section 2.

23. Clarence Thomas, "Be Not Afraid," speech at the American Enterprise Institute, Washington, DC, February 13, 2001, http://www.aei.org/news/newsID.15211/news_detail.asp (accessed February 7, 2004).

24. Ibid.

25. *Lochner v. New York,* 195 U.S. 45 (1905).

26. William J. Brennan, Jr. "The Constitution of the United States; Contemporary Ratification," in David O'Brien, Ed. *Judges on Judging: Views from the Bench* (Chatham, NJ: Chatham House, 1997), p. 204.

27. Ibid.

28. *Beauharnais v. Illinois,* 343 U.S. 250 (1952).

29. *New York v. United States,* 488 U.S. 1041 (1992).

30. *Dred Scott v. Sandford,* 19. How. 393 (1857).

31. See, for example, Abraham Lincoln's comments in Robert W. Johannsen, ed., *The Lincoln-Douglas Debates* (New York: Oxford University Press, 1965), pp. 14–21.

32. *Lochner v. New York,* 198 U.S. 45 (1905). Ellipses deleted from excerpt.

33. *Schechter Poultry Corp. v. United States,* 295 U.S. 495 (1935).

34. John Agresto, *The Supreme Court and Constitutional Democracy* (Ithaca, NY: Cornell University Press, 1984), p. 163.

35. Congressional Research Service, Library of Congress, *The Constitution of the United States of America: Analysis and Interpretation, 2000 Supplement* (Washington, DC: Government Printing Office, 2000).

36. Excerpted with ellipses deleted. Robert A. Dahl, "Decision-Making in a Democracy: The Supreme Court as a National Policy-Maker," *Journal of Public Law* 6 (Fall 1957): 293–294. See also Richard Y. Funston, "The Supreme Court and Critical Elections," *American Political Science Review* 69 (1975): 795–811.

37. James A. Stimson, Michael B. Mackuen, and Robert S. Erikson, "Dynamic Representation," *American Political Science Review* 89 (September 1995): 555. Also see William Mishler and Reginald S. Sheehan, "The Supreme Court as a Counter-Majoritarian Institution? The Impact of Public Opinion on Supreme Court Decisions," *American Political Science Review* 87 (1993): 87–101; and Helmut Norpoth and Jeffery Segal, "Popular Influence on Supreme Court Decisions," *American Political Science Review* 88 (September 1994): 711–724.

38. John C. Jeffries, Jr., *Justice Lewis F. Powell, Jr.: A Biography* (New York: Scribner, 1994), p. 248.

39. Kelly Thornton, "Charges Against Awadallah Dismissed," *San Diego Union Tribune,* May 1, 2002: p. A1.

40. George L. Haskins and Herbert A. Johnson, *History of the Supreme Court of the United States,* Vol. 2, *Foundations of Power: John Marshall 1801–15* (New York: Macmillan, 1981) p. 33.

41. David O'Brien, "Background Paper," in Twentieth Century Fund, *Judicial Roulette* (New York: Priority Press, 1988), p. 37; Sheldon Goldman, "Unpicking Pickering in 2002: Some Thoughts on the Politics of Lower Federal Court Selection and Confirmation," *U.C. Davis Law Review,* 36:695 (February 2003), p. 707.

42. As quoted in Robert A. Carp and Ronald Stidham, *The Federal Courts,* 2nd ed. (Washington, DC: CQ Press, 1991), p. 97.

43. Linda Greenhouse, "Rehnquist Sees a Loss of Prospective Judges," *New York Times,* January 1, 2002: p. A18.

44. Lyle Denniston, "Court Nominee Withdraws in Senate Battle, Democrats Prevail by Way of Filibuster," *Boston Globe,* September 5, 2003: p. A2.

45. Robert A. Carp and Ronald Stidham, *The Federal Courts,* 2nd ed. (Washington, DC: CQ Press, 1991), p. 116; and *U.S. News & World Report,* May 26, 1997: 24.

46. Henning, *Wit and Wisdom,* p. 108.

47. *Martin v. Hunter's Lessee,* 14 U.S. (1 Wheat.) 304 (1816).

48. As quoted in C. Herman Pritchett, *The American Constitution* (New York: McGraw-Hill, 1959), pp. 65, 215.

49. Congressional Research Service, Library of Congress, *The Constitution of the United States of America: Analysis and Interpretation, 1998 Supplement* (Washington, D.C.: U.S. Government Printing Office, 1999).

50. Pritchett, *The American Constitution* (New York: McGraw-Hill, 1959), p. 134.

51. Henning, *Wit and Wisdom,* p. 187.

52. *In re Chapman,* 16 U.S. 661 (1897).

53. Linda Greenhouse, "Legacy of a Term," *New York Times,* July 3, 1996: p. A1.

54. Supreme Court of the United States, *Granted and Noted List – Cases to be Argued, October term 2003* (Washington, DC: U.S. Supreme Court, January 26, 2004).

55. As quoted in Henning, *Wit and Wisdom,* p. 107.

56. Carl B. Swisher, *American Constitutional Development,* 2nd ed. (Boston: Houghton Mifflin, 1954), pp. 1075–1079.

57. Paul Simon, *Advice and Consent* (Washington, D.C.: National Press Books, 1992), p. 275.

58. Henry J. Abraham, *Justices and Presidents: A Political History of Appointments to the Supreme Court,* 3rd ed. (New York: Oxford University Press, 1992).

59. The term *stealth nominee* was coined by Alabama Senator Howell Heflin during nomination hearings for Justice Souter. See Ruth Marcus and Michael Isikoff, "Souter Declines Comment on Abortion," *Washington Post,* September 14, 1990: p. A1.

60. Twentieth Century Fund, *Judicial Roulette* (New York: Priority Press, 1988), pp. 10–11.

61. Jonathan Swift, *Gulliver's Travels* (New York: Penguin, 2003 [1726]), p. 230.

62. *Parts and Electric Motors v. Sterling Electric,* 866 F 2d 288 (1988).

63. Hart Pomerantz, as quoted in Henning, *Wit and Wisdom,* p. 250.

64. H. W. Perry, Jr., *Deciding to Decide: Agenda Setting in the United States Supreme Court* (Cambridge, MA: Harvard University Press, 1991), p. 27.

65. See "Judicial Business of the United States Courts, 2001," Washington, DC: Administrative Office of the U.S. Courts, 2001, Table A-1.

66. Ibid., pp. 218–219.

67. Ibid., p. 99.

68. Address of Chief Justice Vinson before the American Bar Association, September 7, 1949, as quoted in Perry, *Deciding to Decide,* p. 36.

69. *Zelman v. Simmons-Harris,* No. 00-1751 (2002).

70. Jeffries, *Justice Lewis R. Powell, Jr.,* p. 248.

71. Bernard Schwartz, *A History of the Supreme Court* (New York: Oxford University Press, 1993), chap. 13.

72. Linda Cohen and Matthew Spitzer, "The Government Litigant Advantage: Implications for the Law, *Florida State University Law Review* 28 (Fall 2000): 391.

73. Scigliano, *Supreme Court and the Presidency,* p. 162.

74. Jeffrey A. Segal, "*Amicus Curiae* Briefs by the Solicitor General During the Warren and Burger Courts: A Research Note," *Western Political Quarterly* 41 (March 1988): 135–144.

75. Joan Biskupic and Elder Witt, *Guide to the U.S. Supreme Court,* 3rd ed., vol. II, (Washington, DC: Congressional Quarterly Press, 1997), p. 832.

76. Perry, *Deciding to Decide,* p. 71.

77. Schwartz, *History of the Supreme Court,* p. 372.

78. Perry, *Deciding to Decide;* and Schwartz, *History of the Supreme Court,* chap. 16.

79. Biskupic and Witt, *Guide to the U.S. Supreme Court,* p. 828.

80. As quoted in Henning, *Wit and Wisdom,* p. 106.

81. Jeffries, *Justice Lewis F. Powell, Jr.,* p. 247.

82. Ibid., pp. 245–247.

83. *Harris v. Forklift,* 508 U.S. 938 (1993).

84. James F. Simon, *The Center Holds: The Power Struggle Inside the Rehnquist Court* (New York: Simon & Schuster, 1995), pp. 227, 229.

85. Jeffrey A. Segal and Albert D. Cover, "Ideological Values and the Votes of U.S. Supreme Court Justices," *American Political Science Review* 83 (June 1989): 557–565.

86. Henning, *Wit and Wisdom,* p. 250.

87. As quoted by Austin Ranney, "Peltason Created a New Way to Look at What Judges Do," *Public Affairs Report, Institute of Governmental Studies* 36, 6 (November 1995): 7.

88. Excerpted with ellipses deleted. "Federalist 2," edited, and with introduction, by Jacob E. Cooke (Middletown, CT: Wesleyan University Press, 1961), pp. 522–523.

89. Pritchett, *American Constitution,* p. 99.

90. Robert H. Birkby, "The Supreme Court and the Bible Belt: Tennessee Reaction to the 'Shempp Decision,'" *Midwest Journal of Political Science* 10 (August 1966), as reprinted in *The Impact of Supreme Court Decisions,* ed. Theodore L. Becker and Malcolm M. Feeley (New York: Oxford University Press, 1973), p. 114.

91. Steven Lee Myers, "U.S. Judge Upsets Rules to Control How Jails Are Run," *New York Times,* July 24, 1996: p. B2.

92. Abram Chayes, "The Role of the Judge in Public Law Litigation," *Harvard Law Review* 89 (May 1976): 1281–1316.

93. Alexis de Tocqueville, *Democracy in America,* ed. J. P. Mayer (New York: Harper, 1988), p. 270.

94. R. Shep Melnick, *Between the Lines* (Washington, DC: The Brookings Institution, 1994), p. 149.

95. Myron Levin and Henry Weinstein, "Big Tobacco Must Pay Damages in Florida Case," *Los Angeles Times,* April 8, 2000: p. A1.

96. Jerry Hirsch, "Talks to Settle Suit Against Enron, Others, Fail," *Los Angeles Times,* May 2, 2002: part 3, p. 3.

97. Dirk Johnson, "City of Deep Pockets," *Newsweek,* December 15, 2003: 45.

CHAPTER 16

1. See, for example, Washington Post Poll, September 28, 2001, question ID USWASHP.092801, R14B: "As part of the effort to combat terrorism, would you support or oppose . . . allowing court-ordered wiretaps and electronic surveillance to follow a suspect for up to a year, anywhere that person goes in the United States?" 88 percent support.

2. Alison Mitchell and Todd S. Purdum, "Ashcroft, Seeking Broader Powers, Says Congress Must Act Quickly," *New York Times,* October 1, 2001: p. A1.

3. Susan Milligan, "Attorney General Shifts on Liberties," *Boston Globe,* September 26, 2001: p. A9.

4. John Lancaster and Walter Pincus, "Proposed Anti-Terrorism Laws Draw Tough Questions; Lawmakers Express Concerns to Ashcroft, Other Justice Officials About Threat to Civil Liberties," *Washington Post,* September 25, 2001: p. A5.

5. American Civil Liberties Union press release, "Uncle Sam Asks: 'What the Hell is Going On Here?' in New ACLU Print and Radio Advertisements," September 3, 2003, available at http://www.aclu.org/SafeandFree/SafeandFree.cfm?ID=13440 & c=262 (accessed February 21, 2004).

6. Ed Crane and William Niskanen, "Upholding Liberty in America," Washington, DC: Cato Institute, June 24, 2003, http://www.cato.org/research/articles/niskanen-030624.html (accessed February 21, 2004).

7. Center for Constitutional Rights, "The State of Civil Liberties: One Year Later," http://www.ccr-ny.org/v2/whatsnew/report.asp?ObjID=nQdbIRkDgG & Content=153 (accessed February 21, 2004).

8. Adam Clymer, "Threats and Responses: Privacy; Librarians Get Advice on Handling Government Requests for Information on Readers," *New York Times,* December 12, 2002.

9. Susan Schmidt, "Patriot Act Misunderstood, Senators Say," *Washington Post,* October 22, 2003, p. A4.

10. Henry Steele Commager, ed., *Documents of American History,* 6th ed. (New York: Appleton-Century-Crofts, 1958), pp. 125–126. Also see Willi Paul Adams, *The First American Constitutions: Republican Ideology and the Making of the State Constitutions in the Revolutionary Era* (Chapel Hill: University of North Carolina Press, 1980).

11. Charles R. Ritcheson, "'Loyalist Influence' on British Policy Toward the United States After the American Revolution," *Eighteenth Century Studies* 7/1 (Autumn 1973): 1–17. See also Paul A. Smith, "The American Loyalists: Notes on Their Organization and Numerical Strength," *William and Mary Quarterly,* 25, 2 (April 1968): 259–277.

12. Arthur M. Schlesinger, *Prelude to Independence: The Newspaper War on Britain, 1764–1776* (New York: Alfred Knopf, 1958), pp. 297–298.

13. Ibid., p. 299.

14. *Barron v. Baltimore,* 1833, as quoted in C. Herman Pritchett, *Constitutional Civil Liberties* (Englewood Cliffs, NJ: Prentice-Hall, 1984), p. 6.

15. Robert G. McCloskey, revised by Sanford Levinson, *The American Supreme Court,* 3rd ed. (Chicago: University of Chicago Press, 2000), p. 80.

16. *Palko v. Connecticut,* 302 U.S. 319 (1937).

17. Alexander Hamilton, James Madison, and John Jay, "Federalist 10," *The Federalist Papers* (New York: Bantam Books, 1982 [1787–1788]), pp. 45–46.

18. John Dalberg-Acton, 1907, as quoted in John Bartlett, *Familiar Quotations,* 15th ed. (Boston: Little, Brown, 1980), p. 616.

19. John Stuart Mill, *On Liberty* (New York: Norton, 1859/1975), p. 36.

20. David M. Rabban, *Free Speech in Its Forgotten Years* (New York: Cambridge University Press, 1997), p. 193.

21. Robert G. McCloskey, *The American Supreme Court* (Chicago: University of Chicago Press, 1960), p. 224.

22. Quoted in Robert Goldstein, *Political Repression in Modern America: 1870 to the Present* (New York: Schenkman, 1978), p. 565.

23. *Schenck v. United States,* 249 U.S. 47 (1919).

24. *Abrams v. United States,* 250 U.S. 616 (1919).

25. *Stromberg v. California,* 283 U.S. 359 (1931).

26. Goldstein, *Political Repression,* p. 262.

27. *Chaplinsky v. New Hampshire,* 315 U.S. 568 (1942).

28. As quoted in C. Herman Pritchett, *The American Constitution,* 3rd ed. (New York: McGraw-Hill, 1969), p. 375.

29. John Mueller, "Trends in Political Tolerance," *Public Opinion Quarterly* 52, no. 1 (Spring 1988): 1–25; and National Opinion Research Center, General Social Survey 1972–2000 Cumulative File.

30. *United States v. Carolene Products Co.,* 304 U.S. 144 (1938).

31. George Anastaplo, as quoted in Goldstein, *Political Repression,* p. 532.

32. *Papish v. Board of Curators of the University of Missouri,* 410 U.S. 667 (1973).

33. Robert Goldstein, *Saving "Old Glory": The History of the Desecration Controversy* (Boulder, CO: Westview, 1995).

34. *Texas v. Johnson,* 491 U.S. 397 (1989).

35. *Texas v. Johnson,* 491 U.S. 397 (1989).

36. *United States v. Eichman,* 496 U.S. 310, (1990).

37. *R. A. V. v. City of St. Paul, Minnesota,* 112 S Ct. 2541 (1992).

38. Schlesinger, *Prelude to Independence,* pp. 64–65.

39. *Near v. Minnesota,* 283 U.S. 697 (1931).

40. Jonathan Krim, "Congress Acts to Curb Offensive Programs; Senate Panel Proposes Stiff Fines, Delaying Media Consolidation," *Washington Post,* March 10, 2004: p. E1.

41. *NAACP v. Alabama,* 357 U.S. 449 (1958).

42. *Boy Scouts of America v. Dale,* 530 U.S. 640 (2000).

43. *Miller v. California,* 413 U.S. 15 (1973).

44. Linda Greenhouse, "Court, 9-0, Upholds State Laws Prohibiting Assisted Suicide, Protects Speech on Internet," *New York Times,* June 27, 1997: p. A1.

45. *Ashcroft v. American Civil Liberties Union,* 00-1293 (2003).

46. Anthony Lewis, *Make No Law: The Sullivan Case and the First Amendment* (New York: Random House, 1992).

47. Felicity Barringer, "Appeals Court Rejects Damages Against ABC in Food Lion Case," *New York Times,* October 21, 1999: p. 1.

48. As quoted in Charles L. Glenn, Jr., *The Myth of the Common School* (Amherst, MA: University of Massachusetts Press, 1987), p. 84.

49. Diane Ravitch, *The Great School Wars: New York City, 1805–1973* (New York: Basic Books, 1974); and Paul E. Peterson, *The Politics of School Reform, 1870–1940* (Chicago: University of Chicago Press, 1985).

50. *Meek v. Pittenger,* 421 U.S. 349 (1975).

51. *Engel v. Vitale,* 370 U.S. 421 (1962); *School District of Abington Township v. Schempp,* 374 U.S. 273 (1963); and *Wallace v. Jaffree,* 472 U.S. 38 (1985).

52. *Board of Education v. Mergens,* 496 U.S. 226 (1990); see also *Good News Club v. Milford Central School,* 99–2036 (2001).

53. *Mitchell v. Helms,* 98–1648 (2000).

54. *Agostini v. Felton,* 96–552 (1997).

55. *Meyer v. Nebraska,* 262 U.S. 399 (1923). See also *Pierce v. Society of Sisters,* 268 U.S. 510 (1925).

56. *Wisconsin v. Yoder,* 406 U.S. 205 (1972).

57. *Church of the Lukumi Bablu Aye v. City of Hialeah,* 508 U.S. 520 (1993).

58. *Employment Division, Oregon Department of Human Resources v. Smith,* 494 U.S. 872 (1990).

59. Paul E. Peterson, "The New Politics of Choice," in *Learning from the Past,* ed. Diane Ravitch and Maris Vinovskis (Baltimore, MD: Johns Hopkins University Press, 1995).

60. Publius Syrus, as quoted in John Bartlett, *Familiar Quotations,* p. 111.

61. *Olmstead v. United States,* 277 U.S. 438 (1927).

62. *New York Times,* November 12, 1993: p. 1.

63. Senator Joe Biden, as quoted in Chuck Henning, *The Wit and Wisdom of Politics: Expanded Edition* (Golden, CO: Fulcrum Publishing, 1992), p. 47.

64. Justice Potter Stewart, quoted in Bernard Schwartz, *A History of the Supreme Court* (New York: Oxford, 1993), p. 264.

65. Bernard Schwartz, *A History of the Supreme Court* (New York: Oxford, 1993), p. 263.

66. *Chimel v. California,* 395 U.S. 752 (1969).

67. *Mapp v. Ohio,* 167 U.S. 643 (1961).

68. *Mapp v. Ohio,* 167 U.S. 643 (1961).

69. *United States v. Leon,* 468 U.S. 897 (1984).

70. Joan Biskupic, "Police May Stop, Frisk Those Who Flee at Sight of Officer," *Washington Post,* January 13, 2000: p. A10.

71. *Dickerson v. United States,* 99–5525 (2000).

72. Pritchett, *Constitutional Civil Liberties,* p. 78.

73. *Sheppard v. Maxwell,* 384 U.S. 333 (1966).

74. *Nebraska Press Association v. Stuart,* 427 U.S. 539 (1976).

75. Lisa J. McIntyre, *The Public Defender: The Practice of Law in the Shadows of Repute* (Chicago: University of Chicago Press, 1987), p. 162.

76. Robert B. Spangenberg, Marea L. Beeman, and James Downing, "State and County Expenditures for Indigent Defense Services in Fiscal Year 2002" (West Newton, MA: Report prepared for the American Bar Association, September 2003).

77. Jonathan D. Casper, *American Criminal Justice: The Defendant's Perspective* (Englewood Cliffs, NJ: Prentice-Hall, 1972), p. 101.

78. *U.S. v. Lanza,* 260 U.S. 377 (1922).

79. *Hamdi v. Rumsfeld,* 03-6696 (2004); *Rumsfeld v. Padilla,* 03-1027 (2004); *Rasul v. Bush,* 03-334 (2004).

80. Casper, *American Criminal Justice;* and Jerome Skolnick, *Justice Without Trial* (New York: Wiley, 1966).

81. *Santobello v. New York* (1971), as quoted in Lawrence M. Friedman, *Crime and Punishment in American History* (New York: Basic Books, 1993), p. 392.

82. Keith Bradsher, "Boy Who Killed Gets Seven Years; Judge Says Law Is Too Harsh," *New York Times,* January 14, 2000: p. A1.

83. Robert H. Bork, "Neutral Principles and Some First Amendment Problems," *Indiana Law Journal* 47 (1971): 8.

84. *Griswold v. Connecticut,* 381 U.S. 479 (1965).

85. Ibid.

86. *Lawrence v. Texas,* 02-102 (1993).

87. The Gallup Poll: Social and Economic Indicators—Homosexual Relations," http:// www.gallup.com/poll/topics/homosexual.asp (accessed February 18, 2002).

88. *Harris v. McRae,* 448 U.S. 297 (1980).

89. *Webster v. Reproductive Health Services,* 492 U.S. 490 (1989).

90. *Planned Parenthood v. Casey,* 112 S Ct 291 (1992).

91. *Planned Parenthood of Southeastern Pennsylvania v. Casey,* 505 U.S. 833 (1992).

92. David Streitfeld and Charles Pillar, "Big Brother Finds Ally in Once-Wary High-Tech," *Los Angeles Times,* January 19, 2002: p. A1.

93. "Feds, States Work Toward 'National' Driver's License; Plan Is to Improve Existing ID Systems," *San Diego Union Tribune,* January 8, 2002: p. A7.

94. Streitfeld and Piller, "Big Brother Finds Ally."

95. Ibid.

96. Sonia Arrison, "New Anti-Terrorism Law Goes Too Far," *San Diego Union Tribune,* October 31, 2001: p. B9.

97. *Kyllo v. United States,* 99–8508 (2001).

CHAPTER 17

1. Berny Morson, "CU Cookie Caper Gets a Stale Reception; 'Affirmative Action Bake Sale' Met With Protest, Discussion," *Rocky Mountain News,* February 12, 2004, p. 6A.

2. Marcos Mocine-McQueen, "Republicans Raise Little Dough, Some Ire; Bake Sale at CU Spurs Race Debate," *Denver Post,* February 12, 2004: p. B4.

3. Meagan Balink, "Will Students Buy at the 'Bake Sale'?" *Colorado Daily,* February 10, 2004, http://coloradodaily.com/articles/2004/02/10/news/news02.prt (accessed July 21, 2004).

4. Morson, p. 6A.

5. Balink.

6. Ruth Bader Ginsburg, "Employment of the Constitution to Advance the Equal Status of Men and Women," in *The Constitutional Bases of Political and Social Change in the United States,* ed. Shlomo Slonim (New York: Praeger, 1990), p. 188.

7. Martin Luther King, Jr., "Civil Right No. 1: The Right to Vote," in *A Testament of Hope: The Essential Writings and Speeches of Martin Luther King, Jr.,* ed. James M. Washington (New York: HarperCollins, 1986), p. 188.

8. John Agresto, *The Supreme Court and Constitutional Democracy* (Ithaca, NY: Cornell University Press, 1984), p. 27. Ellipses deleted.

9. Philip Converse, "The Nature of Belief Systems in Mass Publics," in David E. Apter, *Ideology and Discontent* (New York: Free Press, 1964), pp. 206–261.

10. John D. Hicks, *The American Nation* (Cambridge, MA: Riverside Press, 1949), p. 21.

11. Eric Foner, *A Short History of Reconstruction* (New York: Harper, 1990).

12. Eric Foner, *Reconstruction, 1863–1877* (New York: Harper & Row, 1988), pp. 425–444.

13. Ibid, p. 428.

14. Richard M. Valelly, "National Parties and Racial Disfranchisement," in *Classifying by Race,* ed. Paul E. Peterson (Princeton, NJ: Princeton University Press, 1995), pp. 188–216.

15. U.S. Commission on Civil Rights, *Report of the Commission on Civil Rights* (Washington, DC: Government Printing Office, 1959), p. 32. Ellipses deleted.

16. V. O. Key, Jr., *Southern Politics* (New York: Random House, 1949).

17. J. Morgan Kousser, *The Shaping of Southern Politics: Suffrage Restriction and the Establishment of the One-Party South, 1880–1910* (New Haven, CT: Yale University Press, 1974), p. 61.

18. Leon F. Litwack, *Trouble in Mind: Black Southerners in the Age of Jim Crow* (New York: Knopf, 1998), p. 229.

19. *Civil Rights Cases,* 109 U.S. 3 (1883).

20. The majority opinion in the Civil Rights Cases suggested that states could ban discrimination in public accommodations, however, and many did so in the 1880s, especially in the North. See Donald G. Nieman, *Promises to Keep: African Americans and the Constitutional Order, 1776 to the Present* (New York: Oxford University Press, 1991), pp. 103–104.

21. *Plessy v. Ferguson,* 163 U.S. 537 (1896).

22. Ibid.

23. Nieman, p. 110.

24. Edward Banfield and James Q. Wilson, *City Politics* (New York: Vintage Books, 1963); and James Q. Wilson, *Negro Politics* (New York: Free Press, 1960). For caveats, see Steven P. Erie, *Rainbow's End: Irish-Americans and the Dilemmas of Urban Machine Politics, 1840–1985* (Berkeley: University of California Press, 1990).

25. Richard A. Keiser, *Subordination or Empowerment? African American Leadership and the Struggle for Urban Political Power* (New York: Oxford University Press, 1997), p. 27.

26. Harold Gosnell, *Negro Politicians* [1935] (Chicago: University of Chicago Press, 1967); Thomas M. Guterbock, *Machine Politics in Transition* (Chicago: University of Chicago Press, 1980); and Ira Katznelson, *Black Men, White Cities* (Chicago: University of Chicago Press, 1976).

27. Oscar DePriest, also of Chicago, had served three terms in the House from 1929 to 1933. As the only African American in Congress at the time, he was a source of inspiration for many blacks—and a point of controversy for some white politicians. See David S. Day, "Herbert Hoover and Racial Politics: The DePriest Incident," *Journal of Negro History* 65, no.1 (Winter 1980), pp. 6–17.

28. David McCullough, *Truman* (New York: Simon & Schuster, 1992), pp. 586–590; and Patricia Gurin, Shirley Hatchett, and James S. Jackson, *Hope and Independence: Blacks' Response to Electoral and Party Politics* (New York: Russell Sage, 1989), pp. 36–38.

29. Gerald N. Rosenberg, *The Hollow Hope: Can Courts Bring About Social Change?* (Chicago: University of Chicago Press, 1991), p. 61.

30. Nieman, pp. 139–40.

31. Hugo Black (1937), Felix Frankfurter (1939), William Douglas (1939), Frank Murphy (1940), and Wiley Rutledge (1943). See Nieman, p. 142.

32. *Smith v. Allwright,* 321 U.S. 649 (1944).

33. *Shelley v. Kraemer,* 334 U.S. 1 (1948).

34. *Cumming v. Richmond County Board of Education,* 357 U.S. 528 (1899).

35. *Missouri ex rel. Gaines v. Canada,* 305 U.S. 337 (1938).

36. *Sweatt v. Painter,* 339 U.S. 629 (1950).

37. *Brown v. Board of Education,* 347 U.S. 483 (1954).

38. *Brown v. Board of Education,* 347 U.S. 483 (1954), note 11. The citation of six psychological and sociological studies in this note led Herbert Garfinkel to charge that the Court was making decisions on the basis of sociology, not law. "Social Science Evidence and the School Segregation Cases," *Journal of Politics* 21 (February 1959): 37–59. Kenneth B. Clar, "Effect of Prejudice and Discrimination on Personality Development" (Midcentury White House Conference on Children and Youth 1950, as cited in note 11 to *Brown*).

39. *San Antonio School District v. Rodriguez,* 411 U.S. 1 (1973). Similar reasoning can be found in Cooper *v.* Aaron 358 U.S. 1 (1958).

40. A. Leon Higgenbotham, Jr., *Shades of Freedom: Racial Politics and Presumptions of the American Legal Process* (New York: Oxford University Press, 1996).

41. A. D. Morris, *Origins of the Civil Rights Movement: Black Communities Organizing for Change* (New York: Free Press, 1984).

42. Ibid., pp. 51–63.

43. Martin Luther King, Jr., "Walk for Freedom," in *A Testament of Hope: The Essential Writings and Speeches of Martin Luther King, Jr.,* ed. James M. Washington, (New York: HarperCollins, 1986), p. 83.

44. Michael Lipsky, "Protest as a Political Resource," *American Political Science Review* LXII (December 1968): 1144–1158.

45. University of Georgia, Carl Vinson Institute of Government, "Historical Documents Related to Georgia," http://www.cviog.uga.edu/Projects/gainfo/gahisdoc.htm (accessed April 6, 2000).

46. Rosenberg, *The Hollow Hope,* p. 50.

47. Taylor Branch, *Parting the Waters: America in the King Years 1954–63* (New York: Simon & Schuster, 1988), p. 375.

48. Martin Luther King, Jr., "I Have a Dream," in *A Testament of Hope: The Essential Writings and Speeches of Martin Luther King, Jr.,* James M. Washington (New York: HarperCollins, 1986), p. 219.

49. Gerald D. Jaynes and Robin M. Williams, Jr., eds., *A Common Destiny: Blacks and American Society* (Washington, DC: National Academy Press, 1989), p. 224.

50. Gerald N. Rosenberg, *The Hollow Hope: Can Courts Bring About Social Change?* (Chicago: University of Chicago Press, 1991), Table 2.1, p. 50.

51. Patricia Gurin, Shirley Hatchett, and James S. Jackson, *Hope and Independence: Blacks' Response to Electoral and Party Politics* (New York: Russell Sage, 1989), pp. 42–49.

52. Jaynes and Williams, *A Common Destiny,* p. 233.

53. Joint Center for Political and Economic Studies, *Focus* (Washington, DC: Joint Center for Political and Economic Studies 1993); and David A. Bositis, *Black Elected Officials: A Statistical Summary, 2000,* (Washington, DC: Joint Center for Political and Economic Studies, 2002), p. 5.

54. William J. Grimshaw, *Bitter Fruit: Black Politics and the Chicago Machine, 1931–1991* (Chicago: University of Chicago Press, 1992).

55. Gary Orfield, *The Reconstruction of Southern Education: The Schools and the 1964 Civil Rights Act* (New York: Wiley, 1969); Gary Orfield, *Must We Bus?* (Washington, DC, The Brookings Institution, 1978); and Jennifer Hochschild, *The New American Dilemma* (New Haven, CT: Yale University Press, 1984).

56. Taylor Branch, *Pillar of Fire: America in the King Years 1963–65* (New York: Simon & Schuster, 1998), p. 549.

57. Katherine Tate, *From Protest to Politics* (Cambridge, MA: Harvard University Press, 1993), chap. 8; see also Edward G. Carmines and James A. Stimson, *Issue Evolution: Race and the Transformation of American Politics* (Princeton, NJ: Princeton University Press, 1989).

58. *Milliken v. Bradley,* I 418 U.S. 717 (1974); 433 U.S. 267 (1977).

59. *Regents of the University of California v. Bakke,* 438 U.S. 265 (1978).

60. *Grutter v. Bollinger,* No. 02-241 (2003).

61. Ibid.

62. *Gratz v. Bollinger,* No. 02-516 (2003).

63. *Grutter v. Bollinger,* No. 02-241 (2003).

64. Linda Greenhouse, "Justices Back Affirmative Action by 5 to 4, But Wider Vote Bans a Racial Point System," *New York Times,* June 24, 2003, p. A1.

65. U.S. Bureau of the Census, *Statistical Abstract of the United States, 2001,* Table 679.

66. U.S. Bureau of the Census, *Statistical Abstract of the United States, 2001,* Table 680.

67. U.S. Bureau of the Census, *Statistical Abstract of the United States, 2001,* Tables 71 and 102.

68. Jennifer L. Hochschild, *Facing Up to the American Dream: Race, Class, and the Soul of the Nation* (Princeton, NJ: Princeton University Press, 1995).

69. Jaynes and Williams, *A Common Destiny,* p. 313.

70. U.S. Bureau of the Census, *Statistical Abstract of the United States, 2003,* Tables 270 and 266.

71. U.S. Bureau of the Census, *Poverty in the United States: 2002,* P60-222 (September 2003) p. 1, poverty rates for previous years obtained from http://www.census.gov/hhes/www/poverty.html, (accessed March 21, 2004).

72. U.S. Bureau of the Census, *Statistical Abstract of the United States, 2001,* Table 569.

73. U.S. Census Bureau 2002 Population Estimates, http://eire.census.gov/popest/data/national/asro.php, (accessed May 24, 2004).

74. Tony Affigne, "Latino Politics in the United States: An Introduction," *PS: Political Science and Politics,* 33, no. 3 (September 2000), pp. 523–527, Table 3.

75. Michael Jones-Correa, *Between Two Nations: The Political Predicament of Latinos in New York City* (Ithaca, NY: Cornell University Press, 1998).

76. National Election Studies, 2000 data.

77. Tyche Hendricks, "Parade, Enthusiastic Crowd Celebrate Cesar Chavez Day," *San Francisco Chronicle,* April 1, 2001: p. A18.

78. *Lau v. Nichols,* 414 U.S. 563 (1974).

79. Bernard Grofman, Lisa Handley, and Richard G. Niemi, *Minority Representation and the Quest for Voting Equality* (New York: Cambridge University Press, 1992), pp. 16–25; also see Thomas Weyr, *Hispanic U.S.A.: Breaking the Melting Pot* (New York: Harper, 1959); and Peter Skerry, *Mexican Americans: The Ambivalent Minority* (New York: Free Press, 1993).

80. Daron Shaw, Rodolfo O. de la Garza, and Jongho Lee, "Examining Latino Turnout in 1996: A Three State, Validated Survey Approach," *American Journal of Political Science* 44, no.2 (April 2000): 332–340.

81. Steven Greenhouse, "About Face; Guess Who's Embracing Immigrants Now?" *New York Times,* March 5, 2000: p. D4.

82. Matthew Dowd, "Doing the Latin Swing; Latino Voters Are the Soccer Moms of the New Decade," *Weekly Standard,* December 3, 2001: 20.

83. James G. Gimpel, "Q: Is the GOP Outreach to Latinos Likely to Succeed?" *Insight on the News,* October 15, 2001: 41.

84. Frank del Olmo, "On the Road to Latino Votes," *Los Angeles Times,* August 19, 2001: p. M5; Ricardo Alonso-Zaldivar, "Bush Would Open U.S. to Guest Workers," *Los Angeles Times,* January 8, 2004: p. A1.

85. http://www.johnkerry.com/issues/immigration/ (accessed March 21, 2004).

86. Ronald Brownstein "Bush and Kerry Have Similar Road Maps to Victory," *Los Angeles Times,* March 19, 2004, p. A25.

87. U.S. Bureau of the Census, *Statistical Abstract of the United States, 1999,* Tables 18 and 57.

88. Stanley Karnow and Nancy Yoshihara, *Asian Americans in Transition* (New York: Asia Society, 1992).

89. Don Nakanishi, "Beyond Electoral Politics: Renewing a Search for a Paradigm of Asian Pacific American Politics," in *Asian Americans and Politics: Perspectives, Experiences, Prospects,* ed. Gordon H. Chang (Washington, DC: Woodrow Wilson Center Press, 2001), pp. 102–129; and William Schneider, "Asian Americans Will Matter More," *National Journal,* August 14, 1999: 2398.

90. Asian Pacific American Institute for Congressional Studies, "Statement from APA Community Organizations," n.d., http://www.apaics.org/statement.html, (accessed April 10, 2000).

91. Robert Goldstein, *Political Repression in Modern America: 1870 to the Present* (New York: Schenkman, 1978), pp. 266–267.

92. *Korematsu v. United States,* 323 U.S. 244 (1944).

93. Nakanishi, p. 121.

94. Angelo Ancheta, *Race, Rights, and the Asian-American Experience* (New Brunswick, NJ: Rutgers University Press, 1997).

95. Timothy Cook, "The Empirical Study of Lesbian, Gay, and Bisexual Politics: Assessing the First Wave of Research," *American Political Science Review* 93, no.3 (September 1999): 679.

96. Shawn Zeller, "Gay Rites: Giving to Democrats," *National Journal,* May 8, 1999: 1241.

97. Donald P. Haider-Markel, "Creating Change—Holding the Line: Agenda Setting on Lesbian and Gay Issues at the National Level," in *Gays and Lesbians in the Democratic Process: Public Policy, Public Opinion, and Political Representation,* ed. Ellen D. B. Riggle and Barry Tadlock (New York: Columbia University Press, 1999), pp. 242–268.

98. From 49 in 1991 to 204 in 2001. Matthew Brelis, "From the Closet to the Campaign Trail; Being Gay Once Defined a Candidate. Now the Issues Do," *Boston Globe,* August 30, 1998: p. E1; and David Phelps, "Out to Win," advocate.com, 2001,

http://www.advocate.com/html/washper/
853_washper.asp (accessed March 4, 2002).

99. Deb Price, "Gays Need Democrats to Win 2000 Elections," *Detroit News,* November 1, 1999: p. A7; and Human Rights Campaign, http://www.hrc.org (accessed March 21, 2004).

100. Dean E. Murphey, "San Francisco Mayor Exults in Move on Gay Marriage," *New York Times,* February 19, 2004, p. A14.

101. Gregory B. Lewis and Marc Rogers, "Does the Public Support Equal Employment Rights for Gays and Lesbians?" in *Gays and Lesbians in the Democratic Process: Public Policy, Public Opinion, and Political Representation,* ed. Ellen D. B. Riggle and Barry Tadlock (New York: Columbia University Press, 1999), pp. 118–145; Steven H. Haeberle, "Gay and Lesbian Rights: Emerging Trends in Public Opinion and Voting Behavior," in Riggle and Tadlock, eds., *Gays and Lesbians in the Democratic Process,* pp. 145–169; and Newsweek Poll February 7, 2004 (Princeton Survey Research Associates, question USPSR.NEW.020704, R14A).

102. Human Rights Campaign, www.hrc.org (accessed March 21, 2004).

103. Vine Deloria, Jr., "The Distinctive Status of Indian Rights," in *The Plains Indians of the Twentieth Century,* ed. Peter Iverson (Norman: University of Oklahoma Press, 1985), p. 241.

104. Ibid., pp. 237–248.

105. U.S. Census, *Poverty in the United States: 2000,* Current Population Reports P60-214, September 2001, p. 7, Table B.

106. Toby Harnden, "Choctaws Take Their Slice of the American Pie," *London Daily Telegraph,* September 2, 2000: p. 15.

107. Deloria, "The Distinctive Status of Indian Rights," p. 237.

108. Agresto, *The Supreme Court and Constitutional Democracy,* pp. 148–149.

109. Theda Skocpol, *Protecting Soldiers and Mothers: The Political Origins of Social Policy in the United States* (Cambridge, MA: Harvard University Press, 1992); and Sara Evans, *Personal Politics: The Roots of Women's Liberation in the Civil Rights Movement and the New Left* (New York: Knopf, 1979).

110. Nancy McGlen and Karen O'Conner, *Women's Rights: The Struggle for Equality in the Nineteenth and Twentieth Centuries* (New York: Praeger, 1983), chap. 9.

111. Jane J. Mansbridge, *Why We Lost the ERA* (Chicago: University of Chicago Press, 1986).

112. Ruth B. Mandel, "The Political Woman," in *American Women in the Nineties: Today's Critical Issues,* ed. Sherri Matteo (Boston: Northeastern University Press, 1993), pp. 34–65.

113. *Hoyt v. Florida,* 368 U.S. 57 (1961).

114. *Craig v. Boren,* 429 U.S. 190 (1976).

115. Ginsburg, *Employment of the Constitution,* p. 191.

116. *Rostker v. Goldberg,* 453 U.S. 65 (1981).

117. Mansbridge, *Why We Lost the ERA,* chap. 7.

118. *Watson v. Fort Worth Bank & Trust,* 487 U.S. 997–999; *New York City Transit Authority v. Beazer,* 440 U.S. at 587, no. 31; and *Griggs v. Duke Power,* 401 U.S. at 432.

119. *Wards Cove v. Antonio,* 490 U.S. 642 (1989).

120. Ibid., p. 661.

121. *Meritor Savings Bank v. Vinson,* 477 U.S. 57 (1986).

122. Catherine S. Manegold, "Women Advance in Politics by Evolution, Not Revolution," *New York Times,* October 21, 1992: p. A1.

123. *Harris v. Forklift Systems,* 510 U.S. 77 (1993).

124. "Hillary's Class," Frontline (PBS television broadcast, No. 15, 1994), as cited in Karla Cooper-Boggs, "The Link Between Private and Public Single-Sex Colleges: Will Wellesley Stand or Fall with the Citadel?" *Indiana Law Review* 29 (1995): 137.

125. Cooper-Boggs, "The Link Between Private and Public Single-Sex Colleges," p. 135.

126. "Bush Aims to Ease Coeducation Rules for Public Schools," *Los Angeles Times,* March 4, 2004, p. A9.

127. *United States v. Virginia,* 116 S Ct. 2264 (1966).

128. United States General Accounting Office, *Women in Management: Analysis of Selected Data from the Current Population Survey,* GAO-02-156 (September 2001).

129. Robin Toner, "Welfare Chief Is Hoping to Promote Marriage," *New York Times,* February 19, 2002: p. A1.

130. Jack McNeil, Americans with Disabilities, 1997: *Household Economic Studies, Current Population Reports,* No. P70-73, (Washington, DC: United States Census, February 2001), Table 4.

131. Laura Trupin, Dorothy P. Rice, and Wendy Max, *Medical Expenditures for People with Disabilities in the United States, 1987* (Washington, DC: U.S. Department of Education, National Institute on Disability and Rehabilitation Research, 1995), Table G (figures updated for 1993 and adjusted for inflation to 2002 dollars).

132. Robert A. Katzman, *Institutional Disability: The Saga of Transportation Policy for the Disabled* (Washington, DC: The Brookings Institution, 1986).

133. Frederick J. Weintraub, ed., *Public Policy and the Education of Exceptional Children* (Washington, DC: Council for Exceptional Children, 1976).

134. Paul E. Peterson, "Background Paper," in Twentieth Century Fund, *Making the Grade: Report of the Twentieth Century Fund Task Force on Federal Elementary and Secondary Education Policy* (New York: Twentieth Century Fund, 1983), chap. 5.

135. Linda Greenhouse, "Justices Hear an Argument for Not Hiring the Disabled," *New York Times,* February 28, 2002: p. A22.

136. *Alabama v. Garrett,* 99–1240 (2001).

137. *Toyota Motor Manufacturing, Kentucky, Inc. v. Williams,* 00-1089 (2002).

138. Gerry Dulac, "Happy for Martin, Unhappy with Ruling," *Pittsburgh Post-Gazette,* May 30, 2001: p. A8.

139. Rufus Browning, Dale Rogers Marshall, and David H. Tabb, *Protest Is Not Enough: The Struggle of Blacks and Hispanics for Equality in Urban Politics* (Berkeley: University of California Press, 1984).

CHAPTER 18

1. Jonathan Weisman, "Deficit Projections Soar with Bush Stimulus Plan; Economists Say a Record Shortfall is Likely," *Washington Post,* January 10, 2003: p. A1.

2. "President Delivers 'State of the Union,'" (The White House: Washington DC, January 28, 2003) http://www.whitehouse.gov/news/releases/2003/01/20030128-19.html (accessed March 30, 2004).

3. Dan Freedman, "Bush Drug Plan Blasted; Groups Say Changes Would Gut Medicare," *Milwaukee Journal Sentinel,* January 30, 2003: p. 2A.

4. Carolyn Lochhead, "Medicare Bill Gives GOP Win on Dems' Turf," *San Francisco Chronicle,* November 26, 2003: p. A4.

5. Vicki Kemper, "Secrecy Probed in Medicare Plan Cost Estimates," *Los Angeles Times,* March 20, 2004: p. A24.

6. Richard Simon, "GOP Gains Feinstein Support on Medicare," *Los Angeles Times,* November 24, 2003: p. A17.

7. John Kingdon, *Agenda, Alternatives and Public Policies* (Boston: Little, Brown, 1984); and Paul Light, *The President's Agenda* (Baltimore, MD: Johns Hopkins University Press, 1991).

8. Arthur Maass, *Congress and the Common Good* (New York: Basic Books, 1983).

9. Eugene Bardach, *The Implementation Game,* 4th ed. (Cambridge, MA: M.I.T. Press, 1982); and Jeffrey L. Pressman and Aaron Wildavsky, *Implementation,* 3rd ed. (Berkeley: University of California Press, 1984).

10. Thomas R. Dye, *Politics, Economics and the Public: Policy Outcomes in the American States* (Chicago: Rand McNally, 1966).

11. Robert Pear, "Despite Sluggish Economy, Welfare Rolls Actually Fell," *New York Times,* March 22, 2004, p. A21.

12. Ibid.

13. Ibid.

14. Timothy Smeeding, Michael O'Higgins, and Lee Rainwater, eds., *Poverty, Inequality and Income Distribution in Comparative Perspective* (New York: Harvester Wheatsheaf, 1990); and Lee Rainwater and Timothy M. Smeeding, "Doing Poorly: The Real Income of American Children in a Comparative Perspective," Maxwell School of Citizenship and Public Affairs, Syracuse University, Syracuse, NY, August 1995, Working Paper No. 127.

15. Neil Howe and Richard Jackson, *Entitlements and the Aging of America* (Washington, DC; National Taxpayers Union Foundation, 1994).

16. Ibid., Chart 4-27, comment.

17. Congressional Budget Office, *Federal Spending on the Elderly and Children,* Summer 2000 (Washington, DC: U.S. Government Printing Office), p. 2.

18. Thomas A. Bailey, *The American Pageant: A History of the Republic* (Boston: D.C. Heath, 1956), p. 840. The figure is in 2004 dollars—the amount was $200 in 1935 dollars.

19. Martha Derthick, *Policymaking for Social Security* (Washington, DC: The Brookings Institution, 1979); and Theda Skocpol, *Protecting Soldiers and Mothers: The Politics of Social Provision in the United States* (Cambridge, MA: Harvard University Press, 1993).

20. R. Kent Weaver, *Automatic Government: The Politics of Indexation* (Washington, DC: The Brookings Institution, 1988).

21. Neil Howe and Richard Jackson, *2001 Chartbook: Entitlements and the Aging of America* (Washington, DC; National Taxpayers' Union Foundation, 2001), Chart 3-23 (figures in 2004 dollars).

22. *Boston Globe,* December 27, 1994: p. 70.

23. As quoted in Chuck Henning, *Wit and Wisdom of Politics,* expanded edition (Golden, CO: Fulcrum, 1992), p. 252.

24. *Strengthening Social Security and Creating Personal Wealth for All Americans,* Report of the President's Commission on Social Security, December 21, 2001, p. 8.

25. As quoted in Henning, *Wit and Wisdom of Politics,* p. 95.

26. Paul Light, *Artful Work: The Politics of Social Security Reform* (New York: Random House, 1985).

27. *Budget of the United States Government, Fiscal Year 2003, Historical Tables* (Washington, DC: Office of Management and Budget, 2002), Table 16.1, p. 297 (figures in constant 2004 dollars).

28. Ibid.

29. Robert Pear, "Many Doctors Shun Patients with Medicare," *New York Times,* March 17, 2002: p. A1.

30. U.S. Bureau of the Census, *Voting and Registration in the Election of November 2000,* February 2002, Table C, p. 12.

31. U.S. Bureau of the Census, *Voting and Registration in the Election of November 2000,* February 2002, Table B, p. 6.

32. Susan A. MacManus, with Patricia A. Turner, *Young v. Old: Generational Combat in the 21st Century* (Boulder, CO: Westview, 1996), pp. 60, 141.

33. AARP Annual Report, 2002, p. 5.

34. Employment and volunteer figures: "AARP: Making the Most of Life After 50," http://www.aarp.org/leadership/Articles/a200 3-01-13-aarphistory.html (accessed March 30, 2004); Expenditure figures: AARP Annual Report, 2002, p. 11.

35. Robert Rector, *Welfare Reform* (Washington, DC: Heritage Foundation, 1996).

36. Michael Lipsky, *Street Level Bureaucracy* (New York: Russell Sage Foundation, 1980); and Theda Skocpol, "Targeting within Universalism: Politically Viable Policies to Combat Poverty in the United States," in *The Urban Underclass,* ed. Christopher Jencks and Paul E. Peterson (Washington, DC: The Brookings Institution, 1991), pp. 411–436.

37. United States Department of Agriculture, Economic Research Service, http://www.ers.usda.gov/Briefing/Food NutritionAssistance/gallery/benefits.htm (accessed March 30, 2004) (2002 figure adjusted for inflation to 2004 dollars).

38. Internal Revenue Service, "2003 1040A Instructions," Earned Income Credit (EIC) Table, p. 46.

39. *2003 SSI Annual Report* (Washington, DC: Social Security Administration, May 2003, p. v).

40. This program is now known as the Housing Choice Voucher Program; see www .hud.gov.

41. Office of Management and Budget, "Budget for Fiscal Year 2005, Historical Tables," Table 16.1, p. 294 (both figures in 2004 dollars).

42. Percentage of monies going for services to the elderly in fiscal year 1993. Marilyn Werber Serafini, "Pinching Pennies," *National Journal* 27/37 (September 16, 1995): 2273. Also see Mark Rom, "Health and Welfare in the

American States," in *Politics in the American States,* 6th ed., ed. Virginia Gray and Herbert Jacob (Washington, DC: CQ Press, 1995).

43. Paul E. Peterson, "An Immodest Proposal," *Daedalus* 121 (Fall 1992): 151–174.

44. U.S. House of Representatives, Committee on Ways and Means, Overview of Entitlement Programs: Background Material and Data on Programs Within the Jurisdiction of the Committee on Ways and Means (otherwise known as the 2004 Green Book) (Washington, DC: U.S. Government Printing Office, 2004), Table I-5, pp. I-9. All subsequent references to this document in this chapter will be simply to the Green Book. They refer to the 2004 edition.

45. Green Book, Table I-5, p. I-9.

46. U.S. Department of Health and Human Services, Administration for Children and Families, Office of Family Assistance, *TANF Selected Provisions of State Plans,* http:// www.acf.dhhs.gov/programs/ofa/provis.htm (accessed July 24, 2000).

47. Joe Garofoli, "Food Stamp Hurdles; For Many, the Hassle Outweighs the Benefits," *San Francisco Chronicle,* February 8, 2002: p. A21.

48. Green Book, Table 7-9, pp. 7-36.

49. Paul E. Peterson and Mark Rom, *Welfare Magnets: A New Case for a National Standard* (Washington, DC: The Brookings Institution, 1990).

50. Rules vary widely by state. See U.S. Department of Health and Human Services, Administration for Children and Families, *Temporary Assistance to Needy Families, Third Annual Report to Congress,* August, 2000, pp. 207–210.

51. Ibid., pp. 204–205.

52. Testimony of Mark H. Greenburg, senior staff attorney, Center for Law and Social Policy, Human Resources Subcommittee, House Committee on Ways and Means, March 7, 2002.

53. "Social Security Penalty on Earnings Is Repealed," *Los Angeles Times,* April 8, 2000: p. A14.

54. Skocpol, *Protecting Soldiers and Mothers.*

55. Charles Murray, *Losing Ground: American Social Policy,* 1950–1980 (New York: Basic Books, 1984).

56. *Statistical Abstract of the United States, 2003,* Table 66.

57. Christopher Jencks, "Is the American Underclass Growing?" in *The Urban Underclass,* ed. Christopher Jencks and Paul E. Peterson (Washington, DC: The Brookings Institution, 1991), pp. 33, 88.

58. *Statistical Abstract of the United States, 2001,* Table 1331.

59. William J. Wilson, *The Truly Disadvantaged: The Inner City, the Underclass, and Public Policy* (Chicago: University of Chicago Press, 1987).

60. U.S. Bureau of the Census, *Current Population Survey, 2000,* Historical Tables, Table A-3; U.S. Census Bureau, "Educational Attainment in the United States: March 2002, Detailed Tables," (PPL-169), Table 8.

61. Associations Unlimited (online database); The Gale Group, 2002.

62. Associations Unlimited, 2002.

63. NPR/Kaiser Family/John F. Kennedy School of Government Survey, May 2001; NBS News/Wall Street Journal Poll, April 28, 1995.

64. Eliza Newlin Carney, "Family Time," *National Journal,* 30 (July 29, 1995): 1947–1949.

65. Jeff Shear, "The Credit Card," *National Journal* 27/32 (August 12, 1995): 2056–2058; and Marilyn W. Serafini, "Turning Up the Heat," *National Journal* 27, no. 32 (August 12, 1995): 2051–2055.

66. Steve Chabot, "Q: Should Congress Close Down the Department of Education? Yes: Give Parents and Communities More Control," *Insight on the News,* August 7, 1995: 18.

67. Paul E. Peterson, "Background Paper," in Twentieth Century Fund Task Force on Federal Elementary and Secondary Education Policy, *Making the Grade* (New York: Twentieth Century Fund, 1983); and *Digest of Education Statistics, 2000,* National Center for Education Statistics, March 2000, Table 158.

68. "Land Ordinance of 1785," in *Documents of American History,* 6th ed., ed. Henry S. Commager (New York: Appleton-Century-Crofts, 1958), p. 124.

69. Charles L. Glenn, Jr., *The Myth of the Common School* (Amherst: University of Massachusetts Press, 1987); Diane Ravitch, *The Great School Wars: New York City, 1805–1973* (New York: Basic Books, 1974); David Tyack and Elizabeth Hansot, *Managers of Virtue: Public School Leadership in America, 1820–1980* New York: Basic Books, 1982); and Paul E. Peterson, *The Politics of School Reform, 1870–1940* (Chicago: University of Chicago Press, 1985).

70. Author's calculation, based on *Digest of Education Statistics, 2000,* National Center for Education Statistics, March 2000, Table 158 (public school revenues); and *Statistical Abstract of the United States: 2001,* Table 640 (GDP figures).

71. Author's calculation, based on *Digest of Education Statistics, 2000,* National Center for Education Statistics, March 2000, Table 75; and *Statistical Abstract of the United States, 2001,* Table 647. Average teacher salaries compared with national per capita personal income, 1970–1999.

72. Eric A Hanushek, "School Resources and Student Performance," in *Does Money Matter? The Effect of School Resources on Student Achievement and Adult Success,* ed. Gary Burtless (Washington, DC: The Brookings Institution, 1996), pp. 43–73.

73. The Gallup Organization, Roper Center for Public Opinion Research Database, Question ID Numbers USGALLUP. 870.Q005A; USGALLUP. 99JNE25R11E, USGALLUP.03JNE09, R02H.

74. David K. Kirkpatrick, *Choice in Schooling: A Case for Tuition Vouchers* (Chicago: Loyola University Press, 1990); and Terry Moe, ed., *Private Vouchers* (Stanford, CA: Hoover Institution Press, 1995).

75. William H. Clune and John F. Witte, eds., *Choice and Control in American Education,* vols. I and II (New York: Falmer Pres, 1990); and Henig, *Rethinking School Choice.*

76. http://www.uscharterschools.org (accessed March 31, 2004).

77. Diane Ravitch, *National Standards in American Education: A Citizen's Guide* (Washington, DC: The Brookings Institution, 1995).

78. John Kerry, "Education Trust Fund," Remarks at Thomas Jefferson High School, Council Bluffs, IA, November 25, 2003, http://www.johnkerry.com (accessed March 31, 2004).

79. Peter W. Cookson, Jr., *School Choice: The Struggle for the Soul of American Education* (New Haven, CT: Yale University Press, 1994); Carnegie Foundation for the Advancement of Teaching, School Choice (Princeton, NJ: Carnegie Foundation, 1992); Larry *v.* Hedges and Rob Greenwald, "Have Times Changed? The Relation Between School Resources and Student Performances," in *Does Money Matter? The Effect of School Resources on Student Achievement and Adult Success,* ed. Gary Burtless (Washington, DC: The Brookings Institution, 1996), pp. 74–92; Amy Gutmann, *Democratic Education* (Princeton, NJ: Princeton University Press, 1987); and Jeffrey Henig, *Rethinking School Choice: Limits of the Market Metaphor* (Princeton, NJ: Princeton University Press, 1994).

80. *Statistical Abstract of the United States, 2001,* Tables 119 and 640.

81. U.S. Department of Education, National Center for Education Statistics, *Digest of Education Statistics, 2000,* May 2001, Tables 158, p. 175; 412, p. 469; and *Statistical Abstract of the United States, 2001,* Table 640.

82. James Peyser & Robert Costrell, "Exploring the Costs of Accountability: Claims That The No Child Left Behind Act Represents An Unfunded Mandate Wilt Under Close Scrutiny," *Education Next,* Spring 2004, pp. 22–29; Paul E. Peterson and Martin R. West, "The Contentious 'No Child' Law II: Money Has *Not* Been Left Behind," *Education Week,* March 17, 2004, http://www.edweek .org (accessed April 10, 2004); Paul E. Peterson and Martin R. West, *No Child Left Behind? The Politics and Practice of School Accountability* (Washington, DC: Brookings Institution Press, 2003).

83. Eric A. Hanushek, "The Economics of Schooling: Production and Efficiency in Public Schools," *Journal of Economic Literature* 24 (September 1986): 1141–1177.

84. Sandra Blakeslee, "Expert Warned that Mad Cow Was Imminent," *New York Times*, December 25, 2003: p. A1.

85. Denise Grady, "U.S. Issues Safety Rules to Protect Food From Mad Cow Disease," *New York Times,* December 31, 2003: p. A1.

86. Craig Petersen, *Business and Government,* 2nd ed. (New York: Harper & Row, 1985), p. 173.

87. *Heart of Atlanta Motel v. United States,* 322 U.S. 533 (1964); and *United States v. South-Eastern Underwriters Association,* 322 U.S. 533 (1944).

88. Jonathan Krim, "Judge Accepts Settlement in Microsoft Case," *Washington Post,* November 2, 2002: p. A1.

89. Gregg Easterbrook, *A Moment on the Earth: The Coming Age of Environmental Optimism* (New York: Penguin, 1995), p. xv. For a more pessimistic view, see Paul R. Ehrlich and Anne H. Ehrlich, *Betrayal of Science and Reason: How Anti-Environmental Rhetoric Threatens Our Future* (Washington, DC: Island Press, 1996).

90. Murray Weidenbaum, "Government Power and Business Performance," in *The United States in the 1980s,* ed. Peter Duignan and Alvin Rabushka (Stanford, CA: Hoover Institution Press, 1990), pp. 197–220.

91. Douglas Jehl, "National Parks Will Ban Recreation Snowmobiling; A Further Curb on the Use of Public Lands," *New York Times,* April 27, 2000: p. A14.

92. T. R. Reid, "For Snowmobiles, An Uncertain Fate," *Washington Post,* March 15, 2004: p. A23.

93. Ibid.

94. Clair Wilcox, *Public Policies Toward Business,* 4th ed. (Homewood, IL: Irwin, 1971), p. 589.

95. Marc K. Landy, Marc J. Roberts, and Stephen R. Thomas, *The Environmental Protection Agency: Asking the Wrong Questions from Nixon to Clinton,* expanded edition (New York: Oxford University Press, 1994).

96. Ibid.

97. Ibid., p. 290.

98. Kenneth Meier, *Regulation: Politics, Bureaucracy, and Economics* (New York: St. Martin's, 1985).

99. Lawrence L. Knutson, "'Rebirth of Our National Symbol'; Bald Eagle Soars Off Endangered List," *Boston Globe,* July 3, 1999: p. A3.

100. Martha Derthick and Paul Quirk, *The Politics of Deregulation* (Washington, DC: The Brookings Institution, 1985); and Mark C. Rom, *Public Spirit in the Thrift Tragedy* (Pittsburgh, PA: University of Pittsburgh Press, 1996).

101. Hardaway, "Transportation Deregulation," p. 143. Another view is given by Paul Dempsey, "The State of the Airline, Airport and Aviation Industries," *Transportation Law Journal* 129 (1992): 130–200.

102. David Monk, "The Lessons of Airline Regulation and Deregulation: Will We Make the Same Mistakes in Space?" *Journal of Air Law and Commerce* 57, no.3 (Spring 1992): 715–753.

103. See, for example, Dennis Carlton and William Landes, "Benefits and Costs of Airline Mergers: A Case Study," *Bell Journal of Economics and Management Science* 65, no.11 (1982): 65–83.

CHAPTER 19

1. United States Bureau of the Census, *Statistical Abstract of the United States, 2001,* Table 643; and *Statistical Abstract of the United States, 1999,* Table 1434.

2. United States Bureau of the Census, *Statistical Abstract of the United States, 1999,* Table 1430; and "Hot Jobs Market Fuels Consumer Confidence," *Los Angeles Times,* May 31, 2000: p. C1.

3. United States Bureau of the Census, *Statistical Abstract of the United States, 1999,* Table 1436.

4. Carolyn Lochhead, "Clinton Cites Economic Expansion; President Warns Bush Not To Ruin Good Times," *San Francisco Chronicle,* January 14, 2001: p. B1.

5. Katherine Hobson, "A Layoff Frenzy?" *U.S. News & World Report,* February 12, 2001: p. 23.

6. Anne E. Kornblut and Sue Kirchhoff, "It Could Be Worse . . . But as Economy Stumbles and Voters Lose Confidence, the Bush Administration Could Be in Political Peril—Making Republicans Worry and Giving Democrats an Opportunity," *Boston Globe,* July 8, 2001: p. E1.

7. Frank Bruni, "Bush Says Rebate Isn't a Substitute for His Tax Plan," *New York Times,* March 28, 2001: p. A1.

8. Byron York, "Bush by the (Poll) Numbers: How Does He Stand, and What's He Doing?" *National Review,* August 6, 2001: 15.

9. Michael Evans, "What Happened to the Recovery?" *Industry Week,* June 2002: 88.

10. A. W. Phillips, "The Relationship Between Unemployment and the Rate of Change of Money Wage Rates in the United Kingdom 1862–1957," *Economica* 25 (1958): 283–299.

11. Morris Fiorina, "Elections and Economics in the 1980s," in *Politics and Economics in the 1980s,* ed. Alberto Alesina and Geoffrey Carliner (Chicago: University of Chicago Press, 1991), pp. 17–38.

12. John Mueller, *Wars, Presidents, and Public Opinion* (New York: Wiley, 1973); and Douglas Hibbs, *The American Political Economy* (Cambridge, MA: Harvard University Press, 1987), chap. 5.

13. For a summary of the relevant literature, see Fiorina, "Elections and Economics in the 1980s."

14. Morris Fiorina, *Retrospective Voting in American National Elections* (New Haven, CT: Yale University Press, 1981), pp. 164–167.

15. Office of Management and Budget, Budget of the United States Government, Fiscal Year 2005, Historical Tables, Table 1.4 (Washington, DC: Office of Management and Budget, 2004); U.S. Department of Commerce, Bureau of Economic Analysis, National Income and Product Accounts, Table 1.1.5, http://www.bea.doc.gov/bea/dn/nipaweb/index.asp (accessed August 25, 2004).

16. Ibid.

17. Paul Peretz, *The Political Economy of Inflation in the United States* (Chicago: University of Chicago, Press, 1983), p. 42.

18. Ibid.

19. "The Genie in the Wings," *The Economist,* June 8, 2002.

20. George W. Bush, State of The Union Address, January 28, 2003, http://www.whitehouse.gov/news/releases/2003/01/20030128-19.html (accessed April 1, 2004).

21. Paul Krugman, *Peddling Prosperity* (New York: Norton, 1994), chaps. 3 and 6.

22. M. Kathryn Eickhoff, Office of Management and Budget, quoted in Peter T. Kilborn, "A $2 Trillion National Debt: Not Just Another Milestone," *New York Times,* September 15, 1985: p. 1.

23. Office of Management and Budget, Budget of the United States Government, Fiscal Year 2005, Historical Tables, Table 10.1, p. 184.

24. Gallup-CNN-USA Today Poll, May 30, 2002, question ID USGALLUP. G02MY28, R07J.

25. Louis Uchitelle, "Ideas and Trends: The Bondholders Are Winning: Why America Won't Boom," *New York Times,* June 12, 1994: p. D4.

26. For a general discussion, see Steven Sheffrin, *Rational Expectations* (London: Cambridge University Press, 1983).

27. Joseph H. Carter, *Never Met a Man I Didn't Like: The Life and Writings of Will Rogers* (New York: Avon Books, 1991), p. 250.

28. *88th Annual Report* (Washington, DC: Board of Governors of the Federal Reserve System, 2001), p. 383.

29. William Greider, *Secrets of the Temple: How the Federal Reserve Runs the Country* (New York: Simon & Schuster, 1987).

30. Schrage, Michael, "It's Time to Put a Transaction Tax on Credit Card Purchases," *Washington Post,* October 17, 1990: p. F3.

31. John Wooley, *Monetary Politics: The Federal Reserve and the Politics of Monetary Policy* (New York: Cambridge University Press, 1984).

32. Alberto Alesina, "Macroeconomics and Politics," in *NBER Macroeconomics Annual, 1988,* ed. Stanley Fischer (Cambridge, MA: MIT Press, 1988), pp. 13–52.

33. Douglas Hibbs, "The Dynamics of Political Support for American Presidents Among Occupational and Partisan Groups," *American Journal of Political Science* 26 (1982): 312–332.

34. Douglas Hibbs, "The Partisan Model of Macroeconomic Cycles: More Theory and Evidence for the United States," *Economics and Politics* 6 (1994): 1–23.

35. Edward Tufte, *Political Control of the Economy* (Princeton, NJ: Princeton University Press, 1978), chap. 2.

36. James Harding, "America's Battleground: Insecurity over Jobs Fuels Voters' Passions in the Election's Crucial Swing States," *Financial Times,* March 11, 2004: p. 19.

37. GDP grew slightly more than 3 percent in non-election years, and slightly more than 4 percent in presidential election years from 1960 to 2001. Analysis by authors of data from U.S. Department of Commerce, Bureau of Economic Analysis, National Accounts Data.

38. Donald Kettl, *Leadership at the Fed* (New Haven, CT: Yale University Press, 1986).

39. "Steady Greenspan; Clinton Plays It Safe on Choice of Fed Chief," *San Diego Union-Tribune,* February 26, 1996: p. B4.

40. David Bradford, *Untangling the Income Tax* (Cambridge, MA: Harvard University Press, 1986).

41. Calculated by the authors from U.S. Bureau of the Census, *Statistical Abstract of the United States, 1999,* Tables 1434 and 1443.

42. Daniel J. Parks with Bill Swindell, "Tax Debate Assured a Long Life As Bush, GOP Press for New Cuts," *CQ Weekly,* June 2, 2001: 1308–1309.

43. Richard W. Stevenson, "Republicans Can't Match Bush's Plan for Tax Cuts," *New York Times,* March 16, 2000: p. A18.

44. http://www.johnkerry.com/issues/economy/index.html (accessed April 1, 2004).

45. Figures on tax expenditures for this and the following tax preferences are drawn from the *Budget of the United States Government, Fiscal Year 2005* (Washington, DC: Office of Management and Budget, 2004), Analytical Perspectives, Table 18-1. College tuition tax credit figures include the Lifetime Learning Tax Credit, the HOPE Tax Credit, exclusion of scholarship and fellowship income, deductibility of student loan interest, deduction for higher education expenses, state prepaid tuition plans, and exclusion of interest on student loan bonds. Charitable contribution figures include charitable contributions to educational and health institutions. Figures are estimates for 2004.

46. William C. Mitchell and Michael Munger, "Economic Models of Interest Groups: An Introductory Survey," *American Journal of Political Science* 35, no. 2 (May,1991) 512–546.

47. Howard Schuman, *Politics and the Budget,* 3rd ed. (Englewood Cliffs, NJ: Prentice-Hall, 1992), p. 121.

48. The specific statistic in the text is for a family of four with median income. Reductions were similar for both higher- and lower-income families. C. Eugene Searle, *The Tax Decade* (Washington, DC: Urban Institute Press, 1985).

49. The intellectual basis of such proposals is usually credited to Robert Hall and Alvin Rabushka, *The Flat Tax* (Stanford, CA: Hoover Institution Press, 1985).

50. Internal Revenue Service, "Taxpayers Receiving Assistance, Paid and Unpaid, Specified Tax Years 1990–2000," *SOI Bulletin,* Winter 2001–2002, Table 23; and Internal Revenue Service, "Projections of Returns To Be Filed in Calendar Years 2001–2008," *SOI Bulletin,* Winter 2001–2002, p. 176.

51. Scott Moody, "The Cost of Tax Compliance" (Washington, DC: Tax Foundation, February 2002), www.taxfoundation.org/compliance2002.html (accessed August 25, 2004).

52. U.S. Bureau of the Census, *Statistical Abstract of the United States, 1999,* Table 1372.

53. Organization for Economic Cooperation and Development, "OECD Standardized Unemployment Rates—January 2004," (Paris: OECD, January 9, 2004).

54. "Judgement Day," *The Economist* (February 18, 1995): 49–51.

55. Study by the McKinsey Global Institute summarized in "How Regulation Kills New Jobs," *The Economist,* November 19, 1994: 78; "Economy Producing Mostly Bad Jobs? Not So Fast," Annenberg Political Fact Check, Annenberg Public Policy Center, University of Pennsylvania, July 9, 2004, www.factcheck.org (accessed August 25, 2004).

56. U.S. Bureau of the Census, *Statistical Abstract of the United States, 1999,* Tables 1432 and 1442.

57. *Digital Economy 2002* (Washington, DC: U.S. Department of Commerce, Economics and Statistics Administration, June 2002), Figure 2.8.

58. For a critical survey, see Krugman, *Peddling Prosperity,* chap. 5.

CHAPTER 20

1. "Transcript of Rice's 9-11 Commission Statement," CNN.com, May 19, 2004, http://www.cnn.com/2004/ALLPOLITICS/04/08/rice.transcript/ (accessed June 21, 2004).

2. Paul Pillar, *Terrorism and U.S. Foreign Policy* (Washington, DC: The Brookings Institution, 2001), p. 125.

3. Joseph Biden, "U.S. Foreign Policy in the 21st Century: Defining Our Interests in a Changing World," Remarks at the National Press Club, September 10, 2001, http://biden.senate.gov/press/speeches/091001.htm (accessed June 21, 2004).

4. Joseph S. Nye, Jr., "Government's Challenge: Getting Serious About Terrorism," in *How Did This Happen? Terrorism and the New War,* ed. James F. Hoge, Jr. and Gideon Rose (New York: Public Affairs, 2001, pp. 199–200).

5. Aaron Wildavsky, "The Two Presidencies," in Steven A. Shull, *The Two Presidencies: A Quarter Century Assessment* (Chicago: Nelson Hall, 1991 [1965]), pp. 11–25.

6. Alexander Hamilton, *The Federalist Papers, No. 70* (Baltimore, MD: Johns Hopkins University Press, 1981), p. 199.

7. Chuck Henning, *The Wit and Wisdom of Politics: Expanded Edition* (Golden, CO: Fulcrum, 1992), p. 56.

8. Wildavsky, "The Two Presidencies," p. 15.

9. John E. Mueller, *War, Presidents and Public Opinion* (New York: Wiley, 1973); and Gary King and Lyn Ragsdale, *The Elusive Executive: Discovering Statistical Patterns in the Presidency* (Washington, DC: CQ Press, 1988).

10. Mueller, *War, Presidents and Public Opinion.*

11. Richard Stevenson, "White House Says Prisoner Policy Set Humane Tone," *New York Times,* June 23, 2004: p. A1.

12. George W. Bush, "Remarks by the President on Iraq and the War on Terror," United States Army War College, Carlisle, PA, May 24, 2004, http://www.whitehouse.gov/news/releases/2004/05/20040524-10.html (accessed June 24, 2004).

13. Wildavksy, "The Two Presidencies," p. 16.

14. James Baker, III, with Thomas M. DeFrank, *The Politics of Diplomacy: Revolution, War, and Peace, 1989–1992* (New York: Putnam, 1995), p. 116.

15. American Israel Public Affairs Committee, "AIPAC Ranked #2 for Second Consecutive Year in *Fortune* Magazine's 'Power 25,'" November 23, 1998 press release.

16. Middle East expert William Quandt, as quoted in Steven Erlanger, "Albright May Be Facing Unfamiliar Tests," *New York Times,* December 7, 1966: p. 5.

17. Wildavksy, "The Two Presidencies," p. 17.

18. Barry M. Blechman, *The Politics of National Security: Congress and U.S. Defense Policy* (New York: Oxford University Press, 1990); Duane M. Oldfield and Aaron Wildavsky, "Reconsidering the Two Presidencies," in *The Two Presidencies: A Quarter Century Assessment,* ed. Steve A. Shull (Chicago: Nelson-Hall, 1991), pp. 181–190; Thomas Franck and Edward Weisband, *Foreign Policy by Congress* (New York: Oxford University Press, 1979); Thomas E. Mann, ed., *A Question of Balance: The President, the Congress and Foreign Policy* (Washington, DC: The Brookings Institution, 1990); and Stephen R. Weissman, *A Culture of Deference: Congress's Failure of Leadership in Foreign Policy* (New York: Basic Books, 1955).

19. Hamilton, "Federalist 2," ellipses deleted.

20. Speech before the House of Representatives, March 7, 1800, as quoted in *Marbury v. Madison,* 5 U.S. (1 Cranch) 137 (1803).

21. As quoted in Henning, *The Wit and Wisdom of Politics,* p. 240.

22. *U.S. v. Curtiss Wright Export Corporation,* 299 U.S. 304 (1936).

23. *Youngstown Sheet & Tube Co. v. Sawyer,* 343 U.S. 579 (1952).

24. Harold Hongju Koh, *The National Security Constitution: Sharing Power After the Iran-Contra Affair* (New Haven, CT: Yale University Press, 1990); Gordon Silverstein, "Judicial Expansion of Presidential Power," in Paul E. Peterson, ed. *The President, Congress, and the Making of Foreign Policy* (Norman, OK: Oklahoma University Press, 1994), pp. 23–48; and Gordon Silverstein, *The Imbalance of Powers: Constitutional Interpretation and the*

Making of American Foreign Policy (New York: Oxford University Press, 1996).

25. Joint Resolution of Congress, H.J. RES 1145, August 7, 1964.

26. Louis Fisher and David Gray Adler, "The War Powers Resolution: Time to Say Goodbye," *Political Science Quarterly* 113, no. 3: 1–20.

27. "A joint resolution to authorize the use of United States Armed Forces against those responsible for the recent attacks launched against the United States," Public Law 107-40, September 18, 2001.

28. "A joint resolution to authorize the use of United States Armed Forces against Iraq," Public Law 107-243, October 16, 2002.

29. United States Senate, "Treaties," http://www.senate.gov/artandhistory/history/common/briefing/Treaties.htm (accessed June 25, 2004).

30. *United States v. Belmont,* 301 U.S. 324 (1937).

31. Ann Devroy, "Pact Reached to Dismantle Ukraine's Nuclear Force; Detailed Plan to Be Signed Friday, Clinton Announces," *Washington Post,* January 11, 1994: p. A1.

32. NSC-68, "United States Objectives and Programs for National Security," National Security Council, April 14, 1950.

33. NSC-68, "United States Objectives and Programs for National Security," National Security Council, April 14, 1950.

34. George F. Kennan, "The Sources of Soviet Conduct," *Foreign Affairs* 25 (July 1947): 566–582.

35. White House National Security Council, "The National Security Strategy of the United States of America," September, 2002.

36. National Commission on Terrorist Attacks Against the United States, "Staff State-ment 17: Improvising a Homeland Defense," (Washington, DC: June 17, 2004), p. 28.

37. George Marshall, secretary of state under Harry Truman, as quoted in Alexander

De Conde, "George C. Marshall," in *An Uncertain Tradition: American Secretaries of State in the Twentieth Century,* ed. Norman A. Graebner (New York: McGraw Hill, 1961), p. 252.

38. Henning, *The Wit and Wisdom of Politics,* p. 69.

39. Ibid., p. 68.

40. Norman A. Graebner, "Dean G. Acheson," in *An Uncertain Tradition: American Secretaries of State in the Twentieth Century,* ed. Norman A. Graebner (New York: McGraw Hill, 1961), p. 13.

41. Don Van Natta, Jr., "President Rewards 43 Members of Fund-Raising Club with Prominent Posts," *New York Times,* March 6, 2002.

42. Barry Rubin, *Secrets of State: The State Department and the Struggle Over U.S. Foreign Policy* (New York: Oxford University Press, 1985), p. 64.

43. Stephen Holmes, "What Russia Teaches Us Now; How Weak States Threaten Freedom," *The American Prospect,* July-August 1997: 30.

44. General Omar Bradley, Chair of Joint Chiefs, Testimony to the Committee on Armed Services, House of Representatives, October 19, 1949, as quoted in John Bartlett, *Familiar Quotations* (Boston: Little, Brown, 1980), p. 824.

45. These points are taken from an insightful analysis of the way in which the Bush Administration changed U. S. counter-terrorism policy. See Abraham D. Sofaer, "The 'War' on Terrorism: Doctrinal Foundations," Hoover Institution, March 2002.

46. Loch K. Johnson, *America's Secret Power: The CIA in a Democratic Society* (New York: Oxford University Press, 1989), pp. 12, 43.

47. Ibid., chap. 2.

48. "Testing Intelligence," *Economist,* October 6, 2001.

49. Ibid.

50. Rubin, *Secrets of State,* p. 50.

51. Speech at the Constitutional Convention, as quoted in Hans J. Morgenthau, *Politics Among Nations,* 4th ed. (New York: Knopf, 1966), p. 12.

52. Speech in Philadelphia, February 22, 1861, as quoted in Morgenthau, *Politics Among Nations,* p. 35.

53. Steve Chapman, "Should We Be in the Balkans Forever?" TownHall.com Columnists, October 26, 2000. Available at www.townhall.com.

54. George W. Bush, "Remarks by the President on Iraq and the War on Terror," United States Army War College, Carlisle, PA, May 24, 2004.

55. Al Gore, "Our Founders and the Unbalance of Power," Remarks to the American Constitution Society for Law and Policy, June 24, 2004.

56. Robert Keohane, *After Hegemony: Cooperation and Discord in the World Political Economy* (Princeton, NJ: Princeton University Press, 1984).

57. Morgenthau, *Politics Among Nations;* Kenneth N. Waltz, *Theory of International Politics* (New York: McGraw Hill, 1979); John J. Mearscheimer, "Back to the Future: Instability in Europe After the Cold War," *International Security* 15, no.1 (Summer 1990): 5–56; and Samuel Huntington, *The Clash of Civilizations* (New York: Simon & Schuster, 1996).

58. Joel R. Paul, "The Geopolitical Constitution: Executive Expediency and Executive Agreements," *California Law Review* 86, no. 671 (July 1998): 749–752.

59. Marcus Noland, "Learning to Love the WTO," *Foreign Affairs,* September-October 1999: 78.

60. "Reactions," *Seattle Times,* December 1, 1999: p. A17.

61. Robert Matthew and Neil King, Jr., "Imposing Steel Tariffs, Bush Buys Some Time for Troubled Industry," *Wall Street Journal,* March 6, 2002: p. 1.

Name Index

Subject Index

Page citations followed by an italicized *t*, *f*, or *b* indicate tables, figures, and boxed material.

Labor, laws designed to protect, and judicial
  review, 404
Labor, U.S. Department of, 377
Laboratories of democracy, states as, 80
Labor unions, 64, 174, 188
  coerced membership in, 178–79
  for government employees, 216–17, 430
Latinos
  civil rights of, 479–81
  in Congress, 300f, 301, 302
  courting vote of, 110b, 480
  as growing minority group, 95f, 115
  as state and local government employees,
    373f
Law(s)
  civil, and criminal code, 397, 398t
  earmarked funds written into, 384, 385b
  enforcement of, by bureaucracies, 365–66
  Jim Crow (segregation), 467
  process by which bill becomes, 327–30
  rights of suspects and, 449–56
Law clerks, Supreme Court, 418–19
Law enforcement, shared functions of, 68
Lawrence v. Texas (2003), 457
Lawsuits. *See* Litigation
Leaders, views of group, 194t
League of Nations, 564, 578
League of Women Voters, 309
Legal counsel, right of, 454
Legal distinction, 416
Legislation
  agency responsibilities written in, 383–84
  checking power of courts with revised,
    422
  civil rights, 180, 466, 467, 473–75
  earmarking funds in, 384, 385b
  challenge to House, from home
    schooling advocates, 172
  process of bills becoming laws, 327–30
Legislative branch of government, 32, 40–41
  Congress and, 314–15 (*see also* Congress,
    U.S.)
  components of, 316t
Legislative Reorganization Act of 1946, 322
Libel, free speech and, 445–46
Liberalism, 97–106
  American individualism and, 98–101
  contemporary explanations of American,
    108–10
  defined, 97
  equality, individualism and, 102–3
  religion and, 103–6
  traditional explanations of American,
    106–7
Liberal political theory on public assistance
  programs, 511
Library of Congress, 315
Lightner, Candy, 181
Lincoln, Abraham, presidency of, 7, 16,
  62–63, 344, 345, 348, 355, 358, 560
Line item veto, 344–45

Literacy test, immigration and, 93
Litigation, 188–89
  affirmative action, 116–18
  civil rights movement and strategies of,
    188, 189, 423–24, 469–72
  enforcing laws by using private, 66
  influencing government by means of,
    188–89
  as political strategy, 423–24
Living-constitution theory of judicial
  review, 402
Lobbying, 182–84
  grassroots, 184
Lobbyist, 181, 183, 184
Local election(s), 4, 78
Local government, 76–79
  domestic expenditures of, 76f
  elections for, 4, 78
  employment in, 365, 366f
  federal grants to, 69–70, 72f, 73f
  limits on, 79
  minorities working in, 372f, 373f
  number of (years 1942-2002), 77f
  popularity of, 78–79
  sovereignty issues and, 57
  types and numbers of, 77–78
Lochner v. New York (1905), 404
Locke, John, political theory of, 32, 97–98
Logrolling, congressional, 325, 326
Louisiana Purchase, 50, 207
Loyalty oaths, 442
"L" states, Republican, 266, 267f

McCain-Feingold Act (2002), 308–9, 310
McCarthyism, 442
McConnell v. FEC (2003), 310
McCulloch v. Maryland (1819), 62, 65, 410
Machine, defined, 209. *See also* Urban
  political machines
McKinley, William, presidency of, 360
Madison, James, presidency of, 344, 560
Magazines, 223–24
Maine, electoral votes of, 266
Majority(ies)
  elections and, 19–20
  freedom of speech, assembly, and press
    and tyranny of, 438–39
  in Senate, 41
  tyranny of, 61
Majority leader, House of Representatives,
  318–19
Majority-minority districts, 302, 303
Mandates, 9
  unfunded, 75, 76
Mapp v. Ohio (1961), 452
Marble-cake federalism, 67–76
Marbury v. Madison (1803), 400
Margolies-Mezvinsky, Marjorie,
  congressional term and reelection
  campaign of, 282
Markup, legislative bill, 329

Maryland, 494
Martin v. Hunter's Lessee (1816), 410
Massachusetts
  compulsory schooling in, 447
  gay marriage and state court ruling in, 411
  social services in Framingham, 79
Massachusetts colony, 27–28
Mass communications
  privacy rights and, 458–59
  rise of, and permanent campaign, 14
  weakening of political parties and, 217
Mass media, defined, 223. *See also* Media
Mass public, defined, 137
Matching funds, defined, 259
Material incentives, 177
Mayflower Compact, 28
Measurement error in polls, defined, 129
Media, 221–48
  Al Jazeera cable network, 240b
  American choices of, for information,
    230
  biases of, 235–41
  coverage of government by, 245–47
  coverage of Senate elections by, 294–95
  cultural issues in electoral politics and,
    251
  development of mass, 223–30
  effects of, 230–35
  electoral politics and, 241–45
  influence of, on nomination of
    presidential candidates, 261–62
  influence of, on presidential elections,
    273–74
  influence of, on public opinion, 125–26
  polling by, 15
  role of, in 1968 Democratic convention
    protests, 222
Medicaid, 72, 73, 75, 277, 508–9
  as component of federal budget, 532, 533f
Medicare, 203, 277
  complexities of, 505–6
  as component of federal budget, 532,
    533f
  defined, 499
  establishment of, 502, 503
  reform of, 380, 498
Meek v. Pittenger (1975), 447
Meritor Savings Bank v. Vinson (1986), 487
Mexican American Legal Defense and
  Education Fund (MALDEF), 480–81
Mexican immigrants, 93, 95, 109
Mexico
  elections in, 6b
  U.S. war with (1846-1848), 560, 571
Microsoft Corporation, 227, 519
  lobbyists of, 181
Military
  gays in, 350, 354
  gender classification and women in, 486,
    487
  response of, to terrorism, 572

Photo Credits